QUARTET
A Book of Stories, Plays, Poems, and Critical Essays

EDITED BY
HAROLD P. SIMONSON
UNIVERSITY OF WASHINGTON

QUARTET

A Book of Stories, Plays, Poems, and Critical Essays

**SECOND
EDITION**

Harper & Row, Publishers, New York/Evanston/San Francisco/London

QUARTET
SECOND EDITION
A Book of Stories, Plays, Poems, and Critical Essays

Copyright © 1973 by Harold P. Simonson

Printed in the United States of America. All rights reserved. No part of this book may be used or reproduced in any manner whatsoever without written permission except in the case of brief quotations embodied in critical articles and reviews. For information address Harper & Row, Publishers, Inc., 10 East 53rd Street, New York, N.Y. 10022

Standard Book Number: 06-046184-5

Library of Congress Catalog Card Number: 72-9402

ACKNOWLEDGMENTS

W. H. AUDEN, "Musée des Beaux Arts," copyright, 1940 and renewed 1968 by W. H. Auden. Reprinted from *The Collected Shorter Poems* of W. H. Auden by permission of Random House, Inc., and Faber & Faber Ltd.

JAMES BALDWIN, "Sonny's Blues," copyright © 1957 by James Baldwin. First appeared in *Partisan Review*, Summer, 1957, Vol. 24, No. 3.

R. P. BLACKMUR, "The Later Poetry of W. B. Yeats," copyright, 1940, by Richard P. Blackmur; renewed, 1968, by The First National Bank of Princeton. Reprinted from *Language as a Gesture* by Richard P. Blackmur by permission of Harcourt Brace Jovanovich, Inc., and George Allen and Unwin Ltd.

ROBERT BLY, "The Executive's Death," copyright © 1960 by Robert Bly; "Watching Television," copyright © 1963 by Robert Bly; "Come with Me," copyright © 1964 by Robert Bly; "Wanting to Experience All Things," copyright © 1967 by Robert Bly. All poems from *The Light Around the Body* by Robert Bly. Reprinted by permission of Harper & Row, Publishers, Inc.

JORGE LUIS BORGES, "The South," from *Ficciones*, translated by Anthony Kerrigan. Reprinted by permission of Grove Press, Inc. Copyright © 1962 by Grove Press, Inc.

CLEANTH BROOKS, "The Heresy of Paraphrase," from *The Well Wrought Urn*, copyright, 1947, by Cleanth Brooks. Reprinted by permission of Harcourt Brace Jovanovich, Inc.

GWENDOLYN BROOKS, "kitchenette building," "a song in the front yard," "the preacher: ruminates behind the sermon," from *Selected Poems* by Gwendolyn Brooks, copyright, 1945 by Gwendolyn Brooks Blakely. "Medgar Evers," copyright © 1964 by Gwendolyn Brooks Blakely; "To a Winter Squirrel," copyright © 1968 by Gwendolyn Brooks Blakely, both from *In the Mecca* by Gwendolyn Brooks. All poems reprinted by permission of Harper & Row, Publishers, Inc.

FREDERICK C. CREWS, "Literature and Psychology." Reprinted by permission of the Modern Language Association of America from *Relations of Literary Study*, edited by James Thorpe (1967). Copyright © 1967 by the Modern Language Association of America.

COUNTEE CULLEN, "Heritage," from *On These I Stand* by Countee Cullen, copyright, 1925 by Harper & Row, Publishers, Inc.; renewed, 1953 by Ida M. Cullen. Reprinted by permission of Harper & Row, Publishers, Inc.

E. E. CUMMINGS, "Buffalo Bill's," and "the Cambridge ladies who live in furnished souls," copyright 1923, 1951 by E. E. Cummings; "the skinny voice," copyright 1925, 1953 by E. E. Cummings; "my sweet old etcetera," copyright 1926 by Horace Liveright; renewed 1954 by E. E. Cummings, "if there are any heavens," copyright 1931, 1959 by E. E. Cummings; "i thank You God for this most amazing," copyright 1950 by E. E. Cummings. All poems reprinted from his volume, *Poems 1923–1954*. All poems reprinted by permission of Harcourt Brace Jovanovich, Inc.

BABETTE DEUTSCH, "A Symposium on Roethke's 'In a Dark Time,'" from *New World Writing 19*. Copyright © 1961 by J. B. Lippincott Company. Reprinted by permission of the publisher and author.

EMILY DICKINSON, "Success Is Counted Sweetest," "Safe in Their Alabaster Chambers," "I Like a Look of Agony," "Because I Could Not Stop for Death," "A Narrow Fellow in the Grass," "The Bustle in a House," "Immortal Is an Ample Word," "Apparently with No Surprise," reprinted by permission of the publishers and the Trustees of Amherst College from Thomas H. Johnson, Editor, *The Poems of Emily Dickinson*, Cambridge, Mass.: The Belknap Press of Harvard University Press. Copyright 1951, 1955, by The President and Fellows of Harvard College.

T. S. ELIOT, "The Love Song of J. Alfred Prufrock," from *Collected Poems 1909–1962* by T. S. Eliot, copyright 1936 by Harcourt Brace Jovanovich, Inc.; copyright, © 1963, 1964, by T. S. Eliot. Reprinted by permission of Harcourt Brace Jovanovich, Inc., and Faber & Faber Ltd. "Tradition and the Individual Talent," from *Selected Essays of T. S. Eliot*, copyright, 1932, 1936, 1950, by Harcourt Brace Jovanovich, Inc.; © 1960, 1964 by T. S. Eliot. Reprinted by permission of Harcourt Brace Jovanovich, Inc., and Faber & Faber Ltd.

WILLIAM FAULKNER, "That Evening Sun," copyright 1931 and renewed 1959 by William Faulkner. Reprinted from *The Collected Stories of William Faulkner* by permission of Random House, Inc.

FRANCIS FERGUSSON, "*Ghosts*: The Theater of Modern Realism," pp. 148–161 from Francis Fergusson, *The Idea of a Theater* (copyright 1949, 1968 by Princeton University Press; Princeton paperback, 1968). Reprinted by permission of Princeton University Press.

NORMAN FOERSTER, "The Esthetic Judgment and the Ethical Judgment," in *The Intent of the Critic*, edited by Donald A. Stauffer et al. (copyright 1941 © 1969 by Princeton University Press), pp. 65–88. Reprinted by permission of Princeton University Press.

ROBERT FROST, "Reluctance," "After Apple-Picking," " 'Out, Out—,' " "Fire and Ice," "Stopping by Woods on a Snowy Evening," "Desert Places," from *Complete Poems of Robert Frost*. Copyright 1916, 1923, 1930, 1934, 1939 by Holt, Rinehart and Winston, Inc. Copyright 1936, 1944, 1951, © 1958, 1962 by Robert Frost. Copyright © 1964, 1967 by Leslie Frost Ballantine. All poems reprinted by permission of Holt, Rinehart and Winston, Inc.

NORTHRUP FRYE, "The Keys to Dreamland," from *The Educated Imagination* by Northrup Frye. Reprinted by permission of Indiana University Press and the author.

LORRAINE HANSBERRY, "A Raisin in the Sun," copyright © 1958, 1959, 1966 by Robert Nemiroff as Executor of the Estate of Lorraine Hansberry. Reprinted by permission of Random House, Inc.

ROBERT HAYDEN, "Mourning Poem for the Queen of Sunday," "The Whipping," "Those Winter Sundays," and "Frederick Douglass," from *Selected Poems*, copyright © 1966 by Robert Hayden. "Monet's 'Waterlilies'," "A Plague of Starlings," from *Words in the Mourning Time*, copyright © 1970 by Robert Hayden. All poems reprinted by permission of October House Inc.

ROBERT B. HEILMAN, "The Full Man and the Fullness Thereof," from *College Composition and Communication* (October 1970). Copyright © 1970 by the National Council of Teachers of English. Reprinted by permission of the publisher and Robert B. Heilman.

ERNEST HEMINGWAY, "Big Two-Hearted River," Parts I and II, reprinted with the permission of Charles Scribner's Sons from *In Our Time* by Ernest Hemingway. Copyright 1925 Charles Scribner's Sons; renewal copyright 1953 Ernest Hemingway.

A. E. HOUSMAN, "Loveliest of Trees," "With rue my heart is laden," "Terence, this is stupid stuff," from "A Shropshire Lad"—Authorized Edition—from

The Collected Poems of A. E. Housman. Copyright 1939, 1940, © 1959 by Holt, Rinehart and Winston, Inc. Copyright © 1967, 1968 by Robert E. Symons. "The chestnut casts his flambeaux," from *The Collected Poems of A. E. Housman*. Copyright 1922 by Holt, Rinehart and Winston, Inc. Copyright 1950 by Barclays Bank Ltd. All poems reprinted by permission of Holt, Rinehart and Winston, Inc. Also reprinted by permission of The Society of Authors as literary representative of the Estate of A. E. Housman, and Messrs. Jonathan Cape Ltd., publishers of A. E. Housman's *Collected Poems*.

HENRIK IBSEN, "Ghosts," translated by Farquharson Sharp. From the book *Ghosts, An Enemy of the People, The Warriors of Helgeland* by Henrik Ibsen. Trans. by R. Farquharson Sharp. Everyman's Library edition published by E. P. Dutton & Co., Inc. Reprinted also by permission of J. M. Dent & Sons Ltd.

EUGENE IONESCO, "The Gap," translated by Rosette Lamont. Reprinted from *The Massachusetts Review*, © 1969 The Massachusetts Review, Inc. "Slime," translated by Rosette Lamont. Reprinted by permission of Grove Press and the translator.

JAMES JOYCE, "Araby," from *Dubliners* by James Joyce. Copyright © 1967 by the Estate of James Joyce. All rights reserved. Reprinted by permission of The Viking Press, Inc.

FRANZ KAFKA, "The Judgment," reprinted by permission of Schocken Books Inc. from *The Penal Colony* by Franz Kafka. Copyright © 1948 by Schocken Books Inc.

STANLEY KUNITZ, "A Symposium on Roethke's 'In a Dark Time,'" from *New World Writing* 19. Copyright © 1961 by J. B. Lippincott Company. Reprinted by permission of the publisher and author.

D. H. LAWRENCE, "The Shades of Spring," from *The Complete Short Stories of D. H. Lawrence*, Volume I. All rights reserved. Reprinted by permission of The Viking Press, Inc.

C. S. LEWIS, "Donne and Love Poetry in the Seventeenth Century," from *Seventeenth-Century Studies Presented to Sir Herbert Grierson*. By permission of The Clarendon Press, Oxford.

ROBERT LOWELL, "Man and Wife," reprinted by permission of Farrar, Straus & Giroux, Inc., from *Life Studies*, copyright © 1958 by Robert Lowell. "A Quaker Graveyard in Nantucket," "The Drunken Fisherman," from *Lord Weary's Castle*, copyright, 1944, 1946, by Robert Lowell. Reprinted by permission of Harcourt Brace Jovanovich, Inc.

GEORG LUKÁCS, "The Ideology of Modernism," from *Realism in Our Time* by Georg Lukács, translated by John and Necke Mander. First published in an English translation under the title *The Meaning of Contemporary Realism*. Copyright © 1962 by Merlin Press Ltd. Reprinted by permission of Harper & Row, Publishers, Inc., and The Merlin Press Ltd.

BERNARD MALAMUD, "Idiots First," reprinted with permission of Farrar, Straus & Giroux, Inc., from *Idiots First*, copyright © 1961 by Bernard Malamud.

CARSON MCCULLERS, "A Tree, A Rock, A Cloud," from *The Ballad of the Sad Cafe*. Copyright 1955 by Carson McCullers. Reprinted by permission of the publisher, Houghton Mifflin Company.

MARIANNE MOORE, "The Fish," "In the Days of Prismatic Colour," reprinted from *Collected Poems* by Marianne Moore. Copyright 1935 by Marianne Moore, renewed 1963 by Marianne Moore and T. S. Eliot. "What Are Years?" reprinted from *Collected Poems* by Marianne Moore. Copyright 1941 by

Marianne Moore. All poems reprinted with permission of The Macmillan Company.

HERBERT J. MULLER, "Pessimism," from *Modern Fiction: A Study of Values* by Herbert J. Muller. By permission of Funk & Wagnalls.

HENRY A. MURRAY, "Bartleby and I," from *Bartleby the Scrivener*, the Melville Society's symposium of 1966. By permission of the Kent State University Press.

FLANNERY O'CONNOR, "Good Country People," from *A Good Man Is Hard to Find and Other Stories*, copyright, 1955, by Flannery O'Connor. Reprinted by permission of Harcourt Brace Jovanovich, Inc.

WALTER J. ONG, "The Jinnee in the Well-Wrought Urn," from *Essays in Criticism*, IV (1954), edited by F. W. Bateson. Reprinted by permission of F. W. Bateson.

SYLVIA PLATH, "Tulips," copyright © 1962 by Ted Hughes; "Poppies in October," "Years," copyright © 1963 by Ted Hughes; "Words," copyright © 1966 by Ted Hughes; from *Ariel* by Sylvia Plath. "Insomniac," "Mirror," (originally appeared in *The New Yorker*), "Whitsun," "Witch Burning," "Crossing the Water," copyright © 1971 by Ted Hughes, from *Crossing the Water* by Sylvia Plath. Reprinted by permission of Harper & Row, Publishers, Inc., and Olwyn Hughes, Literary Agent. *Crossing the Water* also published by Faber & Faber Ltd.

KATHERINE ANNE PORTER, "Flowering Judas," copyright 1930, 1958 by Katherine Anne Porter. Reprinted from her volume, *Flowering Judas and Other Stories* by permission of Harcourt Brace Jovanovich, Inc.

JOHN CROWE RANSOM, "Bells for John Whiteside's Daughter," "Nocturne," copyright, 1924 by Alfred A. Knopf, Inc. and renewed 1952 by John Crowe Ransom; "Blue Girls," copyright 1927 by Alfred A. Knopf, Inc. and renewed 1955 by John Crowe Ransom. All poems reprinted from *Selected Poems* by John Crowe Ransom by permission of the publisher.

THEODORE ROETHKE, "Open House" and "To My Sister," copyright 1941 by Theodore Roethke; "My Papa's Waltz," copyright 1942 by Hearst Magazines, Inc.; "Dolor," copyright 1943 by Modern Poetry Association, Inc.; "Moss-Gathering," copyright 1946 by Editorial Publications, Inc.; lines from "The Lost Son" and from "The Shape of the Fire," copyright 1947 by Theodore Roethke; "Elegy for Jane," copyright 1950 by Theodore Roethke; "The Waking," copyright 1953 by Theodore Roethke; "The Dream," copyright © 1955 by Theodore Roethke; "In a Dark Time," "In Evening Air," "The Sequel," copyright © 1960 by Beatrice Roethke as Administratrix of the Estate of Theodore Roethke. All poems reprinted from *The Collected Poems of Theodore Roethke* by permission of Doubleday & Company, Inc. "Some Self-Analysis," from *On the Poet and His Craft: Selected Prose of Theodore Roethke*, ed. Ralph J. Mills (1965), pp. 3–6. By permission of the University of Washington Press.

PHILIP ROTH, "The Conversion of the Jews," from *Goodbye Columbus* (1959). Copyright © 1959 by Philip Roth. Reprinted by permission of the publisher, Houghton Mifflin Company. Also reprinted by permission of Robert Lantz-Candida Donadio Literary Agency, Inc.

JEAN-PAUL SARTRE, "The Wall," translated by Maria Jolas. Copyright, 1945 by Random House, Inc. Reprinted from *The Bedside Book of Famous French Stories*, edited by Belle Becker and Robert N. Linscott by permission of the publisher. "Existentialism," reprinted by permission of Philosophical Library.

Acknowledgments

WALTER J. SLATOFF, "Varieties of Involvement," reprinted from Walter J. Slatoff: *With Respect to Readers: Dimensions of Literary Response*. Copyright © 1970 by Cornell University. Used by permission of Cornell University Press.

THEODORE SPENCER, "The Central Problem in Literary Criticism," *College English*, December, 1942. Reprinted with the permission of the National Council of Teachers of English and Theodore Spencer.

WILLIAM STAFFORD, "Traveling through the Dark," copyright © 1960 by William Stafford; "The Tillamook Burn," copyright © 1958 by William Stafford; "Vocation," "Requiem," copyright © 1962 by William Stafford. All poems reprinted from *Traveling through the Dark* by William Stafford. "Our City Is Guarded by Automatic Rockets," copyright © 1958 by William E. Stafford, from *The Rescued Year* by William Stafford. All poems reprinted by permission of Harper & Row, Publishers, Inc.

WALLACE STEVENS, "A High-Toned Old Christian Woman," "Disillusionment of Ten O'Clock," "Sunday Morning," copyright 1923 by Wallace Stevens and renewed 1951 by Wallace Stevens. Reprinted from *The Collected Poems of Wallace Stevens* by permission of Alfred A. Knopf, Inc.

AUGUST STRINDBERG, "Miss Julie," from *Six Plays of Strindberg*, translated by Elizabeth Sprigge. Reprinted by permission of Collins-Knowlton-Wing, Inc. Copyright © 1955 by Elizabeth Sprigge. All performance rights strictly reserved. For performing rights in the United States of America and Canada, address inquiries to the author's agents, Collins-Knowlton-Wing, Inc., 60 East 56th Street, New York, N.Y. 10022. For all other countries A. P. Watt & Son, 26–28 Bedford Row, London, W.C. 1, England.

ALLEN TATE, "Ode to the Confederate Dead" is reprinted by permission of Charles Scribner's Sons from *Poems* by Allen Tate. Copyright 1931, 1932, 1937, 1948 Charles Scribner's Sons; renewal copyright © 1959, 1960 Allen Tate.

DYLAN THOMAS, "The Force That Through the Green Fuse," "A Refusal to Mourn the Death of a Child," "Fern Hill," "Do Not Go Gentle into That Good Night," "Death Shall Have No Dominion," from *Collected Poems* by Dylan Thomas. Copyright 1939, 1943, 1946 by New Directions. Copyright 1952 by Dylan Thomas. Reprinted by permission of New Directions Publishing Corporation, J. M. Dent & Sons Ltd., and The Trustees for the Copyrights of the late Dylan Thomas.

E. M. W. TILLYARD, "The Personal Heresy, II," from *The Personal Heresy: A Controversy* by E. M. W. Tillyard and C. S. Lewis, published by Oxford University Press.

LEO TOLSTOY, "The Death of Iván Ilých," from *The Death of Iván Ilých and Other Stories* by Leo Tolstoy, translated by Louise and Aylmer Maude, published by Oxford University Press.

LIONEL TRILLING, "Art and Neurosis," from *The Liberal Imagination* by Lionel Trilling. Copyright 1945 by Lionel Trilling. Reprinted by permission of The Viking Press, Inc.

MIGUEL DE UNAMUNO, "Saint Emmanuel the Good, Martyr," from *Abel Sanchez and Other Stories*, translated by Anthony Kerrigan, 1956. Reprinted by permission of Henry Regnery Company.

RENÉ WELLEK, "Periods and Movements in Literary History," from *English Institute Annual 1940* (New York: Columbia University Press, 1940), pp.

73–93. Reprinted by permission of Columbia University Press and René Wellek.

EUDORA WELTY, "A Worn Path," copyright, 1941, renewed, 1969, by Eudora Welty. Reprinted from her volume, *A Curtain of Green and Other Stories*, by permission of Harcourt Brace Jovanovich, Inc.

PHILIP WHEELWRIGHT, "Poetry, Myth and Reality," by Philip Wheelwright from *The Language of Poetry*, edited by Allen Tate (Princeton University Press, 1942). Reprinted by permission of Princeton University Press.

TENNESSEE WILLIAMS, "The Glass Menagerie," copyright, 1945 by Tennessee Williams. Reprinted from *Six Modern American Plays*, Modern Library Edition, by permission of Random House, Inc.

WILLIAM CARLOS WILLIAMS, "Gulls," "The Red Wheelbarrow," "The Yachts," from William Carlos Williams, *Collected Earlier Poems*. Copyright 1938 by William Carlos Williams. "A Sort of a Song," "Prelude to Winter," "The Pause," from William Carlos Williams, *Collected Later Poems*. Copyright 1944, 1950 by William Carlos Williams. All poems reprinted by permission of New Directions Publishing Corporation.

EDMUND WILSON, "Philoctetes: The Wound and the Bow," from *The Wound and the Bow* (1965), pp. 223–242. By permission of the author.

W. K. WIMSATT and M. C. BEARDSLEY, "The Intentional Fallacy," from *The Verbal Icon*. Reprinted by permission of University of Kentucky Press.

RICHARD WRIGHT, "The Man Who Was Almost a Man." Reprinted by permission of The World Publishing Company from *Eight Men* by Richard Wright. Copyright © 1940, 1961 by Richard Wright.

WILLIAM BUTLER YEATS, "An Irish Airman Foresees His Death," "The Wild Swans at Coole," copyright 1919 by The Macmillan Company, renewed 1947 by Bertha Georgie Yeats; "Easter 1916," "A Prayer for My Daughter," copyright 1924 by The Macmillan Company, renewed 1952 by Bertha Georgie Yeats; "Among School Children," copyright 1928 by The Macmillan Company, renewed 1956 by Georgie Yeats; "Byzantium," "Crazy Jane Talks with the Bishop," copyright 1933 by The Macmillan Company, renewed 1961 by Bertha Georgie Yeats; "The Lake Isle of Innisfree," copyright 1906 by The Macmillan Company, renewed 1934 by William Butler Yeats; "The Magi," copyright 1916 by The Macmillan Company, renewed 1944 by Bertha Georgie Yeats; "The Second Coming," copyright 1924 by The Macmillan Company, renewed 1952 by Bertha Georgie Yeats; "Leda and the Swan," "Sailing to Byzantium," copyright 1928 by The Macmillan Company, renewed 1956 by Georgie Yeats. All poems reprinted from *Collected Poems* by William Butler Yeats with permission of The Macmillan Company.

To Carolyn and the trio

CONTENTS

Preface xxi
Writing About Literature xxiii

Stories

STEPHEN CRANE *The Open Boat* 3
D. H. LAWRENCE *The Shades of Spring* 25
JAMES JOYCE *Araby* 39
WILLIAM FAULKNER *That Evening Sun* 44
RICHARD WRIGHT *The Man Who Was Almost a Man* 59
JAMES BALDWIN *Sonny's Blues* 70
FRANZ KAFKA *The Judgment* 98
PHILIP ROTH *The Conversion of the Jews* 107
FYODOR DOSTOEVSKY *The Grand Inquisitor* 120
EUGENE IONESCO *Slime* 138
ERNEST HEMINGWAY
   Big Two-Hearted River: Part I 152
   Big Two-Hearted River: Part II 159
KATHERINE ANNE PORTER *Flowering Judas* 168
FLANNERY O'CONNOR *Good Country People* 179
MIGUEL DE UNAMUNO *Saint Emmanuel the Good, Martyr* 197
JEAN-PAUL SARTRE *The Wall* 228
JORGE LUIS BORGES *The South* 245
CARSON MCCULLERS *A Tree, A Rock, A Cloud* 251
EUDORA WELTY *A Worn Path* 258
BERNARD MALAMUD *Idiots First* 266
LEO TOLSTOY *The Death of Iván Ilých* 275
HERMAN MELVILLE *Bartleby the Scrivener* 324

Plays

HENRIK IBSEN *Ghosts* 359
AUGUST STRINDBERG *Miss Julie* 416
JOHN MILLINGTON SYNGE *Riders to the Sea* 447
TENNESSEE WILLIAMS *The Glass Menagerie* 457
LORRAINE HANSBERRY *A Raisin in the Sun* 514
EUGENE IONESCO *The Gap* 588

Poems

WILLIAM SHAKESPEARE *Sonnets*
   XVIII *Shall I compare thee to a summer's day* 597
   XXX *When to the sessions of sweet silent thought* 597

    LXXIII *That time of year thou mayst in me behold*   597
    CXVI *Let me not to the marriage of true minds*   598
JOHN DONNE
    Song   599
    The Sun Rising   599
    The Indifferent   600
    The Canonization   601
    The Flea   602
    The Ecstasy   603
    Love's Deity   605
    The Funeral   606
    Holy Sonnets   607
        V *I am a little world made cunningly*   607
        VII *At the round earth's imagined corners*   607
        X *Death, be not proud*   607
        XIV *Batter my heart, three-personed God*   608
GEORGE HERBERT
    The Pulley   609
    The Altar   610
    Easter Wings   610
HENRY VAUGHAN
    The World   611
ROBERT HERRICK
    Delight in Disorder   613
    Corinna's Going A-Maying   613
ANDREW MARVELL
    To His Coy Mistress   616
JOHN MILTON
    To the Nightingale   618
    On His Having Arrived at the Age of Twenty-three   618
    On His Blindness   619
WILLIAM BLAKE
    The Lamb   620
    The Sick Rose   620
    The Tiger   620
    Ah Sun-Flower!   621
    London   622
WILLIAM WORDSWORTH
    Tintern Abbey   623
    Composed upon Westminster Bridge, September 3, 1802   626
    It Is a Beauteous Evening, Calm and Free   627

London, 1802   627
The World Is Too Much with Us; Late and Soon   628
JOHN KEATS
   On First Looking into Chapman's Homer   629
   La Belle Dame Sans Merci   629
   Ode on Melancholy   630
   Ode on a Grecian Urn   631
   Ode to a Nightingale   633
   To Autumn   635
WALT WHITMAN
   Out of the Cradle Endlessly Rocking   637
   A March in the Ranks Hard-Prest, and the Road Unknown   642
   When Lilacs Last in the Dooryard Bloom'd   643
ALFRED, LORD TENNYSON
   Ulysses   651
   Tithonus   652
MATTHEW ARNOLD
   The Buried Life   655
   Requiescat   657
   Dover Beach   658
EMILY DICKINSON
   Success Is Counted Sweetest   659
   Safe in Their Alabaster Chambers   659
   I Like a Look of Agony   660
   Because I Could Not Stop for Death   660
   A Narrow Fellow in the Grass   661
   The Bustle in a House   661
   Immortal Is an Ample Word   662
   Apparently with No Surprise   662
A. E. HOUSMAN
   Loveliest of Trees   663
   With Rue My Heart Is Laden   663
   Terence, This Is Stupid Stuff   663
   The Chestnut Casts His Flambeaux   665
WILLIAM BUTLER YEATS
   The Lake Isle of Innisfree   667
   The Magi   667
   The Wild Swans at Coole   667
   An Irish Airman Foresees His Death   668
   Easter, 1916   669
   The Second Coming   671

    A Prayer for My Daughter   671
    Leda and the Swan   673
    Sailing to Byzantium   674
    Among School Children   675
    Byzantium   677
    Crazy Jane Talks with the Bishop   679
ROBERT FROST
    Reluctance   680
    After Apple-Picking   680
    "Out, Out—"   681
    Fire and Ice   682
    Stopping by Woods on a Snowy Evening   683
    Desert Places   683
WALLACE STEVENS
    A High-Toned Old Christian Woman   684
    Disillusionment of Ten O'Clock   684
    Sunday Morning   685
WILLIAM CARLOS WILLIAMS
    Gulls   689
    The Red Wheelbarrow   689
    The Yachts   690
    A Sort of a Song   691
    Prelude to Winter   691
    The Pause   691
MARIANNE MOORE
    The Fish   692
    In the Days of Prismatic Colour   693
    What Are Years?   694
T. S. ELIOT
    The Love Song of J. Alfred Prufrock   695
JOHN CROWE RANSOM
    Bells for John Whiteside's Daughter   699
    Blue Girls   699
    Nocturne   700
E. E. CUMMINGS
    Buffalo Bill's   701
    the Cambridge ladies   701
    the skinny voice   701
    my sweet old etcetera   702
    if there are any heavens   703
    i thank You God   704

ALLEN TATE
  Ode to the Confederate Dead   705
COUNTEE CULLEN
  Heritage   708
W. H. AUDEN
  Musée des Beaux Arts   711
THEODORE ROETHKE
  Open House   712
  To My Sister   712
  Moss-Gathering   712
  My Papa's Waltz   713
  Dolor   713
  Elegy for Jane   714
  The Waking   714
  The Dream   715
  In a Dark Time   716
  In Evening Air   717
  The Sequel   718
  The Right Thing   719
ROBERT HAYDEN
  Mourning Poem for the Queen of Sunday   720
  The Whipping   721
  Those Winter Sundays   721
  Frederick Douglass   722
  Monet's "Waterlilies"   722
  A Plague of Starlings   723
WILLIAM STAFFORD
  Traveling through the Dark   725
  The Tillamook Burn   725
  Vocation   726
  Requiem   726
  Our City Is Guarded by Automatic Rockets   727
DYLAN THOMAS
  The Force That Through the Green Fuse Drives the Flower   728
  A Refusal to Mourn the Death, by Fire, of a Child in London   728
  Fern Hill   729
  Do Not Go Gentle into That Good Night   730
  And Death Shall Have No Dominion   731
GWENDOLYN BROOKS
  kitchenette building   733
  a song in the front yard   733

    the preacher: ruminates behind the sermon   734
    Medgar Evers   734
    To a Winter Squirrel   735
ROBERT LOWELL
    The Quaker Graveyard in Nantucket   736
    The Drunken Fisherman   740
    Man and Wife   741
ROBERT BLY
    The Executive's Death   742
    Watching Television   742
    Come with Me   743
    Wanting to Experience All Things   743
SYLVIA PLATH
    Tulips   744
    Poppies in October   745
    Years   746
    Words   746
    Insomniac   747
    Mirror   748
    Whitsun   749
    Witch Burning   749
    Crossing the Water   750

Critical Essays

The Writer

THEODORE ROETHKE *Some Self-Analysis*   753
WALTER J. SLATOFF *Varieties of Involvement*   755
ROBERT B. HEILMAN *The Full Man and the Fullness Thereof*   772
EDMUND WILSON *Philoctetes: The Wound and the Bow*   779
LIONEL TRILLING *Art and Neurosis*   793
NORTHROP FRYE *The Keys to Dreamland*   809
HERBERT J. MULLER *Pessimism*   819
JEAN-PAUL SARTRE *Existentialism*   833

Critical Approaches

THEODORE SPENCER *The Central Problem in Literary Criticism*   843
W. K. WIMSATT, JR., and M. C. BEARDSLEY *The Intentional Fallacy*   849
CLEANTH BROOKS *The Heresy of Paraphrase*   862
PHILIP WHEELWRIGHT *Poetry, Myth and Reality*   878

FREDERICK C. CREWS *Literature and Psychology* 896
E. M. W. TILLYARD *The Personal Heresy, II* 907
WALTER J. ONG *The Jinnee in the Well-Wrought Urn* 918
T. S. ELIOT *Tradition and the Individual Talent* 928
GEORG LUKÁCS *The Ideology of Modernism* 935
NORMAN FOERSTER *The Esthetic Judgment and
   the Ethical Judgment* 958
RENÉ WELLEK *Periods and Movements in Literary History* 971

Specific Works

HENRY A. MURRAY *Bartleby and I* 983
FRANCIS FERGUSSON *Ghosts: The Theater of Modern Realism* 1003
C. S. LEWIS *Donne and Love Poetry in the Seventeenth Century* 1014
R. P. BLACKMUR *The Later Poetry of W. B. Yeats* 1032
BABETTE DEUTSCH and STANLEY KUNITZ *A Symposium on Roethke's
   "In a Dark Time"* 1053

Biographical Notes 1065
Index 1089

PREFACE

This second edition of *Quartet* contains abundant fiction, drama, poetry, and criticism for full introductory courses in literature and the humanities, or for a one-quarter or one-semester literary study as part of freshman English programs. The imaginative literature respresents the three main genres, includes a wide range of style and theme, and originates from many different nationalities and ethnic groups. The criticism represents some of this century's finest and most influential critical writing.

Although the fiction loosely follows a thematic sequence from youth to age, all the stories invite readers to explore many levels of experience. The six modern plays open internal worlds of mind and culture. The poems range from Elizabethan to contemporary times, with emphasis favoring poetry of the last hundred years. To encourage concentrated study, four poets—John Donne, William Butler Yeats, Theodore Roethke, and Sylvia Plath—are represented in depth. The critical essays concern the writer—his creative process and relation to the world, critical approaches to literature, and specific literary works found elsewhere in the book.

What continues to distinguish *Quartet* is the unquestioned quality of its literature and criticism. Each story, play, or poem can be studied for its own artistic merits; each critical essay is valuable for its insights. Except in the poetry section, no effort has been made to fit selections into chronological order; and, as for the poetry, I have chosen each poem for its intrinsic worth rather than for its niche in literary history. Choices throughout the book challenge today's student to probe his own experiences. Hopefully, his feelings and attitudes will find expression through these literary works, and his critical insights will be sharpened through his careful reading of major critics.

One additional feature requires comment. Knowing that students who read literature also write about it, I have prepared an introductory essay on the subject, "Writing About Literature." The essay contains a discussion of certain assumptions supporting critical writing; suggests ways students might outline a critical analysis; points out how they might handle such literary problems as plot, setting, point of view, characterization, symbolism, and tone—each relevant to one or more genres; offers modest advice about a student's own writing style; and discusses the experience of literature, or what might be called writing *through* literature.

For assistance in preparing and revising this book I am indebted to my wife, Carolyn, and to Miss Janet Grimes, who kept a good many details straight. To Les Elliott I owe more gratitude than I can ever express. And somewhere in my consciousness I feel indebted to my three children who, in their separate ways, daily confirm the real world.

H. P. S.

WRITING ABOUT LITERATURE

To the Student

Preliminary thoughts

No one denies that the literary artist needs imagination, but we may forget that the reader and the critic need it too. This point must be explicit at the beginning, for the world of literature is ultimately a world only imagination can reach. The essence of art is fiction, not as genre but as vision, in the sense that art is untrue to life; it is neither life itself nor an exact imitation of it. Insofar as imagination is alive in us, we accept this fictional world. We accept it because our imagination encompasses horizons far wider than what is validated by science, logic, and reason. In short, we accept literature because we accept imagination.

In saying this we acknowledge the existence of the artist as creator, as one who brings to life a new synthesis of experience through his thoughts and feelings. Call this synthesis a poem, call it a sonata; we find in it a strange power which quickens our own creative responses, so that in reading the poem or in listening to the sonata we recreate the artist's original experience. In broader terms, we share the experience with all men. Self-realization that comes to us through literature is a losing of self into the larger human element. From this paradoxical experience we gain both pleasure and truth.

But at its fullest, neither pleasure nor truth can come without understanding. It is at this point that the critic's work comes in. Through understanding he accounts for what literature yields. The same process describes your own work as a writer. By analyzing literature, by writing about it, your pleasure is enlarged and the truth to be found is deepened. There should be no mistake about the usefulness of literary analysis—or of what I have called understanding. From it comes all the richness of literary experience. Without it you will have only superficial titillation and only a penny's worth of truth.

Certain assumptions bear closely upon your analysis of literature. In the first place, because literature is imaginative you can neither judge its worth nor validate its meaning by testing its factual details. Whether Keats heard a real nightingale; whether in his sonnet "On First Looking into Chapman's Homer" he mistook Cortez for Balboa; whether Georg in Kafka's "The Judgment" literally drowned; whether Borges links his fantasies to facts doesn't really matter—literal details such as these do not make the stuff of literature. Verisimilitude, yes. Enough credibility that we may willingly suspend our disbelief, yes. But certainly it is not overstating the case to say that imaginative literature calls for an imaginative reader, one who comes to Keats and Kafka and Borges with something more than demands for petty certainties. To read literature, to write about it, demands that one open himself to a world of experience extending beyond literal facts.

Secondly, literature treats private experience. Notwithstanding T. S. Eliot's claim in "Tradition and the Individual Talent" that literature calls for the artist's self-surrender, and for his private voice to be subsumed into a larger literary tradition, we can still insist on the individuality of the author and in his vast subjective world of feeling. More importantly, we can say that literature points to this vast world within each of us. You are aware of this world within yourself, and sometimes you catch glimpses of it in others. Literature intensifies this awareness. Therefore, analysis of literature must take into account this experience, private though it is. This does not mean that you investigate Ibsen's private feelings when you write about *Ghosts*, fruitful though such investigation might be. But it does mean that you pay attention to those feelings of Mrs. Alving, Oswald, and the other characters. It means that you attend to those private feelings of your own. The quality of literature is not judged by the reader's gooseflesh; nevertheless, to shy away from the affective experience is to make literary analysis only a chilly business indeed.

Thirdly, literature is public. It stands alone, separate from the artist who created it and, to a degree, separate from those who respond to it. It is autotelic; it exists by and for itself. Critics have referred to this quality as organic. Accordingly, a poem consists of its interrelated parts, and in this interrelationship it can be said to exist. Writing about literature requires that one identify the parts and explain how they work together. We know that a poem is not merely its rhyme, images, meter, and metaphors; it does contain these parts, but they are the "whatness" of a poem. They function in harmony, and the way this harmony is achieved—the "howness" of the poem—must be considered.

In this kind of analysis you need not mention the poet, his cultural background, or anything "outside" the work itself. Instead, you will analyze such elements as structure, imagery, meter, theme, characterizations, symbols, and their inter-workings. In short, when a work of art synthesizes experience, the work itself is also a synthesis of its own artistic elements.

A fourth assumption is that in writing about literature you hopefully will pass beyond understanding to an appreciation of it. The two words are important, though subtle in their distinction. To understand a literary work is to know its contents and meaning; to appreciate it is to place a value on it, to judge it. Understanding precedes but does not preclude appreciation. Furthermore, whereas understanding necessarily relates to critical judgment, appreciation takes you to the heart of it. Mere taste is never reliable. Somehow, as a literary work engages us, its value has something to do with our involvement. Reading a poem or play becomes an event. The strategy behind your analysis must take into account this event and its value to you. To speculate about a poem's value totally apart from yourself, to use only objective criteria in your judgment, is dull fare. The point is that the judgment you make about the poem is a commitment based upon the experience of pleasure and truth you had in understanding the poem.

Outline for a literary analysis

Your analysis may follow the simple outline of *meaning, structure,* and *style.* You will decide what priority of importance goes to each.

1. To get at the *meaning* or theme of a poem, story, or play, you must look closely at the details. It requires knowing thoroughly the plot or situation. The fact that the strongest man, the oiler, is the one who drowns might seem insignificant in Stephen Crane's story, for Crane apparently gives little importance to the fact. But, of course, such a detail is crucial to the story's meaning. The details of a character's talk, his dress, his gestures, even his name can all be meaningful. Develop the practice of close reading. Be alert to every detail. Only in this way can you recognize what finally is the total meaning of the work. What is called for here is the highest kind of literacy. You must go beyond the literal in order to see how literal details shape the dominant idea. One can assume that every poem, story, or play has a dominant theme, idea, or feeling, rarely explicit but nevertheless present. It is this central configuration of meaning, this figure in the carpet, which the various parts of a work serve.

Perhaps the theme of life's mutability strikes you as dominant in a Shakespearean sonnet; perhaps in Dostoevsky's "The Grand Inquisitor" the central idea concerns the nature of unconditional faith. As abstract truth or meaning, these topics are worth close analysis. You will consider what characters say and do, how they represent opposing ways of looking at life; or, in the case of a short lyric, how its imagery conveys feeling and suggests some intellectual posture, some abstract meaning, inseparable from the work itself, yet subject to discussion and analysis.

2. The meaning of a literary work cannot be divorced from details; neither can details be separated from *structure*. Every literary work has a pattern or structure in which details relate to each other. Actions have causes and consequences. Images evoke tone. Characters come into conflict with themselves and their world. Nothing is static. Writing about literature involves these various patterns—their development, their changes, and finally their overall structure. Granted this demands a lot of work for the critical writer. Patterns can be intricate and subtle, as in a poem by Eliot or a story by William Faulkner. The surface simplicities in Tennessee Williams' *The Glass Menagerie* or William Blake's little poem "The Sick Rose" may hide patterns of profound psychological and artistic consequence. Yet these are the patterns which combine into a unified structure.

Reading a work once over lightly is hardly sufficient for one who seriously analyzes its structure. Only by returning again and again to the work will its details take shape. One remembers, for example, how Melville in *Moby Dick* (chapter 3) described the large oil painting hanging in the Spouter-Inn. He said that its patterns were "so thoroughly besmoked, and every way defaced, that in the unequal cross-lights by which you viewed it, *it was only by diligent study and a series of systematic visits to it*, and careful inquiry of the neighbors, that you could any way arrive at an understanding of its purpose" [my italics]. This is good advice for anyone seeking to discover the structure of a work of art.

3. Literary analysis must consider *style*, again inseparable from structure and meaning. Any skillful artist knows that the "how" affects the "what," that manner affects the matter. Similarly, any skillful critic takes careful note of this relationship in what he reads. As you write literary analysis, notice the author's language. You do not need a large storehouse of terms to discuss his imagery, metaphors, concreteness, irony, sentence patterns, alliteration. Even a fragment of Keats's "Ode on Melancholy" provides ample room for stylistic analysis:

> Veiled Melancholy has her sovran shrine,
>   Though seen of none save him whose strenuous tongue
> Can burst Joy's grape against his palate fine. . . .

Or consider the stylistic qualities in a passage from Joyce's "Araby":

> The space of sky above us was the color
>   of ever-changing violet and towards it the lamps

of the street lifted their feeble lanterns.
The cold air stung us and
we played till our bodies glowed.

Literary analysis calls for the most careful discrimination of meaning, structure, and style, and for an awareness of their interlocking effect. A careful reader discovers what makes the story, play, or poem "work." Your job as one writing about literature is to describe this organic action. But the job is not finished until you consider how the literary piece has worked on you. Your imagination—the living agent in perception—synthesizes the many details and opens you to a literary experience to which you give assent. Underlying all these matters is the assumption that reading literature, and writing about it, is an event in which you have your own important part to play.

Special literary techniques

Unlike other kinds of writing, the task of writing about literature requires one to know special techniques or devices which the artist uses. Each of these can be considered under one or more of the categories mentioned above (meaning, structure, style), and each may be relevant to one or more literary genres (fiction, drama, poetry).

One such device is *plot*. A story, play, or narrative poem has an ordered action based on the author's assumption of causality. Although the incidents may seem to have no logical cause, as in a typical Kafka story, they are not random. They must show artistic causality. That is, separate actions relate to the larger action we call plot. Each of Laura's actions in "Flowering Judas"—each man she encounters, even each thought or dream she has—contributes to the overall, artistically ordered web of action.

The problem in writing about plot is to answer the question, "What happened?" How do incidents contribute to the total sequence of action? Remember, however, that action need not be physical. In Hemingway's "Big Two-Hearted River" the important action may be far more psychological than physical. Of course Nick Adams goes fishing, and in this singular action there may be substantial business for analysis. But Nick's emotional tension, his fear of thinking, his compulsiveness in arranging everything in order—these qualities of Nick's mind may be said to determine what he does.

Like experience itself, plot is rarely simple. To render this complexity the artist uses *conflict*. The oarsmen in Crane's story vie with the sea; Mrs. Alving in Ibsen's play struggles with the ghosts of the past; Unamuno's Don Emmanuel finds himself to be a double, each half fighting to be its honest self. A protagonist confronts his antagonist whether it be nature, the past, his alter-ego, or another person, and this opposition intensifies the plot. Sometimes conflict is artistically achieved through a *double plot* as in "'That Evening Sun" where the Compson children's world overlays Nancy's. Still another technique of plot—one that is used in Tolstoy's "The Death of Iván Ilých"—is the *flashback*, the author's way of interjecting events or scenes of the past to highlight the present. In all these matters *proportion* is of utmost importance. You need to pay attention to how and why the beginning, middle, and end serve the artistic purpose of the whole, how and why events lead to a climax and then to a resolution. This means observing, for example, why Tolstoy opens his story with Iván Ilých's funeral, covered in one narrative section, spends two sections on his life, and then devotes the remaining seven sections to Ilých's dying; or why Eudora Welty spends many paragraphs to describe the land.

Another element in imaginative literature is *setting*. Where an action takes place may be as important as the action itself. It is for good reason that Bartleby the Scrivener transcribes lifeless documents in an office bounded by a white wall and a dark wall; that he is further constricted by an airshaft and screen; and, like the undelivered letters in the Dead Letter office, that he finally ends in the Tombs. The *atmosphere* of place adds an important dimension to the action. The melancholy fisher-folk in Synge's *Riders to the Sea* take on, as it were, the mood of the sea, which is both their sustenance and their doom. In projecting the emotions of the characters, setting establishes an emotional aura for the readers who are thereby drawn into the world of wonder created by the artist. No single detail should be overlooked for its connotative possibilities. What is the season of the year, the time of day, the color of dress, the weather, the landscape, the furniture in a room? All these details, full of connotation, require close attention for what they contribute to setting.

Whatever private feelings an author has, his poem or story may only remotely relate to them. To protect these feelings or, more likely, to detach himself from them, he establishes a *point of view* other than his own. He creates a character on whose consciousness experience is recorded and through whose eyes the world is seen. Such a character may be in fact a mask for the author; the important point, however, is that the character exists in his own right, and his consciousness is independent. This *first person* point of view means that, in the case of Sartre's "The Wall," the central experience is Pablo's; it is *his* consciousness which we enter, no one else's. The same can be said about Sonny's brother in Baldwin's story, Quentin in Faulkner's, and Eliot's J. Alfred Prufrock ("Let us go then, you and I"). In each case, the "I" is a *persona*, a created character detached from his creator who, as James Joyce once said, sits back and pares his fingernails. Even in lyric poetry, supposedly the most personal form of literary expression, the point of view can only safely be said to be that of the "poet" or the "narrator," not that of Robert Burns the man.

The author may choose to establish a *third person limited* point of view: again, a single character whose consciousness provides our means of knowing the world depicted in the work. Instead of the "I" we have the third person "he" or "she," and again our information is restricted to what this single character sees, feels, and thinks. Eudora Welty's "A Worn Path" is an example. If the author wishes to be all-knowing and unrestricted, he establishes a *third person omniscient* point of view. As in drama, he creates multi-consciousness and, even though "omniscient," he fractures reality according to the number of independent perspectives.

Writing about point of view requires that you differentiate the author from his persona or his characters. The world you find presented in the work takes its quality from the consciousness through which this imagined world is seen. To see it fully is to see it from the proper point of view and, in this way, to catch its irony, peace, doom, or whatever reality a certain perspective reveals.

Point of view leads us to *characterization*. A character's consciousness (and unconsciousness) determines the way he confronts reality. Studying point of view is therefore the first step in analyzing characterization. You must attend to what the character thinks and feels, to what he says, and to how he acts. You need to discover what his conflicts are, what choices he faces and does or does not make. You must see him as one to whom things happen or as one who initiates action. All the complexities of personality combine in artistic characterization—all the hidden passions, fears, hopes, as well as all the overt actions. It was Sigmund Freud who argued that all behavior is symptomatic—a slip of the tongue, a lapse of memory, mislaying an object, doodling, and fiddling. Countless trivialities betray some deeper condition. The stories by D. H. Lawrence, Porter, Baldwin, and Joyce are full of such seemingly insignificant details which, in actuality, reveal characters' hidden qualities. These are the complexities you must deal with as you write about characters. Finally, of course, you must judge whether or not the character "lives," whether or not in his particularity he has something of the universal about him. Is he both an individual person and a human being? Are his emotions also ours?

To ask this question leads to the subject of *symbolism* and the problem of abstract meaning conveyed through the concrete object or the individual character. The problem is one of analogy, handled on various levels by metaphor, symbol, and myth. A *metaphor* suggests a likeness between two unlike objects or situations. To say, for example, that disorder in dress "Kindles in clothes a wantonness" (Robert Herrick) is to make analogous disorder and fire ("Kindles"), all the concrete connotations of fire vivifying the abstraction of disorder. A *symbol* is an outward sign, action, or situation embodying some analogous abstraction or signifying another object. For example, in Whitman's "When Lilacs Last in the Dooryard Bloom'd," the lilac symbolizes spring and new birth, the drooping star in the west symbolizes Abraham Lincoln's death and death itself, and the solitary bird symbolizes Whitman and all poets whose song embraces both birth and death. *Myth* externalizes into narrative form some natural or psychological phenomenon, some social, cultural, or religious belief. The abstraction is embodied in a fanciful story, one accounting for our origins and destinies, our age-old experiences of creation, the fall, the lost paradise, the millennial hope. Hemingway, for example, recreates the ancient rites of initiation in "Big Two-Hearted River," a story which can be analyzed mythically.

Upon whatever level of symbolic language we interpret literature, the problem is essentially the same. We are faced with the fact of analogical language; the visible stands for the invisible, the concrete represents the universal, the specific embodies the abstract. The danger is in leaping too quickly to the "meaning-level," in not giving the literal reality a chance to be just that. The young man who goes fishing in "Big Two-Hearted River," one critic says, is not Everyman but Nick Adams, and the river in which he fishes is not the Nile or Ganges but a stream in Upper Michigan. This is fair warning to readers who too quickly become "symbol hunters." The fact remains, however, that fishing may symbolize a quest, as it has from time immemorial, and that the lamb and the tiger in Blake's poems may symbolically point to a dimension of reality entirely trans-literal.

Speculating about symbolic meaning is one of the real pleasures in literary analysis. The ocean in Whitman's "Out of the Cradle Endlessly Rocking," the glass menagerie in Williams' play, the high rooftop in Philip Roth's story are all potential symbols. After reading such critics as Northrop Frye and Philip Wheelwright, you will discover the possibilities inherent in this kind of analysis.

Another major element in literature is *tone*. When we say that the tone of a work is melancholic, joyous, bitter, sad, intimate, we are identifying the author's feeling or attitude toward his subject. To miss the tone is to miss not only an important feature of literary writing but the distinction between this kind of writing and the scientific report or the telephone book. The latter is toneless, feelings do not intrude; whereas literary language expresses countless nuances of feeling.

Your task is to determine what these nuances are and how they are expressed. Is there a pattern of *imagery*, for example, which suggests a certain tone in Strindberg's *Miss Julie*? What feelings are generated in Faulkner's images of darkness—after the evening sun goes down? How does *irony* throughout the stories of Crane and Sartre, or in A. E. Housman's "Terence, This Is Stupid Stuff," convey the author's tone of bitter resignation? What is ironic about the rhyming juxtaposition in Eliot's question:

Should I, after tea and cakes and ices,
Have the strength to force the moment to its crisis?

How does *paradox* suggest divine ineffableness in Donne's sonnet, "Batter my heart, three-personed God"? What tonal coloring does E. E. Cummings' bizarre *versification* bring to his poetry? Important as these technical terms are by themselves, their greater importance is their contribution to tone. These devices serve the writer who, rather than using expository prose to explain his feelings, evokes these feelings so that the reader may experience them also. To connote allows for greater range of expression than to denote. Your responsibility, to repeat, is to understand what the tone of a work is, how this tone carries meaning, and why, in turn, this meaning justifies the tonal color.

Your own expository style

How ironic it is to analyze the literary style of Richard Wright or Wallace Stevens if we neglect stylistic matters in our own writing! Yet through some kind of absent-mindedness or sublime disregard, we often commit this very negligence. Must literary analysis be devoid of tone? Is there no place for the paradoxical, the figurative, the analogical? What I suggest is that you bring the same criteria to bear upon your expository writing that you bring to so-called creative literature. For in a sense the one kind of writing need be no less creative than the other. In both instances the writer can make something new out of his experience. In your case the experience is that of reading a poem, play, or story. What you make of it can be as original, as unique, as infused with tone as the "creative" poem or whatever. Anything less must be mere communication, and even a weather report or train schedule accomplishes this. A few words, then, about your own tone may be helpful.

Certainly no job is more delicate than to establish a tone which reflects your feelings toward both your subject and your reader. You may wish your critical essay to be formal, casual, even slightly playful as Henry A. Murray's essay on "Bartleby the Scrivener." For this effect you must rely only upon words—no smiles, shouts, gestures, or whispers. Clearly, language can never be fully adequate to the task demanded of it, for neither in its grammar nor in its connotation can it contain a person's total expression. Still, you do have the word. Choosing it is your supreme test as a writer. It is also your supreme risk. You cannot always predict what the effect of words will be. You cannot even count upon their sufficiency. All of us know the anxiety of J. Alfred Prufrock who experiences the frustration inherent in one's use of language ("It is impossible to say just what I mean!"). Words are elusive. Yet they do convey thought and feeling, and some general statements can apply to their use.

First of all, you need to remember that using words effectively is not strictly a matter of building a vocabulary. Good writing does not depend upon mastery of such words as *obtund, exuviate, culm, idoneous, vatic*. Much nonsense has been published about the importance of "big" words, as if one's vocabulary becomes stronger in ratio to the number of words one can define. Up to a point the equation is true. Any writer needs a vocabulary, the larger the better. But a large vocabulary does not explain good writing. More important than the number of words a person knows is the imaginative use he makes of the everyday words already at his command. Shakespeare's description of trees in winter—"Bare ruin'd choirs, where late the sweet birds sang"—does not depend upon big words whose definitions only the learned person knows.

Enormous power lies in what words suggest apart from their explicit meanings. Herein is the main distinction between the language of art and that of science. Words for the artist are many-valued, connotative; words for the scientist are one-valued, denotative. In the one case, words send out endless ripples of meaning, finding their way into the emotional recesses of the mind. In the other, words devoid of overtones strike but once, as lead balls upon pavement. Every accomplished writer knows this distinction; he knows too that tone comes not from definitions in a dictionary but from the imagination working upon them. Your own writing is expository, critical, not poetic. Nevertheless, the best writers, poets or otherwise, utilize the range of language, including its connotative possibilities.

Yet the common word must also be the exact word. You will find the dictionary invaluable to save you from confusing the denotative meanings of words. There are important differences between such words as *habits* and *mores*, *effect* and *affect*, *imply* and *infer*. A dictionary will help you understand these differences, as well as the shades of difference among words having the same general meaning. Precision is always necessary. Nothing justifies the use of inaccurate words.

Finally, the common word must be the lean word, fat-free, and vigorous. When agglutinations appear they must be sliced away. There can be little room for either tone or meaning when, for example, *usually* swells to *in the majority of cases*; when *therefore* expands to *in view of the foregoing circumstances*. Imagine how Yeats's line—"An aged man is but a paltry thing"—would strike the reader if it were, instead, "The condition of a senior citizen is likely to be one of enfeeblement."

Using vigorous words is a matter of confidence. The bold writer gets to the point, and he does so knowing that language is his servant, not his master. He is not so uncertain about his own voice that he hides it behind language or allows clichés and gummy phrases to rule his style. He is not dependent upon flamboyant expressions, slang, euphemisms, and smart critical patios to command attention. In short, he knows that the best writers use common words to say uncommon things, and that their highest expression obtains when a lucid style reveals a sensitive consciousness.

This kind of writing is also a matter of honesty. Reading the following words of Theodore Roethke, who was a college undergraduate when he wrote "Some Self-Analysis," might be a profitable experience:

> I have long wondered just what my strength was as a writer. I am often filled with tremendous enthusiasm for a subject, yet my writing about it will seem a sorry attempt. Above all, I possess a driving sincerity,—that prime

virtue of any creative worker. I write only what I believe to be the absolute truth,—even if I must ruin the theme in so doing. In this respect I feel far superior to those glib people in my classes who often garner better grades than I do. They are so often pitiful frauds,—artificial—insincere. They have a line that works. They do not write from the depths of their hearts. Nothing of theirs was ever born of pain. Many an incoherent yet sincere piece of writing has outlived the polished product.

Writing through literature

Roethke's words just quoted deserve re-reading. They suggest the distinction to be made between writing about and writing through literature. I do not mean that the two activities are mutually exclusive but rather that the former when bereft of the latter may result in barren stuff indeed. What then is the distinction? Writing about literature is primarily an analytical exercise. You stand here, the poem stands there, and from this distance you observe and then describe how it works. Nothing is wrong with this kind of writing; at its best it can be intelligent and penetrating. But I would like to think that literature has a certain affective power. When, for example, we get close to it, when we allow ourselves to be affected by it, we discover that it lives in us, is assimilated into us, and that we are changed. Writing through literature means that we do not stop at a safe distance, as if the poem were a bulwark, something then to besiege with critical artillery; but rather that we join with the poem and experience what its language has already shaped. Writing through literature becomes a uniquely creative act because, like the poet, we shape with words what we have discovered with feelings. Through literature we identify our feelings, we find our voice. In short, writing through literature means that in touching the living pulse of literature you experience the agony or the ecstasy inherent in the work and that you write from imaginatively having been through that experience.

The assumption underlying this notion is that literature is essentially personality. I know that T. S. Eliot says it is the "extinction of personality," and that W. K. Wimsatt, Jr. and M. C. Beardsley, insisting that a poem is "detached from the author at birth," warn against the danger of confusing poetic study with biographical study. Then, of course, there is the myth critic who, like Northop Frye, thinks of literature in the context of its Classical and Christian heritage; or the sociological critic, like Georg Lukács, who insists that the writer is primarily a political voice. All these theories, compelling as they are, may fall short of explaining a fundamental premise about words. E. M. W. Tillyard comes close when, in debating C. S. Lewis on the subject of "The Personal Heresy," he makes the telling point that style "suggests the mental pattern of the author, the personality realized in words." There is, says Walter Ong, a "jinnee," a personality, in any well wrought work of art.

What does all this mean to the student reading literature and, hopefully, writing through it? It means, first, that you will penetrate the literary form to find the human feeling and then discover the marriage of the two; and, second, it means that you will appropriate literature to set your own feelings astir and to quicken your own susceptibility to the experiences heightened in the literary expression. More specifically, it means that when you read Yeats's line—"An aged man is but a paltry thing"—you will catch the throb of human feeling in these words and let them kindle responses from which your own words can grow. Whether through a novel, a poem, or a single image, the student who perceives the human element and then writes out of the synthesis that his own thoughts and feelings create, is truly doing something more than standing off and writing about literature. Instead, he is transforming the literary moment into an event, and it is through this event that he writes. In the beginning is his word, but it is a word firmly rooted in personality.

I do not advocate that the "through" take precedence over the "about." You can profitably study and write about the mechanics of literary art, certainly a prerequisite for critical judgments. I only offer another emphasis if not option. Like the artist, you also have windmills to attack and dark journeys to undertake, yes even fathers to slay and whales to hunt. Literary themes are human ones as well. One thinks of the distinction made by Martin Luther, and later by Kierkegaard, between the student of religion and the religious student, or between the person who studies philosophy and the person who philosophizes. From the first is asked commitment of mind; from the second, commitment of mind and heart. As for the critic and the artist, I think we need not settle upon the first as the only model. Write analyses but also write literature. To your surprise you have both the head and the heart for it. If literature has something to do with personality realized in words, then your weekly essay about literature may indeed show that you have also written through literature, and the essay may be no less significant than a precious lyric poem. What you write may cost some pain, as Roethke reminds us, but at least it will not be glib. It may in fact reveal nothing less than your own heart.

QUARTET
A Book of Stories, Plays, Poems, and Critical Essays

STORIES

Stephen Crane
D. H. Lawrence
James Joyce
William Faulkner
Richard Wright
James Baldwin
Franz Kafka
Philip Roth
Fyodor Dostoevsky
Eugene Ionesco
Ernest Hemingway
Katherine Anne Porter
Flannery O'Connor
Miguel de Unamuno
Jean-Paul Sartre
Jorge Luis Borges
Carson McCullers
Eudora Welty
Bernard Malamud
Leo Tolstoy
Herman Melville

The Open Boat

A Tale intended to be after the Fact: Being the Experience of Four Men from the Sunk Steamer Commodore

I

None of them knew the colour of the sky. Their eyes glanced level, and were fastened upon the waves that swept toward them. These waves were of the hue of slate, save for the tops, which were of foaming white, and all of the men knew the colours of the sea. The horizon narrowed and widened, and dipped and rose, and at all times its edge was jagged with waves that seemed thrust up in points like rocks.

Many a man ought to have a bathtub larger than the boat which here rode upon the sea. These waves were most wrongfully and barbarously abrupt and tall, and each froth-top was a problem in small-boat navigation.

The cook squatted in the bottom, and looked with both eyes at the six inches of gunwale which separated him from the ocean. His sleeves were rolled over his fat forearms, and the two flaps of his unbuttoned vest dangled as he bent to bail out the boat. Often he said, "Gawd! that was a narrow clip." As he remarked it he invariably gazed eastward over the broken sea.

The oiler, steering with one of the two oars in the boat, sometimes raised himself suddenly to keep clear of the water that swirled in over the stern. It was a thin little oar, and it seemed often ready to snap.

The correspondent, pulling at the other oar, watched the waves and wondered why he was there.

The injured captain, lying in the bow, was at this time buried in that profound dejection and indifference which come, temporarily at least, to even the bravest and most enduring when, willy-nilly, the firm fails, the army loses, the ship goes down. The mind of the master of a vessel is rooted deep in the timbers of her, though he command for a day or a decade; and this captain had on him the stern impression of a scene in the greys of dawn of seven turned faces, and later a stump of a topmast with a white ball on it, that slashed to and fro at the waves, went low and lower, and down. Thereafter there was something strange in his voice. Although steady, it was deep with mourning, and of a quality beyond oration or tears.

"Keep 'er a little more south, Billie," said he.

"A little more south, sir," said the oiler in the stern.

A seat in this boat was not unlike a seat upon a bucking broncho, and by the same token a broncho is not much smaller. The craft pranced and reared and plunged like an animal. As each wave came, and she rose for it, she seemed like a horse making at a fence outrageously high. The manner of her scramble over these walls of water is a mystic thing, and, moreover, at the top of them were ordinarily these problems in white water, the foam racing down from the summit of each wave requiring a new leap, and a leap from the air. Then, after scornfully bumping a crest, she would slide and race and splash down a long incline, and arrive bobbing and nodding in front of the next menace.

A singular disadvantage of the sea lies in the fact that after successfully surmounting one wave you discover that there is another behind it just as important and just as nervously anxious to do something effective in the way of swamping boats. In a ten-foot dinghy one can get an idea of the resources of the sea in the line of waves that is not probable to the average experience which is never at sea in a dinghy. As each slaty wall of water approached, it shut all else from the view of the men in the boat, and it was not difficult to imagine that this particular wave was the final outburst of the ocean, the last effort of the grim water. There was a terrible grace in the move of the waves, and they came in silence, save for the snarling of the crests.

In the wan light the faces of the men must have been grey. Their eyes must have glinted in strange ways as they gazed steadily astern. Viewed from a balcony, the whole thing would doubtless have been weirdly picturesque. But the men in the boat had no time to see it, and if they had had leisure, there were other things to occupy their minds. The sun swung steadily up the sky, and they knew it was broad day because the colour of the sea changed from slate to emerald green streaked with amber lights, and the foam was like tumbling snow. The process of the breaking day was unknown to them. They were aware only of this effect upon the colour of the waves that rolled toward them.

In disjointed sentences the cook and the correspondent argued as to the difference between a life-saving station and a house of refuge. The cook had said: "There's a house of refuge just north of the Mosquito Inlet Light, and as soon as they see us they'll come off in their boat and pick us up."

"As soon as who see us?" said the correspondent.

"The crew," said the cook.

"Houses of refuge don't have crews," said the correspondent. "As I understand them, they are only places where clothes and grub are stored for the benefit of shipwrecked people. They don't carry crews."

"Oh, yes, they do," said the cook.

"No, they don't," said the correspondent.

"Well, we're not there yet, anyhow," said the oiler, in the stern.

"Well," said the cook, "perhaps it's not a house of refuge that I'm thinking of as being near Mosquito Inlet Light; perhaps it's a lifesaving station."

"We're not there yet," said the oiler in the stern.

II

As the boat bounced from the top of each wave the wind tore through the hair of the hatless men, and as the craft plopped her stern down again the spray slashed past them. The crest of each of these waves was a hill, from the top of which the men surveyed for a moment a broad tumultuous expanse, shining and wind-riven. It was probably splendid, it was probably glorious, this play of the free sea, wild with lights of emerald and white and amber.

"Bully good thing it's an on-shore wind," said the cook. "If not, where would we be? Wouldn't have a show."

"That's right," said the correspondent.

The busy oiler nodded his assent.

Then the captain, in the bow, chuckled in a way that expressed humour, contempt, tragedy, all in one. "Do you think we've got much of a show now, boys?" said he.

Whereupon the three were silent, save for a trifle of hemming and hawing. To express any particular optimism at this time they felt to be childish and stupid, but they all doubtless possessed this sense of the situation in their minds. A young man thinks doggedly at such times. On the other hand, the ethics of their condition was decidedly against any open suggestion of hopelessness. So they were silent.

"Oh, well," said the captain, soothing his children, "we'll get ashore all right."

But there was that in his tone which made them think; so the oiler quoth, "Yes! if this wind holds."

The cook was bailing. "Yes! if we don't catch hell in the surf."

Canton-flannel gulls flew near and far. Sometimes they sat down on the sea, near patches of brown seaweed that rolled over the waves with a movement like carpets on a line in a gale. The birds sat comfortably in groups, and they were envied by some in the dinghy, for the wrath of the sea was no more to them than it was to a covey of prairie chickens a thousand miles inland. Often they came very close and stared at the men with black bead-like eyes. At these times they were uncanny and sinister in their unblinking scrutiny, and the men hooted angrily at them, telling them to be gone. One came, and evidently decided to alight on the top of the captain's head. The bird flew parallel to the boat and did not circle, but made short sidelong jumps in the air in chicken-fashion. His black eyes were wistfully fixed upon the captain's head. "Ugly brute," said the oiler to the bird. "You look as if you were made with a jackknife." The cook and the correspondent swore darkly at the creature. The captain naturally wished to knock it away with the end of the heavy painter, but he did not dare do it, because anything resembling an emphatic gesture would have capsized this freighted boat; and so, with his open hand, the captain gently and carefully waved the gull away. After it had been discouraged from the pursuit the captain breathed easier on account of his hair, and others breathed easier because the bird struck their minds at this time as being somehow gruesome and ominous.

In the meantime the oiler and the correspondent rowed. And also they rowed. They sat together in the same seat, and each rowed an oar. Then the oiler took both oars; then the correspondent took both oars; then the oiler; then the correspondent. They rowed and they rowed. The very ticklish part of the business was when the time came for the reclining one in the stern to take his turn at the oars. By the very last star of truth, it is easier to steal eggs from under a hen than it was to change seats in the dinghy. First the man in the stern slid his hand along the thwart and moved with care, as if he were of Sèvres. Then the man in the rowing-seat slid his hand along the other thwart. It was all done with the most extraordinary care. As the two sidled past each other, the whole party kept watchful eyes on the coming wave, and the captain cried: "Look out, now! Steady, there!"

The brown mats of seaweed that appeared from time to time were like islands, bits of earth. They were traveling, apparently, neither one way nor the other. They were, to all intents, stationary. They informed the men in the boat that it was making progress slowly toward the land.

The captain, rearing cautiously in the bow after the dinghy soared on a great swell, said that he had seen the lighthouse at Mosquito Inlet. Presently the cook remarked that he had seen it. The correspondent was at the oars then, and for some reason he too wished to look at the lighthouse; but his back was toward the far shore, and the waves were important, and for some time he could not seize an opportunity to turn his head. But at last there came a wave more gentle than the others, and when at the crest of it he swiftly scoured the western horizon.

"See it?" said the captain.

"No," said the correspondent, slowly; "I didn't see anything."

"Look again," said the captain. He pointed. "It's exactly in that direction."

At the top of another wave the correspondent did as he was bid, and this time his eyes chanced on a small, still thing on the edge of the swaying horizon. It was precisely like the point of a pin. It took an anxious eye to find a lighthouse so tiny.

"Think we'll make it, Captain?"

"If this wind holds and the boat don't swamp, we can't do much else," said the captain.

The little boat, lifted by each towering sea and splashed viciously by the crests, made progress that in the absence of seaweed was not apparent to those in her. She seemed just a wee thing wallowing, miraculously top up, at the mercy of five oceans. Occasionally a great spread of water, like white flames, swarmed into her.

"Bail her, cook," said the captain, serenely.

"All right, Captain," said the cheerful cook.

III

It would be difficult to describe the subtle brotherhood of men that was here established on the seas. No one said that it was so. No one mentioned it. But it dwelt in the boat, and each man felt it warm him. They were a captain, an oiler, a cook, and a correspondent, and they were friends—friends in a more curiously iron-bound degree than may be common. The hurt captain, lying against the water-jar in the bow, spoke always in a low voice and calmly; but he could never command a more ready and swiftly obedient crew than the motley three of the dinghy. It was more than a mere recognition of what was best for the common safety. There was surely in it a quality that was personal and heart-felt. And after this devotion to the commander of the boat, there was this comradeship, that the correspondent, for instance, who had been taught to be cynical of men, knew even at the time was the best experience of his life. But no one said that it was so. No one mentioned it.

"I wish we had a sail," remarked the captain. "We might try my overcoat on the end of an oar, and give you two boys a chance to rest." So the cook and the correspondent held the mast and spread wide the overcoat; the oiler steered; and the little boat made good way with her new rig. Sometimes the oiler had to scull sharply to keep a sea from breaking into the boat, but otherwise sailing was a success.

Meanwhile the lighthouse had been growing slowly larger. It had now almost assumed colour, and appeared like a little grey shadow on the sky. The man at the oars could not be prevented from turning his head rather often to try for a glimpse of this little grey shadow.

At last, from the top of each wave, the men in the tossing boat could see land. Even as the lighthouse was an upright shadow on the sky, this land seemed but a long black shadow on the sea. It certainly was thinner than paper. "We must be about opposite New Smyrna," said the cook, who had coasted this shore often in schooners. "Captain, by the way, I believe they abandoned that life-saving station there about a year ago."

"Did they?" said the captain.

The wind slowly died away. The cook and the correspondent were not now obliged to slave in order to hold high the oar. But the waves continued their old impetuous swooping at the dinghy, and the little craft, no longer under way, struggled woundily over them. The oiler or the correspondent took the oars again.

Shipwrecks are *àpropos* of nothing. If men could only train for them and have them occur when the men had reached pink condition, there would be less drowning at sea. Of the four in the dinghy none had slept any time worth mentioning for two days and two nights previous to embarking in the dinghy, and in the excitement of clambering about the deck of a foundering ship they had also forgotten to eat heartily.

For these reasons, and for others, neither the oiler nor the correspondent was fond of rowing at this time. The correspondent wondered ingenuously how in the name of all that was sane could there be people who thought it amusing to row a boat. It was not an amusement; it was a diabolical punishment, and even a genius of mental aberrations could never conclude that it was anything but a horror to the muscles and a crime against the back. He mentioned to the boat in general how the amusement of rowing struck him, and the weary-faced oiler smiled in full sympathy. Previously to the foundering, by the way, the oiler had worked a double watch in the engine-room of the ship.

"Take her easy now, boys," said the captain. "Don't spend yourselves. If we have to run a surf you'll need all your strength, because we'll sure have to swim for it. Take your time."

Slowly the land arose from the sea. From a black line it became a line of black and line of white—trees and sand. Finally the captain said that he could make out a house on the shore. "That's the house of refuge, sure," said the cook. "They'll see us before long, and come out after us."

The distant lighthouse reared high. "The keeper ought to be able to make us out now, if he's looking through a glass," said the captain. "He'll notify the life-saving people."

"None of those other boats could have got ashore to give word of this wreck," said the oiler, in a low voice, "else the life-boat would be out hunting us."

Slowly and beautifully the land loomed out of the sea. The wind came again. It had veered from the north-east to the south-east. Finally a new sound struck the ears of the men in the boat. It was the low thunder of the surf on the shore. "We'll never be able to make the lighthouse now," said the captain. "Swing her head a little more north, Billie."

"A little more north, sir," said the oiler.

Whereupon the little boat turned her nose once more down the wind, and all but the oarsman watched the shore grow. Under the influence of this expansion doubt and direful apprehension were leaving the minds of the men. The management of the boat was still most absorbing, but it could not prevent a quiet cheefulness. In an hour, perhaps, they would be ashore.

Their backbones had become thoroughly used to balancing in the boat, and they now rode this wild colt of a dinghy like circus men. The correspondent thought that he had been drenched to the skin, but happening to feel in the top pocket of his coat, he found therein eight cigars. Four of them were soaked with sea-water; four were perfectly scatheless. After a search, somebody produced three dry matches; and thereupon the four waifs rode impudently in their little boat and, with an assurance of an impending rescue shining in their eyes, puffed at the big cigars, and judged well and ill of all men. Everybody took a drink of water.

IV

"Cook," remarked the captain, "there don't seem to be any signs of life about your house of refuge."

"No," replied the cook. "Funny they don't see us!"

A broad stretch of lowly coast lay before the eyes of the men. It was of low dunes topped with dark vegetation. The roar of the surf was plain, and sometimes they could see the white lip of a wave as it spun up the beach. A tiny house was blocked out black upon the sky. Southward, the slim lighthouse lifted its little grey length.

Tide, wind, and waves were swinging the dinghy northward. "Funny they don't see us," said the men.

The surf's roar was here dulled, but its tone was nevertheless thunderous and mighty. As the boat swam over the great rollers the men sat listening to this roar. "We'll swamp sure," said everybody.

It is fair to say here that there was not a life-saving station within twenty miles in either direction; but the men did not know this fact, and in consequence they made dark and opprobrious remarks concerning the eyesight of the nation's life-savers. Four scowling men sat in the dinghy and surpassed records in the invention of epithets.

"Funny they don't see us."

The light-heartedness of a former time had completely faded. To their sharpened minds it was easy to conjure pictures of all kinds of incompetency and blindness and, indeed, cowardice. There was the shore of the populous land, and it was bitter and bitter to them that from it came no sign.

"Well," said the captain, ultimately, "I suppose we'll have to make a try for ourselves. If we stay out here too long, we'll none of us have strength left to swim after the boat swamps."

And so the oiler, who was at the oars, turned the boat straight for the shore. There was a sudden tightening of muscles. There was some thinking.

"If we don't all get ashore," said the captain—"if we don't all get ashore, I suppose you fellows know where to send news of my finish?"

They then briefly exchanged some addresses and admonitions. As for the reflections of the men, there was a great deal of rage in them. Perchance they might be formulated thus: "If I am going to be drowned—if I am going to be drowned—if I am going to be drowned, why, in the name of the seven mad gods who rule the sea, was I allowed to come thus far and contemplate sand and trees? Was I brought here merely to have my nose dragged away as I was about to nibble the sacred cheese of life? It is preposterous. If this old ninny-woman, Fate, cannot do better than this, she should be deprived of the management of men's fortunes. She is an old hen who knows not her intention. If she has decided to drown me, why did she not do it in the beginning and save me all this trouble? The whole affair is absurd.—But no; she cannot mean to drown me. She dare not drown me. She cannot drown me. Not after all this work." Afterward the man might have had an impulse to shake his fist at the clouds. "Just you drown me, now, and then hear what I call you!"

The billows that came at this time were more formidable. They seemed always just about to break and roll over the little boat in a turmoil of foam. There was a preparatory and long growl in the speech of them. No mind unused to the sea would have concluded that the dinghy could ascend these sheer heights in time. The shore was still afar. The oiler was a wily surfman. "Boys," he said swiftly, "she won't live three minutes more, and we're too far out to swim. Shall I take her to sea again, Captain?"

"Yes; go ahead!" said the captain.

This oiler, by a series of quick miracles and fast and steady oarsmanship, turned the boat in the middle of the surf and took her safely to sea again.

There was a considerable silence as the boat bumped over the furrowed sea to deeper water. Then somebody in gloom spoke: "Well, anyhow, they must have seen us from the shore by now."

The gulls went in slanting flight up the wind toward the grey, desolate east. A squall, marked by dingy clouds and clouds brick-red like smoke from a burning building, appeared from the south-east.

"What do you think of those life-saving people? Ain't they peaches?"

"Funny they haven't seen us."

"Maybe they think we're out here for sport! Maybe they think we're fishin'. Maybe they think we're damned fools."

It was a long afternoon. A changed tide tried to force them southward, but wind and wave said northward. Far ahead, where coast-line, sea, and sky formed their mighty angle, there were little dots which seemed to indicate a city on the shore.

"St. Augustine?"

The captain shook his head. "Too near Mosquito Inlet."

And the oiler rowed, and then the correspondent rowed; then the oiler rowed. It was a weary business. The human back can become the seat of more aches and pains than are registered in books for the composite anatomy of a regiment. It is a limited area, but it can become the theatre of innumerable muscular conflicts, tangles, wrenches, knots, and other comforts.

"Did you ever like to row, Billie?" asked the correspondent.

"No," said the oiler; "hang it!"

When one exchanged the rowing-seat for a place in the bottom of the boat, he suffered a bodily depression that caused him to be careless of everything save an obligation to wiggle one finger. There was cold seawater swashing to and fro in the boat, and he lay in it. His head, pillowed on a thwart, was within an inch of the swirl of a wavecrest, and sometimes a particularly obstreperous sea came inboard and drenched him once more. But these matters did not annoy him. It is almost certain that if the boat had capsized he would have tumbled comfortably out upon the ocean as if he felt sure that it was a great soft mattress.

"Look! There's a man on the shore!"

"Where?"

"There! See 'im? See 'im?"

"Yes, sure! He's walking along."

"Now he's stopped. Look! He's facing us!"

"He's waving at us!"

"So he is! By thunder!"

"Ah, now we're all right! Now we're all right! There'll be a boat out here for us in half an hour."

"He's going on. He's running. He's going up to that house there."

The remote beach seemed lower than the sea, and it required a searching glance to discern the little black figure. The captain saw a floating stick, and they rowed to it. A bath towel was by some weird chance in the boat, and, tying this on the stick, the captain waved it. The oarsman did not dare turn his head, so he was obliged to ask questions.

"What's he doing now?"

"He's standing still again. He's looking, I think.—There he goes again—toward the house.—Now he's stopped again."

"Is he waving at us?"

"No, not now; he was, though."

"Look! There comes another man!"

"He's running."

"Look at him go, would you!"

"Why, he's on a bicycle. Now he's met the other man. They're both waving at us. Look!"

"There comes something up the beach."

"What the devil is that thing?"

"Why, it looks like a boat."

"Why, certainly, it's a boat."

"No; it's on wheels."

"Yes, so it is. Well, that must be the life-boat. They drag them along shore on a wagon."

"That's the life-boat, sure."

"No, by God, it's—it's an omnibus."

"I tell you it's a life-boat."

"It is not! It's an omnibus. I can see it plain. See? One of these big hotel omnibuses."

"By thunder, you're right. It's an omnibus, sure as fate. What do you suppose they are doing with an omnibus? Maybe they are going around collecting the life-crew, hey?"

"That's it, likely. Look! There's a fellow waving a little black flag. He's standing on the steps of the omnibus. There come those other two fellows. Now they're all talking together. Look at the fellow with the flag. Maybe he ain't waving it!"

"That ain't a flag, is it? That's his coat. Why, certainly, that's his coat."

"So it is; it's his coat. He's taken it off and is waving it around his head. But would you look at him swing it!"

"Oh, say, there isn't any life-saving station there. That's just a winter-resort hotel omnibus that has brought over some of the boarders to see us drown."

"What's that idiot with the coat mean? What's he signaling, anyhow?"

"It looks as if he were trying to tell us to go north. There must be a life-saving station up there."

"No; he thinks we're fishing. Just giving us a merry hand. See? Ah, there, Willie!"

"Well, I wish I could make something out of those signals. What do you suppose he means?"

"He don't mean anything; he's just playing."

"Well, if he'd just signal us to try the surf again, or to go to sea and wait, or go north, or go south, or go to hell, there would be some reason in it. But look at him! He just stands there and keeps his coat revolving like a wheel. The ass!"

"There come more people."

"Now there's quite a mob. Look! Isn't that a boat?"

"Where? Oh, I see where you mean. No, that's no boat."

"That fellow is still waving his coat."

"He must think we like to see him do that. Why don't he quit it? It don't mean anything."

"I don't know. I think he is trying to make us go north. It must be that there's a life-saving station there somewhere."

"Say, he ain't tired yet. Look at 'im wave!"

"Wonder how long he can keep that up. He's been revolving his coat ever since he caught sight of us. He's an idiot. Why aren't they getting men to bring a boat out? A fishing-boat—one of those big yawls—could come out here all right. Why don't he do something?"

"Oh, it's all right now."

"They'll have a boat out here for us in less than no time, now that they've seen us."

A faint yellow tone came into the sky over the low land. The shadows on the sea slowly deepened. The wind bore coldness with it, and the men began to shiver.

"Holy smoke!" said one, allowing his voice to express his impious mood, "if we keep on monkeying out here! If we've got to flounder out here all night!"

"Oh, we'll never have to stay here all night! Don't you worry. They've seen us now, and it won't be long before they'll come chasing out after us."

The shore grew dusky. The man waving a coat blended gradually into this gloom, and it swallowed in the same manner the omnibus and the group of people. The spray, when it dashed uproariously over the side, made the voyagers shrink and swear like men who were being branded.

"I'd like to catch the chump who waved the coat. I feel like socking him one, just for luck."

"Why? What did he do?"

"Oh, nothing, but then he seemed so damned cheerful."

In the meantime the oiler rowed, and then the correspondent rowed, and then the oiler rowed. Grey-faced and bowed forward, they mechanically, turn by turn, plied the leaden oars. The form of the lighthouse had vanished from the southern horizon, but finally a pale star appeared, just lifting from the sea. The streaked saffron in the west passed before the all-merging darkness, and the sea to the east was black. The land had vanished, and was expressed only by the low and drear thunder of the surf.

"If I am going to be drowned—if I am going to be drowned—if I am going to be drowned, why, in the name of the seven mad gods who rule the sea, was I allowed to come thus far and contemplate sand and trees? Was I brought here merely to have my nose dragged away as I was about to nibble the sacred cheese of life?"

The patient captain, drooped over the water-jar, was sometimes obliged to speak to the oarsman.

"Keep her head up! Keep her head up!"

"Keep her head up, sir." The voices were weary and low.

This was surely a quiet evening. All save the oarsman lay heavily and listlessly in the boat's bottom. As for him, his eyes were just capable of noting the tall black waves that swept forward in a most sinister silence, save for an occasional subdued growl of a crest.

The cook's head was on a thwart, and he looked without interest at the water under his nose. He was deep in other scenes. Finally he spoke. "Billie," he murmured, dreamfully, "what kind of pie do you like best?"

V

"Pie!" said the oiler and the correspondent, agitatedly, "Don't talk about those things, blast you!"

"Well," said the cook, "I was just thinking about ham sandwiches and—"

A night on the sea in an open boat is a long night. As darkness settled finally, the shine of the light, lifting from the sea in the south, changed to full gold. On the northern horizon a new light appeared, a small bluish gleam on the edge of the waters. These two lights were the furniture of the world. Otherwise there was nothing but waves.

Two men huddled in the stern, and distances were so magnificent in the dinghy that the rower was enabled to keep his feet partly warm by thrusting them under his companions. Their legs indeed extended far under the rowing-seat until they touched the feet of the captain forward. Sometimes, despite the efforts of the tired oarsman, a wave came piling into the boat, an icy wave of the night, and the chilling water soaked them anew. They would twist their bodies for a moment and groan, and sleep the dead sleep once more, while the water in the boat gurgled about them as the craft rocked.

The plan of the oiler and the correspondent was for one to row until he lost the ability, and then arouse the other from his sea-water couch in the bottom of the boat.

The oiler plied the oars until his head drooped forward and the overpowering sleep blinded him; and he rowed yet afterward. Then he touched a man in the bottom of the boat, and called his name. "Will you spell me for a little while?" he said, meekly.

"Sure, Billie," said the correspondent, awaking and dragging himself to a sitting position. They exchanged places carefully, and the oiler, cuddling down in the seawater at the cook's side, seemed to go to sleep instantly.

The particular violence of the sea had ceased. The waves came without snarling. The obligation of the man at the oars was to keep the boat headed so that the tilt of the rollers would not capsize her, and to preserve her from filling when the crests rushed past. The black waves were silent and hard to be seen in the darkness. Often one was almost upon the boat before the oarsman was aware.

In a low voice the correspondent addressed the captain. He was not sure that the captain was awake, although this iron man seemed to be always awake. "Captain, shall I keep her making for that light north, sir?"

The same steady voice answered him. "Yes. Keep it about two points off the port bow."

The cook had tied a life-belt around himself in order to get even the warmth which this clumsy cork contrivance could donate, and he seemed almost stove-like when a rower, whose teeth invariably chattered wildly as soon as he ceased his labour, dropped down to sleep.

The correspondent, as he rowed, looked down at the two men sleeping underfoot. The cook's arm was around the oiler's shoulders, and, with their fragmentary clothing and haggard faces, they were the babes of the sea—a grotesque rendering of the old babes in the wood.

Later he must have grown stupid at his work, for suddenly there was a growling of water, and a crest came with a roar and a swash into the boat, and it was a wonder that it did not set the cook afloat in his life-belt. The cook continued to sleep, but the oiler sat up, blinking his eyes and shaking with the new cold.

"Oh, I'm awfully sorry, Billie," said the correspondent, contritely.

"That's all right, old boy," said the oiler, and lay down again and was asleep.

Presently it seemed that even the captain dozed, and the correspondent thought that he was the one man afloat on all the oceans. The wind had a voice as it came over the waves, and it was sadder than the end.

There was a long, loud swishing astern of the boat, and a gleaming trail of phosphorescence, like blue flame, was furrowed on the black waters. It might have been made by a monstrous knife.

Then there came a stillness, while the correspondent breathed with open mouth and looked at the sea.

Suddenly there was another swish and another long flash of bluish light, and this time it was alongside the boat, and might almost have been reached with an oar. The correspondent saw an enormous fin speed like a shadow through the water, hurling the crystalline spray and leaving the long glowing trail.

The correspondent looked over his shoulder at the captain. His face was hidden, and he seemed to be asleep. He looked at the babes of the sea. They certainly were asleep. So, being bereft of sympathy, he leaned a little way to one side and swore softly into the sea.

But the thing did not then leave the vicinity of the boat. Ahead or astern, on one side or the other, at intervals long or short, fled the long sparkling streak, and there was to be heard the *whirroo* of the dark fin. The speed and power of the thing was greatly to be admired. It cut the water like a gigantic and keen projectile.

The presence of this biding thing did not affect the man with the same horror that it would if he had been a picnicker. He simply looked at the sea dully and swore in an undertone.

Nevertheless, it is true that he did not wish to be alone with the thing. He wished one of his companions to awake by chance and keep him company with it. But the captain hung motionless over the water-jar, and the oiler and the cook in the bottom of the boat were plunged in slumber.

VI

"If I am going to be drowned—if I am going to be drowned—if I am going to be drowned, why, in the name of the seven mad gods who rule the sea, was I allowed to come thus far and contemplate sand and trees?"

During this dismal night, it may be remarked that a man would conclude that it was really the intention of the seven mad gods to drown him, despite the abominable injustice of it. For it was certainly an abominable injustice to drown a man who had worked so hard, so hard. The man felt it would be a crime most unnatural. Other people had drowned at sea since galleys swarmed with painted sails, but still—

When it occurs to a man that nature does not regard him as important, and that she feels she would not maim the universe by disposing of him, he at first wishes to throw bricks at the temple, and he hates deeply the fact that there are no bricks and no temples. Any visible expression of nature would surely be pelleted with his jeers.

Then, if there be no tangible thing to hoot, he feels, perhaps, the desire to confront a personification and indulge in pleas, bowed to one knee, and with hands supplicant, saying, "Yes, but I love myself."

A high cold star on a winter's night is the word he feels that she says to him. Thereafter he knows the pathos of his situation.

The men in the dinghy had not discussed these matters, but each had, no doubt, reflected upon them in silence and according to his mind. There was seldom any expression upon their faces save the general one of complete weariness. Speech was devoted to the business of the boat.

To chime the notes of his emotion, a verse mysteriously entered the correspondent's head. He had even forgotten that he had forgotten this verse, but it suddenly was in his mind.

> *A soldier of the Legion lay dying in Algiers;*
> *There was lack of woman's nursing, there was dearth of woman's tears;*
> *But a comrade stood beside him, and he took that comrade's hand,*
> *And he said, "I never more shall see my own, my native land."*

In his childhood the correspondent had been made acquainted with the fact that a soldier of the Legion lay dying in Algiers, but he had never regarded the fact as important. Myriads of his school-fellows had informed him of the soldier's plight, but the dinning had naturally ended by making him perfectly indifferent. He had never considered it his affair that a soldier of the Legion lay dying in Algiers, nor had it appeared to him as a matter for sorrow. It was less to him than the breaking of a pencil's point.

Now, however, it quaintly came to him as a human, living thing. It was no longer merely a picture of a few throes in the breast of a poet, meanwhile drinking tea and warming his feet at the grate; it was an actuality—stern, mournful, and fine.

The correspondent plainly saw the soldier. He lay on the sand with his feet out straight and still. While his pale left hand was upon his chest in an attempt to thwart the going of his life, the blood came between his fingers. In the far Algerian distance, a city of low square forms was set against a sky that was faint with the last sunset hues. The correspondent, plying the oars and dreaming of the slow and slower movements of the lips of the soldier, was moved by a profound and perfectly impersonal comprehension. He was sorry for the soldier of the Legion who lay dying in Algiers.

The thing which had followed the boat and waited had evidently grown bored at the delay. There was no longer to be heard the slash of the cut-water, and there was no longer the flame of the long trail. The light in the north still glimmered, but it was apparently no nearer to the boat. Sometimes the boom of the surf rang in the correspondent's ears, and he turned the craft seaward then and rowed harder. Southward, some one had evidently built a watch-fire on the beach. It was too low and too far to be seen, but it made a shimmering, roseate reflection upon the bluff in back of it, and this could be discerned from the boat. The wind came stronger, and sometimes a wave suddenly raged out like a mountain cat, and there was to be seen the sheen and sparkle of a broken crest.

The captain, in the bow, moved on his water-jar and sat erect. "Pretty long night," he observed to the correspondent. He looked at the shore. "Those life-saving people take their time."

"Did you see that shark playing around?"

"Yes, I saw him. He was a big fellow, all right."

"Wish I had known you were awake."

Later the correspondent spoke into the bottom of the boat. "Billie!" There was a slow and gradual disentanglement. "Billie, will you spell me?"

"Sure," said the oiler.

As soon as the correspondent touched the cold, comfortable sea-water in the bottom of the boat and had huddled close to the cook's life-belt he was deep in sleep, despite the fact that his teeth played all the popular airs. This sleep was so good to him that it was but a moment before he heard a voice call his name in a tone that demonstrated the last stages of exhaustion. "Will you spell me?"

"Sure, Billie."

The light in the north had mysteriously vanished, but the correspondent took his course from the wide-awake captain.

Later in the night they took the boat farther out to sea, and the captain directed the cook to take one oar at the stern and keep the boat facing the seas. He was to call out if he should hear the thunder of the surf. This plan enabled the oiler and the correspondent to get respite together. "We'll give those boys a chance to get into shape again," said the captain. They curled down and, after a few preliminary chatterings and trembles, slept once more the dead sleep. Neither knew they had bequeathed to the cook the company of another shark, or perhaps the same shark.

As the boat carousoused on the waves, spray occasionally bumped over the side and gave them a fresh soaking, but this had no power to break their repose. The ominous slash of the wind and the water affected them as it would have affected mummies.

"Boys," said the cook, with the notes of every reluctance in his voice, "she's drifted in pretty close. I guess one of you had better take her to sea again." The correspondent, aroused, heard the crash of the toppled crests.

As he was rowing, the captain gave him some whisky-and-water, and this steadied the chills out of him. "If I ever get ashore and anybody shows me even a photograph of an oar—"

At last there was a short conversation.

"Billie!—Billie, will you spell me?"

"Sure," said the oiler.

VII

When the correspondent again opened his eyes, the sea and the sky were each of the grey hue of the dawning. Later, carmine and gold was painted upon the waters. The morning appeared finally, in its splendour, with a sky of pure blue, and the sunlight flamed on the tips of the waves.

On the distant dunes were set many little black cottages, and a tall white windmill reared above them. No man, nor dog, nor bicycle appeared on the beach. The cottages might have formed a deserted village.

The voyagers scanned the shore. A conference was held in the boat. "Well," said the captain, "if no help is coming, we might better try a run through the surf right away. If we stay out here much longer we will be too weak to do anything for ourselves at all." The others silently acquiesced in this reasoning. The boat was headed for the beach. The correspondent wondered if none ever ascended the tall wind-tower, and if then they never looked seaward. This tower was a giant, standing with its back to the plight of the ants. It represented in a degree, to the correspondent, the serenity of nature amid the struggles of the individual—nature in the wind, and nature in the vision of men. She did not seem cruel to him then, nor beneficent, nor treacherous, nor wise. But she was indifferent, flatly indifferent. It is, perhaps, plausible that a man in this situation, impressed with the unconcern of the universe, should see the innumerable flaws of his life, and have them taste wickedly in his mind, and wish for another chance. A distinction between right and wrong seems absurdly clear to him, then, in this new ignorance of the grave-edge, and he understands that if he were given another opportunity he would mend his conduct and his words, and be better and brighter during an introduction or at a tea.

"Now, boys," said the captain, "she is going to swamp sure. All we can do is to work her in as far as possible, and then when she swamps, pile out and scramble for the beach. Keep cool now, and don't jump until she swamps sure."

The oiler took the oars. Over his shoulders he scanned the surf. "Captain," he said, "I think I'd better bring her about and keep her head-on to the seas and back her in."

"All right, Billie," said the captain. "Back her in." The oiler swung the boat then, and, seated in the stern, the cook and the correspondent were obliged to look over their shoulders to contemplate the lonely and indifferent shore.

The monstrous inshore rollers heaved the boat high until the men were again enabled to see the white sheets of water scudding up the slanted beach. "We won't get in very close," said the captain. Each time a man could wrest his attention from the rollers, he turned his glance toward the shore, and in the expression of the eyes during this contemplation there was a singular quality. The correspondent, observing the others, knew that they were not afraid, but the full meaning of their glances was shrouded.

As for himself, he was too tired to grapple fundamentally with the fact. He tried to coerce his mind into thinking of it, but the mind was dominated at this time by the muscles, and the muscles said they did not care. It merely occurred to him that if he should drown it would be a shame.

There were no hurried words, no pallor, no plain agitation. The men simply looked at the shore. "Now, remember to get well clear of the boat when you jump," said the captain.

Seaward the crest of a roller suddenly fell with a thunderous crash, and the long white comber came roaring down upon the boat.

"Steady now," said the captain. The men were silent. They turned their eyes from the shore to the comber and waited. The boat slid up the incline, leaped at the furious top, bounced over it, and swung down the long back of the wave. Some water had been shipped, and the cook bailed it out.

But the next crest crashed also. The tumbling, boiling flood of white water caught the boat and whirled it almost perpendicular. Water swarmed in from all sides. The correspondent had his hands on the gunwale at this time, and when the water entered at that place he swiftly withdrew his fingers, as if he objected to wetting them.

The little boat, drunken with this weight of water, reeled and snuggled deeper into the sea.

"Bail her out, cook! Bail her out!" said the captain.

"All right, Captain," said the cook.

"Now, boys, the next one will do for us sure," said the oiler. "Mind to jump clear of the boat."

The third wave moved forward, huge, furious, implacable. It fairly swallowed the dinghy, and almost simultaneously the men tumbled into the sea. A piece of life-belt had lain in the bottom of the boat, and as the correspondent went overboard he held this to his chest with his left hand.

The January water was icy, and he reflected immediately that it was colder than he had expected to find it off the coast of Florida. This appeared to his dazed mind as a fact important enough to be noted at the time. The coldness of the water was sad; it was tragic. This fact was somehow mixed and confused with his opinion of his own situation, so that it seemed almost a proper reason for tears. The water was cold.

When he came to the surface he was conscious of little but the noisy water. Afterward he saw his companions in the sea. The oiler was ahead in the race. He was swimming strongly and rapidly. Off to the correspondent's left, the cook's great white and corked back bulged out of the water; and in the rear the captain was hanging with his one good hand to the keel of the overturned dinghy.

There is a certain immovable quality to a shore, and the correspondent wondered at it amid the confusion of the sea.

It seemed also very attractive; but the correspondent knew that it was a long journey, and he paddled leisurely. The piece of life-preserver lay under him, and sometimes he whirled down the incline of a wave as if he were on a hand-sled.

But finally he arrived at a place in the sea where travel was beset with difficulty. He did not pause swimming to inquire what manner of current had caught him, but there his progress ceased. The shore was set before him like a bit of scenery on a stage, and he looked at it and understood with his eyes each detail of it.

As the cook passed, much farther to the left, the captain was calling to him. "Turn over on your back, cook! Turn over on your back and use the oar."

"All right, sir." The cook turned on his back, and, paddling with an oar, went ahead as if he were a canoe.

Presently the boat also passed to the left of the correspondent, with the captain clinging with one hand to the keel. He would have appeared like a man raising himself to look over a board fence if it were not for the extraordinary gymnastics of the boat. The correspondent marvelled that the captain could still hold to it.

They passed on nearer to the shore—the oiler, the cook, the captain —and following them went the water-jar, bouncing gaily over the seas.

The correspondent remained in the grip of this strange new enemy— a current. The shore, with its white slope of sand and its green bluff topped with little silent cottages, was spread like a picture before him. It was very near to him then, but he was impressed as one who, in a gallery, looks at a scene from Brittany or Algiers.

He thought: "I am going to drown? Can it be possible? Can it be possible? Can it be possible?" Perhaps an individual must consider his own death to be the final phenomenon of nature.

But later a wave perhaps whirled him out of his small deadly current, for he found suddenly that he could again make progress toward the shore. Later still he was aware that the captain, clinging with one hand to the keel of the dinghy, had his face turned away from the shore and toward him, and was calling his name. "Come to the boat! Come to the boat!"

In his struggle to reach the captain and the boat, he reflected that when one gets properly wearied drowning must really be a comfortable arrangement—a cessation of hostilities accompanied by a large degree of relief; and he was glad of it, for the main thing in his mind for some moments had been horror of the temporary agony. He did not wish to be hurt.

Presently he saw a man running along the shore. He was undressing with most remarkable speed. Coat, trousers, shirt, everything flew magically off him.

"Come to the boat!" called the captain.

"All right, Captain." As the correspondent paddled, he saw the captain let himself down to bottom and leave the boat. Then the correspondent performed his one little marvel of the voyage. A large wave caught him and flung him with ease and supreme speed completely over the boat and far beyond it. It struck him even then as an event in gymnastics and a true miracle of the sea. An overturned boat in the surf is not a plaything to a swimming man.

The correspondent arrived in water that reached only to his waist, but his condition did not enable him to stand for more than a moment. Each wave knocked him into a heap, and the undertow pulled at him.

Then he saw the man who had been running and undressing, and undressing and running, come bounding into the water. He dragged ashore the cook, and then waded toward the captain; but the captain waved him away and sent him to the correspondent. He was naked—naked as a tree in winter; but a halo was about his head, and he shone like a saint. He gave a strong pull, and a long drag, and a bully heave at the correspondent's hand. The correspondent, schooled in the minor formulae, said, "Thanks, old man." But suddenly the man cried, "What's that?" He pointed a swift finger. The correspondent said, "Go."

In the shallows, face downward, lay the oiler. His forehead touched sand that was periodically, between each wave, clear of the sea.

The correspondent did not know all that transpired afterward. When he achieved safe ground he fell, striking the sand with each particular part of his body. It was as if he had dropped from a roof, but the thud was grateful to him.

It seemed that instantly the beach was populated with men with blankets, clothes, and flasks, and women with coffee-pots and all the remedies sacred to their minds. The welcome of the land to the men from the sea was warm and generous; but a still and dripping shape was carried slowly up the beach, and the land's welcome for it could only be the different and sinister hospitality of the grave.

When it came night, the white waves paced to and fro in the moonlight, and the wind brought the sound of the great sea's voice to the men on the shore, and they felt that they could then be interpreters.

The Shades of Spring

I

It was a mile nearer through the wood. Mechanically, Syson turned up by the forge and lifted the field-gate. The blacksmith and his mate stood still, watching the trespasser. But Syson looked too much a gentleman to be accosted. They let him go on in silence across the small field to the wood.

There was not the least difference between this morning and those of bright springs, six or eight years back. White and sandy-gold fowls still scratched round the gate, littering the earth and the field with feathers and scratched-up rubbish. Between the two thick holly bushes in the wood-hedge was the hidden gap, whose fence one climbed to get into the wood; the bars were scored just the same by the keeper's boots. He was back in the eternal.

Syson was extraordinarily glad. Like an uneasy spirit he had returned to the country of his past, and he found it waiting for him, unaltered. The hazel still spread glad little hands downwards, the bluebells here were still wan and few, among the lush grass and in shade of the bushes.

The path through the wood, on the very brow of a slope, ran winding easily for a time. All around were twiggy oaks, just issuing their gold, and floor spaces diapered with woodruff, with patches of dog-mercury and tufts of hyacinth. Two fallen trees still lay across the track. Syson jolted down a steep, rough slope, and came again upon the open land, this time looking north as through a great window in the wood. He stayed to gaze over the level fields of the hill-top, at the village which strewed the bare upland as if it had tumbled off the passing waggons of industry, and been forsaken. There was a stiff, modern, grey little church, and block and rows of red dwellings lying at random; at the back, the twinkling headstocks of the pit, and the looming pit-hill. All was naked and out-of-doors, not a tree! It was quite unaltered.

Syson turned, satisfied, to follow the path that sheered downhill into the wood. He was curiously elated, feeling himself back in an enduring vision. He started. A keeper was standing a few yards in front, barring the way.

"Where might you be going this road, sir?" asked the man. The tone of his question had a challenging twang. Syson looked at the fellow with an impersonal, observant gaze. It was a young man of four or five-and-twenty, ruddy and well favoured. His dark blue eyes now stared aggressively at the intruder. His black moustache, very thick, was cropped short over a small, rather soft mouth. In every other respect the fellow was manly and good-looking. He stood just above middle height; the strong forward thrust of his chest, and the perfect ease of his erect, self-sufficient body, gave one the feeling that he was taut with animal life, like the thick jet of a fountain balanced in itself. He stood with the butt of his gun on the ground, looking uncertainly and questioningly at Syson. The dark, restless eyes of the trespasser, examining the man and penetrating into him without heeding his office, troubled the keeper and made him flush.

"Where is Naylor? Have you got his job?" Syson asked.

"You're not from the House, are you?" inquired the keeper. It could not be, since everyone was away.

"No, I'm not from the House," the other replied. It seemed to amuse him.

"Then might I ask where you were making for?" said the keeper, nettled.

"Where I am making for?" Syson repeated. "I am going to Willey-Water Farm."

"This isn't the road."

"I think so. Down this path, past the well, and out by the white gate."

"But that's not the public road."

"I suppose not. I used to come so often, in Naylor's time, I had forgotten. Where is he, by the way?"

"Crippled with rheumatism," the keeper answered reluctantly.

"Is he?" Syson exclaimed in pain.

"And who might you be?" asked the keeper, with a new intonation.

"John Adderley Syson; I used to live in Cordy Lane."

"Used to court Hilda Millership?"

Syson's eyes opened with a pained smile. He nodded. There was an awkward silence.

"And you—who are you?" asked Syson.

"Arthur Pilbeam—Naylor's my uncle," said the other.

"You live here in Nuttall?"

"I'm lodgin' at my uncle's—at Naylor's."

"I see!"

"Did you say you was goin' down to Willey-Water?" asked the keeper.

"Yes."

There was a pause of some moments, before the keeper blurted: "*I'm* courtin' Hilda Millership."

The young fellow looked at the intruder with a stubborn defiance, almost pathetic. Syson opened new eyes.

"Are you?" he said, astonished. The keeper flushed dark.

"She and me are keeping company," he said.

"I didn't know!" said Syson. The other man waited uncomfortably.

"What, is the thing settled?" asked the intruder.

"How, settled?" retorted the other sulkily.

"Are you going to get married soon, and all that?"

The keeper stared in silence for some moments, impotent.

"I suppose so," he said, full of resentment.

"Ah!" Syson watched closely.

"I'm married myself," he added, after a time.

"You are?" said the other incredulously.

Syson laughed in his brilliant, unhappy way.

"This last fifteen months," he said.

The keeper gazed at him with wide, wondering eyes, apparently thinking back, and trying to make things out.

"Why, didn't you know?" asked Syson.

"No, I didn't," said the other sulkily.

There was silence for a moment.

"Ah well!" said Syson, "I will go on. I suppose I may." The keeper stood in silent opposition. The two men hesitated in the open, grassy space, set round with small sheaves of sturdy bluebells; a little open platform on the brow of the hill. Syson took a few indecisive steps forward, then stopped.

"I say, how beautiful!" he cried.

He had come in full view of the downslope. The wide path ran from his feet like a river, and it was full of bluebells, save for a green winding thread down the center, where the keeper walked. Like a stream the path opened into azure shallows at the levels, and there were pools of bluebells, with still the green thread winding through, like a thin current of ice-water through blue lakes. And from under the twig-purple of the bushes swam the shadowed blue, as if the flowers lay in flood water over the woodland.

"Ah, isn't it lovely!" Syson exclaimed; this was his past, the country he had abandoned, and it hurt him to see it so beautiful. Wood-pigeons cooed overhead, and the air was full of the brightness of birds singing.

"If you're married, what do you keep writing to her for, and sending her poetry books and things?" asked the keeper. Syson stared at him, taken aback and humiliated. Then he began to smile.

"Well," he said, "I did not know about you. . . ."

Again the keeper flushed darkly.

"But if you are married—" he charged.

"I am," answered the other cynically.

Then, looking down the blue beautiful path, Syson felt his own humiliation. "What right *have* I to hang on to her?" he thought, bitterly self-contemptuous.

"She knows I'm married and all that," he said.

"But you keep sending her books," challenged the keeper.

Syson, silenced, looked at the other man quizzically, half pitying. Then he turned.

"Good day," he said, and was gone. Now everything irritated him; the two sallows, one all gold and perfume and murmur, one silver-green and bristly, reminded him that here he had taught her about pollination. What a fool he was! What god-forsaken folly it all was!

"Ah well," he said to himself; "the poor devil seems to have a grudge against me. I'll do my best for him." He grinned to himself, in a very bad temper.

II

The farm was less than a hundred yards from the wood's edge. The wall of trees formed the fourth side to the open quadrangle. The house faced the wood. With tangled emotions, Syson noted the plum blossom falling on the profuse, coloured primroses, which he himself had brought here and set. How they had increased! There were thick tufts of scarlet, and pink, and pale purple primroses under the plum trees. He saw somebody glance at him through the kitchen window, heard men's voices.

The door opened suddenly: very womanly she had grown! He felt himself going pale.

"You?—Addy!" she exclaimed, and stood motionless.

"Who?" called the farmer's voice. Men's low voices answered. Those low voices, curious and almost jeering, roused the tormented spirit in the visitor. Smiling brilliantly at her, he waited.

"Myself—why not?" he said.

The flush burned very deep on her cheek and throat.

"We are just finishing dinner," she said.

"Then I will stay outside." He made a motion to show that he would sit on the red earthenware pipkin that stood near the door among the daffodils, and contained the drinking water.

"Oh no, come in," she said hurriedly. He followed her. In the doorway, he glanced swiftly over the family, and bowed. Every one was confused. The farmer, his wife, and the four sons sat at the coarsely laid dinnertable, the men with arms bare to the elbows.

"I am sorry I come at lunch-time," said Syson.

"Hello, Addy!" said the farmer, assuming the old form of address, but his tone cold. "How are you?"

And he shook hands.

"Shall you have a bit?" he invited the young visitor, but taking for granted the offer would be refused. He assumed that Syson was become too refined to eat so roughly. The young man winced at the imputation.

"Have you had any dinner?" asked the daughter.

"No," replied Syson. "It is too early. I shall be back at half-past one."

"You call it lunch, don't you?" asked the eldest son, almost ironical. He had once been an intimate friend of this young man.

"We'll give Addy something when we've finished," said the mother, an invalid, deprecating.

"No—don't trouble. I don't want to give you any trouble," said Syson.

"You could allus live on fresh air an' scenery," laughed the youngest son, a lad of nineteen.

Syson went round the buildings, and into the orchard at the back of the house, where daffodils all along the hedgerow swung like yellow, ruffled birds on their perches. He loved the place extraordinarily, the hills ranging round, with bear-skin woods covering their giant shoulders, and small red farms like brooches clasping their garments; the blue streak of water in the valley, the bareness of the home pasture, the sound of myriad-threaded bird-singing, which went mostly unheard. To his last day, he would dream of this place, when he felt the sun on his face or saw the small handfuls of snow between the winter twigs, or smelt the coming of spring.

Hilda was very womanly. In her presence he felt constrained. She was twenty-nine, as he was, but she seemed to him much older. He felt foolish, almost unreal, beside her. She was so static. As he was fingering some shed plum blossom on a low bough, she came to the back door to shake the tablecloth. Fowls raced from the stackyard, birds rustled from the trees. Her dark hair was gathered up in a coil like a crown on her head. She was very straight, distant in her bearing. As she folded the cloth, she looked away over the hills.

Presently Syson returned indoors. She had prepared eggs and curd cheese, stewed gooseberries and cream.

"Since you will dine tonight," she said, "I have only given you a light lunch."

"It is awfully nice," he said. "You keep a real idyllic atmosphere—your belt of straw and ivy buds."

Still they hurt each other.

He was uneasy before her. Her brief, sure speech, her distant bearing, were unfamiliar to him. He admired again her grey-black eyebrows, and her lashes. Their eyes met. He saw, in the beautiful grey and black of her glance, tears and a strange light, and at the back of all, calm acceptance of herself, and triumph over him.

He felt himself shrinking. With an effort he kept up the ironic manner.

She sent him into the parlour while she washed the dishes. The long low room was refurnished from the Abbey sale, with chairs upholstered in claret-coloured rep, many years old, and an oval table of polished walnut, and another piano, handsome, though still antique. In spite of the strangeness, he was pleased. Opening a high cupboard let into the thickness of the wall, he found it full of his books, his old lesson-books, and volumes of verse he had sent her, English and German. The daffodils in the white window-bottoms shone across the room, he could almost feel their rays. The old glamour caught him again. His youthful watercolours on the wall no longer made him grin; he remembered how fervently he had tried to paint for her, twelve years before.

She entered, wiping a dish, and he saw again the bright, kernel-white beauty of her arms.

"You are quite splendid here," he said, and their eyes met.

"Do you like it?" she asked. It was the old, low, husky tone of intimacy. He felt a quick change beginning in his blood. It was the old, delicious sublimation, the thinning, almost the vaporizing of himself, as if his spirit were to be liberated.

"Aye," he nodded, smiling at her like a boy again. She bowed her head.

"This was the countess's chair," she said in low tones. "I found her scissors down here between the padding."

"Did you? Where are they?"

Quickly, with a lilt in her movement, she fetched her workbasket, and together they examined the long-shanked old scissors.

"I knew you could use them," she said, laughing, as he fitted his fingers into the round loops of the countess's scissors.

"I knew you could use them," she said, with certainty. He looked at his fingers, and at the scissors. She meant his fingers were fine enough for the small-looped scissors.

"That is something to be said for me," he laughed, putting the scissors aside. She turned to the window. He noticed the fine, fair down on her cheek and her upper lip, and her soft, white neck, like the throat of a nettle flower, and her fore-arms, bright as newly blanched kernels. He was looking at her with new eyes, and she was a different person to him. He did not know her. But he could regard her objectively now.

"Shall we go out awhile?" she asked.

"Yes!" he answered. But the predominant emotion, that troubled the excitement and perplexity of his heart, was fear, fear of that which he saw. There was about her the same manner, the same intonation in her voice, now as then, but she was not what he had known her to be. He knew quite well what she had been for him. And gradually he was realizing that she was something quite other, and always had been.

She put no covering on her head, merely took off her apron, saying, "We will go by the larches." As they passed the old orchard, she called him in to show him a blue-tit's nest in one of the apple trees, and a sycock's in the hedge. He rather wondered at her surety, at a certain hardness like arrogance hidden under her humility.

"Look at the apple buds," she said, and he then perceived myriads of little scarlet balls among the drooping boughs. Watching his face, her eyes went hard. She saw the scales were fallen from him, and at last he was going to see her as she was. It was the thing she had most dreaded in the past, and most needed, for her soul's sake. Now he was going to see her as she was. He would not love her, and he would know he never could love her. The old illusion gone, they were strangers, crude and entire. But he would give her her due—she would have her due from him.

She was brilliant as he had not known her. She showed him nests: a jenny wren's in a low bush.

"See this jinty's!" she exclaimed.

He was surprised to hear her use the local name. She reached carefully through the thorns, and put her finger in the nest's round door.

"Five!" she said. "Tiny little things."

She showed him nests of robins, and chaffinches, and linnets, and buntings; of a wagtail beside the water.

"And if we go down, nearer the lake, I will show you a kingfisher's. . . ."

"Among the young fir trees," she said, "there's a throstle's or a blackie's on nearly every bough, every ledge. The first day, when I had seen them all, I felt as if I mustn't go in the wood. It seemed a city of birds: and in the morning, hearing them all, I thought of the noisy early markets. I was afraid to go in my own wood."

She was using the language they had both of them invented. Now it was all her own. He had done with it. She did not mind his silence, but was always dominant, letting him see her wood. As they came along a marshy path where forget-me-nots were opening in a rich blue drift: "We know all the birds, but there are many flowers we can't find out," she said. It was half an appeal to him, who had known the names of things.

She looked dreamily across the open fields that slept in the sun.

"I have a lover as well, you know," she said, with assurance, yet dropping again almost into the intimate tone.

This woke in him the spirit to fight her.

"I think I met him. He is good-looking—also in Arcady."

Without answering, she turned into a dark path that led up-hill, where the trees and undergrowth were very thick.

"They did well," she said at length, "to have various altars to various gods, in old days."

"Ah yes!" he agreed. "To whom is the new one?"

"There are no old ones," she said. "I was always looking for this."

"And whose is it?" he asked.

"I don't know," she looking full at him.

"I'm very glad for your sake," he said, "that you are satisfied."

"Aye—but the man doesn't matter so much," she said. There was a pause.

"No!" he exclaimed, astonished, yet recognizing her as her real self.

"It is one's self that matters," she said. "Whether one is being one's own self and serving one's own God."

There was silence, during which he pondered. The path was almost flowerless, gloomy. At the side, his heels sank into soft clay.

III

"I," she said, very slowly, "I was married the same night as you."

He looked at her.

"Not legally, of course," she replied. "But—actually."

"To the keeper?" he said, not knowing what else to say.

She turned to him.

"You thought I could not?" she said. But the flush was deep in her cheek and throat, for all her assurance.

Still he would not say anything.

"You see"—she was making an effort to explain—"I had to understand also."

"And what does it amount to, this *understanding*?" he asked.

"A very great deal—does it not to you?" she replied. "One is free."

"And you are not disappointed?"

"Far from it!" Her tone was deep and sincere.
"You love him?"
"Yes, I love him."
"Good!" he said.
This silenced her for a while.
"Here, among his things, I love him," she said.
His conceit would not let him be silent.
"It needs this setting?" he asked.
"It does," she cried. "You were always making me to be not myself."
He laughed shortly.
"But is it a matter of surroundings?" he said. He had considered her all spirit.
"I am like a plant," she replied. "I can only grow in my own soil."
They came to a place where the undergrowth shrank away, leaving a bare, brown space, pillared with the brick-red and purplish trunks of pine trees. On the fringe, hung the sombre green of elder trees, with flat flowers in bud, and below were bright, unfurling pennons of fern. In the midst of the bare space stood a keeper's log hut. Pheasant-coops were lying about, some occupied by a clucking hen, some empty.

Hilda walked over the brown pine-needles to the hut, took a key from among the eaves, and opened the door. It was a bare wooden place with a carpenter's bench and form, carpenter's tools, an axe, snares, traps, some skins pegged down, everything in order. Hilda close the door. Syson examined the weird flat coats of wild animals, that were pegged down to be cured. She turned some knotch in the side wall, and disclosed a second, small apartment.

"How romantic!" said Syson.
"Yes. He is very curious—he has some of a wild animal's cunning—in a nice sense—and he is inventive, and thoughtful—but not beyond a certain point."

She pulled back a dark green curtain. The apartment was occupied almost entirely by a large couch of heather and bracken, on which was an ample rabbit-skin rug. On the floor were patchwork rugs of cat-skin, and a red calf-skin, while hanging from the wall were other furs. Hilda took down one which she put on. It was a cloak of rabbit-skin and of white fur, with a hood, apparently of the skins of stoats. She laughed at Syson from out of this barbaric mantle, saying:

"What do you think of it?"
"Ah—! I congratulate you on your man," he replied.
"And look!" she said.

In a little jar on a shelf were some sprays, frail and white, of the first honeysuckle.

"They will scent the place at night," she said.

He looked round curiously.

"Where does he come short, then?" he asked. She gazed at him for a few moments. Then, turning aside:

"The stars aren't the same with him," she said. "You could make them flash and quiver, and the forget-me-nots come up at me like phosphorescence. You could make things *wonderful*. I have it out—it is true. But I have them all for myself, now."

He laughed, saying:

"After all, stars and forget-me-nots are only luxuries. You ought to make poetry."

"Aye," she assented. "But I have them all now."

Again he laughed bitterly at her.

She turned swiftly. He was leaning against the small window of the tiny, obscure room and was watching her, who stood in the doorway, still cloaked in her mantle. His cap was removed, so she saw his face and head distinctly in the dim room. His black, straight, glossy hair was brushed clean back from his brow. His black eyes were watching her, and his face, that was clear and cream, and perfectly smooth, was flickering.

"We are very different," she said bitterly.

Again he laughed.

"I see you disapprove of me," he said.

"I disapprove of what you have become," she said.

"You think we might"—he glanced at the hut—"have been like this—you and I?"

She shook her head.

"You! No; never! You plucked a thing and looked at it till you had found out all you wanted to know about it, then you threw it away," she said.

"Did I?" he asked. "And could your way never have been my way? I suppose not."

"Why should it?" she said. "I am a separate being."

"But surely two people sometimes go the same way," he said.

"You took me away from myself," she said.

He knew he had mistaken her, had taken her for something she was not. That was his fault, not hers.

"And did you always know?" he asked.

"No—you never let me know. You bullied me. I couldn't help myself. I was glad when you left me, really."

"I know you were," he said. But his face went paler, almost deathly luminous.

"Yet," he said, "it was you who sent me the way I have gone."

"I!" she exclaimed, in pride.

"You *would* have me take the Grammar School scholarship—and you would have me foster poor little Botell's fervent attachment to me, till he couldn't live without me—and because Botell was rich and influential. You triumphed in the wine-merchant's offer to send me to Cambridge, to befriend his only child. You wanted me to rise in the world. And all the time you were sending me away from you—every new success of mine put a separation between us, and more for you than for me. You never wanted to come with me: you wanted just to send me to see what it was like. I believe you even wanted me to marry a lady. You wanted to triumph over society in me."

"And I am responsible," she said, with sarcasm.

"I distinguished myself to satisfy you," he replied.

"Ah!" she cried, "you always wanted change, change, like a child."

"Very well! And I am a success, and I know it, and I do some good work. But—I thought you were different. What right have you to a man?"

"What do you want?" she said, looking at him with wide, fearful eyes.

He looked back at her, his eyes pointed, like weapons.

"Why, nothing," he laughed shortly.

There was a rattling at the outer latch, and the keeper entered. The woman glanced round, but remained standing, fur-cloaked, in the inner doorway. Syson did not move.

The other man entered, saw, and turned away without speaking. The two also were silent.

Pilbeam attended to his skins.

"I must go," said Syson.

"Yes," she replied.

"Then I give you 'To our vast and varying fortunes.'" He lifted his hand in pledge.

"'To our vast and varying fortunes,'" she answered gravely, and speaking in cold tones.

"Arthur!" she said.

The keeper pretended not to hear. Syson, watching keenly, began to smile. The woman drew herself up.

"Arthur!" she said again, with a curious upward inflection, which warned the two men that her soul was trembling on a dangerous crisis.

The keeper slowly put down his tool and came to her.

"Yes," he said.

"I wanted to introduce you," she said, trembling.

"I've met him a'ready," said the keeper.

"Have you? It is Addy, Mr. Syson, whom you know about.—This is Arthur, Mr. Pilbeam," she added, turning to Syson. The latter held out his hand to the keeper, and they shook hands in silence.

"I'm glad to have met you," said Syson. "We drop our correspondence, Hilda?"

"Why need we?" she asked.

The two men stood at a loss.

"*Is* there no need?" said Syson.

Still she was silent.

"It is as you will," she said.

They went all three together down the gloomy path.

" 'Qu'il était bleu, le ciel, et grand l'espoir,' " quoted Syson, not knowing what to say.

"What do you mean?" she said. "Besides, *we* can't walk in *our* wild oats—we never sowed any."

Syson looked at her. He was startled to see his young love, his nun, his Botticelli angel, so revealed. It was he who had been the fool. He and she were more separate than any two strangers could be. She only wanted to keep up a correspondence with him—and he, of course, wanted it kept up, so that he could write to her, like Dante to some Beatrice who had never existed save in the man's own brain.

At the bottom of the path she left him. He went along with the keeper, towards the open, towards the gate that closed on the wood. The two men walked almost like friends. They did not broach the subject of their thoughts.

Instead of going straight to the high-road gate, Syson went along the wood's edge, where the brook spread out in a little bog, and under the alder trees, among the reeds, great yellow stools and bosses of marigolds shone. Threads of brown water trickled by, touched with gold from the flowers. Suddenly there was a blue flash in the air, as a kingfisher passed.

Syson was extraordinarily moved. He climbed the bank to the gorse bushes, whose sparks of blossom had not yet gathered into a flame. Lying on the dry brown turf, he discovered sprigs of tiny purple milkwort and pink spots of lousewort. What a wonderful world it was—marvellous, forever new. He felt as if it were underground, like the fields of monotone hell, notwithstanding. Inside his breast was a pain like a wound. He remembered the poem of William Morris, where in the Chapel of Lyonesse, a knight lay wounded, with the truncheon of a spear deep in his breast, lying always as dead, yet did not die, while day after day the coloured sunlight dipped from the painted window across the chancel, and passed away. He knew now it never had been true, that which was between him and her, not for a moment. The truth had stood apart all the time.

Syson turned over. The air was full of the sound of larks, as if the sunshine above were condensing and falling in a shower. Amid this bright sound, voices sounded small and distinct.

"But if he's married, an' quite willing to drop it off, what has ter against it?" said the man's voice.

"I don't want to talk about it now. I want to be alone."

Syson looked through the bushes. Hilda was standing in the wood, near the gate. The man was in the field, loitering by the hedge, and playing with the bees as they settled on the white bramble flowers.

There was silence for a while, in which Syson imagined her will among the brightness of the larks. Suddenly the keeper exclaimed "Ah!" and swore. He was gripping at the sleeve of his coat, near the shoulder. Then he pulled off his jacket, threw it on the ground, and absorbedly rolled up his shirt sleeve right to the shoulder.

"Ah!" he said vindictively, as he picked out the bee and flung it away. He twisted his fine, bright arm, peering awkwardly over his shoulder.

"What is it?" asked Hilda.

"A bee—crawled up my sleeve," he answered.

"Come here to me," she said.

The keeper went to her, like a sulky boy. She took his arm in her hands.

"Here it is—and the sting left in—poor bee!"

She picked out the sting, put her mouth to his arm, and sucked away the drop of poison. As she looked at the red mark her mouth had made, and at his arm, she said, laughing:

"That is the reddest kiss you will ever have."

When Syson next looked up, at the sound of voices, he saw in the shadow the keeper with his mouth on the throat of his beloved, whose head was thrown back, and whose hair had fallen, so that one rough rope of dark brown hair hung across his bare arm.

"No," the woman answered. "I am not upset because he's gone. You won't understand. . . ."

Syson could not distinguish what the man said. Hilda replied, clear and distinct:

"You know I love you, he has gone quite out of my life—don't trouble about him. . . ." He kissed her, murmuring. She laughed hollowly.

"Yes," she said, indulgent. "We will be married, we will be married.

But not just yet." He spoke to her again. Syson heard nothing for a time. Then she said:

"You must go home, now, dear—you will get no sleep."

Again was heard the murmur of the keeper's voice, troubled by fear and passion.

"But why should we be married at once?" she said. "What more would you have, by being married? It is most beautiful as it is."

At last he pulled on his coat and departed. She stood at the gate, not watching him, but looking over the sunny country.

When at last she had gone, Syson also departed, going back to town.

Araby

North Richmond Street, being blind, was a quiet street except at the hour when the Christian Brothers' School set the boys free. An uninhabited house of two stories stood at the blind end, detached from its neighbours in a square ground. The other houses of the street, conscious of decent lives within them, gazed at one another with brown imperturbable faces.

The former tenant of our house, a priest, had died in the back drawingroom. Air, musty from having been long enclosed, hung in all the rooms, and the waste room behind the kitchen was littered with old useless papers. Among these I found a few paper-covered books, the pages of which were curled and damp: *The Abbot*, by Walter Scott, *The Devout Communicant*, and *The Memoirs of Vidocq*. I liked the last best because its leaves were yellow. The wild garden behind the house contained a central apple tree and a few straggling bushes under one of which I found the late tenant's rusty bicycle pump. He had been a very charitable priest; in his will he had left all his money to institutions and the furniture of his house to his sister.

When the short days of winter came dusk fell before we had well eaten our dinners. When we met in the street the houses had grown sombre. The space of sky above us was the colour of ever-changing violet and towards it the lamps of the street lifted their feeble lanterns. The cold air stung us and we played till our bodies glowed. Our shouts echoed in the silent street. The career of our play brought us through the dark muddy lanes behind the houses where we ran the gauntlet of the rough tribes from the cottages, to the back doors of the dark dripping gardens where odours arose from the ash-pits, to the dark odorous stables where a coachman smoothed and combed the horse or shook music from the buckled harness. When we returned to the street, light from the kitchen windows had filled the areas. If my uncle was seen turning the corner we hid in the shadow until we had seen him safely housed. Or if Mangan's sister came out on the doorstep to call her brother in to his tea we watched her from our shadow peer up and down the street. We waited to see whether she would remain or go in and, if she remained, we left our shadow and walked up to Mangan's steps resignedly. She was waiting for us, her figure defined by the light from the half-opened door. Her brother always teased her before he obeyed and I stood by the railings looking at her. Her dress swung as she moved her body and the soft rope of her hair tossed from side to side.

Every morning I lay on the floor in the front parlour watching her door. The blind was pulled down to within an inch of the sash so that I could not be seen. When she came out on the doorstep my heart leaped. I ran to the hall, seized my books and followed her. I kept her brown figure always in my eye and, when we came near the point at which our ways diverged, I quickened my pace and passed her. This happened morning after morning. I had never spoken to her, except for a few casual words, and yet her name was like a summons to all my foolish blood.

Her image accompanied me even in places the most hostile to romance. On Saturday evenings when my aunt went marketing I had to go to carry some of the parcels. We walked through the flaring streets, jostled by drunken men and bargaining women, amid the curses of labourers, the shrill litanies of shop-boys who stood on guard by the barrels of pigs' cheeks, the nasal chanting of street-singers, who sang a *come-all-you* about O'Donovan Rossa, or a ballad about the troubles in our native land. These noises converged in a single sensation of life for me: I imagined that I bore my chalice safely through a throng of foes. Her name sprang to my lips at moments in strange prayers and praises which I myself did not understand. My eyes were often full of tears (I could not tell why) and at times a flood from my heart seemed to pour itself out into my bosom. I thought little of the future. I did not know whether I would ever speak to her or not or, if I spoke to her, how I could tell her of my confused adoration. But my body was like a harp and her words and gestures were like fingers running upon the wires.

One evening I went into the back drawing-room in which the priest had died. It was a dark rainy evening and there was no sound in the house. Through one of the broken panes I heard the rain impinge upon the earth, the fine incessant needles of water playing in the sodden beds. Some distant lamp or lighted window gleamed below me. I was thankful that I could see so little. All my senses seemed to desire to veil themselves and, feeling that I was about to slip from them, I pressed the palms of my hands together until they trembled, murmuring: "*O love! O love!*" many times.

At last she spoke to me. When she addressed the first words to me I was so confused that I did not know what to answer. She asked me was I going to *Araby*. I forgot whether I answered yes or no. It would be a splendid bazaar, she said she would love to go.

"And why can't you?" I asked.

While she spoke she turned a silver bracelet round and round her wrist. She could not go, she said, because there would be a retreat that week in her convent. Her brother and two other boys were fighting for their caps and I was alone at the railings. She held one of the spikes, bowing her head towards me. The light from the lamp opposite our door caught the white curve of her neck, lit up her hair that rested there and, falling, lit up the hand upon the railing. It fell over one side of her dress and caught the white border of a petticoat, just visible as she stood at ease.

"It's well for you," she said.

"If I go," I said, "I will bring you something."

What innumerable follies laid waste my waking and sleeping thoughts after the evening! I wished to annihilate the tedious intervening days. I chafed against the work of school. At night in my bedroom and by day in the classroom her image came between me and the page I strove to read. The syllables of the word *Araby* were called to me through the silence in which my soul luxuriated and cast an Eastern enchantment over me. I asked for leave to go to the bazaar on Saturday night. My aunt was surprised and hoped it was not some Freemason affair. I answered few questions in class. I watched my master's face pass from amiability to sternness; he hoped I was not beginning to idle, I could not call my wandering thoughts together. I had hardly any patience with the serious work of life which, now that it stood between me and my desire, seemed to me child's play, ugly monotonous child's play.

On Saturday morning I reminded my uncle that I wished to go to the bazaar in the evening. He was fussing at the hall-stand, looking for the hat brush, and answered me curtly:

"Yes, boy, I know."

As he was in the hall I could not go into the front parlour and lie at the window. I left the house in bad humour and walked slowly towards the school. The air was pitilessly raw and already my heart misgave me.

When I came home to dinner my uncle had not yet been home. Still it was early. I sat staring at the clock for some time and, when its ticking began to irritate me, I left the room. I mounted the staircase and gained the upper part of the house. The high cold empty gloomy rooms liberated me and I went from room to room singing. From the front window I saw my companions playing below in the street. Their cries reached me weakened and indistinct and, leaning my forehead against the cool glass, I looked over at the dark house where she lived. I may have stood there for an hour, seeing nothing but the brown-clad figure cast by my imagination, touched discreetly by the lamplight at the curved neck, at the hand upon the railings and at the border below the dress.

When I came downstairs again I found Mrs. Mercer sitting at the fire. She was an old garrulous woman, a pawnbroker's widow, who collected used stamps for some pious purpose. I had to endure the gossip of the tea-table. The meal was prolonged beyond an hour and still my uncle did not come. Mrs. Mercer stood up to go: she was sorry she couldn't wait any longer, but it was after eight o'clock and she did not like to be out late, as the night air was bad for her. When she had gone I began to walk up and down the room, clenching my fists. My aunt said:

"I'm afraid you may put off your bazaar for this night of Our Lord."

At nine o'clock I heard my uncle's latchkey in the halldoor. I heard him talking to himself and heard the hallstand rocking when it had received the weight of his overcoat. I could interpret these signs. When he was midway through his dinner I asked him to give me the money to go to the bazaar. He had forgotten.

"The people are in bed and after their first sleep now," he said.

I did not smile. My aunt said to him energetically:

"Can't you give him the money and let him go? You've kept him late enough as it is."

My uncle said he was very sorry he had forgotten. He said he believed in the old saying: "All work and no play makes Jack a dull boy." He asked me where I was going and, when I had told him a second time, he asked me did I know *The Arab's Farewell to his Steed*. When I left the kitchen he was about to recite the opening lines of the piece to my aunt.

I held a florin tightly in my hand as I strode down Buckingham Street towards the station. The sight of the streets thronged with buyers and glaring with gas recalled to me the purpose of my journey. I took my seat in a third-class carriage of a deserted train. After an intolerable delay the train moved out of the station slowly. It crept onward among ruinous houses and over the twinkling river. At Westland Row Station a crowd of people pressed to the carriage doors; but the porters moved them back, saying that it was a special train for the bazaar. I remained alone in the bare carriage. In a few minutes the train drew up beside an improvised wooden platform. I passed out on the road and saw by the lighted dial of a clock that it was ten minutes to ten. In front of me was a large building which displayed the magical name.

I could not find any sixpenny entrance and, fearing that the bazaar would be closed, I passed in quickly through a turnstile, handing a shilling to a weary-looking man. I found myself in a big hall girdled at half its height by a gallery. Nearly all the stalls were closed and the greater part of the hall was in darkness. I recognized a silence like that which pervades a church after a service. I walked into the center of the bazaar timidly. A few people were gathered about the stalls which were still open. Before a curtain, over which the words *Café Chantant* were written in coloured lamps, two men were counting money on a salver. I listened to the fall of the coins.

Remembering with difficulty why I had come I went over to one of the stalls and examined porcelain vases and flowered tea-sets. At the door of the stall a young lady was talking and laughing with two young gentlemen. I remarked their English accents and listened vaguely to their conversation.

"O, I never said such a thing!"

"O, but you did!"

"O, but I didn't!"

"Didn't she say that?"

"Yes. I heard her."

"O, there's a . . . fib!"

Observing me, the young lady came over and asked me did I wish to buy anything. The tone of her voice was not encouraging; she seemed to have spoken to me out of a sense of duty. I looked humbly at the great jars that stood like eastern guards at either side of the dark entrance to the stall and murmured:

"No, thank you."

The young lady changed the position of one of the vases and went back to the two young men. They began to talk of the same subject. Once or twice the young lady glanced at me over her shoulder.

I lingered before her stall, though I knew my stay was useless, to make my interest in her wares seem the more real. Then I turned away slowly and walked down the middle of the bazaar. I allowed the two pennies to fall against the sixpence in my pocket. I heard a voice call from one end of the gallery that the light was out. The upper part of the hall was now completely dark.

Gazing up into the darkness I saw myself as a creature driven and derided by vanity; and my eyes burned with anguish and anger.

That Evening Sun

I

Monday is no different from any other weekday in Jefferson now. The streets are paved now, and the telephone and electric companies are cutting down more and more of the shade trees—the water oaks, the maples and locusts and elms—to make room for iron poles bearing clusters of bloated and ghostly and bloodless grapes, and we have a city laundry which makes the rounds on Monday morning, gathering the bundles of clothes into bright-colored, specially-made motor cars: the soiled wearing of a whole week now flees apparitionlike behind alert and irritable electric horns, with a long diminishing noise of rubber and asphalt like tearing silk, and even the Negro women who still take in white people's washing after the old custom, fetch and deliver it in automobiles.

But fifteen years ago, on Monday morning the quiet, dusty, shady streets would be full of Negro women with, balanced on their steady, turbaned heads, bundles of clothes tied up in sheets, almost as large as cotton bales, carried so without touch of hand between the kitchen door of the white house and the blackened washpot beside a cabin door in Negro Hollow.

Nancy would set her bundle on the top of her head, then upon the bundle in turn she would set the black straw sailor hat which she wore winter and summer. She was tall, with a high, sad face sunken a little where her teeth were missing. Sometimes we would go a part of the way down the lane and across the pasture with her, to watch the balanced bundle and the hat that never bobbed nor wavered, even when she walked down into the ditch and up the other side and stooped through the fence. She would go down on her hands and knees and crawl through the gap, her head rigid, uptilted, the bundle steady as a rock or a balloon, and rise to her feet again and go on.

Sometimes the husbands of the washing women would fetch and deliver the clothes, but Jesus never did that for Nancy, even before father told him to stay away from our house, even when Dilsey was sick and Nancy would come to cook for us.

And then about half the time we'd have to go down the lane to Nancy's cabin and tell her to come on and cook breakfast. We would stop at the ditch, because father told us to not have anything to do with Jesus—he was a short black man, with a razor scar down his face—and we would throw rocks at Nancy's house until she came to the door, leaning her head around it without any clothes on.

"What yawl mean, chunking my house?" Nancy said. "What you little devils mean?"

"Father says for you to come on and get breakfast," Caddy said. "Father says it's over a half an hour now, and you've got to come this minute."

"I aint studying no breakfast," Nancy said. "I going to get my sleep out."

"I bet you're drunk," Jason said. "Father says you're drunk. Are you drunk, Nancy?"

"Who says I is?" Nancy said. "I got to get my sleep out. I aint studying no breakfast."

So after a while we quit chunking the cabin and went back home. When she finally came, it was too late for me to go to school. So we thought it was whisky until that day they arrested her again and they were taking her to jail and they passed Mr Stovall. He was the cashier in the bank and a deacon in the Baptist church, and Nancy began to say:

"When you going to pay me, white man? When you going to pay me, white man? It's been three times now since you paid me a cent—" Mr Stovall knocked her down, but she kept on saying, "When you going to pay me, white man? It's been three times now since—" until Mr Stovall kicked her in the mouth with his heel and the marshal caught Mr Stovall back, and Nancy lying in the street, laughing. She turned her head and spat out some blood and teeth and said, "It's been three times now since he paid me a cent."

That was how she lost her teeth, and all that day they told about Nancy and Mr Stovall, and all that night the ones that passed the jail could hear Nancy singing and yelling. They could see her hands holding to the window bars, and a lot of them stopped along the fence, listening to her and to the jailer trying to make her stop. She didn't shut up until almost daylight, when the jailer began to hear a bumping and a scraping upstairs and he went up there and found Nancy hanging from the window bar. He said that it was cocaine and not whisky, because no nigger would try to commit suicide unless he was full of cocaine, because a nigger full of cocaine wasn't a nigger any longer.

The jailer cut her down and revived her; then he beat her, whipped her. She had hung herself with her dress. She had fixed it all right, but when they arrested her she didn't have on anything except a dress and so she didn't have anything to tie her hands with and she couldn't make her hands let go of the window ledge. So the jailer heard the noise and ran up there and found Nancy hanging from the window, stark naked, her belly already swelling out a little, like a little balloon.

When Dilsey was sick in her cabin and Nancy was cooking for us, we could see her apron swelling out; that was before father told Jesus to stay away from the house. Jesus was in the kitchen, sitting behind the stove, with his razor scar on his black face like a piece of dirty string. He said it was a watermelon that Nancy had under her dress.

"It never come off your vine, though," Nancy said.

"Off of what vine?" Caddy said.

"I can cut down the vine it did come off of," Jesus said.

"What makes you want to talk like that before these chillen?" Nancy said. "Whyn't you go on to work? You done et. You want Mr Jason to catch you hanging around his kitchen, talking that way before these children?"

"Talking what way?" Caddy said. "What vine?"

"I cant hang around white man's kitchen," Jesus said. "But white man can hang around mine. White man can come in my house, but I cant stop him. When white man want to come in my house, I aint got no house. I cant stop him, but he cant kick me outen it. He cant do that."

Dilsey was still sick in her cabin. Father told Jesus to stay off our place. Dilsey was still sick. It was a long time. We were in the library after supper.

"Isn't Nancy through in the kitchen yet?" mother said. "It seems to me that she has had plenty of time to have finished the dishes."

"Let Quentin go and see," father said. "Go and see if Nancy is through, Quentin. Tell her she can go on home."

I went to the kitchen. Nancy was through. The dishes were put away and the fire was out. Nancy was sitting in a chair, close to the cold stove. She looked at me.

"Mother wants to know if you are through," I said.

"Yes," Nancy said. She looked at me. "I done finished." She looked at me.

"What is it?" I said. "What is it?"

"I aint nothing but a nigger," Nancy said. "It aint none of my fault."

She looked at me, sitting in the chair before the cold stove, the sailor hat on her head. I went back to the library. It was the cold stove and all, when you think of a kitchen being warm and busy and cheerful. And with a cold stove and the dishes all put away, and nobody wanting to eat at that hour.

"Is she through?" mother said.

"Yessum," I said.

"What is she doing?" mother said.

"She's not doing anything. She's through."

"I'll go and see," father said.

"Maybe she's waiting for Jesus to come and take her home," Caddy said.

"Jesus is gone," I said. Nancy told us how one morning she woke up and Jesus was gone.

"He quit me," Nancy said. "Done gone to Memphis, I reckon. Dodging them city *po*-lice for a while, I reckon."

"And a good riddance," father said. "I hope he stays there."

"Nancy's scaired of the dark," Jason said.

"So are you," Caddy said.

"I'm not," Jason said.

"Scairy cat," Caddy said.

"I'm not," Jason said.

"You, Candace!" mother said. Father came back.

"I am going to walk down the lane with Nancy," he said. "She says that Jesus is back."

"Has she seen him?" mother said.

"No. Some Negro sent her word that he was back in town. I wont be long."

"You'll leave me alone, to take Nancy home?" mother said. "Is her safety more precious to you than mine?"

"I wont be long," father said.

"You'll leave these children unprotected, with that Negro about?"

"I'm going too," Caddy said. "Let me go, Father."

"What would he do with them, if he were unfortunate enough to have them?" father said.

"I want to go, too," Jason said.

"Jason!" mother said. She was speaking to father. You could tell that by the way she said the name. Like she believed that all day father had been trying to think of doing the thing she wouldn't like the most, and that she knew all the time that after a while he would think of it. I stayed quiet, because father and I both knew that mother would want him to make me stay with her if she just thought of it in time. So father didn't look at me. I was the oldest. I was nine and Caddy was seven and Jason was five.

"Nonsense," father said. "We wont be long."

Nancy had her hat on. We came to the lane. "Jesus always been good to me," Nancy said. "Whenever he had two dollars, one of them was mine." We walked in the lane. "If I can just get through the lane," Nancy said, "I be all right then."

The lane was always dark. "This is where Jason got scared on Hallowe'en," Caddy said.

"I didn't," Jason said.

"Cant Aunt Rachel do anything with him?" father said. Aunt Rachel was old. She lived in a cabin beyond Nancy's, by herself. She had white hair and she smoked a pipe in the door, all day long; she didn't work any more. They said she was Jesus' mother. Sometimes she said she was and sometimes she said she wasn't any kin to Jesus.

"Yes, you did," Caddy said. "You were scairder than Frony. You were scairder than T.P. even. Scairder than niggers."

"Cant nobody do nothing with him," Nancy said. "He say I done woke up the devil in him and aint but one thing going to lay it down again."

"Well, he's gone now," father said. "There's nothing for you to be afraid of now. And if you'd just let white men alone."

"Let what white men alone?" Caddy said. "How let them alone?"

"He aint gone nowhere," Nancy said. "I can feel him. I can feel him now, in this lane. He hearing us talk, every word, hid somewhere, waiting. I aint seen him, and I aint going to see him again but once more, with that razor in his mouth. That razor on that string down his back, inside his shirt. And then I aint going to be even surprised."

"I wasn't scaired," Jason said.

"If you'd behave yourself, you'd have kept out of this," father said. "But it's all right now. He's probably in St. Louis now. Probably got another wife by now and forgot all about you."

"If he has, I better not find out about it," Nancy said. "I'd stand there right over them, and every time he wropped her, I'd cut that arm off. I'd cut his head off and I'd slit her belly and I'd shove—"

"Hush," father said.

"Slit whose belly, Nancy?" Caddy said.

"I wasn't scaired," Jason said. "I'd walk right down this lane by myself."

"Yah," Caddy said. "You wouldn't dare to put your foot down in it if we were not here too."

II

Dilsey was still sick, so we took Nancy home every night until mother said, "How much longer is this going on? I to be left alone in this big house while you take home a frightened Negro?"

We fixed a pallet in the kitchen for Nancy. One night we waked up, hearing the sound. It was not singing and it was not crying, coming up the dark stairs. There was a light in mother's room and we heard father going down the hall, down the back stairs, and Caddy and I went into the hall. The floor was cold. Our toes curled away from it while we listened to the sound. It was like singing and it wasn't like singing, like the sounds that Negroes make.

Then it stopped and we heard father going down the back stairs, and we went to the head of the stairs. Then the sound began again, in the stairway, not loud, and we could see Nancy's eyes halfway up the stairs, against the wall. They looked like cat's eyes do, like a big cat against the wall, watching us. When we came down the steps to where she was, she quit making the sound again, and we stood there until father came back up from the kitchen, with his pistol in his hand. He went back down with Nancy and they came back with Nancy's pallet.

We spread the pallet in our room. After the light in mother's room went off, we could see Nancy's eyes again. "Nancy," Caddy whispered, "are you asleep, Nancy?"

Nancy whispered something. It was oh or no, I dont know which. Like nobody had made it, like it came from nowhere and went nowhere, until it was like Nancy was not there at all; that I had looked so hard at her eyes on the stairs that they had got printed on my eyeballs, like the sun does when you have closed your eyes and there is no sun. "Jesus," Nancy whispered, "Jesus."

"Was it Jesus?" Caddy said. "Did he try to come into the kitchen?"

"Jesus," Nancy said. Like this: Jeeeeeeeeeeeeeeesus, until the sound went out, like a match or a candle does.

"It's the other Jesus she means," I said.

"Can you see us, Nancy?" Caddy whispered. "Can you see your eyes too?"

"I aint nothing but a nigger," Nancy said. "God knows. God knows."

"What did you see down there in the kitchen?" Caddy whispered. "What tried to get in?"

"God knows," Nancy said. We could see her eyes. "God knows."

Dilsey got well. She cooked dinner. "You'd better stay in bed a day or two longer," father said.

"What for?" Dilsey said. "If I had been a day later, this place would be to rack and ruin. Get on out of here now, and let me get my kitchen straight again."

Dilsey cooked supper too. And that night, just before dark, Nancy came into the kitchen.

"How do you know he's back?" Dilsey said. "You aint seen him."

"Jesus is a nigger," Jason said.

"I can feel him," Nancy said. "I can feel him laying yonder in the ditch."

"Tonight?" Dilsey said. "Is he there tonight?"

"Dilsey's a nigger too," Jason said.

"You try to eat something," Dilsey said.

"I dont want nothing," Nancy said.

"I aint a nigger," Jason said.

"Drink some coffee," Dilsey said. She poured a cup of coffee for Nancy. "Do you know he's out there tonight? How come you know it's tonight?"

"I know," Nancy said. "He's there, waiting. I know. I done lived with him too long. I know what he is fixing to do fore he know it himself."

"Drink some coffee," Dilsey said. Nancy held the cup to her mouth and blew into the cup. Her mouth pursed out like a spreading adder's, like a rubber mouth, like she had blown all the color out of her lips with blowing the coffee.

"I aint a nigger," Jason said. "Are you a nigger, Nancy?"

"I hellborn, child," Nancy said. "I wont be nothing soon. I going back where I come from soon."

III

She began to drink the coffee. While she was drinking, holding the cup in both hands, she began to make the sound again. She made the sound into the cup and the coffee sploshed out onto her hands and her dress. Her eyes looked at us and she sat there, her elbows on her knees, holding the cup in both hands, looking at us across the wet cup, making the sound. "Look at Nancy," Jason said. "Nancy cant cook for us now. Dilsey's got well now."

"You hush up," Dilsey said. Nancy held the cup in both hands, looking at us, making the sound, like there were two of them: one looking at us and the other making the sound. "Whynt you let Mr Jason telefoam the marshal?" Dilsey said. Nancy stopped then, holding the cup in her long brown hands. She tried to drink some coffee again, but it sploshed out of the cup, onto her hands and her dress, and she put the cup down. Jason watched her.

"I cant swallow it," Nancy said. "I swallows but it wont go down me."

"You go down to the cabin," Dilsey said. "Frony will fix you a pallet and I'll be there soon."

"Wont no nigger stop him," Nancy said.

"I aint a nigger," Jason said. "Am I, Dilsey?"

"I reckon not," Dilsey said. She looked at Nancy. "I dont reckon so. What you going to do, then?"

Nancy looked at us. Her eyes went fast, like she was afraid there wasn't time to look, without hardly moving at all. She looked at us, at all three of us at one time. "You member that night I stayed in yawls' room?" she said. She told about how we waked up early the next morning, and played. We had to play quiet, on her pallet, until father woke up and it was time to get breakfast. "Go and ask your maw to let me stay here tonight," Nancy said. "I wont need no pallet. We can play some more."

Caddy asked mother. Jason went too. "I cant have Negroes sleeping in the bedrooms," mother said. Jason cried. He cried until mother said he couldn't have any dessert for three days if he didn't stop. Then Jason said he would stop if Dilsey would make a chocolate cake. Father was there.

"Why dont you do something about it?" mother said. "What do we have officers for?"

"Why is Nancy afraid of Jesus?" Caddy said. "Are you afraid of father, mother?"

"What could the officers do?" father said. "If Nancy hasn't seen him, how could the officers find him?"

"Then why is she afraid?" mother said.

"She says he is there. She says she knows he is there tonight."

"Yet we pay taxes," mother said. "I must wait here alone in this big house while you take a Negro woman home."

"You know that I am not lying outside with a razor," father said.

"I'll stop if Dilsey will make a chocolate cake," Jason said. Mother told us to go out and father said he didn't know if Jason would get a chocolate cake or not, but he knew what Jason was going to get in about a minute. We went back to the kitchen and told Nancy.

"Father said for you to go home and lock the door, and you'll be all right," Caddy said. "All right from what, Nancy? Is Jesus mad at you?" Nancy was holding the coffee cup in her hands again, her elbows on her knees and her hands holding the cup between her knees. She was looking into the cup. "What have you done that made Jesus mad?" Caddy said. Nancy let the cup go. It didn't break on the floor, but the coffee spilled out, and Nancy sat there with her hands still making the shape of the cup. She began to make the sound again, not loud. Not singing and not unsinging. We watched her.

"Here," Dilsey said. "You quit that, now. You get aholt of yourself. You wait here. I going to get Versh to walk home with you." Dilsey went out.

We looked at Nancy. Her shoulders kept shaking, but she quit making the sound. We watched her. "What's Jesus going to do to you?" Caddy said. "He went away."

Nancy looked at us. "We had fun that night I stayed in yawls' room, didn't we?"

"I didn't," Jason said. "I didn't have any fun."

"You were asleep in mother's room," Caddy said. "You were not there."

"Let's go down to my house and have some more fun," Nancy said.

"Mother wont let us," I said. "It's too late now."

"Dont bother her," Nancy said. "We can tell her in the morning. She wont mind."

"She wouldn't let us," I said.

"Dont ask her now," Nancy said. "Dont bother her now."

"She didn't say we couldn't go," Caddy said.

"We didn't ask," I said.

"If you go, I'll tell," Jason said.

"We'll have fun," Nancy said. "They won't mind, just to my house. I been working for yawl a long time. They won't mind."

"I'm not afraid to go," Caddy said. "Jason is the one that's afraid. He'll tell."

"I'm not," Jason said.

"Yes, you are," Caddy said. "You'll tell."

"I won't tell," Jason said. "I'm not afraid."

"Jason ain't afraid to go with me," Nancy said. "Is you, Jason?"

"Jason is going to tell," Caddy said. The lane was dark. We passed the pasture gate. "I bet if something was to jump out from behind that gate, Jason would holler."

"I wouldn't," Jason said. We walked down the lane. Nancy was talking loud.

"What are you talking so loud for, Nancy?" Caddy said.

"Who; me?" Nancy said. "Listen at Quentin and Caddy and Jason saying I'm talking loud."

"You talk like there was five of us here," Caddy said. "You talk like father was here too."

"Who; me talking loud, Mr. Jason?" Nancy said.

"Nancy called Jason 'Mister,' " Caddy said.

"Listen how Caddy and Quentin and Jason talk," Nancy said.

"We're not talking loud," Caddy said. "You're the one that's talking like father—"

"Hush," Nancy said; "hush, Mr. Jason."
"Nancy called Jason 'Mister' aguh—"
"Hush," Nancy said. She was talking loud when we crossed the ditch and stooped through the fence where she used to stoop through with the clothes on her head. Then we came to her house. We were going fast then. She opened the door. The smell of the house was like the lamp and the smell of Nancy was like the wick, like they were waiting for one another to begin to smell. She lit the lamp and closed the door and put the bar up. Then she quit talking loud, looking at us.

"What're we going to do?" Caddy said.
"What do yawl want to do?" Nancy said.
"You said we would have some fun," Caddy said.
There was something about Nancy's house; something you could smell besides Nancy and the house. Jason smelled it, even. "I don't want to stay here," he said. "I want to go home."
"Go home, then," Caddy said.
"I don't want to go by myself," Jason said.
"We're going to have some fun," Nancy said.
"How?" Caddy said.
Nancy stood by the door. She was looking at us, only it was like she had emptied her eyes, like she had quit using them. "What do you want to do?" she said.
"Tell us a story," Caddy said. "Can you tell a story?"
"Yes," Nancy said.
"Tell it," Caddy said. We looked at Nancy. "You don't know any stories."
"Yes," Nancy said. "Yes, I do."
She came and sat in a chair before the hearth. There was a little fire there. Nancy built it up, when it was already hot inside. She built a good blaze. She told a story. She talked like her eyes looked, like her eyes watching us and her voice talking to us did not belong to her. Like she was living somewhere else, waiting somewhere else. She was outside the cabin. Her voice was inside and the shape of her, the Nancy that could stoop under a barbed wire fence with a bundle of clothes balanced on her head as though without weight, like a balloon, was there. But that was all. "And so this here queen come walking up to the ditch, where that bad man was hiding. She was walking up to the ditch, and she say, 'If I can just get past this here ditch,' was what she say. . . ."

"What ditch?" Caddy said. "A ditch like that one out there? Why did a queen want to go into a ditch?"

"To get to her house," Nancy said. She looked at us. "She had to cross the ditch to get into her house quick and bar the door."

"Why did she want to go home and bar the door?" Caddy said.

IV

Nancy looked at us. She quit talking. She looked at us. Jason's legs stuck straight out of his pants where he sat on Nancy's lap. "I don't think that's a good story," he said. "I want to go home."

"Maybe we had better," Caddy said. She got up from the floor. "I bet they are looking for us right now." She went toward the door.

"No," Nancy said. "Don't open it." She got up quick and passed Caddy. She didn't touch the door, the wooden bar.

"Why not?" Caddy said.

"Come back to the lamp," Nancy said. "We'll have fun. You don't have to go."

"We ought to go," Caddy said. "Unless we have a lot of fun." She and Nancy came back to the fire, the lamp.

"I want to go home," Jason said. "I'm going to tell."

"I know another story," Nancy said. She stood close to the lamp. She looked at Caddy, like when your eyes look up at a stick balanced on your nose. She had to look down to see Caddy, but her eyes looked like that, like when you are balancing a stick.

"I won't listen to it," Jason said. "I'll bang on the floor."

"It's a good one," Nancy said. "It's better than the other one."

"What's it about?" Caddy said. Nancy was standing by the lamp. Her hand was on the lamp, against the light, long and brown.

"Your hand is on that hot globe," Caddy said. "Don't it feel hot to your hand?"

Nancy looked at her hand on the lamp chimney. She took her hand away, slow. She stood there, looking at Caddy, wringing her long hand as though it were tied to her wrist with a string.

"Let's do something else," Caddy said.

"I want to go home," Jason said.

"I got some popcorn," Nancy said. She looked at Caddy and then at Jason and then at me and then at Caddy again. "I got some popcorn."

"I don't like popcorn," Jason said. "I'd rather have candy."

Nancy looked at Jason. "You can hold the popper." She was still wringing her hand; it was long and limp and brown.

"All right," Jason said. "I'll stay a while if I can do that. Caddy can't hold it. I'll want to go home again if Caddy holds the popper."

Nancy built up the fire. "Look at Nancy putting her hands in the fire," Caddy said. "What's the matter with you, Nancy?"

"I got popcorn," Nancy said. "I got some." She took the popper from under the bed. It was broken. Jason began to cry.

"Now we can't have any popcorn," he said.

"We ought to go home, anyway," Caddy said. "Come on, Quentin."

"Wait," Nancy said; "wait. I can fix it. Don't you want to help me fix it?"

"I don't think I want any," Caddy said. "It's too late now."

"You help me, Jason," Nancy said. "Don't you want to help me?"

"No," Jason said. "I want to go home."

"Hush," Nancy said; "hush. Watch. Watch me. I can fix it so Jason can hold it and pop the corn." She got a piece of wire and fixed the popper.

"It won't hold good," Caddy said.

"Yes, it will," Nancy said. "Yawl watch. Yawl help me shell some corn."

The popcorn was under the bed too. We shelled it into the popper and Nancy helped Jason hold the popper over the fire.

"It's not popping," Jason said. "I want to go home."

"You wait," Nancy said. "It'll begin to pop. We'll have fun then." She was sitting close to the fire. The lamp was turned up so high it was beginning to smoke.

"Why don't you turn it down some?" I said.

"It's all right," Nancy said. "I'll clean it. Yawl wait. The popcorn will start in a minute."

"I don't believe it's going to start," Caddy said. "We ought to start home, anyway. They'll be worried."

"No," Nancy said. "It's going to pop. Dilsey will tell um yawl with me. I been working for yawl long time. They won't mind if yawl at my house. You wait, now. It'll start popping any minute now."

Then Jason got some smoke in his eyes and he began to cry. He dropped the popper into the fire. Nancy got a wet rag and wiped Jason's face, but he didn't stop crying.

"Hush," she said. "Hush." But he didn't hush. Caddy took the popper out of the fire.

"It's burned up," she said. "You'll have to get some more popcorn, Nancy."

"Did you put all of it in?" Nancy said.

"Yes," Caddy said. Nancy looked at Caddy. Then she took the popper and opened it and poured the cinders into her apron and began to sort the grains, her hands long and brown, and we watching her.

"Haven't you got any more?" Caddy said.

"Yes," Nancy said; "yes. Look. This here ain't burnt. All we need to do is—"

"I want to go home," Jason said. "I'm going to tell."

"Hush," Caddy said. We all listened. Nancy's head was already turned toward the barred door, her eyes filled with red lamplight. "Somebody is coming," Caddy said.

Then Nancy began to make that sound again, not loud, sitting there above the fire, her long hands dangling between her knees; all of a sudden water began to come out on her face in big drops, running down her face, carrying in each one a little turning ball of firelight like a spark until it dropped off her chin. "She's not crying." I said.

"I ain't crying," Nancy said. Her eyes were closed. "I ain't crying. Who is it?"

"I don't know," Caddy said. She went to the door and looked out. "We've got to go now," she said. "Here comes father."

"I'm going to tell," Jason said. "Yawl made me come."

The water still ran down Nancy's face. She turned in her chair. "Listen. Tell him. Tell him we going to have fun. Tell him I take good care of yawl until in the morning. Tell him to let me come home with yawl and sleep on the floor. Tell him I won't need no pallet. We'll have fun. You remember last time how we had so much fun?"

"I didn't have fun," Jason said. "You hurt me. You put smoke in my eyes. I'm going to tell."

V

Father came in. He looked at us. Nancy did not get up.

"Tell him," she said.

"Caddy made us come down here," Jason said. "I didn't want to."

Father came to the fire. Nancy looked up at him. "Can't you go to Aunt Rachel's and stay?" he said. Nancy looked up at father, her hands between her knees. "He's not here," father said. "I would have seen him. There's not a soul in sight."

"He in the ditch," Nancy said. "He waiting in the ditch yonder."

"Nonsense," father said. He looked at Nancy. "Do you know he's there?"

"I got the sign," Nancy said.

"What sign?"

"I got it. It was on the table when I come in. It was a hog-bone, with blood meat still on it, laying by the lamp. He's out there. When yawl walk out that door, I gone."

"Gone where, Nancy?" Caddy said.

"I'm not a tattletale," Jason said.

"Nonsense," father said.

"He out there," Nancy said. "He looking through that window this minute, waiting for yawl to go. Then I gone."

"Nonsense," father said. "Lock up your house and we'll take you on to Aunt Rachel's."

" 'Twont do no good," Nancy said. She didn't look at father now, but he looked down at her, at her long, limp, moving hands. "Putting it off wont do no good."

"Then what do you want to do?" father said.

"I don't know," Nancy said. "I can't do nothing. Just put it off. And that don't do no good. I reckon it belong to me. I reckon what I going to get ain't no more than mine."

"Get what?" Caddy said. "What's yours?"

"Nothing," father said. "You all must get to bed."

"Caddy made me come," Jason said.

"Go on to Aunt Rachel's," father said.

"It won't do no good," Nancy said. She sat before the fire, her elbows on her knees, her long hands between her knees. "When even your own kitchen wouldn't do no good. When even if I was sleeping on the floor in the room with your chillen, and the next morning there I am, and blood—"

"Hush," father said. "Lock the door and put out the lamp and go to bed."

"I scared of the dark," Nancy said. "I scared for it to happen in the dark."

"You mean you're going to sit right here with the lamp lighted?" father said. Then Nancy began to make the sound again, sitting before the fire, her long hands between her knees. "Ah, damnation," father said. "Come along, chillen. It's past bedtime."

"When yawl go home, I gone," Nancy said. She talked quieter now, and her face looked quiet, like her hands. "Anyway, I got my coffin money saved up with Mr. Lovelady." Mr. Lovelady was a short, dirty man who collected the Negro insurance, coming around to the cabins or the kitchens every Saturday morning, to collect fifteen cents. He and his wife lived at the hotel. One morning his wife committed suicide.

They had a child, a little girl. He and the child went away. After a week or two he came back alone. We would see him going along the lanes and the back streets on Saturday mornings.

"Nonsense," father said. "You'll be the first thing I'll see in the kitchen tomorrow morning."

"You'll see what you'll see, I reckon," Nancy said. "But it will take the Lord to say what will be."

VI

We left her sitting before the fire.

"Come and put the bar up," father said. But she didn't move. She didn't look at us again, sitting quietly there between the lamp and the fire. From some distance down the lane we could look back and see her through the open door.

"What, Father?" Caddy said. "What's going to happen?"

"Nothing," father said. Jason was on father's back so Jason was the tallest of all of us. We went down into the ditch. I looked at it, quiet. I couldn't see much where the moonlight and the shadows tangled.

"If Jesus is hid here, he can see us, cant he?" Caddy said.

"He's not there," father said. "He went away a long time ago."

"You made me come," Jason said, high; against the sky it looked like father had two heads, a little one and a big one. "I didn't want to."

We went up out of the ditch. We could still see Nancy's house and the open door, but we couldn't see Nancy now, sitting before the fire with the door open, because she was tired. "I just done got tired," she said. "I just a nigger. It ain't no fault of mine."

But we could hear her, because she began just after we came up out of the ditch, the sound that was not singing and not unsinging. "Who will do our washing now, Father?" I said.

"I'm not a nigger," Jason said, high and close above father's head.

"You're worse," Caddy said, "you are a tattletale. If something was to jump out, you'd be scairder than a nigger."

"I wouldn't," Jason said.

"You'd cry," Caddy said.

"Caddy," father said.

"I wouldn't!" Jason said.

"Scairy cat," Caddy said.

"Candace!" father said.

The Man Who Was Almost a Man

Dave struck out across the fields, looking homeward through paling light. Whut's the use talkin wid em niggers in the field? Anyhow, his mother was putting supper on the table. Them niggers can't understan nothing. One of these days he was going to get a gun and practice shooting, then they couldn't talk to him as though he were a little boy. He slowed, looking at the ground. Shucks, Ah ain scareda them even ef they are biggern me! Aw, Ah know whut Ahma do. Ahm going by ol Joe's sto n git that Sears Roebuck catlog n look at them guns. Mebbe Ma will lemme buy one when she gits mah pay from ol man Hawkins. Ahma beg her t gimme some money. Ahm ol ernough to hava gun. Ahm seventeen. Almost a man. He strode, feeling his long loose-jointed limbs. Shucks, a man oughta hava little gun aftah he don worked hard all day.

He came in sight of Joe's store. A yellow lantern glowed on the front porch. He mounted steps and went through the screen door, hearing it bang behind him. There was a strong smell of coal oil and mackerel fish. He felt very confident until he saw fat Joe walk in through the rear door, then his courage began to ooze.

"Howdy, Dave! Whutcha want?"

"How yuh, Mistah Joe? Aw, Ah don wanna buy nothing. Ah jus wanted t see ef yuhd lemme look at tha catlog erwhile."

"Sure! You wanna see it here?"

"Nawsuh. Ah wans t take it home wid me. Ah'll bring it back termorrow when Ah come in from the fiels."

"You plannin on buying something?"

"Yessuh."

"Your ma lettin you have your own money now?"

"Shucks. Mistah Joe, Ahm gittin t be a man like anybody else!"

Joe laughed and wiped his greasy white face with a red bandanna.

"What you plannin on buyin?"

Dave looked at the floor, scratched his head, scratched his thigh, and smiled. Then he looked up shyly.

"Ah'll tell yuh, Mistah Joe, ef yuh promise yuh won't tell."

"I promise."

"Waal, Ahma buy a gun."

"A gun? Whut you want with a gun?"

"Ah wanna keep it."

"You ain't nothing but a boy. You don't need a gun."

"Aw, lemme have the catlog, Mistah Joe. Ah'll bring it back."

Joe walked through the rear door. Dave was elated. He looked around at barrels of sugar and flour. He heard Joe coming back. He craned his neck to see if he were bringing the book. Yeah, he's got it. Gawddog, he's got it!

"Here, but be sure you bring it back. It's the only one I got."

"Sho, Mistah Joe."

"Say, if you wanna buy a gun, why don't you buy one from me? I gotta gun to sell."

"Will it shoot?"

"Sure it'll shoot."

"Whut kind is it?"

"Oh, it's kinda old . . . a left-hand Wheeler. A pistol. A big one."

"Is it got bullets in it?"

"It's loaded."

"Kin Ah see it?"

"Where's your money?"

"Whut yuh wan fer it?"

"I'll let you have it for two dollars."

"Just two dollahs? Shucks, Ah could buy tha when Ah git mah pay."

"I'll have it here when you want it."

"Awright, suh. Ah be in fer it."

He went through the door, hearing it slam again behind him. Ahma git some money from Ma n buy me a gun! Only two dollahs! He tucked the thick catalogue under his arm and hurried.

"Where yuh been, boy?" His mother held a steaming dish of black-eyed peas.

"Aw, Ma, Ah jus stopped down the road t talk wid the boys."

"Yuh know bettah t keep suppah waitin."

He sat down, resting the catalogue on the edge of the table.

"Yuh git up from there and git to the well n wash yosef! Ah ain feedin no hogs in mah house!"

She grabbed his shoulder and pushed him. He stumbled out of the room, then came back to get the catalogue.

"Whut this?"

"Aw, Ma, it's jusa catlog."

"Who yuh git it from?"

"From Joe, down at the sto."

"Waal, thas good. We kin use it in the outhouse."

"Naw, Ma." He grabbed for it. "Gimme ma catlog, Ma."

She held onto it and glared at him.

"Quit hollerin at me! Whut's wrong wid yuh? Yuh crazy?"

"But Ma, please. It ain mine! It's Joe's! He tol me t bring it back t im termorrow."

She gave up the book. He stumbled down the back steps, hugging the thick book under his arm. When he had splashed water on his face and hands, he groped back to the kitchen and fumbled in a corner for the towel. He bumped into a chair; it clattered to the floor. The catalogue sprawled at his feet. When he had dried his eyes he snatched up the book and held it again under his arm. His mother stood watching him.

"Now, ef yuh gonna act a fool over that ol book, Ah'll take it n burn it up."

"Naw, Ma, please."

"Waal, set down n be still!"

He sat down and drew the oil lamp close. He thumbed page after page, unaware of the food his mother set on the table. His father came in. Then his small brother.

"Whutcha got there, Dave?" his father asked.

"Jusa catlog," he answered, not looking up.

"Yeah, here they is!" His eyes glowed at blue-and-black revolvers. He glanced up, feeling sudden guilt. His father was watching him. He eased the book under the table and rested it on his knees. After the blessing was asked, he ate. He scooped up peas and swallowed fat meat without chewing. Buttermilk helped to wash it down. He did not want to mention money before his father. He would do much better by cornering his mother when she was alone. He looked at his father uneasily out of the edge of his eye.

"Boy, how come yuh don quit foolin wid tha book n eat yo suppah?"

"Yessuh."

"How you n ol man Hawkins gitten erlong?"

"Suh?"

"Can't yuh hear? Why don yuh lissen? Ah ast yu how wuz yuh n ol man Hawkins gittin erlong?"

"Oh, swell, Pa. Ah plows mo lan than anybody over there."

"Waal, yuh oughta keep yo mind on whut yuh doin."

"Yessuh."

He poured his plate full of molasses and sopped it up slowly with a chunk of cornbread. When his father and brother had left the kitchen, he still sat and looked again at the guns in the catalogue, longing to muster courage enough to present his case to his mother. Lawd, ef Ah only had tha pretty one! He could almost feel the slickness of the weapon with his fingers. If he had a gun like that he would polish it and keep it shining so it would never rust. N Ah'd keep it loaded, by Gawd!

"Ma?" His voice was hesitant.

"Hunh?"

"Ol man Hawkins give yuh mah money yit?"

"Yeah, but ain no usa yuh thinking bout throwin nona it erway. Ahm keepin tha money sos yuh kin have cloes t go to school this winter."

He rose and went to her side with the open catalogue in his palms. She was washing dishes, her head bent low over a pan. Shyly he raised the book. When he spoke, his voice was husky, faint.

"Ma, Gawd knows Ah wans one of these."

"One of whut?" she asked, not raising her eyes.

"One of these," he said again, not daring even to point. She glanced up at the page, then at him with wide eyes.

"Nigger, is yuh gone plumb crazy?"

"Aw, Ma—"

"Git outta here! Don yuh talk t me bout no gun! Yuh a fool!"

"Ma, Ah kin buy one fer two dollahs."

"Not ef Ah knows it, yuh ain!"

"But yuh promised me one—"

"Ah don care whut Ah promised! Yuh ain nothing but a boy yit!"

"Ma, ef yuh lemme buy one Ah'll *never* ast yuh fer nothing no mo."

"Ah tol yuh t git outta here! Yuh ain gonna toucha penny of tha money fer no gun! Thas how come Ah has Mistah Hawkins t pay yo wages t me, cause Ah knows yuh ain got no sense."

"But, Ma, we needa gun. Pa ain got no gun. We needa gun in the house. Yuh kin never tell whut might happen."

"Now don yuh try to maka fool outta me, boy! Ef we did hava gun, yuh wouldn't have it!"

He laid the catalogue down and slipped his arm around her waist.

"Aw, Ma, Ah done worked hard alla summer n ain ast yuh fer nothin, is Ah, now?"

"Thas whut yuh spose t do!"

"But Ma, Ah wans a gun. Yuh kin lemme have two dollahs outta mah money. Please, Ma. I kin give it to Pa . . . Please, Ma! Ah loves yuh, Ma."

When she spoke her voice came soft and low.

"Whut yu wan wida gun, Dave? Yuh don need no gun. Yuh'll git in trouble. N ef yo pa jus thought Ah let yuh have money t buy a gun he'd hava fit."

"Ah'll hide it, Ma. It ain but two dollahs."

"Lawd, chil, whut's wrong wid yuh?"

"Ain nothin wrong, Ma. Ahm almos a man now. Ah wans a gun."

"Who gonna sell yuh a gun?"

"Ol Joe at the sto."

"N it don cos but two dollahs?"

"Thas all, Ma. Jus two dollahs. Please, Ma."

She was stacking the plates away; her hands moved slowly, reflectively. Dave kept an anxious silence. Finally, she turned to him.

"Ah'll let yuh git tha gun ef yuh promise me one thing."

"Whut's tha, Ma?"

"Yuh bring it straight back t me, yuh hear? It be fer Pa."

"Yessum! Lemme go now, Ma."

She stooped, turned slightly to one side, raised the hem of her dress, rolled down the top of her stocking, and came up with a slender wad of bills.

"Here," she said. "Lawd knows yuh don need no gun. But yer pa does. Yuh bring it right back t me, yuh hear? Ahma put it up. Now ef yuh don, Ahma have yuh pa lick yuh so hard yuh won fergit it."

"Yessum."

He took the money, ran down the steps, and across the yard.

"Dave! Yuuuuuh Daaaaave!"

He heard, but he was not going to stop now. "Naw, Lawd!"

The first movement he made the following morning was to reach under his pillow for the gun. In the gray light of dawn he held it loosely, feeling a sense of power. Could kill a man with a gun like this. Kill anybody, black or white. And if he were holding his gun in his hand, nobody could run over him; they would have to respect him. It was a big gun, with a long barrel and a heavy handle. He raised and lowered it in his hand, marveling at its weight.

He had not come straight home with it as his mother had asked; instead he had stayed out in the fields, holding the weapon in his hand, aiming it now and then at some imaginary foe. But he had not fired it; he had been afraid that his father might hear. Also he was not sure he knew how to fire it.

To avoid surrendering the pistol he had not come into the house until he knew that they were all asleep. When his mother had tiptoed to his bedside late that night and demanded the gun, he had first played possum; then he had told her that the gun was hidden outdoors, that he would bring it to her in the morning. Now he lay turning it slowly in his hands. He broke it, took out the cartridges, felt them, and then put them back.

He slid out of bed, got a long strip of old flannel from a trunk, wrapped the gun in it, and tied it to his naked thigh while it was still loaded. He did not go in to breakfast. Even though it was not yet daylight, he started for Jim Hawkins' plantation. Just as the sun was rising he reached the barns where the mules and plows were kept.

"Hey! That you, Dave?"

He turned. Jim Hawkins stood eying him suspiciously.

"What're yuh doing here so early?"

"Ah didn't know Ah wuz gittin up so early, Mistah Hawkins. Ah wuz fixin t hitch up ol Jenny n take her t the fiels."

"Good. Since you're so early, how about plowing that stretch down by the woods?"

"Suits me, Mistah Hawkins."

"O.K. Go to it!"

He hitched Jenny to a plow and started across the fields. Hot dog! This was just what he wanted. If he could get down by the woods, he could shoot his gun and nobody would hear. He walked behind the plow, hearing the traces creaking, feeling the gun tied tight to his thigh.

When he reached the woods, he plowed two whole rows before he decided to take out the gun. Finally, he stopped, looked in all directions, then untied the gun and held it in his hand. He turned to the mule and smiled.

"Know whut this is, Jenny? Naw, yuh wouldn know! Yuhs jusa ol mule! Anyhow, this is a gun, n it kin shoot, by Gawd!"

He held the gun at arm's length. Whut t hell, Ahma shoot this thing! He looked at Jenny again.

"Lissen here, Jenny! When Ah pull this ol trigger, Ah don wan yuh t run n acka fool now!"

Jenny stood with head down, her short ears pricked straight. Dave walked off about twenty feet, held the gun far out from him at arm's length, and turned his head. Hell, he told himself, Ah ain afraid. The gun felt loose in his fingers; he waved it wildly for a moment. Then he shut his eyes and tightened his forefinger. Bloom! A report half deafened him and he thought his right hand was torn from his arm. He heard Jenny whinnying and galloping over the field, and he found himself on his knees, squeezing his fingers hard between his legs. His hand was numb; he jammed it into his mouth, trying to warm it, trying to stop the pain. The gun lay at his feet. He did not quite know what had happened. He stood up and stared at the gun as though it were a living thing. He gritted his teeth and kicked the gun. Yuh almos broke mah arm! He turned to look for Jenny; she was far over the fields, tossing her head and kicking wildly.

"Hol on there, ol mule!"

When he caught up with her she stood trembling, walling her big white eyes at him. The plow was far away; the traces had broken. Then Dave stopped short, looking, not believing. Jenny was bleeding. Her left side was red and wet with blood. He went closer. Lawd, have mercy! Wondah did Ah shoot this mule? He grabbed for Jenny's mane. She flinched, snorted, whirled, tossing her head.

"Hol on now! Hol on."

Then he saw the hole in Jenny's side, right between the ribs. It was round, wet, red. A crimson stream streaked down the front leg, flowing fast. Good Gawd! Ah wuzn't shootin at tha mule. He felt panic. He knew he had to stop that blood, or Jenny would bleed to death. He had never seen so much blood in all his life. He chased the mule for half a mile, trying to catch her. Finally she stopped, breathing hard, stumpy tail half arched. He caught her mane and led her back to where the plow and gun lay. Then he stooped and grabbed handfuls of damp black earth and tried to plug the bullet hole. Jenny shuddered, whinnied, and broke from him.

"Hol on! Hol on now!"

He tried to plug it again, but blood came anyhow. His fingers were hot and sticky. He rubbed dirt into his palms, trying to dry them. Then again he attempted to plug the bullet hole, but Jenny shied away, kicking her heels high. He stood helpless. He had to do something. He ran at Jenny; she dodged him. He watched a red stream of blood flow down Jenny's leg and form a bright pool at her feet.

"Jenny . . . Jenny," he called weakly.

His lips trembled. She's bleeding t death! He looked in the direction of home, wanting to go back, wanting to get help. But he saw the pistol lying in the damp black clay. He had a queer feeling that if he only did something, this would not be; Jenny would not be there bleeding to death.

When he went to her this time, she did not move. She stood with sleepy, dreamy eyes; and when he touched her she gave a low-pitched whinny and knelt to the ground, her front knees slopping in blood.

"Jenny . . . Jenny . . ." he whispered.

For a long time she held her neck erect; then her head sank, slowly. Her ribs swelled with a mighty heave and she went over.

Dave's stomach felt empty, very empty. He picked up the gun and held it gingerly between his thumb and forefinger. He buried it at the foot of a tree. He took a stick and tried to cover the pool of blood with dirt—but what was the use? There was Jenny lying with her mouth open and her eyes walled and glassy. He could not tell Jim Hawkins he had shot his mule. But he had to tell something. Yeah, Ah'll tell em Jenny started gitten wil n fell on the joint of the plow. . . . But that would hardly happen to a mule. He walked across the field slowly, head down.

It was sunset. Two of Jim Hawkins' men were over near the edge of the woods digging a hole in which to bury Jenny. Dave was surrounded by a knot of people, all of whom were looking down at the dead mule.

"I don't see how in the world it happened," said Jim Hawkins for the tenth time.

The crowd parted and Dave's mother, father, and small brother pushed into the center.

"Where Dave?" his mother called.

"There he is," said Jim Hawkins.

His mother grabbed him.

"What happened, Dave? Whut yuh done?"

"Nothin."

"C mon, boy, talk," his father said.

Dave took a deep breath and told the story he knew nobody believed.

"Waal," he drawled. "Ah brung ol Jenny down here sos Ah could do mah plowin. Ah plowed bout two rows, just like yuh see." He stopped and pointed at the long rows of upturned earth. "Then somethin musta been wrong wid ol Jenny. She wouldn ack right a-tall. She started snortin n kickin her heels. Ah tried t hol her, but she pulled erway, rearin n goin in. Then when the point of the plow was sticking up in the air, she swung erroun n twisted herself back on it . . . She stuck herself n started t bleed. N fo Ah could do anything, she wuz dead."

"Did you ever hear of anything like that in all your life?" asked Jim Hawkins.

There were white and black standing in the crowd. They murmured. Dave's mother came close to him and looked hard into his face. "Tell the truth, Dave," she said.

"Looks like a bullet hole to me," said one man.

"Dave whut yuh do wid the gun?" his mother asked.

The crowd surged in, looking at him. He jammed his hands into his pockets, shook his head slowly from left to right, and backed away. His eyes were wide and painful.

"Did he hava gun?" asked Jim Hawkins.

"By Gawd, Ah tol yuh tha wuz a gun wound," said a man, slapping his thigh.

His father caught his shoulders and shook him till his teeth rattled.

"Tell whut happened, yuh rascal! Tell whut . . ."

Dave looked at Jenny's stiff legs and began to cry.

"What yuh do wid tha gun?" his mother asked.

"What wuz he doin wida gun?" his father asked.

"Come on and tell the truth," said Hawkins. "Ain't nobody going to hurt you . . ."

His mother crowded close to him.

"Did yuh shoot tha mule, Dave?"

Dave cried, seeing blurred white and black faces.

"Ahh ddinn gggo tt sshooot hher . . . Ah ssswear ffo Gawd Ahh ddin. . . Ah wuz a-tryin t sssee ef the old gggun would sshoot—"

"Where yuh git the gun from?" his father asked.

"Ah got it from Joe, at the sto."

"Where yuh git the money?"

"Ma give it t me."

"He kept worryin me, Bob. Ah had t. Ah tol im t bring the gun right back t me . . . It was fer yuh, the gun."

"But how yuh happen to shoot that mule?" asked Jim Hawkins.

"Ah wuzn shootin at the mule, Mistah Hawkins. The gun jumped when Ah pulled the trigger . . . N fo Ah knowed anythin Jenny was there a-bleedin."

Somebody in the crowd laughed. Jim Hawkins walked close to Dave and looked into his face.

"Well, looks like you have bought you a mule, Dave."

"Ah swear fo Gawd, Ah didn go t kill the mule, Mistah Hawkins!"

"But you killed her!"

All the crowd was laughing now. They stood on tiptoe and poked heads over one another's shoulders.

"Well, boy, looks like yuh done bought a dead mule! Hahaha!"

"Ain tha ershame."

"Hohohohoho."

Dave stood, head down, twisting his feet in the dirt.

"Well, you needn't worry about it, Bob," said Jim Hawkins to Dave's father. "Just let the boy keep on working and pay me two dollars a month."

"What yuh wan fer yo mule, Mistah Hawkins?"

Jim Hawkins screwed up his eyes.

"Fifty dollars."

"What yuh do wid the gun?" Dave's father demanded.

Dave said nothing.

"Yuh wan me t take a tree n beat yuh till yuh talk!"

"Nawsuh!"

"What yuh do wid it?"

"Ah throwed it erway."

"Where?"

"Ah . . . Ah throwed it in the creek."

"Waal, c mon home. N firs thing in the mawnin git to tha creek n fin tha gun."

"Yessuh."

"Whut yuh pay fer it?"

"Two dollars."

"Take tha gun n git yo money back n carry it t Mistah Hawkins, yuh hear? N don forgit Ahma lam you black bottom good fer this! Now march yosef on home, suh!"

Dave turned and walked slowly. He heard people laughing. Dave glared, his eyes welling with tears. Hot anger bubbled in him. Then he swallowed and stumbled on.

That night Dave did not sleep. He was glad that he had gotten out of killing the mule so easily, but he was hurt. Something hot seemed to turn over inside him each time he remembered how they had laughed. He tossed on his bed, feeling his hard pillow. N Pa says he's gonna beat me . . . He remembered other beatings, and his back quivered. Naw, naw, Ah sho don wan im t beat me tha way no mo. Dam em all! Nobody ever gave him anything. All he did was work. They treat me like a mule, n then they beat me. He gritted his teeth. N Ma had t tell on me.

Well, if he had to, he would take old man Hawkins that two dollars. But that meant selling the gun. And he wanted to keep that gun. Fifty dollars for a dead mule.

He turned over, thinking how he had fired the gun. He had an itch to fire it again. Ef other men kin shoota gun, by Gawd, Ah kin! He was still, listening. Mebbe they all sleepin now. The house was still. He heard the soft breathing of his brother. Yes, now! He would go down and get that gun and see if he could fire it! He eased out of bed and slipped into overalls.

The moon was bright. He ran almost all the way to the edge of the woods. He stumbled over the ground, looking for the spot where he had buried the gun. Yeah, here it is. Like a hungry dog scratching for a bone, he pawed it up. He puffed his black cheeks and blew dirt from the trigger and barrel. He broke it and found four cartridges unshot. He looked around; the fields were filled with silence and moonlight. He clutched the gun stiff and hard in his fingers. But, as soon as he wanted to pull the trigger, he shut his eyes and turned his head. Naw, Ah can't shoot wid mah eyes closed n mah head turned. With effort he held his eyes open; then he squeezed. *Blooooom!* He was still, not breathing. The gun was still in his hands. Dammit, he'd done it! He fired again. *Blooooom!* He smiled. *Blooooom! Blooooom! Click, click.* There! It was empty. If anybody could shoot a gun, he could. He put the gun into his hip pocket and started across the fields.

When he reached the top of a ridge he stood straight and proud in the moonlight, looking at Jim Hawkins' big white house, feeling the gun sagging in his pocket. Lawd, ef Ah had just one mo bullet Ah'd taka shot at tha house. Ah'd like t scare ol man Hawkins jusa little . . . Jusa enough t let im know Dave Saunders is a man.

To his left the road curved, running to the tracks of the Illinois Central. He perked his head, listening. From far off came a faint *hoooof-hoooof; hoooof-hoooof; hoooof-hoooof.* . . . He stood rigid. Two dallahs a mont. Les see now . . . Tha means it'll take bout two years. Shucks! Ah'll be dam!

He started down the road, toward the tracks. Yeah, here she comes! He stood beside the track and held himself stiffly. Here she comes, erroun the ben . . . C mon, yuh slow poke! C mon! He had his hand on his gun; something quivered in his stomach. Then the train thundered past, the gray and brown box cars rumbling and clinking. He gripped the gun tightly; then he jerked his hand out of his pocket. Ah betcha Bill wouldn't do it! Ah betcha . . . The cars slid past, steel grinding upon steel. Ahm ridin yuh ternight, so hep me Gawd! He was hot all over. He hesitated just a moment; then he grabbed, pulled atop of a car, and lay flat. He felt his pocket; the gun was still there. Ahead the long rails were glinting in the moonlight, stretching away, away to somewhere, somewhere where he could be a man . . .

Sonny's Blues

I read about it in the paper, in the subway, on my way to work. I read it, and I couldn't believe it, and I read it again. Then perhaps I just stared at it, at the newsprint spelling out his name, spelling out the story. I stared at it in the swinging lights of the subway car, and in the faces and bodies of the people, and in my own face, trapped in the darkness which roared outside.

It was not to be believed and I kept telling myself that as I walked from the subway station to the high school. And at the same time I couldn't doubt it. I was scared, scared for Sonny. He became real to me again. A great block of ice got settled in my belly and kept melting there slowly all day long, while I taught my classes algebra. It was a special kind of ice. It kept melting, sending trickles of ice water all up and down my veins, but it never got less. Sometimes it hardened and seemed to expand until I felt my guts were going to come spilling out or that I was going to choke or scream. This would always be at a moment when I was remembering some specific thing Sonny had once said or done.

When he was about as old as the boys in my classes his face had been bright and open, there was a lot of copper in it; and he'd had wonderfully direct brown eyes, and great gentleness and privacy. I wondered what he looked like now. He had been picked up, the evening before, in a raid on an apartment downtown, for peddling and using heroin.

I couldn't believe it: but what I mean by that is that I couldn't find any room for it anywhere inside me. I had kept it outside me for a long time. I hadn't wanted to know. I had had suspicions, but I didn't name them, I kept putting them away. I told myself that Sonny was wild, but he wasn't crazy. And he'd always been a good boy, he hadn't ever turned hard or evil or disrespectful, the way kids can, so quick, so quick, especially in Harlem. I didn't want to believe that I'd ever see my brother going down, coming to nothing, all that light in his face gone out, in the condition I'd already seen so many others. Yet it had happened and here I was, talking about algebra to a lot of boys who might, every one of them for all I knew, be popping off needles every time they went to the head. Maybe it did more for them than algebra could.

I was sure that the first time Sonny had ever had horse, he couldn't have been much older than these boys were now. These boys, now, were living as we'd been living then, they were growing up with a rush and their heads bumped abruptly against the low ceiling of their actual possibilities. They were filled with rage. All they really knew were two darknesses, the darkness of their lives, which was now closing in on them, and the darkness of the movies, which had blinded them to that other darkness, and in which they now, vindictively, dreamed, at once more together than they were at any other time, and more alone.

When the last bell rang, the last class ended, I let out my breath. It seemed I'd been holding it for all that time. My clothes were wet—I may have looked as though I'd been sitting in a steam bath, all dressed up, all afternoon. I sat alone in the classroom a long time. I listened to the boys outside, downstairs, shouting and cursing and laughing. Their laughter struck me for perhaps the first time. It was not the joyous laughter which—God knows why—one associates with children. It was mocking and insular, its intent was to denigrate. It was disenchanted, and in this, also, lay the authority of their curses. Perhaps I was listening to them because I was thinking about my brother and in them I heard my brother. And myself.

One boy was whistling a tune, at once very complicated and very simple, it seemed to be pouring out of him as though he were a bird, and it sounded very cool and moving through all that harsh, bright air, only just holding its own through all those other sounds.

I stood up and walked over to the window and looked down into the courtyard. It was the beginning of the spring and the sap was rising in the boys. A teacher passed through them every now and again, quickly, as though he or she couldn't wait to get out of that courtyard, to get those boys out of their sight and off their minds. I started collecting my stuff. I thought I'd better get home and talk to Isabel.

The courtyard was almost deserted by the time I got downstairs. I saw this boy standing in the shadow of a doorway, looking just like Sonny. I almost called his name. Then I saw that it wasn't Sonny, but somebody we used to know, a boy from around our block. He'd been Sonny's friend. He'd never been mine, having been too young for me, and, anyway, I'd never liked him. And now, even though he was a grown-up man, he still hung around that block, still spent hours on the street corner, was always high and raggy. I used to run into him from time to time and he'd often work around to asking me for a quarter or fifty cents. He always had some real good excuse, too, and I always gave it to him, I don't know why.

But now, abruptly, I hated him. I couldn't stand the way he looked at me, partly like a dog, partly like a cunning child. I wanted to ask him what the hell he was doing in the school courtyard.

He sort of shuffled over to me, and he said, "I see you got the papers. So you already know about it."

"You mean about Sonny? Yes, I already know about it. How come they didn't get you?"

He grinned. It made him repulsive and it also brought to mind what he'd looked like as a kid. "I wasn't there. I stay away from them people."

"Good for you." I offered him a cigarette and I watched him through the smoke. "You come all the way down here just to tell me about Sonny?"

"That's right." He was sort of shaking his head and his eyes looked strange, as though they were about to cross. The bright sun deadened his damp dark brown skin and it made his eyes look yellow and showed up the dirt in his conked hair. He smelled funky. I moved a little away from him and I said, "Well, thanks. But I already know about it and I got to get home."

"I'll walk you a little ways," he said. We started walking. There were a couple of kids still loitering in the courtyard and one of them said good night to me and looked strangely at the boy beside me.

"What're you going to do?" he asked me. "I mean, about Sonny?"

"Look. I haven't seen Sonny for over a year, I'm not sure I'm going to do anything. Anyway, what the hell *can* I do?"

"That's right," he said quickly, "ain't nothing you can do. Can't much help old Sonny no more, I guess."

It was what I was thinking and so it seemed to me he had no right to say it.

"I'm surprised at Sonny, though," he went on—he had a funny way of talking, he looked straight ahead as though he were talking to himself— "I thought Sonny was a smart boy, I thought he was too smart to get hung."

"I guess he thought so too," I said sharply, "and that's how he got hung. And how about you? You're pretty goddamn smart, I bet."

Then he looked directly at me, just for a minute. "I ain't smart," he said. "If I was smart, I'd have reached for a pistol a long time ago."

"Look. Don't tell *me* your sad story, if it was up to me, I'd give you one." Then I felt guilty—guilty, probably, for never having supposed that the poor bastard *had* a story of his own, much less a sad one, and I asked, quickly, "What's going to happen to him now?"

He didn't answer this. He was off by himself some place. "Funny thing," he said, and from his tone we might have been discussing the quickest way to get to Brooklyn, "when I saw the papers this morning, the first thing I asked myself was if I had anything to do with it. I felt sort of responsible."

I began to listen more carefully. The subway station was on the corner, just before us, and I stopped. He stopped, too. We were in front of a bar and he ducked slightly, peering in, but whoever he was looking for didn't seem to be there. The juke box was blasting away with something black and bouncy and I half watched the barmaid as she danced her way from the juke box to her place behind the bar. And I watched her face as she laughingly responded to something someone said to her, still keeping time to the music. When she smiled one saw the little girl, one sensed the doomed, still-struggling woman beneath the battered face of the semi-whore.

"I never *give* Sonny nothing," the boy said finally, "but a long time ago I come to school high and Sonny asked me how it felt." He paused, I couldn't bear to watch him, I watched the barmaid, and I listened to the music which seemed to be causing the pavement to shake. "I told him it felt great." The music stopped, the barmaid paused and watched the juke box until the music began again. "It did."

All this was carrying me some place I didn't want to go. I certainly didn't want to know how it felt. It filled everything, the people, the houses, the music, the dark, quicksilver barmaid, with menace; and this menace was their reality.

"What's going to happen to him now?" I asked again.

"They'll send him away some place and they'll try to cure him." He shook his head. "Maybe he'll even think he's kicked the habit. Then they'll let him loose"—he gestured, throwing his cigarette into the gutter. "That's all."

"What do you mean, that's *all*?"

But I knew what he meant.

"I *mean*, that's *all*." He turned his head and looked at me, pulling down the corners of his mouth. "Don't you know what I mean?" he asked softly.

"How the hell *would* I know what you mean?" I almost whispered it, I don't know why.

"That's right," he said to the air, "how would *he* know what I mean?" He turned toward me again, patient and calm, and yet I somehow felt him shaking, shaking as though he were going to fall apart. I felt that ice in my guts again, the dread I'd felt all afternoon; and again I watched the barmaid, moving about the bar, washing glasses, and singing. "Listen. They'll let him out and then it'll just start all over again. That's what I mean."

"You mean—they'll let him out. And then he'll just start working his way back in again. You mean he'll never kick the habit. Is that what you mean?"

"That's right," he said, cheerfully. "*You* see what I mean."

"Tell me," I said at last, "why does he want to die? He must want to die, he's killing himself, why does he want to die?"

He looked at me in surprise. He licked his lips. "He don't want to die. He wants to live. Don't nobody want to die, ever."

Then I wanted to ask him—too many things. He could not have answered, or if he had, I could not have borne the answers. I started walking. "Well, I guess it's none of my business."

"It's going to be rough on old Sonny," he said. We reached the subway station. "This is your station?" he asked. I nodded. I took one step down. "Damn!" he said, suddenly. I looked up at him. He grinned again. "Damn if I didn't leave all my money home. You ain't got a dollar on you, have you? Just for a couple of days, is all."

All at once something inside gave and threatened to come pouring out of me. I didn't hate him any more. I felt that in another moment I'd start crying like a child.

"Sure," I said. "Don't sweat." I looked in my wallet and didn't have a dollar, I only had a five. "Here," I said. "That hold you?"

He didn't look at it—he didn't want to look at it. A terrible, closed look came over his face, as though he were keeping the number on the bill a secret from him and me. "Thanks," he said, and now he was dying to see me go. "Don't worry about Sonny. Maybe I'll write him or something."

"Sure," I said. "You do that. So long."

"Be seeing you," he said. I went on down the steps.

And I didn't write Sonny or send him anything for a long time. When I finally did, it was just after my little girl died, he wrote me back a letter which made me feel like a bastard.

Here's what he said:

Dear brother,

You don't know how much I needed to hear from you. I wanted to write you many a time but I dug how much I must have hurt you and so I didn't write. But now I feel like a man who's been trying to climb up out of some deep, real deep and funky hole and just saw the sun up there, outside. I got to get outside.

I can't tell you much about how I got here. I mean I don't know how to tell you. I guess I was afraid of something or I was trying to escape from something and you know I have never been very strong in the head (smile). I'm glad Mama and Daddy are dead and can't see what's happened to their son and

I swear if I'd known what I was doing I would never have hurt you so, you and a lot of other fine people who were nice to me and who believed in me.

I don't want you to think it had anything to do with me being a musician. It's more than that. Or maybe less than that. I can't get anything straight in my head down here and I try not to think about what's going to happen to me when I get outside again. Sometime I think I'm going to flip and *never* get outside and sometime I think I'll come straight back. I tell you one thing, though, I'd rather blow my brains out than go through this again. But that's what they all say, so they tell me. If I tell you when I'm coming to New York and if you could meet me, I sure would appreciate it. Give my love to Isabel and the kids and I was sorry to hear about little Gracie. I wish I could be like Mama and say the Lord's will be done, but I don't know it seems to me that trouble is the one thing that never does get stopped and I don't know what good it does to blame it on the Lord. But maybe it does some good if you believe it.

Your brother,
SONNY

Then I kept in constant touch with him and I sent him whatever I could and I went to meet him when he came back to New York. When I saw him many things I thought I had forgotten came flooding back to me. This was because I had begun, finally, to wonder about Sonny, about the life that Sonny lived inside. This life, whatever it was, had made him older and thinner and it had deepened the distant stillness in which he had always moved. He looked very unlike my baby brother. Yet, when he smiled, when we shook hands, the baby brother I'd never known looked out from the depths of his private life, like an animal waiting to be coaxed into the light.

"How you been keeping?" he asked me.

"All right. And you?"

"Just fine." He was smiling all over his face. "It's good to see you again."

"It's good to see you."

The seven years' difference in our ages lay between us like a chasm: I wondered if these years would ever operate between us as a bridge. I was remembering, and it made it hard to catch my breath, that I had been there when he was born; and I had heard the first words he had ever spoken. When he started to walk, he walked from our mother straight to me. I caught him just before he fell when he took the first steps he ever took in this world.

"How's Isabel?"

"Just fine. She's dying to see you."

"And the boys?"

"They're fine, too. They're anxious to see their uncle."

"Oh, come on. You know they don't remember me."

"Are you kidding? Of course they remember you."

He grinned again. We got into a taxi. We had a lot to say to each other, far too much to know how to begin.

As the taxi began to move, I asked, "You still want to go to India?"

He laughed. "You still remember that. Hell, no. This place is Indian enough for me."

"It used to belong to them," I said.

And he laughed again. "They damn sure knew what they were doing when they got rid of it."

Years ago, when he was around fourteen, he'd been all hipped on the idea of going to India. He read books about people sitting on rocks, naked, in all kinds of weather, but mostly bad, naturally, and walking barefoot through hot coals and arriving at wisdom. I used to say that it sounded to me as though they were getting away from wisdom as fast as they could. I think he sort of looked down on me for that.

"Do you mind," he asked, "if we have the driver drive alongside the park? On the west side—I haven't seen the city in so long."

"Of course not," I said. I was afraid that I might sound as though I were humoring him, but I hoped he wouldn't take it that way.

So we drove along, between the green of the park and the stony, lifeless elegance of hotels and apartment buildings, toward the vivid, killing streets of our childhood. These streets hadn't changed, though housing projects jutted up out of them now like rocks in the middle of a boiling sea. Most of the houses in which we had grown up had vanished, as had the stores from which we had stolen, the basements in which we had first tried sex, the rooftops from which we had hurled tin cans and bricks. But houses exactly like the houses of our past yet dominated the landscape, boys exactly like the boys we once had been found themselves smothering in these houses, came down into the streets for light and air and found themselves encircled by disaster. Some escaped the trap, most didn't. Those who got out always left something of themselves behind, as some animals amputate a leg and leave it in the trap. It might be said, perhaps, that I had escaped, after all, I was a school teacher; or that Sonny had, he hadn't lived in Harlem for years. Yet, as the cab moved uptown through streets which seemed, with a rush, to darken with dark people, and as I covertly studied Sonny's face, it came to me that what we both were seeking through our separate cab windows was that part of ourselves which had been left behind. It's always at the hour of trouble and confrontation that the missing member aches.

We hit 110th Street and started rolling up Lenox Avenue. And I'd known this avenue all my life, but it seemed to me again, as it had seemed on the day I'd first heard about Sonny's trouble, filled with a hidden menace which was its very breath of life.

"We almost there," said Sonny.

"Almost." We were both too nervous to say anything more.

We live in a housing project. It hasn't been up long. A few days after it was up it seemed uninhabitably new, now, of course, it's already rundown. It looks like a parody of the good, clean, faceless life—God knows the people who live in it do their best to make it a parody. The beat-looking grass lying around isn't enough to make their lives green, the hedges will never hold out the streets, and they know it. The big windows fool no one, they aren't big enough to make space out of no space. They don't bother with the windows, they watch the TV screen instead. The playground is most popular with the children who don't play at jacks, or skip rope, or roller skate, or swing, and they can be found in it after dark. We moved in partly because it's not too far from where I teach, and partly for the kids; but it's really just like the houses in which Sonny and I grew up. The same things happen, they'll have the same things to remember. The moment Sonny and I started into the house I had the feeling that I was simply bringing him back into the danger he had almost died trying to escape.

Sonny has never been talkative. So I don't know why I was sure he'd be dying to talk to me when supper was over the first night. Everything went fine, the oldest boy remembered him, and the youngest boy liked him, and Sonny had remembered to bring something for each of them; and Isabel, who is really much nicer than I am, more open and giving, had gone to a lot of trouble about dinner and was genuinely glad to see him. And she's always been able to tease Sonny in a way that I haven't. It was nice to see her face so vivid again and to hear her laugh and watch her make Sonny laugh. She wasn't, or, anyway, she didn't seem to be, at all uneasy or embarrassed. She chatted as though there were no subject which had to be avoided and she got Sonny past his first, faint stiffness. And thank God she was there, for I was filled with that icy dread again. Everything I did seemed awkward to me, and everything I said sounded freighted with hidden meaning. I was trying to remember everything I'd heard about dope addiction and I couldn't help watching Sonny for signs. I wasn't doing it out of malice. I was trying to find out something about my brother. I was dying to hear him tell me he was safe.

"Safe!" my father grunted, whenever Mama suggested trying to move to a neighborhood which might be safer for children. "Safe, hell! Ain't no place safe for kids, nor nobody."

He always went on like this, but he wasn't, ever, really as bad as he sounded, not even on weekends, when he got drunk. As a matter of fact, he was always on the lookout for "something a little better," but he died before he found it. He died suddenly, during a drunken weekend in the middle of the war, when Sonny was fifteen. He and Sonny hadn't ever got on too well. And this was partly because Sonny was the apple of his father's eye. It was because he loved Sonny so much and was frightened for him, that he was always fighting with him. It doesn't do any good to fight with Sonny. Sonny just moves back, inside himself, where he can't be reached. But the principal reason that they never hit it off is that they were so much alike. Daddy was big and rough and loud-talking, just the opposite of Sonny, but they both had—that same privacy.

Mama tried to tell me something about this, just after Daddy died. I was home on leave from the army.

This was the last time I ever saw my mother alive. Just the same, this picture gets all mixed up in my mind with pictures I had of her when she was younger. The way I always see her is the way she used to be on a Sunday afternoon, say, when the old folks were talking after the big Sunday dinner. I always see her wearing pale blue. She'd be sitting on the sofa. And my father would be sitting in the easy chair, not far from her. And the living room would be full of church folks and relatives. There they sit, in chairs all around the living room, and the night is creeping up outside, but nobody knows it yet. You can see the darkness growing against the window-panes and you hear the street noises every now and again, or maybe the jangling beat of a tambourine from one of the churches close by, but it's real quiet in the room. For a moment nobody's talking, but every face looks darkening, like the sky outside. And my mother rocks a little from the waist, and my father's eyes are closed. Everyone is looking at something a child can't see. For a minute they've forgotten the children. Maybe a kid is lying on the rung half asleep. Maybe somebody's got a kid on his lap and is absent-mindedly stroking the kid's head. Maybe there's a kid, quiet and big-eyed, curled up in a big chair in the corner. The silence, the darkness coming, and the darkness in the faces frightens the child obscurely. He hopes that the hand which strokes his forehead will never stop—will never die. He hopes that there will never come a time when the old folks won't be sitting around the living room, talking about where they've come from, and what they've seen, and what's happened to them and their kinfolk.

But something deep and watchful in the child knows that this is bound to end, is already ending. In a moment someone will get up and turn on the light. Then the old folks will remember the children and they won't talk any more that day. And when light fills the room, the child is filled with darkness. He knows that every time this happens he's moved just a little closer to that darkness outside. The darkness outside is what the old folks have been talking about. It's what they've come from. It's what they endure. The child knows that they won't talk any more because if he knows too much about what's happened to *them*, he'll know too much too soon, about what's going to happen to *him*.

The last time I talked to my mother, I remember I was restless. I wanted to get out and see Isabel. We weren't married then and we had a lot to straighten out between us.

There Mama sat, in black, by the window. She was humming an old church song, *Lord, you brought me from a long ways off*. Sonny was out somewhere. Mama kept watching the streets.

"I don't know," she said, "if I'll ever see you again, after you go off from here. But I hope you'll remember the things I tried to teach you."

"Don't talk like that," I said, and smiled. "You'll be here a long time yet."

She smiled, too, but she said nothing. She was quiet for a long time. And I said, "Mama, don't you worry about nothing. I'll be writing all the time, and you be getting the checks. . . ."

"I want to talk to you about your brother," she said, suddenly. "If anything happens to me he ain't going to have nobody to look out for him."

"Mama," I said, "ain't nothing going to happen to you *or* Sonny. Sonny's all right. He's a good boy and he's got good sense."

"It ain't a question of his being a good boy," Mama said, "nor of his having good sense. It ain't only the bad ones, nor yet the dumb ones that gets sucked under." She stopped, looking at me. "Your Daddy once had a brother," she said, and she smiled in a way that made me feel she was in pain. "You didn't never know that, did you?"

"No," I said, "I never knew that," and I watched her face.

"Oh, yes," she said, "your Daddy had a brother." She looked out of the window again. "I know you never saw your Daddy cry. But *I* did— many a time, through all these years."

I asked her, "What happened to his brother? How come nobody's ever talked about him?"

This was the first time I ever saw my mother look old.

"His brother got killed," she said, "when he was just a little younger than you are now. I knew him. He was a fine boy. He was maybe a little full of the devil, but he didn't mean nobody no harm."

Then she stopped and the room was silent, exactly as it had sometimes been on those Sunday afternoons. Mama kept looking out into the streets.

"He used to have a job in the mill," she said, "and, like all young folks, he just liked to perform on Saturday nights. Saturday nights, him and your father would drift around to different places, go to dances and things like that, or just sit around with people they knew, and your father's brother would sing, he had a fine voice, and play along with himself on his guitar. Well, this particular Saturday night, him and your father was coming home from some place, and they were both a little drunk and there was a moon that night, it was bright like day. Your father's brother was feeling kind of good, and he was whistling to himself, and he had his guitar slung over his shoulder. They was coming down a hill and beneath them was a road that turned off from the highway. Well, your father's brother, being always kind of frisky, decided to run down this hill, and he did, with that guitar banging and clanging behind him, and he ran across the road, and he was making water behind a tree. And your father was sort of amused at him and he was still coming down the hill, kind of slow. Then he heard a car motor and that same minute his brother stepped from behind the tree, into the road, in the moonlight. And he started to cross the road. And your father started to run down the hill, he says he don't know why. This car was full of white men. They was all drunk, and when they seen your father's brother they let out a great whoop and holler and they aimed the car straight at him. They was having fun, they just wanted to scare him, the way they do sometimes, you know. But they was drunk. And I guess the boy, being drunk, too, and scared, kind of lost his head. By the time he jumped it was too late. Your father says he heard his brother scream when the car rolled over him, and he heard the wood of that guitar when it give, and he heard them strings go flying, and he heard them white men shouting, and the car kept on a-going and it ain't stopped till this day. And, time your father got down the hill, his brother weren't nothing but blood and pulp."

Tears were gleaming on my mother's face. There wasn't anything I could say.

"He never mentioned it," she said, "because I never let him mention it before you children. Your Daddy was like a crazy man that night and for many a night thereafter. He says he never in his life seen anything as dark as that road after the lights of that car had gone away. Weren't nothing, weren't nobody on that road, just your Daddy and his brother and that busted guitar. Oh, yes. Your Daddy never did really get right again. Till the day he died he weren't sure but that every white man he saw was the man that killed his brother."

She stopped and took out her handkerchief and dried her eyes and looked at me.

"I ain't telling you all this," she said, "to make you scared or bitter or to make you hate nobody. I'm telling you this because you got a brother. And the world ain't changed."

I guess I didn't want to believe this. I guess she saw this in my face. She turned away from me, toward the window again, searching those streets.

"But I praise my Redeemer," she said at last, "that He called your Daddy home before me. I ain't saying it to throw no flowers at myself, but, I declare, it keeps me from feeling too cast down to know I helped your father get safely through this world. Your father always acted like he was the roughest, strongest man on earth. And everybody took him to be like that. But if he hadn't had *me* there—to see his tears!"

She was crying again. Still, I couldn't move. I said, "Lord, Lord, Mama, I didn't know it was like that."

"Oh, honey," she said, "there's a lot that you don't know. But you are going to find it out." She stood up from the window and came over to me. "You got to hold on to your brother," she said, "and don't let him fall, no matter what it looks like is happening to him and no matter how evil you gets with him. You going to be evil with him many a time. But don't you forget what I told you, your hear?"

"I won't forget," I said. "Don't you worry, I won't forget. I won't let nothing happen to Sonny."

My mother smiled as though she were amused at something she saw in my face. Then, "You may not be able to stop nothing from happening. But you got to let him know you's *there*."

Two days later I was married, and then I was gone. And I had a lot of things on my mind and I pretty well forgot my promise to Mama until I got shipped home on a special furlough for her funeral.

And, after the funeral, with just Sonny and me alone in the empty kitchen, I tried to find out something about him.

"What do you want to do?" I asked him.

"I'm going to be a musician," he said.

For he had graduated, in the time I had been away, from dancing to the juke box to finding out who was playing what, and what they were doing with it, and he had bought himself a set of drums.

"You mean, you want to be a drummer?" I somehow had the feeling that being a drummer might be all right for other people but not for my brother Sonny.

"I don't think," he said, looking at me very gravely, "that I'll ever be a good drummer. But I think I can play a piano."

I frowned. I'd never played the role of the older brother quite so seriously before, had scarcely ever, in fact, *asked* Sonny a damn thing. I sensed myself in the presence of something I didn't really know how to handle, didn't understand. So I made my frown a little deeper as I asked: "What kind of musician do you want to be?"

He grinned. "How many kinds do you think there are?"

"Be *serious*," I said.

He laughed, throwing his head back, and then looked at me. "I *am* serious."

"Well, then, for Christ's sake, stop kidding around and answer a serious question. I mean, do you want to be a concert pianist, you want to play classical music and all that, or—or what?" Long before I finished he was laughing again. "For Christ's *sake*, Sonny!"

He sobered, but with difficulty. "I'm sorry. But you sound so—*scared!*" and he was off again.

"Well, you may think it's funny now, baby, but it's not going to be so funny when you have to make your living at it, let me tell you *that*." I was furious because I knew he was laughing at me and I didn't know why.

"No," he said, very sober now, and afraid, perhaps, that he'd hurt me, "I don't want to be a classical pianist. That isn't what interests me. I mean"—he paused, looking hard at me, as though his eyes would help me to understand, and then gestured helplessly, as though perhaps his hand would help—"I mean, I'll have a lot of studying to do, and I'll have to study *everything*, but I mean, I want to play *with*—jazz musicians." He stopped. "I want to play jazz," he said.

Well, the word had never before sounded as heavy, as real, as it sounded that afternoon in Sonny's mouth. I just looked at him and I was probably frowning a real frown by this time. I simply couldn't see why on earth he'd want to spend his time hanging around night clubs, clowning around on band-stands, while people pushed each other around a dance floor. It seemed—beneath him, somehow. I had never thought about it before, had never been forced to, but I suppose I had always put jazz musicians in a class with what Daddy called "good-time people."

"Are you *serious?*"

"Hell, *yes*, I'm serious."

He looked more helpless than ever, and annoyed, and deeply hurt.

I suggested, helpfully: "You mean—like Louis Armstrong?"

His face closed as though I'd struck him. "No. I'm not talking about none of that old-time, down home crap."

"Well, look, Sonny, I'm sorry, don't get mad. I just don't altogether get it, that's all. Name somebody—you know, a jazz musician you admire."

"Bird."

"Who?"

"Bird! Charlie Parker! Don't they teach you nothing in the goddamn army?"

I lit a cigarette. I was surprised and then a little amused to discover that I was trembling. "I've been out of touch," I said. "You'll have to be patient with me. Now. Who's this Parker character?"

"He's just one of the greatest jazz musicians alive," said Sonny, sullenly, his hands in his pockets, his back to me. "Maybe *the* greatest," he added, bitterly, "that's probably why *you* never heard of him."

"All right," I said, "I'm ignorant. I'm sorry. I'll go out and buy all the cat's records right away, all right?"

"It don't," said Sonny, with dignity, "make any difference to me. I don't care what you listen to. Don't do me no favors."

I was beginning to realize that I'd never seen him so upset before. With another part of my mind I was thinking that this would probably turn out to be one of those things kids go through and that I shouldn't make it seem important by pushing it too hard. Still, I didn't think it would do any harm to ask: "Doesn't all this take a lot of time? Can you make a living at it?"

He turned back to me and half leaned, half sat, on the kitchen table. "Everything takes time," he said, "and—well, yes, sure, I can make a living at it. But what I don't seem to be able to make you understand is that it's the only thing I want to do."

"Well Sonny," I said, gently, "you know people can't always do exactly what they *want* to do—"

"*No*, I don't know that," said Sonny, surprising me. "I think people *ought* to do what they want to do, what else are they alive for?"

"You getting to be a big boy," I said desperately, "it's time you started thinking about your future."

"I'm thinking about my future," said Sonny, grimly. "I think about it all the time."

I gave up. I decided, if he didn't change his mind, that we could always talk about it later. "In the meantime," I said, "you got to finish school." We had already decided that he'd have to move in with Isabel and her folks. I knew this wasn't the ideal arrangement because Isabel's folks are inclined to be dicty and they hadn't especially wanted Isabel to marry me. But I didn't know what else to do. "And we have to get you fixed up at Isabel's."

There was a long silence. He moved from the kitchen table to the window. "That's a terrible idea. You know it yourself."

"Do you have a *better* idea?"

He just walked up and down the kitchen for a minute. He was as tall as I was. He had started to shave. I suddenly had the feeling that I didn't know him at all.

He stopped at the kitchen table and picked up my cigarettes. Looking at me with a kind of mocking, amused defiance, he put one between his lips. "You mind?"

"You smoking already?"

He lit the cigarette and nodded, watching me through the smoke. "I just wanted to see if I'd have the courage to smoke in front of you." He grinned and blew a great cloud of smoke to the ceiling. "It was easy." He looked at my face. "Come on, now. I bet you was smoking at my age, tell the truth."

I didn't say anything but the truth was on my face, and he laughed. But now there was something very strained in his laugh. "Sure. And I bet that ain't all you was doing."

He was frightening me a little. "Cut the crap," I said. "We already decided that you was going to go and live at Isabel's. Now what's got into you all of a sudden?"

"*You* decided it," he pointed out. "*I* didn't decide nothing." He stopped in front of me, leaning against the stove, arms loosely folded. "Look, brother. I don't want to stay in Harlem no more, I really don't." He was very earnest. He looked at me, then over toward the kitchen window. There was something in his eyes I'd never seen before, some thoughtfulness, some worry all his own. He rubbed the muscle of one arm. "It's time I was getting out of here."

"Where do you want to *go*, Sonny?"

"I want to join the army. Or the navy, I don't care. If I say I'm old enough they'll believe me."

Then I got mad. It was because I was so scared. "You must be crazy. You goddamn fool, what the hell do you want to go and join the *army* for?"

"I just told you. To get out of Harlem."

"Sonny, you haven't even finished *school*. And if you really want to be a musician, how do you expect to study if you're in the *army?*"

He looked at me, trapped, and in anguish. "There's ways. I might be able to work out some kind of deal. Anyway, I'll have the G.I. Bill when I come out."

"*If* you come out." We stared at each other. "Sonny, please. Be reasonable. I know the setup is far from perfect. But we got to do the best we can."

"I ain't learning nothing in school," he said. "Even when I go." He turned away from me and opened the window and threw his cigarette out into the narrow alley. I watched his back. "At least, I ain't learning nothing you'd want me to learn." He slammed the window so hard I thought the glass would fly out, and turned back to me. "And I'm sick of the stink of these garbage cans!"

"Sonny," I said, "I know how you feel. But if you don't finish school now, you're going to be sorry later that you didn't." I grabbed him by the shoulders. "And you only got another year. It ain't so bad. And I'll come back and I swear I'll help you do *whatever* you want to do. Just try to put up with it till I come back. Will you please do that? For me?"

He didn't answer and he wouldn't look at me.

"Sonny. You hear me?"

He pulled away. "I hear you. But you never hear anything *I* say."

I didn't know what to say to that. He looked out of the window and then back at me. "OK," he said, and sighed. "I'll try."

Then I said, trying to cheer him up a little, "They got a piano at Isabel's. You can practice on it."

And as a matter of fact, it did cheer him up for a minute. "That's right," he said to himself. "I forgot that." His face relaxed a little. But the worry, the thoughtfulness, played on it still, the way shadows play on a face which is staring into the fire.

But I thought I'd never hear the end of that piano. At first, Isabel would write me, saying how nice it was that Sonny was so serious about his music and how, as soon as he came in from school, or wherever he had been when he was supposed to be at school, he went straight to that piano and stayed there until suppertime. And, after supper, he went back to that piano and stayed there until everybody went to bed. He was at that piano all day Saturday and all day Sunday. Then he bought a record player and started playing records. He'd play one record over and over again, all day long sometimes, and he'd improvise along with it on the piano. Or he'd play one section of the record, one chord, one change, one progression, then he'd do it on the piano. Then back to the record. Then back to the piano.

Well, I really don't know how they stood it. Isabel finally confessed that it wasn't like living with a person at all, it was like living with sound. And the sound didn't make any sense to her, didn't make any sense to any of them—naturally. They began, in a way, to be afflicted by this presence that was living in their home. It was as though Sonny were some sort of god, or monster. He moved in an atmosphere which wasn't like theirs at all. They fed him and he ate, he washed himself, he walked in and out of their door; he certainly wasn't nasty or unpleasant or rude, Sonny isn't any of those things; but it was as though he were all wrapped up in some cloud, some fire, some vision all his own; and there wasn't any way to reach him.

At the same time, he wasn't really a man yet, he was still a child, and they had to watch out for him in all kinds of ways. They certainly couldn't throw him out. Neither did they dare to make a great scene about that piano because even they dimly sensed, as I sensed, from so many thousands of miles away, that Sonny was at that piano playing for his life.

But he hadn't been going to school. One day a letter came from the school board and Isabel's mother got it—there had, apparently, been other letters but Sonny had torn them up. This day, when Sonny came in, Isabel's mother showed him the letter and asked where he'd been spending his time. And she finally got it out of him that he'd been down in Greenwich Village, with musicians and other characters, in a white girl's apartment. And this scared her and she started to scream at him and what came up, once she began—though she denies it to this day—was what sacrifices they were making to give Sonny a decent home and how little he appreciated it.

Sonny didn't play the piano that day. By evening, Isabel's mother had calmed down but then there was the old man to deal with, and Isabel herself. Isabel says she did her best to be calm but she broke down and started crying. She says she just watched Sonny's face. She could tell, by watching him, what was happening with him. And what was happening was that they penetrated his cloud, they had reached him. Even if their fingers had been a thousand times more gentle than human fingers ever are, he could hardly help feeling that they had stripped him naked and were spitting on that nakedness. For he also had to see that his presence, that music, which was life or death to him, had been torture for them and that they had endured it, not at all for his sake, but only for mine. And

Sonny couldn't take that. He can take it a little better today than he could then but he's still not very good at it and, frankly, I don't know anybody who is.

The silence of the next few days must have been louder than the sound of all the music ever played since time began. One morning, before she went to work, Isabel was in his room for something and she suddenly realized that all of his records were gone. And she knew for certain that he was gone. And he was. He went as far as the navy would carry him. He finally sent me a postcard from some place in Greece and that was the first I knew that Sonny was still alive. I didn't see him any more until we were both back in New York and the war had long been over.

He was a man by then, of course, but I wasn't willing to see it. He came by the house from time to time, but we fought almost every time we met. I didn't like the way he carried himself, loose and dreamlike all the time, and I didn't like his friends, and his music seemed to be merely an excuse for the life he led. It sounded just that weird and disordered.

Then we had a fight, a pretty awful fight, and I didn't see him for months. By and by I looked him up, where he was living, in a furnished room in the Village, and I tried to make it up. But there were lots of other people in the room and Sonny just lay on his bed, and he wouldn't come downstairs with me, and he treated these other people as though they were his family and I weren't. So I got mad and then he got mad, and then I told him that he might just as well be dead as live the way he was living. Then he stood up and he told me not to worry about him any more in life, that he *was* dead as far as I was concerned. Then he pushed me to the door and the other people looked on as though nothing were happening, and he slammed the door behind me. I stood in the hallway, staring at the door. I heard somebody laugh in the room and then the tears came to my eyes. I started down the steps, whistling to keep from crying, I kept whistling to myself, *You going to need me, baby, one of these cold, rainy days.*

I read about Sonny's trouble in the spring. Little Grace died in the fall. She was a beautiful little girl. But she only lived a little over two years. She died of polio and she suffered. She had a slight fever for a couple of days, but it didn't seem like anything and we just kept her in bed. And we would certainly have called the doctor, but the fever dropped, she seemed to be all right. So we thought it had just been a cold. Then, one day, she was up, playing, Isabel was in the kitchen fixing lunch for the two boys when they'd come in from school, and she heard Grace fall down in the living room. When you have a lot of children you don't always start running when one of them falls, unless they start screaming or something. And, this time, Grace was quiet. Yet, Isabel says that when she heard that *thump* and then that silence, something happened in her to make her afraid. And she ran to the living room and there was little Grace on the floor, all twisted up and the reason she hadn't screamed was that she couldn't get her breath. And when she did scream, it was the worst sound, Isabel says, that she'd ever heard in all her life, and she still hears it sometimes in her dreams. Isabel will sometimes wake me up with a low, moaning, strangled sound and I have to be quick to awaken her and hold her to me and where Isabel is weeping against me seems a mortal wound.

I think I may have written Sonny the very day that little Grace was buried. I was sitting in the living room in the dark, by myself, and I suddenly thought of Sonny. My trouble made his real.

One Saturday afternoon, when Sonny had been living with us, or, anyway, been in our house, for nearly two weeks, I found myself wandering aimlessly about the living room, drinking from a can of beer, and trying to work up the courage to search Sonny's room. He was out, he was usually out whenever I was home, and Isabel had taken the children to see their grandparents. Suddenly I was standing still in front of the living room window, watching Seventh Avenue. The idea of searching Sonny's room made me still. I scarcely dared to admit to myself what I'd be searching for. I didn't know what I'd do if I found it. Or if I didn't.

On the sidewalk across from me, near the entrance to a barbecue joint, some people were holding an old-fashioned revival meeting. The barbecue cook, wearing a dirty white apron, his conked hair reddish and metallic in the pale sun, and a cigarette between his lips, stood in the doorway, watching them. Kids and older people paused in their errands and stood there, along with some older men and a couple of very tough-looking women who watched everything that happened on the avenue, as though they owned it, or were maybe owned by it. Well, they were watching this, too. The revival was being carried on by three sisters in black, and a brother. All they had were their voices and their Bibles and a tambourine. The brother was testifying and while he testified two of the sisters stood together, seeming to say, Amen, and the third sister walked around with the tambourine outstretched and a couple of people dropped coins into it. Then the brother's testimony ended and the sister who had been taking up the collection dumped the coins into her palm and transferred them to the pocket of her long black robe. Then she raised both hands, striking the tambourine against the air, and then against one hand, and she started to sing. And the two other sisters and the brother joined in.

It was strange, suddenly, to watch, though I had been seeing these street meetings all my life. So, of course, had everybody else down there. Yet, they paused and watched and listened and I stood still at the window. "Tis the old ship of Zion," they sang, and the sister with the tambourine kept a steady, jangling beat, "It has rescued many a thousand!" Not a soul under the sound of their voices was hearing this song for the first time, not one of them had been rescued. Nor had they seen much in the way of rescue work being done around them. Neither did they especially believe in the holiness of the three sisters and the brother, they knew too much about them, knew where they lived, and how. The woman with the tambourine, whose voice dominated the air, whose face was bright with joy, was divided by very little from the woman who stood watching her, a cigarette between her heavy, chapped lips, her hair a cuckoo's nest, her face scarred and swollen from many beatings, and her black eyes glittering like coal. Perhaps they both knew this, which was why, when, as rarely, they addressed each other, they addressed each other as Sister. As the singing filled the air the watching, listening faces underwent a change, the eyes focusing on something within; the music seemed to soothe a poison out of them; and time seemed, nearly, to fall away from the sullen, belligerent, battered faces, as though they were fleeing back to their first condition, while dreaming of their last. The barbecue cook half shook his head and smiled, and dropped his cigarette and disappeared into his joint. A man fumbled in his pockets for change and stood holding it in his hand impatiently, as though he had just remembered a pressing appointment further up the avenue. He looked furious. Then I saw Sonny, standing on the edge of the crowd. He was carrying a wide, flat notebook with a green cover, and it made him look, from where I was standing, almost like a schoolboy. The coppery sun brought out the copper in his skin, he was very faintly smiling, standing very still. Then the singing stopped, the tambourine turned into a collection plate again. The furious man dropped in his coins and vanished, so did a couple of the women, and Sonny dropped some change in the plate, looking directly at the woman with a little smile. He started across the avenue, toward the house. He has a slow, loping walk, something like the way Harlem hipsters walk, only he's imposed on this his own half-beat. I had never really noticed it before.

I stayed at the window, both relieved and apprehensive. As Sonny disappeared from my sight, they began singing again. And they were still singing when his key turned in the lock.

"Hey," he said.

"Hey, yourself. You want some beer?"

"No. Well, maybe." But he came up to the window and stood beside me, looking out. "What a warm voice," he said.

They were singing *If I could only hear my mother pray again!*

"Yes," I said, "and she can sure beat that tambourine."

"But what a terrible song," he said, and laughed. He dropped his notebook on the sofa and disappeared into the kitchen. "Where's Isabel and the kids?"

"I think they went to see their grandparents. You hungry?"

"No." He came back into the living room with his can of beer. "You want to come some place with me tonight?"

I sensed, I don't know how, that I couldn't possibly say No. "Sure. Where?"

He sat down on the sofa and picked up his notebook and started leafing through it. "I'm going to sit in with some fellows in a joint in the Village."

"You mean, you're going to play, tonight?"

"That's right." He took a swallow of his beer and moved back to the window. He gave me a sidelong look. "If you can stand it."

"I'll try," I said.

He smiled to himself and we both watched as the meeting across the way broke up. The three sisters and the brother, heads bowed, were singing *God be with you till we meet again*. The faces around them were very quiet. Then the song ended. The small crowd dispersed. We watched the three women and the lone man walk slowly up the avenue.

"When she was singing before," said Sonny, abruptly, "her voice reminded me for a minute of what heroin feels like sometimes —when it's in your veins. It makes you feel sort of warm and cool at the same time. And distant. And—and sure." He sipped his beer, very deliberately not looking at me. I watched his face. "It makes you feel—in control. Sometimes you've got to have that feeling."

"Do you?" I sat down slowly in the easy chair.

"Sometimes." He went to the sofa and picked up his notebook again. "Some people do."

"In order," I asked, "to play?" And my voice was very ugly, full of contempt and anger.

"Well"—he looked at me with great, troubled eyes, as though, in fact,

he hoped his eyes would tell me things he could never otherwise say—
"they *think* so. And *if* they think so—!"

"And what do *you* think?" I asked.

He sat on the sofa and put his can of beer on the floor. "I don't know," he said, and I couldn't be sure if he were answering my question or pursuing his thoughts. His face didn't tell me. "It's not so much to *play*. It's to *stand* it, to be able to make it at all. On any level." He frowned and smiled: "In order to keep from shaking to pieces."

"But these friends of yours," I said, "they seem to shake themselves to pieces pretty goddamn fast."

"Maybe." He played with the notebook. And something told me that I should curb my tongue, that Sonny was doing his best to talk, that I should listen. "But of course you only know the ones that've gone to pieces. Some don't—or at least they haven't *yet* and that's just about all *any* of us can say." He paused. "And then there are some who just live, really, in hell, and they know it and they see what's happening and they go right on. I don't know." He sighed, dropped the notebook, folded his arms. "Some guys, you can tell from the way they play, they on something *all* the time. And you can see that, well, it makes something real for them. But of course," he picked up his beer from the floor and sipped it and put the can down again, "they *want* to, too, you've got to see that. Even some of them that say they don't—*some*, not all."

"And what about you?" I asked—I couldn't help it. "What about you? Do *you* want to?"

He stood up and walked to the window and remained silent for a long time. Then he sighed. "Me," he said. Then: "While I was downstairs before, on my way here, listening to that woman sing, it struck me all of a sudden how much suffering she must have had to go through—to sing like that. It's *repulsive* to think you have to suffer that much."

I said: "But there's no way not to suffer—is there, Sonny?"

"I believe not," he said, and smiled, "but that's never stopped anyone from trying." He looked at me. "Has it?" I realized, with this mocking look, that there stood between us, forever, beyond the power of time or forgiveness, the fact that I had held silence—so long!—when he had needed human speech to help him. He turned back to the window. "No, there's no way not to suffer. But you try all kinds of ways to keep from drowning in it, to keep on top of it, and to make it seem—well, like *you*. Like you did something, all right, and now you're suffering for it. You know?" I said nothing. "Well you know," he said, impatiently, "why *do* people suffer? Maybe it's better to do something to give it a reason, *any* reason."

"But we just agreed," I said, "that there's no way not to suffer. Isn't it better, then, just to—take it?"

"But nobody just takes it," Sonny cried, "that's what I'm telling you! *Everybody* tries not to. You're just hung up on the *way* some people try—it's not *your* way!"

The hair on my face began to itch, my face felt wet. "That's not true," I said, "that's not true. I don't give a damn what other people do, I don't even care how they suffer. I just care how *you* suffer." And he looked at me. "Please believe me," I said, "I don't want to see you—die—trying not to suffer."

"I won't," he said, flatly, "die trying not to suffer. At least, not any faster than anybody else."

"But there's no need," I said, trying to laugh, "is there? in killing yourself."

I wanted to say more, but I couldn't. I wanted to talk about will power and how life could be—well, beautiful. I wanted to say that it was all within; but was it? or, rather, wasn't that exactly the trouble? And I wanted to promise that I would never fail him again. But it would all have sounded—empty words and lies.

So I made the promise to myself and prayed that I would keep it.

"It's terrible sometimes, inside," he said, "that's what's the trouble. You walk these streets, black and funky and cold, and there's not really a living ass to talk to, and there's nothing shaking, and there's no way of getting it out—that storm inside. You can't talk it and you can't make love with it, and when you finally try to get with it and play it, you realize *nobody's* listening. So *you've* got to listen. You got to find a way to listen."

And then he walked away from the window and sat on the sofa again, as though all the wind had suddenly been knocked out of him. "Sometimes you'll do *anything* to play, even cut your mother's throat." He laughed and looked at me. "Or your brother's." Then he sobered. "Or your own." Then: "Don't worry. I'm all right now and I think I'll *be* all right. But I can't forget—where I've been. I don't mean just the physical place I've been, I mean where I've *been*. And *what* I've been."

"What have you been, Sonny?" I asked.

He smiled—but sat sideways on the sofa, his elbow resting on the back, his fingers playing with his mouth and chin, not looking at me. "I've been something I didn't recognize, didn't know I could be. Didn't know anybody could be." He stopped, looking inward, looking helplessly young, looking old. "I'm not talking about it now because I feel *guilty* or anything like that—maybe it would be better if I did, I don't know. Anyway, I can't really talk about it. Not to you, not to anybody," and now he turned and faced me. "Sometimes, you know, and it was actually when I was most *out* of the world, I felt that I was in it, that I was *with* it, really, and I could play or I didn't really have to *play*, it just came out of me, it was there. And I don't know how I played, thinking about it now, but I know I did awful things, those times, sometimes, to people. Or it wasn't that I *did* anything to them—it was that they weren't real." He picked up the beer can; it was empty; he rolled it between his palms: "And other times—well, I needed a fix, I needed to find a place to lean, I needed to clear a space to *listen*—and I couldn't find it, and I—went crazy, I did terrible things to *me*, I was terrible *for* me." He began pressing the beer can between his hands, I watched the metal begin to give. It glittered, as he played with it, like a knife, and I was afraid he would cut himself, but I said nothing. "Oh well. I can never tell you. I was all by myself at the bottom of something, stinking and sweating and crying and shaking, and I smelled it, you know? *my* stink, and I thought I'd die if I couldn't get away from it and yet, all the same, I knew that everything I was doing was just locking me in with it. And I didn't know," he paused, still flattening the beer can, "I didn't know, I still *don't* know, something kept telling me that maybe it was good to smell your own stink, but I didn't think that *that* was what I'd been trying to do—and—who can stand it?" and he abruptly dropped the ruined beer can, looking at me with a small, still smile, and then rose, walking to the window as though it were the lodestone rock. I watched his face, he watched the avenue. "I couldn't tell you when Mama died—but the reason I wanted to leave Harlem so bad was to get away from drugs. And then, when I ran away, that's what I was running from—really. When I came back, nothing had changed, *I* hadn't changed, I was just—older." And he stopped, drumming with his fingers on the windowpane. The sun had vanished, soon darkness would fall. I watched his face. "It can come again," he said, almost as though speaking to himself. Then he turned to me. "It can come again," he repeated. "I just want you to know that."

"All right," I said, at last. "So it can come again. All right."

He smiled, but the smile was sorrowful. "I had to try to tell you," he said.

"Yes," I said. "I understand that."

"You're my brother," he said, looking straight at me, and not smiling at all.

"Yes," I repeated, "yes. I understand that."

He turned back to the window, looking out. "All that hatred down there," he said, "all that hatred and misery and love. It's a wonder it doesn't blow the avenue apart."

We went to the only night club on a short, dark street, downtown. We squeezed through the narrow, chattering, jam-packed bar to the entrance of the big room, where the bandstand was. And we stood there for a moment, for the lights were very dim in this room and we couldn't see. Then, "Hello, boy," said a voice and an enormous black man, much older than Sonny or myself, erupted out of all that atmospheric lighting and put an arm around Sonny's shoulder. "I been sitting right here," he said, "waiting for you."

He had a big voice, too, and heads in the darkness turned toward us. Sonny grinned and pulled a little away, and said, "Creole, this is my brother. I told you about him."

Creole shook my hand. "I'm glad to meet you, son," he said, and it was clear that he was glad to meet me *there*, for Sonny's sake. And he smiled, "You got a real musician in *your* family," and he took his arm from Sonny's shoulder and slapped him, lightly, affectionately, with the back of his hand.

"Well. Now I've heard it all," said a voice behind us. This was another musician, and a friend of Sonny's, a coal-black, cheerful-looking man, built close to the ground. He immediately began confiding to me, at the top of his lungs, the most terrible things about Sonny, his teeth gleaming like a lighthouse and his laugh coming up out of him like the beginning of an earthquake. And it turned out that everyone at the bar knew Sonny, or almost everyone; some were musicians, working there, or nearby, or not working, some were simply hangers-on, and some were there to hear Sonny play. I was introduced to all of them and they were all very polite to me. Yet, it was clear that, for them, I was only Sonny's brother. Here, I was in Sonny's world. Or, rather: his kingdom. Here, it was not even a question that his veins bore royal blood.

They were going to play soon and Creole installed me, by myself, at a table in a dark corner. Then I watched them, Creole, and the little black man, and Sonny, and the others, while they horsed around, standing just below the bandstand. The light from the bandstand spilled just a little short of them and, watching them laughing and gesturing and moving about, I had the feeling that they, nevertheless, were being most careful not to step into that circle of light too suddenly: that if they moved into the light too suddenly, without thinking, they would perish in flame. Then, while I watched, one of them, the small, black man, moved into the light and crossed the bandstand and started fooling around with his drums. Then—being funny and being, also, extremely ceremonious—Creole took Sonny by the arm and led him to the piano. A woman's voice called Sonny's name and a few hands started clapping. And Sonny, also being funny and being ceremonious, and so touched, I think, that he could have cried, but neither hiding it nor showing it, riding it like a man, grinned, and put both hands to his heart and bowed from the waist.

Creole then went to the bass fiddle and a lean, very bright-skinned brown man jumped up on the bandstand and picked up his horn. So there they were, and the atmosphere on the bandstand and in the room began to change and tighten. Someone stepped up to the microphone and announced them. Then there were all kinds of murmurs. Some people at the bar shushed others. The waitress ran around, frantically getting in the last orders, guys and chicks got closer to each other, and the lights on the bandstand, on the quartet, turned to a kind of indigo. Then they all looked different there. Creole looked about him for the last time, as though he were making certain that all his chickens were in the coop, and then he—jumped and struck the fiddle. And there they were.

All I know about music is that not many people ever really hear it. And even then, on the rare occasions when something opens within, and the music enters, what we mainly hear, or hear corroborated, are personal private, vanishing evocations. But the man who creates the music is hearing something else, is dealing with the roar rising from the void and imposing order on it as it hits the air. What is evoked in him, then, is of another order, more terrible because it has no words, and triumphant, too, for that same reason. And his triumph, when he triumphs, is ours. I just watched Sonny's face. His face was troubled, he was working hard, but he wasn't with it. And I had the feeling that, in a way, everyone on the bandstand was waiting for him, both waiting for him and pushing him along. But as I began to watch Creole. I realized that it was Creole who held them all back. He had them on a short rein. Up there, keeping the beat with his whole body, wailing on the fiddle, with his eyes half closed, he was listening to everything, but he was listening to Sonny. He was having a dialogue with Sonny. He wanted Sonny to leave the shore line and strike out for the deep water. He was Sonny's witness that deep water and drowning were not the same thing—he had been there, and he knew. And he wanted Sonny to know. He was waiting for Sonny to do the things on the keys which would let Creole know that Sonny was in the water.

And, while Creole listened, Sonny moved, deep within, exactly like someone in torment. I had never before thought of how awful the relationship must be between the musician and his instrument. He has to fill it, this instrument, with the breath of life, his own. He has to make it do what he wants it to do. And a piano is just a piano. It's made out of so much wood and wires and little hammers and big ones, and ivory. While there's only so much you can do with it, the only way to find this out is to try and make it do everything.

And Sonny hadn't been near a piano for over a year. And he wasn't on much better terms with his life, not the life that stretched before him now. He and the piano stammered, started one way, got scared, stopped; started another way, panicked, marked time, started again; then seemed to have found a direction, panicked again, got stuck. And the face I saw on Sonny I'd never seen before. Everything had been burned out of it, and, at the same time, things usually hidden were being burned in, by the fire and fury of the battle which was occurring in him up there.

Yet, watching Creole's face as they neared the end of the first set, I had the feeling that something had happened, something I hadn't heard. Then they finished, there was scattered applause, and then, without an instant's warning, Creole started into something else, it was almost sardonic, it was *Am I Blue*. And, as though he commanded, Sonny began to play. Something began to happen. And Creole let out the reins. The dry, low, black man said something awful on the drums, Creole answered, and the drums talked back. Then the horn insisted, sweet and high, slightly detached perhaps, and Creole listened, commenting now and then, dry, and driving, beautiful and calm and old. Then they all came together again, and Sonny was part of the family again. I could tell this from his face. He seemed to have found, right there beneath his fingers, a damn brand-new piano. It seemed that he couldn't get over it. Then, for awhile, just being happy with Sonny, they seemed to be agreeing with him that brand-new pianos certainly were a gas.

Then Creole stepped forward to remind them that what they were playing was the blues. He hit something in all of them, he hit something in me, myself, and the music tightened and deepened, apprehension began to beat the air. Creole began to tell us what the blues were all about. They were not about anything very new. He and his boys up there were keeping it new, at the risk of ruin, destruction, madness, and death, in order to find new ways to make us listen. For, while the tale of how we suffer, and how we are delighted, and how we may triumph is never new, it always must be heard. There isn't any other tale to tell, it's the only light we've got in all this darkness.

And this tale, according to that face, that body, those strong hands on those strings, has another aspect in every country, and a new depth in every generation. Listen, Creole seemed to be saying, listen. Now these are Sonny's blues. He made the little black man on the drums know it, and the bright, brown man on the horn. Creole wasn't trying any longer to get Sonny in the water. He was wishing him Godspeed. Then he stepped back, very slowly, filling the air with the immense suggestion that Sonny speak for himself.

Then they all gathered around Sonny and Sonny played. Every now and again one of them seemed to say, Amen. Sonny's fingers filled the air with life, his life. But that life contained so many others. And Sonny went all the way back, he really began with the spare, flat statement of the opening phrase of the song. Then he began to make it his. It was very beautiful because it wasn't hurried and it was no longer a lament. I seemed to hear with what burning he had made it his, with what burning we had yet to make it ours, how we could cease lamenting. Freedom lurked around us and I understood, at last, that he could help us to be free if we would listen, that he would never be free until we did. Yet, there was no battle in his face now. I heard what he had gone through, and would continue to go through until he came to rest in earth. He had made it his: that long line, of which we knew only Mama and Daddy. And he was giving it back, as everything must be given back, so that, passing through death, it can live forever. I saw my mother's face again, and felt, for the first time, how the stones of the road she had walked on must have bruised her feet. I saw the moonlit road where my father's brother died. And it brought something else back to me, and carried me past it, I saw my little girl again and felt Isabel's tears again, and I felt my own tears begin to rise. And I was yet aware that this was only a moment, that the world waited outside, as hungry as a tiger, and that trouble stretched above us, longer than the sky.

Then it was over. Creole and Sonny let out their breath, both soaking wet, and grinning. There was a lot of applause and some of it was real. In the dark, the girl came by and I asked her to take drinks to the bandstand. There was a long pause, while they talked up there in the indigo light and after awhile I saw the girl put a Scotch and milk on top of the piano for Sonny. He didn't seem to notice it, but just before they started playing again, he sipped from it and looked toward me, and nodded. Then he put it back on top of the piano. For me, then, as they began to play again, it glowed and shook above my brother's head like the very cup of trembling.

The Judgment

It was a Sunday morning in the very height of spring. Georg Bendemann, a young merchant, was sitting in his own room on the first floor of one of a long row of small, ramshackle houses stretching beside the river which were scarcely distinguishable from each other except in height and coloring. He had just finished a letter to an old friend of his who was now living abroad, had put it into its envelope in a slow and dreamy fashion, and with his elbows propped on the writing table was gazing out of the window at the river, the bridge and the hills on the farther bank with their tender green.

He was thinking about his friend, who had actually run away to Russia some years before, being dissatisfied with his prospects at home. Now he was carrying on a business in St. Petersburg, which had flourished to begin with but had long been going downhill, as he always complained on his increasingly rare visits. So he was wearing himself out to no purpose in a foreign country, the unfamiliar full beard he wore did not quite conceal the face Georg had known so well since childhood, and his skin was growing so yellow as to indicate some latent disease. By his own account he had no regular connection with the colony of his fellow countrymen out there and almost no social intercourse with Russian families, so that he was resigning himself to becoming a permanent bachelor.

What could one write to such a man, who had obviously run off the rails, a man one could be sorry for but could not help. Should one advise him to come home, to transplant himself and take up his old friendships again—there was nothing to hinder him—and in general to rely on the help of his friends? But that was as good as telling him, and the more kindly the more offensively, that all his efforts hitherto had miscarried, that he should finally give up, come back home, and be gaped at by everyone as a returned prodigal, that only his friends knew what was what and that he himself was just a big child who should do what his successful and home-keeping friends prescribed. And was it certain, besides, that all the pain one would have to inflict on him would achieve its object? Perhaps it would not even be possible to get him to come home at all—he said himself that he was now out of touch with commerce in his native country—and then he would still be left an alien in a foreign land embittered by his friends' advice and more than ever estranged from them. But if he did follow their advice and then didn't fit in at home—not out of malice, of course, but through force of circumstances—couldn't get on with his friends or without them, felt humiliated, couldn't be said to have either friends or a country of his own any longer, wouldn't it have been better for him to stay abroad just as he was? Taking all this into account, how could one be sure that he would make a success of life at home?

For such reasons, supposing one wanted to keep up correspondence with him, one could not send him any real news such as could frankly be told to the most distant acquaintance. It was more than three years since his last visit, and for this he offered the lame excuse that the political situation in Russia was too uncertain, which apparently would not permit even the briefest absence of a small business man while it allowed hundreds of thousands of Russians to travel peacefully abroad. But during these three years Georg's own position in life had changed a lot. Two years ago his mother had died, since when he and his father had shared the household together, and his friend had of course been informed of that and had expressed his sympathy in a letter phrased so dryly that the grief caused by such an event, one had to conclude, could not be realized in a distant country. Since that time, however, Georg had applied himself with greater determination to the business as well as to everything else.

Perhaps during his mother's lifetime his father's insistence on having everything his own way in the business had hindered him from developing any real activity of his own, perhaps since her death his father had become less aggressive, although he was still active in the business, perhaps it was mostly due to an accidental run of good fortune—which was very probable indeed—but at any rate during those two years the business had developed in a most unexpected way, the staff had had to be doubled, the turnover was five times as great, no doubt about it, farther progress lay just ahead.

But Georg's friend had no inkling of this improvement. In earlier years, perhaps for the last time in that letter of condolence, he had tried to persuade Georg to emigrate to Russia and had enlarged upon the prospects of success for precisely Georg's branch of trade. The figures quoted were microscopic by comparison with the range of Georg's present operations. Yet he shrank from letting his friend know about his business success, and if he were to do it now retrospectively that certainly would look peculiar.

So Georg confined himself to giving his friend unimportant items of gossip such as rise at random in the memory when one is idly thinking things over on a quiet Sunday. All he desired was to leave undisturbed the idea of the home town which his friend must have built up to his own content during the long interval. And so it happened to Georg that three times in three fairly widely separated letters he had told his friend about the engagement of an unimportant man to an equally unimportant girl, until indeed, quite contrary to his intentions, his friend began to show some interest in this notable event.

Yet Georg preferred to write about things like these rather than to confess that he himself had got engaged a month ago to a Fräulein Frieda Brandenfeld, a girl from a well-to-do family. He often discussed this friend of his with his fiancée and the peculiar relationship that had developed between them in their correspondence. "So he won't be coming to our wedding," said she, "and yet I have a right to get to know all your friends." "I don't want to trouble him," answered Georg, "don't misunderstand me, he would probably come, at least I think so, but he would feel that his hand had been forced and he would be hurt, perhaps he would envy me and certainly he'd be discontented and without being able to do anything about his discontent he'd have to go away again alone. Alone—do you know what that means?" "Yes, but may he not hear about our wedding in some other fashion?" "I can't prevent that, of course, but it's unlikely, considering the way he lives." "Since your friends are like that, Georg, you shouldn't ever have got engaged at all." "Well, we're both to blame for that; but I wouldn't have it any other way now." And when, breathing quickly under his kisses, she still brought out: "All the same, I do feel upset," he thought it could not really involve him in trouble were he to send the news to his friend. "That's the kind of man I am and he'll just have to take me as I am," he said to himself, "I can't cut myself to another pattern that might make a more suitable friend for him."

And in fact he did inform his friend, in the long letter he had been writing that Sunday morning, about his engagement, with these words: "I have saved my best news to the end. I have got engaged to a Fräulein Frieda Brandenfeld, a girl from a well-to-do family, who only came to live here a long time after you went away, so that you're hardly likely to know her. There will be time to tell you more about her later, for today let me just say that I am very happy and as between you and me the only difference in our relationship is that instead of a quite ordinary kind of friend you will now have in me a happy friend. Besides that, you will acquire in my fiancée, who sends her warm greetings and will soon write you herself, a genuine friend of the opposite sex, which is not without importance to a bachelor. I know that there are many reasons why you can't come to see us, but would not my wedding be precisely the right occasion for giving all obstacles the go-by? Still, however that may be, do just as seems good to you without regarding any interests but your own."

With this letter in his hand Georg had been sitting a long time at the writing table, his face turned towards the window. He had barely acknowledged, with an absent smile, a greeting waved to him from the street by a passing acquaintance.

At last he put the letter in his pocket and went out of his room across a small lobby into his father's room, which he had not entered for months. There was in fact no need for him to enter it, since he saw his father daily at business and they took their midday meal together at an eating house; in the evening, it was true, each did as he pleased, yet even then, unless Georg—as mostly happened—went out with friends or, more recently, visited his fiancée, they always sat for a while, each with his newspaper, in their common sitting room.

It surprised Georg how dark his father's room was even on this sunny morning. So it was overshadowed as much as that by the high wall on the other side of the narrow courtyard. His father was sitting by the window in a corner hung with various mementoes of Georg's dead mother, reading a newspaper which he held to one side before his eyes in an attempt to overcome a defect of vision. On the table stood the remains of his breakfast, not much of which seemed to have been eaten.

"Ah, Georg," said his father, rising at once to meet him. His heavy dressing gown swung open as he walked and the skirts of it fluttered around him.—"My father is still a giant of a man," said Georg to himself.

"It's unbearably dark here," he said aloud.

"Yes, it's dark enough," answered his father.

"And you've shut the window, too?"

"I prefer it like that."

"Well, it's quite warm outside," said Georg, as if continuing his previous remark, and sat down.

His father cleared away the breakfast dishes and set them on a chest.

"I really only wanted to tell you," went on Georg, who had been vacantly following the old man's movements, "that I am now sending the news of my engagement to St. Petersburg." He drew the letter a little way from his pocket and let it drop back again.

"To St. Petersburg?" asked his father.

"To my friend there," said Georg, trying to meet his father's eye.— In business hours he's quite different, he was thinking, how solidly he sits here with his arms crossed.

"Oh yes. To your friend," said his father, with peculiar emphasis.

"Well, you know, Father, that I wanted not to tell him about my engagement at first. Out of consideration for him, that was the only reason. You know yourself he's a difficult man. I said to myself that someone else might tell him about my engagement, although he's such a solitary creature that that was hardly likely—I couldn't prevent that—but I wasn't ever going to tell him myself."

"And now you've changed your mind?" asked his father, laying his enormous newspaper on the window sill and on top of it his spectacles, which he covered with one hand.

"Yes, I've been thinking it over. If he's a good friend of mine, I said to myself, my being happily engaged should make him happy too. And so I wouldn't put off telling him any longer. But before I posted the letter I wanted to let you know."

"Georg," said his father, lengthening his toothless mouth, "listen to me! You've come to me about this business, to talk it over with me. No doubt that does you honor. But it's nothing, it's worse than nothing, if you don't tell me the whole truth. I don't want to stir up matters that shouldn't be mentioned here. Since the death of our dear mother certain things have been done that aren't right. Maybe the time will come for mentioning them, and maybe sooner than we think. There's many a thing in the business I'm not aware of, maybe it's not done behind my back— I'm not going to say that it's done behind my back—I'm not equal to things any longer, my memory's failing, I haven't an eye for so many things any longer. That's the course of nature in the first place, and in the second place the death of our dear mother hit me harder than it did you.—But since we're talking about it, about this letter, I beg you, Georg, don't deceive me. It's a trivial affair, it's hardly worth mentioning, so don't deceive me. Do you really have this friend in St. Petersburg?"

Georg rose in embarrassment. "Never mind my friends. A thousand friends wouldn't make up to me for my father. Do you know what I think? You're not taking enough care of yourself. But old age must be taken care of. I can't do without you in the business, you know that very well, but if the business is going to undermine your health, I'm ready to close it down tomorrow forever. And that won't do. We'll have to make a change in your way of living. But a radical change. You sit here in the dark, and in the sitting room you would have plenty of light. You just take a bite of breakfast instead of properly keeping up your strength. You sit by a closed window, and the air would be so good for you. No, father! I'll get the doctor to come, and we'll follow his orders. We'll change your room, you can move into the front room and I'll move in here. You won't notice the change, all your things will be moved with you. But there's time for all that later, I'll put you to bed now for a little, I'm sure you need to rest. Come, I'll help you to take off your things, you'll see I can do it. Or if you would rather go into the front room at once, you can lie down in my bed for the present. That would be the most sensible thing."

Georg stood close beside his father, who had let his head with its unkempt white hair sink on his chest.

"Georg," said his father in a low voice, without moving.

Georg knelt down at once beside his father, in the old man's weary face he saw the pupils, over-large, fixedly looking at him from the corners of the eyes.

"You have no friend in St. Petersburg. You've always been a leg-puller and you haven't even shrunk from pulling my leg. How could you have a friend out there! I can't believe it."

"Just think back a bit, Father," said Georg, lifting his father from the chair and slipping off his dressing gown as he stood feebly enough, "it'll soon be three years since my friend came to see us last. I remember that you used not to like him very much. At least twice I kept you from seeing him, although he was actually sitting with me in my room. I could quite well understand your dislike of him, my friend has his peculiarities. But then, later, you got on with him very well. I was proud because you listened to him and nodded and asked him questions. If you think back you're bound to remember. He used to tell us the most incredible stories of the Russian Revolution. For instance, when he was on a business trip to Kiev and ran into a riot, and saw a priest on a balcony who cut a broad cross in blood on the palm of his hand and held the hand up and appealed to the mob. You've told that story yourself once or twice since."

Meanwhile Georg had succeeded in lowering his father down again and carefully taking off the woollen drawers he wore over his linen underpants and his socks. The not particularly clean appearance of this underwear made him reproach himself for having been neglectful. It should have certainly been his duty to see that his father had clean changes of underwear. He had not yet explicitly discussed with his bride-to-be what arrangements should be made for his father in the future, for they had both of them silently taken it for granted that the old man would go on living alone in the old house. But now he made a quick, firm decision to take him into his own future establishment. It almost looked, on closer inspection, as if the care he meant to lavish there on his father might come too late.

He carried his father to bed in his arms. It gave him a dreadful feeling to notice that while he took the few steps towards the bed the old man on his breast was playing with his watch chain. He could not lay him down on the bed for a moment, so firmly did he hang on to the watch chain.

But as soon as he was laid in bed, all seemed well. He covered himself up and even drew the blankets farther than usual over his shoulders. He looked up at Georg with a not unfriendly eye.

"You begin to remember my friend, don't you?" asked Georg, giving him an encouraging nod.

"Am I well covered up now?" asked his father, as if he were not able to see whether his feet were properly tucked in or not.

"So you find it snug in bed already," said Georg, and tucked the blankets more closely around him.

"Am I well covered up?" asked the father once more, seeming to be strangely intent upon the answer.

"Don't worry, you're well covered up."

"No!" cried his father, cutting short the answer, threw the blankets off with a strength that sent them all flying in a moment and sprang erect in bed. Only one hand lightly touched the ceiling to steady him.

"You wanted to cover me up, I know, my young sprig, but I'm far from being covered up yet. And even if this is the last strength I have, it's enough for you, too much for you. Of course I know your friend. He would have been a son after my own heart. That's why you've been playing him false all these years. Why else? Do you think I haven't been sorry for him? And that's why you had to lock yourself up in your office —the Chief is busy, mustn't be disturbed—just so that you could write your lying letters to Russia. But thank goodness a father doesn't need to be taught how to see through his son. And now that you thought you'd got him down, so far down that you could set your bottom on him and sit on him and he wouldn't move, then my fine son makes up his mind to get married!"

Georg stared at the bogey conjured up by his father. His friend in St. Petersburg, whom his father suddenly knew too well, touched his imagination as never before. Lost in the vastness of Russia he saw him. At the door of an empty, plundered warehouse he saw him. Among the wreckage of his showcases, the slashed remnants of his wares, the falling gas brackets, he was just standing up. Why did he have to go so far away!

"But attend to me!" cried his father, and Georg, almost distracted, ran towards the bed to take everything in, yet came to a stop halfway.

"Because she lifted up her skirts," his father began to flute, "because she lifted her skirts like this, the nasty creature," and mimicking her he lifted his shirt so high that one could see the scar on his thigh from his war wound, "because she lifted her skirts like this and this you made up to her, and in order to make free with her undisturbed you have disgraced your mother's memory, betrayed your friend and stuck your father into bed so that he can't move. But he can move, or can't he?"

And he stood up quite unsupported and kicked his legs out. His insight made him radiant.

Georg shrank into a corner, as far away from his father as possible. A long time ago he had firmly made up his mind to watch closely every least movement so that he should not be surprised by any indirect attack, a pounce from behind or above. At this moment he recalled this long-forgotten resolve and forgot it again, like a man drawing a short thread through the eye of a needle.

"But your friend hasn't been betrayed after all!" cried his father, emphasizing the point with stabs of his forefinger. "I've been representing him here on the spot."

"You comedian!" Georg could not resist the retort, realized at once the harm done and, his eyes starting in his head, bit his tongue back, only too late, till the pain made his knees give.

"Yes, of course I've been playing a comedy! A comedy! That's a good expression! What other comfort was left to a poor old widower? Tell me—and while you're answering me be you still my living son—what else was left to me, in my back room, plagued by a disloyal staff, old to the marrow of my bones? And my son strutting through the world, finishing off deals that I had prepared for him, bursting with triumphant glee and stalking away from his father with the closed face of a respectable business man! Do you think I didn't love you, I, from whom you are sprung?"

Now he'll lean forward, thought Georg, what if he topples and smashes himself! These words went hissing through his mind.

His father leaned forward but did not topple. Since Georg did not come any nearer, as he had expected, he straightened himself again.

"Stay where you are, I don't need you! You think you have strength enough to come over here and that you're only hanging back of your own accord. Don't be too sure! I am still much the stronger of us two. All by myself I might have had to give way, but your mother has given me so much of her strength that I've established a fine connection with your friend and I have your customers here in my pocket!"

"He has pockets even in his shirt!" said Georg to himself, and believed that with this remark he could make him an impossible figure for all the world. Only for a moment did he think so, since he kept on forgetting everything.

"Just take your bride on your arm and try getting in my way! I'll sweep her from your very side, you don't know how!"

Georg made a grimace of disbelief. His father only nodded, confirming the truth of his words, towards Georg's corner.

"How you amused me today, coming to ask me if you should tell your friend about your engagement. He knows it already, you stupid boy, he knows it all! I've been writing to him, for you forgot to take my writing things away from me. That's why he hasn't been here for years, he knows everything a hundred times better than you do yourself, in his left hand he crumples your letters unopened while in his right hand he holds up my letters to read through!"

In his enthusiasm he waved his arm over his head. "He knows everything a thousand times better!" he cried.

"Ten thousand times!" said Georg, to make fun of his father, but in his very mouth the words turned into deadly earnest.

"For years I've been waiting for you to come with some such question! Do you think I concern myself with anything else? Do you think I read my newspapers? Look!" and he threw Georg a newspaper sheet which he had somehow taken to bed with him. An old newspaper, with a name entirely unknown to Georg.

"How long a time you've taken to grow up! Your mother had to die, she couldn't see the happy day, your friend is going to pieces in Russia, even three years ago he was yellow enough to be thrown away, and as for me, you see what condition I'm in. You have eyes in your head for that!"

"So you've been lying in wait for me!" cried Georg.

His father said pityingly, in an offhand manner: "I suppose you wanted to say that sooner. But now it doesn't matter." And in a louder voice: "So now you know what else there was in the world besides yourself, till now you've known only about yourself! An innocent child, yes, that you were, truly, but still more truly have you been a devilish human being!— And therefore take note: I sentence you now to death by drowning!"

Georg felt himself urged from the room, the crash with which his father fell on the bed behind him was still in his ears as he fled. On the staircase, which he rushed down as if its steps were an inclined plane, he ran into his charwoman on her way up to do the morning cleaning of the room. "Jesus!" she cried, and covered her face with her apron, but he was already gone. Out of the front door he rushed, across the roadway, driven towards the water. Already he was grasping at the railings as a starving man clutches food. He swung himself over, like the distinguished gymnast he had once been in his youth, to his parents' pride. With weakening grip he was still holding on when he spied between the railings a motor-bus coming which would easily cover the noise of his fall, called in a low voice: "Dear parents, I have always loved you, all the same," and let himself drop.

At this moment an unending stream of traffic was just going over the bridge.

The Conversion of the Jews

You're a real one for opening your mouth in the first place," Itzie said. "What do you open your mouth all the time for?"

"I didn't bring it up, Itz, I didn't," Ozzie said.

"What do you care about Jesus Christ for anyway?"

"I didn't bring up Jesus Christ. He did. I didn't even know what he was talking about. Jesus is historical, he kept saying. Jesus is historical." Ozzie mimicked the monumental voice of Rabbi Binder.

"Jesus was a person that lived like you and me," Ozzie continued. "That's what Binder said—"

"Yeah? . . . So what! What do I give two cents whether he lived or not. And what do you gotta open your mouth!" Itzie Lieberman favored closed-mouthedness, especially when it came to Ozzie Freedman's questions. Mrs. Freedman had to see Rabbi Binder twice before about Ozzie's questions and this Wednesday at four-thirty would be the third time. Itzie preferred to keep *his* mother in the kitchen; he settled for behind-the-back subtleties such as gestures, faces, snarls and other less delicate barnyard noises.

"He was a real person, Jesus, but he wasn't like God, and we don't believe he is God." Slowly, Ozzie was explaining Rabbi Binder's position to Itzie, who had been absent from Hebrew School the previous afternoon.

"The Catholics," Itzie said helpfully, "they believe in Jesus Christ, that he's God." Itzie Lieberman used "the Catholics" in its broadest sense—to include the Protestants.

Ozzie received Itzie's remark with a tiny head bob, as though it were a footnote, and went on. "His mother was Mary, and his father probably was Joseph," Ozzie said. "But the New Testament says his real father was God."

"His *real* father?"

"Yeah," Ozzie said, "that's the big thing, his father's supposed to be God."

"Bull."

"That's what Rabbi Binder says, that it's impossible—"

"Sure it's impossible. That stuff's all bull. To have a baby you gotta get laid," Itzie theologized. "Mary hadda get laid."

"That's what Binder says: 'The only way a woman can have a baby is to have intercourse with a man.' "

"He said *that*, Ozz?" For a moment it appeared that Itzie had put the theological question aside. "He said that, intercourse?" A little curled smile shaped itself in the lower half of Itzie's face like a pink mustache. "What you guys do, Ozz, you laugh or something?"

"I raised my hand."

"Yeah? Whatja say?"

"That's when I asked the question."

Itzie's face lit up. "Whatja ask about—intercourse?"

"No, I asked the question about God, how if He could create the heaven and earth in six days, and make all the animals and the fish and the light in six days—the light especially, that's what always gets me, that He could make the light. Making fish and animals, that's pretty good—"

"That's damn good." Itzie's appreciation was honest but unimaginative: it was as though God had just pitched a one-hitter.

"But making light . . . I mean when you think about it, it's really something," Ozzie said. "Anyway, I asked Binder if He could make all that in six days, and He could *pick* the six days he wanted right out of nowhere, why couldn't He let a woman have a baby without having intercourse."

"You said intercourse, Ozz, to Binder?"

"Yeah."

"Right in class?"

"Yeah."

Itzie smacked the side of his head.

"I mean, no kidding around," Ozzie said, "that'd really be nothing. After all that other stuff, that'd practically be nothing."

Itzie considered a moment. "What'd Binder say?"

"He started all over again explaining how Jesus was historical and how he lived like you and me but he wasn't God. So I said I under*stood* that. What I wanted to know was different."

What Ozzie wanted to know was always different. The first time he had wanted to know how Rabbi Binder could call the Jews "The Chosen People" if the Declaration of Independence claimed all men to be created equal. Rabbi Binder tried to distinguish for him between political equality and spiritual legitimacy, but what Ozzie wanted to know, he insisted vehemently, was different. That was the first time his mother had to come.

Then there was the plane crash. Fifty-eight people had been killed in a plane crash at La Guardia. In studying a casualty list in the newspaper his mother had discovered among the list of those dead eight Jewish names (his grandmother had nine but she counted Miller as a Jewish name); because of the eight she said the plane crash was "a tragedy."

During free-discussion time on Wednesday Ozzie had brought to Rabbi Binder's attention this matter of "some of his relations" always picking out the Jewish names. Rabbi Binder had begun to explain cultural unity and some other things when Ozzie stood up at his seat and said that what he wanted to know was different. Rabbi Binder insisted that he sit down and it was then that Ozzie shouted that he wished all fifty-eight were Jews. That was the second time his mother came.

"And he kept explaining about Jesus being historical, and so I kept asking him. No kidding, Itz, he was trying to make me look stupid."

"So what he finally do?"

"Finally he starts screaming that I was deliberately simple-minded and a wise guy, and that my mother had to come, and this was the last time. And that I'd never get bar-mitzvahed if he could help it. Then, Itz, then he starts talking in that voice like a statue, real slow and deep, and he says that I better think over what I said about the Lord. He told me to go to his office and think it over." Ozzie leaned his body towards Itzie. "Itz, I thought it over for a solid hour, and now I'm convinced God could do it."

Ozzie had planned to confess his latest transgression to his mother as soon as she came home from work. But it was a Friday night in November and already dark, and when Mrs. Freedman came through the door she tossed off her coat, kissed Ozzie quickly on the face, and went to the kitchen table to light the three yellow candles, two for the Sabbath and one for Ozzie's father.

When his mother lit the candles she would move her two arms slowly towards her, dragging them through the air, as though persuading people whose minds were half made up. And her eyes would get glassy with tears. Even when his father was alive Ozzie remembered that her eyes had gotten glassy, so it didn't have anything to do with his dying. It had something to do with lighting the candles.

As she touched the flaming match to the unlit wick of a Sabbath candle, the phone rang, and Ozzie, standing only a foot from it, plucked it off the receiver and held it muffled to his chest. When his mother lit candles Ozzie felt there should be no noise; even breathing, if you could manage it, should be softened. Ozzie pressed the phone to his breast and watched his mother dragging whatever she was dragging, and he felt his own eyes get glassy. His mother was a round, tired, gray-haired penguin of a woman whose gray skin had begun to feel the tug of gravity and the weight of her own history. Even when she was dressed up she didn't look like a chosen person. But when she lit candles she looked like something better; like a woman who knew momentarily that God could do anything.

After a few mysterious minutes she was finished. Ozzie hung up the phone and walked to the kitchen table where she was beginning to lay the two places for the four-course Sabbath meal. He told her that she would have to see Rabbi Binder next Wednesday at four-thirty, and then he told her why. For the first time in their life together she hit Ozzie across the face with her hand.

All through the chopped liver and chicken soup part of the dinner Ozzie cried; he didn't have any appetite for the rest.

On Wednesday, in the largest of the three basement classrooms of the synagogue, Rabbi Marvin Binder, a tall, handsome, broad-shouldered man of thirty with thick strong-fibered black hair, removed his watch from his pocket and saw that it was four o'clock. At the rear of the room Yakov Blotnik, the seventy-one-year-old custodian, slowly polished the large window, mumbling to himself, unaware that it was four o'clock or six o'clock, Monday or Wednesday. To most of the students Yakov Blotnik's mumbling, along with his brown curly beard, scythe nose, and two heel-trailing black cats, made of him an object of wonder, a foreigner, a relic, towards whom they were alternately fearful and disrespectful. To Ozzie the mumbling had always seemed a monotonous, curious prayer; what made it curious was that old Blotnik had been mumbling so steadily for so many years, Ozzie suspected he had memorized the prayers and forgotten all about God.

"It is now free-discussion time," Rabbi Binder said. "Feel free to talk about any Jewish matter at all—religion, family, politics, sports—"

There was silence. It was a gusty, clouded November afternoon and it did not seem as though there ever was or could be a thing called baseball. So nobody this week said a word about that hero from the past, Hank Greenberg—which limited free discussion considerably.

And the soul-battering Ozzie Freedman had just received from Rabbi Binder had imposed its limitation. When it was Ozzie's turn to read aloud from the Hebrew book the rabbi had asked him petulantly why he didn't read more rapidly. He was showing no progress. Ozzie said he could read faster but that if he did he was sure not to understand what he was reading. Nevertheless, at the rabbi's repeated suggestion Ozzie tried, and showed a great talent, but in the midst of a long passage he stopped short and said he didn't understand a word he was reading, and started in again at a drag-footed pace. Then came the soul-battering.

Consequently when free-discussion time rolled around none of the students felt too free. The rabbi's invitation was answered only by the mumbling of feeble old Blotnik.

"Isn't there any thing at all you would like to discuss?" Rabbi Binder asked again, looking at his watch. "No questions or comments?"

There was a small grumble from the third row. The rabbi requested that Ozzie rise and give the rest of the class the advantage of his thought.

Ozzie rose. "I forget it now," he said, and sat down in his place.

Rabbi Binder advanced a seat towards Ozzie and poised himself on the edge of the desk. It was Itzie's desk and the rabbi's frame only a dagger's-length away from his face snapped him to sitting attention.

"Stand up again, Oscar," Rabbi Binder said calmly, "and try to assemble your thoughts."

Ozzie stood up. All his classmates turned in their seats and watched as he gave an unconvincing scratch to his forehead.

"I can't assemble any," he announced, and plunked himself down.

"Stand up!" Rabbi Binder advanced from Itzie's desk to the one directly in front of Ozzie; when the rabbinical back was turned Itzie gave it five-fingers off the tip of his nose, causing a small titter in the room. Rabbi Binder was too absorbed in squelching Ozzie's nonsense once and for all to bother with titters. "Stand up, Oscar, What's your question about?"

Ozzie pulled a word out of the air. It was the handiest word. "Religion."

"Oh, now you remember?"

"Yes."

"What is it?"

Trapped, Ozzie blurted the first thing that came to him. "Why can't He make anything He wants to make!"

As Rabbi Binder prepared an answer, a final answer, Itzie, ten feet behind him, raised one finger on his left hand, gestured it meaningfully towards the rabbi's back, and brought the house down.

Binder twisted quickly to see what had happened and in the midst of the commotion Ozzie shouted into the rabbi's back what he couldn't have shouted to his face. It was a loud, toneless sound that had the timbre of something stored inside for about six days.

"You don't know! You don't know anything about God!"

The rabbi spun back towards Ozzie. "What?"

"You don't know—you don't—"

"Apologize, Oscar, apologize!" It was a threat.

"You don't—"

Rabbi Binder's hand flicked out at Ozzie's cheek. Perhaps it had only been meant to clamp the boy's mouth shut, but Ozzie ducked and the palm caught him squarely on the nose.

The blood came in a short, red spurt on to Ozzie's shirt front.

The next moment was all confusion. Ozzie screamed, "You bastard, you bastard!" and broke for the classroom door. Rabbi Binder lurched a step backwards, as though his own blood had started flowing violently in the opposite direction, then gave a clumsy lurch forward and bolted out the door after Ozzie. The class followed after the rabbi's huge blue-suited back, and before old Blotnik could turn from his window, the room was empty and everyone was headed full speed up the three flights leading to the roof.

If one should compare the light of day to the life of man: sunrise to birth; sunset—the dropping down over the edge—to death; then as Ozzie Freedman wiggled through the trapdoor of the synagogue roof, his feet kicking backwards bronco-style at Rabbi Binder's outstretched arms—at that moment the day was fifty years old. As a rule, fifty or fifty-five reflects accurately the age of late afternoons in November, for it is in that month, during those hours, that one's awareness of light seems no longer a matter of seeing, but of hearing: light begins clicking away. In fact, as Ozzie locked shut the trapdoor in the rabbi's face, the sharp click of the bolt into the lock might momentarily have been mistaken for the sound of the heavier gray that had just throbbed through the sky.

With all his weight Ozzie kneeled on the locked door; any instant he was certain that Rabbi Binder's shoulder would fling it open, splintering the wood into shrapnel and catapulting his body into the sky. But the door did not move and below him he heard only the rumble of feet, first loud then dim, like thunder rolling away.

A question shot through his brain. "Can this be *me*?" For a thirteen-year-old who had just labeled his religious leader a bastard, twice, it was not an improper question. Louder and louder the question came to him—"Is it me? Is it me?"—until he discovered himself no longer kneeling, but racing crazily towards the edge of the roof, his eyes crying, his throat screaming, and his arms flying everywhichway as though not his own.

"Is it me? Is it me Me ME ME ME! It has to be me—but is it!"

It is the question a thief must ask himself the night he jimmies open his first window, and it is said to be the question with which bridegrooms quiz themselves before the altar.

In the few wild seconds it took Ozzie's body to propel him to the edge of the roof, his self-examination began to grow fuzzy. Gazing down at the street, he became confused as to the problem beneath the question: was it, is-it-me-who-called-Binder-a-bastard? or, is-it-me-prancing-around-on-the-roof? However, the scene below settled all, for there is an instant in any action when whether it is you or somebody else is academic. The thief crams the money in his pockets and scoots out the window. The bridegroom signs the hotel register for two. And the boy on the roof finds a streetful of people gaping at him, necks stretched backwards, faces up, as though he were the ceiling of the Hayden Planetarium. Suddenly you know it's you.

"Oscar! Oscar Freedman!" A voice rose from the center of the crowd, a voice that, could it have been seen, would have looked like the writing on scroll. "Oscar Freedman, get down from there. Immediately!" Rabbi Binder was pointing one arm stiffly up at him; and at the end of that arm, one finger aimed menacingly. It was the attitude of a dictator, but one—the eyes confessed all—whose personal valet had spit neatly in his face.

Ozzie didn't answer. Only for a blink's length did he look towards Rabbi Binder. Instead his eyes began to fit together the world beneath him, to sort out people from places, friends from enemies, participants from spectators. In little jagged starlike clusters his friends stood around Rabbi Binder, who was still pointing. The topmost point on a star compounded not of angels but of five adolescent boys was Itzie. What a world it was, with those stars below, Rabbi Binder below . . . Ozzie, who a moment earlier hadn't been able to control his own body, started to feel the meaning of the word control: he felt Peace and he felt Power.

"Oscar Freedman, I'll give you three to come down."

Few dictators give their subjects three to do anything; but, as always, Rabbi Binder only looked dictatorial.

"Are you ready, Oscar?"

Ozzie nodded his head yes, although he had no intention in the world—the lower one of the celestial one he'd just entered—of coming down even if Rabbi Binder should give him a million.

"All right then," said Rabbi Binder. He ran a hand through his black Samson hair as though it were the gesture prescribed for uttering the first digit. Then, with his other hand cutting a circle out of the small piece of sky around him, he spoke. "One!"

There was no thunder. On the contrary, at that moment, as though "one" was the cue for which he had been waiting, the world's least thunderous person appeared on the synagogue steps. He did not so much come out the synagogue door as lean out, onto the darkening air. He clutched at the doorknob with one hand and looked up at the roof.

"Oy!"

Yakov Blotnik's old mind hobbled slowly, as if on crutches, and though he couldn't decide precisely what the boy was doing on the roof, he knew it wasn't good—that is, it wasn't-good-for-the-Jews. For Yakov Blotnik life had fractionated itself simply: things were either good-for-the-Jews or no-good-for-the-Jews.

He smacked his free hand to his in-sucked cheek, gently. "Oy, Gut!" And then quickly as he was able, he jacked down his head and surveyed the street. There was Rabbi Binder (like a man at an auction with only three dollars in his pocket, he had just delivered a shaky "Two!"); there were the students, and that was all. So far it-wasn't-so-bad-for-the-Jews. But the boy had to come down immediately, before anybody saw. The problem: how to get the boy off the roof?

Anybody who has ever had a cat on the roof knows how to get him down. You call the fire department. Or first you call the operator and you ask her for the fire department. And the next thing there is great jamming of brakes and clanging of bells and shouting of instructions. And then the cat is off the roof. You do the same thing to get a boy off the roof.

That is, you do the same thing if you are Yakov Blotnik and you once had a cat on the roof.

When the engines, all four of them, arrived, Rabbi Binder had four times given Ozzie the count of three. The big hook-and-ladder swung around the corner and one of the firemen leaped from it, plunging headlong towards the yellow fire hydrant in front of the synagogue. With a huge wrench he began to unscrew the top nozzle. Rabbi Binder raced over to him and pulled at his shoulder.

"There's no fire . . ."

The fireman mumbled back over his shoulder and, heatedly, continued working at the nozzle.

"But there's no fire, there's no fire . . ." Binder shouted. When the fireman mumbled again, the rabbi grasped his face with both his hands and pointed it up at the roof.

To Ozzie it looked as though Rabbi Binder was trying to tug the fireman's head out of his body, like a cork from a bottle. He had to giggle at the picture they made: it was a family portrait—rabbi in black skullcap, fireman in red fire hat, and the little yellow hydrant squatting beside like a kid brother, bareheaded. From the edge of the roof Ozzie waved at the portrait, a one-handed, flapping, mocking wave; in doing it his right foot slipped from under him. Rabbi Binder covered his eyes with his hands.

Firemen work fast. Before Ozzie had even regained his balance, a big, round, yellowed net was being held on the synagogue lawn. The firemen who held it looked up at Ozzie with stern, feelingless faces.

One of the firemen turned his head towards Rabbi Binder. "What, is the kid nuts or something?"

Rabbi Binder unpeeled his hands from his eyes, slowly, painfully, as if they were tape. Then he checked: nothing on the sidewalk, no dents in the net.

"Is he gonna jump, or what?" the fireman shouted.

In a voice not at all like a statue, Rabbi Binder finally answered. "Yes, Yes, I think so . . . He's been threatening to . . ."

Threatening to? Why, the reason he was on the roof, Ozzie remembered, was to get away; he hadn't even thought about jumping. He had just run to get away, and the truth was that he hadn't really headed for the roof as much as he'd been chased there.

"What's his name, the kid?"

"Freedman," Rabbi Binder answered. "Oscar Freedman."

The fireman looked up at Ozzie. "What is it with you, Oscar? You gonna jump, or what?"

Ozzie did not answer. Frankly, the question had just arisen.

"Look, Oscar, if you're gonna jump, jump—and if you're not gonna jump, don't jump. But don't waste our time, willya?"

Ozzie looked at the fireman and then at Rabbi Binder. He wanted to see Rabbi Binder cover his eyes one more time.

"I'm going to jump."

And then he scampered around the edge of the roof to the corner, where there was no net below, and he flapped his arms at his sides, swishing the air and smacking his palms to his trousers on the downbeat. He began screaming like some kind of engine, "Wheeeee . . . wheeeeee," and leaning way out over the edge with the upper half of his body. The firemen whipped around to cover the ground with the net. Rabbi Binder mumbled a few words to Somebody and covered his eyes. Everything happened quickly, jerkily, as in a silent movie. The crowd, which had arrived with the fire engines, gave out a long, Fourth-of-July fireworks oooh-aahhh. In the excitement no one had paid the crowd much heed, except, of course, Yakov Blotnik, who swung from the doorknob counting heads. "Fier und tsvansik . . . finf und tsvantsik . . . Oy, Gut!" It wasn't like this with the cat.

Rabbi Binder peeked through his fingers, checked the sidewalk and net. Empty. But there was Ozzie racing to the other corner. The firemen raced with him but were unable to keep up. Whenever Ozzie wanted to he might jump and splatter himself upon the sidewalk, and by the time the firemen scooted to the spot all they could do with their net would be to cover the mess.

"Wheeeee . . . wheeeee . . ."

"Hey, Oscar," the winded fireman yelled, "What the hell is this, a game or something?"

"Wheeeee . . . wheeeee . . ."

"Hey, Oscar—"

But he was off now to the other corner, flapping his wings fiercely. Rabbi Binder couldn't take it any longer—the fire engines from nowhere, the screaming suicidal boy, the net. He fell to his knees, exhausted, and with his hands curled together in front of his chest like a little dome, he pleaded, "Oscar, stop it, Oscar. Don't jump, Oscar. Please come down . . . Please don't jump."

And further back in the crowd a single voice, a single young voice, shouted a lone word to the boy on the roof.

"Jump!"

It was Itzie. Ozzie momentarily stopped flapping.

"Go ahead, Ozz—jump!" Itzie broke off his point of the star and courageously, with the inspiration not of a wise-guy but of a disciple, stood alone. "Jump, Ozz, jump!"

Still on his knees, his hands still curled, Rabbi Binder twisted his body back. He looked at Itzie, then, agonizingly, back to Ozzie.

"Oscar, Don't jump! Please, Don't Jump . . . please please . . ."

"Jump!" This time it wasn't Itzie but another point of the star. By the time Mrs. Freedman arrived to keep her four-thirty appointment with Rabbi Binder, the whole little upside down heaven was shouting and pleading for Ozzie to jump, and Rabbi Binder no longer was pleading with him not to jump, but was crying into the dome of his hands.

Understandably Mrs. Freedman couldn't figure out what her son was doing on the roof. So she asked.

"Ozzie, my Ozzie, what are you doing? My Ozzie, what is it?"

Ozzie stopped wheeeeeing and slowed his arms down to a cruising flap, the kind birds use in soft winds, but he did not answer. He stood against the low, clouded, darkening sky—light clicked down swiftly now, as on a small gear—flapping softly and gazing down at the small bundle of a woman who was his mother.

"What are you doing, Ozzie?" She turned towards the kneeling Rabbi Binder and rushed so close that only a paper-thickness of dusk lay between her stomach and his shoulders.

"What is my baby doing?"

Rabbi Binder gaped up at her but he too was mute. All that moved was the dome of his hands; it shook back and forth like a weak pulse.

"Rabbi, get him down! He'll kill himself. Get him down, my only baby . . ."

"I can't," Rabbi Binder said, "I can't . . ." and he turned his handsome head towards the crowd of boys behind him. "It's them. Listen to them."

And for the first time Mrs. Freedman saw the crowd of boys, and she heard what they were yelling.

"He's doing it for them. He won't listen to me. It's them." Rabbi Binder spoke like one in a trance.

"For them?"

"Yes."

"Why for them?"

"They want him to . . ."

Mrs. Freedman raised her two arms upward as though she were conducting the sky. "For them he's doing it!" And then in a gesture older than pyramids, older than prophets and floods, her arms came slapping down to her sides. "A martyr I have. Look!" She tilted her head to the roof. Ozzie was still flapping softly. "My martyr."

"Oscar, come down, *please*," Rabbi Binder groaned.

In a startlingly even voice Mrs. Freedman called to the boy on the roof. "Ozzie, come down, Ozzie. Don't be a martyr, my baby."

As though it were a litany, Rabbi Binder repeated her words. "Don't be a martyr, my baby. Don't be a martyr."

"Gawhead, Ozz—*be* a Martin!" It was Itzie. "Be a Martin, be a Martin," and all the voices joined in singing for Martindom, whatever *it* was. "Be a Martin, be a Martin . . ."

Somehow when you're on a roof the darker it gets the less you can hear. All Ozzie knew was that two groups wanted two new things: his friends were spirited and musical about what they wanted; his mother and the rabbi were even-toned, chanting, about what they didn't want. The rabbi's voice was without tears now and so was his mother's.

The big net stared up at Ozzie like a sightless eye. The big, clouded sky pushed down. From beneath it looked like a gray corrugated board. Suddenly, looking up into that unsympathetic sky, Ozzie realized all the strangeness of what these people, his friends, were asking: they wanted him to jump, to kill himself; they were singing about it now—it made them that happy. And there was an even greater strangeness: Rabbi

Binder was on his knees, trembling. If there was a question to be asked now it was not "Is it me?" but rather "Is it us? . . . Is it us?"

Being on the roof, it turned out, was a serious thing. If he jumped would the singing become dancing? Would it? What would jumping stop? Yearningly, Ozzie wished he could rip open the sky, plunge his hands through, and pull out the sun; and on the sun, like a coin, would be stamped JUMP or DON'T JUMP.

Ozzie's knees rocked and sagged a little under him as though they were setting him for a dive. His arms tightened, stiffened, froze, from shoulders to fingernails. He felt as if each part of his body were going to vote as to whether he should kill himself or not—and each part as though it were independent of *him*.

The light took an unexpected click down and the new darkness, like a gag, hushed the friends singing for this and the mother and rabbi chanting for that.

Ozzie stopped counting votes, and in a curiously high voice, like one who wasn't prepared for speech, he spoke.

"Mamma?"

"Yes, Oscar."

"Mamma, get down on your knees, like Rabbi Binder."

"Oscar—"

"Get down on your knees," he said, "or I'll jump."

Ozzie heard a whimper, then a quick rustling, and when he looked down where his mother had stood he saw the top of a head and beneath that a circle of dress. She was kneeling beside Rabbi Binder.

He spoke again. "Everybody kneel." There was the sound of everybody kneeling.

Ozzie looked around. With one hand he pointed towards the synagogue entrance. "Make *him* kneel."

There was a noise, not of kneeling, but of body-and-cloth stretching. Ozzie could hear Rabbi Binder saying in a gruff whisper, ". . . or he'll *kill* himself," and when next he looked there was Yakov Blotnik off the doorknob and for the first time in his life upon his knees in the Gentile posture of prayer.

As for the firemen—it is not as difficult as one might imagine to hold a net taut while you are kneeling.

Ozzie looked around again; and then he called to Rabbi Binder.

"Rabbi?"

"Yes, Oscar."

"Rabbi Binder, do you believe in God."

"Yes."

"Do you believe God can do Anything?" Ozzie leaned his head out into the darkness. "Anything?"

"Oscar, I think—"

"Tell me you believe God can do Anything."

There was a second's hesitation. Then: "God can do Anything."

"Tell me you believe God can make a child without intercourse."

"He can."

"Tell me!"

"God," Rabbi Binder admitted, "can make a child without intercourse."

"Mamma, you tell me."

"God can make a child without intercourse," his mother said.

"Make *him* tell me." There was no doubt who *him* was.

In a few moments Ozzie heard an old comical voice say something to the increasing darkness about God.

Next, Ozzie made everybody say it. And then he made them all say they believed in Jesus Christ—first one at a time, then all together.

When the catechizing was through it was the beginning of evening. From the street it sounded as if the boy on the roof might have sighed.

"Ozzie?" A woman's voice dared to speak. "You'll come down now?"

There was no answer, but the woman waited, and when a voice finally did speak it was thin and crying, and exhausted as that of an old man who has just finished pulling the bells.

"Mamma, don't you see—you shouldn't hit me. He shouldn't hit me. You shouldn't hit me about God, Mamma. You should never hit anybody about God—"

"Ozzie, please come down now."

"Promise me, promise me you'll never hit anybody about God."

He had asked only his mother, but for some reason everyone kneeling in the street promised he would never hit anybody about God.

Once again there was silence.

"I can come down now, Mamma," the boy on the roof finally said. He turned his head both ways as though checking the traffic lights. "Now I can come down . . ."

And he did, right into the center of the yellow net that glowed in the evening's edge like an overgrown halo.

FYODOR DOSTOEVSKY

The Grand Inquisitor

Editor's Note:

[Although "The Grand Inquisitor" is chapter 5 in Book V of Dostoevsky's last novel The Brothers Karamazov, it can be read as a complete story in itself. Ivan, the narrator, who represents the intellectual element in the family, calls what he has "written" a "poem in prose." A university student of twenty-four, Ivan wavers between intellectual honesty and moral nihilism, in contrast with his brother Alyosha, four years younger, who as a novice in a nearby monastery accepts in faith the mysteries of the invisible. In juxtaposing the two brothers, Dostoevsky has unforgettably explored the nature of Christian faith, man and God, freedom and suffering. The story, told to Alyosha by his brother Ivan, comes from the New Testament account of Christ's temptations: Matthew 4:1–11 and Luke 4:1–13.]

"Even this must have a preface—that is, a literary preface," laughed Ivan, "and I am a poor hand at making one. You see, my action takes place in the sixteenth century, and at that time, as you probably learnt at school, it was customary in poetry to bring down heavenly powers on earth. Not to speak of Dante, in France, clerks, as well as the monks in the monasteries, used to give regular performances in which the Madonna, the saints, the angels, Christ, and God Himself were brought on the stage. In those days it was done in all simplicity. In Victor Hugo's 'Notre Dame de Paris' an edifying and gratuitous spectacle was provided for the people in the Hotel de Ville of Paris in the reign of Louis XI in honor of the birth of the dauphin. It was called *Le bon jugement de la très sainte et gracieuse Vierge Marie*,[1] and she appears herself on the stage and pronounces her *bon jugement*. Similar plays, chiefly from the Old Testament, were occasionally performed in Moscow too, up to the times of Peter the Great. But besides plays there were all sorts of legends and ballads scattered about the world, in which the saints and angels and all the powers of Heaven took part when required. In our monasteries the monks busied themselves with translating, copying, and even composing such poems—and even under the Tatars. There is, for instance, one such poem (of course, from the Greek), 'The Wanderings of Our

---

[1] *Le . . . Marie:* "The Sound Judgment of the Most Holy and Gracious Virgin Mary" (French).

Lady through Hell,' with descriptions as bold as Dante's. Our Lady visits Hell, and the Archangel Michael leads her through the torments. She sees the sinners and their punishment. There she sees among others one noteworthy set of sinners in a burning lake; some of them sink to the bottom of the lake so that they can't swim out, and 'these God forgets' —an expression of extraordinary depth and force. And so Our Lady, shocked and weeping, falls before the throne of God and begs for mercy for all in Hell—for all she has seen there, indiscriminately. Her conversation with God is immensely interesting. She beseeches Him, she will not desist, and when God points to the hands and feet of her Son, nailed to the Cross, and asks, 'How can I forgive His tormentors?' she bids all the saints, all the martyrs, all the angels and archangels to fall down with her and pray for mercy on all without distinction. It ends by her winning from God a respite of suffering every year from Good Friday till Trinity day, and the sinners at once raise a cry of thankfulness from Hell, chanting, 'Thou art just, O Lord, in this judgment.' Well, my poem would have been of that kind if it had appeared at that time. He comes on the scene in my poem, but He says nothing, only appears and passes on. Fifteen centuries have passed since He promised to come in His glory, fifteen centuries since His prophet wrote, 'Behold, I came quickly'; 'Of that day and that hour knoweth no man, neither the Son, but the Father,' as He Himself predicted on earth. But humanity awaits him with the same faith and with the same love. Oh, with greater faith, for it is fifteen centuries since man has ceased to see signs from Heaven.

> No signs from Heaven come today
> To add to what the heart doth say.

There was nothing left but faith in what the heart doth say. It is true there were many miracles in those days. There were saints who performed miraculous cures; some holy people, according to their biographies, were visited by the Queen of Heaven herself. But the devil did not slumber, and doubts were already arising among men of the truth of these miracles. And just then there appeared in the north of Germany a terrible new heresy. 'A huge star like to a torch' (that is, to a church) 'fell on the sources of the waters and they became bitter.'[2] These heretics began blasphemously denying miracles. But those who remained faithful were all the more ardent in their faith. The tears of humanity rose up to Him as before, awaited His coming, loved Him, hoped for Him, yearned to suffer and die for Him as before. And so many ages mankind had prayed with faith and fervor, 'O Lord our God, hasten Thy coming,' so many ages called upon Him, that in His infinite mercy He deigned to come

[2] Revelation 8:10–11.

down to His servants. Before that day He had come down, He had visited some holy men, martyrs and hermits, as is written in their 'Lives.' Among us, Tyutchev,[3] with absolute faith in the truth of his words, bore witness that

> Bearing the Cross, in slavish dress,
> Weary and worn, the Heavenly King
> Our mother, Russia, came to bless,
> And through our land went wandering.

And that certainly was so, I assure you.

"And behold, He deigned to appear for a moment to the people, to the tortured, suffering people, sunk in iniquity, but loving Him like children. My story is laid in Spain, in Seville, in the most terrible time of the Inquisition, when fires were lighted every day to the glory of God, and 'in the splendid *auto da fé*[4] the wicked heretics were burnt.' Oh, of course, this was not the coming in which He will appear according to His promise at the end of time in all His heavenly glory, and which will be sudden 'as lightning flashing from east to west.' No, He visited His children only for a moment, and there where the flames were crackling round the heretics. In His infinite mercy He came once more among men in that human shape in which He walked among men for three years fifteen centuries ago. He came down to the 'hot pavement' of the southern town in which on the day before almost a hundred heretics had, *ad majorem gloriam Dei*,[5] been burnt by the cardinal, the Grand Inquisitor, in a magnificent *auto da fé*, in the presence of the king, the court, the knights, the cardinals, the most charming ladies of the court, and the whole population of Seville.

"He came softly, unobserved, and yet, strange to say, every one recognized Him. That might be one of the best passages in the poem. I mean, why they recognized Him. The people are irresistibly drawn to Him, they surround Him, they flock about Him, follow Him. He moves silently in their midst with a gentle smile of infinite compassion. The sun of love burns in His heart, light and power shine from His eyes, and their radiance, shed on the people, stirs their hearts with responsive love. He holds out His hands to them, blesses them, and a healing virtue comes from contact with Him, even with His garments. An old man in the crowd, blind from childhood, cries out, 'O Lord, heal me and I shall see Thee!' and, as it were, scales fall from his eyes and the blind man sees

---

[3] *Tyutchev*: a Russian poet. [4] *auto da fé*: "act of faith" (Portuguese). [5] *ad . . . Dei*: "to the greater glory of God" (Latin).

Him. The crowd weeps and kisses the earth under His feet. Children throw flowers before Him, sing, and cry hosannah. 'It is He—it is He!' all repeat. 'It must be He, it can be no one but Him!' He stops at the steps of the Seville cathedral at the moment when the weeping mourners are bringing in a little open white coffin. In it lies a child of seven, the only daughter of a prominent citizen. The dead child lies hidden in flowers. 'He will raise your child,' the crowd shouts to the weeping mother. The priest, coming to meet the coffin, looks perplexed, and frowns, but the mother of the dead child throws herself at His feet with a wail. 'If it is Thou, raise my child!' she cries, holding out her hands to Him. The procession halts, the coffin is laid on the steps at His feet. He looks with compassion, and His lips once more softly pronounce, 'Maiden, arise!'[6] and the maiden arises. The little girl sits up in the coffin and looks round, smiling with wide-open wondering eyes, holding a bunch of white roses they had put in her hand.

"There are cries, sobs, confusion among the people, and at that moment the cardinal himself, the Grand Inquisitor, passes by the cathedral. He is an old man, almost ninety, tall and erect, with a withered face and sunken eyes, in which there is still a gleam of light. He is not dressed in his gorgeous cardinal's robes, as he was the day before, when he was burning the enemies of the Roman Church—at that moment he was wearing his coarse, old, monk's cassock. At a distance behind him come his gloomy assistants and slaves and the 'holy guard.' He stops at the sight of the crowd and watches it from a distance. He sees everything; he sees them set the coffin down at His feet, sees the child rise up, and his face darkens. He knits his thick gray brows and his eyes gleam with a sinister fire. He holds out his finger and bids the guards take Him. And such is his power, so completely are the people cowed into submission and trembling obedience to him, that the crowd immediately make way for the guards, and in the midst of deathlike silence they lay hands on Him and lead Him away. The crowd instantly bows down to the earth, like one man, before the old inquisitor. He blesses the people in silence and passes on. The guards lead their prisoner to the close, gloomy vaulted prison in the ancient palace of the Holy Inquisition and shut Him in it. The day passes and is followed by the dark, burning 'breathless' night of Seville. The air is 'fragrant with laurel and lemon.' In the pitch darkness the iron door of the prison is suddenly opened and the Grand Inquisitor himself comes in with a light in his hand. He is alone; the door is closed at once behind him. He stands in the doorway and for a

[6] See Mark 5:35-43.

minute or two gazes into His face. At last he goes up slowly, sets the light on the table and speaks.

" 'Is it Thou? Thou?' but receiving no answer, he adds at once, 'Don't answer, be silent. What canst Thou say, indeed? I know too well what Thou wouldst say. And Thou hast no right to add anything to what Thou hadst said of old. Why, then, art Thou come to hinder us? For Thou hast come to hinder us, and Thou knowest that. But dost Thou know what will be tomorrow? I know not who Thou art and care not to know whether it is Thou or only a semblance of Him, but tomorrow I shall condemn Thee and burn Thee at the stake as the worst of heretics. And the very people who have today kissed Thy feet, tomorrow at the faintest sign from me will rush to heap up the embers of Thy fire. Knowest Thou that? Yes, maybe Thou knowest it,' he added with thoughtful penetration, never for a moment taking his eyes off the Prisoner."

"I don't quite understand, Ivan. What does it mean?" Alyosha, who had been listening in silence, said with a smile. "Is it simply a wild fantasy, or a mistake on the part of the old man—some impossible *quiproquo*?"[7]

"Take it as the last," said Ivan, laughing, "if you are so corrupted by modern realism and can't stand anything fantastic. If you like it to be a case of mistaken identity, let it be so. It is true," he went on, laughing, "the old man was ninety, and he might well be crazy over his set idea. He might have been struck by the appearance of the Prisoner. It might, in fact, be simply his ravings, the delusion of an old man of ninety, overexcited by the *auto da fé* of a hundred heretics the day before. But does it matter to us after all whether it was a mistake of identity or a wild fantasy? All that matters is that the old man should speak out, should speak openly of what he has thought in silence for ninety years."

"And the Prisoner too is silent? Does He look at him and not say a word?"

"That's inevitable in any case," Ivan laughed again. "The old man has told Him He hasn't the right to add anything to what He has said of old. One may say it is the most fundamental feature of Roman Catholicism, in my opinion at least. 'All has been given by Thee to the Pope," they say, 'and all, therefore, is still in the Pope's hands, and there is no need for Thee to come now at all. Thou must not meddle for the time, at least.' That's how they speak and write too—the Jesuits, at any rate. I have read it myself in the works of their theologians. 'Hast Thou the right to reveal to us one of the mysteries of that world from which Thou

---

[7] *quiproquo:* "one person for another" (Latin).

hast come?' my old man asks Him, and answers the question for Him. 'No, Thou hast not; that Thou mayest not add to what has been said of old, and mayest not take from men the freedom which Thou didst exalt when Thou wast on earth. Whatsoever Thou revealest anew will encroach on men's freedom of faith; for it will be manifest as a miracle, and the freedom of their faith was dearer to Thee than anything in those days fifteen hundred years ago. Didst Thou not often say then, "I will make you free"? But now Thou hast seen these "free" men,' the old man adds suddenly, with a pensive smile. 'Yes, we've paid dearly for it,' he goes on, looking sternly at Him, 'but at last we have completed that work in Thy name. For fifteen centuries we have been wrestling with Thy freedom, but now it is ended and over for good. Dost Thou not believe that it's over for good? Thou lookest meekly at me and deignest not even to be wroth with me. But let me tell Thee that now, today, people are more persuaded than ever that they have perfect freedom, yet they have brought their freedom to us and laid it humbly at our feet. But that has been our doing. Was this what Thou didst? Was this Thy freedom?' "

"I don't understand again," Alyosha broke in. "Is he ironical, is he jesting?"

"Not a bit of it! He claims it as a merit for himself and his Church that at last they have vanquished freedom and have done so to make men happy. 'For now' (he is speaking of the Inquisition, of course) 'for the first time it has become possible to think of the happiness of men. Man was created a rebel; and how can rebels be happy? Thou wast warned,' he says to Him. 'Thou hast had no lack of admonitions and warnings, but Thou didst not listen to those warnings; Thou didst reject the only way by which men might be made happy. But fortunately, departing Thou didst hand on the work to us. Thou hast promised, Thou hast established by Thy word, Thou hast given to us the right to bind and to unbind, and now, of course, Thou canst not think of taking it away. Why, then, hast Thou come to hinder us?' "

"And what's the meaning of 'no lack of admonitions and warnings'?" asked Alyosha.

"Why, that's the chief part of what the old man must say."

" 'The wise and dread spirit, the spirit of self-destruction and non-existence,' the old man goes on, 'the great spirit talked with Thee in the wilderness, and we are told in the books that he "tempted" Thee.[8] Is that so? And could anything truer be said than what he revealed to Thee

---

[8] See Matthew 4:1–11 and Luke 4:1–13.

in three questions and what Thou didst reject, and what in the books is called "the temptation"? And yet if there has ever been on earth a real stupendous miracle, it took place on that day, on the day of the three temptations. The statement of those three questions was itself the miracle. If it were possible to imagine simply for the sake of argument that those three questions of the dread spirit had perished utterly from the books, and that we had to restore them and to invent them anew, and to do so had gathered together all the wise men of the earth—rulers, chief priests, learned men, philosophers, poets—and had set them the task to invent three questions, such as would not only fit the occasion, but express in three words, three human phrases, the whole future history of the world and of humanity—dost Thou believe that all the wisdom of the earth united could have invented anything in depth and force equal to the three questions which were actually put to Thee then by the wise and mighty spirit in the wilderness? From those questions alone, from the miracle of their statement, we can see that we have here to do not with the fleeting human intelligence, but with the absolute and eternal. For in those three questions the whole subsequent history of mankind is, as it were, brought together into one whole, and foretold, and in them are united all the unsolved historical contradictions of human nature. At the time it could not be so clear, since the future was unknown; but now that fifteen hundred years have passed, we see that everything in those three questions was so justly divined and foretold, and has been so truly fulfilled, that nothing can be added to them or taken from them.

" 'Judge Thyself who was right—Thou or he who questioned Thee then? Remember the first questions; its meaning, in other words, was this: "Thou wouldst go into the world, and art going with empty hands, with some promise of freedom which men in their simplicity and their natural unruliness cannot even understand, which they fear and dread— for nothing has ever been more insupportable for a man and a human society than freedom. But seest Thou these stones in this parched and barren wilderness? Turn them into bread, and mankind will run after Thee like a flock of sheep, grateful and obedient, though for ever trembling, lest Thou withdraw Thy hand and deny them Thy bread." But Thou wouldst not deprive man of freedom and didst reject the offer, thinking, what is that freedom worth, if obedience is bought with bread? Thou didst reply that man lives not by bread alone. But dost Thou know that for the sake of that earthly bread the spirit of the earth will rise up against Thee and will strive with Thee and overcome Thee, and all will follow him, crying, "Who can compare with this beast? He has given us fire from heaven!" Dost Thou know that the ages will pass, and humanity will proclaim by the lips of their sages that there is no crime, and therefore no sin; there is only hunger? "Feed men, and then ask of them virtue!" that's what they'll write on the banner, which they will raise against Thee, and with which they will destroy Thy temple. Where Thy temple stood will rise a new building; the terrible tower of Babel will be built again, and though, like the one of old, it will not be finished, yet Thou mightest have prevented that new tower and have cut short the sufferings of men for a thousand years; for they will come back to us after a thousand years of agony with their tower. They will seek us again, hidden underground in the catacombs, for we shall be again persecuted and tortured. They will find us and cry to us, "Feed us, for those who have promised us fire from heaven haven't given it!" And then we shall finish building their tower, for he finishes the building who feeds them. And we alone shall feed them in Thy name, declaring falsely that it is in Thy name. Oh, never, never can they feed themselves without us! No science will give them bread so long as they remain free. In the end they will lay their freedom at our feet, and say to us, "Make us your slaves, but feed us." They will understand themselves, at last, that freedom and bread enough for all are inconceivable together, for never, never will they be able to share between them! They will be convinced, too, that they can never be free, for they are weak, vicious, worthless and rebellious. Thou didst promise them the bread of Heaven, but, I repeat again, can it compare with earthly bread in the eyes of the weak, ever sinful and ignoble race of man? And if for the sake of the bread of Heaven thousands and tens of thousands shall follow Thee, what is to become of the millions and tens of thousands of millions of creatures who will not have the strength to forgo the earthly bread for the sake of the heavenly? Or dost Thou care only for the tens of thousands of the great and strong, while the millions, numerous as the sands of the sea, who are weak but love Thee, must exist only for the sake of the great and strong? No, we care for the weak too. They are sinful and rebellious, but in the end they too will become obedient. They will marvel at us and look on us as gods, because we are ready to endure the freedom which they have found so dreadful and to rule over them—so awful it will seem to them to be free. But we shall tell them that we are Thy servants and rule them in Thy name. We shall deceive them again, for we will not let Thee come to us again. That deception will be our suffering, for we shall be forced to lie.

" 'This is the significance of the first question in the wilderness, and this is what Thou hast rejected for the sake of that freedom which

Thou hast exalted above everything. Yet in this question lies hid the great secret of this world. Choosing "bread," Thou wouldst have satisfied the universal and everlasting craving of humanity—to find some one to worship. So long as man remains free he strives for nothing so incessantly and so painfully as to find some one to worship. But man seeks to worship what is established beyond dispute, so that all men would agree at once to worship it. For these pitiful creatures are concerned not only to find what one or the other can worship, but to find something that all would believe in and worship; what is essential is that all may be *together* in it: This craving for community of worship is the chief misery of every man individually and of all humanity from the beginning of time. For the sake of common worship they've slain each other with the sword. They have set up gods and challenged one another, "Put away your gods and come and worship ours, or we will kill you and your gods!" And so it will be to the end of the world, even when gods disappear from the earth; they will fall down before idols just the same. Thou didst know, Thou couldst not but have known, this fundamental secret of human nature, but Thou didst reject the one infallible banner which was offered Thee to make all men bow down to Thee alone—the banner of earthly bread; and Thou hast rejected it for the sake of freedom and the bread of Heaven. Behold what Thou didst further. And all again in the name of freedom! I tell Thee that man is tormented by no greater anxiety than to find some one quickly to whom he can hand over that gift of freedom with which the ill-fated creature is born. But only one who can appease their conscience can take over their freedom. In bread there was offered Thee an invincible banner; give bread, and man will worship Thee, for nothing is more certain than bread. But if some one else gains possession of his conscience—oh! then he will cast away Thy bread and follow after him who has ensnared his conscience. In that Thou wast right. For the secret of man's being is not only to live but to have something to live for. Without a stable conception of the object of life, man would not consent to go on living, and would rather destroy himself than remain on earth, though he had bread in abundance. That is true. But what happened? Instead of taking men's freedom from them, Thou didst make it greater than ever! Didst Thou forget that man prefers peace, and even death, to freedom of choice in the knowledge of good and evil? Nothing is more seductive for man than his freedom of conscience, but nothing is a greater cause of suffering. And behold, instead of giving a firm foundation for setting the conscience of man at rest for ever, Thou didst choose all that is exceptional, vague and enigmatic; Thou didst choose what was utterly beyond the strength of men, acting as though Thou didst not love them at all—Thou who didst come to give Thy life for them! Instead of taking possession of men's freedom, Thou didst increase it, and burdened the spiritual kingdom of mankind with its sufferings for ever. Thou didst desire man's free love, that he should follow Thee freely, enticed and taken captive by Thee. In place of the rigid ancient law, man must hereafter with free heart decide for himself what is good and what is evil, having only Thy image before him as his guide. But didst Thou not know he would at last reject even Thy image and Thy truth, if he is weighed down with the fearful burden of free choice? They will cry aloud at last that the truth is not in Thee, for they could not have been left in greater confusion and suffering than Thou hast caused, laying upon them so many cares and unanswerable problems.

" 'So that, in truth, Thou didst Thyself lay the foundation for the destruction of Thy kingdom, and no one is more to blame for it. Yet what was offered Thee? There are three powers, three powers alone, able to conquer and to hold captive for ever the conscience of these impotent rebels for their happiness—those forces are miracle, mystery and authority. Thou hast rejected all three and hast set the example for doing so. When the wise and dread spirit set Thee on the pinnacle of the temple and said to Thee, "If Thou wouldst know whether Thou art the Son of God then cast Thyself down, for it is written: the angels shall hold him up lest he fall and bruise himself, and Thou shalt know then whether Thou art the Son of God and shalt prove then how great is Thy faith in Thy Father." But Thou didst refuse and wouldst not cast Thyself down. Oh! of course, Thou didst proudly and well, like God; but the weak, unruly race of men, are they gods? Oh, Thou didst know then that in taking one step, in making one movement to cast Thyself down, Thou wouldst be tempting God and have lost all Thy faith in Him, and wouldst have been dashed to pieces against that earth which Thou didst come to save. And the wise spirit that tempted Thee would have rejoiced. But I ask again, are there many like Thee? And couldst Thou believe for one moment that men, too, could face such a temptation? Is the nature of men such, that they can reject miracle, and at the great moments of their life, the moments of their deepest, most agonizing spiritual difficulties, cling only to the free verdict of the heart? Oh, Thou didst know that Thy deed would be recorded in books, would be handed down to remote times and the utmost ends of the earth, and Thou didst hope that man, following Thee, would cling to God and not ask for a miracle. But Thou didst not know that when man rejects miracle he rejects God too; for man seeks not so much God as the miraculous. And as man cannot bear to be without the miraculous, he will create new miracles of his own for himself, and will worship deeds of sorcery and witchcraft, though he might be a hundred times over a rebel, heretic and infidel. Thou didst not come down from the Cross when they shouted to Thee, mocking and reviling Thee, "Come down from the cross and we will believe that Thou art He." Thou didst not come down, for again Thou wouldst not enslave man by a miracle, and didst crave faith given freely, not based on miracle. Thou didst crave for free love and not the base raptures of the slave before the might that has overawed him for ever. But Thou didst think too highly of men therein, for they are slaves, of course, though rebellious by nature. Look round and judge; fifteen centuries have passed, look upon them. Whom hast Thou raised up to Thyself? I swear, man is weaker and baser by nature than Thou hast believed him! Can he, can he do what Thou didst? By showing him so much respect, Thou didst, as it were, cease to feel for him, for Thou didst ask far too much from him—Thou who hast loved him more than Thyself! Respecting him less, Thou wouldst have asked less of him. That would have been more like love, for his burden would have been lighter. He is weak and vile. What though he is everywhere now rebelling against our power, and proud of his rebellion? It is the pride of a child and a schoolboy. They are little children rioting and barring out the teacher at school. But their childish delight will end; it will cost them dear. They will cast down temples and drench the earth with blood. But they will see at last, the foolish children, that, though they are rebels, they are impotent rebels, unable to keep up their own rebellion. Bathed in their foolish tears, they will recognize at last that He who created them rebels must have meant to mock at them. They will say this in despair, and their utterance will be a blasphemy which will make them more unhappy still, for man's nature cannot bear blasphemy, and in the end always avenges it on itself. And so unrest, confusion and unhappiness—that is the present lot of man after Thou didst bear so much for their freedom! Thy great prophet tells in vision and in image, that he saw all those who took part in the first resurrection and that there were of each tribe twelve thousand.[9] But if there were so many of them, they must have been not men but gods. They had borne Thy cross, they had endured scores of years in the barren, hungry wilderness, living upon locusts and roots—and Thou mayest indeed point with pride at those children of freedom, of free love, of free and splendid sacrifice for Thy name. But remember that they were only some thou-

---

[9] Revelation 7:4–8.

sands; and what of the rest? And how are the other weak ones to blame, because they could not endure what the strong have endured? How is the weak soul to blame that it is unable to receive such terrible gifts? Canst Thou have simply come to the elect and for the elect? But if so, it is a mystery and we cannot understand it. And if it is a mystery, we too have a right to preach a mystery, and to teach them that it's not the free judgment of their hearts, not love that matters, but a mystery which they must follow blindly, even against their conscience. So we have done. We have corrected Thy work and have founded it upon *miracle, mystery* and *authority*. And men rejoiced that they were again led like sheep, and that the terrible gift that had brought them such suffering, was, at last, lifted from their hearts. Were we right teaching them this? Speak! Did we not love mankind, so meekly acknowledging their feebleness, lovingly lightening their burden, and permitting their weak nature even sin with our sanction? Why hast Thou come now to hinder us? And why dost Thou look silently and searchingly at me with Thy mild eyes? Be angry. I don't want Thy love, for I love Thee not. And what use is it for me to hide anything from Thee? Don't I know to Whom I am speaking? All that I can say is known to Thee already. And is it for me to conceal from Thee our mystery? Perhaps it is Thy will to hear it from my lips. Listen, then. We are not working with Thee, but with *him*—that is our mystery. It's long—eight centuries—since we have been on *his* side and not on Thine. Just eight centuries ago, we took from him what Thou didst reject with scorn, that last gift he offered Thee, showing Thee all the kingdoms of the earth. We took from him Rome and the sword of Caesar, and proclaimed ourselves sole rulers of the earth, though hitherto we have not been able to complete our work. But whose fault is that? Oh, the work is only beginning, but it has begun. It has long to await completion and the earth has yet much to suffer, but we shall triumph and shall be Caesars, and then we shall plan the universal happiness of man. But Thou mightest have taken even then the sword of Caesar. Why didst Thou reject that last gift? Hadst Thou accepted that last counsel of the mighty spirit, Thou wouldst have accomplished all that man seeks on earth—that is, some one to worship, some one to keep his conscience, and some means of uniting all in one unanimous and harmonious ant-heap, for the craving for universal unity is the third and last anguish of men. Mankind as a whole has always striven to organize a universal state. There have been many great nations with great histories, but the more highly they were developed the more unhappy they were, for they felt more acutely than other people the craving for worldwide union. The great conquerors, Timours and Ghengis-Khans, whirled like hurricanes over the face of the earth striving to subdue its people, and they too were but the unconscious expression of the same craving for universal unity. Hadst Thou taken the world and Caesar's purple,[10] Thou wouldst have founded the universal state and have given universal peace. For who can rule men if not he who holds their conscience and their bread in his hands? We have taken the sword of Caesar, and in taking it, of course, have rejected Thee and followed *him*. Oh, ages are yet to come of the confusion of free thought, of their science and cannibalism. For having begun to build their tower of Babel without us, they will end, of course, with cannibalism. But then the beast[11] will crawl to us and lick our feet and spatter them with tears of blood. And we shall sit upon the beast and raise the cup, and on it will be written, "Mystery." But then, and only then, the reign of peace and happiness will come for men. Thou art proud of Thine elect, but Thou hast only the elect, while we give rest to all. And besides, how many of those elect, those mighty ones who could become elect, have grown weary waiting for Thee, and have transferred and will transfer the powers of their spirit and the warmth of their heart to the other camp, and end by raising their *free* banner against Thee. Thou didst Thyself lift up that banner. But with us all will be happy and will no more rebel nor destroy one another as under Thy freedom. Oh, we shall persuade them that they will only become free when they renounce their freedom to us and submit to us. And shall we be right or shall we be lying? They will be convinced that we are right, for they will remember the horrors of slavery and confusion to which Thy freedom brought them. Freedom, free thought and science, will lead them into such straits and will bring them face to face with such marvels and insoluble mysteries, that some of them, the fierce and rebellious, will destroy themselves, others, rebellious but weak, will destroy one another, while the rest, weak and unhappy, will crawl fawning to our feet and whine to us: "Yes, you were right, you alone possess His mystery, and we come back to you, save us from ourselves!"

" 'Receiving bread from us, they will see clearly that we take the bread made by their hands from them, to give it to them, without any miracle. They will see that we do not change the stones to bread, but in truth they will be more thankful for taking it from our hands than for the bread itself! For they will remember only too well that in old days, without our help, even the bread they made turned to stones in their hands, while since they have come back to us, the very stones have turned

---

[10] *Caesar's purple*: symbol of absolute power.   [11] *beast*: see Revelation 17.

to bread in their hands. Too, too well they know the value of complete submission! And until men know that, they will be unhappy. Who is most to blame for their not knowing it, speak? Who scattered the flock and sent it astray on unknown paths? But the flock will come together again and will submit once more, and then it will be once for all. Then we shall give them the quiet humble happiness of weak creatures such as they are by nature. Oh, we shall persuade them at last not to be proud, for Thou didst lift them up and thereby taught them to be proud. We shall show them that they are weak, that they are only pitiful children, but that childlike happiness is the sweetest of all. They will become timid and will look to us and huddle close to us in fear, as chicks to the hen. They will marvel at us and will be awe-stricken before us, and will be proud at our being so powerful and clever, that we have been able to subdue such a turbulent flock of thousands of millions. They will tremble impotently before our wrath, their minds will grow fearful, they will be quick to shed tears like women and children, but they will be just as ready at a sign from us to pass to laughter and rejoicing, to happy mirth and childish song. Yes, we shall set them to work, but in their leisure hours we shall make their life like a child's game, with children's songs and innocent dance. Oh, we shall allow them even sin, they are weak and helpless, and they will love us like children because we allow them to sin. We shall tell them that every sin will be expiated, if it is done with our permission, that we allow them to sin because we love them, and the punishment for these sins we take upon ourselves. And we shall take it upon ourselves, and they will adore us as their saviors who have taken on themselves their sins before God. And they will have no secrets from us. We shall allow or forbid them to live with their wives and mistresses, to have or not to have children—according to whether they have been obedient or disobedient—and they will submit to us gladly and cheerfully. The most painful secrets of their conscience, all, all they will bring to us, and we shall have an answer for all. And they will be glad to believe our answer, for it will save them from the great anxiety and terrible agony they endure at present in making a free decision for themselves. And all will be happy, all the millions of creatures except the hundred thousand who rule over them. For only we, we who guard the mystery, shall be unhappy. There will be thousands of millions of happy babes, and a hundred thousand sufferers who have taken upon themselves the curse of the knowledge of good and evil. Peacefully they will die, peacefully they will expire in Thy name, and beyond the grave they will find nothing but death. But we shall keep the secret, and for their happiness we shall allure them with the reward of heaven and eternity. Though if there were anything in the other world, it certainly would not be for such as they. It is prophesied that Thou wilt come again in victory, Thou wilt come with Thy chosen, the proud and strong, but we will say that they have only saved themselves, but we have saved all. We are told that the harlot who sits upon the beast, and holds in her hands the *mystery*, shall be put to shame, that the weak will rise up again, and will rend her royal purple and will strip naked her loathsome body. But then I will stand up and point out to Thee the thousand millions of happy children who have known no sin. And we who have taken their sins upon us for their happiness will stand up before Thee and say: "Judge us if Thou canst and darest." Know that I fear Thee not. Know that I too have been in the wilderness, I too have lived on roots and locusts, I too prized the freedom with which Thou hast blessed men, and I too was striving to stand among Thy elect, among the strong and powerful, thirsting "to make up the number."[12] But I awakened and would not serve madness. I turned back and joined the ranks of those *who have corrected Thy work*. I left the proud and went back to the humble, for the happiness of the humble. What I say to Thee will come to pass, and our dominion will be built up. I repeat, to-morrow Thou shalt see that obedient flock who at a sign from me will hasten to heap up the hot cinders about the pile on which I shall burn Thee for coming to hinder us. For if any one has ever deserved our fires, it is Thou. To-morrow I shall burn Thee. *Dixi.*' "[13]

Ivan stopped. He was carried away as he talked and spoke with excitement; when he had finished, he suddenly smiled.

Alyosha had listened in silence; towards the end he was greatly moved and seemed several times on the point of interrupting, but restrained himself. Now his words came with a rush.

"But . . . that's absurd!" he cried, flushing. "Your poem is in praise of Jesus, not in blame of Him—as you meant it to be. And who will believe you about freedom? Is that the way to understand it? That's not the idea of it in the Orthodox Church . . . That's Rome, and not even the whole of Rome, it's false—those are the worst of the Catholics, the Inquisitors, the Jesuits! . . . And there could not be such a fantastic creature as your Inquisitor. What are these sins of mankind they take on themselves? Who are these keepers of the mystery who have taken some curse upon themselves for the happiness of mankind? When have they been seen? We know the Jesuits, they are spoken ill of, but surely they are not what you describe? They are not that at all, not at all. . . .

---

[12] *To make up the number*: the elect. See Revelation 14. [13] *Dixi*: "I have spoken" (Latin).

They are simply the Romish army for the earthly sovereignty of the world in the future, with the Pontiff of Rome for Emperor . . . that's their ideal, but there's no sort of mystery or lofty melancholy about it. . . . It's simple lust of power, of filthy earthly gain, of domination—something like a universal serfdom with them as masters—that's all they stand for. They don't even believe in God perhaps. Your suffering inquisitor is a mere fantasy."

"Stay, stay," laughed Ivan, "how hot you are! A fantasy you say, let it be so! Of course it's a fantasy. But allow me to say: do you really think that the Roman Catholic movement of the last centuries is actually nothing but the lust of power, of filthy earthly gain? Is that Father Païssy's teaching?"[14]

"No, no, on the contrary, Father Païssy did once say something rather the same as you . . . but of course it's not the same, not a bit the same," Alyosha hastily corrected himself.

"A precious admission, in spite of your 'not a bit the same.' I ask you why your Jesuits and Inquisitors have united simply for vile material gain? Why can there not be among them one martyr oppressed by great sorrow and loving humanity? You see, only suppose that there was one such man among all those who desire nothing but filthy material gain—if there's only one like my old inquisitor, who had himself eaten roots in the desert and made frenzied efforts to subdue his flesh to make himself free and perfect. But yet all his life he loved humanity, and suddenly his eyes were opened, and he saw that it is no great moral blessedness to attain perfection and freedom, if at the same time one gains the conviction that millions of God's creatures have been created as a mockery, that they will never be capable of using their freedom, that these poor rebels can never turn into giants to complete the tower, that it was not for such geese that the great idealist dreamt his dream of harmony. Seeing all that he turned back and joined—the clever people. Surely that could have happened?"

"Joined whom, what clever people?" cried Alyosha, completely carried away. "They have no such great cleverness and no mysteries and secrets. . . . Perhaps nothing but Atheism, that's all their secret. Your inquisitor does not believe in God, that's his secret!"

"What if it is so! At last you have guessed it. It's perfectly true that that's the whole secret, but isn't that suffering, at least for a man like that, who has wasted his whole life in the desert and yet could not shake off his incurable love of humanity? In his old age he reached the clear

---

[14] *Father Païssy:* a monk in *The Brothers Karamazov.*

conviction that nothing but the advice of the great dread spirit could build up any tolerable sort of life for the feeble, unruly, 'incomplete, empirical creatures created in jest.' And so, convinced of this, he sees that he must follow the counsel of the wise spirit, the dread spirit of death and destruction, and therefore accept lying and deception, and lead men consciously to death and destruction, and yet deceive them all the way so that they may not notice where they are being led, that the poor blind creatures may at least on the way think themselves happy. And note, the deception is in the name of Him in Whose ideal the old man had so fervently believed all his life long. Is not that tragic? And if only one such stood at the head of the whole army 'filled with the lust of power only for the sake of filthy gain'—would not one such be enough to make a tragedy? More than that, one such standing at the head is enough to create the actual leading idea of the Roman Church with all its armies and Jesuits, its highest idea. I tell you frankly that I firmly believe that there has always been such a man among those who stood at the head of the movement. Who knows, there may have been some such even among the Roman Popes. Who knows, perhaps the spirit of that accursed old man who loves mankind so obstinately in his own way, is to be found even now in a whole multitude of such old men, existing not by chance but by agreement, as a secret league formed long ago for the guarding of the mystery, to guard it from the weak and the unhappy, so as to make them happy. No doubt it is so, and so it must be indeed. I fancy that even among the Masons there's something of the same mystery at the bottom, and that that's why the Catholics so detest the Masons as their rivals breaking up the unity of the idea, while it is so essential that there should be one flock and one shepherd. . . . But from the way I defend my idea I might be an author impatient of your criticism. Enough of it."

"You are perhaps a Mason yourself!" broke suddenly from Alyosha. "You don't believe in God," he added, speaking this time very sorrowfully. He fancied besides that his brother was looking at him ironically. "How does your poem end?" he asked, suddenly looking down. "Or was it the end?"

"I meant to end it like this. When the Inquisitor ceased speaking he waited some time for his Prisoner to answer him. His silence weighed down upon him. He saw that the Prisoner had listened intently all the time, looking gently in his face and evidently not wishing to reply. The old man longed for Him to say something, however bitter and terrible. But He suddenly approached the old man in silence and softly kissed him on his bloodless aged lips. That was all his answer. The old man shuddered. His lips moved. He went to the door, opened it, and said to Him: 'Go, and come no more . . . come not at all, never, never!' and he let Him out into the dark alleys of the town. The Prisoner went away."

"And the old man?"

"The kiss glows in his heart, but the old man adheres to his idea."

"And you with him, you too?" cried Alyosha, mournfully.

Ivan laughed.

"Why, it's all nonsense, Alyosha. It's only a senseless poem of a senseless student, who could never write two lines of verse. Why do you take it so seriously? Surely you don't suppose I am going straight off to the Jesuits, to join the men who are correcting His work? Good Lord, it's no business of mine."

Slime

I was at the height of my powers, looked well, made a good appearance—tall stature, fine clothes, regular features, energetic expression, the embodiment of health and vigor—when I experienced the first symptoms of my illness. It started with a slight, almost imperceptible fatigue which, though it passed quickly, kept on returning. I went on working, writing often as many as forty business letters a day. Rain or shine, hot or cold, I would take to the road, visiting, inspecting, covering great stretches as I had done for many years. I ate heartily, drank my fill, loved life and nature, was in fact full of vim, vigor and zest, yet, once in a while, I might have to stop to catch my breath. I lingered in restaurants and inns a bit longer than usual, sipping a small glass of orange liqueur. Getting up from the table I felt drowsy, but a couple of steps in the country air, an errand in the suburbs would quickly dispel this numbness. There was nothing noticeable yet.

Then I, who had all my life risen at the crack of dawn, sometimes earlier still, or had taken an ice-cold shower after staying up all night, to go on the rest of the day, began to find it increasingly difficult to wake up in the morning. A soupçon of melancholy pervaded my awakening. I asked them to heat the cold water for my morning toilet.

Till then waking up had always been a triumphant experience: daybreak was a rebirth. The consciousness of living in a universe renewed each day stirred a welling joy in the depths of my being. I would jump out of bed, throw my windows open to look upon a world streaming with light. I drew breath with delight, and drunk with joy would stare at a pristine sea, a victorious city, fields shining with the glory of the first day of creation. Bursting into song I rushed downstairs to take hold of the world with a paean.

Suddenly one morning, and the next, and others still, I had to resort to taking a drink before setting out in order to recapture the indispensable euphoria, the energy, warmth, power of rebirth which I then communicated to the rest of creation. Yet things were no longer the same. Something kept on whispering slyly in my ear that this happiness had been bought unnaturally. With joy no longer invulnerable my energy weakened; colors lost their luster, unable to unfurl as before their bright banner in the light of day; magic was disappearing from the world, something was waning. In the morning everything was as on the preceding day. The universe wore its shirt slightly soiled at the collar. A certain monotony seemed to pervade cities, seasons, and countryside.

I blamed it first on the weather. A rainy summer had caused the crops to rot. Autumn had followed too quickly, and the month of December, dank and dark, was in need of fresh snow.

Without clear-cut reason I developed a pessimistic, melancholy frame of mind. Man's fate filled me with pity. I was vaguely considering what I could do to better his condition when I found myself in the throes of groundless remorse.

My bad conscience made me irritable and aware of having a liver, a weighty stone I carried within my flesh, which spread insolently beyond the confines of this organ. I could feel it from the right shoulder to the navel, the thigh, the kidney, radiating even to the other shoulder. I tried to find solace in the idea that each one of us has a cross to bear. That's the *essensual* nature of man, I punned bitterly, but I could no longer be healed by humor. The bitterness of a sharp tongue spiced my saliva, and only added to the hyperacidity of my stomach. Nor did it alleviate my pain to know that the discomfort was of my own creation, and that objectively, logically, nothing had changed in the world outside. Yet I could recall a time when all seasons had seemed beautiful, all shades of gray luminous. The pleasure of stalking a hare through tilled fields, along dirt roads with the wet brambles catching at my sleeve, my gun slung over my shoulder, was a vivid memory.

I did not have the opportunity to look into this question, as my ills developed, giving me new cares. My sight seemed to be failing. Sometimes I would start to limp. Then this disappeared. More and more frequently I found myself short of breath. I even had to stop in the middle of the road —a thing which would have been inconceivable only a short while back— to rest and breathe. Sometimes, still a long way from town or village gate, far from any hotel or inn, I was forced to lean against a signpost. Having reached my destination, I would collapse, dripping with sweat, so utterly exhausted that I did not have the strength to call for a drink. I would have to start out again, struggling with the desire to do nothing, to sleep. Quite often I felt sleepy in the middle of the day. My lazy stomach would not hold what I was taking in. Everything I drank turned to vinegar, everything I ate to mud, rock, thorny wood. Digestion! What an insoluble problem! I was all the more painful since after lunch I had to climb uphill.

I changed sectors, choosing a flatter plain. However, the work became monotonous. There were few, scattered inns, and I ran the risk of falling asleep on the road. After a while I decided to return to my old hotel. The change had not been beneficial.

Next, I applied myself to figuring out all my moves in order to store up the last bits of energy. In my section there were many inns at short intervals. This was how I lost the habit of walking. The more I stopped the heavier I seemed to get. I was always behind in my work.

However, amazingly enough I still looked healthy. There was nothing obviously wrong: no cough, no fever, no abscess, a regular pulse—only this heavy feeling in my liver, and in one leg.

I embarked upon a strict diet. This decision ought to have been taken earlier. I was too exhausted now for any test of will power. Despite a full stomach, a mouth in which the aftertaste of undigested food lingered forever, a heavy, coated tongue, I was continually hungry. The intestines sent up deleterious gasses to the brain, and these vapors, clouding my mind, made me live in an intellectual fog. I was able to realize however what was happening, so that I stopped eating sausages, patés, lentils, peas, beans, cabbage, bacon, salt, and drinking beer, red wine and cocoa.

At the end of fourteen days something happened. I woke up one morning free of my headache, feeling light; my liver seemed to have shrunk back to normal, my leg to have loosened. Vague stirrings of my former euphoria lifted me up for a moment so that I felt as though I were floating. An ancient grace informed the poplars, touched with a new light. The world's opaqueness was changing to translucence. I couldn't get over it.

This did not last long. For forty-eight hours I was happy—normal—and normally at home in the universe. Then my stomach rebelled. It was hungry, and began to pain me. The intestines soon joined in. Once more the world grew dark; my prostration returned.

I decided to stop eating fruit, butter, carrots, cheese, salad, radishes, mushrooms. I lost weight, weakened, became despondent and gloomy. My aches shifted around: I got a pain in the right shoulder, then the left, then in both at once; my fingers were growing numb while migraine headaches started up in conjunction with neuralgic toothaches. I must have caught cold from perspiring. I felt it best to give up drinking water almost completely; my kidneys hardened like parched earth. It became increasingly difficult to bend down. I was stiff all over, and a dull pain circled my rib cage. Fearing most foods, I had almost stopped eating. As a result I lost more weight; I was fairly melting away. Yet I did not feel lighter, quite the opposite in fact: heaviness seemed to have settled within, once and for all. My legs were giving way under the weight of a stooped, bony body; cramps stiffened the muscles of my calves, my feet were perpetually frozen.

Yet I remained active as though some lingering reflex action like that which sets in motion the limbs of a decapitated frog allowed me to continue functioning. I dragged myself over hill and dale. Breathing itself had become wearing. The surrounding air was as heavy as my arms, and my briefcase leaden. Each step struggled against some invisible, unavoidable barrier.

Noise became unbearable, piercing to the ears. The lightest child's voice rang like a sharp, heartrending cry. Sounds reached me as though reverberated by some solid element. Shrieks cut across my eardrums. Leaves fluttered down with the thud of stones, the rustling of trees rent the air.

In self-defense I grew half deaf. The world of sound receded, turning into a kaleidoscope of drab, mute images. I found myself swathed in cotton while the stifled sounds which reached my ears had no apparent connection with their cause: a swearing coachman emitted chirps through a gaping mouth, the piercing voice of the innkeeper's wife was transformed into a sweet murmuring brook. Often I barely escaped being run over by trucks whose roar had struck my eardrums with the gentle caress of a breeze. The concentration I was forced to use increased my troubles. Whirling round at every stop I found it almost impossible to walk.

I would hurry back to the inn to go to sleep for I was sleepy all the time, at any moment of the day. I found it hard not to fall asleep while walking. I returned late at night no matter how early I would start back, yet I was never too far from home, since I invariably gave up some four hundred paces from the unreachable goal I set for myself each day.

After ten hours of heavy sleep I might wake up with a clearer head, but a conscience as bitter as my mouth filled by a coated, swollen tongue. I found it hard to recall my anguished dreams; fragments of forms, nameless faces, dark glimmering light dissolving in air floated through my mind. My brain was drowned in mist. I had only to get up to become once again the prey of drowsiness and fatigue. I would lie back once more before finally rising with a great effort to walk a road which led nowhere.

As the illness progressed the symptoms changed. My headaches left me, or rather the aches spread all over without a definite spot, not settling in any organ. Pain radiated in a diffuse way through my body which had become an enormous, awkward object, independent of myself. I had no control over my limbs; they seemed to move about in some confused, chaotic fashion. The joints were rusty. A limitless apathy, a passive, biological anarchy, had taken hold of all my organs, which fought one another like intractable enemies. My jaws refused to masticate the staples I occasionally entrusted to them; they let the stomach do the job, and since it was out of commission the undigested food went on to the intestines where it formed petrified mountains, pyramids. My mind struggled, enclosed in a pasty void, yet some part of my brain remained free to formulate lucid yet aimless thoughts, as clear as an empty sky. Half of my head was lead, or something heavier still, the other half aerial.

At night, as I sank into sleep, a desert light seemed to envelop subtle, transparent forms; vaporous images haunted my lethargy. At the core of darkness pale lights flickered, then a white shadow appeared, a clearing, the contour of a rock, a field of snow, a glove, a tower, a wing, a lake. Set against a gray background spots of color shone like droplets of incandescent rain which streamed up instead of falling. All these fragments, these vague images, and evanescent ruins would then be blown away by some dumb, yet violent wind. I might still perceive a whirlwind of russet leaves, then the rest of the world, this luminous dust, disappeared, swallowed up by a dark abyss. These visions did not rob me of consciousness. Some last thing, the remaining living particle of my being, rescued me from the void. I would then awaken in the real darkness of my room at night, and heed the thick silence haunted by memories of noises, steps, the faintly-recalled squeaking of the floor, sighs recaptured.

It was hard to get up at dawn, and take a few faltering steps, clutching on to some pieces of furniture. I wanted to regain my grasp on life, not to let go completely, but after I had covered a distance of three yards in the room this weak desire foundered in an overwhelming torpor. Exhausted, unable to remain standing, with a reeling head I would sink into the armchair next to the window, still clutching one shoe after having pulled on one of my socks. From that spot I could not stir. My face grew thin, my stomach enormous, too heavy to carry. I could no longer leave the room.

Nor would I bother to wash. My beard was growing in, a sad shade of gray. My hands were dirty with black nails. As I had become used to sleeping with my clothes on they were wrinkled with holes at the elbows and had an evil smell.

I spent all my time buried in my armchair, reading the same newspaper which was growing yellower each day. Every morning I read over again the same headlines, and they always appeared new to me since I forgot them five minutes after having read them.

At first people knocked at the door but I did not answer. The letters they slipped in accumulated on the floor, in the dust. Soon the letters stopped coming. People had forgotten me.

I no longer opened the window. I had neither the strength nor the desire. The outside air could only harm me. I despised the memory of the scent of grass, the smell of the woods. This summons from an outside world could only irritate and tire me. Then it was humid. It kept on raining.

Often, as the newspaper escaped from my numb fingers, I stretched out my arm to pick it up, but I did not always succeed in doing so. Peering into the void I escaped into empty daydreams. Thus would I fall asleep and wake up with a start. From time to time—was it day or night?—I would take a swallow of tepid mineral water right from the bottle, and chew on a crust of bread dipped in the water. I might pick on some beef from a can, or suck on a piece of caramel. At rare intervals I would rise from the armchair whose springs were growing weak, and throw myself on the unmade bed with its dirty sheets reeking with cold sweat. Free of desires or regrets I might have been happy in this state of indifference were it not for the leaden weight of my body. I feared one thing only: to be disturbed. But on that score I could be at peace: a unanimity of discretion seemed to be the order of the day.

I had gotten out of the habit of switching on the light. At dusk, wet shadows enveloped the room, drowning out all shapes which silently vanished, swept to the bottom of a boundless ocean of shadows. Then, at dawn, they would reappear, ghostly and wan, absurd, like corpses, or the useless remnants of a shipwreck, still standing in the same spot, yet washed clean of their past, like rocks at low tide.

Daybreak found me in my armchair, chilled through. I would rise cautiously, knowing I had forgotten how to walk, and make my way to the bed between the sharp edges of the objects which cluttered my room. I would slip into bed, huddling under humid blankets. My teeth chattered, and I could not stop shivering. Soon however the congealed sweat on my sheets started to thaw, till I found myself bathing in vapors. I allowed myself to simmer in my lethargy.

It no longer seemed necessary to get up. One week passed, or possibly two. I could not tell for time had been abolished. Morning followed dusk, dusk morning. I hardly noticed the change. Rather than being aware of the passage of time I observed a subtle change in the color of space, or even changes of colors from somewhere beyond space. It even appeared as though the same dusk, followed by the same sunrise, returned ceaselessly detached from any concept of duration.

I was at the center of a circle in which the bed was the immobile point. As I closed and opened my eyes two changeless images alternated: the battered reddish armchair with the discarded paper lying beside it, and, when I lowered my eyelids, a dark disk whirling around an incandescent hub, becoming gradually smaller, then melting away along with me into a heavy sleep.

One night I suddenly woke up with a start, bathed in sweat, and realizing that the shriek I had heard was my own. I could not tell what had frightened me, what signal, instantly forgotten, had drawn my attention to the intense peril of my state, what words of warning had been uttered which now rang only as a distant echo. I stared into the night and saw the nave of the wheel growing larger, then bursting, and splinters of light hitting the walls and sinking into darkness. Shaking with fear I crept up in bed, leaning against the pillows. What did I comprehend in my panic? What had I heard? What supreme warning had thus been given? Nothing lingered in my memory except a burning pit; nothing around it save impenetrable, terrifying darkness, and the smell of decomposition. An irrevocable unavoidable threat hung over me in all its potential doom. Was there something I wanted to protect? Would it be serious to simply give up? Is there such a thing as death? Was I about to suffer an evil death? I was wide awake, crazed with fear. My instinct for survival then took hold of me. I grasped the full implications of the impending disaster, and wished to defend myself. What was I to do? I should have acted sooner; should have reacted earlier. My teeth were chattering, yet I felt that perhaps there was still a little time, a ray of hope.

My hand explored my flabby thighs, my thin chest, my moist, swollen stomach, and I was filled with astonishment at the realization that these belonged to me, were indeed parts of my own body. I rubbed one leg against the other, wiggled my toes, pulled on a corner of the bed sheet, as though to regain awareness of my body, of myself, through the use of my limbs.

I decided to make decisions. But it was necessary to wait till dawn, and I was filled with impatience. This made me conscious of time, a sign of progress. I thought. At the first sign of daylight I was going to resume my work, pick up my usual occupation, go out, take to the road, as I had always done. But I had to proceed methodically, to re-educate myself. It was difficult to decide where to start.

First, I would change my underwear, shave, put on a clean suit, open the windows, and let air, light invade the room and drive out the miasmic vapors. I would ask them to clean up after me, to sweep, to wash the floor, to give me spotless sheets. After all there was help at my hotel, paid for this very purpose.

Then I would come down. Nothing was easier! Hadn't I walked up and down these stairs many times a day, for many years without giving it a thought? Next I would open the doors, step outside, walk across courtyards, meadows, jump over fences, pass the little bridge over the brook, the railway bridge, reach the three roads, take the one to the right which goes up, stand above the old mill, the blue hamlet, the chapel, climb to the top of the hill, beyond the wheat field full of poppies, and emerge into the sunlight, singing! That was it, indeed: I just had to walk uphill, in the abstract as well as the concrete meaning of the expression. This witty remark cheered me up considerably, and I felt a slight exhilaration take hold of me which made me quite forget that this was not harvest time. My weakness, my nervousness, were doubtlessly due to lack of nourishment. I would have to start eating again, a bit of everything. Inaction must have fostered this feeling of exhaustion; the less one works, the more fatigued one feels. This *malaise* was basically moral. From now on I would lead an active life; I would not allow inertia to take hold of me. I would react, I would have will power.

I envisioned myself getting out of bed, pulling on my socks, standing in front of the mirror, a sharp, new razor in my hand. I could see myself putting on my blue-and-white dotted tie walking to the door of the room, picking up the envelopes strewn all over the floor, opening them, reading, sitting down at my desk and composing answers. There would be no delay in my correspondence, I would see to that. Of course I would have to answer my mail in a certain order, the most urgent messages would have to be done first. It would be rather complicated, but that was the way to do it. I would even go to the post office to send some letters special delivery.

I burned with impatience. I wanted to start at once: alas, it was still the middle of the night. I could brook no further delay. I got up, and walked to the armchair, feeling my way, in order to wait there for morning, and jump up at the first ray of light, ready to go. Soon I felt cold, and possibly unable to remain in one spot, walked back to the bed, pulled off a blanket, and returned to the armchair. What a long night, and yet having sketched my project, having "ideally" taken action, I felt as though it had already been accomplished. Life was easy, one need only wish, "when there's a will, there's a way."

In my mind I went over my plan of action for the following day, trying to imprint it on my brain. Tomorrow, as every day from now on, I would first put on my socks, then wash, then write, then drink my cup of coffee in the downstairs dining room, or rather drink my coffee first, and then write; no, first file my letters, then write, no, rather first shave, then file my correspondence, then write; or rather, file, write, shave, and go out; or: shave, go out, come back to my room to file my correspondence after a brisk stroll through the fields. No: get up, put on my socks; no, wash first. No, get up first, pick up the letters, file them, put on my socks, shave, wash; no wash, shave. Or before shaving and washing, ring for my breakfast, and ask them to bring it up to my bed, or I might have it sitting up in the armchair, a hearty breakfast of course. After all I was already in the armchair, so why stir? But I would only have to take one step to reach the door, pick up my mail, one step, or two, or possibly three, not more, that wasn't much. This was not the problem.

The problem was where to start. By putting on my shoes or drinking coffee? Where to begin? Where to commence? I fell asleep, exhausted by all these questions, fell asleep again, then, again, woke up. Would I have enough will power? Did I want to start over again? Which part of me would be the strongest? The one which wanted, or the one which did not want? The part which was trying to regain its footing, or the part which wished to let go? After all I was as ignorant of the reasoning which made one part of me wish to survive, as I was of the reasons another part of me might have not to wish it. Or rather I knew that there were no good reasons for one or the other, that there never is any reason, that one finds them later. There is only an unreasonable, unreasoned will to do this, or that; useful, useless, false problem, what does it all mean? Everything is necessary, everything is superfluous. One must act, and choose spontaneously.

Dawn rose at last over the fields which I could see from my window. It was one of those livid autumn mornings which make you feel like closing your eyes again. I fought against this desire with all my strength. . . . I got up, dragged myself to the armchair, took hold of one of its arms, then, out of breath, took a few lurching steps toward the window to open it: A gloomy landscape, gray bushes, furrows, poplars enclosing a field stretching out under a cloudy sky. I tried to recall the plan of action I had set up. It was all mixed up in my mind. I don't know how I put on my trousers. Then, I slipped my bare feet into my shoes, took my coat, and an old hat. Strengthened by this feat I opened the door, walked over the letters, then went down the flight of stairs as in a dream. The janitor saw me, called his wife, and both of them stared at me with fear and a kind of scorn. They answered my greeting with a shrug and a sneer, and followed me with their eyes. I crossed the yard, opened the gate. The dog growled and backed from me, the cat ran off. Walking toward the bridge which runs over the pond near the old washhouse, I tried to light a cigarette but it went out at once under the rain which had started falling. The badly joined planks of the narrow bridge were rotten. The bridge shook. I got dizzy. However, I reached the other side, and leaning on the humid trunk of one of the poplars looked at the tilled earth on my right and the dirt road ahead of me, enclosed by dripping hedges. I walked through the mud, the puddles, listening to the rustling of the trees, the mournful cry of an animal in the bushes; the mud seeped through my shoes. My overcoat was decidedly not waterproof, nor my hat, for after having walked a hundred paces I was drenched. I had to cover twice that distance to reach a well-kept road which would certainly be drier than this one. There I might meet a farmer riding in a chariot which might take me to Chapelle-Marie, three kilometers away in the direction of the station, or to Beaupré, in the other direction, from where I could proceed to the capital of the borough. What would I do in this township? The borough president had been a school pal of mine. Had he not left his post a long time ago? In Beaupré, friends of mine owned a grocery store. They were merry people. Yes, I would go to visit them, unless chance, incarnated in a peasant and his cart, would take me to Chapelle-Marie where I would take the train. Once you're in a train there are countless possibilities. At the moment however I was laboring hard, slipping, about to fall. I should not have taken this bad road. I knew that it was impracticable in the rainy season. At last I saw a white line in the gray countryside. It was a road, with people, people who would help me, save me. Help was at hand, at hand!! I was about to reach the road when I noticed a great puddle which lay between me and my goal. It was deeper than the others, almost a pond, hard to cross. I went to the edge of the road, trying to by-pass it. One foot of muddy earth separated the puddle from a field of reeds. I clung to a couple of stalks, hailing a man who was driving a cart on the road, a couple of yards away. He did not hear me. The wind had risen, blowing my call in the other direction. I renewed my efforts to go faster, slipped again, and fell on my stomach among the reeds. My hat rolled on the ground, not too far, as it was held by the plants. Since I had fallen and felt tired, I decided that the best thing would be to rest a few moments. One could not feel the wind among the reeds, and if the humidity had been warm it would have been almost perfect. I made an effort to turn over. I succeeded, I was now lying on my back in a much more comfortable position. I sprawled, breathing deeply. Ten minutes of rest would certainly do me a lot of good, give me back my strength. I decided not to think of anything, to make my mind utterly blank as for a vacation of that spirit. That's the only way to relax while waiting to gather strength.

I lost consciousness. When I came back to my senses (after how long?) I saw a dark sky above. A gentle breeze rippled the reeds. To my right I could see a toad sitting on the leaf of a water lily. It looked back at me for a moment, jumped and disappeared. From the depths of the sky a bird of prey swooped upon a sparrow, and vanished. The wind died down, the mist thickened, cleared, thickened again. I was cold. A kind of sigh choked me. Why did I feel like crying? What about? Let's see, someone had died? That was it. I was then mourning this death. But who could it be? Myself, where did I come from? Ah, from the inn. I thought of going back there. Why had I left it? Yes, I had to retrace my steps. I ought never to have attempted this expedition. I tried to get up. I was homesick for my room, for the bed warmed by my fever. I got up on one knee, made another bit of effort, and was able to stand. To get back to the inn one had to walk uphill. How difficult it was!! There was a point where the paths crossed. Where was that? I must have passed this spot so many times a while ago. I walked to the left, right into the reeds, in the hope of finding a short cut. The mud was slowing me down, as well as the exhausting process of spreading the stalks. . . . There was no road to be seen. Still I persisted, advanced. . . .

I walked numbly through the valley all evening, and all night. I walked in my sleep. Then it was daylight once more. Many hours passed, days, minutes. The fog had lifted. There was still rushes, reeds, marshes, two trees, rushes, a barrier, a thicket, a barrier, reeds. My legs carried me somehow. They were taking the lead. The mechanism of walking kept on functioning. Despite total numbness my body felt pain, my shoulders stooped forward, my joints creaked, I had a dull headache, my arms were swinging like a pendulum, my nose kept on running, I was seized with rheumatism.

I tripped, skidding over a wet lump of earth, and fell into the mud. When I got up on my feet I was a walking statue of slime.

The winter had softened. We were in mid-March, perhaps. The world was still the same, except that I was no longer sensitive to smells. I was not cold; I stopped, took a few steps, stopped once more. The air was heavy, compact, resistant as though one had to cut it, or tear it to pass. Suddenly my legs gave way, and I fell again. I tried mechanically to rise, slid, and gave up. After all I was just as well off here as anywhere else. It was a day outside of time. I stretched out on my back, gently. In the void of thoughtlessness I was filled with a profound nostalgia, an intolerable, overwhelming sadness, nameless desires, limitless regrets, a vague kind of remorse, a boundless pity for all those things I had tried to clutch, all those I had held, for what my hands had built, yes, an incurable regret for the soil trodden by my feet, for roads, dwellings, streets and walls, for the forest, the meadows, the valleys, for the high mountain white or green, for sun, colors, red, yellow, blue, for what had grown gray, for the music which had stopped, for the forgotten voices. Once there had been a bell, the whirling of pink petticoats. Once there had been leafy springs, scents, the river, the bridges of a city, and lights in the night. Leaves had moaned in the gentle wind, leaves moaned, and the rain started to fall. How sweet!! Rain is a balm. I could feel its humid fingers on my face. It had happened before, or had I always been here and dreamed all the rest? Or had all this happened to someone else who might have told me this story which I was picking up, reliving in my memory.

Had I really wished to climb a mountain? Once on a clear morning, at the age of thirteen, I had left the house in a hollow of the valley, a stick in hand, a hazelnut stick. At first the road was pebbly and sharp. At each step I ran the risk of a sprain. It was summer. One could see the blue sky through the leaves and the branches. I had emerged at the crossroads between fields . . . a clearing. . . . It must have been in August. The harvest had been gathered, in the fields the stubble pricked my feet, and an old woman coming down one of the roads asked: "Where are you going?" I was to take the road on the other side of the clearing. The trees on either side of that path, which seemed quite rocky, were higher, thicker, drier. Was I accompanied? I believe that suddenly I was left alone with the echo of voices vanishing in the distance. Then, as I walked, the trees grew sparce, spare, small, and the slope hard to climb. I continued, perspiring with fatigue as much as with heat. . . . Yes, I remember, I could recall, or had I been told this story?

An arid land had suddenly appeared. . . . Then abandoned tracks of a funicular, no more trees, stones, rocks, just dry earth. . . . Then, to climb further I had had to hang on to clumps of dry grass, to stones, sand. I had continued to climb on my knees, up, up. . . . Before me I could see the sharp drop of a mountain slope. If only I could have seen the glorious summits! I had continued on bloody hands and knees. But the dryness had grown worse. I did not even sweat. Thirst had dried my throat, my palate, my guts; my ears were buzzing. I knew I should not stop. Before me there was only a rock, an immense vertical desert. Maybe I could still stop for one second, I said to myself. Not to drink, but to imagine a spring, to stop for a while and enjoy the inner vision of an inhabited place, the memory of a room, shady in summer, fresh, in a thick-walled house overgrown with moss, sheltered from this implacable heat. I could go down a bit, take a few steps back toward a hut, a mountain refuge. It was at this moment that the slide down had started. I had let go and I was filled with a voluptuous sensation mingled with remorse. I passed by forests, rolled down slopes edging on waterfalls, then there were brooks, ponds, the humid earth of the plains. Was it a memory? Was it the remembrance of memory? Was it my fall? Was that how I got here where I was lying on my back? Despite the heavy clouds, and the graying light, I could see as though beyond, the night, a starry sky. I had been a child once. My father held me in his arms, and told me a story. We were walking along a fence. It was a country rather than a city suburb. It was night. A sky crowded with stars. I closed my eyes. I could still recall a blue sky, dry, illuminated summits. I opened my eyes, but I no longer knew how many hours, or days, had passed. I had forgotten where I had come from, and I felt no surprise at lying here. The memory of the fall had grown quite vague. Painlessly, my right arm detached itself from my shoulder. It fell in the mud with a soft thud, and then sank slowly into slime. Where the elbow had been there was a muddy puddle, only my hand emerged, white, inert, resting upon a round, flat leaf. Had the elbow dissolved already? Or was it still intact in the brew of water and earth mixed together? A frog leaped toward my hand, looked at it and disappeared. Stiff rushes rustled in the wind. The sight of my right hand with the wedding ring on the ring finger made me smile: it was a kind of animal, or something in between an animal and a plant, which could stretch, dilate. The fingers moved like thick, lazy little snakes. Was it possible that this thing had belonged to me?

The left arm, closer to the heart, was still fastened to my body; the hand hooked to a dirty wrist, the finger nails black. It shuddered once in a while but I did not control the vibrations I communicated. My bloated stomach pressed upon my heart which struggled wildly, like a bad swimmer ready to give up. My liver had enlarged. It had spread to the whole right side of the thorax, had settled at the base of the lung, forcing it up, as though to dislodge it in a slow, continuous process. A few soft ribs had split, and the skin, like a canvas bag giving way under the weight of its load, had split here and there. Pus mixed with humid clay.

As for the rest, I could see from where I was only the surface of my stomach, a strange mound which hid from me the bottom part of my body. I made an effort, was able to move my head to the right; I found that I could see a thick shoe (half hidden in the roots of the rushes) letting a livid toe emerge through a large hole. How far was it from me? A yard? Two? A mile? Was this shoe my own? I could feel neither my feet, nor my legs, nor my pelvis. Only my liver and my stomach still fought for the supremacy of this half-body of mine. I must have bought this shoe once, for I had a kind of vision of a shop and a woman in it. My wife? She had smiled? Was it my wife or my mother? Nothing definite save her smile emerged from the mist. Despite my coated tongue, the penetrating cold, my hyperacidity, I would not have felt too uncomfortable (for a certain numbness invaded the vestiges of my limbs, my trunk, softening physical pain), were it not for the humidity of the wet earth against my back.

Mosquitoes kept on biting my nose and forehead. I could hardly feel their sting upon my swollen flesh, but I disliked hearing them.

The air I breathed in was heavy, but the air I breathed out was heavier still, almost a liquid substance. The mist passed through my vertebrae, swelling my chest, filling my mouth, coming out of my ears. This had been my nourishment for many weeks. I could feel the hairs of my beard growing tough, tight, wet, deeply rooted in my skin. My cranium was still in place, and my eyes were dry. I could see clearly the outline of things: the undulating reeds, and vapors rising over marshes. Only my hand appeared to me as some hazy, moist whiteness, rapping once, twice . . . one two . . . one two . . . as though self-impelled . . . upon the leaf, round as a dish. My ears buzzed again. In order to look in I closed my eyes and watched flames licking empty walls to the rising rhythm of the pulsations of my heart covering inarticulated sobs. I could see burning forests, braziers, and empty land, and hear distant cries. When I opened my eyes again everything was in order. The reeds were there, and the water into which my lips and belly sank, detaching themselves from me once and for all. There was a slight rent, a gurgle followed by an eddy: this must have been heavy! For a moment I identified myself with a kite in flight, a body free of weight, then I found I was still in mist and water. My heart did not beat as fast. My liver could spread without difficulty, having overcome all resistance. Cries, sobs, flames, images of burning blood were growing soft, melting into grayness. I had become a lucid, quiet mind, a pure conscience, registering what was happening. My left arm had detached itself as the remnants of sensitivity and physical pain were disappearing. Where could consciousness dwell? I was there: an eye, a cranium, a heart slowing down. Water, mud must have risen, for all of a sudden I could not see anything, I did not see my body, except for a vague outline where my body must have been. Fear had disappeared long ago, so had desire. No, no, not quite. Of course I had failed, but I would start over again. I will start, everything will start, from birth, from the seed. . . . I will start, I said, closing my eyes. The mist had lifted, and it was with the blue vision of a sky washed clean that I left.

Big Two-Hearted River: Part I

The train went on up the track out of sight, around one of the hills of burnt timber. Nick sat down on the bundle of canvas and bedding the baggage man had pitched out of the door of the baggage car. There was no town, nothing but the rails and the burned-over country. The thirteen saloons that had lined the one street of Seney had not left a trace. The foundations of the Mansion House hotel stuck up above the ground. The stone was chipped and split by the fire. It was all that was left of the town of Seney. Even the surface had been burned off the ground.

Nick looked at the burned-over stretch of hillside, where he had expected to find the scattered houses of the town and then walked down the railroad track to the bridge over the river. The river was there. It swirled against the log spiles of the bridge. Nick looked down into the clear, brown water, colored from the pebbly bottom, and watched the trout keeping themselves steady in the current with wavering fins. As he watched them they changed their positions by quick angles, only to hold steady in the fast water again. Nick watched them a long time.

He watched them holding themselves with their noses into the current, many trout in deep, fast moving water, slightly distorted as he watched far down through the glassy convex surface of the pool, its surface pushing and swelling smooth against the resistance of the log-driven piles of the bridge. At the bottom of the pool were the big trout. Nick did not see them at first. Then he saw them at the bottom of the pool, big trout looking to hold themselves on the gravel bottom in a varying mist of gravel and sand, raised in spurts by the current.

Nick looked down into the pool from the bridge. It was a hot day. A kingfisher flew up the stream. It was a long time since Nick had looked into a stream and seen trout. They were very satisfactory. As the shadow of the kingfisher moved up the stream, a big trout shot upstream in a long angle, only his shadow marking the angle, then lost his shadow as he came through the surface of the water, caught the sun, and then, as he went back into the stream under the surface, his shadow seemed to float down the stream with the current, unresisting, to his post under the bridge where he tightened facing up into the current.

Nick's heart tightened as the trout moved. He felt all the old feeling.

He turned and looked down the stream. It stretched away, pebbly-bottomed with shallows and big boulders and a deep pool as it curved away around the foot of a bluff.

Nick walked back up the ties to where his pack lay in the cinders beside the railway track. He was happy. He adjusted the pack harness around the bundle, pulling straps tight, slung the pack on his back, got his arms through the shoulder straps and took some of the pull off his shoulders by leaning his forehead against the wide band of the tump-line. Still, it was too heavy. It was much too heavy. He had his leather rod-case in his hand and leaning forward to keep the weight of the pack high on his shoulders he walked along the road that paralleled the railway track, leaving the burned town behind in the heat, and then turned off around a hill with a high, fire-scarred hill on either side onto a road that went back into the country. He walked along the road feeling the ache from the pull of the heavy pack. The road climbed steadily. It was hard work walking up-hill. His muscles ached and the day was hot, but Nick felt happy. He felt he had left everything behind, the need for thinking, the need to write, other needs. It was all back of him.

From the time he had gotten down off the train and the baggage man had thrown his pack out of the open car door things had been different. Seney was burned, the country was burned over and changed, but it did not matter. It could not all be burned. He knew that. He hiked along the road, sweating in the sun, climbing to cross the range of hills that separated the railway from the pine plains.

The road ran on, dipping occasionally, but always climbing. Nick went on up. Finally the road after going parallel to the burnt hillside reached the top. Nick leaned back against a stump and slipped out of the pack harness. Ahead of him, as far as he could see, was the pine plain. The burned country stopped off at the left with the range of hills. On ahead islands of dark pine trees rose out of the plain. Far off to the left was the line of the river. Nick followed it with his eye and caught glints of the water in the sun.

There was nothing but the pine plain ahead of him, until the far blue hills that marked the Lake Superior height of land. He could hardly see them, faint and far away in the heat-light over the plain. If he looked too steadily they were gone. But if he only half-looked they were there, the far-off hills of the height of land.

Nick sat down against the charred stump and smoked a cigarette. His pack balanced on the top of the stump, harness holding ready, a hollow molded in it from his back. Nick sat smoking, looking out over the country. He did not need to get his map out. He knew where he was from the position of the river.

As he smoked, his legs stretched out in front of him, he noticed a grasshopper walk along the ground and up onto his woolen sock. The grasshopper was black. As he had walked along the road, climbing, he had started many grasshoppers from the dust. They were all black. They were not the big grasshoppers with yellow and black or red and black wings whirring out from their black wing sheathing as they fly up. These were just ordinary hoppers, but all a sooty black in color. Nick had wondered about them as he walked, without really thinking about them. Now, as he watched the black hopper that was nibbling at the wool of his sock with its fourway lip, he realized that they had all turned black from living in the burned-over land. He realized that the fire must have come the year before, but the grasshoppers were all black now. He wondered how long they would stay that way.

Carefully he reached his hand down and took hold of the hopper by the wings. He turned him up, all his legs walking in the air, and looked at his jointed belly. Yes, it was black too, iridescent where the back and head were dusty.

"Go on, hopper," Nick said, speaking out loud for the first time.. "Fly away somewhere."

He tossed the grasshopper up into the air and watched him sail away to a charcoal stump across the road.

Nick stood up. He leaned his back against the weight of his pack where it rested upright on the stump and got his arms through the shoulder straps. He stood with the pack on his back on the brow of the hill looking out across the country, toward the distant river and then struck down the hillside away from the road. Underfoot the ground was good walking. Two hundred yards down the hillside the fire line stopped. Then it was sweet fern, growing ankle high, to walk through, and clumps of jack pines; a long undulating country with frequent rises and descents, sandy underfoot and the country alive again.

Nick kept his direction by the sun. He knew where he wanted to strike the river and he kept on through the pine plain, mounting small rises to see other rises ahead of him and sometimes from the top of a rise a great solid island of pines off to his right or his left. He broke off some sprigs of the heathery sweet fern, and put them under his pack straps. The chafing crushed it and he smelled it as he walked.

He was tired and very hot, walking across the uneven, shadeless pine plain. At any time he knew he could strike the river by turning off to his left. It could not be more than a mile away. But he kept on toward the north to hit the river as far upstream as he could go in one day's walking.

For some time as he walked Nick had been in sight of one of the big islands of pine standing out above the rolling high ground he was crossing. He dipped down and then as he came slowly up to the crest of the bridge he turned and made toward the pine trees.

There was no underbrush in the island of pine trees. The trunks of the trees went straight up or slanted toward each other. The trunks were straight and brown without branches. The branches were high above. Some interlocked to make a solid shadow on the brown forest floor. Around the grove of trees was a bare space. It was brown and soft underfoot as Nick walked on it. This was the over-lapping of the pine needle floor, extending out beyond the width of the high branches. The trees had grown tall and the branches moved high, leaving in the sun this bare space they had once covered with shadow. Sharp at the edge of this extension of the forest floor commenced the sweet fern.

Nick slipped off his pack and lay down in the shade. He lay on his back and looked up into the pine trees. His neck and back and the small of his back rested as he stretched. The earth felt good against his back. He looked up at the sky, through the branches, and then shut his eyes. He opened them and looked up again. There was a wind high up in the branches. He shut his eyes again and went to sleep.

Nick woke stiff and cramped. The sun was nearly down. His pack was heavy and the straps painful as he lifted it on. He leaned over with the pack on and picked up the leather rod-case and started out from the pine trees across the sweet fern swale, toward the river. He knew it could not be more than a mile.

He came down a hillside covered with stumps into a meadow. At the edge of the meadow flowed the river. Nick was glad to get to the river. He walked upstream through the meadow. His trousers were soaked with the dew as he walked. After the hot day, the dew had come quickly and heavily. The river made no sound. It was too fast and smooth. At the edge of the meadow, before he mounted to a piece of high ground to make camp, Nick looked down the river at the trout rising. They were rising to insects come from the swamp on the other side of the stream when the sun went down. The trout jumped out of water to take them. While Nick walked through the little stretch of meadow alongside the stream, trout had jumped high out of water. Now as he looked down the river, the insects must be settling on the surface, for the trout were feeding steadily all down the stream. As far down the long stretch as he could see, the trout were rising, making circles all down the surface of the water, as though it were starting to rain.

The ground rose, wooded and sandy, to overlook the meadow, the stretch of river and the swamp. Nick dropped his pack and rod-case and looked for a level piece of ground. He was very hungry and he wanted to make his camp before he cooked. Between two jack pines, the ground was quite level. He took the ax out of the pack and chopped out two projecting roots. That leveled a piece of ground large enough to sleep on. He smoothed out the sandy soil with his hand and pulled all the sweet fern bushes by their roots. His hands smelled good from the sweet fern. He smoothed the uprooted earth. He did not want anything making lumps under the blankets. When he had the ground smooth, he spread his three blankets. One he folded double, next to the ground. The other two he spread on top.

With the ax he slit off a bright slab of pine from one of the stumps and split it into pegs for the tent. He wanted them long and solid to hold in the ground. With the tent unpacked and spread on the ground, the pack, leaning against a jackpine, looked much smaller. Nick tied the rope that served the tent for a ridge-pole to the trunk of one of the pine trees and pulled the tent up off the ground with the other end of the rope and tied it to the other pine. The tent hung on the rope like a canvas blanket on a clothesline. Nick poked a pole he had cut up under the back peak of the canvas and then made it a tent by pegging out the sides. He pegged the sides out taut and drove the pegs deep, hitting them down into the ground with the flat of the ax until the rope loops were buried and the canvas was drum tight.

Across the open mouth of the tent Nick fixed cheesecloth to keep out mosquitoes. He crawled inside under the mosquito bar with various things from the pack to put at the head of the bed under the slant of the canvas. Inside the tent the light came through the brown canvas. It smelled pleasantly of canvas. Already there was something mysterious and homelike. Nick was happy as he crawled inside the tent. He had not been unhappy all day. This was different though. Now things were done. There had been this to do. Now it was done. It had been a hard trip. He was very tired. That was done. He had made his camp. He was settled. Nothing could touch him. It was a good place to camp. He was there, in the good place. He was in his home where he had made it. Now he was hungry.

He came out, crawling under the cheesecloth. It was quite dark outside. It was lighter in the tent.

Nick went over to the pack and found, with his fingers, a long nail in a paper sack of nails, in the bottom of the pack. He drove it into the pine tree, holding it close and hitting it gently with the flat of the ax. He hung the pack up on the nail. All his supplies were in the pack. They were off the ground and sheltered now.

Nick was hungry. He did not believe he had ever been hungrier. He opened and emptied a can of pork and beans and a can of spaghetti into the frying pan.

"I've got a right to eat this kind of stuff, if I'm willing to carry it," Nick said. His voice sounded strange in the darkening woods. He did not speak again.

He started a fire with some chunks of pine he got with the ax from a stump. Over the fire he stuck a wire grill, pushing the four legs down into the ground with his boot. Nick put the frying pan on the grill over the flames. He was hungrier. The beans and spaghetti warmed. Nick stirred them and mixed them together. They began to bubble, making little bubbles that rose with difficulty to the surface. There was a good smell. Nick got out a bottle of tomato catchup and cut four slices of bread. The little bubbles were coming faster now. Nick sat down beside the fire and lifted the frying pan off. He poured about half the contents out into the tin plate. It spread slowly on the plate. Nick knew it was too hot. He poured on some tomato catchup. He knew the beans and spaghetti were still too hot. He looked at the fire, then at the tent, he was not going to spoil it all by burning his tongue. For years he had never enjoyed fried bananas because he had never been able to wait for them to cool. His tongue was very sensitive. He was very hungry. Across the river in the swamp, in the almost dark, he saw a mist rising. He looked at the tent once more. All right. He took a full spoonful from the plate.

"Chrise," Nick said. "Geezus Chrise," he said happily.

He ate the whole plateful before he remembered the bread. Nick finished the second plateful with the bread, mopping the plate shiny. He had not eaten since a cup of coffee and a ham sandwich in the station restaurant at St. Ignace. It had been a very fine experience. He had been that hungry before, but had not been able to satisfy it. He could have made camp hours before if he had wanted to. There were plenty of good places to camp on the river. But this was good.

Nick tucked two big chips of pine under the grill. The fire flared up. He had forgotten to get water for the coffee. Out of the pack he got a folding canvas bucket and walked down the hill, across the edge of the meadow, to the stream. The other bank was in the white mist. The grass was wet and cold as he knelt on the bank and dipped the canvas bucket into the stream. It bellied and pulled hard in the current. The water was ice cold. Nick rinsed the bucket and carried it full up to the camp. Up away from the stream it was not so cold.

Nick drove another big nail and hung up the bucket full of water. He dipped the coffee pot half full, put some more chips under the grill onto the fire and put the pot on. He could not remember which way he made coffee. He could remember an argument about it with Hopkins, but not which side he had taken. He decided to bring it to a boil. He remembered now that was Hopkins's way. He had once argued about everything with Hopkins. While he waited for the coffee to boil, he opened a small can of apricots. He liked to open cans. He emptied the can of apricots out into a tin cup. While he watched the coffee on the fire, he drank the juice syrup of the apricots, carefully at first to keep from spilling, then meditatively, sucking the apricots down. They were better than fresh apricots.

The coffee boiled as he watched. The lid came up and coffee and grounds ran down the side of the pot. Nick took it off the grill. It was a triumph for Hopkins. He put sugar in the empty apricot cup and poured some of the coffee out to cool. It was too hot to pour and he used his hat to hold the handle of the coffee pot. He would not let it steep in the pot at all. Not the first cup. It should be straight Hopkins all the way. Hop deserved that. He was a very serious coffee drinker. He was the most serious man Nick had ever known. Not heavy, serious. That was a long time ago. Hopkins spoke without moving his lips. He had played polo. He made millions of dollars in Texas. He had borrowed carfare to go to Chicago, when the wire came that his first big well had come in. He could have wired for money. That would have been too slow. They called Hop's girl the Blonde Venus. Hop did not mind because she was not his real girl. Hopkins said very confidently that none of them would make fun of his real girl. He was right. Hopkins went away when the telegram came. That was on the Black River. It took eight days for the telegram to reach him. Hopkins gave away his .22 caliber Colt automatic pistol to Nick. He gave his camera to Bill. It was to remember him always by. They were all going fishing again next summer. The Hop Head was rich. He would get a yacht and they would all cruise along the north shore of Lake Superior. He was excited but serious. They said good-bye and all felt bad. It broke up the trip. They never saw Hopkins again. That was a long time ago on the Black River.

Nick drank the coffee, the coffee according to Hopkins. The coffee was bitter. Nick laughed. It made a good ending to the story. His mind was starting to work. He knew he could choke it because he was tired enough. He spilled the coffee out of the pot and shook the grounds loose into the fire. He lit a cigarette and went inside the tent. He took off his shoes and trousers, sitting on the blankets, rolled the shoes up inside the trousers for a pillow and got in between the blankets.

Out through the front of the tent he watched the glow of the fire, when the night wind blew on it. It was a quiet night. The swamp was perfectly quiet. Nick stretched under the blanket comfortably. A mosquito hummed close to his ear. Nick sat up and lit a match. The mosquito was on the canvas, over his head. Nick moved the match quickly up to it. The mosquito made a satisfactory hiss in the flame. The match went out. Nick lay down again under the blanket. He turned on his side and shut his eyes. He was sleepy. He felt sleep coming. He curled up under the blanket and went to sleep.

Big Two-Hearted River: Part II

In the morning the sun was up and the tent was starting to get hot. Nick crawled out under the mosquito netting stretched across the mouth of the tent, to look at the morning. The grass was wet on his hands as he came out. He held his trousers and his shoes in his hands. The sun was just up over the hill. There was the meadow, the river and the swamp. There were birch trees in the green of the swamp on the other side of the river.

The river was clear and smoothly fast in the early morning. Down about two hundred yards were three logs all the way across the stream. They made the water smooth and deep above them. As Nick watched, a mink crossed the river on the logs and went into the swamp. Nick was excited. He was excited by the early morning and the river. He was really too hurried to eat breakfast, but he knew he must. He built a little fire and put on the coffee pot.

While the water was heating in the pot he took an empty bottle and went down over the edge of the high ground to the meadow. The meadow was wet with dew and Nick wanted to catch grasshoppers for bait before the sun dried the grass. He found plenty of good grasshoppers. They were at the base of the grass stems. Sometimes they clung to a grass stem. They were cold and wet with the dew, and could not jump until the sun warmed them. Nick picked them up, taking only the medium-sized brown ones, and put them into the bottle. He turned over a log and just under the shelter of the edge were several hundred hoppers. It was a grasshopper lodging house. Nick put about fifty of the medium browns into the bottle. While he was picking up the hoppers the others warmed in the sun and commenced to hop away. They flew when they hopped. At first they made one flight and stayed stiff when they landed, as though they were dead.

Nick knew that by the time he was through with breakfast they would be as lively as ever. Without dew in the grass it would take him all day to catch a bottle full of good grasshoppers and he would have to crush many of them, slamming at them with his hat. He washed his hands at the stream. He was excited to be near it. Then he walked up to the tent. The hoppers were already jumping stiffly in the grass. In the bottle, warmed by the sun, they were jumping in a mass. Nick put in a pine stick as a cork. It plugged the mouth of the bottle enough, so the hoppers could not get out and left plenty of air passage.

He had rolled the log back and knew he could get grasshoppers there every morning.

Nick laid the bottle full of jumping grasshoppers against a pine trunk. Rapidly he mixed some buckwheat flour with water and stirred it smooth, one cup of flour, one cup of water. He put a handful of coffee in the pot and dipped a lump of grease out of a can and slid it sputtering across the hot skillet. On the smoking skillet he poured smoothly the buckwheat batter. It spread like lava, the grease spitting sharply. Around the edges the buckwheat cake began to firm, then brown, then crisp. The surface was bubbling slowly to porousness. Nick pushed under the browned under surface with a fresh pine chip. He shook the skillet sideways and the cake was loose on the surface. I won't try and flop it, he thought. He slid the chip of clean wood all the way under the cake, and flopped it over onto its face. It sputtered in the pan.

When it was cooked Nick regreased the skillet. He used all the batter. It made another big flapjack and one smaller one.

Nick ate a big flapjack and a smaller one, covered with apple butter. He put apple butter on the third cake, folded it over twice, wrapped it in oiled paper and put it in his shirt pocket. He put the apple butter jar back in the pack and cut bread for two sandwiches.

In the pack he found a big onion. He sliced it in two and peeled the silky outer skin. Then he cut one half into slices and made onion sandwiches. He wrapped them in oiled paper and buttoned them in the other pocket of his khaki shirt. He turned the skillet upside down on the grill, drank the coffee, sweetened and yellow brown with the condensed milk in it, and tidied up the camp. It was a good camp.

Nick took his fly rod out of the leather rod-case, jointed it, and shoved the rod-case back into the tent. He put on the reel and threaded the line through the guides. He had to hold it from hand to hand, as he threaded it, or it would slip back through its own weight. It was a heavy, double tapered fly line. Nick had paid eight dollars for it a long time ago. It was made heavy to lift back in the air and come forward flat and heavy and straight to make it possible to cast a fly which has no weight. Nick opened the aluminum leader box. The leaders were coiled between the damp flannel pads. Nick had wet the pads at the water cooler on the train up to St. Ignace. In the damp pads the gut leaders had softened and Nick unrolled one and tied it by a loop at the end to the heavy fly line. He fastened a hook on the end of the leader. It was a small hook; very thin and springy.

Nick took it from his hook book, sitting with the rod across his lap. He tested the knot and the spring of the rod by pulling the line taut. It was a good feeling. He was careful not to let the hook bite into his finger.

He started down to the stream, holding his rod, the bottle of grasshoppers hung from his neck by a thong tied in half hitches around the neck of the bottle. His landing net hung by a hook from his belt. Over his shoulder was a long flour sack tied at each corner into an ear. The cord went over his shoulder. The sack flapped against his legs.

Nick felt awkward and professionally happy with all his equipment hanging from him. The grasshopper bottle swung against his chest. In his shirt the breast pockets bulged against him with the lunch and his fly book.

He stepped into the stream. It was a shock. His trousers clung tight to his legs. His shoes felt the gravel. The water was a rising cold shock.

Rushing, the current sucked against his legs. Where he stepped in, the water was over his knees. He waded with the current. The gravel slid under his shoes. He looked down at the swirl of water below each leg and tipped up the bottle to get a grasshopper.

The first grasshopper gave a jump in the neck of the bottle and went out into the water. He was sucked under in the whirl by Nick's right leg and came to the surface a little way down stream. He floated rapidly, kicking. In a quick circle, breaking the smooth surface of the water, he disappeared. A trout had taken him.

Another hopper poked his face out of the bottle. His antennae wavered. He was gettting his front legs out of the bottle to jump. Nick took him by the head and held him while he threaded the slim hook under his chin, down through his thorax and into the last segments of his abdomen. The grasshopper took hold of the hook with his front feet, spitting tobacco juice on it. Nick dropped him into the water.

Holding the rod in his right hand he let out line against the pull of the grasshopper in the current. He stripped off line from the reel with his left hand and let it run free. He could see the hopper in the little waves of the current. It went out of sight.

There was a tug on the line. Nick pulled against the taut line. It was his first strike. Holding the now living rod across the current, he brought in the line with his left hand. The rod bent in jerks, the trout pumping against the current. Nick knew it was a small one. He lifted the rod straight up in the air. It bowed with the pull.

He saw the trout in the water jerking with his head and body against the shifting tangent of the line in the stream.

Nick took the line in his left hand and pulled the trout, thumping tiredly against the current, to the surface. His back was mottled the clear, water-over-gravel color, his side flashing in the sun. The rod under his right arm, Nick stooped, dipping his right hand into the current. He held the trout, never still, with his moist right hand, while he unhooked the barb from his mouth, then dropped him back into the stream.

He hung unsteadily in the current, then settled to the bottom beside a stone. Nick reached down his hand to touch him, his arm to the elbow under water. The trout was steady in the moving stream, resting on the gravel, beside a stone. As Nick's fingers touched him, touched his smooth, cool, underwater feeling he was gone, gone in a shadow across the bottom of the stream.

He's all right, Nick thought. He was only tired.

He had wet his hand before he touched the trout, so he would not disturb the delicate mucus that covered him. If a trout was touched with a dry hand, a white fungus attacked the unprotected spot. Years before when he had fished crowded streams, with fly fishermen ahead of him and behind him, Nick had again and again come on dead trout, furry with white fungus, drifted against a rock, or floating belly up in some pool. Nick did not like to fish with other men on the river. Unless they were of your party, they spoiled it.

He wallowed down the stream, above his knees in the current, through the fifty yards of shallow water above the pile of logs that crossed the stream. He did not rebait his hook and held it in his hand as he waded. He was certain he could catch small trout in the shallows, but he did not want them. There would be no big trout in the shallows this time of day.

Now the water deepened up his thighs sharply and coldly. Ahead was the smooth damned-back flood of water above the logs. The water was smooth and dark; on the left, the lower edge of the meadow; on the right the swamp.

Nick leaned back against the current and took a hopper from the bottle. He threaded the hopper on the hook and spat on him for good luck. Then he pulled several yards of line from the reel and tossed the hopper out ahead onto the fast, dark water. It floated down towards the log, then the weight of the line pulled the bait under the surface. Nick held the rod in his right hand, letting the line run out through his fingers.

There was a long tug. Nick struck and the rod came alive and dangerous, bent double, the line tightening, coming out of water, tightening, all in a heavy, dangerous, steady pull. Nick felt the moment when the leader would break if the strain increased and let the line go.

The reel ratcheted into a mechanical shriek as the line went out in a rush. Too fast. Nick could not check it, the line rushing out, the reel note rising as the line ran out.

With the core of the reel showing, his heart feeling stopped with the excitement, leaning back against the current that mounted icily his thighs, Nick thumbed the reel hard with his left hand. It was awkward getting his thumb inside the fly reel frame.

As he put on pressure the line tightened into sudden hardness and beyond the logs a huge trout went high out of water. As he jumped, Nick lowered the tip of the rod. But he felt, as he dropped the tip to ease the strain, the moment when the strain was too great; the hardness too tight. Of course, the leader had broken. There was no mistaking the feeling when all spring left the line and it became dry and hard. Then it went slack.

His mouth dry, his heart down, Nick reeled in. He had never seen so big a trout. There was a heaviness, a power not to be held, and then the bulk of him, as he jumped. He looked as broad as a salmon.

Nick's hand was shaky. He reeled in slowly. The thrill had been too much. He felt, vaguely, a little sick, as though it would be better to sit down.

The leader had broken where the hook was tied to it. Nick took it in his hand. He thought of the trout somewhere on the bottom, holding himself steady over the gravel, far down below the light, under the logs, with the hook in his jaw. Nick knew the trout's teeth would cut through the snell of the hook. The hook would imbed itself in his jaw. He'd bet the trout was angry. Anything that size would be angry. That was a trout. He had been solidly hooked. Solid as a rock. He felt like a rock, too, before he started off. By God, he was a big one. By God, he was the biggest one I ever heard of.

Nick climbed out onto the meadow and stood, water running down his trousers and out of his shoes, his shoes squelchy. He went over and sat on the logs. He did not want to rush his sensations any.

He wriggled his toes in the water, in his shoes, and got out a cigarette from his breast pocket. He lit it and tossed the match into the fast water below the logs. A tiny trout rose at the match, as it swung around in the fast current. Nick laughed. He would finish the cigarette.

He sat on the logs, smoking, drying in the sun, the sun warm on his back, the river shallow ahead entering the woods, curving into the woods, shallows, light glittering, big water-smooth rocks, cedars along the bank and white birches, the logs warm in the sun, smooth to sit on, without bark, gray to the touch; slowly the feeling of disappointment left him. It went away slowly, the feeling of disappointment that came sharply after the thrill that made his shoulders ache. It was all right now. His rod lying out on the logs. Nick tied a new hook on the leader, pulling the gut tight until it grimped into itself in a hard knot.

He baited up, then picked up the rod and walked to the far end of the logs to get into the water, where it was not too deep. Under and beyond the logs was a deep pool. Nick walked around the shallow shelf near the swamp shore until he came out on the shallow bed of the stream.

On the left, where the meadow ended and the woods began, a great elm tree was uprooted. Gone over in a storm, it lay back into the woods, its roots clotted with dirt, grass growing in them, rising a solid bank beside the stream. The river cut to the edge of the uprooted tree. From where Nick stood he could see deep channels, like ruts, cut in the shallow bed of the stream by the flow of the current. Pebbly where he stood and pebbly and full of boulders beyond; where it curved near the tree roots, the bed of the stream was marly and between the ruts of deep water green weed fronds swung in the current.

Nick swung the rod back over his shoulder and forward, and the line, curving forward, laid the grasshopper down on one of the deep channels in the weeds. A trout struck and Nick hooked him.

Holding the rod far out toward the uprooted tree and sloshing backward in the current, Nick worked the trout, plunging, the rod bending alive, out of the danger of the weeds into the open river. Holding the rod, pumping alive against the current, Nick brought the trout in. He rushed, but always came, the spring of the rod yielding to the rushes, sometimes jerking under water, but always bringing him in. Nick eased downstream with the rushes. The rod above his head he led the trout over the net, then lifted.

The trout hung heavy in the net, mottled trout back and silver sides in the meshes. Nick unhooked him; heavy sides, good to hold, big undershot jaw, and slipped him, heaving and big sliding, into the long sack that hung from his shoulders in the water.

Nick spread the mouth of the sack against the current and it filled, heavy with water. He held it up, the bottom in the stream, and the water poured out through the sides. Inside at the bottom was the big trout, alive in the water.

Nick moved downstream. The sack out ahead of him sunk heavy in the water, pulling from his shoulders.

It was getting hot, the sun hot on the back of his neck.

Nick had one good trout. He did not care about getting many trout. Now the stream was shallow and wide. There were trees along both banks. The trees of the left bank made short shadows on the current in the forenoon sun. Nick knew there were trout in each shadow. In the afternoon, after the sun had crossed toward the hills, the trout would be in the cool shadows on the other side of the stream.

The very biggest ones would lie up close to the bank. You could always pick them up there on the Black. When the sun was down they all moved out into the current. Just when the sun made the water blinding in the glare before it went down, you were liable to strike a big trout anywhere in the current. It was almost impossible to fish then, the surface of the water was blinding as a mirror in the sun. Of course, you could fish upstream, but in a stream like the Black, or this, you had to wallow against the current and in a deep place, the water piled up on you. It was no fun to fish upstream with this much current.

Nick moved along through the shallow stretch watching the banks for deep holes. A beech tree grew close beside the river, so that the branches hung down into the water. The stream went back in under the leaves. There were always trout in a place like that.

Nick did not care about fishing that hole. He was sure he would get hooked in the branches.

It looked deep though. He dropped the grasshopper so the current took it under water, back in under the overhanging branch. The line pulled hard and Nick struck. The trout threshed heavily, half out of water in the leaves and branches. The line was caught. Nick pulled hard and the trout was off. He reeled in and holding the hook in his hand, walked down the stream.

Ahead, close to the left bank, was a big log. Nick saw it was hollow; pointing up river the current entered it smoothly, only a little ripple spread each side of the log. The water was deepening. The top of the hollow log was gray and dry. It was partly in the shadow.

Nick took the cork out of the grasshopper bottle and a hopper clung to it. He picked him off, hooked him and tossed him out. He held the rod far out so that the hopper on the water moved into the current flowing into the hollow log. Nick lowered the rod and the hopper floated in. There was a heavy strike. Nick swung the rod against the pull. It felt as though he were hooked into the log itself, except for the live feeling.

He tried to force the fish out into the current. It came, heavily.

The line went slack and Nick thought the trout was gone. Then he saw him, very near, in the current, shaking his head, trying to get the hook out. His mouth was clamped shut. He was fighting the hook in the clear flowing current.

Looping in the line with his left hand, Nick swung the rod to make the line taut and tried to lead the trout toward the net, but he was gone, out of sight, the line pumping. Nick fought him against the current, letting him thump in the water against the spring of the rod. He shifted the rod to his left hand, worked the trout upstream, holding his weight, fighting on the rod, and then let him down into the net. He lifted him clear of the water, a heavy half circle in the net, the net dripping, unhooked him and slid him into the sack.

He spread the mouth of the sack and looked down in at the two big trout alive in the water.

Through the deepening water, Nick waded over to the hollow log. He took the sack off, over his head, the trout flopping as it came out of water, and hung it so the trout were deep in the water. Then he pulled himself up on the log and sat, the water from his trouser and boots running down into the stream. He laid his rod down, moved along to the shady end of the log and took the sandwiches out of his pocket. He dipped the sandwiches in the cold water. The current carried away the crumbs. He ate the sandwiches and dipped his hat full of water to drink, the water running out through his hat just ahead of his drinking.

It was cool in the shade, sitting on the log. He took a cigarette out and struck a match to light it. The match sunk into the gray wood, making a tiny furrow. Nick leaned over the side of the log, found a hard place and lit the match. He sat smoking and watching the river.

Ahead the river narrowed and went into a swamp. The river became smooth and deep and the swamp looked solid with cedar trees, their trunks close together, their branches solid. It could not be possible to walk through a swamp like that. The branches grew so low. You would have to keep almost level with the ground to move at all. You could not crash through the branches. That must be why the animals that lived in swamps were built the way they were, Nick thought.

He wished he had brought something to read. He felt like reading. He did not feel like going into the swamp. He looked down the river. A big cedar slanted all the way across the stream. Beyond that the river went into the swamp.

Nick did not want to go in there now. He felt a reaction against deep wading with the water deepening up under his armpits, to hook big trout in places impossible to land them. In the swamp the banks were bare, the big cedars came together overhead, the sun did not come through, except in patches; in the fast deep water, in the half light, the fishing would be tragic. In the swamp fishing was a tragic adventure. Nick did not want it. He did not want to go down the stream any further today.

He took out his knife, opened it and stuck it in the log. Then he pulled up the sack, reached into it and brought out one of the trout. Holding him near the tail, hard to hold, alive, in his hand, he whacked him against the log. The trout quivered, rigid. Nick laid him on the log in the shade and broke the neck of the other fish the same way. He laid them side by side on the log. They were fine trout.

Nick cleaned them, slitting them from the vent to the tip of the jaw. All the insides and the gills and tongue came out in one piece. They were both males; long gray-white strips of milt, smooth and clean. All the insides clean and compact, coming out all together. Nick tossed the offal ashore for the minks to find.

He washed the trout in the stream. When he held them back up in the water they looked like live fish. Their color was not gone yet. He washed his hands and dried them on the log. Then he laid the trout on the sack spread out on the log, rolled them up in it, tied the bundle and put it in the landing net. His knife was still standing, blade stuck in the log. He cleaned it on the wood and put it in his pocket.

Nick stood up on the log, holding his rod, the landing net hanging heavy, then stepped into the water and splashed ashore. He climbed the bank and cut up into the woods, toward the high ground. He was going back to camp. He looked back. The river just showed through the trees. There were plenty of days coming when he could fish the swamp.

Flowering Judas

Braggioni sits heaped upon the edge of a straight-backed chair much too small for him, and sings to Laura in a furry, mournful voice. Laura has begun to find reasons for avoiding her own house until the latest possible moment, for Braggioni is there almost every night. No matter how late she is, he will be sitting there with a surly, waiting expression, pulling at his kinky yellow hair, thumbing the strings of his guitar, snarling a tune under his breath. Lupe the Indian maid meets Laura at the door, and says with a flicker of a glance towards the upper room, "He waits."

Laura wishes to lie down, she is tired of her hairpins and the feel of her long tight sleeves, but she says to him, "Have you a new song for me this evening?" If he says yes, she asks him to sing it. If he says no, she remembers his favorite one, and asks him to sing it again. Lupe brings her a cup of chocolate and plate of rice, and Laura eats at the small table under the lamp, first inviting Braggioni, whose answer is always the same: "I have eaten, and besides, chocolate thickens the voice."

Laura says, "Sing, then," and Braggioni heaves himself into song. He scratches the guitar familiarly as though it were a pet animal, and sings passionately off key, taking the high notes in a prolonged painful squeal. Laura, who haunts the markets listening to the ballad singers, and stops every day to hear the blind boy playing his reed-flute in Sixteenth of September Street, listens to Braggioni with pitiless courtesy, because she dares not smile at his miserable performance. Nobody dares to smile at him. Braggioni is cruel to everyone, with a kind of specialized insolence, but he is so vain of his talents, and so sensitive to slights, it would require a cruelty and vanity greater than his own to lay a finger on the vast cureless wound of his self-esteem. It would require courage, too, for it is dangerous to offend him, and nobody has this courage.

Braggioni loves himself with such tenderness and amplitude and eternal charity that his followers—for he is a leader of men, a skilled revolutionist, and his skin has been punctured in honorable warfare—warm themselves in the reflected glow, and say to each other: "He has a real nobility, a love of humanity raised above mere personal affections." The excess of this self-love has flowed out, inconveniently for her, over Laura, who, with so many others, owes her comfortable situation and her salary to him. When he is in a very good humor, he tells her, "I am tempted to forgive you for being a *gringa*. *Gringita!*"[1] and Laura, burning,

---

[1] *Gringa*: a disparaging term used by Spanish Americans in referring to foreigners, especially Americans and English.

imagines herself leaning forward suddenly, and with a sound back-handed slap wiping the suety smile from his face. If he notices her eyes at these moments he gives no sign.

She knows what Braggioni would offer her, and she must resist tenaciously without appearing to resist, and if she could avoid it she would not admit even to herself the slow drift of his intention. During these long evenings which have spoiled a long month for her, she sits in her deep chair with an open book on her knees, resting her eyes on the consoling rigidity of the printed page when the sight and sound of Braggioni singing threaten to identify themselves with all her remembered afflictions and to add their weight to her uneasy premonitions of the future. The gluttonous bulk of Braggioni has become a symbol of her many disillusions, for a revolutionist should be lean, animated by heroic faith, a vessel of abstract virtues. This is nonsense, she knows it now and is ashamed of it. Revolution must have leaders, and leadership is a career for energetic men. She is, her comrades tell her, full of romantic error, for what she defines as cynicism in them is merely "a developed sense of reality." She is almost too willing to say, "I am wrong, I suppose I don't really understand the principles," and afterward she makes a secret truce with herself, determined not to surrender her will to such expedient logic. But she cannot help feeling that she has been betrayed irreparably by the disunion between her way of living and her feeling of what life should be, and at times she is almost contented to rest in this sense of grievance as a private store of consolation. Sometimes she wishes to run away, but she stays. Now she longs to fly out of this room, down the narrow stairs, and into the street where the houses lean together like conspirators under a single mottled lamp, and leave Braggioni singing to himself.

Instead she looks at Braggioni, frankly and clearly, like a good child who understands the rules of behavior. Her knees cling together under sound blue serge, and her round white collar is not purposely nun-like. She wears the uniform of an idea, and has renounced vanities. She was born Roman Catholic, and in spite of her fear of being seen by someone who might make a scandal of it, she slips now and again into some crumbling little church, kneels on the chilly stone, and says a Hail Mary on the gold rosary she bought in Tehuantepec. It is no good and she ends by examining the altar with its tinsel flowers and ragged brocades, and feels tender about the battered doll-shape of some male saint whose white, lace-trimmed drawers hang limply around his ankles below the hieratic dignity of his velvet robe. She has encased herself in a set of principles derived from her early training, leaving no detail of gesture or of personal taste untouched, and for this reason she will not wear lace made on machines. This is her private heresy, for in her special group the machine is sacred, and will be the salvation of the workers. She loves fine lace, and there is a tiny edge of fluted cobweb on this collar, which is one of twenty precisely alike, folded in blue tissue paper in the upper drawer of her clothes chest.

Braggioni catches her glance solidly as if he had been waiting for it, leans forward, balancing his paunch between his spread knees, and sings with tremendous emphasis, weighing his words. He has, the song relates, no father and no mother, nor even a friend to console him; lonely as a wave of the sea he comes and goes, lonely as a wave. His mouth opens round and yearns sideways, his balloon cheeks grow oily with the labor of song. He bulges marvelously in his expensive garments. Over his lavender collar, crushed upon a purple necktie, held by a diamond hoop: over his ammunition belt of tooled leather worked in silver, buckled cruelly around his gasping middle: over the tops of his glossy yellow shoes Braggioni swells with ominous ripeness, his mauve silk hose stretched taut, his ankles bound with the stout leather thongs of his shoes.

When he stretches his eyelids at Laura she notes again that his eyes are the true tawny yellow cat's eyes. He is rich, not in money, he tells her, but in power, and this power brings with it the blameless ownership of things, and the right to indulge his love of small luxuries. "I have a taste for the elegant refinements," he said once, flourishing a yellow silk handkerchief before her nose. "Smell that? It is Jockey Club, imported from New York." Nonetheless he is wounded by life. He will say so presently. "It is true everything turns to dust in the hand, to gall on the tongue." He sighs and his leather belt creaks like a saddle girth. "I am disappointed in everything as it comes. Everything." He shakes his head. "You, poor thing, you will be disappointed too. You are born for it. We are more alike than you realize in some things. Wait and see. Some day you will remember what I have told you, you will know that Braggioni was your friend."

Laura feels a slow chill, a purely physical sense of danger, a warning in her blood that violence, mutilation, a shocking death, wait for her with lessening patience. She has translated this fear into something homely, immediate, and sometimes hesitates before crossing the street. "My personal fate is nothing, except as the testimony of a mental attitude," she reminds herself, quoting from some forgotten philosophic primer, and is sensible enough to add, "Anyhow, I shall not be killed by an automobile if I can help it."

"It may be true I am as corrupt, in another way, as Braggioni," she thinks in spite of herself, "as callous, as incomplete," and if this is so, any kind of death seems preferable. Still she sits quietly, she does not run. Where could she go? Uninvited she has promised herself to this place; she can no longer imagine herself as living in another country, and there is no pleasure in remembering her life before she came here.

Precisely what is the nature of this devotion, its true motives, and what are its obligations? Laura cannot say. She spends part of her days in Xochimilco, near by, teaching Indian children to say in English, "The cat is on the mat." When she appears in the classroom they crowd about her with smiles on their wise, innocent, clay-colored faces, crying, "Good morning, my titcher!" in immaculate voices, and they make of her desk a fresh garden of flowers every day.

During her leisure she goes to union meetings and listens to busy important voices quarreling over tactics, methods, internal politics. She visits prisoners of her own political faith in their cells, where they entertain themselves with counting cockroaches, repenting of their indiscretions, composing their memoirs, writing out manifestoes and plans for their comrades who are still walking about free, hands in pockets, sniffing fresh air. Laura brings them food and cigarettes and a little money, and she brings messages disguised in equivocal phrases from the men outside who dare not set foot in the prison for fear of disappearing into the cells kept empty for them. If the prisoners confuse night and day, and complain, "Dear little Laura, time doesn't pass in this infernal hole, and I won't know when it is time to sleep unless I have a reminder," she brings them their favorite narcotics, and says in a tone that does not wound them with pity, "Tonight will really be night for you," and though her Spanish amuses them, they find her comforting, useful. If they lose patience and all faith, and curse the slowness of their friends in coming to their rescue with money and influence, they trust her not to repeat everything, and if she inquires, "Where do you think we can find money, or influence?" they are certain to answer, "Well, there is Braggioni, why doesn't he do something?"

She smuggles letters from headquarters to men hiding from firing squads in back streets in mildewed houses, where they sit in tumbled beds and talk bitterly as if all Mexico were at their heels, when Laura knows positively they might appear at the band concert in the Alameda on Sunday morning, and no one would notice them. But Braggioni says, "Let them sweat a little. The next time they may be careful. It is very restful to have them out of the way for a while." She is not afraid to knock on any door in any street after midnight, and enter in the darkness, and say to one of these men who is really in danger: "They will be looking for you—seriously—tomorrow morning after six. Here is some money from Vicente. Go to Vera Cruz and wait."

She borrows money from the Roumanian agitator to give to his bitter enemy the Polish agitator. The favor of Braggioni is their disputed territory, and Braggioni holds the balance nicely, for he can use them both. The Polish agitator talks love to her over café tables, hoping to exploit what he believes is her secret sentimental preference for him, and he gives her misinformation which he begs her to repeat as the solemn truth to certain persons. The Roumanian is more adroit. He is generous with his money in all good causes, and lies to her with an air of ingenuous candor, as if he were her good friend and confidant. She never repeats anything they may say. Braggioni never asks questions. He has other ways to discover all that he wishes to know about them.

Nobody touches her, but all praise her gray eyes, and the soft, round under lip which promises gayety, yet is always grave, nearly always firmly closed: and they cannot understand why she is in Mexico. She walks back and forth on her errands, with puzzled eyebrows, carrying her little folder of drawings and music and school papers. No dancer dances more beautifully than Laura walks, and she inspires some amusing, unexpected ardors, which cause little gossip, because nothing comes of them. A young captain who had been a soldier in Zapata's army attempted, during a horseback ride near Cuernavaca, to express his desire for her with the noble simplicity befitting a rude folk-hero: but gently, because he was gentle. This gentleness was his defeat, for when he alighted, and removed her foot from the stirrup, and essayed to draw her down into his arms, her horse, ordinarily a tame one, shied fiercely, reared and plunged away. The young hero's horse careered blindly after his stablemate, and the hero did not return to the hotel until rather late that evening. At breakfast he came to her table in full charro dress, gray buckskin jacket and trousers with strings of silver buttons down the leg, and he was in a humorous, careless mood. "May I sit with you?" and "You are a wonderful rider. I was terrified that you might be thrown and dragged. I should never have forgiven myself. But I cannot admire you enough for your riding!"

"I learned to ride in Arizona," said Laura.

"If you will ride with me again this morning, I promise you a horse that will not shy with you," he said. But Laura remembered that she must return to Mexico City at noon.

Next morning the children made a celebration and spent their playtime writing on the blackboard, "We lov ar ticher," and with tinted chalks they drew wreaths of flowers around the words. The young hero wrote her a letter: "I am a very foolish, wasteful, impulsive man. I should have first said I love you, and then you would not have run away. But you shall see me again." Laura thought, "I must send him a box of colored crayons," but she was trying to forgive herself for having spurred her horse at the wrong moment.

A brown, shock-haired youth came and stood in her patio one night and sang like a lost soul for two hours, but Laura could think of nothing to do about it. The moonlight spread a wash of gauzy silver over the clear spaces of the garden, and the shadows were cobalt blue. The scarlet blossoms of the Judas tree were dull purple, and the names of the colors repeated themselves automatically in her mind, while she watched not the boy, but his shadow, fallen like a dark garment across the fountain rim, trailing in the water. Lupe came silently and whispered expert counsel in her ear: "If you will throw him one little flower, he will sing another song or two and go away." Laura threw the flower, and he sang a last song and went away with the flower tucked in the band of his hat. Lupe said, "He is one of the organizers of the Typographers Union, and before that he sold corridos in the Merced market, and before that, he came from Guanajuato, where I was born. I would not trust any man, but I trust least those from Guanajuato."

She did not tell Laura that he would be back again the next night, and the next, nor that he would follow her at a certain fixed distance around the Merced market, through the Zócolo, up Francisco I. Madero Avenue, and so along the Paseo de la Reforma to Chapultepec Park, and into the Philosopher's Footpath, still with that flower withering in his hat, and an indivisible attention in his eyes.

Now Laura is accustomed to him, it means nothing except that he is nineteen years old and is observing a convention with all propriety, as though it were founded on a law of nature, which in the end it might well prove to be. He is beginning to write poems which he prints on a wooden press, and he leaves them stuck like handbills in her door. She is pleasantly disturbed by the abstract, unhurried watchfulness of his black eyes which will in time turn easily towards another object. She tells herself that throwing the flower was a mistake, for she is twenty-two years old and knows better; but she refuses to regret it, and persuades herself that her negation of all external events as they occur is a sign that she is gradually perfecting herself in the stoicism she strives to cultivate against that disaster she fears, though she cannot name it.

She is not at home in the world. Every day she teaches children who remain strangers to her, though she loves their tender round hands and their charming opportunist savagery. She knocks at unfamiliar doors not knowing whether a friend or a stranger shall answer, and even if a known face emerges from the sour gloom of that unknown interior, still it is the face of a stranger. No matter what this stranger says to her, nor what her message to him, the very cells of her flesh reject knowledge and kinship in one monotonous word. No. No. No. She draws her strength from this one holy talismanic word which does not suffer her to be led into evil. Denying everything, she may walk anywhere in safety, she looks at everything without amazement.

No, repeats this firm unchanging voice of her blood; and she looks at Braggioni without amazement. He is a great man, he wishes to impress this simple girl who covers her great round breasts with thick dark cloth, and who hides long, invaluably beautiful legs under a heavy skirt. She is almost thin except for the incomprehensible fullness of her breasts, like a nursing mother's, and Braggioni, who considers himself a judge of women, speculates again on the puzzle of her notorious virginity, and takes the liberty of speech which she permits without a sign of modesty, indeed, without any sort of sign, which is disconcerting.

"You think you are so cold, *gringita!* Wait and see. You will surprise yourself some day! May I be there to advise you!" He stretches his eyelids at her, and his ill-humored cat's eyes waver in a separate glance for the two points of light marking the opposite ends of a smoothly drawn path between the swollen curve of her breasts. He is not put off by that blue serge, nor by her resolutely fixed gaze. There is all the time in the world. His cheeks are bellying with the wind of song. "O girl with the dark eyes," he sings, and reconsiders. "But yours are not dark. I can change all that. O girl with the green eyes, you have stolen my heart away!" then his mind wanders to the song, and Laura feels the weight of his attention being shifted elsewhere. Singing thus, he seems harmless, he is quite harmless, there is nothing to do but sit patiently and say "No," when the moment comes. She draws a full breath, and her mind wanders also, but not far. She dares not wander too far.

Not for nothing has Braggioni taken pains to be a good revolutionist and a professional lover of humanity. He will never die of it. He has the malice, the cleverness, the wickedness, the sharpness of wit, the hardness of heart, stipulated for loving the world profitably. *He will never die of it.* He will live to see himself kicked out from his feeding trough by other hungry world-saviors. Traditionally he must sing in spite of his life which drives him to bloodshed, he tells Laura, for his father was a Tuscany peasant who drifted to Yucatan and married a Maya woman: a woman of race, an aristocrat. They gave him the love and knowledge of music, thus: and under the rip of his thumbnail, the strings of the instrument complain like exposed nerves.

Once he was called Delgadito by all the girls and married women who ran after him; he was so scrawny all his bones showed under his thin cotton clothing, and he could squeeze his emptiness to the very backbone with his two hands. He was a poet and the revolution was only a dream then; too many women loved him and sapped away his youth, and he could never find enough to eat anywhere, anywhere! Now he is a leader of men, crafty men who whisper in his ear, hungry men who wait for hours outside his office for a word with him, emaciated men with wild faces who waylay him at the street gate with a timid, "Comrade, let me tell you . . ." and they blow the foul breath from their empty stomachs in his face.

He is always sympathetic. He gives them handfuls of small coins from his own pocket, he promises them work, there will be demonstrations, they must join the unions and attend meetings, above all they must be on the watch for spies. They are closer to him than his own brothers, without them he can do nothing—until tomorrow, comrade!

Until tomorrow. "They are stupid, they are lazy, they are treacherous, they would cut my throat for nothing," he says to Laura. He has good food and abundant drink, he hires an automobile and drives in the Paseo on Sunday morning, and enjoys plenty of sleep in a soft bed beside a wife who dares not disturb him; and he sits pampering his bones in easy billows of fat, singing to Laura, who knows and thinks these things about him. When he was fifteen, he tried to drown himself because he loved a girl, his first love, and she laughed at him. "A thousand women have paid for that," and his tight little mouth turns down at the corners. Now he perfumes his hair with Jockey Club, and confides to Laura: "One woman is really as good as another for me, in the dark. I prefer them all."

His wife organizes unions among the girls in the cigarette factories, and walks in picket lines, and even speaks at meetings in the evening. But she cannot be brought to acknowledge the benefits of true liberty. "I tell her I must have my freedom, net. She does not understand my point of view." Laura has heard this many times. Braggioni scratches the guitar and meditates. "She is an instinctively virtuous woman, pure gold, no doubt of that. If she were not, I should lock her up, and she knows it."

His wife, who works so hard for the good of the factory girls, employs part of her leisure lying on the floor weeping because there are so many women in the world, and only one husband for her, and she never knows where nor when to look for him. He told her: "Unless you can learn to cry when I am not here, I must go away for good." That day he went away and took a room at the Hotel Madrid.

It is this month of separation for the sake of higher principles that has been spoiled not only for Mrs. Braggioni, whose sense of reality is beyond criticism, but for Laura, who feels herself bogged in a nightmare. Tonight Laura envies Mrs. Braggioni, who is alone, and free to weep as much as she pleases about a concrete wrong. Laura has just come from a visit to the prison, and she is waiting for tomorrow with a bitter anxiety as if tomorrow may not come, but time may be caught immovably in this hour, with herself transfixed, Braggioni singing on forever, and Eugenio's body not yet discovered by the guard.

Braggioni says: "Are you going to sleep?" Almost before she can shake her head, he begins telling her about the May-day disturbances coming on in Morelia, for the Catholics hold a festival in honor of the Blessed Virgin, and the Socialists celebrate their martyrs on that day. "There will be two independent processions, starting from either end of town, and they will march until they meet, and the rest depends . . ." He asks her to oil and load his pistols. Standing up, he unbuckles his ammunition belt, and spreads it laden across her knees. Laura sits with the shells slipping through the cleaning cloth dipped in oil, and he says again he cannot understand why she works so hard for the revolutionary idea unless she loves some man who is in it. "Are you not in love with someone?" "No," says Laura. "And no one is in love with you?" "No." "Then it is your own fault. No woman need go begging. Why, what is the matter with you? The legless beggar woman in the Alameda has a perfectly faithful lover. Did you know that?"

Laura peers down the pistol barrel and says nothing, but a long, slow faintness rises and subsides in her; Braggioni curves his swollen fingers around the throat of the guitar and softly smothers the music out of it, and when she hears him again he seems to have forgotten her, and is speaking in the hypnotic voice he uses when talking in small rooms to a listening, close-gathered crowd. Some day this world, now seemingly so composed and eternal, to the edges of every sea shall be merely a tangle of gaping trenches, or crashing walls and broken bodies. Everything must be torn from its accustomed place where it has rotted for centuries, hurled skyward and distributed, cast down again clean as rain, without separate identity. Nothing shall survive that the stiffened hands of poverty have created for the rich and no one shall be left alive except the elect spirits destined to procreate a new world cleansed of cruelty and injustice, ruled by benevolent anarchy: "Pistols are good, I love them, cannon are even better, but in the end I pin my faith to good dynamite," he concludes, and strokes the pistol lying in her hands. "Once I dreamed of destroying this city, in case it offered resistance to General Ortíz, but it fell into his hands like an overripe pear."

He is made restless by his own words, rises and stands waiting. Laura holds up the belt to him: "Put that on and go kill somebody in Morelia, and you will be happier," she says softly. The presence of death in the room makes her bold. "Today, I found Eugenio going into a stupor. He refused to allow me to call the prison doctor. He had taken all the tablets I brought him yesterday. He said he took them because he was bored."

"He is a fool, and his death is his own business," says Braggioni, fastening his belt carefully.

"I told him if he had waited only a little while longer, you would have got him set free," says Laura. "He said he did not want to wait."

"He is a fool and we are well rid of him," says Braggioni, reaching for his hat.

He goes away. Laura knows his mood has changed, she will not see him any more for a while. He will send word when he needs her to go on errands into strange streets, to speak to the strange faces that will appear, like clay masks with the power of human speech, to mutter their thanks to Braggioni for his help. Now she is free, and she thinks, I must run while there is time. But she does not go.

Braggioni enters his own house where for a month his wife has spent many hours every night weeping and tangling her hair upon her pillow. She is weeping now, and she weeps more at the sight of him, the cause of all her sorrows. He looks about the room. Nothing is changed, the smells are good and familiar, he is well acquainted with the woman who comes toward him with no reproach except grief on her face. He says to her tenderly: "You are so good, please don't cry any more, you dear good creature." She says, "Are you tired, my angel? Sit here and I will wash your feet." She brings a bowl of water, and kneeling, unlaces his shoes, and when from her knees she raises her sad eyes under her blackened lids, he is sorry for everything, and bursts into tears. "Ah, yes, I am hungry, I am tired, let us eat something together," he says, between sobs. His wife leans her head on his arm and says, "Forgive me!" and this time he is refreshed by the solemn, endless rain of her tears.

Laura takes off her serge dress and puts on a white linen nightgown and goes to bed. She turns her head a little to one side, and lying still, reminds herself that it is time to sleep. Numbers tick in her brain like little clocks, soundless doors close of themselves around her. If you would sleep, you must not remember anything, the children will say tomorrow, good morning, my teacher, the poor prisoners who come every day bringing flowers to their jailor. 1–2–3–4–5—it is monstrous to confuse love with revolution, night with day, life with death—ah, Eugenio!

The tolling of the midnight bell is a signal, but what does it mean? Get up, Laura, and follow me: come out of your sleep, out of your bed, out of this strange house. What are you doing in this house? Without a word, without fear she rose and reached for Eugenio's hand, but he eluded her with a sharp, sly smile and drifted away. This is not all, you shall see—Murderer, he said, follow me, I will show you a new country, but it is far away and we must hurry. No, said Laura, not unless you take my hand, no; and she clung first to the stair rail, and then to the topmost branch of the Judas tree that bent down slowly and set her upon the earth, and then to the rocky ledge of a cliff, and then to the jagged wave of a sea that was not water but a desert of crumbling stone. Where are you taking me, she asked in wonder but without fear. To death, and it is a long way off, and we must hurry, said Eugenio. No, said Laura, not unless you take my hand. Then eat these flowers, poor prisoner, said Eugenio in a voice of pity, take and eat: and from the Judas tree he stripped the warm bleeding flowers, and held them to her lips. She saw that his hand was fleshless, a cluster of small white petrified branches, and his eye sockets were without light, but she ate the flowers greedily for they satisfied both hunger and thirst. Murderer! said Eugenio, and Cannibal! This is my body and my blood. Laura cried No! and at the sound of her own voice, she awoke trembling, and was afraid to sleep again.

Good Country People

Besides the neutral expression that she wore when she was alone, Mrs. Freeman had two others, forward and reverse, that she used for all her human dealings. Her forward expression was steady and driving like the advance of a heavy truck. Her eyes never swerved to left or right but turned as the story turned as if they followed a yellow line down the center of it. She seldom used the other expression because it was not often necessary for her to retract a statement, but when she did, her face came to a complete stop, there was an almost imperceptible movement of her black eyes, during which they seemed to be receding, and then the observer would see that Mrs. Freeman, though she might stand there as real as several grain sacks thrown on top of each other, was no longer there in spirit. As for getting anything across to her when this was the case, Mrs. Hopewell had given it up. She might talk her head off. Mrs. Freeman could never be brought to admit herself wrong on any point. She would stand there and if she could be brought to say anything, it was something like, "Well, I wouldn't of said it was and I wouldn't of said it wasn't," or letting her gaze range over the top kitchen shelf where there was an assortment of dusty bottles, she might remark, "I see you ain't ate many of them figs you put up last summer."

They carried on their most important business in the kitchen at breakfast. Every morning Mrs. Hopewell got up at seven o'clock and lit her gas heater and Joy's. Joy was her daughter, a large blonde girl who had an artificial leg. Mrs. Hopewell thought of her as a child though she was thirty-two years old and highly educated. Joy would get up while her mother was eating and lumber into the bathroom and slam the door, and before long, Mrs. Freeman would arrive at the back door. Joy would hear her mother call, "Come on in," and then they would talk for a while in low voices that were indistinguishable in the bathroom. By the time Joy came in, they had usually finished the weather report and were on one or the other of Mrs. Freeman's daughters, Glynese or Carramae. Joy called them Glycerin and Caramel. Glynese, a redhead, was eighteen and had many admirers; Carramae, a blonde, was only fifteen but already married and pregnant. She could not keep anything on her stomach. Every morning Mrs. Freeman told Mrs. Hopewell how many times she had vomited since the last report.

Mrs. Hopewell liked to tell people that Glynese and Carramae were two of the finest girls she knew and that Mrs. Freeman was a *lady* and that she was never ashamed to take her anywhere or introduce her to anybody they might meet. Then she would tell how she had happened to hire the

Freemans in the first place and how they were a godsend to her and how she had had them four years. The reason for her keeping them so long was that they were not trash. They were good country people. She had telephoned the man whose name they had given as a reference and he had told her that Mr. Freeman was a good farmer but that his wife was the nosiest woman ever to walk the earth. "She's got to be into everything," the man said. "If she don't get there before the dust settles, you can bet she's dead, that's all. She'll want to know all your business. I can stand him real good," he had said, "but me nor my wife neither could have stood that woman one more minute on this place." That had put Mrs. Hopewell off for a few days.

She had hired them in the end because there were no other applicants but she had made up her mind beforehand exactly how she would handle the woman. Since she was the type who had to be into everything, then, Mrs. Hopewell had decided, she would not only let her be into everything, she would *see to it* that she was into everything—she would give her the responsibility of everything, she would put her in charge. Mrs. Hopewell had no bad qualities of her own but she was able to use other people's in such a constructive way that she never felt the lack. She had hired the Freemans and she had kept them four years.

Nothing is perfect. This was one of Mrs. Hopewell's favorite sayings. Another was: that is life! And still another, the most important, was: well, other people have their opinions too. She would make these statements, usually at the table, in a tone of gentle insistence as if no one held them but her, and the large hulking Joy, whose constant outrage had obliterated every expression from her face, would stare just a little to the side of her, her eyes icy blue, with the look of someone who has achieved blindness by an act of will and means to keep it.

When Mrs. Hopewell said to Mrs. Freeman that life was like that, Mrs. Freeman would say, "I always said so myself." Nothing had been arrived at by anyone that had not first been arrived at by her. She was quicker than Mr. Freeman. When Mrs. Hopewell said to her after they had been on the place a while, "You know, you're the wheel behind the wheel," and winked, Mrs. Freeman had said, "I know it. I've always been quick. It's some that are quicker than others."

"Everybody is different," Mrs. Hopewell said.
"Yes, most people is," Mrs. Freeman said.
"It takes all kinds to make the world."
"I always said it did myself."

The girl was used to this kind of dialogue for breakfast and more of it for dinner; sometimes they had it for supper too. When they had no guest they ate in the kitchen because that was easier. Mrs. Freeman always managed to arrive at some point during the meal and to watch them finish it. She would stand in the doorway if it were summer but in the winter she would stand with one elbow on top of the refrigerator and look down on them, or she would stand by the gas heater, lifting the back of her skirt slightly. Occasionally she would stand against the wall and roll her head from side to side. At no time was she in any hurry to leave. All this was very trying on Mrs. Hopewell but she was a woman of great patience. She realized that nothing is perfect and that in the Freemans she had good country people and that if, in this day and age, you get good country people, you had better hang onto them.

She had had plenty of experience with trash. Before the Freemans she had averaged one tenant family a year. The wives of these farmers were not the kind you would want to be around you for very long. Mrs. Hopewell, who had divorced her husband long ago, needed someone to walk over the fields with her; and when Joy had to be impressed for these services, her remarks were usually so ugly and her face so glum that Mrs. Hopewell would say, "If you can't come pleasantly, I don't want you at all," to which the girl, standing square and rigid-shouldered with her neck thrust slightly forward, would reply, "If you want me, here I am—LIKE I AM."

Mrs. Hopewell excused this attitude because of the leg (which had been shot off in a hunting accident when Joy was ten). It was hard for Mrs. Hopewell to realize that her child was thirty-two now and that for more than twenty years she had had only one leg. She thought of her still as a child because it tore her heart to think instead of the poor stout girl in her thirties who had never danced a step or had any *normal* good times. Her name was really Joy but as soon as she was twenty-one and away from home, she had had it legally changed. Mrs. Hopewell was certain that she had thought and thought until she had hit upon the ugliest name in any language. Then she had gone and had the beautiful name, Joy, changed without telling her mother until after she had done it. Her legal name was Hulga.

When Mrs. Hopewell thought the name, Hulga, she thought of the broad blank hull of a battleship. She would not use it. She continued to call her Joy to which the girl responded but in a purely mechanical way.

Hulga had learned to tolerate Mrs. Freeman who saved her from taking walks with her mother. Even Glynese and Carramae were useful when they occupied attention that might otherwise have been directed at her. At first she had thought she could not stand Mrs. Freeman for she had found that it was not possible to be rude to her. Mrs. Freeman would take on strange resentments and for days together she would be sullen but the source of her displeasure was always obscure; a direct attack, a positive leer, blatant ugliness to her face—these never touched her. And without warning one day, she began calling her Hulga.

She did not call her that in front of Mrs. Hopewell who would have been incensed but when she and the girl happened to be out of the house together, she would say something and add the name Hulga to the end of it, and the big spectacled Joy-Hulga would scowl and redden as if her privacy had been intruded upon. She considered the name her personal affair. She had arrived at it first purely on the basis of its ugly sound and then the full genius of its fitness had struck her. She had a vision of the name working like the ugly sweating Vulcan who stayed in the furnace and to whom, presumably, the goddess had come when called. She saw it as the name of her highest creative act. One of her major triumphs was that her mother had not been able to turn her dust into Joy, but the greater one was that she had been able to turn it herself into Hulga. However, Mrs. Freeman's relish for using the name only irritated her. It was as if Mrs. Freeman's beady steel-pointed eyes had penetrated far enough behind her face to reach some secret fact. Something about her seemed to fascinate Mrs. Freeman and then one day Hulga realized that it was the artificial leg. Mrs. Freeman had a special fondness for the details of secret infections, hidden deformities, assaults upon children. Of diseases, she preferred the lingering or incurable. Hulga had heard Mrs. Hopewell give her the details of the hunting accident, how the leg had been literally blasted off, how she had never lost consciousness. Mrs. Freeman could listen to it any time as if it had happened an hour ago.

When Hulga stumped into the kitchen in the morning (she could walk without making the awful noise but she made it—Mrs. Hopewell was certain—because it was ugly-sounding), she glanced at them and did not speak. Mrs. Hopewell would be in her red kimono with her hair tied around her head in rags. She would be sitting at the table, finishing her breakfast and Mrs. Freeman would be hanging by her elbow outward from the refrigerator, looking down at the table. Hulga always put her eggs on the stove to boil and then stood over them with her arms folded, and Mrs. Hopewell would look at her—a kind of indirect gaze divided between her and Mrs. Freeman—and would think that if she would only keep herself up a little, she wouldn't be so bad looking. There was nothing wrong with her face that a pleasant expression wouldn't help. Mrs. Hopewell said that people who looked on the bright side of things would be beautiful even if they were not.

Whenever she looked at Joy this way, she could not help but feel that it would have been better if the child had not taken the Ph.D. It had certainly not brought her out any and now that she had it, there was no more excuse for her to go to school again. Mrs. Hopewell thought it was nice for girls to go to school to have a good time but Joy had "gone through." Anyhow, she would not have been strong enough to go again. The doctors had told Mrs. Hopewell that with the best of care, Joy might see forty-five. She had a weak heart. Joy had made it plain that if it had not been for this condition, she would be far from these red hills and good country people. She would be in a university lecturing to people who knew what she was talking about. And Mrs. Hopewell could very well picture her there, looking like a scarecrow and lecturing to more of the same. Here she went about all day in a six-year-old skirt and a yellow sweat shirt with a faded cowboy on a horse embossed on it. She thought this was funny; Mrs. Hopewell thought it was idiotic and showed simply that she was still a child. She was brilliant but she didn't have a grain of sense. It seemed to Mrs. Hopewell that every year she grew less like other people and more like herself—bloated, rude, and squint-eyed. And she said such strange things! To her own mother she had said—without warning, without excuse, standing up in the middle of a meal with her face purple and her mouth half full—"Woman! do you ever look inside? Do you ever look inside and see what you are *not*? God!" she had cried sinking down again and staring at her plate, "Malebranche was right: we are not our own light. We are not our own light!" Mrs. Hopewell had no idea to this day what brought that on. She had only made the remark, hoping Joy would take it in, that a smile never hurt anyone.

The girl had taken the Ph.D. in philosophy and this left Mrs. Hopewell at a complete loss. You could say, "My daughter is a nurse," or "My daughter is a school teacher," or even, "My daughter is a chemical engineer." You could not say, "My daughter is a philosopher." That was something that had ended with the Greeks and Romans. All day Joy sat on her neck in a deep chair, reading. Sometimes she went for walks but she didn't like dogs or cats or birds or flowers or nature or nice young men. She looked at nice young men as if she could smell their stupidity.

One day Mrs. Hopewell had picked up one of the books the girl had just put down and opening it at random, she read, "Science, on the other hand, has to assert its soberness and seriousness afresh and declare that it is concerned solely with what-is. Nothing—how can it be for science anything but a horror and a phantasm? If science is right, then one thing stands firm: science wishes to know nothing of nothing. Such is after all the strictly scientific approach to Nothing. We know it by wishing to know nothing of Nothing." These words had been underlined with a blue pencil and they worked on Mrs. Hopewell like some evil incantation in gibberish. She shut the book quickly and went out of the room as if she were having a chill.

This morning when the girl came in, Mrs. Freeman was on Carramae. "She thrown up four times after supper," she said, "and was up twice in the night after three o'clock. Yesterday she didn't do nothing but ramble in the bureau drawer. All she did. Stand up there and see what she could run up on."

"She's got to eat," Mrs. Hopewell muttered, sipping her coffee, while she watched Joy's back at the stove. She was wondering what the child had said to the Bible salesman. She could not imagine what kind of a conversation she could possibly have had with him.

He was a tall gaunt hatless youth who had called yesterday to sell them a Bible. He had appeared at the door, carrying a large black suitcase that weighted him so heavily on one side that he had to brace himself against the door facing. He seemed on the point of collapse but he said in a cheerful voice, "Good morning, Mrs. Cedars!" and set the suitcase down on the mat. He was not a bad-looking young man though he had on a bright blue suit and yellow socks that were not pulled up far enough. He had prominent face bones and a streak of sticky-looking brown hair falling across his forehead.

"I'm Mrs. Hopewell," she said.

"Oh!" he said, pretending to look puzzled but with his eyes sparkling, "I saw it said 'The Cedars,' on the mailbox so I thought you was Mrs. Cedars!" and he burst out in a pleasant laugh. He picked up the satchel and under cover of a pant, he fell forward into her hall. It was rather as if the suitcase had moved first, jerking him after it. "Mrs. Hopewell!" he said and grabbed her hand. "I hope you are well!" and he laughed again and then all at once his face sobered completely. He paused and gave her a straight earnest look and said, "Lady, I've come to speak of serious things."

"Well, come in," she muttered, none too pleased because her dinner was almost ready. He came into the parlor and sat down on the edge of a straight chair and put the suitcase between his feet and glanced around the room as if he were sizing her up by it. Her silver gleamed on the two sideboards; she decided he had never been in a room as elegant as this.

"Mrs. Hopewell," he began, using he name in a way that sounded almost intimate, "I know you believe in Chrustian service."

"Well yes," she murmured.

"I know," he said and paused, looking very wise with his head cocked on one side, "that you're a good woman. Friends have told me."

Mrs. Hopewell never liked to be taken for a fool. "What are you selling?" she asked.

"Bibles," the young man said and his eye raced around the room before he added, "I see you have no family Bible in your parlor, I see that is the one lack you got!"

Mrs. Hopewell could not say, "My daughter is an atheist and won't let me keep the Bible in the parlor." She said, stiffening slightly, "I keep my Bible by my bedside." This was not the truth. It was in the attic somewhere.

"Lady," he said, "the word of God ought to be in the parlor."

"Well, I think that's a matter of taste," she began. "I think . . ."

"Lady," he said, "for a Chrustian, the word of God ought to be in every room in the house besides in his heart. I know you're a Chrustian because I can see it in every line of your face."

She stood up and said, "Well, young man, I don't want to buy a Bible and I smell my dinner burning."

He didn't get up. He began to twist his hands and looking down at them, he said softly, "Well lady, I'll tell you the truth—not many people want to buy one nowadays and besides, I know I'm real simple. I don't know how to say a thing but to say it. I'm just a country boy." He glanced up into her unfriendly face. "People like you don't like to fool with country people like me!"

"Why!" she cried, "good country people are the salt of the earth! Besides, we all have different ways of doing, it takes all kinds to make the world go 'round. That's life!"

"You said a mouthful," he said.

"Why, I think there aren't enough good country people in the world!" she said, stirred. "I think that's what's wrong with it!"

His face had brightened. "I didn't intraduce myself," he said. "I'm Manley Pointer from out in the country around Willohobie, not even from a place, just from near a place."

"You wait a minute," she said. "I have to see about my dinner." She went out to the kitchen and found Joy standing near the door where she had been listening.

"Get rid of the salt of the earth," she said, "and let's eat."

Mrs. Hopewell gave her a pained look and turned the heat down under the vegetables. "*I* can't be rude to anybody," she murmured and went back into the parlor.

He had opened the suitcase and was sitting with a Bible on each knee.

"You might as well put those up," she told him. "I don't want one."

"I appreciate your honesty," he said. "You don't see any more real honest people unless you go way out in the country."

"I know," she said, "real genuine folks!" Through the crack in the door she heard a groan.

"I guess a lot of boys come telling you they're working their way through college," he said, "but I'm not going to tell you that. Somehow," he said, "I don't want to go to college. I want to devote my life to Chrustian service. See," he said, lowering his voice, "I got this heart condition. I may not live long. When you know it's something wrong with you and you may not live long, well then, lady . . ." He paused, with his mouth open, and stared at her.

He and Joy had the same condition! She knew that her eyes were filling with tears but she collected herself quickly and murmured, "Won't you stay for dinner? We'd love to have you!" and was sorry the instant she heard herself say it.

"Yes mam," he said in an abashed voice, "I would sher love to do that!"

Joy had given him one look on being introduced to him and then throughout the meal had not glanced at him again. He had addressed several remarks to her, which she had pretended not to hear. Mrs. Hopewell could not understand deliberate rudeness, although she lived with it, and she felt she had always to overflow with hospitality to make up for Joy's lack of courtesy. She urged him to talk about himself and he did. He said he was the seventh child of twelve and that his father had been crushed under a tree when he himself was eight year old. He had been crushed very badly, in fact, almost cut in two and was practically not recognizable. His mother had got along the best she could by hard working and she had always seen that her children went to Sunday School and that they read the Bible every evening. He was now nineteen year old and he had been selling Bibles for four months. In that time he had sold seventy-seven Bibles and had the promise of two more sales. He wanted to become a missionary because he thought that was the way you could do most for people. "He who losest his life shall find it," he said simply and he was so sincere, so genuine and earnest that Mrs. Hopewell would not for the world have smiled. He prevented his peas from sliding onto the table by blocking them with a piece of bread which he later cleaned his plate with. She could see Joy observing sidewise how he handled his knife and fork and she saw too that every few minutes, the boy would dart a keen appraising glance at the girl as if he were trying to attract her attention.

After dinner Joy cleared the dishes off the table and disappeared and

Mrs. Hopewell was left to talk with him. He told her again about his childhood and his father's accident and about various things that had happened to him. Every five minutes or so she would stifle a yawn. He sat for two hours until finally she told him she must go because she had an appointment in town. He packed his Bibles and thanked her and prepared to leave, but in the doorway he stopped and wrung her hand and said that not on any of his trips had he met a lady as nice as her and he asked if he could come again. She had said she would always be happy to see him.

Joy had been standing in the road, apparently looking at something in the distance, when he came down the steps toward her, bent to the side with his heavy valise. He stopped where she was standing and confronted her directly. Mrs. Hopewell could not hear what he said but she trembled to think what Joy would say to him. She could see that after a minute Joy said something and that then the boy began to speak again, making an excited gesture with his free hand. After a minute Joy said something else at which the boy began to speak once more. Then to her amazement, Mrs. Hopewell saw the two of them walk off together, toward the gate. Joy had walked all the way to the gate with him and Mrs. Hopewell could not imagine what they had said to each other, and she had not yet dared to ask.

Mrs. Freeman was insisting upon her attention. She had moved from the refrigerator to the heater so that Mrs. Hopewell had to turn and face her in order to seem to be listening. "Glynese gone out with Harvey Hill again last night," she said. "She had this sty."

"Hill," Mrs. Hopewell said absently, "is that the one who works in the garage?"

"Nome, he's the one that goes to chiropracter school," Mrs. Freeman said. "She had this sty. Been had it two days. So she says when he brought her in the other night he says, 'Lemme get rid of that sty for you,' and she says, 'How?' and he says, 'You just lay yourself down acrost the seat of that car and I'll show you.' So she done it and he popped her neck. Kept on a-popping it several times until she made him quit. This morning," Mrs. Freeman said, "she ain't got no sty. She ain't got no traces of a sty."

"I never heard of that before," Mrs. Hopewell said.

"He ast her to marry him before the Ordinary," Mrs. Freeman went on, "and she told him she wasn't going to be married in no *office*."

"Well, Glynese is a fine girl," Mrs. Hopewell said. "Glynese and Carramae are both fine girls."

"Carramae said when her and Lyman was married Lyman said it sure felt sacred to him. She said he said he wouldn't take five hundred dollars for being married by a preacher."

"How much would he take?" the girl asked from the stove.

"He said he wouldn't take five hundred dollars," Mrs. Freeman repeated.

"Well we all have work to do," Mrs. Hopewell said.

"Lyman said it just felt more sacred to him," Mrs. Freeman said. "The doctor wants Carramae to eat prunes. Says instead of medicine. Says them cramps is coming from pressure. You know where I think it is?"

"She'll be better in a few weeks," Mrs. Hopewell said.

"In the tube," Mrs. Freeman said. "Else she wouldn't be as sick as she is."

Hulga had cracked her two eggs into a saucer and was bringing them to the table along with a cup of coffee that she had filled too full. She sat down carefully and began to eat, meaning to keep Mrs. Freeman there by questions if for any reason she showed an inclination to leave. She could perceive her mother's eye on her. The first roundabout question would be about the Bible salesman and she did not wish to bring it on. "How did he pop her neck?" she asked.

Mrs. Freeman went into a description of how he had popped her neck. She said he owned a '55 Mercury but that Glynese said she would rather marry a man with only a '36 Plymouth who would be married by a preacher. The girl asked what if he had a '32 Plymouth and Mrs. Freeman said what Glynese had said was a '36 Plymouth.

Mrs. Hopewell said there were not many girls with Glynese's common sense. She said what she admired in those girls was their common sense. She said that reminded her that they had had a nice visitor yesterday, a young man selling Bibles. "Lord," she said, "he bored me to death but he was so sincere and genuine I couldn't be rude to him. He was just good country people, you know," she said, "—just the salt of the earth."

"I seen him walk up," Mrs. Freeman said, "and then later—I seen him walk off," and Hulga could feel the slight shift in her voice, the slight insinuation, that he had not walked off alone, had he? Her face remained expressionless but the color rose into her neck and she seemed to swallow it down with the next spoonful of egg. Mrs. Freeman was looking at her as if they had a secret together.

"Well, it takes all kinds of people to make the world go 'round," Mrs. Hopewell said. "It's very good we aren't all alike."

"Some people are more alike than others," Mrs. Freeman said.

Hulga got up and stumped, with about twice the noise that was necessary, into her room and locked the door. She was to meet the Bible salesman at ten o'clock at the gate. She had thought about it half the night. She had started thinking of it as a great joke and then she had begun to see profound implications in it. She had lain in bed imagining dialogues for them that were insane on the surface but that reached below to depths that no Bible salesman would be aware of. Their conversation yesterday had been of this kind.

He had stopped in front of her and had simply stood there. His face was bony and sweaty and bright, with a little pointed nose in the center of it, and his look was different from what it had been at the dinner table. He was gazing at her with open curiosity, with fascination, like a child watching a new fantastic animal at the zoo, and he was breathing as if he had run a great distance to reach her. His gaze seemed somehow familiar but she could not think where she had been regarded with it before. For almost a minute he didn't say anything. Then on what seemed an insuck of breath, he whispered, "You ever ate a chicken that was two days old?"

The girl looked at him stonily. He might have just put this question up for consideration at the meeting of a philosophical association. "Yes," she presently replied as if she had considered it from all angles.

"It must have been mighty small!" he said triumphantly and shook all over with little nervous giggles, getting very red in the face, and subsiding finally into his gaze of complete admiration, while the girl's expression remained exactly the same.

"How old are you?" he asked softly.

She waited some time before she answered. Then in a flat voice she said, "Seventeen."

His smiles came in succession like waves breaking on the surface of a little lake. "I see you got a wooden leg," he said. "I think you're real brave. I think you're real sweet."

The girl stood blank and solid and silent.

"Walk to the gate with me," he said. "You're a brave sweet little thing and I liked you the minute I seen you walk in the door."

Hulga began to move forward.

"What's your name?" he asked, smiling down on the top of her head.

"Hulga," she said.

"Hulga," he murmured, "Hulga. Hulga. I never heard of anybody name Hulga before. You're shy, aren't you, Hulga?" he asked.

She nodded, watching his large red hand on the handle of the giant valise.

"I like girls that wear glasses," he said. "I think a lot. I'm not like these people that a serious thought don't ever enter their heads. It's because I may die."

"I may die too," she said suddenly and looked up at him. His eyes were very small and brown, glittering feverishly.

"Listen," he said, "don't you think some people was meant to meet on account of what all they got in common and all? Like they both think serious thoughts and all?" He shifted the valise to his other hand so that the hand nearest her was free. He caught hold of her elbow and shook it a little. "I don't work on Saturday," he said. "I like to walk in the woods and see what Mother Nature is wearing. O'er the hills and far away. Picnics and things. Couldn't we go on a pic-nic tomorrow? Say yes, Hulga," he said and gave her a dying look as if he felt his insides about to drop out of him. He had even seemed to sway slightly toward her.

During the night she had imagined that she seduced him. She imagined that the two of them walked on the place until they came to the storage barn beyond the two back fields and there, she imagined, that things came to such a pass that she very easily seduced him and that then, of course, she had to reckon with his remorse. True genius can get an idea across even to an inferior mind. She imagined that she took his remorse in hand and changed it into a deeper understanding of life. She took all his shame away and turned it into something useful.

She set off for the gate at exactly ten o'clock, escaping without drawing Mrs. Hopewell's attention. She didn't take anything to eat, forgetting that food is usually taken on a picnic. She wore a pair of slacks and a dirty white shirt, and as an afterthought, she had put some Vapex on the collar of it since she did not own any perfume. When she reached the gate no one was there.

She looked up and down the empty highway and had the furious feeling that she had been tricked, that he had only meant to make her walk to the gate after the idea of him. Then suddenly he stood up, very tall, from behind a bush on the opposite embankment. Smiling, he lifted his hat which was new and wide-brimmed. He had not worn it yesterday and she wondered if he had bought it for the occasion. It was toast-colored with a red and white band around it and was slightly too large for him. He stepped from behind the bush still carrying the black valise. He had on the same suit and the same yellow socks sucked down in his shoes from walking. He crossed the highway and said, "I knew you'd come!"

The girl wondered acidly how he had known this. She pointed to the valise and asked, "Why did you bring your Bibles?"

He took her elbow, smiling down on her as if he could not stop. "You can never tell when you'll need the word of God, Hulga," he said. She had a moment in which she doubted that this was actually happening and then they began to climb the embankment. They went down into the pasture toward the woods. The boy walked lightly by her side, bouncing on his toes. The valise did not seem to be heavy today; he even swung it. They crossed half the pasture without saying anything and then, putting his hand easily on the small of her back, he asked softly, "Where does your wooden leg join on?"

She turned an angry red and glared at him and for an instant the boy looked abashed. "I didn't mean you no harm," he said. "I only meant you're so brave and all. I guess God takes care of you."

"No," she said, looking forward and walking fast, "I don't even believe in God."

At this he stopped and whistled. "No!" he exclaimed as if he were too astonished to say anything else.

She walked on and in a second he was bouncing at her side, fanning with his hat. "That's very unusual for a girl," he remarked, watching her out of the corner of his eye. When they reached the edge of the wood, he put his hand on her back again and drew her against him without a word and kissed her heavily.

The kiss, which had more pressure than feeling behind it, produced that extra surge of adrenalin in the girl that enables one to carry a packed trunk out of a burning house, but in her, the power went at once to the brain. Even before he released her, her mind, clear and detached and ironic anyway, was regarding him from a great distance, with amusement but with pity. She had never been kissed before and she was pleased to discover that it was an unexceptional experience and all a matter of the mind's control. Some people might enjoy drain water if they were told it was vodka. When the boy, looking expectant but uncertain, pushed her gently away, she turned and walked on, saying nothing as if such business, for her, were common enough.

He came along panting at her side, trying to help her when he saw a root that she might trip over. He caught and held back the long swaying blades of thorn vine until she had passed beyond them. She led the way and he came breathing heavily behind her. Then they came out on a sunlit hillside, sloping softly into another one a little smaller. Beyond, they could see the rusted top of the old barn where the extra hay was stored.

The hill was sprinkled with small pink weeds. "Then you ain't saved?" he asked suddenly, stopping.

The girl smiled. It was the first time she had smiled at him at all. "In my economy," she said, "I'm saved and you are damned but I told you I didn't believe in God."

Nothing seemed to destroy the boy's look of admiration. He gazed at her now as if the fantastic animal at the zoo had put its paw through the bars and giving him a loving poke. She thought he looked as if he wanted to kiss her again and she walked on before he had the chance.

"Ain't there somewheres we can sit down sometime?" he murmured, his voice softening toward the end of the sentence.

"In that barn," she said.

They made for it rapidly as if it might slide away like a train. It was a large two-story barn, cool and dark inside. The boy pointed up the ladder that led into the loft and said, "It's too bad we can't go up there."

"Why can't we?" she asked.

"Yer leg," he said reverently.

The girl gave him a contemptuous look and putting both hands on the ladder, she climbed it while he stood below, apparently awestruck. She pulled herself expertly through the opening and then looked down at him and said, "Well, come on if you're coming," and he began to climb the ladder, awkwardly bringing the suitcase with him.

"We won't need the Bible," she observed.

"You never can tell," he said, panting. After he had got into the loft, he was a few seconds catching his breath. She had sat down on a pile of straw. A wide sheath of sunlight, filled with dust particles, slanted over her. She lay back against a bale, her face turned away, looking out the front opening of the barn where hay was thrown from a wagon into the loft. The two pink-speckled hillsides lay back against a dark ridge of woods. The sky was cloudless and cold blue. The boy dropped down by her side and put one arm under her and the other over her and began methodically kissing her face, making little noises like a fish. He did not remove his hat but it was pushed far enough back not to interfere. When her glasses got in his way, he took them off of her and slipped them into his pocket.

The girl as first did not return any of the kisses but presently she began to and after she had put several on his cheek, she reached his lips and remained there, kissing him again and again as if she were trying to draw all the breath out of him. His breath was clear and sweet like a child's and the kisses were sticky like a child's. He mumbled about loving her and about knowing when he first seen her that he loved her, but the mumbling was like the sleepy fretting of a child being put to sleep by his mother. Her mind, throughout this, never stopped or lost itself for a second to her feelings. "You ain't said you loved me none," he whispered finally, pulling back from her. "You got to say that."

She looked away from him off into the hollow sky and then down at a black ridge and then down farther into what appeared to be two green swelling lakes. She didn't realize he had taken her glasses but this landscape could not seem exceptional to her for she seldom paid any close attention to her surroundings.

"You got to say it," he repeated. "You got to say you love me."

She was always careful how she committed herself. "In a sense," she began, "if you use the word loosely, you might say that. But it's not a word I use. I don't have illusions. I'm one of those people who see *through* to nothing."

The boy was frowning. "You got to say it. I said it and you got to say it," he said.

The girl looked at him almost tenderly. "You poor baby," she murmured. "It's just as well you don't understand," and she pulled him by the neck, face-down, against her. "We are all damned," she said, "but some of us have taken off our blindfolds and see that there's nothing to see. It's a kind of salvation."

The boy's astonished eyes looked blankly through the ends of her hair. "Okay," he almost whined, "but do you love me or don'tcher?"

"Yes," she said and added, "in a sense. But I must tell you something. There mustn't be anything dishonest between us." She lifted his head and looked him in the eye. "I am thirty years old," she said. "I have a number of degrees."

The boy's look was irritated but dogged. "I don't care," he said. "I don't care a thing about what all you done. I just want to know if you love me or don'tcher?" and he caught her to him and wildly planted her face with kisses until she said, "Yes, yes."

"Okay then," he said, letting her go. "Prove it."

She smiled, looking dreamily out on the shifty landscape. She had seduced him without even making up her mind to try. "How?" she asked, feeling that he should be delayed a little.

He leaned over and put his lips to her ear. "Show me where your wooden leg joins on," he whispered.

The girl uttered a sharp little cry and her face instantly drained of color. The obscenity of the suggestion was not what shocked her. As a child she had sometimes been subject to feelings of shame but education had removed the last traces of that as a good surgeon scrapes for cancer; she would no more have felt it over what he was asking than she would have believed in his Bible. But she was as sensitive about the artificial leg as a peacock about his tail. No one ever touched it but her. She took care of it as someone else would his soul, in private and almost with her own eyes turned away. "No," she said.

"I known it," he muttered, sitting up. "You're just playing me for a sucker."

"Oh no no!" she cried. "It joins on at the knee. Only at the knee. Why do you want to see it?"

The boy gave her a long penetrating look. "Because," he said, "it's what makes you different. You ain't like anybody else."

She sat staring at him. There was nothing about her face or her round freezing-blue eyes to indicate that this had moved her; but she felt as if her heart had stopped and left her mind to pump her blood. She decided that for the first time in her life she was face to face with real innocence. This boy, with an instinct that came from beyond wisdom, had touched the truth about her. When after a minute, she said in a hoarse high voice, "All right," it was like surrendering to him completely. It was like losing her own life and finding it again, miraculously, in his.

Very gently he began to roll the slack leg up. The artificial limb, in a white sock and brown flat shoe, was bound in a heavy material like canvas and ended in an ugly jointure where it was attached to the stump. The boy's face and his voice were entirely reverent as he uncovered it and said, "Now show me how to take it off and on."

She took it off for him and put it back on again and then he took it off himself, handling it as tenderly as if it were a real one. "See!" he said with a delighted child's face. "Now I can do it myself!"

"Put it back on," she said. She was thinking that she would run away with him and that every night he would take the leg off and every morning put it back on again. "Put it back on," she said.

"Not yet," he murmured, setting it on its foot out of her reach. "Leave it off for a while. You got me instead."

She gave a little cry of alarm but he pushed her down and began to kiss her again. Without the leg she felt entirely dependent on him. Her brain seemed to have stopped thinking altogether and to be about some other function that it was not very good at. Different expressions raced back and forth over her face. Every now and then the boy, his eyes like two steel spikes, would glance behind him where the leg stood. Finally she pushed him off and said, "Put it back on me now."

"Wait," he said. He leaned the other way and pulled the valise toward him and opened it. It had a pale blue spotted lining and there were only two Bibles in it. He took one of these out and opened the cover of it. It was hollow and contained a pocket flask of whiskey, a pack of cards, and a small blue box with printing on it. He laid these out in front of her one at a time in an evenly-spaced row, like one presenting offerings at the shrine of a goddess. He put the blue box in her hand. THIS PRODUCT TO BE USED ONLY FOR THE PREVENTION OF DISEASE, she read, and dropped it. The boy was unscrewing the top of the flask. He stopped and pointed, with a smile, to the deck of cards. It was not an ordinary deck but one with an obscene picture on the back of each card. "Take a swig," he said, offering her the bottle first. He held it in front of her, but like one mesmerized, she did not move.

Her voice when she spoke had an almost pleading sound. "Aren't you," she murmured, "aren't you just good country people?"

The boy cocked his head. He looked as if he were just beginning to understand that she might be trying to insult him. "Yeah," he said, curling his lip slightly, "but it ain't held me back none. I'm as good as you any day in the week."

"Give me my leg," she said.

He pushed it farther away with his foot. "Come on now, let's begin to have us a good time," he said coaxingly. "We ain't got to know one another good yet."

"Give me my leg!" she screamed and tried to lunge for it but he pushed her down easily.

"What's the matter with you all of a sudden?" he asked, frowning as he screwed the top on the flask and put it quickly back inside the Bible. "You just a while ago said you didn't believe in nothing. I thought you was some girl!"

Her face was almost purple. "You're a Christian!" she hissed. "You're a fine Christian! You're just like them all—say one thing and do another. You're a perfect Christian you're . . ."

The boy's mouth was set angrily. "I hope you don't think," he said in a lofty indignant tone, "that I believe in that crap! I may sell Bibles but I know which end is up and I wasn't born yesterday and I know where I'm going!"

"Give me my leg!" she screeched. He jumped up so quickly that she barely saw him sweep the cards and the blue box back into the Bible and throw the Bible into the valise. She saw him grab the leg and then she saw it for an instant slanted forlornly across the inside of the suitcase with a Bible at either side of its opposite ends. He slammed the lid shut and snatched up the valise and swung it down the hole and then stepped through himself.

When all of him had passed but his head, he turned and regarded her with a look that no longer had any admiration in it. "I've gotten a lot of interesting things," he said. "One time I got a woman's glass eye this way. And you needn't to think you'll catch me because Pointer ain't really my name. I use a different name at every house I call at and don't stay nowhere long. And I'll tell you another thing, Hulga," he said, using the name as if he didn't think much of it, "you ain't so smart. I been believing in nothing ever since I was born!" and then the toast-colored hat disappeared down the hole and the girl was left, sitting on the straw in the dusty sunlight. When she turned her churning face toward the opening, she saw his blue figure struggling successfully over the green speckled lake.

Mrs. Hopewell and Mrs. Freeman, who were in the back pasture, digging up onions, saw him emerge a little later from the woods and head across the meadow toward the highway. "Why, that looks like that nice dull young man that tried to sell me a Bible yesterday," Mrs. Hopewell said, squinting. "He must have been selling them to the Negroes back in there. He was so simple," she said, "but I guess the world would be better off if we were all that simple."

Mrs. Freeman's gaze drove forward and just touched him before he disappeared under the hill. Then she returned her attention to the evil-smelling onion shoot she was lifting from the ground. "Some can't be that simple," she said. "I know I never could."

MIGUEL DE UNAMUNO

Saint Emmanuel the Good, Martyr

If with this life only in view we have had hope in Christ, we are of all men the most to be pitied. —SAINT PAUL: I COR. 15:19.

Now that the bishop of the diocese of Renada, to which this my beloved village of Valverde de Lucerna belongs, is seeking (according to rumor), to initiate the process of beatification of our Don Manuel, or more correctly, Saint Emmanuel the Good, who was parish priest here, I want to state in writing, by way of confession (although to what end only God, and not I can say), all that I can vouch for and remember of that matriarchal man who pervaded the most secret life of my soul, who was my true spiritual father, the father of my spirit, the spirit of myself, Angela Carballino.

The other, my flesh-and-blood temporal father, I scarcely knew, for he died when I was still a very young girl. I know that he came to Valverde de Lucerna from the outside world—that he was a stranger—and that he settled here when he married my mother. He had brought a number of books with him: *Don Quixote*, some plays from the classic theatre, some novels, a few histories, the *Bertoldo*, everything all mixed together. From these books (practically the only ones in the entire village), I nurtured dreams as a young girl, dreams which in turn devoured me. My good mother gave me very little account either of the words or the deeds of my father. For the words and deeds of Don Manuel, whom she worshipped, of whom she was enamored, in common with all the rest of the village—in an exquisitely chaste manner, of course—had obliterated the memory of the words and deeds of her husband; him she commended to God, with full fervor, as she said her daily rosary.

Don Emmanuel I remember as if it were yesterday, from the time when I was a girl of ten, just before I was taken to the convent school in the cathedral city of Renada. At that time Don Emmanuel, our saint, must have been about thirty-seven years old. He was tall, slender, erect; he carried himself the way our Buitre Peak carries its crest, and his eyes had all the blue depth of our lake. As he walked he commanded all eyes, and not only the eyes but the hearts of all; gazing round at us he seemed to look through our flesh as through glass and penetrate our hearts. We all of us loved him, especially the children. And the things he said to us! Not words, things! The villagers could scent the odor of sanctity, they were intoxicated with it.

It was at this time that my brother Lazarus, who was in America, from where he regularly sent us money with which we lived in decent leisure, had my mother send me to the convent school, so that my education might be completed outside the village; he suggested this move despite the fact that he had no special fondness for the nuns. "But since, as far as I know," he wrote us, "there are no lay schools there yet,—especially not for young ladies—we will have to make use of the ones that do exist. The important thing is for Angelita to receive some polish and not be forced to continue among village girls." And so I entered the convent school. At one point I even thought I would become a teacher; but pedagogy soon palled upon me.

At school I met girls from the city and I made friends with some of them. But I still kept in touch with people in our village, and I received frequent reports and sometimes a visit.

And the fame of the parish priest reached as far as the school, for he was beginning to be talked of in the cathedral city. The nuns never tired of asking me about him.

Ever since early youth I had been endowed, I don't very well know from where, with a large degree of curiosity and restlessness, due at least in part to that jumble of books which my father had collected, and these qualities were stimulated at school, especially in the course of a relationship which I developed with a girl friend, who grew excessively attached to me. At times she proposed that we enter the same convent together, swearing to an everlasting "sisterhood"—and even that we seal the oath in blood. At other times she talked to me, with eyes half closed, of sweethearts and marriage adventures. Strangely enough, I have never heard of her since, or of what became of her, despite the fact that whenever our Don Manuel was spoken of, or when my mother wrote me something about him in her letters—which happened in almost every letter—and I read it to her, this girl would exclaim, as if in rapture: "What luck, my dear, to be able to live near a saint like that, a live saint, of flesh and blood, and to be able to kiss his hand; when you go back to your village write me everything, everything, and tell me about him."

Five years passed at school, five years which now have evanesced in memory like a dream at dawn, and when I became fifteen I returned to my own Valverde de Lucerna. By now everything revolved around Don Emmanuel: Don Emmanuel, the lake and the mountain. I arrived home anxious to know him, to place myself under his protection, and hopeful he would set me on my path in life.

It was rumored that he had entered the seminary to become a priest so that he might thus look after the sons of a sister recently widowed and provide for them in place of their father; that in the seminary his keen mind and his talents had distinguished him and that he had subsequently turned down opportunities for a brilliant career in the church because he wanted to remain exclusively a part of his Valverde de Lucerna, of his remote village which lay like a brooch between the lake and the mountain reflected in it.

How he did love his people! His life consisted in salvaging wrecked marriages, in forcing unruly sons to submit to their parents, or reconciling parents to their sons, and, above all, of consoling the embittered and the weary in spirit; meanwhile he helped everyone to die well.

I recall, among other incidents, the occasion when the unfortunate daughter of old aunt Rabona returned to our town. She had been in the city and lost her virtue there; now she returned unmarried and castoff, and she brought back a little son. Don Emmanuel did not rest until he had persuaded an old sweetheart, Perote by name, to marry the poor girl and, moreover, to legitimize the little creature with his own name. Don Emmanuel told Perote:

"Come now, give this poor waif a father, for he hasn't got one except in heaven."

"But, Don Emmanuel, it's not my fault . . . !"

"Who knows, my son, who knows . . . ! And besides, it's not a question of guilt."

And today, poor Perote, inspired on that occasion to saintliness by Don Emmanuel, and now a paralytic and invalid, has for staff and consolation of his life the son he accepted as his own when the boy was not his at all.

On Midsummer's Night, the shortest night of the year, it was a local custom here (and still is) for all the old crones, and a few old men, who thought they were possessed or bewitched (hysterics they were, for the most part, or in some cases epileptics) to flock to the lake. Don Emmanuel undertook to fulfill the same function as the lake, to serve as a pool of healing, to treat his charges and even, if possible, to cure them. And such was the effect of his presence, of his gaze, and above all of his voice—the miracle of his voice!—and the infinitely sweet authority of his words, that he actually did achieve some remarkable cures. Whereupon his fame increased, drawing all the sick of the environs to our lake and our priest. And yet once when a mother came to ask for a miracle in behalf of her son, he answered her with a sad smile:

"Ah, but I don't have my bishop's permission to perform miracles."

He was particularly interested in seeing that all the villagers kept themselves clean. If he chanced upon someone with a torn garment he would send him to the church: "Go and see the sacristan, and let him mend that tear." The sacristan was a tailor, and when, on the first day of the year, everyone went to congratulate him on his saint's day—his holy patron was Our Lord Jesus Himself—it was by Don Emmanuel's wish that everyone appeared in a new shirt, and those that had none received the present of a new one from Don Emmanuel himself.

He treated everyone with the greatest kindness; if he favored anyone, it was the most unfortunate, and especially those who rebelled. There was a congenital idiot in the village, the fool Blasillo, and it was toward him that Don Emmanuel chose to show the greatest love and concern; as a consequence he succeeded in miraculously teaching him things which had appeared beyond the idiot's comprehension. The fact was that the embers of understanding feebly glowing in the idiot were kindled whenever, like a pitiable monkey, he imitated his Don Emmanuel.

The marvel of the man was his voice; a divine voice which brought one close to weeping. Whenever he officiated at Solemn High Mass and intoned the prelude, a tremor ran through the congregation and all within sound of his voice were moved to the depths of their being. The sound of his chanting, overflowing the church, went on to float over the lake and settle at the foot of the mountain. And when on Good Friday he intoned "My God, my God, my God, why hast Thou forsaken me?" a profound shudder swept through the multitude, like the lash of a northeaster across the waters of the lake. It was as if these people heard the Lord Jesus Christ himself, as if the voice sprang from the ancient crucifix, at the foot of which generations of mothers had offered up their sorrows. And it happened that on one occasion his mother heard him and was unable to contain herself, and cried out to him right in the church, "My son!," calling her child. And the entire congregation was visibly affected. It was as if the mother's cry had issued from the half-open lips of the Mater Dolorosa—her heart transfixed by seven swords—which stood on one of the chapels of the nave. Afterwards, the fool Blasillo went about piteously repeating, as if he were an echo, "My God, my God, my God, why hast Thou forsaken me?" with such effect that everyone who heard him was moved to tears, to the great satisfaction of the fool, who prided himself on this triumph of imitation.

The priest's effect on people was such that no one ever dared to tell him a lie, and everyone confessed themselves to him without need of a confessional. So true was this that on one occasion, when a revolting crime had been committed in a neighboring village, the judge—a dull fellow who badly misunderstood Don Emmanuel—called on the priest and said:

"Let us see, Don Manuel, if you can get this bandit to admit the truth."

"So that afterwards you may punish him?" asked the saintly man.
"No, Judge, no; I will not extract from any man a truth which could be the death of him. That is a matter between him and his God. . . . Human justice is none of my affair. 'Judge not that ye be not judged,' said our Lord."

"But the fact is, Father, that I, a Judge . . ."

"I understand. You, Judge, must render unto Caesar that which is Caesar's, while I shall render unto God that which is God's."

And, as Don Emmanuel departed, he gazed at the suspected criminal and said:

"Make sure, only, that God forgives you, for that is all that matters."

Everyone went to Mass in the village, even if it were only to hear him and see him at the altar, where he appeared to be transfigured, his countenance lit from within. He introduced one holy practice to the popular cult; it consisted in assembling the whole town inside the church, men and women, ancients and youths, some thousand persons; there we recited the Creed, in unison, so that it sounded like a single voice: "I believe in God, the Almighty Father, Creator of heaven and earth . . ." and all the rest. It was not a chorus, but a single voice, a simple united voice, all the voices based on one on which they formed a kind of mountain, whose peak, lost at times in the clouds, was Don Emmanuel. As we reached the section "I believe in the resurrection of the flesh and life everlasting," the voice of Don Emmanuel was submerged, drowned in the voice of the populace as in a lake. In truth, he was silent. And I could hear the bells of that city which is said hereabouts to be at the bottom of the lake—bells which are also said to be audible on Midsummer's Night—the bells of the city which is submerged in the spiritual lake of our populace; I was hearing the voice of our dead, resurrected in us by the communion of saints. Later, when I had learned the secret of our saint, I understood that it was as if a caravan crossing the desert lost its leader as they approached the goal of their trek, whereupon his people lifted him on their shoulders to bring his lifeless body into the promised land.

When it came to dying themselves, most of the villagers refused to die unless they were holding on to Don Emmanuel's hand, as if to an anchor chain.

In his sermons he never inveighed against unbelievers, Masons, liberals or heretics. What for, when there were none in the village? Nor did it occur to him to speak against the wickedness of the press. On the other hand, one of his most frequent themes was gossip, against which he lashed out.

"Envy," he liked to repeat, "envy is nurtured by those who prefer to think they are envied, and most persecutions are the result of a persecution complex rather than of an impulse to persecute."

"But Don Emmanuel, just listen to what that fellow was trying to tell me . . ."

"We should concern ourselves less with what people are trying to tell us than with what they tell us without trying . . ."

His life was active rather than contemplative, and he constantly fled from idleness, even from leisure. Whenever he heard it said that idleness was the mother of all the vices, he added: "And also of the greatest vice of them all, which is to think idly." Once I asked him what he meant and he answered: "Thinking idly is thinking as a substitute for doing, or thinking too much about what is already done instead of about what must be done. What's done is done and over with, and one must go on to something else, for there is nothing worse than remorse without possible relief." Action! Action! Even in those early days I had already begun to realize that Don Emmanuel fled from being left to think in solitude, and I guessed that some obsession haunted him.

And so it was that he was always occupied, sometimes even occupied in searching for occupations. He wrote very little on his own, so that he scarcely left us anything in writing, even notes; on the other hand, he acted as scrivener for everyone else, especially mothers, for whom he composed letters to their absent sons.

He also worked with his hands, pitching in to help with some of the village tasks. At threshing time he reported to the threshing floor to flair and winnow, meanwhile teaching and entertaining the workers by turn. Sometimes he took the place of a worker who had fallen sick. One day in the dead of winter he came upon a child, shivering with the bitter cold. The child's father had sent him into the woods to bring back a strayed calf.

"Listen," he said to the child, "you go home and get warm, and tell your father that I am bringing back the calf." On the way back with the animal he ran into the father, who had come out to meet him, thoroughly ashamed of himself.

In winter he chopped wood for the poor. When a certain magnificent walnut tree died—"that matriarchal walnut," he called it, a tree under whose shade he had played as a boy and whose fruit he had eaten for so many years—he asked for the trunk, carried it to his house and, after he had cut six planks from it, which he put away at the foot of his bed, he made firewood of the rest to warm the poor. He also was in the habit of making handballs for the boys and a goodly number of toys for the younger children.

Often he used to accompany the doctor on his rounds, adding his presence and prestige to the doctor's prescriptions. Most of all he was interested in maternity cases and the care of children; it was his opinion that the old wives' sayings "from the cradle to heaven" and the other one about "little angels belong in heaven" were nothing short of blasphemy.[1] The death of a child moved him deeply.

"A child stillborn," I once heard him say, "or one who dies soon after birth, is the most terrible of mysteries to me. It's as if it were a suicide. Or as if the child were crucified."

And once, when a man had taken his own life and the father of the suicide, an outsider, asked Don Emmanuel if his son could be buried in consecrated ground, the priest answered:

"Most certainly, for at the last moment, in the very last throes, he must certainly have repented. There is no doubt of it whatsoever in my mind."

From time to time he would visit the local school to help the teacher, to teach alongside him—and not only the catechism. The simple truth was that he fled relentlessly from idleness and from solitude. He went so far in this desire of his to mingle with the villagers, especially the youth and the children, that he even attended the village dances. And more than once he played the drum to keep time for the young men and women dancing; this kind of activity, which in another priest would have seemed like a grotesque mockery of his calling, in him somehow took on the appearance of a holy and religious exercise. When the Angelus would ring out, he would put down the drum and sticks, take off his hat (all the others doing the same) and pray: "The angel of the Lord declared unto Mary: Hail Mary . . ." And afterwards: "Now, let us rest until tomorrow."

"First of all," he would say, "the village must be happy; everyone must be happy to be alive. To be satisfied with life is of first importance. No one should want to die until it is God's will."

"I want to die now," a recently widowed woman once told him, "I want to be with my husband . . ."

"And why now?" he asked. "Stay here and pray God for his soul."

One of his well-loved remarks was made at a wedding: "Ah, if I could only change all the water in our lake into wine, into a dear little wine

---

[1] "Teta y gloria" and "angelitos al cielo."

which, no matter how much of it one drank, would always make one joyful without intoxicating . . . or, if intoxicating, would make one joyfully drunk."

Once upon a time a band of poor acrobats came through the village. The leader—who arrived on the scene with a gravely ill and pregnant wife and three sons to help him—played the clown. While he was in the village square making all the children, and even some of the adults, laugh with glee, his wife suddenly fell desperately ill and had to leave; she went off accompanied by a look of anguish from the clown and a howl of laughter from the children. Don Emmanuel hurried after, and, a little later, in a corner of the inn's stable, he helped her give up her soul in a state of grace. When the performance was over and the villagers and the clown learned of the tragedy, they came to the inn, and there the poor bereaved clown, in a voice choked with tears, told Don Emmanuel, as he took his hand and kissed it: "They are quite right, Father, when they say you are a saint." Don Emmanuel took the clown's hand in his and replied before everyone:

"It's you who are the saint, good clown. I watched you at your work and understand that you do it not only to provide bread for your children, but also to give joy to the children of others. And I tell you now that your wife, the mother of your children, whom I sent to God while you worked to give joy, is at rest in the Lord, and that you will join her there, and that the angels, whom you will make laugh with happiness in heaven, will reward you with their laughter."

And everyone present wept, children and elders alike, as much from sorrow as from a mysterious joy in which all sorrow was drowned. Later, recalling that solemn hour, I have come to realize that the imperturbable joyousness of Don Emmanuel was merely the temporal, earthly form of an infinite, eternal sadness which the priest concealed from the eyes and ears of the world with heroic saintliness.

His constant activity, his ceaseless intervention in the tasks and diversions of everyone, had the appearance, in short, of a flight from himself, of a flight from solitude. He confirmed this suspicion: "I have a fear of solitude," he would say. And still, from time to time he would go off by himself, along the shores of the lake, to the ruins of the abbey where the souls of pious Cistercians seem still to repose, although history has long since buried them in oblivion. There, the cell of the so-called Father-Captain can still be found, and it is said that the drops of blood spattered on the walls as he flagellated himself can still be seen. What thoughts occupied our Don Emmanuel as he walked there? I remember a conversation we held once in which I asked him, as he was speaking of the abbey, why it had never occurred to him to enter a monastery, and he answered me:

"It is not at all because of the fact that my sister is a widow and I have her children and herself to support—for God looks after the poor—but rather because I simply was not born to be a hermit, an anchorite; the solitude would crush my soul; and, as far as a monastery is concerned, my monastery is Valverde de Lucerna. I was not meant to live alone, or die alone. I was meant to live for my village, and die for it too. How should I save my soul if I were not to save the soul of my village as well?"

"But there have been saints who were hermits, solitaries . . ." I said.

"Yes, the Lord gave them the grace of solitude which He has denied me, and I must resign myself. I must not throw away my village to win my soul. God made me that way. I would not be able to resist the temptations of the desert. I would not be able, alone, to carry the cross of birth . . ."

I have summoned up all these recollections, from which my faith was fed, in order to portray our Don Emmanuel as he was when I, a young girl of sixteen, returned from the convent of Renada to our "monastery of Valverde de Lucerna," once more to kneel at the feet of our "abbot."

"Well, here is the daughter of Simona," he said as soon as he saw me, "made into a young woman, and knowing French, and how to play the piano, and embroider, and heaven knows what else besides! Now you must get ready to give us a family. And your brother Lazarus; when does he return? Is he still in the New World?"

"Yes, Father, he is still in the New World."

"The New World! And we in the Old. Well then, when you write him, tell him for me, on behalf of the parish priest, that I should like to know when he is returning from the New World to the Old, to bring us the latest from over there. And tell him that he will find the lake and the mountain as he left them."

When I first went to him for confession, I became so confused that I could not enunciate a word. I recited the "Forgive me, Father, for I have sinned," in a stammer, almost a sob. And he, observing this, said:

"Good heavens, my dear, what are you afraid of, or of whom are you afraid? Certainly you're not trembling now under the weight of your sins, nor in fear of God. No, you're trembling because of me, isn't that so?"

At this point I burst into tears.

"What have they been telling you about me? What fairy tales? Was it your mother, perhaps? Come, come, please be calm, you must imagine you are talking to your brother . . ."

At this I plucked up courage and began to tell him of my anxieties, doubts and sorrows.

"Bah! Where did you read all this, Miss Intellectual. All this is literary nonsense. Don't succumb to everything you read just yet, not even to Saint Theresa. If you need to amuse yourself, read the *Bertoldo*, as your father before you did."

I came away from my first confession to that holy man deeply consoled. The initial fear—simple fright more than respect—with which I had approached him, turned into a profound pity. I was at that time a very young woman, almost a girl still; and yet, I was beginning to be a woman, in my innermost being I felt the juice and stirrings of maternity, and when I found myself in the confessional at the side of the saintly priest, I sensed a kind of unspoken confession on his part in the soft murmur of his voice. And I remembered how when he had intoned in the church the words of Jesus Christ: "My God, my God, why hast Thou forsaken me?" his own mother had cried out in the congregation: "My son!"; and I could hear the cry that had rent the silence of the temple. And I went to him again for confession—and to comfort him.

Another time in the confessional I told him of a doubt which assailed me, and he responded:

"As to that, you know what the catechism says. Don't question me about it, for I am ignorant; in Holy Mother Church there are learned doctors of theology who will know how to answer you."

"But you are the learned doctor here."

"Me? A learned doctor? Not even in thought! I, my little doctress, am only a poor country priest. And those questions, . . . do you know who whispers them into your ear? Well . . . . the Devil does!"

Then, making bold, I asked him point-blank:

"And suppose he were to whisper these questions to you?"

"Who? To me? The Devil? No, we don't even know each other, my daughter, we haven't met at all."

"But if he did whisper them? . . ."

"I wouldn't pay any attention. And that's enough of that; let's get on, for there are some people, really sick people, waiting for me."

I went away thinking, I don't know why, that our Don Emmanuel, so famous for curing the bedeviled, didn't really even believe in the Devil. As I started home, I ran into the fool Blasillo, who had probably been hovering around outside; as soon as he saw me, and by way of treating me to a display of his virtuosity, he began the business of repeating— and in what a manner!—"My God, my God, why hast Thou forsaken me?" I arrived home utterly saddened and locked myself in my room to cry, until finally my mother arrived.

"With all these confessions, Angelita, you will end by going off to a nunnery."

"Don't worry, Mother," I answered her. "I have plenty to do here, in the village, and it will be my only convent."

"Until you marry."

"I don't intend to," I rejoined.

The next time I saw Don Emmanuel I asked him, looking straight into his eyes:

"Is there really a Hell, Don Emmanuel?"

And he, without altering his expression, answered:

"For you, my daughter, no."

"For others, then?"

"Does it matter to you, if you are not to go there?"

"It matters for the others, in any case. Is there a Hell?"

"Believe in Heaven, the Heaven we can see. Look at it there"—and he pointed to the heavens above the mountain, and then down into the lake, to the reflection.

"But we are supposed to believe in Hell as well as in Heaven," I said.

"That's true. We must believe everything believed and taught by our Holy Mother Church, Catholic, Apostolic, and Roman. And now, that will do!"

I thought I read a deep unknown sadness in his eyes, eyes which were as blue as the waters of the lake.

Those years passed as if in a dream. Within me, a reflected image of Don Emmanuel was unconsciously taking form. He was an ordinary enough man in many ways, of such daily use as the daily bread we asked for in our Paternoster. I helped him whenever I could with his tasks, visiting the sick, his sick, the girls at school, and helping, too, with the church linen and the vestments; I served in the role, as he said, of his deaconess. Once I was invited to the city for a few days by a school friend, but I had to hurry home, for the city stifled me—something was missing, I was thirsty for a sight of the waters of the lake, hungry for a sight of the peaks of the mountain; and even more, I missed my Don Emmanuel, as if his absence called to me, as if he were endangered by my being so far away, as if he were in need of me. I began to feel a kind of maternal affection for my spiritual father; I longed to help him bear the cross of birth.

My twenty-fourth birthday was approaching when my brother Lazarus came back from America with the small fortune he had saved up. He came back to Valverde de Lucerna with the intention of taking me and my mother to live in a city, perhaps even Madrid.

"In the country," he said, "in these villages, a person becomes stupefied, brutalized and spiritually impoverished." And he added: "Civilization is the very opposite of everything countryfied. The idiocy of village life! No, that's not for us; I didn't have you sent away to school so that later you might spoil here, among these ignorant peasants."

I said nothing, though I was disposed to resist emigration. But our mother, already past sixty, took a firm stand from the start: "Change pastures at my age?" she demanded at once. A little later she made it quite clear that she could not live out of sight of her lake, her mountain, and, above all, of her Don Emmanuel.

"The two of you are like those cats that get attached to houses," my brother muttered.

When he realized the complete sway exercised over the entire village—especially over my mother and myself—by the saintly priest, my brother began to resent him. He saw in this situation an example of the obscurantist theocracy which, according to him, smothered Spain. And he commenced to spout the old anti-clerical commonplaces, to which he added anti-religious and "progressive" propaganda brought back from the New World.

"In the Spain of sloth and flabby useless men, the priests manipulate the women, and the women manipulate the men. Not to mention the idiocy of the country, and this feudal backwater!"

"Feudal," to him, meant something frightful. "Feudal" and "medieval" were the epithets he employed to condemn something completely.

The failure of his diatribes to move us and their total lack of effect upon the village—where they were listened to with respectful indifference—disconcerted him no end. "The man does not exist who could move these clods." But, he soon began to understand—for he was an intelligent man, and therefore a good one—the kind of influence exercised over the village by Don Emmanuel, and he came to appreciate the effect of the priest's work in the village.

"This priest is not like the others," he announced. "He is, in fact, a saint."

"How do you know what the others are like," I asked. To which he answered:

"I can imagine."

In any case, he did not set foot inside the church nor did he miss an opportunity to parade his incredulity—though he always exempted Don Emmanuel from his scorning accusations. In the village, an unconscious expectancy began to build up, the anticipation of a kind of duel between my brother Lazarus and Don Emmanuel—in short, it was expected that Don Emmanuel would convert my brother. No one doubted but that in the end the priest would bring him into the fold. On his side, Lazarus was eager (he told me so himself, later) to go and hear Don Emmanuel, to see and hear him in the church, to get to know him and to talk with him, so that he might learn the secret of his spiritual hold over our souls. And he let himself be coaxed to this end, so that finally— "out of curiosity," as he said—he went to hear the preacher.

"Now, this is something else again," he told me as soon as he came from hearing Don Emmanuel for the first time. "He's not like the others; still, he doesn't fool me, he's too intelligent to believe everything he must teach."

"You mean you think he's a hypocrite?"

"A hypocrite . . . no! But he has a job by which he must live."

As for me, my brother undertook to see that I read the books he brought me, and others which he urged me to buy.

"So your brother Lazarus wants you to read," Don Emmanuel queried. "Well, read, my daughter, read and make him happy by doing so. I know you will read only worthy books. Read even if only novels; they are as good as the books which deal with so-called 'reality.' You are better off reading than concerning yourself with village gossip and old wives' tales. Above all, though, you will do well to read devotional books which will bring you contentment in life, a quiet, gentle contentment, and peace."

And he, did he enjoy such contentment?

It was about this time that our mother fell mortally sick and died. In her last days her one wish was that Don Emmanuel should convert Lazarus, whom she expected to see again in heaven, in some little corner among the stars from where they could see the lake and the mountain of Valverde de Lucerna. She felt she was going there now, to see God.

"You are not going anywhere," Don Emmanuel would tell her; "you are staying right here. Your body will remain here, in this land, and your soul also, in this house, watching and listening to your children though they do not see or hear you."

"But, Father," she said, "I am going to see God."

"God, my daughter, is all around us, and you will see Him from here, right from here. And all of us in Him, and He in all of us."

"God bless you," I whispered to him.

"The peace in which your mother dies will be her eternal life," he told me.

And, turning to my brother Lazarus: "Her heaven is to go on seeing you, and it is at this moment that she must be saved. Tell her you will pray for her."

"But—"

"But what? . . . Tell her you will pray for her, to whom you owe your life. And I know that once you promise her, you *will* pray, and I know that once you pray . . ."

My brother, his eyes filled with tears, drew near our dying mother and gave her his solemn promise to pray for her.

"And I, in heaven, will pray for you, for all of you," my mother responded. And then, kissing the crucifix and fixing her eyes on Don Emmanuel, she gave up her soul to God.

"Into Thy hands I commend my spirit," prayed the priest.

My brother and I stayed on in the house alone. What had happened at the time of my mother's death had established a bond between Lazarus and Don Emmanuel. The latter seemed even to neglect some of his charges, his patients and his other needy to look after my brother. In the afternoons, they would go for a stroll together, walking along the lake or toward the ruins, overgrown with ivy, of the old Cistercian abbey.

"He's an extraordinary man," Lazarus told me. "You know the story they tell of how there is a city at the bottom of the lake, submerged beneath the water, and that on Midsummer's Night at midnight the sound of its church bells can be heard . . ."

"Yes, a city 'feudal and medieval' . . ."

"And I believe," he went on, "that at the bottom of Don Emmanuel's soul there is a city, submerged and inundated, and that sometimes the sound of its bells can be heard . . ."

"Yes . . . And this city submerged in Don Emmanuel's soul, and perhaps—why not?—in yours as well, is certainly the cemetery of the souls of our ancestors, the ancestors of our Valverde de Lucerna . . . 'feudal and medieval'!"

In the end, my brother began going to Mass. He went regularly to hear Don Emmanuel. When it became known that he was prepared to comply with his annual duty of receiving Communion, that he would receive when the others received, an intimate joy ran through the town, which felt that by this act he was restored to his people. The rejoicing was of such nature, moreover, so openhanded and honest, that Lazarus never did feel that he had been "vanquished" or "overcome."

The day of his Communion arrived; of Communion before the entire village, with the entire village. When it came time for my brother's turn, I saw Don Emmanuel—white as January snow on the mountain, and moving like the surface of the lake when it is stirred by the northeast wind—come up to him with the holy wafer in his hand, which trembled violently as it reached out to Lazarus's mouth; at that moment the priest had an instant of faintness and the wafer dropped to the ground. My brother himself recovered it and placed it in his mouth. The people saw the tears on Don Emmanuel's face, and everyone wept, saying: "What great love he bears!" And then, because it was dawn, a cock crowed.

On returning home I locked myself in with my brother; alone with him I put my arms around his neck and kissed him.

"Lazarus, Lazarus, what joy you have given us all today; the entire village, the living and the dead, and especially our mother. Did you see how Don Emmanuel wept for joy? What joy you have given us all!"

"It was for that reason that I did what I did," he answered me.

"For what? To give us pleasure? Surely you did it for your own sake, first of all; because of your conversion."

And then Lazarus, my brother, grown as pale and tremulous as Don Emmanuel when he was giving Communion, bade me sit down, in the very chair where our mother used to sit. He took a deep breath, and, in the intimate tone of a familiar and domestic confession, he told me:

"Angelita, the time has come when I must tell you the truth, the absolute truth, and I shall tell you because I must, because I cannot, I ought not, conceal it from you, and because, sooner or later, you are bound to intuit it anyway, if only halfway—which would be worse."

Thereupon, serenely and tranquilly, in a subdued voice, he recounted a tale that drowned me in a lake of sorrow. He told how Don Emmanuel had appealed to him, particularly during the walks to the ruins of the old Cistercian abbey, to set a good example, to avoid scandalizing the townspeople, to take part in the religious life of the community, to feign belief even if he did not feel any, to conceal his own ideas—all this without attempting in any way to catechize him, to instruct him in religion, or to effect a true conversion.

"But is it possible?" I asked in consternation.

"Possible and true. When I said to him: 'Is this you, the priest, who suggests I dissimulate?' he replied, hesitatingly: 'Dissimulate? Not at all!

That is not dissimulation. "Dip your fingers in holy water, and you will end by believing," as someone said.' And I, gazing into his eyes, asked him: 'And you, celebrating the Mass, have you ended by believing?' He looked away and stared out at the lake, until his eyes filled with tears. And it was in this way that I came to understand his secret."

"Lazarus!" I cried out, incapable of another word.

At that moment the fool Blasillo came along our street, crying out his: "My God, my God, why hast Thou forsaken me?" And Lazarus shuddered, as if he had heard the voice of Don Emmanuel, or of Christ.

"It was then," my brother at length continued, "that I really understood his motives and his saintliness; for a saint he is, Sister, a true saint. In trying to convert me to his holy cause—for it is a holy cause, a most holy cause—he was not attempting to score a triumph, but rather was doing it to protect the peace, the happiness, the illusions, perhaps, of his charges. I understood that if he thus deceives them—if it *is* deceit—it is not for his own advantage. I submitted to his logic,—and that was my conversion.

"I shall never forget the day on which I said to him: 'But, Don Emmanuel, the truth, the truth, above all!'; and he, all a-tremble, whispered in my ear—though we were all alone in the middle of the countryside —'The truth? The truth, Lazarus, is perhaps something so unbearable, so terrible, something so deadly, that simple people could not live with it!'

"'And why do you show me a glimpse of it now, here, as if we were in the confessional?' I asked. And he said: 'Because if I did not, I would be so tormented by it, so tormented, that I would finally shout it in the middle of the plaza, which I must never, never, never do . . . I am put here to give life to the souls of my charges, to make them happy, to make them dream they are immortal—and not to destroy them. The important thing is that they live sanely, in concord with each other,—and with the truth, with my truth, they could not live at all. Let them live. That is what the Church does, it lets them live. As for true religion, all religions are true as long as they give spiritual life to the people who profess them, as long as they console them for having been born only to die. And for each people the truest religion is their own, the religion that made them . . . And mine? Mine consists in consoling myself by consoling others, even though the consolation I give them is not ever mine.' I shall never forget his words."

"But then this Communion of yours has been a sacrilege," I dared interrupt, regretting my words as soon as I said them.

"Sacrilege? What about the priest who gave it to me? And his Masses?"

"What martyrdom!" I exclaimed.

"And now," said my brother, "there is one more person to console the people."

"To deceive them, you mean?" I said.

"Not at all," he replied, "but rather to confirm them in their faith."

"And they, the people, do they really believe, do you think?"

"About that, I know nothing! . . . They probably believe without trying, from force of habit, tradition. The important thing is not to stir them up. To let them live from their thin sentiments, without acquiring the torments of luxury. Blessed are the poor in spirit!"

"That then is the sentiment you have learned from Don Emmanuel. . . . And tell me, do you feel you have carried out your promise to our mother on her deathbed, when you promised to pray for her?"

"Do you think I *could* fail her? What do you take me for, sister? Do you think I would go back on my word, my solemn promise made at the hour of death to a mother?"

"I don't know. . . . You might have wanted to deceive her so she could die in peace."

"The fact is, though, that if I had not lived up to my promise, I would be totally miserable."

"And . . ."

"I carried out my promise and I have not neglected for a single day to pray for her."

"Only for her?"

"Well, now, for whom else?"

"For yourself! And now, for Don Emmanuel."

We parted and went to our separate rooms. I to weep through the night, praying for the conversion of my brother and of Don Emmanuel. And Lazarus, to what purpose, I know not.

From that day on I was fearful of finding myself alone with Don Emmanuel, whom I continued to aid in his pious works. And he seemed to sense my inner state and to guess at its cause. When at last I came to him in the confessional's penitential tribunal (who was the judge, and who the offender?) the two of us, he and I, bowed our heads in silence and began to cry. It was he, finally, Don Emmanuel, who broke the terrible silence, with a voice which seemed to issue from the tomb:

"Angelita, you have the same faith you had when you were ten, don't you? You believe, don't you?"

"I believe, Father."

"Then go on believing. And if doubts come to torment you, suppress them utterly, even to yourself. The main thing is to live . . ."

I summoned up courage, and dared to ask, trembling:

"But, Father, do you believe?"

For a brief moment he hesitated, and then, mastering himself, he said: "I believe!"

"In what, Father, in what? Do you believe in the after life? Do you believe that in dying we do not die in every way, completely? Do you believe that we will see each other again, that we will love each other in a world to come? Do you believe in another life?"

The poor saint was sobbing.

"My child, leave off, leave off!"

Now, when I come to write this memoir, I ask myself: Why did he not deceive me? Why did he not deceive me as he deceived the others? Why did he afflict himself? Why could he not deceive himself, or why could he not deceive me? And I want to believe that he was afflicted because he could not deceive himself into deceiving me.

"And now," he said, "pray for me, for your brother, and for yourself —for all of us. We must go on living. And giving life."

And, after a pause:

"Angelita, why don't you marry?"

"You know why I do not."

"No, no; you must marry. Lazarus and I will find you a suitor. For it would be good for you to marry, and rid yourself of these obsessions."

"Obsessions, Don Emmanuel?"

"I know well enough what I am saying. You should not torment yourself for the sake of others, for each of us has more than enough to do answering for himself."

"That it should be you, Don Emmanuel, who says this! That you should advise me to marry and answer for myself alone and not suffer over others! That it should be you!"

"Yes, you are right, Angelita. I am no longer sure of what I say. I am no longer sure of what I say since I began to confess to you. Only, one must go on living. Yes! One must live!"

And when I rose to leave the church, he asked me:

"Now, Angelita, in the name of the people, do you absolve me?"

I felt pierced by a mysterious and priestly prompting and said:

"In the name of the Father, the Son and the Holy Ghost, I absolve you, Father."

We quitted the church, and as I went out I felt the quickening of maternity within me.

My brother, now totally devoted to the work of Don Emmanuel, had become his closest and most zealous collaborator and companion. They were bound together, moreover, by their common secret. Lazarus accompanied the priest on his visits to the sick, and to schools, and he placed his resources at the disposition of the saintly man. A little more zeal, and he would have learned to help celebrate Mass. All the while he was sounding deeper in the unfathomable soul of the priest.

"What manliness!" he exclaimed to me once. "Yesterday, as we walked along the lake he said: 'There lies my direst temptation.' When I interrogated him with my eyes, he went on: 'My poor father, who was close to ninety when he died, was tormented all his life, as he confessed to me himself, by a temptation to suicide, by an instinct to self-destruction which had come to him from a time before memory—from birth, from his *nation*, as he said—and was forced to fight against it always. And this fight grew to be his life. So as not to succumb to this temptation he was forced to take precautions, to guard his life. He told me of terrible episodes. His urge was a form of madness,—and I have inherited it. How that water beckons me in its deep quiet! . . . an apparent quietude reflecting the sky like a mirror—and beneath it the hidden current! My life, Lazarus, is a kind of continual suicide, or a struggle against suicide, which is the same thing. . . . Just so long as our people go on living!' And then he added: 'Here the river eddies to form a lake, so that later, flowing down the plateau, it may form into cascades, waterfalls, and torrents, hurling itself through gorges and chasms. Thus does life eddy in the village; and the temptation to suicide is the greater beside the still waters which at night reflect the stars, than it is beside the crashing falls which drive one back in fear. Listen, Lazarus, I have helped poor villagers to die well, ignorant, illiterate villagers, who had scarcely ever been out of their village, and I have learned from their own lips, or divined it when they were silent, the real cause of their sickness unto death, and there at the head of their deathbed I have been able to see into the black abyss of their life-weariness. A weariness a thousand times worse than hunger! For our part, Lazarus, let us go on with our kind of suicide of working for the people, and let them dream their life as the lake dreams the heavens.'

"Another time," said my brother, "as we were coming back, we spied a country girl, a goatherd, standing erect on a height of the mountain slope overlooking the lake and she was singing in a voice fresher than its waters. Don Emmanuel took hold of me, and pointing to her said: 'Look, it's as though time had stopped, as though this country girl had always been there just as she is, singing in the way she is, and as though she would always be there, as she was before my consciousness began, as she will be when it is past. That girl is a part of nature—not of history —along with the rocks, the clouds, the trees, and the waters.' He has such a subtle feeling for nature, he infuses it with spirit!

"I shall not forget the day when snow was falling and he asked me: 'Have you ever seen a greater mystery, Lazarus, than the snow falling, and dying, in the lake, while a hood is laid upon the mountain?' "

Don Emmanuel had to moderate and temper my brother's zeal and his neophyte's rawness. As soon as he heard that Lazarus was going about inveighing against some of the popular superstitions he told him forcefully:

"Leave them alone! it's difficult enough making them understand where orthodox belief leaves off and where superstition begins. It's hard enough, especially for us. Leave them alone, then, as long as they get some comfort. . . . It's better for them to believe everything, even things that contradict one another, than to believe nothing. The idea that someone who believes too much ends by not believing in anything is a Protestant notion. Let us not protest! Protestation destroys contentment and peace."

My brother told me, too, about one moonlit night when they were returning to town along the lake (whose surface a mountain breeze was stirring, so that the moonbeams topped the whitecaps), Don Emmanuel turned to him and said:

"Look, the water is reciting the litany and saying: *ianua caeli, ora pro nobis*; gate of heaven, pray for us."

Two evanescent tears fell from his lashes to the grass, where the light of the full moon shone upon them like dew.

And time went hurrying by, and my brother and I began to notice that Don Emmanuel's spirits were failing, that he could no longer control completely the deep rooted sadness which consumed him; perhaps some treacherous illness was undermining his body and soul. In an effort to rouse his interest, Lazarus spoke to him of the good effect the organization of a type of Catholic agrarian syndicate would have.

"A syndicate?" Don Emmanuel repeated sadly. "A syndicate? And what is that? The Church is the only syndicate I know. And you have certainly heard 'My kingdom is not of this world.' Our kingdom, Lazarus, is not of this world . . ."

"And of the other?"

Don Emmanuel bowed his head:

"The other is here. Two kingdoms exist in this world. Or rather, the other world. . . . Ah, I don't really know what I'm saying. But as for the syndicate, that's a vestige from your days of 'progressivism.' No, Lazarus, no; religion does not exist to resolve the economic or political conflicts of this world, which God handed over to men for their disputes. Let men think and act as they will, let them console themselves for having been born, let them live as happily as possible in the illusion that all this has a purpose. I don't propose to advise the poor to submit to the rich, nor to suggest to the rich that they subordinate themselves to the poor; but rather to preach resignation in everyone, and charity toward everyone. For even the rich man must resign himself—to his riches, and to life; and the poor man must show charity—even to the rich. The Social Question? Ignore it, for it is none of our business. So, a new society is on the way, in which there will be neither rich nor poor, in which wealth will be justly divided, in which everything will belong to everyone—and so, what then? Won't this general well-being and comfort lead to even greater tedium and weariness of life? I know well enough that one of those chiefs of what they call the Social Revolution has already said that religion is the opium of the people. Opium . . . Opium . . . Yes, opium it is. We should give them opium, and help them sleep, and dream. I, myself, with my mad activity, give myself opium. And still I don't manage to sleep well, let alone dream well. . . . What a fearful nightmare! . . . I, too, can say, with the Divine Master: 'My soul is weary unto death.' No, Lazarus, no; no syndicates for us. If *they* organize them, well and good—they would be distracting themselves in that way. Let them play at syndicates, if that makes them happy."

The entire village began to realize that Don Emmanuel's spirit was weakening, that his strength was waning. His very voice—that miracle of a voice—acquired a kind of quaking. Tears came into his eyes for any reason whatever—or for no reason. Whenever he spoke to people about the other world, about the other life, he was compelled to pause at frequent intervals, and he would close his eyes. "It is a vision," people would say, "he has a vision of what lies ahead." At such moments the fool Blasillo was the first to break into tears. He wept copiously these days, crying now more than he laughed, and even his laughter had the sound of tears.

The last Easter Week which Don Emmanuel was to celebrate among us, in this world, in this village of ours, arrived, and all the village sensed the impending end of tragedy. And how the words did strike home when for the last time Don Emmanuel cried out before us: "My God, my God, why hast Thou forsaken me?"! And when he repeated the words of the Lord to the Good Thief ("All thieves are good," Don Emmanuel used to tell us): "Tomorrow shalt thou be with me in Paradise." . . . ! And then, the last general Communion which our saint was to give! When he came to my brother to give him the Host— his hand steady this time—, just after the liturgical ". . . *in vitam aeternam,*" he bent down and whispered to him: "There is no other life but this, no life more eternal . . . let them dream it eternal . . . let it be eternal for a few years . . ."

And when he came to me he said: "Pray, my child, pray for us all." And then, something so extraordinary happened that I carry it now in my heart as the greatest of mysteries: he bent over and said, in a voice which seemed to belong to the other world: ". . . and pray, too, for our Lord Jesus Christ."

I stood up, going weak as I did so, like a somnambulist. Everything around me seemed dream-like. And I thought: "Am I to pray, too, for the lake and the mountain?" And next: "Am I bewitched, then?" Home at last, I took up the crucifix my mother had held in her hands when she had given up her soul to God, and, gazing at it through my tears and recalling the "My God, my God, why hast Thou forsaken me?" of our two Christs, the one of this earth and the other of this village, I prayed: "Thy will be done on earth as it is in heaven," and then, "And lead us not into temptation. Amen." After this I turned to the statue of the Mater Dolorosa—her heart transfixed by seven swords—which had been my poor mother's most sorrowful comfort, and I prayed again: "Holy Mary, Mother of God, pray for us sinners, now and in the hour of our death. Amen." I had scarcely finished the prayer, when I asked myself: "Sinners? Sinners are we? And what is our sin, what is it?" And all day I brooded over the question.

The next day I presented myself before Don Emmanuel—Don Emmanuel now in the full sunset of his magnificent religiosity—and I said to him:

"Do you remember, my Father, years ago when I asked you a certain question you answered: 'That question you must not ask me; for I am ignorant; there are learned doctors of the Holy Mother Church who will know how to answer you'?"

"Do I remember? . . . Of course. And I remember I told you those were questions put to you by the Devil."

"Well, then, Father, I have come again, bedeviled, to ask you another question put to me by my Guardian Devil."

"Ask it."

"Yesterday, when you gave me Communion, you asked me to pray for all of us, and even for . . ."

"That's enough! . . . Go on."

"I arrived home and began to pray; when I came to the part 'Pray for us sinners, now and at the hour of our death,' a voice in me asked: 'Sinners? Sinners are we? And what is our sin?' What is our sin, Father?"

"Our sin?" he replied. "A great doctor of the Spanish Catholic Apostolic Church has already explained it; the great doctor of *Life is a Dream* has written 'The greatest sin of man is to have been born.' That, my child, is our sin; to have been born."

"Can it be atoned, Father?"

"Go and pray again. Pray once more for us sinners, now and at the hour of our death. . . . Yes, at length the dream is atoned . . . at length life is atoned . . . at length the cross of birth is expiated and atoned, and the drama comes to an end. . . . And as Calderón said, to have done good, to have feigned good, even in dreams, is something which is not lost."

The hour of his death arrived at last. The entire village saw it come. And he made it his finest lesson. For he would not die alone or at rest. He died preaching to his people in the church. But first, before being carried to the church (his paralysis made it impossible for him to move), he summoned Lazarus and me to his bedside. Alone there, the three of us together, he said:

"Listen to me: watch over these poor sheep; find some comfort for them in living, and let them believe what I could not. And Lazarus, when your hour comes, die as I die, as Angela will die, in the arms of the Holy Mother Church, Catholic, Apostolic, and Roman; that is to say, of the Holy Mother Church of Valverde de Lucerna. And now, farewell; until we never meet again, for this dream of life is coming to an end . . ."

"Father, Father," I cried out.

"Do not grieve, Angela, only go on praying for all sinners, for all who have been born. Let them dream, let them dream . . . O, what a longing I have to sleep, to sleep, sleep without end, sleep for all eternity, and never dream! Forgetting this dream! . . . When they go to bury me, let it be in a box made from the six planks I cut from the old walnut tree—poor old tree!—in whose shade I played as a child, when I began the dream. . . . In those days, I did really believe in life everlasting. That is to say, it seems to me now that I believed. For a child, to believe is the same as to dream. And for a people, too. . . . You'll find those six planks I cut at the foot of the bed."

He was seized by a sudden fit of choking, and then, composing himself once more, he went on:

"You will recall that when we prayed together, animated by a common sentiment, a community of spirit, and we came to the final verse of the Creed, you will remember that I would fall silent. . . . When the Israelites were coming to the end of their wandering in the desert, the Lord told Aaron and Moses that because they had not believed in Him they would not set foot in the Promised Land with their people; and he bade them climb the heights of Mount Hor, where Moses ordered Aaron stripped of his garments, so that Aaron died there, and then Moses went up from the plains of Moab to Mount Nebo, to the top of Pisgah, looking into Jericho, and the Lord showed him all of the land promised to His people, but said to him: 'You will not go there.' And there Moses died, and no one knew his grave. And he left Joshua to be chief in his place. You, Lazarus, must be my Joshua, and if you can make the sun stand still, make it stop, and never mind progress. Like Moses, I have seen the face of God—our supreme dream—face to face, and as you already know, and as the Scripture says, he who sees God's face, he who sees the eyes of the dream, the eyes with which He looks at us, will die inexorably and forever. And therefore, do not let our people, so long as thy live, look into the face of God. Once dead, it will no longer matter, for then they will see nothing . . ."

"Father, Father, Father," I cried again.

And he said:

"Angela, you must pray always, so that all sinners may go on dreaming, until they die, of the resurrection of the flesh and the life everlasting . . ."

I was expecting "and who knows it might be . . ." But instead, Don Emmanuel had another attack of coughing.

"And now," he finally went on, "and now, in the hour of my death, it is high time to have me brought, in this very chair, to the church, so that I may take leave there of my people, who await me."

He was carried to the church and brought, in his armchair, into the chancel, to the foot of the altar. In his hands he held a crucifix. My brother and I stood close to him, but the fool Blasillo wanted to stand even closer. He wanted to grasp Don Emmanuel by the hand, so that he could kiss it. When some of the people nearby tried to stop him, Don Emmanuel rebuked them and said:

"Let him come closer. . . . Come, Blasillo, give me your hand."

The fool cried for joy. And then Don Emmanuel spoke:

"I have very few words left, my children; I scarcely feel I have strength enough left to die. And then, I have nothing new to tell you, either. I have already said everything I have to say. Live with each other in peace and contentment, in the hope that we will all see each other again some day, in that other Valverde de Lucerna up there among the nighttime stars, the stars which the lake reflects over the image of the reflected mountain. And pray, pray to the Most Blessed Mary, and to our Lord. Be good . . . that is enough. Forgive me whatever wrong I may have done you inadvertently or unknowingly. After I give you my blessing, let us pray together, let us say the Paternoster, the Ave Maria, the Salve, and the Creed."

Then he gave his blessing to the whole village, with the crucifix held in his hand, while the women and children cried and even some of the men wept softly. Almost at once the prayers were begun. Don Emmanuel listened to them in silence, his hand in the hand of Blasillo the fool, who began to fall asleep to the sound of the praying. First the Paternoster with its "Thy will be done on earth as it is in heaven"; then the Ave Maria, with its "Pray for us sinners, now and in the hour of our death"; followed by the Salve, with its "mourning and weeping in this vale of tears"; and finally, the Creed. On reaching "The resurrection of the flesh and life everlasting" the people sensed that their saint had yielded up his soul to God. It was not necessary to close his eyes even, for he died with them closed. When an attempt was made to wake Blasillo, it was found that he, too, had fallen asleep in the Lord forever. So that later there were two bodies to be buried.

The village immediately repaired en masse to the house of the saint to carry away holy relics, to divide up pieces of his garments among themselves, to carry off whatever they could find as a memento of the blessed martyr. My brother preserved his breviary, between the pages of which he discovered a carnation, dried as in a herbarium and mounted on a piece of paper, and upon the paper a cross and a certain date.

No one in the village seemed able to believe that Don Emmanuel was dead; everyone expected to see him—perhaps some of them did—taking his daily walk along the side of the lake, his figure mirrored in the water, or silhouetted against the background of the mountain. They continued to hear his voice, and they all visited his grave, around which a veritable cult sprang up, old women "possessed by devils" came to touch the cross of walnut, made with his own hands from the tree which had yielded the six planks of his casket.

The ones who least of all believed in his death were my brother and I. Lazarus carried on the tradition of the saint, and he began to compile a record of the priest's words. Some of the conversations in this account of mine were made possible by his notes.

"It was he," said my brother, "who made me into a new man. I was a true Lazarus whom he raised from the dead. He gave me faith."

"Ah, faith . . ."

"Yes, faith, faith in the charity of life, in life's joy. It was he who cured me of my delusion of 'progress,' of my belief in its political implications. For there are, Angela, two types of dangerous and harmful men: those who, convinced of life beyond the grave, of the resurrection of the flesh, torment other people—like the inquisitors they are—so that they will despise this life as a transitory thing and work for the other life; and then, there are those who, believing only in this life . . ."

"Like you, perhaps . . ."

"Yes, and like Don Emmanuel. Believing only in this world, this second group looks forward to some vague future society and exerts every effort to prevent the populace finding consoling joy from belief in another world . . ."

"And so . . ."

"The people should be allowed to live with their illusion."

The poor priest who came to the parish to replace Don Emmanuel found himself overwhelmed in Valverde de Lucerna by the memory of the saint, and he put himself in the hands of my brother and myself for guidance. He wanted only to follow in the footsteps of the saint. And my brother told him: "Very little theology, Father, very little theology. Religion, religion, religion." Listening to him, I smiled to myself wondering if this was not a kind of theology, too.

I had by now begun to fear for my poor brother. From the time Don Emmanuel died it could scarcely be said that he lived. Daily he went to the priest's tomb; for hours on end he stood gazing into the lake. He was filled with nostalgia for deep, abiding peace.

"Don't stare into the lake so much," I begged him.

"Don't worry. It's not this lake which draws me, nor the mountain. Only, I cannot live without his help."

"And the joy of living, Lazarus, what about the joy of living?"

"That's for others. Not for those of us who have seen God's face, those of us on whom the Dream of Life has gazed with His eyes."

"What; are you preparing to go and see Don Emmanuel?"

"No, sister, no. Here at home now, between the two of us, the whole truth—bitter as it may be, bitter as the sea into which the sweet waters of our lake flow—the whole truth for you, who are so set against it . . ."

"No, no, Lazarus. You are wrong. Your truth is not the truth."

"It's my truth."

"Yours, perhaps, but surely not . . ."

"His, too."

"No, Lazarus. Not now, it isn't. Now, he must believe otherwise; now he must believe . . ."

"Listen, Angela, once Don Emmanuel told me that there are truths which, though one reveals them to oneself, must be kept from others; and I told him that telling me was the same as telling himself. And then he said, he confessed to me, that he thought that more than one of the great saints, perhaps the very greatest himself, had died without believing in the other life."

"Is it possible?"

"All too possible! And now, sister, you must be careful that here, among the people, no one even suspects our secret . . ."

"Suspect it?" I cried in amazement. "Why even if I were to try, in a fit of madness, to explain it to them, they wouldn't understand it. The people do not understand your words, they understand your actions much better. To try and explain all this to them would be like reading some pages from Saint Thomas Aquinas to eight-year-old children, in Latin."

"All the better. In any case, when I am gone, pray for me and for him and for all of us."

At length, his own time came. A sickness which had been eating away at his robust nature seemed to flare with the death of Don Emmanuel.

"I don't so much mind dying," he said to me in his last days, "as the fact that with me another piece of Don Emmanuel dies too. The remainder of him must live on with you. Until, one day, even we dead will die forever."

When he lay in the throes of death, the people of the village came in to bid him farewell (as is customary in our towns) and they commended his soul to the care of Don Emmanuel the Good, Martyr. My brother said nothing to them; he had nothing more to say. He had already said everything there was to say. He had become a link between the two Valverde de Lucernas—the one at the bottom of the lake and the one reflected in its surface. He was already one more of us who had died of life, and, in his way, one more of our saints.

I was desolate, more than desolate; but I was, at least, among my own people, in my own village. Now, having lost my Saint Emmanuel, the father of my soul, and my own Lazarus, my more than carnal brother, my spiritual brother, now it is I realize that I have aged. But, have I really lost them then? Have I grown old? Is my death approaching?

I must live! And he taught me to live, he taught us to live, to feel life, to feel the meaning of life, to merge with the soul of the mountain, with the soul of the lake, with the soul of the village, to lose ourselves in them so as to remain in them forever. He taught me by his life to lose myself in the life of the people of my village, and I no longer felt the passing of the hours, and the days, and the years, any more than I felt the passage of the water in the lake. It began to seem that my life would always be thus. I no longer felt myself growing old. I no longer lived in myself, but in my people, and my people lived in me. I tried to speak as they spoke, as they spoke without trying. I went into the street—it was the one highway—and, since I knew everyone, I lived in them and forgot myself (while, on the other hand, in Madrid, where I went once with my brother, I had felt a terrible loneliness, since I knew no one, and had been tortured by the sight of so many unknown people).

Now, as I write this memoir, this confession of my experience with saintliness, with a saint, I am of the opinion that Don Emmanuel the Good, my Don Emmanuel, and my brother, too, died believing they did not believe, but that, without believing in their belief, they actually believed, with resignation and in desolation.

But why, I have asked myself repeatedly, did not Don Emmanuel attempt to convert my brother deceitfully, with a lie, pretending to be a believer himself without being one? And I have finally come to think that Don Emmanuel realized he would not be able to delude him, that with him a fraud would not do, that only through the truth, with his truth, would he be able to convert him; that he knew he would accomplish nothing if he attempted to enact the comedy—the tragedy, rather—which he played out for the benefit of the people. And thus did he win him over, in effect, to his pious fraud; thus did he win him over to the cause of life with the truth of death. And thus did he win me, who never permitted anyone to see through his divine, his most saintly, game. For I believed then, and I believe now, that God—as part of I know not what sacred and inscrutable purpose—caused them to believe they were unbelievers. And that at the moment of their passing, perhaps, the blindfold was removed.

And I, do I believe?

As I write this—here in my mother's old house, and I past my fiftieth year and my memories growing as dim and blanched as my hair—outside it is snowing, snowing upon the lake, snowing upon the mountain, upon the memory of my father, the stranger, upon the memory of my mother, my brother Lazarus, my people, upon the memory of my Saint Emmanuel, and even on the memory of the poor fool Blasillo, my Saint Blasillo—and may he help me in heaven! The snow effaces corners and blots out shadows, for even in the night it shines and illuminates. Truly, I do not know what is true and what is false, nor what I saw and what I merely dreamt—or rather, what I dreamt and what I merely saw—, nor what I really knew or what I merely believed true. Neither do I know whether or not I am transferring to this paper, white as the snow outside, my consciousness, for it to remain in writing, leaving me without it. But why, any longer, cling to it?

Do I really understand any of it? Do I really believe in any of it? Did what I am writing about here actually take place, and did it take place in just the way I tell it? Is it possible for such things to happen? Is it possible that all this is more than a dream dreamed within another dream? Can it be that I, Angela Carballino, a woman in her fifties, am the only one in this village to be assailed by far-fetched thoughts, thoughts unknown to everyone else? And the others, those around me, do they believe? And what does it mean, to believe? At least they go on living. And now they believe in Saint Emmanuel the Good, Martyr, who, with no hope of immortality for himself, preserved their hope in it.

It appears that our most illustrious bishop, who set in motion the process for beatifying our saint from Valverde de Lucerna, is intent on writing an account of Don Emmanuel's life, something which would serve as a guide for the perfect parish priest, and with this end in mind he is gathering information of every sort. He has repeatedly solicited information from me; more than once he has come to see me; and I have supplied him with all sorts of facts. But I have never revealed the tragic secret of Don Emmanuel and my brother. And it is curious that he has never suspected. I trust that what I have set down here will never come to his knowledge. For, all temporal authorities are to be avoided; I fear all authorities on this earth—even when they are church authorities.

But this is an end to it. Let its fate be what it will . . .

• • •

How, you ask, did this document, this memoir of Angela Carballino fall into my hands? That, reader, is something I must keep secret. I have transcribed it for you just as it is written, just as it came to me, with only a few, a very few editorial emendations. It recalls to you other things I have written? This fact does not gainsay its objectivity, its originality. Moreover, for all I know, perhaps I created real, actual beings, independent of me, beyond my control, characters with immortal souls. For all I know, Augusto Perez in my novel Mist[2] was right when he claimed to be more real, more objective than I myself, who had thought to have invented him. As for the reality of this Saint Emmanuel the Good, Martyr—as he is revealed to me by his disciple and spiritual daughter Angela Carballino—of his reality it has not occurred to me to doubt. I believe in it more than the saint himself did. I believe in it more than I do in my own reality.

And now, before I bring this epilogue to a close, I wish to recall to your mind, patient reader, the ninth verse of the Epistle of the forgotten Apostle, Saint Judas—what power in a name!—where we are told how my heavenly patron, St. Michael Archangel (Mičhael means "Who such as God?" and archangel means arch-messenger) disputed with the Devil (Devil means accuser, prosecutor) over the body of Moses, and would not allow him to carry it off as a prize, to damnation. Instead, he told the Devil: "May the Lord rebuke thee." And may he who wishes to understand, understand!

I would like also, since Angela Carballino injected her own feelings into her narrative—I don't know how it could have been otherwise—to comment on her statement to the effect that if Don Emmanuel and his disciple Lazarus had confessed their convictions to the people, they, the people, would not have understood. Nor, I should like to add, would they have believed the pair. They would have believed in their works and not their words. And works stand by themselves, and need no words to back them up. In a village like Valverde de Lucerna one makes one's confession by one's conduct.

And as for faith, the people scarce know what it is, and care less.

I am well aware of the fact that no action takes place in this narrative, this *novelistic* narrative, if you will—the novel is, after all, the most intimate, the truest history, so that I scarcely understand why some people are outraged to have the Bible called a novel, when such a designa-

---

[2] In the denouement of Mist, the protagonist Augusto Perez turns on Unamuno, and tells him that he, a creation of human thought and genius, is more real than his author, a product of blind animality.

tion actually sets it above some mere chronicle or other. In short, nothing happens. But I hope that this is because everything that takes place happens, and, instead of coming to pass, and passing away, remains forever, like the lakes and the mountains and the blessed simple souls fixed firmly beyond faith and despair, the blessed souls who, in the lakes and the mountains, outside history, in their divine novel, take refuge.

The Wall

They pushed us into a large white room and my eyes began to blink because the light hurt them. Then I saw a table and four fellows seated at the table, civilians, looking at some papers. The other prisoners were herded together at one end and we were obliged to cross the entire room to join them. There were several I knew, and others who must have been foreigners. The two in front of me were blond with round heads. They looked alike. I imagine they were French. The smaller one kept pulling at his trousers, out of nervousness.

This lasted about three hours. I was dog-tired and my head was empty. But the room was well-heated, which struck me as rather agreeable; we had not stopped shivering for twenty-four hours. The guards led the prisoners in one after the other in front of the table. Then the four fellows asked them their names and what they did. Most of the time that was all—or perhaps from time to time they would ask such questions as: "Did you help sabotage the munitions?" or, "Where were you on the morning of the ninth and what were you doing?" They didn't even listen to the replies, or at least they didn't seem to. They just remained silent for a moment and looked straight ahead, then they began to write. They asked Tom if it was true he had served in the International Brigade. Tom couldn't say he hadn't because of the papers they had found in his jacket. They didn't ask Juan anything, but after he told them his name, they wrote for a long while.

"It's my brother José who's the anarchist," Juan said. "You know perfectly well he's not here now. I don't belong to any party. I never did take part in politics." They didn't answer.

Then Juan said, "I didn't do anything. And I'm not going to pay for what the others did."

His lips were trembling. A guard told him to stop talking and led him away. It was my turn.

"Your name is Pablo Ibbieta?"

I said yes.

The fellow looked at his papers and said, "Where is Ramon Gris?"

"I don't know."

"You hid him in your house from the sixth to the nineteenth."

"I did not."

They continued to write for a moment and the guards led me away. In the hall, Tom and Juan were waiting between two guards. We started walking. Tom asked one of the guards, "Was that just the preliminary questioning, or was that the trial?" "That was the trial," the guard said.

"So now what? What are they going to do with us?" The guard answered drily, "The verdict will be told you in your cell."

In reality, our cell was one of the cellars of the hospital. It was terribly cold there because it was very drafty. We had been shivering all night long and it had hardly been any better during the day. I had spent the preceding five days in a cellar in the archbishop's palace, a sort of dungeon that must have dated back to the Middle Ages. There were lots of prisoners and not much room, so they housed them just anywhere. But I was not homesick for my dungeon. I hadn't been cold there, but I had been alone, and that gets to be irritating. In the cellar I had company. Juan didn't say a word; he was afraid, and besides, he was too young to have anything to say. But Tom was a good talker and knew Spanish well.

In the cellar there were a bench and four straw mattresses. When they led us back we sat down and waited in silence. After a while Tom said, "Our goose is cooked."

"I think so too," I said. "But I don't believe they'll do anything to the kid."

Tom said, "They haven't got anything on him. He's the brother of a fellow who's fighting, and that's all."

I looked at Juan. He didn't seem to have heard.

Tom continued, "You know what they do in Saragossa? They lay the guys across the road and then they drive over them with trucks. It was a Moroccan deserter who told us that. They say it's just to save ammunition."

I said, "Well, it doesn't save gasoline."

I was irritated with Tom; he shouldn't have said that.

He went on, "There are officers walking up and down the roads with their hands in their pockets, smoking, and they see that it's done right. Do you think they'd put 'em out of their misery? Like hell they do. They just let 'em holler. Sometimes as long as an hour. The Moroccan said the first time he almost puked."

"I don't believe they do that here," I said, "unless they really are short of ammunition."

The daylight came in through four air vents and a round opening that had been cut in the ceiling, to the left, and which opened directly onto the sky. It was through this hole, which was ordinarily closed by means of a trapdoor, that they unloaded coal into the cellar. Directly under the hole, there was a big pile of coal dust; it had been intended for heating the hospital, but at the beginning of the war they had evacuated the patients and the coal had stayed there unused; it even got rained on from time to time, when they forgot to close the trapdoor.

Tom started to shiver. "God damn it," he said, "I'm shivering. There, it is starting again."

He rose and began to do gymnastic exercises. At each movement, his shirt opened and showed his white, hairy chest. He lay down on his back, lifted his legs in the air and began to do the scissors movement. I watched his big buttocks tremble. Tom was tough, but he had too much fat on him. I kept thinking that soon bullets and bayonet points would sink into that mass of tender flesh as though it were a pat of butter.

I wasn't exactly cold, but I couldn't feel my shoulders or my arms. From time to time, I had the impression that something was missing and I began to look around for my jacket. Then I would suddenly remember they hadn't given me a jacket. It was rather awkward. They had taken our clothes to give them to their own soldiers and had left us only our shirts and these cotton trousers the hospital patients wore in mid-summer. After a moment, Tom got up and sat down beside me, breathless.

"Did you get warmed up?"

"Damn it, no. But I'm all out of breath."

Around eight o'clock in the evening, a Major came in with two falangists.

"What are the names of those three over there?" he asked the guard.

"Steinbock, Ibbieta and Mirbal," said the guard.

The Major put on his glasses and examined his list.

"Steinbock—Steinbock. . . . Here it is. You are condemned to death. You'll be shot tomorrow morning."

He looked at his list again.

"The other two, also," he said.

"That's not possible," said Juan. "Not me."

The Major looked at him with surprise. "What's your name?"

"Juan Mirbal."

"Well, your name is here," said the Major, "and you're condemned to death."

"I didn't do anything," said Juan.

The Major shrugged his shoulders and turned toward Tom and me.

"You are both Basque?"

"No, nobody's Basque."

He appeared exasperated.

"I was told there were three Basques. I'm not going to waste my time running after them. I suppose you don't want a priest?"

We didn't even answer.

Then he said, "A Belgian doctor will be around in a little while. He has permission to stay with you all night."

He gave a military salute and left.

"What did I tell you?" Tom said. "We're in for something swell."

"Yes," I said. "It's a damned shame for the kid."

I said that to be fair, but I really didn't like the kid. His face was too refined and it was disfigured by fear and suffering, which had twisted all his features. Three days ago, he was just a kid with a kind of affected manner some people like. But now he looked like an aging fairy, and I thought to myself he would never be young again, even if they let him go. It wouldn't have been a bad thing to show him a little pity, but pity makes me sick, and besides, I couldn't stand him. He hadn't said anything more, but he had turned gray. His face and hands were gray. He sat down again and stared, round-eyed, at the ground. Tom was goodhearted and tried to take him by the arm, but the kid drew himself away violently and made an ugly face. "Leave him alone," I said quietly. "Can't you see he's going to start to bawl?" Tom obeyed regretfully. He would have liked to console the kid; that would have kept him occupied and he wouldn't have been tempted to think about himself. But it got on my nerves. I had never thought about death, for the reason that the question had never come up. But now it had come up, and there was nothing else to do but think about it.

Tom started talking. "Say, did you ever bump anybody off?" he asked me. I didn't answer. He started to explain to me that he had bumped off six fellows since August. He hadn't yet realized what we were in for, and I saw clearly he didn't *want* to realize it. I myself hadn't quite taken it in. I wondered if it hurt very much. I thought about the bullets; I imagined their fiery hail going through my body. All that was beside the real question; but I was calm, we had all night in which to realize it. After a while Tom stopped talking and I looked at him out of the corner of my eye. I saw that he, too, had turned gray and that he looked pretty miserable. I said to myself, "It's starting." It was almost dark, a dull light filtered through the air vents across the coal pile and made a big spot under the sky. Through the hole in the ceiling I could already see a star. The night was going to be clear and cold.

The door opened and two guards entered. They were followed by a blond man in a tan uniform. He greeted us.

"I'm the doctor," he said. "I've been authorized to give you any assistance you may require in these painful circumstances."

He had an agreeable, cultivated voice.

I said to him, "What are you going to do here?"

"Whatever you want me to do. I shall do everything in my power to lighten these few hours."

"Why did you come to us? There are lots of others: the hospital's full of them."

"I was sent here," he answered vaguely. "You'd probably like to smoke, wouldn't you?" he added suddenly. "I've got some cigarettes and even some cigars."

He passed around some English cigarettes and some *puros*, but we refused them. I looked him straight in the eye and he appeared uncomfortable.

"You didn't come here out of compassion," I said to him. "In fact, I know who you are. I saw you with some fascists in the barracks yard the day I was arrested."

I was about to continue, when all at once something happened to me which surprised me: the presence of this doctor had suddenly ceased to interest me. Usually, when I've got hold of a man I don't let go. But somehow the desire to speak had left me. I shrugged my shoulders and turned away. A little later, I looked up and saw he was watching me with an air of curiosity. The guards had sat down on one of the mattresses. Pedro, the tall thin one, was twiddling his thumbs, while the other one shook his head occasionally to keep from falling asleep.

"Do you want some light?" Pedro suddenly asked the doctor. The other fellow nodded, "Yes." I think he was not over-intelligent, but doubtless he was not malicious. As I looked at his big, cold, blue eyes, it seemed to me the worst thing about him was his lack of imagination. Pedro went out and came back with an oil lamp which he set on the corner of the bench. It gave a poor light, but it was better than nothing; the night before we had been left in the dark. For a long while I stared at the circle of light the lamp threw on the ceiling. I was fascinated. Then, suddenly, I came to, the light circle paled, and I felt as if I were being crushed under an enormous weight. It wasn't the thought of death, and it wasn't fear; it was something anonymous. My cheeks were burning hot and my head ached.

I roused myself and looked at my two companions. Tom had his head in his hands and only the fat, white nape of his neck was visible. Juan was by far worst off; his mouth was wide open and his nostrils were trembling. The doctor came over to him and touched him on the shoulder, as though to comfort him; but his eyes remained cold. Then I saw the Belgian slide his hand furtively down Juan's arm to his wrist. Indifferent, Juan let himself be handled. Then, as though absent-mindedly, the Belgian laid three fingers over his wrist; at the same time, he drew away somewhat and managed to turn his back to me. But I leaned over backward and saw him take out his watch and look at it a moment before relinquishing the boy's wrist. After a moment, he let the inert hand fall and went and leaned against the wall. Then, as if he had suddenly remembered something very important that had to be noted down immediately, he took a notebook from his pocket and wrote a few lines in it. "The son-of-a-bitch," I thought angrily. "He better not come and feel my pulse; I'll give him a punch in his dirty jaw."

He didn't come near me, but I felt he was looking at me. I raised my head and looked back at him. In an impersonal voice, he said, "Don't you think it's frightfully cold here?"

He looked purple with cold.

"I'm not cold," I answered him.

He kept looking at me with a hard expression. Suddenly I understood, and I lifted my hands to my face. I was covered with sweat. Here, in this cellar, in mid-winter, right in a draft, I was sweating. I ran my fingers through my hair, which was stiff with sweat; at the same time, I realized my shirt was damp and sticking to my skin. I had been streaming with perspiration for an hour, at least, and had felt nothing. But this fact hadn't escaped that Belgian swine. He had seen the drops rolling down my face and had said to himself that it showed an almost pathological terror; and he himself had felt normal and proud of it because he was cold. I wanted to get up and go punch his face in, but I had hardly started to make a move before my shame and anger had disappeared. I dropped back onto the bench with indifference.

I was content to rub my neck with my handkerchief because now I felt the sweat dripping from my hair onto the nape of my neck and that was disagreeable. I soon gave up rubbing myself, however, for it didn't do any good; my handkerchief was already wringing wet and I was still sweating. My buttocks, too, were sweating, and my damp trousers stuck to the bench.

Suddenly, Juan said, "You're a doctor, aren't you?"

"Yes," said the Belgian.

"Do people suffer—very long?"

"Oh! When . . . ? No, no," said the Belgian, in a paternal voice, "it's quickly over."

His manner was as reassuring as if he had been answering a paying patient.

"But I . . . Somebody told me—they often have to fire two volleys."

"Sometimes," said the Belgian, raising his head, "it just happens that the first volley doesn't hit any of the vital organs."

"So then they have to reload their guns and aim all over again?" Juan thought for a moment, then added hoarsely, "But that takes time!"

He was terribly afraid of suffering. He couldn't think about anything else, but that went with his age. As for me, I hardly thought about it any more and it certainly was not fear of suffering that made me perspire.

I rose and walked toward the pile of coal dust. Tom gave a start and looked at me with a look of hate. I irritated him because my shoes squeaked. I wondered if my face was as putty-colored as his. Then I noticed that he, too, was sweating. The sky was magnificent; no light at all came into our dark corner and I had only to lift my head to see the Big Bear. But it didn't look the way it had looked before. Two days ago, from my cell in the archbishop's palace, I could see a big patch of sky and each time of day brought back a different memory. In the morning, when the sky was a deep blue, and light, I thought of beaches along the Atlantic; at noon, I could see the sun, and I remembered a bar in Seville where I used to drink manzanilla and eat anchovies and olives; in the afternoon, I was in the shade, and I thought of the deep shadow which covers half of the arena while the other half gleams in the sunlight: it really gave me a pang to see the whole earth reflected in the sky like that. Now, however, no matter how much I looked up in the air, the sky no longer recalled anything. I liked it better that way. I came back and sat down next to Tom. There was a long silence.

Then Tom began to talk in a low voice. He had to keep talking, otherwise he lost his way in his own thoughts. I believe he was talking to me, but he didn't look at me. No doubt he was afraid to look at me, because I was gray and sweating. We were both alike and worse than mirrors for each other. He looked at the Belgian, the only one who was alive.

"Say, do you understand? I don't."

Then I, too, began to talk in a low voice. I was watching the Belgian.

"Understand what? What's the matter?"

"Something's going to happen to us that I don't understand."

There was a strange odor about Tom. It seemed to me that I was more sensitive to odors than ordinarily. With a sneer, I said, "You'll understand, later."

"That's not so sure," he said stubbornly. "I'm willing to be courageous, but at least I ought to know. . . . Listen, they're going to take us out into the courtyard. All right. The fellows will be standing in line in front of us. How many of them will there be?"

"Oh, I don't know. Five, or eight. Not more."

"That's enough. Let's say there'll be eight of them. Somebody will shout 'Shoulder arms!' and I'll see all eight rifles aimed at me. I'm sure I'm going to feel like going through the wall. I'll push against the wall as hard as I can with my back, and the wall won't give in. The way it is in a nightmare. . . . I can imagine all that. Ah, if you only knew how well I can imagine it!"

"Skip it!" I said. "I can imagine it too."

"It must hurt like the devil. You know they aim at your eyes and mouth so as to disfigure you," he added maliciously. "I can feel the wounds already. For the last hour I've been having pains in my head and neck. Not real pains—it's worse still. They're the pains I'll feel tomorrow morning. And after that, then what?"

I understood perfectly well what he meant, but I didn't want to seem to understand. As for the pains, I, too, felt them all through my body, like a lot of little gashes. I couldn't get used to them, but I was like him, I didn't think they were very important.

"After that," I said roughly, "you'll be eating daisies."

He started talking to himself, not taking his eyes off the Belgian, who didn't seem to be listening to him. I knew what he had come for, and that what we were thinking didn't interest him. He had come to look at our bodies, our bodies which were dying alive.

"It's like in a nightmare," said Tom. "You want to think of something, you keep having the impression you've got it, that you're going to understand, and then it slips away from you, it eludes you and it's gone again. I say to myself, afterwards, there won't be anything. But I don't really understand what that means. There are moments when I almost do—and then it's gone again. I start to think of the pains, the bullets, the noise of the shooting. I am a materialist, I swear it; and I'm not going crazy, either. But there's something wrong. I see my own corpse. That's not hard, but it's *I* who see it, with *my* eyes. I'll have to get to the point where I think—where I think I won't see anything more. I won't hear anything more, and the world will go on for the others. We're not made to think that way, Pablo. Believe me, I've already stayed awake all night waiting for something. But this is not the same thing. This will grab us from behind, Pablo, and we won't be ready for it."

"Shut up," I said. "Do you want me to call a father confessor?"

He didn't answer. I had already noticed that he had a tendency to prophesy and call me "Pablo" in a kind of pale voice. I didn't like that very much, but it seems all the Irish are like that. I had a vague impression that he smelled of urine. Actually, I didn't like Tom very much, and I didn't see why, just because we were going to die together, I should like him any better. There are certain fellows with whom it would be different—with Ramon Gris, for instance. But between Tom and Juan, I felt alone. In fact, I liked it better that way. With Ramon I might have grown soft. But I felt terribly hard at that moment, and I wanted to stay hard.

Tom kept on muttering, in a kind of absent-minded way. He was certainly talking to keep from thinking. Naturally, I agreed with him, and I could have said everything he was saying. It's not *natural* to die. And since I was going to die, nothing seemed natural any more: neither the coal pile, nor the bench, nor Pedro's dirty old face. Only it was disagreeable for me to think the same things Tom thought. And I knew perfectly well that all night long, within five minutes of each other, we would keep on thinking things at the same time, sweating or shivering at the same time. I looked at him sideways and, for the first time, he seemed strange to me. He had death written on his face. My pride was wounded. For twenty-four hours I had lived side by side with Tom, I had listened to him, I had talked to him, and I knew we had nothing in common. And now we were as alike as twin brothers, simply because we were going to die together. Tom took my hand without looking at me.

"Pablo, I wonder . . . I wonder if it's true that we just cease to exist."

I drew my hand away.

"Look between your feet, you dirty dog."

There was a puddle between his feet and water was dripping from his trousers.

"What's the matter?" he said, frightened.

"You're wetting your pants," I said to him.

"It's not true," he said furiously. "I can't be . . . I don't feel anything."

The Belgian had come closer to him. With an air of false concern, he asked, "Aren't you feeling well?"

Tom didn't answer. The Belgian looked at the puddle without comment.

"I don't know what that is," Tom said savagely, "but I'm not afraid. I swear to you, I'm not afraid."

The Belgian made no answer. Tom rose and went to the corner. He came back, buttoning his fly, and sat down, without a word. The Belgian was taking notes.

We were watching the doctor. Juan was watching him too. All three of us were watching him because he was alive. He had the gestures of a living person, the interests of a living person; he was shivering in this cellar the way living people shiver; he had an obedient, well-fed body. We, on the other hand, didn't feel our bodies any more—not the same way, in any case. I felt like touching my trousers, but I didn't dare to. I looked at the Belgian, well-planted on his two legs, master of his muscles—and able to plan for tomorrow. We were like three shadows deprived of blood; we were watching him and sucking his life like vampires.

Finally he came over to Juan. Was he going to lay his hand on the nape of Juan's neck for some professional reason, or had he obeyed a charitable impulse? If he had acted out of charity, it was the one and only time during the whole night. He fondled Juan's head and the nape of his neck. The kid let him do it, without taking his eyes off him. Then, suddenly, he took hold of the doctor's hand and looked at it in a funny way. He held the Belgian's hand between his own two hands and there was nothing pleasing about them, those two gray paws squeezing that fat red hand. I sensed what was going to happen and Tom must have sensed it, too. But all the Belgian saw was emotion, and he smiled paternally. After a moment, the kid lifted the big red paw to his mouth and started to bite it. The Belgian drew back quickly and stumbled toward the wall. For a second, he looked at us with horror. He must have suddenly understood that we were not men like himself. I began to laugh, and one of the guards started up. The other had fallen asleep with his eyes wide open, showing only the whites.

I felt tired and over-excited at the same time. I didn't want to think any more about what was going to happen at dawn—about death. It didn't make sense, and I never got beyond just words, or emptiness. But whenever I tried to think about something else I saw the barrels of rifles aimed at me. I must have lived through my execution twenty times in succession; one time I thought it was the real thing; I must have dozed off for a moment. They were dragging me toward the wall and I was resisting; I was imploring their pardon. I woke with a start and looked at the Belgian. I was afraid I had cried out in my sleep. But he was smoothing his mustache; he hadn't noticed anything. If I had wanted to, I believe I could have slept for a while. I had been awake for the last forty-eight hours, and I was worn out. But I didn't want to lose two hours of life. They would have had to come and wake me at dawn. I would have followed them, drunk with sleep, and I would have gone off without so much as "Gosh!" I didn't want it that way, I didn't want to die like an animal. I wanted to understand. Besides, I was afraid of having nightmares. I got up and began to walk up and down and, so as to think about something else, I began to think about my past life. Memories crowded in on me, helter-skelter. Some were good and some were bad— at least that was how I had thought of them *before*. There were faces and happenings. I saw the face of a little *novilero* who had gotten himself horned during the *Feria*, in Valencia. I saw the face of one of my uncles, of Ramon Gris. I remembered all kinds of things that had happened: how I had been on strike for three months in 1926, and had almost died of hunger. I recalled a night I had spent on a bench in Granada; I hadn't eaten for three days, I was nearly wild, I didn't want to give up the sponge. I had to smile. With what eagerness I had run after happiness, and women, and liberty! And to what end? I had wanted to liberate Spain, I admired Py Margall, I had belonged to the anarchist movement, I had spoken at public meetings. I took everything as seriously as if I had been immortal.

At that time I had the impression that I had my whole life before me, and I thought to myself, "It's all a god-damned lie." Now it wasn't worth anything because it was finished. I wondered how I had ever been able to go out and have a good time with girls. I wouldn't have lifted my little finger if I had ever imagined that I would die like this. I saw my life before me, finished, closed, like a bag, and yet what was inside was not finished. For a moment I tried to appraise it. I would have liked to say to myself, "It's been a good life." But it couldn't be appraised, it was only an outline. I had spent my time writing checks on eternity, and had understood nothing. Now, I didn't miss anything. There were a lot of things I might have missed: the taste of manzanilla, for instance, or the swims I used to take in summer in a little creek near Cadiz. But death had taken the charm out of everything.

Suddenly the Belgian had a wonderful idea.

"My friends," he said to us, "if you want me to—and providing the military authorities give their consent—I could undertake to deliver a word or some token from you to your loved ones. . . ."

Tom growled, "I haven't got anybody."

I didn't answer. Tom waited for a moment, then he looked at me with curiosity. "Aren't you going to send any message to Concha?"

"No."

I hated that sort of sentimental conspiracy. Of course, it was my fault, since I had mentioned Concha the night before, and I should have kept my mouth shut. I had been with her for a year. Even as late as last night, I would have cut my arm off with a hatchet just to see her again for five minutes. That was why I had mentioned her. I couldn't help it. Now I didn't care any more about seeing her. I hadn't anything more to say to her. I didn't even want to hold her in my arms. I loathed my body because it had turned gray and was sweating—and I wasn't even sure that I didn't loathe hers too. Concha would cry when she heard about my death; for months she would have no more interest in life. But still it was I who was going to die. I thought of her beautiful, loving eyes. When she looked at me something went from her to me. But I thought to myself that it was all over; if she looked at me *now* her gaze would not leave her eyes, it would not reach out to me. I was alone.

Tom too, was alone, but not the same way. He was seated astride his chair and had begun to look at the bench with a sort of smile, with surprise, even. He reached out his hand and touched the wood cautiously, as though he were afraid of breaking something, then he drew his hand back hurriedly, and shivered. I wouldn't have amused myself touching that bench, if I had been Tom, that was just some more Irish play-acting. But somehow it seemed to me too that the different objects had something funny about them. They seemed to have grown paler, less massive than before. I had only to look at the bench, the lamp or the pile of coal dust to feel I was going to die. Naturally, I couldn't think clearly about my death, but I saw it everywhere, even on the different objects, the way they had withdrawn and kept their distance, tactfully, like people talking at the bedside of a dying person. It was *his own death* Tom had just touched on the bench.

In the state I was in, if they had come and told me I could go home quietly, that my life would be saved, it would have left me cold. A few hours, or a few years of waiting are all the same, when you've lost the illusion of being eternal. Nothing mattered to me any more. In a way, I was calm. But it was a horrible kind of calm—because of my body. My body—I saw with its eyes and I heard with its ears, but it was no longer I. It sweat and trembled independently, and I didn't recognize it any longer. I was obliged to touch it and look at it to know what was happening to it, just as if it had been someone else's body. At times I still felt it, I felt a slipping, a sort of headlong plunging, as in a falling airplane, or else I heard my heart beating. But this didn't give me confidence. In fact, everything that came from my body had something damned dubious about it. Most of the time it was silent, it stayed put and I didn't feel anything other than a sort of heaviness, a loathsome presence against me. I had the impression of being bound to an enormous vermin.

The Belgian took out his watch and looked at it.

"It's half-past three," he said.

The son-of-a-bitch! He must have done it on purpose. Tom jumped up. We hadn't yet realized the time was passing. The night surrounded us like a formless, dark mass; I didn't even remember it had started.

Juan started to shout. Wringing his hands, he implored, "I don't want to die! I don't want to die!"

He ran the whole length of the cellar with his arms in the air, then he dropped down onto one of the mattresses, sobbing. Tom looked at him with dismal eyes and didn't even try to console him any more. The fact was, it was no use; the kid made more noise than we did, but he was less affected, really. He was like a sick person who defends himself against his malady with a high fever. When there's not even any fever left, it's much more serious.

He was crying. I could tell he felt sorry for himself; he was thinking about death. For one second, one single second, I too felt like crying, crying out of pity for myself. But just the contrary happened. I took one look at the kid, saw his thin, sobbing shoulders, and I felt I was inhuman. I couldn't feel pity either for these others or for myself. I said to myself, "I want to die decently."

Tom had gotten up and was standing just under the round opening looking out for the first signs of daylight. I was determined, I wanted to die decently, and I only thought about that. But underneath, ever since the doctor had told us the time, I felt time slipping, flowing by, one drop at a time.

It was still dark when I heard Tom's voice.

"Do you hear them?"

"Yes."

People were walking in the courtyard.

"What the hell are they doing? After all, they can't shoot in the dark."

After a moment, we didn't hear anything more. I said to Tom, "There's the daylight."

Pedro got up yawning, and came and blew out the lamp. He turned to the man beside him. "It's hellish cold."

The cellar had grown gray. We could hear shots at a distance.

"It's about to start," I said to Tom. "That must be in the back courtyard."

Tom asked the doctor to give him a cigarette. I didn't want any; I didn't want either cigarettes or alcohol. From that moment on, the shooting didn't stop.

"Can you take it in?" Tom said.

He started to add something, then he stopped and began to watch the door. The door opened and a lieutenant came in with four soldiers. Tom dropped his cigarette.

"Steinbock?"

Tom didn't answer. Pedro pointed him out.

"Juan Mirbal?"

"He's the one on the mattress."

"Stand up," said the Lieutenant.

Juan didn't move. Two soldiers took hold of him by the armpits and stood him up on his feet. But as soon as they let go of him he fell down.

The soldiers hesitated a moment.

"He's not the first one to get sick," said the Lieutenant. "You'll have to carry him, the two of you. We'll arrange things when we get there." He turned to Tom. "All right, come along."

Tom left between two soldiers. Two other soldiers followed, carrying the kid by his arms and legs. He was not unconscious; his eyes were wide open and tears were rolling down his cheeks. When I started to go out, the Lieutenant stopped me.

"Are you Ibbieta?"

"Yes."

"You wait here. They'll come and get you later on."

They left. The Belgian and the two jailers left too, and I was alone. I didn't understand what had happened to me, but I would have liked it better if they had ended it all right away. I heard the volleys at almost regular intervals; at each one, I shuddered. I felt like howling and tearing my hair. But instead, I gritted my teeth and pushed my hands deep into my pockets, because I wanted to stay decent.

An hour later, they came to fetch me and took me up to the first floor in a little room which smelt of cigar smoke and was so hot it seemed to me suffocating. Here there were two officers sitting in comfortable chairs, smoking, with papers spread out on their knees.

"Your name is Ibbieta?"

"Yes."

"Where is Ramon Gris?"

"I don't know."

The man who questioned me was small and stocky. He had hard eyes behind his glasses.

"Come nearer," he said to me.

I went nearer. He rose and took me by the arms, looking at me in a way calculated to make me go through the floor. At the same time he pinched my arms with all his might. He didn't mean to hurt me; it was quite a game; he wanted to dominate me. He also seemed to think it was necessary to blow his fetid breath right into my face. We stood like that for a moment, only I felt more like laughing than anything else. It takes a lot more than that to intimidate a man who's about to die: it didn't work. He pushed me away violently and sat down again.

"It's your life or his," he said. "You'll be allowed to go free if you tell us where he is."

After all, these two bedizened fellows with their riding crops and boots were just men who were going to die one day. A little later than I, perhaps, but not a great deal. And there they were, looking for names among their papers, running after other men in order to put them in prison or do away with them entirely. They had their opinions on the future of Spain and on other subjects. Their petty activities seemed to me to be offensive and ludicrous. I could no longer put myself in their place. I had the impression they were crazy.

The little fat fellow kept looking at me, tapping his boots with his riding crop. All his gestures were calculated to make him appear like a spirited, ferocious animal.

"Well? Do you understand?"

"I don't know where Gris is," I said. "I thought he was in Madrid."

The other officer lifted his pale hand indolently. This indolence was also calculated. I saw through all their little tricks, and I was dumbfounded that men should still exist who took pleasure in that kind of thing.

"You have fifteen minutes to think it over," he said slowly. "Take him to the linen-room, and bring him back here in fifteen minutes. If he continues to refuse, he'll be executed at once."

They knew what they were doing. I had spent the night waiting. After that, they had made me wait another hour in the cellar, while they shot Tom and Juan, and now they locked me in the linen-room. They must have arranged the whole thing the night before. They figured that sooner or later people's nerves wear out and they hoped to get me that way.

They made a big mistake. In the linen-room I sat down on a ladder because I felt very weak, and I began to think things over. Not their proposition, however. Naturally I knew where Gris was. He was hiding in his cousins' house, about two miles outside of the city. I knew, too, that I would not reveal his hiding place, unless they tortured me (but they didn't seem to be considering that). All that was definitely settled and didn't interest me in the least. Only I would have liked to understand the reasons for my own conduct. I would rather die than betray Gris. Why? I no longer liked Ramon Gris. My friendship for him had died shortly before dawn along with my love for Concha, along with my own desire to live. Of course I still admired him—he was hard. But it was not for that reason that I was willing to die in his place; his life was no more valuable than mine. No life was of any value. A man was going to be stood up against a wall and fired at till he dropped dead. It didn't make any difference whether it was I or Gris or somebody else. I knew perfectly well he was more useful to the Spanish cause than I was, but I didn't give a God damn about Spain or anarchy, either; nothing had any importance now. And yet, there I was. I could save my skin by betraying Gris and I refused to do it. It seemed more ludicrous to me than anything else; it was stubbornness.

I thought to myself, "Am I hard-headed!" And I was seized with a strange sort of cheerfulness.

They came to fetch me and took me back to the two officers. A rat darted out under our feet and that amused me. I turned to one of the falangists and said to him, "Did you see that rat?"

He made no reply. He was gloomy, and took himself very seriously. As for me, I felt like laughing, but I restrained myself because I was afraid that if I started, I wouldn't be able to stop. The falangist wore mustaches. I kept after him, "You ought to cut off those mustaches, you fool."

I was amused by the fact that he let hair grow all over his face while he was still alive. He gave me a kind of half-hearted kick, and I shut up.

"Well," said the fat officer, "have you thought things over?"

I looked at them with curiosity, like insects of a very rare species.

"I know where he is," I said. "He's hiding in the cemetery. Either in one of the vaults, or in the gravediggers' shack."

I said that just to make fools of them. I wanted to see them get up and fasten their belts and bustle about giving orders.

They jumped to their feet.

"Fine. Moles, go ask Lieutenant Lopez for fifteen men. And as for you," the little fat fellow said to me, "if you've told the truth, I don't go back on my word. But you'll pay for this, if you're pulling our leg."

They left noisily and I waited in peace, still guarded by the falangists. From time to time I smiled at the thought of the face they were going to make. I felt dull and malicious. I could see them lifting up the gravestones, or opening the doors of the vaults one by one. I saw the whole situation as though I were another person: the prisoner determined to play the hero, the solemn falangists with their mustaches and the men in uniform running around among the graves. It was irresistibly funny.

After half an hour, the little fat fellow came back alone. I thought he had come to give the order to execute me. The others must have stayed in the cemetery.

The officer looked at me. He didn't look at all foolish.

"Take him out in the big courtyard with the others," he said. "When military operations are over, a regular tribunal will decide his case."

I thought I must have misunderstood.

"So they're not—they're not going to shoot me?" I asked.

"Not now, in any case. Afterwards, that doesn't concern me."
I still didn't understand.
"But why?" I said to him.
He shrugged his shoulders without replying, and the soldiers led me away. In the big courtyard there were a hundred or so prisoners, women, children and a few old men. I started to walk around the grass plot in the middle. I felt absolutely idiotic. At noon we were fed in the dining hall. Two or three fellows spoke to me. I must have known them, but I didn't answer. I didn't even know where I was.

Toward evening, about ten new prisoners were pushed into the courtyard. I recognized Garcia, the baker.

He said to me, "Lucky dog! I didn't expect to find you alive."

"They condemned me to death," I said, "and then they changed their minds. I don't know why."

"I was arrested at two o'clock," Garcia said.

"What for?"

Garcia took no part in politics.

"I don't know," he said. "They arrest everybody who doesn't think the way they do."

He lowered his voice.

"They got Gris."

I began to tremble.

"When?"

"This morning. He acted like a damned fool. He left his cousins' house Tuesday because of a disagreement. There were any number of fellows who would have hidden him, but he didn't want to be indebted to anybody any more. He said, 'I would have hidden at Ibbieta's, but since they've got him, I'll go hide in the cemetery.' "

"In the cemetery?"

"Yes. It was the god-damnedest thing. Naturally they passed by there this morning; that had to happen. They found him in the gravediggers' shack. They opened fire at him and they finished him off."

"In the cemetery!"

Everything went around in circles, and when I came to I was sitting on the ground. I laughed so hard the tears came to my eyes.

JORGE LUIS BORGES

The South

The man who landed in Buenos Aires in 1871 bore the name of Johannes Dahlmann and he was a minister in the Evangelical Church. In 1939, one of his grandchildren, Juan Dahlmann, was secretary of a municipal library on Calle Córdoba, and he considered himself profoundly Argentinian. His maternal grandfather had been that Francisco Flores, of the Second Line-Infantry Division, who had died on the frontier of Buenos Aires, run through with a lance by Indians from Catriel; in the discord inherent between his two lines of descent, Juan Dahlmann (perhaps driven to it by his Germanic blood) chose the line represented by his romantic ancestor, his ancestor of the romantic death. An old sword, a leather frame containing the daguerreotype of a blank-faced man with a beard, the dash and grace of certain music, the familiar strophes of *Martín Fierro*, the passing years, boredom and solitude, all went to foster this voluntary, but never ostentatious nationalism. At the cost of numerous small privations, Dahlmann had managed to save the empty shell of a ranch in the South which had belonged to the Flores family; he continually recalled the image of the balsamic eucalyptus trees and the great rose-colored house which had once been crimson. His duties, perhaps even indolence, kept him in the city. Summer after summer he contented himself with the abstract idea of possession and with the certitude that his ranch was waiting for him on a precise site in the middle of the plain. Late in February, 1939, something happened to him.

Blind to all fault, destiny can be ruthless at one's slightest distraction. Dahlmann had succeeded in acquiring, on that very afternoon, an imperfect copy of Weil's edition of *The Thousand and One Nights*. Avid to examine this find, he did not wait for the elevator but hurried up the stairs. In the obscurity, something brushed by his forehead: a bat, a bird? On the face of the woman who opened the door to him he saw horror engraved, and the hand he wiped across his face came away red with blood. The edge of a recently painted door which someone had forgotten to close had caused this wound. Dahlmann was able to fall asleep, but from the moment he awoke at dawn the savor of all things was atrociously poignant. Fever wasted him and the pictures in *The Thousand and One Nights* served to illustrate nightmares. Friends and relatives paid him visits and, with exaggerated smiles, assured him that they thought he looked fine. Dahlmann listened to them with a kind of feeble stupor and he marveled at their not knowing that he was in hell. A week, eight days passed, and they were like eight centuries. One afternoon, the usual doctor appeared, accompanied by a new doctor, and they carried him off to a sanitarium on the Calle Ecuador, for it was necessary to X-ray him. Dahlmann, in the hackney coach which bore them away, thought that he would, at last, be able to sleep in a room different from his own. He felt happy and communicative. When he arrived at his destination, they undressed him, shaved his head, bound him with metal fastenings to a stretcher; they shone bright lights on him until he was blind and dizzy, auscultated him, and a masked man stuck a needle into his arm. He awoke with a feeling of nausea, covered with a bandage, in a cell with something of a well about it; in the days and nights which followed the operation he came to realize that he had merely been, up until then, in a suburb of hell. Ice in his mouth did not leave the least trace of freshness. During these days Dahlmann hated himself in minute detail: he hated his identity, his bodily necessities, his humiliation, the beard which bristled upon his face. He stoically endured the curative measures, which were painful, but when the surgeon told him he had been on the point of death from septicemia, Dahlmann dissolved in tears of self-pity for his fate. Physical wretchedness and the incessant anticipation of horrible nights had not allowed him time to think of anything so abstract as death. On another day, the surgeon told him he was healing and that, very soon, he would be able to go to his ranch for convalescence. Incredibly enough, the promised day arrived.

Reality favors symmetries and slight anachronisms: Dahlmann had arrived at the sanitarium in a hackney coach and now a hackney coach was to take him to the Constitución station. The first fresh tang of autumn, after the summer's oppressiveness, seemed like a symbol in nature of his rescue and release from fever and death. The city, at seven in the morning, had not lost that air of an old house lent it by the night; the streets seemed like long vestibules, the plazas were like patios. Dahlmann recognized the city with joy on the edge of vertigo: a second before his eyes registered the phenomena themselves, he recalled the corners, the billboards, the modest variety of Buenos Aires. In the yellow light of the new day, all things returned to him.

Every Argentine knows that the South begins at the other side of Rivadavia. Dahlmann was in the habit of saying that this was no mere convention, that whoever crosses this street enters a more ancient and sterner world. From inside the carriage he sought out, among the new buildings, the iron grill window, the brass knocker, the arched door, the entrance way, the intimate patio.

At the railroad station he noted that he still had thirty minutes. He quickly recalled that in a café on the Calle Brazil (a few dozen feet from Yrigoyen's house) there was an enormous cat which allowed itself to be caressed as if it were a disdainful divinity. He entered the café. There was the cat, asleep. He ordered a cup of coffee, slowly stirred the sugar, sipped it (this pleasure had been denied him in the clinic), and thought, as he smoothed the cat's black coat, that this contact was an illusion and that the two beings, man and cat, were as good as separated by a glass, for man lives in time, in succession, while the magical animal lives in the present, in the eternity of the instant.

Along the next to the last platform the train lay waiting. Dahlmann walked through the coaches until he found one almost empty. He arranged his baggage in the network rack. When the train started off, he took down his valise and extracted, after some hesitation, the first volume of *The Thousand and One Nights*. To travel with this book, which was so much a part of the history of his ill-fortune, was a kind of affirmation that his ill-fortune had been annulled; it was a joyous and secret defiance of the frustrated forces of evil.

Along both sides of the train the city dissipated into suburbs; this sight, and then a view of the gardens and villas, delayed the beginning of his reading. The truth was that Dahlmann read very little. The magnetized mountain and the genie who swore to kill his benefactor are—who would deny it?—marvelous, but not so much more than the morning itself and the mere fact of being. The joy of life distracted him from paying attention to Scheherezade and her superfluous miracles. Dahlmann closed his book and allowed himself to live.

Lunch—the bouillon served in shining metal bowls, as in the remote summers of childhood—was one more peaceful and rewarding delight.

Tomorrow I'll wake up at the ranch, he thought, and it was as if he was two men at a time: the man who traveled through the autumn day and across the geography of the fatherland, and the other one, locked up in a sanitarium and subject to methodical servitude. He saw unplastered brick houses, long and angled, timelessly watching the trains go by; he saw horsemen along the dirt roads; he saw gullies and lagoons and ranches; he saw great luminous clouds that resembled marble; and all these things were accidental, casual, like dreams of the plain. He also thought he recognized trees and crop fields; but he would not have been able to name them, for his actual knowledge of the countryside was quite inferior to his nostalgic and literary knowledge.

From time to time he slept, and his dreams were animated by the impetus of the train. The intolerable white sun of high noon had already become the yellow sun which precedes nightfall, and it would not be long before it would turn red. The railroad car was now also different; it was not the same as the one which had quit the station siding at Constitución; the plain and the hours had transfigured it. Outside, the moving shadow of the railroad car stretched toward the horizon. The elemental earth was not perturbed either by settlements or other signs of humanity. The country was vast but at the same time intimate and, in some measure, secret. The limitless country sometimes contained only a solitary bull. The solitude was perfect, perhaps hostile, and it might have occurred to Dahlmann that he was traveling into the past and not merely south. He was distracted from these considerations by the railroad inspector who, on reading his ticket, advised him that the train would not let him off at the regular station but at another: an earlier stop, one scarcely known to Dahlmann. (The man added an explanation which Dahlmann did not attempt to understand, and which he hardly heard, for the mechanism of events did not concern him.)

The train laboriously ground to a halt, practically in the middle of the plain. The station lay on the other side of the tracks; it was not much more than a siding and a shed. There was no means of conveyance to be seen, but the station chief supposed that the traveler might secure a vehicle from a general store and inn to be found some ten or twelve blocks away.

Dahlmann accepted the walk as a small adventure. The sun had already disappeared from view, but a final splendor exalted the vivid and silent plain, before the night erased its color. Less to avoid fatigue than to draw out his enjoyment of these sights, Dahlmann walked slowly, breathing in the odor of clover with sumptuous joy.

The general store at one time had been painted a deep scarlet, but the years had tempered this violent color for its own good. Something in its poor architecture recalled a steel engraving, perhaps one from an old edition of *Paul et Virginie*. A number of horses were hitched up to the paling. Once inside, Dahlmann thought he recognized the shopkeeper. Then he realized that he had been deceived by the man's resemblance to one of the male nurses in the sanitarium. When the shopkeeper heard Dahlmann's request, he said he would have the shay made up. In order to add one more event to that day and to kill time, Dahlmann decided to eat at the general store.

Some country louts, to whom Dahlmann did not at first pay any attention, were eating and drinking at one of the tables. On the floor, and hanging on to the bar, squatted an old man, immobile as an object. His years had reduced and polished him as water does a stone or the generations of men do a sentence. He was dark, dried up, diminutive, and seemed outside time, situated in eternity. Dahlmann noted with satisfaction the kerchief, the thick poncho, the long *chiripá*, and the colt boots, and told himself, as he recalled futile discussions with people from the Northern counties or from the province of Entre Rios, that gauchos like this no longer existed outside the South.

Dahlmann sat down next to the window. The darkness began overcoming the plain, but the odor and sound of the earth penetrated the iron bars of the window. The shop owner brought him sardines, followed by some roast meat. Dahlmann washed the meal down with several glasses of red wine. Idling, he relished the tart savor of the wine, and let his gaze, now grown somewhat drowsy, wander over the shop. A kerosene lamp hung from a beam. There were three customers at the other table: two of them appeared to be farm workers; the third man, whose features hinted at Chinese blood, was drinking with his hat on. Of a sudden, Dahlmann felt something brush lightly against his face. Next to the heavy glass of turbid wine, upon one of the stripes in the table cloth, lay a spit ball of breadcrumb. That was all: but someone had thrown it there.

The men at the other table seemed totally cut off from him. Perplexed, Dahlmann decided that nothing had happened, and he opened the volume of *The Thousand and One Nights*, by way of suppressing reality. After a few moments another little ball landed on his table, and now the *peones* laughed outright. Dahlmann said to himself that he was not frightened, but he reasoned that it would be a major blunder if he, a convalescent, were to allow himself to be dragged by strangers into some chaotic quarrel. He determined to leave, and had already gotten to his feet when the owner came up and exhorted him in an alarmed voice:

"*Señor* Dahlmann, don't pay any attention to those lads; they're half high."

Dahlmann was not surprised to learn that the other man, now, knew his name. But he felt that these conciliatory words served only to aggravate the situation. Previous to this moment, the *peones*' provocation was directed against an unknown face, against no one in particular, almost against no one at all. Now it was an attack against him, against his name, and his neighbors knew it. Dahlmann pushed the owner aside, confronted the *peones*, and demanded to know what they wanted of him.

The tough with a Chinese look staggered heavily to his feet. Almost in Juan Dahlmann's face he shouted insults, as if he had been a long way off. His game was to exaggerate his drunkenness, and this extravagance constituted a ferocious mockery. Between curses and obscenities, he threw a long knife into the air, followed it with his eyes, caught and juggled it, and challenged Dahlmann to a knife fight. The owner objected in a tremulous voice, pointing out that Dahlmann was unarmed. At this point, something unforeseeable occurred.

From a corner of the room, the old ecstatic gaucho—in whom Dahlmann saw a summary and cipher of the South (his South)—threw him a naked dagger, which landed at his feet. It was as if the South had resolved that Dahlmann should accept the duel. Dahlmann bent over to pick up the dagger, and felt two things. The first, that this almost instinctive act bound him to fight. The second, that the weapon, in his torpid hand, was no defense at all, but would merely serve to justify his murder. He had once played with a poniard, like all men, but his idea of fencing and knife-play did not go further than the notion that all strokes should be directed upwards, with the cutting edge held inwards. *They would not have allowed such things to happen to me in the sanitarium,* he thought.

"Let's get on our way," said the other man.

They went out and if Dahlmann was without hope, he was also without fear. As he crossed the threshold, he felt that to die in a knife fight, under the open sky, and going forward to the attack, would have been a liberation, a joy, and a festive occasion, on the first night in the sanitarium, when they stuck him with the needle. He felt that if he had been able to choose, then, or to dream his death, this would have been the death he would have chosen or dreamt.

Firmly clutching his knife, which he perhaps would not know how to wield, Dahlmann went out into the plain.

A Tree, A Rock, A Cloud

It was raining that morning, and still very dark. When the boy reached the streetcar café he had almost finished his route and he went in for a cup of coffee. The place was an all-night café owned by a bitter and stingy man called Leo. After the raw, empty street, the café seemed friendly and bright; along the counter there were a couple of soldiers, three spinners from the cotton mill, and in a corner a man who sat hunched over with his nose and half his face down in a beer mug. The boy wore a helmet such as aviators wear. When he went into the café he unbuckled the chin strap and raised the right flap up over his pink little ear; often as he drank his coffee someone would speak to him in a friendly way. But this morning Leo did not look into his face and none of the men were talking. He paid and was leaving the café when a voice called out to him:

"Son! Hey Son!"

He turned back and the man in the corner was crooking his finger and nodding to him. He had brought his face out of the beer mug and he seemed suddenly very happy. The man was long and pale, with a big nose and faded orange hair.

"Hey Son!"

The boy went toward him. He was an undersized boy of about twelve, with one shoulder drawn higher than the other because of the weight of the paper sack. His face was shallow, freckled, and his eyes were round child eyes.

"Yeah Mister?"

The man laid one hand on the paper boy's shoulders, then grasped the boy's chin and turned his face slowly from one side to the other. The boy shrank back uneasily.

"Say! What's the big idea?"

The boy's voice was shrill; inside the café it was suddenly very quiet.

The man said slowly, "I love you."

All along the counter the men laughed. The boy, who had scowled and sidled away, did not know what to do. He looked over the counter at Leo, and Leo watched him with a weary, brittle jeer. The boy tried to laugh also. But the man was serious and sad.

"I did not mean to tease you, Son," he said. "Sit down and have a beer with me. There is something I have to explain."

Cautiously, out of the corner of his eye, the paper boy questioned the men along the counter to see what he should do. But they had gone back to their beer or their breakfast and did not notice him. Leo put a cup of coffee on the counter and a little jug of cream.

"He is a minor," Leo said.

The paper boy slid himself up onto the stool. His ear beneath the upturned flap of the helmet was very small and red. The man was nodding at him soberly. "It is important," he said. Then he reached in his hip pocket and brought out something which he held up in the palm of his hand for the boy to see.

"Look very carefully," he said.

The boy stared, but there was nothing to look at very carefully. The man held in his big, grimy palm a photograph. It was the face of a woman, but blurred, so that only the hat and the dress she was wearing stood out clearly.

"See?" the man asked.

The boy nodded and the man placed another picture in his palm. The woman was standing on a beach in a bathing suit. The suit made her stomach very big, and that was the main thing you noticed.

"Got a good look?" He leaned over closer and finally asked: "You ever seen her before?"

The boy sat motionless, staring slantwise at the man. "Not so I know of."

"Very well." The man blew on the photographs and put them back into his pocket. "That was my wife."

"Dead?" the boy asked.

Slowly the man shook his head. He pursed his lips as though about to whistle and answered in a long-drawn way: "Nuuu—" he said. "I will explain."

The beer on the counter before the man was in a large brown mug. He did not pick it up to drink. Instead he bent down and, putting his face over the rim, he rested there for a moment. Then with both hands he tilted the mug and sipped.

"Some night you'll go to sleep with your big nose in a mug and drown," said Leo. "Prominent transient drowns in beer. That would be a cute death."

The paper boy tried to signal to Leo. While the man was not looking he screwed up his face and worked his mouth to question soundlessly: "Drunk?" But Leo only raised his eyebrows and turned away to put some pink strips of bacon on the grill. The man pushed the mug away from him, straightened himself, and folded his loose crooked hands on the counter. His face was sad as he looked at the paper boy. He did not blink, but from time to time the lids closed down with delicate gravity over his pale green eyes. It was nearing dawn and the boy shifted the weight of the paper sack.

"I am talking about love," the man said. "With me it is a science."

The boy half slid down from the stool. But the man raised his forefinger, and there was something about him that held the boy and would not let him go away.

"Twelve years ago I married the woman in the photograph. She was my wife for one year, nine months, three days, and two nights. I loved her. Yes. . . ." He tightened his blurred, rambling voice and said again: "I loved her. I thought also that she loved me. I was a railroad engineer. She had all home comforts and luxuries. It never crept into my brain that she was not satisfied. But do you know what happened?"

"Mgneeow!" said Leo.

The man did not take his eyes from the boy's face. "She left me. I came in one night and the house was empty and she was gone. She left me."

"With a fellow?" the boy asked.

Gently the man placed his palm down on the counter. "Why, naturally, Son. A woman does not run off like that alone."

The café was quiet, the soft rain black and endless in the street outside. Leo pressed down the frying bacon with the prongs of his long fork. "So you have been chasing the floozie for eleven years. You frazzled old rascal!"

For the first time the man glanced at Leo. "Please don't be vulgar. Besides, I was not speaking to you." He turned back to the boy and said in a trusting and secretive undertone, "Let's not pay any attention to him. O.K.?"

The paper boy nodded doubtfully.

"It was like this," the man continued. "I am a person who feels many things. All my life one thing after another has impressed me. Moonlight. The leg of a pretty girl. One thing after another. But the point is that when I had enjoyed anything there was a peculiar sensation as though it was laying around loose in me. Nothing seemed to finish itself up or fit in with the other things. Women? I had my portion of them. The same. Afterwards laying around loose in me. I was a man who had never loved."

Very slowly he closed his eyelids, and the gesture was like a curtain drawn at the end of a scene in a play. When he spoke again his voice was excited and the words came fast—the lobes of his large, loose ears seemed to tremble.

"Then I met this woman. I was fifty-one years old and she always said she was thirty. I met her at a filling station and we were married within three days. And do you know what it was like? I just can't tell you. All I had ever felt was gathered together around this woman. Nothing lay around loose in me any more but was finished up by her."

The man stopped suddenly and stroked his long nose. His voice sank down to a steady and reproachful undertone: "I'm not explaining this right. What happened was this. There were these beautiful feelings and loose little pleasures inside me. And this woman was something like an assembly line for my soul. I run these little pieces of myself through her and I come out complete. Now do you follow me?"

"What was her name?" the boy asked.

"Oh," he said. "I called her Dodo. But that is immaterial."

"Did you try to make her come back?"

The man did not seem to hear. "Under the circumstances you can imagine how I felt when she left me."

Leo took the bacon from the grill and folded two strips of it between a bun. He had a gray face, with slitted eyes, and a pinched nose saddled by faint blue shadows. One of the mill workers signaled for more coffee and Leo poured it. He did not give refills on coffee free. The spinner ate breakfast there every morning, but the better Leo knew his customers the stingier he treated them. He nibbled his own bun as though he grudged it to himself.

"And you never got hold of her again?"

The boy did not know what to think of the man, and his child's face was uncertain with mingled curiosity and doubt. He was new on the paper route; it was still strange to him to be out in the town in the black, queer early morning.

"Yes," the man said. "I took a number of steps to get her back. I went around trying to locate her. I went to Tulsa where she had folks. And to Mobile. I went to every town she had ever mentioned to me, and I hunted down every man she had formerly been connected with. Tulsa, Atlanta, Chicago, Cheehaw, Memphis. . . . For the better part of two years I chased around the country trying to lay hold of her."

"But the pair of them had vanished from the face of the earth!" said Leo.

"Don't listen to him," the man said confidentially. "And also just forget those two years. They are not important. What matters is that around the third year a curious thing begun to happen to me."

"What?" the boy asked.

The man leaned down and tilted his mug to take a sip of beer. But as he hovered over the mug his nostrils fluttered slightly; he sniffed the staleness of the beer and did not drink. "Love is a curious thing to begin with. At first I thought only of getting her back. It was a kind of mania. But then as time went on I tried to remember her. But do you know what happened?"

"No," the boy said.

"When I laid myself down on a bed and tried to think about her my mind became a blank. I couldn't see her. I would take out her pictures and look. No good. Nothing doing. A blank. Can you imagine it?"

"Say Mac!" Leo called down the counter. "Can you imagine this bozo's mind a blank?"

Slowly, as though fanning away flies, the man waved his hand. His green eyes were concentrated and fixed on the shallow little face of the paper boy.

"But a sudden piece of glass on a sidewalk. Or a nickel tune in a music box. A shadow on a wall at night. And I would remember. It might happen in a street and I would cry or bang my head against a lamppost. You follow me?"

"A piece of glass . . ." the boy said.

"Anything. I would walk around and I had no power of how and when to remember her. You think you can put up a kind of shield. But remembering don't come to a man face forward—it corners around sideways. I was at the mercy of everything I saw and heard. Suddenly instead of me combing the countryside to find her she began to chase me around in my very soul. *She* chasing *me*, mind you! and in my soul."

The boy asked finally: "What part of the country were you in then?"

"Ooh," the man groaned, "I was a sick mortal. It was like smallpox. I confess, Son, that I boozed. I fornicated. I committed any sin that suddenly appealed to me. I am loath to confess it but I will do so. When I recall that period it is all curdled in my mind, it was so terrible."

The man leaned his head down and tapped his forehead on the counter. For a few seconds he stayed bowed over in this position, the back of his stringy neck covered with orange furze, his hands with their long warped fingers held palm to palm in an attitude of prayer. Then the man straightened himself; he was smiling and suddenly his face was bright and tremulous and old.

"It was in the fifth year that it happened," he said. "And with it I started my science."

Leo's mouth jerked with a pale, quick grin. "Well none of we boys are getting any younger," he said. Then with sudden anger he balled up a dishcloth he was holding and threw it down hard on the floor. "You draggle-tailed old Romeo!"

"What happened?" the boy asked.

The old man's voice was high and clear: "Peace," he answered.

"Huh?"

"It is hard to explain scientifically, Son," he said. "I guess the logical explanation is that she and I had fleed around from each other for so long that finally we just got tangled up together and lay down and quit. Peace. A queer and beautiful blankness. It was spring in Portland and the rain came every afternoon. All evening I just stayed there on my bed in the dark. And that is how the science come to me."

The windows in the streetcar were pale blue with light. The two soldiers paid for their beers and opened the door—one of the soldiers combed his hair and wiped off his muddy puttees before they went outside. The three mill workers bent silently over their breakfasts. Leo's clock was ticking on the wall.

"It is this. And listen carefully. I meditated on love and reasoned it out. I realized what is wrong with us. Men fall in love for the first time. And what do they fall in love with?"

The boy's soft mouth was partly open and he did not answer.

"A woman," the old man said. "Without science, with nothing to go by, they undertake the most dangerous and sacred experience in God's earth. They fall in love with a woman. Is that correct, Son?"

"Yeah," the boy said faintly.

"They start at the wrong end of love. They begin at the climax. Can you wonder it is so miserable? Do you know how men should love?"

The old man reached over and grasped the boy by the collar of his leather jacket. He gave him a gentle shake and his green eyes gazed down unblinking and grave.

"Son, do you know how love should be begun?"

The boy sat small and listening and still. Slowly he shook his head. The old man leaned closer and whispered:

"A tree. A rock. A cloud."

It was still raining outside in the street: a mild, gray, endless rain. The mill whistle blew for the six o'clock shift and the three spinners paid and went away. There was no one in the café but Leo, the old man, and the little paper boy.

"The weather was like this in Portland," he said. "At the time my science was begun. I meditated and I started very cautious. I would pick up something from the street and take it home with me. I bought a goldfish and I concentrated on the goldfish and I loved it. I graduated from one thing to another. Day by day I was getting this technique. On the road from Portland to San Diego——"

"Aw shut up!" screamed Leo suddenly. "Shut up! Shut up!"

The old man still held the collar of the boy's jacket; he was trembling and his face was earnest and bright and wild. "For six years now I have gone around by myself and built up my science. And now I am a master.

Son, I can love anything. No longer do I have to think about it even. I see a street full of people and a beautiful light comes in me. I watch a bird in the sky. Or I meet a traveler on the road. Everything, Son. And anybody. All strangers and all loved! Do you realize what a science like mine can mean?"

The boy held himself stiffly, his hands curled tight around the counter edge. Finally he asked: "Did you ever really find that lady?"

"What? What say, Son?"

"I mean," the boy asked timidly. "Have you fallen in love with a woman again?"

The old man loosened his grasp on the boy's collar. He turned away and for the first time his green eyes had a vague and scattered look. He lifted his mug from the counter, drank down the yellow beer. His head was shaking slowly from side to side. Then finally he answered: "No, Son. You see that is the last step in my science. I go cautious. And I am not quite ready yet."

"Well!" said Leo. "Well well well!"

The old man stood in the open doorway. "Remember," he said. Framed there in the gray damp light of the early morning he looked shrunken and seedy and frail. But his smile was bright. "Remember I love you," he said with a last nod. And the door closed quietly behind him.

The boy did not speak for a long time. He pulled down the bangs on his forehead and slid his grimy little forefinger around the rim of his empty cup. Then without looking at Leo he finally asked:

"Was he drunk?"

"No," said Leo shortly.

The boy raised his clear voice higher. "Then was he a dope fiend?"

"No."

The boy looked up at Leo, and his flat little face was desperate, his voice urgent and shrill. "Was he crazy? Do you think he was a lunatic?" The paper boy's voice dropped suddenly with doubt. "Leo?" Or not?"

But Leo would not answer him. Leo had run a night café for fourteen years, and he held himself to be a critic of craziness. There were the town characters and also the transients who roamed in from the night. He knew the manias of all of them. But he did not want to satisfy the questions of the waiting child. He tightened his pale face and was silent.

So the boy pulled down the right flap of his helmet and as he turned to leave he made the only comment that seemed safe to him, the only remark that could not be laughed down and despised:

"He sure has done a lot of traveling."

A Worn Path

It was December—a bright frozen day in the early morning. Far out in the country there was an old Negro woman with her head tied in a red rag, coming along a path through the pinewoods. Her name was Phoenix Jackson. She was very old and small and she walked slowly in the dark pine shadows, moving a little from side to side in her steps, with the balanced heaviness and lightness of a pendulum in a grandfather clock. She carried a thin, small cane made from an umbrella, and with this she kept tapping the frozen earth in front of her. This made a grave and persistent noise in the still air, that seemed meditative like the chirping of a solitary little bird.

She wore a dark striped dress reaching down to her shoe tops, and an equally long apron of bleached sugar sacks, with a full pocket: all neat and tidy, but every time she took a step she might have fallen over her shoelaces, which dragged from her unlaced shoes. She looked straight ahead. Her eyes were blue with age. Her skin had a pattern all its own of numberless branching wrinkles and as though a whole little tree stood in the middle of her forehead, but a golden color ran underneath, and the two knobs of her cheeks were illumined by a yellow burning under the dark. Under the red rag her hair came down on her neck in the frailest of ringlets, still black, and with an odor like copper.

Now and then there was a quivering in the thicket. Old Phoenix said, "Out of my way, all you foxes, owls, beetles, jack rabbits, coons and wild animals! . . . Keep out from under these feet, little bob-whites. . . . Keep the big wild hogs out of my path. Don't let none of these come running my direction. I got a long way." Under her small black-freckled hand her cane, limber as a buggy whip, would switch at the brush as if to rouse up any hiding things.

On she went. The woods were deep and still. The sun made the pine needles almost too bright to look at, up where the wind rocked. The cones dropped as light as feathers. Down in the hollow was the mourning dove —it was not too late for him.

The path ran up a hill. "Seem like there is chains about my feet, time I get this far," she said, in the voice of argument old people keep to use with themselves. "Something always take a hold of me on this hill—pleads I should stay."

After she got to the top she turned and gave a full, severe look behind her where she had come. "Up through pines," she said at length. "Now down through oaks."

Her eyes opened their widest, and she started down gently. But before she got to the bottom of the hill a bush caught her dress.

Her fingers were busy and intent, but her skirts were full and long, so that before she could pull them free in one place they were caught in another. It was not possible to allow the dress to tear. "I in the thorny bush," she said. "Thorns, you doing your appointed work. Never want to let folks pass, no sir. Old eyes thought you was a pretty little *green* bush."

Finally, trembling all over, she stood free, and after a moment dared to stoop for her cane.

"Sun so high!" she cried, leaning back and looking, while the thick tears went over her eyes. "The time getting all gone here."

At the foot of this hill was a place where a log was laid across the creek. "Now comes the trial," said Phoenix.

Putting her right foot out, she mounted the log and shut her eyes. Lifting her skirt, leveling her cane fiercely before her, like a festival figure in some parade, she began to march across. Then she opened her eyes and she was safe on the other side.

"I wasn't as old as I thought," she said.

But she sat down to rest. She spread her skirts on the bank around her and folded her hands over her knees. Up above her was a tree in a pearly cloud of mistletoe. She did not dare to close her eyes, and when a little boy brought her a plate with a slice of marble-cake on it she spoke to him. "That would be acceptable," she said. But when she went to take it there was just her own hand in the air.

So she left that tree, and had to go through a barbed-wire fence. There she had to creep and crawl, spreading her knees and stretching her fingers like a baby trying to climb the steps. But she talked loudly to herself: she could not let her dress be torn now, so late in the day, and she could not pay for having her arm or her leg sawed off if she got caught fast where she was.

At last she was safe through the fence and risen up out in the clearing. Big dead trees, like black men with one arm, were standing in the purple stalks of the withered cotton field. There sat a buzzard.

"Who you watching?"

In the furrow she made her way along.

"Glad this not the season for bulls," she said, looking sideways, "and the good Lord made his snakes to curl up and sleep in the winter. A pleasure I don't see no two-headed snake coming around that tree, where it come once. It took a while to get by him, back in the summer."

She passed through the old cotton and went into a field of dead corn. It whispered and shook and was taller than her head. "Through the maze now," she said, for there was no path.

Then there was something tall, black, and skinny there, moving before her.

At first she took it for a man. It could have been a man dancing in the field. But she stood still and listened, and it did not make a sound. It was as silent as a ghost.

"Ghost," she said sharply, "who be you the ghost of? For I have heard of nary death close by."

But there was no answer—only the ragged dancing in the wind.

She shut her eyes, reached out her hand, and touched a sleeve. She found a coat and inside that an emptiness, cold as ice.

"You scarecrow," she said. Her face lighted. "I ought to be shut up for good," she said with laughter. "My senses is gone. I too old. I the oldest people I ever know. Dance, old scarecrow," she said, "while I dancing with you."

She kicked her foot over the furrow, and with mouth drawn down, shook her head once or twice in a little strutting way. Some husks blew down and whirled in streamers about her skirts.

Then she went on, parting her way from side to side with the cane, through the whispering field. At last she came to the end, to a wagon track where the silver grass blew between the red ruts. The quail were walking around like pullets, seeming all dainty and unseen.

"Walk pretty," she said. "This the easy place. This the easy going."

She followed the track, swaying through the quiet bare fields, through the little strings of trees silver in their dead leaves, past cabins silver from weather, with the doors and windows boarded shut, all like old women under a spell sitting there. "I walking in their sleep," she said, nodding her head vigorously.

In a ravine she went where a spring was silently flowing through a hallow log. Old Phoenix bent and drank. "Sweet-gum makes the water sweet," she said, and drank more. "Nobody know who made this well, for it was here when I was born."

The track crossed a swampy part where the moss hung as white as lace from every limb. "Sleep on, alligators, and blow your bubbles." Then the track went into the road.

Deep, deep the road went down between the high green-colored banks. Overhead the live-oaks met, and it was as dark as a cave.

A black dog with a lolling tongue came up out of the weeds by the ditch. She was meditating, and not ready, and when he came at her she only hit him a little with her cane. Over she went in the ditch, like a little puff of milkweed.

Down there, her senses drifted away. A dream visited her, and she reached her hand up, but nothing reached down and gave her a pull. So she lay there and presently went to talking. "Old woman," she said to herself, "that black dog come up out of the weeds to stall your off, and now there he sitting on his fine tail, smiling at you."

A white man finally came along and found her—a hunter, a young man, with his dog on a chain.

"Well, Granny!" he laughed. "What are you doing there?"

"Lying on my back like a June-bug waiting to be turned over, mister," she said, reaching up her hand.

He lifted her up, gave her a swing in the air, and set her down. "Anythink broken, Granny?"

"No sir, them old dead weeds is springy enough," said Phoenix, when she had got her breath. "I thank you for your trouble."

"Where do you live, Granny?" he asked, while the two dogs were growling at each other.

"Away back yonder, sir, behind the ridge. You can't even see it from here."

"On your way home?"

"No sir, I going to town."

"Why, that's too far! That's as far as I walk when I come out myself, and I get something for my trouble." He patted the stuffed bag he carried, and there hung down a little closed claw. It was one of the bob-whites, with its beak hooked bitterly to show it was dead. "Now you go on home, Granny!"

"I bound to go to town, mister," said Phoenix. "The time come around."

He gave another laugh, filling the whole landscape. "I know you old colored people! Wouldn't miss going to town to see Santa Claus!"

But something held old Phoenix very still. The deep lines in her face went into a fierce and different radiation. Without warning, she had seen with her own eyes a flashing nickel fall out of the man's pocket onto the ground.

"How old are you, Granny?" he was saying.

"There is no telling, mister," she said, "no telling."

Then she gave a little cry and clapped her hands and said, "Git on away from here, dog! Look! Look at that dog!" She laughed as if in admiration. "He ain't scared of nobody. He a big black dog." She whispered, "Sic him!"

"Watch me get rid of that cur," said the man. "Sic him, Pete! Sic him!"

Phoenix heard the dogs fighting, and heard the man running and throwing sticks. She even heard a gunshot. But she was slowly bending forward by that time, further and further forward, the lids stretched down over her eyes, as if she were doing this in her sleep. Her chin was lowered almost to her knees. The yellow palm of her hand came out from the fold of her apron. Her fingers slid down and along the ground under the piece of money with the grace and care they would have in lifting an egg from under a setting hen. Then she slowly straightened up, she stood erect, and the nickel was in her apron pocket. A bird flew by. Her lips moved. "God watching me the whole time. I come to stealing."

The man came back, and his own dog panted about them. "Well, I scared him off that time," he said, and then he laughed and lifted his gun and pointed it at Phoenix.

She stood straight and faced him.

"Doesn't the gun scare you?" he said, still pointing it.

"No, sir, I seen plenty go off closer by, in my day, and for less than what I done," she said, holding utterly still.

He smiled, and shouldered the gun. "Well, Granny," he said, "you must be a hundred years old, and scared of nothing. I'd give you a dime if I had any money with me. But you take my advice and stay home, and nothing will happen to you."

"I bound to go on my way, mister," said Phoenix. She inclined her head in the red rag. Then they went in different directions, but she could hear the gun shooting again and again over the hill.

She walked on. The shadows hung from the oak trees to the road like curtains. Then she smelled wood-smoke, and smelled the river, and she saw a steeple and the cabins on their steep steps. Dozens of little black children whirled around her. There ahead was Natchez shining. Bells were ringing. She walked on.

In the paved city it was Christmas time. There were red and green electric lights strung and crisscrossed everywhere, and all turned on in the daytime. Old Phoenix would have been lost if she had not distrusted her eyesight and depended on her feet to know where to take her.

She paused quietly on the sidewalk where people were passing by. A lady came along in the crowd, carrying an armful of red-, green- and silver-wrapped presents; she gave off perfume like red roses in hot summer, and Phoenix stopped her.

"Please, missy, will you lace up my shoe?" She held up her foot.

"What do you want, Grandma?"

"See my shoe," said Phoenix. "Do all right for out in the country, but wouldn't look right to go in a big building."

"Stand still then, Grandma," said the lady. She put her packages down on the sidewalk beside her and laced and tied both shoes tightly.

"Can't lace 'em with a cane," said Phoenix. "Thank you, missy. I doesn't mind asking a nice lady to tie up my shoe, when I gets out on the street."

Moving slowly and from side to side, she went into the big building, and into a tower of steps, where she walked up and around and around until her feet knew to stop.

She entered a door, and there she saw nailed up on the wall the document that had been stamped with the gold seal and framed in the gold frame, which matched the dream that was hung up in her head.

"Here I be," she said. There was a fixed and ceremonial stiffness over her body.

"A charity case, I suppose," said an attendant who sat at the desk before her.

But Phoenix only looked above her head. There was sweat on her face, the wrinkles in her skin shone like a bright net.

"Speak up, Grandma," the woman said. "What's your name? We must have your history, you know. Have you been here before? What seems to be the trouble with you?"

Old Phoenix only gave a twitch to her face as if a fly were bothering her.

"Are you deaf?" cried the attendant.

But then the nurse came in.

"Oh, that's just old Aunt Phoenix," she said. "She doesn't come for herself—she has a little grandson. She makes these trips just as regular as clockwork. She lives away back off the Old Natchez Trace." She bent down. "Well, Aunt Phoenix, why don't you just take a seat? We won't keep you standing after your long trip." She pointed.

The old woman sat down, bolt upright in the chair.

"Now, how is the boy?" asked the nurse.

Old Phoenix did not speak.

"I said, how is the boy?"

But Phoenix only waited and stared straight ahead, her face very solemn and withdrawn into rigidity.

"Is his throat any better?" asked the nurse. "Aunt Phoenix, don't you hear me? Is your grandson's throat any better since the last time you came for the medicine?"

With her hands on her knees, the old woman waited, silent, erect and motionless, just as if she were in armor.

"You mustn't take up our time this way, Aunt Phoenix," the nurse said. "Tell us quickly about your grandson, and get it over. He isn't dead, is he?"

At last there came a flicker and then a flame of comprehension across her face, and she spoke.

"My grandson. It was my memory had left me. There I sat and forgot why I made my long trip."

"Forgot?" The nurse frowned. "After you came so far?"

Then Phoenix was like an old woman begging a dignified forgiveness for waking up frightened in the night. "I never did go to school, I was too old at the Surrender," she said in a soft voice. "I'm an old woman without an education. It was my memory fail me. My little grandson, he is just the same, and I forgot it in the coming."

"Throat never heals, does it?" said the nurse, speaking in a loud, sure voice to old Phoenix. By now she had a card with something written on it, a little list. "Yes. Swallowed lye. When was it?—January—two-three years ago—"

Phoenix spoke unasked now. "No, missy, he not dead, he just the same. Every little while his throat begin to close up again, and he not able to swallow. He not get his breath. He not able to help himself. So the time come around, and I go on another trip for the soothing medicine."

"All right. The doctor said as long as you came to get it, you could have it," said the nurse. "But it's an obstinate case."

"My little grandson, he sit up there in the house all wrapped up, waiting by himself," Phoenix went on. "We is the only two left in the world. He suffer and it don't seem to put him back at all. He got a sweet look. He going to last. He wear a little patch quilt and peep out holding his mouth open like a little bird. I remembers so plain now. I not going to forget him again, no, the whole enduring time. I could tell him from all the others in creation."

"All right." The nurse was trying to hush her now. She brought her a bottle of medicine. "Charity," she said, making a check mark in a book.

Old Phoenix held the bottle close to her eyes, and then carefully put it into her pocket.

"I thank you," she said.

"It's Christmas time, Grandma," said the attendant. "Could I give you a few pennies out of my purse?"

"Five pennies is a nickel," said Phoenix stiffly.

"Here's a nickel," said the attendant.

Phoenix rose carefully and held out her hand. She received the nickel and then fished the other nickel out of her pocket and laid it beside the new one. She stared at her palm closely, with her head on one side.

Then she gave a tap with her cane on the floor.

"This is what come to me to do," she said. "I going to the store and buy my child a little windmill they sells, made out of paper. He going to find it hard to believe there such a thing in the world. I'll march myself back where he waiting, holding it straight up in this hand."

She lifted her free hand, gave a little nod, turned around, and walked out of the doctor's office. Then her slow step began on the stairs, going down.

Idiots First

The thick ticking of the tin clock stopped. Mendel, dozing in the dark, awoke in fright. The pain returned as he listened. He drew on his cold embittered clothing, and wasted minutes sitting at the edge of the bed.

"Isaac," he ultimately sighed.

In the kitchen, Isaac, his astonished mouth open, held six peanuts in his palm. He placed each on the table. "One . . . two . . . nine."

He gathered each peanut and appeared in the doorway. Mendel, in loose hat and long overcoat, still sat on the bed. Isaac watched with small eyes and ears, thick hair graying the sides of his head.

"Schlaf," he nasally said.

"No," muttered Mendel. As if stifling he rose. "Come, Isaac."

He wound his old watch though the sight of the stopped clock nauseated him.

Isaac wanted to hold it to his ear.

"No, it's late." Mendel put the watch carefully away. In the drawer he found the little paper bag of crumpled ones and fives and slipped it into his overcoat pocket. He helped Isaac on with his coat.

Isaac looked at one dark window, then at the other. Mendel stared at both blank windows.

They went slowly down the darkly lit stairs, Mendel first, Isaac watching the moving shadows on the wall. To one long shadow he offered a peanut.

"Hungrig."

In the vestibule the old man gazed through the thin glass. The November night was cold and bleak. Opening the door he cautiously thrust his head out. Though he saw nothing he quickly shut the door.

"Ginzburg, that he came to see me yesterday," he whispered in Isaac's ear.

Isaac sucked air.

"You know who I mean?"

Isaac combed his chin with his fingers.

"That's the one, with the black whiskers. Don't talk to him or go with him if he asks you."

Isaac moaned.

"Young people he don't bother so much," Mendel said in afterthought.

It was suppertime and the street was empty but the store windows dimly lit their way to the corner. They crossed the deserted street and went on.

Isaac, with a happy cry, pointed to the three golden balls. Mendel smiled but was exhausted when they got to the pawnshop.

The pawnbroker, a red-bearded man with black horn-rimmed glasses, was eating a whitefish at the rear of the store. He craned his head, saw them, and settled back to sip his tea.

In five minutes he came forward, patting his shapeless lips with a large white handkerchief.

Mendel, breathing heavily, handed him the worn gold watch. The pawnbroker, raising his glasses, screwed in his eyepiece. He turned the watch over once. "Eight dollars."

The dying man wet his cracked lips. "I must have thirty-five."

"So go to Rothschild."

"Cost me myself sixty."

"In 1905." The pawnbroker handed back the watch. It had stopped ticking. Mendel wound it slowly. It ticked hollowly.

"Isaac must go to my uncle that he lives in California."

"It's a free country," said the pawnbroker.

Isaac, watching a banjo, snickered.

"What's the matter with him?" the pawnbroker asked.

"So let be eight dollars," muttered Mendel, "but where will I get the rest till tonight?"

"How much for my hat and coat?" he asked.

"No sale." The pawnbroker went behind the cage and wrote out a ticket. He locked the watch in a small drawer but Mendel still heard it ticking.

In the street he slipped the eight dollars into the paper bag, then searched in his pockets for a scrap of writing. Finding it, he strained to read the address by the light of the street lamp.

As they trudged to the subway, Mendel pointed to the sprinkled sky.

"Isaac, look how many stars are tonight."

"Eggs," said Isaac.

"First we will go to Mr. Fishbein, after we will eat."

They got off the train in upper Manhattan and had to walk several blocks before they located Fishbein's house.

"A regular palace," Mendel murmured, looking forward to a moment's warmth.

Isaac stared uneasily at the heavy door of the house.

Mendel rang. The servant, a man with long sideburns, came to the door and said Mr. and Mrs. Fishbein were dining and could see no one.

"He should eat in peace but we will wait till he finishes."

"Come back tomorrow morning. Tomorrow morning Mr. Fishbein will talk to you. He don't do business or charity at this time of the night."

"Charity I am not interested—"

"Come back tomorrow."

"Tell him it's life or death—"

"Whose life or death?"

"So if not his, then mine."

"Don't be such a big smart aleck."

"Look me in my face," said Mendel, "and tell me if I got time till tomorrow morning?"

The servant stared at him, then at Isaac, and reluctantly let them in.

The foyer was a vast high-ceilinged room with many oil paintings on the walls, voluminous silken draperies, a thick flowered rug at foot, and a marble staircase.

Mr. Fishbein, a paunchy bald-headed man with hairy nostrils and small patent leather feet, ran lightly down the stairs, a large napkin tucked under a tuxedo coat button. He stopped on the fifth step from the bottom and examined his visitors.

"Who comes on Friday night to a man that he has guests, to spoil him his supper?"

"Excuse me that I bother you, Mr. Fishbein," Mendel said. "If I didn't come now I couldn't come tomorrow."

"Without more preliminaries, please state your business. I'm a hungry man."

"Hungrig," wailed Isaac.

Fishbein adjusted his pince-nez. "What's the matter with him?"

"This is my son Isaac. He is like this all his life."

Isaac mewled.

"I am sending him to California."

"Mr. Fishbein don't contribute to personal pleasure trips."

"I am a sick man and he must go tonight on the train to my Uncle Leo."

"I never give to unorganized charity," Fishbein said, "but if you are hungry I will invite you downstairs in my kitchen. We having tonight chicken with stuffed derma."

"All I ask is thirty-five dollars for the train ticket to my uncle in California. I have already the rest."

"Who is your uncle? How old a man?"

"Eighty-one years, a long life to him."

Fishbein burst into laughter. "Eighty-one years and you are sending him this halfwit."

Mendel, flailing both arms, cried, "Please, without names."

Fishbein politely conceded.

"Where is open the door there we go in the house," the sick man said. "If you will kindly give me thirty-five dollars, God will bless you. What is thirty-five dollars to Mr. Fishbein? Nothing. To me, for my boy, is everything."

Fishbein drew himself up to his tallest height.

"Private contributions I don't make—only to institutions. This is my fixed policy."

Mendel sank to his creaking knees on the rug.

"Please, Mr. Fishbein, if not thirty-five, give maybe twenty."

"Levinson!" Fishbein angrily called.

The servant with the long sideburns appeared at the top of the stairs.

"Show this party where is the door—unless he wishes to partake food before leaving the premises."

"For what I got chicken won't cure it," Mendel said.

"This way if you please," said Levinson, descending.

Isaac assisted his father up.

"Take him to an institution," Fishbein advised over the marble balustrade. He ran quickly up the stairs and they were at once outside, buffeted by winds.

The walk to the subway was tedious. The wind blew mournfully. Mendel, breathless, glanced furtively at shadows. Isaac, clutching his peanuts in his frozen fist, clung to his father's side. They entered a small park to rest for a minute on a stone bench under a leafless two-branched tree. The thick right branch was raised, the thin left one hung down. A very pale moon rose slowly. So did a stranger as they approached the bench.

"Gut yuntif," he said hoarsely.

Mendel, drained of blood, waved his wasted arms. Isaac yowled sickly. Then a bell chimed and it was only ten. Mendel let out a piercing anguished cry as the bearded stranger disappeared into the bushes. A policeman came running, and though he beat the bushes with his nightstick, could turn up nothing. Mendel and Isaac hurried out of the little park. When Mendel glanced back the dead tree had its thin arm raised, the thick one down. He moaned.

They boarded a trolley, stopping at the home of a former friend, but he had died years ago. On the same block they went into a cafeteria and ordered two fried eggs for Isaac. The tables were crowded except where a heavy-set man sat eating soup with kasha. After one look at him they left in haste, although Isaac wept.

Mendel had another address on a slip of paper but the house was too far away, in Queens, so they stood in a doorway shivering.

What can I do, he frantically thought, in one short hour?

He remembered the furniture in the house. It was junk but might bring a few dollars. "Come, Isaac." They went once more to the pawnbroker's to talk to him, but the shop was dark and an iron gate—rings and gold watches glinting through it—was drawn tight across his place of business.

They huddled behind a telephone pole, both freezing. Isaac whimpered.

"See the big moon, Isaac. The whole sky is white."

He pointed but Isaac wouldn't look.

Mendel dreamed for a minute of the sky lit up, long sheets of light in all directions. Under the sky, in California, sat Uncle Leo drinking tea with lemon. Mendel felt warm but woke up cold.

Across the street stood an ancient brick synagogue.

He pounded on the huge door but no one appeared. He waited till he had breath and desperately knocked again. At last there were footsteps within, and the synagogue door creaked open on its massive brass hinges.

A darkly dressed sexton, holding a dripping candle, glared at them.

"Who knocks this time of night with so much noise on the synagogue door?"

Mendel told the sexton his troubles. "Please, I would like to speak to the rabbi."

"The rabbi is an old man. He sleeps now. His wife won't let you see him. Go home and come back tomorrow."

"To tomorrow I said goodbye already. I am a dying man."

Though the sexton seemed doubtful he pointed to an old wooden house next door. "In there he lives." He disappeared into the synagogue with his lit candle casting shadows around him.

Mendel, with Isaac clutching his sleeve, went up the wooden steps and rang the bell. After five minutes a big-faced, gray-haired bulky woman came out on the porch with a torn robe thrown over her nightdress. She emphatically said the rabbi was sleeping and could not be waked.

But as she was insisting, the rabbi himself tottered to the door. He listened a minute and said, "Who wants to see me let them come in."

They entered a cluttered room. The rabbi was an old skinny man with bent shoulders and a wisp of white beard. He wore a flannel nightgown and black skullcap; his feet were bare.

"Vey is mir," his wife muttered. "Put on shoes or tomorrow comes sure pneumonia." She was a woman with a big belly, years younger than her husband. Staring at Isaac, she turned away.

Mendel apologetically related his errand. "All I need more is thirty-five dollars."

"Thirty-five?" said the rabbi's wife. "Why not thirty-five thousand? Who has so much money? My husband is a poor rabbi. The doctors take away every penny."

"Dear friend," said the rabbi, "if I had I would give you."

"I got already seventy," Mendel said, heavy-hearted. "All I need more is thirty-five."

"God will give you," said the rabbi.

"In the grave," said Mendel. "I need tonight. Come, Isaac."

"Wait," called the rabbi.

He hurried inside, came out with a fur-lined caftan, and handed it to Mendel.

"Yascha," shrieked his wife, "not your new coat!"

"I got my old one. Who needs two coats for one body?"

"Yascha, I am screaming—"

"Who can go among poor people, tell me, in a new coat?"

"Yascha," she cried, "what can this man do with your coat? He needs tonight the money. The pawnbrokers are asleep."

"So let him wake them up."

"No." She grabbed the coat from Mendel.

He held on to a sleeve, wrestling her for the coat. Her I know, Mendel thought. "Shylock," he muttered. Her eyes glittered.

The rabbi groaned and tottered dizzily. His wife cried out as Mendel yanked the coat from her hands.

"Run," cried the rabbi.

"Run, Isaac."

They ran out of the house and down the steps.

"Stop, you thief," called the rabbi's wife.

The rabbi pressed both hands to his temples and fell to the floor.

"Help!" his wife wept. "Heart attack! Help!"

But Mendel and Isaac ran through the streets with the rabbi's new fur-lined caftan. After them noiselessly ran Ginzburg.

It was very late when Mendel bought the train ticket in the only booth open.

There was no time to stop for a sandwich so Isaac ate his peanuts and they hurried to the train in the vast deserted station.

"So in the morning," Mendel gasped as they ran, "there comes a man that he sells sandwiches and coffee. Eat but get change. When reaches California the train, will be waiting for you on the station Uncle Leo. If you don't recognize him he will recognize you. Tell him I send best regards."

But when they arrived at the gate to the platform it was shut, the light out.

Mendel, groaning, beat on the gate with his fists.

"Too late," said the uniformed ticket collector, a bulky, bearded man with hairy nostrils and a fishy smell.

He pointed to the station clock. "Already past twelve."

"But I see standing there still the train," Mendel said, hopping in his grief.

"It just left—in one more minute."

"A minute is enough. Just open the gate."

"Too late I told you."

Mendel socked his bony chest with both hands. "With my whole heart I beg you this little favor."

"Favors you had enough already. For you the train is gone. You shoulda been dead already at midnight. I told you that yesterday. This is the best I can do."

"Ginzburg!" Mendel shrank from him.

"Who else?" The voice was metallic, eyes glittered, the expression amused.

"For myself," the old man begged, "I don't ask a thing. But what will happen to my boy?"

Ginzburg shrugged slightly. "What will happen happens. This isn't my responsibility. I got enough to think about without worrying about somebody on one cylinder."

"What then is your responsibility?"

"To create conditions. To make happen what happens. I ain't in the anthropomorphic business."

"Whatever business you in, where is your pity?"

"This ain't my commodity. The law is the law."

"Which law is this?"

"The cosmic universal law, goddamit, the one I got to follow myself."

"What kind of a law is it?" cried Mendel. "For God's sake, don't you understand what I went through in my life with this poor boy? Look at him. For thirty-nine years, since the day he was born, I wait for him to grow up, but he don't. Do you understand what this means in a father's heart? Why don't you let him go to his uncle?" His voice had risen and he was shouting.

Isaac mewled loudly.

"Better calm down or you'll hurt somebody's feelings," Ginzburg said with a wink toward Isaac.

"All my life," Mendel cried, his body trembling, "what did I have? I was poor. I suffered from my health. When I worked I worked too hard. When I didn't work was worse. My wife died a young woman. But I didn't ask from anybody nothing. Now I ask a small favor. Be so kind, Mr. Ginzburg."

The ticket collector was picking his teeth with a match stick.

"You ain't the only one, my friend, some got it worse than you. That's how it goes in this country."

"You dog you." Mendel lunged at Ginzburg's throat and began to choke. "You bastard, don't you understand what it means human?"

They struggled nose to nose, Ginzburg, though his astonished eyes bulged, began to laugh. "You pipsqueak nothing. I'll freeze you to pieces."

His eyes lit in rage and Mendel felt an unbearable cold like an icy dagger invading his body, all of his parts shriveling.

Now I die without helping Isaac.

A crowd gathered. Isaac yelped in fright.

Clinging to Ginzburg in his last agony, Mendel saw reflected in the ticket collector's eyes the depth of his terror. But he saw that Ginzburg, staring at himself in Mendel's eyes, saw mirrored in them the extent of his own awful wrath. He beheld a shimmering, starry, blinding light that produced darkness.

Ginzburg looked astounded. "Who me?"

His grip on the squirming old man slowly loosened, and Mendel, his heart barely beating, slumped to the ground.

"Go." Ginzburg muttered, "take him to the train."

"Let pass," he commanded a guard.

The crowd parted. Isaac helped his father up and they tottered down the steps to the platform where the train waited, lit and ready to go.

Mendel found Isaac a coach seat and hastily embraced him. "Help Uncle Leo, Isaakil. Also remember your father and mother."

"Be nice to him," he said to the conductor. "Show him where everything is."

He waited on the platform until the train began slowly to move. Isaac sat at the edge of his seat, his face strained in the direction of his journey. When the train was gone, Mendel ascended the stairs to see what had become of Ginzburg.

LEO TOLSTOY

The Death of Iván Ilých

I

During an interval in the Melvínski trial in the large building of the Law Courts the members and public prosecutor met in Iván Egórobich Shébek's private room, where the conversation turned on the celebrated Krasóvski case. Fëdor Vasílievich warmly maintained that it was not subject to their jurisdiction, Iván Egórovich maintained the contrary, while Peter Ivánovich, not having entered into the discussion at the start, took no part in it but looked through the *Gazette* which had just been handed in.

"Gentlemen," he said, "Iván Ilých has died!"

"You don't say so!"

"Here, read it yourself," replied Peter Ivánovich, handing Fëdor Vasílievich the paper still damp from the press. Surrounded by a black border were the words: "Praskóvya Fëdorovna Goloviná, with profound sorrow, informs relatives and friends of the demise of her beloved husband Iván Ilých Golovín, Member of the Court of Justice, which occurred on February the 4th of this year 1882. The funeral will take place on Friday at one o'clock in the afternoon."

Iván Ilých had been a colleague of the gentlemen present and was liked by them all. He had been ill for some weeks with an illness said to be incurable. His post had been kept open for him, but there had been conjectures that in case of his death Alexéev might receive his appointment, and that either Vínnikov or Shtábel would succeed Alexéev. So on receiving the news of Iván Ilých's death the first thought of each of the gentlemen in that private room was of the changes and promotions it might occasion among themselves or their acquaintances.

"I shall be sure to get Shtábel's place or Vínnikov's," thought Fëdor Vasílievich. "I was promised that long ago, and the promotion means an extra eight hundred rubles a year for me besides the allowance."

"Now I must apply for my brother-in-law's transfer from Kalúga," thought Peter Ivánovich. "My wife will be very glad, and then she won't be able to say that I never do anything for her relations."

"I thought he would never leave his bed again," said Peter Ivánovich aloud. "It's very sad."

"But what really was the matter with him?"

"The doctors couldn't say—at least they could, but each of them said something different. When last I saw him I thought he was getting better."

"And I haven't been to see him since the holidays. I always meant to go."

"Had he any property?"

"I think his wife had a little—but something quite trifling."

"We shall have to go to see her, but they live so terribly far away."

"Far away from you, you mean. Everything's far away from your place."

"You see, he never can forgive my living on the other side of the river," said Peter Ivánovich, smiling at Shébek. Then, still talking of the distances between different parts of the city, they returned to the Court.

Besides considerations as to the possible transfers and promotions likely to result from Iván Ilých's death, the mere fact of the death of a near acquaintance aroused, as usual, in all who heard of it the complacent feeling that, "it is he who is dead and not I."

Each one thought or felt, "Well, he's dead but I'm alive!" But the more intimate of Iván Ilých's acquaintances, his so-called friends, could not help thinking also that they would now have to fulfill the very tiresome demands of propriety by attending the funeral service and paying a visit of condolence to the widow.

Fëdor Vasílievich and Peter Ivánovich had been his nearest acquaintances. Peter Ivánovich had studied law with Iván Ilých and had considered himself to be under obligations to him.

Having told his wife at dinner-time of Iván Ilých's death, and of his conjecture that it might be possible to get her brother transferred to their circuit, Peter Ivánovich sacrificed his usual nap, put on his evening clothes, and drove to Iván Ilých's house.

At the entrance stood a carriage and two cabs. Leaning against the wall in the hall downstairs near the cloak-stand was a coffin-lid covered with cloth of gold, ornamented with gold cord and tassels, that had been polished up with metal powder. Two ladies in black were taking off their fur cloaks. Peter Ivánovich recognized one of them as Iván Ilých's sister, but the other was a stranger to him. His colleague Schwartz was just coming downstairs, but on seeing Peter Ivánovich enter he stopped and winked at him, as if to say: "Iván Ilých has made a mess of things—not like you and me."

Schwartz's face with his Piccadilly whiskers, and his slim figure in evening dress, had as usual an air of elegant solemnity which contrasted with the playfulness of his character and had a special piquancy here, or so it seemed to Peter Ivánovich.

Peter Ivánovich allowed the ladies to precede him and slowly followed them upstairs. Schwartz did not come down but remained where he was, and Peter Ivánovich understood that he wanted to arrange where they should play bridge that evening. The ladies went upstairs to the widow's room, and Schwartz with seriously compressed lips but a playful look in his eyes, indicated by a twist of his eyebrows the room to the right where the body lay.

Peter Ivánovich, like everyone else on such occasions, entered feeling uncertain what he would have to do. All he knew was that at such times it is always safe to cross oneself. But he was not quite sure whether one should make obeisances while doing so. He therefore adopted a middle course. On entering the room he began crossing himself and made a slight movement resembling a bow. At the same time, as far as the motion of his head and arm allowed, he surveyed the room. Two young men—apparently nephews, one of whom was a high-school pupil—were leaving the room, crossing themselves as they did so. An old woman was standing motionless, and a lady with strangely arched eyebrows was saying something to her in a whisper. A vigorous, resolute Church Reader, in a frock-coat, was reading something in a loud voice with an expression that precluded any contradiction. The butler's assistant, Gerásim, stepping lightly in front of Peter Ivánovich, was strewing something on the floor. Noticing this, Peter Ivánovich was immediately aware of a faint odour of a decomposing body.

The last time he had called on Iván Ilých, Peter Ivánovich had seen Gerásim in the study. Iván Ilých had been particularly fond of him and he was performing the duty of a sick-nurse.

Peter Ivánovich continued to make the sign of the cross slightly inclining his head in an intermediate direction between the coffin, the Reader, and the icons on the table in a corner of the room. Afterwards, when it seemed to him that this movement of his arm in crossing himself had gone on too long, he stopped and began to look at the corpse.

The dead man lay, as dead men always lie, in a specially heavy way, his rigid limbs sunk in the soft cushions of the coffin, with the head forever bowed on the pillow. His yellow waxen brow with bald patches over his sunken temples was thrust up in the way peculiar to the dead, the protruding nose seeming to press on the upper lip. He was much changed and had grown even thinner since Peter Ivánovich had last seen him, but, as is always the case with the dead, his face was handsomer and above all more dignified than when he was alive. The expression on the face said that what was necessary had been accomplished, and accomplished rightly. Besides this there was in that expression a reproach and a warning to the living. This warning seemed to Peter Ivánovich out of place, or at least not applicable to him. He felt a certain discomfort and so he hurriedly crossed himself once more and turned and went out of the door—too hurriedly and too regardless of propriety, as he himself was aware.

Schwartz was waiting for him in the adjoining room with legs spread wide apart and both hands toying with his top-hat behind his back. The mere sight of that playful, well-groomed, and elegant figure refreshed Peter Ivánovich. He felt that Schwartz was above all these happenings and would not surrender to any depressing influences. His very look said that this incident of a church service for Iván Ilých could not be a sufficient reason for infringing the order of the session—in other words, that it would certainly not prevent his unwrapping a new pack of cards and shuffling them that evening while a footman placed four fresh candles on the table: in fact, there was no reason for supposing that this incident would hinder their spending the evening agreeably. Indeed he said this in a whisper as Peter Ivánovich passed him, proposing that they should meet for a game at Fëdor Vasílievich's. But apparently Peter Ivánovich was not destined to play bridge that evening. Praskóvya Fëdorovna (a short, fat woman who despite all efforts to the contrary had continued to broaden steadily from her shoulders downwards and who had the same extraordinarily arched eyebrows as the lady who had been standing by the coffin), dressed all in black, her head covered with lace, came out of her own room with some other ladies, conducted them to the room where the dead body lay, and said: "The service will begin immediately. Please go in."

Schwartz, making an indefinite bow, stood still, evidently neither accepting nor declining this invitation. Praskóvya Fëdorovna recognizing Peter Ivánovich, sighed, went close up to him, took his hand, and said: "I know you were a true friend to Iván Ilých . . ." and looked at him awaiting some suitable response. And Peter Ivánovich knew that, just as it had been the right thing to cross himself in that room, so what he had to do here was to press her hand, sigh, and say, "Believe me . . ." So he did all this and as he did it felt that the desired result had been achieved: that both he and she were touched.

"Come with me. I want to speak to you before it begins," said the widow. "Give me your arm."

Peter Ivánovich gave her his arm and they went to the inner rooms, passing Schwartz who winked at Peter Ivánovich compassionately.

"That does for our bridge! Don't object if we find another player. Perhaps you can cut in when you do escape," said his playful look.

Peter Ivánovich sighed still more deeply and despondently, and Praskóvya Fëdorovna pressed his arm gratefully. When they reached the drawing-room, upholstered in pink cretonne and lighted by a dim lamp, they sat down at the table—she on a sofa and Peter Ivánovich on a low pouffe, the springs of which yielded spasmodically under his weight. Praskóvya Fëdorovna had been on the point of warning him to take another seat, but felt that such a warning was out of keeping with her present condition and so changed her mind. As he sat down on the pouffe Peter Ivánovich recalled how Iván Ilých had arranged this room and had consulted him regarding this pink cretonne with green leaves. The whole room was full of furniture and knick-knacks, and on her way to the sofa the lace of the widow's black shawl caught on the carved edge of the table. Peter Ivánovich rose to detach it, and the springs of the pouffe, relieved of his weight, rose also and gave him a push. The widow began detaching her shawl herself, and Peter Ivánovich again sat down, suppressing the rebellious springs of the pouffe under him. But the widow had not quite freed herself and Peter Ivánovich got up again, and again the pouffe rebelled and even creaked. When this was all over she took out a clean cambric handkerchief and began to weep. The episode with the shawl and the struggle with the pouffe had cooled Peter Ivánovich's emotions and he sat there with a sullen look on his face. This awkward situation was interrupted by Sokolóv, Iván Ilých's butler, who came to report that the plot in the cemetery that Praskóvya Fëdorovna had chosen would cost two hundred rubles. She stopped weeping and, looking at Peter Ivánovich with the air of a victim, remarked in French that it was very hard for her. Peter Ivánovich made a silent gesture signifying his full conviction that it must indeed be so.

"Please smoke," she said in a magnanimous yet crushed voice, and turned to discuss with Sokolóv the price of the plot for the grave.

Peter Ivánovich while lighting his cigarette heard her inquiring very circumstantially into the price of different plots in the cemetery and finally decide which she would take. When that was done she gave instructions about engaging the choir. Sokolóv then left the room.

"I look after everything myself," she told Peter Ivánovich, shifting the albums that lay on the table; and noticing that the table was endangered by his cigarette-ash, she immediately passed him an ashtray, saying as she did so: "I consider it an affectation to say that my grief prevents my attending to practical affairs. On the contrary, if anything can—I won't say console me, but—distract me, it is seeing to everything concerning him." She again took out her handkerchief as if preparing to cry, but suddenly, as if mastering her feeling, she shook herself and began to speak calmly. "But there is something I want to talk to you about."

Peter Ivánovich bowed, keeping control of the springs of the pouffe, which immediately began quivering under him.

"He suffered terribly the last few days."

"Did he?" said Peter Ivánovich.

"Oh, terribly! He screamed unceasingly, not for minutes but for hours. For the last three days he screamed incessantly. It was unendurable. I cannot understand how I bore it; you could hear him three rooms off. Oh, what I have suffered!"

"Is it possible that he was conscious all that time?" asked Peter Ivánovich.

"Yes," she whispered. "To the last moment. He took leave of us a quarter of an hour before he died, and asked us to take Volódya away."

The thought of the sufferings of this man he had known so intimately, first as a merry little boy, then as a school-mate, and later as a grown-up colleague, suddenly struck Peter Ivánovich with horror, despite an unpleasant consciousness of his own and this woman's dissimulation. He again saw that brow, and that nose pressing down on the lip, and felt afraid for himself.

"Three days of frightful suffering and then death! Why, that might suddenly, at any time, happen to me," he thought, and for a moment felt terrified. But—he did not himself know how—the customary reflection at once occurred to him that this had happened to Iván Ilých and not to him, and that it should not and could not happen to him, and that to think that it could would be yielding to depression which he ought not to do, as Schwartz's expression plainly showed. After which reflection Peter Ivánovich felt reassured, and began to ask with interest about the details of Iván Ilých's death, as though death was an accident natural to Iván Ilých but certainly not to himself.

After many details of the really dreadful physical sufferings Iván Ilých had endured (which details he learnt only from the effect those sufferings had produced on Praskóvya Fëdorovna's nerves) the widow apparently found it necessary to get to business.

"Oh, Peter Ivánovich, how hard it is! How terribly, terribly hard!" and she again began to weep.

Peter Ivánovich sighed and waited for her to finish blowing her nose. When she had done so he said, "Believe me . . ." and she again began talking and brought out what was evidently her chief concern with him —namely, to question him as to how she could obtain a grant of money from the government on the occasion of her husband's death. She made it appear that she was asking Peter Ivánovich's advice about her pension, but he soon saw that she already knew about that to the minutest detail, more even than he did himself. She knew how much could be got out of the government in consequence of her husband's death, but wanted to find out whether she could not possibly extract something more. Peter Ivánovich tried to think of some means of doing so, but after reflecting for a while and, out of propriety, condemning the government for its niggardliness, he said he thought that nothing more could be got. Then she sighed and evidently began to devise means of getting rid of her visitor. Noticing this, he put out his cigarette, rose, pressed her hand, and went out into the anteroom.

In the dining-room where the clock stood that Iván Ilých had liked so much and had bought at an antique shop, Peter Ivánovich met a priest and a few acquaintances who had come to attend the service, and he recognized Iván Ilých's daughter, a handsome young woman. She was in black and her slim figure appeared slimmer than ever. She had a gloomy, determined, almost angry expression, and bowed to Peter Ivánovich as though he were in some way to blame. Behind her, with the same offended look, stood a wealthy young man, an examining magistrate, whom Peter Ivánovich also knew and who was her fiancé, as he had heard. He bowed mournfully to them and was about to pass into the death-chamber, when from under the stairs appeared the figure of Iván Ilých's schoolboy son, who was extremely like his father. He seemed a little Iván Ilých, such as Peter Ivánovich remembered when they studied law together. His tear-stained eyes had in them the look that is seen in the eyes of boys of thirteen or fourteen who are not pure-minded. When he saw Peter Ivánovich he scowled morosely and shamefacedly. Peter Ivánovich nodded to him and entered the death-chamber. The service began: candles, groans, incense, tears, and sobs. Peter Ivánovich stood looking gloomily down at his feet. He did not look once at the dead man, did not yield to any depressing influence, and was one of the first to leave the room. There was no one in the anteroom, but Gerásim darted out of the dead man's room, rummaged with his strong hands among the fur coats to find Peter Ivánovich's and helped him on with it.

"Well, friend Gerásim," said Peter Ivánovich, so as to say something. "It's a sad affair, isn't it?"

"It's God's will. We shall all come to it some day," said Gerásim, displaying his teeth—the even, white teeth of a healthy peasant—and, like a man in the thick of urgent work, he briskly opened the front door, called the coachman, helped Peter Ivánovich into the sledge, and sprang back to the porch as if in readiness for what he had to do next.

Peter Ivánovich found the fresh air particularly pleasant after the smell of incense, the dead body, and carbolic acid.

"Where to, sir?" asked the coachman.

"It's not too late even now. . . . I'll call round on Fëdor Vasílievich."

He accordingly drove there and found them just finishing the first rubber, so that it was quite convenient for him to cut in.

II

Iván Ilých's life had been most simple and most ordinary and therefore most terrible.

He had been a member of the Court of Justice, and died at the age of forty-five. His father had been an official who after serving in various ministries and departments in Petersburg had made the sort of career which brings men to positions from which by reason of their long service they cannot be dismissed, though they are obviously unfit to hold any responsible position, and for whom therefore posts are specially created, which though fictitious carry salaries of from six to ten thousand rubles that are not fictitious, and in receipt of which they live on to a great age.

Such was the Privy Councillor and superfluous member of various superfluous institutions, Ilyá Epímovich Golovín.

He had three sons, of whom Iván Ilých was the second. The eldest son was following in his father's footsteps only in another department, and was already approaching that stage in the service at which a similar sinecure would be reached. The third son was a failure. He had ruined his prospects in a number of positions and was now serving in the railway department. His father and brothers, and still more their wives, not merely disliked meeting him, but avoided remembering his existence unless compelled to do so. His sister had married Baron Greff, a Petersburg official of her father's type. Iván Ilých was *le phénix de la famille* as people said. He was neither as cold and formal as his elder brother nor as wild as the younger, but was a happy mean between them—an intelligent, polished, lively and agreeable man. He had studied with his younger brother at the School of Law, but the latter had failed to complete the course and was expelled when he was in the fifth class. Iván Ilých finished the course well. Even when he was at the School of Law he was just what he remained for the rest of his life: a capable, cheerful, good-natured, and sociable man, though strict in the fulfilment of what he considered to be his duty: and he considered his duty to be what was so considered by those in authority. Neither as a boy nor as a man was he a toady, but from early youth was by nature attracted to people of high station as a fly is drawn to the light, assimilating their ways and views of life and establishing friendly relations with them. All the enthusiasms of childhood and youth passed without leaving much trace on him; he succumbed to sensuality, to vanity, and latterly among the highest classes to liberalism, but always within limits which his instinct unfailingly indicated to him as correct.

At school he had done things which had formerly seemed to him very horrid and made him feel disgusted with himself when he did them; but when later on he saw that such actions were done by people of good position and that they did not regard them as wrong, he was able not exactly to regard them as right, but to forget about them entirely or not be at all troubled at remembering them.

Having graduated from the School of Law and qualified for the tenth rank of the civil service, and having received money from his father for his equipment, Iván Ilých ordered himself clothes at Scharmer's, the fashionable tailor, hung a medallion inscribed *respice finem* on his watch-chain, took leave of his professor and the prince who was patron of the school, had a farewell dinner with his comrades at Donon's first-class restaurant, and with his new and fashionable portmanteau, linen, clothes, shaving and other toilet appliances, and a travelling rug, all purchased at the best shops, he set off for one of the provinces where, through his father's influence, he had been attached to the Governor as an official for special service.

In the province Iván Ilých soon arranged as easy and agreeable a position for himself as he had had at the School of Law. He performed his official tasks, made his career, and at the same time amused himself pleasantly and decorously. Occasionally he paid official visits to country districts, where he behaved with dignity both to his superiors and inferiors, and performed the duties entrusted to him, which related chiefly to the sectarians, with an exactness and incorruptible honesty of which he could not but feel proud.

In official matters, despite his youth and taste for frivolous gaiety, he was exceedingly reserved, punctilious, and even severe; but in society he was often amusing and witty, and always good-natured, correct in his manner, and *bon enfant*, as the governor and his wife—with whom he was like one of the family—used to say of him.

In the provinces he had an affair with a lady who made advances to the elegant young lawyer, and there was also a milliner; and there were carousals with aides-de-camp who visited the district, and after-supper visits to a certain outlying street of doubtful reputation; and there was too some obsequiousness to his chief and even to his chief's wife, but all this was done with such a tone of good breeding that no hard names could be applied to it. It all came under the heading of the French saying: *"Il faut que jeunesse se passe."* It was all done with clean hands, in clean linen, with French phrases, and above all among people of the best society and consequently with the approval of people of rank.

So Iván Ilých served for five years and then came a change in his official life. The new and reformed judicial institutions were introduced, and new men were needed. Iván Ilých became such a new man. He was offered the post of Examining Magistrate, and he accepted it though the post was in another province and obliged him to give up the connexions he had formed and to make new ones. His friends met to give him a send-off; they had a group-photograph taken and presented him with a silver cigarette-case, and he set off to his new post.

As examining magistrate Iván Ilých was just as *comme il faut* and decorous a man, inspiring general respect and capable of separating his official duties from his private life, as he had been when acting as an official on special service. His duties now as examining magistrate were far more interesting and attractive than before. In his former position it had been pleasant to wear an undress uniform made by Scharmer, and to pass through the crowd of petitioners and officials who were timorously awaiting an audience with the governor, and who envied him as with free and easy gait he went straight into his chief's private room to have a cup of tea and a cigarette with him. But not many people had then been directly dependent on him—only police officials and the sectarians when he went on special missions—and he liked to treat them politely, almost as comrades, as if he were letting them feel that he who had the power to crush them was treating them in this simple, friendly way. There were then but few such people. But now, as an examining magistrate, Iván Ilých felt that everyone without exception, even the most important and self-satisfied, was in his power, and that he need only write a few words on a sheet of paper with a certain heading, and this or that important, self-satisfied person would be brought before him in the role of an accused person or a witness, and if he did not choose to allow him to sit down, would have to stand before him and answer his questions. Iván Ilých never abused his power; he tried on the contrary to soften its expression, but the consciousness of it and of the possibility of softening its effect, supplied the chief interest and attraction of his office. In his work itself, especially in his examinations, he very soon acquired a method of eliminating all considerations irrelevant to the legal aspect of the case, and reducing even the most complicated case to a form in which it would be presented on paper only in its externals, completely excluding his personal opinion of the matter, while above all observing every prescribed formality. The work was new and Iván Ilých was one of the first men to apply the new Code of 1864.[1]

On taking up the post of examining magistrate in a new town, he made new acquaintances and connexions, placed himself on a new footing, and assumed a somewhat different tone. He took up an attitude of rather dignified aloofness towards the provincial authorities, but picked out the best circle of legal gentlemen and wealthy gentry living in the town and assumed a tone of slight dissatisfaction with the government, of moderate liberalism, and of enlightened citizenship. At the same time, without at all altering the elegance of his toilet, he ceased shaving his chin and allowed his beard to grow as it pleased.

Iván Ilých settled down very pleasantly in this new town. The society there, which inclined towards opposition to the Governor, was friendly, his salary was larger, and he began to play *vint* [a form of bridge], which he found added not a little to the pleasure of life, for he had a capacity for cards, played good-humouredly, and calculated rapidly and astutely, so that he usually won.

After living there for two years he met his future wife, Praskóvya Fëdorovna Míkhel, who was the most attractive, clever, and brilliant girl of the set in which he moved, and among other amusements and relaxation from his labours as examining magistrate, Iván Ilých established light and playful relations with her.

While he had been an official on special service he had been accustomed to dance, but now as an examining magistrate it was exceptional for him to do so. If he danced now, he did it as if to show that though he served under the reformed order of things, and had reached the fifth official rank, yet when it came to dancing he could do it better than most people. So at the end of an evening he sometimes danced with Praskóvya Fëdorovna, and it was chiefly during these dances that he captivated her. She fell in love with him. Iván Ilých had at first no definite intention of

---

[1] The emancipation of the serfs in 1861 was followed by a thorough all-round reform of judicial proceedings.—Aylmer Maud [translator].

marrying, but when the girl fell in love with him he said to himself: "Really, why shouldn't I marry?"

Praskóvya Fëdorovna came of a good family, was not bad looking, and had some little property. Iván Ilých might have aspired to a more brilliant match, but even this was good. He had his salary, and she, he hoped, would have an equal income. She was well connected, and was a sweet, pretty, and thoroughly correct young woman. To say that Iván Ilých married because he fell in love with Praskóvya Fëdorovna and found that she sympathized with his views of life would be as incorrect as to say that he married because his social circle approved of the match. He was swayed by both these considerations: the marriage gave him personal satisfaction, and at the same time it was considered the right thing by the most highly placed of his associates.

So Iván Ilých got married.

The preparations for marriage and the beginning of married life, with its conjugal caresses, the new furniture, new crockery, and new linen, were very pleasant until his wife became pregnant—so that Iván Ilých had begun to think that marriage would not impair the easy, agreeable, gay and always decorous character of his life, approved of by society and regarded by himself as natural, but would even improve it. But from the first months of his wife's pregnancy, something new, unpleasant, depressing, and unseemly, and from which there was no way of escape, unexpectedly showed itself.

His wife, without any reason—*de gaieté de coeur* as Iván Ilých expressed it to himself—began to disturb the pleasure and propriety of their life. She began to be jealous without any cause, expected him to devote his whole attention to her, found fault with everything, and made coarse and ill-mannered scenes.

At first Iván Ilých hoped to escape from the unpleasantness of this state of affairs by the same easy and decorous relation to life that had served him heretofore: he tried to ignore his wife's disagreeable moods, continued to live in his usual easy and pleasant way, invited friends to his house for a game of cards, and also tried going out to his club or spending his evenings with friends. But one day his wife began upbraiding him so vigorously, using such coarse words, and continued to abuse him every time he did not fulfil her demands, so resolutely and with such evident determination not to give way till he submitted—that is, till he stayed at home and was bored just as she was—that he became alarmed. He now realized that matrimony—at any rate with Praskóvya Fëdorovna—was not always conducive to the pleasures and amenities of life but on the contrary often infringed both comfort and propriety, and that he must therefore entrench himself against such infringement. And Iván Ilých began to seek for means of doing so. His official duties were the one thing that imposed upon Praskóvya Fëdorovna, and by means of his official work and the duties attached to it he began struggling with his wife to secure his own independence.

With the birth of their child, the attempts to feed it and the various failures in doing so, and with the real and imaginary illnesses of mother and child, in which Iván Ilých's sympathy was demanded but about which he understood nothing, the need of securing for himself an existence outside his family life became still more imperative.

As his wife grew more irritable and exacting and Iván Ilých transferred the centre of gravity of his life more and more to his official work, so did he grow to like his work better and became more ambitious than before.

Very soon, within a year of his wedding, Iván Ilých had realized that marriage, though it may add some comforts to life, is in fact a very intricate and difficult affair towards which in order to perform one's duty, that is, to lead a decorous life approved of by society, one must adopt a definite attitude just as towards one's official duties.

And Iván Ilých evolved such an attitude towards married life. He only required of it those conveniences—dinner at home, housewife, and bed—which it could give him, and above all that propriety of external forms required by public opinion. For the rest he looked for light-hearted pleasure and propriety, and was very thankful when he found them, but if he met with antagonism and querulousness he at once retired into his separate fenced-off world of official duties, where he found satisfaction.

Iván Ilých was esteemed a good official, and after three years was made Assistant Public Prosecutor. His new duties, their importance, the possibility of indicting and imprisoning anyone he chose, the publicity his speeches received, and the success he had in all these things, made his work still more attractive.

More children came. His wife became more and more querulous and ill-tempered, but the attitude Iván Ilých had adopted towards his home life rendered him almost impervious to her grumbling.

After seven years' service in that town he was transferred to another province as Public Prosecutor. They moved, but were short of money and his wife did not like the place they moved to. Though the salary was higher the cost of living was greater, besides which two of their children died and family life became still more unpleasant for him.

Praskóvya Fëdorovna blamed her husband for every inconvenience they encountered in their new home. Most of the conversations between husband and wife, especially as to the children's education, led to topics which recalled former disputes, and those disputes were apt to flare up at any moment. There remained only those rare periods of amorousness which still came to them at times but did not last long. These were islets at which they anchored for a while and then again set out upon that ocean of veiled hostility which showed itself in their aloofness from one another. This aloofness might have grieved Iván Ilých had he considered that it ought not to exist, but he now regarded the position as normal, and even made it the goal at which he aimed in family life. His aim was to free himself more and more from those unpleasantnesses and to give them a semblance of harmlessness and propriety. He attained this by spending less and less time with his family, and when obliged to be at home he tried to safeguard his position by the presence of outsiders. The chief thing however was that he had his official duties. The whole interest of his life now centred in the official world and that interest absorbed him. The consciousness of his power, being able to ruin anybody he wished to ruin, the importance, even the external dignity of his entry into court, or meetings with his subordinates, his success with superiors and inferiors, and above all his masterly handling of cases, of which he was conscious—all this gave him pleasure and filled his life, together with chats with his colleagues, dinners, and bridge. So that on the whole Iván Ilých's life continued to flow as he considered it should do—pleasantly and properly.

So things continued for another seven years. His eldest daughter was already sixteen, another child had died, and only one son was left, a schoolboy and a subject of dissension. Iván Ilých wanted to put him in the School of Law, but to spite him Praskóvya Fëdorovna entered him at the High School. The daughter had been educated at home and had turned out well: the boy did not learn badly either.

III

So Iván Ilých lived for seventeen years after his marriage. He was already a Public Prosecutor of long standing, and had declined several proposed transfers while awaiting a more desirable post, when an unanticipated occurrence quite upset the peaceful course of his life. He was expecting to be offered the post of presiding judge in a University town, but Happe somehow came to the front and obtained the appointment instead. Iván Ilých became irritable, reproached Happe, and quarrelled both with him and with his immediate superiors—who became colder to him and again passed him over when other appointments were made.

This was in 1880, the hardest year of Iván Ilých's life. It was then that it became evident on the one hand that his salary was insufficient for them to live on, and on the other that he had been forgotten, and not only this, but that what was for him the greatest and most cruel injustice appeared to others a quite ordinary occurrence. Even his father did not consider it his duty to help him. Iván Ilých felt himself abandoned by everyone, and that they regarded his position with a salary of 3,500 rubles [about $2,000] as quite normal and even fortunate. He also knew that with the consciousness of the injustices done him, with his wife's incessant nagging, and with the debts he had contracted by living beyond his means, his position was far from normal.

In order to save money that summer he obtained leave of absence and went with his wife to live in the country at her brother's place.

In the country, without his work, he experienced *ennui* for the first time in his life, and not only *ennui* but intolerable depression, and he decided that it was impossible to go on living like that, and that it was necessary to take energetic measures.

Having passed a sleepless night pacing up and down the veranda, he decided to go to Petersburg and bestir himself, in order to punish those who had failed to appreciate him and to get transferred to another ministry.

Next day, despite many protests from his wife and her brother, he started for Petersburg with the sole object of obtaining a post with a salary of five thousand rubles a year. He was no longer bent on any particular department, or tendency, or kind of activity. All he now wanted was an appointment to another post with a salary of five thousand rubles, either in the administration, in the banks, with the railways, in one of the Empress Márya's Institutions, or even in the customs—but it had to carry with it a salary of five thousand rubles and be in a ministry other than that in which they had failed to appreciate him.

And this quest of Iván Ilých's was crowned with remarkable and unexpected success. At Kursk an acquaintance of his, F. I. Ilyín, got into the first-class carriage, sat down beside Iván Ilých, and told him of a telegram just received by the Governor of Kursk announcing that a change was about to take place in the ministry: Peter Ivánovich was to be superseded by Iván Semënovich.

The proposed change, apart from its significance for Russia, had a special significance for Iván Ilých, because by bringing forward a new man, Peter Petróvich, and consequently his friend Zachár Ivánovich, it was highly favourable for Iván Ilých, since Zachár Ivánovich was a friend and colleague of his.

In Moscow this news was confirmed, and on reaching Petersburg

Iván Ilých found Zachár Ivánovich and received a definite promise of an appointment in his former Department of Justice.

A week later he telegraphed to his wife: "Zachár in Miller's place. I shall receive appointment on presentation of report."

Thanks to this change of personnel, Iván Ilých had unexpectedly obtained an appointment in his former ministry which placed him two stages above his former colleagues besides giving him five thousand rubles salary and three thousand five hundred rubles for expenses connected with his removal. All his ill humour towards his former enemies and the whole department vanished, and Iván Ilých was completely happy.

He returned to the country more cheerful and contented than he had been for a long time. Praskóvya Fëdorovna also cheered up and a truce was arranged between them. Iván Ilých told of how he had been fêted by everybody in Petersburg, how all those who had been his enemies were put to shame and now fawned on him, how envious they were of his appointment, and how much everybody in Petersburg had liked him.

Praskóvya Fëdorovna listened to all this and appeared to believe it. She did not contradict anything, but only made plans for their life in the town to which they were going. Iván Ilých saw with delight that these plans were his plans, that he and his wife agreed, and that, after a stumble, his life was regaining its due and natural character of pleasant lightheartedness and decorum.

Iván Ilých had come back for a short time only, for he had to take up his new duties on the 10th of September. Moreover, he needed time to settle into the new place, to move all his belongings from the province, and to buy and order many additional things: in a word, to make such arrangements as he had resolved on, which were almost exactly what Praskóvya Fëdorovna too had decided on.

Now that everything had happened so fortunately, and that he and his wife were at one in their aims and moreover saw so little of one another, they got on together better than they had done since the first years of marriage. Iván Ilých had thought of taking his family away with him at once, but the insistence of his wife's brother and her sister-in-law, who had suddenly become particularly amiable and friendly to him and his family, induced him to depart alone.

So he departed, and the cheerful state of mind induced by his success and by the harmony between his wife and himself, the one intensifying the other, did not leave him. He found a delightful house, just the thing both he and his wife had dreamt of. Spacious, lofty reception rooms in the old style, a convenient and dignified study, rooms for his wife and daughter, a study for his son—it might have been specially built for them. Iván Ilých himself superintended the arrangements, chose the wall-papers, supplemented the furniture (preferably with antiques which he considered particularly *comme il faut*), and supervised the upholstering. Everything progressed and progressed and approached the ideal he had set for himself: even when things were only half completed they exceeded his expectations. He saw what a refined and elegant character, free from vulgarity, it would all have when it was ready. On falling asleep he pictured to himself how the reception-room would look. Looking at the yet unfinished drawing-room he could see the fireplace, the screen, the what-not, the little chairs dotted here and there, the dishes and plates on the walls, and the bronzes, as they would be when everything was in place. He was pleased by the thought of how his wife and daughter, who shared his taste in this matter, would be impressed by it. They were certainly not expecting as much. He had been particularly successful in finding, and buying cheaply, antiques which gave a particularly aristocratic character to the whole place. But in his letters he intentionally understated everything in order to be able to surprise them. All this so absorbed him that his new duties—though he liked his official work—interested him less than he had expected. Sometimes he even had moments of absent-mindedness during the Court Sessions, and would consider whether he should have straight or curved cornices for his curtains. He was so interested in it all that he often did things himself, rearranging the furniture, or rehanging the curtains. Once when mounting a step-ladder to show the upholsterer, who did not understand, how he wanted the hangings draped, he made a false step and slipped, but being a strong and agile man he clung on and only knocked his side against the knob of the window frame. The bruised place was painful but the pain soon passed, and he felt particularly bright and well just then. He wrote: "I feel fifteen years younger." He thought he would have everything ready by September, but it dragged on till mid-October. But the result was charming not only in his eyes but to everyone who saw it.

In reality it was just what is usually seen in the houses of people of moderate means who want to appear rich, and therefore succeed only in resembling others like themselves: there were damasks, dark wood, plants, rugs, and dull and polished bronzes—all the things people of a certain class have in order to resemble other people of that class. His house was so like the others that it would never have been noticed, but to him it all seemed to be quite exceptional. He was very happy when he met his family at the station and brought them to the newly furnished house all lit up, where a footman in a white tie opened the door into the hall decorated with plants, and when they went on into the drawing-room and the study uttering exclamations of delight. He conducted them everywhere, drank in their praises eagerly, and beamed with pleasure. At tea that evening, when Praskóvya Fëdorovna among other things asked him about his fall, he laughed, and showed them how he had gone flying and had frightened the upholsterer.

"It's a good thing I'm a bit of an athlete. Another man might have been killed, but I merely knocked myself, just here; it hurts when it's touched, but it's passing off already—it's only a bruise."

So they began living in their new home—in which, as always happens, when they got thoroughly settled in they found they were just one room short—and with the increased income, which as always was just a little (some five hundred rubles) too little, but it was all very nice.

Things went particularly well at first, before everything was finally arranged and while something had still to be done: this thing bought, that thing ordered, another thing moved, and something else adjusted. Though there were some disputes between husband and wife, they were both so well satisfied and had so much to do that it all passed off without any serious quarrels. When nothing was left to arrange it became rather dull and something seemed to be lacking, but they were then making acquaintances, forming habits, and life was growing fuller.

Iván Ilých spent his mornings at the law court and came home to dinner, and at first he was generally in a good humour, though he occasionally became irritable just on account of his house. (Every spot on the tablecloth or the upholstery, and every broken window-blind string, irritated him. He had devoted so much trouble to arranging it all that every disturbance of it distressed him.) But on the whole his life ran its course as he believed life should do: easily, pleasantly, and decorously.

He got up at nine, drank his coffee, read the paper, and then put on his undress uniform and went to the law courts. There the harness in which he worked had already been stretched to fit him and he donned it without a hitch: petitioners, inquiries at the chancery, the chancery itself, and the sittings public and administrative. In all this the thing was to exclude everything fresh and vital, which always disturbs the regular course of official business, and to admit only official relations with people, and then only on official grounds. A man would come, for instance, wanting some information. Iván Ilých, as one in whose sphere the matter did not lie, would have nothing to do with him: but if the man had some business with him in his official capacity, something that could be expressed on officially stamped paper, he would do everything, positively everything he could within the limits of such relations, and in doing so would maintain the semblance of friendly human relations, that is, would observe the courtesies of life. As soon as the official relations ended, so did everything else. Iván Ilých possessed this capacity to separate his real life from the official side of affairs and not mix the two, in the highest degree, and by long practice and natural aptitude had brought it to such a pitch that sometimes, in the manner of a virtuoso, he would even allow himself to let the human and official relations mingle. He let himself do this just because he felt that he could at any time he chose resume the strictly official attitude again and drop the human relation. And he did it all easily, pleasantly, correctly, and even artistically. In the intervals between the sessions he smoked, drank tea, chatted a little about politics, a little about general topics, a little about cards, but most of all about official appointments. Tired, but with the feelings of a virtuoso—one of the first violins who has played his part in an orchestra with precision—he would return home to find that his wife and daughter had been out paying calls, or had a visitor, and that his son had been to school, had done his homework with his tutor, and was duly learning what is taught at High Schools. Everything was as it should be. After dinner, if they had no visitors, Iván Ilých sometimes read a book that was being much discussed at the time, and in the evening settled down to work, that is, read official papers, compared the depositions of witnesses, and noted paragraphs of the Code applying to them. This was neither dull nor amusing. It was dull when he might have been playing bridge, but if no bridge was available it was at any rate better than doing nothing or sitting with his wife. Iván Ilých's chief pleasure was giving little dinners to which he invited men and women of good social position, and just as his drawing-room resembled all other drawing-rooms so did his enjoyable little parties resemble all other such parties.

Once they even gave a dance. Iván Ilých enjoyed it and everything went off well, except that it led to a violent quarrel with his wife about the cakes and sweets. Praskóvya Fëdorovna had made her own plans, but Iván Ilých insisted on getting everything from an expensive confectioner and ordered too many cakes, and the quarrel occurred because some of those cakes were left over and the confectioner's bill came to forty-five rubles. It was a great and disagreeable quarrel. Praskóvya Fëdorovna called him "a fool and an imbecile," and he clutched at his head and made angry allusions to divorce.

But the dance itself had been enjoyable. The best people were there, and Iván Ilých had danced with Princess Trúfonova, a sister of the distinguished founder of the Society "Bear by Burden."

The pleasures connected with his work were pleasure of ambition; his social pleasures were those of vanity; but Iván Ilých's greatest pleasure was playing bridge. He acknowledged that whatever disagreeable incident happened in his life, the pleasure that beamed like a ray of light above everything else was to sit down to bridge with good players, not noisy partners, and of course to four-handed bridge (with five players it was annoying to have to stand out, though one pretended not to mind), to play a clever and serious game (when the cards allowed it) and then to have supper and drink a glass of wine. After a game of bridge, especially if he had won a little (to win a large sum was unpleasant), Iván Ilých went to bed in specially good humour.

So they lived. They formed a circle of acquaintances among the best people and were visited by people of importance and by young folk. In their views as to their acquaintances, husband, wife and daughter were entirely agreed, and tacitly and unanimously kept at arm's length and shook off the various shabby friends and relations who, with much show of affection, gushed into the drawing-room with its Japanese plates on the walls. Soon these shabby friends ceased to obtrude themselves and only the best people remained in the Golovíns' set.

Young men made up to Lisa, and Petríshchev, an examining magistrate and Dmítri Ivánovich Petríshchev's son and sole heir, began to be so attentive to her that Iván Ilých had already spoken to Praskóvya Fëdorovna about it, and considered whether they should not arrange a party for them, or get up some private theatricals.

So they lived, and all went well, without change, and life flowed pleasantly.

IV

They were all in good health. It could not be called ill health if Iván Ilých sometimes said that he had a queer taste in his mouth and felt some discomfort in his left side.

But this discomfort increased and, though not exactly painful, grew into a sense of pressure in his side accompanied by ill humor. And his irritability became worse and worse and began to mar the agreeable, easy, and correct life that had established itself in the Golovín family. Quarrels between husband and wife became more and more frequent, and soon the ease and amenity disappeared and even the decorum was rarely maintained. Scenes again became frequent, and very few of those islets remained on which husband and wife could meet without an explosion. Praskóvya Fëdorovna now had good reason to say that her husband's temper was trying. With characteristic exaggeration she said he had always had a dreadful temper, and that it had needed all her good nature to put up with it for twenty years. It was true that now the quarrels were started by him. His bursts of temper always came just before dinner, often just as he began to eat his soup. Sometimes he noticed that a plate or dish was chipped, or the food was not right, or his son put his elbow on the table, or his daughter's hair was not done as he liked it, and for all this he blamed Praskóvya Fëdorovna. At first she retorted and said disagreeable things to him, but once or twice he fell into such a rage at the beginning of dinner that she realized it was due to some physical derangement brought on by taking food, and so she restrained herself and did not answer, but only hurried to get the dinner over. She regarded this self-restraint as highly praiseworthy. Having come to the conclusion that her husband had a dreadful temper and made her life miserable, she began to feel sorry for herself, and the more she pitied herself the more she hated her husband. She began to wish he would die; yet she did not want him to die because then his salary would cease. And this irritated her against him still more. She considered herself dreadfully unhappy just because not even his death could save her, and though she concealed her exasperation, that hidden exasperation of hers increased his irritation also.

After one scene in which Iván Ilých had been particularly unfair and after which he had said in explanation that he certainly was irritable but that it was due to his not being well, she said that if he was ill it should be attended to, and insisted on his going to see a celebrated doctor.

He went. Everything took place as he had expected and as it always does. There was the usual waiting and the important air assumed by the doctor, with which he was so familiar (resembling that which he himself assumed in court), and the sounding and listening, and the questions which called for answers that were foregone conclusions and were evidently unnecessary, and the look of importance which implied that "if only you put yourself in our hands we will arrange everything—we know indubitably how it has to be done, always in the same way for everybody alike." It was all just as it was in the law courts. The doctor put on just the same air towards him as he himself put on towards an accused person.

The doctor said that so-and-so indicated that there was so-and-so inside the patient, but if the investigation of so-and-so did not confirm this, then he must assume that and that. If he assumed that and that, then . . . and so on. To Iván Ilých only one question was important: was his case serious or not? But the doctor ignored that inappropriate question. From his point of view it was not the one under consideration, the real question was to decide between a floating kidney, chronic catarrh, or appendicitis. It was not a question of Iván Ilých's life or death, but one between a floating kidney and appendicitis. And that question the doctor solved brilliantly, as it seemed to Iván Ilých, in favour of the appendix, with the reservation that should an examination of the urine give fresh indications the matter would be reconsidered. All this was just what Iván Ilých had himself brilliantly accomplished a thousand times in dealing with men on trial. The doctor summed up just as brilliantly, looking over his spectacles triumphantly and even gaily at the accused. From the doctor's summing up Iván Ilých concluded that things were bad, but that for the doctor, and perhaps for everybody else, it was a matter of indifference, though for him it was bad. And this conclusion struck him painfully, arousing in him a great feeling of pity for himself and of bitterness towards the doctor's indifference to a matter of such importance.

He said nothing of this, but rose, placed the doctor's fee on the table, and remarked with a sigh: "We sick people probably often put inappropriate questions. But tell me, in general, is this complaint dangerous, or not? . . ."

The doctor looked at him sternly over his spectacles with one eye, as if to say: "Prisoner, if you will not keep to the questions put to you, I shall be obliged to have you removed from the court."

"I have already told you what I consider necessary and proper. The analysis may show something more." And the doctor bowed.

Iván Ilých went out slowly, seated himself disconsolately in his sledge, and drove home. All the way home he was going over what the doctor had said, trying to translate those complicated, obscure, scientific phrases into plain language and find in them an answer to the question: "Is my condition bad? Is it very bad? Or is there as yet nothing much wrong?" And it seemed to him that the meaning of what the doctor had said was that it was very bad. Everything in the streets seemed depressing. The cabmen, the houses, the passers-by, and the shops, were dismal. His ache, this dull gnawing ache that never ceased for a moment, seemed to have acquired a new and more serious significance from the doctor's dubious remarks. Iván Ilých now watched it with a new and oppressive feeling.

He reached home and began to tell his wife about it. She listened, but in the middle of his account his daughter came in with her hat on, ready to go out with her mother. She sat down reluctantly to listen to this tedious story, but could not stand it long, and her mother too did not hear him to the end.

"Well, I am very glad," she said. "Mind now to take your medicine regularly. Give me the prescription and I'll send Gerásim to the chemist's." And she went to get ready to go out.

While she was in the room Iván Ilých had hardly taken time to breathe, but he sighed deeply when she left it.

"Well," he thought, "perhaps it isn't so bad after all."

He began taking his medicine and following the doctor's directions, which had been altered after the examination of the urine. But then it happened that there was a contradiction between the indications drawn from the examination of the urine and the symptoms that showed themselves. It turned out that what was happening differed from what the doctor had told him, and that he had either forgotten, or blundered, or hidden something from him. He could not, however, be blamed for that, and Iván Ilých still obeyed his orders implicitly and at first derived some comfort from doing so.

From the time of his visit to the doctor, Iván Ilých's chief occupation was the exact fulfilment of the doctor's instructions regarding hygiene and the taking of medicine, and the observation of his pain and his excretions. His chief interests came to be people's ailments and people's health. When sickness, deaths, or recoveries, were mentioned in his presence, especially when the illness resembled his own, he listened with agitation which he tried to hide, asked questions, and applied what he heard to his own case.

The pain did not grow less, but Iván Ilých made efforts to force himself to think that he was better. And he could do this so long as nothing agitated him. But as soon as he had any unpleasantness with his wife, any lack of success in his official work, or held bad cards at bridge, he was at once acutely sensible of his disease. He had formerly borne such mischances, hoping soon to adjust what was wrong, to master it and attain success, or make a grand slam. But now every mischance upset him and plunged him into despair. He would say to himself: "There now, just as I was beginning to get better and the medicine had begun to take effect, comes this accursed misfortune, or unpleasantness. . . ." And he was furious with the mishap, or with the people who were causing the unpleasantness and killing him, for he felt that his fury was killing him but could not restrain it. One would have thought that it should have been clear to him that this exasperation with circumstances and people aggravated his illness, and that he ought therefore to ignore unpleasant occurrences. But he drew the very opposite conclusion: he said that he needed peace, and he watched for everything that might disturb it and became irritable at the slightest infringement of it. His condition was rendered worse by the fact that he read medical books and consulted doctors. The progress of his disease was so gradual that he could deceive himself when comparing one day with another—the difference was so slight. But when he consulted the doctors it seemed to him that he was getting worse, and even very rapidly. Yet despite this he was continually consulting them.

That month he went to see another celebrity, who told him almost the same as the first had done but put his questions rather differently, and the interview with this celebrity only increased Iván Ilých's doubts and fears. A friend of a friend of his, a very good doctor, diagnosed his illness again quite differently from the others, and though he predicted recovery, his questions and suppositions bewildered Iván Ilých still more and increased his doubts. A homoeopathist diagnosed the disease in yet another way, and prescribed medicine which Iván Ilých took secretly for a week. But after a week, not feeling any improvement and having lost confidence both in the former doctor's treatment and in this one's, he became still more despondent. One day a lady acquaintance mentioned a cure effected by a wonder-working icon. Iván Ilých caught himself listening attentively and beginning to believe that it had occurred. This incident alarmed him. "Has my mind really weakened to such an extent?" he asked himself. "Nonsense! It's all rubbish. I mustn't give way to nervous fears but having chosen a doctor must keep strictly to his treatment. That is what I will do. Now it's all settled. I won't think about it, but will follow the treatment seriously till summer, and then we shall see. From now there must be no more of this wavering!" This was easy to say but impossible to carry out. The pain in his side oppressed him and seemed to grow worse and more incessant, while the taste in his mouth grew stranger and stranger. It seemed to him that his breath had a disgusting smell, and he was conscious of a loss of appetite and strength. There was no deceiving himself: something terrible, new, and more important than anything before in his life, was taking place within him of which he alone was aware. Those about him did not understand or would not understand it, but thought everything in the world was going on as usual. That tormented Iván Ilých more than anything. He saw that his household, especially his wife and daughter who were in a perfect whirl of visiting, did not understand anything of it and were annoyed that he was so depressed and so exacting, as if he were to blame for it. Though they tried to disguise it he saw that he was an obstacle in their path, and that his wife had adopted a definite line in regard to his illness and kept to it regardless of anything he said or did. Her attitude was this: "You know," she would say to her friends, "Iván Ilých can't do as other people do, and keep to the treatment prescribed for him. One day he'll take his drops and keep strictly to his diet and go to bed in good time, but the next day unless I watch him he'll suddenly forget his medicine, eat sturgeon—which is forbidden—and sit up playing cards till one o'clock in the morning."

"Oh, come, when was that?" Iván Ilých would ask in vexation. "Only once at Peter Ivánovich's."

"And yesterday with Shébek."

"Well, even if I hadn't stayed up, this pain would have kept me awake."

"Be that as it may you'll never get well like that, but will always make us wretched."

Praskóvya Fëdorovna's attitude to Iván Ilých's illness, as she expressed it both to others and to him, was that it was his own fault and was another of the annoyances he caused her. Iván Ilých felt that this opinion escaped her involuntarily—but that did not make it easier for him.

At the law courts too, Iván Ilých noticed, or thought he noticed, a strange attitude towards himself. It sometimes seemed to him that people were watching him inquisitively as a man whose place might soon be vacant. Then again, his friends would suddenly begin to chaff him in a friendly way about his low spirits, as if the awful, horrible, and unheard-of thing that was going on within him, incessantly gnawing at him and irresistibly drawing him away, was a very agreeable subject for jests. Schwartz in particular irritated him by his jocularity, vivacity, and *savoir-faire*, which reminded him of what he himself had been ten years ago.

Friends came to make up a set and they sat down to cards. They dealt, bending the new cards to soften them, and he sorted the diamonds in his hand and found he had seven. His partner said "No trumps" and supported him with two diamonds. What more could be wished for? It ought to be jolly and lively. They would make a grand slam. But suddenly Iván Ilých was conscious of that gnawing pain, that taste in his mouth, and it seemed ridiculous that in such circumstances he should be pleased to make a grand slam.

He looked at his partner Mikháil Mikháylovich, who rapped the table with his strong hand and instead of snatching up the tricks pushed the cards courteously and indulgently towards Iván Ilých that he might have the pleasure of gathering them up without the trouble of stretching out his hand for them. "Does he think I am too weak to stretch out my arm?" thought Iván Ilých, and forgetting what he was doing he overtrumped his partner, missing the grand slam by three tricks. And what was most awful of all was that he saw how upset Mikháil Mikháylovich was about it but did not himself care. And it was dreadful to realize why he did not care.

They all saw that he was suffering, and said: "We can stop if you are tired. Take a rest." Lie down? No, he was not at all tired, and he finished the rubber. All were gloomy and silent. Iván Ilých felt that he had diffused this gloom over them and could not dispel it. They had supper and went away, and Iván Ilých was left alone with the consciousness that his life was poisoned and was poisoning the lives of others, and that this poison did not weaken but penetrated more and more deeply into his whole being.

With this consciousness, and with physical pain besides the terror, he must go to bed, often to lie awake the greater part of the night. Next morning he had to get up again, dress, go to the law courts, speak, and write; or if he did not go out, spend at home those twenty-four hours a day each of which was a torture. And he had to live thus all alone on the brink of an abyss, with no one who understood or pitied him.

V

So one month passed and then another. Just before the New Year his brother-in-law came to town and stayed at their house. Iván Ilých was at the law courts and Praskóvya Fëdorovna had gone shopping. When Iván Ilých came home and entered his study he found his brother-in-law there—a healthy, florid man—unpacking his portmanteau himself. He raised his head on hearing Iván Ilých's footsteps and looked up at him for a moment without a word. That stare told Iván Ilých everything. His brother-in-law opened his mouth to utter an exclamation of surprise but checked himself, and that action confirmed it all.

"I have changed, eh?"

"Yes, there is a change."

And after that, try as he would to get his brother-in-law to return to the subject of his looks, the latter would say nothing about it. Praskóvya Fëdorovna came home and her brother went out to her. Iván Ilých locked the door and began to examine himself in the glass, first full face, then in profile. He took up a portrait of himself taken with his wife, and compared it with what he saw in the glass. The change in him was immense. Then he bared his arms to the elbow, looked at them, drew the sleeves down again, sat down on an ottoman, and grew blacker than night.

"No, no, this won't do!" he said to himself, and jumped up, went to the table, took up some law papers and began to read them, but could not continue. He unlocked the door and went into the reception-room. The door leading to the drawing-room was shut. He approached it on tiptoe and listened.

"No, you are exaggerating!" Praskóvya Fëdorovna was saying.

"Exaggerating! Don't you see it? Why, he's a dead man! Look at his eyes—there's no light in them. But what is it that is wrong with him?"

"No one knows. Nikoláevich [that was another doctor] said something, but I don't know what. And Leshchetítsky [this was the celebrated specialist] said quite the contrary. . . ."

Iván Ilých walked away, went to his own room, lay down, and began musing: "The kidney, a floating kidney." He recalled all the doctors had told him of how it detached itself and swayed about. And by an effort of imagination he tried to catch that kidney and arrest it and support it. So little was needed for this, it seemed to him. "No, I'll go to see Peter Ivánovich again." [That was the friend whose friend was a doctor.] He rang, ordered the carriage, and got ready to go.

"Where are you going, Jean?" asked his wife, with a specially sad and exceptionally kind look.

This exceptionally kind look irritated him. He looked morosely at her.

"I must go to see Peter Ivánovich."

He went to see Peter Ivánovich, and together they went to see his friend, the doctor. He was in, and Iván Ilých had a long talk with him.

Reviewing the anatomical and physiological details of what in the doctor's opinion was going on inside him, he understood it all.

There was something, a small thing, in the vermiform appendix. It might all come right. Only stimulate the energy of one organ and check the activity of another, then absorption would take place and everything would come right. He got home rather late for dinner, ate his dinner, and conversed cheerfully, but could not for a long time bring himself to go back to work in his room. At last, however, he went to his study and did what was necessary, but the consciousness that he had put something aside—an important, intimate matter which he would revert to when his work was done—never left him. When he had finished his work he remembered that this intimate matter was the thought of his vermiform appendix. But he did not give himself up to it, and went to the drawing-room for tea. There were callers there, including the examining magistrate who was a desirable match for his daughter, and they were conversing, playing the piano and singing. Iván Ilých, as Praskóvya Fëdorovna remarked, spent that evening more cheerfully than usual, but he never for a moment forgot that he had postponed the important matter of the appendix. At eleven o'clock he said good-night and went to his bedroom. Since his illness he had slept alone in a small room next to his study. He undressed and took up a novel by Zola, but instead of reading it he fell into thought, and in his imagination that desired improvement in the vermiform appendix occurred. There was the absorption and evacuation and the re-establishment of normal activity. "Yes, that's it" he said to himself. "One need only assist nature, that's all." He remembered his medicine, rose, took it, and lay down on his back watching for the beneficent action of the medicine and for it to lessen the pain. "I need only take it regularly and avoid all injurious influences. I am already feeling better, much better." He began touching his side: it was not painful to the touch. "There, I really don't feel it. It's much better already." He put out the light and turned on his side . . . "The appendix is getting better, absorption is occurring." Suddenly he felt the old familiar, dull, gnawing pain, stubborn and serious. There was the same familiar loathsome taste in his mouth. His heart sank and he felt dazed. "My God! My God!" he muttered. "Again, again; And it will never cease." And suddenly the matter presented itself in a quite different aspect. "Vermiform appendix; Kidney!" he said to himself. "It's not a question of appendix or kidney, but of life . . . and death. Yes, life was there and now it is going, going and I cannot stop it. Yes. Why deceive myself? Isn't it obvious to everyone but me that I'm dying, and that it's only a question of weeks, days . . . it may happen this moment. There was light and now there is darkness. I was here and now I'm going there! Where?" A chill came over him, his breathing ceased, and he felt only the throbbing of his heart.

"When I am not, what will there be? There will be nothing. Then where shall I be when I am no more? Can this be dying? No, I don't want to!" He jumped up and tried to light the candle, felt for it with trembling hands, dropped candle and candlestick on the floor, and fell back on his pillow.

"What's the use? It makes no difference," he said to himself, staring with wide-open eyes into the darkness. "Death. Yes, death. And none of them know or wish to know it, and they have no pity for me. Now they are playing." (He heard through the door the distant sound of a song and its accompaniment.) "It's all the same to them, but they will die too! Fools! I first, and they later, but it will be the same for them. And now they are merry . . . the beasts!"

Anger choked him and he was agonizingly, unbearably miserable. "It is impossible that all men have been doomed to suffer this awful horror!" He raised himself.

"Something must be wrong. I must calm myself—must think it all over from the beginning." And he again began thinking. "Yes, the beginning of my illness: I knocked my side, but I was still quite well that day and the next. It hurt a little, then rather more. I saw the doctors, then followed despondency and anguish, more doctors, and I drew nearer to the abyss. My strength grew less and I kept coming nearer and nearer, and now I have wasted away and there is no light in my eyes. I think of the appendix—but this is death! I think of mending the appendix, and all the while here is death! Can it really be death?" Again terror seized him and he gasped for breath. He leant down and began feeling for the matches, pressing with his elbow on the stand beside the bed. It was in his way and hurt him, he grew furious with it, pressed on it still harder, and upset it. Breathless and in despair he fell on his back, expecting death to come immediately.

Meanwhile the visitors were leaving. Praskóvya Fëdorovna was seeing them off. She heard something fall and came in.

"What has happened?"

"Nothing. I knocked it over accidentally."

She went out and returned with a candle. He lay there panting heavily, like a man who has run a thousand yards, and stared upwards at her with a fixed look.

"What is it, Jean?"

"No . . . o . . . thing. I upset it." ("Why speak of it? She won't understand," he thought.)

And in truth she did not understand. She picked up the stand, lit his candle, and hurried away to see another visitor off. When she came back he still lay on his back, looking upwards.

"What is it? Do you feel worse?"

"Yes."

She shook her head and sat down.

"Do you know, Jean, I think we must ask Leshchetítsky to come and see you here."

This meant calling in the famous specialist, regardless of expense. He smiled malignantly and said "No." She remained a little longer and then went up to him and kissed his forehead.

While she was kissing him he hated her from the bottom of his soul and with difficulty refrained from pushing her away.
"Good-night. Please God you'll sleep."
"Yes."

VI

Iván Ilých saw that he was dying, and he was in continual despair.

In the depth of his heart he knew he was dying, but not only was he not accustomed to the thought, he simply did not and could not grasp it.

The syllogism he had learnt from Kiezewetter's Logic: "Caius is a man, men are mortal, therefore Caius is mortal," had always seemed to him correct as applied to Caius, but certainly not as applied to himself. That Caius—man in the abstract—was mortal, was perfectly correct, but he was not Caius, not an abstract man, but a creature quite, quite separate from all others. He had been little Ványa, with a mamma and a papa, with Mitya and Volódya, with the toys, a coachman and a nurse, afterwards with Kátenka and with all the joys, griefs, and delights of childhood, boyhood, and youth. What did Caius know of the smell of that striped leather ball Ványa had been so fond of? Had Caius kissed his mother's hand like that, and did the silk of her dress rustle so for Caius? Had he rioted like that at school when the pastry was bad? Had Caius been in love like that? Could Caius preside at a session as he did? "Caius really was mortal, and it was right for him to die; but for me, little Ványa, Iván Ilých, with all my thoughts and emotions, it's altogether a different matter. It cannot be that I ought to die. That would be too terrible."

Such was his feeling.

"If I had to die like Caius I should have known it was so. An inner voice would have told me so, but there was nothing of the sort in me and I and all my friends felt that our case was quite different from that of Caius. And now here it is!" he said to himself. "It can't be. It's impossible! But here it is. How is this? How is one to understand it?"

He could not understand it, and tried to drive this false, incorrect, morbid thought away and to replace it by other proper and healthy thoughts. But that thought, and not the thought only but the reality itself, seemed to come and confront him.

And to replace that thought he called up a succession of others, hoping to find in them some support. He tried to get back into the former current of thoughts that had once screened the thought of death from him. But strange to say, all that had formerly shut off, hidden, and destroyed, his consciousness of death, no longer had that effect. Iván Ilých now spent most of his time in attempting to re-establish that old current. He would say to himself: "I will take up my duties again—after all I used to live by them." And banishing all doubts he would go to the law courts, enter into conversation with his colleagues, and sit carelessly as was his wont, scanning the crowd with a thoughtful look and leaning both his emaciated arms on the arms of his oak chair; bending over as usual to a colleague and drawing his papers nearer he would interchange whispers with him, and then suddenly raising his eyes and sitting erect would pronounce certain words and open the proceedings. But suddenly in the midst of those proceedings the pain in his side, regardless of the stage the proceedings had reached, would begin its own gnawing work. Iván Ilých would turn his attention to it and try to drive the thought of it away, but without success. *It* would come and stand before him and look at him, and he would be petrified and the light would die out of his eyes, and he would again begin asking himself whether *It* alone was true. And his colleagues and subordinates would see with surprise and distress that he, the brilliant and subtle judge, was becoming confused and making mistakes. He would shake himself, try to pull himself together, manage somehow to bring the sitting to a close, and return home with the sorrowful consciousness that his judicial labours could not as formerly hide from him what he wanted them to hide, and could not deliver him from *It*. And what was worst of all was that *It* drew his attention to itself not in order to make him take some action but only that he should look at *It*, look it straight in the face: look at it and without doing anything, suffer inexpressibly.

And to save himself from this condition Iván Ilých looked for consolations—new screens—and new screens were found and for a while seemed to save him, but then they immediately fell to pieces or rather became transparent, as if *It* penetrated them and nothing could veil *It*.

In these latter days he would go into the drawing-room he had arranged—that drawing-room where he had fallen and for the sake of which (how bitterly ridiculous it seemed) he had sacrificed his life—for he knew that his illness originated with that knock. He would enter and see that something had scratched the polished table. He would look for the cause of this and find that it was the bronze ornamentation of an album, that had got bent. He would take up the expensive album which he had lovingly arranged, and feel vexed with his daughter and her friends for their untidiness—for the album was torn here and there and some of the photographs turned upside down. He would put it carefully in order and bend the ornamentation back into position. Then it would occur to him to place all those things in another corner of the room, near the plants. He would call the footman, but his daughter or wife would come to help him. They would not agree, and his wife would contradict him, and he would dispute and grow angry. But that was all right, for then he did not think about *It*. *It* was invisible.

But then, when he was moving something himself, his wife would say: "Let the servants do it. You will hurt yourself again." And suddenly *It* would flash through the screen and he would see it. *It* was just a flash, and he hoped it would disappear, but he would involuntarily pay attention to his side. "It sits there as before, gnawing just the same!" And he could no longer forget *It*, but could distinctly see it looking at him from behind the flowers. "What is it all for?"

"It really is so! I lost my life over that curtain as I might have done when storming a fort. Is that possible? How terrible and how stupid. It can't be true! It can't, but it is."

He would go to his study, lie down, and again be alone with *It*: face to face with *It*. And nothing could be done with *It* except to look at it and shudder.

VII

How it happened it is impossible to say because it came about step by step, unnoticed, but in the third month of Iván Ilých's illness, his wife, his daughter, his son, his acquaintances, the doctors, the servants, and above all he himself, were aware that the whole interest he had for other people was whether he would soon vacate his place, and at last release the living from the discomfort caused by his presence and be himself released from his sufferings.

He slept less and less. He was given opium and hypodermic injections of morphine, but this did not relieve him. The dull depression he experienced in a somnolent condition at first gave him a little relief, but only as something new, afterwards it became as distressing as the pain itself or even more so.

Special foods were prepared for him by the doctors' orders, but all those foods became increasingly distasteful and disgusting to him.

For his excretions also special arrangements had to be made, and this was a torment to him every time—a torment from the uncleanliness, the unseemliness, and the smell, and from knowing that another person had to take part in it.

But just through this most unpleasant matter Iván Ilých obtained comfort. Gerásim, the butler's young assistant, always came in to carry the things out. Gerásim was a clean, fresh peasant lad, grown stout on town food and always cheerful and bright. At first the sight of him, in his clean Russian peasant costume, engaged on that disgusting task embarrassed Iván Ilých.

Once when he got up from the commode too weak to draw up his trousers, he dropped into a soft armchair and looked with horror at his bare, enfeebled thighs with the muscles so sharply marked on them.

Gerásim with a firm light tread, his heavy boots emitting a pleasant smell of tar and fresh winter air, came in wearing a clean Hessian apron, the sleeves of his print shirt tucked up over his strong bare young arms; and refraining from looking at his sick master out of consideration for his feelings, and restraining the joy of life that beamed from his face, went up to the commode.

"Gerásim!" said Iván Ilých in a weak voice.

Gerásim started, evidently afraid he might have committed some blunder, and with a rapid movement turned his fresh, kind, simple young face which just showed the first downy signs of a beard.

"Yes, sir?"

"That must be very unpleasant for you. You must forgive me. I am helpless."

"Oh, why, sir," and Gerásim's eyes beamed and he showed his glistening white teeth, "what's a little trouble? It's a case of illness with you, sir."

And his deft strong hands did their accustomed task, and he went out of the room stepping lightly. Five minutes later he as lightly returned.

Iván Ilých was still sitting in the same position in the armchair.

"Gerásim," he said when the latter had replaced the freshly-washed utensil. "Please come here and help me." Gerásim went up to him. "Lift me up. It is hard for me to get up, and I have sent Dmítri away."

Gerásim went up to him, grasped his master with his strong arms deftly but gently, in the same way that he stepped—lifted him, supported him with one hand, and with the other drew up his trousers and would have set him down again, but Iván Ilých asked to be led to the sofa. Gerásim, without an effort and without apparent pressure, led him, almost lifting him, to the sofa and placed him on it.

"Thank you. How easily and well you do it all!"

Gerásim smiled again and turned to leave the room. But Iván Ilých felt his presence such a comfort that he did not want to let him go.

"One thing more, please move up that chair. No, the other one—under my feet. It is easier for me when my feet are raised."

Gerásim brought the chair, set it down gently in place, and raised Iván

Ilých's legs on to it. It seemed to Iván Ilých that he felt better while Gerásim was holding up his legs.

"It's better when my legs are higher," he said. "Place that cushion under them."

Gerásim did so. He again lifted the legs and placed them, and again Iván Ilých felt better while Gerásim held his legs. When he set them down Iván Ilých fancied he felt worse.

"Gerásim," he said. "Are you busy now?"

"Not at all, sir," said Gerásim, who had learnt from the townsfolk how to speak to gentlefolk.

"What have you still to do?"

"What have I to do? I've done everything except chopping the logs for to-morrow."

"Then hold my legs up a bit higher, can you?"

"Of course I can. Why not?" And Gerásim raised his master's legs higher and Iván Ilých thought that in that position he did not feel any pain at all.

"And how about the logs?"

"Don't trouble about that, sir. There's plenty of time."

Iván Ilých told Gerásim to sit down and hold his legs, and began to talk to him. And strange to say it seemed to him that he felt better while Gerásim held his legs up.

After that Iván Ilých would sometimes call Gerásim and get him to hold his legs on his shoulders, and he liked talking to him. Gerásim did it all easily, willingly, simply, and with a good nature that touched Iván Ilých. Health, strength, and vitality in other people were offensive to him, but Gerásim's strength and vitality did not mortify but soothed him.

What tormented Iván Ilých most was the deception, the lie, which for some reason they all accepted, that he was not dying but was simply ill, and that he only need keep quiet and undergo a treatment and then something very good would result. He however knew that do what they would nothing would come of it, only still more agonizing suffering and death. This deception tortured him—their not wishing to admit what they all knew and what he knew, but wanting to lie to him concerning his terrible condition, and wishing and forcing him to participate in that lie. Those lies—lies enacted over him on the eve of his death and destined to degrade this awful, solemn act to the level of their visitings, their curtains, their sturgeon for dinner—were a terrible agony for Iván Ilých. And strangely enough, many times when they were going through their antics over him he had been within a hairbreadth of calling out to them: "Stop lying! You know and I know that I am dying. Then at least stop lying about it!" But he had never had the spirit to do it. The awful, terrible act of his dying was, he could see, reduced by those about him to the level of a casual, unpleasant, and almost indecorous incident (as if someone entered a drawing-room diffusing an unpleasant odour) and this was done by that very decorum which he had served all his life long. He saw that no one felt for him, because no one even wished to grasp his position. Only Gerásim recognized it and pitied him. And so Iván Ilých felt at ease only with him. He felt comforted when Gerásim supported his legs (sometimes all night long) and refused to go to bed, saying: "Don't you worry, Iván Ilých. I'll get sleep enough later on," or when he suddenly became familiar and exclaimed: "If you weren't sick it would be another matter, but as it is, why should I grudge a little trouble?" Gerásim alone did not lie; everything showed that he alone understood the facts of the case and did not consider it necessary to disguise them, but simply felt sorry for his emaciated and enfeebled master. Once when Iván Ilých was sending him away he even said straight out: "We shall all of us die, so why should I grudge a little trouble?"—expressing the fact that he did not think his work burdensome, because he was doing it for a dying man and hoped someone would do the same for him when his time came.

Apart from this lying, or because of it, what most tormented Iván Ilých was that no one pitied him as he wished to be pitied. At certain moments after prolonged suffering he wished most of all (though he would have been ashamed to confess it) for someone to pity him as a sick child is pitied. He longed to be petted and comforted. He knew he was an important functionary, that he had a beard turning grey, and that therefore what he longed for was impossible, but still he longed for it. And in Gerásim's attitude towards him there was something akin to what he wished for, and so that attitude comforted him. Iván Ilých wanted to weep, wanted to be petted and cried over, and then his colleague Shébek would come, and instead of weeping and being petted, Iván Ilých would assume a serious, severe, and profound air, and by force of habit would express his opinion on a decision of the Court of Cassation and would stubbornly insist on that view. This falsity around him and within him did more than anything else to poison his last days.

VIII

It was morning. He knew it was morning because Gerásim had gone, and Peter the footman had come and put out the candles, drawn back one of the curtains, and begun quietly to tidy up. Whether it was morning or evening, Friday or Sunday, made no difference, it was all just the same: the gnawing, unmitigated, agonizing pain, never ceasing for an instant, the consciousness of life inexorably waning but not yet extinguished, that approach of that ever dreaded and hateful Death which was the only reality, and always the same falsity. What were days, weeks, hours, in such a case?

"Will you have some tea, sir?"

"He wants things to be regular, and wishes the gentlefolk to drink tea in the morning," thought Iván Ilých, and only said "No."

"Wouldn't you like to move onto the sofa, sir?"

"He wants to tidy up the room, and I'm in the way. I am uncleanliness and disorder," he thought, and said only:

"No, leave me alone."

The man went on bustling about. Iván Ilých stretched out his hand. Peter came up, ready to help.

"What is it, sir?"

"My watch."

Peter took the watch which was close at hand and gave it to his master.

"Half-past eight. Are they up?"

"No sir, except Vladímir Ivánich" (the son) "who has gone to school. Praskóvya Fëdorovna ordered me to wake her if you asked for her. Shall I do so?"

"No, there's no need to." "Perhaps I'd better have some tea," he thought, and added aloud: "Yes, bring me some tea."

Peter went to the door but Iván Ilých dreaded being left alone. "How can I keep him here? Oh yes, my medicine." "Peter, give me my medicine." "Why not? Perhaps it may still do me some good." He took a spoonful and swallowed it. "No, it won't help. It's all tomfoolery, all deception," he decided as soon as he became aware of the familiar, sickly, hopeless taste. "No, I can't believe in it any longer. But the pain, why this pain? If it would only cease just for a moment!" And he moaned. Peter turned towards him. "It's all right. Go and fetch me some tea."

Peter went out. Left alone Iván Ilých groaned not so much with pain, terrible though that was, as from mental anguish. Always and for ever the same, always these endless days and nights. If only it would come quicker! If only *what* would come quicker? Death, darkness? . . . No, no! Anything rather than death!

When Peter returned with the tea on a tray, Iván Ilých stared at him for a time in perplexity, not realizing who and what he was. Peter was disconcerted by that look and his embarrassment brought Iván Ilých to himself.

"Oh, tea! All right, put it down. Only help me to wash and put on a clean shirt."

And Iván Ilých began to wash. With pauses for rest, he washed his hands and then his face, cleaned his teeth, brushed his hair, and looked in the glass. He was terrified by what he saw, especially by the limp way in which his hair clung to his pallid forehead.

While his shirt was being changed he knew that he would be still more frightened at the sight of his body, so he avoided looking at it. Finally he was ready. He drew on a dressing-gown, wrapped himself in a plaid, and sat down in the armchair to take his tea. For a moment he felt refreshed, but as soon as he began to drink the tea he was again aware of the same taste, and the pain also returned. He finished it with an effort, and then lay down stretching out his legs, and dismissed Peter.

Always the same. Now a spark of hope flashes up, then a sea of despair rages, and always pain; always pain, always despair, and always the same. When alone he had a dreadful and distressing desire to call someone, but he knew beforehand that with others present it would be still worse. "Another dose of morphine—to lose consciousness. I will tell him, the doctor, that he must think of something else. It's impossible, impossible, to go on like this."

An hour and another pass like that. But now there is a ring at the door bell. Perhaps it's the doctor? It is. He comes in fresh, hearty, plump, and cheerful, with that look on his face that seems to say: "There now, you're in a panic about something, but we'll arrange it all for you directly!" The doctor knows this expression is out of place here, but he has put it on once for all and can't take it off—like a man who has put on a frock-coat in the morning to pay a round of calls.

The doctor rubs his hands vigorously and reassuringly.

"Brr! How cold it is! There's such a sharp frost; just let me warm myself!" he says, as if it were only a matter of waiting till he was warm, and then he would put everything right.

"Well now, how are you?"

Iván Ilých feels that the doctor would like to say: "Well, how are our affairs?" but that even he feels that this would not do, and says instead: "What sort of a night have you had?"

Iván Ilých looks at him as much as to say: "Are you really never ashamed of lying?" But the doctor does not wish to understand this question, and Iván Ilých says: "Just as terrible as ever. The pain never leaves me and never subsides. If only something. . . ."

"Yes, you sick people are always like that. . . . There, now I think I am warm enough. Even Praskóvya Fëdorovna, who is so particular, could find no fault with my temperature. Well, now I can say good-morning," and the doctor presses his patient's hand.

Then, dropping his former playfulness, he begins with a most serious face to examine the patient, feeling his pulse and taking his temperature, and then begins the sounding and auscultation.

Iván Ilých knows quite well and definitely that all this is nonsense and pure deception, but when the doctor, getting down on his knee, leans over him, putting his ear first higher then lower, and performs various gymnastic movements over him with a significant expression on his face, Iván Ilých submits to it all as he used to submit to the speeches of the lawyers, though he knew very well that they were all lying and why they were lying.

The doctor, kneeling on the sofa, is still sounding him when Praskóvya Fëdorovna's silk dress rustles at the door and she is heard scolding Peter for not having let her know of the doctor's arrival.

She comes in, kisses her husband, and at once proceeds to prove that she has been up a long time already, and only owing to a misunderstanding failed to be there when the doctor arrived.

Iván Ilých looks at her, scans her all over, sets against her the whiteness and plumpness and cleanness of her hands and neck, the gloss of her hair, and the sparkle of her vivacious eyes. He hates her with his whole soul. And the thrill of hatred he feels for her makes him suffer from her touch.

Her attitude towards him and his disease is still the same. Just as the doctor had adopted a certain relation to his patient which he could not abandon, so had she formed one towards him—that he was not doing something he ought to do and was himself to blame, and that she reproached him lovingly for this—and she could not now change that attitude.

"You see he doesn't listen to me and doesn't take his medicine at the proper time. And above all he lies in a position that is no doubt bad for him—with his legs up."

She described how he made Gerásim hold his legs up.

The doctor smiled with a contemptuous affability that said: "What's to be done? These sick people do have foolish fancies of that kind, but we must forgive them."

When the examination was over the doctor looked at his watch, and then Praskóvya Fëdorovna announced to Iván Ilých that it was of course as he pleased, but she had sent to-day for a celebrated specialist who would examine him and have a consultation with Michael Danílovich (their regular doctor).

"Please don't raise any objections. I am doing this for my own sake," she said ironically, letting it be felt that she was doing it all for his sake and only said this to leave him no right to refuse. He remained silent, knitting his brows. He felt that he was so surrounded and involved in a mesh of falsity that it was hard to unravel anything.

Everything she did for him was entirely for her own sake, and she told him she was doing for herself what she actually was doing for herself, as if that was so incredible that he must understand the opposite.

At half-past eleven the celebrated specialist arrived. Again the sounding began and the significant conversations in his presence and in another room, about the kidneys and the appendix, and the questions and answers, with such an air of importance that again, instead of the real question of life and death which now alone confronted him, the question arose of the kidney and appendix which were not behaving as they ought to and would now be attacked by Michael Danílovich and the specialist and forced to amend their ways.

The celebrated specialist took leave of him with a serious though not hopeless look, and in reply to the timid question Iván Ilých, with eyes glistening with fear and hope, put to him as to whether there was a chance of recovery, said that he could not vouch for it but there was a possibility. The look of hope with which Iván Ilých watched the doctor out was so pathetic that Praskóvya Fëdorovna, seeing it, even wept as she left the room to hand the doctor his fee.

The gleam of hope kindled by the doctor's encouragement did not last long. The same room, the same pictures, curtains, wall-paper, medicine bottles, were all there, and the same aching suffering body, and Iván Ilých began to moan. They gave him a subcutaneous injection and he sank into oblivion.

It was twilight when he came to. They brought him his dinner and he swallowed some beef tea with difficulty, and then everything was the same again and night was coming on.

After dinner, at seven o'clock, Praskóvya Fëdorovna came into the room in evening dress, her full bosom pushed up by her corset, and with traces of powder on her face. She had reminded him in the morning that they were going to the theatre. Sarah Bernhardt was visiting the town and they had a box, which he had insisted on their taking. Now he had forgotten about it and her toilet offended him, but he concealed his vexation when he remembered that he had himself insisted on their securing a box and going because it would be an instructive and aesthetic pleasure for the children.

Praskóvya Fëdorovna came in, self-satisfied but yet with a rather guilty air. She sat down and asked how he was but, as he saw, only for the sake of asking and not in order to learn about it, knowing that there was nothing to learn—and then went on to what she really wanted to say: that she would not on any account have gone but that the box had been taken and Helen and their daughter were going, as well as Petríshchev (the examining magistrate, their daughter's fiancé) and that it was out of the question to let them go alone; but that she would have much preferred to sit with him for a while; and he must be sure to follow the doctor's orders while she was away.

"Oh, and Fëdor Petróvich" (the fiancé) "would like to come in. May he? And Lisa?"

"All right."

Their daughter came in in full evening dress, her fresh young flesh exposed (making a show of that very flesh which in his own case caused so much suffering), strong, healthy, evidently in love, and impatient with illness, suffering, and death, because they interfered with her happiness.

Fëdor Petróvich came in too, in evening dress, his hair curled *à la Capoul*, a tight still collar round his long sinewy neck, an enormous white shirt-front and narrow black trousers tightly stretched over his strong thighs. He had one white glove tightly drawn on, and was holding his opera hat in his hand.

Following him the schoolboy crept in unnoticed, in a new uniform, poor little fellow, and wearing gloves. Terribly dark shadows showed under his eyes, the meaning of which Iván Ilých knew well.

His son had always seemed pathetic to him, and now it was dreadful to see the boy's frightened look of pity. It seemed to Iván Ilých that Vásya was the only one besides Gerásim who understood and pitied him.

They all sat down and again asked how he was. A silence followed. Lisa asked her mother about the opera-glasses, and there was an altercation between mother and daughter as to who had taken them and where they had been put. This occasioned some unpleasantness.

Fëdor Petróvich inquired of Iván Ilých whether he had ever seen Sarah Bernhardt. Iván Ilých did not at first catch the question, but then replied: "No, have you seen her before?"

"Yes, in *Adrienne Lecouvreur*."

Praskóvya Fëdorovna mentioned some rôles in which Sarah Bernhardt was particularly good. Her daughter disagreed. Conversation sprang up as to the elegance and realism of her acting—the sort of conversation that is always repeated and is always the same.

In the midst of the conversation Fëdor Petróvich glanced at Iván Ilých and became silent. The others also looked at him and grew silent. Iván Ilých was staring with glittering eyes straight before him, evidently indignant with them. This had to be rectified, but it was impossible to do so. The silence had to be broken, but for a time no one dared to break it and they all became afraid that the conventional deception would suddenly become obvious and the truth become plain to all. Lisa was the first to pluck up courage and break that silence, but by trying to hide what everybody was feeling, she betrayed it.

"Well, if we are going it's time to start," she said, looking at her watch, a present from her father, and with a faint and significant smile at Fëdor Petróvich relating to something known only to them. She got up with a rustle of her dress.

They all rose, said good-night, and went away.

When they had gone it seemed to Iván Ilých that he felt better; the falsity had gone with them. But the pain remained—that same pain and that same fear that made everything monotonously alike, nothing harder and nothing easier. Everything was worse.

Again minute followed minute and hour followed hour. Everything remained the same and there was no cessation. And the inevitable end of it all became more and more terrible.

"Yes, send Gerásim here," he replied to a question Peter asked.

IX

His wife returned late at night. She came in on tiptoe, but he heard her, opened his eyes, and made haste to close them again. She wished to send Gerásim away and to sit with him herself, but he opened his eyes and said: "No, go away."

"Are you in great pain?"

"Always the same."

"Take some opium."

He agreed and took some. She went away.

Till about three in the morning he was in a state of stupefied misery. It seemed to him that he and his pain were being thrust into a narrow, deep black sack, but though they were pushed further and further in they could not be pushed to the bottom. And this, terrible enough in itself, was accompanied by suffering. He was frightened yet wanted to fall through the sack, he struggled but yet co-operated. And suddenly he broke through, fell, and regained consciousness. Gerásim was sitting at the foot of the bed dozing quietly and patiently, while he himself lay with his emaciated stockinged legs resting on Gerásim's shoulders; the same shaded candle was there and the same unceasing pain.

"Go away, Gerásim," he whispered.

"It's all right, sir. I'll stay a while."

"No. Go away."

He removed his legs from Gerásim's shoulders, turned sideways onto his arm, and felt sorry for himself. He only waited till Gerásim had gone into the next room and then restrained himself no longer but wept like a child. He wept on account of his helplessnes, his terrible loneliness, the cruelty of man, the cruelty of God, and the absence of God.

"Why hast Thou done all this? Why hast Thou brought me here? Why, why dost Thou torment me so terribly?"

He did not expect an answer and yet wept because there was no answer and could be none. The pain again grew more acute, but he did not stir and did not call. He said to himself: "Go on! Strike me! But what is it for? What have I done to Thee? What is it for?"

Then he grew quiet and not only ceased weeping but even held his breath and became all attention. It was as though he were listening not to an audible voice but to the voice of his soul, to the current of thoughts arising within him.

"What is it you want?" was the first clear conception capable of expression in words, that he heard.

"What do you want? What do you want?" he repeated to himself.

"What do I want? To live and not to suffer," he answered.

And again he listened with such concentrated attention that even his pain did not distract him.

"To live? How?" asked his inner voice.

"Why, to live as I used to—well and pleasantly."

"As you lived before, well and pleasantly?" the voice repeated.

And in imagination he began to recall the best moments of his pleasant life. But strange to say none of these best moments of his pleasant life now seemed at all what they had then seemed—none of them except the first recollections of childhood. There, in childhood, there had been something really pleasant with which it would be possible to live if it could return. But the child who had experienced that happiness existed no longer, it was like a reminiscence of somebody else.

As soon as the period began which had produced the present Iván Ilých, all that had then seemed joys now melted before his sight and turned into something trivial and often nasty.

And the further he departed from childhood and the nearer he came to the present the more worthless and doubtful were the joys. This began with the School of Law. A little that was really good was still found there—there was light-heartedness, friendship, and hope. But in the upper classes there had already been fewer of such good moments. Then during the first years of his official career, when he was in the service of the Governor, some pleasant moments again occurred: they were the memories of love for a woman. Then all became confused and there was still less of what was good; later on again there was still less that was good, and the further he went the less there was. His marriage, a mere accident, then the disenchantment that followed it, his wife's bad breath and the sensuality and hypocrisy: then that deadly official life and those preoccupations about money, a year of it, and two, and ten, and twenty, and always the same thing. And the longer it lasted the more deadly it became. "It is as if I had been going downhill while I imagined I was going up. And that is really what it was. I was going up in public opinion, but to the same extent life was ebbing away from me. And now it is all done and there is only death."

"Then what does it mean? Why? It can't be that life is so senseless and horrible. But if it really has been so horrible and senseless, why must I die in agony? There is something wrong!"

"Maybe I did not live as I ought to have done," it suddenly occurred to him. "But how could that be, when I did everything properly?" he replied, and immediately dismissed from his mind this, the sole solution of all the riddles of life and death, as something quite impossible.

"Then what do you want now? To live: Live how? Live as you lived in the law courts when the usher proclaimed "The judge is coming!" "The judge is coming, the judge!" he repeated to himself. "Here he is, the judge. But I am not guilty!" he exclaimed angrily. "What is it for?" And he ceased crying, but turning his face to the wall continued to ponder on the same question: Why, and for what purpose, is there all this horror? But however much he pondered he found no answer. And whenever the thought occurred to him, as it often did, that it all resulted from his not having lived as he ought to have done, he at once recalled the correctness of his whole life and dismissed so strange an idea.

X

Another fortnight passed. Iván Ilých now no longer left his sofa. He would not lie in bed but lay on the sofa, facing the wall nearly all the time. He suffered ever the same unceasing agonies and in his loneliness pondered always on the same insoluble question: "What is this? Can it be that it is Death?" And the inner voice answered: "Yes, it is Death."

"Why these sufferings?" And the voice answered, "For no reason—they just are so." Beyond and besides this there was nothing.

From the very beginning of his illness, ever since he had first been to see the doctor, Iván Ilých's life had been divided between two contrary and alternating moods: now it was despair and the expectation of this uncomprehended and terrible death, and now hope and an intently interested observation of the functioning of his organs. Now before his eyes there was only a kidney or an intestine that temporarily evaded its duty, and now only that incomprehensible and dreadful death from which it was impossible to escape.

These two states of mind had alternated from the very beginning of his illness, but the further it progressed the more doubtful and fantastic became the conception of the kidney, and the more real the sense of impending death.

He had but to call to mind what he had been three months before and what he was now, to call to mind with what regularity he had been going downhill, for every possibility of hope to be shattered.

Latterly during that loneliness in which he found himself as he lay facing the back of the sofa, a loneliness in the midst of a populous town and surrounded by numerous acquaintances and relations but that yet could not have been more complete anywhere—either at the bottom of the sea or under the earth—during that terrible loneliness Iván Ilých had lived only in memories of the past. Pictures of his past rose before him one after another. They always began with what was nearest in time and then went back to what was most remote—to his childhood—and rested there. If he thought of the stewed prunes that had been offered him that day, his mind went back to the raw shrivelled French plums of his childhood, their peculiar flavour and the flow of saliva when he sucked their stones, and along with the memory of that taste came a whole series of memories of those days: his nurse, his brother, and their toys. "No, I mustn't think of that. . . . It is too painful," Iván Ilých said to himself, and brought himself back to the present—to the button on the back of the sofa and the creases in its morocco. "Morocco is expensive, but it does not wear well: there had been a quarrel about it. It was a different kind of quarrel and a different kind of morocco that time when we tore father's portfolio and were punished, and mamma brought us some tarts. . . ." And again his thoughts dwelt on his childhood, and again it was painful and he tried to banish them and fix his mind on something else.

Then again together with that chain of memories another series passed through his mind—of how his illness had progressed and grown worse. There also the further back he looked the more life there had been. There had been more of what was good in life and more of life itself. The two merged together. "Just as the pain went on getting worse and worse so my life grew worse and worse," he thought. "There is one bright spot there at the back, at the beginning of life, and afterwards all becomes blacker and blacker and proceeds more and more rapidly—in inverse ratio to the square of the distance from death," thought Iván Ilých. And the example of a stone falling downwards with increasing velocity entered his mind. Life, a series of increasing sufferings, flies further and further towards its end—the most terrible suffering. "I am flying. . . . " He shuddered, shifted himself, and tried to resist, but was already aware that resistance was impossible, and again with eyes weary of gazing but unable to cease seeing what was before them, he stared at the back of the sofa and waited—awaiting that dreadful fall and shock and destruction.

"Resistance is impossible!" he said to himself. "If I could only understand what it is all for! But that too is impossible. An explanation would be possible if it could be said that I have not lived as I ought to. But it is impossible to say that," and he remembered all the legality, correctitude, and propriety of his life. "That at any rate can certainly not be admitted," he thought, and his lips smiled ironically as if someone could see that smile and be taken in by it. "There is no explanation! Agony, death. . . . What for?"

XI

Another two weeks went by in this way and during that fortnight an event occurred that Iván Ilých and his wife had desired. Petríschev formally proposed. It happened in the evening. The next day Praskóvya Fëdorovna came into her husband's room considering how best to inform him of it, but that very night there had been a fresh change for the worse in his condition. She found him still lying on the sofa but in a different position. He lay on his back, groaning and staring fixedly straight in front of him.

She began to remind him of his medicines, but he turned his eyes towards her with such a look that she did not finish what she was saying; so great an animosity, to her in particular, did that look express.

"For Christ's sake, let me die in peace!" he said.

She would have gone away, but just then their daughter came in and went up to say good morning. He looked at her as he had done at his wife, and in reply to her inquiry about his health said dryly that he would soon free them all of himself. They were both silent and after sitting with him for a while went away.

"Is it our fault?" Lisa said to her mother. "It's as if we were to blame! I am sorry for papa, but why should we be tortured?"

The doctor came at his usual time. Iván Ilých answered "Yes" and "No," never taking his angry eyes from him, and at last said: "You know you can do nothing for me, so leave me alone."

"We can ease your sufferings."

"You can't even do that. Let me be."

The doctor went into the drawing-room and told Praskóvya Fëdorovna that the case was very serious and that the only resource left was opium to allay her husband's sufferings, which must be terrible.

It was true, as the doctor said, that Iván Ilých's physical sufferings were terrible, but worse than the physical sufferings were his mental sufferings which were his chief torture.

His mental sufferings were due to the fact that that night, as he looked at Gerásim's sleepy, good-natured face with its prominent cheekbones, the question suddenly occurred to him: "What if my whole life has really been wrong?"

It occurred to him that what appeared perfectly impossible before, namely that he had not spent his life as he should have done, might after all be true. It occurred to him that his scarcely perceptible attempts to struggle against what was considered good by the most highly placed people, those scarcely noticeable impulses which he had immediately suppressed, might have been the real thing, and all the rest false. And his professional duties and the whole arrangement of his life and of his family, and all his social and official interests, might all have been false. He tried to defend all those things to himself and suddenly felt the weakness of what he was defending. There was nothing to defend.

"But if that is so," he said to himself, "and I am leaving this life with the consciousness that I have lost all that was given me and it is impossible to rectify it—what then?"

He lay on his back and began to pass his life in review in quite a new way. In the morning when he saw first his footman, then his wife, then his daughter, and then the doctor, their every word and movement confirmed to him the awful truth that had been revealed to him during the night. In them he saw himself—all that for which he had lived—

and saw clearly that it was not real at all, but a terrible and huge deception which had hidden both life and death. This consciousness intensified his physical suffering tenfold. He groaned and tossed about, and pulled at his clothing which choked and stifled him. And he hated them on that account.

He was given a large dose of opium and became unconscious, but at noon his sufferings began again. He drove everybody away and tossed from side to side.

His wife came to him and said:

"Jean, my dear, do this for me. It can't do any harm and often helps. Healthy people often do it."

He opened his eyes wide.

"What? Take communion? Why? It's unnecessary! However. . . ."

She began to cry.

"Yes, do, my dear. I'll send for our priest. He is such a nice man."

"All right. Very well," he muttered.

When the priest came and heard his confession, Iván Ilých was softened and seemed to feel a relief from his doubts and consequently from his sufferings, and for a moment there came a ray of hope. He again began to think of the vermiform appendix and the possibility of correcting it. He received the sacrament with tears in his eyes.

When they laid him down again afterwards he felt a moment's ease, and the hope that he might live awoke in him again. He began to think of the operation that had been suggested to him. "To live! I want to live!" he said to himself.

His wife came in to congratulate him after his communion, and when uttering the usual conventional words she added:

"You feel better, don't you?"

Without looking at her he said "Yes."

Her dress, her figure, the expression of her face, the tone of her voice, all revealed the same thing. "This is wrong, it is not as it should be. All you have lived for and still live for is falsehood and deception, hiding life and death from you." And as soon as he admitted that thought, his hatred and his agonizing physical suffering again sprang up, and with that suffering a consciousness of the unavoidable, approaching end. And to this was added a new sensation of grinding shooting pain and a feeling of suffocation.

The expression of his face when he uttered that "yes" was dreadful. Having uttered it, he looked her straight in the eyes, turned on his face with a rapidity extraordinary in his weak state and shouted:

"Go away! Go away and leave me alone!"

XII

From that moment the screaming began that continued for three days, and was so terrible that one could not hear it through two closed doors without horror. At the moment he answered his wife he realized that he was lost, that there was no return, that the end had come, the very end, and his doubts were still unsolved and remained doubts.

"Oh! Oh! Oh!" he cried in various intonations. He had begun by screaming "I won't!" and continued screaming on the letter "o."

For three whole days, during which time did not exist for him, he struggled in that black sack into which he was being thrust by an invisible, resistless force. He struggled as a man condemned to death struggles in the hands of the executioner, knowing that he cannot save himself. And every moment he felt that despite all his efforts he was drawing nearer and nearer to what terrified him. He felt that his agony was due to his being thrust into that black hole and still more to his not being able to get right into it. He was hindered from getting into it by his conviction that his life had been a good one. That very justification of his life held him fast and prevented his moving forward, and it caused him most torment of all.

Suddenly some force struck him in the chest and side, making it still harder to breathe, and he fell through the hole and there at the bottom was a light. What had happened to him was like the sensation one sometimes experiences in a railway carriage when one thinks one is going backwards while one is really going forwards and suddenly becomes aware of the real direction.

"Yes, it was all not the right thing," he said to himself, "but that's no matter. It can be done. But what *is* the right thing?" he asked himself, and suddenly grew quiet.

This occurred at the end of the third day, two hours before his death. Just then his schoolboy son had crept softly in and gone up to the bedside. The dying man was still screaming desperately and waving his arms. His hand fell on the boy's head, and the boy caught it, pressed it to his lips, and began to cry.

At that very moment Iván Ilých fell through and caught sight of the light, and it was revealed to him that though his life had not been what it should have been, this could still be rectified. He asked himself, "What *is* the right thing?" and grew still, listening. Then he felt that someone was kissing his hand. He opened his eyes, looked at his son, and felt sorry for him. His wife came up to him and he glanced at her. She was gazing at him open-mouthed, with undried tears on her nose and cheek and a despairing look on her face. He felt sorry for her too.

"Yes, I am making them wretched," he thought. "They are sorry, but it will be better for them when I die." He wished to say this but had not the strength to utter it. "Besides, why speak? I must act," he thought. With a look at his wife he indicated his son and said: "Take him away . . . sorry for him . . . sorry for you too. . . ." He tried to add, "forgive me," but said "forego" and waved his hand, knowing that He whose understanding mattered would understand.

And suddenly it grew clear to him that what had been oppressing him and would not leave him was all dropping away at once from two sides, from ten sides, and from all sides. He was sorry for them, he must act so as not to hurt them: release them and free himself from these sufferings. "How good and how simple!" he thought. "And the pain?" he asked himself. "What has become of it? Where are you, pain?"

He turned his attention to it.

"Yes, here it is. Well, what of it? Let the pain be."

"And death . . . where is it?"

He sought his former accustomed fear of death and did not find it. "Where is it? What death?" There was no fear because there was no death.

In place of death there was light.

"So that's what it is!" he suddenly exclaimed aloud. "What joy!"

To him all this happened in a single instant, and the meaning of that instant did not change. For those present his agony continued for another two hours. Something rattled in his throat, his emaciated body twitched, then the gasping and rattle became less and less frequent.

"It is finished!" said someone near him.

He heard these words and repeated them in his soul.

"Death is finished," he said to himself. "It is no more!"

He drew in a breath, stopped in the midst of a sigh, stretched out, and died.

Bartleby the Scrivener

I am a rather elderly man. The nature of my avocations, for the last thirty years, has brought me into more than ordinary contact with what would seem an interesting and somewhat singular set of men, of whom, as yet, nothing, that I know of, has ever been written—I mean, the law-copyists, or scriveners. I have known very many of them, professionally and privately, and, if I pleased, could relate divers histories, at which good-natured gentlemen might smile, and sentimental souls might weep. But I waive the biographies of all other scriveners, for a few passages in the life of Bartleby, who was a scrivener, the strangest I ever saw, or heard of. While, of other law-copyists, I might write the complete life, of Bartleby nothing of that sort can be done. I believe that no materials exist, for a full and satisfactory biography of this man. It is an irreparable loss to literature. Bartleby was one of those beings of whom nothing is ascertainable, except from the original sources, and, in his case, those are very small. What my own astonished eyes saw of Bartleby, *that* is all I know of him, except, indeed, one vague report, which will appear in the sequel.

Ere introducing the scrivener, as he first appeared to me, it is fit I make some mention of myself, my *employés*, my business, my chambers, and general surroundings; because some such description is indispensable to an adequate understanding of the chief character about to be presented. Imprimis: I am a man who, from his youth upwards, has been filled with a profound conviction that the easiest way of life is the best. Hence, though I belong to a profession proverbially energetic and nervous, even to turbulence, at times, yet nothing of that sort have I ever suffered to invade my peace. I am one of those unambitious lawyers who never addresses a jury, or in any way draws down public applause; but, in the cool tranquillity of a snug retreat, do a snug business among rich men's bonds, and mortgages, and title-deeds. All who know me, consider me an eminently *safe* man. The late John Jacob Astor, a personage little given to poetic enthusiasm, had no hesitation in pronouncing my first grand point to be prudence; my next, method. I do not speak it in vanity, but simply record the fact, that I was not unemployed in my profession by the late John Jacob Astor,[1] a name which, I admit, I love to repeat; for it hath a rounded and orbicular sound to it, and rings like unto bullion. I will freely add, that I was not insensible to the late John Jacob Astor's good opinion.

---

[1] *John Jacob Astor:* (1763–1848) an American fur trader and financier.

Some time prior to the period at which this little history begins, my avocations had been largely increased. The good old office, now extinct in the State of New York, of a Master in Chancery, had been conferred upon me. It was not a very arduous office, but very pleasantly remunerative. I seldom lose my temper; much more seldom indulge in dangerous indignation at wrongs and outrages; but, I must be permitted to be rash here, and declare, that I consider the sudden and violent abrogation of the office of Master in Chancery, by the new Constitution, as a —— premature act; inasmuch as I had counted upon a life-lease of the profits, whereas I only received those of a few short years. But this is by the way.

My chambers were up stairs, at No. —— Wall Street. At one end, they looked upon the white wall of the interior of a spacious sky-light shaft, penetrating the building from top to bottom.

This view might have been considered rather tame than otherwise, deficient in what landscape painters call "life." But, if so, the view from the other end of my chambers offered, at least, a contrast, if nothing more. In that direction, my windows commanded an unobstructed view of a lofty brick wall, black by age and everlasting shade; which wall required no spy-glass to bring out its lurking beauties, but, for the benefit of all near-sighted spectators, was pushed up to within ten feet of my window panes. Owing to the great height of the surrounding buildings, and my chambers being on the second floor, the interval between this wall and mine not a little resembled a huge square cistern.

At the period just preceding the advent of Bartleby, I had two persons as copyists in my employment, and a promising lad as an office-boy. First, Turkey; second, Nippers; third, Ginger Nut. These may seem names, the like of which are not usually found in the Directory. In truth, they were nicknames, mutually conferred upon each other by my three clerks, and were deemed expressive of their respective persons or characters. Turkey was a short, pursy Englishman, of about my own age—that is, somewhere not far from sixty. In the morning, one might say, his face was of a fine florid hue, but after twelve o'clock, meridian—his dinner hour— it blazed like a grate full of Christmas coals; and continued blazing— but, as it were, with a gradual wane—till six o'clock, P.M., or thereabouts; after which, I saw no more of the proprietor of the face, which, gaining its meridian with the sun, seemed to set with it, to rise, culminate, and decline the following day, with the like regularity and undiminished glory. There are many singular coincidences I have known in the course of my life, not the least among which was the fact, that, exactly when Turkey displayed his fullest beams from his red and radiant countenance, just then, too, at that critical moment, began the daily period when I considered his business capacities as seriously disturbed for the remainder of the twenty-four hours. Not that he was absolutely idle, or averse to business, then; far from it. The difficulty was, he was apt to be altogether too energetic. There was a strange, inflamed, flurried, flighty recklessness of activity about him. He would be incautious in dipping his pen into his inkstand. All his blots upon my documents were dropped there after twelve o'clock, meridian. Indeed, not only would he be reckless, and sadly given to making blots in the afternoon, but, some days, he went further, and was rather noisy. At such times, too, his face flamed with augmented blazonry, as if cannel coal had been heaped on anthracite. He made an unpleasant racket with his chair; spilled his sand-box; in mending his pens, impatiently split them all to pieces, and threw them on the floor in a sudden passion; stood up, and leaned over his table, boxing his papers about in a most indecorous manner, very sad to behold in an elderly man like him. Nevertheless, as he was in many ways a most valuable person to me, and all the time before twelve o'clock, meridian, was the quickest, steadiest creature, too, accomplishing a great deal of work in a style not easily to be matched—for these reasons, I was willing to overlook his eccentricities, though, indeed, occasionally, I remonstrated with him. I did this very gently, however, because, though the civilest, nay, the blandest and most reverential of men in the morning, yet, in the afternoon, he was disposed, upon provocation, to be slightly rash with his tongue—in fact, insolent. Now, valuing his morning services as I did, and resolved not to lose them—yet, at the same time, made uncomfortable by his inflamed ways after twelve o'clock—and being a man of peace, unwilling by my admonitions to call forth unseemly retorts from him, I took upon me, one Saturday noon (he was always worse on Saturdays) to hint to him, very kindly, that, perhaps, now that he was growing old, it might be well to abridge his labors; in short, he need not come to my chambers after twelve o'clock, but, dinner over, had best go home to his lodgings, and rest himself till tea-time. But no; he insisted upon his afternoon devotions. His countenance became intolerably fervid, as he oratorically assured me—gesticulating with a long ruler at the other end of the room—that if his services in the morning were useful, how indispensable, then, in the afternoon?

"With submission, sir," said Turkey, on this occasion, "I consider myself your right-hand man. In the morning I but marshal and deploy my columns; but in the afternoon I put myself at their head, and gallantly charge the foe, thus"—and he made a violent thrust with the ruler.

"But the blots, Turkey," intimated I.

"True; but, with submission, sir, behold these hairs! I am getting old.

Surely, sir, a blot or two of a warm afternoon is not to be severely urged against gray hairs. Old age—even if it blot the page—is honorable. With submission, sir, we *both* are getting old."

This appeal to my fellow-feeling was hardly to be resisted. At all events, I saw that go he would not. So, I made up my mind to let him stay, resolving, nevertheless, to see to it that, during the afternoon, he had to do with my less important papers.

Nippers, the second on my list, was a whiskered, sallow, and, upon the whole, rather piratical-looking young man, of about five and twenty. I always deemed him the victim of two evil powers—ambition and indigestion. The ambition was evinced by a certain impatience of the duties of a mere copyist, an unwarrantable usurpation of strictly professional affairs, such as the original drawing up of legal documents. The indigestion seemed betokened in an occasional nervous testiness and grinning irritability, causing the teeth to audibly grind together over mistakes committed in copying; unnecessary maledictions, hissed, rather than spoken, in the heat of business; and especially by a continual discontent with the height of the table where he worked. Though of a very ingenious mechanical turn, Nippers could never get this table to suit him. He put chips under it, blocks of various sorts, bits of pasteboard, and at last went so far as to attempt an exquisite adjustment, by final pieces of folded blotting-paper. But no invention would answer. If, for the sake of easing his back, he brought the table lid at a sharp angle well up towards his chin, and wrote there like a man using the steep roof of a Dutch house for his desk, then he declared that it stopped the circulation in his arms. If now he lowered the table to his waistbands, and stooped over it in writing, then there was a sore aching in his back. In short, the truth of the matter was, Nippers knew not what he wanted. Or, if he wanted anything, it was to be rid of a scrivener's table altogether. Among the manifestations of his diseased ambition was a fondness he had for receiving visits from certain ambiguous-looking fellows in seedy coats, whom he called his clients. Indeed, I was aware that not only was he, at times, considerable of a ward-politician, but he occasionally did a little business at the Justices' courts, and was not unknown on the steps of the Tombs. I have good reason to believe, however, that one individual who called upon him at my chambers, and who, with a grand air, he insisted was his client, was no other than a dun, and the alleged title-deed, a bill. But, with all his failings, and the annoyances he caused me, Nippers, like his compatriot Turkey, was a very useful man to me; wrote a neat, swift hand; and, when he chose, was not deficient in a gentlemanly sort of deportment. Added to this, he always dressed in a gentlemanly sort of way; and so, incidentally, reflected credit upon my chambers. Whereas, with respect to Turkey, I had much ado to keep him from being a reproach to me. His clothes were apt to look oily, and smell of eating-houses. He wore his pantaloons very loose and baggy in summer. His coats were execrable; his hat not to be handled. But while the hat was a thing of indifference to me, inasmuch as his natural civility and deference, as a dependent Englishman, always led him to doff it the moment he entered the room, yet his coat was another matter. Concerning his coats, I reasoned with him; but with no effect. The truth was, I suppose, that a man with so small an income could not afford to sport such a lustrous face and a lustrous coat at one and the same time. As Nippers once observed, Turkey's money went chiefly for red ink. One winter day, I presented Turkey with a highly respectable-looking coat of my own—a padded gray coat, of a most comfortable warmth, and which buttoned straight up from the knee to the neck. I thought Turkey would appreciate the favor, and abate his rashness and obstreperousness of afternoons. But no; I verily believe that buttoning himself up in so downy and blanket-like a coat had a pernicious effect upon him—upon the same principle that too much oats are bad for horses. In fact, precisely as a rash, restive horse is said to feel his oats, so Turkey felt his coat. It made him insolent. He was a man whom prosperity harmed.

Though, concerning the self-indulgent habits of Turkey, I had my own private surmises, yet, touching Nippers, I was well persuaded that, whatever might be his faults in other respects, he was, at least, a temperate young man. But, indeed, nature herself seemed to have been his vintner, and, at his birth, charged him so thoroughly with an irritable, brandy-like disposition, that all subsequent potations were needless. When I consider how, amid the stillness of my chambers, Nippers would sometimes impatiently rise from his seat, and stooping over his table, spread his arms wide apart, seize the whole desk, and move it, and jerk it, with a grim, grinding motion on the floor, as if the table were a perverse voluntary agent, intent on thwarting and vexing him, I plainly perceive that, for Nippers, brandy-and-water were altogether superfluous.

It was fortunate for me that, owing to its peculiar cause—indigestion—the iritability and consequent nervousness of Nippers were mainly observable in the morning, while in the afternoon he was comparatively mild. So that, Turkey's paroxysms only coming on about twelve o'clock, I never had to do with their eccentricities at one time. Their fits relieved each other, like guards. When Nippers' was on, Turkey's was off; and *vice versa*. This was a good natural arrangement, under the circumstances.

Ginger Nut, the third on my list, was a lad, some twelve years old.

His father was a car-man, ambitious of seeing his son on the bench instead of a cart, before he died. So he sent him to my office, as student at law, errand-boy, cleaner and sweeper, at the rate of one dollar a week. He had a little desk to himself, but he did not use it much. Upon inspection, the drawer exhibited a great array of the shells of various sorts of nuts. Indeed, to this quick-witted youth, the whole noble science of the law was contained in a nut-shell. Not the least among the employments of Ginger Nut, as well as one which he discharged with the most alacrity, was his duty as cake and apple purveyor for Turkey and Nippers. Copying law-papers being proverbially a dry, husky sort of business, my two scriveners were fain to moisten their mouths very often with Spitzenbergs, to be had at the numerous stalls nigh the Custom House and Post Office. Also, they sent Ginger Nut very frequently for that peculiar cake—small, flat, round, and very spicy—after which he had been named by them. Of a cold morning, when business was but dull, Turkey would gobble up scores of these cakes, as if they were mere wafers—indeed, they sell them at the rate of six or eight for a penny—the scrape of his pen blending with the crunching of the crisp particles in his mouth. Of all the fiery afternoon blunders and flurried rashnesses of Turkey, was his once moistening a ginger-cake between his lips, and clapping it on to a mortgage, for a seal. I came within an ace of dismissing him then. But he mollified me by making an oriental bow, and saying—

"With submission, sir, it was generous of me to find you in stationery on my own account."

Now my original business—that of a conveyancer and title hunter, and drawer-up of recondite documents of all sorts—was considerably increased by receiving the master's office. There was now great work for scriveners. Not only must I push the clerks already with me, but I must have additional help.

In answer to my advertisement, a motionless young man one morning stood upon my office threshold, the door being open, for it was summer. I can see that figure now—pallidly neat, pitiably respectable, incurably forlorn! It was Bartleby.

After a few words touching his qualifications, I engaged him, glad to have among my corps of copyists a man of so singularly sedate an aspect, which I thought might operate beneficially upon the flighty temper of Turkey, and the fiery one of Nippers.

I should have stated before that ground glass folding-doors divided my premises into two parts, one of which was occupied by my scriveners, the other by myself. According to my humor, I threw open these doors, or closed them. I resolved to assign Bartleby a corner by the folding-doors, but on my side of them, so as to have this quiet man within easy call, in case any trifling thing was to be done. I placed his desk close up to a small side-window in that part of the room, a window which originally had afforded a lateral view of certain grimy backyards and bricks, but which, owing to subsequent erections, commanded at present no view at all, though it gave some light. Within three feet of the panes was a wall, and the light came down from far above, between two lofty buildings, as from a very small opening in a dome. Still further to a satisfactory arrangement, I procured a high green folding screen, which might entirely isolate Bartleby from my sight, though not remove him from my voice. And thus, in a manner, privacy and society were conjoined.

At first, Bartleby did an extraordinary quantity of writing. As if long famishing for something to copy, he seemed to gorge himself on my documents. There was no pause for digestion. He ran a day and night line, copying by sun-light and by candle-light. I should have been quite delighted with his application, had he been cheerfully industrious. But he wrote on silently, palely, mechanically.

It is, of course, an indispensable part of a scrivener's business to verify the accuracy of his copy, word by word. Where there are two or more scriveners in an office, they assist each other in this examination, one reading from the copy, the other holding the original. It is a very dull, wearisome, and lethargic affair. I can readily imagine that, to some sanguine temperaments, it would be altogether intolerable. For example, I cannot credit that the mettlesome poet, Byron, would have contentedly sat down with Bartleby to examine a law document of, say five hundred pages, closely written in a crimpy hand.

Now and then, in the haste of business, it had been my habit to assist in comparing some brief document myself, calling Turkey or Nippers for this purpose. One object I had, in placing Bartleby so handy to me behind the screen, was, to avail myself of his services on such trivial occasions. It was on the third day, I think, of his being with me, and before any necessity had arisen for having his own writing examined, that, being much hurried to complete a small affair I had in hand, I abruptly called to Bartleby. In my haste and natural expectancy of instant compliance, I sat with my head bent over the original on my desk, and my right hand sideways, and somewhat nervously extended with the copy, so that, immediately upon emerging from his retreat, Bartleby might snatch it and proceed to business without the least delay.

In this very attitude did I sit when I called to him, rapidly stating what it was I wanted him to do—namely, to examine a small paper with me. Imagine my surprise, nay, my consternation, when, without moving from his privacy, Bartleby, in a singularly mild, firm voice, replied, "I would prefer not to."

I sat awhile in perfect silence, rallying my stunned faculties. Immediately it occurred to me that my ears had deceived me, or Bartleby had entirely misunderstood my meaning. I repeated my request in the clearest tone I could assume; but in quite as clear a one came the previous reply, "I would prefer not to."

"Prefer not to," echoed I, rising in high excitement, and crossing the room with a stride. "What do you mean? Are you moon-struck? I want you to help me compare this sheet here—take it," and I thrust it towards him.

"I would prefer not to," said he.

I looked at him steadfastly. His face was leanly composed; his gray eye dimly calm. Not a wrinkle of agitation rippled him. Had there been the least uneasiness, anger, impatience or impertinence in his manner; in other words, had there been any thing ordinarily human about him, doubtless I should have violently dismissed him from the premises. But as it was, I should have as soon thought of turning my pale plaster-of-paris bust of Cicero out of doors. I stood gazing at him awhile, as he went on with his own writing, and then reseated myself at my desk. This is very strange, thought I. What had one best do? But my business hurried me. I concluded to forget the matter for the present, reserving it for my future leisure. So calling Nippers from the other room, the paper was speedily examined.

A few days after this, Bartleby concluded four lengthy documents, being quadruplicates of a week's testimony taken before me in my High Court of Chancery. It became necessary to examine them. It was an important suit, and great accuracy was imperative. Having all things arranged, I called Turkey, Nippers, and Ginger Nut, from the next room, meaning to place the four copies in the hands of my four clerks, while I should read from the original. Accordingly, Turkey, Nippers, and Ginger Nut had taken their seats in a row, each with his document in his hand, when I called to Bartleby to join this interesting group.

"Bartleby! quick, I am waiting."

I heard a slow scrape of his chair legs on the uncarpeted floor, and soon he appeared standing at the entrance of his hermitage.

"What is wanted?" said he, mildly.

"The copies, the copies," said I, hurriedly. "We are going to examine them. There"—and I held towards him the fourth quadruplicate.

"I would prefer not to," he said, and gently disappeared behind the screen.

For a few moments I was turned into a pillar of salt, standing at the head of my seated column of clerks. Recovering myself, I advanced towards the screen, and demanded the reason for such extraordinary conduct.

"*Why* do you refuse?"

"I would prefer not to."

With any other man I should have flown outright into a dreadful passion, scorned all further words, and thrust him ignominiously from my presence. But there was something about Bartleby that not only strangely disarmed me, but, in a wonderful manner, touched and disconcerted me. I began to reason with him.

"These are your own copies we are about to examine. It is labor saving to you, because one examination will answer for your four papers. It is common usage. Every copyist is bound to help examine his copy. Is it not so? Will you not speak? Answer!"

"I prefer not to," he replied in a flutelike tone. It seemed to me that, while I had been addressing him, he carefully revolved every statement that I made; fully comprehended the meaning; could not gainsay the irresistible conclusion; but, at the same time, some paramount consideration prevailed with him to reply as he did.

"You are decided, then, not to comply with my request—a request made according to common usage and common sense?"

He briefly gave me to understand, that on that point my judgment was sound. Yes: his decision was irreversible.

It is not seldom the case that, when a man is browbeaten in some unprecedented and violently unreasonable way, he begins to stagger in his own plainest faith. He begins, as it were, vaguely to surmise that, wonderful as it may be, all the justice and all the reason is on the other side. Accordingly, if any disinterested persons are present, he turns to them for some reinforcement of his own faltering mind.

"Turkey," said I, "what do you think of this? Am I not right?"

"With submission, sir," said Turkey, in his blandest tone, "I think that you are."

"Nippers," said I, "what do *you* think of it?"

"I think I should kick him out of the office."

(The reader, of nice perceptions, will here perceive that, it being morning, Turkey's answer is couched in polite and tranquil terms, but Nippers' replies in ill-tempered ones. Or, to repeat a previous sentence, Nippers' ugly mood was on duty, and Turkey's off.)

"Ginger Nut," said I, willing to enlist the smallest suffrage in my behalf, "what do *you* think of it?"

"I think, sir, he's a little *luny*," replied Ginger Nut, with a grin.

"You hear what they say," said I, turning towards the screen, "come forth and do your duty."

But he vouchsafed no reply. I pondered a moment in sore perplexity. But once more business hurried me. I determined again to postpone the consideration of this dilemma to my future leisure. With a little trouble we made out to examine the papers without Bartleby, though at every page or two Turkey deferentially dropped his opinion, that this proceeding was quite out of the common; while Nippers, twitching in his chair with a dyspeptic nervousness, ground out, between his set teeth, occasional hissing maledictions against the stubborn oaf behind the screen. And for his (Nippers') part, this was the first and the last time he would do another man's business without pay.

Meanwhile Bartleby sat in his hermitage, oblivious to everything but his own peculiar business there.

Some days passed, the scrivener being employed upon another lengthy work. His late remarkable conduct led me to regard his ways narrowly. I observed that he never went to dinner; indeed, that he never went anywhere. As yet I had never, of my personal knowledge, known him to be outside of my office. He was a perpetual sentry in the corner. At about eleven o'clock though, in the morning, I noticed that Ginger Nut would advance toward the opening in Bartleby's screen, as if silently beckoned thither by a gesture invisible to me where I sat. The boy would then leave the office, jingling a few pence, and reappear with a handful of gingernuts, which he delivered in the hermitage, receiving two of the cakes for his trouble.

He lives, then, on ginger-nuts, thought I; never eats a dinner, properly speaking; he must be a vegetarian, then; but no; he never eats even vegetables, he eats nothing but ginger-nuts. My mind then ran on in reveries concerning the probable effects upon the human constitution of living entirely on ginger-nuts. Ginger-nuts are so called, because they contain ginger as one of their peculiar constituents, and the final flavoring one. Now, what was ginger? A hot, spicy thing. Was Bartleby hot and spicy? Not at all. Ginger, then, had no effect upon Bartleby. Probably he preferred it should have none.

Nothing so aggravates an earnest person as a passive resistance. If the individual so resisted be of a not inhumane temper, and the resisting one perfectly harmless in his passivity, then, in the better moods of the former, he will endeavor charitably to construe to his imagination what proves impossible to be solved by his judgment. Even so, for the most part, I regarded Bartleby and his ways. Poor fellow! thought I, he means no mischief; it is plain he intends no insolence; his aspect sufficiently evinces that his eccentricities are involuntary. He is useful to me. I can get along with him. If I turn him away, the chances are he will fall in with some less-indulgent employer, and then he will be rudely treated, and perhaps driven forth miserably to starve. Yes. Here I can cheaply purchase a delicious self-approval. To befriend Bartleby; to humor him in his strange willfulness, will cost me little or nothing, while I lay up in my soul what will eventually prove a sweet morsel for my conscience. But this mood was not invariable with me. The passiveness of Bartleby sometimes irritated me. I felt strangely goaded on tō encounter him in new opposition—to elicit some angry spark from him answerable to my own. But, indeed, I might as well have essayed to strike fire with my knuckles against a bit of Windsor soap. But one afternoon the evil impulse in me mastered me, and the following little scene ensued:

"Bartleby," said I, "when those papers are all copied, I will compare them with you."

"I would prefer not to."

"How? Surely you do not mean to persist in that mulish vagary?"

No answer.

I threw open the folding-doors near by, and, turning upon Turkey and Nippers, exclaimed:

"Bartleby a second time says, he won't examine his papers. What do you think of it, Turkey?"

It was afternoon, be it remembered. Turkey sat glowing like a brass boiler; his bald head steaming; his hands reeling among his blotted papers.

"Think of it?" roared Turkey; "I think I'll just step behind his screen, and black his eyes for him!"

So saying, Turkey rose to his feet and threw his arms into a pugilistic position. He was hurrying away to make good his promise, when I detained him, alarmed at the effect of incautiously rousing Turkey's combativeness after dinner.

"Sit down, Turkey," said I, "and hear what Nippers has to say. What do you think of it, Nippers? Would I not be justified in immediately dismissing Bartleby?"

"Excuse me, that is for you to decide, sir. I think his conduct quite unusual, and, indeed, unjust, as regards Turkey and myself. But it may only be a passing whim."

"Ah," exclaimed I, "you have strangely changed your mind, then—you speak very gently of him now."

"All beer," cried Turkey; "gentleness is effects of beer—Nippers and

I dined together to-day. You see how gentle *I* am, sir. Shall I go and black his eyes?"

"You refer to Bartleby, I suppose. No, not to-day, Turkey," I replied; "pray, put up your fists."

I closed the doors, and again advanced towards Bartleby. I felt additional incentives tempting me to my fate. I burned to be rebelled against again. I remember that Bartleby never left the office.

"Bartleby," said I, "Ginger Nut is away; just step around to the Post Office, won't you? (it was but a three minutes' walk), and see if there is anything for me."

"I would prefer not to."

"You *will* not?"

"I *prefer* not."

I staggered to my desk, and sat there in a deep study. My blind inveteracy returned. Was there any other thing in which I could procure myself to be ignominiously repulsed by this lean, penniless wight?—my hired clerk? What added thing is there, perfectly reasonable, that he will be sure to refuse to do?

"Bartleby!"

No answer.

"Bartleby," in a louder tone.

No answer.

"Bartleby," I roared.

Like a very ghost, agreeably to the laws of magical invocation, at the third summons, he appeared at the entrance of his hermitage.

"Go to the next room, and tell Nippers to come to me."

"I prefer not to," he respectfully and slowly said, and mildly disappeared.

"Very good, Bartleby," said I, in a quiet sort of serenely-severe self-possessed tone, intimating the unalterable purpose of some terrible retribution very close at hand. But upon the whole, as it was drawing towards my dinner-hour, I thought it best to put on my hat and walk home for the day, suffering much from perplexity and distress of mind.

Shall I acknowledge it? The conclusion of this whole business was, that it soon became a fixed fact of my chambers, that a pale young scrivener, by the name of Bartleby, had a desk there; that he copied for me at the usual rate of four cents a folio (one hundred words); but he was permanently exempt from examining the work done by him, that duty being transferred to Turkey and Nippers, out of compliment, doubtless, to their superior acuteness; moreover, said Bartleby was never, on any account, to be dispatched on the most trivial errand of any sort; and that even if entreated to take upon him such a matter, it was generally understood that he would "prefer not to"—in other words, that he would refuse point-blank.

As days passed on, I became considerably reconciled to Bartleby. His steadiness, his freedom from all dissipation, his incessant industry (except when he chose to throw himself into a standing revery behind his screen), his great stillness, his unalterableness of demeanor under all circumstances, made him a valuable acquisition. One prime thing was this—*he was always there*—first in the morning, continually through the day, and the last at night. I had a singular confidence in his honesty. I felt my most precious papers perfectly safe in his hands. Sometimes, to be sure, I could not, for the very soul of me, avoid falling into sudden spasmodic passions with him. For it was exceeding difficult to bear in mind all the time those strange peculiarities, privileges, and unheard of exemptions, forming the tacit stipulations on Bartleby's part under which he remained in my office. Now and then, in the eagerness of dispatching pressing business, I would inadvertently summon Bartleby, in a short, rapid tone, to put his finger, say, on the incipient tie of a bit of red tape with which I was about compressing some papers. Of course, from behind the screen the usual answer, "I prefer not to," was sure to come; and then, how could a human creature, with the common infirmities of our nature, refrain from bitterly exclaiming upon such perverseness—such unreasonableness. However, every added repulse of this sort which I received only tended to lessen the probability of my repeating the inadvertence.

Here it must be said, that according to the custom of most legal gentlemen occupying chambers in densely-populated law buildings, there were several keys to my door. One was kept by a woman residing in the attic, which person weekly scrubbed and daily swept and dusted my apartments. Another was kept by Turkey for convenience sake. The third I sometimes carried in my own pocket. The fourth I knew not who had.

Now, one Sunday morning I happened to go to Trinity Church, to hear a celebrated preacher, and finding myself rather early on the ground I thought I would walk around to my chambers for a while. Luckily I had my key with me; but upon applying it to the lock, I found it resisted by something inserted from the inside. Quite surprised, I called out; when to my consternation a key was turned from within; and thrusting his lean visage at me, and holding the door ajar, the apparition of Bartleby appeared, in his shirt sleeves, and otherwise in a strangely tattered deshabille, saying quietly that he was sorry, but he was deeply engaged just then, and—preferred not admitting me at present. In a brief word or two, he moreover added, that perhaps I had better walk around the block two or three times, and by that time he would probably have concluded his affairs.

Now, the utterly unsurmised appearance of Bartleby, tenanting my law-chambers of a Sunday morning, with his cadaverously gentlemanly *nonchalance*, yet withal firm and self-possessed, had such a strange effect upon me, that incontinently I slunk away from my own door, and did as desired. But not without sundry twinges of impotent rebellion against the mild effrontery of this unaccountable scrivener. Indeed, it was his wonderful mildness chiefly, which not only disarmed me, but unmanned me as it were. For I consider that one, for the time, is somehow unmanned when he tranquilly permits his hired clerk to dictate to him, and order him away from his own premises. Furthermore, I was full of uneasiness as to what Bartleby could possibly be doing in my office in his shirt sleeves, and in an otherwise dismantled condition of a Sunday morning. Was anything amiss going on? Nay, that was out of the question. It was not to be thought of for a moment that Bartleby was an immoral person. But what could he be doing there?—copying? Nay again, whatever might be his eccentricities, Bartleby was an eminently decorous person. He would be the last man to sit down to his desk in any state approaching to nudity. Besides, it was Sunday; and there was something about Bartleby that forbade the supposition that he would by any secular occupation violate the proprieties of the day.

Nevertheless, my mind was not pacified; and full of a restless curiosity, at last I returned to the door. Without hindrance I inserted my key, opened it, and entered. Bartleby was not to be seen. I looked round anxiously, peeped behind his screen; but it was very plain that he was gone. Upon more closely examining the place, I surmised that for an indefinite period Bartleby must have ate, dressed, and slept in my office, and that, too, without plate, mirror, or bed. The cushioned seat of a rickety old sofa in one corner bore the faint impress of a lean, reclining form. Rolled away under his desk, I found a blanket; on a chair, a tin basin, with soap and a ragged towel; in a newspaper a few crumbs of ginger-nuts and a morsel of cheese. Yes, thought I, it is evident enough that Bartleby has been making his home here, keeping bachelor's hall all by himself. Immediately then the thought came sweeping across me, what miserable friendlessness and loneliness are here revealed! His poverty is great; but his solitude, how horrible! Think of it. Of a Sunday, Wall Street is deserted as Petra;[2] and every night of every day it is an

---

[2] Petra: ancient city in Syria.

emptiness. This building, too, which of week-days hums with industry and life, at nightfall echoes with sheer vacancy, and all through Sunday is forlorn. And here Bartleby makes his home; sole spectator of a solitude which he has seen all populous—a sort of innocent and transformed Marius brooding among the ruins of Carthage!

For the first time in my life a feeling of over-powering stinging melancholy seized me. Before, I had never experienced aught but a not unpleasing sadness. The bond of a common humanity now drew me irresistibly to gloom. A fraternal melancholy! For both I and Bartleby were sons of Adam. I remembered the bright silks and sparkling faces I had seen that day, in gala trim, swan-like sailing down the Mississippi of Broadway; and I contrasted them with the pallid copyist, and thought to myself, Ah, happiness courts the light, so we deem the world is gay; but misery hides aloof, so we deem that misery there is none. These sad fancyings—chimeras, doubtless, of a sick and silly brain—led on to other and more special thoughts, concerning the eccentricities of Bartleby. Presentiments of strange discoveries hovered round me. The scrivener's pale form appeared to me laid out, among uncaring strangers, in its shivering winding sheet.

Suddenly I was attracted by Bartleby's closed desk, the key in open sight left in the lock.

I mean no mischief, seek the gratification of no heartless curiosity, thought I; besides, the desk is mine, and its contents, too, so I will make bold to look within. Everything was methodically arranged, the papers smoothly placed. The pigeon holes were deep, and removing the files of documents, I groped into their recesses. Presently I felt something there, and dragged it out. It was an old bandanna handkerchief, heavy and knotted. I opened it, and saw it was a saving's bank.

I now recalled all the quiet mysteries which I had noted in the man. I remembered that he never spoke but to answer; that, though at intervals he had considerable time to himself, yet I had never seen him reading—no, not even a newspaper; that for long periods he would stand looking out, at his pale window behind the screen, upon the dead brick wall; I was quite sure he never visited any refectory or eating house; while his pale face clearly indicated that he never drank beer like Turkey, or tea and coffee even, like other men; that he never went anywhere in particular that I could learn; never went out for a walk, unless, indeed, that was the case at present; that he had declined telling who he was, or whence he came, or whether he had any relatives in the world; that though so thin and pale, he never complained of ill health. And more than all, I remembered a certain unconscious air of pallid—how shall I call it?—of pallid haughtiness, say, or rather an austere reserve about him, which had positively awed me into my tame compliance with his eccentricities, when I had feared to ask him to do the slightest incidental thing for me, even though I might know, from his long-continued motionlessness, that behind his screen he must be standing in one of those dead-wall reveries of his.

Revolving all these things, and coupling them with the recently discovered fact, that he made my office his constant abiding place and home, and not forgetful of his morbid moodiness; revolving all these things, a prudential feeling began to steal over me. My first emotions had been those of pure melancholy and sincerest pity; but just in proportion as the forlornness of Bartleby grew and grew to my imagination, did that same melancholy merge into fear, that pity into repulsion. So true it is, and so terrible, too, that up to a certain point the thought or sight of misery enlists our best affections; but, in certain special cases, beyond that point it does not. They err who would assert that invariably this is owing to the inherent selfishness of the human heart. It rather proceeds from a certain hopelessness of remedying excessive and organic ill. To a sensitive being, pity is not seldom pain. And when at last it is perceived that such pity cannot lead to effectual succor, common sense bids the soul be rid of it. What I saw that morning persuaded me that the scrivener was the victim of innate and incurable disorder. I might give alms to his body; but his body did not pain him; it was his soul that suffered, and his soul I could not reach.

I did not accomplish the purpose of going to Trinity Church that morning. Somehow, the things I had seen disqualified me for the time from church-going. I walked homeward, thinking what I would do with Bartleby. Finally, I resolved upon this—I would put certain calm questions to him the next morning, touching his history, etc., and if he declined to answer them openly and unreservedly (and I supposed he would prefer not), then to give him a twenty dollar bill over and above whatever I might owe him, and tell him his services were no longer required; but that if in any other way I could assist him, I would be happy to do so, especially if he desired to return to his native place, wherever that might be, I would willingly help to defray the expenses. Moreover, if, after reaching home, he found himself at any time in want of aid, a letter from him would be sure of a reply.

The next morning came.

"Bartleby," said I, gently calling to him behind his screen.

No reply.

"Bartleby," said I, in a still gentler tone, "come here; I am not going to ask you to do anything you would prefer not to do—I simply wish to speak to you."

Upon this he noiselessly slid into view.

"Will you tell me, Bartleby, where you were born?"

"I would prefer not to."

"Will you tell me *anything* about yourself?"

"I would prefer not to."

"But what reasonable objection can you have to speak to me? I feel friendly towards you."

He did not look at me while I spoke, but kept his glance fixed upon my bust of Cicero, which, as I then sat, was directly behind me, some six inches above my head.

"What is your answer, Bartleby," said I, after waiting a considerable time for a reply, during which his countenance remained immovable, only there was the faintest conceivable tremor of the white attenuated mouth.

"At present I prefer to give no answer," he said, and retired into his hermitage.

It was rather weak in me I confess, but his manner, on this occasion, nettled me. Not only did there seem to lurk in it a certain calm disdain, but his perverseness seemed ungrateful, considering the undeniable good usage and indulgence he had received from me.

Again I sat ruminating what I should do. Mortified as I was at his behavior, and resolved as I had been to dismiss him when I entered my office, nevertheless I strangely felt something superstitious knocking at my heart, and forbidding me to carry out my purpose, and denouncing me for a villain if I dared to breathe one bitter word against this forlornest of mankind. At last, familiarly drawing my chair behind his screen, I sat down and said: "Bartleby, never mind, then, about revealing your history; but let me entreat you, as a friend, to comply as far as may be with the usages of this office. Say now, you will help to examine papers to-morrow or next day: in short, say now, that in a day or two you will begin to be a little reasonable:—say so, Bartleby."

"At present I would prefer not to be a little reasonable," was his mildly cadaverous reply.

Just then the folding-doors opened, and Nippers approached. He seemed suffering from an unusually bad night's rest, induced by severer indigestion than common. He overheard those final words of Bartleby.

"*Prefer not*, eh?" gritted Nippers—"I'd *prefer* him, if I were you, sir," addressing me—"I'd *prefer* him; I'd give him preferences, the stubborn mule! What is it, sir, pray, that he *prefers* not to do now?"

Bartleby moved not a limb.

"Mr. Nippers," said I, "I'd prefer that you would withdraw for the present."

Somehow, of late, I had got into the way of involuntarily using this word "prefer" upon all sorts of not exactly suitable occasions. And I trembled to think that my contact with the scrivener had already and seriously affected me in a mental way. And what further and deeper aberration might it not yet produce? This apprehension had not been without efficacy in determining me to summary measures.

As Nippers, looking very sour and sulky, was departing, Turkey blandly and deferentially approached.

"With submission, sir," said he, "yesterday I was thinking about Bartleby here, and I think that if he would but prefer to take a quart of good ale every day, it would do much towards mending him, and enabling him to assist in examining his papers."

"So you have got the word, too," said I, slightly excited.

"With submission, what word, sir," asked Turkey, respectfully crowding himself into the contracted space behind the screen, and by so doing, making me jostle the scrivener. "What word, sir?"

"I would prefer to be left alone here," said Bartleby, as if offended at being mobbed in his privacy.

"*That's* the word, Turkey," said I—"*that's* it."

"Oh, *prefer?* oh yes—queer word. I never use it myself. But, sir, as I was saying, if he would but prefer—"

"Turkey," interrupted I, "you will please withdraw."

"Oh, certainly, sir, if you prefer that I should."

As he opened the folding-door to retire, Nippers at his desk caught a glimpse of me, and asked whether I would prefer to have a certain paper copied on blue paper or white. He did not in the least roguishly accent the word prefer. It was plain that it involuntarily rolled from his tongue. I thought to myself, surely I must get rid of a demented man, who already has in some degree turned the tongues, if not the heads of myself and clerks. But I thought it prudent not to break the dismission at once.

The next day I noticed that Bartleby did nothing but stand at his window in his dead-wall revery. Upon asking him why he did not write, he said that he had decided upon doing no more writing.

"Why, how now? what next?" exclaimed I, "do no more writing?"

"No more."

"And what is the reason?"

"Do you not see the reason for yourself," he indifferently replied.

I looked steadfastly at him, and perceived that his eyes looked dull and glazed. Instantly it occurred to me, that his unexampled diligence in copying by his dim window for the first few weeks of his stay with me might have temporarily impaired his vision.

I was touched. I said something in condolence with him. I hinted that of course he did wisely in abstaining from writing for a while; and urged him to embrace that opportunity of taking wholesome exercise in the open air. This, however, he did not do. A few days after this, my other clerks being absent, and being in a great hurry to dispatch certain letters by the mail, I thought that, having nothing else earthly to do, Bartleby would surely be less inflexible than usual, and carry these letters to the post-office. But he blankly declined. So, much to my inconvenience, I went myself.

Still added days went by. Whether Bartleby's eyes improved or not, I could not say. To all appearance, I thought they did. But when I asked him if they did, he vouchsafed no answer. At all events, he would do no copying. At last, in reply to my urgings, he informed me that he had permanently given up copying.

"What!" exclaimed I; "suppose your eyes should get entirely well—better than ever before—would you not copy then?"

"I have given up copying," he answered, and slid aside.

He remained as ever, a fixture in my chamber. Nay—if that were possible—he became still more of a fixture than before. What was to be done? He would do nothing in the office; why should he stay there? In plain fact, he had now become a millstone to me, not only useless as a necklace, but afflictive to bear. Yet I was sorry for him. I speak less than truth when I say that, on his own account, he occasioned me uneasiness. If he would but have named a single relative or friend, I would instantly have written, and urged their taking the poor fellow away to some convenient retreat. But he seemed alone, absolutely alone in the universe. A bit of wreck in the mid Atlantic. At length, necessities connected with my business tyrannized over all other considerations. Decently as I could, I told Bartleby that in six days time he must unconditionally leave the office. I warned him to take measures, in the interval, for procuring some other abode. I offered to assist him in this endeavor, if he himself would but take the first step towards a removal. "And when you finally quit me, Bartleby," added I, "I shall see that you go not away entirely unprovided. Six days from this hour, remember."

At the expiration of that period, I peeped behind the screen, and lo! Bartleby was there.

I buttoned up my coat, balanced myself; advanced slowly towards him, touched his shoulder, and said, "The time has come; you must quit this place; I am sorry for you; here is money; but you must go."

"I would prefer not," he replied, with his back still towards me.

"You *must*."

He remained silent.

Now I had an unbounded confidence in this man's common honesty. He had frequently restored to me sixpences and shillings carelessly dropped upon the floor, for I am apt to be very reckless in such shirt-button affairs. The proceeding, then, which followed will not be deemed extraordinary.

"Bartleby," said I, "I owe you twelve dollars on account; here are thirty-two; the odd twenty are yours—Will you take it?" and I handed the bills towards him.

But he made no motion.

"I will leave them here, then," putting them under a weight on the table. Then taking my hat and cane and going to the door, I tranquilly turned and added—"After you have removed your things from these offices, Bartleby, you will of course lock the door—since every one is now gone for the day but you—and if you please, slip your key underneath the mat, so that I may have it in the morning. I shall not see you again; so good-bye to you. If, hereafter, in your new place of abode, I can be of any service to you, do not fail to advise me by letter. Good-by, Bartleby, and fare you well."

But he answered not a word; like the last column of some ruined temple, he remained standing mute and solitary in the middle of the otherwise deserted room.

As I walked home in a pensive mood, my vanity got the better of my pity. I could not but highly plume myself on my masterly management in getting rid of Bartleby. Masterly I call it, and such it must appear to any dispassionate thinker. The beauty of my procedure seemed to consist in its perfect quietness. There was no vulgar bullying, no bravado of any sort, no choleric hectoring, and striding to and fro across the apartment, jerking out vehement commands for Bartleby to bundle himself off with his beggarly traps. Nothing of the kind. Without loudly bidding Bartleby depart—as an inferior genius might have done—I *assumed* the ground that depart he must; and upon that assumption built all I had to say. The more I thought over my procedure, the more I was charmed with it. Nevertheless, next morning, upon awakening, I had my doubts—I had somehow slept off the fumes of vanity. One of the coolest and wisest hours a man has, is just after he awakes in the morning. My procedure seemed as sagacious as ever—but only in theory. How it would prove in practice—there was the rub. It was truly a beautiful thought to have assumed Bartleby's departure; but, after all, that assumption was simply my own, and none of Bartleby's. The great point was, not whether I had assumed that he would quit me, but whether he would prefer so to do. He was more a man of preferences than assumptions.

After breakfast, I walked down town, arguing the probabilities *pro* and *con*. One moment I thought it would prove a miserable failure, and Bartleby would be found all alive at my office as usual; the next moment it seemed certain that I should find his chair empty. And so I kept veering about. At the corner of Broadway and Canal Street, I saw quite an excited group of people standing in earnest conversation.

"I'll take odds he doesn't," said a voice as I passed.

"Doesn't go?—done!" said I, "put up your money."

I was instinctively putting my hand in my pocket to produce my own, when I remembered that this was an election day. The words I had overheard bore no reference to Bartleby, but to the success or nonsuccess of some candidate for the mayoralty. In my intent frame of mind, I had, as it were, imagined that all Broadway shared in my excitement, and were debating the same question with me. I passed on, very thankful that the uproar of the street screened my momentary absent-mindedness.

As I had intended, I was earlier than usual at my office door. I stood listening for a moment. All was still. He must be gone. I tried the knob. The door was locked. Yes, my procedure had worked to a charm; he indeed must be vanished. Yet a certain melancholy mixed with this: I was almost sorry for my brilliant success. I was fumbling under the door mat for the key, which Bartleby was to have left there for me, when accidentally my knee knocked against a panel, producing a summoning sound, and in response a voice came to me from within—"Not yet; I am occupied."

It was Bartleby.

I was thunderstruck. For an instant I stood like the man who, pipe in mouth, was killed one cloudless afternoon long ago in Virginia, by summer lightning; at his own warm open window he was killed, and remained leaning out there upon the dreamy afternoon, till some one touched him, when he fell.

"Not gone!" I murmured at last. But again obeying that wondrous ascendancy which the inscrutable scrivener had over me, and from which ascendancy, for all my chafing, I could not completely escape, I slowly went down stairs and out into the street, and while walking round the block, considered what I should next do in this unheard-of perplexity. Turn the man out by an actual thrusting I could not; to drive him away by calling him hard names would not do; calling in the police was an unpleasant idea; and yet, permit him to enjoy his cadaverous triumph over me—this, too, I could not think of. What was to be done? or, if nothing could be done, was there anything further that I could *assume* in the matter? Yes, as before I had prospectively assumed that Bartleby would depart, so now I might retrospectively assume that departed he was. In the legitimate carrying out of this assumption, I might enter my office in a great hurry, and pretending not to see Bartleby at all, walk straight against him as if he were air. Such a proceeding would in a singular degree have the appearance of a home-thrust. It was hardly possible that Bartleby could withstand such an application of the doctrine of assumptions. But upon second thoughts the success of the plan seemed rather dubious. I resolved to argue the matter over with him again.

"Bartleby," said I, entering the office, with a quietly severe expression, "I am seriously displeased. I am pained, Bartleby. I had thought better of you. I had imagined you of such a gentlemanly organization, that in any delicate dilemma a slight hint would suffice—in short, an assumption. But it appears I am deceived. Why," I added, unaffectedly starting, "you have not even touched that money yet," pointing to it, just where I had left it the evening previous.

He answered nothing.

"Will you, or will you not, quit me?" I now demanded in a sudden passion, advancing close to him.

"I would prefer *not* to quit you," he replied, gently emphasizing the *not*.

"What earthly right have you to stay here? Do you pay any rent? Do you pay my taxes? Or is this property yours?"

He answered nothing.

"Are you ready to go on and write now? Are your eyes recovered? Could you copy a small paper for me this morning? or help examine a few lines? or step round to the post-office? In a word, will you do anything at all, to give a coloring to your refusal to depart the premises?"

He silently retired into his hermitage.

I was now in such a state of nervous resentment that I thought it but prudent to check myself at present from further demonstrations. Bartleby and I were alone. I remembered the tragedy of the unfortunate Adams and the still more unfortunate Colt in the solitary office of the latter; and how poor Colt, being dreadfully incensed by Adams, and imprudently permitting himself to get wildly excited, was at unawares hurried into his fatal act—an act which certainly no man could possibly deplore more than the actor himself. Often it had occurred to me in my ponderings upon the subject, that had that altercation taken place in the public street, or at a private residence, it would not have terminated as it did. It was the circumstance of being alone in a solitary office, up stairs, of a building entirely unhallowed by humanizing domestic associations— an uncarpeted office, doubtless, of a dusty, haggard sort of appearance— this it must have been, which greatly helped to enhance the irritable desperation of the hapless Colt.[3]

But when this old Adam of resentment rose in me and tempted me concerning Bartleby, I grappled him and threw him. How? Why, simply by recalling the divine injunction: "A new commandment give I unto you, that ye love one another." Yes, this it was that saved me. Aside from higher considerations, charity often operates as a vastly wise and prudent principle—a great safeguard to its possessor. Men have committed murder for jealousy's sake, and anger's sake, and hatred's sake, and selfishness' sake, and spiritual pride's sake; but no man, that ever I heard of, ever committed a diabolical murder for sweet charity's sake. Mere self-interest, then, if no better motive can be enlisted, should, especially with high-tempered men, prompt all beings to charity and philanthropy. At any rate, upon the occasion in question, I strove to drown my exasperated feelings towards the scrivener by benevolently construing his conduct. Poor fellow, poor fellow! thought I, he don't mean anything; and besides, he has seen hard times, and ought to be indulged.

I endeavored, also, immediately to occupy myself, and at the same time to comfort my despondency. I tried to fancy, that in the course of the morning, at such time as might prove agreeable to him, Bartleby, of his own free accord, would emerge from his hermitage and take up some decided line of march in the direction of the door. But no. Half-past twelve o'clock came; Turkey began to glow in the face, overturn his inkstand, and become generally obstreperous; Nippers abated down into quietude and courtesy; Ginger Nut munched his noon apple; and Bartleby remained standing at his window in one of his profoundest dead-wall reveries. Will it be credited? Ought I to acknowledge it? That afternoon I left the office without saying one further word to him.

Some days now passed, during which, at leisure intervals I looked a little into "Edwards on the Will," and "Priestly on Necessity." Under

---

[3] *Adams . . . Colt*: a widely publicized murder-case in which John C. Colt killed Samuel Adams, in New York City, in January, 1842.

the circumstances, those books induced a salutary feeling. Gradually I slid into the persuasion that these troubles of mine, touching the scrivener, had been all predestinated from eternity, and Bartleby was billeted upon me for some mysterious purpose of an allwise Providence, which it was not for a mere mortal like me to fathom. Yes, Bartleby, stay there behind your screen, thought I; I shall persecute you no more; you are harmless and noiseless as any of these old chairs; in short, I never feel so private as when I know you are here. At last I see it, I feel it; I penetrate to the predestinated purpose of my life. I am content. Others may have loftier parts to enact; but my mission in this world, Bartleby, is to furnish you with office-room for such period as you may see fit to remain.

I believe that this wise and blessed frame of mind would have continued with me, had it not been for the unsolicited and uncharitable remarks obtruded upon me by my professional friends who visited the rooms. But thus it often is, that the constant friction of illiberal minds wears out at last the best resolves of the more generous. Though to be sure, when I reflected upon it, it was not strange that people entering my office should be struck by the peculiar aspect of the unaccountable Bartleby, and so be tempted to throw out some sinister observations concerning him. Sometimes an attorney, having business with me, and calling at my office, and finding no one but the scrivener there, would undertake to obtain some sort of precise information from him touching my whereabouts; but without heeding his idle talk, Bartleby would remain standing immovable in the middle of the room. So after contemplating him in that position for a time, the attorney would depart, no wiser than he came.

Also, when a reference was going on, and the room full of lawyers and witnesses, and business driving fast, some deeply-occupied legal gentleman present, seeing Bartleby wholly unemployed, would request him to run round to his (the legal gentleman's) office and fetch some papers for him. Thereupon, Bartleby would tranquilly decline, and yet remain idle as before. Then the lawyer would give a great stare, and turn to me. And what could I say? At last I was made aware that all through the circle of my professional acquaintance, a whisper of wonder was running round, having reference to the strange creature I kept at my office. This worried me very much. And as the idea came upon me of his possibly turning out a long-lived man, and keep occupying my chambers, and denying my authority; and perplexing my visitors; and scandalizing my professional reputation; and casting a general gloom over the premises; keeping soul and body together to the last upon his savings (for doubtless he spent but half a dime a day), and in the end perhaps outlive me, and claim possession of my office by right of his perpetual occupancy: as all these dark anticipations crowded upon me more and more, and my friends continually intruded their relentless remarks upon the apparition in my room; a great change was wrought in me. I resolved to gather all my faculties together, and forever rid me of this intolerable incubus.

Ere revolving any complicated project, however, adapted to this end, I first simply suggested to Bartleby the propriety of his permanent departure. In a calm and serious tone, I commended the idea to his careful and mature consideration. But, having taken three days to meditate upon it, he apprised me, that his original determination remained the same; in short, that he still preferred to abide with me.

What shall I do? I now said to myself, buttoning up my coat to the last button. What shall I do? what ought I to do? what does conscience say I *should* do with this man, or, rather, ghost. Rid myself of him, I must; go, he shall. But how? You will not thrust him, the poor, pale, passive mortal—you will not thrust such a helpless creature out of your door? you will not dishonor yourself by such cruelty? No, I will not, I cannot do that. Rather would I let him live and die here, and then mason up his remains in the wall. What, then, will you do? For all your coaxing, he will not budge. Bribes he leaves under your own paper-weight on your table; in short, it is quite plain that he prefers to cling to you.

Then something severe, something unusual must be done. What! surely you will not have him collared by a constable, and commit his innocent pallor to the common jail? And upon what ground could you procure such a thing to be done?—a vagrant, is he? What! he a vagrant, a wanderer, who refuses to budge? It is because he will *not* be a vagrant, then, that you seek to count him *as* a vagrant. That is too absurd. No visible means of support: there I have him. Wrong again: for indubitably he *does* support himself, and that is the only unanswerable proof that any man can show of his possessing the means so to do. No more, then. Since he will not quit me, I must quit him. I will change my offices; I will move elsewhere, and give him fair notice, that if I find him on my new premises I will then proceed against him as a common trespasser.

Acting accordingly, next day I thus addressed him: "I find these chambers too far from the City Hall; the air is unwholesome. In a word, I propose to remove my offices next week, and shall no longer require your services. I tell you this now, in order that you may seek another place."

He made no reply, and nothing more was said.

On the appointed day I engaged carts and men, proceeded to my chambers, and, having but little furniture, everything was removed in a few hours. Throughout, the scrivener remained standing behind the screen, which I directed to be removed the last thing. It was withdrawn; and, being folded up like a huge folio, left him the motionless occupant of a naked room. I stood in the entry watching him a moment, while something from within me upbraided me.

I re-entered, with my hand in my pocket—and—and my heart in my mouth.

"Good-by, Bartleby; I am going—good-by, and God some way bless you; and take that," slipping something in his hand. But it dropped upon the floor, and then—strange to say—I tore myself from him whom I had so longed to be rid of.

Established in my new quarters, for a day or two I kept the door locked, and started at every footfall in the passages. When I returned to my rooms, after any little absence, I would pause at the threshold for an instant, and attentively listen, ere applying my key. But these fears were needless. Bartleby never came nigh me.

I thought all was going well, when a perturbed-looking stranger visited me, inquiring whether I was the person who had recently occupied rooms at No. — Wall Street.

Full of forebodings, I replied that I was.

"Then, sir," said the stranger, who proved a lawyer, "you are are responsible for the man you left there. He refuses to do any copying; he refuses to do anything; he says he prefers not to; and he refuses to quit the premises."

"I am very sorry, sir," said I, with assumed tranquillity, but an inward tremor, "but, really, the man you allude to is nothing to me—he is no relation or apprentice of mine, that you should hold me responsible for him."

"In mercy's name, who is he?"

"I certainly cannot inform you. I know nothing about him. Formerly I employed him as a copyist; but he has done nothing for me now for some time past."

"I shall settle him, then—good morning, sir."

Several days passed, and I heard nothing more; and, though I often felt a charitable prompting to call at the place and see poor Bartleby, yet a certain squeamishness, of I know not what, withheld me.

All is over with him, by this time, thought I, at last, when, through another week, no further intelligence reached me. But, coming to my room the day after, I found several persons waiting at my door in a high state of nervous excitement.

"That's the man—here he comes," cried the foremost one, whom I recognized as the lawyer who had previously called upon me alone.

"You must take him away, sir, at once," cried a portly person among them, advancing upon me, and whom I knew to be the landlord of No. — Wall Street. "These gentlemen, my tenants, cannot stand it any longer; Mr. B——," pointing to the lawyer, "has turned him out of his room, and he now persists in haunting the building generally, sitting upon the banisters of the stairs by day, and sleeping in the entry by night. Everybody is concerned; clients are leaving the offices; some fears are entertained of a mob; something you must do, and that without delay."

Aghast at this torrent, I fell back before it, and would fain have locked myself in my new quarters. In vain I persisted that Bartleby was nothing to me—no more than to any one else. In vain—I was the last person known to have anything to do with him, and they held me to the terrible account. Fearful, then, of being exposed in the papers (as one person present obscurely threatened), I considered the matter, and, at length, said, that if the lawyer would give me a confidential interview with the scrivener, in his (the lawyer's) own room, I would, that afternoon, strive my best to rid them of the nuisance they complained of.

Going up stairs to my old haunt, there was Bartleby silently sitting upon the banister at the landing.

"What are you doing here, Bartleby?" said I.

"Sitting upon the banister," he mildly replied.

I motioned him into the lawyer's room, who then left us.

"Bartleby," said I, "are you aware that you are the cause of great tribulation to me, by persisting in occupying entry after being dismissed from the office?"

No answer.

"Now one of two things must take place. Either you must do something, or something must be done to you. Now what sort of business would you like to engage in? Would you like to re-engage in copying for some one?"

"No; I would prefer not to make any change."

"Would you like a clerkship in a dry-goods store?"

"There is too much confinement about that. No, I would not like a clerkship; but I am not particular."

"Too much confinement," I cried, "why you keep yourself confined all the time!"

"I would prefer not to take a clerkship," he rejoined, as if to settle that little item at once.

"How would a bar-tender's business suit you? There is no trying of the eye-sight in that."

"I would not like it at all; though, as I said before, I am not particular."

His unwonted wordiness inspirited me. I returned to the charge.

"Well, then, would you like to travel through the country collecting bills for the merchants? That would improve your health."

"No, I would prefer to be doing something else."

"How, then, would going as a companion to Europe, to entertain some young gentleman with your conversation—how would that suit you?"

"Not at all. It does not strike me that there is anything definite about that. I like to be stationary. But I am not particular."

"Stationary you shall be, then," I cried, now losing all patience, and, for the first time in all my exasperating connection with him, fairly flying into a passion. "If you do not go away from these premises before night, I shall feel bound—indeed, I *am* bound—to—to—to quit the premises myself!" I rather absurdly concluded, knowing not with what possible threat to try to frighten his immobility into compliance. Despairing of all further efforts, I was precipitately leaving him, when a final thought occurred to me—one which had not been wholly unindulged before.

"Bartleby," said I, in the kindest tone I could assume under such exciting circumstances, "will you go home with me now—not to my office, but my dwelling—and remain there till we can conclude upon some convenient arrangement for you at our leisure? Come, let us start now, right away."

"No: at present I would prefer not to make any change at all."

I answered nothing; but, effectually dodging every one by the suddenness and rapidity of my flight, rushed from the building, ran up Wall Street towards Broadway, and, jumping into the first omnibus, was soon removed from pursuit. As soon as tranquillity returned, I distinctly perceived that I had now done all that I possibly could, both in respect to the demands of the landlord and his tenants, and with regard to my own desire and sense of duty, to benefit Bartleby, and shield him from rude persecution. I now strove to be entirely care-free and quiescent; and my conscience justified me in the attempt; though, indeed, it was not so successful as I could have wished. So fearful was I of being again hunted out by the incensed landlord and his exasperated tenants, that, surrendering my business to Nippers, for a few days, I drove about the upper part of the town and through the suburbs, in my rockaway; crossed over to Jersey City and Hoboken, and paid fugitive visits to Manhattan-ville and Astoria. In fact, I almost lived in my rockaway for the time.

When again I entered my office, lo, a note from the landlord lay upon the desk. I opened it with trembling hands. It informed me that the writer had sent to the police, and had Bartleby removed to the Tombs as a vagrant. Moreover, since I knew more about him than any one else, he wished me to appear at that place, and make a suitable statement of the facts. These tidings had a conflicting effect upon me. At first I was indignant; but, at last, almost approved. The landlord's energetic, summary disposition, had led him to adopt a procedure which I do not think I would have decided upon myself; and yet, as a last resort, under such peculiar circumstances, it seemed the only plan.

As I afterwards learned, the poor scrivener, when told that he must be conducted to the Tombs, offered not the slightest obstacle, but, in his pale, unmoving way, silently acquiesced.

Some of the compassionate and curious bystanders joined the party; and headed by one of the constables arm in arm with Bartleby, the silent procession filed its way through all the noise, and heat, and joy of the roaring thoroughfares at noon.

The same day I received the note, I went to the Tombs, or, to speak more properly, the Halls of Justice. Seeking the right officer, I stated the purpose of my call, and was informed that the individual I described was, indeed, within. I then assured the functionary that Bartleby was a perfectly honest man, and greatly to be compassionated, however unaccountably eccentric. I narrated all I knew, and closed by suggesting the idea of letting him remain in as indulgent confinement as possible, till something less harsh might be done—though, indeed, I hardly knew what. At all events, if nothing else could be decided upon, the almshouse must receive him. I then begged to have an interview.

Being under no disgraceful charge, and quite serene and harmless in all his ways, they had permitted him freely to wander about the prison, and, especially, in the inclosed grass-platted yards thereof. And so I found him there, standing all alone in the quietest of the yards, his face towards a high wall, while all around, from the narrow slits of the jail windows, I thought I saw peering out upon him the eyes of murderers and thieves.

"Bartleby!"

"I know you," he said, without looking round—"and I want nothing to say to you."

"It was not I that brought you here, Bartleby," said I, keenly pained at his implied suspicion. "And to you, this should not be so vile a place. Nothing reproachful attaches to you by being here. And see, it is not so sad a place as one might think. Look, there is the sky, and here is the grass."

"I know where I am," he replied, but would say nothing more, and so I left him.

As I entered the corridor again, a broad meat-like man, in an apron, accosted me, and, jerking his thumb over his shoulder, said—"Is that your friend?"

"Yes."

"Does he want to starve? If he does, let him live on the prison fare, that's all."

"Who are you?" asked I, not knowing what to make of such an unofficially speaking person in such a place.

"I am the grub-man. Such gentlemen as have friends here, hire me to provide them with something good to eat."

"Is this so?" said I, turning to the turnkey.

He said it was.

"Well, then," said I, slipping some silver into the grub-man's hands (for so they called him), "I want you to give particular attention to my friend there; let him have the best dinner you can get. And you must be as polite to him as possible."

"Introduce me, will you?" said the grub-man, looking at me with an expression which seemed to say he was all impatience for an opportunity to give a specimen of his breeding.

Thinking it would prove of benefit to the scrivener, I acquiesced; and, asking the grub-man his name, went up with him to Bartleby.

"Bartleby, this is a friend; you will find him very useful to you."

"Your sarvant, sir, your sarvant," said the grub-man, making a low salutation behind his apron. "Hope you find it pleasant here, sir; nice grounds—cool apartments—hope you'll stay with us sometime—try to make it agreeable. What will you have for dinner to-day?"

"I prefer not to dine to-day," said Bartleby, turning away. "It would disagree with me; I am unused to dinners." So saying, he slowly moved to the other side of the inclosure, and took up a position fronting the dead-wall.

"How's this?" said the grub-man, addressing me with a stare of astonishment, "He's odd, ain't he?"

"I think he is a little deranged," said I, sadly.

"Deranged? deranged is it? Well, now, upon my word, I thought that friend of yourn was a gentleman forger; they are always pale and genteel-like, them forgers. I can't help pity 'em—can't help it, sir. Did you know Monroe Edwards?" he added, touchingly, and paused. Then, laying his hand piteously on my shoulder, sighed, "he died of consumption at Sing-Sing. So you weren't acquainted with Monroe?"

"No, I was never socially acquainted with any forgers. But I cannot stop longer. Look to my friend yonder. You will not lose by it. I will see you again."

Some few days after this, I again obtained admission to the Tombs, and went through the corridors in quest of Bartleby; but without finding him.

"I saw him coming from his cell not long ago," said a turnkey, "may be he's gone to loiter in the yards."

So I went in that direction.

"Are you looking for the silent man?" said another turnkey, passing me. "Yonder he lies—sleeping in the yard there. 'Tis not twenty minutes since I saw him lie down."

The yard was entirely quiet. It was not accessible to the common prisoners. The surrounding walls, of amazing thickness, kept off all sounds behind them. The Egyptian character of the masonry weighed upon me with its gloom. But a soft imprisoned turf grew under foot. The heart of the eternal pyramids, it seemed, wherein, by some strange magic, through the clefts, grass-seed, dropped by birds, had sprung.

Strangely huddled at the base of the wall, his knees drawn up, and lying on his side, his head touching the cold stones, I saw the wasted Bartleby. But nothing stirred. I paused; then went close up to him; stooped over, and saw that his dim eyes were open; otherwise he seemed profoundly sleeping. Something prompted me to touch him. I felt his hand, when a tingling shiver ran up my arm and down my spine to my feet.

The round face of the grub-man peered upon me now. "His dinner is ready. Won't he dine to-day, either? Or does he live without dining?"

"Lives without dining," said I, and closed the eyes.

"Eh!—He's asleep, ain't he?"

"With kings and counselors," murmured I.

• • •

There would seem little need for proceeding further in this history. Imagination will readily supply the meagre recital of poor Bartleby's interment. But, ere parting with the reader, let me say, that if this little narrative has sufficiently interested him, to awaken curiosity as to who Bartleby was, and what manner of life he led prior to the present narrator's making his acquaintance, I can only reply, that in such curiosity

I fully share, but am wholly unable to gratify it. Yet here I hardly know whether I should divulge one little item of rumor, which came to my ear a few months after the scrivener's decease. Upon what basis it rested, I could never ascertain; and hence, how true it is I cannot now tell. But, inasmuch as this vague report has not been without a certain suggestive interest to me, however sad, it may prove the same with some others; and so I will briefly mention it. The report was this: that Bartleby had been a subordinate clerk in the Dead Letter Office at Washington, from which he had been suddenly removed by a change in the administration. When I think over this rumor, hardly can I express the emotions which seize me. Dead letters! does it not sound like dead men? Conceive a man by nature and misfortune prone to a pallid hopelessness, can any business seem more fitted to heighten it than that of continually handling these dead letters, and assorting them for the flames? For by the cartload they are annually burned. Sometimes from out the folded paper the pale clerk takes a ring—the finger it was meant for, perhaps, moulders in the grave; a bank-note sent in swiftest charity—he whom it would relieve, nor eats nor hungers any more; pardon for those who died despairing; hope for those who died unhoping; good tidings for those who died stifled by unrelieved calamities. On errands of life, these letters speed to death.

Ah, Bartleby! Ah, humanity!

PLAYS

Henrik Ibsen
August Strindberg
John Millington Synge
Tennessee Williams
Lorraine Hansberry
Eugene Ionesco

Ghosts

Characters

MRS. ALVING *a widow*
OSWALD ALVING *her son, an artist*
MANDERS *the Pastor of the parish*
ENGSTRAND *a carpenter*
REGINA ENGSTRAND *his daughter, in Mrs. Alving's service*

The action takes place at MRS. ALVING'S *house on one of the larger fjords of western Norway.*

Act I

Scene: *A large room looking upon a garden. A door in the left-hand wall, and two in the right. In the middle of the room, a round table with chairs set about it, and books, magazines, and newspapers upon it. In the foreground on the left, a window, by which is a small sofa with a work-table in front of it. At the back the room opens into a conservatory rather smaller than the room. From the right-hand side of this a door leads to the garden. Through the large panes of glass that form the outer wall of the conservatory, a gloomy fjord landscape can be discerned, half obscured by steady rain.*
ENGSTRAND *is standing close up to the garden door. His left leg is slightly deformed, and he wears a boot with a clump of wood under the sole.* REGINA, *with an empty garden-syringe in her hand, is trying to prevent his coming in.*

REGINA [*below her breath*] What is it you want? Stay where you are. The rain is dripping off you.
ENGSTRAND God's good rain, my girl.
REGINA The Devil's own rain, that's what it is!
ENGSTRAND Lord, how you talk, Regina. [*Takes a few limping steps forward*] What I wanted to tell you was this—
REGINA Don't clump about like that, stupid! The young master is lying asleep upstairs.
ENGSTRAND Asleep still? In the middle of the day?
REGINA Well, it's no business of yours.
ENGSTRAND Yes, we are poor weak mortals, my girl—
REGINA We are indeed.

ENGSTRAND —and the temptations of the world are manifold, you know—but, for all that, here I was at my work at half-past five this morning.

REGINA Yes, yes, but make yourself scarce now. I am not going to stand here as if I had a *rendez-vous* with you.

ENGSTRAND As if you had a what?

REGINA I am not going to have any one find you here; so now you know, and you can go.

ENGSTRAND [*coming a few steps nearer*] Not a bit of it! Not before we have had a little chat. This afternoon I shall have finished my job down at the school house, and I shall be off home to town by to-night's boat.

REGINA [*mutters*] Pleasant journey to you!

ENGSTRAND Thanks, my girl. To-morrow is the opening of the Orphanage, and I expect there will be a fine kick-up here and plenty of good strong drink, don't you know. And no one shall say of Jacob Engstrand that he can't hold off when temptation comes in his way.

REGINA Oho!

ENGSTRAND Yes, because there will be a lot of fine folk here to-morrow. Parson Manders is expected from town, too.

REGINA What is more, he's coming to-day.

ENGSTRAND There you are! And I'm going to be precious careful he doesn't have anything to say against me, do you see?

REGINA Oh, that's your game, is it?

ENGSTRAND What do you mean?

REGINA [*with a significant look at him*] What is it you want to humbug Mr. Manders out of, this time?

ENGSTRAND Sh! Sh! Are you crazy? Do you suppose *I* would want to humbug Mr. Manders? No, no—Mr. Manders has always been too kind a friend for me to do that. But what I wanted to talk to you about, was my going back home to-night.

REGINA The sooner you go, the better I shall be pleased.

ENGSTRAND Yes, only I want to take you with me, Regina.

REGINA [*open-mouthed*] You want to take me—? What did you say?

ENGSTRAND I want to take you home with me, I said.

REGINA [*contemptuously*] You will never get me home with you.

ENGSTRAND Ah, we shall see about that.

REGINA Yes, you can be quite certain we *shall* see about that. I, who have been brought up by a lady like Mrs. Alving?—I, who have been treated almost as if I were her own child?—do you suppose I am going home with *you?*—to such a house as yours? Not likely!

ENGSTRAND What the devil do you mean? Are you setting yourself up against your father, you hussy?

REGINA [*mutters, without looking at him*] You have often told me I was none of yours.
ENGSTRAND Bah!—why do you want to pay any attention to that?
REGINA Haven't you many and many a time abused me and called me a—? For shame!
ENGSTRAND I'll swear I never used such an ugly word.
REGINA Oh, it doesn't matter what word you used.
ENGSTRAND Besides, that was only when I was a bit fuddled—hm! Temptations are manifold in this world, Regina.
REGINA Ugh!
ENGSTRAND And it was when your mother was in a nasty temper. I had to find some way of getting my knife into her, my girl. She was always so precious genteel [*Mimicking her*] "Let go, Jacob! Let me be! Please to remember that I was three years with the Alvings at Rosenvold, and they were people who went to Court!" [*Laughs*] Bless my soul, she never could forget that Captain Alving got a Court appointment while she was in service here.
REGINA Poor mother—you worried her into her grave pretty soon.
ENGSTRAND [*shrugging his shoulders*] Of course, of course; I have got to take the blame for everything.
REGINA [*beneath her breath, as she turns away*] Ugh—that leg, too!
ENGSTRAND What are you saying, my girl?
REGINA *Pied de mouton.*
ENGSTRAND Is that English?
REGINA Yes.
ENGSTRAND You have had a good education out here, and no mistake; and it may stand you in good stead now, Regina.
REGINA [*after a short silence*] And what was it you wanted me to come to town for?
ENGSTRAND Need you ask why a father wants his only child? Ain't I a poor lonely widower?
REGINA Oh, don't come to me with that tale. Why do you want me to go?
ENGSTRAND Well, I must tell you I am thinking of taking up a new line now.
REGINA [*whistles*] You have tried that so often—but it has always proved a fool's errand.
ENGSTRAND Ah, but this time you will just see, Regina! Strike me dead if—
REGINA [*stamping her feet*] Stop swearing!
ENGSTRAND Sh! Sh!—you're quite right, my girl, quite right! What I wanted to say was only this, that I have put by a tidy penny out of what I have made by working at this new Orphanage up here.

REGINA Have you? All the better for you.

ENGSTRAND What is there for a man to spend his money on, out here in the country?

REGINA Well, what then?

ENGSTRAND Well, you see, I thought of putting the money into something that would pay. I thought of some kind of an eating-house for seafaring folk—

REGINA Heavens!

ENGSTRAND Oh, a high-class eating-house, of course,—not a pigsty for common sailors. Damn it, no; it would be a place ships' captains and first mates would come to; really good sort of people, you know.

REGINA And what should I—?

ENGSTRAND You would help there. But only to make a show, you know. You wouldn't find it hard work, I can promise you, my girl. You should do exactly as you liked.

REGINA Oh, yes, quite so!

ENGSTRAND But we must have some women in the house; that is as clear as daylight. Because in the evening we must make the place a little attractive—some singing and dancing, and that sort of thing. Remember they are sea-folk—wayfarers on the waters of life! [*Coming nearer to her*] Now don't be a fool and stand in your own way, Regina. What good are you going to do here? Will this education, that your mistress has paid for, be of any use? You are to look after the children in the new Home, I hear. Is that the sort of work for you? Are you so frightfully anxious to go and wear out your health and strength for the sake of these dirty brats?

REGINA No, if things were to go as I want them to, then—. Well, it may happen!

ENGSTRAND What may happen?

REGINA Never you mind. Is it much that you have put by, up here?

ENGSTRAND Taking it all round, I should say about forty or fifty pounds.

REGINA That's not so bad.

ENGSTRAND It's enough to make a start with, my girl.

REGINA Don't you mean to give me any of the money?

ENGSTRAND No, I'm hanged if I do.

REGINA Don't you mean to send me as much as a dress-length of stuff, just for once?

ENGSTRAND Come and live in the town with me and you shall have plenty of dresses.

REGINA Pooh!—I can get that much for myself, if I have a mind to.

ENGSTRAND But it's far better to have a father's guiding hand, Regina. Just now I can get a nice house in Little Harbour Street. They don't want much money down for it—and we could make it like a sort of seamen's home, don't you know.

REGINA But I have no intention of living with you! I have nothing whatever to do with you. So now, be off!

ENGSTRAND You wouldn't be living with me long, my girl. No such luck—not if you knew how to play your cards. Such a fine wench as you have grown this last year or two—

REGINA Well—?

ENGSTRAND It wouldn't be very long before some first mate came along—or perhaps a captain.

REGINA I don't mean to marry a man of that sort. Sailors have no *savoir-vivre*.

ENGSTRAND What haven't they got?

REGINA I know what sailors are, I tell you. They aren't the sort of people to marry.

ENGSTRAND Well, don't bother about marrying them. You can make it pay just as well. [*More confidentially*] That fellow—the Englishman—the one with the yacht—he gave seventy pounds, he did; and she wasn't a bit prettier than you.

REGINA [*advancing towards him*] Get out!

ENGSTRAND [*stepping back*] Here! here!—you're not going to hit me, I suppose?

REGINA Yes, if you talk like that of mother, I will hit you. Get out, I tell you! [*Pushes him up to the garden door*] And don't bang the doors. Young Mr. Alving—

ENGSTRAND Is asleep—I know. It's funny how anxious you are about young Mr. Alving. [*In a lower tone*] Oho! is it possible that it is *he* that—?

REGINA Get out, and be quick about it! Your wits are wandering, my good man. No, don't go that way; Mr. Manders is just coming along. Be off down the kitchen stairs.

ENGSTRAND [*moving towards the right*] Yes, yes—all right. But have a bit of a chat with him that's coming along. He's the chap to tell you what a child owes to its father. For I am your father, anyway, you know. I can prove it by the Register.

[*He goes out through the farther door which* REGINA *has opened. She shuts it after him, looks hastily at herself in the mirror, fans herself with her handkerchief and sets her collar straight; then busies herself with the flowers.* MANDERS *enters the conservatory through the garden* door. *He wears an overcoat, carries an umbrella and has a small travelling-bag slung over his shoulder on a strap*]

MANDERS Good morning, Miss Engstrand.

REGINA [*turning round with a look of pleased surprise*] Oh, Mr. Manders, good morning. The boat is in, then?

MANDERS Just in. [*Comes into the room*] It is most tiresome, this rain every day.

REGINA [*following him in*] It's a splendid rain for the farmers, Mr. Manders.

MANDERS Yes, you are quite right. We town-folk think so little about that. [*Begins to take off his overcoat*]

REGINA Oh, let me help you. That's it. Why, how wet it is! I will hang it up in the hall. Give me your umbrella, too; I will leave it open, so that it will dry.

[*She goes out with the things by the farther door on the right.* MANDERS *lays his bag and his hat down on a chair.* REGINA *re-enters*]

MANDERS Ah, it's very pleasant to get indoors. Well, is everything going on well here?

REGINA Yes, thanks.

MANDERS Properly busy, though, I expect, getting ready for to-morrow?

REGINA Oh, yes, there is plenty to do.

MANDERS And Mrs. Alving is at home, I hope?

REGINA Yes, she is. She has just gone upstairs to take the young master his chocolate.

MANDERS Tell me—I heard down at the pier that Oswald had come back.

REGINA Yes, he came the day before yesterday. We didn't expect him till to-day.

MANDERS Strong and well, I hope?

REGINA Yes, thank you, well enough. But dreadfully tired after his journey. He came straight from Paris without a stop—I mean, he came all the way without breaking his journey. I fancy he is having a sleep now, so we must talk a little bit more quietly, if you don't mind.

MANDERS All right, we will be very quiet.

REGINA [*while she moves an armchair up to the table*] Please sit down, Mr. Manders, and make yourself at home. [*He sits down; she puts a footstool under his feet*] There! Is that comfortable?

MANDERS Thank you, thank you. That is most comfortable. [*Looks at her*] I'll tell you what, Miss Engstrand, I certainly think you have grown since I saw you last.

REGINA Do you think so? Mrs. Alving says, too, that I have developed.

MANDERS Developed? Well, perhaps a little—just suitably.
[*A short pause*]
REGINA Shall I tell Mrs. Alving you are here?
MANDERS Thanks, there is no hurry, my dear child.—Now tell me, Regina my dear, how has your father been getting on here?
REGINA Thank you, Mr. Manders, he is getting on pretty well.
MANDERS He came to see me, the last time he was in town.
REGINA Did he? He is always so glad when he can have a chat with you.
MANDERS And I suppose you have seen him pretty regularly every day?
REGINA I? Oh, yes, I do—whenever I have time, that is to say.
MANDERS Your father has not a very strong character, Miss Engstrand. He sadly needs a guiding hand.
REGINA Yes, I can quite believe that.
MANDERS He needs someone with him that he can cling to, someone whose judgment he can rely on. He acknowledged that freely himself, the last time he came to see me.
REGINA Yes, he has said something of the same sort to me. But I don't know whether Mrs. Alving could do without me—most of all just now, when we have the new Orphanage to see about. And I should be dreadfully unwilling to leave Mrs. Alving, too; she has always been so good to me.
MANDERS But a daughter's duty, my good child—. Naturally we should have to get your mistress' consent first.
REGINA Still I don't know whether it would be quite the thing, at my age, to keep house for a single man.
MANDERS What!! My dear Miss Engstrand, it is your own father we are speaking of!
REGINA Yes, I dare say, but still—. Now, if it were in a good house and with a real gentleman—
MANDERS But, my dear Regina—
REGINA —one whom I could feel an affection for, and really feel in the position of a daughter to—
MANDERS Come, come—my dear good child—
REGINA I should like very much to live in town. Out here it is terribly lonely; and you know yourself, Mr. Manders, what it is to be alone in the world. And, though I say it, I really am both capable and willing. Don't you know any place that would be suitable for me, Mr. Manders?
MANDERS I? No, indeed I don't.
REGINA But, dear Mr. Manders—at any rate don't forget me, in case—

MANDERS [*getting up*] No, I won't forget you, Miss Engstrand.
REGINA Because, if I—
MANDERS Perhaps you will be so kind as to let Mrs. Alving know I am here?
REGINA I will fetch her at once, Mr. Manders.

[*Goes out to the left.* MANDERS *walks up and down the room once or twice, stands for a moment at the farther end of the room with his hands behind his back and looks out into the garden. Then he comes back to the table, takes up a book and looks at the title page, gives a start and looks at some of the others*]

MANDERS Hm!—Really!

[MRS. ALVING *comes in by the door on the left. She is followed by* REGINA, *who goes out again at once through the nearer door on the right*]

MRS. ALVING [*holding out her hand*] I am very glad to see you, Mr. Manders.
MANDERS How do you do, Mrs. Alving. Here I am, as I promised.
MRS. ALVING Always punctual!
MANDERS Indeed, I was hard put to it to get away. What with vestry meetings and committees—
MRS. ALVING It was all the kinder of you to come in such good time; we can settle our busines before dinner. But where is your luggage?
MANDERS [*quickly*] My things are down at the village shop. I am going to sleep there to-night.
MRS. ALVING [*repressing a smile*] Can't I really persuade you to stay the night here this time?
MANDERS No, no; many thanks all the same; I will put up there, as usual. It is so handy for getting on board the boat again.
MRS. ALVING Of course you shall do as you please. But it seems to me quite another thing, now we are two old people—
MANDERS Ha! ha! You will have your joke! And it's natural you should be in high spirits to-day—first of all there is the great event to-morrow, and also you have got Oswald home.
MRS. ALVING Yes, am I not a lucky woman! It is more than two years since he was home last, and he has promised to stay the whole winter with me.
MANDERS Has he, really? That is very nice and filial of him; because there must be many more attractions in his life in Rome or in Paris, I should think.
MRS. ALVING Yes, but he has his mother here, you see. Bless the dear boy, he has got a corner in his heart for his mother still.

MANDERS Oh, it would be very sad if absence and preoccupation with such a thing as Art were to dull the natural affections.

MRS. ALVING It would, indeed. But there is no fear of that with him, I am glad to say. I am quite curious to see if you recognise him again. He will be down directly; he is just lying down for a little on the sofa upstairs. But do sit down, my dear friend.

MANDERS Thank you. You are sure I am not disturbing you?

MRS. ALVING Of course not.

[*She sits down at the table*]

MANDERS Good. Then I will show you—. [*He goes to the chair where his bag is lying and takes a packet of papers from it; then sits down at the opposite side of the table and looks for a clear space to put the papers down*] Now first of all, here is—[*breaks off*] Tell me, Mrs. Alving, what are these books doing here?

MRS. ALVING These books? I am reading them.

MANDERS Do you read this sort of thing?

MRS. ALVING Certainly I do.

MANDERS Do you feel any the better or the happier for reading books of this kind?

MRS. ALVING I think it makes me, as it were, more self-reliant.

MANDERS That is remarkable. But why?

MRS. ALVING Well, they give me an explanation or a confirmation of lots of different ideas that have come into my own mind. But what surprises me, Mr. Manders, is that, properly speaking, there is nothing at all new in these books. There is nothing more in them than what most people think and believe. The only thing is, that most people either take no account of it or won't admit it to themselves.

MANDERS But, good heavens, do you seriously think that most people—?

MRS. ALVING Yes, indeed, I do.

MANDERS But not here in the country at any rate? Not here amongst people like ourselves?

MRS. ALVING Yes, amongst people like ourselves too.

MANDERS Well, really, I must say—!

MRS. ALVING But what is the particular objection that you have to these books?

MANDERS What objection? You surely don't suppose that I take any particular interest in such productions?

MRS. ALVING In fact, you don't know anything about what you are denouncing?

MANDERS I have read quite enough about these books to disapprove of them.

MRS. ALVING Yes, but your own opinion—

MANDERS My dear Mrs. Alving, there are many occasions in life when one has to rely on the opinion of others. That is the way in this world, and it is quite right that it should be so. What would become of society, otherwise?

MRS. ALVING Well, you may be right.

MANDERS Apart from that, naturally I don't deny that literature of this kind may have a considerable attraction. And I cannot blame you, either, for wishing to make yourself acquainted with the intellectual tendencies which I am told are at work in the wider world in which you have allowed your son to wander for so long. But—

MRS. ALVING But—?

MANDERS [*lowering his voice*] But one doesn't talk about it, Mrs. Alving. One certainly is not called upon to account to every one for what one reads or thinks in the privacy of one's own room.

MRS. ALVING Certainly not. I quite agree with you.

MANDERS Just think of the consideration you owe to this Orphanage, which you decided to build at a time when your thoughts on such subjects were very different from what they are now—as far as I am able to judge.

MRS. ALVING Yes, I freely admit that. But it was about the Orphanage—

MANDERS It was about the Orphanage we were going to talk; quite so. Well—walk warily, dear Mrs. Alving! And now let us turn to the business in hand. [*Opens an envelope and takes out some papers*] You see these?

MRS. ALVING The deeds?

MANDERS Yes, the whole lot—and everything in order. I can tell you it has been no easy matter to get them in time. I had positively to put pressure on the authorities; they are almost painfully conscientious when it is a question of settling property. But here they are at last. [*Turns over the papers*] Here is the deed of conveyance of that part of the Rosenvold estate known as the Solvik property, together with the building newly erected thereon—the school, the masters' houses and the chapel. And here is the legal sanction for the statutes of the institution. Here, you see—[*reads*] "Statutes for the Captain Alving Orphanage."

MRS. ALVING [*after a long look at the papers*] That seems all in order.

MANDERS I thought "Captain" was the better title to use, rather than your husband's Court title of "Chamberlain." "Captain" seems less ostentatious.

MRS. ALVING Yes, yes; just as you think best.

MANDERS And here is the certificate for the investment of the capital in the bank, the interest being earmarked for the current expenses of the Orphanage.

MRS. ALVING Many thanks; but I think it will be most convenient if you will kindly take charge of them.

MANDERS With pleasure. I think it will be best to leave the money in the bank for the present. The interest is not very high, it is true; four per cent at six months' call. Later on, if we can find some good mortgage—of course it must be a first mortgage and on unexceptionable security—we can consider the matter further.

MRS. ALVING Yes, yes, my dear Mr. Manders, you know best about all that.

MANDERS I will keep my eye on it, anyway. But there is one thing in connection with it that I have often meant to ask you about.

MRS. ALVING What is that?

MANDERS Shall we insure the buildings, or not?

MRS. ALVING Of course we must insure them.

MANDERS Ah, but wait a moment, dear lady. Let us look into the matter a little more closely.

MRS. ALVING Everything of mine is insured—the house and its contents, my livestock—everything.

MANDERS Naturally. They are your own property. I do exactly the same, of course. But this, you see, is quite a different case. The Orphanage is, so to speak, dedicated to higher uses.

MRS. ALVING Certainly, but—

MANDERS As far as I am personally concerned, I can conscientiously say that I don't see the smallest objection to our insuring ourselves against all risks.

MRS. ALVING That is exactly what I think.

MANDERS But what about the opinion of the people hereabouts?

MRS. ALVING Their opinion—?

MANDERS Is there any considerable body of opinion here—opinion of some account, I mean—that might take exception to it?

MRS. ALVING What, exactly, do you mean by opinion of some account?

MANDERS Well, I was thinking particularly of persons of such independent and influential position that one could hardly refuse to attach weight to their opinion.

MRS. ALVING There are a certain number of such people here, who might perhaps take exception to it if we—

MANDERS That's just it, you see. In town there are lots of them. All my fellow-clergymen's congregations, for instance! It would be so extremely easy for them to interpret it as meaning that neither you nor I had a proper reliance on Divine protection.

MRS. ALVING But as far as you are concerned, my dear friend, you have at all events the consciousness that—

MANDERS Yes, I know, I know; my own mind is quite easy about it, it is true. But we should not be able to prevent a wrong and injurious interpretation of our action. And that sort of thing, moreover, might very easily end in exercising a hampering influence on the work of the Orphanage.

MRS. ALVING Oh, well, if that is likely to be the effect of it—

MANDERS Nor can I entirely overlook the difficult—indeed, I may say, painful—position I might possibly be placed in. In the best circles in town the matter of this Orphanage is attracting a great deal of attention. Indeed the Orphanage is to some extent built for the benefit of the town too, and it is to be hoped that it may result in the lowering of our poor-rate by a considerable amount. But as I have been your adviser in the matter and have taken charge of the business side of it, I should be afraid that it would be I that spiteful persons would attack first of all—

MRS. ALVING Yes, you ought not to expose yourself to that.

MANDERS Not to mention the attacks that would undoubtedly be made upon me in certain newspapers and reviews—

MRS. ALVING Say no more about it, dear Mr. Manders; that quite decides it.

MANDERS Then you don't wish it to be insured?

MRS. ALVING No, we will give up the idea.

MANDERS [leaning back in his chair] But suppose, now, that some accident happened?—one can never tell—would you be prepared to make good the damage?

MRS. ALVING No; I tell you quite plainly I would not do so under any circumstances.

MANDERS Still, you know, Mrs. Alving—after all, it is a serious responsibility that we are taking upon ourselves.

MRS. ALVING But do you think we can do otherwise?

MANDERS No, that's just it. We really can't do otherwise. We ought not to expose ourselves to a mistaken judgment; and we have no right to do anything that will scandalise the community.

MRS. ALVING You ought not to, as a clergyman, at any rate.

MANDERS And, what is more, I certainly think that we may count upon our enterprise being attended by good fortune—indeed, that it will be under a special protection.

MRS. ALVING Let us hope so, Mr. Manders.
MANDERS Then we will leave it alone?
MRS. ALVING Certainly.
MANDERS Very good. As you wish. [*Makes a note*] No insurance, then.
MRS. ALVING It's a funny thing that you should just have happened to speak about that to-day—
MANDERS I have often meant to ask you about it—
MRS. ALVING —because yesterday we very nearly had a fire up there.
MANDERS Do you mean it!
MRS. ALVING Oh, as a matter of fact it was nothing of any consequence. Some shavings in the carpenter's shop caught fire.
MANDERS Where Engstrand works?
MRS. ALVING Yes. They say he is often so careless with matches.
MANDERS He has so many things on his mind, poor fellow—so many anxieties. Heaven be thanked, I am told he is really making an effort to live a blameless life.
MRS. ALVING Really? Who told you so?
MANDERS He assured me himself that it is so. He's a good workman, too.
MRS. ALVING Oh, yes, when he is sober.
MANDERS Ah, that sad weakness of his! But the pain in his poor leg often drives him to it, he tells me. The last time he was in town, I was really quite touched by him. He came to my house and thanked me so gratefully for getting him work here, where he could have the chance of being with Regina.
MRS. ALVING He doesn't see very much of her.
MANDERS But he assured me that he saw her every day.
MRS. ALVING Oh well, perhaps he does.
MANDERS He feels so strongly that he needs some one who can keep a hold on him when temptations assail him. That is the most winning thing about Jacob Engstrand; he comes to one like a helpless child and accuses himself and confesses his frailty. The last time he came and had a talk with me—. Suppose now, Mrs. Alving, that it were really a necessity of his existence to have Regina at home with him again—
MRS. ALVING [*standing up suddenly*] Regina!
MANDERS —you ought not to set yourself against him.
MRS. ALVING Indeed, I set myself very definitely against that. And, besides, you know Regina is to have a post in the Orphanage.
MANDERS But consider, after all he is her father—
MRS. ALVING I know best what sort of a father he has been to her. No, she shall never go to him with my consent.

MANDERS [*getting up*] My dear lady, don't judge so hastily. It is very sad how you misjudge poor Engstrand. One would really think you were afraid—

MRS. ALVING [*more calmly*] That is not the question. I have taken Regina into my charge, and in my charge she remains. [*Listens.*] Hush, dear Mr. Manders, don't say any more about it. [*Her face brightens with pleasure*] Listen! Oswald is coming downstairs. We will only think about him now.

[OSWALD ALVING, *in a light overcoat, hat in hand and smoking a big meerschaum pipe, comes in by the door on the left*]

OSWALD [*standing in the doorway*] Oh, I beg your pardon, I thought you were in the office. [*Comes in*] Good morning, Mr. Manders.

MANDERS [*staring at him*] Well! It's most extraordinary—

MRS. ALVING Yes, what do you think of him, Mr. Manders?

MANDERS I—I—no, can it possibly be—?

OSWALD Yes, it really is the prodigal son, Mr. Manders.

MANDERS Oh, my dear young friend—

OSWALD Well, the son come home, then.

MRS. ALVING Oswald is thinking of the time when you were so opposed to the idea of his being a painter.

MANDERS We are only fallible, and many steps seem to us hazardous at first, that afterwards—[*grasps his hand*] Welcome, welcome! Really, my dear Oswald—may I still call you Oswald?

OSWALD What else would you think of calling me?

MANDERS Thank you. What I mean, my dear Oswald, is that you must not imagine that I have any unqualified disapproval of the artist's life. I admit that there are many who, even in that career, can keep the inner man free from harm.

OSWALD Let us hope so.

MRS. ALVING [*beaming with pleasure*] I know one who has kept both the inner and the outer man free from harm. Just take a look at him, Mr. Manders.

OSWALD [*walks across the room*] Yes, yes, mother dear, of course.

MANDERS Undoubtedly—no one can deny it. And I hear you have begun to make a name for yourself. I have often seen mention of you in the papers—and extremely favourable mention, too. Although, I must admit, latterly I have not seen your name so often.

OSWALD [*going towards the conservatory*] I haven't done so much painting just lately.

MRS. ALVING An artist must take a rest sometimes, like other people.

MANDERS Of course, of course. At those times the artist is preparing and strengthening himself for a greater effort.
OSWALD Yes. Mother, will dinner soon be ready?
MRS. ALVING In half an hour. He has a fine appetite, thank goodness.
MANDERS And a liking for tobacco, too.
OSWALD I found father's pipe in the room upstairs, and—
MANDERS Ah, that is what it was!
MRS. ALVING What?
MANDERS When Oswald came in at that door with the pipe in his mouth, I thought for the moment it was his father in the flesh.
OSWALD Really?
MRS. ALVING How can you say so! Oswald takes after me.
MANDERS Yes, but there is an expression about the corners of his mouth—something about the lips—that reminds me so exactly of Mr. Alving—especially when he smokes.
MRS. ALVING I don't think so at all. To my mind, Oswald has much more of a clergyman's mouth.
MANDERS Well, yes—a good many of my colleagues in the church have a similar expression.
MRS. ALVING But put your pipe down, my dear boy. I don't allow any smoking in here.
OSWALD [puts down his pipe] All right, I only wanted to try it, because I smoked it once when I was a child.
MRS. ALVING You?
OSWALD Yes; it was when I was quite a little chap. And I can remember going upstairs to father's room one evening when he was in very good spirits.
MRS. ALVING Oh, you can't remember anything about those days.
OSWALD Yes, I remember plainly that he took me on his knee and let me smoke his pipe. "Smoke, my boy," he said, "have a good smoke, boy!" And I smoked as hard as I could, until I felt I was turning quite pale and the perspiration was standing in great drops on my forehead. Then he laughed—such a hearty laugh—
MANDERS It was an extremely odd thing to do.
MRS. ALVING Dear Mr. Manders, Oswald only dreamt it.
OSWALD No indeed, mother, it was no dream. Because—don't you remember—you came into the room and carried me off to the nursery, where I was sick, and I saw that you were crying. Did father often play such tricks?
MANDERS In his young days he was full of fun—

OSWALD And, for all that, he did so much with his life—so much that was good and useful, I mean—short as his life was.

MANDERS Yes, my dear Oswald Alving, you have inherited the name of a man who undoubtedly was both energetic and worthy. Let us hope it will be a spur to your energies—

OSWALD It ought to be, certainly.

MANDERS In any case it was nice of you to come home for the day that is to honour his memory.

OSWALD I could do no less for my father.

MRS. ALVING And to let me keep him so long here—that's the nicest part of what he has done.

MANDERS Yes, I hear you are going to spend the winter at home.

OSWALD I am here for an indefinite time, Mr. Manders.—Oh, it's good to be at home again!

MRS. ALVING [*beaming*] Yes, isn't it!

MANDERS [*looking sympathetically at him*] You went out into the world very young, my dear Oswald.

OSWALD I did. Sometimes I wonder if I wasn't too young.

MRS. ALVING Not a bit of it. It is the best thing for an active boy, and especially for an only child. It's a pity when they are kept at home with their parents and get spoilt.

MANDERS That is a very debatable question, Mrs. Alving. A child's own home is, and always must be, his proper place.

OSWALD There I agree entirely with Mr. Manders.

MANDERS Take the case of your own son. Oh yes, we can talk about it before him. What has the result been in his case? He is six or seven and twenty, and has never yet had the opportunity of learning what a well-regulated home means.

OSWALD Excuse me, Mr. Manders, you are quite wrong there.

MANDERS Indeed? I imagined that your life abroad had practically been spent entirely in artistic circles.

OSWALD So it has.

MANDERS And chiefly amongst the younger artists.

OSWALD Certainly.

MANDERS But I imagined that those gentry, as a rule, had not the means necessary for family life and the support of a home.

OSWALD There are a considerable number of them who have not the means to marry, Mr. Manders.

MANDERS That is exactly my point.

OSWALD But they can have a home of their own, all the same; a good

many of them have. And they are very well-regulated and very comfortable homes, too.
[MRS. ALVING, *who has listened to him attentively, nods assent, but says nothing*]
MANDERS Oh, but I am not talking of bachelor establishments. By a home I mean family life—the life a man lives with his wife and children.
OSWALD Exactly, or with his children and his children's mother.
MANDERS [*starts and clasps his hands*] Good heavens!
OSWALD What is the matter?
MANDERS Lives with—with—his children's mother!
OSWALD Well, would you rather he should repudiate his children's mother?
MANDERS Then what you are speaking of are those unprincipled conditions known as irregular unions!
OSWALD I have never noticed anything particularly unprincipled about these people's lives.
MANDERS But do you mean to say that it is possible for a man of any sort of bringing up, and a young woman, to reconcile themselves to such a way of living—and to make no secret of it, either?
OSWALD What else are they to do? A poor artist, and a poor girl—it costs a good deal to get married. What else are they to do?
MANDERS What are they to do? Well, Mr. Alving, I will tell you what they ought to do. They ought to keep away from each other from the very beginning—that is what they ought to do!
OSWALD That advice wouldn't have much effect upon hot-blooded young folk who are in love.
MRS. ALVING No, indeed it wouldn't.
MANDERS [*persistently*] And to think that the authorities tolerate such things! That they are allowed to go on, openly! [*Turns to* MRS. ALVING] Had I so little reason, then, to be sadly concerned about your son? In circles where open immorality is rampant—where, one may say, it is honoured—
OSWALD Let me tell you this, Mr. Manders. I have been a constant Sunday guest at one or two of these "irregular" households—
MANDERS On Sunday, too!
OSWALD Yes, that is the day of leisure. But never have I heard one objectionable word there, still less have I ever seen anything that could be called immoral. No; but do you know when and where I *have* met with immorality in artists' circles?
MANDERS No, thank heaven, I don't!

OSWALD Well, then, I shall have the pleasure of telling you. I have met with it when some one or other of your model husbands and fathers have come out there to have a bit of a look round on their own account, and have done the artists the honour of looking them up in their humble quarters. Then we had a chance of learning something, I can tell you. These gentlemen were able to instruct us about places and things that we had never so much as dreamt of.

MANDERS What? Do you want me to believe that honourable men when they get away from home will—

OSWALD Have you never, when these same honourable men come home again, heard them deliver themselves on the subject of the prevalence of immorality abroad?

MANDERS Yes, of course, but—

MRS. ALVING I have heard them, too.

OSWALD Well, you take their word for it, unhesitatingly. Some of them are experts in the matter. [*Putting his hands to his head*] To think that the glorious freedom of the beautiful life over there should be so besmirched!

MRS. ALVING You mustn't get too heated, Oswald; you gain nothing by that.

OSWALD No, you are quite right, mother. Besides, it isn't good for me. It's because I am so infernally tired, you know. I will go out and take a turn before dinner. I beg your pardon, Mr. Manders. It is impossible for you to realise the feeling; but it takes me that way.
[*Goes out by the farther door on the right*]

MRS. ALVING My poor boy!

MANDERS You may well say so. This is what it has brought him to! [MRS. ALVING *looks steadily at him, but does not speak*] He called himself the prodigal son. It's only too true, alas—only too true! [MRS. ALVING *looks steadily at him*] And what do you say to all this?

MRS. ALVING I say that Oswald was right in every single word he said.

MANDERS Right? Right? To hold such principles as that?

MRS. ALVING In my loneliness here I have come to just the same opinions as he, Mr. Manders. But I have never presumed to venture upon such topics in conversation. Now there is no need; my boy shall speak for me.

MANDERS You deserve the deepest pity, Mrs. Alving. It is my duty to say an earnest word to you. It is no longer your business man and adviser, no longer your old friend and your dead husband's old friend, that stands before you now. It is your priest that stands before you, just as he did once at the most critical moment of your life.

MRS. ALVING And what is it that my priest has to say to me?

MANDERS First of all I must stir your memory. The moment is well chosen. To-morrow is the tenth anniversary of your husband's death; to-morrow the memorial to the departed will be unveiled; to-morrow I shall speak to the whole assembly that will be met together. But to-day I want to speak to you alone.

MRS. ALVING Very well, Mr. Manders, speak!

MANDERS Have you forgotten that after barely a year of married life you were standing at the very edge of a precipice?—that you forsook your house and home?—that you ran away from your husband—yes, Mrs. Alving, ran away, ran away—and refused to return to him in spite of his requests and entreaties?

MRS. ALVING Have you forgotten how unspeakably unhappy I was during that first year?

MANDERS To crave for happiness in this world is simply to be possessed by a spirit of revolt. What right have we to happiness? No! we must do our duty, Mrs. Alving. And your duty was to cleave to the man you had chosen and to whom you were bound by a sacred bond.

MRS. ALVING You know quite well what sort of a life my husband was living at that time—what excesses he was guilty of.

MANDERS I know only too well what rumour used to say of him; and I should be the last person to approve of his conduct as a young man, supposing that rumour spoke the truth. But it is not a wife's part to be her husband's judge. You should have considered it your bounden duty humbly to have borne the cross that a higher will had laid upon you. But, instead of that, you rebelliously cast off your cross, you deserted the man whose stumbling footsteps you should have supported, you did what was bound to imperil your good name and reputation, and came very near to imperilling the reputation of others into the bargain.

MRS. ALVING Of others? Of one other, you mean.

MANDERS It was the height of imprudence, your seeking refuge with me.

MRS. ALVING With our priest? With our intimate friend?

MANDERS All the more on that account. You should thank God that I possessed the necessary strength of mind—that I was able to turn you from your outrageous intention, and that it was vouchsafed to me to succeed in leading you back into the path of duty and back to your lawful husband.

MRS. ALVING Yes, Mr. Manders, that certainly was your doing.

MANDERS I was but the humble instrument of a higher power. And is it not true that my having been able to bring you again under the yoke of duty and obedience sowed the seeds of a rich blessing on all the rest of your life? Did things not turn out as I foretold to you? Did not your husband turn from straying in the wrong path as a man should? Did he not, after all, live a life of love and good report with you all his days? Did he not become a benefactor to the neighbourhood? Did he not so raise you up to his level, so that by degrees you became his fellow-worker in all his undertakings—and a noble fellow-worker, too, I know, Mrs. Alving; that praise I will give you.—But now I come to the second serious false step in your life.

MRS. ALVING What do you mean?

MANDERS Just as once you forsook your duty as a wife, so, since then, you have forsaken your duty as a mother.

MRS. ALVING Oh—!

MANDERS You have been overmastered all your life by a disastrous spirit of wilfulness. All your impulses have led you towards what is undisciplined and lawless. You have never been willing to submit to any restraint. Anything in life that has seemed irksome to you, you have thrown aside recklessly and unscrupulously, as if it were a burden that you were free to rid yourself of if you would. It did not please you to be a wife any longer, and so you left your husband. Your duties as a mother were irksome to you, so you sent your child away among strangers.

MRS. ALVING Yes, that is true; I did that.

MANDERS And that is why you have become a stranger to him.

MRS. ALVING No, no, I am not that!

MANDERS You are; you must be. And what sort of a son is it that you have got back? Think over it seriously, Mrs. Alving. You erred grievously in your husband's case—you acknowledged as much, by erecting this memorial to him. Now you are bound to acknowledge how much you have erred in your son's case; possibly there may still be time to reclaim him from the paths of wickedness. Turn over a new leaf, and set yourself to reform what there may still be that is capable of reformation in him. Because [*with uplifted forefinger*] in very truth, Mrs. Alving, you are a guilty mother!—That is what I have thought it my duty to say to you.

[*A short silence*]

MRS. ALVING [*speaking slowly and with self-control*] You have had your say, Mr. Manders, and to-morrow you will be making a public speech in memory of my husband. I shall not speak to-morrow. But now I wish to speak to you for a little, just as you have been speaking to me.

MANDERS By all means; no doubt you wish to bring forward some excuses for your behaviour—

MRS. ALVING No. I only want to tell you something.

MANDERS Well?

MRS. ALVING In all that you said just now about me and my husband, and about our life together after you had, as you put it, led me back into the path of duty—there was nothing that you knew at first hand. From that moment you never again set foot in our house—you, who had been our daily companion before that.

MANDERS Remember that you and your husband moved out of town immediately afterwards.

MRS. ALVING Yes, and you never once came out here to see us in my husband's lifetime. It was only the business in connection with the Orphanage that obliged you to come and see me.

MANDERS [*in a low and uncertain voice*] Helen—if that is a reproach, I can only beg you to consider—

MRS. ALVING—the respect you owed to your calling?—yes. All the more as I was a wife who had tried to run away from her husband. One can never be too careful to have nothing to do with such reckless women.

MANDERS My dear—Mrs. Alving, you are exaggerating dreadfully—

MRS. ALVING Yes, yes,—very well. What I mean is this, that when you condemn my conduct as a wife you have nothing more to go upon than ordinary public opinion.

MANDERS I admit it. What then?

MRS. ALVING Well—now, Mr. Manders, now I am going to tell you the truth. I had sworn to myself that you should know it one day—you, and you only!

MANDERS And what may the truth be?

MRS. ALVING The truth is this, that my husband died just as great a profligate as he had been all his life.

MANDERS [*feeling for a chair*] What are you saying?

MRS. ALVING After nineteen years of married life, just as profligate—in his desires at all events—as he was before you married us.

MANDERS And can you talk of his youthful indiscretions—his irregularities—his excesses, if you like—as a profligate life!

MRS. ALVING That was what the doctor who attended him called it.

MANDERS I don't understand what you mean.

MRS. ALVING It is not necessary you should.

MANDERS It makes my brain reel. To think that your marriage—all the years of wedded life you spent with your husband—were nothing but a hidden abyss of misery.

MRS. ALVING That and nothing else. Now you know.

MANDERS This—this bewilders me. I can't understand it! I can't grasp it! How in the world was it possible—? How could such a state of things remain concealed?

MRS. ALVING That was just what I had to fight for incessantly, day after day. When Oswald was born, I thought I saw a slight improvement. But it didn't last long. And after that I had to fight doubly hard—fight a desperate fight so that no one should know what sort of a man my child's father was. You know quite well what an attractive manner he had; it seemed as if people could believe nothing but good of him. He was one of those men whose mode of life seems to have no effect upon their reputations. But at last, Mr. Manders—you must hear this too—at last something happened more abominable than everything else.

MANDERS More abominable than what you have told me!

MRS. ALVING I had borne with it all, though I knew only too well what he indulged in in secret, when he was out of the house. But when it came to the point of the scandal coming within our four walls—

MANDERS Can you mean it! Here?

MRS. ALVING Yes, here, in our own home. It was in there [*pointing to the nearer door on the right*] in the dining-room that I got the first hint of it. I had something to do in there and the door was standing ajar. I heard our maid come up from the garden with water for the flowers in the conservatory.

MANDERS Well—?

MRS. ALVING Shortly afterwards I heard my husband come in too. I heard him say something to her in a low voice. And then I heard—[*with a short laugh*]—oh, it rings in my ears still, with its mixture of what was heartbreaking and what was so ridiculous—I heard my own servant whisper: "Let me go, Mr. Alving! Let me be!"

MANDERS What unseemly levity on his part! But surely nothing more than levity, Mrs. Alving, believe me.

MRS. ALVING I soon knew what to believe. My husband had his will of the girl—and that intimacy had consequences, Mr. Manders.

MANDERS [*as if turned to stone*] And all that in this house! In this house!

MRS. ALVING I have suffered a good deal in this house. To keep him at home in the evening—and at night—I have had to play the part of boon companion in his secret drinking-bouts in his room up there. I have had to sit there alone with him, have had to hobnob and drink with him, have had to listen to his ribald senseless talk, have had to fight with brute force to get him to bed—

MANDERS [*trembling*] And you were able to endure all this!

MRS. ALVING I had my little boy, and endured it for his sake. But when the crowning insult came—when my own servant—then I made up my mind that there should be an end of it. I took the upper hand in the house, absolutely—both with him and all the others. I had a weapon to use against him, you see; he didn't dare to speak. It was then that Oswald was sent away. He was about seven then, and was beginning to notice things and ask questions as children will. I couldn't endure all that, my friend. It seemed to me that the child would be poisoned if he breathed the air of this polluted house. That was why I sent him away. And now you understand, too, why he never set foot here as long as his father was alive. No one knows what it meant to me.

MANDERS You have indeed had a pitiable experience.

MRS. ALVING I could never have gone through with it, if I had not had my work. Indeed, I can boast that I have worked. All the increase in the value of the property, all the improvements, all the useful arrangement that my husband got the honour and glory of—do you suppose that he troubled himself about any of them? He, who used to lie the whole day on the sofa reading old Official Lists! No, you may as well know that too. It was I that kept him up to the mark when he had his lucid intervals; it was I that had to bear the whole burden of it when he began his excesses again or took to whining about his miserable condition.

MANDERS And this is the man you are building a memorial to!

MRS. ALVING There you see the power of an uneasy conscience.

MANDERS An uneasy conscience? What do you mean?

MRS. ALVING I had always before me the fear that it was impossible that the truth should not come out and be believed. That is why the Orphanage is to exist, to silence all rumours and clear away all doubt.

MANDERS You certainly have not fallen short of the mark in that, Mrs. Alving.

MRS. ALVING I had another very good reason. I did not wish Oswald, my own son, to inherit a penny that belonged to his father.

MANDERS Then it is with Mr. Alving's property—

MRS. ALVING Yes. The sums of money that, year after year, I have given towards this Orphanage, make up the amount of property—I have reckoned it carefully—which in the old days made Lieutenant Alving a catch.

MANDERS I understand.

MRS. ALVING That was my purchase money. I don't wish it to pass into Oswald's hands. My son shall have everything from me, I am determined.

[OSWALD *comes in by the farther door on the right. He has left his hat and coat outside*]

MRS. ALVING Back again, my own dear boy?

OSWALD Yes, what can one do outside in this everlasting rain? I hear dinner is nearly ready. That's good!

[REGINA *comes in from the dining-room, carrying a parcel*]

REGINA This parcel has come for you, ma'am.

[*Gives it to her*]

MRS. ALVING [*glancing at* MANDERS] The ode to be sung to-morrow, I expect.

MANDERS Hm—!

REGINA And dinner is ready.

MRS. ALVING Good. We will come in a moment. I will just—[*begins to open the parcel*].

REGINA [*to* OSWALD] Will you drink white or red wine, sir?

OSWALD Both, Miss Engstrand.

REGINA *Bien*—very good, Mr. Alving.

[*Goes into the dining-room*]

OSWALD I may as well help you to uncork it—.

[*Follows her into the dining-room, leaving the door ajar after him*]

MRS. ALVING Yes, I thought so. Here is the ode, Mr. Manders.

MANDERS [*clasping his hands*] How shall I ever have the courage to-morrow to speak the address that—

MRS. ALVING Oh, you will get through it.

MANDERS [*in a low voice, fearing to be heard in the dining-room*] Yes, we must raise no suspicions.

MRS. ALVING [*quietly but firmly*] No; and then this long dreadful comedy will be at an end. After to-morrow, I shall feel as if my dead husband had never lived in this house. There will be no one else here then but my boy and his mother.

[*From the dining-room is heard the noise of a chair falling; then* REGINA'S *voice is heard in a loud whisper*: Oswald! Are you mad? Let me go!]

MRS. ALVING [*starting in horror*] Oh—!

[*She stares wildly at the half-open door.* OSWALD *is heard coughing and humming, then the sound of a bottle being uncorked*]

MANDERS [*in an agitated manner*] What's the matter? What is it, Mrs. Alving?

MRS. ALVING [*hoarsely*] Ghosts. The couple in the conservatory—over again.
MANDERS What are you saying! Regina—? Is she—?
MRS. ALVING Yes. Come. Not a word—!
[*Grips* MANDERS *by the arm and walks unsteadily with him into the dining-room*]

Act II

The same scene. The landscape is still obscured by mist. MANDERS *and* MRS. ALVING *come in from the dining-room.*

MRS. ALVING [*calls into the dining-room from the doorway*] Aren't you coming in here, Oswald?
OSWALD No, thanks; I think I will go out for a bit.
MRS. ALVING Yes, do; the weather is clearing a little. [*She shuts the dining-room door, then goes to the hall door and calls*] Regina!
REGINA [*from without*] Yes, ma'am?
MRS. ALVING Go down into the laundry and help with the garlands.
REGINA Yes, ma'am.
[MRS. ALVING *satisfies herself that she has gone, then shuts the door*]
MANDERS I suppose he can't hear us?
MRS. ALVING Not when the door is shut. Besides, he is going out.
MANDERS I am still quite bewildered. I don't know how I managed to swallow a mouthful of your excellent dinner.
MRS. ALVING [*walking up and down, and trying to control her agitation*] Nor I. But what are we to do?
MANDERS Yes, what are we to do? Upon my word I don't know; I am so completely unaccustomed to things of this kind.
MRS. ALVING I am convinced that nothing serious has happened yet.
MANDERS Heaven forbid! But it is most unseemly behaviour, for all that.
MRS. ALVING It is nothing more than a foolish jest of Oswald's, you may be sure.
MANDERS Well, of course, as I said, I am quite inexperienced in such matters; but it certainly seems to me—
MRS. ALVING Out of the house she shall go—and at once. That part of it it as clear as daylight—
MANDERS Yes, that is quite clear.
MRS. ALVING But where is she to go? We should not be justified in—
MANDERS Where to? Home to her father, of course.
MRS. ALVING To whom, did you say?

MANDERS To her—. No, of course Engstrand isn't—. But, great heavens, Mrs. Alving, how is such a thing possible? You surely may have been mistaken, in spite of everything.
MRS. ALVING There was no chance of mistake, more's the pity. Joanna was obliged to confess it to me—and my husband couldn't deny it. So there was nothing else to do but to hush it up.
MANDERS No, that was the only thing to do.
MRS. ALVING The girl was sent away at once, and was given a tolerably liberal sum to hold her tongue. She looked after the rest herself when she got to town. She renewed an old acquaintance with the carpenter Engstrand; gave him a hint, I suppose, of how much money she had got, and told him some fairy tale about a foreigner who had been here in his yacht in the summer. So she and Engstrand were married in a great hurry. Why, you married them yourself!
MANDERS I can't understand it—. I remember clearly Engstrand's coming to arrange about the marriage. He was full of contrition, and accused himself bitterly for the light conduct he and his fiancée had been guilty of.
MRS. ALVING Of course he had to take the blame on himself.
MANDERS But the deceitfulness of it! And with me, too! I positively would not have believed it of Jacob Engstrand. I shall most certainly give him a serious talking to.—And the immorality of such a marriage! Simply for the sake of the money—! What sum was it that the girl had?
MRS. ALVING It was seventy pounds.
MANDERS Just think of it—for a paltry seventy pounds to let yourself be bound in marriage to a fallen woman!
MRS. ALVING What about myself, then?—I let myself be bound in marriage to a fallen man.
MANDERS Heaven forgive you! what are you saying? A fallen man?
MRS. ALVING Do you suppose my husband was any purer, when I went with him to the altar, than Joanna was when Engstrand agreed to marry her?
MANDERS The two cases are as different as day from night—
MRS. ALVING Not so very different, after all. It is true there was a great difference in the price paid, between a paltry seventy pounds and a whole fortune.
MANDERS How can you compare such totally different things! I presume you consulted your own heart—and your relations.
MRS. ALVING [*looking away from him*] I thought you understood where what you call my heart had strayed to at that time.

MANDERS [*in a constrained voice*] If I had understood anything of the kind, I would not have been a daily guest in your husband's house.
MRS. ALVING Well, at any rate this much is certain, that I didn't consult myself in the matter at all.
MANDERS Still you consulted those nearest to you, as was only right—your mother, your two aunts.
MRS. ALVING Yes, that is true. The three of them settled the whole matter for me. It seems incredible to me now, how clearly they made out that it would be sheer folly to reject such an offer. If my mother could only see what all that fine prospect has led to!
MANDERS No one can be responsible for the result of it. Anyway, there is this to be said, that the match was made in complete conformity with law and order.
MRS. ALVING [*going to the window*] Oh, law and order! I often think it is that that is at the bottom of all the misery in the world.
MANDERS Mrs. Alving, it is very wicked of you to say that.
MRS. ALVING That may be so; but I don't attach importance to those obligations and considerations any longer. I cannot! I must struggle for my freedom.
MANDERS What do you mean?
MRS. ALVING [*tapping on the window panes*] I ought never to have concealed what sort of a life my husband led. But I had not the courage to do otherwise then—for my own sake, either. I was too much of a coward.
MANDERS A coward?
MRS. ALVING If others had known anything of what happened, they would have said: "Poor man, it is natural enough that he should go astray, when he has a wife that has run away from him."
MANDERS They would have had a certain amount of justification for saying so.
MRS. ALVING [*looking fixedly at him*] If I had been the woman I ought, I would have taken Oswald into my confidence and said to him: "Listen, my son, your father was a dissolute man"—
MANDERS Miserable woman—
MRS. ALVING —and I would have told him all I have told you, from beginning to end.
MANDERS I am almost shocked at you, Mrs. Alving.
MRS. ALVING I know. I know quite well! I am shocked at myself when I think of it. [*Comes away from the window*] I am coward enough for that.

MANDERS Can you call it cowardice that you simply did your duty! Have you forgotten that a child should love and honour his father and mother?

MRS. ALVING Don't let us talk in such general terms. Suppose we say: "Ought Oswald to love and honour Mr. Alving?"

MANDERS You are a mother—isn't there a voice in your heart that forbids you to shatter your son's ideals?

MRS. ALVING And what about the truth?

MANDERS What about his ideals?

MRS. ALVING Oh—ideals, ideals! If only I were not such a coward as I am!

MANDERS Do not spurn ideals, Mrs. Alving—they have a way of avenging themselves cruelly. Take Oswald's own case, now. He hasn't many ideals, more's the pity. But this much I have seen, that his father is something of an ideal to him.

MRS. ALVING You are right there.

MANDERS And his conception of his father is what you inspired and encouraged by your letters.

MRS. ALVING Yes, I was swayed by duty and consideration for others; that was why I lied to my son, year in and year out. Oh, what a coward—what a coward I have been!

MANDERS You have built up a happy illusion in your son's mind, Mrs. Alving—and that is a thing you certainly ought not to undervalue.

MRS. ALVING Ah, who knows if that is such a desirable thing after all!—But anyway I don't intend to put up with any goings on with Regina. I am not going to let him get the poor girl into trouble.

MANDERS Good heavens, no—that would be a frightful thing!

MRS. ALVING If only I knew whether he meant it seriously, and whether it would mean happiness for him—

MANDERS In what way? I don't understand.

MRS. ALVING But that is impossible; Regina is not equal to it, unfortunately.

MANDERS I don't understand. What do you mean?

MRS. ALVING If I were not such a miserable coward, I would say to him: "Marry her, or make any arrangement you like with her—only let there be no deceit in the matter."

MANDERS Heaven forgive you! Are you actually suggesting anything so abominable, so unheard of, as a marriage between them!

MRS. ALVING Unheard of, do you call it? Tell me honestly, Mr. Manders, don't you suppose there are plenty of married couples out here in the country that are just as nearly related as they are?

MANDERS I am sure I don't understand you.

MRS. ALVING Indeed you do.
MANDERS I suppose you are thinking of cases where possibly—. It is only too true, unfortunately, that family life is not always as stainless as it should be. But as for the sort of thing you hint at—well, it's impossible to tell, at all events with any certainty. Here, on the other hand—for you, a mother, to be willing to allow your—
MRS. ALVING But I am not willing to allow it. I would not allow it for anything in the world; that is just what I was saying.
MANDERS No, because you are a coward, as you put it. But, supposing you were not a coward—! Great heavens—such a revolting union!
MRS. ALVING Well, for the matter of that, we are all descended from a union of that description, so we are told. And who was it that was responsible for this state of things, Mr. Manders?
MANDERS I can't discuss such questions with you, Mrs. Alving; you are by no means in the right frame of mind for that. But for you to dare to say that it is cowardly of you—!
MRS. ALVING I will tell you what I mean by that. I am frightened and timid, because I am obsessed by the presence of ghosts that I never can get rid of.
MANDERS The presence of what?
MRS. ALVING Ghosts. When I heard Regina and Oswald in there, it was just like seeing ghosts before my eyes. I am half inclined to think we are all ghosts, Mr. Manders. It is not only what we have inherited from our fathers and mothers that exists again in us, but all sorts of old dead ideas and all kinds of old dead beliefs and things of that kind. They are not actually alive in us; but there they are dormant, all the same, and we can never be rid of them. Whenever I take up a newspaper and read it, I fancy I see ghosts creeping between the lines. There must be ghosts all over the world. They must be as countless as the grains of the sands, it seems to me. And we are so miserably afraid of the light, all of us.
MANDERS Ah!—there we have the outcome of your reading. Fine fruit it has borne—this abominable, subversive, free-thinking literature!
MRS. ALVING You are wrong there, my friend. You are the one who made me begin to think; and I owe you my best thanks for it.
MANDERS I!
MRS. ALVING Yes, by forcing me to submit to what you called my duty and my obligations; by praising as right and just what my whole soul revolted against, as it would against something abominable. That was what led me to examine your teachings critically. I only wanted to unravel one point in them; but as soon as I had got that unravelled, the

whole fabric came to pieces. And then I realised that it was only machine-made.

MANDERS [*softly, and with emotion*] Is that all I accomplished by the hardest struggle of my life?

MRS. ALVING Call it rather the most ignominious defeat of your life.

MANDERS It was the greatest victory of my life, Helen; victory over myself.

MRS. ALVING It was a wrong done to both of us.

MANDERS A wrong?—wrong for me to entreat you as a wife to go back to your lawful husband, when you came to me half distracted and crying: "Here I am, take me!" Was that a wrong?

MRS. ALVING I think it was.

MANDERS We two do not understand one another.

MRS. ALVING Not now, at all events.

MANDERS Never—even in my most secret thoughts—have I for a moment regarded you as anything but the wife of another.

MRS. ALVING Do you believe what you say?

MANDERS Helen—!

MRS. ALVING One so easily forgets one's own feelings.

MANDERS Not I. I am the same as I always was.

MRS. ALVING Yes, yes—don't let us talk any more about the old days. You are buried up to your eyes now in committees and all sorts of business; and I am here, fighting with ghosts both without and within me.

MANDERS I can at all events help you to get the better of those without you. After all that I have been horrified to hear from you to-day, I cannot conscientiously allow a young defenceless girl to remain in your house.

MRS. ALVING Don't you think it would be best if we could get her settled?—by some suitable marriage, I mean.

MANDERS Undoubtedly. I think, in any case, it would have been desirable for her. Regina is at an age now that—well, I don't know much about these things, but—

MRS. ALVING Regina developed very early.

MANDERS Yes, didn't she. I fancy I remember thinking she was remarkably well developed, bodily, at the time I prepared her for Confirmation. But, for the time being she must in any case go home. Under her father's care—no, but of course Engstrand is not—. To think that he, of all men, could so conceal the truth from me!

[*A knock is heard at the hall door*]

MRS. ALVING Who can that be? Come in!
[ENGSTRAND, *dressed in his Sunday clothes, appears in the doorway*]
ENGSTRAND I humbly beg pardon, but—
MANDERS Aha! Hm!—
MRS. ALVING Oh, it's you, Engstrand!
ENGSTRAND There were none of the maids about, so I took the great liberty of knocking.
MRS. ALVING That's all right. Come in. Do you want to speak to me?
ENGSTRAND [*coming in*] No, thank you very much, ma'am. It was Mr. Manders I wanted to speak to for a moment.
MANDERS [*walking up and down*] Hm!—do you. You want to speak to me, do you?
ENGSTRAND Yes, sir, I wanted so very much to—
MANDERS [*stopping in front of him*] Well, may I ask what it is you want?
ENGSTRAND It's this way, Mr. Manders. We are being paid off now. And many thanks to you, Mrs. Alving. And now the work is quite finished, I thought it would be so nice and suitable if all of us, who have worked so honestly together all this time, were to finish up with a few prayers this evening.
MANDERS Prayers? Up at the Orphanage?
ENGSTRAND Yes, sir, but if it isn't agreeable to you, then—
MANDERS Oh, certainly—but—hm!—
ENGSTRAND I have made a practice of saying a few prayers there myself each evening—
MRS. ALVING Have you?
ENGSTRAND Yes, ma'am, now and then—just as a little edification, so to speak. But I am only a poor common man, and haven't rightly the gift, alas—and so I thought that as Mr. Manders happened to be here, perhaps—
MANDERS Look here, Engstrand. First of all I must ask you a question. Are you in a proper frame of mind for such a thing? Is your conscience free and untroubled?
ENGSTRAND Heaven have mercy on me a sinner! My conscience isn't worth our speaking about, Mr. Manders.
MANDERS But it is just what we must speak about. What do you say to my question?
ENGSTRAND My conscience? Well—it's uneasy sometimes, of course.
MANDERS Ah, you admit that at all events. Now will you tell me, without any concealment—what is your relationship to Regina?
MRS. ALVING [*hastily*] Mr. Manders!

MANDERS [*calming her*] Leave it to me!

ENGSTRAND With Regina? Good Lord, how you frightened me! [*Looks at* MRS. ALVING] There is nothing wrong with Regina, is there?

MANDERS Let us hope not. What I want to know is, what is your relationship to her? You pass as her father, don't you?

ENGSTRAND [*unsteadily*] Well—hm!—you know, sir, what happened between me and my poor Joanna.

MANDERS No more distortion of the truth! Your late wife made a full confession to Mrs. Alving, before she left her service.

ENGSTRAND What!—do you mean to say—? Did she do that after all?

MANDERS You see it has all come out, Engstrand.

ENGSTRAND Do you mean to say that she, who gave me her promise and solemn oath—

MANDERS Did she take an oath?

ENGSTRAND Well, no—she only gave me her word, but as seriously as a woman could.

MANDERS And all these years you have been hiding the truth from me —from me, who have had such complete and absolute faith in you.

ENGSTRAND I am sorry to say I have, sir.

MANDERS Did I deserve that from you, Engstrand? Haven't I been always ready to help you in word and deed as far as lay in my power? Answer me! Is it not so?

ENGSTRAND Indeed there's many a time I should have been very badly off without you, sir.

MANDERS And this is the way you repay me—by causing me to make false entries in the church registers, and afterwards keeping back from me for years the information which you owed it both to me and to your sense of the truth to divulge. Your conduct has been absolutely inexcusable, Engstrand, and from to-day everything is at an end between us.

ENGSTRAND [*with a sigh*] Yes, I can see that's what it means.

MANDERS Yes, because how can you possibly justify what you did?

ENGSTRAND Was the poor girl to go and increase her load of shame by talking about it? Just suppose, sir, for a moment that your reverence was in the same predicament as my poor Joanna—

MANDERS I!

ENGSTRAND Good Lord, sir, I don't mean the same predicament. I mean, suppose there were something your reverence were ashamed of in the eyes of the world, so to speak. We men oughtn't to judge a poor woman too hardly, Mr. Manders.

MANDERS But I am not doing so at all. It is you I am blaming.

ENGSTRAND Will your reverence grant me leave to ask you a small question?
MANDERS Ask away.
ENGSTRAND Shouldn't you say it was right for a man to raise up the fallen?
MANDERS Of course it is.
ENGSTRAND And isn't a man bound to keep his word of honour?
MANDERS Certainly he is; but—
ENGSTRAND At the time when Joanna had her misfortune with this Englishman—or maybe he was an American or a Russian, as they call 'em—well, sir, then she came to town. Poor thing, she had refused me once or twice before; she only had eyes for good-looking men in those days, and I had this crooked leg then. Your reverence will remember how I had ventured up into a dancing-saloon where seafaring men were revelling in drunkenness and intoxication, as they say. And when I tried to exhort them to turn from their evil ways—
MRS. ALVING [*coughs from the window*] Ahem!
MANDERS I know, Engstrand, I know—the rough brutes threw you downstairs. You have told me about that incident before. The affliction to your leg is a credit to you.
ENGSTRAND I don't want to claim credit for it, your reverence. But what I wanted to tell you was that she came then and confided in me with tears and gnashing of teeth. I can tell you, sir, it went to my heart to hear her.
MANDERS Did it, indeed, Engstrand? Well, what then?
ENGSTRAND Well, then I said to her: "The American is roaming about on the high seas, he is. And you, Joanna," I said, "you have committed a sin and are a fallen woman. But here stands Jacob Engstrand," I said, "on two strong legs"—of course that was only speaking in a kind of metaphor, as it were, your reverence.
MANDERS I quite understand. Go on.
ENGSTRAND Well, sir, that was how I rescued her and made her my lawful wife, so that no one should know how recklessly she had carried on with the stranger.
MANDERS That was all very kindly done. The only thing I cannot justify was your bringing yourself to accept the money—
ENGSTRAND Money? I? Not a farthing.
MANDERS [*to* MRS. ALVING, *in a questioning tone*] But—
ENGSTRAND Ah, yes!—wait a bit; I remember now. Joanna did have a trifle of money, you are quite right. But I didn't want to know anything about that. "Fie," I said, "on the mammon of unrighteous-

ness, it's the price of your sin; as for this tainted gold"—or notes, or whatever it was—"we will throw it back in the American's face," I said. But he had gone away and disappeared on the stormy seas, your reverence.

MANDERS Was that how it was, my good fellow?

ENGSTRAND It was, sir. So then Joanna and I decided that the money should go towards the child's bringing-up, and that's what became of it; and I can give a faithful account of every single penny of it.

MANDERS This alters the complexion of the affair very considerably.

ENGSTRAND That's how it was, your reverence. And I make bold to say that I have been a good father to Regina—as far as was in my power—for I am a poor erring mortal, alas!

MANDERS There, there, my dear Engstrand—

ENGSTRAND Yes, I do make bold to say that I brought up the child, and made my poor Joanna a loving and careful husband, as the Bible says we ought. But it never occurred to me to go to your reverence and claim credit for it or boast about it because I had done one good deed in this world. No; when Jacob Engstrand does a thing like that, he holds his tongue about it. Unfortunately it doesn't often happen, I know that only too well. And whenever I do come to see your reverence, I never seem to have anything but trouble and wickedness to talk about. Because, as I said just now—and I say it again—conscience can be very hard on us sometimes.

MANDERS Give me your hand, Jacob Engstrand.

ENGSTRAND Oh, sir, I don't like—

MANDERS No nonsense. [*Grasps his hand*] That's it!

ENGSTRAND And may I make bold humbly to beg your reverence's pardon—

MANDERS You? On the contrary it is for me to beg your pardon—

ENGSTRAND Oh no, sir.

MANDERS Yes, certainly it is, and I do it with my whole heart. Forgive me for having so much misjudged you. And I assure you that if I can do anything for you to prove my sincere regret and my goodwill towards you—

ENGSTRAND Do you mean it, sir?

MANDERS It would give me the greatest pleasure.

ENGSTRAND As a matter of fact, sir, you could do it now. I am thinking of using the honest money I have put away out of my wages up here, in establishing a sort of Sailors' Home in the town.

MRS. ALVING You?

ENGSTRAND Yes, to be a sort of Refuge, as it were. There are such manifold temptations lying in wait for sailor men when they are roaming about on shore. But my idea is that in this house of mine they should have a sort of parental care looking after them.

MANDERS What do you say to that, Mrs. Alving!

ENGSTRAND I haven't much to begin such a work with, I know; but Heaven might prosper it, and if I found any helping hand stretched out to me, then—

MANDERS Quite so; we will talk over the matter further. Your project attracts me enormously. But in the meantime go back to the Orphanage and put everything tidy and light the lights, so that the occasion may seem a little solemn. And then we will spend a little edifying time together, my dear Engstrand, for now I am sure you are in a suitable frame of mind.

ENGSTRAND I believe I am, sir, truly. Good-bye, then, Mrs. Alving, and thank you for all your kindness; and take good care of Regina for me. [*Wipes a tear from his eye*] Poor Joanna's child—it is an extraordinary thing, but she seems to have grown into my life and to hold me by the heartstrings. That's how I feel about it, truly.
[*Bows and goes out*]

MANDERS Now then, what do you think of him, Mrs. Alving! That was quite another explanation that he gave us.

MRS. ALVING It was, indeed.

MANDERS There, you see how exceedingly careful we ought to be in condemning our fellow-men. But at the same time it gives one genuine pleasure to find that one was mistaken. Don't you think so?

MRS. ALVING What I think is that you are, and always will remain, a big baby, Mr. Manders.

MANDERS I?

MRS. ALVING [*laying her hands on his shoulders*] And I think that I should like very much to give you a good hug.

MANDERS [*drawing back hastily*] No, no, good gracious! What an idea!

MRS. ALVING [*with a smile*] Oh, you needn't be afraid of me.

MANDERS [*standing by the table*] You choose such an extravagant way of expressing yourself sometimes. Now I must get these papers together and put them in my bag. [*Does so*] That's it. And now good-bye, for the present. Keep your eyes open when Oswald comes back. I will come back and see you again presently.
[*He takes his hat and goes out by the hall door.* MRS. ALVING *sighs, glances out of the window, puts one or two things tidy in the room and turns to go into the dining-room. She stops in the doorway with a stifled cry*]

MRS. ALVING Oswald, are you still sitting at table!
OSWALD [*from the dining-room*] I am only finishing my cigar.
MRS. ALVING I thought you had gone out for a little turn.
OSWALD [*from within the room*] In weather like this? [*A glass is heard clinking.* MRS ALVING *leaves the door open and sits down with her knitting on the couch by the window*] Wasn't that Mr. Manders that went out just now?
MRS. ALVING Yes, he has gone over to the Orphanage.
OSWALD Oh.
[*The clink of a bottle on a glass is heard again*]
MRS ALVING [*with an uneasy expression*] Oswald, dear, you should be careful with that liqueur. It is strong.
OSWALD It's a good protective against the damp.
MRS. ALVING Wouldn't you rather come in here?
OSWALD You know you don't like smoking in there.
MRS ALVING You may smoke a cigar in here, certainly.
OSWALD All right; I will come in then. Just one drop more. There! [*Comes in, smoking a cigar, and shuts the door after him. A short silence*] Where has the parson gone?
MRS. ALVING I told you he had gone over to the Orphanage.
OSWALD Oh, so you did.
MRS. ALVING You shouldn't sit so long at table, Oswald.
OSWALD [*holding his cigar behind his back*] But it's so nice and cosy, mother dear. [*Caresses her with one hand*] Think what it means to me—to have come home; to sit at my mother's own table, in my mother's own room and to enjoy the charming meals she gives me.
MRS. ALVING My dear, dear boy!
OSWALD [*a little impatiently, as he walks up and down smoking*] And what else is there for me to do here? I have no occupation—
MRS. ALVING No occupation?
OSWALD Not in this ghastly weather, when there isn't a blink of sunshine all day long. [*Walks up and down the floor*] Not to be able to work, it's—!
MRS. ALVING I don't believe you were wise to come home.
OSWALD Yes, mother; I had to.
MRS. ALVING Because I would ten times rather give up the happiness of having you with me, sooner than that you should—
OSWALD [*standing still by the table*] Tell me, mother—is it really such a great happiness for you to have me at home?
MRS. ALVING Can you ask?
OSWALD [*crumpling up a newspaper*] I should have thought it would have been pretty much the same to you whether I were here or away.

MRS. ALVING Have you the heart to say that to your mother, Oswald?
OSWALD But you have been quite happy living without me so far.
MRS. ALVING Yes, I have lived without you—that is true.
[*A silence. The dusk falls by degrees.* OSWALD *walks restlessly up and down. He has laid aside his cigar*]
OSWALD [*stopping beside* MRS. ALVING] Mother, may I sit on the couch beside you?
MRS. ALVING Of course, my dear boy.
OSWALD [*sitting down*] Now I must tell you something, mother.
MRS. ALVING [*anxiously*] What?
OSWALD [*staring in front of him*] I can't bear it any longer.
MRS. ALVING Bear what? What do you mean?
OSWALD [*as before*] I couldn't bring myself to write to you about it; and since I have been at home—
MRS. ALVING [*catching him by the arm*] Oswald, what is it?
OSWALD Both yesterday and to-day I have tried to push my thoughts away from me—to free myself from them. But I can't.
MRS. ALVING [*getting up*] You must speak plainly, Oswald!
OSWALD [*drawing her down to her seat again*] Sit still, and I will try and tell you. I have made a great deal of the fatigue I felt after my journey—
MRS. ALVING Well, what of that?
OSWALD But that isn't what is the matter. It is no ordinary fatigue—
MRS. ALVING [*trying to get up*] You are not ill, Oswald!
OSWALD [*pulling her down again*] Sit still, mother. Do take it quietly. I am not exactly ill—not ill in the usual sense. [*Takes his head in his hands*] Mother, it's my mind that has broken down—gone to pieces—I shall never be able to work any more!
[*Buries his face in his hands and throws himself at her knees in an outburst of sobs*]
MRS. ALVING [*pale and trembling*] Oswald! Look at me! No, no, it isn't true!
OSWALD [*looking up with a distracted expression*] Never to be able to work any more! Never—never! A living death! Mother, can you imagine anything so horrible!
MRS. ALVING My poor unhappy boy! How has this terrible thing happened?
OSWALD [*sitting up again*] That is just what I cannot possibly understand. I have never lived recklessly, in any sense. You must believe that of me, mother! I have never done that.
MRS. ALVING I haven't a doubt of it, Oswald.
OSWALD And yet this comes upon me all the same!—this terrible disaster!

MRS. ALVING Oh, but it will all come right again, my dear precious boy. It is nothing but overwork. Believe me, that is so.
OSWALD [*dully*] I thought so too, at first; but it isn't so.
MRS. ALVING Tell me about it.
OSWALD Yes, I will.
MRS. ALVING When did you first feel anything?
OSWALD It was just after I had been home last time and had got back to Paris. I began to feel the most violent pains in my head—mostly at the back, I think. It was as if a tight band of iron was pressing on me from my neck upwards.
MRS. ALVING And then?
OSWALD At first I thought it was nothing but the headaches I always used to be so much troubled with while I was growing.
MRS. ALVING Yes, yes—
OSWALD But it wasn't; I soon saw that. I couldn't work any longer. I would try and start some big new picture; but it seemed as if all my faculties had forsaken me, as if all my strength were paralysed. I couldn't manage to collect my thoughts; my head seemed to swim—everything went round and round. It was a horrible feeling! At last I sent for a doctor—and from him I learnt the truth.
MRS. ALVING In what way, do you mean?
OSWALD He was one of the best doctors there. He made me describe what I felt, and then he began to ask me a whole heap of questions which seemed to me to have nothing to do with the matter. I couldn't see what he was driving at—
MRS. ALVING Well?
OSWALD At last he said: "You have had the canker of disease in you practically from your birth"—the actual word he used was "*vermoulu*."
MRS. ALVING [*anxiously*] What did he mean by that?
OSWALD I couldn't understand, either—and I asked him for a clearer explanation. And then the old cynic said—[*clenching his fist*] Oh!
MRS. ALVING What did he say?
OSWALD He said: "The sins of the fathers are visited on the children."
MRS. ALVING [*getting up slowly*] The sins of the fathers—!
OSWALD I nearly struck him in the face—
MRS. ALVING [*walking across the room*] The sins of the fathers—!
OSWALD [*smiling sadly*] Yes, just imagine! Naturally I assured him that what he thought was impossible. But do you think he paid any heed to me? No, he persisted in his opinion; and it was only when I got out your letters and translated to him all the passages that referred to my father—

MRS. ALVING Well, and then?

OSWALD Well, then of course he had to admit that he was on the wrong track; and then I learnt the truth—the incomprehensible truth! I ought to have had nothing to do with the joyous happy life I had lived with my comrades. It had been too much for my strength. So it was my own fault!

MRS. ALVING No, no, Oswald! Don't believe that!

OSWALD There was no other explanation of it possible, he said. That is the most horrible part of it. My whole life incurably ruined—just because of my own imprudence. All that I wanted to do in the world—not to dare to think of it any more—not to be *able* to think of it! Oh! if only I could live my life over again—if only I could undo what I have done!

[*Throws himself on his face on the couch.* MRS. ALVING *wrings her hands and walks up and down silently fighting with herself*]

OSWALD [*looks up after a while, raising himself on his elbows*] If only it had been something I had inherited—something I could not help. But, instead of that, to have disgracefully, stupidly, thoughtlessly thrown away one's happiness, one's health, everything in the world—one's future, one's life—

MRS. ALVING No, no, my darling boy; that is impossible! [*Bending over him*] Things are not so desperate as you think.

OSWALD Ah, you don't know—. [*Springs up*] And to think, mother, that I should bring all this sorrow upon you! Many a time I have almost wished and hoped that you really did not care so very much for me.

MRS. ALVING I, Oswald? My only son! All that I have in the world! The only thing I care about!

OSWALD [*taking hold of her hands and kissing them*] Yes, yes, I know that is so. When I am at home I know that is true. And that is one of the hardest parts of it to me. But now you know all about it; and now we won't talk any more about it to-day. I can't stand thinking about it long at a time. [*Walks across the room*] Let me have something to drink, mother!

MRS. ALVING To drink? What do you want?

OSWALD Oh, anything you like. I suppose you have got some punch in the house.

MRS. ALVING Yes, but my dear Oswald—!

OSWALD Don't tell me I mustn't, mother. Do be nice! I must have something to drown these gnawing thoughts. [*Goes into the conservatory*] And how—how gloomy it is here! [MRS. ALVING *rings the bell*] And this incessant rain. It may go on week after week—a whole month.

Never a ray of sunshine. I don't remember ever having seen the sun shine once when I have been at home.

MRS. ALVING Oswald—you are thinking of going away from me!

OSWALD Hm!—[*sighs deeply*] I am not thinking about anything. I can't think about anything! [*in a low voice*] I have to let that alone.

REGINA [*coming from the dining-room*] Did you ring, ma'am?

MRS. ALVING Yes, let us have the lamp in.

REGINA In a moment, ma'am; it is all ready lit.

[*Goes out*]

MRS. ALVING [*going up to* OSWALD] Oswald, don't keep anything back from me.

OSWALD I don't, mother. [*Goes to the table*] It seems to me I have told you a good lot.

[REGINA *brings the lamp and puts it upon the table*]

MRS. ALVING Regina, you might bring us a small bottle of champagne.

REGINA Yes ma'am.

[*Goes out*]

OSWALD [*taking hold of his mother's face*] That's right. I knew my mother wouldn't let her son go thirsty.

MRS. ALVING My poor dear boy, how could I refuse you anything now?

OSWALD [*eagerly*] Is that true, mother? Do you mean it?

MRS. ALVING Mean what?

OSWALD That you couldn't deny me anything?

MRS. ALVING My dear Oswald—

OSWALD Hush!

[REGINA *brings in a tray with a small bottle of champagne and two glasses, which she puts on the table*]

REGINA Shall I open the bottle?

OSWALD No, thank you, I will do it.

[REGINA *goes out*]

MRS. ALVING [*sitting down at the table*] What did you mean, when you asked if I could refuse you nothing?

OSWALD [*busy opening the bottle*] Let us have a glass first—or two.

[*He draws the cork, fills one glass and is going to fill the other*]

MRS. ALVING [*holding her hand over the second glass*] No, thanks—not for me.

OSWALD Oh, well, for me then!

[*He empties his glass, fills it again and empties it; then sits down at the table*]

MRS. ALVING [*expectantly*] Now, tell me.

OSWALD [*without looking at her*] Tell me this; I thought you and Mr. Manders seemed so strange—so quiet—at dinner.

MRS. ALVING Did you notice that?

OSWALD Yes. Ahem! [*After a short pause*] Tell me—what do you think of Regina?

MRS. ALVING What do I think of her?

OSWALD Yes, isn't she splendid!

MRS. ALVING Dear Oswald, you don't know her as well as I do—

OSWALD What of that?

MRS. ALVING Regina was too long at home, unfortunately. I ought to have taken her under my charge sooner.

OSWALD Yes, but isn't she splendid to look at, mother?
[*Fills his glass*]

MRS. ALVING Regina has many serious faults—

OSWALD Yes, but what of that?
[*Drinks*]

MRS. ALVING But I am fond of her, all the same; and I have made myself responsible for her. I wouldn't for the world she should come to any harm.

OSWALD [*jumping up*] Mother, Regina is my only hope of salvation!

MRS. ALVING [*getting up*] What do you mean?

OSWALD I can't go on bearing all this agony of mind alone.

MRS. ALVING Haven't you your mother to help you to bear it?

OSWALD Yes, I thought so; that was why I came home to you. But it is no use; I see that it isn't. I cannot spend my life here.

MRS. ALVING Oswald!

OSWALD I must live a different sort of life, mother; so I shall have to go away from you. I don't want you watching it.

MRS. ALVING My unhappy boy! But, Oswald, as long as you are ill like this—

OSWALD If it was only a matter of feeling ill, I would stay with you, mother. You are the best friend I have in the world.

MRS. ALVING Yes, I am that, Oswald, am I not?

OSWALD [*walking restlessly about*] But all this torment—the regret, the remorse—and the deadly fear. Oh—this horrible fear!

MRS. ALVING [*following him*] Fear? Fear of what? What do you mean?

OSWALD Oh, don't ask me any more about it. I don't know what it is. I can't put it into words. [MRS. ALVING *crosses the room and rings the bell*] What do you want?

MRS. ALVING I want my boy to be happy, that's what I want. He mustn't brood over anything. [*To* REGINA, *who has come to the door*] More champagne—a large bottle.

OSWALD Mother!

MRS. ALVING Do you think we country people don't know how to live?

OSWALD Isn't she splendid to look at? What a figure! And the picture of health!

MRS. ALVING [*sitting at the table*] Sit down, Oswald, and let us have a quiet talk.

OSWALD [*sitting down*] You don't know, mother, that I owe Regina a little reparation.

MRS. ALVING You!

OSWALD Oh, it was only a little thoughtlessness—call it what you like. Something quite innocent, anyway. The last time I was home—

MRS. ALVING Yes?

OSWALD —she used often to ask me questions about Paris, and I told her one thing and another about the life there. And I remember saying one day: "Wouldn't you like to go there yourself?"

MRS. ALVING Well?

OSWALD I saw her blush, and she said: "Yes, I should like to very much." "All right," I said, "I daresay it might be managed"—or something of that sort.

MRS. ALVING And then?

OSWALD I naturally had forgotten all about it; but the day before yesterday I happened to ask her if she was glad I was to be so long at home—

MRS. ALVING Well?

OSWALD —and she looked so queerly at me, and asked: "But what is to become of my trip to Paris?"

MRS. ALVING Her trip!

OSWALD And then I got it out of her that she had taken the thing seriously, and had been thinking about me all the time, and had set herself to learn French—

MRS. ALVING So that was why—

OSWALD Mother—when I saw this fine, splendid, handsome girl standing there in front of me—I had never paid any attention to her before then—but now, when she stood there as if with open arms ready for me to take her to myself—

MRS. ALVING Oswald!

OSWALD —then I realised that my salvation lay in her, for I saw the joy of life in her.

MRS. ALVING [*starting back*] The joy of life—? Is there salvation in that?

REGINA [*coming in from the dining-room with a bottle of champagne*] Excuse me for being so long; but I had to go to the cellar.
[*Puts the bottle down on the table*]
OSWALD Bring another glass, too.
REGINA [*looking at him in astonishment*] The mistress's glass is there, sir.
OSWALD Yes, but fetch one for yourself, Regina. [REGINA *starts, and gives a quick shy glance at* MRS. ALVING] Well?
REGINA [*in a low and hesitating voice*] Do you wish me to, ma'am?
MRS. ALVING Fetch the glass, Regina.
[REGINA *goes into the dining-room*]
OSWALD [*looking after her*] Have you noticed how well she walks?—so firmly and confidently!
MRS. ALVING It cannot be, Oswald.
OSWALD It is settled. You must see that. It is no use forbidding it.
[REGINA *comes in with a glass, which she holds in her hand*] Sit down, Regina.
[REGINA *looks questioningly at* MRS. ALVING]
MRS. ALVING Sit down. [REGINA *sits down on a chair near the dining-room door, still holding the glass in her hand*] Oswald, what was it you were saying about the joy of life?
OSWALD Ah, mother—the joy of life! You don't know very much about that at home here. I shall never realise it here.
MRS. ALVING Not even when you are with me?
OSWALD Never at home. But you can't understand that.
MRS. ALVING Yes, indeed I almost think I do understand you—now.
OSWALD That—and the joy of work. They are really the same thing at bottom. But you don't know anything about that either.
MRS. ALVING Perhaps you are right. Tell me some more about it, Oswald.
OSWALD Well, all I mean is that here people are brought up to believe that work is a curse and a punishment for sin, and that life is a state of wretchedness and that the sooner we can get out of it the better.
MRS. ALVING A vale of tears, yes. And we quite conscientiously make it so.
OSWALD But the people over there will have none of that. There is no one there who really believes doctrines of that kind any longer. Over there the mere fact of being alive is thought to be a matter for exultant happiness. Mother, have you noticed that everything I have painted has turned upon the joy of life?—always upon the joy of life, unfailingly. There is light there, and sunshine, and a holiday feeling—and people's faces beaming with happiness. That is why I am afraid to stay at home here with you.

MRS. ALVING Afraid? What are you afraid of here, with me?
OSWALD I am afraid that all these feelings that are so strong in me would degenerate into something ugly here.
MRS. ALVING [*looking steadily at him*] Do you think that is what would happen?
OSWALD I am certain it would. Even if one lived the same life at home here, as over there—it would never really be the same life.
MRS. ALVING [*who has listened anxiously to him, gets up with a thoughtful expression and says*] Now I see clearly how it all happened.
OSWALD What do you see?
MRS. ALVING I see it now for the first time. And now I can speak.
OSWALD [*getting up*] Mother, I don't understand you.
REGINA [*who has got up also*] Perhaps I had better go.
MRS. ALVING No, stay here. Now I can speak. Now, my son, you shall know the whole truth. Oswald! Regina!
OSWALD Hush!—here is the parson—
[MANDERS *comes in by the hall door*]
MANDERS Well, my friends, we have been spending an edifying time over there.
OSWALD So have we.
MANDERS Engstrand must have help with his Sailors' Home. Regina must go home with him and give him her assistance.
REGINA No, thank you, Mr. Manders.
MANDERS [*perceiving her for the first time*] What—? you in here?—and with a wineglass in your hand!
REGINA [*putting down the glass hastily*] I beg your pardon—!
OSWALD Regina is going away with me, Mr. Manders.
MANDERS Going away! With you!
OSWALD Yes, as my wife—if she insists on that.
MANDERS But, good heavens—!
REGINA It is not my fault, Mr. Manders.
OSWALD Or else she stays here if I stay.
REGINA [*involuntarily*] Here!
MANDERS I am amazed at you, Mrs. Alving.
MRS. ALVING Neither of those things will happen, for now I can speak openly.
MANDERS But you won't do that! No, no, no!
MRS. ALVING Yes, I can and I will. And without destroying any one's ideals.
OSWALD Mother, what is it that is being concealed from me?
REGINA [*listening*] Mrs. Alving! Listen! They are shouting outside.
[*Goes into the conservatory and looks out*]

OSWALD [*going to the window on the left*] What can be the matter? Where does that glare come from?
REGINA [*calls out*] The Orphanage is on fire!
MRS. ALVING [*going to the window*] On fire?
MANDERS On fire? Impossible. I was there just a moment ago.
OSWALD Where is my hat? Oh, never mind that. Father's Orphanage—!
[*Runs out through the garden door*]
MRS. ALVING My shawl, Regina! The whole place is in flames.
MANDERS How terrible! Mrs. Alving, that fire is a judgment on this house of sin!
MRS. ALVING Quite so. Come, Regina.
[*She and* REGINA *hurry out*]
MANDERS [*clasping his hands*] And no insurance!
[*Follows them out*]

Act III

The same scene. All the doors are standing open. The lamp is still burning on the table. It is dark outside, except for a faint glimmer of light seen through the windows at the back. MRS. ALVING, *with a shawl over her head, is standing in the conservatory, looking out.* REGINA, *also wrapped in a shawl, is standing a little behind her.*

MRS. ALVING Everything burnt—down to the ground.
REGINA It is burning still in the basement.
MRS. ALVING I can't think why Oswald doesn't come back. There is no chance of saving anything.
REGINA Shall I go and take his hat to him?
MRS. ALVING Hasn't he even got his hat?
REGINA [*pointing to the hall*] No, there it is, hanging up.
MRS. ALVING Never mind. He is sure to come back soon. I will go and see what he is doing.
[*Goes out by the garden door.* MANDERS *comes in from the hall*]
MANDERS Isn't Mrs. Alving here?
REGINA She has just this moment gone down into the garden.
MANDERS I have never spent such a terrible night in my life.
REGINA Isn't it a shocking misfortune, sir!
MANDERS Oh, don't speak about it. I scarcely dare to think about it.
REGINA But how can it have happened?
MANDERS Don't ask me, Miss Engstrand! How should I know? Are you going to suggest too—? Isn't it enough that your father—?
REGINA What has he done?
MANDERS He has nearly driven me crazy.

ENGSTRAND [*coming in from the hall*] Mr. Manders—!

MANDERS [*turning round with a start*] Have you even followed me here!

ENGSTRAND Yes, God help us all—! Great heavens! What a dreadful thing, your reverence!

MANDERS [*walking up and down*] Oh dear, oh dear!

REGINA What do you mean?

ENGSTRAND Our little prayer-meeting was the cause of it all, don't you see? [*Aside, to* REGINA] Now we've got the old fool, my girl. [*Aloud*] And to think it is my fault that Mr. Manders should be the cause of such a thing!

MANDERS I assure you, Engstrand—

ENGSTRAND But there was no one else carrying a light there except you, sir.

MANDERS [*standing still*] Yes, so you say. But I have no clear recollection of having had a light in my hand.

ENGSTRAND But I saw quite distinctly your reverence take a candle and snuff it with your fingers and throw away the burning bit of wick among the shavings.

MANDERS Did you see that?

ENGSTRAND Yes, distinctly.

MANDERS I can't understand it at all. It is never my habit to snuff a candle with my fingers.

ENGSTRAND Yes, it wasn't like you to do that, sir. But who would have thought it could be such a dangerous thing to do?

MANDERS [*walking restlessly backwards and forwards*] Oh, don't ask me!

ENGSTRAND [*following him about*] And you hadn't insured it either, had you, sir?

MANDERS No, no, no; you heard me say so.

ENGSTRAND You hadn't insured it—and then went and set light to the whole place! Good Lord, what bad luck!

MANDERS [*wiping the perspiration from his forehead*] You may well say so, Engstrand.

ENGSTRAND And that it should happen to a charitable institution that would have been of service both to the town and the country, so to speak! The newspapers won't be very kind to your reverence, I expect.

MANDERS No, that is just what I am thinking of. It is almost the worst part of the whole thing. The spiteful attacks and accusations—it is horrible to think of!

MRS. ALVING [*coming in from the garden*] I can't get him away from the fire.

MANDERS Oh, there you are, Mrs. Alving.

MRS. ALVING You will escape having to make your inaugural address now, at all events, Mr. Manders.

MANDERS Oh, I would so gladly have—

MRS. ALVING [*in a dull voice*] It is just as well it has happened. This Orphanage would never have come to any good.

MANDERS Don't you think so?

MRS. ALVING Do you?

MANDERS But it is none the less an extraordinary piece of ill luck.

MRS. ALVING We will discuss it simply as a business matter.—Are you waiting for Mr. Manders, Engstrand?

ENGSTRAND [*at the hall door*] Yes, I am.

MRS. ALVING Sit down then, while you are waiting.

ENGSTRAND Thank you, I would rather stand.

MRS. ALVING [*to* MANDERS] I suppose you are going by the boat?

MANDERS Yes. It goes in about an hour.

MRS. ALVING Please take all the documents back with you. I don't want to hear another word about the matter. I have something else to think about now—

MANDERS Mrs. Alving—

MRS. ALVING Later on I will send you a power of attorney to deal with it exactly as you please.

MANDERS I shall be most happy to undertake that. I am afraid the original intention of the bequest will have to be entirely altered now.

MRS. ALVING Of course.

MANDERS Provisionally, I should suggest this way of disposing of it. Make over the Solvik property to the parish. The land is undoubtedly not without a certain value; it will always be useful for some purpose or another. And as for the interest on the remaining capital that is on deposit in the bank, possibly I might make suitable use of that in support of some undertaking that promises to be of use to the town.

MRS. ALVING Do exactly as you please. The whole thing is a matter of indifference to me now.

ENGSTRAND You will think of my Sailors' Home, Mr. Manders?

MANDERS Yes, certainly, that is a suggestion. But we must consider the matter carefully.

ENGSTRAND [*aside*] Consider!—devil take it! Oh Lord.

MANDERS [*sighing*] And unfortunately I can't tell how much longer I may have anything to do with the matter—whether public opinion may not force me to retire from it altogether. That depends entirely upon the result of the inquiry into the cause of the fire.

MRS. ALVING What do you say?

MANDERS And one cannot in any way reckon upon the result beforehand.
ENGSTRAND [*going nearer to him*] Yes, indeed one can; because here stand I, Jacob Engstrand.
MANDERS Quite so, but—
ENGSTRAND [*lowering his voice*] And Jacob Engstrand isn't the man to desert a worthy benefactor in the hour of need, as the saying is.
MANDERS Yes, but, my dear fellow—how—?
ENGSTRAND You might say Jacob Engstrand is an angel of salvation, so to speak, your reverence.
MANDERS No, no, I couldn't possibly accept that.
ENGSTRAND That's how it will be, all the same. I know some one who has taken the blame for some one else on his shoulders before now, I do.
MANDERS Jacob! [*Grasps his hand*] You are one in a thousand! You shall have assistance in the matter of your Sailors' Home, you may rely upon that.
[ENGSTRAND *tries to thank him, but is prevented by emotion*]
MANDERS [*hanging his wallet over his shoulder*] Now we must be off. We will travel together.
ENGSTRAND [*by the dining-room door, says aside to* REGINA] Come with me, you hussy! You shall be as cosy as the yolk in an egg!
REGINA [*tossing her head*] Merci!
[*She goes out into the hall and brings back* MANDERS' *luggage*]
MANDERS Good-bye, Mrs. Alving! And may the spirit of order and of what is lawful speedily enter into this house.
MRS. ALVING Good-bye, Mr. Manders.
[*She goes into the conservatory, as she sees* OSWALD *coming in by the garden door*]
ENGSTRAND [*as he and* REGINA *are helping* MANDERS *on with his coat*] Good-bye, my child. And if anything should happen to you, you know where Jacob Engstrand is to be found. [*Lowering his voice*] Little Harbour Street, ahem—! [*to* MRS. ALVING *and* OSWALD] And my house for poor seafaring men shall be called the "Alving Home," it shall. And, if I can carry out my own ideas about it, I shall make bold to hope that it may be worthy of bearing the late Mr. Alving's name.
MANDERS [*at the door*] Ahem—ahem! Come along, my dear Engstrand. Good-bye—good-bye!
[*He and* ENGSTRAND *go out by the hall door*]
OSWALD [*going to the table*] What house was he speaking about?
MRS. ALVING I believe it is some sort of a Home that he and Mr. Manders want to start.
OSWALD It will be burnt up just like this one.

MRS. ALVING What makes you think that?
OSWALD Everything will be burnt up; nothing will be left that is in memory of my father. Here am I being burnt up, too.
[REGINA *looks at him in alarm*]
MRS. ALVING Oswald! You should not have stayed so long over there, my boy.
OSWALD [*sitting down at the table*] I almost believe you are right.
MRS. ALVING Let me dry your face, Oswald; you are all wet.
[*Wipes his face with her handkerchief*]
OSWALD [*looking straight before him with no expression in his eyes*] Thank you, mother.
MRS. ALVING And aren't you tired, Oswald? Don't you want to go to sleep?
OSWALD [*uneasily*] No, no—not to sleep! I never sleep; I only pretend to. [*Gloomily*] That will come soon enough.
MRS. ALVING [*looking at him anxiously*] Anyhow you are really ill, my darling boy.
REGINA [*intently*] Is Mr. Alving ill?
OSWALD [*impatiently*] And do shut all the doors! This deadly fear—
MRS. ALVING Shut the doors, Regina. [REGINA *shuts the doors and remains standing by the hall door.* MRS. ALVING *takes off her shawl;* REGINA *does the same.* MRS. ALVING *draws up a chair near to* OSWALD'S *and sits down beside him*] That's it! Now I will sit beside you—
OSWALD Yes, do. And Regina must stay in here too. Regina must always be near me. You must give me a helping hand, you know, Regina. Won't you do that?
REGINA I don't understand—
MRS. ALVING A helping hand?
OSWALD Yes—when there is need for it.
MRS. ALVING Oswald, have you not your mother to give you a helping hand?
OSWALD You? [*Smiles*] No, mother, you will never give me the kind of helping hand I mean. [*Laughs grimly*] You? Ha, ha! [*Looks gravely at her*] After all, you have the best right. [*Impetuously*] Why don't you call me by my Christian name, Regina? Why don't you say Oswald?
REGINA [*in a low voice*] I did not think Mrs. Alving would like it.
MRS. ALVING It will not be long before you have the right to do it. Sit down here now beside us, too. [REGINA *sits down quietly and hesitatingly at the other side of the table*] And now, my poor tortured boy, I am going to take the burden off your mind—

OSWALD You, mother?

MRS. ALVING —all that you call remorse and regret and self-reproach.

OSWALD And you think you can do that?

MRS. ALVING Yes, now I can, Oswald. A little while ago you were talking about the joy of life, and what you said seemed to shed a new light upon everything in my whole life.

OSWALD [*shaking his head*] I don't in the least understand what you mean.

MRS. ALVING You should have known your father in his young days in the army. He was full of the joy of life, I can tell you.

OSWALD Yes, I know.

MRS. ALVING It gave me a holiday feeling only to look at him, full of irrepressible energy and exuberant spirits.

OSWALD What then?

MRS. ALVING Well, then this boy, full of the joy of life—for he was just like a boy, then—had to make his home in a second-rate town which had none of the joy of life to offer him, but only dissipations. He had to come out here and live an aimless life; he had only an official post. He had no work worth devoting his whole mind to; he had nothing more than official routine to attend to. He had not a single companion capable of appreciating what the joy of life meant; nothing but idlers and tipplers—

OSWALD Mother—!

MRS. ALVING And so the inevitable happened!

OSWALD What was the inevitable?

MRS. ALVING You said yourself this evening what would happen in your case if you stayed at home.

OSWALD Do you mean by that, that father—?

MRS. ALVING Your poor father never found any outlet for the overmastering joy of life that was in him. And I brought no holiday spirit into his home, either.

OSWALD You didn't either?

MRS. ALVING I had been taught about duty, and the sort of thing that I believed in so long here. Everything seemed to turn upon duty—my duty, or his duty—and I am afraid I made your poor father's home unbearable to him, Oswald.

OSWALD Why did you never say anything about it to me in your letters?

MRS. ALVING I never looked at it as a thing I could speak of to you, who were his son.

OSWALD What way did you look at it, then?

MRS. ALVING I only saw the one fact, that your father was a lost man before ever you were born.
OSWALD [*in a choking voice*] Ah—!
[*He gets up and goes to the window*]
MRS. ALVING And then I had the one thought in my mind, day and night, that Regina in fact had as good a right in this house—as my own boy had.
OSWALD [*turns round suddenly*] Regina—?
REGINA [*gets up and asks in choking tones*] I—?
MRS. ALVING Yes, now you both know it.
OSWALD Regina!
REGINA [*to herself*] So mother was one of that sort too.
MRS. ALVING Your mother had many good qualities, Regina.
REGINA Yes, but she was one of that sort too, all the same. I have even thought so myself, sometimes, but—. Then, if you please, Mrs. Alving, may I have permission to leave at once?
MRS. ALVING Do you really wish to, Regina?
REGINA Yes, indeed, I certainly wish to.
MRS. ALVING Of course you shall do as you like, but—
OSWALD [*going to* REGINA] Leave now? This is your home.
REGINA *Merci*, Mr. Alving—oh, of course I may say Oswald now, but that is not the way I thought it would become allowable.
MRS. ALVING Regina, I have not been open with you—
REGINA No, I can't say you have! If I had known Oswald was ill—. And now that there can never be anything serious between us—. No, I really can't stay here in the country and wear myself out looking after invalids.
OSWALD Not even for the sake of one who has so near a claim on you?
REGINA No, indeed I can't. A poor girl must make some use of her youth, otherwise she may easily find herself out in the cold before she knows where she is. And I have got the joy of life in me, too, Mrs. Alving!
MRS. ALVING Yes, unfortunately; but don't throw yourself away, Regina.
REGINA Oh, what's going to happen will happen. If Oswald takes after his father, it is just as likely I take after my mother, I expect.—May I ask, Mrs. Alving, whether Mr. Manders knows this about me?
MRS. ALVING Mr. Manders knows everything.
REGINA [*putting on her shawl*] Oh, well then, the best thing I can do is to get away by the boat as soon as I can. Mr. Manders is such a nice gentleman to deal with; and it certainly seems to me that I have just as much right to some of that money as he—as that horrid carpenter.
MRS. ALVING You are quite welcome to it, Regina.

REGINA [*looking at her fixedly*] You might as well have brought me up like a gentleman's daughter; it would have been more suitable. [*Tosses her head*] Oh, well—never mind! [*With a bitter glance at the unopened bottle*] I daresay some day I shall be drinking champagne with gentlefolk, after all.

MRS. ALVING If ever you need a home, Regina, come to me.

REGINA No, thank you, Mrs. Alving. Mr. Manders takes an interest in me, I know. And if things should go very badly with me, I know one house at any rate where I shall feel at home.

MRS. ALVING Where is that?

REGINA In the "Alving Home."

MRS. ALVING Regina—I can see quite well—you are going to your ruin!

REGINA Pooh!—good-bye.

[*She bows to them and goes out through the hall*]

OSWALD [*standing by the window and looking out*] Has she gone?

MRS. ALVING Yes.

OSWALD [*muttering to himself*] I think it's all wrong.

MRS. ALVING [*going up to him from behind and putting her hands on his shoulders*] Oswald, my dear boy—has it been a great shock to you?

OSWALD [*turning his face towards her*] All this about father, do you mean?

MRS. ALVING Yes, about your unhappy father. I am so afraid it may have been too much for you.

OSWALD What makes you think that? Naturally it has taken me entirely by surprise; but, after all, I don't know that it matters much to me.

MRS. ALVING [*drawing back her hands*] Doesn't matter!—that your father's life was such a terrible failure!

OSWALD Of course I can feel sympathy for him, just as I would for anyone else, but—

MRS. ALVING No more than that! For your own father!

OSWALD [*impatiently*] Father—father! I never knew anything of my father. I don't remember anything else about him except that he once made me sick.

MRS. ALVING It is dreadful to think of!—But surely a child should feel some affection for his father, whatever happens?

OSWALD When the child has nothing to thank his father for? When he has never known him? Do you really cling to that antiquated superstition—you, who are so broadminded in other things?

MRS. ALVING You call it nothing but a superstition!

OSWALD Yes, and you can see that for yourself quite well, mother. It is one of those beliefs that are put into circulation in the world, and—

MRS. ALVING Ghosts of beliefs!
OSWALD [*walking across the room*] Yes, you might call them ghosts.
MRS. ALVING [*with an outburst of feeling*] Oswald—then you don't love me either.
OSWALD You I know, at any rate—
MRS. ALVING You know me, yes: but is that all?
OSWALD And I know how fond you are of me, and I ought to be grateful to you for that. Besides, you can be so tremendously useful to me, now that I am ill.
MRS. ALVING Yes, can't I, Oswald! I could almost bless your illness, as it has driven you home to me. For I see quite well that you are not my very own yet; you must be won.
OSWALD [*impatiently*] Yes, yes, yes; all that is just a way of talking. You must remember I am a sick man, mother. I can't concern myself much with anyone else; I have enough to do, thinking about myself.
MRS. ALVING [*gently*] I will be very good and patient.
OSWALD And cheerful too, mother!
MRS. ALVING Yes, my dear boy, you are quite right. [*Goes up to him*] Now have I taken away all your remorse and self-reproach?
OSWALD Yes, you have done that. But who will take away the fear?
MRS. ALVING The fear?
OSWALD [*crossing the room*] Regina would have done it for one kind word.
MRS. ALVING I don't understand you. What fear do you mean—and what has Regina to do with it?
OSWALD Is it very late, mother?
MRS. ALVING It is early morning. [*Looks out through the conservatory windows*] The dawn is breaking already on the heights. And the sky is clear, Oswald. In a little while you will see the sun.
OSWALD I am glad of that. After all, there may be many things yet for me to be glad of and to live for—
MRS. ALVING I should hope so!
OSWALD Even if I am not able to work—
MRS. ALVING You will soon find you are able to work again now, my dear boy. You have no longer all those painful depressing thoughts to brood over.
OSWALD No, it is a good thing that you have been able to rid me of those fancies. If only, now, I could overcome this one thing—. [*Sits down on the couch*] Let us have a little chat, mother.
MRS. ALVING Yes, let us.
[*Pushes an armchair near to the couch and sits down beside him*]

OSWALD The sun is rising—and you know all about it; so I don't feel the fear any longer.

MRS. ALVING I know all about what?

OSWALD [*without listening to her*] Mother, isn't it the case that you said this evening there was nothing in the world you would not do for me if I asked you?

MRS. ALVING Yes, certainly I said so.

OSWALD And will you be as good as your word, mother?

MRS. ALVING You may rely upon that, my own dear boy. I have nothing else to live for, but you.

OSWALD Yes, yes; well, listen to me, mother. You are very strong-minded, I know. I want you to sit quite quiet when you hear what I am going to tell you.

MRS. ALVING But what is this dreadful thing—?

OSWALD You mustn't scream. Do you hear? Will you promise me that? We are going to sit and talk it over quite quietly. Will you promise me that, mother?

MRS. ALVING Yes, yes, I promise—only tell me what it is.

OSWALD Well, then, you must know that this fatigue of mine—and my not being able to think about my work—all that is not really the illness itself—

MRS. ALVING What is the illness itself?

OSWALD What I am suffering from is hereditary; it—[*touches his forehead, and speaks very quietly*]—it lies here.

MRS. ALVING [*almost speechless*] Oswald! no—no!

OSWALD Don't scream; I can't stand it. Yes, I tell you, it lies here, waiting. And any time, any moment, it may break out.

MRS. ALVING How horrible—!

OSWALD Do keep quiet. That is the state I am in—

MRS. ALVING [*springing up*] It isn't true, Oswald! It is impossible! It can't be that!

OSWALD I had one attack while I was abroad. It passed off quickly. But when I learnt the condition I had been in, then this dreadful haunting fear took possession of me.

MRS. ALVING That was the fear, then—

OSWALD Yes, it is so indescribably horrible, you know. If only it had been an ordinary mortal disease—. I am not so much afraid of dying; though, of course, I should like to live as long as I can.

MRS. ALVING Yes, yes, Oswald, you must!

OSWALD But this is so appallingly horrible. To become like a helpless child again—to have to be fed, to have to be— Oh, it's unspeakable!

MRS. ALVING My child has his mother to tend him.
OSWALD [*jumping up*] No, never; that is just what I won't endure! I dare not think what it would mean to linger on like that for years—to get old and grey like that. And you might die before I did. [*Sits down in* MRS. ALVING's *chair*] Because it doesn't necessarily have a fatal end quickly, the doctor said. He called it a kind of softening of the brain—or something of that sort. [*Smiles mournfully*] I think that expression sounds so nice. It always makes me think of cherry-coloured velvet curtains—something that is soft to stroke.
MRS. ALVING [*with a scream*] Oswald!
OSWALD [*jumps up and walks about the room*] And now you have taken Regina from me! If I had only had her. She would have given me a helping hand, I know.
MRS. ALVING [*going up to him*] What do you mean, my darling boy? Is there any help in the world I would not be willing to give you?
OSWALD When I had recovered from the attack I had abroad, the doctor told me that when it recurred—and it will recur—there would be no more hope.
MRS. ALVING And he was heartless enough to—
OSWALD I insisted on knowing. I told him I had arrangements to make—. [*Smiles cunningly*] And so I had. [*Takes a small box from his inner breast-pocket*] Mother, do you see this?
MRS. ALVING What is it?
OSWALD Morphia powders.
MRS. ALVING [*looking at him in terror*] Oswald—my boy!
OSWALD I have twelve of them saved up—
MRS. ALVING [*snatching at it*] Give me the box, Oswald!
OSWALD Not yet, mother.
[*Puts it back in his pocket*]
MRS. ALVING I shall never get over this!
OSWALD You must. If I had Regina here now, I would have told her quietly how things stand with me—and asked her to give me this last helping hand. She would have helped me, I am certain.
MRS. ALVING Never!
OSWALD If this horrible thing had come upon me and she had seen me lying helpless, like a baby, past help, past saving, past hope—with no chance of recovering—
MRS. ALVING Never in the world would Regina have done it.
OSWALD Regina would have done it. Regina was so splendidly light-hearted. And she would very soon have tired of looking after an invalid like me.

MRS. ALVING Then thank heaven Regina is not here!
OSWALD Well, now you have got to give me that helping hand, mother.
MRS. ALVING [*with a loud scream*] I!
OSWALD Who has a better right than you?
MRS. ALVING I? Your mother!
OSWALD Just for that reason.
MRS. ALVING I, who gave you your life!
OSWALD I never asked you for life. And what kind of a life was it that you gave me? I don't want it! You shall take it back!
MRS. ALVING Help! Help!
[*Runs into the hall*]
OSWALD [*following her*] Don't leave me! Where are you going?
MRS. ALVING [*in the hall*] To fetch the doctor to you, Oswald! Let me out!
OSWALD [*going into the hall*] You shan't go out. And no one shall come in. [*Turns the key in the lock*]
MRS. ALVING [*coming in again*] Oswald! Oswald!—my child!
OSWALD [*following her*] Have you a mother's heart—and can bear to see me suffering this unspeakable terror?
MRS. ALVING [*controlling herself, after a moment's silence*] There is my hand on it.
OSWALD Will you—?
MRS. ALVING If it becomes necessary. But it shan't become necessary. No, no—it is impossible it should!
OSWALD Let us hope so. And let us live together as long as we can. Thank you, mother.
[*He sits down in the armchair, which* MRS. ALVING *had moved beside the couch. Day is breaking; the lamp is still burning on the table*]
MRS. ALVING [*coming cautiously nearer*] Do you feel calmer now?
OSWALD Yes.
MRS. ALVING [*bending over him*] It has only been a dreadful fancy of yours, Oswald. Nothing but fancy. All this upset has been bad for you. But now you will get some rest, at home with your own mother, my darling boy. You shall have everything you want, just as you did when you were a little child.—There, now. The attack is over. You see how easily it passed off! I knew it would.—And look, Oswald, what a lovely day we are going to have? Brilliant sunshine. Now you will be able to see your home properly.
[*She goes to the table and puts out the lamp. It is sunrise. The glaciers and peaks in the distance are seen bathed in bright morning light*]

OSWALD [*who has been sitting motionless in the armchair, with his back to the scene outside, suddenly says*] Mother, give me the sun.
MRS. ALVING [*standing at the table, and looking at him in amazement*] What do you say?
OSWALD [*repeats in a dull, toneless voice*] The sun—the sun.
MRS. ALVING [*going up to him*] Oswald, what is the matter with you? [OSWALD *seems to shrink up in the chair; all his muscles relax; his face loses its expression, and his eyes stare stupidly.* MRS. ALVING *is trembling with terror*] What is it! [*Screams*] Oswald! What is the matter with you! [*Throws herself on her knees beside him and shakes him*] Oswald! Oswald! Look at me! Don't you know me!
OSWALD [*in an expressionless voice, as before*] The sun—the sun.
MRS. ALVING [*jumps up despairingly, beats her head with her hands, and screams*] I can't bear it! [*Whispers as though paralysed with fear*] I can't bear it! Never! [*Suddenly*] Where has he got it? [*Passes her hand quickly over his coat*] Here! [*Draws back a little way and cries*] No, no, no!—Yes!—no, no!
[*She stands a few steps from him, her hands thrust into her hair, and stares at him in speechless terror*]
OSWALD [*sitting motionless, as before*] The sun—the sun.

Miss Julie

Characters

MISS JULIE *aged 25*
JEAN *the valet, aged 30*
KRISTIN *the cook, aged 35*

Scene: *The large kitchen of a Swedish manor house in a country district in the eighties.*
Midsummer eve.
The kitchen has three doors, two small ones into JEAN's *and* KRISTIN's *bedrooms, and a large, glass-fronted double one, opening on to a courtyard. This is the only way to the rest of the house.*
Through these glass doors can be seen part of a fountain with a cupid, lilac bushes in flower and the tops of some Lombardy poplars. On one wall are shelves edged with scalloped paper on which are kitchen utensils of copper, iron and tin.
To the left is the corner of a large tiled range and part of its chimney-hood, to the right the end of the servants' dinner table with chairs beside it.
The stove is decorated with birch boughs, the floor strewn with twigs of juniper. On the end of the table is a large Japanese spice jar full of lilac.
There are also an ice-box, a scullery table and a sink. Above the double door hangs a big old-fashioned bell; near it is a speaking-tube.
A fiddle can be heard from the dance in the barn near-by. KRISTIN *is standing at the stove, frying something in a pan. She wears a light-coloured cotton dress and a big apron.*
JEAN *enters, wearing livery and carrying a pair of large riding-boots with spurs, which he puts in a conspicuous place.*

JEAN Miss Julie's crazy again to-night, absolutely crazy.
KRISTIN Oh, so you're back, are you?
JEAN When I'd taken the Count to the station, I came back and dropped in at the Barn for a dance. And who did I see there but our young lady leading off with the gamekeeper. But the moment she sets eyes on me, up she rushes and invites me to waltz with her. And how she waltzed—I've never seen anything like it! She's crazy.
KRISTIN Always has been, but never so bad as this last fortnight since the engagement was broken off.

JEAN Yes, that was a pretty business, to be sure. He's a decent enough chap, too, even if he isn't rich. Oh, but they're choosy! [*Sits down at the end of the table*] In any case, it's a bit odd that our young—er—lady would rather stay at home with the yokels than go with her father to visit her relations.

KRISTIN Perhaps she feels a bit awkward, after that bust-up with her fiancé.

JEAN Maybe. That chap had some guts, though. Do you know the sort of thing that was going on, Kristin? I saw it with my own eyes, though I didn't let on I had.

KRISTIN You saw them . . . ?

JEAN Didn't I just! Came across the pair of them one evening in the stable-yard. Miss Julie was doing what she called "training" him. Know what that was? Making him jump over her riding-whip—the way you teach a dog. He did it twice and got a cut each time for his pains, but when it came to the third go, he snatched the whip out of her hand and broke it into smithereens. And then he cleared off.

KRISTIN What goings on! I never did!

JEAN Well, that's how it was with that little affair . . . Now, what have you got for me, Kristin? Something tasty?

KRISTIN [*serving from the pan to his plate*] Well, it's just a little bit of kidney I cut off their joint.

JEAN [*smelling it*] Fine! That's my special delice. [*Feels the plate*] But you might have warmed the plate.

KRISTIN When you choose to be finicky you're worse than the Count himself. [*Pulls his hair affectionately*]

JEAN [*crossly*] Stop pulling my hair. You know how sensitive I am.

KRISTIN There, there! It's only love, you know.

[JEAN *eats.* KRISTIN *brings a bottle of beer*]

JEAN Beer on Midsummer Eve? No thanks! I've got something better than that. [*From a drawer in the table brings out a bottle of red wine with a yellow seal*] Yellow seal, see! Now get me a glass. You use a glass with a stem of course when you're drinking it straight.

KRISTIN [*giving him a wine-glass*] Lord help the woman who gets you for a husband, you old fusser! [*She puts the beer in the ice-box and sets a small saucepan on the stove*]

JEAN Nonsense! You'll be glad enough to get a fellow as smart as me. And I don't think it's done you any harm people calling me your fiancé. [*Tastes the wine*] Good. Very good indeed. But not quite warmed enough. [*Warms the glass in his hand*] We bought this in

Dijon. Four francs the litre without the bottle, and duty on top of that. What are you cooking now? It stinks.

KRISTIN Some bloody muck Miss Julie wants for Diana.

JEAN You should be more refined in your speech, Kristin. But why should you spend a holiday cooking for that bitch? Is she sick or what?

KRISTIN Yes, she's sick. She sneaked out with the pug at the lodge and got in the usual mess. And that, you know, Miss Julie won't have.

JEAN Miss Julie's too high-and-mighty in some respects, and not enough in others, just like her mother before her. The Countess was more at home in the kitchen and cowsheds than anywhere else, but would she ever go driving with only one horse? She went round with her cuffs filthy, but she had to have the coronet on the cuff-links. Our young lady—to come back to her—hasn't any proper respect for herself or her position. I mean she isn't refined. In the Barn just now she dragged the gamekeeper away from Anna and made him dance with her—no waiting to be asked. We wouldn't do a thing like that. But that's what happens when the gentry try to behave like the common people—they become common . . . Still she's a fine girl. Smashing! What shoulders! And what—er—etcetera!

KRISTIN Oh come off it! I know what Clara says, and she dresses her.

JEAN Clara? Pooh, you're all jealous! But I've been out riding with her . . . and as for her dancing!

KRISTIN Listen, Jean. You will dance with me, won't you, as soon as I'm through.

JEAN Of course I will.

KRISTIN Promise?

JEAN Promise? When I say I'll do a thing I do it. Well, thanks for the supper. It was a real treat. [*Corks the bottle*]

[JULIE *appears in the doorway, speaking to someone outside*]

JULIE I'll be back in a moment. Don't wait.

[JEAN *slips the bottle into the drawer and rises respectfully.* JULIE *enters and joins* KRISTIN *at the stove*]

Well, have you made it? [KRISTIN *signs that* JEAN *is near them*]

JEAN [*gallantly*] Have you ladies got some secret?

JULIE [*flipping his face with her handkerchief*] You're very inquisitive.

JEAN What a delicious smell! Violets.

JULIE [*coquettishly*] Impertinence! Are you an expert of scent too? I must say you know how to dance. Now don't look. Go away. [*The music of a schottische begins*]

JEAN [*with impudent politeness*] Is it some witches' brew you're cooking on Midsummer Eve? Something to tell your stars by, so you can see your future?

JULIE [*sharply*] If you could see that you'd have good eyes. [*To* KRISTIN] Put it in a bottle and cork it tight. Come and dance this schottische with me, Jean.

JEAN [*hesitating*] I don't want to be rude, but I've promised to dance this one with Kristin.

JULIE Well, she can have another, can't you, Kristin? You'll lend me Jean, won't you?

KRISTIN [*bottling*] It's nothing to do with me. When you're so condescending, Miss, it's not his place to say no. Go on, Jean, and thank Miss Julie for the honour.

JEAN Frankly speaking, Miss, and no offence meant, I wonder if it's wise for you to dance twice running with the same partner, specially as those people are so ready to jump to conclusions.

JULIE [*flaring up*] What did you say? What sort of conclusions? What do you mean?

JEAN [*meekly*] As you choose not to understand, Miss Julie, I'll have to speak more plainly. It looks bad to show a preference for one of your retainers when they're all hoping for the same unusual favour.

JULIE Show a preference! The very idea! I'm surprised at you. I'm doing the people an honour by attending their ball when I'm mistress of the house, but if I'm really going to dance, I mean to have a partner who can lead and doesn't make me look ridiculous.

JEAN If those are your orders, Miss, I'm at your service.

JULIE [*gently*] Don't take it as an order. To-night we're all just people enjoying a party. There's no question of class. So now give me your arm. Don't worry, Kristin. I shan't steal your sweetheart.

[JEAN *gives* JULIE *his arm and leads her out*]

[*Left alone,* KRISTIN *plays her scene in an unhurried, natural way, humming to the tune of the schottische, played on a distant violin. She clears* JEAN's *place, washes up and puts things away, then takes off her apron, brings out a small mirror from a drawer, props it against the jar of lilac, lights a candle, warms a small pair of tongs and curls her fringe. She goes to the door and listens, then turning back to the table finds* MISS JULIE's *forgotten handkerchief. She smells it, then meditatively smooths it out and folds it*]

[*Enter* JEAN]

JEAN She really *is* crazy. What a way to dance! With people standing grinning at her too from behind the doors. What's got into her, Kristin?

KRISTIN Oh, it's just her time coming on. She's always queer then. Are you going to dance with me now?

JEAN Then you're not wild with me for cutting that one.

KRISTIN You know I'm not—for a little thing like that. Besides, I know my place.
JEAN [*putting his arm round her waist*] You're a sensible girl, Kristin, and you'll make a very good wife . . .
[*Enter* JULIE, *unpleasantly surprised*]
JULIE [*with forced gaiety*] You're a fine beau—running away from your partner.
JEAN Not away, Miss Julie, but as you see back to the one I deserted.
JULIE [*changing her tone*] You really can dance, you know. But why are you wearing your livery on a holiday. Take it off at once.
JEAN Then I must ask you to go away for a moment, Miss. My black coat's here. [*Indicates it hanging on the door to his room*]
JEAN Are you so shy of me—just over changing a coat? Go into your room then—or stay here and I'll turn my back.
JEAN Excuse me then, Miss. [*He goes to his room and is partly visible as he changes his coat*]
JULIE Tell me, Kristin, is Jean your fiancé? You seem very intimate.
KRISTIN My fiancé? Yes, if you like. We call it that.
JULIE Call it?
KRISTIN Well, you've had a fiancé yourself, Miss, and . . .
JULIE But we really were engaged.
KRISTIN All the same it didn't come to anything.
[JEAN *returns in his black coat*]
JULIE Très gentil, Monsieur Jean. Très gentil.
JEAN Vous voulez plaisanter, Madame.
JULIE Et vous voulez parler français. Where did you learn it?
JEAN In Switzerland, when I was sommelier at one of the biggest hotels in Lucerne.
JULIE You look quite the gentleman in that get-up. Charming.
[*Sits at the table*]
JEAN Oh, you're just flattering me!
JULIE [*annoyed*] Flattering you?
JEAN I'm too modest to believe you would pay real compliments to a man like me, so I must take it you are exaggerating—that this is what's known as flattery.
JULIE Where on earth did you learn to make speeches like that? Perhaps you've been to the theatre a lot.
JEAN That's right. And travelled a lot too.
JULIE But you come from this neighbourhood, don't you?
JEAN Yes, my father was a labourer on the next estate—the District Attorney's place. I often used to see you, Miss Julie, when you were little, though you never noticed me.

JULIE Did you really?
JEAN Yes. One time specially I remember . . . but I can't tell you about that.
JULIE Oh do! Why not? This is just the time.
JEAN No, I really can't now. Another time perhaps.
JULIE Another time means never. What harm in now?
JEAN No harm, but I'd rather not. [*Points to* KRISTIN, *now fast asleep*] Look at her.
JULIE She'll make a charming wife, won't she? I wonder if she snores.
JEAN No, she doesn't, but she talks in her sleep.
JULIE [*cynically*] How do you know she talks in her sleep?
JEAN [*brazenly*] I've heard her. [*Pause. They look at one another*]
JULIE Why don't you sit down?
JEAN I can't take such a liberty in your presence.
JULIE Supposing I order you to.
JEAN I'll obey.
JULIE Then sit down. No, wait a minute. Will you get me a drink first?
JEAN I don't know what's in the ice-box. Only beer, I expect.
JULIE There's no only about it. My taste is so simple I prefer it to wine.
[JEAN *takes a bottle from the ice-box, fetches a glass and plate and serves the beer*]
JEAN At your service.
JULIE Thank you. Won't you have some yourself?
JEAN I'm not really a beer-drinker, but if it's an order . . .
JULIE Order? I should have thought it was ordinary manners to keep your partner company.
JEAN That's a good way of putting it. [*He opens another bottle and fetches a glass*]
JULIE Now drink my health. [*He hesitates*] I believe the man really is shy.
[JEAN *kneels and raises his glass with mock ceremony*]
JEAN To the health of my lady!
JULIE Bravo! Now kiss my shoe and everything will be perfect. [*He hesitates, then boldly takes hold of her foot and lightly kisses it*] Splendid. You ought to have been an actor.
JEAN [*rising*] We can't go on like this, Miss Julie. Someone might come in and see us.
JULIE Why would that matter?
JEAN For the simple reason that they'd talk. And if you knew the way their tongues were wagging out there just now, you . . .
JULIE What were they saying? Tell me. Sit down.
JEAN [*sitting*] No offence meant, Miss, but . . . well, their language

wasn't nice, and they were hinting . . . oh, you know quite well what. You're not a child, and if a lady's seen drinking alone at night with a man—and a servant at that—then . . .
JULIE Then what? Besides, we're not alone. Kristin's here.
JEAN Yes, asleep.
JULIE I'll wake her up. [*Rises*] Kristin, are you asleep? [KRISTIN *mumbles in her sleep*] Kristin! Goodness, how she sleeps!
KRISTIN [*in her sleep*] The Count's boots are cleaned—put the coffee on—yes, yes, at once . . . [*Mumbles incoherently*]
JULIE [*tweaking her nose*] Wake up, can't you!
JEAN [*sharply*] Let her sleep.
JULIE What?
JEAN When you've been standing at the stove all day you're likely to be tired at night. And sleep should be respected.
JULIE [*changing her tone*] What a nice idea. It does you credit. Thank you for it. [*Holds out her hand to him*] Now come out and pick some lilac for me.
[*During the following* KRISTIN *goes sleepily in to her bedroom*]
JEAN Out with you, Miss Julie?
JULIE Yes.
JEAN It wouldn't do. It really wouldn't.
JULIE I don't know what you mean. You can't possibly imagine that . . .
JEAN I don't, but others do.
JULIE What? That I'm in love with the valet?
JEAN I'm not a conceited man, but such a thing's been known to happen, and to these rustics nothing's sacred.
JULIE You, I take it, are an aristocrat.
JEAN Yes, I am.
JULIE And I am coming down in the world.
JEAN Don't come down, Miss Julie. Take my advice. No one will believe you came down of your own accord. They'll all say you fell.
JULIE I have a higher opinion of our people than you. Come and put it to the test. Come on. [*Gazes into his eyes*]
JEAN You're very strange, you know.
JULIE Perhaps I am, but so are you. For that matter everything is strange. Life, human beings, everything, just scum drifting about on the water until it sinks—down and down. That reminds me of a dream I sometimes have, in which I'm on top of a pillar and can't see any way of getting down. When I look down I'm dizzy; I have to get down but I haven't the courage to jump. I can't stay there and I long to fall, but I don't fall. There's no respite. There can't be any peace at all

for me until I'm down, right down on the ground. And if I did get to the ground I'd want to be under the ground . . . Have you ever felt like that?

JEAN No. In my dream I'm lying under a great tree in a dark wood. I want to get up, up to the top of it, and look out over the bright landscape where the sun is shining and rob that high nest of its golden eggs. And I climb and climb, but the trunk is so thick and smooth and it's so far to the first branch. But I know if I can once reach that first branch I'll go to the top just as if I'm on a ladder. I haven't reached it yet, but I shall get there, even if only in my dreams.

JULIE Here I am chattering about dreams with you. Come on. Only into the park. [*She takes his arm and they go towards the door*]

JEAN We must sleep on nine midsummer flowers tonight; then our dreams will come true, Miss Julie. [*They turn at the door. He has a hand to his eye*]

JULIE Have you got something in your eye? Let me see.

JEAN Oh, it's nothing. Just a speck of dust. It'll be gone in a minute.

JULIE My sleeve must have rubbed against you. Sit down and let me see to it. [*Takes him by the arm and makes him sit down, bends his head back and tries to get the speck out with the corner of her handkerchief*] Keep still now, quite still. [*Slaps his hand*] Do as I tell you. Why, I believe you're trembling, big, strong man though you are! [*Feels his biceps*] What muscles!

JEAN [*warning*] Miss Julie!

JULIE Yes, Monsieur Jean?

JEAN Attention. Je ne suis qu'un homme.

JULIE Will you stay still! There now. It's out. Kiss my hand and say thank you.

JEAN [*rising*] Miss Julie, listen. Kristin's gone to bed now. Will you listen?

JULIE Kiss my hand first.

JEAN Very well, but you'll have only yourself to blame.

JULIE For what?

JEAN For what! Are you still a child at twenty-five? Don't you know it's dangerous to play with fire?

JULIE Not for me. I'm insured.

JEAN [*bluntly*] No, you're not. And even if you are, there's still stuff here to kindle a flame.

JULIE Meaning yourself?

JEAN Yes. Not because I'm me, but because I'm a man and young and . . .

JULIE And good-looking? What incredible conceit! A Don Juan perhaps? Or a Joseph? Good Lord, I do believe you are a Joseph!
JEAN Do you?
JULIE I'm rather afraid so.
[JEAN *goes boldly up and tries to put his arms round her and kiss her. She boxes his ears*]
How dare you!
JEAN Was that in earnest or a joke?
JULIE In earnest.
JEAN Then what went before was in earnest too. You take your games too seriously and that's dangerous. Anyhow I'm tired of playing now and beg leave to return to my work. The Count will want his boots first thing and it's past midnight now.
JULIE Put those boots down.
JEAN No. This is my work, which it's my duty to do. But I never undertook to be your playfellow and I never will be. I consider myself too good for that.
JULIE You're proud.
JEAN In some ways—not all.
JULIE Have you ever been in love?
JEAN We don't put it that way, but I've been gone on quite a few girls. And once I went sick because I couldn't have the one I wanted. Sick, I mean, like those princes in the Arabian Nights who couldn't eat or drink for love.
JULIE Who was she? [*No answer*] Who was she?
JEAN You can't force me to tell you that.
JULIE If I ask as an equal, ask as a—friend? Who was she?
JEAN You.
JULIE [*sitting*] How absurd!
JEAN Yes, ludicrous if you like. That's the story I wouldn't tell you before, see, but now I will . . . Do you know what the world looks like from below? No, you don't. No more than the hawks and falcons do whose backs one hardly ever sees because they're always soaring up aloft. I lived in a labourer's hovel with seven other children and a pig, out in the grey fields where there isn't a single tree. But from the window I could see the wall round the Count's park with apple-trees above it. That was the Garden of Eden, guarded by many terrible angels with flaming swords. All the same I and the other boys managed to get to the tree of life. Does all this make you despise me?
JULIE Goodness, all boys steal apples!
JEAN You say that now, but all the same you do despise me. However,

one time I went into the Garden of Eden with my mother to weed the onion beds. Close to the kitchen garden there was a Turkish pavilion hung all over with jasmine and honeysuckle. I hadn't any idea what it was used for, but I'd never seen such a beautiful building. People used to go in and then come out again, and one day the door was left open. I crept up and saw the walls covered with pictures of kings and emperors, and the windows had red curtains with fringes —you know now what the place was, don't you? I . . . [*Breaks off a piece of lilac and holds it for* JULIE *to smell. As he talks, she takes it from him*] I had never been inside the manor, never seen anything but the church, and this was more beautiful. No matter where my thoughts went, they always came back—to that place. The longing went on growing in me to enjoy it fully, just once. Enfin, I sneaked in, gazed and admired. Then I heard someone coming. There was only one way out for the gentry, but for me there was another and I had no choice but to take it. [JULIE *drops the lilac on the table*] Then I took to my heels, plunged through the raspberry canes, dashed across the strawberry beds and found myself on the rose terrace. There I saw a pink dress and a pair of white stockings—it was you. I crawled into a weed pile and lay there right under it among prickly thistles and damp rank earth. I watched you walking among the roses and said to myself: "If it's true that a thief can get to heaven and be with the angels, it's pretty strange that a labourer's child here on God's earth mayn't come in the park and play with the Count's daughter."

JULIE [*sentimentally*] Do you think all poor children feel the way you did?

JEAN [*taken aback, then rallying*] All poor children? . . . Yes, of course they do. Of course.

JULIE It must be terrible to be poor.

JEAN [*with exaggerated distress*] Oh yes, Miss Julie, yes. A dog may lie on the Countess's sofa, a horse may have his nose stroked by a young lady, but a servant . . . [*change of tone*] well, yes, now and then you meet one with guts enough to rise in the world, but how often? Anyhow, do you know what I did? Jumped in the millstream with my clothes on, was pulled out and got a hiding. But the next Sunday, when Father and all the rest went to Granny's, I managed to get left behind. Then I washed with soap and hot water, put my best clothes on and went to church so as to see you. I did see you and went home determined to die. But I wanted to die beautifully and peacefully, without any pain. Then I remembered it was dangerous to sleep under an elder bush. We had a big one in full bloom, so I stripped it and climbed into the oats-bin with the flowers. Have you ever noticed how smooth oats are? Soft to touch as human skin . . . Well, I closed the lid and shut my eyes, fell asleep, and when they woke me I was very ill. But I didn't die, as you see. What I meant by all that I don't know. There was no hope of winning you—you were simply a symbol of the hopelessness of ever getting out of the class I was born in.

JULIE You put things very well, you know. Did you go to school?

JEAN For a while. But I've read a lot of novels and been to the theatre. Besides, I've heard educated folk talking—that's what's taught me most.

JULIE Do you stand round listening to what we're saying?

JEAN Yes, of course. And I've heard quite a bit too! On the carriage box or rowing the boat. Once I heard you, Miss Julie, and one of your young lady friends . . .

JULIE Oh! Whatever did you hear?

JEAN Well, it wouldn't be nice to repeat it. And I must say I was pretty startled. I couldn't think where you had learnt such words. Perhaps, at bottom, there isn't as much difference between people as one's led to believe.

JULIE How dare you! We don't behave as you do when we're engaged.

JEAN [*looking hard at her*] Are you sure? It's no use making out so innocent to me.

JULIE The man I gave my love to was a rotter.

JEAN That's what you always say—afterwards.

JULIE Always?

JEAN I think it must be always. I've heard the expression several times in similar circumstances.

JULIE What circumstances?

JEAN Like those in question. The last time . . .

JULIE [*rising*] Stop. I don't want to hear any more.

JEAN Nor did *she*—curiously enough. May I go to bed now please?

JULIE [*gently*] Go to bed on Midsummer Eve?

JEAN Yes. Dancing with that crowd doesn't really amuse me.

JULIE Get the key of the boathouse and row me out on the lake. I want to see the sun rise.

JEAN Would that be wise?

JULIE You sound as though you're frightened for your reputation.

JEAN Why not? I don't want to be made a fool of, nor to be sent packing without a character when I'm trying to better myself. Besides, I have Kristin to consider.

JULIE So now it's Kristin.

JEAN Yes, but it's you I'm thinking about too. Take my advice and go to bed.

JULIE Am I to take orders from you?

JEAN Just this once, for your own sake. Please. It's very late and sleepiness goes to one's head and makes one rash. Go to bed. What's more, if my ears don't deceive me, I hear people coming this way. They'll be looking for me, and if they find us here, you're done for.

[*The* CHORUS *approaches, singing. During the following dialogue the song is heard in snatches, and in full when the peasants enter*]

Out of the wood two women came,
Tridiri-ralla, tridiri-ra.
The feet of one were bare and cold,
Tridiri-ralla-la.

The other talked of bags of gold,
Tridiri-ralla, tridiri-ra.
But neither had a sou to her name,
Tridiri-ralla-la.

The bridal wreath I give to you,
Tridiri-ralla, tridiri-ra.
But to another I'll be true,
Tridiri-ralla-la.

JULIE I know our people and I love them, just as they do me. Let them come. You'll see.

JEAN No, Miss Julie, they don't love you. They take your food, then spit at it. You must believe me. Listen to them, just listen to what they're singing . . . No, don't listen.

JULIE [*listening*] What are they singing?

JEAN They're mocking—you and me.

JULIE Oh no! How horrible! What cowards!

JEAN A pack like that's always cowardly. But against such odds there's nothing we can do but run away.

JULIE Run away? Where to? We can't get out and we can't go into Kristin's room.

JEAN Into mine then. Necessity knows no rules. And you can trust me. I really am your true and devoted friend.

JULIE But supposing . . . supposing they were to look for you in there?

JEAN I'll bolt the door, and if they try to break in I'll shoot. Come on.
[*Pleading*] Please come.
JULIE [*tensely*] Do you promise . . . ?
JEAN I swear!
  [JULIE *goes quickly into his room and he excitedly follows her*]
  [*Led by the fiddler, the peasants enter in festive attire with flowers in their hats. They put a barrel of beer and a keg of spirits, garlanded with leaves, on the table, fetch glasses and begin to carouse. The scene becomes a ballet. They form a ring and dance and sing and mime:* "Out of the wood two women came." *Finally they go out, still singing*]
  [JULIE *comes in alone. She looks at the havoc in the kitchen, wrings her hands, then takes out her powder puff and powders her face*]
  [JEAN *enters in high spirits*]
JEAN Now you see! And you heard, didn't you? Do you still think it's possible for us to stay here?
JULIE No, I don't. But what can we do?
JEAN Run away. Far away. Take a journey.
JULIE Journey? But where to?
JEAN Switzerland. The Italian lakes. Ever been there?
JULIE No. Is it nice?
JEAN Ah! Eternal summer, oranges, evergreens . . . ah!
JULIE But what would we do there?
JEAN I'll start a hotel. First-class accommodation and first-class customers.
JULIE Hotel?
JEAN There's life for you. New faces all the time, new languages—no time for nerves or worries, no need to look for something to do—work rolling up of its own accord. Bells ringing night and day, trains whistling, buses coming and going, and all the time gold pieces rolling on to the counter. There's life for you!
JULIE For *you*. And I?
JEAN Mistress of the house, ornament of the firm. With your looks, and your style . . . oh, it's bound to be a success! Terrific! You'll sit like a queen in the office and set your slaves in motion by pressing an electric button. The guests will file past your throne and nervously lay their treasure on your table. You've no idea the way people tremble when they get their bills. I'll salt the bills and you'll sugar them with your sweetest smiles. Ah, let's get away from here! [*Produces a timetable*] At once, by the next train. We shall be at Malmö at six-thirty, Hamburg eight-forty next morning, Frankfurt-Basle the following

day, and Como by the St. Gothard pass in—let's see—three days. Three days!

JULIE That's all very well. But Jean, you must give me courage. Tell me you love me. Come and take me in your arms.

JEAN [*reluctantly*] I'd like to, but I daren't. Not again in this house. I love you—that goes without saying. You can't doubt that, Miss Julie, can you?

JULIE [*shyly, very feminine*] Miss? Call me Julie. There aren't any barriers between us now. Call me Julie.

JEAN [*uneasily*] I can't. As long as we're in this house, there *are* barriers between us. There's the past and there's the Count. I've never been so servile to anyone as I am to him. I've only got to see his gloves on a chair to feel small. I've only to hear his bell and I shy like a horse. Even now, when I look at his boots, standing there so proud and stiff, I feel my back beginning to bend. [*Kicks the boots*] It's those old, narrow-minded notions drummed into us as children . . . but they can soon be forgotten. You've only got to get to another country, a republic, and people will bend themselves double before my porter's livery. Yes, double they'll bend themselves, but I shan't. I wasn't born to bend. I've got guts, I've got character, and once I reach that first branch, you'll watch me climb. Today I'm valet, next year I'll be proprietor, in ten years I'll have made a fortune, and then I'll go to Roumania, get myself decorated and I may, I only say *may*, mind you, end up as a Count.

JULIE [*sadly*] That would be very nice.

JEAN You see in Roumania one can buy a title, and then you'll be a Countess after all. My Countess.

JULIE What do I care about all that? I'm putting those things behind me. Tell me you love me, because if you don't . . . if you don't, what am I?

JEAN I'll tell you a thousand times over—later. But not here. No sentimentality now or everything will be lost. We must consider this thing calmly like reasonable people. [*Takes a cigar, cuts and lights it*] You sit down there and I'll sit here and we'll talk as if nothing has happened.

JULIE My God, have you no feelings at all?

JEAN Nobody has more. But I know how to control them.

JULIE A short time ago you were kissing my shoe. And now . . .

JEAN [*harshly*] Yes, that was then. Now we have something else to think about.

JULIE Don't speak to me so brutally.

JEAN I'm not. Just sensibly. One folly's been committed, don't let's have more. The Count will be back at any moment and we've got to settle our future before that. Now, what do you think of my plans? Do you approve?
JULIE It seems a very good idea—but just one thing. Such a big undertaking would need a lot of capital. Have you got any?
JEAN [*chewing his cigar*] I certainly have. I've got my professional skill, my wide experience and my knowledge of foreign languages. That's capital worth having, it seems to me.
JULIE But it won't buy even one railway ticket.
JEAN Quite true. That's why I need a backer to advance some ready cash.
JULIE How could you get that at a moment's notice?
JEAN You must get it, if you want to be my partner.
JULIE I can't. I haven't any money of my own. [*Pause*]
JEAN Then the whole thing's off.
JULIE And . . . ?
JEAN We go on as we are.
JULIE Do you think I'm going to stay under this roof as your mistress? With everyone pointing at me. Do you think I can face my father after this? No. Take me away from here, away from this shame, this humiliation. Oh my God, what have I done? My God, my God! [*Weeps*]
JEAN So that's the tune now, is it? What have you done? Same as many before you.
JULIE [*hysterically*] And now you despise me. I'm falling, I'm falling.
JEAN Fall as far as me and I'll lift you up again.
JULIE Why was I so terribly attracted to you? The weak to the strong, the falling to the rising? Or was it love? Is that love? Do you know what love is?
JEAN Do I? You bet I do. Do you think I never had a girl before?
JULIE The things you say, the things you think!
JEAN That's what life's taught me, and that's what I am. It's no good getting hysterical or giving yourself airs. We're both in the same boat now. Here, my dear girl, let me give you a glass of something special. [*Opens the drawer, takes out the bottle of wine and fills two used glasses*]
JULIE Where did you get that wine?
JEAN From the cellar.
JULIE My father's burgundy.
JEAN Why not, for his son-in-law?
JULIE And I drink beer.

JEAN That only shows your taste's not so good as mine.
JULIE Thief!
JEAN Are you going to tell on me?
JULIE Oh, God! The accomplice of a petty thief! Was I blind drunk? Have I dreamt this whole night? Midsummer Eve, the night for innocent merrymaking.
JEAN Innocent, eh?
JULIE Is anyone on earth as wretched as I am now?
JEAN Why should *you* be? After such a conquest. What about Kristin in there? Don't you think she has any feelings?
JULIE I did think so, but I don't any longer. No. A menial is a menial . . .
JEAN And a whore is a whore.
JULIE [*falling to her knees, her hands clasped*] O God in heaven, put and end to my miserable life! Lift me out of this filth in which I'm sinking. Save me! Save me!
JEAN I must admit I'm sorry for you. When I was in the onion bed and saw you up there among the roses, I . . . yes, I'll tell you now . . . I had the same dirty thoughts as all boys.
JULIE You, who wanted to die because of me?
JEAN In the oats-bin? That was just talk.
JULIE Lies, you mean.
JEAN [*getting sleepy*] More or less. I think I read a story in some paper about a chimney-sweep who shut himself up in a chest full of lilac because he'd been summonsed for not supporting some brat . . .
JULIE So this is what you're like.
JEAN I had to think up something. It's always the fancy stuff that catches the women.
JULIE Beast!
JEAN Merde!
JULIE Now you have seen the falcon's back.
JEAN Not exactly its *back*.
JULIE I was to be the first branch.
JEAN But the branch was rotten.
JULIE I was to be a hotel sign.
JEAN And I the hotel.
JULIE Sit at your counter, attract your clients and cook their accounts.
JEAN I'd have done that myself.
JULIE That any human being can be so steeped in filth!
JEAN Clean it up then.
JULIE Menial! Lackey! Stand up when I speak to you.
JEAN Menial's whore, lackey's harlot, shut your mouth and get out of

here! Are you the one to lecture me for being coarse? Nobody of my kind would ever be as coarse as you were tonight. Do you think any servant girl would throw herself at a man that way? Have you ever seen a girl of my class asking for it like that? I haven't. Only animals and prostitutes.

JULIE [*broken*] Go on. Hit me, trample on me—it's all I deserve. I'm rotten. But help me! If there's any way out at all, help me.

JEAN [*more gently*] I'm not denying myself a share in the honour of seducing you, but do you think anybody in my place would have dared look in your direction if you yourself hadn't asked for it? I'm still amazed . . .

JULIE And proud.

JEAN Why not? Though I must admit the victory was too easy to make me lose my head.

JULIE Go on hitting me.

JEAN [*rising*] No. On the contrary I apologise for what I've said. I don't hit a person who's down—least of all a woman. I can't deny there's a certain satisfaction in finding that what dazzled one below was just moonshine, that that falcon's back is grey after all, that there's powder on the lovely cheek, that polished nails can have black tips, that the handkerchief is dirty although it smells of scent. On the other hand it hurts to find that what I was struggling to reach wasn't high and isn't real. It hurts to see you fallen so low you're far lower than your own cook. Hurts like when you see the last flowers of summer lashed to pieces by rain and turned to mud.

JULIE You're talking as if you're already my superior.

JEAN I am. I might make you a Countess, but you could never make me a Count, you know.

JULIE But I am the child of a Count, and you could never be that.

JEAN True, but I might be the father of Counts if . . .

JULIE You're a thief. I'm not.

JEAN There are worse things than being a thief—much lower. Besides, when I'm in a place I regard myself as a member of the family to some extent, as one of the children. You don't call it stealing when children pinch a berry from overladen bushes. [*His passion is roused again*] Miss Julie, you're a glorious woman, far too good for a man like me. You were carried away by some kind of madness, and now you're trying to cover up your mistake by persuading yourself you're in love with me. You're not, although you may find me physically attractive, which means your love's no better than mine. But I wouldn't be satisfied with being nothing but an animal for you, and I could never make you love me.

JULIE Are you sure?

JEAN You think there's a chance? Of my loving you, yes, of course. You're beautiful, refined—[*takes her hand*]—educated, and you can be nice when you want to be. The fire you kindle in a man isn't likely to go out. [*Puts his arm round her*] You're like mulled wine, full of spices, and your kisses . . . [*He tries to pull her to him, but she breaks away*]

JULIE Let go of me! You won't win me that way.

JEAN Not that way, how then? Not by kisses and fine speeches, not by planning the future and saving you from shame? How then?

JULIE How? How? I don't know. There isn't any way. I loathe you—loathe you as I loathe rats, but I can't escape from you.

JEAN Escape with me.

JULIE [*pulling herself together*] Escape? Yes, we must escape. But I'm so tired. Give me a glass of wine. [*He pours it out. She looks at her watch*] First we must talk. We still have a little time. [*Empties the glass and holds it out for more*]

JEAN Don't drink like that. You'll get tipsy.

JULIE What's that matter?

JEAN What's it matter? It's vulgar to get drunk. Well, what have you got to say?

JULIE We've got to run away, but we must talk first—or rather, I must, for so far you've done all the talking. You've told me about your life, now I want to tell you about mine, so that we really know each other before we begin this journey together.

JEAN Wait. Excuse my saying so, but don't you think you may be sorry afterwards if you give away your secrets to me?

JULIE Aren't you my friend?

JEAN On the whole. But don't rely on me.

JULIE You can't mean that. But anyway everyone knows my secrets. Listen. My mother wasn't well-born; she came of quite humble people, and was brought up with all those new ideas of sex-equality and women's rights and so on. She thought marriage was quite wrong. So when my father proposed to her, she said she would never become his *wife* . . . but in the end she did. I came into the world, as far as I can make out, against my mother's will, and I was left to run wild, but I had to do all the things a boy does—to prove women are as good as men. I had to wear boys' clothes; I was taught to handle horses—and I wasn't allowed in the dairy. She made me groom and harness and go out hunting; I even had to try to plough. All the men on the estate were given the women's jobs, and the women the men's, until the whole place went to rack and ruin and we were the laughing-stock of

the neighbourhood. At last my father seems to have come to his senses and rebelled. He changed everything and ran the place his own way. My mother got ill—I don't know what was the matter with her, but she used to have strange attacks and hide herself in the attic or the garden. Sometimes she stayed out all night. Then came the great fire which you have heard people talking about. The house and the stables and the barns—the whole place burnt to the ground. In very suspicious circumstances. Because the accident happened the very day the insurance had to be renewed, and my father had sent the new premium, but through some carelessness of the messenger it arrived too late.
[*Refills her glass and drinks*]

JEAN Don't drink any more.

JULIE Oh, what does it matter? We were destitute and had to sleep in the carriages. My father didn't know how to get money to rebuild, and then my mother suggested he should borrow from an old friend of hers, a local brick manufacturer. My father got the loan and, to his surprise, without having to pay interest. So the place was rebuilt. [*Drinks*] Do you know who set fire to it?

JEAN Your lady mother.

JULIE Do you know who the brick manufacturer was?

JEAN Your mother's lover?

JULIE Do you know whose the money was?

JEAN Wait . . . no, I don't know that.

JULIE It was my mother's.

JEAN In other words the Count's, unless there was a settlement.

JULIE There wasn't any settlement. My mother had a little money of her own which she didn't want my father to control, so she invested it with her—friend.

JEAN Who grabbed it.

JULIE Exactly. He appropriated it. My father came to know all this. He couldn't bring an action, couldn't pay his wife's lover, nor prove it was his wife's money. That was my mother's revenge because he made himself master in his own house. He nearly shot himself then—at least there's a rumour he tried and didn't bring it off. So he went on living, and my mother had to pay dearly for what she'd done. Imagine what those five years were like for me. My natural sympathies were with my father, yet I took my mother's side, because I didn't know the facts. I'd learnt from her to hate and distrust men—you know how she loathed the whole male sex. And I swore to her I'd never become the slave of any man.

JEAN And so you got engaged to that attorney.

JULIE So that he should be my slave.
JEAN But he wouldn't be.
JULIE Oh yes, he wanted to be, but he didn't have the chance. I got bored with him.
JEAN Is that what I saw—in the stable-yard?
JULIE What did you see?
JEAN What I saw was him breaking off the engagement.
JULIE That's a lie. It was I who broke it off. Did he say it was him? The cad.
JEAN He's not a cad. Do you hate men, Miss Julie?
JULIE Yes . . . most of the time. But when that weakness comes, oh . . . the shame!
JEAN Then do you hate me?
JULIE Beyond words. I'd gladly have you killed like an animal.
JEAN Quick as you'd shoot a mad dog, eh?
JULIE Yes.
JEAN But there's nothing here to shoot with—and there isn't a dog. So what do we do now?
JULIE Go abroad.
JEAN To make each other miserable for the rest of our lives?
JULIE No, to enjoy ourselves for a day or two, for a week, for as long as enjoyment lasts, and then—to die . . .
JEAN Die? How silly! I think it would be far better to start a hotel.
JULIE [*without listening*] . . . die on the shores of Lake Como, where the sun always shines and at Christmas time there are green trees and glowing oranges.
JEAN Lake Como's a rainy hole and I didn't see any oranges outside the shops. But it's a good place for tourists. Plenty of villas to be rented by—er—honeymoon couples. Profitable business that. Know why? Because they all sign a lease for six months and all leave after three weeks.
JULIE [*naïvely*] After three weeks? Why?
JEAN They quarrel, of course. But the rent has to be paid just the same. And then it's let again. So it goes on and on, for there's plenty of love although it doesn't last long.
JULIE You don't want to die with me?
JEAN I don't want to die at all. For one thing I like living and for another I consider suicide's a sin against the Creator who gave us life.
JULIE You believe in God—*you?*
JEAN Yes, of course. And I go to church every Sunday. Look here, I'm tired of all this. I'm going to bed.

JULIE Indeed! And do you think I'm going to leave things like this? Don't you know what you owe the woman you've ruined?

JEAN [*taking out his purse and throwing a silver coin on the table*] There you are. I don't want to be in anybody's debt.

JULIE [*pretending not to notice the insult*] Don't you know what the law is?

JEAN There's no law unfortunately that punishes a woman for seducing a man.

JULIE But can you see anything for it but to go abroad, get married and then divorce?

JEAN What if I refuse this mésalliance?

JULIE Mésalliance?

JEAN Yes, for me. I'm better bred than you, see! Nobody in my family committed arson.

JULIE How do you know?

JEAN Well, you can't prove otherwise, because we haven't any family records outside the Registrar's office. But I've seen your family tree in that book on the drawing-room table. Do you know who the founder of your family was? A miller who let his wife sleep with the King one night during the Danish war. I haven't any ancestors like that. I haven't any ancestors at all, but I might become one.

JULIE This is what I get for confiding in someone so low, for sacrificing my family honour . . .

JEAN Dishonour! Well, I told you so. One shouldn't drink, because then one talks. And one shouldn't talk.

JULIE Oh, how ashamed I am, how bitterly ashamed! If at least you loved me!

JEAN Look here—for the last time—what do you want? Am I to burst into tears? Am I to jump over your riding whip? Shall I kiss you and carry you off to Lake Como for three weeks, after which . . . What am I to do? What do you want? This is getting unbearable, but that's what comes of playing around with women. Miss Julie, I can see how miserable you are; I know you're going through hell, but I don't understand you. We don't have scenes like this; we don't go in for hating each other. We make love for fun in our spare time, but we haven't all day and all night for it like you. I think you must be ill. I'm sure you're ill.

JULIE Then you must be kind to me. You sound almost human now.

JEAN Well, be human yourself. You spit at me, then won't let me wipe it off—on you.

JULIE Help me, help me! Tell me what to do, where to go.

JEAN Jesus, as if I knew!
JULIE I've been mad, raving mad, but there must be a way out.
JEAN Stay here and keep quiet. Nobody knows anything.
JULIE I can't. People do know. Kristin knows.
JEAN They don't know and they wouldn't believe such a thing.
JULIE [*hesitating*] But—it might happen again.
JEAN That's true.
JULIE And there might be—consequences.
JEAN [*in panic*] Consequences! Fool that I am I never thought of that. Yes, there's nothing for it but to go. At once. I can't come with you. That would be a complete giveaway. You must go alone—abroad—anywhere.
JULIE Alone? Where to? I can't.
JEAN You must. And before the Count gets back. If you stay, we know what will happen. Once you've sinned you feel you might as well go on, as the harm's done. Then you get more and more reckless and in the end you're found out. No. You must go abroad. Then write to the Count and tell him everything, except that it was me. He'll never guess that—and I don't think he'll want to.
JULIE I'll go if you come with me.
JEAN Are you crazy, woman? "Miss Julie elopes with valet." Next day it would be in the headlines, and the Count would never live it down.
JULIE I can't go. I can't stay. I'm so tired, so completely worn out. Give me orders. Set me going. I can't think any more, can't act . . .
JEAN You see what weaklings you are. Why do you give yourselves airs and turn up your noses as if you're the lords of creation? Very well, I'll give you your orders. Go upstairs and dress. Get money for the journey and come down here again.
JULIE [*softly*] Come up with me.
JEAN To your room? Now you've gone crazy again. [*Hesitates a moment*] No! Go along at once. [*Takes her hand and pulls her to the door*]
JULIE [*as she goes*] Speak kindly to me, Jean.
JEAN Orders always sound unkind. Now you know. Now you know. [*Left alone,* JEAN *sighs with relief, sits down at the table, takes out a note-book and pencil and adds up figures, now and then aloud. Dawn begins to break.* KRISTIN *enters dressed for church, carrying his white dickey and tie*]
KRISTIN Lord Jesus, look at the state the place is in! What have you been up to? [*Turns out the lamp*]
JEAN Oh, Miss Julie invited the crowd in. Did you sleep through it? Didn't you hear anything?

KRISTIN I slept like a log.
JEAN And dressed for church already.
KRISTIN Yes, you promised to come to Communion with me today.
JEAN Why, so I did. And you've got my bib and tucker, I see. Come on then. [*Sits.* KRISTIN *begins to put his things on. Pause. Sleepily*] What's the lesson today?
KRISTIN It's about the beheading of John the Baptist, I think.
JEAN That's sure to be horribly long. Hi, you're choking me! Oh Lord, I'm so sleepy, so sleepy!
KRISTIN Yes, what have you been doing up all night? You look absolutely green.
JEAN Just sitting here talking with Miss Julie.
KRISTIN She doesn't know what's proper, that one. [*Pause*]
JEAN I say, Kristin.
KRISTIN What?
JEAN It's queer really, isn't it, when you come to think of it? Her.
KRISTIN What's queer?
JEAN The whole thing. [*Pause*]
KRISTIN [*looking at the half-filled glasses on the table*] Have you been drinking together too?
JEAN Yes.
KRISTIN More shame you. Look me straight in the face.
JEAN Yes.
KRISTIN Is it possible? Is it possible?
JEAN [*after a moment*] Yes, it is.
KRISTIN Oh! This I would never have believed. How low!
JEAN You're not jealous of her, surely?
KRISTIN No, I'm not. If it had been Clara or Sophie I'd have scratched your eyes out. But not of her. I don't know why; that's how it is though. But it's disgusting.
JEAN You're angry with her then.
KRISTIN No. With you. It was wicked of you, very very wicked. Poor girl. And, mark my words, I won't stay here any longer now—in a place where one can't respect one's employers.
JEAN Why should one respect them?
KRISTIN You should know since you're so smart. But you don't want to stay in the service of people who aren't respectable, do you? I wouldn't demean myself.
JEAN But it's rather a comfort to find out they're no better than us.
KRISTIN I don't think so. If they're no better there's nothing for us to live up to. Oh and think of the Count! Think of him. He's been

through so much already. No, I won't stay in the place any longer. A fellow like you too! If it had been that attorney now or somebody of her own class . . .
JEAN Why, what's wrong with . . .
KRISTIN Oh, you're all right in your own way, but when all's said and done there is a difference between one class and another. No, this is something I'll never be able to stomach. That our young lady who was so proud and so down on men you'd never believe she'd let one come near her should go and give herself to one like you. She who wanted to have poor Diana shot for running after the lodge-keeper's pug. No, I must say . . . ! Well, I won't stay here any longer. On the twenty-fourth of October I quit.
JEAN And then?
KRISTIN Well, since you mention it, it's about time you began to look around, if we're ever going to get married.
JEAN But what am I to look for? I shan't get a place like this when I'm married.
KRISTIN I know you won't. But you might get a job as porter or caretaker in some public institution. Government rations are small but sure, and there's a pension for the widow and children.
JEAN That's all very fine, but it's not in my line to start thinking at once about dying for my wife and children. I must say I had rather bigger ideas.
KRISTIN You and your ideas! You've got obligations too, and you'd better start thinking about them.
JEAN Don't *you* start pestering me about obligations. I've had enough of that. [*Listens to a sound upstairs*] Anyway we've plenty of time to work things out. Go and get ready now and we'll be off to church.
KRISTIN Who's that walking about upstairs?
JEAN Don't know—unless it's Clara.
KRISTIN [*going*] You don't think the Count could have come back without our hearing him?
JEAN [*scared*] The Count? No, he can't have. He'd have rung for me.
KRISTIN God help us! I've never known such goings on.
[*Exit*]
[*The sun has now risen and is shining on the treetops. The light gradually changes until it slants in through the windows.* JEAN *goes to the door and beckons.* JULIE *enters in travelling clothes, carrying a small bird-cage covered with a cloth which she puts on a chair*]
JULIE I'm ready.
JEAN Hush! Kristin's up.

JULIE [*in a very nervous state*] Does she suspect anything?
JEAN Not a thing. But, my God, what a sight you are!
JULIE Sight? What do you mean?
JEAN You're white as a corpse and—pardon me—your face is dirty.
JULIE Let me wash then. [*Goes to the sink and washes her face and hands*] There. Give me a towel. Oh! The sun is rising!
JEAN And that breaks the spell.
JULIE Yes. The spell of Midsummer Eve . . . But listen, Jean. Come with me. I've got the money.
JEAN [*sceptically*] Enough?
JULIE Enough to start with. Come with me. I can't travel alone today. It's Midsummer Day, remember. I'd be packed into a suffocating train among crowds of people who'd all stare at me. And it would stop at every station while I yearned for wings. No, I can't do that, I simply can't. There will be memories too; memories of Midsummer Days when I was little. The leafy church—birch and lilac—the gaily spread dinner table, relatives, friends—evening in the park—dancing and music and flowers and fun. Oh, however far you run away—there'll always be memories in the baggage car—and remorse and guilt.
JEAN I will come with you, but quickly now then, before it's too late. At once.
JULIE Put on your things. [*Picks up the cage*]
JEAN No luggage mind. That would give us away.
JULIE No, only what we can take with us in the carriage.
JEAN [*fetching his hat*] What on earth have you got there? What is it?
JULIE Only my greenfinch. I don't want to leave it behind.
JEAN Well, I'll be damned! We're to take a bird-cage along, are we? You're crazy. Put that cage down.
JULIE It's the only thing I'm taking from my home. The only living creature who cares for me since Diana went off like that. Don't be cruel. Let me take it.
JEAN Put that cage down, I tell you—and don't talk so loud. Kristin will hear.
JULIE No, I won't leave it in strange hands. I'd rather you killed it.
JEAN Give the little beast here then and I'll wring its neck.
JULIE But don't hurt it, don't . . . no, I can't.
JEAN Give it here. I *can*.
JULIE [*taking the bird out of the cage and kissing it*] Dear little Serena, must you die and leave your mistress?
JEAN Please don't make a scene. It's *your* life and future we're worrying about. Come on, quick now!

[*He snatches the bird from her, puts it on a board and picks up a*

chopper. JULIE *turns away*]
You should have learnt how to kill chickens instead of target-shooting. Then you wouldn't faint at a drop of blood.

JULIE [*screaming*] Kill me too! Kill me! You who can butcher an innocent creature without a quiver. Oh, how I hate you, how I loathe you! There is blood between us now. I curse the hour I first saw you. I curse the hour I was conceived in my mother's womb.

JEAN What's the use of cursing. Let's go.

JULIE [*going to the chopping-block as if drawn against her will*] No, I won't go yet. I can't . . . I must look. Listen! There's a carriage. [*Listens without taking her eyes off the board and chopper*] You don't think I can bear the sight of blood. You think I'm so weak. Oh, how I should like to see your blood and your brains on a chopping-block! I'd like to see the whole of your sex swimming like that in a sea of blood. I think I could drink out of your skull, bathe my feet in your broken breast and eat your heart roasted whole. You think I'm weak. You think I love you, that my womb yearned for your seed and I want to carry your offspring under my heart and nourish it with my blood. You think I want to bear your child and take your name. By the way, what is your name? I've never heard your surname. I don't suppose you've got one. I should be "Mrs. Hovel" or "Madam Dunghill." You dog wearing my collar, you lackey with my crest on your buttons! I share you with my cook; I'm my own servant's rival! Oh! Oh! Oh! . . . You think I'm a coward and will run away. No, now I'm going to stay—and let the storm break. My father will come back . . . find his desk broken open . . . his money gone. Then he'll ring that bell—twice for the valet—and then he'll send for the police . . . and I shall tell everything. Everything. Oh how wonderful to make an end of it all—a real end! He has a stroke and dies and that's the end of all of us. Just peace and quietness . . . eternal rest. The coat of arms broken on the coffin and the Count's line extinct . . . But the valet's line goes on in an orphanage, wins laurels in the gutter and ends in jail.

JEAN There speaks the noble blood! Bravo, Miss Julie. But now, don't let the cat out of the bag.
[KRISTIN *enters dressed for church, carrying a prayer-book.* JULIE *rushes to her and flings herself into her arms for protection*]

JULIE Help me, Kristin! Protect me from this man!

KRISTIN [*unmoved and cold*] What goings-on for a feast day morning! [*Sees the board*] And what a filthy mess. What's it all about? Why are you screaming and carrying on so?

JULIE Kristin, you're a woman and my friend. Beware of that scoundrel!

JEAN [*embarrassed*] While you ladies are talking things over, I'll go and shave. [*Slips into his room*]
JULIE You must understand. You must listen to me.
KRISTIN I certainly don't understand such loose ways. Where are you off to in those travelling clothes? And he had his hat on, didn't he, eh?
JULIE Listen, Kristin. Listen, I'll tell you everything.
KRISTIN I don't want to know anything.
JULIE You must listen.
KRISTIN What to? Your nonsense with Jean? I don't care a rap about that; it's nothing to do with me. But if you're thinking of getting him to run off with you, we'll soon put a stop to that.
JULIE [*very nervously*] Please try to be calm, Kristin, and listen. I can't stay here, nor can Jean—so we must go abroad.
KRISTIN Hm, hm!
JULIE [*brightening*] But you see, I've had an idea. Supposing we all three go—abroad—to Switzerland and start a hotel together . . . I've got some money, you see . . . and Jean and I could run the whole thing—and I thought you would take charge of the kitchen. Wouldn't that be splendid? Say yes, do. If you come with us everything will be fine. Oh do say yes! [*Puts her arms round* KRISTIN]
KRISTIN [*coolly thinking*] Hm, hm.
JULIE [*presto tempo*] You've never travelled, Kristin. You should go abroad and see the world. You've no idea how nice it is travelling by train—new faces all the time and new countries. On our way through Hamburg we'll go to the zoo—you'll love that—and we'll go to the theatre and the opera too . . . and when we get to Munich there'll be the museums, dear, and pictures by Rubens and Raphael—the great painters, you know . . . You've heard of Munich, haven't you? Where King Ludwig lived—you know, the king who went mad. . . . We'll see his castles—some of his castles are still just like in fairy-tales . . . and from there it's not far to Switzerland—and the Alps. Think of the Alps, Kristin dear, covered with snow in the middle of summer . . . and there are oranges there and trees that are green the whole year round . . .
[JEAN *is seen in the door of his room, sharpening his razor on a strop which he holds with his teeth and his left hand. He listens to the talk with satisfaction and now and then nods approval.* JULIE *continues, tempo prestissimo*]
And then we'll get a hotel . . . and I'll sit at the desk, while Jean receives the guests and goes out marketing and writes letters . . . There's life for you! Trains whistling, buses driving up, bells ringing

upstairs and downstairs . . . and I shall make out the bills—and I shall cook them too . . . you've no idea how nervous travellers are when it comes to paying their bills. And you—you'll sit like a queen in the kitchen . . . of course there won't be any standing at the stove for you. You'll always have to be nicely dressed and ready to be seen, and with your looks—no, I'm not flattering you—one fine day you'll catch yourself a husband . . . some rich Englishman, I shouldn't wonder—they're the ones who are easy—[*slowing down*]—to catch . . . and then we'll get rich and build ourselves a villa on Lake Como . . . of course it rains there a little now and then—but—[*dully*]—the sun must shine there too sometimes—even though it seems gloomy—and if not—then we can come home again—come back—[*pause*]—here—or somewhere else . . .

KRISTIN Look here, Miss Julie, do you believe all that yourself?

JULIE [*exhausted*] Do I believe it?

KRISTIN Yes.

JULIE [*wearily*] I don't know. I don't believe anything any more. [*Sinks down on the bench; her head in her arms on the table*] Nothing. Nothing at all.

KRISTIN [*turning to* JEAN] So you meant to beat it, did you?

JEAN [*disconcerted, putting the razor on the table*] Beat it? What are you talking about? You've heard Miss Julie's plan, and though she's tired now with being up all night, it's a perfectly sound plan.

KRISTIN Oh, is it? If you thought I'd work for that . . .

JEAN [*interrupting*] Kindly use decent language in front of your mistress. Do you hear?

KRISTIN Mistress?

JEAN Yes.

KRISTIN Well, well, just listen to that!

JEAN Yes, it would be a good thing if you did listen and talked less. Miss Julie is your mistress and what's made you lose your respect for her now ought to make you feel the same about yourself.

KRISTIN I've always had enough self-respect—

JEAN To despise other people.

KRISTIN —not to go below my own station. Has the Count's cook ever gone with the groom or the swineherd? Tell me that.

JEAN No, you were lucky enough to have a high-class chap for your beau.

KRISTIN High-class all right—selling the oats out of the Count's stable.

JEAN You're a fine one to talk—taking a commission on the groceries and bribes from the butcher.

KRISTIN What the devil . . . ?

JEAN And now you can't feel any respect for your employers. You, you!

KRISTIN Are you coming to church with me? I should think you need a good sermon after your fine deeds.

JEAN No, I'm not going to church today. You can go alone and confess your own sins.

KRISTIN Yes, I'll do that and bring back enough forgiveness to cover yours too. The Saviour suffered and died on the cross for all our sins, and if we go to Him with faith and a penitent heart, He takes all our sins upon Himself.

JEAN Even grocery thefts?

JULIE Do you believe that, Kristin?

KRISTIN That is my living faith, as sure as I stand here. The faith I learnt as a child and have kept ever since, Miss Julie. "But where sin abounded, grace did much more abound."

JULIE Oh, if I had your faith! Oh, if . . .

KRISTIN But you see you can't have it without God's special grace, and it's not given to all to have that.

JULIE Who is it given to then?

KRISTIN That's the great secret of the workings of grace, Miss Julie. God is no respecter of persons, and with Him the last shall be first . . .

JULIE Then I suppose He does respect the last.

KRISTIN [continuing] . . . and it is easier for a camel to go through the eye of a needle than for a rich man to enter into the kingdom of God. That's how it is, Miss Julie. Now I'm going—alone, and on my way I shall tell the groom not to let any of the horses out, in case anyone should want to leave before the Count gets back. Goodbye. [Exit]

JEAN What a devil! And all on account of a greenfinch.

JULIE [wearily] Never mind the greenfinch. Do you see any way out of this, any end to it?

JEAN [pondering] No.

JULIE If you were in my place, what would you do?

JEAN In your place? Wait a bit. If I was a woman—a lady of rank who had—fallen. I don't know. Yes, I do know now.

JULIE [picking up the razor and making a gesture] This?

JEAN Yes. But I wouldn't do it, you know. There's a difference between us.

JULIE Because you're a man and I'm a woman? What is the difference?

JEAN The usual difference—between man and woman.

JULIE [holding the razor] I'd like to. But I can't. My father couldn't either, that time he wanted to.

JEAN No, he didn't want to. He had to be revenged first.
JULIE And now my mother is revenged again, through me.
JEAN Didn't you ever love your father, Miss Julie?
JULIE Deeply, but I must have hated him too—unconsciously. And he let me be brought up to despise my own sex, to be half woman, half man. Whose fault is what's happened? My father's, my mother's or my own? My own? I haven't anything that's my own. I haven't one single thought that I didn't get from my father, one emotion that didn't come from my mother, and as for this last idea—about all people being equal—I got that from him, my fiancé—that's why I call him a cad. How can it be my fault? Push the responsibility on to Jesus, like Kristin does? No, I'm too proud and—thanks to my father's teaching—too intelligent. As for all that about a rich person not being able to get into heaven, it's just a lie, but Kristin, who has money in the savings-bank, will certainly not get in. Whose fault is it? What does it matter whose fault it is? In any case I must take the blame and bear the consequences.
JEAN Yes, but . . . [*There are two sharp rings on the bell.* JULIE *jumps to her feet.* JEAN *changes into his livery*] The Count is back. Supposing Kristin . . . [*Goes to the speaking-tube, presses it and listens*]
JULIE Has he been to his desk yet?
JEAN This is Jean, sir. [*Listens*] Yes, sir. [*Listens*] Yes, sir, very good, sir. [*Listens*] At once, sir? [*Listens*] Very good, sir. In half an hour.
JULIE [*in panic*] What did he say? My God, what did he say?
JEAN He ordered his boots and his coffee in half an hour.
JULIE Then there's half an hour . . . Oh, I'm so tired! I can't do anything. Can't be sorry, can't run away, can't stay, can't live—can't die. Help me. Order me, and I'll obey like a dog. Do me this last service—save my honour, save his name. You know what I ought to do, but haven't the strength to do. Use your strength and order me to do it.
JEAN I don't know why—I can't now—I don't understand . . . It's just as if this coat made me—I can't give you orders—and now that the Count has spoken to me—I can't quite explain, but . . . well, that devil of a lackey is bending my back again. I believe if the Count came down now and ordered me to cut my throat, I'd do it on the spot.
JULIE Then pretend you're him and I'm you. You did some fine acting before, when you knelt to me and played the aristocrat. Or . . . Have you ever seen a hypnotist at the theatre? [*He nods*] He says to the person "Take the broom," and he takes it. He says "Sweep," and he sweeps . . .

JEAN But the person has to be asleep.
JULIE [*as if in a trance*] I am asleep already . . . the whole room has turned to smoke—and you look like a stove—a stove like a man in black with a tall hat—your eyes are glowing like coals when the fire is low—and your face is a white patch like ashes. [*The sunlight has now reached the floor and lights up* JEAN] How nice and warm it is! [*She holds out her hands as though warming them at a fire*] And so light—and so peaceful.
JEAN [*putting the razor in her hand*] Here is the broom. Go now while it's light—out to the barn—and . . . [*Whispers in her ear*]
JULIE [*waking*] Thank you. I am going now—to rest. But just tell me that even the first can receive the gift of grace.
JEAN The first? No, I can't tell you that. But wait . . . Miss Julie, I've got it! You aren't one of the first any longer. You're one of the last.
JULIE That's true. I'm one of the very last. I *am* the last. Oh! . . . But now I can't go. Tell me again to go.
JEAN No, I can't now either. I can't.
JULIE And the first shall be last.
JEAN Don't think, don't think. You're taking my strength away too and making me a coward. What's that? I thought I saw the bell move . . . To be so frightened of a bell! Yes, but it's not just a bell. There's somebody behind it—a hand moving it—and something else moving the hand—and if you stop your ears—if you stop your ears—yes, then it rings louder than ever. Rings and rings until you answer—and then it's too late. Then the police come and . . . and . . . [*The bell rings twice loudly.* JEAN *flinches, then straightens himself up*] It's horrible. But there's no other way to end it . . . Go! [JULIE *walks firmly out through the door*]

CURTAIN

Riders to the Sea

A Play in One Act

Characters

MAURYA *an old woman*
BARTLEY *her son*
CATHLEEN *her daughter*
NORA *a younger daughter*
MEN AND WOMEN

Scene: *An Island off the West of Ireland.* [*Cottage kitchen, with nets, oil-skins, spinning wheel, some new boards standing by the wall, etc. Cathleen, a girl of about twenty, finishes kneading cake, and puts it down in the pot-oven by the fire; then wipes her hands, and begins to spin at the wheel.* NORA, *a young girl, puts her head in at the door*]

NORA [*In a low voice*] Where is she?
CATHLEEN She's lying down, God help her, and may be sleeping, if she's able.
   [NORA *comes in softly, and takes a bundle from under her shawl*]
CATHLEEN [*Spinning the wheel rapidly*] What is it you have?
NORA The young priest is after bringing them. It's a shirt and a plain stocking were got off a drowned man in Donegal.
   [CATHLEEN *stops her wheel with a sudden movement, and leans out to listen*]
NORA We're to find out if it's Michael's they are, some time herself will be down looking by the sea.
CATHLEEN How would they be Michael's, Nora? How would he go the length of that way to the far north?
NORA The young priest says he's known the like of it. "If it's Michael's they are," says he, "you can tell herself he's got a clean burial by the grace of God, and if they're not his, let no one say a word about them, for she'll be getting her death," says he, "with crying and lamenting."
   [*The door which* NORA *half closed is blown open by a gust of wind*]
CATHLEEN [*Looking out anxiously*] Did you ask him would he stop Bartley going this day with the horses to the Galway fair?
NORA "I won't stop him," says he, "but let you not be afraid. Herself does be saying prayers half through the night, and the Almighty God won't leave her destitute," says he, "with no son living."

CATHLEEN Is the sea bad by the white rocks, Nora?
NORA Middling bad, God help us. There's a great roaring in the west, and it's worse it'll be getting when the tide's turned to the wind. [*She goes over to the table with the bundle*] Shall I open it now?
CATHLEEN Maybe she'd wake up on us, and come in before we'd done. [*Coming to the table*] It's a long time we'll be, and the two of us crying.
NORA [*Goes to the inner door and listens*] She's moving about on the bed. She'll be coming in a minute.
CATHLEEN Give me the ladder, and I'll put them up in the turf-loft, the way she won't know of them at all, and maybe when the tide turns she'll be going down to see would he be floating from the east.
[*They put the ladder against the gable of the chimney;* CATHLEEN *goes up a few steps and hides the bundle in the turf-loft.* MAURYA *comes from the inner room*]
MAURYA [*Looking up at* CATHLEEN *and speaking querulously*] Isn't it turf enough you have for this day and evening?
CATHLEEN There's a cake baking at the fire for a short space [*Throwing down the turf*] and Bartley will want it when the tide turns if he goes to Connemara.
[NORA *picks up the turf and puts it round the pot-oven*]
MAURYA [*Sitting down on a stool at the fire*] He won't go this day with the wind rising from the south and west. He won't go this day, for the young priest will stop him surely.
NORA He'll not stop him, mother, and I heard Eamon Simon and Stephen Pheety and Colum Shawn saying he would go.
MAURYA Where is he itself?
NORA He went down to see would there be another boat sailing in the week, and I'm thinking it won't be long till he's here now, for the tide's turning at the green head, and the hooker's tacking from the east.
CATHLEEN I hear some one passing the big stones.
NORA [*Looking out*] He's coming now, and he in a hurry.
BARTLEY [*Comes in and looks round the room. Speaking sadly and quietly*] Where is the bit of new rope, Cathleen, was bought in Connemara?
CATHLEEN [*Coming down*] Give it to him, Nora; it's on a nail by the white boards. I hung it up this morning, for the pig with the black feet was eating it.
NORA [*Giving him a rope*] Is that it, Bartley?

MAURYA You'd do right to leave that rope, Bartley, hanging by the boards [*Bartley takes the rope*]. It will be wanting in this place, I'm telling you, if Michael is washed up tomorrow morning, or the next morning, or any morning in the week, for it's a deep grave we'll make him by the grace of God.

BARTLEY [*Beginning to work with the rope*] I've no halter the way I can ride down on the mare, and I must go now quickly. This is the one boat going for two weeks or beyond it, and the fair will be a good fair for horses I heard them saying below.

MAURYA It's a hard thing they'll be saying below if the body is washed up and there's no man in it to make the coffin, and I after giving a big price for the finest white boards you'd find in Connemara.
[*She looks round at the boards*]

BARTLEY How would it be washed up, and we after looking each day for nine days, and a strong wind blowing a while back from the west and south?

MAURYA If it wasn't found itself, that wind is raising the sea, and there was a star up against the moon, and it rising in the night. If it was a hundred horses, or a thousand horses you had itself, what is the price of a thousand horses against a son where there is one son only?

BARTLEY [*Working at the halter, to* CATHLEEN] Let you go down each day, and see the sheep aren't jumping in on the rye, and if the jobber comes you can sell the pig with the black feet if there is a good price going.

MAURYA How would the like of her get a good price for a pig?

BARTLEY [*To* CATHLEEN] If the west wind holds with the last bit of the moon let you and Nora get up weed enough for another cock for the kelp. It's hard set we'll be from this day with no one in it but one man to work.

MAURYA It's hard set we'll be surely the day you're drownd'd with the rest. What way will I live and the girls with me, and I an old woman looking for the grave?
[BARTLEY *lays down the halter, takes off his old coat, and puts on a newer one of the same flannel*]

BARTLEY [*To* NORA] Is she coming to the pier?

NORA [*Looking out*] She's passing the green head and letting fall her sails.

BARTLEY [*Getting his purse and tobacco*] I'll have half an hour to go down, and you'll see me coming again in two days, or in three days, or maybe in four days if the wind is bad.

MAURYA [*Turning round to the fire, and putting her shawl over her head*] Isn't it a hard and cruel man won't hear a word from an old woman, and she holding him from the sea?

CATHLEEN It's the life of a young man to be going on the sea, and who would listen to an old woman with one thing and she saying it over?

BARTLEY [*Taking the halter*] I must go now quickly. I'll ride down on the red mare, and the gray pony'll run behind me . . . The blessing of God on you.

[*He goes out*]

MAURYA [*Crying out as he is in the door*] He's gone now, God spare us, and we'll not see him again. He's gone now, and when the black night is falling I'll have no son left me in the world.

CATHLEEN Why wouldn't you give him your blessing and he looking round in the door? Isn't it sorrow enough is on every one in this house without your sending him out with an unlucky word behind him, and a hard word in his ear?

[MAURYA *takes up the tongs and begins raking the fire aimlessly without looking round*]

NORA [*Turning towards her*] You're taking away the turf from the cake.

CATHLEEN [*Crying out*] The Son of God forgive us, Nora, we're after forgetting his bit of bread.

[*She comes over to the fire*]

NORA And it's destroyed he'll be going till dark night, and he after eating nothing since the sun went up.

CATHLEEN [*Turning the cake out of the oven*] It's destroyed he'll be, surely. There's no sense left on any person in a house where an old woman will be talking for ever.

[MAURYA *sways herself on her stool*]

CATHLEEN [*Cutting off some of the bread and rolling it in a cloth; to* MAURYA] Let you go down now to the spring well and give him this and he passing. You'll see him then and the dark word will be broken, and you can say "God speed you," the way he'll be easy in his mind.

MAURYA [*Taking the bread*] Will I be in it as soon as himself?

CATHLEEN If you go now quickly.

MAURYA [*Standing up unsteadily*] It's hard set I am to walk.

CATHLEEN [*Looking at her anxiously*] Give her the stick, Nora, or maybe she'll slip on the big stones.

NORA What stick?

CATHLEEN The stick Michael brought from Connemara.

MAURYA [*Taking a stick* NORA *gives her*] In the big world the old people do be leaving things after them for their sons and children, but in this place it is the young men do be leaving things behind for them that do be old.

[*She goes out slowly.* NORA *goes over to the ladder*]

CATHLEEN Wait, Nora, maybe she'd turn back quickly. She's that sorry, God help her, you wouldn't know the thing she'd do.

NORA Is she gone round by the bush?

CATHLEEN [*Looking out*] She's gone now. Throw it down quickly, for the Lord knows when she'll be out of it again.

NORA [*Getting the bundle from the loft*] The young priest said he'd be passing tomorrow, and we might go down and speak to him below if it's Michael's they are surely.

CATHLEEN [*Taking the bundle*] Did he say what way they were found?

NORA [*Coming down*] "There were two men," says he, "and they rowing round with poteen before the cocks crowed, and the oar of one of them caught the body, and they passing the black cliffs of the north."

CATHLEEN [*Trying to open the bundle*] Give me a knife, Nora, the string's perished with the salt water, and there's a black knot on it you wouldn't loosen in a week.

NORA [*Giving her a knife*] I've heard tell it was a long way to Donegal.

CATHLEEN [*Cutting the string*] It is surely. There was a man in here a while ago—the man sold us that knife—and he said if you set off walking from the rocks beyond, it would be seven days you'd be in Donegal.

NORA And what time would a man take, and he floating?

[*Cathleen opens the bundle and takes out a bit of a stocking. They look at them eagerly*]

CATHLEEN [*In a low voice*] The Lord spare us, Nora! isn't it a queer hard thing to say if it's his they are surely?

NORA I'll get his shirt off the hook the way we can put the one flannel on the other [*she looks through some clothes hanging in the corner*]. It's not with them, Cathleen, and where will it be?

CATHLEEN I'm thinking Bartley put it on him in the morning, for his own shirt was heavy with the salt in it [*pointing to the corner*]. There's a bit of a sleeve was of the same stuff. Give me that and it will do.

[NORA *brings it to her and they compare the flannel*]

CATHLEEN It's the same stuff, Nora; but if it is itself aren't there great rolls of it in the shops of Galway, and isn't it many another man may have a shirt of it as well as Michael himself?

NORA [*Who has taken up the stocking and counted the stitches, crying out*] It's Michael, Cathleen, it's Michael; God spare his soul, and what will herself say when she hears this story, and Bartley on the sea?

CATHLEEN [*Taking the stocking*] It's a plain stocking.

NORA It's the second one of the third pair I knitted, and I put up three score stitches, and I dropped four of them.

CATHLEEN [*Counts the stitches*] It's that number is in it [*crying out*]. Ah, Nora, isn't it a bitter thing to think of him floating that way to the far north, and no one to keen him but the black hags that do be flying on the sea?

NORA [*Swinging herself round, and throwing out her arms on the clothes*] And isn't it a pitiful thing when there is nothing left of a man who was a great rower and fisher, but a bit of an old shirt and a plain stocking?

CATHLEEN [*After an instant*] Tell me is herself coming, Nora? I hear a little sound on the path.

NORA [*Looking out*] She is, Cathleen. She's coming up to the door.

CATHLEEN Put these things away before she'll come in. Maybe it's easier she'll be after giving her blessing to Bartley, and we won't let on we've heard anything the time he's on the sea.

NORA [*Helping* CATHLEEN *to close the bundle*] We'll put them here in the corner.

[*They put them into a hole in the chimney corner.* CATHLEEN *goes back to the spinning-wheel*]

NORA Will she see it was crying I was?

CATHLEEN Keep your back to the door the way the light'll not be on you.
[NORA *sits down at the chimney corner, with her back to the door.* MAURYA *comes in very slowly, without looking at the girls, and goes over to her stool at the other side of the fire. The cloth with the bread is still in her hand. The girls look at each other, and Nora points to the bundle of bread*]

CATHLEEN [*After spinning for a moment*] You didn't give him his bit of bread?

[MAURYA *begins to keen softly, without turning round*]

CATHLEEN Did you see him riding down?

[MAURYA *goes on keening*]

CATHLEEN [*A little impatiently*] God forgive you; isn't it a better thing to raise your voice and tell what you seen, than to be making lamentation for a thing that's done? Did you see Bartley, I'm saying to you.

MAURYA [*With a weak voice*] My heart's broken from this day.

CATHLEEN [*As before*] Did you see Bartley?

MAURYA I seen the fearfulest thing.
CATHLEEN [*Leaves her wheel and looks out*] God forgive you; he's riding the mare now over the green head, and the gray pony behind him.
MAURYA [*Starts, so that her shawl falls back from her head and shows her white tossed hair. With a frightened voice*] The gray pony behind him.
CATHLEEN [*Coming to the fire*] What is it ails you, at all?
MAURYA [*Speaking very slowly*] I've seen the fearfulest thing any person has seen, since the day Bride Dara seen the dead man with the child in his arms.
CATHLEEN and NORA Uah. [*They crouch down in front of the old woman at the fire*]
NORA Tell us what it is you seen.
MAURYA I went down to the spring well, and I stood there saying a prayer to myself. Then Bartley came along, and he riding on the red mare with the gray pony behind him [*she puts up her hands, as if to hide something from her eyes*] The Son of God spare us, Nora!
CATHLEEN What is it you seen?
MAURYA I seen Michael himself.
CATHLEEN [*Speaking softly*] You did not, mother; it wasn't Michael you seen, for his body is after being found in the far north, and he's got a clean burial by the grace of God.
MAURYA [*A little defiantly*] I'm after seeing him this day, and he riding and galloping. Bartley came first on the red mare; and I tried to say "God speed you," but something choked the words in my throat. He went by quickly; and "the blessing of God on you," says he, and I could say nothing. I looked up then, and I crying, at the gray pony, and there was Michael upon it—with fine clothes on him, and new shoes on his feet.
CATHLEEN [*Begins to keen*] It's destroyed we are from this day. It's destroyed, surely.
NORA Didn't the young priest say the Almighty God wouldn't leave her destitute with no son living?
MAURYA [*In a low voice, but clearly*] It's little the like of him knows of the sea. . . . Bartley will be lost now, and let you call in Eamon and make me a good coffin out of the white boards, for I won't live after them. I've had a husband, and a husband's father, and six sons in this house—six fine men, though it was a hard birth I had with every one of them and they coming to the world—and some of them were found and some of them were not found, but they're gone now the lot of them. . . . There were Stephen, and Shawn, were lost in the

great wind, and found after in the Bay of Gregory of the Golden Mouth, and carried up the two of them on the one plank, and in by that door.

[*She pauses for a moment, the girls start as if they heard something through the door that is half open behind them*]

NORA [*In a whisper*] Did you hear that, Cathleen? Did you hear a noise in the north-east?

CATHLEEN [*In a whisper*] There's some one after crying out by the seashore.

MAURYA [*Continues without hearing anything*] There was Sheamus and his father, and his own father again, were lost in a dark night, and not a stick or sign was seen of them when the sun went up. There was Patch after was drowned out of a curagh that turned over. I was sitting here with Bartley, and he a baby, lying on my two knees, and I seen two women, and three women, and four women coming in, and they crossing themselves, and not saying a word. I looked out then, and there were men coming after them, and they holding a thing in the half of a red sail, and water dripping out of it—it was a dry day, Nora—and leaving a track to the door.

[*She pauses again with her hand stretched out towards the door. It opens softly and old women begin to come in, crossing themselves on the threshold, and kneeling down in front of the stage with red petticoats over their heads*]

MAURYA [*Half in a dream, to* CATHLEEN] Is it Patch, or Michael, or what is it at all?

CATHLEEN Michael is after being found in the far north, and when he is found there how could he be here in this place?

MAURYA There does be a power of young men floating round in the sea, and what way would they know if it was Michael they had, or another man like him, for when a man is nine days in the sea, and the wind blowing, it's hard set his own mother would be to say what man was it.

CATHLEEN It's Michael, God spare him, for they're after sending us a bit of his clothes from the far north.

[*She reaches out and hands* MAURYA *the clothes that belonged to Michael.* MAURYA *stands up slowly, and takes them in her hands.* NORA *looks out*]

NORA They're carrying a thing among them and there's water dripping out of it and leaving a track by the big stones.

CATHLEEN [*In a whisper to the women who have come in*] Is it Bartley it is?

ONE OF THE WOMEN It is surely, God rest his soul. [*Two younger women come in and pull out the table. Then men carry in the body of Bartley, laid on a plank, with a bit of a sail over it, and lay it on the table*]

CATHLEEN [*To the women, as they are doing so*] What way was he drowned?

ONE OF THE WOMEN The gray pony knocked him into the sea, and he was washed out where there is a great surf on the white rocks.

[MAURYA *has gone over and knelt down at the head of the table. The women are keening softly and swaying themselves with a slow movement.* CATHLEEN *and* NORA *kneel at the other end of the table. The men kneel near the door*]

MAURYA [*Raising her head and speaking as if she did not see the people around her*] They're all gone now, and there isn't anything more the sea can do to me. . . . I'll have no call now to be up crying and praying when the wind breaks from the south, and you can hear the surf is in the east, and the surf is in the west, making a great stir with the two noises, and they hitting one on the other. I'll have no call now to be going down and getting Holy Water in the dark nights after Samhain, and I won't care what way the sea is when the other women will be keening. [*To* NORA] Give me the Holy Water, Nora, there's a small sup still on the dresser.

[NORA *gives it to her*]

MAURYA [*Drops Michael's clothes across Bartley's feet, and sprinkles the Holy Water over him*] It isn't that I haven't prayed for you, Bartley, to the Almighty God. It isn't that I haven't said prayers in the dark night till you wouldn't know what I'd be saying; but it's a great rest I'll have now, and it's time surely. It's a great rest I'll have now, and great sleeping in the long nights after Samhain, if it's only a bit of wet flour we do have to eat, and maybe a fish that would be stinking.

[*She kneels down again, crossing herself, and saying prayers under her breath*]

CATHLEEN [*To an old man*] Maybe yourself and Eamon would make a coffin when the sun rises. We have fine white boards herself bought, God help her, thinking Michael would be found, and I have a new cake you can eat while you'll be working.

THE OLD MAN [*Looking at the boards*] Are there nails with them?

CATHLEEN There are not, Colum; we didn't think of the nails.

ANOTHER MAN It's a great wonder she wouldn't think of the nails, and all the coffins she's seen made already.

CATHLEEN It's getting old she is, and broken.

[MAURYA *stands up again very slowly and spreads out the pieces of Michael's clothes beside the body, sprinkling them with the last of the Holy Water*]

NORA [*In a whisper to* CATHLEEN] She's quiet now and easy; but the day Michael was drowned you could hear her crying out from this to the spring well. It's fonder she was of Michael, and would any one have thought that?

CATHLEEN [*Slowly and clearly*] An old woman will be soon tired with anything she will do, and isn't it nine days herself is after crying and keening, and making great sorrow in the house?

MAURYA [*Puts the empty cup mouth downwards on the table, and lays her hands together on* BARTLEY's *feet*] They're all together this time, and the end is come. May the Almighty God have mercy on Bartley's soul, and on Michael's soul, and on the souls of Sheamus and Patch, and Stephen and Shawn [*bending her head*]; and may He have mercy on my soul, Nora, and on the soul of every one is left living in the world.

[*She pauses, and the keen rises a little more loudly from the women, then sinks away*]

MAURYA [*Continuing*] Michael has a clean burial in the far north, by the grace of the Almighty God. Bartley will have a fine coffin out of the white boards, and a deep grave surely. What more can we want than that? No man at all can be living for ever, and we must be satisfied.

[*She kneels down again and the curtain falls slowly*]

The Glass Menagerie

The Author's Production Notes:

[Being a "memory play," The Glass Menagerie can be presented with unusual freedom of convention. Because of its considerably delicate or tenuous material, atmospheric touches and subtleties of direction play a particularly important part. Expressionism and all other unconventional techniques in drama have only one valid aid, and that is a closer approach to truth. When a play employs unconventional techniques, it is not, or certainly shouldn't be, trying to escape its responsibility of dealing with reality, or interpreting experience, but is actually or should be attempting to find a closer approach, a more penetrating and vivid expression of things as they are. The straight realistic play with its genuine frigidaire and authentic ice-cubes, its characters that speak exactly as its audience speaks, corresponds to the academic landscape and has the same virtue of a photographic likeness. Everyone should know nowadays the unimportance of the photographic in art: that truth, life, or reality is an organic thing which the poetic imagination can represent or suggest, in essence, only through transformation, through changing into other forms than those which were merely present in appearance.

These remarks are not meant as a preface only to this particular play. They have to do with a conception of a new, plastic theatre which must take the place of the exhausted theatre of realistic conventions if the theatre is to resume vitality as a part of our culture.

THE SCREEN DEVICE

There *is* only one important difference between the original and acting version of the play *and that is the omission in the latter of the device which I tentatively included in my original script.* This device was the use of a screen on which were projected magic-lantern slides bearing images or titles. I do not regret the omission of this device from the present Broadway production. The extraordinary power of Miss [Laurette] Taylor's performance made it suitable to have the utmost simplicity in the physical production. But I think it may be interesting to some readers to see how this device was conceived. So I am putting it into the published manuscript. These images and legends, projected from behind, were cast on a section of wall between the front-room and dining-room areas, which should be indistinguishable from the rest when not in use.

The purpose of this will probably be apparent. It is to give accent to certain values in each scene. Each scene contains a particular point (or several) which is structurally the most important. In an episodic play, such as this, the basic structure or narrative line may be obscured from the audience; the effect may seem fragmentary rather than architectural. This may not be the fault of the play so much as a lack of attention in the audience. The legend or image upon the screen will strengthen the effect of what is merely allusion in the writing and allow the primary point to be made more simply and lightly than if the entire responsibility were on the spoken lines. Aside from this structural value, I think the screen will have a definite emotional appeal, less definable but just as important. An imaginative producer or director may invent many other uses for this device than those indicated in the present script. In fact the possibilities of the device seem much larger to me than the instance of this play can possibly utilize.

THE MUSIC

Another extra-literary accent in this play is provided by the use of music. A single recurring tune, "The Glass Menagerie," is used to give emotional emphasis to suitable passages. This tune is like circus music, not when you are on the grounds or in the immediate vicinity of the parade, but when you are at some distance and very likely thinking of something else. It seems under those circumstances to continue almost interminably and it weaves in and out of your preoccupied consciousness; then it is the lightest, most delicate music in the world and perhaps the saddest. It expresses the surface vivacity of life with the underlying strain of immutable and inexpressible sorrow. When you look at a piece of delicately spun glass you think of two things: how beautiful it is and how easily it can be broken. Both of those ideas should be woven into the recurring tune, which dips in and out of the play as if it were carried on a wind that changes. It serves as a thread of connection and allusion between the narrator with his separate point in time and space and the subject of his story. Between each episode it returns as reference to the emotion, nostalgia, which is the first condition of the play. It is primarily Laura's music and therefore comes out most clearly when the play focuses upon her and the lovely fragility of glass which is her image.

THE LIGHTING

The lighting in the play is not realistic. In keeping with the atmosphere of memory, the stage is dim. Shafts of light are focused on selected areas or actors, sometimes in contradistinction to what is the apparent center. For instance, in the quarrel scene between Tom and Amanda, in which Laura has no active part, the clearest pool of light is on her figure. This is also true of the supper scene, when her silent figure on the sofa should remain the visual center. The light upon Laura should be distinct from the others, having a peculiar pristine clarity such as light used in early religious portraits of female saints or madonnas. A certain correspondence to light in religious paintings, such as El Greco's, where the figures are radiant in atmosphere that is relatively dusky, could be effectively used throughout the play. (It will also permit a more effective use of the screen.) A free, imaginative use of light can be of enormous value in giving a mobile, plastic quality to plays of a more or less static nature.]

Characters

AMANDA WINGFIELD *the mother*
 A little woman of great but confused vitality clinging frantically to another time and place. Her characterization must be carefully created, not copied from type. She is not paranoiac, but her life is paranoia. There is much to admire in Amanda, and as much to love and pity as there is to laugh at. Certainly she has endurance and a kind of heroism, and though her foolishness makes her unwittingly cruel at times, there is tenderness in her slight person.

LAURA WINGFIELD *her daughter*
 Amanda, having failed to establish contact with reality, continues to live vitally in her illusions, but Laura's situation is even graver. A childhood illness has left her crippled, one leg slightly shorter than the other, and held in a brace. This defect need not be more than suggested on the stage. Stemming from this, Laura's separation increases till she is like a piece of her own glass collection, too exquisitely fragile to move from the shelf.

TOM WINGFIELD *her son*
 And the narrator of the play. A poet with a job in a warehouse. His nature is not remorseless, but to escape from a trap he has to act without pity.

JIM O'CONNOR *the gentleman caller*
 A nice, ordinary, young man.

Scene: *An Alley in St. Louis*
Part I: *Preparation for a Gentleman Caller.*
Part II: *The Gentleman calls.*
Time: *Now and the Past.*

Scene I

The Wingfield apartment is in the rear of the building, one of those vast hive-like conglomerations of cellular living-units that flower as warty growths in overcrowded urban centers of lower middle-class population and are symptomatic of the impulse of this largest and fundamentally enslaved section of American society to avoid fluidity and differentiation and to exist and function as one interfused mass of automatism.

The apartment faces an alley and is entered by a fire-escape, a structure whose name is a touch of accidental poetic truth, for all of these huge buildings are always burning with the slow and implacable fires of human desperation. The fire-escape is included in the set—that is, the landing of it and steps descending from it.

The scene is memory and is therefore nonrealistic. Memory takes a lot of poetic license. It omits some details; others are exaggerated, according to the emotional value of the articles it touches, for memory is seated predominantly in the heart. The interior is therefore rather dim and poetic.

At the rise of the curtain, the audience is faced with the dark, grim rear wall of the Wingfield tenement. This building, which runs parallel to the footlights, is flanked on both sides by dark, narrow alleys which run into murky canyons of tangled clotheslines, garbage cans and the sinister lattice-work of neighboring fire-escapes. It is up and down these side alleys that exterior entrances and exits are made, during the play. At the end of TOM's opening commentary, the dark tenement wall slowly reveals (by means of a transparency) the interior of the ground floor Wingfield apartment.

Downstage is the living room, which also serves as a sleeping room for LAURA, the sofa unfolding to make her bed. Upstage, center, and divided by a wide arch or second proscenium with transparent faded portieres (or second curtain), is the dining room. In an old-fashioned what-not in the living room are seen scores of transparent glass animals. A blown-up photograph of the father hangs on the wall of the living room, facing the audience, to the left of the archway. It is the face of a very handsome young man in a doughboy's First World War cap. He is gallantly smiling, ineluctably smiling, as if to say, "I will be smiling forever."

The audience hears and sees the opening scene in the dining room through both the transparent fourth wall of the building and the transparent gauze portieres of the dining-room arch. It is during this revealing *scene that the fourth wall slowly ascends out of sight. This transparent exterior wall is not brought down again until the very end of the play, during* TOM's *final speech.*

The narrator is an undisguised convention of the play. He takes whatever license with dramatic convention as is convenient to his purposes.

TOM *enters dressed as a merchant sailor from alley, stage left, and strolls across the front of the stage to the fire-escape. There he stops and lights a cigarette. He addresses the audience.*

TOM Yes, I have tricks in my pocket, I have things up my sleeve. But I am the opposite of a stage magician. He gives you illusion that has the appearance of truth. I give you truth in the pleasant disguise of illusion.

To begin with, I turn back time. I reverse it to that quaint period, the thirties, when the huge middle class of America was matriculating in a school for the blind. Their eyes had failed them, or they had failed their eyes, and so they were having their fingers pressed forcibly down on the fiery Braille alphabet of a dissolving economy.

In Spain there was revolution. Here there was only shouting and confusion.

In Spain there was Guernica.[1] Here there were disturbances of labor, sometimes pretty violent, in otherwise peaceful cities such as Chicago, Cleveland, Saint Louis . . .

This is the social background of the play.

[*Music*]

The play is memory.

Being a memory play, it is dimly lighted, it is sentimental, it is not realistic.

In memory everything seems to happen to music. That explains the fiddle in the wings.

I am the narrator of the play, and also a character in it.

The other characters are my mother, Amanda, my sister, Laura, and a gentleman caller who appears in the final scenes.

He is the most realistic character in the play, being an emissary from a world of reality that we were somehow set apart from.

But since I have a poet's weakness for symbols, I am using this character also as a symbol; he is the long delayed but always expected something that we live for.

There is a fifth character in the play who doesn't appear except in

---

[1] *Guernica*: symbolic of modern war's inhumanity, this town in northern Spain was mercilessly bombed in the Spanish Civil War.

this larger-than-life-size photograph over the mantel.
This is our father who left us a long time ago.
He was a telephone man who fell in love with long distances; he gave up his job with the telephone company and skipped the light fantastic out of town . . .
The last we heard of him was a picture post-card from Mazatlan, on the Pacific coast of Mexico, containing a message of two words—
"Hello—Good-bye!" and no address.

[AMANDA's *voice becomes audible through the portieres*]

[*Legend on screen: "Où sont les neiges"*]

[*He divides the portieres and enters the upstage area.* AMANDA *and* LAURA *are seated at a drop-leaf table. Eating is indicated by gestures without food or utensils.* AMANDA *faces the audience.* TOM *and* LAURA *are seated in profile. The interior has lit up softly and through the scrim we see* AMANDA *and* LAURA *seated at the table in the upstage area*]

AMANDA [*calling*] Tom?

TOM Yes, Mother.

AMANDA We can't say grace until you come to the table!

TOM Coming, Mother. [*He bows slightly and withdraws, reappearing a few moments later in his place at the table*]

AMANDA [*to her son*]. Honey, don't *push* with your *fingers*. If you have to push with something, the thing to push with is a crust of bread. And chew—chew! Animals have secretions in their stomachs which enable them to digest food without mastication, but human beings are supposed to chew their food before they swallow it down. Eat food leisurely, son, and really enjoy it. A well-cooked meal has lots of delicate flavors that have to be held in the mouth for appreciation. So chew your food and give your salivary glands a chance to function! [TOM *deliberately lays his imaginary fork down and pushes his chair back from the table*]

TOM I haven't enjoyed one bite of this dinner because of your constant directions on how to eat it. It's you that make me rush through meals with your hawk-like attention to every bite I take. Sickening—spoils my appetite—all this discussion of animal's secretion—salivary glands—mastication!

AMANDA [*lightly*]. Temperament like a Metropolitan star! [*He rises and crosses downstage*] You're not excused from the table.

TOM I'm getting a cigarette.

AMANDA You smoke too much.

[LAURA *rises*]

LAURA I'll bring in the blanc mange.
[*He remains standing with his cigarette by the portieres during the following*]
AMANDA [*rising*] No, sister, no, sister—you be the lady this time and I'll be the darky.
LAURA I'm already up.
AMANDA Resume your seat, little sister—I want you to stay fresh and pretty—for gentlemen callers!
LAURA I'm not expecting any gentlemen callers.
AMANDA [*crossing out to kitchenette. Airily*] Sometimes they come when they are least expected! Why I remember one Sunday afternoon in Blue Mountain—
[*Enters kitchenette*]
TOM I know what's coming!
LAURA Yes. But let her tell it.
TOM Again?
LAURA She loves to tell it.
[AMANDA *returns with bowl of dessert*]
AMANDA One Sunday afternoon in Blue Mountain—your mother received—*seventeen*—gentlemen callers! Why, sometimes there weren't chairs enough to accommodate them all. We had to send the nigger over to bring in folding chairs from the parish house.
TOM [*remaining at portieres*] How did you entertain those gentlemen callers?
AMANDA I understood the art of conversation.
TOM I bet you could talk.
AMANDA Girls in those days *knew* how to talk, I can tell you.
TOM Yes?
[*Image:* AMANDA *as a girl on a porch, greeting callers*]
AMANDA They knew how to entertain their gentleman callers. It wasn't enough for a girl to be possessed of a pretty face and a graceful figure—although I wasn't slighted in either respect. She also needed to have a nimble wit and a tongue to meet all occasions.
TOM What did you talk about?
AMANDA Things of importance going on in the world! Never anything coarse or common or vulgar. [*She addresses* TOM *as though he were seated in the vacant chair at the table though he remains by portieres. He plays this scene as though he held the book*] My callers were gentlemen—all! Among my callers were some of the most prominent young planters of the Mississippi Delta—planters and sons of planters!
[TOM *motions for music and a spot of light on* AMANDA. *Her eyes lift,*

her face glows, her voice becomes rich and elegiac]
[*Screen legend: "Où sont les neiges"*]
   There was young Champ Laughlin who later became vice-president of the Delta Planters Bank.
   Hadley Stevenson who was drowned in Moon Lake and left his widow one hundred and fifty thousand in Government bonds.
   There were the Cutrere brothers, Wesley and Bates. Bates was one of my bright particular beaux! He got in a quarrel with that wild Wainwright boy. They shot it out on the floor of Moon Lake Casino. Bates was shot through the stomach. Died in the ambulance on his way to Memphis. His widow was also well-provided for, came into eight or ten thousand acres, that's all. She married him on the rebound—never loved her—carried my picture on him the night he died!
   And there was that boy that every girl in the Delta had set her cap for! That beautiful, brilliant young Fitzhugh boy from Greene County!

TOM What did he leave his widow?

AMANDA He never married! Gracious, you talk as though all of my old admirers had turned up their toes to the daises!

TOM Isn't his the first you've mentioned that still survives?

AMANDA That Fitzhugh boy went North and made a fortune—came to be known as the Wolf of Wall Street! He had the Midas touch, whatever he touched turned to gold!
   And I could have been Mrs. Duncan J. Fitzhugh, mind you! But —I picked your *father*!

LAURA [*rising*] Mother, let me clear the table.

AMANDA No, dear, you go in front and study your typewriter chart. Or practice your shorthand a little. Stay fresh and pretty!—It's almost time for our gentlemen callers to start arriving. [*She flounces girlishly toward the kitchenette*] How many do you suppose we're going to entertain this afternoon?

[TOM *throws down the paper and jumps up with a groan*]

LAURA [*alone in the dining room*] I don't believe we're going to receive any, Mother.

AMANDA [*reappearing, airily*] What? No one—not one? You must be joking! [LAURA *nervously echoes her laugh. She slips in a fugitive manner through the half-opened portieres and draws them gently behind her. A shaft of very clear light is thrown on her face against the faded tapestry of the curtains. Music: "The Glass Menagerie" under faintly. Lightly*] Not one gentleman caller? It can't be true! There must be a flood, there must have been a tornado!

LAURA It isn't a flood, it's not a tornado, Mother. I'm just not popular like you were in Blue Mountain. . . . [TOM *utters another groan.* LAURA *glances at him with a faint apologetic smile. Her voice catching a little*] Mother's afraid I'm going to be an old maid.
[*The scene dims out with "Glass Menagerie" music*]

Scene II

"Laura, Haven't You Ever Liked Some Boy?"
On the dark stage the screen is lighted with the image of blue roses. Gradually LAURA's figure becomes apparent and the screen goes out. The music subsides.
LAURA *is seated in the delicate ivory chair at the small clawfoot table. She wears a dress of soft violet material for a kimono—her hair is tied back from her forehead with a ribbon. She is washing and polishing her collection of glass.*
AMANDA *appears on the fire-escape steps. At the sound of her ascent,* LAURA *catches her breath, thrusts the bowl of ornaments away and seats herself stiffly before the diagram of the typewriter keyboard as though it held her spellbound. Something has happened to* AMANDA. *It is written in her face as she climbs to the landing: a look that is grim and hopeless and a little absurd. She has on one of those cheap or imitation velvety-looking cloth coats with imitation fur collar. Her hat is five or six years old, one of those dreadful cloche hats that were worn in the late twenties and she is clasping an enormous black patent-leather pocketbook with nickel clasps and initials. This is her full-dress outfit, the one she usually wears to the D.A.R. Before entering she looks through the door. She purses her lips, opens her eyes very wide, rolls them upward and shakes her head. Then she slowly lets herself in the door. Seeing her mother's expression* LAURA *touches her lips with a nervous gesture.*

LAURA Hello, Mother, I was—[*She makes a nervous gesture toward the chart on the wall.* AMANDA *leans against the shut door and stares at* LAURA *with a martyred look*]
AMANDA Deception? Deception? [*She slowly removes her hat and gloves, continuing the sweet suffering stare. She lets the hat and gloves fall on the floor—a bit of acting*]
LAURA [*shakily*] How was the D.A.R. meeting? [AMANDA *slowly opens her purse and removes a dainty white handkerchief which she shakes out delicately and delicately touches to her lips and nostrils*] Didn't you go to the D.A.R. meeting, Mother?

AMANDA [*faintly, almost inaudibly*] —No.—No. [*Then more forcibly*] I did not have the strength—to go to the D.A.R. In fact, I did not have the courage! I wanted to find a hole in the ground and hide myself in it forever! [*She crosses slowly to the wall and removes the diagram of the typewriter keyboard. She holds it in front of her for a second, staring at it sweetly and sorrowfully—then bites her lips and tears it in two pieces*]

LAURA [*faintly*] Why did you do that, Mother? [AMANDA *repeats the same procedure with the chart of the Gregg Alphabet*] Why are you—

AMANDA Why? Why? How old are you, Laura?

LAURA Mother, you know my age.

AMANDA I thought that you were an adult; it seems that I was mistaken. [*She crosses slowly to the sofa and sinks down and stares at* LAURA]

LAURA Please don't stare at me, Mother.

[AMANDA *closes her eyes and lowers her head. Count ten*]

AMANDA What are we going to do, what is going to become of us, What is the future?

[*Count ten*]

LAURA Has something happened, Mother? [AMANDA *draws a long breath and takes out the handkerchief again. Dabbing process*] Mother, has—something happened?

AMANDA I'll be all right in a minute. I'm just bewildered—[*Count five*]—by life....

LAURA Mother, I wish that you would tell me what's happened!

AMANDA As you know, I was supposed to be inducted into my office at the D.A.R. this afternoon. [*Image: a swarm of typewriters*] But I stopped off at Rubicam's Business College to speak to your teachers about your having a cold and ask them what progress they thought you were making down there.

LAURA Oh....

AMANDA I went to the typing instructor and introduced myself as your mother. She didn't know who you were. Wingfield, she said. We don't have any such student enrolled at the school!

I assured her she did, that you have been going to classes since early in January.

"I wonder," she said, "if you could be talking about that terribly shy little girl who dropped out of school after only a few days' attendance?"

"No," I said, "Laura, my daughter, has been going to school every day for the past six weeks!"

"Excuse me," she said. She took the attendance book out and there was your name, unmistakably printed, and all the dates you were absent until they decided that you had dropped out of school.

I still said, "No, there must have been some mistake! There must have been some mix-up in the records!"

And she said, "No—I remember her perfectly now. Her hands shook so that she couldn't hit the right keys! The first time we gave a speed-test, she broke down completely—was sick at the stomach and almost had to be carried into the wash-room! After that morning she never showed up any more. We phoned the house but never got any answer"—while I was working at Famous and Barr, I suppose, demonstrating those—Oh!

I felt so weak I could barely keep on my feet!

I had to sit down while they got me a glass of water!

Fifty dollars' tuition, all of our plans—my hopes and ambitions for you—just gone up the spout, just gone up the spout like that.

[LAURA *draws a long breath and gets awkwardly to her feet. She crosses to the victrola and winds it up*] What are you doing?

LAURA Oh! [*She releases the handle and returns to her seat*]

AMANDA Laura, where have you been going when you've gone out pretending that you were going to business college?

LAURA I've just been going out walking.

AMANDA That's not true.

LAURA It is. I just went walking.

AMANDA Walking? Walking? In winter? Deliberately courting pneumonia in that light coat? Where did you walk to, Laura?

LAURA All sorts of places—mostly in the park.

AMANDA Even after you'd started catching that cold?

LAURA It was the lesser of two evils, Mother. [*Image: Winter scene in park*] I couldn't go back up. I—threw up—on the floor!

AMANDA From half past seven till after five every day you mean to tell me you walked around in the park, because you wanted to make me think you were still going to Rubicam's Business College?

LAURA It wasn't as bad as it sounds. I went inside places to get warmed up.

AMANDA Inside where?

LAURA I went in the art museum and the birdhouses at the Zoo. I visited the penguins every day! I did without lunch and went to the movies. Lately I've been spending most of my afternoons in the Jewel-box, that big glass house where they raise the tropical flowers.

AMANDA You did all this to deceive me, just for deception? [LAURA *looks down*] Why?

LAURA Mother, when you're disappointed, you get that awful suffering

look on your face, like the picture of Jesus' mother in the museum!
AMANDA Hush!
LAURA I couldn't face it.
   [*Pause. A whisper of strings*]
   [*Legend: "The Crust of Humility"*]
AMANDA [*hopelessly fingering the huge pocketbook*] So what are we going to do the rest of our lives? Stay home and watch the parades go by? Amuse ourselves with the glass menagerie, darling? Eternally play those worn-out phonograph records your father left as a painful reminder of him?

   We won't have a business career—we've given that up because it gave us nervous indigestion! [*Laughs wearily*] What is there left but dependency all our lives? I know so well what becomes of unmarried women who aren't prepared to occupy a position. I've seen such pitiful cases in the South—barely tolerated spinsters living upon the grudging patronage of sister's husband or brother's wife!—stuck away in some little mouse-trap of a room—encouraged by one in-law to visit another—little birdlike women without any nest—eating the crust of humility all their life!

   Is that the future that we've mapped out for ourselves?
   I swear it's the only alternative I can think of!
   It isn't a very pleasant alternative, is it?
   Of course—some girls *do marry*.
   [LAURA *twists her hands nervously*]
   Haven't you ever liked some boy?
LAURA Yes, I liked one once. [*Rises*] I came across his picture a while ago.
AMANDA [*with some interest*] He gave you his picture?
LAURA No, it's in the year-book.
AMANDA [*disappointed*] Oh—a high-school boy.
   [*Screen image:* JIM *as high-school hero bearing a silver cup*]
LAURA Yes. His name was Jim. [LAURA *lifts the heavy annual from the claw-foot table*] Here he is in *The Pirates of Penzance*.
AMANDA [*absently*] The what?
LAURA The operetta the senior class put on. He had a wonderful voice and we sat across the aisle from each other Mondays, Wednesdays and Fridays in the Aud. Here he is with the silver cup for debating! See his grin?
AMANDA [*absently*] He must have had a jolly disposition.
LAURA He used to call me—Blue Roses.
   [*Image: Blue roses*]
AMANDA Why did he call you such a name as that?
LAURA When I had that attack of pleurosis—he asked me what was the

matter when I came back. I said pleurosis—he thought that I said Blue Roses! So that's what he always called me after that. Whenever he saw me, he'd holler, "Hello, Blue Roses!" I didn't care for the girl that he went out with. Emily Meisenbach. Emily was the best-dressed girl at Soldan. She never struck me, though, as being sincere . . . It says in the Personal Section—they're engaged. That's —six years ago! They must be married by now.

AMANDA Girls that aren't cut out for business careers usually wind up married to some nice man. [*Gets up with a spark of revival*] Sister, that's what you'll do!

[LAURA *utters a startled, doubtful laugh. She reaches quickly for a piece of glass*]

LAURA But, Mother—

AMANDA Yes? [*Crossing to photograph*]

LAURA [*in a tone of frightened apology*] I'm—crippled!

[*Image: screen*]

AMANDA Nonsense! Laura, I've told you never, never to use that word. Why, you're not crippled, you just have a little defect—hardly noticeable, even! When people have some slight disadvantage like that, they cultivate other things to make up for it—develop charm—and vivacity—and—*charm!* That's all you have to do! [*She turns again to the photograph*] One thing your father had *plenty of*—was *charm!*

[TOM *motions to the fiddle in the wings*]

[*The scene fades out with music*]

Scene III

Legend on screen: "After the fiasco—"
TOM *speaks from the fire-escape landing.*

TOM After the fiasco at Rubicam's Business College, the idea of getting a gentleman caller for Laura began to play a more and more important part in Mother's calculations.

It became an obsession. Like some archetype of the universal unconscious, the image of the gentleman caller haunted our small apartment. . . .

[*Image: Young man at door with flowers*]

An evening at home rarely passed without some allusion to this image, this spectre, this hope. . . .

Even when he wasn't mentioned, his presence hung in Mother's preoccupied look and in my sister's frightened, apologetic manner—hung like a sentence passed upon the Wingfields!

Mother was a woman of action as well as words.
She began to take logical steps in the planned direction.
Late that winter and in the early spring—realizing that extra money would be needed to properly feather the nest and plume the bird—she conducted a vigorous campaign on the telephone, roping in subscribers to one of those magazines for matrons called *The Homemaker's Companion,* the type of journal that features the serialized sublimations of ladies of letters who think in terms of delicate cuplike breasts, slim, tapering waists, rich, creamy thighs, eyes like woodsmoke in autumn, fingers that soothe and caress like strains of music, bodies as powerful as Etruscan sculpture.

[*Screen image: Glamor magazine cover*]

[AMANDA *enters with phone on long extension cord. She is spotted in the dim stage*]

AMANDA Ida Scott? This is Amanda Wingfield! We *missed* you at the D.A.R. last Monday!

I said to myself: She's probably suffering with that sinus condition! How is that sinus condition?

Horrors! Heaven have mercy!—You're a Christian martyr, yes, that's what you are, a Christian martyr!

Well, I just now happen to notice that your subscription to the *Companion's* about to expire! Yes, it expires with the next issue, honey!—just when that wonderful new serial by Bessie Mae Hopper is getting off to such an exciting start. Oh, honey, it's something that you can't miss! You remember how *Gone With the Wind* took everybody by storm? You simply couldn't go out if you hadn't read it. All everybody *talked* was Scarlett O'Hara. Well, this is a book that critics already compare to *Gone With the Wind.* It's the *Gone With the Wind* of the post-World War generation!—What?—Burning?—Oh, honey, don't let them burn, go take a look in the oven and I'll hold the wire! Heavens—I think she's hung up!

[*Dim out*]

[*Legend on screen: "You think I'm in love with Continental Shoemakers?"*]

[*Before the stage is lighted, the violent voices of* TOM *and* AMANDA *are heard. They are quarreling behind the portieres. In front of them stands* LAURA *with clenched hands and panicky expression. A clear pool of light on her figure throughout this scene*]

TOM What in Christ's name am I—

AMANDA [*shrilly*] Don't you use that—

TOM Supposed to do!

AMANDA Expression! Not in my—
TOM Ohhh!
AMANDA Presence! Have you gone out of your senses?
TOM I have, that's true, *driven* out!
AMANDA What is the matter with you, you—big—big—IDIOT!
TOM Look!—I've got *no thing*, no single thing—
AMANDA Lower your voice!
TOM In my life here that I can call my OWN! Everything is—
AMANDA Stop that shouting!
TOM Yesterday you confiscated my books! You had the nerve to—
AMANDA I took that horrible novel back to the library—yes! That hideous book by that insane Mr. Lawrence. [TOM *laughs wildly*] I cannot control the output of diseased minds or people who cater to them— [TOM *laughs still more wildly*] BUT I WON'T ALLOW SUCH FILTH BROUGHT INTO MY HOUSE! No, no, no, no, no!
TOM House, house! Who pays rent on it, who makes a slave of himself to—
AMANDA [*fairly screeching*] Don't you DARE to—
TOM No, no, I mustn't say things! I've got to just—
AMANDA Let me tell you—
TOM I don't want to hear any more! [*He tears the portieres open. The upstage area is lit with a turgid smoky red glow*]
[AMANDA's *hair is in metal curlers and she wears a very old bathrobe, much too large for her slight figure, a relic of the faithless Mr. Wingfield. An upright typewriter and a wild disarray of manuscripts is on the drop-leaf table. The quarrel was probably precipitated by* AMANDA's *interruption of his creative labor. A chair lying overthrown on the floor. Their gesticulating shadows are cast on the ceiling by the fiery glow*]
AMANDA You *will* hear more, you—
TOM No, I won't hear more, I'm going out!
AMANDA You come right back in—
TOM Out, out, out! Because I'm—
AMANDA Come back here, Tom Wingfield! I'm not through talking to you!
TOM Oh, go—
LAURA [*desperately*]—Tom!
AMANDA You're going to listen, and no more insolence from you! I'm at the end of my patience!
[*He comes back toward her*]
TOM What do you think I'm at? Aren't I supposed to have any patience

to reach the end of, Mother? I know, I know. It seems unimportant to you, what I'm *doing*—what I *want* to do—having a little *difference* between them! You don't think that—
AMANDA I think you've been doing things that you're ashamed of. That's why you act like this. I don't believe that you go every night to the movies. Nobody goes to the movies night after night. Nobody in their right minds goes to the movies as often as you pretend to. People don't go to the movies at nearly midnight, and movies don't let out at two A.M. Come in stumbling. Muttering to yourself like a maniac! You get three hours' sleep and then go to work. Oh, I can picture the way you're doing down there. Moping, doping, because you're in no condition.
TOM [*wildly*] No, I'm in no condition!
AMANDA What right have you got to jeopardize your job? Jeopardize the security of us all? How do you think we'd manage if you were—
TOM Listen! You think I'm crazy *about* the *warehouse*? [*He bends fiercely toward her slight figure*] You think I'm in love with the Continental Shoemakers? You think I want to spend fifty-five *years* down there in that—*celotex interior!* with—*fluorescent—tubes!* Look! I'd rather somebody picked up a crowbar and battered out my brains—than go back mornings! I *go!* Every time you come in yelling that God damn "*Rise and Shine!*" "*Rise and Shine!*" I say to myself, "How *lucky dead* people are!" But I get up. *I go!* For sixty-five dollars a month I give up all that I dream of doing and being *ever!* And you say self—*self's* all I ever think of. Why, listen, if self is what I thought of, Mother, I'd be where he is—GONE! [*Pointing to father's picture*] As far as the system of transportation reaches! [*He starts past her. She grabs his arm*] Don't grab at me, Mother!
AMANDA Where are you going?
TOM I'm going to the *movies!*
AMANDA I don't believe that lie!
TOM [*crouching toward her, overtowering her tiny figure. She backs away, gasping*] I'm going to opium dens! Yes, opium dens, dens of vice and criminals' hang-outs, Mother. I've joined the Hogan gang, I'm a hired assassin, I carry a tommy-gun in a violin case! I run a string of cat-houses in the Valley! They call me Killer, Killer Wingfield, I'm leading a double-life, a simple, honest warehouse worker by day, by night a dynamic *czar* of the *underworld*, *Mother*. I go to gambling casinos, I spin away fortunes on the roulette table! I wear a patch over one eye and a false mustache, sometimes I put on green whiskers. On those occasions they call me—*El Diablo!* Oh, I could tell you

things to make you sleepless! My enemies plan to dynamite this place. They're going to blow us all sky-high some night! I'll be glad, very happy, and so will you! You'll go up, up on a broomstick, over Blue Mountain with seventeen gentlemen callers! You ugly—babbling old—witch. . . . [*He goes through a series of violent, clumsy movements, seizing his overcoat, lunging to the door pulling it fiercely open. The women watch him, aghast. His arm catches in the sleeve of the coat as he struggles to pull it on. For a moment he is pinioned by the bulky garment. With an outraged groan he tears the coat off again, splitting the shoulder of it, and hurls it across the room. It strikes against the shelf of* LAURA's *glass collection, there is a tinkle of shattering glass.* LAURA *cries out as if wounded*]
[*Music. Legend: "The Glass Menagerie"*]
LAURA [*shrilly*] My glass!—menagerie. . . . [*She covers her face and turns away*]
[*But* AMANDA *is still stunned and stupefied by the "ugly witch" so that she barely notices this occurrence. Now she recovers her speech*]
AMANDA [*in an awful voice*] I won't speak to you—until you apologize! [*She crosses through portieres and draws them together behind her.* TOM *is left with* LAURA. LAURA *clings weakly to the mantel with her face averted.* TOM *stares at her stupidly for a moment. Then he crosses to shelf. Drops awkwardly on his knees to collect the fallen glass, glancing at* LAURA *as if he would speak but couldn't*]
[*"The Glass Menagerie" steals in as the scene dims out*]

Scene IV

The interior is dark. Faint light in the alley. A deep-voiced bell in a church is tolling the hour of five as the scene commences.
TOM *appears at the top of the alley. After each solemn boom of the bell in the tower, he shakes a little noise-maker or rattle as if to express the tiny spasm of man in contrast to the sustained power and dignity of the Almighty. This and the unsteadiness of his advance make it evident that he has been drinking. As he climbs the few steps to the fire-escape landing light steals up inside.* LAURA *appears in night-dress, observing* TOM's *empty bed in the front room.* TOM *fishes in his pockets for door-key, removing a motley assortment of articles in the search, including a perfect shower of movie-ticket stubs and an empty bottle. At last he finds the key, but just as he is about to insert it, it slips from his fingers. He strikes a match and crouches below the door.*

TOM [*bitterly*] One crack—and it falls through!
[LAURA *opens the door*]
LAURA Tom! Tom, what are you doing?
TOM Looking for a door-key.
LAURA Where have you been all this time?
TOM I have been to the movies.
LAURA All this time at the movies?
TOM There was a very long program. There was a Garbo picture and a Mickey Mouse and a travelogue and a newsreel and a preview of coming attractions. And there was an organ solo and a collection for the milk-fund—simultaneously—which ended up in a terrible fight between a fat lady and an usher!
LAURA [*innocently*] Did you have to stay through everything?
TOM Of course! And, oh, I forgot! There was a big stage show! The headliner on this stage show was Malvolio the Magician. He performed wonderful tricks, many of them, such as pouring water back and forth between pitchers. First it turned to wine and then it turned to beer and then it turned to whiskey. I know it was whiskey it finally turned into because he needed somebody to come up out of the audience to help him, and I came up—both shows! It was Kentucky Straight Bourbon. A very generous fellow, he gave souvenirs. [*He pulls from his back pocket a shimmering rainbow-colored scarf*] He gave me this. This is his magic scarf. You can have it, Laura. You wave it over a canary cage and you get a bowl of gold-fish. You wave it over the gold-fish bowl and they fly away canaries. . . . But the wonderfullest trick of all was the coffin trick. We nailed him into a coffin and he got out of the coffin without removing one nail. [*He has come inside*] There is a trick that would come in handy for me—get me out of this 2 by 4 situation. [*Flops onto bed and starts removing shoes*]
LAURA Tom—shhh!
TOM What're you shushing me for?
LAURA You'll wake up Mother.
TOM Goody, goody! Pay 'er back for all those "Rise an' Shines." [*Lies down, groaning*] You know it don't take much intelligence to get yourself into a nailed-up coffin, Laura. But who in hell ever got himself out of one without removing one nail?
[*As if in answer, the father's grinning photograph lights up*]
[*Scene dims out*]
[*Immediately following: The church bell is heard striking six. At the sixth stroke the alarm clock goes off in* AMANDA's *room, and after a few moments we hear her calling:* "Rise and Shine! Rise and Shine! LAURA, *go tell your brother to rise and shine!*"]

TOM [*sitting up slowly*] I'll rise—but I won't shine.
[*The light increases*]
AMANDA Laura, tell your brother his coffee is ready.
[LAURA *slips into front room*]
LAURA Tom!—It's nearly seven. Don't make Mother nervous. [*He stares at her stupidly. Beseechingly*] Tom, speak to Mother this morning. Make up with her, apologize, speak to her!
TOM She won't to me. It's her that started not speaking.
LAURA If you just say you're sorry she'll start speaking.
TOM Her not speaking—is that such a tragedy?
LAURA Please—please!
AMANDA [*calling from kitchenette*] Laura, are you going to do what I asked you to do, or do I have to get dressed and go out myself?
LAURA Going, going—soon as I get on my coat! [*She pulls on a shapeless felt hat with nervous, jerky movement, pleadingly glancing at* TOM. *Rushes awkwardly for coat. The coat is one of* AMANDA's, *inaccurately made-over, the sleeves too short for* LAURA] Butter and what else?
AMANDA [*Entering upstage*] Just butter. Tell them to charge it.
LAURA Mother, they make such faces when I do that.
AMANDA Sticks and stones can break our bones, but the expression on Mr. Garfinkel's face won't harm us! Tell your brother his coffee is getting cold.
LAURA [*at door*] Do what I asked you, will you, will you, Tom?
[*He looks sullenly away*]
AMANDA Laura, go now or just don't go at all!
LAURA [*rushing out*] Going—going! [*A second later she cries out.* TOM *springs up and crosses to door.* AMANDA *rushes anxiously in.* TOM *opens the door*]
TOM Laura?
LAURA I'm all right. I slipped, but I'm all right.
AMANDA [*peering anxiously after her*] If anyone breaks a leg on those fire-escape steps, the landlord ought to be sued for every cent he possesses! [*She shuts door. Remembers she isn't speaking and returns to other room*]
[*As* TOM *enters listlessly for his coffee, she turns her back to him and stands rigidly facing the window on the gloomy gray vault of the areaway. Its light on her face with its aged but childish features is cruelly sharp, satirical as a Daumier print*]
[*Music under:* "*Ave Maria*"]
[TOM *glances sheepishly but sullenly at her averted figure and slumps at the table. The coffee is scalding hot; he sips it and gasps and spits it back in the cup. At his gasp,* AMANDA *catches her breath and*

half turns. Then catches herself and turns back to window. TOM *blows on his coffee, glancing sidewise at his mother. She clears her throat.* TOM *clears his. He starts to rise. Sinks back down again, scratches his head, clears his throat again.* AMANDA *coughs.* TOM *raises his cup in both hands to blow on it, his eyes staring over the rim of it at his mother for several moments. Then he slowly sets the cup down and awkwardly and hesitantly rises from the chair]*

TOM [*hoarsely*] Mother. I—I apologize, Mother. [AMANDA *draws a quick, shuddering breath. Her face works grotesquely. She breaks into childlike tears*] I'm sorry for what I said, for everything that I said, I didn't mean it.

AMANDA [*sobbingly*] My devotion has made me a witch and so I make myself hateful to my children!

TOM No, you *don't*.

AMANDA I worry so much, don't sleep, it makes me nervous!

TOM [*gently*] I understand that.

AMANDA I've had to put up a solitary battle all these years. But you're my right-hand bower! Don't fall down, don't fail!

TOM [*gently*] I try, Mother.

AMANDA [*with great enthusiasm*] Try and you will SUCCEED! [*The notion makes her breathless*] Why, you—you're just *full* of natural endowments! Both of my children—they're *unusual* children! Don't you think I know it? I'm so—*proud!* Happy and—feel I've—so much to be thankful for but—Promise me one thing, Son!

TOM What, Mother?

AMANDA Promise, son, you'll—never be a drunkard!

TOM [*turns to her grinning*] I will never be a drunkard, Mother.

AMANDA That's what frightened me so, that you'd be drinking! Eat a bowl of Purina!

TOM Just coffee, Mother.

AMANDA Shredded wheat biscuit?

TOM No. No, Mother, just coffee.

AMANDA You can't put in a day's work on an empty stomach. You've got ten minutes—don't gulp! Drinking too-hot liquids makes cancer of the stomach. . . . Put cream in.

TOM No, thank you.

AMANDA To cool it.

TOM No! No, thank you, I want it black.

AMANDA I know, but it's not good for you. We have to do all that we can to build ourselves up. In these trying times we live in, all that we have to cling to is—each other. . . . That's why it's so important

to—Tom, I—I sent out your sister so I could discuss something with you. If you hadn't spoken I would have spoken to you. [*Sits down*]
TOM [*gently*] What is it, Mother, that you want to discuss?
AMANDA *Laura!*
[TOM *puts his cup down slowly*]
[*Legend on screen: "Laura"*]
[*Music: "The Glass Menagerie"*]
TOM —Oh.—Laura . . .
AMANDA [*touching his sleeve*] You know how Laura is. So quiet but—still water runs deep! She notices things and I think she—broods about them. [TOM *looks up*] A few days ago I came in and she was crying.
TOM What about?
AMANDA You.
TOM Me?
AMANDA She has an idea that you're not happy here.
TOM What gave her that idea?
AMANDA What gives her any idea? However, you do act strangely. I—I'm not criticizing, understand *that!* I know your ambitions do not lie in the warehouse, that like everybody in the whole wide world—you've had to—make sacrifices, but—Tom—Tom—life's not easy, it calls for—Spartan endurance! There's so many things in my heart that I cannot describe to you! I've never told you but I—*loved* your father. . . .
TOM [*gently*] I know that, Mother.
AMANDA And you—when I see you taking after his ways! Staying out late—and—well, you *had* been drinking the night you were in that—terrifying condition! Laura says that you hate the apartment and that you go out nights to yet away from it! Is that true, Tom?
TOM No. You say there's so much in your heart that you can't describe to me. That's true of me, too. There's so much in my heart that I can't describe to *you!* So let's respect each other's—
AMANDA But, why—*why*, Tom—are you always so *restless?* Where do you *go* to, nights?
TOM I—go to the movies.
AMANDA Why do you go to the movies so much, Tom?
TOM I go to the movies because—I like adventure. Adventure is something I don't have much of at work, so I go to the movies.
AMANDA But, Tom, you go to the movies *entirely too much!*
TOM I like a lot of adventure.
[AMANDA *looks baffled, then hurt. As the familiar inquisition resumes*

he becomes hard and impatient again. AMANDA *slips back into her querulous attitude toward him*]
[*Image on screen: Sailing vessel with Jolly Roger*]
AMANDA Most young men find adventure in their careers.
TOM Then most young men are not employed in a warehouse.
AMANDA The world is full of young men employed in warehouses and offices and factories.
TOM Do all of them find adventure in their careers?
AMANDA They do or they do without it! Not everybody has a craze for adventure.
TOM Man is by instinct a lover, a hunter, a fighter, and none of those instincts are given much play at the warehouse!
AMANDA Man is by instinct! Don't quote instinct to me! Instinct is something that people have got away from! It belongs to animals! Christian adults don't want it!
TOM What do Christian adults want, then, Mother?
AMANDA Superior things! Things of the mind and the spirit! Only animals have to satisfy instincts! Surely your aims are somewhat higher than theirs! Than monkeys—pigs—
TOM I reckon they're not.
AMANDA You're joking. However, that isn't what I wanted to discuss.
TOM [*rising*] I haven't much time.
AMANDA [*pushing his shoulders*] Sit down.
TOM You want me to punch in red at the warehouse, Mother?
AMANDA You have five minutes. I want to talk about Laura.
[*Legend: "Plans and provisions"*]
TOM All right! What about Laura?
AMANDA We have to be making some plans and provisions for her. She's older than you, two years, and nothing has happened. She just drifts along doing nothing. It frightens me terribly how she just drifts along.
TOM I guess she's the type that people call home girls.
AMANDA There's no such type, and if there is, it's a pity! That is unless the home is hers, with a husband!
TOM What?
AMANDA Oh, I can see the handwriting on the wall as plain as I see the nose in front of my face! It's terrifying! More and more you remind me of your father! He was out all hours without explanation!—Then *left! Good-bye!* And me with the bag to hold. I saw that letter you got from the Merchant Marine. I know what you're dreaming of. I'm not standing here blindfolded. Very well, then. Then *do* it! But not till there's somebody to take your place.

TOM What do you mean?

AMANDA I mean that as soon as Laura has got somebody to take care of her, married, a home of her own, independent—why, then you'll be free to go wherever you please, on land, on sea, whichever way the wind blows you! But until that time you've got to look out for your sister. I don't say me because I'm old and don't matter! I say for your sister because she's young and dependent. I put her in business college—a dismal failure! Frightened her so it made her sick at the stomach. I took her over to the Young People's League at the church. Another fiasco. She spoke to nobody, nobody spoke to her. Now all she does is fool with those pieces of glass and play those worn-out records. What kind of a life is that for a girl to lead?

TOM What can I do about it?

AMANDA Overcome selfishness! Self, self, self is all that you ever think of! [TOM *springs up and crosses to get his coat. It is ugly and bulky. He pulls on a cap with earmuffs*] Where is your muffler? Put your wool muffler on! [*He snatches it angrily from the closet and tosses it around his neck and pulls both ends tight*] Tom! I haven't said what I had in mind to ask you.

TOM I'm too late to—

AMANDA [*catching his arm—very importunately. Then shyly*]. Down at the warehouse, aren't there some—nice young men?

TOM No!

AMANDA There *must* be—*some* . . .

TOM Mother—[*Gesture*]

AMANDA Find out one that's clean-living—doesn't drink and—ask him out for sister!

TOM What?

AMANDA For *sister!* To *meet!* Get *acquainted!*

TOM [*stamping to door*] Oh, my go-osh!

AMANDA Will you? [*He opens door. Imploringly*] Will you? [*He starts down*] Will you? *Will* you, dear?

TOM [*calling back*] YES!

[AMANDA *closes the door hesitantly and with a troubled but faintly hopeful expression*]

[*Screen image: Glamor magazine cover*]

[*Spot* AMANDA *at phone*]

AMANDA Ella Cartwright? This is Amanda Wingfield! How are you, honey? How is that kidney condition? [*Count five*] Horrors! [*Count five*] You're a Christian martyr, yes, honey, that's what you are, a Christian martyr! Well, I just now happened to notice in my little red book that your subscription to the *Companion* has just run out!

I knew that you wouldn't want to miss out on the wonderful serial starting in this new issue. It's by Bessie Mae Hopper, the first thing she's written since *Honeymoon for Three.* Wasn't that a strange and interesting story? Well, this one is even lovelier, I believe. It has a sophisticated, society background. It's all about the horsey set on Long Island!
[*Fade out*]

Scene V

Legend on screen: "Annunciation." Fade with music.
It is early dusk of a spring evening. Supper has just been finished in the Wingfield apartment. AMANDA *and* LAURA *in light-colored dresses are removing dishes from the table, in the upstage area, which is shadowy, their movements formalized almost as a dance or ritual, their moving forms as pale and silent as moths.* TOM, *in white shirt and trousers, rises from the table and crosses toward the fire-escape.*

AMANDA [*as he passes her*] Son, will you do me a favor?
TOM What?
AMANDA Comb your hair! You look so pretty when your hair is combed! [TOM *slouches on sofa with evening paper. Enormous caption "Franco Triumphs"*] There is only one respect in which I would like you to emulate your father.
TOM What respect is that?
AMANDA The care he always took of his appearance. He never allowed himself to look untidy. [*He throws down the paper and crosses to fire-escape*] Where are you going?
TOM I'm going out to smoke.
AMANDA You smoke too much. A pack a day at fifteen cents a pack. How much would that amount to in a month? Thirty times fifteen is how much, Tom? Figure it out and you will be astounded at what you could save. Enough to give you a night-school course in accounting at Washington U! Just think what a wonderful thing that would be for you, Son!
[TOM *is unmoved by the thought*]
TOM I'd rather smoke. [*He steps out on landing, letting the screen door slam*]
AMANDA [*sharply*] I know! That's the tragedy of it. . . . [*Alone, she turns to look at her husband's picture*]
[*Dance music: "All the World Is Waiting for the Sunrise!"*]

TOM [*to the audience*] Across the alley from us was the Paradise Dance Hall. On evenings in spring the windows and doors were open and the music came outdoors. Sometimes the lights were turned out except for a large glass sphere that hung from the ceiling. It would turn slowly about and filter the dusk with delicate rainbow colors. Then the orchestra played a waltz or a tango, something that had a slow and sensuous rhythm. Couples would come outside, to the relative privacy of the alley. You could see them kissing behind ash-pits and telephone poles. This was the compensation for lives that passed like mine, without any change or adventure. Adventure and change were imminent in this year. They were waiting around the corner for all these kids. Suspended in the mist over Berchtesgaden,[2] caught in the folds of Chamberlain's[3] umbrella—In Spain there was Guernica![4] But here there was only hot swing music and liquor, dance halls, bars, and movies, and sex that hung in the gloom like a chandelier and flooded the world with brief, deceptive rainbows. . . . All the world was waiting for bombardments!

[AMANDA *turns from the picture and comes outside*].

AMANDA [*sighing*] A fire-escape landing's a poor excuse for a porch. [*She spreads a newspaper on a step and sits down, gracefully and demurely as if she were settling into a swing on a Mississippi veranda*] What are you looking at?

TOM The moon.

AMANDA Is there a moon this evening?

TOM It's rising over Garfinkel's Delicatessen.

AMANDA So it is! A little silver slipper of a moon. Have you made a wish on it yet?

TOM Um-hum.

AMANDA What did you wish for?

TOM That's a secret.

AMANDA A secret, huh? Well, I won't tell mine either. I will be just as mysterious as you.

TOM I bet I can guess what yours is.

AMANDA Is my head so transparent?

TOM You're not a sphinx.

AMANDA No, I don't have secrets. I'll tell you what I wished for on the moon. Success and happiness for my precious children! I wish for

---

[2] *Berchtesgaden:* town in Bavarian Alps where Adolf Hitler had his vacation headquarters. [3] *Chamberlain:* Arthur Neville Chamberlain (1869–1940), England's Prime Minister at the start of World War II. [4] *Guernica:* see note p. 524.

that whenever there's a moon, and when there isn't a moon I wish for it, too.

TOM I thought perhaps you wished for a gentleman caller.

AMANDA Why do you say that?

TOM Don't you remember asking me to fetch one?

AMANDA I remember suggesting that it would be nice for your sister if you brought home some nice young man from the warehouse. I think that I've made that suggestion more than once.

TOM Yes, you have made it repeatedly.

AMANDA Well?

TOM We are going to have one.

AMANDA *What?*

TOM A gentleman caller!

[*The annunciation is celebrated with music*]
[AMANDA *rises*]
[*Image on screen: Caller with bouquet*]

AMANDA You mean you have asked some nice young man to come over?

TOM Yep. I've asked him to dinner.

AMANDA You really did?

TOM I did!

AMANDA You did, and did he—*accept?*

TOM He did!

AMANDA Well, well—well, well! That's—lovely!

TOM I thought that you would be pleased.

AMANDA It's definite, then?

TOM Very definite.

AMANDA Soon?

TOM Very soon.

AMANDA For heaven's sake, stop putting on and tell me some things, will you?

TOM What things do you want me to tell you?

AMANDA *Naturally* I would like to know when he's *coming!*

TOM He's coming tomorrow.

AMANDA *Tomorrow?*

TOM Yep. Tomorrow.

AMANDA But; Tom!

TOM Yes, Mother?

AMANDA Tomorrow gives me no time!

TOM Time for what?

AMANDA Preparation! Why didn't you phone me at once, as soon as you asked him, the minute that he accepted? Then, don't you see, I could have been getting ready!

TOM You don't have to make any fuss.

AMANDA Oh, Tom, Tom, Tom, of course I have to make a fuss! I want things nice, not sloppy! Not thrown together. I'll certainly have to do some fast thinking, won't I?

TOM I don't see why you have to think at all.

AMANDA You just don't know. We can't have a gentleman caller in a pig-sty. All my wedding silver has to be polished, the monogrammed table linen ought to be laundered! The windows have to be washed and fresh curtains put up. And how about clothes? We have to *wear* something, don't we?

TOM Mother, this boy is no one to make a fuss over!

AMANDA Do you realize he's the first young man we've introduced to your sister? It's terrible, dreadful, disgraceful that poor little sister has never received a single gentleman caller! Tom, come inside! [*She opens the screen door*]

TOM What for?

AMANDA I want to ask you some things.

TOM If you're going to make such a fuss, I'll call it off, I'll tell him not to come!

AMANDA You certainly won't do anything of the kind. Nothing offends people worse than broken engagements. It simply means I'll have to work like a Turk! We won't be brilliant, but we will pass inspection. Come on inside. [TOM *follows, groaning*] Sit down.

TOM Any particular place you would like me to sit?

AMANDA Thank heavens I've got that new sofa! I'm also making payments on a floor lamp I'll have sent out! And put the chintz covers on, they'll brighten things up! Of course I'd hoped to have these walls re-papered. . . . What is the young man's name?

TOM His name is O'Connor.

AMANDA That, of course, means fish—tomorrow is Friday! I'll have that salmon loaf—with Durkee's dressing! What does he do? He works at the warehouse?

TOM Of course! How else would I—

AMANDA Tom, he—doesn't drink?

TOM Why do you ask me that?

AMANDA Your father *did!*

TOM Don't get started on that!

AMANDA He *does* drink, then?

TOM Not that I know of!

AMANDA Make sure, be certain! The last thing I want for my daughter's a boy who drinks!

TOM Aren't you being a little bit premature? Mr. O'Connor has not yet appeared on the scene!

AMANDA But will tomorrow. To meet your sister, and what do I know about his character? Nothing! Old maids are better off than wives of drunkards!

TOM Oh, my God!

AMANDA Be still!

TOM [*leaning forward to whisper*] Lots of fellows meet girls whom they don't marry!

AMANDA Oh, talk sensibly, Tom—and don't be sarcastic! [*She has gotten a hairbrush*]

TOM What are you doing?

AMANDA I'm brushing that cow-lick down! What is this young man's position at the warehouse?

TOM [*submitting grimly to the brush and the interrogation*] This young man's position is that of a shipping clerk, Mother.

AMANDA Sounds to me like a fairly responsible job, the sort of a job *you* would be in if you just had more *get-up*.

What is his salary? Have you any idea?

TOM I would judge it to be approximately eighty-five dollars a month.

AMANDA Well—not princely, but—

TOM Twenty more than I make.

AMANDA Yes, how well I know! But for a family man, eighty-five dollars a month is not much more than you can just get by on. . . .

TOM Yes, but Mr. O'Connor is not a family man.

AMANDA He might be, mightn't he? Some time in the future?

TOM I see. Plans and provisions.

AMANDA You are the only young man that I know of who ignores the fact that the future becomes the present, the present the past, and the past turns into everlasting regret if you don't plan for it!

TOM I will think that over and see what I can make of it.

AMANDA Don't be supercilious with your mother! Tell me some more about this—what do you call him?

TOM James D. O'Connor. The D. is for Delaney.

AMANDA Irish on *both* sides! *Gracious!* And doesn't drink?

TOM Shall I call him up and ask him right this minute?

AMANDA The only way to find out about those things is to make discreet inquiries at the proper moment. When I was a girl in Blue Mountain and it was suspected that a young man drank, the girl whose attentions he had been receiving, if any girl was, would sometimes speak to the minister of his church, or rather her father would if her father was living, and sort of feel him out on the young man's character. That is the way such things are discreetly handled to keep a young woman from making a tragic mistake!

TOM Then how did you happen to make a tragic mistake?

AMANDA That innocent look of your father's had everyone fooled! He *smiled*—the world was *enchanted!* No girl can do worse than put herself at the mercy of a handsome appearance! I hope that Mr. O'Connor is not too good-looking.

TOM No, he's not too good-looking. He's covered with freckles and hasn't too much of a nose.

AMANDA He's not right-down homely, though?

TOM Not right-down homely. Just medium homely, I'd say.

AMANDA Character's what to look for in a man.

TOM That's what I've always said, Mother.

AMANDA You've never said anything of the kind and I suspect you would never give it a thought.

TOM Don't be so suspicious of me.

AMANDA At least I hope he's the type that's up and coming.

TOM I think he really goes in for self-improvement.

AMANDA What reason have you to think so?

TOM He goes to night school.

AMANDA [*beaming*] Splendid! What does he do, I mean study?

TOM Radio engineering and public speaking!

AMANDA Then he has visions of being advanced in the world! Any young man who studies public speaking is aiming to have an executive job some day! And radio engineering? A thing for the future! Both of these facts are very illuminating. Those are the sort of things that a mother should know concerning any young man who comes to call on her daughter. Seriously or—not.

TOM One little warning. He doesn't know about Laura. I didn't let on that we had dark ulterior motives. I just said, why don't you come and have dinner with us? He said okay and that was the whole conversation.

AMANDA I bet it was! You're eloquent as an oyster. However, he'll know about Laura when he gets here. When he sees how lovely and sweet and pretty she is, he'll thank his lucky stars he was asked to dinner.

TOM Mother, you mustn't expect too much of Laura.

AMANDA What do you mean?

TOM Laura seems all those things to you and me because she's ours and we love her. We don't even notice she's crippled any more.
AMANDA Don't say crippled. You know that I never allow that word to be used!
TOM But face facts, Mother. She is and—that's not all—
AMANDA What do you mean "not all"?
TOM Laura is very different from other girls.
AMANDA I think the difference is all to her advantage.
TOM Not quite all—in the eyes of others—strangers—she's terribly shy and lives in a world of her own and those things make her seem a little peculiar to people outside the house.
AMANDA Don't say peculiar.
TOM Face the facts. She is.
[*The dance-hall music changes to a tango that has a minor and somewhat ominous tone*]
AMANDA In what way is she peculiar—may I ask?
TOM [*gently*] She lives in a world of her own—a world of—little glass ornaments, Mother. . . . [*Gets up.* AMANDA *remains holding brush, looking at him, troubled*] She plays old phonograph records and—that's about all—[*He glances at himself in the mirror and crosses to door*]
AMANDA [*sharply*] Where are you going?
TOM I'm going to the movies. [*Out screen door*]
AMANDA Not to the movies, every night to the movies! [*Follows quickly to screen door*] I don't believe you always go to the movies! [*He is gone.* AMANDA *looks worriedly after him for a moment. Then vitality and optimism return and she turns from the door. Crossing to portieres*] Laura! Laura! [LAURA *answers from kitchenette*]
LAURA Yes, Mother.
AMANDA Let those dishes go and come in front! [LAURA *appears with dish towel. Gaily*] Laura, come here and make a wish on the moon! [*Screen image: Moon*]
LAURA [*entering*] Moon—moon?
AMANDA A little silver slipper of a moon. Look over your left shoulder, Laura, and make a wish! [LAURA *looks faintly puzzled as if called out of sleep.* AMANDA *seizes her shoulders and turns her at an angle by the door*] Now! Now, darling, *wish!*
LAURA What shall I wish for, Mother?
AMANDA [*her voice trembling and her eyes suddenly filling with tears*] Happiness! Good fortune!

[*The violin rises and the stage dims out*]
[*Curtain*]

Scene VI

[*Image: High school hero*]

TOM And so the following evening I brought Jim home to dinner. I had known Jim slightly in high school. In high school Jim was a hero. He had tremendous Irish good nature and vitality with the scrubbed and polished look of white chinaware. He seemed to move in a continual spotlight. He was a star in basketball, captain of the debating club, president of the senior class and the glee club and he sang the male lead in the annual light operas. He was always running or bounding, never just walking. He seemed always at the point of defeating the law of gravity. He was shooting with such velocity through his adolescence that you would logically expect him to arrive at nothing short of the White House by the time he was thirty. But Jim apparently ran into more interference after his graduation from Soldan. His speed had definitely slowed. Six years after he left high school he was holding a job that wasn't much better than mine.

[*Image: Clerk*]

He was the only one at the warehouse with whom I was on friendly terms. I was valuable to him as someone who could remember his former glory, who had seen him win basketball games and the silver cup in debating. He knew of my secret practice of retiring to a cabinet of the wash-room to work on poems when business was slack in the warehouse. He called me Shakespeare. And while the other boys in the warehouse regarded me with suspicious hostility, Jim took a humorous attitude toward me. Gradually his attitude affected the others, their hostility wore off and they also began to smile at me as people smile at an oddly fashioned dog who trots across their path at some distance.

I knew that Jim and Laura had known each other at Soldan, and I had heard Laura speak admiringly of his voice. I didn't know if Jim remembered her or not. In high school Laura had been as unobtrusive as Jim had been astonishing. If he did remember Laura, it was not as my sister, for when I asked him to dinner, he grinned and said, "You know, Shakespeare, I never thought of you as having folks!"

He was about to discover that I did. . . .

[*Light up stage*]

[*Legend on screen: "The accent of a coming foot"*]
[*Friday evening. It is about five o'clock of a late spring evening which comes "scattering poems in the sky." A delicate lemony light is in the Wingfield apartment.* AMANDA *has worked like a Turk in preparation for the gentleman caller. The results are astonishing. The new floor lamp with its rose-silk shade is in place, a colored paper lantern conceals the broken light-fixture in the ceiling, new billowing white curtains are at the windows, chintz covers are on chairs and sofa, a pair of new sofa pillows make their initial appearance. Open boxes and tissue paper are scattered on the floor.* LAURA *stands in the middle with lifted arms while* AMANDA *crouches before her, adjusting the hem of the new dress, devout and ritualistic. The dress is colored and designed by memory. The arrangement of* LAURA's *hair is changed: it is softer and more becoming. A fragile, unearthly prettiness has come out in* LAURA: *she is like a piece of translucent glass touched by light, given a momentary radiance, not actual, not lasting*]

AMANDA [*impatiently*] Why are you trembling?
LAURA Mother, you've made me so nervous!
AMANDA How have I made you nervous?
LAURA By all this fuss! You make it seem so important!
AMANDA I don't understand you, Laura. You couldn't be satisfied with just sitting home, and yet whenever I try to arrange something for you, you seem to resist it. [*She gets up*] Now take a look at yourself. No, wait! Wait just a moment—I have an idea!
LAURA What is it now?
[AMANDA *produces two powder puffs which she wraps in handkerchiefs and stuffs in* LAURA's *bosom*]
LAURA Mother, what are you doing?
AMANDA They call them "Gay Deceivers"!
LAURA I won't wear them!
AMANDA You will!
LAURA Why should I?
AMANDA Because, to be painfully honest, your chest is flat.
LAURA You make it seem like we were setting a trap.
AMANDA All pretty girls are a trap, a pretty trap, and men expect them to be. [*Legend: "A pretty trap"*] Now look at yourself, young lady. This is the prettiest you will ever be! I've got to fix myself now! You're going to be surprised by your mother's appearance! [*She crosses through portieres, humming gaily.* LAURA *moves slowly to the long mirror and*

stares solemnly at herself. A wind blows the white curtains inward in a slow, graceful motion and with a faint, sorrowful sighing]

AMANDA [*off stage*] It isn't dark enough yet. [*She turns slowly before the mirror with a troubled look*]

[*Legend on screen: "This is my sister: celebrate her with strings!" Music*]

AMANDA [*laughing, off*] I'm going to show you something. I'm going to make a spectacular appearance!

LAURA What is it, Mother?

AMANDA Possess your soul in patience—you will see! Something I've resurrected from that old trunk! Styles haven't changed so terribly much after all. . . . [*She parts the portieres*] Now just look at your mother! [*She wears a girlish frock of yellowed voile with a blue silk sash. She carries a bunch of jonquils—the legend of her youth is nearly revived. Feverishly*] This is the dress in which I led the cotillion. Won the cakewalk twice at Sunset Hill, wore one spring to the Governor's ball in Jackson! See how I sashayed around the ballroom, Laura? [*She raises her skirt and does a mincing step around the room*] I wore it on Sundays for my gentlemen callers! I had it on the day I met your father—I had malaria fever all that spring. The change of climate from East Tennessee to the Delta—weakened resistance—I had a little temperature all the time—not enough to be serious—just enough to make me restless and giddy!—Invitations poured in—parties all over the Delta!—"Stay in bed," said Mother, "you have fever!"—but I just wouldn't.—I took quinine but kept on going, going!—Evenings, dances!—Afternoons, long, long rides! Picnics—lovely!—So lovely, that country in May.—All lacy with dogwood, literally flooded with jonquils!—That was the spring I had the craze for jonquils. Jonquils became an absolute obsession. Mother said "Honey, there's no more room for jonquils." And still I kept on bringing in more jonquils. Whenever, wherever I saw them, I'd say, "Stop! Stop! I see jonquils!" I made the young men help me gather the jonquils! It was a joke, Amanda and her jonquils! Finally there were no more vases to hold them, every available space was filled with jonquils. No vases to hold them? All right, I'll hold them myself! And then I—[*She stops in front of the picture. Music*] met your father! Malaria fever and jonquils and then—this—boy. . . . [*She switches on the rose-colored lamp*] I hope they get here before it starts to rain. [*She crosses upstage and places the jonquils in bowl on table*] I gave your brother a little extra change so he and Mr. O'Connor could take the service car home.

LAURA [*with altered look*] What did you say his name was?

AMANDA O'Connor.
LAURA What is his first name?
AMANDA I don't remember. Oh, yes, I do. It was—Jim!
  [LAURA *sways slightly and catches hold of a chair*]
  [*Legend on screen: "Not Jim!"*]
LAURA [*faintly*] Not—Jim!
AMANDA Yes, that was it, it was Jim! I've never known a Jim that wasn't nice!
  [*Music: Ominous*]
LAURA Are you sure his name is Jim O'Connor?
AMANDA Yes. Why?
LAURA Is he the one that Tom used to know in high school?
AMANDA He didn't say so. I think he just got to know him at the warehouse.
LAURA There was a Jim O'Connor we both knew in high school— [*Then, with effort*] If that is the one that Tom is bringing to dinner— you'll have to excuse me. I won't come to the table.
AMANDA What sort of nonsense is this?
LAURA You asked me once if I'd ever liked a boy. Don't you remember I showed you this boy's picture?
AMANDA You mean the boy you showed me in the year book?
LAURA Yes, that boy.
AMANDA Laura, Laura, were you in love with that boy?
LAURA I don't know, Mother. All I know is I couldn't sit at the table if it was him!
AMANDA It won't be him! It isn't the least bit likely. But whether it is or not, you will come to the table. You will not be excused.
LAURA I'll have to be, Mother.
AMANDA I don't intend to humor your silliness, Laura. I've had too much from you and your brother, both! So just sit down and compose yourself till they come. Tom has forgotten his key so you'll have to let them in, when they arrive.
LAURA [*panicky*] Oh, Mother—*you* answer the door!
AMANDA [*lightly*] I'll be in the kitchen—busy!
LAURA Oh, Mother, please answer the door, don't make me do it!
AMANDA [*crossing into kitchenette*] I've got to fix the dressing for the salmon. Fuss, fuss—silliness!—over a gentleman caller!
  [*Door swings shut.* LAURA *is left alone*]
  [*Legend: "Terror!"*]
  [*She utters a low moan and turns off the lamp—sits stiffly on the edge of the sofa, knotting her fingers together*]

[*Legend on screen: "The opening of a door!"*]
[TOM *and* JIM *appear on the fire-escape steps and climb to landing. Hearing their approach,* LAURA *rises with a panicky gesture. She retreats to the portieres. The doorbell.* LAURA *catches her breath and touches her throat. Low drums*]
AMANDA [*calling*] Laura, sweetheart! The door! [LAURA *stares at it without moving*]
JIM I think we just beat the rain.
TOM Uh-huh. [*He rings again, nervously.* JIM *whistles and fishes for a cigarette*]
AMANDA [*very, very gaily*] Laura, that is your brother and Mr. O'Connor! Will you let them in, darling?
[LAURA *crosses toward kitchenette door*]
LAURA [*breathlessly*] Mother—you go to the door!
[AMANDA *steps out of kitchenette and stares furiously at* LAURA. *She points imperiously at the door*]
LAURA Please, please!
AMANDA [*in a fierce whisper*] What is the matter with you, you silly thing?
LAURA [*desperately*] Please, you answer it, *please!*
AMANDA I told you I wasn't going to humor you, Laura. Why have you chosen this moment to lose your mind?
LAURA Please, please, please, you go!
AMANDA You'll have to go to the door because I can't!
LAURA [*despairingly*] I can't either!
AMANDA *Why?*
LAURA I'm *sick!*
AMANDA I'm sick, too—of your nonsense! Why can't you and your brother be normal people? Fantastic whim and behavior? [TOM *gives a long ring*] Preposterous goings on! Can you give me one reason—[*Calls out lyrically*] Coming! Just one second!—why you should be afraid to open a door? Now you answer it, Laura!
LAURA Oh, oh, oh . . . [*She returns through the portieres. Darts to the victrola and winds it frantically and turns it on*]
AMANDA Laura Wingfield, you march right to that door!
LAURA Yes—yes, Mother!
[*A faraway, scratchy rendition of "Dardanella" softens the air and gives her strength to move through it. She slips to the door and draws it cautiously open.* TOM *enters with the caller,* JIM O'CONNOR]
TOM Laura, this is Jim. Jim, this is my sister, Laura.
JIM [*stepping inside*] I didn't know that Shakespeare had a sister!

LAURA [*retreating stiff and trembling from the door*] How—how do you do?

JIM [*heartily extending his hand*] Okay! [LAURA *touches it hesitantly with hers*]

JIM Your hand's *cold*, Laura!

LAURA Yes, well—I've been playing the victrola. . . .

JIM Must have been playing classical music on it! You ought to play a little hot swing music to warm you up!

LAURA Excuse me—I haven't finished playing the victrola. . . . [*She turns awkwardly and hurries into the front room. She pauses a second by the victrola. Then catches her breath and darts through the portieres like a frightened deer*]

JIM [*grinning*] What was the matter?

TOM Oh—with Laura? Laura is—terribly shy.

JIM Shy, huh? It's unusual to meet a shy girl nowadays. I don't believe you ever mentioned you had a sister.

TOM Well, now you know. I have one. Here is the *Post Dispatch*. You want a piece of it?

JIM Uh-huh.

TOM What piece? The comics?

JIM Sports! [*Glances at it*] Ole Dizzy Dean is on his bad behavior.

TOM [*disinterest*] Yeah? [*Lights cigarette and crosses back to fire-escape door*]

JIM Where are *you* going?

TOM I'm going out on the terrace.

JIM [*goes after him*] You know, Shakespeare—I'm going to sell you a bill of goods!

TOM What goods?

JIM A course I'm taking.

TOM Huh?

JIM In public speaking! You and me, we're not the warehouse type.

TOM Thanks—that's good news. But what has public speaking got to do with it?

JIM It fits you for—executive positions!

TOM Awww.

JIM I tell you it's done a helluva lot for me.

[*Image: Executive at desk*]

TOM In what respect?

JIM In every! Ask yourself what is the difference between you an' me and men in the office down front? Brains?—No!—Ability?—No! Then what? Just one little thing—

TOM What is that one little thing?

JIM Primarily it amounts to—social poise! Being able to square up to people and hold your own on any social level!
AMANDA [*off stage*] Tom?
TOM Yes, Mother?
AMANDA Is that you and Mr. O'Connor?
TOM Yes, Mother.
AMANDA Ask Mr. O'Connor if he would like to wash his hands.
JIM Aw, no—no—thank you—I took care of that at the warehouse. Tom—
TOM Yes?
JIM Mr. Mendoza was speaking to me about you.
TOM Favorably?
JIM What do you think?
TOM Well—
JIM You're going to be out of a job if you don't wake up.
TOM I am waking up—
JIM You show no signs.
TOM The signs are interior.

[*Image on screen: The sailing vessel with Jolly Roger again*]

TOM I'm planning to change. [*He leans over the rail speaking with quiet exhilaration. The incandescent marquees and signs of the first-run movie houses light his face from across the alley. He looks like a voyager*] I'm right at the point of committing myself to a future that doesn't include the warehouse and Mr. Mendoza or even a night-school course in public speaking.
JIM What are you gassing about?
TOM I'm tired of the movies.
JIM Movies!
TOM Yes, movies! Look at them—[*A wave toward the marvels of Grand Avenue*] All of those glamorous people—having adventures—hogging it all, gobbling the whole thing up! You know what happens? People go to the *movies* instead of *moving*! Hollywood characters are supposed to have all the adventures for everybody in America, while everybody in America sits in a dark room and watches them have them! Yes, until there's a war. That's when adventure becomes available to the masses! *Everyone's* dish, not only Gable's! Then the people in the dark room come out of the dark room to have some adventures themselves—Goody, goody!—It's our turn now, to go to the South Sea Island—to make a safari—to be exotic, far-off!—but I'm not patient. I don't want to wait till then. I'm tired of the *movies* and I am *about* to *move!*
JIM [*incredulously*] Move?

TOM Yes.
JIM When?
TOM Soon!
JIM Where? Where?
   [*Theme three music seems to answer the question, while* TOM *thinks it over. He searches among his pockets*]
TOM I'm starting to boil inside. I know I seem dreamy, but inside—well, I'm boiling!—Whenever I pick up a shoe, I shudder a little thinking how short life is and what I am doing!—Whatever that means, I know it doesn't mean shoes—except as something to wear on a traveler's feet! [*Finds paper*] Look—
JIM What?
TOM I'm a member.
JIM [*reading*] The Union of Merchant Seamen.
TOM I paid my dues this month, instead of the light bill.
JIM You will regret it when they turn the lights off.
TOM I won't be here.
JIM How about your mother?
TOM I'm like my father. The bastard son of a bastard! See how he grins? And he's been absent going on sixteen years!
JIM You're just talking, you drip. How does your mother feel about it?
TOM Shhh!—Here comes Mother! Mother is not acquainted with my plans!
AMANDA [*enters portieres*] Where are you all?
TOM On the terrace, Mother.
   [*They start inside. She advances to them.* TOM *is distinctly shocked at her appearance. Even* JIM *blinks a little. He is making his first contact with girlish Southern vivacity and in spite of the night-school course in public speaking is somewhat thrown off the beam by the unexpected outlay of social charm. Certain responses are attempted by* JIM *but are swept aside by* AMANDA's *gay laughter and chatter.* TOM *is embarrassed but after the first shock* JIM *reacts very warmly. Grins and chuckles, is altogether won over*]
   [*Image:* AMANDA *as a girl*]
AMANDA [*coyly smiling, shaking her girlish ringlets*] Well, well, well, so this is Mr. O'Connor. Introductions entirely unnecessary. I've heard so much about you from my boy. I finally said to him, Tom—good gracious!—why don't you bring this paragon to supper? I'd like to meet this nice young man at the warehouse!—Instead of just hearing him sing your praises so much!
   I don't know why my son is so stand-offish—that's not Southern behavior!

Let's sit down and—I think we could stand a little more air in here! Tom, leave the door open. I felt a nice fresh breeze a moment ago. Where has it gone to?

Mmm, so warm already! And not quite summer, even. We're going to burn up when summer really gets started.

However, we're having—we're having a very light supper. I think light things are better fo' this time of year. The same as light clothes are. Light clothes an' light food are what warm weather calls fo'. You know our blood gets so thick during th' winter—it takes a while fo' us to *adjust* ou'selves!—when the season changes . . .

It's come so quick this year. I wasn't prepared. All of a sudden—heavens! Already summer!—I ran to the trunk an' pulled out this light dress—Terribly old! Historical almost! But feels so good—so good an' co-ol, y'know. . . .

TOM Mother—

AMANDA Yes, honey?

TOM How about—supper?

AMANDA Honey, you go ask Sister if supper is ready! You know that Sister is in full charge of supper!

Tell her you hungry boys are waiting for it. [*To* JIM] Have you met Laura?

JIM She—

AMANDA Let you in? Oh, good, you've met already! It's rare for a girl as sweet an' pretty as Laura to be domestic! But Laura is, thank heavens, not only pretty but also very domestic. I'm not at all. I never was a bit. I never could make a thing but angel-food cake. Well, in the South we had so many servants. Gone, gone, gone. All vestige of gracious living! Gone completely! I wasn't prepared for what the future brought me. All of my gentlemen callers were sons of planters and so of course I assumed that I would be married to one and raise my family on a large piece of land with plenty of servants. But man proposes—and woman accepts the proposal!—To vary that old, old saying a little bit—I married no planter! I married a man who worked for the telephone company!—That gallantly smiling gentleman over there! [*Points to the picture*] A telephone man who—fell in love with long-distance!—Now he travels and I don't even know where!—But what am I going on for about my tribulations? Tell me yours—I hope you don't have any! Tom?

TOM [*returning*] Yes, Mother?

AMANDA Is supper nearly ready?

TOM It looks to me like supper is on the table.

AMANDA Let me look—[*She rises prettily and looks through portieres*]

Oh, lovely!—But where is Sister?
TOM Laura is not feeling well and she says that she thinks she'd better not come to the table.
AMANDA What?—Nonsense!—Laura? Oh, Laura!
LAURA [off stage, faintly] Yes, Mother.
AMANDA You really must come to the table. We won't be seated until you come to the table! Come in, Mr. O'Connor. You sit over there, and I'll—Laura? Laura Wingfield! You're keeping us waiting, honey! We can't say grace until you come to the table!
[The back door is pushed weakly open and LAURA comes in. She is obviously quite faint, her lips trembling, her eyes wide and staring. She moves unsteadily toward the table]
[Legend: "Terror!"]
[Outside a summer storm is coming abruptly. The white curtains billow inward at the windows and there is a sorrowful murmur and deep blue dusk. LAURA suddenly stumbles—she catches at a chair with a faint moan]
TOM Laura!
AMANDA Laura! [There is a clap of thunder. Legend: "Ah!" Despairingly] Why, Laura, you *are* sick, darling! Tom, help your sister into the living room, dear! Sit in the living room, Laura—rest on the sofa. Well! [To the gentleman caller] Standing over the hot stove made her ill!— I told her that it was just too warm this evening, but—[TOM comes back in. LAURA is on the sofa] Is Laura all right now?
TOM Yes.
AMANDA What *is* that? Rain? A nice cool rain has come up! [She gives the gentleman caller a frightened look] I think we may—have grace— now. . . . [TOM looks at her stupidly] Tom, honey—you say grace!
TOM Oh . . . "For these and all thy mercies—" [They bow their heads, AMANDA stealing a nervous glance at JIM. In the living room LAURA, stretched on the sofa, clenches her hand to her lips, to hold back a shuddering sob] God's Holy Name be praised—
[The scene dims out]

Scene VII

A Souvenir.
Half an hour later. Dinner is just being finished in the upstage area which is concealed by the drawn portieres. As the curtain rises LAURA *is still huddled upon the sofa, her feet drawn under her, her head resting on a pale blue pillow, her eyes wide and mysteriously watchful. The new floor lamp with its shade of rose-colored silk gives a soft, becoming light*

to her face, bringing out the fragile, unearthly prettiness which usually escapes attention. There is a steady murmur of rain, but it is slackening and stops soon after the scene begins; the air outside becomes pale and luminous as the moon breaks out. A moment after the curtain rises, the lights in both rooms flicker and go out.

JIM Hey, there, Mr. Light Bulb!
   [AMANDA *laughs nervously*]
   [*Legend: "Suspension of a public service"*]
AMANDA Where was Moses when the lights went out? Ha-ha. Do you know the answer to that one, Mr. O'Connor?
JIM No, Ma'am, what's the answer?
AMANDA In the dark! [JIM *laughs appreciatively*] Everybody sit still. I'll light the candles. Isn't it lucky we have them on the table? Where's a match? Which of you gentlemen can provide a match?
JIM Here.
AMANDA Thank you, sir.
JIM Not at all, Ma'am!
AMANDA I guess the fuse has burnt out. Mr. O'Connor, can you tell a burnt-out fuse? I know I can't and Tom is a total loss when it comes to mechanics. [*Sound: Getting up: Voices recede a little to kitchenette*] Oh, be careful you don't bump into something. We don't want our gentleman caller to break his neck. Now wouldn't that be a fine howdy-do?
JIM Ha-ha! Where is the fuse-box?
AMANDA Right here next to the stove. Can you see anything?
JIM Just a minute.
AMANDA Isn't electricity a mysterious thing? Wasn't it Benjamin Franklin who tied a key to a kite? We live in such a mysterious universe, don't we? Some people say that science clears up all the mysteries for us. In my opinion it only creates more!
   Have you found it yet?
JIM No, Ma'am. All these fuses look okay to me.
AMANDA Tom!
TOM Yes, Mother?
AMANDA That light bill I gave you several days ago. The one I told you we got the notices about?
   [*Legend: "Ha!"*]
TOM Oh.—Yeah.
AMANDA You didn't neglect to pay it by any chance?
TOM Why, I—
AMANDA Didn't! I might have known it!

JIM Shakespeare probably wrote a poem on that light bill, Mrs. Wingfield.
AMANDA I might have known better than to trust him with it! There's such a high price for negligence in this world!
JIM Maybe the poem will win a ten-dollar prize.
AMANDA We'll just have to spend the remainder of the evening in the nineteenth century, before Mr. Edison made the Mazda lamp!
JIM Candlelight is my favorite kind of light.
AMANDA That shows you're romantic! But that's no excuse for Tom. Well, we got through dinner. Very considerate of them to let us get through dinner before they plunged us into everlasting darkness, wasn't it, Mr. O'Connor?
JIM Ha-ha!
AMANDA Tom, as a penalty for your carelessness you can help me with the dishes.
JIM Let me give you a hand.
AMANDA Indeed you will not!
JIM I ought to be good for something.
AMANDA Good for something? [*Her tone is rhapsodic*] You? Why, Mr. O'Connor, nobody, *nobody's* given me this much entertainment in years—as you have!
JIM Aw, now, Mrs. Wingfield!
AMANDA I'm not exaggerating, not one bit! But Sister is all by her lonesome. You go keep her company in the parlor!
   I'll give you this lovely old candelabrum that used to be on the altar at the church of the Heavenly Rest. It was melted a little out of shape when the church burnt down. Lightning struck it one spring. Gypsy Jones was holding a revival at the time and he intimated that the church was destroyed because the Episcopalians gave card parties.
JIM Ha-ha.
AMANDA And how about you coaxing Sister to drink a little wine? I think it would be good for her! Can you carry both at once?
JIM Sure. I'm Superman!
AMANDA Now, Thomas, get into this apron!
[*The door of the kitchenette swings closed on* AMANDA's *gay laughter; the flickering light approaches the portieres.* LAURA *sits up nervously as he enters. Her speech at first is low and breathless from the almost intolerable strain of being alone with a stranger*]
[*The legend: "I don't suppose you remember me at all!"*]
[*In her first speeches in this scene, before* JIM's *warmth overcomes her paralyzing shyness,* LAURA's *voice is thin and breathless as though she has just run up a steep flight of stairs.* JIM's *attitude is gently*

humorous. In playing this scene it should be stressed that while the incident is apparently unimportant, it is to LAURA *the climax of her secret life*]

JIM Hello, there, Laura.

LAURA [*faintly*] Hello. [*She clears her throat*]

JIM How are you feeling now? Better?

LAURA Yes. Yes, thank you.

JIM This is for you. A little dandelion wine. [*He extends it toward her with extravagant gallantry*]

LAURA Thank you.

JIM Drink it—but don't get drunk! [*He laughs heartily.* LAURA *takes the glass uncertainly; laughs shyly*] Where shall I set the candles?

LAURA Oh—oh, anywhere . . .

JIM How about here on the floor? Any objections?

LAURA No.

JIM I'll spread a newspaper under to catch the drippings. I like to sit on the floor. Mind if I do?

LAURA Oh, no.

JIM Give me a pillow?

LAURA What?

JIM A pillow!

LAURA Oh . . . [*Hands him one quickly*]

JIM How about you? Don't you like to sit on the floor?

LAURA Oh—yes.

JIM Why don't you then?

LAURA I—will.

JIM Take a pillow! [LAURA *does. Sits on the other side of the candelabrum.* JIM *crosses his legs and smiles engagingly at her*] I can't hardly see you sitting way over there.

LAURA I can—see you.

JIM I know, but that's not fair, I'm in the limelight. [*Laura moves her pillow closer*] Good! Now I can see you! Comfortable?

LAURA Yes.

JIM So am I. Comfortable as a cow! Will you have some gum?

LAURA No, thank you.

JIM I think that I will indulge, with your permission. [*Musingly unwraps it and holds it up*] Think of the fortune made by the guy that invented the first piece of chewing gum. Amazing, huh? The Wrigley Building is one of the sights of Chicago.—I saw it summer before last when I went up to the Century of Progress. Did you take in the Century of Progress?

LAURA No, I didn't.
JIM Well, it was quite a wonderful exposition. What impressed me most was the Hall of Science. Gives you an idea of what the future will be in America, even more wonderful than the present time is! [*Pause. Smiling at her*] Your brother tells me you're shy. Is that right, Laura?
LAURA I—don't know.
JIM I judge you to be an old-fashioned type of girl. Well, I think that's a pretty good type to be. Hope you don't think I'm being too personal—do you?
LAURA [*hastily, out of embarrassment*] I believe I *will* take a piece of gum, if you—don't mind. [*Clearing her throat*] Mr. O'Connor, have you—kept up with your singing?
JIM Singing? Me?
LAURA Yes. I remember what a beautiful voice you had.
JIM When did you hear me sing?
[*Voice off stage in the pause*]
VOICE [*off stage*]

> O blow, ye winds, heigh-ho,
> A-roving I will go!
>   I'm off to my love
>   With a boxing glove—
> Ten thousand miles away!

JIM You say you've heard me sing?
LAURA Oh, yes! Yes, very often . . . I—don't suppose—you remember me—at all?
JIM [*smiling doubtfully*] You know I have an idea I've seen you before. I had that idea as soon as you opened the door. It seemed almost like I was about to remember your name. But the name I started to call you—wasn't a name! And so I stopped myself before I said it.
LAURA Wasn't it—Blue Roses?
JIM [*springs up. Grinning*] Blue Roses!—My gosh, yes—Blue Roses! That's what I had on my tongue when you opened the door! Isn't it funny what tricks your memory plays? I didn't connect you with high school somehow or other. But that's where it was; it was high school. I didn't even know you were Shakespeare's sister! Gosh, I'm sorry.
LAURA I didn't expect you to. You—barely knew me!
JIM But we did have a speaking acquaintance, huh?
LAURA Yes, we—spoke to each other.
JIM When did you recognize me?
LAURA Oh, right away!
JIM Soon as I came in the door?

LAURA When I heard your name I thought it was probably you. I knew that Tom used to know you a little in high school. So when you came in the door—Well, then I was—sure.
JIM Why didn't you *say* something, then?
LAURA [*breathlessly*] I didn't know what to say, I was—too surprised!
JIM For goodness' sakes! You know, this sure is funny!
LAURA Yes! Yes, isn't it, though . . .
JIM Didn't we have a class in something together?
LAURA Yes, we did.
JIM What class was that?
LAURA It was—singing—Chorus!
JIM Aw!
LAURA I sat across the aisle from you in the Aud.
JIM Aw.
LAURA Mondays, Wednesdays and Fridays.
JIM Now I remember—you always came in late.
LAURA Yes, it was so hard for me, getting upstairs. I had that brace on my leg—it clumped so loud!
JIM I never heard any clumping.
LAURA [*wincing at the recollection*] To me it sounded like—thunder!
JIM Well, well, well, I never even noticed.
LAURA And everybody was seated before I came in. I had to walk in front of all those people. My seat was in the back row. I had to go clumping all the way up the aisle with everyone watching!
JIM You shouldn't have been self-conscious.
LAURA I know, but I was. It was always such a relief when the singing started.
JIM Aw, yes, I've placed you now! I used to call you Blue Roses. How was it that I got started calling you that?
LAURA I was out of school a little while with pleurosis. When I came back you asked me what was the matter. I said I had pleurosis—you thought I said Blue Roses. That's what you always called me after that!
JIM I hope you didn't mind.
LAURA Oh, no—I liked it. You see, I wasn't acquainted with many—people. . . .
JIM As I remember you sort of stuck by yourself.
LAURA I—I—never have had much luck at—making friends.
JIM I don't see why you wouldn't.
LAURA Well, I—started out badly.
JIM You mean being—
LAURA Yes, it sort of—stood between me—
JIM You shouldn't have let it!

LAURA I know, but it did, and—
JIM You were shy with people!
LAURA I tried not to be but never could—
JIM Overcome it?
LAURA No, I—I never could!
JIM I guess being shy is something you have to work out of kind of gradually.
LAURA [*sorrowfully*] Yes—I guess it—
JIM Takes time!
LAURA Yes—
JIM People are not so dreadful when you know them. That's what you have to remember! And everybody has problems, not just you, but practically everybody has got some problems. You think of yourself as having the only problems, as being the only one who is disappointed. But just look around you and you will see lots of people as disappointed as you are. For instance, I hoped when I was going to high school that I would be further along at this time, six years later, than I am now—You remember that wonderful write-up I had in *The Torch*?
LAURA Yes! [*She rises and crosses to table*]
JIM It said I was bound to succeed in anything I went into! [LAURA *returns with the annual*] Holy Jeez! *The Torch*! [*He accepts it reverently. They smile across it with mutual wonder.* LAURA *crouches beside him and they begin to turn through it.* LAURA's *shyness is dissolving in his warmth*]
LAURA Here you are in *The Pirates of Penzance*!
JIM [*wistfully*] I sang the baritone lead in that operetta.
LAURA [*raptly*] So—*beautifully*!
JIM [*protesting*] Aw—
LAURA Yes, yes—beautifully—beautifully!
JIM You heard me?
LAURA All three times!
JIM No!
LAURA Yes!
JIM All three performances?
LAURA [*looking down*] Yes.
JIM Why?
LAURA I—wanted to ask you to—autograph my program.
JIM Why didn't you ask me to?
LAURA You were always surrounded by your own friends so much that I never had a chance to.
JIM You should have just—

LAURA Well, I—thought you might think I was—
JIM Thought I might think you was—what?
LAURA Oh—
JIM [*with reflective relish*] I was beleaguered by females in those days.
LAURA You were terribly popular!
JIM Yeah—
LAURA You had such a—friendly way—
JIM I was spoiled in high school.
LAURA Everybody—liked you!
JIM Including you?
LAURA I—yes, I did, too—[*She gently closes the book in her lap*]
JIM Well, well, well!—Give me that program, Laura. [*She hands it to him. He signs it with a flourish*] There you are—better late than never!
LAURA Oh, I—what a—surprise!
JIM My signature isn't worth very much right now. But some day—maybe—it will increase in value! Being disappointed is one thing and being discouraged is something else. I am disappointed but I am not discouraged. I'm twenty-three years old. How old are you?
LAURA I'll be twenty-four in June.
JIM That's not old age!
LAURA No, but—
JIM You finished high school?
LAURA [*with difficulty*] I didn't go back.
JIM You mean you dropped out?
LAURA I made bad grades in my final examinations. [*She rises and replaces the book and the program. Her voice strained*] How is—Emily Meisenbach getting along?
JIM Oh, that kraut-head!
LAURA Why do you call her that?
JIM That's what she was.
LAURA You're not still—going with her?
JIM I never see her.
LAURA It said in the Personal Section that you were—engaged!
JIM I know, but I wasn't impressed by that—propaganda!
LAURA It wasn't—the truth?
JIM Only in Emily's optimistic opinion!
LAURA Oh—
  [Legend: "*What have you done since high school?*"]
  [JIM *lights a cigarette and leans indolently back on his elbows smiling at* LAURA *with a warmth and charm which lights her inwardly with altar candles. She remains by the table and turns in her hands a piece of glass to cover her tumult*]

JIM [*after several reflective puffs on a cigarette*] What have you done since high school? [*She seems not to hear him*] Huh? [LAURA *looks up*] I said what have you done since high school, Laura?
LAURA Nothing much.
JIM You must have been doing something these six long years.
LAURA Yes.
JIM Well, then, such as what?
LAURA I took a business course at business college—
JIM How did that work out?
LAURA Well, not very—well—I had to drop out, it gave me—indigestion—
[JIM *laughs gently*]
JIM What are you doing now?
LAURA I don't do anything—much. Oh, please don't think I sit around doing nothing! My glass collection takes up a good deal of time. Glass is something you have to take good care of.
JIM What did you say—about glass?
LAURA Collection I said—I have one—[*She clears her throat and turns away again, acutely shy*]
JIM [*abruptly*] You know what I judge to be the trouble with you? Inferiority complex! Know what that is? That's what they call it when someone low-rates himself! I understand it because I had it, too. Although my case was not so aggravated as yours seems to be. I had it until I took up public speaking, developed my voice, and learned that I had an aptitude for science. Before that time I never thought of myself as being outstanding in any way whatsoever! Now I've never made a regular study of it, but I have a friend who says I can analyze people better than doctors that make a profession of it. I don't claim that to be necessarily true, but I can sure guess a person's psychology, Laura! [*Takes out his gum*] Excuse me, Laura. I always take it out when the flavor is gone. I'll use this scrap of paper to wrap it in. I know how it is to get it stuck on a shoe. Yep—that's what I judge to be your principal trouble. A lack of confidence in yourself as a person. You don't have the proper amount of faith in yourself. I'm basing that fact on a number of your remarks and also on certain observations I've made. For instance that clumping you thought was so awful in high school. You say you even dreaded to walk into class. You see what you did? You dropped out of school, you gave up an education because of a clump, which as far as I know was practically non-existent! A little physical defect is what you have. Hardly noticeable even! Magnified thousands of times by imagination! You know what my strong advice to you is? Think of yourself as *superior* in some way!

LAURA In what way would I think?

JIM Why, man alive, Laura! Just look about you a little. What do you see? A world full of common people! All of 'em born and all of 'em going to die! Which of them has one-tenth of your good points! Or mine! Or anyone else's, as far as that goes—Gosh! Everybody excels in some one thing. Some in many! [*Unconsciously glances at himself in the mirror*] All you've got to do is discover in what! Take me, for instance. [*He adjusts his tie at the mirror*] My interest happens to lie in electro-dynamics. I'm taking a course in radio engineering at night school, Laura, on top of a fairly responsible job at the warehouse. I'm taking that course and studying public speaking.

LAURA Ohhhh.

JIM Because I believe in the future of television! [*Turning back to her*] I wish to be ready to go up right along with it. Therefore I'm planning to get in on the ground floor. In fact I've already made the right connections and all that remains is for the industry to get under way! Full steam—[*His eyes are starry*] Knowledge—Zzzzzp! Money—Zzzzzzp!—Power! That's the cycle democracy is built on! [*His attitude is convincingly dynamic.* LAURA *stares at him, even her shyness eclipsed in her absolute wonder. He suddenly grins*] I guess you think I think a lot of myself!

LAURA No—o-o-o, I—

JIM Now how about you? Isn't there something you take more interest in than anything else?

LAURA Well, I do—as I said—have my—glass collection—
[*A peal of girlish laughter from the kitchen*]

JIM I'm not right sure I know what you're talking about. What kind of glass is it?

LAURA Little articles of it, they're ornaments mostly! Most of them are little animals made out of glass, the tiniest little animals in the world. Mother calls them a glass menagerie! Here's an example of one, if you'd like to see it! This is one of the oldest. It's nearly thirteen. [*Music: "The Glass Menagerie." He stretches out his hand*] Oh, be careful—if you breathe, it breaks!

JIM I'd better not take it. I'm pretty clumsy with things.

LAURA Go on, I trust you with him! [*Places it in his palm*] There now—you're holding him gently! Hold him over the light, he loves the light! You see how the light shines through him?

JIM It sure does shine!

LAURA I shouldn't be partial, but he is my favorite one.

JIM What kind of a thing is this one supposed to be?

LAURA Haven't you noticed the single horn on his forehead?

JIM A unicorn, huh?

LAURA Mmm-hmmm!

JIM Unicorns, aren't they extinct in the modern world?

LAURA I know!

JIM Poor little fellow, he must feel sort of lonesome.

LAURA [smiling] Well, if he does he doesn't complain about it. He stays on a shelf with some horses that don't have horns and all of them seem to get along nicely together.

JIM How do you know?

LAURA [lightly] I haven't heard any arguments among them!

JIM [grinning] No arguments, huh? Well, that's a pretty good sign! Where shall I set him?

LAURA Put him on the table. They all like a change of scenery once in a while!

JIM [stretching] Well, well, well, well—Look how big my shadow is when I stretch!

LAURA Oh, oh, yes—it stretches across the ceiling!

JIM [crossing to door] I think it's stopped raining. [Opens fire-escape door] Where does the music come from?

LAURA From the Paradise Dance Hall across the alley.

JIM How about cutting the rug a little, Miss Wingfield?

LAURA Oh, I—

JIM Or is your program filled up? Let me have a look at it. [Grasps imaginary card] Why, every dance is taken! I'll just have to scratch some out. [Waltz music: "La Golondrina"] Ahhh, a waltz! [He executes some sweeping turns by himself then holds his arms toward LAURA]

LAURA [breathlessly] I—can't dance!

JIM There you go, that inferiority stuff!

LAURA I've never danced in my life!

JIM Come on, try!

LAURA Oh, but I'd step on you!

JIM I'm not made out of glass.

LAURA How—how—how do we start?

JIM Just leave it to me. You hold your arms out a little.

LAURA Like this?

JIM A little bit higher. Right. Now don't tighten up, that's the main thing about it—relax.

LAURA [laughing breathlessly] It's hard not to.

JIM Okay.

LAURA I'm afraid you can't budge me.

JIM What do you bet I can't? [*He swings her into motion*]
LAURA Goodness, yes, you can!
JIM Let yourself go, now, Laura, just let yourself go.
LAURA I'm—
JIM Come on!
LAURA Trying!
JIM Not so stiff—Easy does it!
LAURA I know but I'm—
JIM Loosen th' backbone! There now, that's a lot better.
LAURA Am I?
JIM Lots, lots better! [*He moves her about the room in a clumsy waltz*]
LAURA Oh, my!
JIM Ha-ha!
LAURA Oh, my goodness!
JIM Ha-ha-ha! [*They suddenly bump into the table.* JIM *stops*] What did we hit on?
LAURA Table.
JIM Did something fall off it? I think—
LAURA Yes.
JIM I hope that it wasn't the little glass horse with the horn!
LAURA Yes.
JIM Aw, aw, aw. Is it broken?
LAURA Now it is just like all the other horses.
JIM It's lost its—
LAURA Horn! It doesn't matter. Maybe it's a blessing in disguise.
JIM You'll never forgive me. I bet that that was your favorite piece of glass.
LAURA I don't have favorites much. It's no tragedy, Freckles. Glass breaks so easily. No matter how careful you are. The traffic jars the shelves and things fall off them.
JIM Still I'm awfully sorry that I was the cause.
LAURA [*smiling*] I'll just imagine he had an operation. The horn was removed to make him feel less—freakish! [*They both laugh*] Now he will feel more at home with the other horses, the ones that don't have horns . . .
JIM Ha-ha, that's very funny! [*Suddenly serious*] I'm glad to see that you have a sense of humor.
    You know—you're—well—very different! Surprisingly different from anyone else I know! [*His voice becomes soft and hesitant with a genuine feeling*] Do you mind me telling you that? [LAURA *is abashed beyond speech*] I mean it in a nice way . . . [LAURA *nods shyly,*

looking away] You make me feel sort of—I don't know how to put it! I'm usually pretty good at expressing things, but—This is something that I don't know how to say! [LAURA *touches her throat and clears it—turns the broken unicorn in her hands. Even softer*] Has anyone ever told you that you were pretty? [*Pause: music.* LAURA *looks up slowly, with wonder, and shakes her head*] Well, you are! In a very different way from anyone else. And all the nicer because of the difference too. [*His voice becomes low and husky.* LAURA *turns away, nearly faint with the novelty of her emotions*] I wish that you were my sister. I'd teach you to have some confidence in yourself. The different people are not like other people, but being different is nothing to be ashamed of. Because other people are not such wonderful people. They're one hundred times one thousand. You're one times one! They walk all over the earth. You just stay here. They're common as—weeds, but—you—well, you're—*Blue Roses!*
[*Image on screen: Blue roses*]
[*Music changes*]
LAURA But blue is wrong for—roses . . .
JIM It's right for you!—You're—pretty!
LAURA In what respect am I pretty?
JIM In all respects—believe me! Your eyes—your hair—are pretty! Your hands are pretty! [*He catches hold of her hand*] You think I'm making this up because I'm invited to dinner and have to be nice. Oh, I could do that! I could put on an act for you, Laura, and say lots of things without being very sincere. But this time I am. I'm talking to you sincerely. I happened to notice you had this inferiority complex that keeps you from feeling comfortable with people. Somebody needs to build your confidence up and make you proud instead of shy and turning away and—blushing—Somebody—ought to—ought to—*kiss* you, Laura! [*His hand slips slowly up her arm to her shoulder. Music swells tumultuously. He suddenly turns her about and kisses her on the lips. When he releases her,* LAURA *sinks on the sofa with a bright, dazed look.* JIM *backs away and fishes in his pocket for a cigarette. Legend on screen: "Souvenir"*] Stumble-john! [*He lights the cigarette, avoiding her look. There is a peal of girlish laughter from* AMANDA *in the kitchen.* LAURA *slowly raises and opens her hand. It still contains the little broken glass animal. She looks at it with a tender, bewildered expression*] Stumble-john! I shouldn't have done that—That was way off the beam. You don't smoke, do you? [*She looks up, smiling, not hearing the question. He sits beside her a little gingerly. She looks at him speechlessly—waiting. He coughs decorously and moves a little farther aside as he considers the situation and senses her feelings,*

dimly, with perturbation. Gently] Would you—care for a—mint? [*She doesn't seem to hear him but her look grows brighter even*] Peppermint—Life-Saver? My pocket's a regular drug store—wherever I go . . . [*He pops a mint in his mouth. Then gulps and decides to make a clean breast of it. He speaks slowly and gingerly*] Laura, you know, if I had a sister like you, I'd do the same thing as Tom. I'd bring out fellows and—introduce her to them. The right type of boys of a type to—appreciate her. Only—well—he made a mistake about me. Maybe I've got no call to be saying this. That may not have been the idea in having me over. But what if it was? There's nothing wrong about that. The only trouble is that in my case—I'm not in a situation to—do the right thing.

I can't take down your number and say I'll phone. I can't call up next week and—ask for a date. I thought I had better explain the situation in case you—misunderstood it and—hurt your feelings. . . . [*Pause. Slowly, very slowly,* LAURA's *look changes, her eyes returning slowly from his to the ornaments in her palm.* AMANDA *utters another gay laugh in the kitchen*]

LAURA [*faintly*] You—won't—call again?

JIM No, Laura, I can't. [*He rises from the sofa*] As I was just explaining, I've—got strings on me. Laura, I've—been going steady! I go out all the time with a girl named Betty. She's a home-girl like you, and Catholic, and Irish, and in a great many ways we—get along fine. I met her last summer on a moonlight boat trip up the river to Alton, on the *Majestic*. Well—right away from the start it was—love! [*Legend: Love!* LAURA *sways slightly forward and grips the arm of the sofa. He fails to notice, now enrapt in his own comfortable being*] Being in love has made a new man of me! [*Leaning stiffly forward, clutching the arm of the sofa,* LAURA *struggles visibly with her storm. But* JIM *is oblivious, she is a long way off*] The power of love is really pretty tremendous! Love is something that—changes the whole world, Laura! [*The storm abates a little and* LAURA *leans back. He notices her again*] It happened that Betty's aunt took sick, she got a wire and had to go to Centralia. So Tom—when he asked me to dinner—I naturally just accepted the invitation, not knowing that you—that he—that I—[*He stops awkwardly*] Huh—I'm a stumble-john! [*He flops back on the sofa. The holy candles in the altar of* LAURA's *face have been snuffed out. There is a look of almost infinite desolation.* JIM *glances at her uneasily*] I wish that you would—say something. [*She bites her lip which was trembling and then bravely smiles. She opens her hand again on the broken glass ornament. Then she gently takes his hand and raises it level with her own. She care-*

fully places the unicorn in the palm of his hand, then pushes his fingers closed upon it] What are you—doing that for? You want me to have him?—Laura? [She nods] What for?

LAURA A—souvenir . . . [She rises unsteadily and crouches beside the victrola to wind it up]

[Legend on screen: "Things have a way of turning out so badly!"]
[Or image: "Gentleman caller waving good-bye!—gaily"]
[At this moment AMANDA rushes brightly back in the front room. She bears a pitcher of fruit punch in an old-fashioned cut-glass pitcher and a plate of macaroons. The plate has a gold border and poppies painted on it]

AMANDA Well, well, well! Isn't the air delightful after the shower? I've made you children a little liquid refreshment. [Turns gaily to the gentleman caller] Jim, do you know that song about lemonade?

Lemonade, lemonade
Made in the shade and stirred with a spade—
Good enough for any old maid!

JIM [uneasily] Ha-ha! No—I never heard it.
AMANDA Why, Laura! You look so serious!
JIM We were having a serious conversation.
AMANDA Good! Now you're better acquainted!
JIM [uncertainly] Ha-ha! Yes.
AMANDA You modern young people are much more serious-minded than my generation. I was so gay as a girl!
JIM You haven't changed, Mrs. Wingfield.
AMANDA Tonight I'm rejuvenated! The gaiety of the occasion, Mr. O'Connor! [She tosses her head with a peal of laughter. Spills lemonade] Oooo! I'm baptizing myself!
JIM Here—let me—
AMANDA [setting the pitcher down] There now. I discovered we had some maraschino cherries. I dumped them in, juice and all!
JIM You shouldn't have gone to that trouble, Mrs. Wingfield.
AMANDA Trouble, trouble? Why, it was loads of fun! Didn't you hear me cutting up in the kitchen? I bet your ears were burning! I told Tom how out-done with him I was for keeping you to himself so long a time! He should have brought you over much, much sooner! Well, now that you've found your way, I want you to be a very frequent caller! Not just occasional but all the time. Oh, we're going to have a lot of gay times together! I see them coming! Mmmm, just breathe that air! So fresh, and the moon's so pretty! I'll skip back out—I know where my place is when young folks are having a—serious conversation!

JIM Oh, don't go out, Mrs. Wingfield. The fact of the matter is I've got to be going.
AMANDA Going, now? You're joking! Why, it's only the shank of the evening, Mr. O'Connor!
JIM Well, you know how it is.
AMANDA You mean you're a young workingman and have to keep workingmen's hours. We'll let you off early tonight. But only on the condition that next time you stay later. What's the best night for you? Isn't Saturday night the best night for you workingmen?
JIM I have a couple of time-clocks to punch, Mrs. Wingfield. One at morning, another one at night!
AMANDA My, but you *are* ambitious! You work at night, too?
JIM No, Ma'am, not work but—Betty! [*He crosses deliberately to pick up his hat. The band at the Paradise Dance Hall goes into a tender waltz*]
AMANDA Betty? Betty? Who's—Betty! [*There is an ominous cracking sound in the sky*]
JIM Oh, just a girl. The girl I go steady with! [*He smiles charmingly. The sky falls*]
[*Legend: "The sky falls"*]
AMANDA [*a long-drawn exhalation*] Ohhhh . . . Is it a serious romance, Mr. O'Connor?
JIM We're going to be married the second Sunday in June.
AMANDA Ohhhh—how nice! Tom didn't mention that you were engaged to be married.
JIM The cat's not out of the bag at the warehouse yet. You know how they are. They call you Romeo and stuff like that. [*He stops at the oval mirror to put on his hat. He carefully shapes the brim and the crown to give a discreetly dashing effect*] It's been a wonderful evening, Mrs. Wingfield. I guess this is what they mean by Southern hospitality.
AMANDA It really wasn't anything at all.
JIM I hope it don't seem like I'm rushing off. But I promised Betty I'd pick her up at the Wabash depot, an' by the time I get my jalopy down there her train'll be in. Some women are pretty upset if you keep 'em waiting.
AMANDA Yes, I know—The tyranny of women! [*Extends her hand*] Good-bye, Mr. O'Connor. I wish you luck—and happiness—and success! All three of them, and so does Laura!—Don't you, Laura?
LAURA Yes!
JIM [*taking her hand*] Good-bye, Laura. I'm certainly going to treasure that souvenir. And don't you forget the good advice I gave you.

[*Raises his voice to a cheery shout*] So long, Shakespeare! Thanks again, ladies—Good night! [*He grins and ducks jauntily out. Still bravely grimacing,* AMANDA *closes the door on the gentleman caller. Then she turns back to the room with a puzzled expression. She and* LAURA *don't dare to face each other.* LAURA *crouches beside the victrola to wind it*]

AMANDA [*faintly*] Things have a way of turning out so badly. I don't believe that I would play the victrola. Well, well—well—Our gentleman caller was engaged to be married! Tom!

TOM [*from back*] Yes, Mother?

AMANDA Come in here a minute. I want to tell you something awfully funny.

TOM [*enters with macaroon and a glass of the lemonade*] Has the gentleman caller gotten away already?

AMANDA The gentleman caller has made an early departure. What a wonderful joke you played on us!

TOM How do you mean?

AMANDA You didn't mention that he was engaged to be married.

TOM Jim? Engaged?

AMANDA That's what he just informed us.

TOM I'll be jiggered! I didn't know about that.

AMANDA That seems very peculiar.

TOM What's peculiar about it?

AMANDA Didn't you call him your best friend down at the warehouse?

TOM He is, but how did I know?

AMANDA It seems extremely peculiar that you wouldn't know your best friend was going to be married!

TOM The warehouse is where I work, not where I know things about people!

AMANDA You don't know things anywhere! You live in a dream; you manufacture illusions! [*He crosses to door*] Where are you going?

TOM I'm going to the movies.

AMANDA That's right, now that you've had us make such fools of ourselves. The effort, the preparations, all the expense! The new floor lamp, the rug, the clothes for Laura! All for what? To entertain some other girl's fiancé! Go to the movies, go! Don't think about us, a mother deserted, an unmarried sister who's crippled and has no job! Don't let anything interfere with your selfish pleasure! Just go, go, go—to the movies!

TOM All right, I will! The more you shout about my selfishness to me the quicker I'll go, and I won't go to the movies!

AMANDA Go, then! Then go to the moon—you selfish dreamer!
[TOM smashes his glass on the floor. He plunges out on the fire-escape, slamming the door. LAURA screams—cut by door. Dance-hall music up. TOM goes to the rail and grips it desperately, lifting his face in the chill white moonlight penetrating the narrow abyss of the alley]
[Legend on screen: "And so good-bye . . ."]
[TOM's closing speech is timed with the interior-pantomime. The interior scene is played as though viewed through soundproof glass. AMANDA appears to be making a comforting speech to LAURA who is huddled upon the sofa. Now that we cannot hear the mother's speech, her silliness is gone and she has dignity and tragic beauty. LAURA's dark hair hides her face until at the end of the speech she lifts it to smile at her mother. AMANDA's gestures are slow and graceful, almost dance-like, as she comforts the daughter. At the end of her speech she glances a moment at the father's picture—then withdraws through the portieres. At close of TOM's speech, LAURA blows out the candles, ending the play]
TOM I didn't go to the moon, I went much further—for time is the longest distance between two places—Not long after that I was fired for writing a poem on the lid of a shoe-box. I left Saint Louis. I descended the steps of this fire-escape for a last time and followed, from then on, in my father's footsteps, attempting to find in motion what was lost in space—I traveled around a great deal. The cities swept about me like dead leaves, leaves that were brightly colored but torn away from the branches. I would have stopped, but I was pursued by something. It always came upon me unawares, taking me altogether by surprise. Perhaps it was a familiar bit of music. Perhaps it was only a piece of transparent glass—Perhaps I am walking along a street at night, in some strange city, before I have found companions. I pass the lighted window of a shop where perfume is sold. The window is filled with pieces of colored glass, tiny transparent bottles in delicate colors, like bits of a shattered rainbow. Then all at once my sister touches my shoulder. I turn around and look into her eyes . . . Oh, Laura, Laura, I tried to leave you behind me, but I am more faithful than I intended to be! I reach for a cigarette, I cross the street, I run into the movies or a bar, I buy a drink, I speak to the nearest stranger—anything that can blow your candles out! [LAURA bends over the candles]—for nowadays the world is lit by lightning! Blow out your candles, Laura—and so good-bye. . . . [She blows the candles out]
[The scene dissolves]

A Raisin in the Sun

To Mama: in gratitude for the dream

> *What happens to a dream deferred?*
> *Does it dry up*
> *Like a raisin in the sun?*
> *Or fester like a sore—*
> *And then run?*
> *Does it stink like rotten meat?*
> *Or crust and sugar over—*
> *Like a syrupy sweet?*
>
> *Maybe it just sags*
> *Like a heavy load.*
>
> *Or does it explode?*
>
> —Langston Hughes

Characters

RUTH YOUNGER
TRAVIS YOUNGER
WALTER LEE YOUNGER (*brother*)
BENEATHA YOUNGER
LENA YOUNGER (*mama*)
JOSEPH ASAGAI
GEORGE MURCHISON
KARL LINDNER
BOBO
MOVING MEN

The action of the play is set in Chicago's Southside, sometime between World War II and the present.

Act One
Scene 1: *Friday morning.*
Scene 2: *The following morning.*

Act Two
Scene 1: *Later, the same day.*
Scene 2: *Friday night, a few weeks later.*
Scene 3: *Moving day, one week later.*

Act Three
An hour later.

Act I
Scene One

The YOUNGER living room would be a comfortable and well-ordered room if it were not for a number of indestructible contradictions to this state of being. Its furnishings are typical and undistinguished and their primary feature now is that they have clearly had to accommodate the living of too many people for too many years—and they are tired. Still, we can see that at some time, a time probably no longer remembered by the family (except perhaps for MAMA) the furnishings of this room were actually selected with care and love and even hope—and brought to this apartment and arranged with taste and pride. That was a long time ago. Now the once loved pattern of the couch upholstery has to fight to show itself from under acres of crocheted doilies and couch covers which have themselves finally come to be more important than the upholstery. And here a table or a chair has been moved to disguise the worn places in the carpet; but the carpet has fought back by showing its weariness, with depressing uniformity, elsewhere on its surface. Weariness has, in fact, won in this room. Everything has been polished, washed, sat on, used, scrubbed too often. All pretenses but living itself have long since vanished from the very atmosphere of this room.

Moreover, a section of this room, for it is not really a room unto itself, though the landlord's lease would make it seem so, slopes backward to provide a small kitchen area, where the family prepares the meals that are eaten in the living room proper, which must also serve as dining room. The single window that has been provided for these "two" rooms is located in this kitchen area. The sole natural light the family may enjoy in the course of a day is only that which fights its way through this little window.

At left, a door leads to a bedroom which is shared by MAMA and her daughter, BENEATHA. At right, opposite, is a second room (which in the beginning of the life of this apartment was probably a breakfast room) which serves as a bedroom for WALTER and his wife, RUTH.

Time: Sometime between World War II and the present.

Place: Chicago's Southside.

At Rise: It is morning dark in the living room. TRAVIS is asleep on the make-down bed at center. An alarm clock sounds from within the bedroom *at right, and presently* RUTH *enters from that room and closes the door behind her. She crosses sleepily toward the window. As she passes her sleeping son she reaches down and shakes him a little. At the window she raises the shade and a dusky Southside morning light comes in feebly. She fills a pot with water and puts it on to boil. She calls to the boy, between yawns, in a slightly muffled voice.*

RUTH *is about thirty. We can see that she was a pretty girl, even exceptionally so, but now it is apparent that life has been little that she expected, and disappointment has already begun to hang in her face. In a few years, before thirty-five even, she will be known among her people as a "settled woman."*

She crosses to her son and gives him a good, final, rousing shake.

RUTH Come on now, boy, it's seven thirty! [*Her son sits up at last, in a stupor of sleepiness*] I say hurry up, Travis! You ain't the only person in the world got to use a bathroom! [*The child, a sturdy, handsome little boy of ten or eleven, drags himself out of the bed and almost blindly takes his towels and "today's clothes" from drawers and a closet and goes out to the bathroom, which is in an outside hall and which is shared by another family or families on the same floor.* RUTH *crosses to the bedroom door at right and opens it and calls in to her husband*] Walter Lee! . . . It's after seven thirty! Lemme see you do some waking up in there now! [*She waits*] You better get up from there, man! It's after seven thirty I tell you. [*She waits again*] All right, you just go ahead and lay there and next thing you know Travis be finished and Mr. Johnson'll be in there and you'll be fussing and cussing round here like a mad man! And be late too! [*She waits, at the end of patience*] Walter Lee—it's time for you to get up!

[*She waits another second and then starts to go into the bedroom, but is apparently satisfied that her husband has begun to get up. She stops, pulls the door to, and returns to the kitchen area. She wipes her face with a moist cloth and runs her fingers through her sleep-disheveled hair in a vain effort and ties an apron around her housecoat. The bedroom door at right opens and her husband stands in the doorway in his pajamas, which are rumpled and mismated. He is a lean, intense young man in his middle thirties, inclined to quick nervous movements and erratic speech habits—and always in his voice there is a quality of indictment*]

WALTER Is he out yet?

RUTH What you mean *out?* He ain't hardly got in there good yet.

WALTER [*Wandering in, still more oriented to sleep than to a new day*] Well, what was you doing all that yelling for if I can't even get in there yet? [*Stopping and thinking*] Check coming today?

RUTH They *said* Saturday and this is just Friday and I hopes to God you ain't going to get up here first thing this morning and start talking to me 'bout no money—'cause I 'bout don't want to hear it.

WALTER Something the matter with you this morning?

RUTH No—I'm just sleepy as the devil. What kind of eggs you want?

WALTER Not scrambled. [RUTH *starts to scramble eggs*] Paper come? [RUTH *points impatiently to the rolled up* Tribune *on the table, and he gets it and spreads it out and vaguely reads the front page*] Set off another bomb yesterday.

RUTH [*Maximum indifference*] Did they?

WALTER [*Looking up*] What's the matter with you?

RUTH Ain't nothing the matter with me. And don't keep asking me that this morning.

WALTER Ain't nobody bothering you. [*Reading the news of the day absently again*] Say Colonel McCormick is sick.

RUTH [*Affecting tea-party interest*] Is he now? Poor thing.

WALTER [*Sighing and looking at his watch*] Oh, me. [*He waits*] Now what is that boy doing in that bathroom all this time? He just going to have to start getting up earlier. I can't be going late to work on account of him fooling around in there.

RUTH [*Turning on him*] Oh, no he ain't going to be getting up no earlier no such thing! It ain't his fault that he can't get to bed no earlier nights 'cause he got a bunch of crazy good-for-nothing clowns sitting up running their mouths in what is supposed to be his bedroom after ten o'clock at night . . .

WALTER That's what you mad about, ain't it? The things I want to talk about with my friends just couldn't be important in your mind, could they?

[*He rises and finds a cigarette in her handbag on the table and crosses to the little window and looks out, smoking and deeply enjoying this first one*]

RUTH [*Almost matter of factly, a complaint too automatic to deserve emphasis*] Why you always got to smoke before you eat in the morning?

WALTER [*At the window*] Just look at 'em down there . . . Running and racing to work . . . [*He turns and faces his wife and watches her a moment at the stove, and then, suddenly*] You look young this morning, baby.

RUTH [*Indifferently*] Yeah?
WALTER Just for a second—stirring them eggs. It's gone now—just for a second it was—you looked real young again. [*Then, drily*] It's gone now—you look like yourself again.
RUTH Man, if you don't shut up and leave me alone.
WALTER [*Looking out to the street again*] First thing a man ought to learn in life is not to make love to no colored woman first thing in the morning. You all some evil people at eight o'clock in the morning.
[TRAVIS *appears in the hall doorway, almost fully dressed and quite wide awake now, his towels and pajamas across his shoulders. He opens the door and signals for his father to make the bathroom in a hurry*]
TRAVIS [*Watching the bathroom*] Daddy, come on!
[WALTER *gets his bathroom utensils and flies out to the bathroom*]
RUTH Sit down and have your breakfast, Travis.
TRAVIS Mama, this is Friday. [*Gleefully*] Check coming tomorrow, huh?
RUTH You get your mind off money and eat your breakfast.
TRAVIS [*Eating*] This is the morning we supposed to bring the fifty cents to school.
RUTH Well, I ain't got no fifty cents this morning.
TRAVIS Teacher say we have to.
RUTH I don't care what teacher say. I ain't got it. Eat your breakfast, Travis.
TRAVIS I *am* eating.
RUTH Hush up now and just eat!
[*The boy gives her an exasperated look for her lack of understanding, and eats grudgingly*]
TRAVIS You think Grandmama would have it?
RUTH No! And I want you to stop asking your grandmother for money, you hear me?
TRAVIS [*Outraged*] Gaaaleee! I don't ask her, she just gimme it sometimes!
RUTH Travis Willard Younger—I got too much on me this morning to be—
TRAVIS Maybe Daddy—
RUTH *Travis!*
[*The boy hushes abruptly. They are both quiet and tense for several seconds*]
TRAVIS [*Presently*] Could I maybe go carry some groceries in front of the supermarket for a little while after school then?
RUTH Just hush, I said. [TRAVIS *jabs his spoon into his cereal bowl viciously, and rests his head in anger upon his fists*] If you through eating, you can get over there and make up your bed.
[*The boy obeys stiffly and crosses the room, almost mechanically, to the*

bed and more or less carefully folds the covering. He carries the bedding into his mother's room and returns with his books and cap]
TRAVIS [*Sulking and standing apart from her unnaturally*] I'm gone.
RUTH [*Looking up from the stove to inspect him automatically*] Come here. [*He crosses to her and she studies his head*] If you don't take this comb and fix this here head, you better! [TRAVIS *puts down his books with a great sigh of oppression, and crosses to the mirror. His mother mutters under her breath about his "slubbornness"*] 'Bout to march out of here with that head looking like chickens slept in it! I just don't know where you get your stubborn ways . . . And get your jacket, too. Looks chilly out this morning.
TRAVIS [*With conspicuously brushed hair and jacket*] I'm gone.
RUTH Get carfare and milk money—[*Waving one finger*]—and not a single penny for no caps, you hear me?
TRAVIS [*With sullen politeness*] Yes'm.
[*He turns in outrage to leave. His mother watches after him as in his frustration he approaches the door almost comically. When she speaks to him, her voice has become a very gentle tease*]
RUTH [*Mocking; as she thinks he would say it*] Oh, Mama makes me so mad sometimes, I don't know what to do! [*She waits and continues to his back as he stands stock-still in front of the door*] I wouldn't kiss that woman good-bye for nothing in this world this morning! [*The boy finally turns around and rolls his eyes at her, knowing the mood has changed and he is vindicated; he does not, however, move toward her yet*] Not for nothing in this world! [*She finally laughs aloud at him and holds out her arms to him and we see that it is a way between them, very old and practiced. He crosses to her and allows her to embrace him warmly but keeps his face fixed with masculine rigidity. She holds him back from her presently and looks at him and runs her fingers over the features of his face. With utter gentleness—*] Now—whose little old angry man are you?
TRAVIS [*The masculinity and gruffness start to fade at last*] Aw gaalee—Mama . . .
RUTH [*Mimicking*] Aw—gaaaaalleeeee, Mama! [*She pushes him, with rough playfulness and finality, toward the door*] Get on out of here or you going to be late.
TRAVIS [*In the face of love, new aggressiveness*] Mama, could I *please* go carry groceries?
RUTH Honey, it's starting to get so cold evenings.
WALTER [*Coming in from the bathroom and drawing a make-believe gun from a make-believe holster and shooting at his son*] What is it he wants to do?

RUTH Go carry groceries after school at the supermarket.
WALTER Well, let him go . . .
TRAVIS [*Quickly, to the ally*] I *have* to—she won't gimme the fifty cents . . .
WALTER [*To his wife only*] Why not?
RUTH [*Simply, and with flavor*] 'Cause we don't have it.
WALTER [*To* RUTH *only*] What you tell the boy things like that for?
[*Reaching down into his pants with a rather important gesture*] Here, son—
[*He hands the boy the coin, but his eyes are directed to his wife's.* TRAVIS *takes the money happily*]
TRAVIS Thanks, Daddy.
[*He starts out.* RUTH *watches both of them with murder in her eyes.* WALTER *stands and stares back at her with defiance, and suddenly reaches into his pocket again on an afterthought*]
WALTER [*Without even looking at his son, still staring hard at his wife*] In fact, here's another fifty cents . . . Buy yourself some fruit today—or take a taxicab to school or something!
TRAVIS Whoopee—
[*He leaps up and clasps his father around the middle with his legs, and they face each other in mutual appreciation; slowly* WALTER LEE *peeks around the boy to catch the violent rays from his wife's eyes and draws his head back as if shot*]
WALTER You better get down now—and get to school, man.
TRAVIS [*At the door*] O.K. Good-bye.
[*He exits*]
WALTER [*After him, pointing with pride*] That's *my* boy. [*She looks at him in disgust and turns back to her work*] You know what I was thinking 'bout in the bathroom this morning?
RUTH No.
WALTER How come you always try to be so pleasant!
RUTH What is there to be pleasant 'bout!
WALTER You want to know what I was thinking 'bout in the bathroom or not!
RUTH I know what you thinking 'bout.
WALTER [*Ignoring her*] 'Bout what me and Willy Harris was talking about last night.
RUTH [*Immediately—a refrain*] Willie Harris is a good-for-nothing loud mouth.
WALTER Anybody who talks to me has got to be a good-for-nothing loud mouth, ain't he? And what you know about who is just a good-for-

nothing loud mouth? Charlie Atkins was just a "good-for-nothing loud mouth" too, wasn't he! When he wanted me to go in the dry-cleaning business with him. And now—he's grossing a hundred thousand a year. A hundred thousand dollars a year! You still call *him* a loud mouth!

RUTH [*Bitterly*] Oh, Walter Lee . . .

[*She folds her head on her arms over the table*]

WALTER [*Rising and coming to her and standing over her*] You tired, ain't you? Tired of everything. Me, the boy, the way we live—this beat-up hole—everything. Ain't you? [*She doesn't look up, doesn't answer*] So tired—moaning and groaning all the time, but you wouldn't do nothing to help, would you? You couldn't be on my side that long for nothing, could you?

RUTH Walter, please leave me alone.

WALTER A man needs for a woman to back him up . . .

RUTH Walter—

WALTER Mama would listen to you. You know she listen to you more than she do me and Bennie. She think more of you. All you have to do is just sit down with her when you drinking your coffee one morning and talking 'bout things like you do and—[*He sits down beside her and demonstrates graphically what he thinks her methods and tone should be*]—you just sip your coffee, see, and say easy like that you been thinking 'bout that deal Walter Lee is so interested in, 'bout the store and all, and sip some more coffee, like what you saying ain't really that important to you—And the next thing you know, she be listening good and asking you questions and when I come home—I can tell her the details. This ain't no fly-by-night proposition, baby. I mean we figured it out, me and Willy and Bobo.

RUTH [*With a frown*] Bobo?

WALTER Yeah. You see, this little liquor store we got in mind cost seventy-five thousand and we figured the initial investment on the place be 'bout thirty thousand, see. That be ten thousand each. Course, there's a couple of hundred you got to pay so's you don't spend your life just waiting for them clowns to let your license get approved—

RUTH You mean graft?

WALTER [*Frowning impatiently*] Don't call it that. See there, that just goes to show you what women understand about the world. Baby, don't *nothing* happen for you in this world 'less you pay *somebody* off!

RUTH Walter, leave me alone! [*She raises her head and stares at him vigorously—then says, more quietly*] Eat your eggs, they gonna be cold.

WALTER [*Straightening up from her and looking off*] That's it. There you are. Man say to his woman: I got me a dream. His woman say: Eat your eggs. [*Sadly, but gaining in power*] Man say: I got to take hold of this here world, baby! And a woman will say: Eat your eggs and go to work. [*Passionately now*] Man say: I got to change my life, I'm choking to death, baby! And his woman say—[*In utter anguish as he brings his fists down on his thighs*]—Your eggs is getting cold!

RUTH [*Softly*] Walter, that ain't none of our money.

WALTER [*Not listening at all or even looking at her*] This morning, I was lookin' in the mirror and thinking about it . . . I'm thirty-five years old; I been married eleven years and I got a boy who sleeps in the living room—[*Very, very quietly*]—and all I got to give him is stories about how rich white people live . . .

RUTH Eat your eggs, Walter.

WALTER *Damn my eggs . . . damn all the eggs that ever was!*

RUTH Then go to work.

WALTER [*Looking up at her*] See—I'm trying to talk to you 'bout myself—[*Shaking his head with the repetition*]—and all you can say is eat them eggs and go to work.

RUTH [*Wearily*] Honey, you never say nothing new. I listen to you every day, every night and every morning, and you never say nothing new. [*Shrugging*] So you would rather *be* Mr. Arnold than be his chauffeur. So—I would *rather* be living in Buckingham Palace.

WALTER That is just what is wrong with the colored woman in this world . . . Don't understand about building their men up and making 'em feel like they somebody. Like they can do something.

RUTH [*Drily, but to hurt*] There *are* colored men who do things.

WALTER No thanks to the colored woman.

RUTH Well, being a colored woman, I guess I can't help myself none. [*She rises and gets the ironing board and sets it up and attacks a huge pile of rough-dried clothes, sprinkling them in preparation for the ironing and then rolling them into tight fat balls*]

WALTER [*Mumbling*] We one group of men tied to a race of women with small minds.

[*His sister* BENEATHA *enters. She is about twenty, as slim and intense as her brother. She is not as pretty as her sister-in-law, but her lean, almost intellectual face has a handsomeness of its own. She wears a bright-red flannel nightie, and her thick hair stands wildly about her head. Her speech is a mixture of many things; it is different from the rest of the family's insofar as education has permeated her sense of English—and perhaps the Midwest rather than the South has finally—at last—won out in her inflection; but not altogether, because over all of it is a soft slurring and transformed use of vowels which is the decided in-*

fluence of the Southside. *She passes through the room without looking at either* RUTH *or* WALTER *and goes to the outside door and looks, a little blindly, out to the bathroom. She sees that it has been lost to the Johnsons. She closes the door with a sleepy vengeance and crosses to the table and sits down a little defeated*]

BENEATHA I am going to start timing those people.

WALTER You should get up earlier.

BENEATHA [*Her face in her hands. She is still fighting the urge to go back to bed*] Really—would you suggest dawn? Where's the paper?

WALTER [*Pushing the paper across the table to her as he studies her almost clinically, as though he has never seen her before*] You a horrible-looking chick at this hour.

BENEATHA [*Drily*] Good morning, everybody.

WALTER [*Senselessly*] How is school coming?

BENEATHA [*In the same spirit*] Lovely. Lovely. And you know, biology is the greatest. [*Looking up at him*] I dissected something that looked just like you yesterday.

WALTER I just wondered if you've made up your mind and everything.

BENEATHA [*Gaining in sharpness and impatience*] And what did I answer yesterday morning—and the day before that?

RUTH [*From the ironing board, like someone disinterested and old*] Don't be so nasty, Bennie.

BENEATHA [*Still to her brother*] And the day before that and the day before that!

WALTER [*Defensively*] I'm interested in you. Something wrong with that? Ain't many girls who decide—

WALTER *and* BENEATHA [*In unison*] —"to be a doctor."

[*Silence*]

WALTER Have we figured out yet just exactly how much medical school is going to cost?

RUTH Walter Lee, why don't you leave that girl alone and get out of here to work?

BENEATHA [*Exits to the bathroom and bangs on the door*] Come on out of there, please!

[*She comes back into the room*]

WALTER [*Looking at his sister intently*] You know the check is coming tomorrow.

BENEATHA [*Turning on him with a sharpness all her own*] That money belongs to Mama, Walter, and it's for her to decide how she wants to use it. I don't care if she wants to buy a house or a rocket ship or just nail it up somewhere and look at it. It's hers. Not ours—*hers*.

WALTER [*Bitterly*] Now ain't that fine! You just got your mother's interest at heart, ain't you, girl? You such a nice girl—but if Mama got that money she can always take a few thousand and help you through school too—can't she?

BENEATHA I have never asked anyone around here to do anything for me!

WALTER No! And the line between asking and just accepting when the time comes is big and wide—ain't it!

BENEATHA [*With fury*] What do you want from me, Brother—that I quit school or just drop dead, which!

WALTER I don't want nothing but for you to stop acting holy 'round here. Me and Ruth done made some sacrifices for you—why can't you do something for the family?

RUTH Walter, don't be dragging me in it.

WALTER You are in it—Don't you get up and go work in somebody's kitchen for the last three years to help put clothes on her back?

RUTH Oh, Walter—that's not fair . . .

WALTER It ain't that nobody expects you to get on your knees and say thank you, Brother; thank you, Ruth; thank you, Mama—and thank you, Travis, for wearing the same pair of shoes for two semesters—

BENEATHA [*Dropping to her knees*] Well—I *do*—all right?—thank everybody . . . and forgive me for ever wanting to be anything at all . . . forgive me, forgive me!

RUTH Please stop it! Your mama'll hear you.

WALTER Who the hell told you you had to be a doctor? If you so crazy 'bout messing 'round with sick people—then go be a nurse like other women—or just get married and be quiet . . .

BENEATHA Well—you finally got it said . . . It took you three years but you finally got it said. Walter, give up; leave me alone—it's Mama's money.

WALTER *He was my father, too!*

BENEATHA So what? He was mine, too—and Travis' grandfather—but the insurance money belongs to Mama. Picking on me is not going to make her give it to you to invest in any liquor stores—[*Underbreath, dropping into a chair*]—and I for one say, God bless Mama for that!

WALTER [*To Ruth*] See—did you hear? Did you hear!

RUTH Honey, please go to work.

WALTER Nobody in this house is ever going to understand me.

BENEATHA Because you're a nut.

WALTER Who's a nut?

BENEATHA You—you are a nut. Thee is mad, boy.

WALTER [*Looking at his wife and his sister from the door, very sadly*] The world's most backward race of people, and that's a fact.

BENEATHA [*Turning slowly in her chair*] And then there are all those prophets who would lead us out of the wilderness—[WALTER *slams out of the house*]—into the swamps!
RUTH Bennie, why you always gotta be pickin' on your brother? Can't you be a little sweeter sometimes? [*Door opens.* WALTER *walks in*]
WALTER [*To Ruth*] I need some money for carfare.
RUTH [*Looks at him, then warms; teasing, but tenderly*] Fifty cents? [*She goes to her bag and gets money*] Here, take a taxi.
[WALTER *exits.* MAMA *enters. She is a woman in her early sixties, full-bodied and strong. She is one of those women of a certain grace and beauty who wear it so unobtrusively that it takes a while to notice. Her dark-brown face is surrounded by the total whiteness of her hair, and, being a woman who has adjusted to many things in life and overcome many more, her face is full of strength. She has, we can see, wit and faith of a kind that keep her eyes lit and full of interest and expectancy. She is, in a word, a beautiful woman. Her bearing is perhaps most like the noble bearing of the women of the Hereros of Southwest Africa—rather as if she imagines that as she walks she still bears a basket or a vessel upon her head. Her speech, on the other hand, is as careless as her carriage is precise—she is inclined to slur everything—but her voice is perhaps not so much quiet as simply soft*]
MAMA Who that 'round here slamming doors at this hour?
[*She crosses through the room, goes to the window, opens it, and brings in a feeble little plant growing doggedly in a small pot on the window sill. She feels the dirt and puts it back out*]
RUTH That was Walter Lee. He and Bennie was at it again.
MAMA My children and they tempers. Lord, if this little old plant don't get more sun than it's getting it ain't going to see spring again. [*She turns from the window*] What's the matter with you this morning, Ruth? You looks right peaked. You aiming to iron all them things? Leave some for me. I'll get to 'em this afternoon. Bennie honey, it's too drafty for you to be sitting 'round half dressed. Where's your robe?
BENEATHA In the cleaners.
MAMA Well, go get mine and put it on.
BENEATHA I'm not cold, Mama, honest.
MAMA I know—but you so thin . . .
BENEATHA [*Irritably*] Mama, I'm not cold.
MAMA [*Seeing the make-down bed as* TRAVIS *has left it*] Lord have mercy, look at that poor bed. Bless his heart—he tries, don't he?
[*She moves to the bed* TRAVIS *has sloppily made up*]
RUTH No—he don't half try at all 'cause he knows you going to come along behind him and fix everything. That's just how come he don't

know how to do nothing right now—you done spoiled that boy so.
MAMA Well—he's a little boy. Ain't supposed to know 'bout housekeeping. My baby, that's what he is. What you fix for his breakfast this morning?
RUTH [Angrily] I feed my son, Lena!
MAMA I ain't meddling—[Underbreath; busy-bodyish] I just noticed all last week he had cold cereal, and when it starts getting this chilly in the fall a child ought to have some hot grits or something when he goes out in the cold—
RUTH [Furious] I gave him hot oats—is that all right!
MAMA I ain't meddling. [Pause] Put a lot of nice butter on it? [RUTH shoots her an angry look and does not reply] He likes lots of butter.
RUTH [Exasperated] Lena—
MAMA [To BENEATHA. MAMA is inclined to wander conversationally sometimes] What was you and your brother fussing 'bout this morning?
BENEATHA It's not important, Mama.
[She gets up and goes to look out at the bathroom, which is apparently free, and she picks up her towels and rushes out]
MAMA What was they fighting about?
RUTH Now you know as well as I do.
MAMA [Shaking her head] Brother still worrying hisself sick about that money?
RUTH You know he is.
MAMA You had breakfast?
RUTH Some coffee.
MAMA Girl, you better start eating and looking after yourself better. You almost thin as Travis.
RUTH Lena—
MAMA Un-hunh?
RUTH What are you going to do with it?
MAMA Now don't you start, child. It's too early in the morning to be talking about money. It ain't Christian.
RUTH It's just that he got his heart set on that store—
MAMA You mean that liquor store that Willy Harris want him to invest in?
RUTH Yes—
MAMA We ain't no business people, Ruth. We just plain working folks.
RUTH Ain't nobody business people till they go into business. Walter Lee say colored people ain't never going to start getting ahead till they start gambling on some different kinds of things in the world—investments and things.
MAMA What done got into you, girl? Walter Lee done finally sold you on investing.

RUTH No. Mama, something is happening between Walter and me. I don't know what it is—but he needs something—something I can't give him any more. He needs this chance, Lena.

MAMA [*Frowning deeply*] But liquor, honey—

RUTH Well—like Walter say—I spec people going to always be drinking themselves some liquor.

MAMA Well—whether they drinks it or not ain't none of my business. But whether I go into business selling it to 'em *is*, and I don't want that on my ledger this late in life. [*Stopping suddenly and studying her daughter-in-law*] Ruth Younger, what's the matter with you today? You look like you could fall over right there.

RUTH I'm tired.

MAMA Then you better stay home from work today.

RUTH I can't stay home. She'd be calling up the agency and screaming at them, "My girl didn't come in today—send me somebody! My girl didn't come in!" Oh, she just have a fit . . .

MAMA Well, let her have it. I'll just call her up and say you got the flu—

RUTH [*Laughing*] Why the flu?

MAMA 'Cause it sounds respectable to 'em. Something white people get, too. They know 'bout the flu. Otherwise they think you been cut up or something when you tell 'em you sick.

RUTH I got to go in. We need the money.

MAMA Somebody would of thought my children done all but starved to death the way they talk about money here late. Child, we got a great big old check coming tomorrow.

RUTH [*Sincerely, but also self-righteously*] Now that's your money. It ain't got nothing to do with me. We all feel like that—Walter and Bennie and me—even Travis.

MAMA [*Thoughtfully, and suddenly very far away*] Ten thousand dollars—

RUTH Sure is wonderful.

MAMA Ten thousand dollars.

RUTH You know what you should do, Miss Lena? You should take yourself a trip somewhere. To Europe or South America or someplace—

MAMA [*Throwing up her hands at the thought*] Oh, child!

RUTH I'm serious. Just pack up and leave! Go on away and enjoy yourself some. Forget about the family and have yourself a ball for once in your life—

MAMA [*Drily*] You sound like I'm just about ready to die. Who'd go with me? What I look like wandering 'round Europe by myself?

RUTH Shoot—these here rich white women do it all the time. They don't think nothing of packing up they suitcases and piling on one of them big steamships and—swoosh!—they gone, child.

MAMA Something always told me I wasn't no rich white woman.
RUTH Well—what are you going to do with it then?
MAMA I ain't rightly decided. [*Thinking. She speaks now with emphasis*] Some of it got to be put away for Beneatha and her schoolin'—and ain't nothing going to touch that part of it. Nothing. [*She waits several seconds, trying to make up her mind about something, and looks at* RUTH *a little tentatively before going on*] Been thinking that we maybe could meet the notes on a little old two-story somewhere, with a yard where Travis could play in the summertime, if we use part of the insurance for a down payment and everybody kind of pitch in. I could maybe take on a little day work again, few days a week—
RUTH [*Studying her mother-in-law furtively and concentrating on her ironing, anxious to encourage without seeming to*] Well, Lord knows, we've put enough rent into this here rat trap to pay for four houses by now . . .
MAMA [*Looking up at the words "rat trap" and then looking around and leaning back and sighing—in a suddenly reflective mood—*] "Rat trap" —yes, that's all it is. [*Smiling*] I remember just as well the day me and Big Walter moved in here. Hadn't been married but two weeks and wasn't planning on living here no more than a year. [*She shakes her head at the dissolved dream*] We was going to set away, little by little, don't you know, and buy a little place out in Morgan Park. We had even picked out the house. [*Chuckling a little*] Looks right dumpy today. But Lord, child, you should know all the dreams I had 'bout buying that house and fixing it up and making me a little garden in the back—[*She waits and stops smiling*] And didn't none of it happen. [*Dropping her hands in a futile gesture*]
RUTH [*Keeps her head down, ironing*] Yes, life can be a barrel of disappointments, sometimes.
MAMA Honey, Big Walter would come in here some nights back then and slump down on that couch there and just look at the rug, and look at me and look at the rug and then back at me—and I'd know he was down then . . . really down. [*After a second very long and thoughtful pause; she is seeing back to times that only she can see*] And then, Lord, when I lost that baby—little Claude—I almost thought I was going to lose Big Walter too. Oh, that man grieved hisself! He was one man to love his children.
RUTH Ain't nothin' can tear at you like losin' your baby.
MAMA I guess that's how come that man finally worked hisself to death like he done. Like he was fighting his own war with this here world that took his baby from him.

RUTH He sure was a fine man, all right. I always liked Mr. Younger.
MAMA Crazy 'bout his children! God knows there was plenty wrong with Walter Younger—hard-headed, mean, kind of wild with women—plenty wrong with him. But he sure loved his children. Always wanted them to have something—be something. That's where Brother gets all these notions, I reckon. Big Walter used to say, he'd get right wet in the eyes sometimes, lean his head back with the water standing in his eyes and say, "Seem like God didn't see fit to give the black man nothing but dreams—but He did give us children to make them dreams seem worth while." [*She smiles*] He could talk like that, don't you know.
RUTH Yes, he sure could. He was a good man, Mr. Younger.
MAMA Yes, a fine man—just couldn't never catch up with his dreams, that's all.
[BENEATHA *comes in, brushing her hair and looking up to the ceiling, where the sound of a vacuum cleaner has started up*]
BENEATHA What could be so dirty on that woman's rugs that she has to vacuum them every single day?
RUTH I wish certain young women 'round here who I could name would take inspiration about certain rugs in a certain apartment I could also mention.
BENEATHA [*Shrugging*] How much cleaning can a house need, for Christ's sakes.
MAMA [*Not liking the Lord's name used thus*] Bennie!
RUTH Just listen to her—just listen!
BENEATHA Oh, God!
MAMA If you use the Lord's name just one more time—
BENEATHA [*A bit of a whine*] Oh, Mama—
RUTH Fresh—just fresh as salt, this girl!
BENEATHA [*Drily*] Well—if the salt loses its savor—
MAMA Now that will do. I just ain't going to have you 'round here reciting the scriptures in vain—you hear me?
BENEATHA How did I manage to get on everybody's wrong side by just walking into a room?
RUTH If you weren't so fresh—
BENEATHA Ruth, I'm twenty years old.
MAMA What time you be home from school today?
BENEATHA Kind of late. [*With enthusiasm*] Madeline is going to start my guitar lessons today.
[MAMA *and* RUTH *look up with the same expression*]
MAMA Your *what* kind of lessons?

BENEATHA Guitar.
RUTH Oh, Father!
MAMA How come you done taken it in you mind to learn to play the guitar?
BENEATHA I just want to, that's all.
MAMA [*Smiling*] Lord, child, don't you know what to do with yourself? How long it going to be before you get tired of this now—like you got tired of that little play-acting group you joined last year? [*Looking at Ruth*] And what was it the year before that?
RUTH The horseback-riding club for which she bought that fifty-five-dollar riding habit that's been hanging in the closet ever since!
MAMA [*To* BENEATHA] Why you got to flit so from one thing to another, baby?
BENEATHA [*Sharply*] I just want to learn to play the guitar. Is there anything wrong with that?
MAMA Ain't nobody trying to stop you. I just wonders sometimes why you has to flit so from one thing to another all the time. You ain't never done nothing with all that camera equipment you brought home—
BENEATHA I don't flit! I—I experiment with different forms of expression—
RUTH Like riding a horse?
BENEATHA —People have to express themselves one way or another.
MAMA What is it you want to express?
BENEATHA [*Angrily*] Me! [MAMA *and* RUTH *look at each other and burst into raucous laughter*] Don't worry—I don't expect you to understand.
MAMA [*To change the subject*] Who you going out with tomorrow night?
BENEATHA [*With displeasure*] George Murchison again.
MAMA [*Pleased*] Oh—you getting a little sweet on him?
RUTH You ask me, this child ain't sweet on nobody but herself—[*Underbreath*] Express herself!
[*They laugh*]
BENEATHA Oh—I like George all right, Mama. I mean I like him enough to go out with him and stuff, but—
RUTH [*For devilment*] What does *and stuff* mean?
BENEATHA Mind your own business.
MAMA Stop picking at her now, Ruth. [*A thoughtful pause, and then a suspicious sudden look at her daughter as she turns in her chair for emphasis*] What *does* it mean?
BENEATHA [*Wearily*] Oh, I just mean I couldn't ever really be serious about George. He's—he's so shallow.
RUTH Shallow—what do you mean he's shallow? He's *Rich!*
MAMA Hush, Ruth.

BENEATHA I know he's rich. He knows he's rich, too.
RUTH Well—what other qualities a man got to have to satisfy you, little girl?
BENEATHA You wouldn't even begin to understand. Anybody who married Walter could not possibly understand.
MAMA [*Outraged*] What kind of way is that to talk about your brother?
BENEATHA Brother is a flip—let's face it.
MAMA [*To* RUTH, *helplessly*] What's a flip?
RUTH [*Glad to add kindling*] She's saying he's crazy.
BENEATHA Not crazy. Brother isn't really crazy yet—he—he's an elaborate neurotic.
MAMA Hush your mouth!
BENEATHA As for George. Well. George looks good—he's got a beautiful car and he takes me to nice places and, as my sister-in-law says, he is probably the richest boy I will ever get to know and I even like him sometimes—but if the Youngers are sitting around waiting to see if their little Bennie is going to tie up the family with the Murchisons, they are wasting their time.
RUTH You mean you wouldn't marry George Murchison if he asked you someday? That pretty, rich thing? Honey, I knew you was odd—
BENEATHA No I would not marry him if all I felt for him was what I feel now. Besides, George's family wouldn't really like it.
MAMA Why not?
BENEATHA Oh, Mama—The Murchisons are honest-to-God-real-*live*-rich colored people, and the only people in the world who are more snobbish than rich white people are rich colored people. I thought everybody knew that. I've met Mrs. Murchison. She's a scene!
MAMA You must not dislike people 'cause they well off, honey.
BENEATHA Why not? It makes just as much sense as disliking people 'cause they are poor, and lots of people do that.
RUTH [*A wisdom-of-the-ages manner. To* MAMA] Well, she'll get over some of this—
BENEATHA Get over it? What are you talking about, Ruth? Listen, I'm going to be a doctor. I'm not worried about who I'm going to marry yet—if I ever get married.
MAMA *and* RUTH *If!*
MAMA Now, Bennie—
BENEATHA Oh, I probably will . . . but first I'm going to be a doctor, and George, for one, still thinks that's pretty funny. I couldn't be bothered with that. I am going to be a doctor and everybody around here better understand that!
MAMA [*Kindly*] 'Course you going to be a doctor, honey, God willing.

BENEATHA [*Drily*] God hasn't got a thing to do with it.
MAMA Beneatha—that just wasn't necessary.
BENEATHA Well—neither is God. I get sick of hearing about God.
MAMA Beneatha!
BENEATHA I mean it! I'm just tired of hearing about God all the time. What has He got to do with anything? Does he pay tuition?
MAMA You 'bout to get you fresh little jaw slapped!
RUTH That's just what she needs, all right!
BENEATHA Why? Why can't I say what I want to around here, like everybody else?
MAMA It don't sound nice for a young girl to say things like that—you wasn't brought up that way. Me and your father went to trouble to get you and Brother to church every Sunday.
BENEATHA Mama, you don't understand. It's all a matter of ideas, and God is just one idea I don't accept. It's not important. I am not going out and be immoral or commit crimes because I don't believe in God. I don't even think about it. It's just that I get tired of Him getting credit for all the things the human race achieves through its own stubborn effort. There simply is no blasted God—there is only man and it is he who makes miracles!
[MAMA *absorbs this speech, studies her daughter and rises slowly and crosses to* BENEATHA *and slaps her powerfully across the face. After, there is only silence and the daughter drops her eyes from her mother's face, and* MAMA *is very tall before her*]
MAMA Now—you say after me, in my mother's house there is still God.
[*There is a long pause and* BENEATHA *stares at the floor wordlessly.* MAMA *repeats the phrase with precision and cool emotion*] In my mother's house there is still God.
BENEATHA In my mother's house there is still God.
[*A long pause*]
MAMA [*Walking away from* BENEATHA, *too disturbed for triumphant posture. Stopping and turning back to her daughter*] There are some ideas we ain't going to have in this house. Not long as I am at the head of this family.
BENEATHA Yes, ma'am.
[MAMA *walks out of the room*]
RUTH [*Almost gently, with profound understanding*] You think you a woman, Bennie—but you still a little girl. What you did was childish—so you got treated like a child.
BENEATHA I see. [*Quietly*] I also see that everybody thinks it's all right for Mama to be a tyrant. But all the tyranny in the world will never put a God in the heavens!

[*She picks up her books and goes out*]

RUTH [*Goes to* MAMA'*s door*] She said she was sorry.

MAMA [*Coming out, going to her plant*] They frightens me, Ruth. My children.

RUTH You got good children, Lena. They just a little off sometimes—but they're good.

MAMA No—there's something come down between me and them that don't let us understand each other and I don't know what it is. One done almost lost his mind thinking 'bout money all the time and the other done commence to talk about things I can't seem to understand in no form or fashion. What is it that's changing, Ruth?

RUTH [*Soothingly, older than her years*] Now . . . you taking it all too seriously. You just got strong-willed children and it takes a strong woman like you to keep 'em in hand.

MAMA [*Looking at her plant and sprinkling a little water on it*] They spirited all right, my children. Got to admit they got spirit—Bennie and Walter. Like this little old plant that ain't never had enough sunshine or nothing—and look at it . . .

[*She has her back to* RUTH, *who has had to stop ironing and lean against something and put the back of her hand to her forehead*]

RUTH [*Trying to keep* MAMA *from noticing*] You . . . sure . . . loves that little old thing, don't you? . . .

MAMA Well, I always wanted me a garden like I used to see sometimes at the back of the houses down home. This plant is close as I ever got to having one. [*She looks out of the window as she replaces the plant*] Lord, ain't nothing as dreary as the view from this window on a dreary day, is there? Why ain't you singing this morning, Ruth? Sing that "No Ways Tired." That song always lifts me up so—[*She turns at last to see that* RUTH *has slipped quietly into a chair, in a state of semiconsciousness*] Ruth! Ruth honey—what's the matter with you . . . Ruth!

Curtain

Scene Two

It is the following morning; a Saturday morning, and house cleaning is in progress at the YOUNGERS. *Furniture has been shoved hither and yon and* MAMA *is giving the kitchen-area walls a washing down.* BENEATHA, *in dungarees, with a handkerchief tied around her face, is spraying insecticide into the cracks in the walls. As they work, the radio is on and a Southside disk-jockey program is inappropriately filling the house with a rather exotic saxophone blues.* TRAVIS, *the sole idle one, is leaning on his arms, looking out of the window.*

TRAVIS Grandmama, that stuff Bennie is using smells awful. Can I go downstairs, please?
MAMA Did you get all them chores done already? I ain't seen you doing much.
TRAVIS Yes'm—finished early. Where did Mama go this morning?
MAMA [*Looking at* BENEATHA] She had to go on a little errand.
TRAVIS Where?
MAMA To tend to her business.
TRAVIS Can I go outside then?
MAMA Oh, I guess so. You better stay right in front of the house, though . . . and keep a good lookout for the postman.
TRAVIS Yes'm. [*He starts out and decides to give his* AUNT BENEATHA *a good swat on the legs as he passes her*] Leave them poor little old cockroaches alone, they ain't bothering you none.
[*He runs as she swings the spray gun at him both viciously and playfully.* WALTER *enters from the bedroom and goes to the phone*]
MAMA Look out there, girl, before you be spilling some of that stuff on that child!
TRAVIS [*Teasing*] That's right—look out now!
[*He exits*]
BENEATHA [*Drily*] I can't imagine that it would hurt him—it has never hurt the roaches.
MAMA Well, little boys' hides ain't as tough as Southside roaches.
WALTER [*Into phone*] Hello—Let me talk to Willy Harris.
MAMA You better get over there behind the bureau. I seen one marching out of there like Napoleon yesterday.
WALTER Hello, Willy? It ain't come yet. It'll be here in a few minutes. Did the lawyer give you the papers?
BENEATHA There's really only one way to get rid of them, Mama—
MAMA How?
BENEATHA Set fire to this building.
WALTER Good. Good. I'll be right over.
BENEATHA Where did Ruth go, Walter?
WALTER I don't know.
[*He exits abruptly*]
BENEATHA Mama, where did Ruth go?
MAMA [*Looking at her with meaning*] To the doctor, I think.
BENEATHA The doctor? What's the matter? [*They exchange glances*] You don't think—

MAMA [*With her sense of drama*] Now I ain't saying what I think. But I aint never been wrong 'bout a woman neither.
[*The phone rings*]
BENEATHA [*At the phone*] Hay-lo . . . [*Pause, and a moment of recognition*] Well—when did you get back! . . . And how was it? . . . Of course I've missed you—in my way . . . This morning? No . . . house cleaning and all that and Mama hates it if I let people come over when the house is like this . . . You *have*? Well, that's different . . . What is it—Oh, what the hell, come on over . . . Right, see you then.
[*She hangs up*]
MAMA [*Who has listened vigorously, as is her habit*] Who is that you inviting over here with this house looking like this? You ain't got the pride you was born with!
BENEATHA Asagai doesn't care how houses look, Mama—he's an intellectual.
MAMA Who?
BENEATHA Asagai—Joseph Asagai. He's an African boy I met on campus. He's been studying in Canada all summer.
MAMA What's his name?
BENEATHA Asagai, Joseph. Ah-sah-guy . . . He's from Nigeria.
MAMA Oh, that's the little country that was founded by slaves way back . . .
BENEATHA No, Mama—that's Liberia.
MAMA I don't think I never met no African before.
BENEATHA Well, do me a favor and don't ask him a whole lot of ignorant questions about Africans. I mean, do they wear clothes and all that—
MAMA Well, now, I guess if you think we so ignorant 'round here maybe you shouldn't bring your friends here—
BENEATHA It's just that people ask such crazy things. All anyone seems to know about when it comes to Africa is Tarzan—
MAMA [*Indignantly*] Why should I know anything about Africa?
BENEATHA Why do you give money at church for the missionary work?
MAMA Well, that's to help save people.
BENEATHA You mean save them from *heathenism*—
MAMA [*Innocently*] Yes.
BENEATHA I'm afraid they need more salvation from the British and the French.
[RUTH *comes in forlornly and pulls off her coat with dejection. They both turn to look at her*]
RUTH [*Dispiritedly*] Well, I guess from all the happy faces—everybody knows.
BENEATHA You pregnant?

MAMA Lord have mercy, I sure hope it's a little old girl. Travis ought to have a sister.
[BENEATHA *and* RUTH *give her a hopeless look for this grandmotherly enthusiasm*]
BENEATHA How far along are you?
RUTH Two months.
BENEATHA Did you mean to? I mean did you plan it or was it an accident?
MAMA What do you know about planning or not planning?
BENEATHA Oh, Mama.
RUTH [*Wearily*] She's twenty years old, Lena.
BENEATHA Did you plan it, Ruth?
RUTH Mind your own business.
BENEATHA It is my business—where is he going to live, on the roof? [*There is silence following the remark as the three women react to the sense of it*] Gee—I didn't mean that, Ruth, honest. Gee, I don't feel like that at all. I—I think it is wonderful.
RUTH [*Dully*] Wonderful.
BENEATHA Yes—really.
MAMA [*Looking at* RUTH, *worried*] Doctor say everything to be all right?
RUTH [*Far away*] Yes—she says everything is going to be fine . . .
MAMA [*Immediately suspicious*] "She"—What doctor you went to?
[RUTH *folds over, near hysteria*]
MAMA [*Worriedly hovering over* RUTH] Ruth honey—what's the matter with you—you sick?
[RUTH *has her fists clenched on her thighs and is fighting hard to suppress a scream that seems to be rising in her*]
BENEATHA What's the matter with her, Mama?
MAMA [*Working her fingers in* RUTH'S *shoulders to relax her*] She be all right. Woman gets right depressed sometimes when they get her way. [*Speaking softly, expertly, rapidly*] Now you just relax. That's right . . . just lean back, don't think 'bout nothing at all . . . nothing at all—
RUTH I'm all right . . .
[*The glassy-eyed look melts and then she collapses into a fit of heavy sobbing. The bell rings*]
BENEATHA Oh, my God—that must be Asagai.
MAMA [*To* RUTH] Come on now, honey. You need to lie down and rest awhile . . . then have some nice hot food.
[*They exit,* RUTH'S *weight on her mother-in-law.* BENEATHA, *herself profoundly disturbed, opens the door to admit a rather dramatic-looking young man with a large package*]
ASAGAI Hello, Alaiyo—

BENEATHA [*Holding the door open and regarding him with pleasure*] Hello . . . [*Long pause*] Well—come in. And please excuse everything. My mother was very upset about my letting anyone come here with the place like this.
ASAGAI [*Coming into the room*] You look disturbed too . . . Is something wrong?
BENEATHA [*Still at the door, absently*] Yes . . . we've all got acute ghetto-itus. [*She smiles and comes toward him, finding a cigarette and sitting*] So—sit down! How was Canada?
ASAGAI [*A sophisticate*] Canadian.
BENEATHA [*Looking at him*] I'm very glad you are back.
ASAGAI [*Looking back at her in turn*] Are you really?
BENEATHA Yes—very.
ASAGAI Why—you were quite glad when I went away. What happened?
BENEATHA You went away.
ASAGAI Ahhhhhhhh.
BENEATHA Before—you wanted to be so serious before there was time.
ASAGAI How much time must there be before one knows what one feels?
BENEATHA [*Stalling this particular conversation. Her hands pressed together, in a deliberately childish gesture*] What did you bring me?
ASAGAI [*Handing her the package*] Open it and see.
BENEATHA [*Eagerly opening the package and drawing out some records and the colorful robes of a Nigerian woman*] Oh, Asagai! . . . You got them for me! . . . How beautiful . . . and the records too! [*She lifts out the robes and runs to the mirror with them and holds the drapery up in front of herself*]
ASAGAI [*Coming to her at the mirror*] I shall have to teach you how to drape it properly. [*He flings the material about her for the moment and stands back to look at her*] Ah—Oh-pay-gay-day, oh-gbah-mu-shay. [*A Yoruba exclamation for admiration*] You wear it well . . . very well . . . mutilated hair and all.
BENEATHA [*Turning suddenly*] My hair—what's wrong with my hair?
ASAGAI [*Shrugging*] Were you born with it like that?
BENEATHA [*Reaching up to touch it*] No . . . of course not.
[*She looks back to the mirror, disturbed*]
ASAGAI [*Smiling*] How then?
BENEATHA You know perfectly well how . . . as crinkly as yours . . . thats how.
ASAGAI And it is ugly to you that way?
BENEATHA [*Quickly*] Oh, no—not ugly . . . [*More slowly, apologetically*] But it's so hard to manage when it's, well—raw.

ASAGAI And so to accommodate that—you mutilate it every week?
BENEATHA It's not mutilation!
ASAGAI [*Laughing aloud at her seriousness*] Oh . . . please! I am only teasing you because you are so very serious about these things. [*He stands back from her and folds his arms across his chest as he watches her pulling at her hair and frowning in the mirror*] Do you remember the first time you met me at school? . . . [*He laughs*] You came up to me and you said—and I thought you were the most serious little thing I had ever seen—you said: [*He imitates her*] "Mr. Asagai—I want very much to talk with you. About Africa. You see, Mr. Asagai, I am looking for my *identity!*"
[*He laughs*]
BENEATHA [*Turning to him, not laughing*] Yes—
[*Her face is quizzical, profoundly disturbed*]
ASAGAI [*Still teasing and reaching out and taking her face in his hands and turning her profile to him*] Well . . . it is true that this is not so much a profile of a Hollywood queen as perhaps a queen of the Nile—[*A mock dismissal of the importance of the question*] But what does it matter? Assimilationism is so popular in your country.
BENEATHA [*Wheeling, passionately, sharply*] I am not an assimilationist!
ASAGAI [*The protest hangs in the room for a moment and* ASAGAI *studies her, his laughter fading*] Such a serious one. [*There is a pause*] So—you like the robes? You must take excellent care of them—they are from my sister's personal wardrobe.
BENEATHA [*With incredulity*] You—you sent all the way home—for me?
ASAGAI [*With charm*] For you—I would do much more . . . Well, that is what I came for. I must go.
BENEATHA Will you call me Monday?
ASAGAI Yes . . . We have a great deal to talk about. I mean about identity and time and all that.
BENEATHA Time?
ASAGAI Yes. About how much time one needs to know what one feels.
BENEATHA You never understood that there is more than one kind of feeling which can exist between a man and a woman—or, at least, there should be.
ASAGAI [*Shaking his head negatively but gently*] No. Between a man and a woman there need be only one kind of feeling. I have that for you . . . Now even . . . right this moment . . .
BENEATHA I know—and by itself—it won't do. I can find that anywhere.
ASAGAI For a woman it should be enough.
BENEATHA I know—because that's what it says in all the novels that men write. But it isn't. Go ahead and laugh—but I'm not interested in being

someone's little episode in America or—[*With feminine vengeance*]—one of them! [ASAGAI *has burst into laughter again*] That's funny as hell, huh!

ASAGAI It's just that every American girl I have known has said that to me. White—black—in this you are all the same. And the same speech, too!

BENEATHA [*Angrily*] Yuk, yuk, yuk!

ASAGAI It's how you can be sure that the world's most liberated women are not liberated at all. You all talk about it too much!

[MAMA *enters and is immediately all social charm because of the presence of a guest*]

BENEATHA Oh—Mama—this is Mr. Asagai.

MAMA How do you do?

ASAGAI [*Total politeness to an elder*] How do you do, Mrs. Younger. Please forgive me for coming at such an outrageous hour on a Saturday.

MAMA Well, you are quite welcome. I just hope you understand that our house don't always look like this. [*Chatterish*] You must come again. I would love to hear about—[*Not sure of the name*]—your country. I think it's so sad the way our American Negroes don't know nothing about Africa 'cept Tarzan and all that. And all that money they pour into these churches when they ought to be helping you people over there drive out them French and Englishmen done taken away your land.

[*The mother flashes a slightly superior look at her daughter upon completion of the recitation*]

ASAGAI [*Taken aback by this sudden and acutely unrelated expression of sympathy*] Yes . . . yes . . .

MAMA [*Smiling at him suddenly and relaxing and looking him over*] How many miles is it from here to where you come from?

ASAGAI Many thousands.

MAMA [*Looking at him as she would* WALTER] I bet you don't half look after yourself, being away from your mama either. I spec you better come 'round here from time to time and get yourself some decent home-cooked meals . . .

ASAGAI [*Moved*] Thank you. Thank you very much. [*They are all quiet, then—*] Well . . . I must go. I will call you Monday, Alaiyo.

MAMA What's that he call you?

ASAGAI Oh—"Alaiyo." I hope you don't mind. It is what you would call a nickname, I think. It is a Yoruba word. I am a Yoruba.

MAMA [*Looking at* BENEATHA] I—I thought he was from—

ASAGAI [*Understanding*] Nigeria is my country. Yoruba is my tribal origin—

BENEATHA You didn't tell us what Alaiyo means . . . for all I know, you might be calling me Little Idiot or something . . .

ASAGAI Well . . . let me see . . . I do not know how just to explain it . . . The sense of a thing can be so different when it changes languages.
BENEATHA You're evading.
ASAGAI No—really it is difficult . . . [*Thinking*] It means . . . it means One for Whom Bread—Food—Is Not Enough. [*He looks at her*] Is that all right?
BENEATHA [*Understanding, softly*] Thank you.
MAMA [*Looking from one to the other and not understanding any of it*] Well . . . that's nice . . . You must come see us again—Mr.—
ASAGAI Ah-sah-guy . . .
MAMA Yes . . . Do come again.
ASAGAI Good-bye.

[*He exits*]

MAMA [*After him*] Lord, that's a pretty thing just went out here! [*Insinuatingly, to her daughter*] Yes, I guess I see why we done commence to get so interested in Africa 'round here. Missionaries my aunt Jenny! [*She exits*]
BENEATHA Oh, Mama! . . .

[*She picks up the Nigerian dress and holds it up to her in front of the mirror again. She sets the headdress on haphazardly and then notices her hair again and clutches at it and then replaces the headdress and frowns at herself. Then she starts to wriggle in front of the mirror as she thinks a Nigerian woman might.* TRAVIS *enters and regards her*]

TRAVIS You cracking up?
BENEATHA Shut up.

[*She pulls the headdress off and looks at herself in the mirror and clutches at her hair again and squinches her eyes as if trying to imagine something. Then suddenly, she gets her raincoat and kerchief and hurriedly prepares for going out*]

MAMA [*Coming back into the room*] She's resting now. Travis, baby, run next door and ask Miss Johnson to please let me have a little kitchen cleanser. This here can is empty as Jacob's kettle.
TRAVIS I just came in.
MAMA Do as you told. [*He exits and she looks at her daughter*] Where you going?
BENEATHA [*Halting at the door*] To become a queen of the Nile!

[*She exits in a breathless blaze of glory.* RUTH *appears in the bedroom doorway*]

MAMA Who told you to get up?
RUTH Ain't nothing wrong with me to be lying in no bed for. Where did Bennie go?

MAMA [*Drumming her fingers*] Far as I could make out—to Egypt. [RUTH *just looks at her*] What time is it getting to?
RUTH Ten twenty. And the mailman going to ring that bell this morning just like he done every morning for the last umpteen years.
[TRAVIS *comes in with the cleanser can*]
TRAVIS She say to tell you that she don't have much.
MAMA [*Angrily*] Lord, some people I could name sure is tight-fisted! [*Directing her grandson*] Mark two cans of cleanser down on the list there. If she that hard up for kitchen cleanser, I sure don't want to forget to get her none!
RUTH Lena—maybe the woman is just short on cleanser—
MAMA [*Not listening*]—Much baking powder as she done borrowed from me all these years, she could of done gone into the baking business!
[*The bell sounds suddenly and sharply and all three are stunned— serious and silent—mid-speech. In spite of all the other conversations and distractions of the morning, this is what they have been waiting for, even* TRAVIS, *who looks helplessly from his mother to his grandmother.* RUTH *is the first to come to life again*]
RUTH [*To* TRAVIS] Get down them steps, boy!
[TRAVIS *snaps to life and flies out to get the mail*]
MAMA [*Her eyes wide, her hand to her breast*] You mean it done really come?
RUTH [*Excited*] Oh, Miss Lena!
MAMA [*Collecting herself*] Well . . . I don't know what we all so excited about 'round here for. We knowed it was coming for months.
RUTH That's a whole lot different from having it come and being able to hold it in your hands . . . a piece of paper worth ten thousand dollars . . .
[TRAVIS *bursts back into the room. He holds the envelope high above his head, like a little dancer, his face is radiant and he is breathless. He moves to his grandmother with sudden slow ceremony and puts the envelope into her hands. She accepts it, and then merely holds it and looks at it*] Come on! Open it . . . Lord have mercy, I wish Walter Lee was here!
TRAVIS Open it, Grandmama!
MAMA [*Staring at it*] Now you all be quiet. It's just a check.
RUTH Open it . . .
MAMA [*Still staring at it*] Now don't act silly . . . We ain't never been no people to act silly 'bout no money—
RUTH [*Swiftly*] We ain't never had none before—open it!
[MAMA *finally makes a good strong tear and pulls out the thin blue slice*

of paper and inspects it closely. The boy and his mother study it raptly over MAMA's *shoulders*]

MAMA Travis! [*She is counting off with doubt*] Is that the right number of zeros.

TRAVIS Yes'm . . . ten thousand dollars. Gaalee, Grandmama, you rich.

MAMA [*She holds the check away from her, still looking at it. Slowly her face sobers into a mask of unhappiness*] Ten thousand dollars. [*She hands it to* RUTH] Put it away somewhere, Ruth. [*She does not look at* RUTH; *her eyes seem to be seeing something somewhere very far off*] Ten thousand dollars they give you. Ten thousand dollars.

TRAVIS [*To his mother, sincerely*] What's the matter with Grandmama—don't she want to be rich?

RUTH [*Distractedly*] You go on out and play now, baby. [TRAVIS *exits.* MAMA *starts wiping dishes absently, humming intently to herself.* RUTH *turns to her, with kind exasperation*] You've gone and got yourself upset.

MAMA [*Not looking at her*] I spec if it wasn't for you all . . . I would just put that money away or give it to the church or something.

RUTH Now what kind of talk is that. Mr. Younger would just be plain mad if he could hear you talking foolish like that.

MAMA [*Stopping and staring off*] Yes . . . he sure would. [*Sighing*] We got enough to do with that money, all right. [*She halts then, and turns and looks at her daughter-in-law;* RUTH *avoids her eyes and* MAMA *wipes her hands with finality and starts to speak firmly to* RUTH] Where did you go today, girl?

RUTH To the doctor.

MAMA [*Impatiently*] Now, Ruth . . . you know better than that. Old Doctor Jones is strange enough in his way but there ain't nothing 'bout him make somebody slip and call him "she"—like you done this morning.

RUTH Well, that's what happened—my tongue slipped.

MAMA You went to see that woman, didn't you?

RUTH [*Defensively, giving herself away*] What woman you talking about?

MAMA [*Angrily*] That woman who—
[WALTER *enters in great excitement*]

WALTER Did it come?

MAMA [*Quietly*] Can't you give people a Christian greeting before you start asking about money?

WALTER [*To Ruth*] Did it come? [RUTH *unfolds the check and lays it quietly before him, watching him intently with thoughts of her own.* WALTER *sits down and grasps it close and counts off the zeros*] Ten thousand dollars—[*He turns suddenly, frantically to his mother and*

draws some papers out of his breast pocket] Mama—look. Old Willy Harris put everything on paper—
MAMA Son—I think you ought to talk to your wife . . . I'll go on out and leave you alone if you want—
WALTER I can talk to her later—Mama, look—
MAMA Son—
WALTER WILL SOMEBODY PLEASE LISTEN TO ME TODAY!
MAMA [*Quietly*] I don't 'low no yellin' in this house, Walter Lee, and you know it—[WALTER *stares at them in frustration and starts to speak several times*] And there ain't going to be no investing in no liquor stores. I don't aim to have to speak on that again.
[*A long pause*]
WALTER Oh—so you don't aim to have to speak on that again? So *you* have decided . . . [*Crumpling his papers*] Well, *you* tell that to my boy tonight when you put him to sleep on the living-room couch . . . [*Turning to* MAMA *and speaking directly to her*] Yeah—and tell it to my wife, Mama, tomorrow when she has to go out of here to look after somebody else's kids. And tell it to *me*, Mama, every time we need a new pair of curtains and I have to watch *you* go out and work in somebody's kitchen. Yeah, you tell me then!
[WALTER *starts out*]
RUTH Where you going?
WALTER I'm going out!
RUTH Where?
WALTER Just out of this house somewhere—
RUTH [*Getting her coat*] I'll come too.
WALTER I don't want you to come!
RUTH I got something to talk to you about, Walter.
WALTER That's too bad.
MAMA [*Still quietly*] Walter Lee—[*She waits and he finally turns and looks at her*] Sit down.
WALTER I'm a grown man, Mama.
MAMA Ain't nobody said you wasn't grown. But you still in my house and my presence. And as long as you are—you'll talk to your wife civil. Now sit down.
RUTH [*Suddenly*] Oh, let him go out and drink himself to death! He makes me sick to my stomach! [*She flings her coat against him*]
WALTER [*Violently*] And you turn mine too, baby! [RUTH *goes into their bedroom and slams the door behind her*] That was my greatest mistake—
MAMA [*Still quietly*] Walter, what is the matter with you?
WALTER Matter with me? Ain't nothing the matter with *me!*

MAMA Yes there is. Something eating you up like a crazy man. Something more than me not giving you this money. The past few years I been watching it happen to you. You get all nervous acting and kind of wild in the eyes—[WALTER *jumps up impatiently at her words*] I said sit there now, I'm talking to you!

WALTER Mama—I don't need no nagging at me today.

MAMA Seem like you getting to a place where you always tied up in some kind of knot about something. But if anybody ask you 'bout it you just yell at 'em and bust out the house and go out and drink somewheres. Walter Lee, people can't live with that. Ruth's a good, patient girl in her way—but you getting to be too much. Boy, don't make the mistake of driving that girl away from you.

WALTER Why—what she do for me?

MAMA She loves you.

WALTER Mama—I'm going out. I want to go off somewhere and be by myself for a while.

MAMA I'm sorry 'bout your liquor store, son. It just wasn't the thing for us to do. That's what I want to tell you about—

WALTER I got to go out, Mama—

[*He rises*]

MAMA It's dangerous, son.

WALTER What's dangerous?

MAMA When a man goes outside his home to look for peace.

WALTER [*Beseechingly*] Then why can't there never be no peace in this house then?

MAMA You done found it in some other house?

WALTER No—there ain't no woman! Why do women always think there's a woman somewhere when a man gets restless. [*Coming to her*] Mama—Mama—I want so many things . . .

MAMA Yes, son—

WALTER I want so many things that they are driving me kind of crazy . . . Mama—look at me.

MAMA I'm looking at you. You a good-looking boy. You got a job, a nice wife, a fine boy and—

WALTER A job. [*Looks at her*] Mama, a job? I open and close car doors all day long. I drive a man around in his limousine and I say, "Yes, sir; no, sir; very good, sir; shall I take the Drive, sir?" Mama, that ain't no kind of job . . . that ain't nothing at all. [*Very quietly*] Mama, I don't know if I can make you understand.

MAMA Understand what, baby?

WALTER [*Quietly*] Sometimes it's like I can see the future stretched out in front of me—just plain as day. The future, Mama. Hanging over there at the edge of my days. Just waiting for me—a big, looming blank space —full of *nothing*. Just waiting for *me*. [*Pause*] Mama—sometimes when I'm downtown and I pass them cool, quiet-looking restaurants where them white boys are sitting back and talking 'bout things . . . sitting there turning deals worth millions of dollars . . . sometimes I see guys don't look much older than me—

MAMA Son—how come you talk so much 'bout money?

WALTER [*With immense passion*] Because it is life, Mama!

MAMA [*Quietly*] Oh—[*Very quietly*] So now it's life. Money is life. Once upon a time freedom used to be life—now it's money. I guess the world really do change . . .

WALTER No—it was always money, Mama. We just didn't know about it.

MAMA No . . . something has changed. [*She looks at him*] You something new, boy. In my time we was worried about not being lynched and getting to the North if we could and how to stay alive and still have a pinch of dignity too . . . Now here come you and Beneatha—talking 'bout things we ain't never even thought about hardly, me and your daddy. You ain't satisfied or proud of nothing we done. I mean that you had a home; that we kept you out of trouble till you was grown; that you don't have to ride to work on the back of nobody's streetcar—You my children—but how different we done become.

WALTER You just don't understand, Mama, you just don't understand.

MAMA Son—you know your wife is expecting another baby? [WALTER *stands, stunned, and absorbs what his mother has said*] That's what she wanted to talk to you about. [WALTER *sinks down into a chair*] This ain't for me to be telling—but you ought to know. [*She waits*] I think Ruth is thinking 'bout getting rid of that child.

WALTER [*Slowly understanding*] No—no—Ruth wouldn't do that.

MAMA When the world gets ugly enough—a woman will do anything for her family. *The part that's already living.*

WALTER You don't know Ruth, Mama, if you think she would do that.

[RUTH *opens the bedroom door and stands there a little limp*]

RUTH [*Beaten*] Yes I would too, Walter [*Pause*] I gave her a five-dollar down payment.

[*There is total silence as the man stares at his wife and the mother stares at her son*]

MAMA [*Presently*] Well—[*Tightly*] Well—son, I'm waiting to hear you say something . . . I'm waiting to hear how you be your father's son. Be the man he was . . . [*Pause*] Your wife say she going to destroy your child. And I'm waiting to hear you talk like him and say we a people who give children life, not who destroys them—[*She rises*] I'm waiting to see you stand up and look like your daddy and say we done give up one baby to poverty and that we ain't going to give up nary another one . . . I'm waiting.

WALTER Ruth—

MAMA If you a son of mine, tell her! (WALTER *turns, looks at her and can say nothing. She continues, bitterly*) You . . . you are a disgrace to your father's memory. Somebody get me my hat.

Curtain

Act II
Scene One

Time: *Later the same day*.

At rise: RUTH *is ironing again. She has the radio going. Presently* BENEATHA's *bedroom door opens and* RUTH's *mouth falls and she puts down the iron in fascination.*

RUTH What have we got on tonight!

BENEATHA [*Emerging grandly from the doorway so that we can see her thoroughly robed in the costume Asagai brought*] You are looking at what a well-dressed Nigerian woman wears—[*She parades for* RUTH, *her hair completely hidden by the headdress; she is coquettishly fanning herself with an ornate oriental fan, mistakenly more like Butterfly than any Nigerian that ever was*] Isn't it beautiful? [*She promenades to the radio and, with an arrogant flourish, turns off the good loud blues that is playing*] Enough of this assimilationist junk! [RUTH *follows her with her eyes as she goes to the phonograph and puts on a record and turns and waits ceremoniously for the music to come up. Then, with a shout—*] OCOMOGOSIAY!

[RUTH *jumps. The music comes up, a lovely Nigerian melody.* BENEATHA *listens, enraptured, her eyes far away—"back to the past." She begins to dance.* RUTH *is dumfounded*]

RUTH What kind of dance is that?

BENEATHA A folk dance.

RUTH [*Pearl Bailey*] What kind of folks do that, honey?

BENEATHA It's from Nigeria. It's a dance of welcome.

RUTH Who you welcoming?

BENEATHA The men back to the village.

RUTH Where they been?

BENEATHA How should I know—out hunting or something. Anyway, they are coming back now . . .

RUTH Well, that's good.

BENEATHA [*With the record*]

*Alundi, alundi
Alundi alunya
Jop pu a jeepua
Ang gu sooooooooooo*

*Ai yai yae . . .
Ayehaye—alundi . . .*

[WALTER *comes in during this performance; he has obviously been drinking. He leans against the door heavily and watches his sister, at first with distaste. Then his eyes look off—"back to the past"—as he lifts both his fists to the roof, screaming*]

WALTER YEAH . . . AND ETHIOPIA STRETCH FORTH HER HANDS AGAIN! . . .

RUTH [*Drily, looking at him*] Yes—and Africa sure is claiming her own tonight. [*She gives them both up and starts ironing again*]

WALTER [*All in a drunken, dramatic shout*] Shut up! . . . I'm digging them drums . . . them drums move me! . . . [*He makes his weaving way to his wife's face and leans in close to her*] In my heart of hearts— [*He thumps his chest*]—I am much warrior!

RUTH [*Without even looking up*] In your heart of hearts you are much drunkard.

WALTER [*coming away from her and starting to wander around the room, shouting*] Me and Jomo . . . [*Intently, in his sister's face. She has stopped dancing to watch him in this unknown mood*] That's my man, Kenyatta. [*Shouting and thumping his chest*] FLAMING SPEAR! HOT DAMN! [*He is suddenly in possession of an imaginary spear and actively spearing enemies all over the room*] OCOMOGOSIAY . . . THE LION IS WAKING . . . OWIMOWEH! [*He pulls his shirt open and leaps up on a table and gestures with his spear. The bell rings.* RUTH *goes to answer*]

BENEATHA [*To encourage* WALTER, *thoroughly caught up with this side of him*] OCOMOGOSIAY, FLAMING SPEAR!

WALTER [*On the table, very far gone, his eyes pure glass sheets. He sees what we cannot, that he is a leader of his people, a great chief, a descendant of Chaka, and that the hour to march has come*] Listen, my black brothers—

BENEATHA OCOMOGOSIAY!

WALTER —Do you hear the waters rushing against the shores of the coastlands—

BENEATHA OCOMOGOSIAY!

WALTER —Do you hear the screeching of the cocks in yonder hills beyond where the chiefs meet in council for the coming of the mighty war—
BENEATHA OCOMOGOSIAY!
WALTER —Do you hear the beating of the wings of the birds flying low over the mountains and the low places of our land—
[RUTH *opens the door.* GEORGE MURCHISON *enters*]
BENEATHA OCOMOGOSIAY!
WALTER —Do you hear the singing of the women, singing the war songs of our fathers to the babies in the great houses . . . singing the sweet war songs? OH, DO YOU HEAR, MY BLACK BROTHERS!
BENEATHA [*Completely gone*] We hear you, Flaming Spear—
WALTER Telling us to prepare for the greatness of the time—[*To* GEORGE] Black Brother!
[*He extends his hand for the fraternal clasp*]
GEORGE Black Brother, hell!
RUTH [*Having had enough, and embarrassed for the family*] Beneatha, you got company—what's the matter with you? Walter Lee Younger, get down off that table and stop acting like a fool . . .
[WALTER *comes down off the table suddenly and makes a quick exit to the bathroom*]
RUTH He's had a little to drink . . . I don't know what her excuse is.
GEORGE [*To* BENEATHA] Look honey, we're going *to* the theatre—we're not going to be *in* it . . . so go change, huh?
RUTH You expect this boy to go out with you looking like that?
BENEATHA [*Looking at* GEORGE] That's up to George. If he's ashamed of his heritage—
GEORGE Oh, don't be so proud of yourself, Bennie—just because you look eccentric.
BENEATHA How can something that's natural be eccentric?
GEORGE That's what being eccentric means—being natural. Get dressed.
BENEATHA I don't like that, George.
RUTH Why must you and your brother make an argument out of everything people say?
BENEATHA Because I hate assimilationist Negroes!
RUTH Will somebody please tell me what assimila-who-ever means!
GEORGE Oh, it's just a college girl's way of calling people Uncle Toms—but that isn't what it means at all.
RUTH Well, what does it mean?
BENEATHA [*Cutting* GEORGE *off and staring at him as she replies to* RUTH] It means someone who is willing to give up his own culture and sub-

merge himself completely in the dominant, and in this case, *oppressive* culture!

GEORGE Oh, dear, dear, dear! Here we go! A lecture on the African past! On our Great West African Heritage! In one second we will hear all about the great Ashanti empires; the great Songhay civilizations; and the great sculpture of Bénin—and then some poetry in the Bantu—and the whole monologue will end with the word *heritage!* [*Nastily*] Let's face it, baby, your heritage is nothing but a bunch of raggedy-assed spirituals and some grass huts!

BENEATHA *Grass huts!* [RUTH *crosses to her and forcibly pushes her toward the bedroom*] See there . . . you are standing there in your splendid ignorance talking about people who were the first to smelt iron on the face of the earth! [RUTH *is pushing her through the door*] The Ashanti were performing surgical operations when the English—[RUTH *pulls the door to, with* BENEATHA *on the other side, and smiles graciously at* GEORGE. BENEATHA *opens the door and shouts the end of the sentence defiantly at* GEORGE]—were still tattooing themselves with blue dragons . . . [*She goes back inside*]

RUTH Have a seat, George. [*They both sit.* RUTH *folds her hands rather primly on her lap, determined to demonstrate the civilization of the family*] Warm, ain't it? I mean for September. [*Pause*] Just like they always say about Chicago weather: If it's too hot or cold for you, just wait a minute and it'll change. [*She smiles happily at this cliché of clichés*] Everybody say it's got to do with them bombs and things they keep setting off. [*Pause*] Would you like a nice cold beer?

GEORGE No, thank you. I don't care for beer. [*He looks at his watch*] I hope she hurries up.

RUTH What time is the show?

GEORGE It's an eight-thirty curtain. That's just Chicago, though. In New York standard curtain time is eight forty.

[*He is rather proud of this knowledge*]

RUTH [*Properly appreciating it*] You get to New York a lot?

GEORGE [*Offhand*] Few times a year.

RUTH Oh—that's nice. I've never been to New York.

[WALTER *enters. We feel he has relieved himself, but the edge of unreality is still with him*]

WALTER New York ain't got nothing Chicago ain't. Just a bunch of hustling people all squeezed up together—being "Eastern."

[*He turns his face into a screw of displeasure*]

GEORGE Oh—you've been?

WALTER Plenty of times.

RUTH [*Shocked at the lie*] Walter Lee Younger!
WALTER [*Staring her down*] Plenty! [*Pause*] What we got to drink in this house? Why don't you offer this man some refreshment. [*To* GEORGE] They don't know how to entertain people in this house, man.
GEORGE Thank you—I don't really care for anything.
WALTER [*Feeling his head; soberly coming*] Where's Mama?
RUTH She ain't come back yet.
WALTER [*Looking* MURCHISON *over from head to toe, scrutinizing his carefully casual tweed sports jacket over cashmere V-neck sweater over soft eyelet shirt and tie, and soft slacks, finished off with white buckskin shoes*] Why all you college boys wear them fairyish-looking white shoes?
RUTH Walter Lee!

[GEORGE MURCHISON *ignores the remark*]

WALTER [*To* RUTH] Well, they look crazy as hell—white shoes, cold as it is.
RUTH [*Crushed*] You have to excuse him—
WALTER No he don't! Excuse me for what? What you always excusing me for! I'll excuse myself when I needs to be excused! [*A pause*] They look as funny as them black knee socks Beneatha wears out of here all the time.
RUTH It's the college *style*, Walter.
WALTER Style, hell. She looks like she got burnt legs or something!
RUTH Oh, Walter—
WALTER [*An irritable mimic*] Oh, Walter! Oh, Walter! [*To* MURCHISON] How's your old man making out? I understand you all going to buy that big hotel on the Drive? [*He finds a beer in the refrigerator, wanders over to* MURCHISON, *sipping and wiping his lips with the back of his hand, and straddling a chair backwards to talk to the other man*] Shrewd move. Your old man is all right, man. [*Tapping his head and half winking for emphasis*] I mean he knows how to operate. I mean he thinks *big*, you know what I mean, I mean for a *home*, you know? But I think he's kind of running out of ideas now. I'd like to talk to him. Listen, man, I got some plans that could turn this city upside down. I mean I think like he does. *Big*. Invest big, gamble big, hell, lose *big* if you have to, you know what I mean. It's hard to find a man on this whole Southside who understands my kind of thinking—you dig? [*He scrutinizes* MURCHISON *again, drinks his beer, squints his eyes and leans in close, confidential, man to man*] Me and you ought to sit down and talk sometimes, man. Man, I got me some ideas . . .
MURCHISON [*With boredom*] Yeah—sometimes we'll have to do that, Walter.
WALTER [*Understanding the indifference, and offended*] Yeah—well, when you get the time, man. I know you a busy little boy.

RUTH Walter, please—
WALTER [*Bitterly, hurt*] I know ain't nothing in this world as busy as you colored college boys with your fraternity pins and white shoes . . .
RUTH [*Covering her face with humiliation*] Oh, Walter Lee—
WALTER I see you all the time—with the books tucked under your arms—going to your [*British A—a mimic*] "clahsses." And for what! What the hell you learning over there? Filling up your heads—[*Counting off on his fingers*]—with the sociology and the psychology—but they teaching you how to be a man? How to take over and run the world? They teaching you how to run a rubber plantation or a steel mill? Naw—just to talk proper and read books and wear white shoes . . .
GEORGE [*Looking at him with distaste, a little above it all*] You're all wacked up with bitterness, man.
WALTER [*Intently, almost quietly, between the teeth, glaring at the boy*] And you—ain't you bitter, man? Ain't you just about had it yet? Don't you see no stars gleaming that you can't reach out and grab? You happy?—You contented son-of-a-bitch—you happy? You got it made? Bitter? Man, I'm a volcano. Bitter? Here I am a giant—surrounded by ants! Ants who can't even understand what it is the giant is talking about.
RUTH [*Passionately and suddenly*] Oh, Walter—ain't you with nobody!
WALTER [*Violently*] No! 'Cause ain't nobody with me! Not even my own mother!
RUTH Walter, that's a terrible thing to say!
[BENEATHA *enters, dressed for the evening in a cocktail dress and earrings*]
GEORGE Well—hey, you look great.
BENEATHA Let's go, George. See you all later.
RUTH Have a nice time.
GEORGE Thanks. Good night. [*To* WALTER, *sarcastically*] Good night, Prometheus.
[BENEATHA *and* GEORGE *exit*]
WALTER [*To* RUTH] Who is Prometheus?
RUTH I don't know. Don't worry about it.
WALTER [*In fury, pointing after* GEORGE] See there—they get to a point where they can't insult you man to man—they got to go talk about something ain't nobody never heard of!
RUTH How do you know it was an insult? [*To humor him*] Maybe Prometheus is a nice fellow.
WALTER Prometheus! I bet there ain't even no such thing! I bet that simple-minded clown—
RUTH Walter— [*She stops what she is doing and looks at him*]

WALTER [*Yelling*] Don't start!
RUTH Start what?
WALTER Your nagging! Where was I? Who was I with? How much money did I spend?
RUTH [*Plaintively*] Walter Lee—why don't we just try to talk about it . . .
WALTER [*Not listening*] I been out talking with people who understand me. People who care about the things I got on my mind.
RUTH [*Wearily*] I guess that means people like Willy Harris.
WALTER Yes, people like Willy Harris.
RUTH [*With a sudden flash of impatience*] Why don't you all just hurry up and go into the banking business and stop talking about it!
WALTER Why? You want to know why? 'Cause we all tied up in a race of people that don't know how to do nothing but moan, pray and have babies!

[*The line is too bitter even for him and he looks at her and sits down*]
RUTH Oh, Walter . . . [*Softly*] Honey, why can't you stop fighting me?
WALTER [*Without thinking*] Who's fighting you? Who even cares about you?

[*This line begins the retardation of his mood*]
RUTH Well—[*She waits a long time, and then with resignation starts to put away her things*] I guess I might as well go on to bed . . . [*More or less to herself*] I don't know where we lost it . . . but we have . . . [*Then, to him*] I—I'm sorry about this new baby, Walter. I guess maybe I better go on and do what I started . . . I guess I just didn't realize how bad things was with us . . . I guess I just didn't really realize—[*She starts out to the bedroom and stops*] You want some hot milk?
WALTER Hot milk?
RUTH Yes— hot milk.
WALTER Why hot milk?
RUTH 'Cause after all that liquor you come home with you ought to have something hot in your stomach.
WALTER I don't want no milk.
RUTH You want some coffee then?
WALTER No, I don't want no coffee. I don't want nothing hot to drink. [*Almost plaintively*] Why you always trying to give me something to eat?
RUTH [*Standing and looking at him helplessly*] What else can I give you, Walter Lee Younger?

[*She stands and looks at him and presently turns to go out again. He lifts his head and watches her going away from him in a new mood which began to emerge when he asked her "Who cares about you?"*]

WALTER It's been rough, ain't it, baby? [*She hears and stops but does not turn around and he continues to her back*] I guess between two people there ain't never as much understood as folks generally thinks there is. I mean like between me and you—[*She turns to face him*] How we gets to the place where we scared to talk softness to each other. [*He waits, thinking hard himself*] Why you think it got to be like that? [*He is thoughtful, almost as a child would be*] Ruth, what is it gets into people ought to be close?

RUTH I don't know, honey. I think about it a lot.

WALTER On account of you and me, you mean? The way things are with us. The way something done come down between us.

RUTH There ain't so much between us, Walter . . . Not when you come to me and try to talk to me. Try to be with me . . . a little even.

WALTER [*Total honesty*] Sometimes . . . sometimes . . . I don't even know how to try.

RUTH Walter—

WALTER Yes?

RUTH [*Coming to him, gently and with misgiving, but coming to him*] Honey . . . life don't have to be like this. I mean sometimes people can do things so that things are better . . . You remember how we used to talk when Travis was born . . . about the way we were going to live . . . the kind of house . . . [*She is stroking his head*] Well, it's all starting to slip away from us . . .

[MAMA *enters, and* WALTER *jumps up and shouts at her*]

WALTER Mama, where have you been?

MAMA My—them steps is longer than they used to be. Whew! [*She sits down and ignores him*] How you feeling this evening, Ruth?

[RUTH *shrugs, disturbed some at having been prematurely interrupted and watching her husband knowingly*]

WALTER Mama, where have you been all day?

MAMA [*Still ignoring him and leaning on the table and changing to more comfortable shoes*] Where's Travis?

RUTH I let him go out earlier and he ain't come back yet. Boy, is he going to get it!

WALTER Mama!

MAMA [*As if she has heard him for the first time*] Yes, son?

WALTER Where did you go this afternoon?

MAMA I went downtown to tend to some business that I had to tend to.

WALTER What kind of business?

MAMA You know better than to question me like a child, Brother.

WALTER [*Rising and bending over the table*] Where were you, Mama? [*Bringing his fists down and shouting*] Mama, you didn't go do some-

thing with that insurance money, something crazy?
[*The front door opens slowly, interrupting him, and* TRAVIS *peeks his head in, less than hopefully*]

TRAVIS [*To his mother*] Mama, I—

RUTH "Mama I" nothing! You're going to get it, boy! Get on in that bedroom and get yourself ready!

TRAVIS But I—

MAMA Why don't you all never let the child explain hisself.

RUTH Keep out of it now, Lena.

[MAMA *clamps her lips together, and* RUTH *advances toward her son menacingly*]

RUTH A thousand times I have told you not to go off like that—

MAMA [*Holding out her arms to her grandson*] Well—at least let me tell him something. I want him to be the first one to hear . . . Come here, Travis. [*The boy obeys, gladly*] Travis—[*She takes him by the shoulder and looks into his face*]—you know that money we got in the mail this morning?

TRAVIS Yes'm—

MAMA Well—what you think your grandmama gone and done with that money?

TRAVIS I don't know, Grandmama.

MAMA [*Putting her finger on his nose for emphasis*] She went out and she bought you a house! [*The explosion comes from* WALTER *at the end of the revelation and he jumps up and turns away from all of them in a fury.* MAMA *continues, to* TRAVIS] You glad about the house? It's going to be yours when you get to be a man.

TRAVIS Yeah—I always wanted to live in a house.

MAMA All right, gimme some sugar then—[TRAVIS *puts his arms around her neck as she watches her son over the boy's shoulder. Then, to* TRAVIS, *after the embrace*] Now when you say your prayers tonight, you thank God and your grandfather—'cause it was him who give you the house—in his way.

RUTH [*Taking the boy from* MAMA *and pushing him toward the bedroom*] Now you get out of here and get ready for your beating.

TRAVIS Aw, Mama—

RUTH Get on in there—[*Closing the door behind him and turning radiantly to her mother-in-law*] So you went and did it!

MAMA [*Quietly, looking at her son with pain*] Yes, I did.

RUTH [*Raising both arms classically*] Praise God! [*Looks at* WALTER *a moment, who says nothing. She crosses rapidly to her husband*] Please, honey—let me be glad . . . you be glad too. [*She has laid her hands on*

his shoulders, but he shakes himself free of her roughly, without turning to face her] Oh, Walter . . . a home . . . *a home.* [*She comes back to* MAMA] Well—where is it? How big is it? How much it going to cost?
MAMA Well—
RUTH When we moving?
MAMA [*Smiling at her*] First of the month.
RUTH [*Throwing back her head with jubilance*] Praise God!
MAMA [*Tentatively, still looking at her son's back turned against her and* RUTH] It's—it's a nice house too . . . [*She cannot help speaking directly to him. An imploring quality in her voice, her manner, makes her almost like a girl now*] Three bedrooms—nice big one for you and Ruth. . . . Me and Beneatha still have to share our room, but Travis have one of his own—and [*With difficulty*] I figure if the—new baby—is a boy, we could get one of them double-decker outfits . . . And there's a yard with a little patch of dirt where I could maybe get to grow me a few flowers . . . And a nice big basement . . .
RUTH Walter honey, be glad—
MAMA [*Still to his back, fingering things on the table*] 'Course I don't want to make it sound fancier than it is . . . It's just a plain little old house—but it's made good and solid—and it will be *ours.* Walter Lee—it makes a difference in a man when he can walk on floors that belong to *him* . . .
RUTH Where is it?
MAMA [*Frightened at this telling*] Well—well—it's out there in Clybourne Park—
[RUTH's *radiance fades abruptly, and* WALTER *finally turns slowly to face his mother with incredulity and hostility*]
RUTH Where?
MAMA [*Matter-of-factly*] Four o six Clybourne Street, Clybourne Park.
RUTH Clybourne Park? Mama, there ain't no colored people living in Clybourne Park.
MAMA [*Almost idiotically*] Well, I guess there's going to be some now.
WALTER [*Bitterly*] So that's the peace and comfort you went out and bought for us today!
MAMA [*Raising her eyes to meet his finally*] Son—I just tried to find the nicest place for the least amount of money for my family.
RUTH [*Trying to recover from the shock*] Well—well—'course I ain't one never been 'fraid of no crackers, mind you—but—well, wasn't there no other houses nowhere?
MAMA Them houses they put up for colored in them areas way out all seem to cost twice as much as other houses. I did the best I could.

RUTH [*Struck senseless with the news, in its various degrees of goodness and trouble, she sits a moment, her fists propping her chin in thought, and then she starts to rise, bringing her fists down with vigor, the radiance spreading from cheek to cheek again*] Well—well!—All I can say is—if this is my time in life—*my time*—to say good-bye—[*And she builds with momentum as she starts to circle the room with an exuberant, almost tearfully happy release*]—to these Goddamned cracking walls!—[*She pounds the walls*]—and these marching roaches!—[*She wipes at an imaginary army of marching roaches*]—and this cramped little closet which ain't now or never was no kitchen! . . . then I say it loud and good, Hallelujah! and good-bye misery . . . I don't never want to see your ugly face again! [*She laughs joyously, having practically destroyed the apartment, and flings her arms up and lets them come down happily, slowly, reflectively, over her abdomen, aware for the first time perhaps that the life therein pulses with happiness and not despair*] Lena?

MAMA [*Moved, watching her happiness*] Yes, honey?

RUTH [*Looking off*] Is there—is there a whole lot of sunlight?

MAMA [*Understanding*] Yes, child, there's a whole lot of sunlight.

[*Long pause*]

RUTH [*Collecting herself and going to the door of the room* TRAVIS *is in*] Well—I guess I better see 'bout Travis. [*To* MAMA] Lord, I sure don't feel like whipping nobody today!

[*She exits*]

MAMA [*The mother and son are left alone now and the mother waits a long time, considering deeply, before she speaks*] Son—you—you understand what I done, don't you? [WALTER *is silent and sullen*] I—I just seen my family falling apart today . . . just falling to pieces in front of my eyes . . . We couldn't of gone on like we was today. We was going backwards 'stead of forwards—talking 'bout killing babies and wishing each other was dead . . . When it gets like that in life—you just got to do something different, push on out and do something bigger . . . [*She waits*] I wish you say something, son . . . I wish you'd say how deep inside you you think I done the right thing—

WALTER [*Crossing slowly to his bedroom door and finally turning there and speaking measuredly*] What you need me to say you done right for? *You* the head of this family. You run our lives like you want to. It was your money and you did what you wanted with it. So what you need for me to say it was all right for? [*Bitterly, to hurt her as deeply as he knows is possible*] So you butchered up a dream of mine—you—who always talking 'bout your children's dreams . . .

MAMA Walter Lee—
[*He just closes the door behind him.* MAMA *sits alone, thinking heavily*]
Curtain

Scene Two

Time: *Friday night. A few weeks later.*

At rise: *Packing crates mark the intention of the family to move.* BENEATHA *and* GEORGE *come in, presumably from an evening out again.*

GEORGE O.K. . . . O.K., whatever you say . . . [*They both sit on the couch. He tries to kiss her. She moves away*] Look, we've had a nice evening; let's not spoil it, huh? . . .
[*He again turns her head and tries to nuzzle in and she turns away from him, not with distaste but with momentary lack of interest; in a mood to pursue what they were talking about*]
BENEATHA I'm *trying* to talk with you.
GEORGE We always talk.
BENEATHA Yes—and I love to talk.
GEORGE [*Exasperated; rising*] I know it and I don't mind it sometimes . . . I want you to cut it out, see—The moody stuff, I mean. I don't like it. You're a nice-looking girl . . . all over. That's all you need, honey, forget the atmosphere. Guys aren't going to go for the atmosphere—they're going to go for what they see. Be glad for that. Drop the Garbo routine. It doesn't go with you. As for myself, I want a nice—[*Groping*]—simple [*Thoughtfully*]—sophisticated girl . . . not a poet—O.K.?
[*She rebuffs him again and he starts to leave*]
BENEATHA Why are you angry?
GEORGE Because this is stupid! I don't go out with you to discuss the nature of "quiet desperation" or to hear all about your thoughts—because the world will go on thinking what it thinks regardless—
BENEATHA Then why read books? Why go to school?
GEORGE [*With artificial patience, counting on his fingers*] It's simple. You read books—to learn facts—to get grades—to pass the course—to get a degree. That's all—it has nothing to do with thoughts.
[*A long pause*]
BENEATHA I see. [*A longer pause as she looks at him*] Good night, George.
[GEORGE *looks at her a little oddly, and starts to exit. He meets* MAMA *coming in*]
GEORGE Oh—hello, Mrs. Younger.

MAMA Hello, George, how you feeling?
GEORGE Fine—fine, how are you?
MAMA Oh, a little tired. You know them steps can get you after a day's work. You all have a nice time tonight?
GEORGE Yes—a fine time. Well, good night.
MAMA Good night. [*He exits.* MAMA *closes the door behind her*] Hello, honey. What you sitting like that for?
BENEATHA I'm just sitting.
MAMA Didn't you have a nice time?
BENEATHA No.
MAMA No? What's the matter?
BENEATHA Mama, George is a fool—honest. [*She rises*]
MAMA [*Hustling around unloading the packages she has entered with. She stops*] Is he, baby?
BENEATHA Yes.

[BENEATHA *makes up* TRAVIS' *bed as she talks*]

MAMA You sure?
BENEATHA Yes.
MAMA Well—I guess you better not waste your time with no fools.

[BENEATHA *looks up at her mother, watching her put groceries in the refrigerator. Finally she gathers up her things and starts into the bedroom. At the door she stops and looks back at her mother*]

BENEATHA Mama—
MAMA Yes, baby—
BENEATHA Thank you.
MAMA For what?
BENEATHA For understanding me this time.

[*She exits quickly and the mother stands, smiling a little, looking at the place where* BENEATHA *just stood.* RUTH *enters*]

RUTH Now don't you fool with any of this stuff, Lena—
MAMA Oh, I just thought I'd sort a few things out.

[*The phone rings.* RUTH *answers*]

RUTH [*At the phone*] Hello—Just a minute. [*Goes to door*] Walter, it's Mrs. Arnold. [*Waits. Goes back to the phone. Tense*] Hello. Yes, this is his wife speaking . . . He's lying down now. Yes . . . well, he'll be in tomorrow. He's been very sick. Yes—I know we should have called, but we were so sure he'd be able to come in today. Yes—yes, I'm very sorry. Yes . . . Thank you very much. [*She hangs up.* WALTER *is standing in the doorway of the bedroom behind her*] That was Mrs. Arnold.
WALTER [*Indifferently*] Was it?
RUTH She said if you don't come in tomorrow that they are getting a new man . . .

WALTER Ain't that sad—ain't that crying sad.
RUTH She said Mr. Arnold has had to take a cab for three days . . . Walter, you ain't been to work for three days! [*This is a revelation to her*] Where you been, Walter Lee Younger? [WALTER *looks at her and starts to laugh*] You're going to lose your job.
WALTER That's right . . .
RUTH Oh, Walter, and with your mother working like a dog every day—
WALTER That's sad too—Everything is sad.
MAMA What you been doing for these three days, son?
WALTER Mama—you don't know all the things a man what got leisure can find to do in this city . . . What's this—Friday night? Well—Wednesday I borrowed Willy Harris' car and I went for a drive . . . just me and myself and I drove and drove . . . Way out . . . way past South Chicago, and I parked the car and I sat and looked at the steel mills all day long. I just sat in the car and looked at them big black chimneys for hours. Then I drove back and I went to the Green Hat. [*Pause*] And Thursday—Thursday I borrowed the car again and I got in it and I pointed it the other way and I drove the other way—for hours—way, way up to Wisconsin, and I looked at the farms. I just drove and looked at the farms. Then I drove back and I went to the Green Hat. [*Pause*] And today—today I didn't get the car. Today I just walked. All over the Southside. And I looked at the Negroes and they looked at me and finally I just sat down on the curb at Thirty-ninth and South Parkway and I just sat there and watched the Negroes go by. And then I went to the Green Hat. You all sad? You all depressed? And you know where I am going right now—

[RUTH *goes out quietly*]

MAMA Oh, Big Walter, is this the harvest of our days?
WALTER You know what I like about the Green Hat? [*He turns the radio on and a steamy, deep blues pours into the room*] I like this little cat they got there who blows a sax . . . He blows. He talks to me. He ain't but 'bout five feet tall and he's got a conked head and his eyes is always closed and he's all music—
MAMA [*Rising and getting some papers out of her handbag*] Walter—
WALTER And there's this other guy who plays the piano . . . and they got a sound. I mean they can work on some music . . . They got the best little combo in the world in the Green Hat . . . You can just sit there and drink and listen to them three men play and you realize that don't nothing matter worth a damn, just being there—
MAMA I've helped do it to you, haven't I, son? Walter, I been wrong.
WALTER Naw—you ain't never been wrong about nothing, Mama.
MAMA Listen to me, now. I say I been wrong, son. That I been doing to

you what the rest of the world been doing to you. [*She stops and he looks up slowly at her and she meets his eyes pleadingly*] Walter—what you ain't never understood is that I ain't got nothing, don't own nothing, ain't never really wanted nothing that wasn't for you. There ain't nothing as precious to me . . . There ain't nothing worth holding on to, money, dreams, nothing else—if it means—if it means it's going to destroy my boy. [*She puts her papers in front of him and he watches her without speaking or moving*] I paid the man thirty-five hundred dollars down on the house. That leaves sixty-five hundred dollars. Monday morning I want you to take this money and take three thousand dollars and put it in a savings account for Beneatha's medical schooling. The rest you put in a checking account—with your name on it. And from now on any penny that come out of it or that go in it is for you to look after. For you to decide. [*She drops her hands a little helplessly*] It ain't much, but it's all I got in the world and I'm putting it in your hands. I'm telling you to be the head of this family from now on like you supposed to be.

WALTER [*Stares at the money*] You trust me like that, Mama?

MAMA I ain't never stop trusting you. Like I ain't never stop loving you.
[*She goes out, and* WALTER *sits looking at the money on the table as the music continues in its idiom, pulsing in the room. Finally, in a decisive gesture, he gets up, and, in mingled joy and desperation, picks up the money. At the same moment,* TRAVIS *enters for bed*]

TRAVIS What's the matter, Daddy? You drunk?

WALTER [*Sweetly, more sweetly than we have even known him*] No, Daddy ain't drunk. Daddy ain't going to never be drunk again. . . .

TRAVIS Well, Good night, Daddy.
[*The* FATHER *has come from behind the couch and leans over, embracing his son*]

WALTER Son, I feel like talking to you tonight.

TRAVIS About what?

WALTER Oh, about a lot of things. About you and what kind of man you going to be when you grow up. . . . Son—son, what do you want to be when you grow up?

TRAVIS A bus driver.

WALTER [*Laughing a little*] A what? Man, that ain't nothing to want to be!

TRAVIS Why not!

WALTER 'Cause, man—it ain't big enough—you know what I mean.

TRAVIS I don't know then. I can't make up my mind. Sometimes Mama asks me that too. And sometimes when I tell you I just want to be like you—she says she don't want me to be like that and sometimes she says she does. . . .

WALTER [*Gathering him up in his arms*] You know what, Travis? In seven years you going to be seventeen years old. And things is going to be very different with us in seven years, Travis. . . . One day when you are seventeen I'll come home—home from my office downtown somewhere—
TRAVIS You don't work in no office, Daddy.
WALTER No—but after tonight. After what your daddy gonna do tonight, there's going to be offices—a whole lot of offices. . . .
TRAVIS What you gonna do tonight, Daddy?
WALTER You wouldn't understand yet, son, but your daddy's gonna make a transaction . . . a business transaction that's going to change our lives. . . . That's how come one day when you 'bout seventeen years old I'll come home and I'll be pretty tired, you know what I mean, after a day of conferences and secretaries getting things wrong the way they do . . . 'cause an executive's life is hell, man—[*The more he talks the farther away he gets*] And I'll pull the car up on the driveway . . . just a plain black Chrysler, I think, with white walls—no—black tires. More elegant. Rich people don't have to be flashy . . . though I'll have to get something a little sportier for Ruth—maybe a Cadillac convertible to do her shopping in. . . . And I'll come up the steps to the house and the gardener will be clipping away at the hedges and he'll say, "Good evening, Mr. Younger." And I'll say, "Hello, Jefferson, how are you this evening?" And I'll go inside and Ruth will come downstairs and meet me at the door and we'll kiss each other and she'll take my arm and we'll go up to your room to see you sitting on the floor with the catalogues of all the great schools in America around you. . . . All the great schools in the world! And—and I'll say, all right son—it's your seventeenth birthday, what is it you've decided? . . . Just tell me where you want to go to school and you'll go. Just tell me, what it is you want to be—and you'll *be* it. . . . Whatever you want to be— Yessir! [*He holds his arms open for* TRAVIS] You just name it, son . . . [TRAVIS *leaps into them*] and I hand you the world!
[WALTER's *voice has risen in pitch and hysterical promise and on the last line he lifts* TRAVIS *high*]

Blackout

Scene Three

Time: *Saturday, moving day, one week later.*
Before the curtain rises, RUTH's *voice, a strident, dramatic church alto, cuts through the silence.*
It is, in the darkness, a triumphant surge, a penetrating statement of ex-

pectation: "Oh, Lord, I don't feel no ways tired! Children, oh, glory hallelujah!"
As the curtain rises we see that RUTH is alone in the living room, finishing up the family's packing. It is moving day. She is nailing crates and tying cartons. BENEATHA enters, carrying a guitar case, and watches her exuberant sister-in-law.

RUTH Hey!
BENEATHA [Putting away the case] Hi.
RUTH [Pointing at a package] Honey—look in that package there and see what I found on sale this morning at the South Center. [RUTH gets up and moves to the package and draws out some curtains] Lookahere—handturned hems!
BENEATHA How do you know the window size out there?
RUTH [Who hadn't thought of that] Oh—Well, they bound to fit something in the whole house. Anyhow, they was too good a bargain to pass up. [RUTH slaps her head, suddenly remembering something] Oh, Bennie—I meant to put a special note on that carton over there. That's your mama's good china and she wants 'em to be very careful with it.
BENEATHA I'll do it.
[BENEATHA finds a piece of paper and starts to draw large letters on it]
RUTH You know what I'm going to do soon as I get in that new house?
BENEATHA What?
RUTH Honey—I'm going to run me a tub of water up to here . . . [With her fingers practically up to her nostrils] And I'm going to get in it—and I am going to sit . . . and sit . . . and sit in that hot water and the first person who knocks to tell *me* to hurry up and come out—
BENEATHA Gets shot at sunrise.
RUTH [Laughing happily] You said it, sister! [Noticing how large BENEATHA is absent-mindedly making the note] Honey, they ain't going to read that from no airplane.
BENEATHA [Laughing herself] I guess I always think things have more emphasis if they are big, somehow.
RUTH [Looking up at her and smiling] You and your brother seem to have that as a philosophy of life. Lord, that man—done changed so 'round here. You know—you know what we did last night? Me and Walter Lee?
BENEATHA What?
RUTH [Smiling to herself] We went to the movies. [Looking at BENEATHA to see if she understands] We went to the movies. You know the last time me and Walter went to the movies together?

BENEATHA No.
RUTH Me neither. That's how long it been. [*Smiling again*] But we went last night. The picture wasn't much good, but that didn't seem to matter. We went—and we held hands.
BENEATHA Oh, Lord!
RUTH We held hands—and you know what?
BENEATHA What?
RUTH When we come out of the show it was late and dark and all the stores and things was closed up . . . and it was kind of chilly and there wasn't many people on the streets . . . and we was still holding hands, me and Walter.
BENEATHA You're killing me.
[WALTER *enters with a large package. His happiness is deep in him; he cannot keep still with his new-found exuberance. He is singing and wiggling and snapping his fingers. He puts his package in a corner and puts a phonograph record, which he has brought in with him, on the record player. As the music comes up he dances over to* RUTH *and tries to get her to dance with him. She gives in at last to his raunchiness and in a fit of giggling allows herself to be drawn into his mood and together they deliberately burlesque an old social dance of their youth*]
BENEATHA [*Regarding them a long time as they dance, then drawing in her breath for a deeply exaggerated comment which she does not particularly mean*] Talk about—olddddddddddd-fashioneddddddddd—Negroes!
WALTER [*Stopping momentarily*] What kind of Negroes?
[*He says this in fun. He is not angry with her today, nor with anyone. He starts to dance with his wife again*]
BENEATHA Old-fashioned.
WALTER [*As he dances with* RUTH] You know, when these *New Negroes* have their convention—[*Pointing at his sister*]—that is going to be the chairman of the Committee on Unending Agitation. [*He goes on dancing, then stops*] Race, race, race! . . . Girl, I do believe you are the first person in the history of the entire human race to successfully brainwash yourself. [BENEATHA *breaks up and he goes on dancing. He stops again, enjoying his tease*] Damn, even the N double A C P takes a holiday sometimes! [BENEATHA *and* RUTH *laugh. He dances with* RUTH *some more and starts to laugh and stops and pantomimes someone over an operating table*] I can just see that chick someday looking down at some poor cat on an operating table before she starts to slice him, saying . . . [*Pulling his sleeves back maliciously*] "By the way, what are your views on civil rights down there? . . ."

[*He laughs at her again and starts to dance happily. The bell sounds*]

BENEATHA Sticks and stones may break my bones but . . . words will never hurt me!

[BENEATHA *goes to the door and opens it as* WALTER *and* RUTH *go on with the clowning.* BENEATHA *is somewhat surprised to see a quiet-looking middle-aged white man in a business suit holding his hat and a briefcase in his hand and consulting a small piece of paper*]

MAN Uh—how do you do, miss. I am looking for a Mrs.—[*He looks at the slip of paper*] Mrs. Lena Younger?

BENEATHA [*Smoothing her hair with slight embarrassment*] Oh—yes, that's my mother. Excuse me [*She closes the door and turns to quiet the other two*] Ruth! Brother! Somebody's here. [*Then she opens the door. The man casts a curious quick glance at all of them*] Uh—come in please.

MAN [*Coming in*] Thank you.

BENEATHA My mother isn't here just now. Is it business?

MAN Yes . . . well, of a sort.

WALTER [*Freely, the Man of the House*] Have a seat. I'm Mrs. Younger's son. I look after most of her business matters.

[RUTH *and* BENEATHA *exchange amused glances*]

MAN [*Regarding* WALTER, *and sitting*] Well—My name is Karl Lindner . . .

WALTER [*Stretching out his hand*] Walter Younger. This is my wife— [RUTH *nods politely*]—and my sister.

LINDNER How do you do.

WALTER [*Amiably, as he sits himself easily on a chair, leaning with interest forward on his knees and looking expectantly into the newcomer's face*] What can we do for you, Mr. Lindner!

LINDNER [*Some minor shuffling of the hat and briefcase on his knees*] Well—I am a representative of the Clybourne Park Improvement Association—

WALTER [*Pointing*] Why don't you sit your things on the floor?

LINDNER Oh—yes. Thank you. [*He slides the briefcase and hat under the chair*] And as I was saying—I am from the Clybourne Park Improvement Association and we have had it brought to our attention at the last meeting that you people—or at least your mother—has bought a piece of residential property at—[*He digs for the slip of paper again*]—four o six Clybourne Street. . . .

WALTER That's right. Care for something to drink? Ruth, get Mr. Lindner a beer.

LINDNER [*Upset for some reason*] Oh—no, really. I mean thank you very much, but no thank you.

RUTH [*Innocently*] Some coffee?

LINDNER Thank you, nothing at all.

[BENEATHA *is watching the man carefully*]

LINDNER Well, I don't know how much you folks know about our organization. [*He is a gentle man, thoughtful and somewhat labored in his manner*] It is one of these community organizations set up to look after —oh, you know, things like block upkeep and special projects and we also have what we call our New Neighbors Orientation Committee . . .

BENEATHA [*Drily*] Yes—and what do they do?

LINDNER [*Turning a little to her and then returning the main force to* WALTER] Well—it's what you might call a sort of welcoming committee, I guess. I mean they, we, I'm the chairman of the committee—go around and see the new people who move into the neighborhood and sort of give them the lowdown on the way we do things out in Clybourne Park.

BENEATHA [*With appreciation of the two meanings, which escape* RUTH *and* WALTER] Un-huh.

LINDNER And we also have the category of what the association calls—[*He looks elsewhere*]—uh—special community problems . . .

BENEATHA Yes—and what are some of those?

WALTER Girl, let the man talk.

LINDNER [*With understated relief*] Thank you. I would sort of like to explain this thing in my own way. I mean I want to explain to you in a certain way.

WALTER Go ahead.

LINDNER Yes. Well. I'm going to try to get right to the point. I'm sure we'll all appreciate that in the long run.

BENEATHA Yes.

WALTER Be still now!

LINDNER Well—

RUTH [*Still innocently*] Would you like another chair—you don't look comfortable.

LINDNER [*More frustrated than annoyed*] No, thank you very much. Please. Well—to get right to the point I—[*A great breath, and he is off at last*] I am sure you people must be aware of some of the incidents which have happened in various parts of the city when colored people have moved into certain areas—[BENEATHA *exhales heavily and starts tossing a piece of fruit up and down in the air*] Well—because we have what I think is going to be a unique type of organization in American community life—not only do we deplore that kind of thing—but we are trying to do something about it. [BENEATHA *stops tossing and turns with a new and quizzical interest to the man*] We feel—[*gaining confidence in his mission because of the interest in the faces of the people he is talking to*]—we feel that most of the trouble in this world, when you come right down to it—[*He hits his knee for emphasis*]—most of the trouble exists because people just don't sit down and talk to each other.

RUTH [*Nodding as she might in church, pleased with the remark*] You can say that again, mister.

LINDNER [*More encouraged by such affirmation*] That we don't try hard enough in this world to understand the other fellow's problem. The other guy's point of view.

RUTH Now that's right.

[BENEATHA *and* WALTER *merely watch and listen with genuine interest*]

LINDNER Yes—that's the way we feel out in Clybourne Park. And that's why I was elected to come here this afternoon and talk to you people. Friendly like, you know, the way people should talk to each other and see if we couldn't find some way to work this thing out. As I say, the whole business is a matter of *caring* about the other fellow. Anybody can see that you are a nice family of folks, hard working and honest I'm sure. [BENEATHA *frowns slightly, quizzically, her head tilted regarding him*] Today everybody knows what it means to be on the outside of *something*. And of course, there is always somebody who is out to take the advantage of people who don't always understand.

WALTER What do you mean?

LINDNER Well—you see our community is made up of people who've worked hard as the dickens for years to build up that little community. They're not rich and fancy people; just hard-working, honest people who don't really have much but those little homes and a dream of the kind of community they want to raise their children in. Now, I don't say we are perfect and there is a lot wrong in some of the things they want. But you've got to admit that a man, right or wrong, has the right to want to have the neighborhood he lives in a certain kind of way. And at the moment the overwhelming majority of our people out there feel that people get along better, take more of a common interest in the life of the community, when they share a common background. I want you to believe me when I tell you that race prejudice simply doesn't enter into it. It is a matter of the people of Clybourne Park believing, rightly or wrongly, as I say, that for the happiness of all concerned that our Negro families are happier when they live in their *own* communities.

BENEATHA [*With a grand and bitter gesture*] This, friends, is the Welcoming Committee!

WALTER [*Dumfounded, looking at* LINDNER] Is this what you came marching all the way over here to tell us?

LINDNER Well, now we've been having a fine conversation. I hope you'll hear me all the way through.
WALTER [*Tightly*] Go ahead, man.
LINDNER You see—in the face of all things I have said, we are prepared to make your family a very generous offer . . .
BENEATHA Thirty pieces and not a coin less!
WALTER Yeah!
LINDNER [*Putting on his glasses and drawing a form out of the briefcase*] Our association is prepared, through the collective effort of our people, to buy the house from you at a financial gain to your family.
RUTH Lord have mercy, ain't this the living gall!
WALTER All right, you through?
LINDNER Well, I want to give you the exact terms of the financial arrangement—
WALTER We don't want to hear no exact terms of no arrangements. I want to know if you got any more to tell us 'bout getting together?
LINDNER [*Taking off his glasses*] Well—I don't suppose that you feel . . .
WALTER Never mind how I feel—you got any more to say 'bout how people ought to sit down and talk to each other? . . . Get out of my house, man.
[*He turns his back and walks to the door*]
LINDNER [*Looking around at the hostile faces and reaching and assembling his hat and briefcase*] Well—I don't understand why you people are reacting this way. What do you think you are going to gain by moving into a neighborhood where you just aren't wanted and where some elements—well—people can get awful worked up when they feel that their whole way of life and everything they've ever worked for is threatened.
WALTER Get out.
LINDNER [*At the door, holding a small card*] Well—I'm sorry it went like this.
WALTER Get out.
LINDNER [*Almost sadly regarding* WALTER] You just can't force people to change their hearts, son.
[*He turns and puts his card on a table and exits.* WALTER *pushes the door to with stinging hatred, and stands looking at it.* RUTH *just sits and* BENEATHA *just stands. They say nothing.* MAMA *and* TRAVIS *enter*]
MAMA Well—this all the packing got done since I left out of here this morning. I testify before God that my children got all the energy of the dead. What time the moving men due?
BENEATHA Four o'clock. You had a caller, Mama. [*She is smiling, teasingly*]

MAMA Sure enough—who?
BENEATHA [*Her arms folded saucily*] The Welcoming Committee.
[WALTER *and* RUTH *giggle*]
MAMA [*Innocently*] Who?
BENEATHA The Welcoming Committee. They said they're sure going to be glad to see you when you get there.
WALTER [*Devilishly*] Yeah, they said they can't hardly wait to see your face. [*Laughter*]
MAMA [*Sensing their facetiousness*] What's the matter with you all?
WALTER Ain't nothing the matter with us. We just telling you 'bout the gentleman who came to see you this afternoon. From the Clybourne Park Improvement Association.
MAMA What he want?
RUTH [*In the same mood as* BENEATHA *and* WALTER] To welcome you, honey.
WALTER He said they can't hardly wait. He said the one thing they don't have, that they just *dying* to have out there is a fine family of colored people!
[*To* RUTH *and* BENEATHA] Ain't that right!
RUTH *and* BENEATHA [*Mockingly*] Yeah! He left his card in case—
[*They indicate the card, and* MAMA *picks it up and throws it on the floor—understanding and looking off as she draws her chair up to the table on which she has put her plant and some sticks and some cord*]
MAMA Father, give us strength. [*Knowingly—and without fun*] Did he threaten us?
BENEATHA Oh—Mama—they don't do it like that any more. He talked Brotherhood. He said everybody ought to learn how to sit down and hate each other with good Christian fellowship.
[*She and* WALTER *shake hands to ridicule the remark*]
MAMA [*Sadly*] Lord, protect us . . .
RUTH You should hear the money those folks raised to buy the house from us. All we paid and then some.
BENEATHA What they think we going to do—eat 'em?
RUTH No, honey, marry 'em.
MAMA [*Shaking her head*] Lord, Lord, Lord . . .
RUTH Well—that's the way the crackers crumble. Joke.
BENEATHA [*Laughingly noticing what her mother is doing*] Mama, what are you doing?
MAMA Fixing my plant so it won't get hurt none on the way . . .
BENEATHA Mama, you going to take *that* to the new house?
MAMA Un-huh—
BENEATHA That raggedy-looking old thing?

MAMA [*Stopping and looking at her*] It expresses me.
RUTH [*With delight, to* BENEATHA] So there, Miss Thing!
[WALTER *comes to* MAMA *suddenly and bends down behind her and squeezes her in his arms with all his strength. She is overwhelmed by the suddenness of it and, though delighted, her manner is like that of* RUTH *with* TRAVIS]
MAMA Look out now, boy! You make me mess up my thing here!
WALTER [*His face lit, he slips down on his knees beside her, his arms still about her*] Mama . . . you know what it means to climb up in the chariot?
MAMA [*Gruffly, very happy*] Get on away from me now . . .
RUTH [*Near the gift-wrapped package, trying to catch* WALTER'S *eye*] Psst—
WALTER What the old song say, Mama . . .
RUTH Walter—Now?
 [*She is pointing at the package*]
WALTER [*Speaking the lines, sweetly, playfully, in his mother's face*]

I got wings . . . you got wings . . .
All God's Children got wings . . .

MAMA Boy— get out of my face and do some work . . .
WALTER

When I get to heaven gonna put on my wings,
Gonna fly all over God's heaven . . .

BENEATHA [*Teasingly, from across the room*] Everybody talking 'bout heaven ain't going there!
WALTER [*To* RUTH, *who is carrying the box across to them*] I don't know, you think we ought to give her that . . . Seems to me she ain't been very appreciative around here.
MAMA [*Eying the box, which is obviously a gift*] What is that?
WALTER [*Taking it from* RUTH *and putting it on the table in front of* MAMA] Well—what you all think? Should we give it to her?
RUTH Oh—she was pretty good today.
MAMA I'll good you—
 [*She turns her eyes to the box again*]
BENEATHA Open it, Mama.
 [*She stands up, looks at it, turns and looks at all of them, and then presses her hands together and does not open the package*]
WALTER [*Sweetly*] Open it, Mama. It's for you. [MAMA *looks in his eyes. It is the first present in her life without its being Christmas. Slowly she*

opens her package and lifts out, one by one, a brand-new sparkling set of gardening tools. WALTER *continues, prodding*] Ruth made up the note—read it . . .

MAMA [*Picking up the card and adjusting her glasses*] "To our own Mrs. Miniver—Love from Brother, Ruth and Beneatha." Ain't that lovely . . .

TRAVIS [*Tugging at his father's sleeve*] Daddy, can I give her mine now?

WALTER All right, son. [TRAVIS *flies to get his gift*] Travis didn't want to go in with the rest of us, Mama. He got his own. [*Somewhat amused*] We don't know what it is . . .

TRAVIS [*Racing back in the room with a large hatbox and putting it in front of his grandmother*] Here!

MAMA Lord have mercy, baby. You done gone and bought your grandmother a hat?

TRAVIS [*Very proud*] Open it!

[*She does and lifts out an elaborate, but very elaborate, wide gardening hat, and all the adults break up at the sight of it*]

RUTH Travis, honey, what is that?

TRAVIS [*Who thinks it is beautiful and appropriate*] It's a gardening hat! Like the ladies always have on in the magazines when they work in their gardens.

BENEATHA [*Giggling fiercely*] Travis—we are trying to make Mama Mrs. Miniver—not Scarlett O'Hara!

MAMA [*Indignantly*] What's the matter with you all! This here is a beautiful hat! [*Absurdly*] I always wanted me one just like it!

[*She pops it on her head to prove it to her grandson, and the hat is ludicrous and considerably oversized*]

RUTH Hot dog! Go, Mama!

WALTER [*Doubled over with laughter*] I'm sorry, Mama—but you look like you ready to go out and chop you some cotton sure enough!

[*They all laugh except* MAMA, *out of deference to* TRAVIS' *feelings*]

MAMA [*Gathering the boy up to her*] Bless your heart—this is the prettiest hat I ever owned—[WALTER, RUTH *and* BENEATHA *chime in—noisily, festively and insincerely congratulating* TRAVIS *on his gift*] What are we all standing around here for? We ain't finished packin' yet. Bennie, you ain't packed one book.

[*The bell rings*]

BENEATHA That couldn't be the movers . . . it's not hardly two good yet—

[BENEATHA *goes into her room.* MAMA *starts for door*]

WALTER [*Turning, stiffening*] Wait—wait—I'll get it.

[*He stands and looks at the door*]

MAMA You expecting company, son?
WALTER [*Just looking at the door*] Yeah—yeah . . .
[MAMA *looks at* RUTH, *and they exchange innocent and unfrightened glances*]
MAMA [*Not understanding*] Well, let them in, son.
BENEATHA [*From her room*] We need some more string.
MAMA Travis—you run to the hardware and get me some string cord.
[MAMA *goes out and* WALTER *turns and looks at* RUTH. TRAVIS *goes to a dish for money*]
RUTH Why don't you answer the door, man?
WALTER [*Suddenly bounding across the floor to her*] 'Cause sometimes it hard to let the future begin! [*Stooping down in her face*]

I got wings! You got wings!
All Gods children got wings!

[*He crosses to the door and throws it open. Standing there is a very slight little man in a not too prosperous business suit and with haunted frightened eyes and a hat pulled down tightly, brim up, around his forehead.* TRAVIS *passes between the men and exits. Walter leans deep in the man's face, still in his jubilance*]

When I get to heaven gonna put on my wings,
Gonna fly all over God's heaven . . .

[*The little man just stares at him*]

Heaven—

[*Suddenly he stops and looks past the little man into the empty hallway*]
Where's Willy, man?
BOBO He ain't with me.
WALTER [*Not disturbed*] Oh—come on in. You know my wife.
BOBO [*Dumbly, taking off his hat*] Yes—h'you, Miss Ruth.
RUTH [*Quietly, a mood apart from her husband already, seeing* BOBO] Hello, Bobo.
WALTER You right on time today . . . Right on time. That's the way!
[*He slaps* BOBO *on his back*] Sit down . . . lemme hear.
[RUTH *stands stiffly and quietly in back of them, as though somehow she senses death, her eyes fixed on her husband*]
BOBO [*His frightened eyes on the floor, his hat in his hands*] Could I please

get a drink of water, before I tell you about it, Walter Lee.
[WALTER *does not take his eyes off the man.* RUTH *goes blindly to the tap and gets a glass of water and brings it to* BOBO]

WALTER There ain't nothing wrong, is there?

BOBO Lemme tell you—

WALTER Man—didn't nothing go wrong?

BOBO Lemme tell you—Walter Lee. [*Looking at* RUTH *and talking to her more than to* WALTER] You know how it was. I got to tell you how it was. I mean first I got to tell you how it was all the way . . . I mean about the money I put in, Walter Lee . . .

WALTER [*With taut agitation now*] What about the money you put in?

BOBO Well—it wasn't much as we told you—me and Willy—[*He stops*] I'm sorry, Walter. I got a bad feeling about it. I got a real bad feeling about it . . .

WALTER Man, what you telling me about all this for? . . . Tell me what happened in Springfield . . .

BOBO Springfield.

RUTH [*Like a dead woman*] What was supposed to happen in Springfield?

BOBO [*To her*] This deal that me and Walter went into with Willy—Me and Willy was going to go down to Springfield and spread some money 'round so's we wouldn't have to wait so long for the liquor license . . . That's what we were going to do. Everybody said that was the way you had to do, you understand, Miss Ruth?

WALTER Man—what happened down there?

BOBO [*A pitiful man, near tears*] I'm trying to tell you, Walter.

WALTER [*Screaming at him suddenly*] THEN TELL ME, GODDAMMIT . . . WHAT'S THE MATTER WITH YOU?

BOBO Man . . . I didn't go to no Springfield, yesterday.

WALTER [*Halted, life hanging in the moment*] Why not?

BOBO [*The long way, the hard way to tell*] 'Cause I didn't have no reasons to . . .

WALTER Man, what are you talking about!

BOBO I'm talking about the fact that when I got to the train station yesterday morning—eight o'clock like we planned . . . Man—*Willy didn't never show up.*

WALTER Why . . . where was he . . . where is he?

BOBO That's what I'm trying to tell you . . . I don't know . . . I waited six hours . . . I called his house . . . and I waited . . . six hours . . . I waited in that train station six hours . . . [*Breaking into tears*] That was all the extra money I had in the world . . . [*Looking up at* WALTER *with the tears running down his face*] Man, *Willy is gone.*

WALTER Gone, what you mean Willy is gone? Gone where? You mean he went by himself. You mean he went off to Springfield by himself—to take care of getting the license—[*Turns and looks anxiously at* RUTH] You mean maybe he didn't want too many people in on the business down there? [*Looks to* RUTH *again, as before*] You know Willy got his own ways. [*Looks back to* BOBO] Maybe you was late yesterday and he just went on down there without you. Maybe—maybe—he's been callin' you at home tryin' to tell you what happened or something. Maybe—maybe—he just got sick. He's somewhere—he's got to be somewhere. We just got to find him—me and you got to find him. [*Grabs* BOBO *senselessly by the collar and starts to shake him*] We got to!

BOBO [*In sudden angry, frightened agony*] What's the matter with you, Walter! When a cat take off with your money he don't leave you no maps!

WALTER [*Turning madly, as though he is looking for* WILLY *in the very room*] Willy! . . . Willy . . . don't do it . . . Please don't do it . . . Man, not with that money . . . Man, please, not with that money . . . Oh, God . . . Don't let it be true . . . [*He is wandering around, crying out for* WILLY *and looking for him or perhaps for help from God*] Man . . . I trusted you . . . Man, I put my life in your hands . . . [*He starts to crumple down on the floor as* RUTH *just covers her face in horror.* MAMA *opens the door and comes into the room, with* BENEATHA *behind her*] Man . . . [*He starts to pound the floor with his fists, sobbing wildly*] That money is made out of my father's flesh . . .

BOBO [*Standing over him helplessly*] I'm sorry, Walter . . . [*Only* WALTER'S *sobs reply.* BOBO *puts on his hat*] I had my life staked on this deal, too . . .

[*He exits*]

MAMA [*To* WALTER] Son—[*She goes to him, bends down to him, talks to his bent head*] Son . . . Is it gone? Son, I gave you sixty-five hundred dollars. Is it gone? All of it? Beneatha's money too?

WALTER [*Lifting his head slowly*] Mama . . . I never . . . went to the bank at all . . .

MAMA [*Not wanting to believe him*] You mean . . . your sister's school money . . . you used that too . . . Walter? . . .

WALTER Yessss! . . . All of it . . . It's all gone . . .

[*There is total silence.* RUTH *stands with her face covered with her hands;* BENEATHA *leans forlornly against a wall, fingering a piece of red ribbon from the mother's gift.* MAMA *stops and looks at her son without recognition and then, quite without thinking about it, starts to beat him*

senselessly in the face. BENEATHA *goes to them and stops it*]
BENEATHA Mama!
[MAMA *stops and looks at both of her children and rises slowly and wanders vaguely, aimlessly away from them*]
MAMA I seen . . . him . . . night after night . . . come in . . . and look at that rug . . . and then look at me . . . the red showing in his eyes . . . the veins moving in his head . . . I seen him grow thin and old before he was forty . . . working and working and working like somebody's old horse . . . killing himself . . . and you—you give it all away in a day . . .
BENEATHA Mama—
MAMA Oh, God . . . [*She looks up to Him*] Look down here—and show me the strength.
BENEATHA Mama—
MAMA [*Folding over*] Strength . . .
BENEATHA [*Plaintively*] Mama . . .
MAMA Strength!

Curtain

Act III

An hour later.
At curtain, there is a sullen light of gloom in the living room, gray light not unlike that which began the first scene of Act One. At left we can see WALTER *within his room, alone with himself. He is stretched out on the bed, his shirt out and open, his arms under his head. He does not smoke, he does not cry out, he merely lies there, looking up at the ceiling, much as if he were alone in the world.*
In the living room BENEATHA *sits at the table, still surrounded by the now almost ominous packing crates. She sits looking off. We feel that this is a mood struck perhaps an hour before, and it lingers now, full of the empty sound of profound disappointment. We see on a line from her brother's bedroom the sameness of their attitudes. Presently the bell rings and* BENEATHA *rises without ambition or interest in answering. It is* ASAGAI, *smiling broadly, striding into the room with energy and happy expectation and conversation.*

ASAGAI I came over . . . I had some free time. I thought I might help with the packing. Ah, I like the look of packing crates! A household in preparation for a journey! It depresses some people . . . but for me . . . it is another feeling. Something full of the flow of life, do you understand? Movement, progress . . . It makes me think of Africa.

BENEATHA Africa!

ASAGAI What kind of a mood is this? Have I told you how deeply you move me?

BENEATHA He gave away the money, Asagai . . .

ASAGAI Who gave away what money?

BENEATHA The insurance money. My brother gave it away.

ASAGAI Gave it away?

BENEATHA He made an investment! With a man even Travis wouldn't have trusted.

ASAGAI And it's gone?

BENEATHA Gone!

ASAGAI I'm very sorry . . . And you, now?

BENEATHA Me? . . . Me? . . . Me I'm nothing . . . Me. When I was very small . . . we used to take our sleds out in the wintertime and the only hills we had were the ice-covered stone steps of some houses down the street. And we used to fill them in with snow and make them smooth and slide down them all day . . . and it was very dangerous you know . . . far too steep . . . and sure enough one day a kid named Rufus came down too fast and hit the sidewalk . . . and we saw his face just split open right there in front of us . . . And I remember standing there looking at his bloody open face thinking that was the end of Rufus. But the ambulance came and they took him to the hospital and they fixed the broken bones and they sewed it all up . . . and the next time I saw Rufus he just had a little line down the middle of his face . . . I never got over that . . .

[WALTER *sits up, listening on the bed. Throughout this scene it is important that we feel his reaction at all times, that he visibly respond to the words of his sister and* ASAGAI]

ASAGAI What?

BENEATHA That that was what one person could do for another, fix him up—sew up the problem, make him all right again. That was the most marvelous thing in the world . . . I wanted to do that. I always thought it was the one concrete thing in the world that a human being could do. Fix up the sick, you know—and make them whole again. This was truly being God . . .

ASAGAI You wanted to be God?

BENEATHA No—I wanted to cure. It used to be so important to me. I wanted to cure. It used to matter. I used to care. I mean about people and how their bodies hurt . . .

ASAGAI And you've stopped caring?

BENEATHA Yes—I think so.

ASAGAI Why?

[WALTER *rises, goes to the door of his room and is about to open it, then stops and stands listening, leaning on the door jamb*]

BENEATHA Because it doesn't seem deep enough, close enough to what ails mankind—I mean this thing of sewing up bodies or administering drugs. Don't you understand? It was a child's reaction to the world. I thought that doctors had the secret to all the hurts. . . . That's the way a child sees things—or an idealist.

ASAGAI Children see things very well sometimes—and idealists even better.

BENEATHA I know that's what you think. Because you are still where I left off—you still care. This is what you see for the world, for Africa. You with the dreams of the future will patch up all Africa—you are going to cure the Great Sore of colonialism with Independence—

ASAGAI Yes!

BENEATHA Yes—and you think that one word is the penicillin of the human spirit: "Independence!" But then what?

ASAGAI That will be the problem for another time. First we must get there.

BENEATHA And where does it end?

ASAGAI End? Who even spoke of an end? To life? To living?

BENEATHA An end to misery!

ASAGAI [*Smiling*] You sound like a French intellectual.

BENEATHA No! I sound like a human being who just had her future taken right out of her hands! While I was sleeping in my bed in there, things were happening in this world that directly concerned me—and nobody asked me, consulted me—they just went out and did things—and changed my life. Don't you see there isn't any real progress, Asagai, there is only one large circle that we march in, around and around, each of us with our own little picture—in front of us—our own little mirage that we think is the future.

ASAGAI That is the mistake.

BENEATHA What?

ASAGAI What you just said—about the circle. It isn't a circle—it is simply a long line—as in geometry, you know, one that reaches into infinity. And because we cannot see the end—we also cannot see how it changes. And it is very odd but those who see the changes are called "idealists" —and those who cannot, or refuse to think, they are the "realists." It is very strange, and amusing too, I think.

BENEATHA You—you are almost religious.

ASAGAI Yes . . . I think I have the religion of doing what is necessary in the world—and of the worshipping man—because he is so marvelous, you see.

BENEATHA Man is foul! And the human race deserves its misery!

ASAGAI You see: *you* have become the religious one in the old sense. Already, and after such a small defeat, you are worshipping despair.
BENEATHA From now on, I worship the truth—and the truth is that people are puny, small and selfish. . . .
ASAGAI Truth? Why is it that you despairing ones always think that only you have the truth? I never thought to see *you* like that, You! Your brother made a stupid, childish mistake—and you are grateful to him. So that now you can give up the ailing human race on account of it. You talk about what good is struggle; what good is anything? Where are we all going? And why are we bothering?
BENEATHA *And you cannot answer it!* All your talk and dreams about Africa and Independence. Independence and then what? What about all the crooks and petty thieves and just plain idiots who will come into power to steal the plunder the same as before—only now they will be black and do it in the name of the new Independence—You cannot answer that.
ASAGAI [*Shouting over her*] I live the answer! [*Pause*] In my village at home it is the exceptional man who can even read a newspaper . . . or who ever *sees* a book at all. I will go home and much of what I have to say will seem strange to the people of my village . . . But I will teach and work and things will happen, slowly and swiftly. At times it will seem that nothing changes at all . . . and then again . . . the sudden dramatic events which make history leap into the future. And then quiet again. Retrogression even. Guns, murder, revolution. And I even will have moments when I wonder if the quiet was not better than all that death and hatred. But I will look about my village at the illiteracy and disease and ignorance and I will not wonder long. And perhaps . . . perhaps I will be a great man . . . I mean perhaps I will hold on to the substance of truth and find my way always with the right course . . . and perhaps for it I will be butchered in my bed some night by the servants of empire . . .
BENEATHA *The martyr!*
ASAGAI . . . or perhaps I shall live to be a very old man, respected and esteemed in my new nation . . . And perhaps I shall hold office and this is what I'm trying to tell you, Alaiyo; perhaps the things I believe now for my country will be wrong and outmoded, and I will not understand and do terrible things to have things my way or merely to keep my power. Don't you see that there will be young men and women, not British soldiers then, but my own black countrymen . . . to step out of the shadows some evening and slit my then useless throat? Don't you see they have always been there . . . that they always will be. And that

such a thing as my own death will be an advance? They who might kill me even . . . actually replenish me!

BENEATHA Oh, Asagai, I know all that.

ASAGAI Good! Then stop moaning and groaning and tell me what you plan to do.

BENEATHA Do?

ASAGAI I have a bit of a suggestion.

BENEATHA What?

ASAGAI [*Rather quietly for him*] That when it is all over—that you come home with me—

BENEATHA [*Slapping herself on the forehead with exasperation born of misunderstanding*] Oh—Asagai—at this moment you decide to be romantic!

ASAGAI [*Quickly understanding the misunderstanding*] My dear, young creature of the New World—I do not mean across the city—I mean across the ocean; home—to Africa.

BENEATHA [*Slowly understanding and turning to him with murmured amazement*] To—to Nigeria?

ASAGAI Yes! . . . [*Smiling and lifting his arms playfully*] Three hundred years later the African Prince rose up out of the seas and swept the maiden back across the middle passage over which her ancestors had come—

BENEATHA [*Unable to play*] Nigeria?

ASAGAI Nigeria. Home. [*Coming to her with genuine romantic flippancy*] I will show you our mountains and our stars; and give you cool drinks from gourds and teach you the old songs and the ways of our people—and, in time, we will pretend that—[*Very softly*]—you have only been away for a day—

[*She turns her back to him, thinking. He swings her around and takes her full in his arms in a long embrace which proceeds to passion*]

BENEATHA [*Pulling away*] You're getting me all mixed up—

ASAGAI Why?

BENEATHA Too many things—too many things have happened today. I must sit down and think. I don't know what I feel about anything right this minute.

[*She promptly sits down and props her chin on her fist*]

ASAGAI [*Charmed*] All right, I shall leave you. No—don't get up. [*Touching her, gently, sweetly*] Just sit awhile and think . . . Never be afraid to sit awhile and think. [*He goes to door and looks at her*] How often I have looked at you and said, "Ah—so this is what the New World hath finally wrought . . ."

[*He exits.* BENEATHA *sits on alone. Presently* WALTER *enters from his*

room and starts to rummage through things, feverishly looking for something. She looks up and turns in her seat]
BENEATHA [*Hissingly*] Yes—just look at what the New World hath wrought! . . . Just look! [*She gestures with bitter disgust*] There he is! Monsieur le petit bourgeois noir—himself! There he is—Symbol of a Rising Class! Entrepreneur! Titan of the system! [*Walter ignores her completely and continues frantically and destructively looking for something and hurling things to floor and tearing things out of their place in his search.* BENEATHA *ignores the eccentricity of his actions and goes on with the monologue of insult*] Did you dream of yachts on Lake Michigan, Brother? Did you see yourself on that Great Day sitting down at the Conference Table, surrounded by all the mighty baldheaded men in America? All halted, waiting, breathless, waiting for your pronouncements on industry? Waiting for you—Chairman of the Board? [WALTER *finds what he is looking for—a small piece of white paper—and pushes it in his pocket and puts on his coat and rushes out without ever having looked at her. She shouts after him*] I look at you and I see the final triumph of stupidity in the world!
[*The door slams and she returns to just sitting again.* RUTH *comes quickly out of* MAMA's *room*]
RUTH Who was that?
BENEATHA Your husband.
RUTH Where did he go?
BENEATHA Who knows—maybe he has an appointment at U. S. Steel.
RUTH [*Anxiously, with frightened eyes*] You didn't say nothing bad to him, did you?
BENEATHA Bad? Say anything bad to him? No—I told him he was a sweet boy and full of dreams and everything is strictly peachy keen, as the ofay kids say!
[MAMA *enters from her bedroom. She is lost, vague, trying to catch hold, to make some sense of her former command of the world, but it still eludes her. A sense of waste overwhelms her gait; a measure of apology rides on her shoulders. She goes to her plant, which has remained on the table, looks at it, picks it up and takes it to the window sill and sits it outside, and she stands and looks at it a long moment. Then she closes the window, straightens her body with effort and turns around to her children*]
MAMA Well—ain't it a mess in here, though? [*A false cheerfulness, a beginning of something*] I guess we all better stop moping around and get some work done. All this unpacking and everything we got to do. [RUTH *raises her head slowly in response to the sense of the line; and* BENEATHA *in similar manner turns very slowly to look at her mother*] One of you

all better call the moving people and tell 'em not to come.
RUTH Tell 'em not to come?
MAMA Of course, baby. Ain't no need in 'em coming all the way here and having to go back. They charges for that too. [*She sits down, fingers to her brow, thinking*] Lord, ever since I was a little girl. I always remembers people saying, "Lena—Lena Eggleston, you aims too high all the time. You needs to slow down and see life a little more like it is. Just slow down some." That's what they always used to say down home—"Lord, that Lena Eggleston is a high-minded thing. She'll get her due one day!"
RUTH No, Lena . . .
MAMA Me and Big Walter just didn't never learn right.
RUTH Lena, no! We gotta go. Bennie—tell her . . . [*She rises and crosses to* BENEATHA *with her arms outstretched*. BENEATHA *doesn't respond*] Tell her we can still move . . . the notes ain't but a hundred and twenty-five a month. We got four grown people in this house—we can work . . .
MAMA [*To herself*] Just aimed too high all the time—
RUTH [*Turning and going to* MAMA *fast—the words pouring out with urgency and desperation*] Lena—I'll work . . . I'll work twenty hours a day in all the kitchens in Chicago . . . I'll strap my baby on my back if I have to and scrub all the floors in America and wash all the sheets in America if I have to—but we got to move . . . We got to get out of here . . .
[MAMA *reaches out absently and pats* RUTH's *hand*]
MAMA No—I sees things differently now. Been thinking 'bout some of the things we could do to fix this place up some. I seen a second-hand bureau over on Maxwell Street just the other day that could fit right there. [*She points to where the new furniture might go*. RUTH *wanders away from her*] Would need some new handles on it and then a little varnish and then it look like something brand-new. And—we can put up them new curtains in the kitchen . . . Why this place be looking fine. Cheer us all up so that we forget trouble ever came . . . [*To Ruth*] And you could get some nice screens to put up in your room round the baby's bassinet . . . [*She looks at both of them, pleadingly*] Sometimes you just got to know when to give up some things . . . and hold on to what you got.
[WALTER *enters from the outside, looking spent and leaning against the door, his coat hanging from him*]
MAMA Where you been, son?
WALTER [*Breathing hard*] Made a call.
MAMA To who, son?

WALTER To The Man.

MAMA What man, baby?

WALTER The Man, Mama. Don't you know who The Man is?

RUTH Walter Lee?

WALTER *The Man.* Like the guys in the streets say—The Man. Captain Boss— Mistuh Charlie . . . Old Captain Please Mr. Bossman . . .

BENEATHA [*Suddenly*] Lindner!

WALTER That's right! That's good. I told him to come right over.

BENEATHA [*Fiercely, understanding*] For what? What do you want to see him for!

WALTER [*Looking at his sister*] We going to do business with him.

MAMA What you talking 'bout, son?

WALTER Talking 'bout life, Mama. You all always telling me to see life like it is. Well—I laid in there on my back today . . . and I figured it out. Life just like it is. Who gets and who don't get. [*He sits down with his coat on and laughs*] Mama, you know it's all divided up. Life is. Sure enough. Between the takers and the "tooken." [*He laughs*] I've figured it out finally. [*He looks around at them*] Yeah. Some of us always getting "tooken." [*He laughs*] People like Willy Harris, they don't never get "tooken." And you know why the rest of us do? 'Cause we all mixed up. Mixed up bad. We get to looking 'round for the right and the wrong; and we worry about it and cry about it and stay up nights trying to figure out 'bout the wrong and the right of things all the time . . . And all the time, man, them takers is out there operating, just taking and taking. Willy Harris? Shoot—Willy Harris don't even count. He don't even count in the big scheme of things. But I'll say one thing for old Willy Harris . . . he's taught me something. He's taught me to keep my eye on what counts in this world. Yeah—[*Shouting out a little*] Thanks, Willy!

RUTH What did you call that man for, Walter Lee?

WALTER Called him to tell him to come on over to the show. Gonna put on a show for the man. Just what he wants to see. You see, Mama, the man came here today and he told us that them people out there where you want us to move—well they so upset they willing to pay us not to move out there. [*He laughs again*] And—and oh, Mama—you would of been proud of the way me and Ruth and Bennie acted. We told him to get out . . . Lord have mercy! We told the man to get out. Oh, we was some proud folks this afternoon, yeah. [*He lights a cigarette*] We were still full of that old-time stuff . . .

RUTH [*Coming toward him slowly*] You talking 'bout taking them people's money to keep us from moving in that house?

WALTER I ain't just talking 'bout it, baby—I'm telling you that's what's going to happen.

BENEATHA Oh, God! Where is the bottom! Where is the real honest-to-God bottom so he can't go any farther!

WALTER See—that's the old stuff. You and that boy that was here today. You all want everybody to carry a flag and a spear and sing some marching songs, huh? You wanna spend your life looking into things and trying to find the right and the wrong part, huh? Yeah. You know what's going to happen to that boy someday—he'll find himself sitting in a dungeon, locked in forever—and the takers will have the key! Forget it, baby! There ain't no causes—there ain't nothing but taking in this world, and he who takes most is smartest—and it don't make a damn bit of difference *how*.

MAMA You making something inside me cry, son. Some awful pain inside me.

WALTER Don't cry, Mama. Understand. That white man is going to walk in that door able to write checks for more money than we ever had. It's important to him and I'm going to help him . . . I'm going to put on the show, Mama.

MAMA Son—I come from five generations of people who was slaves and sharecroppers—but ain't nobody in my family never let nobody pay 'em no money that was a way of telling us we wasn't fit to walk the earth. We ain't never been that poor. [*Raising her eyes and looking at him*] We ain't never been that dead inside.

BENEATHA Well—we are dead now. All the talk about dreams and sunlight that goes on in this house. All dead.

WALTER What's the matter with you all! I didn't make this world! It was give to me this way! Hell, yes, I want me some yachts someday! Yes, I want to hang some real pearls 'round my wife's neck. Ain't she supposed to wear no pearls? Somebody tell me—tell me, who decides which women is suppose to wear pearls in this world. I tell you I am a *man*—and I think my wife should wear some pearls in this world!

[*This last line hangs a good while and* WALTER *begins to move about the room. The word "Man" has penetrated his consciousness; he mumbles it to himself repeatedly between strange agitated pauses as he moves about*]

MAMA Baby, how you going to feel on the inside?

WALTER Fine! . . . Going to feel fine . . . a man . . .

MAMA You won't have nothing left then, Walter Lee

WALTER [*Coming to her*] I'm going to feel fine, Mama. I'm going to look that son-of-a-bitch in the eyes and say—[*He falters*]—and say, "All right, Mr. Lindner—[*He falters even more*]—that's your neighborhood out there. You got the right to keep it like you want. You got the right to have it like you want. Just write the check and—the house is yours." And, and I am going to say—[*His voice almost breaks*] And you—you people just put the money in my hand and you won't have to live next to this bunch of stinking niggers! . . . [*He straightens up and moves away from his mother, walking around the room*] Maybe—maybe I'll just get down on my black knees . . . [*He does so;* RUTH *and* BENNIE *and* MAMA *watch him in frozen horror*] Captain, Mistuh, Bossman. [*He starts crying*] A-hee-hee-hee! [*Wringing his hands in profoundly anguished imitation*] Yasssssuh! Great White Father, just gi' ussen de money, fo' God's sake, and we's ain't gwine come out deh and dirty up yo' white folks neighborhood . . .

[*He breaks down completely, then gets up and goes into the bedroom*]

BENEATHA That is not a man. That is nothing but a toothless rat.

MAMA Yes—death done come in this here house. [*She is nodding, slowly, reflectively*] Done come walking in my house. On the lips of my children. You what supposed to be my beginning again. You—what supposed to be my harvest. [*To* BENEATHA] You—you mourning your brother?

BENEATHA He's no brother of mine.

MAMA What you say?

BENEATHA I said that that individual in that room is no brother of mine.

MAMA That's what I thought you said. You feeling like you better than he is today? [BENEATHA *does not answer*] Yes? What you tell him a minute ago? That he wasn't a man? Yes? You give him up for me? You done wrote his epitaph too—like the rest of the world? Well, who give you the privilege?

BENEATHA Be on my side for once! You saw what he just did, Mama! You saw him—down on his knees. Wasn't it you who taught me—to despise any man who would do that. Do what he's going to do.

MAMA Yes—I taught you that. Me and your daddy. But I thought I taught you something else too . . . I thought I taught you to love him.

BENEATHA Love him? There is nothing left to love.

MAMA There is always something left to love. And if you ain't learned that, you ain't learned nothing. [*Looking at her*] Have you cried for that boy today? I don't mean for yourself and for the family 'cause we lost the money. I mean for him; what he been through and what it done to him. Child, when do you think is the time to love somebody the most; when they done good and made things easy for everybody? Well then, you ain't through learning—because that ain't the time at all. It's when he's at his lowest and can't believe in hisself 'cause the world done whipped him so. When you starts measuring somebody, measure him right, child,

measure him right. Make sure you done taken into account what hills and valleys he come through before he got to wherever he is.
[TRAVIS *bursts into the room at the end of the speech, leaving the door open*]
TRAVIS Grandmama—the moving men are downstairs! The truck just pulled up.
MAMA [*Turning and looking at him*] Are they, baby? They downstairs? [*She sighs and sits.* LINDNER *appears in the doorway. He peers in and knocks lightly, to gain attention, and comes in. All turn to look at him*]
LINDNER [*Hat and briefcase in hand*] Uh—hello . . . [RUTH *crosses mechanically to the bedroom door and opens it and lets it swing open freely and slowly as the lights come up on* WALTER *within, still in his coat, sitting at the far corner of the room. He looks up and out through the room to* LINDNER]
RUTH He's here.
[*A long minute passes and* WALTER *slowly gets up*]
LINDNER [*Coming to the table with efficiency, putting his briefcase on the table and starting to unfold papers and unscrew fountain pens*] Well, I certainly was glad to hear from you people. [WALTER *has begun the trek out of the room, slowly and awkwardly, rather like a small boy, passing the back of his sleeve across his mouth from time to time*] Life can really be so much simpler than people let it be most of the time. Well —with whom do I negotiate? You, Mrs. Younger, or your son here? [MAMA *sits with her hands folded on her lap and her eyes closed as* WALTER *advances.* TRAVIS *goes closer to* LINDNER *and looks at the papers curiously*] Just some official papers, sonny.
RUTH Travis, you go downstairs.
MAMA [*Opening her eyes and looking into* WALTER'S] No. Travis, you stay right here. And you make him understand what you doing, Walter Lee. You teach him good. Like Willy Harris taught you. You show where our five generations done come to. Go ahead, son—
WALTER [*Looks down into his boy's eyes.* TRAVIS *grins at him merrily and* WALTER *draws him beside him with his arm lightly around his shoulders*] Well, Mr. Lindner. [BENEATHA *turns away*] We called you— [*There is a profound, simple groping quality in his speech*]—because, well, me and my family [*He looks around and shifts from one foot to the other*] Well—we are very plain people . . .
LINDNER Yes—
WALTER I mean—I have worked as a chauffeur most of my life—and my wife here, she does domestic work in people's kitchens. So does my mother. I mean—we are plain people . . .

LINDNER Yes, Mr. Younger—
WALTER [*Really like a small boy, looking down at his shoes and then up at the man*] And—uh—well, my father, well, he was a laborer most of his life.
LINDNER [*Absolutely confused*] Uh, yes—
WALTER [*Looking down at his toes once again*] My father almost beat a man to death once because this man called him a bad name or something, you know what I mean?
LINDNER No, I'm afraid I don't.
WALTER [*Finally straightening up*] Well, what I mean is that we come from people who had a lot of pride. I mean—we are very proud people. And that's my sister over there and she's going to be a doctor—and we are very proud—
LINDNER Well—I am sure that is very nice, but—
WALTER [*Starting to cry and facing the man eye to eye*] What I am telling you is that we called you over here to tell you that we are very proud and that this is—this is my son, who makes the sixth generation of our family in this country, and that we have all thought about your offer and we have decided to move into our house because my father—my father—he earned it. [MAMA *has her eyes closed and is rocking back and forth as though she were in church, with her head nodding the amen yes*] We don't want to make no trouble for nobody or fight no causes—but we will try to be good neighbors. That's all we got to say. [*He looks the man absolutely in the eyes*] We don't want your money.
[*He turns and walks away from the man*]
LINDNER [*Looking around at all of them*] I take it then that you have decided to occupy.
BENEATHA That's what the man said.
LINDNER [*To* MAMA *in her reverie*] Then I would like to appeal to you, Mrs. Younger. You are older and wiser and understand things better I am sure . . .
MAMA [*Rising*] I am afraid you don't understand. My son said we was going to move and there ain't nothing left for me to say. [*Shaking her head with double meaning*] You know how these young folks is nowadays, mister. Can't do a thing with 'em. Good-bye.
LINDNER [*Folding up his materials*] Well—if you are that final about it . . . There is nothing left for me to say. [*He finishes. He is almost ignored by the family, who are concentrating on* WALTER LEE. *At the door* LINDNER *halts and looks around*] I sure hope you people know what you're doing.
[*He shakes his head and exits*]

RUTH [*Looking around and coming to life*] Well, for God's sake—if the moving men are here—LET'S GET THE HELL OUT OF HERE!

MAMA [*Into action*] Ain't it the truth. Look at all this here mess. Ruth, put Travis' good jacket on him . . . Walter Lee, fix your tie and tuck your shirt in, you look just like somebody's hoodlum. Lord have mercy, where is my plant? [*She flies to get it amid the general bustling of the family, who are deliberately trying to ignore the nobility of the past moment*] You all start on down . . . Travis child, don't go empty-handed . . . Ruth, where did I put that box with my skillets in it? I want to be in charge of it myself . . . I'm going to make us the biggest dinner we ever ate tonight . . . Beneatha, what's the matter with them stockings? Pull them things up, girl . . .

[*The family starts to file out as two moving men appear and begin to carry out the heavier pieces of furniture, bumping into the family as they move about*]

BENEATHA Mama, Asagai—asked me to marry him today and go to Africa—

MAMA [*In the middle of her getting-ready activity*] He did? You ain't old enough to marry nobody—[*Seeing the moving men lifting one of her chairs precariously*] Darling, that ain't no bale of cotton, please handle it so we can sit in it again. I had that chair twenty-five years . . .

[*The movers sigh with exasperation and go on with their work*]

BENEATHA [*Girlishly and unreasonably trying to pursue the conversation*] To go to Africa, Mama—be a doctor in Africa . . .

MAMA [*Distracted*] Yes, baby—

WALTER Africa! What he want you to go to Africa for?

BENEATHA To practice there . . .

WALTER Girl, if you don't get all them silly ideas out your head! You better marry yourself a man with some loot . . .

BENEATHA [*Angrily, precisely as in the first scene of the play*] What have you got to do with who I marry!

WALTER Plenty. Now I think George Murchison—

[*He and* BENEATHA *go out yelling at each other vigorously;* BENEATHA *is heard saying that she would not marry* GEORGE MURCHISON *if he were Adam and she were Eve, etc. The anger is loud and real till their voices diminish.* RUTH *stands at the door and turns to* MAMA *and smiles knowingly*]

MAMA [*Fixing her hat at last*] Yeah—they something all right, my children . . .

RUTH Yeah—they're something. Let's go, Lena.

MAMA [*Stalling, starting to look around at the house*] Yes—I'm coming. Ruth—

RUTH Yes?

MAMA [*Quietly, woman to woman*] He finally come into his manhood today, didn't he? Kind of like a rainbow after the rain . . .

RUTH [*Biting her lip lest her own pride explode in front of* MAMA] Yes, Lena.

[WALTER'S *voice calls for them raucously*]

MAMA [*Waving* RUTH *out vaguely*] All right, honey—go on down. I be down directly.

[RUTH *hesitates, then exits.* MAMA *stands, at last alone in the living room, her plant on the table before her as the lights start to come down. She looks around at all the walls and ceilings and suddenly, despite herself, while the children call below, a great heaving thing rises in her and she puts her fist to her mouth, takes a final desperate look, pulls her coat about her, pats her hat and goes out. The lights dim down. The door opens and she comes back in, grabs her plant, and goes out for the last time*]

Curtain

EUGENE IONESCO

The Gap

Translated by Rosette Lamont

Cast of Characters

THE FRIEND
THE ACADEMICIAN
THE ACADEMICIAN'S WIFE
THE MAID

Scene: *A rich bourgeois living room with artistic pretensions. One or two sofas, a number of armchairs, among which, a green, Régence style one, right in the middle of the room. The walls are covered with framed diplomas. One can make out, written in heavy script at the top of a particularly large one, "Doctor Honoris causa." This is followed by an almost illegible Latin inscription. Another equally impressive diploma states: "Doctorat honoris causa," again followed by a long, illegible text. There is an abundance of smaller diplomas, each of which bears a clearly written "doctorate."*
A door to the right of the audience.
As the curtain rises, one can see the academician's wife dressed in a rather crumpled robe. She has obviously just gotten out of bed, and has not had time to dress. The friend faces her. He is well dressed: hat, umbrella in hand, stiff collar, black jacket and striped trousers, shiny black shoes.

THE WIFE Dear friend, tell me all.
THE FRIEND I don't know what to say.
THE WIFE I know.
THE FRIEND I heard the news last night. I did not want to call you. At the same time I couldn't wait any longer. Please forgive me for coming 'so early with such terrible news.
THE WIFE He didn't make it! How terrible! We were still hoping. . . .
THE FRIEND It's hard, I know. He still had a chance. Not much of one. We had to expect it.
THE WIFE I didn't expect it. He was always so successful. He could always manage somehow, at the last moment.
THE FRIEND In that state of exhaustion. You shouldn't have let him!
THE WIFE What can we do, what can we do! . . . How awful!
THE FRIEND Come on, dear friend, be brave. That's life.

THE WIFE I feel faint: I'm going to faint. [*She falls in one of the armchairs*]
THE FRIEND [*holding her, gently slapping her cheeks and hands*]. I shouldn't have blurted it out like that. I'm sorry.
THE WIFE No, you were right to do so. I had to find out somehow or other.
THE FRIEND I should have prepared you, carefully.
THE WIFE I've got to be strong. I can't help thinking of him, the wretched man. I hope they won't put it in the papers. Can we count on the journalists' discretion?
THE FRIEND Close your door. Don't answer the telephone. It will still get around. You could go to the country. In a couple of months, when you are better, you'll come back, you'll go on with your life. People forget such things.
THE WIFE People won't forget so fast. That's all they were waiting for. Some friends will feel sorry, but the others, the others. . . . [THE ACADEMICIAN *comes in, fully dressed: uniform, chest covered with decorations, his sword on his side.*]
THE ACADEMICIAN Up so early, my dear? [*To* THE FRIEND] You've come early too. What's happening? Do you have the final results?
THE WIFE What a disgrace!
THE FRIEND You mustn't crush him like this, dear friend. [*To* THE ACADEMICIAN] You have failed.
THE ACADEMICIAN Are you quite sure?
THE FRIEND You should never have tried to pass the baccalaureate examination.
THE ACADEMICIAN They failed me. The rats! How dare they do this to me!
THE FRIEND The marks were posted late in the evening.
THE ACADEMICIAN Perhaps it was difficult to make them out in the dark. How could you read them?
THE FRIEND They had set up spotlights.
THE ACADEMICIAN They're doing everything to ruin me.
THE FRIEND I passed by in the morning; the marks were still up.
THE ACADEMICIAN You could have bribed the concierge into pulling them down.
THE FRIEND That's exactly what I did. Unfortunately the police were there. Your name heads the list of those who failed. Everyone's standing in line to get a look. There's an awful crush.
THE ACADEMICIAN Who's there? The parents of the candidates?
THE FRIEND Not only they.
THE WIFE All your rivals, all your colleagues must be there. All those you

attacked in the press for ignorance: your undergraduates, your graduate students, all those who failed when you were chairman of the board of examiners.

THE ACADEMICIAN I am discredited! But I won't let them. There must be some mistake.

THE FRIEND I saw the examiners. I spoke with them. They gave me your marks. Zero in mathematics.

THE ACADEMICIAN I had no scientific training.

THE FRIEND Zero in Greek, zero in Latin.

THE WIFE [*to her husband*]. You, a humanist, the spokesman for humanism, the author of that famous treatise "The Defense of Poesy and Humanism."

THE ACADEMICIAN I beg your pardon, but my book concerns itself with twentieth century humanism [*To* THE FRIEND] What about composition? What grade did I get in composition?

THE FRIEND Nine hundred. You have nine hundred points.

THE ACADEMICIAN That's perfect. My average must be all the way up.

THE FRIEND Unfortunately not. They're marking on the basis of two thousand. The passing grade is one thousand.

THE ACADEMICIAN They must have changed the regulations.

THE WIFE They didn't change them just for you. You have a frightful persecution complex.

THE ACADEMICIAN I tell you they changed them.

THE FRIEND They went back to the old ones, back to the time of Napoleon.

THE ACADEMICIAN Utterly outmoded. Besides, when did they make those changes? It isn't legal. I'm chairman of the Baccalaureate Commission of the Ministry of Public Education. They didn't consult me, and they cannot make any changes without my approval. I'm going to expose them. I'm going to bring government charges against them.

THE WIFE Darling, you don't know what you're doing. You're in your dotage. Don't you recall handing in your resignation just before taking the examination so that no one could doubt the complete objectivity of the board of examiners?

THE ACADEMICIAN I'll take it back.

THE WIFE You should never have taken that test. I warned you. After all, it's not as if you needed it. But you have to collect all the honors, don't you? You're never satisfied. What did you need this diploma for? Now all is lost. You have your Doctorate, your Master's, your high school diploma, your elementary school certificate, and even the first part of the baccalaureate.

THE ACADEMICIAN There was a gap.

THE WIFE No one suspected it.
THE ACADEMICIAN But I knew it. Others might have found out. I went to the office of the Registrar and asked for a transcript of my record. They said to me: "Certainly Professor, Mr. President, Your Excellency. . . ." Then they looked up my file, and the Chief Registrar came back looking embarrassed, most embarrassed indeed. He said: "There's something peculiar, very peculiar. You have your Master's, certainly, but it's no longer valid." I asked him why, of course. He answered: "There's a gap behind your Master's. I don't know how it happened. You must have registered and been accepted at the University without having passed the second part of the baccalaureate examination."
THE FRIEND And then?
THE WIFE Your Master's degree is no longer valid?
THE ACADEMICIAN No, not quite. It's suspended. "The duplicate you are asking for will be delivered to you upon completion of the baccalaureate. Of course you will pass the examination with no trouble." That's what I was told, so you see now that I had to take it.
THE FRIEND Your husband, dear friend, wanted to fill the gap. He's a conscientious person.
THE WIFE It's clear you don't know him as I do. That's not it at all. He wants fame, honors. He never has enough. What does one diploma more or less matter? No one notices them anyway, but he sneaks in at night, on tiptoe, into the living room, just to look at them, and count them.
THE ACADEMICIAN What else can I do when I have insomnia?
THE FRIEND The questions asked at the baccalaureate are usually known in advance. You were admirably situated to get this particular information. You could also have sent in a replacement to take the test for you. One of your students, perhaps. Or if you wanted to take the test without people realizing that you already knew the questions, you could have sent your maid to the black market, where one can buy them.
THE ACADEMICIAN I don't understand how I could have failed in my composition. I filled three sheets of paper. I treated the subject fully, taking into account the historical background. I interpreted the situation accurately . . . at least plausibly I didn't deserve a bad grade.
THE FRIEND Do you recall the subject?
THE ACADEMICIAN Hum . . . let's see. . . .
THE FRIEND He doesn't even remember what he discussed.
THE ACADEMICIAN I do. . . wait . . . hum.
THE FRIEND The subject to be treated was the following: "Discuss the influence of Renaissance painters on novelists of the Third Republic." I

have here a photostatic copy of your examination paper. Here is what you wrote.

THE ACADEMICIAN [*grabbing the photostat and reading*]. "The trial of Benjamin. After Benjamin was tried and acquitted, the assessors holding a different opinion from that of the President murdered him, and condemned Benjamin to the suspension of his civic rights, imposing on him a fine of nine hundred francs. . . ."

THE FRIEND That's where the nine hundred points come from.

THE ACADEMICIAN "Benjamin appealed his case . . . Benjamin appealed his case. . . ." I can't make out the rest. I've always had bad handwriting. I ought to have taken a typewriter along with me.

THE WIFE Horrible handwriting, scribbling and crossing out; ink spots didn't help you much.

THE ACADEMICIAN [*goes on with his reading after having retrieved the text his wife had pulled out of his hand*]. "Benjamin appealed his case. Flanked by policemen dressed in zouave uniforms . . . in zouave uniforms. . . ." It's getting dark. I can't see the rest. . . . I don't have my glasses.

THE WIFE What you've written has nothing to do with the subject.

THE FRIEND Your wife's quite right, friend. It has nothing to do with the subject.

THE ACADEMICIAN Yes, it has. Indirectly.

THE FRIEND Not even indirectly.

THE ACADEMICIAN Perhaps I chose the second question.

THE FRIEND There was only one.

THE ACADEMICIAN Even if there was only that one, I treated another quite adequately. I went to the end of the story. I stressed the important points, explaining the motivations of the characters, highlighting their behavior. I explained the mystery, making it plain and clear. There was even a conclusion at the end. I can't make out the rest. [*To* THE FRIEND] Can you read it?

THE FRIEND It's illegible. I don't have my glasses either.

THE WIFE [*taking the text*] It's illegible and I have excellent eyes. You pretended to write. Mere scribbling.

THE ACADEMICIAN That's not true. I've even provided a conclusion. It's clearly marked here in heavy print: "Conclusion or sanction . . . Conclusion or sanction. . . ." They can't get away with it. I'll have this examination rendered null and void.

THE WIFE Since you treated the wrong subject, and treated it badly, setting down only titles, and writing nothing in between, the mark you received is justified. You'd lose your case.

THE FRIEND You'd most certainly lose. Drop it. Take a vacation.
THE ACADEMICIAN You're always on the side of the Others.
THE WIFE After all, these professors know what they're doing. They haven't been granted their rank for nothing. They passed examinations, received serious training. They know the rules of composition.
THE ACADEMICIAN Who was on the board of examiners?
THE FRIEND For Mathematics, a movie star. For Greek, one of the Beatles. For Latin, the champion of the automobile race, and many others.
THE ACADEMICIAN But these people aren't any more qualified than I am. And for composition?
THE FRIEND A woman, a secretary in the editorial division of the review *Yesterday, the Day Before Yesterday, and Today*.
THE ACADEMICIAN Now I know. This wretch gave me a poor grade out of spite because I never joined her political party. It's an act of vengeance. But I have ways and means of rendering the examination null and void. I'm going to call the President.
THE WIFE Don't! You'll make yourself look even more ridiculous. [*To* THE FRIEND] Please try to restrain him. He listens to you more than to me. [THE FRIEND *shrugs his shoulders, unable to cope with the situation.* THE WIFE *turns to her husband, who has just lifted the receiver off the hook.*] Don't call!
THE ACADEMICIAN [On the telephone] Hello, John? It is I . . . What? . . . What did you say? . . . But, listen, my dear friend . . . but, listen to me . . . Hello! Hello! [*Puts down the receiver.*]
THE FRIEND What did he say?
THE ACADEMICIAN He said . . . He said . . . , "I don't want to talk to you. My mummy won't let me make friends with boys at the bottom of the class." Then he hung up on me.
THE WIFE You should have expected it. All is lost. How could you do this to me? How could you do this to me?
THE ACADEMICIAN Think of it! I lectured at the Sorbonne, at Oxford, at American universities. Ten thousand theses have been written on my work; hundreds of critics have analyzed it. I hold an *honoris causa* doctorate from Amsterdam as well as a secret university Chair with the Duchy of Luxembourg. I received the Nobel Prize three times. The King of Sweden himself was amazed by my erudition. A doctorate *honoris causa, honoris causa* . . . and I failed the baccalaureate examination!
THE WIFE Everyone will laugh at us!
[THE ACADEMICIAN *takes off sword and breaks it on his knee.*]
THE FRIEND [*picking up the two pieces*]. I wish to preserve these in

memory of our ancient glory.

[THE ACADEMICIAN *meanwhile in a fit of rage is tearing down his decorations, throwing them on the floor, and stepping on them.*]

THE WIFE [*trying to salvage the remains*]. Don't do this! Don't! That's all we've got left.

[*Curtain.*]

POEMS

William Shakespeare
John Donne
George Herbert
Henry Vaughan
Robert Herrick
Andrew Marvell
John Milton
William Blake
William Wordsworth
John Keats
Walt Whitman
Alfred, Lord Tennyson
Matthew Arnold
Emily Dickinson
A. E. Housman
William Butler Yeats
Robert Frost
Wallace Stevens
William Carlos Williams
Marianne Moore
T. S. Eliot
John Crowe Ransom
E. E. Cummings
Allen Tate
Countee Cullen
W. H. Auden
Theodore Roethke
Robert Hayden
William Stafford
Dylan Thomas
Gwendolyn Brooks
Robert Lowell
Robert Bly
Sylvia Plath

Sonnets

XVIII

Shall I compare thee to a summer's day?
Thou art more lovely and more temperate:
Rough winds do shake the darling buds of May,
And summer's lease hath all too short a date:
Sometime too hot the eye of heaven shines,
And often is his gold complexion dimm'd;
And every fair from fair sometimes declines,
By chance, or nature's changing course, untrimm'd;
But thy eternal summer shall not fade
Nor lose possession of that fair thou ow'st,
Nor shall Death brag thou wand'rest in his shade
When in eternal lines[1] to time thou grow'st:
    So long as men can breathe or eyes can see,
    So long lives this, and this gives life to thee.

XXX

When to the sessions of sweet silent thought
I summon up remembrance of things past,
I sigh the lack of many a thing I sought
And with old woes new wail my dear time's waste;
Then can I drown an eye unus'd to flow,
For precious friends hid in death's dateless night,
And weep afresh love's long since cancell'd woe,
And moan th' expense of many a vanish'd sight;
Then can I grieve at grievances foregone,
And heavily from woe to woe tell o'er
The sad account of fore-bemoaned moan,
Which I new pay as if not paid before:
    But if the while I think on thee, dear friend,
    All losses are restor'd and sorrows end.

LXXIII

That time of year thou mayst in me behold
When yellow leaves, or none, or few, do hang
Upon those boughs which shake against the cold,
Bare ruin'd choirs, where late the sweet birds sang:

---

[1] *eternal lines:* these verses.

In me thou see'st the twilight of such day 5
As after sunset fadeth in the west;
Which by and by black night doth take away,
Death's second self,[2] that seals up all in rest:
In me thou see'st the glowing of such fire,
That on the ashes of his[3] youth doth lie, 10
As the death-bed whereon it must expire,
Consum'd with that which it was nourish'd by.
    This thou perceiv'st, which makes thy love more strong,
    To love that well which thou must leave ere long.

CXVI

Let me not to the marriage of true minds
Admit impediments. Love is not love
Which alters when it alteration finds,
Or bends with the remover[4] to remove:
O no! it is an ever fixed mark,[5] 5
That looks on tempests and is never shaken;
It is the star to every wandering bark,
Whose worth's unknown, although his height be taken.
Love's not Time's fool,[6] though rosy lips and cheeks
Within his bending sickle's compass come; 10
Love alters not with his brief hours and weeks,
But bears it out even to the edge of doom:
    If this be error and upon me proved,
    I never writ, nor no man ever loved.

---

[2] *Death's second self:* sleep.   [3] *his:* its.   [4] *bends with the remover:* changes with the plotting of another person.   [5] *mark:* beacon.   [6] *fool:* plaything.

Song

Go and catch a falling star,
   Get with child a mandrake[1] root,
Tell me where all past years are,
   Or who cleft the devil's foot,
Teach me to hear mermaids singing,
   Or to keep off envy's stinging,
       And find
       What wind
Serves to advance an honest mind.

If thou be'st born to strange sights,
   Things invisible to see,
Ride ten thousand days and nights,
   Till age snow white hairs on thee,
Thou, when thou return'st, wilt tell me
   All strange wonders that befell thee,
       And swear
       Nowhere
Lives a woman true, and fair.

If thou find'st one, let me know;
   Such a pilgrimage were sweet.
Yet do not; I would not go,
   Though at next door we might meet.
Though she were true when you met her,
   And last till you write your letter,
       Yet she
       Will be
False, ere I come, to two or three.

The Sun Rising

   Busy old fool, unruly sun,
      Why dost thou thus
Through windows and through curtains call on us?
Must to thy motions lovers' seasons run?
   Saucy pedantic wretch, go chide
   Late schoolboys and sour prentices,

---

[1] *mandrake*: an herb which, when eaten, supposedly promotes conception: its forked root resembles the human shape.

    Go tell court-huntsmen that the king will ride,
    Call country ants to harvest offices;
Love, all alike, no season knows, nor clime,
Nor hours, days, months, which are the rags of time.

    Thy beams, so reverend, and strong
        Why shouldst thou think?
I could eclipse and cloud them with a wink,
But that I would not lose her sight so long;
    If her eyes have not blinded thine,
        Look, and tomorrow late tell me
Whether both the Indias of spice and mine[2]
Be where thou left'st them, or lie here with me.
Ask for those kings whom thou saw'st yesterday,
And thou shalt hear, all here in one bed lay.

    She is all states, and all princes I;
        Nothing else is.
Princes do but play us; compared to this,
All honor's mimic, all wealth alchemy.
    Thou, sun, art half as happy as we,
        In that the world's contracted thus;
    Thine age asks ease, and since thy duties be
    To warm the world, that's done in warming us.
Shine here to us, and thou art everywhere;
This bed thy center is, these walls thy sphere.

The Indifferent

I can love both fair and brown;
Her whom abundance melts, and her whom want betrays;
Her who loves loneness best, and her who masks and plays;
Her whom the country formed, and whom the town;
Her who believes, and her who tries;[3]
Her who still weeps with spongy eyes,
And her who is dry cork and never cries.
I can love her, and her, and you, and you;
I can love any, so she be not true.

Will no other vice content you?
Will it not serve your turn to do as did your mothers?

[2] *mine:* mines of precious stones.   [3] *tries:* tests.

Or have you all old vices spent, and now would find out others?
Or doth a fear that men are true torment you?
Oh, we are not; be not you so;
Let me, and do you, twenty know. 15
Rob me, but bind me not, and let me go.
Must I, who came to travail thorough[4] you,
Grow your fixed subject because you are true?

Venus heard me sigh this song,
And by love's sweetest part, variety, she swore 20
She heard not this till now, and that it should be so no more.
She went, examined, and returned ere long,
And said, "Alas! some two or three
Poor heretics in love there be,
Which think to 'stablish dangerous constancy. 25
But I have told them, 'Since you will be true,
You shall be true to them who are false to you.'"

The Canonization

For God's sake hold your tongue, and let me love;
   Or chide my palsy, or my gout,
My five grey hairs, or ruined fortune flout;
     With wealth your state, your mind with arts improve,
        Take you a course, get you a place, 5
        Observe his Honor, or his Grace,
Or the king's real, or his stamped[5] face
   Contemplate; what you will, approve,
   So you will let me love.

Alas, alas, who's injured by my love? 10
   What merchant's ships have my sighs drowned?
Who says my tears have overflowed his ground?
     When did my colds a forward spring remove?[6]
        When did the heats which my veins fill
        Add one more to the plaguy bill?[7] 15
Soldiers find wars, and lawyers find out still
   Litigious men, which quarrels move,
   Though she and I do love.

Call us what you will, we are made such by love;
   Call her one, me another fly, 20

---

[4] *thorough*: through. [5] *stamped*: on coins. [6] *colds . . . remove*: chills delay spring. [7] *plaguy bill*: weekly list of plague victims.

We're tapers too, and at our own cost die,
    And we in us find the eagle and the dove.[8]
        The phoenix[9] riddle hath more wit
        By us; we two being one, are it.
So, to one neutral thing both sexes fit.
    We die and rise the same, and prove
    Mysterious by this love.

We can die by it, if not live by love,
    And if unfit for tombs and hearse
Our legend be, it will be fit for verse;
    And if no piece of chronicle we prove,
        We'll build in sonnets pretty rooms;
        As well a well-wrought urn becomes
The greatest ashes, as half-acre tombs,
    And by these hymns all shall approve
    Us canonized for love,

And thus invoke us: "You whom reverend love
    Made one another's hermitage;
You, to whom love was peace, that now is rage;
    Who did the whole world's soul contract, and drove
        Into the glasses of your eyes
        (So made such mirrors, and such spies,
That they did all to you epitomize)
    Countries, towns, courts; beg from above
    A pattern of your love!"

The Flea

Mark but this flea, and mark in this
How little that which thou deny'st me is;
It sucked me first, and now sucks thee,
And in this flea our two bloods mingled be;
Thou know'st that this cannot be said
A sin, nor shame, nor loss of maidenhead;
    Yet this enjoys before it woo,
    And pampered swells with one blood made of two,
    And this, alas, is more than we would do.

Oh stay, three lives in one flea spare,
Where we almost, yea, more than married are.

---

[8] *eagle ... dove*: wisdom and gentleness.   [9] *phoenix*: legendary bird consumed by fire and resurrected from its own ashes.

This flea is you and I, and this
Our marriage bed and marriage temple is;
Though parents grudge, and you, we're met,
And cloistered in these living walls of jet.
   Though use make you apt to kill me,
   Let not to that, self-murder added be,
   And sacrilege: three sins in killing three.

Cruel and sudden, hast thou since
Purpled thy nail in blood of innocence?
Wherein could this flea guilty be,
Except in that drop which it sucked from thee?
Yet thou triumph'st and say'st that thou
Find'st not thyself nor me the weaker now;
   'Tis true. Then learn how false fears be:
   Just so much honor, when thou yield'st to me,
   Will waste, as this flea's death took life from thee.

The Ecstasy

Where, like a pillow on a bed,
   A pregnant bank swelled up to rest
The violet's reclining head,
   Sat we two, one another's best.
Our hands were firmly cemented
   With a fast balm, which thence did spring;
Our eye-beams twisted, and did thread
   Our eyes upon one double string.
So to intergraft our hands, as yet
   Was all the means to make us one;
And pictures in our eyes to get
   Was all our propagation.
As, 'twixt two equal armies, fate
   Suspends uncertain victory,
Our souls, which to advance their state
   Were gone out, hung 'twixt her and me.
And whilst our souls negotiate there,
   We like sepulchral statues[10] lay;
All day the same our postures were,
   And we said nothing, all the day.
If any, so by love refined
   That he soul's language understood,

---

[10] *sepulchral statues*: sculptured figures decorating burial vaults.

And by good love were grown all mind,[11]
    Within convenient distance stood,
He, though he knew not which soul spake,
    Because both meant, both spake, the same,
Might thence a new concoction take,
    And part far purer than he came.[12]
This ecstasy doth unperplex
    (We said) and tell us what we love;
We see by this it was not sex;
    We see, we saw not what did move,
But as all several souls contain
    Mixture of things, they know not what,
Love these mixed souls doth mix again
    And makes both one, each this and that.
A single violet transplant,
    The strength, the color, and the size,
All which before was poor and scant,
    Redoubles still and multiplies.
When love with one another so
    Interinanimates two souls,
That abler soul, which thence doth flow,
    Defects of loneliness controls.
We then, who are this new soul, know
    Of what we are composed and made,
For the atomies[13] of which we grow
    Are souls, whom no change can invade.
But, O alas! so long, so far,
    Our bodies why do we forbear?
They are ours, though they are not we; we are
    The intelligences,[14] they the sphere.
We owe them thanks, because they thus
    Did us, to us, at first convey,
Yielded their forces, sense, to us,
    Nor are dross to us, but allay.[15]
On man heaven's influence works not so,
    But that it first imprints the air;
So soul into the soul may flow,
    Though it to body first repair.[16]

---

[11] *If ... mind*: the Platonist whose devotion to the ideal ("all mind") excludes sensuous love. [12] *concoction ... came*: the Platonic lover should, paradoxically, experience a better love than one which is "all mind." [13] *atomies*: atoms. [14] *intelligences*: in medieval teaching the heavenly bodies were moved by angels or intelligences. [15] *allay*: alloy. [16] *So ... repair*: the body is the medium through which souls of lovers unite.

As our blood labors to beget
   Spirits as like souls as it can,
Because such fingers need to knit
   That subtle knot which makes us man,
So must pure lovers' souls descend   65
   To affections, and to faculties,
Which sense may reach and apprehend;
   Else a great prince in prison lies.[17]
To our bodies turn we then, that so
   Weak men on love revealed may look;   70
Love's mysteries in souls do grow,
   But yet the body is his book.
And if some lover, such as we,
   Have heard this dialogue of one,
Let him still mark us; he shall see   75
   Small change when we are to bodies gone.

Love's Deity

I long to talk with some old lover's ghost,
   Who died before the god of love was born.
I cannot think that he, who then loved most,
   Sunk so low as to love one which did scorn.
But since this god produced a destiny,   5
And that vice-nature, custom, lets it be,
   I must love her that loves not me.

Sure, they which made him god meant not so much,
   Nor he in his young godhead practiced it;
But when an even flame two hearts did touch,   10
   His office was indulgently to fit
Actives to passives.[18] Correspondency
Only his subject was, it cannot be
   Love till I love her that loves me.

But every modern god will now extend   15
   His vast prerogative as far as Jove.

---

[17] *So . . . lies*: lovers' souls must "descend" to senses (union of bodies) to perfect the love relation. Otherwise, love ("a great prince") remains locked up.
[18] *Actives to passives*: lovers capable of acting; objects capable of receiving the effects of the action. This relationship is one of "correspondency."

To rage, to lust, to write to, to commend,
  All is the purlieu[19] of the god of love.
Oh, were we wakened by this tyranny
To ungod this child again, it could not be   20
  I should love her who loves not me.

Rebel and atheist too, why murmur I,
  As though I felt the worst that love could do?
Love might make me leave loving, or might try
  A deeper plague, to make her love me too;   25
Which, since she loves before, I am loth to see.
Falsehood is worse than hate; and that must be
  If she whom I love should love me.

The Funeral

Whoever comes to shroud me, do not harm
  Nor question much
That subtle wreath of hair which crowns my arm;
The mystery, the sign you must not touch,
  For 'tis my outward soul,   5
Viceroy to that, which, then to heaven being gone,
  Will leave this to control,
And keep these limbs, her provinces, from dissolution.

For if the sinewy thread[20] my brain lets fall
  Through every part   10
Can tie those parts, and make me one of all,
These hairs which upward grew, and strength and art
  Have from a better brain,
Can better do it; except she meant that I
  By this should know my pain,   15
As prisoners then are manacled, when they're condemned to die.

Whate'er she meant by it, bury it with me,
  For since I am
Love's martyr, it might breed idolatry
If into other hands these relics came;   20
  As 'twas humility
To afford to it all that a soul can do,
  So, 'tis some bravery,
That since you would have none of me, I bury some of you.

[19] *purlieu:* domain. [20] *sinewy thread:* spinal cord.

Holy Sonnets

V

I am a little world made cunningly
Of elements, and an angelic sprite;[21]
But black sin hath betrayed to endless night
My world's both parts, and, oh, both parts must die.
You which beyond that heaven which was most high
Have found new spheres, and of new lands can write,
Pour new seas in mine eyes, that so I might
Drown my world with my weeping earnestly,
Or wash it if it must be drowned no more:[22]
But oh it must be burnt![23] Alas, the fire
Of lust and envy have burnt it heretofore,
And made it fouler; let their flames retire,
And burn me, O Lord, with a fiery zeal
Of Thee and Thy house, which doth in eating heal.

VII

At the round earth's imagined corners blow
Your trumpets, angels, and arise, arise
From death, you numberless infinities
Of souls, and to your scattered bodies go;
All whom the flood did, and fire shall o'erthrow;
All whom war, dearth, age, agues, tyrannies,
Despair, law, chance, hath slain, and you whose eyes
Shall behold God, and never taste death's woe.
But let them sleep, Lord, and me mourn a space,
For, if above all these, my sins abound,
'Tis late to ask abundance of Thy grace,
When we are there; here on this lowly ground,
Teach me how to repent; for that's as good
As if Thou hadst sealed my pardon, with Thy blood.

X

Death, be not proud, though some have callèd thee
Mighty and dreadful, for thou art not so;

---

[21] *sprite:* spirit. [22] *if . . . more:* the Divine promise (Genesis 9:11) that the earth will not again be destroyed by flood. [23] *But . . . burnt:* the Day of Judgment (II Peter 3:5–7).

For those whom thou think'st thou dost overthrow
Die not, poor Death, nor yet canst thou kill me.
From rest and sleep, which but thy pictures be,
Much pleasure, then from thee much more must flow,
And soonest our best men with thee do go,
Rest of their bones and souls' delivery.
Thou art slave to fate, chance, kings, and desperate men,
And dost with poison, war, and sickness dwell,
And poppy, or charms can make us sleep as well,
And better than thy stroke; why swell'st thou then?
One short sleep past, we wake eternally,
And Death shall be no more; Death, thou shalt die.

XIV

Batter my heart, three-personed God; for You
As yet but knock, breathe, shine, and seek to mend;
That I may rise, and stand, o'erthrow me, and bend
Your force, to break, blow, burn, and make me new.
I, like an usurped town to another due,
Labor to admit You, but oh! to no end;
Reason, Your viceroy in me, me should defend,
But is captived and proves weak or untrue.
Yet dearly I love You, and would be lovèd fain,
But am betrothed unto Your enemy.
Divorce me, untie, or break that knot again,
Take me to You, imprison me, for I
Except You enthrall me, never shall be free;
Nor ever chaste, except You ravish me.

The Pulley[1]

    When God at first made man,
Having a glass of blessings standing by,
"Let us," said He, "pour on him all we can.
Let the world's riches, which dispersèd lie,
    Contract into a span."

    So strength first made a way;
Then beauty flowed, then wisdom, honor, pleasure.
When almost all was out, God made a stay,
Perceiving that, alone of all His treasure,
    Rest in the bottom lay.

    "For if I should," said He,
"Bestow this jewel also on My creature,
He would adore My gifts instead of Me
And rest in nature, not the God of nature;
    So both should losers be.

    "Yet let him keep the rest,
But keep them with repining restlessness.
Let him be rich and weary, that at last,
If goodness lead him not, yet weariness
    May toss him to My breast."

---

[1] Emblem of restlessness.

The Altar[2]

A broken altar, Lord, Thy servant rears,
Made of a heart and cemented with tears;
   Whose parts are as Thy hand did frame;
   No workman's tool hath touched the same.
        A heart alone
        Is such a stone
        As nothing but
        Thy power doth cut
        Wherefore each part
        Of my hard heart
        Meets in this frame
        To praise thy name
   That if I chance to hold my peace,
   These stones to praise Thee may not cease.
Oh, let Thy blessed sacrifice be mine,
And sanctify this altar to be Thine.

Easter Wings

Lord, who createdst man in wealth and store,[3]
  Though foolishly he lost the same,
    Decaying more and more
      Till he became
        Most poor:
      With Thee
    O let me rise
  As larks, harmoniously,
And sing this day Thy victories:
Then shall the fall further the flight in me.

My tender age in sorrow did begin:
And still with sicknesses and shame
  Thou didst so punish sin
    That I became
      Most thin.
    With thee
  Let me combine,
And feel this day Thy victory;
For, if I imp[4] my wing on Thine
Affliction shall advance the flight in me.

[2] Pictorial poems were common in the seventeenth century.   [3] *store:* abundance.   [4] *imp:* graft.

The World

I saw eternity the other night
Like a great ring[1] of pure and endless light,
   All calm as it was bright;
And round beneath it, time, in hours, days, years,
   Driven by the spheres,   5
Like a vast shadow moved, in which the world
   And all her train were hurled.
The doting lover in his quaintest strain
   Did there complain;
Near him, his lute, his fancy, and his flights,   10
   Wit's sour delights,
With gloves and knots,[2] the silly snares of pleasure,
   Yet his dear treasure,
All scattered lay, while he his eyes did pour
   Upon a flower.   15

The darksome statesman, hung with weights and woe,
Like a thick midnight fog, moved there so slow
   He did not stay nor go;
Condemning thoughts, like mad eclipses, scowl
   Upon his soul,   20
And crowds of crying witnesses without
   Pursued him with one shout.
Yet digged the mole, and lest his ways be found,
   Worked under ground,
Where he did clutch his prey. But one did see   25
   That policy:
Churches and altars fed him; perjuries
   Were gnats and flies;[3]
It rained about him blood and tears; but he
   Drank them as free.[4]   30

The fearful miser on a heap of rust
Sat pining all his life there, did scarce trust
   His own hands with the dust;
Yet would not place one piece[5] above, but lives
   In fear of thieves.   35
Thousands there were as frantic as himself,
   And hugged each one his pelf:

---

[1] *ring: primum mobile* or utmost sphere in Ptolemaic cosmology.   [2] *knots:* love knots.   [3] *gnats and flies:* i.e., of little importance.   [4] *free:* freely.   [5] *piece:* coin.

The downright epicure placed heaven in sense,
   And scorned pretense;
While others, slipped into a wide excess,   40
   Said little less;
The weaker sort, slight trivial wares enslave,
   Who think them brave;[6]
And poor, despisèd Truth sat counting by[7]
   Their victory.   45

Yet some, who all this while did weep and sing,
And sing and weep, soared up into the ring;
   But most would use no wing.
"O fools!" said I, "thus to prefer dark night
   Before true light!   50
To live in grots and caves, and hate the day
   Because it shows the way,
The way which from this dead and dark abode
   Leads up to God;
A way where you might tread the sun and be   55
   More bright than he!"
But, as I did their madness so discuss,
   One whispered thus:
"This ring the Bridegroom did for none provide,
   But for His bride."[8]

---

[6] *brave:* costly.   [7] *counting by:* observing.   [8] *Bridegroom ... bride:* see Revelation 21:9.

Delight in Disorder

A sweet disorder in the dress
Kindles in clothes a wantonness.
A lawn[1] about the shoulders thrown
Into a fine distraction;
An erring lace, which here and there   5
Enthralls the crimson stomacher;[2]
A cuff neglectful, and thereby
Ribbons to flow confusedly;
A winning wave, deserving note,
In the tempestuous petticoat;   10
A careless shoe-string, in whose tie
I see a wild civility;
Do more bewitch me than when art
Is too precise in every part.

Corinna's Going A-Maying

Get up! get up for shame! the blooming morn
Upon her wings presents the god unshorn.[3]
    See how Aurora[4] throws her fair
    Fresh-quilted colors through the air:
    Get up, sweet slug-a-bed, and see   5
    The dew bespangling herb and tree.
Each flower has wept and bowed toward the east
Above an hour since, yet you not dressed;
    Nay, not so much as out of bed?
    When all the birds have matins[5] said,   10
    And sung their thankful hymns, 'tis sin,
    Nay, profanation to keep in,
When as a thousand virgins on this day
Spring, sooner than the lark, to fetch in May.

Rise and put on your foliage, and be seen   15
To come forth, like the springtime, fresh and green,
    And sweet as Flora.[6] Take no care
    For jewels for your gown or hair;

---

[1] *lawn:* shawl.   [2] *stomacher:* ornamental part worn in front of dress.
[3] *god unshorn:* Apollo, the sun god, often depicted with long, flowing hair.
[4] *Aurora:* goddess of the dawn.   [5] *matins:* morning prayers.   [6] *Flora:* flower goddess.

Fear not, the leaves will strew
  Gems in abundance upon you;   20
Besides, the childhood of the day has kept,
Against[7] you come, some orient pearls unwept;[8]
  Come and receive them while the light
  Hangs on the dew-locks of the night,
  And Titan[9] on the eastern hill   25
  Retires himself, or else stands still
Till you come forth. Wash, dress, be brief in praying:
Few beads[10] are best when once we go a-Maying.

Come, my Corinna, come; and, coming, mark
How each field turns a street, each street a park   30
  Made green and trimmed with trees; see how
  Devotion gives each house a bough
  Or branch: each porch, each door ere this,
  An ark, a tabernacle is,
Made up of white-thorn neatly interwove,   35
As if here were those cooler shades of love.
  Can such delights be in the street
  And open fields, and we not see't?
  Come, we'll abroad; and let's obey
  The proclamation made for May,   40
And sin no more, as we have done, by staying;
But, my Corinna, come, let's go a-Maying.

There's not a budding boy or girl this day
But is got up and gone to bring in May;
  A deal of youth, ere this, is come   45
  Back, and with white-thorn laden home.
  Some have dispatched their cakes and cream
  Before that we have left to dream;
And some have wept, and wooed, and plighted troth,
And chose their priests, ere we can cast off sloth. 50
  Many a green gown has been given,[11]
  Many a kiss, both odd and even;
  Many a glance, too, has been sent
  From out the eye, love's firmament;
Many a jest told of the keys betraying   55
This night, and locks picked; yet we're not a-Maying.

---

[7] *Against*: for the time when.   [8] *orient ... unwept*: dewdrops still on the grass.   [9] *Titan*: the sun god Helios representing the physical sun, not its spiritual manifestation represented by Apollo.   [10] *beads*: prayer beads, rosary.   [11] *Many ... given*: many a gown stained by the grass.

Come, let us go while we are in our prime,
And take the harmless folly of the time.
   We shall grow old apace, and die
   Before we know our liberty.
   Our life is short, and our days run
   As fast away as does the sun;
And, as a vapor or a drop of rain
Once lost, can ne'er be found again;
   So when or you or I are made
   A fable, song, or fleeting shade,
   All love, all liking, all delight
   Lies drowned with us in endless night.
Then while time serves, and we are but decaying,
Come, my Corinna, come, let's go a-Maying.

To His Coy Mistress

    Had we but world enough, and time,
This coyness, Lady, were no crime.
We would sit down, and think which way
To walk, and pass our long love's day.
Thou by the Indian Ganges' side
Shouldst rubies find; I by the tide
Of Humber[1] would complain. I would
Love you ten years before the Flood,
And you should, if you please, refuse
Till the conversion of the Jews.
My vegetable[2] love should grow
Vaster than empires and more slow;
An hundred years should go to praise
Thine eyes, and on thy forehead gaze;
Two hundred to adore each breast,
But thirty thousand to the rest;
An age at least to every part,
And the last age should show your heart.
For, Lady, you deserve this state,
Nor would I love at lower rate.
    But at my back I always hear
Time's wingèd chariot hurrying near;
And yonder all before us lie
Deserts of vast eternity.
Thy beauty shall no more be found,
Nor, in thy marble vault, shall sound
My echoing song; then worms shall try
That long-preserved virginity,
And your quaint honor turn to dust,
And into ashes all my lust:
The grave's a fine and private place,
But none, I think, do there embrace.
    Now therefore, while the youthful hue
Sits on thy skin like morning lew,[3]
And while thy willing soul transpires[4]
At every pore with instant fires,
Now let us sport us while we may,
And now, like amorous birds of prey,
Rather at once our time devour
Than languish in his slow-chapped[5] power.

---

[1] *Humber:* river in England.   [2] *vegetable:* growing.
[3] *lew:* warmth.   [4] *transpires:* emerges.   [5] *chapped:* jawed.

Let us roll all our strength and all
Our sweetness up into one ball,
And tear our pleasures with rough strife
Through the iron gates of life;
Thus, though we cannot make our sun 45
Stand still, yet we will make him run.

JOHN MILTON

To the Nightingale

O Nightingale that on yon bloomy spray
   Warblest at eve, when all the woods are still,
   Thou with fresh hope the lover's heart dost fill,
   While the jolly hours[1] lead on propitious May.
Thy liquid notes that close the eye of day,   5
   First heard before the shallow cuckoo's bill,
   Portend success in love.[2] O, if Jove's will
   Have linked that amorous power to thy soft lay,
Now timely sing, ere the rude bird of hate[3]
   Foretell my hopeless doom, in some grove nigh   10
   As thou from year to year hast sung too late
For my relief, yet hadst no reason why.
   Whether the Muse or Love call thee his mate,
   Both them I serve, and of their train am I.

On His Having Arrived at the Age of Twenty-three

How soon hath Time, the subtle thief of youth,
   Stolen on his wing my three-and-twentieth year!
   My hasting days fly on with full career,
   But my late spring no bud or blossom shew'th.
Perhaps my semblance might deceive the truth[4]   5
   That I to manhood am arrived so near;
   And inward ripeness doth much less appear,
   That some more timely-happy spirits endu'th.[5]
Yet, be it less or more, or soon or slow,
   It shall be still in strictest measure even   10
   To that same lot, however means or high,
Toward which Time leads me, and the will of Heaven.
   All is, if I have grace to use it so,
   As ever in my great Task-Master's eye.

---

[1] *the jolly hours:* group of goddesses personifying times and seasons, especially those that are propitious.   [2] *Thy ... love:* hearing the nightingale in spring before the cuckoo supposedly foretells success in love.   [3] *rude ... hate:* the cuckoo as contrasted with the nightingale, the bird of tenderness and love.
[4] *my ... truth:* my youthful appearance might belie the fact.   [5] *endu'th:* endows.

On His Blindness[6]

When I consider how my light is spent[7]
   Ere half my days,[8] in this dark world and wide,
   And that one talent[9] which is death to hide
   Lodged with me useless, though my soul more bend
To serve therewith my Maker, and present 5
   My true account, lest he returning chide,
   "Doth God exact day-labour, light denied?"
   I fondly[10] ask. But Patience, to prevent
That murmur, soon replies, "God doth not need
   Either man's work or his own gifts. Who best 10
   Bear his mild yoke, they serve him best. His state
Is kingly: thousands[11] at his bidding speed,
   And post o'er land and ocean without rest;
   They also serve who only stand and wait."

---

[6] *On His Blindness:* in 1652, when he was 44, Milton went totally blind.
[7] *light ... spent:* eyesight is gone. [8] *Ere ... days:* before half the normal age of man. [9] *talent:* allusion to the parable in Matthew 25:14–30. [10] *fondly:* foolishly. [11] *thousands:* angels of God; divine messengers.

The Lamb

    Little Lamb, who made thee?
    Dost thou know who made thee?
Gave thee life and bid thee feed,
By the stream and o'er the mead;
Gave thee clothing of delight,   5
Softest clothing, wooly, bright;
Gave thee such a tender voice,
Making all the vales rejoice?
    Little Lamb, who made thee?
    Dost thou know who made thee?   10

    Little Lamb, I'll tell thee,
    Little Lamb, I'll tell thee:
He is callèd by thy name,
For he calls himself a Lamb.
He is meek, and he is mild;   15
He became a little child.
I a child, and thou a lamb,
We are called by his name.
    Little Lamb, God bless thee!
    Little Lamb, God bless thee!   20

The Sick Rose

O Rose, thou art sick!
The invisible worm,
That flies in the night
In the howling storm,
Has found out thy bed   5
Of crimson joy;
And his dark secret love
Does thy life destroy.

The Tiger

Tiger! Tiger! burning bright
In the forests of the night:
What immortal hand or eye,
Could frame thy fearful symmetry?

In what distant deeps or skies
Burnt the fire of thine eyes?
On what wings dare he aspire?
What the hand dare seize the fire?

And what shoulder, and what art,
Could twist the sinews of thy heart?
And when thy heart began to beat,
What dread hand? and what dread feet?

What the hammer? what the chain?
In what furnace was thy brain?
What the anvil? what dread grasp
Dare its deadly terrors clasp?

When the stars threw down their spears,
And watered heaven with their tears,[1]
Did he smile his work to see?
Did he who made the Lamb make thee?

Tiger! Tiger! burning bright
In the forests of the night:
What immortal hand or eye,
Dare frame thy fearful symmetry?

Ah Sun-Flower!

Ah Sun-flower! weary of time,
Who countest the steps of the sun;
Seeking after that sweet golden clime
Where the traveller's journey is done:

Where the youth pined away with desire,
And the pale virgin shrouded in snow,
Arise from their graves, and aspire[2]
Where my Sun-flower wishes to go.

---

[1] *When . . . tears:* defeat of rebel angels ("stars") which symbolize reason.
[2] *aspire:* soar.

London

I wander through each chartered[3] street,
Near where the chartered Thames does flow,
And mark in every face I meet
Marks of weakness, marks of woe.

In every cry of every man
In every infant's cry of fear,
In every voice, in every ban,[4]
The mind-forged manacles I hear.

How the chimney-sweeper's cry
Every black'ning church appalls;
And the hapless soldier's sigh
Runs in blood down palace walls.

But most through midnight streets I hear
How the youthful harlot's curse
Blasts[5] the new-born infant's tear,
And blights with plagues the marriage hearse.[6]

---

[3] *chartered*: mapped. [4] *ban*: curse. [5] *Blasts*: dries up. [6] *blights . . . hearse*: turns marriage bed into disease-ridden hearse.

Tintern Abbey[1]

Five years have past; five summers, with the length
Of five long winters! and again I hear
These waters, rolling from their mountain-springs
With a soft inland murmur.—Once again
Do I behold these steep and lofty cliffs,
That on a wild secluded scene impress
Thoughts of more deep seclusion; and connect
The landscape with the quiet of the sky.
The day is come when I again repose
Here, under this dark sycamore, and view
These plots of cottage-ground, these orchard-tufts,
Which at this season, with their unripe fruits,
Are clad in one green hue, and lose themselves
'Mid groves and copses. Once again I see
These hedge-rows, hardly hedge-rows, little lines
Of sportive wood run wild: these pastoral farms,
Green to the very door; and wreaths of smoke
Sent up, in silence, from among the trees!
With some uncertain notice, as might seem
Of vagrant dwellers in the houseless woods,
Or of some hermit's cave, where by his fire
The hermit sits alone.
                  These beauteous forms,
Through a long absence, have not been to me
As is a landscape to a blind man's eye:
But oft, in lonely rooms, and 'mid the din
Of towns and cities, I have owed to them
In hours of weariness, sensations sweet,
Felt in the blood, and felt along the heart;
And passing even into my purer mind,
With tranquil restoration:—feelings too
Of unremembered pleasure: such, perhaps,
As have no slight or trivial influence
On that best portion of a good man's life,
His little, nameless, unremembered acts
Of kindness and of love. Nor less, I trust,
To them I may have owed another gift,
Of aspect more sublime; that blessed mood,
In which the burthen of the mystery,
In which the heavy and the weary weight
Of all this unintelligible world,

[1] A beautiful ruin by the river Wye in southwest England.

Is lightened;—that serene and blessed mood,
In which the affections gently lead us on,—
Until, the breath of this corporeal frame
And even the motion of our human blood   45
Almost suspended, we are laid asleep
In body, and become a living soul:
While with an eye made quiet by the power
Of harmony, and the deep power of joy,
We see into the life of things.   50
                            If this
Be but a vain belief, yet, oh! how oft—
In darkness and amid the many shapes
Of joyless daylight; when the fretful stir
Unprofitable, and the fever of the world,   55
Have hung upon the beatings of my heart—
How oft, in spirit, have I turned to thee,
O sylvan Wye! thou wanderer thro' the woods,
How often has my spirit turned to thee!

    And now, with gleams of half-extinguished thought, 60
With many recognitions dim and faint,
And somewhat of a sad perplexity,
The picture of the mind revives again:
While here I stand, not only with the sense
Of present pleasure, but with pleasing thoughts   65
That in this moment there is life and food
For future years. And so I dare to hope,
Though changed, no doubt, from what I was when first
I came among these hills; when like a roe
I bounded o'er the mountains, by the sides   70
Of the deep rivers, and the lonely streams,
Wherever nature led: more like a man
Flying from something that he dreads, than one
Who sought the thing he loved. For nature then
(The coarser pleasures of my boyish days,   75
And their glad animal movements all gone by)
To me was all in all.—I cannot paint
What then I was. The sounding cataract
Haunted me like a passion: the tall rock,
The mountain, and the deep and gloomy wood,   80
Their colours and their forms, were then to me
An appetite; a feeling and a love,
That had no need of a remoter charm,
By thought supplied, nor any interest
Unborrowed from the eye.—That time is past,   85

And all its aching joys are now no more,
And all its dizzy raptures. Not for this
Faint I, nor mourn nor murmur; other gifts
Have followed; for such loss, I would believe,
Abundant recompense. For I have learned
To look on nature, not as in the hour
Of thoughtless youth; but hearing oftentimes
The still, sad music of humanity,
Nor harsh nor grating, though of ample power
To chasten and subdue. And I have felt
A presence that disturbs me with the joy
Of elevated thoughts; a sense sublime
Of something far more deeply interfused,
Whose dwelling is the light of setting suns,
And the round ocean and the living air,
And the blue sky, and in the mind of man:
A motion and a spirit, that impels
All thinking things, all objects of all thought,
And rolls through all things. Therefore am I still
A lover of the meadows and the woods,
And mountains; and of all that we behold
From this green earth; of all the mighty world
Of eye, and ear,—both what they half create,
And what perceive; well pleased to recognise
In nature and the language of the sense,
The anchor of my purest thoughts, the nurse,
The guide, the guardian of my heart, and soul
Of all my moral being.
                Nor perchance,
If I were not thus taught, should I the more
Suffer my genial spirits to decay:
For thou art with me here upon the banks
Of this fair river; thou my dearest friend,
My dear, dear friend; and in thy voice I catch
The language of my former heart, and read
My former pleasures in the shooting lights
Of thy wild eyes. Oh! yet a little while
May I behold in thee what I was once,
My dear, dear sister! and this prayer I make,
Knowing that Nature never did betray
The heart that loved her; 'tis her privilege,
Through all the years of this our life, to lead
From joy to joy: for she can so inform
The mind that is within us, so impress
With quietness and beauty, and so feed

With lofty thoughts, that neither evil tongues,
Rash judgments, nor the sneers of selfish men,
Nor greetings where no kindness is, nor all
The dreary intercourse of daily life,
Shall e'er prevail against us, or disturb   135
Our cheerful faith, that all which we behold
Is full of blessings. Therefore let the moon
Shine on thee in thy solitary walk;
And let the misty mountain-winds be free
To blow against thee: and, in after years,   140
When these wild ecstasies shall be matured
Into a sober pleasure; when thy mind
Shall be a mansion for all lovely forms,
Thy memory be as a dwelling-place
For all sweet sounds and harmonies; oh! then,   145
If solitude, or fear, or pain, or grief,
Should be thy portion, with what healing thoughts
Of tender joy wilt thou remember me,
And these my exhortations! Nor, perchance—
If I should be where I no more can hear   150
Thy voice, nor catch from thy wild eyes these gleams
Of past existence—wilt thou then forget
That on the banks of this delightful stream
We stood together; and that I, so long
A worshipper of Nature, hither came   155
Unwearied in that service: rather say
With warmer love—oh! with far deeper zeal
Of holier love. Nor wilt thou then forget,
That after many wanderings, many years
Of absence, these steep woods and lofty cliffs,   160
And this green pastoral landscape, were to me
More dear, both for themselves and for thy sake!

Composed upon Westminster Bridge, September 3, 1802

Earth has not anything to show more fair:
Dull would he be of soul who could pass by
A sight so touching in its majesty:
This City now doth, like a garment, wear
The beauty of the morning; silent, bare,   5
Ships, towers, domes, theatres, and temples lie
Open unto the fields, and to the sky;
All bright and glittering in the smokeless air.

Never did sun more beautifully steep
In his first splendour, valley, rock, or hill;
Ne'er saw I, never felt, a calm so deep!
The river glideth at his own sweet will:
Dear God! the very houses seem asleep;
And all that mighty heart is lying still!

It Is a Beauteous Evening, Calm and Free

It is a beauteous evening, calm and free,
The holy time is quiet as a Nun
Breathless with adoration; the broad sun
Is sinking down in its tranquillity;
The gentleness of heaven broods o'er the Sea:
Listen! the mighty Being is awake,
And doth with his eternal motion make
A sound like thunder—everlastingly.
Dear Child![2] dear Girl; that walkest with me here,[3]
If thou appear untouched by solemn thought,
Thy nature is not therefore less divine:
Thou liest in Abraham's bosom all the year;
And worship'st at the temple's inner shrine,
God being with thee when we know it not.

London, 1802

Milton! thou shouldst be living at this hour:
England hath need of thee: she is a fen
Of stagnant waters: altar, sword, and pen,
Fireside, the heroic wealth of hall and bower,
Have forfeited their ancient English dower
Of inward happiness. We are selfish men;
Oh! raise us up, return to us again;
And give us manners, virtue, freedom, power.
Thy soul was like a star, and dwelt apart;
Thou hadst a voice whose sound was like the sea:
Pure as the naked heavens, majestic, free,
So didst thou travel on life's common way,
In cheerful godliness; and yet thy heart
The lowliest duties on herself did lay.

[2] *Dear Child*: Wordsworth's daughter. [3] *here*: Calais Beach.

The World Is Too Much with Us; Late and Soon

The world is too much with us; late and soon,
Getting and spending, we lay waste our powers:
Little we see in Nature that is ours;
We have given our hearts away, a sordid boon!
This sea that bares her bosom to the moon; 5
The winds that will be howling at all hours,
And are up-gathered now like sleeping flowers;
For this, for everything, we are out of tune;
It moves us not.—Great God! I'd rather be
A Pagan suckled in a creed outworn; 10
So might I, standing on this pleasant lea,
Have glimpses that would make me less forlorn;
Have sight of Proteus rising from the sea;
Or hear old Triton blow his wreathèd horn.

On First Looking into Chapman's[1] Homer

Much have I travelled in the realms of gold,
And many goodly states and kingdoms seen;
Round many western islands have I been
Which bards in fealty to Apollo hold.
Oft of one wide expanse had I been told
That deep-browed Homer ruled as his demesne;[2]
Yet did I never breathe its pure serene
Till I heard Chapman speak out loud and bold:
Then felt I like some watcher of the skies
When a new planet swims into his ken;
Or like stout Cortez[3] when with eagle eyes
He stared at the Pacific—and all his men
Looked at each other with a wild surmise—
Silent, upon a peak in Darien.[4]

La Belle Dame Sans Merci

O what can ail thee, knight at arms,
   Alone and palely loitering?
The sedge has withered from the lake
   And no birds sing!

O what can ail thee, knight at arms,
   So haggard and so woe-begone?
The squirrel's granary is full,
   And the harvest's done.

I see a lily on thy brow,
   With anguish moist and fever dew;
And on thy cheeks a fading rose
   Fast withereth too.

I met a lady in the meads,
   Full beautiful, a faery's child;
Her hair was long, her foot was light
   And her eyes were wild.

I made a garland for her head,
   And bracelets, too, and fragrant zone;

---

[1] George Chapman, Elizabethan translator of Homer.   [2] *demesne:* domain.
[3] Balboa, not Cortez, discovered the Pacific in 1513.   [4] *Darien:* Panama.

She looked at me as she did love
   And made sweet moan.

I set her on my pacing steed,
   And nothing else saw, all day long;
For sidelong would she bend, and sing
   A faery's song.

She found me roots of relish sweet,
   And honey wild, and manna dew;
And sure in language strange she said,
   "I love thee true."

She took me to her elfin grot,
   And there she wept and sighed full sore;
And there I shut her wild, wild eyes
   With kisses four.

And there she lullèd me asleep
   And there I dreamed, Ah woe betide!
The latest dream I ever dreamt
   On the cold hill side.

I saw pale kings, and princes too
   Pale warriors, death pale were they all;
They cried, "La belle dame sans merci
   Thee hath in thrall!"

I saw their starved lips in the gloam
   With horrid warning gapèd wide,
And I awoke, and found me here
   On the cold hill's side.

And this is why I sojourn here
   Alone and palely loitering;
Though the sedge is withered from the lake
   And no birds sing.

Ode on Melancholy

No, no! go not to Lethe,[5] neither twist
   Wolf's-bane,[6] tight-rooted, for its poisonous wine;

---

[5] *Lethe:* river of forgetfulness.   [6] *Wolf's-bane:* a poisonous plant.

Nor suffer thy pale forehead to be kiss'd
  By nightshade,[7] ruby grape of Proserpine;
Make not your rosary of yew-berries,[8]
  Nor let the beetle,[9] nor the death-moth[10] be
    Your mournful Psyche,[11] nor the downy owl
A partner in your sorrow's mysteries;
  For shade to shade will come too drowsily,
    And drown the wakeful anguish of the soul.

But when the melancholy fit shall fall
  Sudden from heaven like a weeping cloud,
That fosters the droop-headed flowers all,
  And hides the green hill in an April shroud;
Then glut thy sorrow on a morning rose,
  Or on the rainbow of the salt sand-wave,
    Or on the wealth of globèd peonies;
Or if thy mistress some rich anger shows,
  Emprison her soft hand, and let her rave,
    And feed deep, deep upon her peerless eyes.

She dwells with Beauty—Beauty that must die;
  And Joy, whose hand is ever at his lips
Bidding adieu; and aching Pleasure nigh,
  Turning to poison while the bee-mouth sips:
Ay, in the very temple of Delight
  Veiled Melancholy has her sovran shrine,
    Though seen of none save him whose strenuous tongue
Can burst Joy's grape against his palate fine;
  His soul shall taste the sadness of her might,
    And be among her cloudy trophies hung.

Ode on a Grecian Urn

Thou still unravished bride of quietness,
  Thou foster-child of silence and slow time,
Sylvan historian, who canst thus express
  A flowery tale more sweetly than our rhyme:

---

[7] *nightshade:* a poisonous plant. [8] *yew:* a tree associated with mourning. [9] *beetle:* in Egypt, a symbol of resurrection. [10] *death-moth:* a moth whose markings resemble a human skull. [11] *Psyche:* soul, symbolized by the butterfly or moth.

What leaf-fringed legend haunts about thy shape
   Of deities or mortals, or of both,
     In Tempe or the dales of Arcady?
  What men or gods are these? What maidens loth?
What mad pursuit? What struggles to escape?
   What pipes and timbrels? What wild ecstasy?

Heard melodies are sweet, but those unheard
   Are sweeter; therefore, ye soft pipes, play on;
Not to the sensual ear, but, more endeared,
   Pipe to the spirit ditties of no tone:
Fair youth, beneath the trees, thou canst not leave
   Thy song, nor ever can those trees be bare;
     Bold Lover, never, never canst thou kiss,
Though winning near the goal—yet, do not grieve;
     She cannot fade, though thou hast not thy bliss,
For ever wilt thou love, and she be fair!

Ah, happy, happy boughs! that cannot shed
   Your leaves, nor ever bid the Spring adieu;
And, happy melodist, unwearièd,
   For ever piping songs for ever new;
More happy love! more happy, happy love!
   For ever warm and still to be enjoyed,
     For ever panting, and for ever young;
All breathing human passion far above,
     That leaves a heart high-sorrowful and cloyed,
       A burning forehead, and a parching tongue.

Who are these coming to the sacrifice?
   To what green altar, O mysterious priest,
Lead'st thou that heifer lowing at the skies,
   And all her silken flanks with garlands drest?
What little town by river or sea shore,
   Or mountain-built with peaceful citadel,
     Is emptied of this folk, this pious morn?
And, little town, thy streets for evermore
   Will silent be; and not a soul to tell
     Why thou art desolate, can e'er return.

O Attic[12] shape! Fair attitude! with brede[13]
   Of marble men and maidens overwrought,

---

[12] *Attic:* Attica, the Greek state (whose capital was Athens) in which Greece reached its purest artistic expression.   [13] *brede:* embroidery.

With forest branches and the trodden weed;
   Thou, silent form, dost tease us out of thought
As doth eternity: Cold Pastoral!
     When old age shall this generation waste,
       Thou shalt remain, in midst of other woe
Than ours, a friend to man, to whom thou say'st,
"Beauty is truth, truth beauty"—that is all
     Ye know on earth, and all ye need to know.

Ode to a Nightingale

My heart aches, and a drowsy numbness pains
   My sense, as though of hemlock[14] I had drunk,
Or emptied some dull opiate to the drains
   One minute past, and Lethe-wards[15] had sunk:
'Tis not through envy of thy happy lot,
   But being too happy in thine happiness,—
     That thou, light-wingèd Dryad of the trees,
       In some melodious plot
   Of beechen green, and shadows numberless,
     Singest of summer in full-throated ease.

O, for a draught of vintage! that hath been
   Cool'd a long age in the deep-delvèd earth,
Tasting of Flora and the country green,
   Dance, and Provençal song, and sunburnt mirth!
O for a beaker full of the warm South,
   Full of the true, the blushful Hippocrene,[16]
     With beaded bubbles winking at the brim,
       And purple-stainèd mouth;
   That I might drink, and leave the world unseen,
     And with thee fade away into the forest dim:

Fade far away, dissolve, and quite forget
   What thou among the leaves hast never known,
The weariness, the fever, and the fret
   Here, where men sit and hear each other groan;
Where palsy shakes a few, sad, last gray hairs,
   Where youth grows pale, and spectre-thin, and dies;

---

[14] *hemlock:* poison.   [15] *Lethe:* river of forgetfulness.   [16] *Hippocrene:* a fountain on Mt. Helicon in Greece; its waters inspired poets.

>   Where but to think is to be full of sorrow
>   And leaden-eyed despairs,
>   Where Beauty cannot keep her lustrous eyes,
>   Or new Love pine at them beyond tomorrow.   30
>
> Away! away! for I will fly to thee,
>   Not charioted by Bacchus and his pards,[17]
> But on the viewless wings of Poesy,
>   Though the dull brain perplexes and retards:
> Already with thee! tender is the night,   35
>   And haply the Queen-Moon is on her throne,
>   Clustered around by all her starry fays;
>   But here there is no light,
>   Save what from heaven is with the breezes blown
>   Through verdurous glooms and winding mossy ways.   40
>
> I cannot see what flowers are at my feet,
>   Nor what soft incense hangs upon the boughs,
> But, in embalmèd[18] darkness, guess each sweet
>   Wherewith the seasonable month endows
> The grass, the thicket, and the fruit-tree wild;   45
>   White hawthorn, and the pastoral eglantine;
>   Fast fading violets covered up in leaves;
>   And mid-May's eldest child,
>   The coming musk-rose, full of dewy wine,
>   The murmurous haunt of flies on summer eves.   50
>
> Darkling I listen; and for many a time
>   I have been half in love with easeful Death,
> Called him soft names in many a musèd rhyme,
>   To take into the air my quiet breath;
> Now more than ever seems it rich to die,   55
>   To cease upon the midnight with no pain,
>   While thou art pouring forth thy soul abroad
>   In such an ecstasy!
>   Still wouldst thou sing, and I have ears in vain—
>   To thy high requiem become a sod.   60
>
> Thou wast not born for death, immortal Bird!
>   No hungry generations tread thee down;
> The voice I hear this passing night was heard
>   In ancient days by emperor and clown:
> Perhaps the self-same song that found a path   65

[17] *pards*: leopards.   [18] *embalmèd*: balmy, sweet-smelling.

Through the sad heart of Ruth,[19] when, sick for home,
   She stood in tears amid the alien corn;
     The same that oft-times hath
Charmed magic casements, opening on the foam
   Of perilous seas, in faery lands forlorn.   70

Forlorn! the very word is like a bell
   To toll me back from thee to my sole self!
Adieu! the fancy cannot cheat so well
   As she is famed to do, deceiving elf.
Adieu! adieu! thy plaintive anthem fades   75
   Past the near meadows, over the still stream,
     Up the hill-side; and now 'tis buried deep
       In the next valley-glades:
   Was it a vision, or a waking dream?
     Fled is that music:—Do I wake or sleep?   80

To Autumn

Season of mists and mellow fruitfulness,
   Close bosom-friend of the maturing sun;
Conspiring with him how to load and bless
   With fruit the vines that round the thatch-eves run;
To bend with apples the mossed cottage-trees,   5
   And fill all fruit with ripeness to the core;
     To swell the gourd, and plump the hazel shells
With a sweet kernel; to set budding more,
   And still more, later flowers for the bees,
   Until they think warm days will never cease,   10
     For Summer has o'er-brimmed their clammy cells.

Who hath not seen thee oft amid thy store?
   Sometimes whoever seeks abroad may find
Thee sitting careless on a granary floor,
   Thy hair soft-lifted by the winnowing wind;   15
Or on a half-reaped furrow sound asleep,
   Drowsed with the fume of poppies, while thy hook
     Spares the next swath and all its twinèd flowers:
And sometimes like a gleaner thou dost keep
   Steady thy laden head across a brook;   20
   Or by a cider-press, with patient look,
     Thou watchest the last oozings hours by hours.

[19] See Ruth 2.

Where are the songs of Spring? Ay, where are they?
　　Think not of them, thou hast thy music too,—
While barrèd clouds bloom the soft-dying day,
　　And touch the stubble-plains with rosy hue;
Then in a wailful choir the small gnats mourn
　　　Among the river sallows,[20] borne aloft
　　　　Or sinking as the light wind lives or dies;
And full-grown lambs loud bleat from hilly bourn;[21]
　　Hedge-crickets sing; and now with treble soft
　　The red-breast whistles from a garden-croft;
　　　And gathering swallows twitter in the skies.

---

[20] *sallows:* willows.　　[21] *bourn:* boundary.

WALT WHITMAN

Out of the Cradle Endlessly Rocking

Out of the cradle endlessly rocking,
Out of the mocking-bird's throat, the musical shuttle,
Out of the Ninth-month[1] midnight,
Over the sterile sands and the fields beyond, where the child leaving his bed wander'd alone, bareheaded, barefoot,
Down from the shower'd halo,
Up from the mystic play of shadows twining and twisting as if they were alive,
Out from the patches of briers and blackberries,
From the memories of the bird that chanted to me,
From your memories sad brother, from the fitful risings and fallings I heard,
From under that yellow half-moon late-risen and swollen as if with tears,
From those beginning notes of yearning and love there in the mist,
From the thousand responses of my heart never to cease,
From the myriad thence-arous'd words,
From the word stronger and more delicious than any,
From such as now they start the scene revisiting,
As a flock, twittering, rising, or overhead passing,
Borne hither, ere all eludes me, hurriedly,
A man, yet by these tears a little boy again,
Throwing myself on the sand, confronting the waves,
I, chanter of pains and joys, uniter of here and hereafter,
Taking all hints to use them, but swiftly leaping beyond them,
A reminiscence sing.

Once Paumanok,[2]
When the lilac-scent was in the air and Fifth-month grass was growing,
Up this seashore in some briers,
Two feather'd guests from Alabama, two together,
And their nest, and four light-green eggs spotted with brown,
And every day the he-bird to and fro near at hand,
And every day the she-bird crouch'd on her nest, silent, with bright eyes,
And every day I, a curious boy, never too close, never disturbing them,
Cautiously peering, absorbing, translating.

---

[1] *Ninth-month:* September; also term of pregnancy.   [2] *Paumanok:* Indian name for Long Island.

Shine! shine! shine!
Pour down your warmth, great sun!
While we bask, we two together.

Two together!
Winds blow south, or winds blow nórth,
Day come white, or night come black,
Home, or rivers and mountains from home,
Singing all time, minding no time,
While we two keep together.

Till of a sudden,
May-be kill'd, unknown to her mate,
One forenoon the she-bird crouch'd not on the nest,
Nor return'd that afternoon, nor the next,
Nor ever appear'd again.

And thenceforward all summer in the sound of the sea,
And at night under the full of the moon in calmer weather,
Over the hoarse surging of the sea,
Or flitting from brier to brier by day,
I saw, I heard at intervals the remaining one, the he-bird,
The solitary guest from Alabama.

Blow! blow! blow!
Blow up sea-winds along Paumanok's shore;
I wait and I wait till you blow my mate to me.

Yes, when the stars glisten'd,
All night long on the prong of a moss-scallop'd stake,
Down almost amid the slapping waves,
Sat the lone singer wonderful causing tears.

He call'd on his mate,
He pour'd forth the meanings which I of all men know.

Yes my brother I know,
The rest might not, but I have treasur'd every note,
For more than once dimly down to the beach gliding,
Silent, avoiding the moonbeams, blending myself with the shadows,
Recalling now the obscure shapes, the echoes, the sounds and sights
    after their sorts,
The white arms out in the breakers tirelessly tossing,
I, with bare feet, a child, the wind wafting my hair,
Listen'd long and long.

Listen'd to keep, to sing, now translating the notes,
Following you my brother.

Soothe! soothe! soothe!
Close on its wave soothes the wave behind,
And again another behind embracing and lapping, every one close,
But my love soothes not me, not me.

Low hangs the moon, it rose late,
It is lagging—O I think it is heavy with love, with love.

O madly the sea pushes upon the land,
With love, with love.

O night! do I not see my love fluttering out among the breakers?
What is that little black thing I see there in the white?

Loud! loud! loud!
Loud I call to you, my love!

High and clear I shoot my voice over the waves,
Surely you must know who is here, is here,
You must know who I am, my love.

Low-hanging moon!
What is that dusky spot in your brown yellow?
O it is the shape, the shape of my mate!
O moon do not keep her from me any longer.

Land! land! O land!
Whichever way I turn, O I think you could give me my mate back
  again if you only would,
For I am almost sure I see her dimly whichever way I look.

O rising stars!
Perhaps the one I want so much will rise, will rise with some of you.

O throat! O trembling throat!
Sound clearer through the atmosphere!
Pierce the woods, the earth,
Somewhere listening to catch you must be the one I want.

Shake out carols!
Solitary here, the night's carols!
Carols of lonesome love! death's carols!

Carols under that lagging, yellow, waning moon!
O under that moon where she droops almost down into the sea!
O reckless despairing carols.

But soft! sink low! 105
Soft! let me just murmur,
And do you wait a moment you husky-nois'd sea,
For somewhere I believe I heard my mate responding to me,
So faint, I must be still, be still to listen,
But not altogether still, for then she might not come immediately
   to me. 110

Hither my love!
Here I am! here!
With this just-sustain'd note I announce myself to you,
This gentle call is for you my love, for you.

Do not be decoy'd elsewhere, 115
That is the whistle of the wind, it is not my voice,
That is the fluttering, the fluttering of the spray,
Those are the shadows of leaves.

O darkness! O in vain!
O I am very sick and sorrowful. 120

O brown halo in the sky near the moon, drooping upon the sea!
O troubled reflection in the sea!
O throat! O throbbing heart!
And I singing uselessly, uselessly all the night.

O past! O happy life! O songs of joy! 125
In the air, in the woods, over fields,
Loved! loved! loved! loved! loved!
But my mate no more, no more with me!
We two together no more.

The aria sinking, 130
All else continuing, the stars shining,
The winds blowing, the notes of the bird continuous echoing,
With angry moans the fierce old mother incessantly moaning,
On the sands of Paumanok's shore gray and rustling,
The yellow half-moon enlarged, sagging down, drooping, the
   face of the sea almost touching, 135
The boy ecstatic, with his bare feet the waves, with his hair the
   atmosphere dallying,

The love in the heart long pent, now loose, now at last
    tumultuously bursting,
The aria's meaning, the ears, the soul, swiftly depositing,
The strange tears down the cheeks coursing,
The colloquy there, the trio, each uttering, 140
The undertone, the savage old mother incessantly crying,
To the boy's soul's questions sullenly timing, some drown'd
    secret hissing,
To the outsetting bard.

Demon or bird! (said the boy's soul,)
Is it indeed toward your mate you sing? or is it really to me? 145
For I, that was a child, my tongue's use sleeping, now I have
    heard you,
Now in a moment I know what I am for, I awake,
And already a thousand singers, a thousand songs, clearer, louder
    and more sorrowful than yours,
A thousand warbling echoes have started to life within me,
    never to die.

O you singer solitary, singing by yourself, projecting me, 150
O solitary me listening, never more shall I cease perpetuating you,
Never more shall I escape, never more the reverberations,
Never more the cries of unsatisfied love be absent from me,
Never again leave me to be the peaceful child I was before what there
    in the night,
By the sea under the yellow and sagging moon, 155
The messenger there arous'd, the fire, the sweet hell within,
The unknown want, the destiny of me.
O give me the clew! (it lurks in the night here somewhere,)
O if I am to have so much, let me have more!

A word then, (for I will conquer it,) 160
The word final, superior to all,
Subtle, sent up—what is it?—I listen;
Are you whispering it, and have been all the time, you sea waves?
Is that it from your liquid rims and wet sands?

Whereto answering, the sea, 165
Delaying not, hurrying not,
Whisper'd me through the night, and very plainly before daybreak,
Lisp'd to me the low and delicious word death,
And again death, death, death, death,
Hissing melodious, neither like the bird nor like my arous'd child's
    heart, 170

But edging near as privately for me rustling at my feet,
Creeping thence steadily up to my ears and laving me softly all over,
Death, death, death, death, death.

Which I do not forget,
But fuse the song of my dusky demon and brother, 175
That he sang to me in the moonlight on Paumanok's gray beach,
With the thousand responsive songs at random,
My own songs awaked from that hour,
And with them the key, the word up from the waves,
The word of the sweetest song and all songs, 180
That strong and delicious word which, creeping to my feet,
(Or like some old crone rocking the cradle, swathed in sweet
  garments, bending aside,)
The sea whisper'd me.

A March in the Ranks Hard-Prest, and the Road Unknown

A march in the ranks hard-prest, and the road unknown,
A route through a heavy wood with muffled steps in the darkness,
Our army foil'd with loss severe, and the sullen remnant retreating,
Till after midnight glimmer upon us the lights of a dim-lighted
  building,
We come to an open space in the woods, and halt by the dim-lighted
  building, 5
'Tis a large old church at the crossing roads, now an impromptu
  hospital,
Entering but for a minute I see a sight beyond all the pictures and
  poems ever made,
Shadows of deepest, deepest black, just lit by moving candles and
  lamps,
And by one great pitchy torch stationary with wild red flame and
  clouds of smoke,
By these, crowds, groups of forms vaguely I see on the floor, some in
  the pews laid down, 10
At my feet more distinctly a soldier, a mere lad, in danger of bleeding
  to death, (he is shot in the abdomen,)
I stanch the blood temporarily, (the youngster's face is white as a lily,)
Then before I depart I sweep my eyes o'er the scene fain to absorb it all,
Faces, varieties, postures beyond description, most in obscurity, some
  of them dead,
Surgeons operating, attendants holding lights, the smell of ether, the
  odor of blood, 15

The crowd, O the crowd of the bloody forms, the yard outside also
   fill'd,
Some on the bare ground, some on planks or stretchers, some in the
   death-spasm sweating,
An occasional scream or cry, the doctor's shouted orders or calls,
The glisten of the little steel instruments catching the glint of the
   torches,
These I resume as I chant, I see again the forms, I smell the odor,   20
Then hear outside the orders given, *Fall in, my men, fall in;*
But first I bend to the dying lad, his eyes open, a half-smile gives he
   me,
Then the eyes close, calmly close, and I speed forth to the darkness,
Resuming, marching, ever in darkness marching, on in the ranks,
The unknown road still marching.   25

When Lilacs Last in the Dooryard Bloom'd

1

When lilacs last in the dooryard bloom'd,
And the great star early droop'd in the western sky in the night,
I mourn'd, and yet shall mourn with ever-returning spring.

Ever-returning spring, trinity sure to me you bring,
Lilac blooming perennial and drooping star in the west,   5
And thought of him[3] I love.

2

O powerful western star!
O shades of night—O moody, tearful night!
O great star disappear'd—O the black murk that hides the star!
O cruel hands that hold me powerless—O helpless soul of me!   10
O harsh surrounding cloud that will not free my soul.

3

In the dooryard fronting an old farm-house near the white-wash'd
   palings,
Stands the lilac-bush tall-growing with heart-shaped leaves of rich green,

---

[3] *him:* Abraham Lincoln.

With many a pointed blossom rising delicate, with the perfume strong I love,
With every leaf a miracle—and from this bush in the dooryard,   15
With delicate-color'd blossoms and heart-shaped leaves of rich green,
A sprig with its flower I break.

4

In the swamp in secluded recesses,
A shy and hidden bird is warbling a song.
Solitary the thrush,   20
The hermit withdrawn to himself, avoiding the settlements,
Sings by himself a song.

Song of the bleeding throat,
Death's outlet song of life, (for well dear brother I know,
If thou wast not granted to sing thou would'st surely die.)   25

5

Over the breast of the spring, the land, amid cities,
Amid lanes and through old woods, where lately the violets peep'd from the ground, spotting the gray debris,
Amid the grass in the fields each side of the lanes, passing the endless grass,
Passing the yellow-spear'd wheat, every grain from its shroud in the dark-brown fields uprisen,
Passing the apple-tree blows of white and pink in the orchards,   30
Carrying a corpse to where it shall rest in the grave,
Night and day journeys a coffin.

6

Coffin that passes through lanes and streets,
Through day and night with the great cloud darkening the land,
With the pomp of the inloop'd flags with the cities draped in black,   35
With the show of the States themselves as of crepe-veil'd women standing,
With processions long and winding and the flambeaus of the night,
With countless torches lit, with the silent sea of faces and the unbared heads,
With the waiting depot, the arriving coffin, and the sombre faces,
With dirges through the night, with the thousand voices rising strong and solemn,   40

With all the mournful voices of the dirges pour'd around the coffin,
The dim-lit churches and the shuddering organs—where amid these you
    journey,
With the tolling tolling bells' perpetual clang,
Here, coffin that slowly passes,
I give you my sprig of lilac.   45

7

(Nor for you, for one alone,
Blossoms and branches green to coffins all I bring,
For fresh as the morning, thus would I chant a song for you O sane
    and sacred death.

All over bouquets of roses,
O death, I cover you over with roses and early lilies,   50
But mostly and now the lilac that blooms the first,
Copious I break, I break the sprigs from the bushes,
With loaded arms I come, pouring for you,
For you and the coffins all of you O death.)

8

O western orb sailing the heaven,   55
Now I know what you must have meant as a month since I walk'd,
As I walk'd in silence the transparent shadowy night,
As I saw you had something to tell as you bent to me night after night,
As you droop'd from the sky low down as if to my side, (while the
    other stars all look'd on,)
As we wander'd together the solemn night, (for something I know not
    what kept me from sleep,)   60
As the night advanced, and I saw on the rim of the west how full you
    were of woe,
As I stood on the rising ground in the breeze in the cool transparent
    night,
As I watch'd where you pass'd and was lost in the netherward black
    of the night,
As my soul in its trouble dissatisfied sank, as where you sad orb,
Concluded, dropt in the night, and was gone.   65

9

Sing on there in the swamp,
O singer bashful and tender, I hear your notes, I hear your call,
I hear, I come presently, I understand you,

But a moment I linger, for the lustrous star has detain'd me,
The star my departing comrade holds and detains me. 70

10

O how shall I warble myself for the dead one there I loved?
And how shall I deck my song for the large sweet soul that has gone?
And what shall my perfume be for the grave of him I love?

Sea-winds blown from east and west,
Blown from the Eastern sea and blown from the Western sea, till there on the prairies meeting, 75
These and with these and the breath of my chant,
I'll perfume the grave of him I love.

11

O what shall I hang on the chamber walls?
And what shall the pictures be that I hang on the walls,
To adorn the burial-house of him I love? 80

Pictures of growing spring and farms and homes,
With the Fourth-month eve at sundown, and the gray smoke lucid and bright,
With floods of the yellow gold of the gorgeous, indolent, sinking sun, burning, expanding the air,
With the fresh sweet herbage under foot, and the pale green leaves of the trees prolific,
In the distance the flowering glaze, the breast of the river, with a wind-dapple here and there, 85
With ranging hills on the banks, with many a line against the sky, and shadows,
And the city at hand with dwellings so dense, and stacks of chimneys,
And all the scenes of life and the workshops, and the workmen homeward returning.

12

Lo, body and soul—this land,
My own Manhattan with spires, and the sparkling and hurrying tides, and the ships, 90
The varied and ample land, the South and the North in the light, Ohio's shores and flashing Missouri,
And ever the far-spreading prairies cover'd with grass and corn.

Lo, the most excellent sun so calm and haughty,
The violet and purple morn with just-felt breezes,
The gentle soft-born measureless light,
The miracle spreading bathing all, the fulfill'd noon,
The coming eve delicious, the welcome night and the stars,
Over my cities shining all, enveloping man and land.

13

Sing on, sing on you gray-brown bird,
Sing from the swamps, the recesses, pour your chant from the bushes,
Limitless out of the dusk, out of the cedars and pines.

Sing on dearest brother, warble your reedy song,
Loud human song, with voice of uttermost woe.

O liquid and free and tender!
O wild and loose to my soul—O wondrous singer!
You only I hear—yet the star holds me, (but will soon depart,)
Yet the lilac with mastering odor holds me.

14

Now while I sat in the day and look'd forth,
In the close of the day with its light and the fields of spring, and the farmers preparing their crops,
In the large unconscious scenery of my land with its lakes and forests,
In the heavenly aerial beauty, (after the perturb'd winds and the storms,)
Under the arching heavens of the afternoon swift passing, and the voices of children and women,
The many-moving sea-tides, and I saw the ships how they sail'd,
And the summer approaching with richness, and the fields all busy with labor,
And the infinite separate houses, how they all went on, each with its meals and minutia of daily usages,
And the streets how their throbbings throbb'd, and the cities pent—lo, then and there,
Falling upon them all and among them all, enveloping me with the rest,
Appear'd the cloud, appear'd the long black trail,
And I knew death, its thought, and the sacred knowledge of death.

Then with the knowledge of death as walking one side of me,
And the thought of death close-walking the other side of me,
And I in the middle as with companions, and as holding the hands of companions,
I fled forth to the hiding receiving night that talks not,
Down to the shores of the water, the path by the swamp in the dimness,   125
To the solemn shadowy cedars and ghostly pines so still.

And the singer so shy to the rest receiv'd me,
The gray-brown bird I know receiv'd us comrades three,
And he sang the carol of death, and a verse for him I love.

From deep secluded recesses,   130
From the fragrant cedars and the ghostly pines so still,
Came the carol of the bird.
And the charm of the carol rapt me,
As I held as if by their hands my comrades in the night,
And the voice of my spirit tallied the song of the bird.   135

Come lovely and soothing death,
Undulate round the world, serenely arriving, arriving,
In the day, in the night, to all, to each,
Sooner or later delicate death.

Prais'd be the fathomless universe,   140
For life and joy, and for objects and knowledge curious,
And for love, sweet love—but praise! praise! praise!
For the sure-enwinding arms of cool-enfolding death.

Dark mother always gliding near with soft feet,
Have none chanted for thee a chant of fullest welcome?   145
Then I chant it for thee, I glorify thee above all,
I bring thee a song that when thou must indeed come, come unfalteringly.

Approach strong deliveress,
When it is so, when thou hast taken them I joyously sing the dead,
Lost in the loving floating ocean of thee,   150
Laved in the flood of thy bliss O death.

From me to thee glad serenades,
Dances for thee I propose saluting thee, adornments and feastings for thee,
And the sights of the open landscape and the high-spread sky are fitting,
And life and the fields, and the huge and thoughtful night.   155

The night in silence under many a star,
The ocean shore and the husky whispering wave whose voice I know,
And the soul turning to thee O vast and well-veil'd death,
And the body gratefully nestling close to thee.

Over the tree-tops I float thee a song,
Over the rising and sinking waves, over the myriad fields and the
   prairies wide,
Over the dense-pack'd cities all and the teeming wharves and ways,
I float this carol with joy, with joy to thee O death.

15

To the tally of my soul,
Loud and strong kept up the gray-brown bird,
With pure deliberate notes spreading filling the night.

Loud in the pines and cedars dim,
Clear in the freshness moist and the swamp-perfume,
And I with my comrades there in the night.

While my sight that was bound in my eyes unclosed,
As to long panoramas of visions.

And I saw askant the armies,
I saw as in noiseless dreams hundreds of battle-flags,
Borne through the smoke of the battles and pierc'd with missiles I saw
   them,
And carried hither and yon through the smoke, and torn and
   bloody,
And at last but a few shreds left on the staffs, (and all in silence,)
And the staffs all splinter'd and broken.

I saw battle-corpses, myriads of them,
And the white skeletons of young men, I saw them,
I saw the debris and debris of all the slain soldiers of the war,
But I saw they were not as was thought,
They themselves were fully at rest, they suffer'd not,
The living remain'd and suffer'd, the mother suffer'd,
And the wife and the child and the musing comrade suffer'd,
And the armies that remain'd suffer'd.

16

Passing the visions, passing the night,
Passing, unloosing the hold of my comrades' hands,

Passing the song of the hermit bird and the tallying song of my soul,
Victorious song, death's outlet song, yet varying ever-altering song,
As low and wailing, yet clear the notes, rising and falling, flooding the night,   190
Sadly sinking and fainting, as warning and warning, and yet again bursting with joy,
Covering the earth and filling the spread of the heaven,
As that powerful psalm in the night I heard from recesses,
Passing, I leave thee lilac with heart-shaped leaves,
I leave thee there in the dooryard, blooming, returning with spring.   195

I cease from my song for thee,
From my gaze on thee in the west, fronting the west, communing with thee,
O comrade lustrous with silver face in the night.

Yet each to keep and all, retrievements out of the night,
The song, the wondrous chant of the gray-brown bird,   200
And the tallying chant, the echo arous'd in my soul,
With the lustrous and drooping star with the countenance full of woe,
With the holders holding my hand nearing the call of the bird,
Comrades mine and I in the midst, and their memory ever to keep, for the dead I loved so well,   205
For the sweetest, wisest soul of all my days and lands—and this for his dear sake,
Lilac and star and bird twined with the chant of my soul,
There in the fragrant pines and the cedars dusk and dim.

Ulysses[1]

It little profits that an idle king,
By this still hearth, among these barren crags,
Match'd with an aged wife,[2] I mete and dole
Unequal laws unto a savage race,
That hoard, and sleep, and feed, and know not me.   5

I cannot rest from travel: I will drink
Life to the lees: all times I have enjoy'd
Greatly, have suffer'd greatly, both with those
That loved me, and alone; on shore, and when
Thro' scudding drifts the rainy Hyades[3]   10
Vext the dim sea: I am become a name;
For always roaming with a hungry heart
Much have I seen and known; cities of men
And manners, climates, councils, governments,
Myself not least, but honour'd of them all;   15
And drunk delight of battle with my peers,
Far on the ringing plains of windy Troy.
I am a part of all that I have met;
Yet all experience is an arch wherethro'
Gleams that untravell'd world, whose margin fades   20
For ever and for ever when I move.

How dull it is to pause, to make an end,
To rust unburnish'd, not to shine in use!
As tho' to breathe were life. Life piled on life
Were all too little, and of one to me   25
Little remains: but every hour is saved
From that eternal silence, something more,
A bringer of new things; and vile it were
For some three suns to store and hoard myself,
And this gray spirit yearning in desire   30
To follow knowledge like a sinking star,
Beyond the utmost bound of human thought.

    This is my son, mine own Telemachus,
To whom I leave the sceptre and the isle—
Well-loved of me, discerning to fulfil   35
This labour, by slow prudence to make mild

---

[1] *Ulysses*: or Odysseus, ruler of Ithaca and hero of the Trojan War.   [2] *wife*: Penelope.   [3] *Hyades*: group of stars supposed to have signaled rain when they arose with the sun.

A rugged people, and thro' soft degrees
Subdue them to the useful and the good.
Most blameless is he, centred in the sphere
Of common duties, decent not to fail   40
In offices of tenderness, and pay
Meet adoration to my household gods,
When I am gone. He works his work, I mine.

   There lies the port; the vessel puffs her sail:
There gloom the dark broad seas. My mariners,   45
Souls that have toil'd, and wrought, and thought with me—
That ever with a frolic welcome took
The thunder and the sunshine, and opposed
Free hearts, free foreheads—you and I are old;
Old age hath yet his honour and his toil;   50
Death closes all: but something ere the end,
Some work of noble note, may yet be done,
Not unbecoming men that strove with Gods.
The lights begin to twinkle from the rocks:
The long day wanes: the slow moon climbs: the deep   55
Moans round with many voices. Come, my friends,
'Tis not too late to seek a newer world.
Push off, and sitting well in order smite
The sounding furrows; for my purpose holds
To sail beyond the sunset, and the baths[4]   60
Of all the western stars, until I die.
It may be that the gulfs[5] will wash us down:
It may be we shall touch the Happy Isles,[6]
And see the great Achilles,[7] whom we knew.
Tho' much is taken, much abides; and tho'   65
We are not now that strength which in old days
Moved earth and heaven; that which we are, we are;
One equal temper of heroic hearts,
Made weak by time and fate, but strong in will
To strive, to seek, to find, and not to yield.   70

Tithonus[8]

The woods decay, the woods decay and fall,
The vapours weep their burthen[9] to the ground,

---

[4] *baths:* the seas into which the stars descend.   [5] *gulfs:* whirlpools.   [6] *Happy Isles:* Elysium or paradise.   [7] *Achilles:* mighty Greek warrior who slew the Trojan Hector.   [8] *Tithonus:* beloved by Aurora, goddess of the dawn, who gave him

Man comes and tills the field and lies beneath,
And after many a summer dies the swan.
Me only cruel immortality
Consumes: I wither slowly in thine arms,
Here at the quiet limit of the world,
A white-hair'd shadow roaming like a dream
The ever-silent spaces of the East,
Far-folded mists, and gleaming halls of morn.

   Alas! for this gray shadow, once a man—
So glorious in his beauty and thy choice,
Who madest him thy chosen, that he seem'd
To his great heart none other than a God!
I ask'd thee, 'Give me immortality.'
Then didst thou grant mine asking with a smile,
Like wealthy men who care not how they give.
But thy strong Hours indignant work'd their wills,
And beat me down and marr'd and wasted me,
And tho' they could not end me, left me maim'd
To dwell in presence of immortal youth,
Immortal age beside immortal youth,
And all I was, in ashes. Can thy love,
Thy beauty, make amends, tho' even now,
Close over us, the silver star,[10] thy guide,
Shines in those tremulous eyes that fill with tears
To hear me? Let me go: take back thy gift:
Why should a man desire in any way
To vary from the kindly race of men,
Or pass beyond the goal of ordinance[11]
Where all should pause, as is most meet[12] for all?

   A soft air fans the cloud apart; there comes
A glimpse of that dark world where I was born.
Once more the old mysterious glimmer steals
From thy pure brows, and from thy shoulders pure,
And bosom beating with a heart renew'd.
Thy cheek begins to redden thro' the gloom,
Thy sweet eyes brighten slowly close to mine,
Ere yet they blind the stars, and the wild team
Which love thee, yearning for thy yoke, arise,
And shake the darkness from their loosen'd manes,
And beat the twilight into flakes of fire.

---

eternal life but not eternal youth. He grew old and infirm, and as he could not die, according to legend, he was turned into a grasshopper—*Tennyson.*
[9] *burthen:* burden. [10] *star:* Venus. [11] *the ... ordinance:* appointed limit.
[12] *meet:* suitable.

Lo! ever thus thou growest beautiful
In silence, then before thine answer given
Departest, and thy tears are on my cheek.   45

Why wilt thou ever scare me with thy tears,
And make me tremble lest a saying learnt,
In days far-off, on that dark earth, be true?
'The Gods themselves cannot recall their gifts.'

Ay me! ay me! with what another heart   50
In days far-off, and with what other eyes
I used to watch—if I be he that watch'd—
The lucid outline forming round thee; saw
The dim curls kindle into sunny rings;
Changed with thy mystic change, and felt my blood   55
Glow with the glow that slowly crimson'd all
Thy presence and thy portals, while I lay,
Mouth, forehead, eyelids, growing dewy-warm
With kisses balmier than half-opening buds
Of April, and could hear the lips that kiss'd   60
Whispering I knew not what of wild and sweet,
Like that strange song I heard Apollo[13] sing,
While Ilion[14] like a mist rose into towers.

Yet hold me not for ever in thine East:
How can my nature longer mix with thine?   65
Coldly thy rosy shadows bathe me, cold
Are all thy lights, and cold my wrinkled feet
Upon thy glimmering thresholds, when the steam[15]
Floats up from those dim fields about the homes
Of happy men that have the power to die,   70
And grassy barrows of the happier dead.
Release me, and restore me to the ground;
Thou seest all things, thou wilt see my grave:
Thou wilt renew thy beauty morn by morn;
I earth in earth[16] forget these empty courts,   75
And thee returning on thy silver wheels.

---

[13] *Apollo:* Greek god of manly youth, poetry, music.   [14] *Ilion:* Troy.   [15] *steam:* morning mist.   [16] *I . . . earth:* "*Terra in terra*" (Dante); *forget:* will forget.

The Buried Life

Light flows our war of mocking words, and yet,
Behold, with tears my eyes are wet!
I feel a nameless sadness o'er me roll.
Yes, yes, we know that we can jest,
We know, we know that we can smile!
But there's a something in this breast
To which thy light words bring no rest,
And thy gay smiles no anodyne.
Give me thy hand, and hush awhile,
And turn those limpid eyes on mine,
And let me read there, love! thy inmost soul.

Alas, is even love too weak
To unlock the heart and let it speak?
Are even lovers powerless to reveal
To one another what indeed they feel?
I knew the mass of men conceal'd
Their thoughts, for fear that if reveal'd
They would by other men be met
With blank indifference, or with blame reproved;
I knew they lived and moved
Trick'd in disguises, alien to the rest
Of men, and alien to themselves—and yet
    The same heart beats in every human breast!

But we, my love!—doth a like spell benumb
Our hearts, our voices?—must we too be dumb?

Ah, well for us, if even we,
Even for a moment, can get free
Our heart, and have our lips unchain'd;
For that which seals them hath been deep ordain'd.

Fate, which foresaw
How frivolous a baby man would be—
By what distractions he would be possess'd,
How he would pour himself in every strife,
And well-nigh change his own identity—
That it might keep from his capricious play
His genuine self, and force him to obey
Even in his own despite his being's law,
Bade, through the deep recesses of our breast,
The unregarded river of our life

Pursue with indiscernible flow its way;　　　　　　　　　　40
And that we should not see
The buried stream, and seem to be
Eddying about in blind uncertainty,
Though driving on with it eternally.

But often, in the world's most crowded streets,　　　　　45
But often, in the din of strife,
There rises an unspeakable desire
After knowledge of our buried life;
A thirst to spend our fire and restless force
In tracking out our true, original course;　　　　　　　　50
A longing to inquire
Into the mystery of this heart that beats
So wild, so deep in us—to know
Whence our thoughts come and where they go.
And many a man in his own breast then delves,　　　　55
But deep enough, alas! none ever mines.
And we have been on many thousand lines,
And we have shown, on each, spirit and power,
But hardly have we, for one little hour,
Been on our own line, have we been ourselves　　　　　60
Hardly had skill to utter one of all
The nameless feelings that course through our breast,
But they course on for ever unexpress'd.
And long we try in vain to speak and act
Our hidden self, and what we say and do　　　　　　　65
Is eloquent, is well—but 'tis not true!
And then we will no more be rack'd
With inward striving, and demand
Of all the thousand nothings of the hour
Their stupefying power;　　　　　　　　　　　　　　70
Ah yes, and they benumb us at our call!
Yet still, from time to time, vague and forlorn,
From the soul's subterranean depth upborne
As from an infinitely distant land,
Come airs, and floating echoes, and convey　　　　　　75
A melancholy into all our day.

Only—but this is rare—
When a beloved hand is laid in ours,
When, jaded with the rush and glare
Of the interminable hours,　　　　　　　　　　　　　80
Our eyes can in another's eyes read clear,

When our world-deafen'd ear
Is by the tones of a loved voice caress'd—
A bolt is shot back somewhere in our breast
And a lost pulse of feeling stirs again. 85
The eye sinks inward, and the heart lies plain.
And what we mean, we say, and what we would, we know.
A man becomes aware of his life's flow
And hears its winding murmur, and he sees
The meadows where it glides, the sun, the breeze. 90

And there arrives a lull in the hot race
Wherein he doth for ever chase
That flying and elusive shadow, rest.
And an unwonted calm pervades his breast. 95
And then he thinks he knows
The hills where his life rose,
And the sea where it goes.

Requiescat [1]

Strew on her roses, roses,
    And never a spray of yew![2]
In quiet she reposes:
    Ah! would that I did too!

Her mirth the world required: 5
    She bathed it in smiles of glee.
But her heart was tired, tired,
    And now they let her be.

Her life was turning, turning,
    In mazes of heat and sound. 10
But for peace her soul was yearning,
    And now peace laps her round.

Her cabin'd,[3] ample spirit,
    It flutter'd and fail'd for breath.
To-night it doth inherit 15
    The vasty hall of death.

---

[1] *Requiescat:* may she rest (*in pace*—in peace, understood). [2] *yew:* a tree associated with mourning. [3] *cabin'd:* confined (by its mortality).

Dover Beach

The sea is calm to-night.
The tide is full, the moon lies fair
Upon the straits;—on the French coast, the light
Gleams, and is gone; the cliffs of England stand,
Glimmering and vast, out in the tranquil bay.
Come to the window, sweet is the night air!
Only, from the lone line of spray
Where the sea meets the moon-blanch'd land,
Listen! you hear the grating roar
Of pebbles which the waves draw back, and fling,
At their return, up the high strand,
Begin, and cease, and then again begin,
With tremulous cadence slow, and bring
The eternal note of sadness in.

Sophocles[4] long ago
Heard it on the Ægæan, and it brought
Into his mind the turbid ebb and flow
Of human misery; we
Find also in the sound a thought,
Hearing it by this distant northern sea.

The Sea of Faith
Was once, too, at the full, and round earth's shore
Lay like the folds of a bright girdle furl'd.
But now I only hear
Its melancholy, long, withdrawing roar,
Retreating, to the breath
Of the night-wind down the vast edges drear
And naked shingles of the world.

Ah, love, let us be true
To one another! for the world, which seems
To lie before us like a land of dreams,
So various, so beautiful, so new,
Hath really neither joy, nor love, nor light,
Nor certitude, nor peace, nor help for pain;
And we are here as on a darkling plain
Swept with confused alarms of struggle and flight,
Where ignorant armies clash by night.

[4] *Sophocles:* Greek dramatist.

EMILY DICKINSON

Success Is Counted Sweetest

Success is counted sweetest
By those who ne'er succeed.
To comprehend a nectar
Requires sorest need.

Not one of all the purple Host 5
Who took the Flag today
Can tell the definition
So clear of Victory

As he defeated—dying—
On whose forbidden ear 10
The distant strains of triumph
Burst agonized and clear!

Safe in Their Alabaster Chambers—

Safe in their Alabaster Chambers—
Untouched by Morning
And untouched by Noon—
Sleep the meek members of the Resurrection—
Rafter of satin, 5
And Roof of stone.

Light laughs the breeze
In her Castle above them—
Babbles the Bee in a stolid Ear,
Pipe the Sweet Birds in ignorant cadence— 10
Ah, what sagacity perished here!
      version of 1859

Safe in their Alabaster Chambers—
Untouched by Morning—
And untouched by Noon—
Lie the meek members of the Resurrection—
Rafter of Satin—and Roof of Stone! 5

Grand go the Years—in the Crescent—above them—
Worlds scoop their Arcs—
And Firmaments—row—

Diadems—drop—and Doges—surrender—
Soundless as dots—on a Disc of Snow—
                              version of 1861

I Like a Look of Agony

I like a look of Agony,
Because I know it's true—
Men do not sham Convulsion,
Nor simulate, a Throe—

The Eyes glaze once—and that is Death—
Impossible to feign
The Beads upon the Forehead
By homely Anguish strung.

Because I Could Not Stop for Death—

Because I could not stop for Death—
He kindly stopped for me—
The Carriage held but just Ourselves—
And Immortality.

We slowly drove—He knew no haste
And I had put away
My labor and my leisure too,
For his Civility—

We passed the School, where Children strove
At Recess—in the Ring—
We passed the Fields of Gazing Grain—
We passed the Setting Sun—

Or rather—He passed Us—
The Dews drew quivering and chill—
For only Gossamer, my Gown—
My Tippet[1]—only Tulle[2]—

We paused before a House that seemed
A Swelling of the Ground—
The Roof was scarcely visible—
The Cornice—in the Ground—

---

[1] *Tippet:* scarf.   [2] *Tulle:* a thin fine net.

Since then—'tis Centuries—and yet
Feels shorter than the Day
I first surmised the Horses Heads
Were toward Eternity—

A Narrow Fellow in the Grass

A narrow Fellow in the Grass
Occasionally rides—
You may have met Him—did you not
His notice sudden is—

The Grass divides as with a Comb—
A spotted shaft is seen—
And then it closes at your feet
And opens further on—

He likes a Boggy Acre
A Floor too cool for Corn—
Yet when a Boy, and Barefoot—
I more than once at Noon
Have passed, I thought, a Whip lash
Unbraiding in the Sun
When stooping to secure it
It wrinkled, and was gone—

Several of Nature's People
I know, and they know me—
I feel for them a transport
Of cordiality—

But never met this Fellow
Attended, or alone
Without a tighter breathing
And Zero at the Bone—

The Bustle in a House

The Bustle in a House
The Morning after Death
Is solemnest of industries
Enacted upon Earth—

The Sweeping up the Heart
And putting Love away
We shall not want to use again
Until Eternity

Immortal Is an Ample Word

Immortal is an ample word
When what we need is by
But when it leaves us for a time
'Tis a necessity.

Of Heaven above the firmest proof
We fundamental know
Except for its[3] marauding Hand
It had been Heaven below.

Apparently with No Surprise

Apparently with no surprise
To any happy Flower
The Frost beheads it at its[3] play—
In accidental power—
The blonde Assassin passes on—
The Sun proceeds unmoved
To measure off another Day
For an Approving God.

---

[3] *its*: original spelling, *it's*.

Loveliest of Trees

Loveliest of trees, the cherry now
Is hung with bloom along the bough,
And stands about the woodland ride,
Wearing white for Eastertide.

Now, of my threescore years and ten,
Twenty will not come again,
And take from seventy springs a score,
It only leaves me fifty more.

And since to look at things in bloom
Fifty springs are little room,
About the woodlands I will go
To see the cherry hung with snow.

With Rue My Heart Is Laden

With rue my heart is laden
   For golden friends I had,
For many a rose-lipt maiden
   And many a lightfoot lad.

By brooks too broad for leaping
   The lightfoot boys are laid;
The rose-lipt girls are sleeping
   In fields where roses fade.

Terence, This Is Stupid Stuff

'Terence, this is stupid stuff:
You eat your victuals fast enough;
There can't be much amiss, 'tis clear,
To see the rate you drink your beer.
But oh, good Lord, the verse you make,
It gives a chap the belly-ache.
The cow, the old cow, she is dead;
It sleeps well, the horned head:
We poor lads, 'tis our turn now
To hear such tunes as killed the cow.

Pretty friendship 'tis to rhyme
Your friends to death before their time
Moping melancholy mad:
Come, pipe a tune to dance to, lad.'

   Why, if 'tis dancing you would be,   15
There's brisker pipes than poetry.
Say for what were hop-yards meant,
Or why was Burton[1] built on Trent?
Oh many a peer of England brews
Livelier liquor than the Muse,   20
And malt does more than Milton can
To justify God's ways to man.
Ale, man, ale's the stuff to drink
For fellows whom it hurts to think:
Look into the pewter pot   25
To see the world as the world's not.
And faith 'tis pleasant till 'tis past:
The mischief is that 'twill not last.
Oh I have been to Ludlow fair
And left my necktie God knows where,   30
And carried halfway home, or near,
Pints and quarts of Ludlow beer:
Then the world seemed none so bad,
And I myself a sterling lad;
And down in lovely muck I've lain,   35
Happy till I woke again.
Then I saw the morning sky:
Heigho, the tale was all a lie;
The world it was the old world yet,
I was I, my things were wet,   40
And nothing now remained to do
But begin the game anew.

   Therefore, since the world has still
Much good, but much less good than ill,
And while the sun and moon endure   45
Luck's a chance but trouble's sure,
I'd face it as a wise man would,
And train for ill and not for good.
'Tis true, the stuff I bring for sale
Is not so brisk a brew as ale: 50
Out of a stem that scored the hand

---

[1] *Burton:* English town famous for its breweries.

I wrung it in a weary land.
But take it: if the smack is sour,
The better for the embittered hour;
It should do good to heart and head
When your soul is in my soul's stead;
And I will friend you, if I may,
In the dark and cloudy day.

   There was a king reigned in the East:
There, when kings will sit to feast,
They get their fill before they think
With poisoned meat and poisoned drink.
He gathered all that springs to birth
From the many-venomed earth;
First a little, thence to more,
He sampled all her killing store;
And easy, smiling, seasoned sound,
Sate the king when healths went round.
They put arsenic in his meat
And stared aghast to watch him eat;
They poured strychnine in his cup
And shook to see him drink it up:
They shook, they stared as white's their shirt:
Them it was their poison hurt.
—I tell the tale that I heard told.
Mithridates,[2] he died old.

The Chestnut Casts His Flambeaux

The chestnut casts his flambeaux, and the flowers
    Stream from the hawthorn on the wind away,
The doors clap to, the pane is blind with showers.
    Pass me the can, lad; there's an end of May.

There's one spoilt spring to scant our mortal lot,
    One season ruined of our little store.
May will be fine next year as like as not:
    Oh ay, but then we shall be twenty-four.

We for certainty are not the first
    Have sat in taverns while the tempest hurled

---

[2] *Mithridates:* king of ancient Pontus in Asia Minor.

Their hopeful plans to emptiness, and cursed
    Whatever brute and blackguard made the world.

It is in truth iniquity on high
    To cheat our sentenced souls of aught they crave,
And mar the merriment as you and I
    Fare on our long fool's-errand to the grave.

Iniquity it is; but pass the can.
    My lad, no pair of kings our mothers bore;
Our only portion is the estate of man:
    We want the moon, but we shall get no more.

If here to-day the cloud of thunder lours
    To-morrow it will hie on far behests;
The flesh will grieve on other bones than ours
    Soon, and the soul will mourn in other breasts.

The troubles of our proud and angry dust
    Are from eternity and shall not fail.
Bear them we can, and if we can we must.
    Shoulder the sky, my lad, and drink your ale.

The Lake Isle of Innisfree

I will arise and go now, and go to Innisfree,
And a small cabin build there, of clay and wattles made:
Nine bean rows will I have there, a hive for the honey bee,
    And live alone in the bee-loud glade.

And I shall have some peace there, for peace comes dropping slow,   5
Dropping from the veils of the morning to where the cricket sings;
There midnight's all a glimmer, and noon a purple glow,
    And evening full of the linnet's wings.

I will arise and go now, for always night and day
I hear lake water lapping with low sounds by the shore;   10
While I stand on the roadway, or on the pavements gray,
    I hear it in the deep heart's core.

The Magi

Now as at all times I can see in the mind's eye,
In their stiff, painted clothes, the pale unsatisfied ones
Appear and disappear in the blue depth of the sky
With all their ancient faces like rain-beaten stones,
And all their helms of silver hovering side by side,   5
And all their eyes still fixed, hoping to find once more,
Being by Calvary's turbulence unsatisfied,
The uncontrollable mystery on the bestial floor.

The Wild Swans at Coole

The trees are in their autumn beauty,
The woodland paths are dry,
Under the October twilight the water
Mirrors a still sky;
Upon the brimming water among the stones   5
Are nine-and-fifty swans.

The nineteenth autumn has come upon me
Since I first made my count;

I saw, before I had well finished,
All suddenly mount
And scatter wheeling in great broken rings
Upon their clamorous wings.

I have looked upon those brilliant creatures,
And now my heart is sore.
All's changed since I, hearing at twilight,
The first time on this shore,
The bell-beat of their wings above my head,
Trod with a lighter tread.

Unwearied still, lover by lover,
They paddle in the cold
Companionable streams or climb the air;
Their hearts have not grown old;
Passion or conquest, wander where they will,
Attend upon them still.

But now they drift on the still water
Mysterious, beautiful;
Among what rushes will they build,
By what lake's edge or pool
Delight men's eyes when I awake some day
To find they have flown away?

An Irish Airman Foresees His Death

I know that I shall meet my fate
Somewhere among the clouds above;
Those that I fight I do not hate,
Those that I guard I do not love;
My country is Kiltartan Cross,
No likely end could bring them loss
Or leave them happier than before.
Nor law, nor duty bade me fight,
Nor public men, nor cheering crowds,
A lonely impulse of delight
Drove to this tumult in the clouds;
I balanced all, brought all to mind,
The years to come seemed waste of breath,
A waste of breath the years behind
In balance with this life, this death.

Easter, 1916[1]

I have met them at close of day
Coming with vivid faces
From counter or desk among grey
Eighteenth-century houses.
I have passed with a nod of the head
Or polite meaningless words,
Or have lingered awhile and said
Polite meaningless words,
And thought before I had done
Of a mocking tale or a gibe
To please a companion
Around the fire at the club,
Being certain that they and I
But lived where motley is worn:
All changed, changed utterly:
A terrible beauty is born.

That woman's[2] days were spent
In ignorant good-will,
Her nights in argument
Until her voice grew shrill.
What voice more sweet than hers
When, young and beautiful,
She rode to harriers?
This man[3] had kept a school
And rode our wingèd horse;
This other[4] his helper and friend
Was coming into his force;
He might have won fame in the end,
So sensitive his nature seemed,
So daring and sweet his thought.
This other man[5] I had dreamed
A drunken, vainglorious lout.
He had done most bitter wrong
To some who are near my heart,

---

[1] The day of the Easter Rebellion of the Irish Republicans. [2] *That woman's:* Constance Markievicz, one of the insurgents. [3] *This man:* Patrick Pearse, another insurgent. [4] *This other:* James Connolly, the leader of the Easter Rebellion. [5] *This other man:* John MacBride, a major in the Irish Brigade which fought against the British in the Boer War; the husband of Maud Gonne, Yeats' early love.

Yet I number him in the song;
He, too, has resigned his part
In the casual comedy;
He, too, has been changed in his turn,
Transformed utterly:
A terrible beauty is born.

Hearts with one purpose alone
Through summer and winter seem
Enchanted to a stone
To trouble the living stream.
The horse that comes from the road,
The rider, the birds that range
From cloud to tumbling cloud,
Minute by minute they change;
A shadow of cloud on the stream
Changes minute by minute;
A horse-hoof slides on the brim,
And a horse plashes within it;
The long-legged moor-hens dive,
And hens to moor-cocks call;
Minute by minute they live:
The stone's in the midst of all.

Too long a sacrifice
Can make a stone of the heart.
O when may it suffice?
That is Heaven's part, our part
To murmur name upon name,
As a mother names her child
When sleep at last has come
On limbs that had run wild.
What is it but nightfall?
No, no, not night but death;
Was it needless death after all?
For England may keep faith
For all that is done and said.
We know their dream; enough
To know they dreamed and are dead;
And what if excess of love
Bewildered them till they died?
I write it out in a verse—
MacDonagh[6] and MacBride
And Connolly and Pearse

[6] *MacDonagh*: Thomas MacDonagh, poet.

Now and in time to be,
Whatever green is worn,
Are changed, changed utterly:
A terrible beauty is born.

The Second Coming

Turning and turning in the widening gyre
The falcon cannot hear the falconer;
Things fall apart; the centre cannot hold;
Mere anarchy is loosed upon the world,
The blood-dimmed tide is loosed, and everywhere
The ceremony of innocence is drowned;
The best lack all conviction, while the worst
Are full of passionate intensity.

Surely some revelation is at hand;
Surely the Second Coming is at hand.
The Second Coming! Hardly are those words out
When a vast image out of *Spiritus Mundi*[7]
Troubles my sight: somewhere in sands of the desert
A shape with lion body and the head of a man,
A gaze blank and pitiless as the sun,
Is moving its slow thighs, while all about it
Reel shadows of the indignant desert birds.
The darkness drops again; but now I know
That twenty centuries of stony sleep
Were vexed to nightmare by a rocking cradle,
And what rough beast,[8] its hour come round at last,
Slouches towards Bethlehem to be born?

A Prayer for My Daughter

Once more the storm is howling, and half hid
Under this cradle-hood and coverlid
My child sleeps on. There is no obstacle
But Gregory's wood and one bare hill
Whereby the haystack- and roof-levelling wind,
Bred on the Atlantic, can be stayed;

---

[7] *Spiritus Mundi*: world-spirit or collective imagination. [8] *rough beast*: the Antichrist (see I John 2:18) establishing the title's irony.

And for an hour I have walked and prayed
Because of the great gloom that is in my mind.

I have walked and prayed for this young child an hour
And heard the sea-wind scream upon the tower,
And under the arches of the bridge, and scream
In the elms above the flooded stream;
Imagining in excited reverie
That the future years had come,
Dancing to a frenzied drum,
Out of the murderous innocence of the sea.

May she be granted beauty and yet not
Beauty to make a stranger's eye distraught,
Or hers before a looking-glass, for such,
Being made beautiful overmuch,
Consider beauty a sufficient end,
Lose natural kindness and maybe
The heart-revealing intimacy
That chooses right, and never find a friend.

Helen being chosen found life flat and dull
And later had much trouble from a fool,
While that great Queen, that rose out of the spray,
Being fatherless could have her way
Yet chose a bandy-legged smith for man.
It's certain that fine women eat
A crazy salad with their meat
Whereby the Horn of Plenty is undone.

In courtesy I'd have her chiefly learned;
Hearts are not had as a gift but hearts are earned
By those that are not entirely beautiful;
Yet many, that have played the fool
For beauty's very self, has charm made wise,
And many a poor man that has roved,
Loved and thought himself beloved,
From a glad kindness cannot take his eyes.

May she become a flourishing hidden tree
That all her thoughts may like the linnet be,
And have no business but dispensing round
Their magnanimities of sound,
Nor but in merriment begin a chase,
Nor but in merriment a quarrel.
O may she live like some green laurel
Rooted in one dear perpetual place.

My mind, because the minds that I have loved,
The sort of beauty that I have approved,
Prosper but little, has dried up of late,
Yet knows that to be choked with hate
May well be of all evil chances chief.
If there's no hatred in a mind
Assault and battery of the wind
Can never tear the linnet from the leaf.

An intellectual hatred is the worst,
So let her think opinions are accursed.
Have I not seen the loveliest woman born
Out of the mouth of Plenty's horn,
Because of her opinionated mind
Barter that horn and every good
By quiet natures understood
For an old bellows full of angry wind?

Considering that, all hatred driven hence,
The soul recovers radical innocence
And learns at last that it is self-delighting,
Self-appeasing, self-affrighting,
And that its own sweet will is Heaven's will;
She can, though every face should scowl
And every windy quarter howl
Or every bellows burst, be happy still.

And may her bridegroom bring her to a house
Where all's accustomed, ceremonious;
For arrogance and hatred are the wares
Peddled in the thoroughfares.
How but in custom and in ceremony
Are innocence and beauty born?
Ceremony's a name for the rich horn,
And custom for the spreading laurel tree.

Leda[9] and the Swan[10]

A sudden blow: the great wings beating still
Above the staggering girl, her thighs caressed

[9] *Leda:* wife of Tyndareus, king of Sparta. [10] *the Swan:* disguise of Zeus when he made love to Leda.

By the dark webs, her nape caught in his bill,
He holds her helpless breast upon his breast.

How can those terrified vague fingers push
The feathered glory from her loosening thighs?
And how can body, laid in that white rush,
But feel the strange heart beating where it lies?

A shudder in the loins engenders[11] there
The broken wall, the burning roof and tower
And Agamemnon[12] dead.
      Being so caught up,
So mastered by the brute blood of the air,
Did she put on his knowledge with his power
Before the indifferent beak could let her drop?

Sailing to Byzantium

I

That is no country for old men. The young
In one another's arms, birds in the trees
—Those dying generations—at their song,
The salmon-falls, the mackerel-crowded seas,
Fish, flesh, or fowl, commend all summer long
Whatever is begotten, born, and dies.
Caught in that sensual music all neglect
Monuments of unaging intellect.

II

An aged man is but a paltry thing,
A tattered coat upon a stick, unless
Soul clap its hands and sing, and louder sing
For every tatter in its mortal dress,
Nor is there singing school but studying
Monuments of its own magnificence;

---

[11] *engenders:* born of this union were Helen and Pollux; line 10: destruction of Troy. [12] *Agamemnon:* slain upon his return from the Trojan War by Clytemnestra, his wife who was also Helen's half-sister; his brother was Menelaus, Helen's husband.

And therefore I have sailed the seas and come 15
To the holy city of Byzantium.[13]

III

O sages standing in God's holy fire
As in the gold mosaic of a wall,
Come from the holy fire, perne[14] in a gyre,
And be the singing-masters of my soul. 20
Consume my heart away; sick with desire
And fastened to a dying animal
It knows not what it is; and gather me
Into the artifice of eternity.

IV

Once out of nature I shall never take 25
My bodily form from any natural thing,
But such a form as Grecian goldsmiths make[15]
Of hammered gold and gold enamelling
To keep a drowsy Emperor awake;
Or set upon a golden bough to sing 30
To lords and ladies of Byzantium
Of what is past, or passing, or to come.

Among School Children

I

I walk through the long schoolroom questioning;
A kind old nun in a white hood replies;
The children learn to cipher and to sing,
To study reading-books and history,
To cut and sew, be neat in everything 5
In the best modern way—the children's eyes
In momentary wonder stare upon
A sixty-year-old smiling public man.

---

[13] *the holy city of Byzantium*: capital of the Roman Empire after 330 A.D. and, literally, the Holy City of the Eastern Church; later called Constantinople, now Istanbul. Byzantium epitomized for Yeats man's highest achievement in art and religion. [14] *perne*: revolve. [15] Artificial birds sang from golden trees in Emperor's garden.

II

I dream of a Ledaean body, bent
Above a sinking fire, a tale that she
Told of a harsh reproof, or trivial event
That changed some childish day to tragedy—
Told, and it seemed that our two natures blent
Into a sphere from youthful sympathy,
Or else, to alter Plato's parable,[16]
Into the yolk and white of the one shell.

III

And thinking of that fit of grief or rage
I look upon one child or t'other there
And wonder if she stood so at that age—
For even daughters of the swan can share
Something of every paddler's heritage—
And had that colour upon cheek or hair,
And thereupon my heart is driven wild:
She stands before me as a living child.

IV

Her present image floats into the mind—
Did Quattrocento[17] finger fashion it
Hollow of cheek as though it drank the wind
And took a mess of shadows for its meat?
And I though never of Ledaean kind
Had pretty plumage once—enough of that,
Better to smile on all that smile, and show
There is a comfortable kind of old scarecrow.

V

What youthful mother, a shape upon her lap
Honey of generation had betrayed,
And that must sleep, shriek, struggle to escape
As recollection or the drug decide,
Would think her son, did she but see that shape
With sixty or more winters on its head,

---

[16] *Plato's parable*: Plato's *Symposium*.   [17] *Quattrocento*: fifteenth century.

A compensation for the pang of his birth,
Or the uncertainty of his setting forth?

VI

Plato thought nature but a spume that plays
Upon a ghostly paradigm of things;
Solider Aristotle played the taws
Upon the bottom of a king of kings;[18]
World-famous golden-thighed Pythagoras[19]
Fingered upon a fiddle-stick or strings
What a star sang and careless Muses heard:
Old clothes upon old sticks to scare a bird.

VII

Both nuns and mothers worship images,
But those the candles light are not as those
That animate a mother's reveries,
But keep a marble or a bronze repose.
And yet they too break hearts—O Presences
That passion, piety or affection knows,
And that all heavenly glory symbolise—
O self-born mockers of man's enterprise;

VIII

Labour is blossoming or dancing where
The body is not bruised to pleasure soul,
Nor beauty born out of its own despair,
Nor blear-eyed wisdom out of midnight oil.
O chestnut tree, great rooted blossomer,
Are you the leaf, the blossom or the bole?
O body swayed to music, O brightening glance,
How can we know the dancer from the dance?

Byzantium

The unpurged images of day recede;
The Emperor's drunken soldiery are abed;

---

[18] *Solider Aristotle ... king of kings:* Aristotle whipped ("played the taws") his pupil who later became Alexander the Great. [19] *golden-thighed Pythagoras:* pre-Socratic philosopher, reported as having a thigh of gold.

Night resonance recedes, night-walkers' song
After great cathedral gong;
A starlit or a moonlit dome disdains
All that man is,
All mere complexities,
The fury and the mire of human veins.

Before me floats an image, man or shade,
Shade more than man, more image than a shade;
For Hades' bobbin bound in mummy-cloth
May unwind the winding path;
A mouth that has no moisture and no breath
Breathless mouths may summon;
I hail the superhuman;
I call it death-in-life and life-in-death.

Miracle, bird or golden handiwork,
More miracle than bird or handiwork,
Planted on the star-lit golden bough,
Can like the cocks of Hades crow,
Or, by the moon embittered, scorn aloud
In glory of changeless metal
Common bird or petal
And all complexities of mire or blood.

At midnight on the Emperor's pavement flit
Flames that no faggot feeds, nor steel has lit,
Nor storm disturbs, flames begotten of flame,
Where blood-begotten spirits come
And all complexities of fury leave,
Dying into a dance,
An agony of trance,
An agony of flame that cannot singe a sleeve.

Astraddle on the dolphin's mire and blood,
Spirit after spirit! The smithies break the flood,
The golden smithies of the Emperor!
Marbles of the dancing floor
Break bitter furies of complexity,
Those images that yet
Fresh images beget,
That dolphin-torn, that gong-tormented sea.

Crazy Jane Talks with the Bishop

I met the Bishop on the road
And much said he and I.
'Those breasts are flat and fallen now,
Those veins must soon be dry;
Live in a heavenly mansion,
Not in some foul sty.'

'Fair and foul are near of kin,
And fair needs foul,' I cried.
'My friends are gone, but that's a truth
Nor grave nor bed denied,
Learned in bodily lowliness
And in the heart's pride.

'A woman can be proud and stiff
When on love intent;
But Love has pitched his mansion in
The place of excrement;
For nothing can be sole or whole
That has not been rent.'

Reluctance

Out through the fields and the woods
    And over the walls I have wended;
I have climbed the hills of view
    And looked at the world, and descended;
I have come by the highway home,
    And lo, it is ended.

The leaves are all dead on the ground,
    Save those that the oak is keeping
To ravel them one by one
    And let them go scraping and creeping
Out over the crusted snow,
    When others are sleeping.

And the dead leaves lie huddled and still,
    No longer blown hither and thither;
The last lone aster is gone;
    The flowers of the witch-hazel wither;
The heart is still aching to seek,
    But the feet question "Whither?"

Ah, when to the heart of man
    Was it ever less than a treason
To go with the drift of things,
    To yield with a grace to reason,
And bow and accept the end
    Of a love or a season?

After Apple-Picking

My long two-pointed ladder's sticking through a tree
Toward heaven still,
And there's a barrel that I didn't fill
Beside it, and there may be two or three
Apples I didn't pick upon some bough.
But I am done with apple-picking now.
Essence of winter sleep is on the night,
The scent of apples: I am drowsing off.
I cannot rub the strangeness from my sight
I got from looking through a pane of glass
I skimmed this morning from the drinking trough

And held against the world of hoary grass.
It melted, and I let it fall and break.
But I was well
Upon my way to sleep before it fell,
And I could tell
What form my dreaming was about to take.
Magnified apples appear and disappear,
Stem end and blossom end,
And every fleck of russet showing clear.
My instep arch not only keeps the ache,
It keeps the pressure of a ladder-round.
I feel the ladder sway as the boughs bend.
And I keep hearing from the cellar bin
The rumbling sound
Of load on load of apples coming in.
For I have had too much
Of apple-picking: I am overtired
Of the great harvest I myself desired.
There were ten thousand thousand fruit to touch,
Cherish in hand, lift down, and not let fall.
For all
That struck the earth,
No matter if not bruised or spiked with stubble,
Went surely to the cider-apple heap
As of no worth.
One can see what will trouble
This sleep of mine, whatever sleep it is.
Were he not gone,
The woodchuck could say whether it's like his
Long sleep, as I describe its coming on,
Or just some human sleep.

"Out, Out—"[1]

The buzz saw snarled and rattled in the yard
And made dust and dropped stove-length sticks of wood,
Sweet-scented stuff when the breeze drew across it.
And from there those that lifted eyes could count
Five mountain ranges one behind the other
Under the sunset far into Vermont.
And the saw snarled and rattled, snarled and rattled,

[1] "Out, Out—": see Macbeth V, v, 19–28.

As it ran light, or had to bear a load.
And nothing happened: day was all but done.
Call it a day, I wish they might have said   10
To please the boy by giving him the half hour
That a boy counts so much when saved from work.
His sister stood beside them in her apron
To tell them "Supper." At the word, the saw,
As if to prove saws knew what supper meant,   15
Leaped out at the boy's hand, or seemed to leap—
He must have given the hand. However it was,
Neither refused the meeting. But the hand!
The boy's first outcry was a rueful laugh,
As he swung toward them holding up the hand   20
Half in appeal, but half as if to keep
The life from spilling. Then the boy saw all—
Since he was old enough to know, big boy
Doing a man's work, though a child at heart—
He saw all spoiled. "Don't let him cut my hand off— 25
The doctor, when he comes. Don't let him, sister!"
So. But the hand was gone already.
The doctor put him in the dark of ether.
He lay and puffed his lips out with his breath.
And then—the watcher at his pulse took fright.   30
No one believed. They listened at his heart.
Little—less—nothing!—and that ended it.
No more to build on there. And they, since they
Were not the one dead, turned to their affairs.

Fire and Ice

Some say the world will end in fire,
Some say in ice.
From what I've tasted of desire
I hold with those who favor fire.
But if it had to perish twice,   5
I think I know enough of hate
To say that for destruction ice
Is also great
And would suffice.

Stopping by Woods on a Snowy Evening

Whose woods these are I think I know.
His house is in the village though;
He will not see me stopping here
To watch his woods fill up with snow.

My little horse must think it queer
To stop without a farmhouse near
Between the woods and frozen lake
The darkest evening of the year.

He gives his harness bells a shake
To ask if there is some mistake.
The only other sound's the sweep
Of easy wind and downy flake.

The woods are lovely, dark and deep,
But I have promises to keep,
And miles to go before I sleep,
And miles to go before I sleep.

Desert Places

Snow falling and night falling fast, oh, fast
In a field I looked into going past,
And the ground almost covered smooth in snow,
But a few weeds and stubble showing last.

The woods around it have it—it is theirs.
All animals are smothered in their lairs.
I am too absent-spirited to count;
The loneliness includes me unawares.

And lonely as it is that loneliness
Will be more lonely ere it will be less—
A blanker whiteness of benighted snow
With no expression, nothing to express.

They cannot scare me with their empty spaces
Between stars—on stars where no human race is.
I have it in me so much nearer home
To scare myself with my own desert places.

A High-Toned Old Christian Woman

Poetry is the supreme fiction, madame.
Take the moral law and make a nave of it
And from the nave build haunted heaven. Thus,
The conscience is converted into palms,
Like windy citherns[1] hankering for hymns.   5
We agree in principle. That's clear. But take
The opposing law and make a peristyle,[2]
And from the peristyle project a masque[3]
Beyond the planets. Thus, our bawdiness,
Unpurged by epitaph, indulged at last,   10
Is equally converted into palms,
Squiggling like saxophones. And palm for palm,
Madame, we are where we began. Allow,
Therefore, that in the planetary scene
Your disaffected flagellants, well-stuffed,   15
Smacking their muzzy bellies in parade,
Proud of such novelties of the sublime,
Such tink and tank and tunk-a-tunk-tunk,
May, merely may, madame, whip from themselves
A jovial hullabaloo among the spheres.   20
This will make widows wince. But fictive things
Wink as they will. Wink most when widows wince.

Disillusionment of Ten O'Clock

The houses are haunted
By white night-gowns.
None are green,
Or purple with green rings,
Or green with yellow rings,   5
Or yellow with blue rings.
None of them are strange,
With socks of lace
And beaded ceintures.[4]
People are not going   10
To dream of baboons and periwinkles.

---

[1] *citherns:* medieval lutelike instruments. [2] *peristyle:* a system of roof-supporting columns. [3] *masque:* a head or face, often grotesque, used as an adornment.
[4] *ceintures:* belts or sashes.

Only, here and there, an old sailor,
Drunk and asleep in his boots,
Catches tigers
In red weather.   15

Sunday Morning

I

Complacencies of the peignoir, and late
Coffee and oranges in a sunny chair,
And the green freedom of a cockatoo
Upon a rug mingle to dissipate
The holy hush of ancient sacrifice.   5
She dreams a little, and she feels the dark
Encroachment of that old catastrophe,
As a calm darkens among water-lights.
The pungent oranges and bright, green wings
Seem things in some procession of the dead,   10
Winding across wide water, without sound.
The day is like wide water, without sound,
Stilled for the passing of her dreaming feet
Over the seas, to silent Palestine,
Dominion of the blood and sepulchre.   15

II

Why should she give her bounty to the dead?
What is divinity if it can come
Only in silent shadows and in dreams?
Shall she not find in comforts of the sun,
In pungent fruit and bright, green wings, or else   20
In any balm or beauty of the earth,
Things to be cherished like the thought of heaven?
Divinity must live within herself:
Passions of rain, or moods in falling snow;
Grievings in loneliness, or unsubdued   25
Elations when the forest blooms; gusty
Emotions on wet roads on autumn nights;
All pleasures and all pains, remembering
The bough of summer and the winter branch.
These are the measures destined for her soul.   30

III

Jove in the clouds had his inhuman birth.
No mother suckled him, no sweet land gave
Large-mannered motions to his mythy mind.
He moved among us, as a muttering king,
Magnificent, would move among his hinds,
Until our blood, commingling, virginal,
With heaven, brought such requital to desire
The very hinds discerned it, in a star.
Shall our blood fail? Or shall it come to be
The blood of paradise? And shall the earth
Seem all of paradise that we shall know?
The sky will be much friendlier then than now,
A part of labor and a part of pain,
And next in glory to enduring love,
Not this dividing and indifferent blue.

IV

She says, "I am content when wakened birds,
Before they fly, test the reality
Of misty fields, by their sweet questioning;
But when the birds are gone, and their warm fields
Return no more, where, then, is paradise?"
There is not any haunt of prophecy,
Nor any old chimera of the grave,
Neither the golden underground, nor isle
Melodious, where spirits gat them home,
Nor visionary south, nor cloudy palm
Remote on heaven's hill, that has endured
As April's green endures; or will endure
Like her remembrance of awakened birds,
Or her desire for June and evening, tipped
By the consummation of the swallow's wings.

V

She says, "But in contentment I still feel
The need of some imperishable bliss."
Death is the mother of beauty; hence from her,
Alone, shall come fulfillment to our dreams
And our desires. Although she strews the leaves
Of sure obliteration on our paths,

The path sick sorrow took, the many paths
Where triumph rang its brassy phrase, or love
Whispered a little out of tenderness,
She makes the willow shiver in the sun
For maidens who were wont to sit and gaze
Upon the grass, relinquished to their feet.
She causes boys to pile new plums and pears
On disregarded plate. The maidens taste
And stray impassioned in the littering leaves.

VI

Is there no change of death in paradise?
Does ripe fruit never fall? Or do the boughs
Hang always heavy in that perfect sky,
Unchanging, yet so like our perishing earth,
With rivers like our own that seek for seas
They never find, the same receding shores
That never touch with inarticulate pang?
Why set the pear upon those river-banks
Or spice the shores with odors of the plum?
Alas, that they should wear our colors there,
The silken weavings of our afternoons,
And pick the strings of our insipid lutes!
Death is the mother of beauty, mystical,
Within whose burning bosom we devise
Our earthly mothers waiting, sleeplessly.

VII

Supple and turbulent, a ring of men
Shall chant in orgy on a summer morn
Their boisterous devotion to the sun,
Not as a god, but as a god might be,
Naked among them, like a savage source.
Their chant shall be a chant of paradise,
Out of their blood, returning to the sky;
And in their chant shall enter, voice by voice,
The windy lake wherein their lord delights,
The trees, like serafin, and echoing hills,
That choir among themselves long afterward.
They shall know well the heavenly fellowship
Of men that perish and of summer morn.
And whence they came and whither they shall go
The dew upon their feet shall manifest.

VIII

She hears, upon that water without sound,
A voice that cries, "The tomb in Palestine
Is not the porch of spirits lingering.
It is the grave of Jesus, where he lay."
We live in an old chaos of the sun, 110
Or old dependency of day and night,
Or island solitude, unsponsored, free,
Of that wide water, inescapable.
Deer walk upon our mountains, and the quail
Whistle about us their spontaneous cries; 115
Sweet berries ripen in the wilderness;
And, in the isolation of the sky,
At evening, casual flocks of pigeons make
Ambiguous undulations as they sink,
Downward to darkness, on extended wings. 120

Gulls

My townspeople, beyond in the great world,
are many with whom it were far more
profitable for me to live than here with you.
These whirr about me calling, calling!
and for my own part I answer them, loud as I can,
but they, being free, pass!
I remain! Therefore, listen!
For you will not soon have another singer.

First I say this: You have seen
the strange birds, have you not, that sometimes
rest upon our river in winter?
Let them cause you to think well then of the storms
that drive many to shelter. These things
do not happen without reason.

And the next thing I say is this:
I saw an eagle once circling against the clouds
over one of our principal churches—
Easter, it was—a beautiful day!
three gulls came from above the river
and crossed slowly seaward!
Oh, I know you have your own hymns, I have heard them—
and because I knew they invoked some great protector
I could not be angry with you, no matter
how much they outraged true music—

You see, it is not necessary for us to leap at each other,
and, as I told you, in the end
the gulls moved seaward very quietly.

The Red Wheelbarrow

so much depends
upon

a red wheel
barrow

glazed with rain
water

beside the white
chickens.

The Yachts

contend in a sea which the land partly encloses
shielding them from the too-heavy blows
of an ungoverned ocean which when it chooses

tortures the biggest hulls, the best man knows
to pit against its beatings, and sinks them pitilessly.
Mothlike in mists, scintillant in the minute

brilliance of cloudless days, with broad bellying sails
they glide to the wind tossing green water
from their sharp prows while over them the crew crawls

ant-like, solicitously grooming them, releasing,
making fast as they turn, lean far over and having
caught the wind again, side by side, head for the mark.

In a well guarded arena of open water surrounded by
lesser and greater craft which, sycophant, lumbering
and flittering follow them, they appear youthful, rare

as the light of a happy eye, live with the grace
of all that in the mind is fleckless, free and
naturally to be desired. Now the sea which holds them

is moody, lapping their glossy sides, as if feeling
for some slightest flaw but fails completely.
Today no race. Then the wind comes again. The yachts

move, jockeying for a start, the signal is set and they
are off. Now the waves strike at them but they are too
well made, they slip through, though they take in canvas.

Arms with hands grasping seek to clutch at the prows.
Bodies thrown recklessly in the way are cut aside.
It is a sea of faces about them in agony, in despair

until the horror of the race dawns staggering the mind,
the whole sea become an entanglement of watery bodies
lost to the world bearing what they cannot hold. Broken,

beaten, desolate, reaching from the dead to be taken up
they cry out, failing, failing! their cries rising
in waves still as the skillful yachts pass over.

A Sort of a Song

Let the snake wait under
his weed
and the writing
be of words, slow and quick, sharp
to strike, quiet to wait,
sleepless.

—through metaphor to reconcile
the people and the stones.
Compose. (No ideas
but in things) Invent!
Saxifrage is my flower that splits
the rocks.

Prelude to Winter

The moth under the eaves
with wings like
the bark of a tree, lies
symmetrically still—

And love is a curious
soft-winged thing
unmoving under the eaves
when the leaves fall.

The Pause

Values are split, summer, the fierce
jet an axe would not sever, spreads out
at lengths, of its own weight, a rainbow
over the lake of memory—the hard
stem of pure speed broken. Autumn
comes, fruit of many contours, that
glistening tegument painters love hiding
the soft pulp of the insidious reason,
dormant, for worm to nibble or for woman.
But there, within the seed, shaken by
fear as by a sea, it wakes again! to
drive upward, presently, from that soft
belly such a stem as will crack quartz.

The Fish

wade
through black jade.
   Of the crow-blue mussel-shells, one keeps
   adjusting the ash-heaps;
      opening and shutting itself like

an
injured fan.
   The barnacles which encrust the side
   of the wave, cannot hide
      there for the submerged shafts of the

sun,
split like spun
   glass, move themselves with spotlight swiftness
   into the crevices—
      in and out, illuminating

the
turquoise sea
   of bodies. The water drives a wedge
   of iron through the iron edge
      of the cliff; whereupon the stars,

pink
rice-grains, ink-
   bespattered jelly-fish, crabs like green
   lilies, and submarine
      toadstools, slide each on the other.

All
external
   marks of abuse are present on this
   defiant edifice—
      all the physical features of

ac-
cident—lack
   of cornice, dynamite grooves, burns, and
   hatchet strokes, these things stand
      out on it; the chasm-side is

dead.
Repeated
    evidence has proved that it can live
  on what can not revive
      its youth. The sea grows old in it.   40

In the Days of Prismatic Colour

not in the days of Adam and Eve, but when Adam
  was alone; when there was no smoke and colour was
fine, not with the refinement
  of early civilization art, but because
of its originality; with nothing to modify it but the   5

mist that went up, obliqueness was a variation of the perpendicular, plain to see and
to account for: it is no
  longer that; nor did the blue-red-yellow band
of incandescence that was colour keep its stripe: it also is
    one of   10

those things into which much that is peculiar can be
  read; complexity is not a crime, but carry
it to the point of murki-
  ness and nothing is plain. Complexity,
moreover, that has been committed to darkness, instead of
    granting it-   15

self to be the pestilence that it is, moves all a-
  bout as if to bewilder us with the dismal
fallacy that insistence
  is the measure of achievement and that all
truth must be dark. Principally throat, sophistication is as
    it al-   20

ways has been—at the antipodes from the initial great truths. 'Part of it was crawling, part of it
was about to crawl, the rest
  was torpid in its lair.' In the short-legged, fitful advance, the gurgling and all the minutiae—we have
    the classic   25

multitude of feet. To what purpose! Truth is no Apollo
    Belvedere,[1] no formal thing. The wave may go over it if
        it likes.
Know that it will be there when it says,
    'I shall be there when the wave has gone by.'   30

What Are Years?

What is our innocence,
what is our guilt? All are
    naked, none is safe. And whence
is courage: the unanswered question,
the resolute doubt,—   5
dumbly calling, deafly listening—that
in misfortune, even death,
        encourages others
        and in its defeat, stirs

the soul to be strong? He   10
sees deep and is glad, who
    accedes to mortality
and in his imprisonment rises
upon himself as
the sea in a chasm, struggling to be   15
free and unable to be,
        in its surrendering
        finds its continuing.

So he who strongly feels,
behaves. The very bird,   20
    grown taller as he sings, steels
his form straight up. Though he is captive,
his mighty singing
says, satisfaction is a lowly
thing, how pure a thing is joy.   25
        This is mortality.
        this is eternity.

---

[1] *Apollo Belvedere:* more correctly, Apollo of the Belvedere, a Greco-Roman statue considered as ideally perfect form of man.

The Love Song of J. Alfred Prufrock

S'io credesse che mia risposta fosse
A persona che mai tornasse al mondo,
Questa fiamma staria senza piu scosse.
Ma perciocche giammai di questo fondo
Non torno vivo alcun, s'i' odo il vero,
Senza tema d'infamia ti rispondo.[1]

Let us go then, you and I,
When the evening is spread out against the sky
Like a patient etherised upon a table;
Let us go, through certain half-deserted streets,
The muttering retreats 5
Of restless nights in one-night cheap hotels
And sawdust restaurants with oyster-shells:
Streets that follow like a tedious argument
Of insidious intent
To lead you to an overwhelming question . . . 10
Oh, do not ask, "What is it?"
Let us go and make our visit.

In the room the women come and go
Talking of Michelangelo.

The yellow fog that rubs its back upon the window-panes, 15
The yellow smoke that rubs its muzzle on the window-panes
Licked its tongue into the corners of the evening,
Lingered upon the pools that stand in drains,
Let fall upon its back the soot that falls from chimneys,
Slipped by the terrace, made a sudden leap, 20
And seeing that it was a soft October night,
Curled once about the house, and fell asleep.

And indeed there will be time
For the yellow smoke that slides along the street,
Rubbing its back upon the window-panes; 25
There will be time, there will be time
To prepare a face to meet the faces that you meet;
There will be time to murder and create,
And time for all the works and days of hands

---

[1] Epigraph from Dante's *Inferno*, Canto 27: "If I thought my answer were/to one who ever would return to the world,/this flame should shake no more./But since none from this depth/ever did return alive, if what I hear be true,/without fear of infamy I answer thee."

That lift and drop a question on your plate;
Time for you and time for me,
And time yet for a hundred indecisions,
And for a hundred visions and revisions,
Before the taking of a toast and tea.

In the room the women come and go
Talking of Michelangelo.

And indeed there will be time
To wonder, "Do I dare?" and, "Do I dare?"
Time to turn back and descend the stair,
With a bald spot in the middle of my hair—
[They will say: "How his hair is growing thin!"]
My morning coat, my collar mounting firmly to the chin,
My necktie rich and modest, but asserted by a simple pin—
[They will say: "But how his arms and legs are thin!"]
Do I dare
Disturb the universe?
In a minute there is time
For decisions and revisions which a minute will reverse.

For I have known them all already, known them all—
Have known the evenings, mornings, afternoons,
I have measured out my life with coffee spoons;
I know the voices dying with a dying fall
Beneath the music from a farther room.
  So how should I presume?

And I have known the eyes already, known them all:—
The eyes that fix you in a formulated phrase,
And when I am formulated, sprawling on a pin,
When I am pinned and wriggling on the wall,
Then how should I begin
To spit out all the butt-ends of my days and ways?
  And how should I presume?

And I have known the arms already, known them all—
Arms that are braceleted and white and bare
[But in the lamplight, downed with light brown hair!]
Is it perfume from a dress
That makes me so digress?
Arms that lie along a table, or wrap about a shawl.
  And should I then presume?
  And how should I begin?

           . . . .

Shall I say, I have gone at dusk through narrow streets   70
And watched the smoke that rises from the pipes
Of lonely men in shirt-sleeves, leaning out of windows? . . .

I should have been a pair of ragged claws
Scuttling across the floors of silent seas.
          . . . .
And the afternoon, the evening, sleeps so peacefully!   75
Smoothed by long fingers,
Asleep . . . tired . . . or it malingers,
Stretched on the floor, here beside you and me.
Should I, after tea and cakes and ices,
Have the strength to force the moment to its crisis?   80
But though I have wept and fasted, wept and prayed,
Though I have seen my head [grown slightly bald] brought in upon a platter,
I am no prophet[2]—and here's no great matter;
I have seen the moment of my greatness flicker,
And I have seen the eternal Footman hold my coat, and snicker,   85
And in short, I was afraid.

And would it have been worth it, after all,
After the cups, the marmalade, the tea,
Among the porcelain, among some talk of you and me,
Would it have been worth while,   90
To have bitten off the matter with a smile,
To have squeezed the universe into a ball
To roll it toward some overwhelming question,
To say: "I am Lazarus,[3] come from the dead,
Come back to tell you all, I shall tell you all"—   95
If one, settling a pillow by her head,
  Should say: "That is not what I meant at all.
  That is not it, at all."

And would it have been worth it, after all,
Would it have been worth while,   100
After the sunsets and the dooryards and the sprinkled streets,
After the novels, after the teacups, after the skirts that trail along the floor—
And this, and so much more?—
It is impossible to say just what I mean!
But as if a magic lantern threw the nerves in patterns on a screen:
                                                                 105

---

[2] See Matthew 14:3–11.   [3] See John 11.

Would it have been worth while
If one, settling a pillow or throwing off a shawl,
And turning toward the window, should say:
    "That is not it at all,
    That is not what I meant, at all." 110
       . . . .

No! I am not Prince Hamlet, nor was meant to be;
Am an attendant lord, one that will do
To swell a progress,[4] start a scene or two,
Advise the prince; no doubt, an easy tool,
Deferential, glad to be of use, 115
Politic, cautious, and meticulous;
Full of high sentence, but a bit obtuse;
At times, indeed, almost ridiculous—
Almost, at times, the Fool.

I grow old . . . I grow old . . . 120
I shall wear the bottoms of my trousers rolled.[5]

Shall I part my hair behind? Do I dare to eat a peach?
I shall wear white flannel trousers, and walk upon the beach.
I have heard the mermaids singing, each to each.

I do not think that they will sing to me. 125

I have seen them riding seaward on the waves
Combing the white hair of the waves blown back
When the wind blows the water white and black.

We have lingered in the chambers of the sea
By sea-girls wreathed with seaweed red and brown 130
Till human voices wake us, and we drown.

---

[4] *swell a progress:* increase a prince's retinue on a journey.   [5] *rolled:* cuffed.

Bells for John Whiteside's Daughter

There was such speed in her little body,
And such lightness in her footfall,
It is no wonder that her brown study
Astonishes us all.

Her wars were bruited in our high window.
We looked among orchard trees and beyond,
Where she took arms against her shadow,
Or harried unto the pond

The lazy geese, like a snow cloud
Dripping their snow on the green grass,
Tricking and stopping, sleepy and proud,
Who cried in goose, Alas,

For the tireless heart within the little
Lady with rod that made them rise
From their noon apple dreams, and scuttle
Goose-fashion under the skies!

But now go the bells, and we are ready;
In one house we are sternly stopped
To say we are vexed at her brown study,
Lying so primly propped.

Blue Girls

Twirling your blue skirts, travelling the sward
Under the towers of your seminary,
Go listen to your teachers old and contrary
Without believing a word.

Tie the white fillets then about your hair
And think no more of what will come to pass
Than bluebirds that go walking on the grass
And chattering on the air.

Practice your beauty, blue girls, before it fail;
And I will cry with my loud lips and publish
Beauty which all our power shall never establish,
It is so frail.

For I could tell you a story which is true;
I know a lady with a terrible tongue,
Blear eyes fallen from blue, 15
All her perfections tarnished—yet it is not long
Since she was lovelier than any of you.

Nocturne

Where now is the young Adam, sultry in his Aiden?[1]
And where is the goat-footed,[2] pursuing his naked maiden?
Our man shall cut few capers in his dark seersucker coat,
His grave eye subduing the outrageous red tie at his throat,
Considering if he should carry his dutiful flesh to the ball, 5
Rather than open his book, which is flat, and metaphysical.

The centuries have blown hard, and dried his blood
Unto this dark quintessence of manhood;
Much water has passed the bridges, fretfully,
And borne his boats of passion to the sea; 10
There is no storm in this dusk, but a distant flash
Over the foamy sea where the great floods wash.

But still the plum-tree blooms, despite the rocks at its root,
Despite that everyone knows by now its wizened and little fruit,
And the white moon plunges wildly, it is a most ubiquitous ghost, 15
Always seeking her own old people that are a long time lost—
Till he is almost persuaded, and perhaps he would go to the ball,
If he had the heart, and the head, for a furious antique bacchanal.

---

[1] *Aiden:* Eden. [2] *goat-footed:* Pan, the Greek god of flocks and pastures.

Buffalo Bill's

Buffalo Bill's
defunct
          who used to
          ride a watersmooth-silver
                                        stallion
and break onetwothreefourfive pigeonsjustlikethat
                                                    Jesus
he was a handsome man
                        and what i want to know is
how do you like your blueeyed boy
Mister Death

the Cambridge ladies

the Cambridge ladies who live in furnished souls
are unbeautiful and have comfortable minds
(also, with the church's protestant blessings
daughters, unscented shapeless spirited)
they believe in Christ and Longfellow, both dead,
are invariably interested in so many things—
at the present writing one still finds
delighted fingers knitting for the is it Poles?
perhaps. While permanent faces coyly bandy
scandal of Mrs. N and Professor D
. . . . the Cambridge ladies do not care, above
Cambridge if sometimes in its box of
sky lavender and cornerless, the
moon rattles like a fragment of angry candy

the skinny voice

the skinny voice

of the leatherfaced
woman with the crimson
nose and coquettishly-
cocked bonnet

having ceased   the

captain
announces that as three
dimes seven nickels and ten
pennies have been deposited upon

the drum   there is need

of just twenty five cents
dear friends
to make it an even
dollar   whereupon

the Divine Average who was

attracted by the inspired
sister's howling moves
off
will anyone tell him why he should

blow two bits for the coming of Christ Jesus

?
??
???
!

nix, kid

my sweet old etcetera

my sweet old etcetera
aunt lucy during the recent

war[1] could and what
is more did tell you just
what everybody was fighting

for,
my sister
isabel created hundreds
(and

[1] *war*: World War I.

hundreds)of socks not to
mention shirts fleaproof earwarmers

etcetera wristers etcetera,my
mother hoped that

i would die etcetera
bravely of course my father used
to become hoarse talking about how it was
a privilege and if only he
could meanwhile my

self etcetera lay quietly
in the deep mud et

cetera
(dreaming,
et
   cetera,of
Your smile
eyes knees and of your Etcetera)

if there are any heavens

if there are any heavens my mother will(all by herself)have
one.   It will not be a pansy heaven nor
a fragile heaven of lilies-of the-valley but
it will be a heaven of blackred roses

my father will be(deep like a rose
tall like a rose)

standing near my

swaying over her
silent)
with eyes which are really petals and see

nothing with the face of a poet really which
is a flower and not a face with
hands
which whisper
This is my beloved my

                        (suddenly in sunlight
he will bow,

& the whole garden will bow)

i thank You God

i thank You God for most this amazing
day:for the leaping greenly spirits of trees
and a blue true dream of sky;and for everything
which is natural which is infinite which is yes

(i who have died am alive again today,
and this is the sun's birthday;this is the birth
day of life and of love and wings:and of the gay
great happening illimitably earth)

how should tasting touching hearing seeing
breathing any—lifted from the no
of all nothing—human merely being
doubt unimaginable You?

(now the ears of my ears awake and
now the eyes of my eyes are opened)

Ode to the Confederate Dead

Row after row with strict impunity
The headstones yield their names to the element,
The wind whirrs without recollection;
In the riven troughs the splayed leaves
Pile up, of nature the casual sacrament
To the seasonal eternity of death;
Then driven by the fierce scrutiny
Of heaven to their election in the vast breath,
They sough the rumor of mortality.

Autumn is desolation in the plot
Of a thousand acres where these memories grow
From the inexhaustible bodies that are not
Dead, but feed the grass row after rich row.
Think of the autumns that have come and gone!
Ambitious November with the humors of the year,
With a particular zeal for every slab,
Staining the uncomfortable angels that rot
On the slabs, a wing chipped here, an arm there:
The brute curiosity of an angel's stare
Turns you, like them, to stone,
Transforms the heaving air
Till plunged to a heavier world below
You shift your sea-space blindly
Heaving, turning like the blind crab.

    Dazed by the wind, only the wind
    The leaves flying, plunge

You know who have waited by the wall
The twilight certainty of an animal,
Those midnight restitutions of the blood
You know—the immitigable pines, the smoky frieze
Of the sky, the sudden call: you know the rage,
The cold pool left by the mounting flood,
Of muted Zeno and Parmenides.[1]
You who have waited for the angry resolution
Of those desires that should be yours tomorrow,
You know the unimportant shrift of death
And praise the vision
And praise the arrogant circumstance

[1] Greek philosophers who believed that all change and development is a delusion.

Of those who fall
Rank upon rank, hurried beyond decision—
Here by the sagging gate, stopped by the wall.

    Seeing, seeing only the leaves
    Flying, plunge and expire

Turn your eyes to the immoderate past,
Turn to the inscrutable infantry rising
Demons out of the earth—they will not last.
Stonewall, Stonewall and the sunken fields of hemp,
Shiloh, Antietam, Malvern Hill, Bull Run[2]
Lost in that orient of the thick and fast
You will curse the setting sun.

    Cursing only the leaves crying
    Like an old man in a storm

You hear the shout, the crazy hemlocks point
With troubled fingers to the silence which
Smothers you, a mummy, in time.

    The hound bitch
    Toothless and dying, in a musty cellar
    Hears the wind only.

    Now that the salt of their blood
Stiffens the saltier oblivion of the sea,
Seals the malignant purity of the flood,
What shall we who count our days and bow
Our heads with a commemorial woe
In the ribboned coats of grim felicity,
What shall we say of the bones, unclean,
Whose verdurous anonymity will grow?

The ragged arms, the ragged heads and eyes
Lost in these acres of the insane green?
The gray lean spiders come, they come and go;
In a tangle of willows without light
The singular screech-owl's tight
Invisible lyric seeds the mind
With the furious murmur of their chivalry.

[2] Civil War battles.

        We shall say only the leaves
        Flying, plunge and expire

We shall say only the leaves whispering
In the improbable mist of nightfall
That flies on multiple wing:
Night is the beginning and the end
And in between the ends of distraction
Waits mute speculation, the patient curse
That stones the eyes, or like the jaguar leaps
For his own image in a jungle pool, his victim.

What shall we say who have knowledge
Carried to the heart? Shall we take the act
To the grave? Shall we, more hopeful, set up the grave
In the house? The ravenous grave?

            Leave now
The shut gate and the decomposing wall:
The gentle serpent, green in the mulberry bush,
Riots with his tongue through the hush—
Sentinel of the grave who counts us all!

Heritage

(For Harold Jackman)

What is Africa to me:
Copper sun or scarlet sea,
Jungle star or jungle track,
Strong bronzed men, or regal black
Women from whose loins I sprang   5
When the birds of Eden sang?
One three centuries removed
From the scenes his fathers loved,
Spicy grove, cinnamon tree,
What is Africa to me?   10

So I lie, who all day long
Want no sound except the song
Sung by wild barbaric birds
Goading massive jungle herds,
Juggernauts of flesh that pass   15
Trampling tall defiant grass
Where young forest lovers lie,
Plighting troth beneath the sky.
So I lie, who always hear,
Though I cram against my ear   20
Both my thumbs, and keep them there,
Great drums throbbing through the air.
So I lie, whose fount of pride,
Dear distress, and joy allied,
Is my somber flesh and skin,   25
With the dark blood dammed within
Like great pulsing tides of wine
That, I fear, must burst the fine
Channels of the chafing net
Where they surge and foam and fret.   30

Africa? A book one thumbs
Listlessly, till slumber comes.
Unremembered are her bats
Circling through the night, her cats
Crouching in the river reeds,   35
Stalking gentle flesh that feeds
By the river brink; no more
Does the bugle-throated roar
Cry that monarch claws have leapt
From the scabbards where they slept.   40

Silver snakes that once a year
Doff the lovely coats you wear,
Seek no covert in your fear
Lest a mortal eye should see;
What's your nakedness to me?
Here no leprous flowers rear
Fierce corollas in the air;
Here no bodies sleek and wet,
Dripping mingled rain and sweat,
Tread the savage measures of
Jungle boys and girls in love.
What is last year's snow to me,
Last year's anything? The tree
Budding yearly must forget
How its past arose or set—
Bough and blossom, flower, fruit,
Even what shy bird with mute
Wonder at her travail there,
Meekly labored in its hair.
*One three centuries removed
From the scenes his fathers loved,
Spicy grove, cinnamon tree,
What is Africa to me?*

So I lie, who find no peace
Night or day, no slight release
From the unremittant beat
Made by cruel padded feet
Walking through my body's street.
Up and down they go, and back,
Treading out a jungle track.
So I lie, who never quite
Safely sleep from rain at night—
I can never rest at all
When the rain begins to fall;
Like a soul gone mad with pain
I must match its weird refrain;
Ever must I twist and squirm,
Writhing like a baited worm,
While its primal measures drip
Through my body, crying, "Strip!
Doff this new exuberance.
Come and dance the Lover's Dance!"
In an old remembered way
Rain works on me night and day.

Quaint, outlandish heathen gods
Black men fashion out of rods,
Clay, and brittle bits of stone,
In a likeness like their own,
My conversion came high-priced;
I belong to Jesus Christ,
Preacher of humility;
Heathen gods are naught to me.

Father, Son, and Holy Ghost,
So I make an idle boast;
Jesus of the twice-turned cheek,
Lamb of God, although I speak
With my mouth thus, in my heart
Do I play a double part.
Ever at Thy glowing altar
Must my heart grow sick and falter,
Wishing He I served were black,
Thinking then it would not lack
Precedent of pain to guide it,
Let who would or might deride it;
Surely then this flesh would know
Yours had borne a kindred woe.
Lord, I fashion dark gods, too,
Daring even to give You
Dark despairing features where,
Crowned with dark rebellious hair,
Patience wavers just so much as
Mortal grief compels, while touches
Quick and hot, of anger, rise
To smitten cheek and weary eyes.
Lord, forgive me if my need
Sometimes shapes a human creed.
All day long and all night through,
One thing only must I do:
Quench my pride and cool my blood,
Lest I perish in the flood.
Lest a hidden ember set
Timber that I thought was wet
Burning like the dryest flax,
Melting like the merest wax,
Lest the grave restore its dead.
Not yet has my heart or head
In the least way realized
They and I are civilized.

W. H. AUDEN

Musée des Beaux Arts

About suffering they were never wrong,
The Old Masters: how well they understood
Its human position; how it takes place
While someone else is eating or opening a window or just walking
    dully along;
How, when the aged are reverently, passionately waiting   5
For the miraculous birth, there always must be
Children who did not specially want it to happen, skating
On a pond at the edge of the wood:
They never forgot
That even the dreadful martyrdom must run its course   10
Anyhow in a corner, some untidy spot
Where the dogs go on with their doggy life and the torturer's horse
Scratches its innocent behind on a tree.

In Brueghel's *Icarus*,[1] for instance: how everything turns away
Quite leisurely from the disaster; the ploughman may   15
Have heard the splash, the forsaken cry,
But for him it was not an important failure; the sun shone
As it had to on the white legs disappearing into the green
Water; and the expensive delicate ship that must have seen
Something amazing, a boy falling out of the sky,   20
Had somewhere to get to and sailed calmly on.

---

[1] *Brueghel:* Pieter Brueghel, a sixteenth-century Flemish painter. *Icarus:* the painting is entitled "The Fall of Icarus" and depicts Icarus plunging into the sea, the wax on his wings having melted from his having soared too near the sun.

Open House

My secrets cry aloud.
I have no need for tongue.
My heart keeps open house,
My doors are widely swung.
An epic of the eyes
My love, with no disguise.

My truths are all foreknown,
This anguish self-revealed.
I'm naked to the bone,
With nakedness my shield.
Myself is what I wear:
I keep the spirit spare.

The anger will endure,
The deed will speak the truth
In language strict and pure.
I stop the lying mouth:
Rage warps my clearest cry
To witless agony.

To My Sister

O my sister remember the stars the tears the trains
The woods in spring the leaves the scented lanes
Recall the gradual dark the snow's unmeasured fall
The naked fields the cloud's immaculate folds
Recount each childhood pleasure: the skies of azure
The pageantry of wings the eye's bright treasure.

Keep faith with present joys refuse to choose
Defer the vice of flesh the irrevocable choice
Cherish the eyes the proud incredible poise
Walk boldly my sister but do not deign to give
Remain secure from pain preserve thy hate thy heart.

Moss-Gathering

To loosen with all ten fingers held wide and limber
And lift up a patch, dark-green, the kind for lining cemetery baskets,
Thick and cushiony, like an old-fashioned doormat,

The crumbling small hollow sticks on the underside mixed with roots,
And wintergreen berries and leaves still stuck to the top,— 5
That was moss-gathering.
But something always went out of me when I dug loose those carpets
Of green, or plunged to my elbows in the spongy yellowish moss of the
    marshes:
And afterwards I always felt mean, jogging back over the logging road,
As if I had broken the natural order of things in that swampland; 10
Disturbed some rhythm, old and of vast importance,
By pulling off flesh from the living planet;
As if I had committed, against the whole scheme of life, a desecration.

My Papa's Waltz

The whiskey on your breath
Could make a small boy dizzy;
But I hung on like death:
Such waltzing was not easy.

We romped until the pans 5
Slid from the kitchen shelf;
My mother's countenance
Could not unfrown itself.

The hand that held my wrist
Was battered on one knuckle; 10
At every step you missed
My right ear scraped a buckle.

You beat time on my head
With a palm caked hard by dirt,
Then waltzed me off to bed 15
Still clinging to your shirt.

Dolor

I have known the inexorable sadness of pencils,
Neat in their boxes, dolor of pad and paper-weight,
All the misery of manila folders and mucilage,
Desolation in immaculate public places,
Lonely reception room, lavatory, switchboard, 5
The unalterable pathos of basin and pitcher,

Ritual of multigraph, paper-clip, comma,
Endless duplication of lives and objects.
And I have seen dust from the walls of institutions,
Finer than flour, alive, more dangerous than silica,   10
Sift, almost invisible, through long afternoons of tedium,
Dropping a fine film on nails and delicate eyebrows,
Glazing the pale hair, the duplicate gray standard faces.

Elegy for Jane

My Student, Thrown by a Horse

I remember the neckcurls, limp and damp as tendrils;
And her quick look, a sidelong pickerel smile;
And how, once startled into talk, the light syllables leaped for her,
And she balanced in the delight of her thought,
A wren, happy, tail into the wind,   5
Her song trembling the twigs and small branches.
The shade sang with her;
The leaves, their whispers turned to kissing;
And the mold sang in the bleached valleys under the rose.

Oh, when she was sad, she cast herself down into such a pure depth,   10
Even a father could not find her:
Scraping her cheek against straw;
Stirring the clearest water.

My sparrow, you are not here,
Waiting like a fern, making a spiny shadow.   15
The sides of wet stones cannot console me,
Nor the moss, wound with the last light.

If only I could nudge you from this sleep,
My maimed darling, my skittery pigeon.
Over this damp grave I speak the words of my love: 20
I, with no rights in this matter,
Neither father nor lover.

The Waking

I wake to sleep, and take my waking slow.
I feel my fate in what I cannot fear.
I learn by going where I have to go.

We think by feeling. What is there to know?
I hear my being dance from ear to ear.
I wake to sleep, and take my waking slow.

Of those so close beside me, which are you?
God bless the Ground! I shall walk softly there,
And learn by going where I have to go.

Light takes the Tree: but who can tell us how?
The lowly worm climbs up a winding stair;
I wake to sleep, and take my waking slow.

Great Nature has another thing to do
To you and me; so take the lively air,
And, lovely, learn by going where to go.

This shaking keeps me steady. I should know.
What falls away is always. And is near.
I wake to sleep, and take my waking slow.
I learn by going where I have to go.

The Dream

1

I met her as a blossom on a stem
Before she ever breathed, and in that dream
The mind remembers from a deeper sleep:
Eye learned from eye, cold lip from sensual lip.
My dream divided on a point of fire;
Light hardened on the water where we were;
A bird sang low; the moonlight sifted in;
The water rippled, and she rippled on.

2

She came toward me in the flowing air,
A shape of change, encircled by its fire.
I watched her there, between me and the moon;
The bushes and the stones danced on and on;
I touched her shadow when the light delayed;
I turned my face away, and yet she stayed.
A bird sang from the center of a tree;
She loved the wind because the wind loved me.

3

Love is not love until love's vulnerable.
She slowed to sigh, in that long interval.
A small bird flew in circles where we stood;
The deer came down, out of the dappled wood.
All who remember, doubt. Who calls that strange?
I tossed a stone, and listened to its plunge.
She knew the grammar of least motion, she
Lent me one virtue, and I live thereby.

4

She held her body steady in the wind;
Our shadows met, and slowly swung around;
She turned the field into a glittering sea;
I played in flame and water like a boy
And I swayed out beyond the white seafoam;
Like a wet log, I sang within a flame.
In that last while, eternity's confine,
I came to love, I came into my own.

In a Dark Time

In a dark time, the eye begins to see,
I meet my shadow in the deepening shade;
I hear my echo in the echoing wood—
A lord of nature weeping to a tree.
I live between the heron and the wren,
Beasts of the hill and serpents of the den.

What's madness but nobility of soul
At odds with circumstance? The day's on fire!
I know the purity of pure despair,
My shadow pinned against a sweating wall.
That place among the rocks—is it a cave,
Or winding path? The edge is what I have.

A steady storm of correspondences!
A night flowing with birds, a ragged moon,
And in broad day the midnight come again!
A man goes far to find out what he is—

Death of the self in a long, tearless night,
All natural shapes blazing unnatural light.

Dark, dark my light, and darker my desire.
My soul, like some heat-maddened summer fly,
Keeps buzzing at the sill. Which I is I?
A fallen man, I climb out of my fear.
The mind enters itself, and God the mind,
And one is One, free in the tearing wind.

In Evening Air

1

A dark theme keeps me here,
Though summer blazes in the vireo's eye.
Who would be half possessed
By his own nakedness?
Waking's my care—
I'll make a broken music, or I'll die.

2

Ye littles, lie more close!
Make me, O Lord, a last, a simple thing
Time cannot overwhelm.
Once I transcended time:
A bud broke to a rose,
And I rose from a last diminishing.

3

I look down the far light
And I behold the dark side of a tree
Far down a billowing plain,
And when I look again,
It's lost upon the night—
Night I embrace, a dear proximity.

4

I stand by a low fire
Counting the wisps of flame, and I watch how

Light shifts upon the wall.
I bid stillness be still.
I see, in evening air,
How slowly dark comes down on what we do.

The Sequel

1

Was I too glib about eternal things,
An intimate of air and all its songs?
Pure aimlessness pursued and yet pursued
And all wild longings of the insatiate blood
Brought me down to my knees. O who can be
Both moth and flame? The weak moth blundering by.
Whom do we love? I thought I knew the truth;
Of grief I died, but no one knew my death.

2

I saw a body dancing in the wind,
A shape called up out of my natural mind;
I heard a bird stir in its true confine;
A nestling sighed—I called that nestling mine;
A partridge drummed; a minnow nudged its stone;
We danced, we danced, under a dancing moon;
And on the coming of the outrageous dawn,
We danced together, we danced on and on.

3

Morning's a motion in a happy mind:
She stayed in light, as leaves live in the wind,
Swaying in air, like some long water weed.
She left my body, lighter than a seed;
I gave her body full and grave farewell.
A wind came close, like a shy animal.
A light leaf on a tree, she swayed away
To the dark beginnings of another day.

4

Was nature kind? The heart's core tractable?
All waters waver, and all fires fail.

Leaves, leaves, lean forth and tell me what I am;
This single tree turns into purest flame.
I am a man, a man at intervals
Pacing a room, a room with dead-white walls; 30
I feel the autumn fail—all that slow fire
Denied in me, who has denied desire.

The Right Thing

Let others probe the mystery if they can.
Time-harried prisoners of *Shall* and *Will*—
The right thing happens to the happy man.

The bird flies out, the bird flies back again;
The hill becomes the valley, and is still; 5
Let others delve that mystery if they can.

God bless the roots!—Body and soul are one!
The small become the great, the great the small;
The right thing happens to the happy man.

Child of the dark, he can out leap the sun, 10
His being single, and that being all:
The right thing happens to the happy man.

Or if he sits still, a solid figure when
The self-destructive shake the common wall;
Takes to himself what mystery he can, 15

And praising change as the slow night comes on,
Wills what he would, surrendering his will
Till mystery is no more: No more he can.
The right thing happens to the happy man.

Mourning Poem for the Queen of Sunday

    Lord's lost Him His mockingbird,
    His fancy warbler;
    Satan sweet-talked her,
    four bullets hushed her.
    Who would have thought
    she'd end that way?

Four bullets hushed her. And the world a-clang with evil.
Who's going to make old hardened sinner men tremble now
and the righteous rock?
Oh who and oh who will sing Jesus down
to help with struggling and doing without and being colored
all through blue Monday?
Till way next Sunday?

    All those angels
    in their cretonne clouds and finery
    the true believer saw
    when she rared back her head and sang,
    all those angels are surely weeping.
    Who would have thought
    she'd end that way?

Four holes in her heart. The gold works wrecked.
But she looks so natural in her big bronze coffin
among the Broken Hearts and Gates-Ajar,
it's as if any moment she'd lift her head
from its pillow of chill gardenias
and turn this quiet into shouting Sunday
and make folks forget what she did on Monday.

    Oh, Satan sweet-talked her,
    and four bullets hushed her.
    Lord's lost Him His diva,
    His fancy warbler's gone.
    Who would have thought,
    who would have thought she'd end that way?

The Whipping

The old woman across the way
    is whipping the boy again
and shouting to the neighborhood
    her goodness and his wrongs.

Wildly he crashes through elephant ears,
    pleads in dusty zinnias,
while she in spite of crippling fat
    pursues and corners him.

She strikes and strikes the shrilly circling
    boy till the stick breaks
in her hand. His tears are rainy weather
    to woundlike memories:

My head gripped in bony vise
    of knees, the writhing struggle
to wrench free, the blows, the fear
    worse than blows that hateful

Words could bring, the face that I
    no longer knew or loved . . .
Well, it is over now, it is over,
    and the boy sobs in his room,

And the woman leans muttering against
    a tree, exhausted, purged—
avenged in part for lifelong hidings
    she has had to bear.

Those Winter Sundays

Sundays too my father got up early
and put his clothes on in the blueblack cold,
then with cracked hands that ached
from labor in the weekday weather made
banked fires blaze. No one ever thanked him.

I'd wake and hear the cold splintering, breaking.
When the rooms were warm, he'd call,
and slowly I would rise and dress,
fearing the chronic angers of that house,

Speaking indifferently to him,
who had driven out the cold
and polished my good shoes as well.
What did I know, what did I know
of love's austere and lonely offices?

Frederick Douglass

When it is finally ours, this freedom, this liberty, this beautiful
and terrible thing, needful to man as air,
usable as earth; when it belongs at last to all,
when it is truly instinct, brain matter, diastole, systole,
reflex action; when it is finally won; when it is more
than the gaudy mumbo jumbo of politicians:
this man, this Douglass, this former slave, this Negro
beaten to his knees, exiled, visioning a world
where none is lonely, none hunted, alien,
this man, superb in love and logic, this man
shall be remembered. Oh, not with statues' rhetoric,
not with legends and poems and wreaths of bronze alone,
but with the lives grown out of his life, the lives
fleshing his dream of the beautiful, needful thing.

Monet's "Waterlilies"

(for Bill and Sonja)

Today as the news from Selma and Saigon
poisons the air like fallout,
     I come again to see
the serene great picture that I love
and flames disfigured once
     and efficient evil may yet destroy.

Here space and time exist in light
the eye like the eye of faith believes.
     The seen, the known
dissolve in irridescence, become
illusive flesh of light
     that was not, was, forever is.

O light beheld as through refracting tears.
Here is the aura of that world
    each of us has lost.
Here is the shadow of its joy.

A Plague of Starlings

(*Fisk Campus*)

Evenings I hear
the workmen fire
into the stiff
magnolia leaves,
routing the starlings
gathered noisy and
befouling there.

Their scissoring
terror like glass
coins spilling breaking
the birds explode
into mica sky
raggedly fall
to ground rigid
in clench of cold.

The spared return,
when the guns are through,
to the spoiled trees
like choiceless poor
to a dangerous
dwelling place,
chitter and quarrel
in the piercing dark
above the killed.

Mornings, I pick
my way past death's
black droppings:
on campus lawns
and streets
the troublesome
starlings

frost-salted lie,
troublesome still.

And if not careful
I shall tread
upon carcasses
carcasses when I
go mornings now
to lecture on
what Socrates,
the hemlock hour nigh,
told sorrowing
Phaedo and the rest
about the migratory
habits of the soul.

Traveling through the Dark

Traveling through the dark I found a deer
dead on the edge of the Wilson River road.
It is usually best to roll them into the canyon:
that road is narrow; to swerve might make more dead.

By glow of the tail-light I stumbled back of the car
and stood by the heap, a doe, a recent killing;
she had stiffened already, almost cold.
I dragged her off; she was large in the belly.

My fingers touching her side brought me the reason—
her side was warm; her fawn lay there waiting,
alive, still, never to be born.
Beside that mountain road I hesitated.

The car aimed ahead its lowered parking lights;
under the hood purred the steady engine.
I stood in the glare of the warm exhaust turning red;
around our group I could hear the wilderness listen.

I thought hard for us all—my only swerving—,
then pushed her over the edge into the river.

The Tillamook Burn

These mountains have heard God;
they burned for weeks. He spoke
in a tongue of flame from sawmill trash
and you can read His word down to the rock.

In milky rivers the steelhead
butt upstream to spawn
and find a world with depth again,
starting from stillness and water across gray stone.

Inland along the canyons
all night weather smokes
past the deer and the widow-makers—
trees too dead to fall till again He speaks,

Mowing the criss-cross trees and the listening peaks.

Vocation

This dream the world is having about itself
includes a trace on the plains of the Oregon trail,
a groove in the grass my father showed us all
one day while meadowlarks were trying to tell
something better about to happen.

I dreamed the trace to the mountains, over the hills,
and there a girl who belonged wherever she was.
But then my mother called us back to the car:
she was afraid; she always blamed the place,
the time, anything my father planned.

Now both of my parents, the long line through the plain,
the meadowlarks, the sky, the world's whole dream
remain, and I hear him say while I stand between the two,
helpless, both of them part of me:
"Your job is to find what the world is trying to be."

Requiem

Mother is gone. Bird songs wouldn't let her breathe.
The skating bug broke through the eternal veil.
A tree in the forest fell; the air remembered.
Two rocks clinked in the night to signal some meaning.

Traveler north, beyond where you can return,
hearing above you the last of the razor birds whizz
over the drift of dust that bore your name,
there's a kind of waiting you teach us—the art of not knowing.

Suicidal gestures of nobility driven to the wrist,
our molten bodies remembering some easier form,
we feel the bones assert the rites of yesterday
and the flow of angular events becoming destiny.

Summer and locusts own the elm part of town;
on the millpond moss is making its cream.
Our duty is just a certain high kind of waiting;
beyond our hearing is the hearing of the community.

Our City Is Guarded by Automatic Rockets

1

Breaking every law except the one
for Go, rolling its porpoise way, the rocket
staggers on its course; its feelers lock
a stranglehold ahead; and—rocking—finders
whispering "Target, Target," back and forth,
relocating all its meaning in the dark,
it freezes on the final stage. I know
that lift and pour, the flick out of the sky
and then the power. Power is not enough.

2

Bough touching bough, touching . . . till the shore,
a lake, an undecided river, and a lake again
saddling the divide: a world that won't be wise
and let alone, but instead is found outside
by little channels, linked by chance, not stern;
and then when once we're sure we hear a guide
it fades away toward the opposite end of the road
from home—the world goes wrong in order to have revenge.
Our lives are an amnesty given us.

3

There is a place behind our hill so real
it makes me turn my head, no matter. There
in the last thicket lies the cornered cat
saved by its claws, now ready to spend
all there is left of the wilderness, embracing
its blood. And that is the way that I will spit
life, at the end of any trail where I smell any hunter,
because I think our story should not end—
or go on in the dark with nobody listening.

The Force That Through the Green Fuse Drives the Flower

The force that through the green fuse drives the flower
Drives my green age; that blasts the roots of trees
Is my destroyer.
And I am dumb[1] to tell the crooked rose
My youth is bent by the same wintry fever.

The force that drives the water through the rocks
Drives my red blood; that dries the mouthing streams
Turns mine to wax.
And I am dumb to mouth unto my veins
How at the mountain spring the same mouth sucks.

The hand that whirls the water in the pool
Stirs the quicksand; that ropes the blowing wind
Hauls my shroud sail.
And I am dumb to tell the hanging man
How of my clay is made the hangman's lime.

The lips of time leech to the fountain head;
Love drips and gathers, but the fallen blood
Shall calm her sores.
And I am dumb to tell a weather's wind
How time has ticked a heaven round the stars.

And I am dumb to tell the lover's tomb
How at my sheet goes the same crooked worm.

A Refusal to Mourn the Death, by Fire, of a Child in London

Never until the mankind making
Bird beast and flower
Fathering and all humbling darkness
Tells with silence the last light breaking
And the still hour
Is come of the sea tumbling in harness

And I must enter again the round
Zion of the water bead

---

[1] *dumb*: speechless.

And the synagogue of the ear of corn
Shall I let pray the shadow of a sound
Or sow my salt seed
In the least valley of sackcloth to mourn

The majesty and burning of the child's death.
I shall not murder
The mankind of her going with a grave truth
Nor blaspheme down the stations of the breath
With any further
Elegy of innocence and youth.

Deep with the first dead lies London's daughter,
Robed in the long friends,
The grains beyond age, the dark veins of her mother,
Secret by the unmourning water
Of the riding Thames.
After the first death, there is no other.

Fern Hill

Now as I was young and easy under the apple boughs
About the lilting house and happy as the grass was green,
   The night above the dingle starry,
     Time let me hail and climb
   Golden in the heydays of his eyes,
And honoured among wagons I was prince of the apple towns
And once below a time I lordly had the trees and leaves
     Trail with daisies and barley
   Down the rivers of the windfall light.

And as I was green and carefree, famous among the barns
About the happy yard and singing as the farm was home,
   In the sun that is young once only,
     Time let me play and be
   Golden in the mercy of his means,
And green and golden I was huntsman and herdsman, the calves
Sang to my horn, the foxes on the hills barked clear and cold,
     And the sabbath rang slowly
   In the pebbles of the holy streams.

All the sun long it was running, it was lovely, the hay
Fields high as the house, the tunes from the chimneys, it was air

>   And playing, lovely and watery
>   And fire green as grass.
>   And nightly under the simple stars
> As I rode to sleep the owls were bearing the farm away,
> All the moon long I heard, blessed among stables, the nightjars
>   Flying with the ricks, and horses
>   Flashing into the dark.
>
> And then to awake, and the farm, like a wanderer white
> With the dew, come back, the cock on his shoulder: it was all
>   Shining, it was Adam and maiden,
>   The sky gathered again
>   And the sun grew round that very day.
> So it must have been after the birth of the simple light
> In the first, spinning place, the spellbound horses walking warm
>   Out of the whinnying green stable
>   On to the fields of praise.
>
> And honoured among foxes and pheasants by the gay house
> Under the new made clouds and happy as the heart was long
>   In the sun born over and over,
>   I ran my heedless ways,
>   My wishes raced through the house high hay
> And nothing I cared, at my sky blue trades, that time allows
> In all his tuneful turning so few and such morning songs
>   Before the children green and golden
>   Follow him out of grace.
>
> Nothing I cared, in the lamb white days, that time would take me
> Up to the swallow thronged loft by the shadow of my hand,
>   In the moon that is always rising,
>   Nor that riding to sleep
>   I should hear him fly with the high fields
> And wake to the farm forever fled from the childless land.
> Oh as I was young and easy in the mercy of his means,
>   Time held me green and dying
>   Though I sang in my chains like the sea.

Do Not Go Gentle into That Good Night

> Do not go gentle into that good night,
> Old age should burn and rave at close of day;
> Rage, rage against the dying of the light.

Though wise men at their end know dark is right,
Because their words had forked no lightning they
Do not go gentle into that good night.

Good men, the last wave by, crying how bright
Their frail deeds might have danced in a green bay,
Rage, rage against the dying of the light.

Wild men who caught and sang the sun in flight,
And learn, too late, they grieved it on its way,
Do not go gentle into that good night.

Grave men, near death, who see with blinding sight
Blind eyes could blaze like meteors and be gay,
Rage, rage against the dying of the light.

And you, my father, there on the sad height,
Curse, bless, me now with your fierce tears, I pray.
Do not go gentle into that good night.
Rage, rage against the dying of the light.

And Death Shall Have No Dominion

And death shall have no dominion.
Dead men naked they shall be one
With the man in the wind and the west moon;
When their bones are picked clean and the clean bones gone,
They shall have stars at elbow and foot;
Though they go mad they shall be sane,
Though they sink through the sea they shall rise again;
Though lovers be lost love shall not;
And death shall have no dominion.

And death shall have no dominion.
Under the windings of the sea
They lying long shall not die windily;
Twisting on racks when sinews give way,
Strapped to a wheel, yet they shall not break;
Faith in their hands shall snap in two,
And the unicorn evils run them through;
Split all ends up they shan't crack;
And death shall have no dominion.

And death shall have no dominion.
No more may gulls cry at their ears
Or waves break loud on the seashores;
Where blew a flower may a flower no more
Lift its head to the blows of the rain;
Though they be mad and dead as nails,
Heads of the characters hammer through daisies;
Break in the sun till the sun breaks down,
And death shall have no dominion.

kitchenette building

We are things of dry hours and the involuntary plan,
Grayed in, and gray. "Dream" makes a giddy sound, not strong
Like "rent," "feeding a wife," "satisfying a man."

But could a dream send up through onion fumes
Its white and violet, fight with fried potatoes
And yesterday's garbage ripening in the hall,
Flutter, or sing an aria down these rooms

Even if we were willing to let it in,
Had time to warm it, keep it very clean,
Anticipate a message, let it begin?

We wonder. But not well! not for a minute!
Since Number Five is out of the bathroom now,
We think of lukewarm water, hope to get in it.

a song in the front yard

I've stayed in the front yard all my life.
I want a peek at the back
Where it's rough and untended and hungry weed grows.
A girl gets sick of a rose.

I want to go in the back yard now
And maybe down the alley,
To where the charity children play.
I want a good time today.

They do some wonderful things.
They have some wonderful fun.
My mother sneers, but I say it's fine
How they don't have to go in at quarter to nine.
My mother, she tells me that Johnnie Mae
Will grow up to be a bad woman.
That George'll be taken to jail soon or late
(On account of last winter he sold our back gate).

But I say it's fine. Honest, I do.
And I'd like to be a bad woman, too,
And wear the brave stockings of night-black lace
And strut down the streets with paint on my face.

the preacher: ruminates behind the sermon

I think it must be lonely to be God.
Nobody loves a master. No. Despite
The bright hosannas, bright dear-Lords, and bright
Determined reverence of Sunday eyes.

Picture Jehovah striding through the hall
Of His importance, creatures running out
From servant-corners to acclaim, to shout
Appreciation of His merit's glare.

But who walks with Him?—dares to take His arm,
To slap Him on the shoulder, tweak His ear,
Buy Him a Coca-Cola or a beer,
Pooh-pooh His politics, call Him a fool?

Perhaps—who knows?—He tires of looking down.
Those eyes are never lifted. Never straight.
Perhaps sometimes He tires of being great
In solitude. Without a hand to hold.

Medgar Evers

For Charles Evers

The man whose height his fear improved he
arranged to fear no further. The raw
intoxicated time was time for better birth or
a final death.

Old styles, old tempos, all the engagement of
the day—the sedate, the regulated fray—
the antique light, the Moral rose, old gusts,
tight whistlings from the past, the mothballs
in the Love at last our man forswore.

Medgar Evers annoyed confetti and assorted
brands of businessmen's eyes.

The shows came down: to maxims and surprise.
And palsy.

Roaring no rapt arise-ye to the dead, he
leaned across tomorrow. People said that
he was holding clean globes in his hands.

To a Winter Squirrel

That is the way God made you.
And what is wrong with it? Why, nothing.
Except that you are cold and cannot cook.

Merdice can cook. Merdice
of murdered heart and docked sarcastic soul,
Merdice
the bolted nomad, on a winter noon
cooks guts; and sits in gas. (She has no shawl, her landlord has
no coal.)

You out beyond the shellac of her look
and of her sill!
She envies you your furry
buffoonery
that enfolds your silver skill.
She thinks you are a mountain and a star, unbaffleable;
with sentient twitch and scurry.

The Quaker Graveyard in Nantucket

For Warren Winslow, Dead at Sea

Let man have dominion over the fishes
of the sea and the fowls of the air
and the beasts and the whole earth,
and every creeping creature that
moveth upon the earth.[1]

I

A brackish reach of shoal off Madaket,[2]—
The sea was still breaking violently and night
Had steamed into our North Atlantic Fleet,
When the drowned sailor clutched the drag-net. Light
Flashed from his matted head and marble feet,   5
He grappled at the net
With the coiled, hurdling muscles of his thighs:
The corpse was bloodless, a botch of reds and whites,
Its open, staring eyes
Were lustreless dead-lights   10
Or cabin-windows on a stranded hulk
Heavy with sand. We weight the body, close
Its eyes and heave it seaward whence it came,
Where the heel-headed dogfish barks its nose
On Ahab's[3] void and forehead; and the name   15
Is blocked in yellow chalk.
Sailors, who pitch this portent at the sea
Where dreadnaughts shall confess
Its hell-bent deity,
When you are powerless   20
To sand-bag this Atlantic bulwark, faced
By the earth-shaker, green, unwearied, chaste
In his steel scales: ask for no Orphean lute
To pluck life back. The guns of the steeled fleet
Recoil and then repeat   25
The hoarse salute.

II

Whenever winds are moving and their breath
Heaves at the roped-in bulwarks of this pier,

---

[1] See Genesis 1:26.   [2] *Madaket*: a town on Nantucket Island.   [3] *Ahab*: captain of the Pequod which sailed from Nantucket in Melville's *Moby Dick*.

The terns and sea-gulls tremble at your death
In these home waters. Sailor, can you hear
The Pequod's sea wings, beating landward, fall
Headlong and break on our Atlantic wall
Off 'Sconset,[4] where the yawing S-boats splash
The bellbuoy, with ballooning spinnakers,
As the entangled, screeching mainsheet clears
The blocks: off Madaket, where lubbers lash
The heavy surf and throw their long lead squids
For blue-fish? Sea-gulls blink their heavy lids
Seaward. The winds' wings beat upon the stones,
Cousin, and scream for you and the claws rush
At the sea's throat and wring it in the slush
Of this old Quaker graveyard where the bones
Cry out in the long night for the hurt beast
Bobbing by Ahab's whaleboats in the East.

III

All you recovered from Poseidon died
With you, my cousin, and the harrowed brine
Is fruitless on the blue beard of the god,
Stretching beyond us to the castles in Spain,
Nantucket's westward haven. To Cape Cod
Guns, cradled on the tide,
Blast the eelgrass about a waterclock
Of bilge and backwash, roil the salt and sand
Lashing earth's scaffold, rock
Our warships in the hand
Of the great God, where time's contrition blues
Whatever it was these Quaker sailors lost
In the mad scramble of their lives. They died
When time was open-eyed,
Wooden and childish; only bones abide
There, in the nowhere, where their boats were tossed
Sky-high, where mariners had fabled news
Of IS, the whited monster. What it cost
Them is their secret. In the sperm-whale's slick
I see the Quakers drown and hear their cry:
"If God himself had not been on our side,
If God himself had not been on our side
When the Atlantic rose against us, why,
Then it had swallowed us up quick."

---

[4] *'Sconset*: Siasconset, a town on Nantucket Island.

IV

This is the end of the whaleroad and the whale
Who spewed Nantucket bones on the thrashed swell   70
And stirred the troubled waters to whirlpools
To send the Pequod packing off to hell:
This is the end of them, three-quarters fools,
Snatching at straws to sail
Seaward and seaward on the turntail whale,   75
Spouting out blood and water as it rolls,
Sick as a dog to these Atlantic shoals:
Clamavimus,[5] O depths. Let the sea-gulls wail

For water, for the deep where the high tide
Mutters to its hurt self, mutters and ebbs.   80
Waves wallow in their wash, go out and out,
Leave only the death-rattle of the crabs,
The beach increasing, its enormous snout
Sucking the ocean's side.
This is the end of running on the waves;   85
We are poured out like water. Who will dance
The mast-lashed master of Leviathans
Up from this field of Quakers in their unstoned graves?

V

When the whale's viscera go and the roll
Of its corruption overruns this world   90
Beyond tree-swept Nantucket and Wood's Hole
And Martha's Vineyard,[6] Sailor, will your sword
Whistle and fall and sink into the fat?
In the great ash-pit of Jehoshaphat[7]
The bones cry for the blood of the white whale,   95
The fat flukes arch and whack about its ears,
The death-lance churns into the sanctuary, tears
The gun-blue swingle, heaving like a flail,
And hacks the coiling life out: it works and drags
And rips the sperm-whale's midriff into rags,   100
Gobbets of blubber spill to wind and weather,
Sailor, and gulls go round the stoven timbers

---

[5] *Clamavimus:* "We have cried out" (Latin).   [6] *Martha's Vineyard:* an island west of Nantucket.   [7] *Jehoshaphat:* the place of the Last Judgment, according to the Book of Joel (ch. 3).

Where the morning stars sing out together
And thunder shakes the white surf and dismembers
The red flag hammered in the mast-head. Hide,
Our steel, Jonas Messias, in Thy side.

VI *Our Lady of Walsingham*[8]

There once the penitents took off their shoes
And then walked barefoot the remaining mile;
And the small trees, a stream and hedgerows file
Slowly along the munching English lane,
Like cows to the old shrine, until you lose
Track of your dragging pain.
The stream flows down under the druid tree,
Shiloah's whirlpools[9] gurgle and make glad
The castle of God. Sailor, you were glad
And whistled Sion[10] by that stream. But see:
Our Lady, too small for her canopy,
Sits near the altar. There's no comeliness
At all or charm in that expressionless
Face with its heavy eyelids. As before,
This face, for centuries a memory,
Non est species, neque decor,[11]
Expressionless, expresses God: it goes
Past castled Sion.[10] She knows what God knows,
Not Calvary's Cross nor crib at Bethlehem
Now, and the world shall come to Walsingham.

VII

The empty winds are creaking and the oak
Splatters and splatters on the cenotaph,
The boughs are trembling and a gaff
Bobs on the untimely stroke
Of the greased wash exploding on a shoal-bell
In the old mouth of the Atlantic. It's well;
Atlantic, you are fouled with the blue sailors,
Sea-monsters, upward angel, downward fish:
Unmarried and corroding, spare of flesh,
Mart once of supercilious, wing'd clippers;

---

[8] *Walsingham*: village in Norfolk, England, and site of Walsingham Abbey, a great medieval shrine. [9] *Shiloah's whirlpools*: Shiloah, a fountain in Jerusalem. See Isaiah 8:5-7. [10] *Sion*: Zion. [11] *Non . . . decor*: "There is no form nor comeliness" (Latin). See Isaiah 53:2.

Atlantic, where your bell-trap guts its spoil
You could cut the brackish winds with a knife
Here in Nantucket, and cast up the time
When the Lord God formed man from the sea's slime   140
And breathed into his face the breath of life,
And blue-lung'd combers lumbered to the kill.
The Lord survives the rainbow of his will.

The Drunken Fisherman

Wallowing in this bloody sty,
I cast for fish that pleased my eye
(Truly Jehovah's bow suspends
No pots of gold to weight its ends);
Only the blood-mouthed rainbow trout   5
Rose to my bait. They flopped about
My canvas creel until the moth
Corrupted its unstable cloth.

A calendar to tell the day;
A handkerchief to wave away   10
The gnats; a couch unstuffed with storm
Pouching a bottle in one arm;
A whiskey bottle full of worms;
And bedroom slacks; are these fit terms
To mete the worm whose molten rage   15
Boils in the belly of old age?

Once fishing was a rabbit's foot—
O wind blow cold, O wind blow hot,
Let suns stay in or suns step out:
Life danced a jig on the sperm-whale's spout—   20
The fisher's fluent and obscene
Catches kept his conscience clean.
Children, the raging memory drools
Over the glory of past pools.

Now the hot river, ebbing, hauls   25
Its bloody waters into holes;
A grain of sand inside my shoe
Mimics the moon that might undo
Man and Creation too; remorse,
Stinking, has puddled up its source;   30

Here tantrums thrash to a whale's rage.
This is the pot-hole of old age.

Is there no way to cast my hook
Out of this dynamited brook?
The Fisher's sons must cast about   35
When shallow waters peter out.
I will catch Christ with a greased worm,
And when the Prince of Darkness stalks
My bloodstream to its Stygian term . . .
On water the Man-Fisher walks.   40

Man and Wife

Tamed by *Miltown*, we lie on Mother's bed;
the rising sun in war paint dyes us red;
in broad daylight her gilded bed-posts shine,
abandoned, almost Dionysian.
At last the trees are green on Marlborough Street,   5
blossoms on our magnolia ignite
the morning with their murderous five days' white.
All night I've held your hand,
as if you had
a fourth time faced the kingdom of the mad—   10
its hackneyed speech, its homicidal eye—
and dragged me home alive. . . . Oh my *Petite*,
clearest of all God's creatures, still all air and nerve:
you were in your twenties, and I,
once hand on glass   15
and heart in mouth,
outdrank the Rahvs in the heat
of Greenwich Village, fainting at your feet—
too boiled and shy
and poker-faced to make a pass,   20
while the shrill verve
of your invective scorched the traditional South.

Now twelve years later, you turn your back.
Sleepless, you hold
your pillow to your hollows like a child;   25
your old-fashioned tirade—
loving, rapid, merciless—
breaks like the Atlantic Ocean on my head.

The Executive's Death

Merchants have multiplied more than the stars of heaven.
Half the population are like the long grasshoppers
That sleep in the bushes in the cool of the day:
The sound of their wings is heard at noon, muffled, near the earth.
The crane handler dies, the taxi driver dies, slumped over
In his taxi. Meanwhile, high in the air, executives
Walk on cool floors, and suddenly fall:
Dying, they dream they are lost in a snowstorm in mountains,
On which they crashed, carried at night by great machines.
As he lies on the wintry slope, cut off and dying,
A pine stump talks to him of Goethe and Jesus.
Commuters arrive in Hartford at dusk like moles
Or hares flying from a fire behind them,
And the dusk in Hartford is full of their sighs;
Their trains come through the air like a dark music,
Like the sound of horns, the sound of thousands of small wings.

Watching Television

Sounds are heard too high for ears,
From the body cells there is an answering bay;
Soon the inner streets fill with a chorus of barks.

We see the landing craft coming in,
The black car sliding to a stop,
The Puritan killer loosening his guns.

Wild dogs tear off noses and eyes
And run off with them down the street—
The body tears off its own arms and throws them into the air.

The detective draws fifty-five million people into his revolver,
Who sleep restlessly as in an air raid in London;
Their backs become curved in the sloping dark.

The filaments of the soul slowly separate:
The spirit breaks, a puff of dust floats up,
Like a house in Nebraska that suddenly explodes.

Come with Me

Come with me into those things that have felt this despair for so long—
Those removed Chevrolet wheels that howl with a terrible loneliness,
Lying on their backs in the cindery dirt, like men drunk, and naked,
Staggering off down a hill at night to drown at last in the pond.
Those shredded inner tubes abandoned on the shoulders of thruways,
Black and collapsed bodies, that tried and burst,
And were left behind;
And the curly steel shavings, scattered about on garage benches,
Sometimes still warm, gritty when we hold them,
Who have given up, and blame everything on the government,
And those roads in South Dakota that feel around in the darkness . . .

Wanting to Experience All Things

The blind horse among the cherry trees—
And bones, sticking from cool earth.
The heart leaps
Almost up to the sky! But laments
And filaments pull us back into the darkness.
We cannot see—
But a paw
Comes out of the dark
To light the road. Suddenly I am flying,
I follow my own fiery traces through the night!

Tulips

The tulips are too excitable, it is winter here.
Look how white everything is, how quiet, how snowed-in.
I am learning peacefulness, lying by myself quietly
As the light lies on these white walls, this bed, these hands.
I am nobody; I have nothing to do with explosions.
I have given my name and my day-clothes up to the nurses
And my history to the anaesthetist and my body to surgeons.

They have propped my head between the pillow and the sheet-cuff
Like an eye between two white lids that will not shut.
Stupid pupil, it has to take everything in.
The nurses pass and pass, they are no trouble,
They pass the way gulls pass inland in their white caps,
Doing things with their hands, one just the same as another,
So it is impossible to tell how many there are.

My body is a pebble to them, they tend it as water
Tends to the pebbles it must run over, smoothing them gently.
They bring me numbness in their bright needles, they bring me sleep.
Now I have lost myself I am sick of baggage—
My patent leather overnight case like a black pillbox,
My husband and child smiling out of the family photo;
Their smiles catch onto my skin, little smiling hooks.

I have let things slip, a thirty-year-old cargo boat
Stubbornly hanging on to my name and address.
They have swabbed me clear of my loving associations.
Scared and bare on the green plastic-pillowed trolley
I watched my tea-set, my bureaus of linen, my books
Sink out of sight, and the water went over my head.
I am a nun now, I have never been so pure.

I didn't want any flowers, I only wanted
To lie with my hands turned up and be utterly empty.
How free it is, you have no idea how free—
The peacefulness is so big it dazes you,
And it asks nothing, a name tag, a few trinkets.
It is what the dead close on, finally; I imagine them
Shutting their mouths on it, like a Communion tablet.

The tulips are too red in the first place, they hurt me.
Even through the gift paper I could hear them breathe
Lightly, through their white swaddlings, like an awful baby.
Their redness talks to my wound, it corresponds.

They are subtle: they seem to float, though they weigh me down,   40
Upsetting me with their sudden tongues and their colour,
A dozen red lead sinkers round my neck.

Nobody watched me before, now I am watched.
The tulips turn to me, and the window behind me
Where once a day the light slowly widens and slowly thins,   45
And I see myself, flat, ridiculous, a cut-paper shadow
Between the eye of the sun and the eyes of the tulips,
And I have no face, I have wanted to efface myself.
The vivid tulips eat my oxygen.

Before they came the air was calm enough,   50
Coming and going, breath by breath, without any fuss.
Then the tulips filled it up like a loud noise.
Now the air snags and eddies round them the way a river
Snags and eddies round a sunken rust-red engine.
They concentrate my attention, that was happy   55
Playing and resting without committing itself.

The walls, also, seem to be warming themselves.
The tulips should be behind bars like dangerous animals;
They are opening like the mouth of some great African cat,
And I am aware of my heart: it opens and closes   60
Its bowl of red blooms out of sheer love of me.
The water I taste is warm and salt, like the sea,
And comes from a country far away as health.

Poppies in October

Even the sun-clouds this morning cannot manage such skirts.
Nor the woman in the ambulance
Whose red heart blooms through her coat so astoundingly—

A gift, a love gift
Utterly unasked for   5
By a sky

Palely and flamily
Igniting its carbon monoxides, by eyes
Dulled to a halt under bowlers.

O my God, what am I   10
That these late mouths should cry open
In a forest of frost, in a dawn of cornflowers.

Years

They enter as animals from the outer
Space of holly where spikes
Are not the thoughts I turn on, like a Yogi,
But greenness, darkness so pure
They freeze and are.

O God, I am not like you
In your vacuous black,
Stars stuck all over, bright stupid confetti.
Eternity bores me,
I never wanted it.

What I love is
The piston in motion—
My soul dies before it.
And the hooves of the horses,
Their merciless churn.

And you, great Stasis—
What is so great in that!
Is it a tiger this year, this roar at the door?
Is it a Christus,
The awful

God-bit in him
Dying to fly and be done with it?
The blood berries are themselves, they are very still.

The hooves will not have it,
In blue distance the pistons hiss.

Words

Axes
After whose stroke the wood rings,
And the echoes!
Echoes travelling
Off from the centre like horses.

The sap
Wells like tears, like the
Water striving
To re-establish its mirror
Over the rock

That drops and turns,
A white skull,
Eaten by weedy greens.
Years later I
Encounter them on the road—

Words dry and riderless,
The indefatigable hoof-taps.
While
From the bottom of the pool, fixed stars
Govern a life.

Insomniac

The night sky is only a sort of carbon paper,
Blueblack, with the much-poked periods of stars
Letting in the light, peephole after peephole—
A bonewhite light, like death, behind all things.
Under the eyes of the stars and the moon's rictus
He suffers his desert pillow, sleeplessness
Stretching its fine, irritating sand in all directions.

Over and over the old, granular movie
Exposes embarrassments—the mizzling days
Of childhood and adolescence, sticky with dreams,
Parental faces on tall stalks, alternately stern and tearful,
A garden of buggy rose that made him cry.
His forehead is bumpy as a sack of rocks.
Memories jostle each other for face-room like obsolete film stars.

He is immune to pills: red, purple, blue—
How they lit the tedium of the protracted evening!
Those sugary planets whose influence won for him
A life baptized in no-life for a while,
And the sweet, drugged waking of a forgetful baby.
Now the pills are worn-out and silly, like classical gods.
Their poppy-sleepy colors do him no good.

His head is a little interior of grey mirrors.
Each gesture flees immediately down an alley
Of diminishing perspectives, and its significance
Drains like water out the hole at the far end. 25
He lives without privacy in a lidless room,
The bald slots of his eyes stiffened wide-open
On the incessant heat-lightning flicker of situations.

Nightlong, in the granite yard, invisible cats
Have been howling like women, or damaged instruments. 30
Already he can feel daylight, his white disease,
Creeping up with her hatful of trivial repetitions.
The city is a map of cheerful twitters now,
And everywhere people, eyes mica-silver and blank,
Are riding to work in rows, as if recently brainwashed. 35

Mirror

I am silver and exact. I have no preconceptions.
Whatever I see I swallow immediately
Just as it is, unmisted by love or dislike.
I am not cruel, only truthful—
The eye of a little god, four-cornered. 5
Most of the time I meditate on the opposite wall.
It is pink, with speckles. I have looked at it so long
I think it is a part of my heart. But it flickers.
Faces and darkness separate us over and over.

Now I am a lake. A woman bends over me, 10
Searching my reaches for what she really is.
Then she turns to those liars, the candles or the moon.
I see her back, and reflect it faithfully.
She rewards me with tears and an agitation of hands.
I am important to her. She comes and goes. 15
Each morning it is her face that replaces the darkness.
In me she has drowned a young girl, and in me an old woman
Rises toward her day after day, like a terrible fish.

Whitsun

This is not what I meant:
Stucco arches, the banked rocks sunning in rows,
Bald eyes or petrified eggs,
Grownups coffined in stockings and jackets,
Lard-pale, sipping the thin
Air like a medicine.

The stopped horse on his chromium pole
Stares through us; his hooves chew the breeze.
Your shirt of crisp linen
Bloats like a spinnaker. Hat-brims
Deflect the watery dazzle; the people idle
As if in hospital.

I can smell the salt, all right.
At our feet, the weed-mustachioed sea
Exhibits its glaucous silks,
Bowing and truckling like an old-school oriental.
You're no happier than I about it.
A policeman points out a vacant cliff

Green as a pool table, where cabbage butterflies
Peel off to sea as gulls do,
And we picnic in the death-stench of a hawthorn.
The waves pulse and pulse like hearts.
Beached under the spumy blooms, we lie
Seasick and fever-dry.

Witch Burning

In the marketplace they are piling the dry sticks.
A thicket of shadows is a poor coat. I inhabit
The wax image of myself, a doll's body.
Sickness begins here: I am a dartboard for witches.
Only the devil can eat the devil out.
In the month of red leaves I climb to a bed of fire.

It is easy to blame the dark: the mouth of a door,
The cellar's belly. They've blown my sparkler out.
A black-sharded lady keeps me in a parrot cage.
What large eyes the dead have!
I am intimate with a hairy spirit.
Smoke wheels from the beak of this empty jar.

If I am a little one, I can do no harm.
If I don't move about, I'll knock nothing over. So I said,
Sitting under a potlid, tiny and inert as a rice grain.
They are turning the burners up, ring after ring.
We are full of starch, my small white fellows. We grow.
It hurts at first. The red tongues will teach the truth.

Mother of beetles, only unclench your hand:
I'll fly through the candle's mouth like a singeless moth.
Give me back my shape. I am ready to construe the days
I coupled with dust in the shadow of a stone.
My ankles brighten. Brightness ascends my thighs.
I am lost, I am lost, in the robes of all this light.

Crossing the Water

Black lake, black boat, two black, cut-paper people.
Where do the black trees go that drink here?
Their shadows must cover Canada.

A little light is filtering from the water flowers.
Their leaves do not wish us to hurry:
They are round and flat and full of dark advice.

Cold worlds shake from the oar.
The spirit of blackness is in us, it is in the fishes.
A snag is lifting a valedictory, pale hand;

Stars open among the lilies.
Are you not blinded by such expressionless sirens?
This is the silence of astounded souls.

CRITICAL ESSAYS

Theodore Roethke
Walter J. Slatoff
Robert B. Heilman
Edmund Wilson
Lionel Trilling
Northrop Frye
Herbert J. Muller
Jean-Paul Sartre
Theodore Spencer
W. K. Wimsatt, Jr.
M. C. Beardsley
Cleanth Brooks
Philip Wheelwright
Frederick C. Crews
E. M. W. Tillyard
Walter J. Ong
T. S. Eliot
Georg Lukács
Norman Foerster
René Wellek
Henry A. Murray
Francis Fergusson
C. S. Lewis
R. P. Blackmur
Babette Deutsch
Stanley Kunitz

THE WRITER

THEODORE ROETHKE

Some Self-Analysis[1]

I expect this course to open my eyes to story material, to unleash my too dormant imagination, to develop that quality utterly lacking in my nature—a sense of form. I do not expect to acquire much technique. I expect to be able to seize upon the significant, reject the trivial. I hope to acquire a greater love for humanity in all its forms.

I have long wondered just what my strength was as a writer. I am often filled with tremendous enthusiasm for a subject, yet my writing about it will seem a sorry attempt. Above all, I possess a driving sincerity,—that prime virtue of any creative worker. I write only what I believe to be the absolute truth,—even if I must ruin the theme in so doing. In this respect I feel far superior to those glib people in my classes who often garner better grades than I do. They are so often pitiful frauds,—artificial—insincere. They have a line that works. They do not write from the depths of their hearts. Nothing of theirs was ever born of pain. Many an incoherent yet sincere piece of writing has outlived the polished product.

I write only about people and things that I know thoroughly. Perhaps I have become a mere reporter, not a writer. Yet I feel that this is all my present abilities permit. I will open my eyes in my youth and store this raw, living material. Age may bring the fire that molds experience into artistry.

I have a genuine love of nature. It is not the least bit affected, but an integral and powerful part of my life. I know that Cooper is a fraud—that he doesn't give a true sense of the sublimity of American scenery. I know that Muir and Thoreau and Burroughs speak the truth.

I can sense the moods of nature almost instinctively. Ever since I could walk, I have spent as much time as I could in the open. A perception of nature—no matter how delicate, how subtle, how evanescent,—remains with me forever.

I am influenced too much, perhaps, by natural objects. I seem bound by the very room I'm in. I've associated so long with prosaic people that I've dwarfed myself spiritually. When I get alone under an open sky where man isn't too evident—then I'm tremendously exalted and a thousand vivid ideas and sweet visions flood my consciousness.

I think that I possess story material in abundance. I have had an un-

[1] Written as an undergraduate at the University of Michigan.

usual upbringing. I was let alone, thank God! My mother insisted upon two things,—that I strive for perfection in whatever I did and that I always try to be a gentleman. I played with Italians, with Russians, Poles, and the "sissies" on Michigan avenue. I was carefully watched, yet allowed to follow my own inclinations. I have seen a good deal of life that would never have been revealed to an older person. Up to the time I came to college then I had seen humanity in diverse forms. Now I'm cramped and unhappy. I don't feel that these idiotic adolescents are worth writing about. In the summer, I turn animal and work for a few weeks in a factory. Then I'm happy.

My literary achievements have been insignificant. At fourteen, I made a speech which was translated into twenty-six languages and used as Red Cross propaganda. When I was younger, it seemed that everything I wrote was eminently successful. I always won a prize when I entered an essay contest. In college, I've been able to get only one "A" in four rhetoric courses. I feel this keenly. If I can't write, what can I do? I wonder.

When I was a freshman, I told Carleton Wells that I knew I could write whether he thought so or not. On my next theme he wrote "You can Write!" How I have cherished that praise!

It is bad form to talk about grades, I know. If I don't get an "A" in this course, it wouldn't be because I haven't tried. I've made a slow start. I'm going to spend Christmas vacation writing. A "B" symbolizes defeat to me. I've been beaten too often.

I do wish that we were allowed to keep our stories until we felt that we had worked them into the best possible form.

I do not have the divine urge to write. There seems to be something surging within,—a profound undercurrent of emotion. Yet there is none of that fertility of creation which distinguishes the real writer.

Nevertheless, I have faith in myself. I'm either going to be a good writer or a poor fool.

Varieties of Involvement

I want to worry first about some dimensions of the literary experience that have received so little investigation that I scarcely know how to begin. The area is suggested but not defined by the questions: In what sense is reading a personal activity? What kinds of involvement does reading entail? Where can we move or stand between or beyond the equally unsatisfactory positions of the aesthetic theorists who insist that one's relation to a work of art both can and should be impersonal and detached and who argue that personal responses are irrelevant and even contaminating, and those who argue that the only valid and important responses are what they call personal ones?

It would be naïve to expect that we will ever achieve very satisfactory understanding of a matter which draws in the concepts of objectivity and subjectivity and lies finally in the mystery of man's perception and comprehension of any external object or event. But we can do better than we have. If nothing else, we might throw out the arbitrary maps and recognize the complexity of the terrain.

In two very obvious senses actual reading is always a personal activity. It is an act performed by an individual person and the experience occurs within the mind and sensibilities of an individual person. Not only is the act personal, but one has the sense that it is, and draws satisfaction in part because, unlike most of our activities, it is personal, a kind of being with oneself, albeit in a peculiarly rich and exciting way. One is alone, yet in intimate relationship with something else. It combines some of the pleasures of solitary drinking, friendship, introspection, keyhole peeping, drug taking, walking, and puzzle doing. Moreover, the experience is not only personal but private in that it is essentially invisible to others and cannot be fully communicated.

One can explore works in seminars and discussion groups, one can attend to and make use of the experiences and observations of others, and gain new insights and ways of responding, but a reading, and the insights and responses, for that matter, can occur only in an individual consciousness. There is nowhere else for them to occur. This is true not only of the moment-to-moment sequential movement through the work that we usually call reading, but of the fuller experience of it that comes from repeated readings or patient exploration.

These statements seem innocuous enough until we recall that they throw the problem of defining full or proper response or full understanding back within the limits of individual consciousness. There, if one is not merely to be a storehouse, all the relevant responses and awarenesses that groups and critics need only accumulate and point to must come into relation and interact with one another. There, if it is to occur at all, must take place that mysterious fusion of knowledge, judgment, sensory comprehension, and emotional response toward which we hope our teaching and scholarship labor. But there, even apart from individual differences, the experience will always involve a selectivity, an incredibly complex distribution between the centers of attention and emotion and the peripheries. There certain responses will by their intensity inevitably diminish, blur, or entirely inhibit others. There, on the other hand, an effort to respond to or be aware of too many aspects of a work may prevent intensities of focus and concentration which are also required by the work. There, responses are not merely appropriate or proper or valid or informed or educated, but possess textures, colors, and relative degrees of intensity and depth and significance that we can scarcely begin to describe, much less prescribe, in proper proportion. Consider, for example, the difficulty in defining what might be called a "sufficient" or "full" response to any particular work. I am not yet talking about individual differences, but merely the complexity and mystery of any good reader's experience per se, the sense in which reading is personal because it is done by the single consciousness of a person rather than by a group or a machine or a library, or by the ideal reader sometimes invoked as a critical aid.

When we begin to contemplate the extent to which individual differences shape literary experiences it becomes understandable why we have clutched so desperately at theories and ways of talking which permit us to ignore those differences and have tried to relegate them to provinces labeled "psychology" or "taste." On the sensory level alone, our experiences differ more from one another than it is comfortable to reckon with. We differ not only in the thresholds of response of our various senses (in what might be called "innate sensitivity"), but in the prominence of our senses in relation to one another. Some readers are moles; others are transparent eyeballs. Some readers have a virtual painting in their heads as they read the words "a pair of ragged claws/ Scuttling across the floors of silent seas." Others are most acutely aware of the sounds. Still others experience chiefly a kinesthetic scuttling. Probably no two readers experience the rhythms, sounds, and images of a poem in precisely the same proportion. And as I. A. Richards and others have pointed out, we vary remarkably in the extent to which we feel and think in images of any sort. Some readers can scarcely apprehend anything without forming quite specific images of some variety. Others apparently can have rich and detailed experience employing only the sketchiest images, if any at all.[1] This does not imply that we cannot educate our senses to greater awareness or ought not to try to attune them as much as possible to the intent of the particular work. It does mean, however, that the apprehension of a work is to an important extent personal and that while we might talk sensibly of a normal range and proportion of sensory responses to any work and class some responses as inappropriate, we cannot talk meaningfully about an ideal or correct sensory response. Nor can we suppose that when any two readers has learned to give the same nomenclature, say, to Hopkins' rhythms and sounds, they are having the same experience of them. It suggests, too, that some of our tastes, preferences, and even evaluations may well be grounded in these personal sensory differences and that it might be worth trying to find out something about how large a part they play in such choices.[2] Something of their role and their variation is suggested by the extent to which we find such variations among writers themselves.

If one is to experience the rhythms, sounds, and images of a work, and not merely to identify them in accordance with a crude and only moderately expedient nomenclature, one simply cannot leave one's particular sensory organization behind. No matter how much one respects the literary work itself, and how diligently one seeks to experience *its* shape and emphasis, no matter how well one learns to control one's aberrant or idiosyncratic sensory responses, the reading must be an engagement between the work and a particular organism.

When we go beyond the sensory level and consider our variations in sex, age, experience, values, attitudes, temperaments, and habits of mind, conscious and unconscious, to say nothing of the variations in both the con-

---

[1] For more detailed discussion of these and other sensory matters, see I. A. Richards, *Principles of Literary Criticism* (London: Routledge & Kegan Paul Ltd., 1926), pp. 92–133, and his *Practical Criticism* (London: Routledge & Kegan Paul Ltd., 1929), pp. 235–236, 362–364.

[2] Such an inquiry, of course, faces obvious difficulties and can lead to such atrocities as hooking up subjects to elaborate electrical apparatus. But, as with most questions, if we attend to the matter, we can get somewhere through careful self-examination and careful questioning of others. It would not be too difficult, for example, to discover something interesting about one's own or another's intensities and proportions of visual, aural, and kinesthetic response to such lines as "The plowman homeward plods his weary way," "The woods are lovely, dark, and deep," or "Over the bent world broods with warm breast and with ah! bright wings." And one might, by examining responses to a few more carefully chosen lines, discover degrees of sensitivity to (and delight in) particular varieties of alliteration and assonance or to marked or sudden caesurae.

scious and unconscious purposes for which we read—all of which go into shaping and proportioning our experience of a work—it seems wonderful that we can achieve as much communication and agreement as we do about the meaning and worth of any particular work. One might consider, as a single example, the inevitable differences in the response to King Lear's predicament of a confident eighteen-year-old and a weary old man, of a bachelor and a married man, of a daughter who feels close to her father and one who doesn't, of a man who has experienced and recognized a serious betrayal and one who hasn't, of an equable man and a hot-tempered one, to say nothing of the minor differences which might occur between any two people in any one of those categories. Or if one begins to think about the limits of a "proper" or even "adequate" response or experience, one might wonder whether such an experience would be possible for either an unshaken eighteen-year-old or an old man who had just been disowned by his children, a man who is in Lear's shoes, so to speak. Such a man might well feel unbearably involved in and moved by the play; but would he be responding to *Lear's* predicament? I hope to show later that the answer to this question is less obvious than it has usually seemed. My intent here is simply to emphasize the importance of individual differences.

Despite this bewildering variety of individual response we do, of course, manage a considerable degree of communication. We achieve this, in part, by learning to submit ourselves as much as possible to the work itself, by letting our responses be directed and limited as much as possible by it, and, in part, by restricting our discussion largely to those matters about which we can communicate easily or what we sometimes call objectively. This is fine and we must never stop trying to do it. Otherwise we invite and celebrate chaos. At the same time, however, we must recognize how much we oversimplify and disregard by this procedure and try to find ways of moving intelligibly into the disregarded territories. Most important, we need to stop pretending that the sort of discussion we do have at all covers the total ground of our experience of a book.

One measure of how far we have to go is the fact that virtually no critic even admits—in print, at any rate—that his reading of a work may in any way be affected by his own nature, experience, training, temperament, values, biases, or motive for reading. Another measure is the incredible crudity of our language when we do venture to talk about readers' responses. Scholars and critics who would distinguish carefully between various sorts of Neo-Platonism, or examine in minute detail the structure of a chapter or the transmutations of a prevailing metaphor, or trace the full nuances of a topical allusion, will settle happily for mere labels like distance, involvement, identification, detachment, emotional impact, intensity, powerful effect, sympathetic, unsympathetic, deeply felt—labels just about as precise as the term "romantic." Apart from brief general discussions of "Objective and Subjective" and "Connotation and Denotation" and a very brief comment on "Empathy and Sympathy," M. H. Abrams' excellent A *Glossary of Literary Terms* has almost no entries which refer directly to matters of readers' responses. An even more recent glossary contains not a single such entry.

I have no new terminology or full-blown theory to propose. But I would like to begin to look more closely at some of these loosely labeled areas of response. Before we can even begin to look, however, we must try to escape from a set of related polarities and dichotomies which have seriously limited our thinking and observation: objective-subjective, clear thinking-emotional involvement, judgment-sympathy, impersonal-personal, accurate-impressionistic, knowledge-appreciation. In each of these polarities and others like them an activity associated with emotion, feeling, or involvement is seen as some kind of distortion or enemy of proper understanding. Very often the "subjective" pole is equated with irresponsibility and self-indulgence. Now, we need not settle the ultimate questions about the nature of reality and man's perception of it to recognize that such dichotomies and value judgments are particularly inadequate and inappropriate for understanding responses to literature. For one thing, literary works, unlike natural objects, are designed to affect the emotions and to compel various sorts of involvement. Conrad, for example, views the artist as one who "speaks to our capacity for delight and wonder, to the sense of mystery surrounding our lives; to our sense of pity, and beauty, and pain; to the latent feeling of fellowship with all creation—and to the subtle but invincible conviction of solidarity that knits together the loneliness of innumerable hearts, to the solidarity in dreams, in joy, in sorrow, in aspirations, in illusions, in hope, in fear, which binds men to each other." He goes on to say that the "task which I am trying to achieve is, by the power of the written word to make you hear, to make you feel—it is above all, to make you *see*."[3] Coleridge wished poetry to bring the whole soul of man into activity. Scarcely a writer or critic has doubted—in words at any rate —that literature aims to involve something approaching man's whole being.

Moreover, the very meaning of a literary work depends on emotional responses. Most works could scarcely be comprehended at all by a reader who lacked all human emotions. Nor are emotional responses inherently

---

[3] "Preface," *The Nigger of the Narcissus, Conrad's Prefaces* (London: J. M. Dent & Sons, 1937), pp. 50, 52.

less responsible than intellectual ones. One can read as irresponsibly intellectually as one can emotionally, exploit a text to satisfy intellectual needs as easily as to satisfy emotional ones. To respect a text doesn't mean to read impersonally or unemotionally any more than to respect another person means holding him at arm's length. Respect demands a giving of self and bringing of self to bear.

All this seems too obvious to be worth saying until one recalls the incredible extent to which those who care about art have overreacted in act and theory to the general public's tendency to celebrate and trust only emotional response and recalls the strength of the view that finds it a worthy activity to dwell on intellectual responses to a work and a self-indulgence to savor emotional ones. Again and again we are told to think and worry about the prevalence and dangers of inappropriate responses—about the naïve playgoer who rushes onstage to strangle Iago, about the reader who likes or dislikes a character or portrait because the character reminds him of his Aunt Sally, about the unworthiness of books which leave one feeling one ought to join an organization or write a check. From my colleagues I have heard ten thousand stories of their students' foolish and appropriate responses and I have told many such stories of my own. Rarely does one hear a word about the danger of insufficient responses—about the playgoer who never even feels like rushing onstage, about the reader who never lets a character or work connect in any way with his personal experience, about the reader who never feels guilty or never reexamines himself or his responsibilities after finishing a book, about those for whom literary works have become little more than puzzles, games, historical items, or storehouses of images, symbols, myths, or archetypes. Scarcely a word has been addressed to the problem of what in general or specific instances constitutes a full or adequate as opposed to merely appropriate response. Until the subjective, personal, and emotional are seen as inevitable and essential parts of reading and not as intrusions and fallacies, the problem cannot even be recognized. Nor can we begin to talk meaningfully about what does go on or should go on in the actual encounter between a man and a book.

The single most important thing to observe about our emotional transactions with a literary work is that they do not occur along single continuums nor are they in accord with the dimensions of any one metaphor. Even the most limited reader is capable of maintaining several simultaneous states of relation and feeling toward a work, and most readers could say with André Gide that they "have the gift of combining at the same moment two states of mind as different, as contradictory, as passion and lucidity, or as the fever, the delirium, the inward tremor or lyricism, and the chill of reason."[4] Most of us can simultaneously react, identify, and empathize and watch and even feel ourselves doing so. At one and the same moment we can be moved enough to weep and remain cool enough to fight the tears or to be ashamed of them. We can share the experience of a Gulliver, say, feel that experience, and at the same time view him with detachment and view with detachment the part of ourselves that is identifying. We can sympathize with a character despite an author's clear indications that we are not to do so, recognize this, and go on sympathizing. We are just as capable of juxtoposing and keeping in suspension feelings as we are ideas.

It has been recognized, of course, though by no means widely enough, that much reading does put the reader in a generally dual condition of being at once a participant in the action and a detached spectator of it.[5] And there has been quite extensive and thoughtful discussion of the complexities of the unconscious and "primitive" aspects of our participation in literary works. But there has been little recognition, even on the part of these psychologically oriented critics, of the multiplicities and complexities of our involvement in a work or of the inadequacies of our usual concept of a detachment-involvement continuum or of a distance continuum.[6] Most people and most critics, when they touch upon the matter at all, speak as though detachment and involvement were simple opposites and as though readers were simply more or less involved or detached or more or less distant. Apart from its failure to recognize the reader's ability to experience multiple or opposing responses in this respect, such a view lumps together under the label "involvement" a variety of qualitatively different literary experiences. It fails, if nothing else, to distinguish between an experience which simply arouses one's emotions, that is, in which

[4] Roger Martin du Gard, *Recollections of André Gide* (New York: The Viking Press, 1953), p. 96; quoted in Bacon and Breen, *Literature as Experience* (New York: McGraw-Hill, 1959), p. 48.
[5] See, for example, Simon Lesser, *Fiction and the Unconscious* (New York: Vintage Books, 1962), pp. 142–143; Bacon and Breen, pp. 48–49.
[6] I am grateful to Douglas Park, a graduate student of mine, for calling my attention to one article which does indeed recognize some of these multiplicities and complexities: D. W. Harding's "Psychological Processes in the Reading of Fiction," *British Journal of Aesthetics*, II (1962), 133–147. Harding relates the role and responses of readers to those of listeners to gossip and those of onlookers at actual events. He concludes that the terms "identification" and "vicarious experience" designate too great a variety of responses to be very useful and points out some of the ways in which readers both imaginatively share the experience of characters and at the same time, or immediately afterward, contemplate them as fellow beings.

one responds emotionally, and an experience entailing some kind of personal participation in the story or characters. Obviously these experiences are not always easy to separate, but surely we are sometimes moved deeply by characters and events we are essentially observing from the outside and surely this kind of experience can be quite different from the involvement that comes through empathy and identification. In the first instance, one may say that one feels an emotion, say pity, and thereby becomes involved. In the second, one becomes involved and thereby experiences the emotion. But even this division is grossly inadequate, as I shall try to show in a few moments.

The single continuum fails also to make an important distinction between a high degree of something we might call attention or fascination (a condition in which we might describe ourselves as engrossed, carried away, absorbed, gripped, etc.) and a condition of real caring or real concern. These may sometimes go hand in hand, but not necessarily. A high degree of suspense, for example, or of primitive identification, may cause one to read with intense anxiety and concentration, may blot out all one's sense of anything but the world of the book (as in a good detective thriller), and in that sense "involve" one; but one may still in important ways feel utterly unconnected with the characters and events; one cares desperately, but not deeply. On the other hand, one may read a novel like *Middlemarch* or *The Ambassadors* with far greater sense of distance, and yet feel deeply and inextricably involved in the events and characters, be far less gripped or carried away than by the thriller, but far more deeply moved. One might try to explain this sort of difference by saying that the thriller provides more primitive, childlike, unconscious, and therefore superficially more powerful sorts of participation or empathy or identification while the more sophisticated works lead to more mature and conscious and therefore more controlled and restrained connections, but I suspect this is at best a small part of the explanation.

The single dimension of involvement or distance fails also to allow for distinctions between sympathy and empathy or implies that empathy is the more "involved" state of the two, an implication by no means necessarily true. In one case my viscera and muscles are involved; in the other my mind and heart. In Faulkner's *Absalom, Absalom!* for example, I am intensely involved in an empathetic way as Quentin and Shreve themselves empathize with the galloping Charles Bon and Henry Sutpen to the point where no longer four but two are galloping alone; but I am much more fully and deeply shaken and involved at the end when poor Quentin cries out his ambivalence toward the South. At this point I experience some empathy from Faulkner's emphasis on Quentin's painting but surely the chief and most powerful feeling is one of sympathy toward a bewildered and suffering creature who is very clearly not myself.

Nor does the simple continuum help us to distinguish between empathy, which is essentially a lending of oneself to the character, and projection, which is a substitution of the self or part of the self for the character. These responses might seem alike insofar as both can be called forms of identification and both involve a loss of distance and detachment; yet, as I hope will be entirely clear later, they represent very different kinds of experience and relation to the work.

We might distinguish also between what could be labeled "voyeuristic" and "anodynic" involvements, between feeling a delicious personal excitement as a tormented character like Eugene Gant bloodies his fists against the wall of his bedroom and feeling how wonderful it is to be such a suffering hero. The voyeur does not so much share the character's experience as watch it, feed upon it, and use it to activate passions and sensations of his own. Despite the intensity of his response and its intimate connection with what he is observing (which leads one to use the term "involvement"), he is in some respects quite cold and detached. "Anodynic" involvement is closer to the activity of imagining oneself dead in order to enjoy the pain of the bereaved and forgetting that death would preclude such enjoyment. In such involvement one forgets that it hurts to suffer and that one will not be contemplating one's own suffering but experiencing it. In neither of these sorts of "involvement" is there much sympathy or recognition of the "otherness" of the characters being observed. Like projection, and unlike empathy and sympathy, these two forms of "involvement" would seem to be exploitations of works rather than experiences of them, since the reader's attention is on himself rather than on the work. And such responses would seem to be inappropriate since few writers or works—few good ones at any rate—presumably intend such effects. Yet one need not go all the way to De Sade to find moments of content and tone which announce the author's own voyeuristic involvement and compel one's own. One can find such moments, surely, in Flaubert, Dostoevsky, Dickens, Conrad, Kafka, Faulkner, Greene, and Nabokov, to name only a few. Nor is it merely the reader's own romanticism that leads him to stand too comfortably in the shoes of such characters as Eugene Gant, Paul Morel, Stephen Dedalus, and Jake Barnes, for in each case the author is proud of the fact that his semi-autobiographic hero has suffered so much and invests the suffering with a kind of glamor that encourages the reader to overlook the painfulness of the pain.

We might distinguish also between involvements in which the reader experiences a sense of support or nourishment and those in which he or his faiths or values are threatened. Most works, no doubt, instill some degree of anxiety, conscious or unconscious, but surely there is an enormous difference between that warm rush of assent we are likely to feel in the symphony chapter of *Moby-Dick* as Ahab for a moment yearns for human connection and the quality of our assent as he casts his final spear, or between our experience as Macomber finally stands up to the lion and our experience as Ole Anderson turns his face to the wall. And there is an enormous difference in the way it feels vicariously to inhabit the worlds, say, of *Middlemarch* and *Vanity Fair* or even *Jude the Obscure* or *Ulysses*, in which we at least know where we are, and the mystifying worlds of *The Castle*, *The Waves*, or *Catch-22*, to say nothing of those produced by Beckett, Burroughs, or Barthelme. Another distinction of special contemporary relevance would be one between the more usual sorts of identification, concern, sympathy, and empathy and a condition in which one feels not merely involved but implicated or accused, as one does in Brecht's *Threepenny Opera* or Genet's *The Blacks*. In these last cases, we should note, we are involved not at all through a loss of self or distance but as ourselves and as spectators.

The foregoing are but a few of the cruder distinctions which might be made and explored,[7] and they, themselves, are unsatisfactory insofar as they are dichotomous and classificatory rather than descriptive. The important thing is not to name them but to stop using a simple scale so that the actual experiences, whatever they are, can be talked about in whatever terms prove most appropriate or illuminating.

As may already have become apparent, perhaps the most serious difficulty with the notion of a continuum from detachment to involvement, as well as with the whole concept of aesthetic distance, is that it obscures the fascinating question of the place of self and self-awareness with respect to involvement and detachment.

Traditional aesthetic theory makes a division between a normal workaday state of mind in which we presumably look at things solely in terms of their relationship to ourselves and our needs and an aesthetic state of mind or attitude in which we contemplate objects for what they are in themselves, in which we are presumably detached, objective, impersonal, uninvolved. One can see the logic in such a division, and yet in some respects the dichotomy seems not only an oversimplification but almost the reverse of the actual case. It seems to me that our normal condition

[7] How numerous both the varieties and degrees of involvement can be even for a single work will be apparent to anyone who reflects on his experience, say, of Faulkner's *As I Lay Dying* or Ford's *The Good Soldier*.

is one in which we use objects and people but are not really involved with them or in relation to them, for we are not in possession of ourselves. We and they are parts of a machine or an activity. If I am busy I may be unconscious of my companion's grimace of pain, but I will probably also be unaware of my own headache. If I happen to look out of the window and notice a tree, I see that tree as an object utterly separate from me, objectively, with detachment. It is irrelevant to my activity and to me. Or if I see it and think I could sell it for lumber, I am seeing it in relation to my needs but not in relation to myself. It is when I am contemplating it, just looking at it, really *seeing* it, its shape, color, texture, etc., that I am most aware of my own relation to it. I am not merely looking at it, but am feeling the act of observing it, am acutely aware of where I am in relation to it both physically and psychically. Similarly, if I adopt what is called the aesthetic attitude toward, let us say, a student sitting in my office taking an exam, I am more aware not only of his shape and movements, but of my own presence, location, state of being, and relation to him. Part of the awareness in both cases, it is true, is a sense of distance or separation from the object contemplated, but it is the distance or separation between *us*. I am very much there, very much involved, more involved in a sense than when I am busy giving him directions.

Moreover, I suspect that the fullest and deepest experiences of literary involvement may bring about a heightened sense of self. While reading *Parktilden Village* by George P. Elliott, a novel which particularly compelled my deepest attention, identification, empathy, and emotional and intellectual involvement, I was acutely conscious that I was lying on the floor in my own living room, that I was brimming with anxiety and emotion, and that I was deeply and frighteningly implicated—all this at the same time that I was attending with special care to the characters and events in the book. Unquestionably, much of the power of the experience resided in some terrible tension between my involvement and self-awareness. Perhaps part of the explanation for this sort of phenomenon is that when one is powerfully moved, one's attention is drawn to oneself by the very sensation of being moved, the tightening of the heart or the gathering of tears, which is happening in the self rather than in the book. I suspect something similar occurs even in the most physical or physiological sorts of empathy, that as one vaults with the pole vaulter or gathers one's forces with the discus thrower, one is more conscious of the state of one's own body than when one watches with what is normally thought of as detachment.

A fuller explanation, however, of these complex combinations of involvement and self-consciousness surely has to do with fundamental relations between separation and connection that single-continuum notions of distance and involvement fail to take into account. On the very simplest level, one might say that one can't connect with something one isn't separate from. The very notion of connection or involvement implies some separation, some distance to be crossed. In fact, in many instances when there is connection, the sense of its poignance or importance increases as the distance increases. Thus absence makes the heart grow fonder; thus a handclasp or embrace over barbed wire or at the moment of death is peculiarly powerful. Thus when a writer wishes to establish an especially strong sense of connection he may magnify or stress the distance which has been crossed. Faulkner does this with particular frequency and effect.

> You know again now that there is no time: no space: no distance: . . . there is the clear undistanced voice as though out of the delicate antenna-skeins of radio, further than empress's throne, than splendid insatiation, even than matriarch's peaceful rocking chair, across the vast instantaneous intervention, from the long long time ago: *"Listen, stranger, this was myself: this was I."*[8]

Thus lonely romantics like Thomas Wolfe's Eugene Gant or George Webber are likely to feel they are most poignantly involved with mankind when they are looking at it from behind the separation of a train window, and a character like Stephen Dedalus is most likely to experience epiphanies when he is feeling most lonely and isolated. On the most purely physical level, one cannot even see an object or being one has no distance from. If one has taken the place of the object (fully identified with it) or is even shoved right up against it, it ceases to be visible. A somewhat similar inability to see can occur when distance has been sharply reduced by familiarity or even love, as happens sometimes between husband and wife and as is recognized only when some form of separation has brought them into focus for each other, as separate and distinct beings. Other sorts of closeness to an object can reduce as well as heighten one's sense of relation with it. Witness the effect of some Degas paintings or movie close-ups of a kiss or sexual act, or the effect of the undistanced descriptions of a writer like Zola. Or consider Gulliver's feelings as he gazes into the cavernous pores of the Brobdingnagian maiden's breast. The microscope, so to speak, can increase psychic distance at the same time that it, in effect, reduces physical distance. It may be that the revulsion we feel at some of these sorts of close-ups is more akin to empathy than detachment, but in other respects the experience hardly seems one of connection and

---

[8] *Requiem for a Nun* (New York: Random House, 1950), pp. 261–262.

closeness. It may well be that we are most likely to feel closest to objects and people in some sort of middle distance.

On a somewhat different plane, what I am saying is that many important kinds of involvement require, and even derive from, a sense of self and a recognition that the other is not-me. (One could, I suppose, call this recognition a form of detachment, but only if we come to understand that detachment is not an opposite of involvement and remove from the word its connotations of disinterest, coldness, and impersonality.) Paradoxically, such a recognition can allow one more fully to understand and even share another's plight and point of view, as it exists for him, than the unself-conscious participation or projection that often passes for involvement.

It can even be argued, and has been so argued by John Bayley[9] and others, that true connection, or love, can only occur when the otherness and separateness of the object is fully recognized, and that writers like Chaucer, Shakespeare, and Dickens, who are in one sense detached from and separate from their characters, love them, while writers like Lawrence and Thomas Wolfe, who seem to be more deeply involved in their characters, exhibit only self-love since their characters are mainly projections of themselves. The same might be said for readers.

If what I am saying is true, if the fullest being-within, for author and reader alike, requires a simultaneous being-without, the distinctions between involvement and detachment, between empathy and sympathy, and even between sympathy and judgment become less pronounced. Not only can they occur simultaneously but harmoniously as well. Shakespeare can be Lear and at the same time pity and judge him, and so can the reader. Merely to be Lear would be neither to see him or know him nor even to be involved with him.

Anyone with children who doubts our capacity for these intense double relations might consider what happens when one sees one's own child being hurt. One feels the pain as though it were one's own and is, I suppose, as fully involved emotionally as it is possible to be. Yet one immediately uses one's separateness and adult self to offer help and one is acutely conscious of the separate selves and of the connection between them.

In general, I think, psychologists, aestheticians, and critics alike have assumed too easily that intense caring or emotional concern comes only from some form of identification or projection, some form of participation, as it were, and have underestimated our capacity to be deeply concerned

[9] *The Characters of Love: A Study in the Literature of Personality* (New York: Basic Books, 1961).

about, anxious about, and moved by the predicaments of others without performing any act of identification. It may be that the little child initially learns to feel sympathy for another hurt creature by imagining himself in the same condition, and it may be that the only way one can teach people to be more sympathetic is to help them to imagine themselves in other's shoes, but I think that many of us become capable of responding sympathetically without performing that intermediate act (or if we do perform it, we do it so automatically and unconsciously as to make it unrecognizable). Just as few of us would remain unmoved if we were merely to hear the sound of groaning or weeping or of joyous laughter coming from an unknown creature in an adjacent room, a creature whom we have no means of identifying or identifying with, so most of us can be moved by and concerned about the evidences of the emotional states of fictional characters without in any way sharing or experiencing these conditions. And I think most of us become capable of moving directly from an intellectual comprehension of a character's predicament to an actual feeling of sympathy for him. As we come to understand, for example, the full dimensions of Casaubon's plight in *Middlemarch*, we learn, as Dorothea does, to feel for him as we might toward some pathetic "lamed creature," and we are terribly glad that she has not, so to speak, struck him, but rather taken his hand. Few of us, however, in any way, could be said to identify with Casaubon. I am not even sure that the deeper sympathy we feel in that scene for Dorothea depends on anything which we could properly call identification.

Perhaps much of the confusion and oversimplification in this area have come about because no distinction is ever made between identifying with a character and seeing or feeling something from his point of view. Few would deny that we can understand the point of view of another without identifying with him, but there seems to have been no recognition that we are also capable of feeling from another's point of view without in any real sense becoming that character. This may seem to be a quibble in that one might define identification as including any act of perception from another's point of view or might say that identification merely means the seeing and feeling of another's point of view. But I think not only that the distinction is valid psychologically—that it directs attention to two quite distinct sorts of experience (I identify with Marlow; I feel for and with Lord Jim)—but that it also has profound implications of several sorts. If the only way we can deeply comprehend or feel the experience of another is through identification, our range of response is limited by our ability to empathize; if we can feel for and with merely by understanding another's predicament and point of view we can probably have a wider range of experience. A limitation of many readers is that they can only sympathize when they do identify and covet only vicarious experience. If one can feel for another without having to put *oneself* in his shoes or without doing unto him as one would wish done unto oneself, one can perhaps know better what it is like for *him* to be in his shoes and what *he* would like done unto *himself*. This notion is similar, of course, to Bayley's insistence that true connection or love can only occur when the otherness and separateness of the object are fully recognized and accepted.

Another source of difficulty in discussing these matters is the sharp dichotomy which is often made between intellectual and emotional involvement and the implication that involvement is essentially an emotional matter. We can sometimes think without feeling and feel without thinking and the two do frequently get in each other's way; but more often our experiences are deeply interwoven mixtures of the two. At the very least we know that we often think something because we feel something and feel something because we think something, and we are about as hard put to know which came first as we are with the chicken and the egg. We know also that we can care deeply, even violently, about ideas, and I think few would disagree with John Dewey's assertion that "different ideas have their different 'feels,' their immediate qualitative aspects, just as much as anything else. One who is thinking his way through a complicated problem finds direction on his way by means of this property of ideas." Moreover, most good literature is designed to engage, and does engage, both mind and emotion and does engender responses in which thought and feeling are particularly inseparable. I cannot say in *Middlemarch*, for example, and would not wish to, to what extent I care deeply about Dorothea because of my interest in the ethical and moral questions with which she and the novel are concerned and to what extent I care deeply about those questions because of my interest in Dorothea. As nearly as I can tell, the two are inextricably mingled and my very attempt to distinguish between them sounds silly.

A more helpful distinction, if we had some way of making it, might be one which got at the extent to which a response or experience—whether intellectual or emotional—was a full and significant interaction with the work; which got at how much of the reader's being was involved and how significantly, at the extent to which the reader would properly be described as having had an experience as opposed to a mere passing encounter or exercise. And neither a rush of tears nor a rush of thought nor a solemnly pontificated "How true!" or "How tragic!" in itself proves that more than an encounter has taken place. To attempt to define in a general way what might be called full and significant interaction is probably futile and pointless, but we can say that it is something more than either a carefully controlled intellectual response or an emotional orgy, and that, if it is to be achieved, literary works must be viewed as something more than mental and emotional gymnasiums.

One further source of difficulty has been the tendency of most aestheticians and critics to speak as though there were only two sorts of readers: the absolutely particular, individual human being with all his prejudices, idiosyncrasies, personal history, knowledge, needs, and anxieties, who experiences the work of art in solely "personal" terms, and the ideal or universal reader whose response is impersonal and aesthetic. Most actual readers, except for the most naïve, I think, transform themselves as they read into beings somewhere between these extremes. They learn, that is, to set aside many of the particular conditions, concerns, and idiosyncrasies which help to define them in everyday affairs, but they still retain the intellectual and emotional experience and structures, and the temperaments and values, of particular individuals and respond largely in accord with that make-up. When I read, for example, the self that responds is not quite Walter J. Slatoff, Professor of English, third-generation mostly assimilated Jew, aged 48, married, father of Joan and Donald, aged 18 and 16, soldier in World War II, etc., etc. And that self which reads does not say I sympathize with Jake Barnes because I know what war is like but resent Hemingway's treatment of Cohn because I, too, am Jewish and in other ways resemble Cohn more than I do Jake. But at the same time, that reading self is by no means an ideal or impersonal entity. He is mostly over 35 and under 50, has experienced war, marriage, and the responsibility of children, belongs in part to some kind of minority group, is male and not female, and shares most of Slatoff's general ways of thinking and feeling. His experience in the war does affect his feelings toward Jake and he cannot view Cohn as he might if he were the reading self of Lyndon B. Johnson, Henry Miller, Lord David Cecil, or Ernest Hemingway. Because I am a gardener of sorts I do not, as I read "April is the cruelest month," say merely, "How true. He's talking about plants," but I probably do think more about the rebirth of bulbs and plants than the average city apartment dweller. This reading self tends to overreact to certain kinds of moral and psychological situations—to authority questions and pain, for example—much as I do in life, but also recognizes this tendency and resists and watches it, but only up to a point.

This reading self, though more universalized than my fully defined personal self, is by no means an abstraction. It is still an individual self and feels like one, and the experiences it has are very much personal experiences.

If this sounds unduly obvious (and is what we usually mean by the term "educated reader") it is not so in most critical and theoretical discussion. Apart from occasional consideration of the problems of the modern reader confronting older works or the dilemma of a nonbeliever confronting doctrinaire religious works, scarcely ever does a critic even suggest that his reading or evaluation is in any way related to his personal qualities even in this generalized or universalized sense. And although we really know better, we have almost always talked and taught as though there were no middle ground between the impressionist and the definitionless theoretical or ideal reader. And we have supposed that the proper or true or best reading of a work would be that provided either by this theoretical reader or by a chameleon-like reader who became as nearly identical as possible with the consciousness which created and informed the novel. Or, of course, we have pretended that the work can have a "reading" without a reader.

If we were to acknowledge that all good readings are, in fact, performed by only partly depersonalized beings, and were to reckon with this fact in what we call criticism, or even to base criticism on this fact, we would, of course, run against problems (some of which I consider in my next chapter) that ideal readers and literary *objects* allow to remain in hiding. But we would also allow ourselves to get beyond disgracefully oversimple notions of the personal and the impersonal and of detachment and involvement; and we might, paradoxically, move closer to full objective truth about the works we read.

ROBERT B. HEILMAN

The Full Man and the Fullness Thereof

In a more nearly ideal academic world no one, presumably, would think it necessary to say that there is something to be said for reading. But some of us have begun to wonder whether, in an age which takes increasing pride in electronic machinery of all kinds, the printed page is not in danger of becoming an archaeological curiosity. To use this phrase is not to adopt a tactical hyperbole. Readers of the *New York Times*, for instance, were able to read, in the spring of 1969, about a group of writers—yes, under thirty—who said quite candidly that they had given up reading. They only went to the movies. It is an extraordinary phenomenon—writing for others to read but refusing to read what others write. Perhaps it is a phenomenon of selflessness—giving one's self away to others but never nourishing or restoring that self. Of course, a less generous observer might interpret differently. He might see, in this all giving and no receiving, a traditional ailment—a way of playing god. Or non-reading might seem only a venial slip, rather common in romantic days of genial trust in whatever pops or pours out from within. Ben Jonson describes it in commenting on the poet who learns "only . . . of himself"; this self-taught maker, Jonson says, "confesseth his ever having a fool to his master." The non-reading writer might, by his example, have an unusual educational impact on his readers: he might turn them into non-writing non-readers. To canvass these alternatives is to take ourselves right into Sartre's *No Exit*, where an absence of books is one of the defining characteristics of hell (the characteristic destination of the man who would be god).

If this tale of persumably literate people who go to movies but do not read is representative, then we have a problem. But I find no confrontation at all between reading and electronic experience as long as they are supplementary and not competitive. In our day we have plenty of time for both—in life generally and on the campus. A real issue arises only if the electronic begins to supplant reading—in the culture or on the campus. We do not have plenty of classroom time for both, and we should be concerned only when reading and the use of reading material get shortchanged. I in no way challenge the pedagogical use of electronic materials when and where it does something that reading cannot do. I do distrust the diversion of time, in college and university literature classes, from the printed page to records, tapes, films, and the like. This development shows an unconscious distrust of reading, and a failure to grasp the value of the complex experience it affords. Hence I tend to be a little offish when I see an advertisement captioned "Games + Movies + Records = a New Kind of Education," for I suspect that we tend to get, not education, but games, movies, and records: the means becomes ends in themselves.

Insofar as the electronic is a threat to the printed page, either in the culture or on the campus, its position gains strength from three habits of thought that are strong with us. They are summed up in three words that in common usage do not denote neutral entities but connote good things to be admired or sought after: the words *change, experience,* and *gut reaction.* Let us look at the impact of these; as we do so, we may also act as the defense attorney for reading.

Change is a magic word with us, and it may seem mad to have doubts about it. For we all know that change will take place, whether we welcome it or just endure it. What is bad is to assume that change is always good, that we are the better for it, and that passion for it is the hallmark of good guys. Our most characteristic mode of change is to technologize and specifically to electronicize what we once did by hand, body, mind, or imagination. This may be splendid, or regrettable, or something of both. It is not always easy to distinguish changes which are beneficent from those which are not. Hence we tend, in a few cases, to resist stubbornly, or more generally, to fall in with the powerful dogma that change is always an improvement. Since the movement from reading to the electronic is a change, we tend half-consciously to go along with it as a good thing.

A more central problem in the pressure of the electronic upon reading is revealed by the key word of a professor of English explaining why he devotes class time to tapes, records, and films. He says, "I want the kids to have the experience." "The experience" is the key. Subtly this particular kind of experience tends to become the sole experience, as if the audio-visual were the real thing, and reading were either non-experiential or not significantly experiential. No one, of course, can oppose the kind of aesthetic experience offered by a poet's reading, an actor's presentation, or an electronic reproduction of these (in fact, a poet's reading, since most poets read very badly, is hardly likely to seduce a reader from reading). The point is that we are deprived of something important if the audio-visual becomes the sole or chief experience and thus preempts the time and place for reading. For these are two different kinds of experience, and if we lose the one afforded by reading, we will lose something I do not think we can do without.

For one thing, we would lose our way into a very considerable part of the literary realm. While electronics may in time translate all literature into its own idiom, for the moment it seems largely restricted to poems and plays. So far as I know, it does not endeavor to present artistic nonfictional prose. There are, of course, plenty of films of long fictions, but these are essentially different works of art—useful as illustrations of the original but not substitutes for it.

But suppose there were always electronic options, what can be said for experiencing the work by reading the printed page? In reading we have one sense directly engaged, sight, and what we see is a set of arbitrary symbols that denote, of course, not only the worlds of all the senses but all the non-sensory or extrasensory worlds. To use a Platonic metaphor, we are at two removes from the reality being presented to us. But since our problem is not one of cognition, we need not be afraid of this intervening space. Rather it affords an advantage in aesthetic perception: it makes possible a partial detachment in which the critical impulse profitably resists the hypnotic force of the work. This is an important kind of engagement with the work. The key word is *resists,* and this does not mean *triumph* over: the value lies in a tension between two modes of response, between, if you will, disbelief and the suspension of disbelief. If disbelief actually triumphs, the result is a skepticism which voids the experience; if belief triumphs, we simply become slaves of certain stimuli. In reading, one is in the experience represented, and yet has a critical perspective on it; he may be enslaved, but he is also free. I do not mean that all the pressures designed to get one into the work should (in some way) be restrained or denied; the more effective they are, the more the work is given that ultimate term of praise—"powerful." But the stimuli brought to bear upon the recipient are aimed not so much at his sensory apparatus as at his imagination. The verbal symbols do not beat upon him like fragments of actuality but encourage and invite him to transport himself into many other realms of existence. He is drawn into otherness, whether for enrichment or understanding or sympathy or self-knowledge. The value of this outward movement into other realities, or deeper movement into his own reality, is surely axiomatic. But in reading one is not experiencing total immersion; one is in the stream and yet out of it, suspending disbelief and yet practicing it, managing to be both participant and judge, or at least observer of the thing participated in and of the process of participation.

In contrast there is the kind of aesthetic experience that strives to resemble actual experience or even surpass it in impact and intensity. This happens when the verbal symbols, which make possible both distance and, by stimulated imagination, closeness, are replaced by sensory symbols that greatly heighten the immediacy of the experience presented and tend to make it surround and overcome us. In wide areas of art we can detect a tendency to imitate life, not by mirroring it, but by becoming it, with all the pungency, incoherence, disturbingness, and shock of an actual life of conflict. Some sound-and-light shows, one judges, are as overwhelming as battlefield experience. It is in this direction, I believe, that the electronic tends to take us, by a perfectly natural development of its own rich technical resources. For the seeing of words that leads us to imagine human action it substitutes the seeing of bodies in action. For the seeing of words that leads us to imagine sounds we substitute the hearing of sounds. There would seem to be no limit to the extension of this direct sensory experience. Aldous Huxley suggested that it is only a step from the talkies to the feelies. We can surmise the arrival of the tasties and, more easily, the smellies. It may be possible to devise a kinesthetic mode of experience: to have walkies as well as talkies.

All I am trying to do is suggest, and perhaps not hyperbolically, a drive in the aesthetic world itself away from the imaginative and interpretative and toward direct sensation and emotion, the physical responsiveness to strenuous, almost compulsive stimuli. The respondent is mastered by the medium instead of moving through it to the kind of mastery in which warm participation is mysteriously joined with cool detachment. Here, of course, I am describing an ultimate development, one that we may have to learn to live with. But however well we learn it, we will be in serious trouble if we do not retain reading as an alternative way into literary experience. In a 1969 essay J. B. Priestley remarks that "it would be disastrous if and when television-viewing entirely replaces reading for pleasure. There are signs already that some committed viewers and non-readers, of all ages, are beginning to suffer from a blunting of imagination, a kind of curious new anaesthesia"—anaesthesia as the natural aftermath of the hyperaesthesia of electronic stimulation. This is exactly borne out by one of the non-reading writers in New York who says, "It's just easier to go to a movie and let it all wash over you." Wash, precisely: be drowned in it. For the ultimate effects of total sensory overwash, another writing non-reader says that every young writer knows "that he's more consistently moved by what he sees on the screen than [by] what he reads." What he records as a fact is really a debility: we may call it softening of the imagination.

He admits a craving for the "most powerful images" of the cinema. In this he illustrates the third of the three anti-reading forces that I have been surveying. The first is worship of change; the second is the passion for making aesthetic experience simulate actual experience, the third is veneration for what we call the gut reaction. This also helps push us toward the multi-sensory, direct-impact version of literary art. In some quarters the gut reaction tends to become an ultimate source of value. Historically, of course, we are compensating—actually over-compensating—for our nineteenth-century forebears' diffidence about the gut; to be sure that we are not as they, we try to keep our feet firmly planted in the gut. Note that this metaphor makes it silly to invoke the idea of discrimination by asking "Whose gut?" as if we wanted to make a choice among gut reactions. Gut is the great undifferentiated gut, the last-layer bottom of things, the fundament of brute commonplaceness, irresponsible and unquestionable. Gut reaction is a humorless age's heavy substitute for the belly laugh. That age is not likely to be very hospitable to reading, in which the gut is called on too, but no more than the other elements of personality that act as critics of the gut.

In our relations with reality we can think of a spectrum of multiple possibilities. At one extreme we are immersed in reality itself, living in pressures, tensions, drives, passions, engaged physically, socially, emotionally. At the other extreme we are disengaged critics: this is the world of detached analysis or of the printed page in its cognitive dimension—the prose of descriptive or analytical abstraction. Midway between these extremes is the reading of literature: it uniquely draws upon the activities of both extremes, making possible at once a plunge into reality and a separation from it, an empathic entry into the world and a nonpassionate observation of it, an imaginative participation in polymorphous experience, and a maintenance of the partial exile where meanings may be grasped. In this view, reading is not a pre-electronic make-do, a temporary practice appropriate to the printing phase of technological advancement, but an essential human activity, with an intrinsic function that cannot be superseded. Yet one can see its central position always subject to threats, as central positions are, from pendular swings at different moments of history when one extreme or another seems to have the better grasp of truth and hence draws the middle toward it. Much eighteenth-century literature—there are notable exceptions—feels the impact of the rational-critical-separatist extreme; the pressure of that extreme magnifies the abstractive and commentative and inhibits imaginative engagement. In our day, however, the center feels the opposite pressure: what we call life calls to art and says, "Be me." The art that responds to this call of the wild inhibits disengagement. It presses us to total responsiveness, sensory and emotive submission; to be overcome, dispossessed, in a literal sense panicked, that is, merged with all. What I am saying is that this general tendency of our age moves faster and goes further because of the electronic skills which are also characteristic of our age.

I have been drifting in and out of the classroom, but my main point has been that the substitution of electronic experience, in the classroom, for the study of the printed page is open to question. It tends to reduce the amount of reading by creating a thirst for the greater immediate excitement of sound and light. It will curtail the time for the critical inspection of what is read that completes the reading process and makes for better reading the next time. The classroom is for criticism; the critical experience is valuable; and it cannot be wise to attenuate it by the substitution of sensory experience which the age already supplies in excess and which even the literature read is, in our day, eager to approximate or simulate.

Reading allows the recipient of artistic impressions much greater freedom than does a multi-sensory stimulation which tends to envelop him. It lets him be both a critical outsider and an imaginative insider. Besides, if he that runs may read, he that reads may stop. He may stop at any time—to assimilate, absorb, meditate, clarify, refresh, sharpen up or correct impressions, and, above all, to compare related passages, to discover connections, to perceive structure and form. These are the ultimate activities in the study of literature, and it is the printed page that serves them especially well. It permits a continual breaking off of continuity without an essential rupture of continuity, which is held on to imaginatively; while stopping a record or tape or film seems a barbarous breaking off of what by its nature is meant to keep going. Finally, we need reading, as I have said, for all the kinds of literature that do not lend themselves to sound and light. Here I want to stress especially the long works that are not amenable to electronic representation without being transmuted into something else—the epics, the long poems of many kinds, the long novels, the fictional and dramatic trilogies. On the one hand, reading is the most interruptible of the experiences of art that go on in time; on the other hand, it is the most extendable. On the one hand, the pause that makes for refreshment or reflection does not damage the whole; on the other, the whole is not circumscribed by the limits that seem inescapable in the audio-visual domain. With the printed page you can isolate the moment without really stopping the clock or ruining the hour; or you can go on for hour after hour, or for as much time as you have available, in one day or a series of days.

In works of length the printed page offers the on-going, prolonged imaginative engagement which I cannot help believing to be valuable in itself: an experience or even discipline in the long haul, the sticking with it, the evolving and inclusive vision; the having to go beyond the brief episode, the fleeting excitement, the quickly mounting tension, the fast-acting catharsis of love and hate. If literature is a form of knowledge, then that knowledge ought in some part to come through the large work that comprehends more of life, in its duration, with its variations of tone, its diversities of incident, its conflicts of thought, its multiple patterns of feeling and conduct—with all the roughness and contradictions of actuality concretely present, and yet in the end surmounted by a formal power that, in its long tension with chaos, has neither a factitious triumph nor a failure that invalidates art. Hence I like to think that the formed long work may act through the imagination to contribute to the formed life. Or, alternatively, the long exercise, the one that goes on, with whatever inevitable intermissions, from one reading to another, may itself enhance the competence of the imagination—to be discontented with the facile stimulation of the hasty conclusion, to endure the succession of contradictions, to embrace the more readily those whole representations in which dualities and inconsistencies are ever present but never finally obscure the ordering vision of human breadth and depth. This is one way of saying that reading maketh a full man, and of trying to define the fullness.

For these reasons I hope that we do not divorce ourselves from reading. However, I am not proposing that we take a vow of chastity against the seductions of electronic enchantresses. We can perhaps get by with bigamy if we keep our different loves in the right places. I should be worried only if the electronic mistress were to drive us entirely away from reading, which has the virtues of the durable spouse, so that we gave it up entirely or deprived it of needed time in class. The electronic enchantress has an advantage over the printed page in our day because she appeals to that terrible fickleness in us which leads us to imagine that all change is a good thing; because she offers experience of a powerful new sensory kind and tries to make us think that that old homebody, reading, despite the durable and complex imaginative fare that she always offers, is a bit tepid and dull, and really does not provide experience at all; and because she tells us that that gut reaction which she evokes really gets to the bottom of things, and should be trusted, and not really modified by critical second thoughts. She has now helped create this new shaggy anti-reading type whom we may call, a little academically, non-legistic man, the latest incarnation of neo-barbarism. But that she is charming does not mean that she is sinister. Obviously she offers a great deal of pleasure. We can enjoy it, as long as we don't let it eliminate other very substantial and very durable pleasures. She is the kind of girl we should have an occasional date with, but not elope with.

Philoctetes: The Wound and the Bow

The *Philoctetes* of Sophocles is far from being his most popular play. The myth itself has not been one of those which have excited the modern imagination. The idea of Philoctetes' long illness and his banishment to the bleak island is dreary or distasteful to the young, who like to identify themselves with men of action—with Heracles or Perseus or Achilles; and for adults the story told by Sophocles fails to set off such emotional charges as are liberated by the crimes of the Atreidai and the tragedies of the siege of Troy. Whatever may have been dashing in the legend has been lost with the other plays and poems that dealt with it. Philoctetes is hardly mentioned in Homer; and we have only an incomplete account of the plays by Aeschylus and Euripides, which hinged on a critical moment of the campaign of the Greeks at Troy and which seem to have exploited the emotions of Greek patriotism. We have only a few scattered lines and phrases from that other play by Sophocles on the subject, the *Philoctetes at Troy*, in which the humiliated hero was presumably to be cured of his ulcer and to proceed to his victory over Paris.

There survives only this one curious drama which presents Philoctetes in exile—a drama which does not supply us at all with what we ordinarily expect of Greek tragedy, since it culminates in no catastrophe, and which indeed resembles rather our modern idea of a comedy (though the record of the lost plays of Sophocles show that there must have been others like it). Its interest depends almost as much on the latent interplay of character, on a gradual psychological conflict, as that of *Le Misanthrope*. And it assigns itself, also, to a category even more special and less generally appealing through the fact (though this, again, was a feature not uncommon with Sophocles) that the conflict is not even allowed to take place between a man and a woman. Nor does it even put before us the spectacle—which may be made exceedingly thrilling—of the individual in conflict with his social group, which we get in such plays devoid of feminine interest as *Coriolanus* and *An Enemy of the People*. Nor is the conflict even a dual one, as most dramatic conflicts are—so that our emotions seesaw up and down between two opposed persons or groups: though Philoctetes and Odysseus struggle for the loyalty of Neoptolemus, he himself emerges more and more distinctly as representing an independent point of view, so that the contrast becomes a triple affair which makes more complicated demands on our sympathies.

A French dramatist of the seventeenth century, Chateaubrun, found the subject so inconceivable that, in trying to concoct an adaptation which would be acceptable to the taste of his time, he provided Philoctetes with a daughter named Sophie with whom Neoptolemus was to fall in love and thus bring the drama back to the reliable and eternal formula of Romeo and Juliet and the organizer who loves the factory-owner's daughter. And if we look for the imprint of the play on literature since the Renaissance, we shall find a very meager record: a chapter of Fénelon's *Télémaque*, a discussion in Lessing's *Laocoön*, a sonnet of Wordsworth's, a little play by André Gide, an adaptation by John Jay Chapman—this is all, so far as I know, that has any claim to interest.

And yet the play itself *is* most interesting, as some of these writers have felt; and it is certainly one of Sophocles' masterpieces. If we come upon it in the course of reading him, without having heard it praised, we are surprised to be so charmed, so moved—to find ourselves in the presence of something that is so much less crude in its subtlety than either a three-cornered modern comedy like *Candida* or *La Parisienne* or an underplayed affair of male loyalty in a story by Ernest Hemingway, to both of which it has some similarity. It is as if having the three men on the lonely island has enabled the highly sophisticated Sophocles to get further away from the framework of the old myths on which he has to depend and whose barbarities, anomalies and absurdities, tactfully and realistically though he handles them, seem sometimes almost as much out of place as they would in a dialogue by Plato. The people of the *Philoctetes* seem to us more familiar than they do in most of the other Greek tragedies;[1] and they take on for us a more intimate meaning. Philoctetes remains in our mind, and his incurable wound and his invincible bow recur to us with a special insistence. But what is it they mean? How is it possible for Sophocles to make us accept them so naturally? Why do we enter with scarcely a stumble into the situation of people who are preoccupied with a snakebite that lasts forever and a weapon that cannot fail?

Let us first take account of the peculiar twist which Sophocles seems to have given the legend, as it had come to him from the old epics and the dramatists who had used it before him.

The main outline of the story ran as follows: The demigod Heracles had been given by Apollo a bow that never missed its mark. When, poisoned by Deianeira's robe, he had had himself burned on Mount

---

[1] 'Apropos of the rare occasions when the ancients seem just like us, it always has seemed to me that a wonderful example was the repentance of the lad in the (*Philoctetes?*) play of Sophocles over his deceit, and the restoration of the bow.' —Mr. Justice Holmes to Sir Frederick Pollock, October 2, 1921.

Oeta, he had persuaded Philoctetes to light the pyre and had rewarded him by bequeathing to him this weapon. Philoctetes had thus been formidably equipped when he had later set forth against Troy with Agamemnon and Menelaus. But on the way they had to stop off at the tiny island of Chrysè to sacrifice to the local deity. Philoctetes approached the shrine first, and he was bitten in the foot by a snake. The infection became peculiarly virulent; and the groans of Philoctetes made it impossible to perform the sacrifice, which would be spoiled by ill-omened sounds; the bite began to suppurate with so horrible a smell that his companions could not bear to have him near them. They removed him to Lemnos, a neighboring island which was much larger than Chrysè and inhabited, and sailed away to Troy without him.

Philoctetes remained there ten years. The mysterious wound never healed. In the meantime, the Greeks, hard put to it at Troy after the deaths of Achilles and Ajax and baffled by the confession of their soothsayer that he was unable to advise them further, had kidnaped the soothsayer of the Trojans and had forced him to reveal to them that they could never win till they had sent for Neoptolemus, the son of Achilles, and given him his father's armor, and till they had brought Philoctetes and his bow.

Both these things were done. Philoctetes was healed at Troy by the son of the physician Asclepius; and he fought Paris in single combat and killed him. Philoctetes and Neoptolemus became the heroes of the taking of Troy.

Both Aeschylus and Euripides wrote plays on this subject long before Sophocles did; and we know something about them from a comparison of the treatments by the three different dramatists which was written by Dion Chrysostom, a rhetorician of the first century A.D. Both these versions would seem to have been mainly concerned with the relation of Philoctetes to the success of the Greek campaign. All three of the plays dealt with the same episode: the visit of Odysseus to Lemnos for the purpose of getting the bow; and all represented Odysseus as particularly hateful to Philoctetes (because he had been one of those responsible for abandoning him on the island), and obliged to resort to cunning. But the emphasis of Sophocles' treatment appears fundamentally to have differed from that of the other two. In the drama of Aeschylus, we are told, Odysseus was not recognized by Philoctetes, and he seems simply to have stolen the bow. In Euripides, he was disguised by Athena in the likeness of another person, and he pretended that he had been wronged by the Greeks as Philoctetes had been. He had to compete with a delegation of Trojans, who had been sent to get the bow for their side and who arrived at the same time as he; and we do not know precisely what happened. But Dion Chrysostom regarded the play as 'a masterpiece of declamation' and 'a model of ingenious debate,' and Jebb thinks it probable that Odysseus won the contest by an appeal to Philoctetes' patriotism. Since Odysseus was pretending to have been wronged by the Greeks, he could point to his own behavior in suppressing his personal resentments in the interests of saving Greek honor. The moral theme thus established by Aeschylus and Euripides both would have been simply, like the theme of the wrath of Achilles, the conflict between the passions of an individual—in this case, an individual suffering from a genuine wrong—and the demands of duty to a common cause.

This conflict appears also in Sophocles; but it takes on a peculiar aspect. Sophocles, in the plays of his we have, shows himself particularly successful with people whose natures have been poisoned by narrow fanatical hatreds. Even allowing for the tendency of Greek heroes, in legend and history both, to fly into rather childish rages, we still feel on Sophocles' part some sort of special point of view, some sort of special sympathy, for these cases. Such people—Electra and the embittered old Oedipus—suffer as much as they hate: it is because they suffer they hate. They horrify, but they waken pity. Philoctetes is such another: a man obsessed by a grievance, which in his case he is to be kept from forgetting by an agonizing physical ailment; and for Sophocles his pain and hatred have a dignity and an interest. Just as it is by no means plain to Sophocles that in the affair of Antigone *versus* Creon it is the official point of view of Creon, representing the interests of his victorious faction, which should have the last word against Antigone, infuriated by a personal wrong; so it is by no means plain to him that the morality of Odysseus, who is lying and stealing for the fatherland, necessarily deserves to prevail over the animus of the stricken Philoctetes.

The contribution of Sophocles to the story is a third person who will sympathize with Philoctetes. This new character is Neoptolemus, the young son of Achilles, who, along with Philoctetes, is indispensable to the victory of the Greeks and who has just been summoned to Troy. Odysseus is made to bring him to Lemnos for the purpose of deceiving Philoctetes and shanghai-ing him abroad the ship.

The play opens with a scene between Odysseus and the boy, in which the former explains the purpose of their trip. Odysseus will remain in hiding in order not to be recognized by Philoctetes, and Neoptolemus will go up to the cave in which Philoctetes lives and win his confidence by pretending that the Greeks have robbed him of his father's armor, so that he, too, has a grievance against them. The youth in his innocence and candor objects when he is told what his rôle is to be, but Odysseus persuades him by reminding him that they can only take Troy through his obedience and that once they have taken Troy, he will be glorified for his bravery and wisdom. 'As soon as we have won,' Odysseus assures him, 'we shall conduct ourselves with perfect honesty. But for one short day of dishonesty, allow me to direct you what to do—and then forever after you will be known as the most righteous of men.' The line of argument adopted by Odysseus is one with which the politics of our time have made us very familiar. 'Isn't it base, then, to tell falsehoods?' Neoptolemus asks. 'Not,' Odysseus replies, 'when a falsehood will bring our salvation.'

Neoptolemus goes to talk to Philoctetes. He finds him in the wretched cave—described by Sophocles with characteristic realism: the bed of leaves, the crude wooden bowl, the filthy bandages drying in the sun—where he has been living in rags for ten years, limping out from time to time to shoot wild birds or to get himself wood and water. The boy hears the harrowing story of Philoctetes' desertion by the Greeks and listens to his indignation. The ruined captain begs Neoptolemus to take him back to his native land, and the young man pretends to consent. (Here and elsewhere I am telescoping the scenes and simplifying a more complex development.) But just as they are leaving for the ship, the ulcer on Philoctetes' foot sets up an ominous throbbing in preparation for one of its periodical burstings: 'She returns from time to time,' says the invalid, 'as if she were sated with her wanderings.' In a moment he is stretched on the ground, writhing in abject anguish and begging the young man to cut off his foot. He gives Neoptolemus the bow, telling him to take care of it till the seizure is over. A second spasm, worse than the first, reduces him to imploring the boy to throw him into the crater of the Lemnian volcano: so he himself, he says, had lit the fire which consumed the tormented Heracles and had got in return these arms, which he is now handing on to Neoptolemus. The pain abates a little; 'It comes and goes,' says Philoctetes; and he entreats the young man not to leave him. 'Don't worry about that. We'll stay.' 'I shan't even make you swear it, my son.' 'It would not be right to leave you' (it would not be right, of course, even from the Greeks' point of view). They shake hands on it. A third paroxysm twists the cripple; now he asks Neoptolemus to carry him to the cave, but shrinks from his grasp and struggles. At last the abscess bursts, the dark blood begins to flow. Philoctetes, faint and sweating, falls asleep.

The sailors who have come with Neoptolemus urge him to make off with the bow. 'No,' the young man replies. 'He cannot hear us; but I am sure that it will not be enough for us to recapture the bow without him. It is he who is to have the glory—it was he the god told us to bring.'

While they are arguing, Philoctetes awakes and thanks the young man with emotion: 'Agamemnon and Menelaus were not so patient and loyal.' But now they must get him to the ship, and the boy will have to see him undeceived and endure his bitter reproaches. 'The men will carry you down,' says Neoptolemus. 'Don't trouble them: just help me up,' Philoctetes replies. 'It would be too disagreeable for them to take me all the way to the ship.' The smell of the suppuration has been sickening. The young man begins to hesitate. The other sees that he is in doubt about something: 'You're not so overcome with disgust at my disease that you don't think you can have me on the ship with you?'—

οὐ δή σε δυσχέρεια τοῦ νοσήματος
ἔπεισεν ὥστε μή μ' ἄγειν ναύτην ἔτι;

The answer is one of the most effective of those swift and brief speeches of Sophocles which for the first time make a situation explicit (my attempts to render this dialogue colloquially do no justice to the feeling and point of the verse):

ἅπαντα δυσχέρεια, τὴν αὑτοῦ φύσιν
ὅταν λιπών τις δρᾷ τὰ μὴ προσεικότα.

'Everything becomes disgusting when you are false to your own nature and behave in an unbecoming way.'

He confesses his real intentions; and a painful scene occurs. Philoctetes denounces the boy in terms that would be appropriate for Odysseus; he sees himself robbed of his bow and left to starve on the island. The young man is deeply worried: 'Why did I ever leave Scyros?' he asks himself. 'Comrades, what shall I do?'

At this moment, Odysseus, who has been listening, pops out from his hiding place. With a lash of abuse at Neoptolemus, he orders him to hand over the arms. The young man's spirit flares up: when Odysseus invokes the will of Zeus, he tells him that he is degrading the gods by lending them his own lies. Philoctetes turns on Odysseus with an invective which cannot fail to impress the generous Neoptolemus: Why have they come for him now? he demands. Is he not still just as ill-omened and loathsome as he had been when they made him an outcast?

They have only come back to get him because the gods have told them they must.

The young man now defies his mentor and takes his stand with Philoctetes. Odysseus threatens him: if he persists, he will have the whole Greek army against him, and they will see to it that he is punished for his treason. Neoptolemus declares his intention of taking Philoctetes home; he gives him back his bow. Odysseus tries to intervene; but Philoctetes has got the bow and aims an arrow at him. Neoptolemus seizes his hand and restrains him. Odysseus, always prudent, beats a quiet retreat.

Now the boy tries to persuade the angry man that he should, nevertheless, rescue the Greeks. 'I have proved my good faith,' says Neoptolemus; 'you know that I am not going to coerce you. Why be so wrong-headed? When the gods afflict us, we are obliged to bear our misfortunes; but must people pity a man who suffers through his own choice? The snake that bit you was an agent of the gods, it was the guardian of the goddess's shrine, and I swear to you by Zeus that the sons of Asclepius will cure you if you let us take you to Troy.' Philoctetes is incredulous, refuses. 'Since you gave me your word,' he says, 'take me home again.' 'The Greeks will attack me and ruin me.' 'I'll defend you.' 'How can you?' 'With my bow.' Neoptolemus is forced to consent.

But now Heracles suddenly appears from the skies and declares to Philoctetes that what the young man says is true, and that it is right for him to go to Troy. He and the son of Achilles shall stand together like lions and shall gloriously carry the day.—The *deus ex machina* here may of course figure a change of heart which has taken place in Philoctetes as the result of his having found a man who recognizes the wrong that has been done him and who is willing to champion his cause in defiance of all the Greek forces. His patron, the chivalrous Heracles, who had himself performed so many generous exploits, asserts his influence over his heir. The long hatred is finally exorcised.

In a fine lyric utterance which ends the play, Philoctetes says farewell to the cavern, where he has lain through so many nights listening to the deep-voiced waves as they crashed against the headland, and wetted by the rain and the spray blown in by the winter gales. A favorable wind has sprung up; and he sails away to Troy.

It is possible to guess at several motivations behind the writing of the *Philoctetes*. The play was produced in 409, when—if the tradition of his longevity be true—Sophocles would have been eighty-seven; and it is supposed to have been followed by the *Oedipus Coloneus*, which is assigned to 405 or 406. The latter deals directly with old age; but it would appear that the *Philoctetes* anticipates this theme in another form. Philoctetes, like the outlawed Oedipus, is impoverished, humbled, abandoned by his people, exacerbated by hardship and chagrin. He is accursed: Philoctetes' ulcer is an equivalent for the abhorrent sins of Oedipus, parricide and incest together, which have made of the ruler a pariah. And yet somehow both are sacred persons who have acquired superhuman powers, and who are destined to be purged of their guilt. One passage from the earlier play is even strikingly repeated in the later. The conception of the wave-beaten promontory and the sick man lying in his cave assailed by the wind and rain turns up in the *Oedipus Coloneus* (Coloneus was Sophocles' native deme) with a figurative moral value. So the ills of old age assail Oedipus. Here are the lines, in A. E. Housman's translation:

This man, as me, even so,
Have the evil days overtaken;
And like as a cape sea-shaken
With tempest at earth's last verges
And shock of all winds that blow,
His head the seas of woe,
The thunders of awful surges
Ruining overflow;
Blown from the fall of even,
  Blown from the dayspring forth,
Blown from the noon in heaven,
  Blown from night and the North.

But Oedipus has endured as Philoctetes has endured in the teeth of all the cold and the darkness, the screaming winds and the bellowing breakers: the blind old man is here in his own person the headland that stands against the storm.

We may remember a widely current story about the creator of these two figures. It is said that one of Sophocles' sons brought him into court in his advanced old age on the complaint that he was no longer competent to manage his property. The old poet is supposed to have recited a passage from the play which he had been writing: the chorus in praise of Coloneus, with its clear song of nightingales, its wine-dark ivy, its crocus glowing golden and its narcissus moist with dew, where the stainless stream of the Cephisus wanders through the broad-swelling plain and where the gray-leaved olive grows of itself beneath the gaze of the gray-eyed Athena—shining Colonus, breeder of horses and of oarsmen whom the Nereids lead. The scene had been represented on the stage and Sophocles had been made to declare: 'If I am

Sophocles, I am not mentally incapable; if I am mentally incapable, I am not Sophocles.' In any case, the story was that the tribunal, composed of his fellow clansmen, applauded and acquitted the poet and censored the litigating son. The ruined and humiliated heroes of Sophocles' later plays are still persons of mysterious virtue, whom their fellows are forced to respect.

There is also a possibility, even a strong probability, that Sophocles intended Philoctetes to be identified with Alcibiades. This brilliant and unique individual, one of the great military leaders of the Athenians, had been accused by political opponents of damaging the sacred statues of Hermes and burlesquing the Eleusinian mysteries, and had been summoned to stand trial at Athens while he was away on his campaign against Sicily. He had at once gone over to the Spartans, commencing that insolent career of shifting allegiances which ended with his returning to the Athenian side. At a moment of extreme danger, he had taken over a part of the Athenian fleet and had defeated the Spartans in two sensational battles in 411 and 410, thus sweeping them out of the Eastern Aegean and enabling the Athenians to dominate the Hellespont. The *Philoctetes* was produced in 409, when the Athenians already wanted him back and were ready to cancel the charges against him and to restore him to citizenship. Alcibiades was a startling example of a bad character who was indispensable. Plutarch says that Aristophanes well describes the Athenian feeling about Alcibiades when he writes: 'They miss him and hate him and long to have him back.' And the malady of Philoctetes may have figured his moral defects: the unruly and unscrupulous nature which, even though he seems to have been innocent of the charges brought against him, had given them a certain plausibility. It must have looked to the Athenians, too, after the victories of Abydos and Cyzicus, as if he possessed an invincible bow. Plutarch says that the men who had served under him at the taking of Cyzicus did actually come to regard themselves as undefeatable and refused to share quarters with other soldiers who had fought in less successful engagements.

Yet behind both the picture of old age and the line in regard to Alcibiades, one feels in the *Philoctetes* a more general and fundamental idea: the conception of superior strength as inseparable from disability.

For the superiority of Philoctetes does not reside merely in the enchanted bow. When Lessing replied to Winckelmann, who had referred to Sophocles' cripple as if he were an example of the conventional idea of impassive classical fortitude, he pointed out that, far from exemplifying impassivity, Philoctetes becomes completely demoralized every time he has one of his seizures, and yet that this only heightens our admiration for the pride which prevents him from escaping at the expense of helping those who have deserted him. 'We despise,' say the objectors, 'any man from whom bodily pain extorts a shriek. Ay, but not always; not for the first time, nor if we see that the sufferer strains every nerve to stifle the expression of his pain; not if we know him otherwise to be a man of firmness; still less if we witness evidences of his firmness in the very midst of his sufferings, and observe that, although pain may have extorted a shriek, it has extorted nothing else from him, but that on the contrary he submits to the prolongation of his pain rather than renounce one iota of his resolutions, even where such a concession would promise him the termination of his misery.'

For André Gide, in his *Philoctète*, the obstinacy of the invalid hermit takes on a character almost mystical. By persisting in his bleak and lonely life, the Philoctetes of Gide wins the love of a more childlike Neoptolemus and even compels the respect of a less hard-boiled Odysseus. He is practicing a kind of virtue superior not only to the virtue of the latter, with his code of obedience to the demands of the group, but also to that of the former, who forgets his patriotic obligations for those of a personal attachment. There is something above the gods, says the Philoctetes of Gide; and it is virtue to devote oneself to this. But what is it? asks Neoptolemus. I do not know, he answers; oneself! The misfortune of his exile on the island has enabled him to perfect himself: 'I have learned to express myself better,' he tells them, 'now that I am no longer with men. Between hunting and sleeping, I occupy myself with thinking. My ideas, since I have been alone so that nothing, not even suffering, disturbs them, have taken a subtle course which sometimes I can hardly follow. I have come to know more of the secrets of life than my masters had ever revealed to me. And I took to telling the story of my sufferings, and if the phrase was very beautiful, I was by so much consoled; I even sometimes forgot my sadness by uttering it. I came to understand that words inevitably become more beautiful from the moment they are no longer put together in response to the demands of others. . . .' The Philoctetes of Gide is, in fact, a literary man: at once a moralist and an artist, whose genius becomes purer and deeper in ratio to his isolation and outlawry. In the end, he lets the intruders steal the bow after satisfying himself that Neoptolemus can handle it, and subsides into a blissful tranquillity, much relieved that there is no longer any reason for people to seek him out.

With Gide we come close to a further implication, which even Gide does not fully develop but which must occur to the modern reader: the idea that genius and disease, like strength and mutilation, may be inextricably bound up together. It is significant that the only two writers of our time who have especially interested themselves in Philoctetes—André Gide and John Jay Chapman—should both be persons who have not only, like the hero of the play, stood at an angle to the morality of society and defended their position with stubbornness, but who have suffered from psychological disorders which have made them, in Gide's case, ill-regarded by his fellows; in Chapman's case, excessively difficult. Nor is it perhaps accidental that Charles Lamb, with his experience of his sister's insanity, should in his essay on *The Convalescent* choose the figure of Philoctetes as a symbol for his own 'nervous fever.'

And we must even, I believe, grant Sophocles some special insight into morbid psychology. The tragic themes of all three of the great dramatists—the madnesses, the murders and the incests—may seem to us sufficiently morbid. The hero with an incurable wound was even a stock subject of myth not confined to the Philoctetes legend: there was also the story of Telephus, also wounded and also indispensable, about which both Sophocles and Euripides wrote plays. But there is a difference between the treatment that Sophocles gives to these conventional epic subjects and the treatments of the other writers. Aeschylus is more religious and philosophical; Euripides more romantic and sentimental. Sophocles by comparison is clinical. Arthur Platt, who had a special interest in the scientific aspect of the classics, says that Sophocles was scrupulously up-to-date in the physical science of his time. He was himself closely associated by tradition with the cult of the healer Asclepius, whose son is to cure Philoctetes: Lucian had read a poem which he had dedicated to the doctor-god; and Plutarch reports that Asclepius was supposed to have visited his hearth. He is said also to have been actually a priest of another of the medical cults. Platt speaks particularly of his medical knowledge—which is illustrated by the naturalism and precision of his description of Philoctetes' infected bite.

But there is also in Sophocles a cool observation of the behavior of psychological derangements. The madness of Ajax is a genuine madness, from which he recovers to be horrified at the realization of what he has done. And it was not without good reason that Freud laid

Sophocles under contribution for the naming of the Oedipus complex—since Sophocles had not only dramatized the myth that dwelt with the violation of the incest taboo, but had exhibited the suppressed impulse behind it in the speech in which he makes Jocasta attempt to reassure Oedipus by reminding him that it was not uncommon for men to dream about sleeping with their mothers—'and he who thinks nothing of this gets through his life most easily.' Those who do not get through life so easily are presented by Sophocles with a very firm grasp on the springs of their abnormal conduct. Electra is what we should call nowadays schizophrenic: the woman who weeps over the urn which is supposed to contain her brother's ashes is not 'integrated,' as we say, with the fury who prepares her mother's murder. And certainly the fanaticism of Antigone—'fixated,' like Electra, on her brother—is intended to be abnormal, too. The banishment by Jebb from Sophocles' text of the passage in which Antigone explains the unique importance of a brother and his juggling of the dialogue in the scene in which she betrays her indifference to the feelings of the man she is supposed to marry are certainly among the curiosities of Victorian scholarship—though he was taking his cue from the complaint of Goethe that Antigone had been shown by Sophocles as acting from trivial motives and Goethe's hope that her speech about her brother might some day be shown to be spurious. Aristotle had cited this speech of Antigone's as an outstanding example of the principle that if anything peculiar occurs in a play the cause must be shown by the dramatist. It was admitted by Jebb that his rewriting of these passages had no real textual justification; and in one case he violates glaringly the convention of the one-line dialogue. To accept his emendation would involve the assumption that Aristotle did not know what the original text had been and was incapable of criticizing the corrupted version. No: Antigone forgets her fiancé and kills herself for her brother. Her timid sister (like Electra's timid sister) represents the normal feminine point of view. Antigone's point of view is peculiar, as Aristotle says. (The real motivation of the Antigone has been retraced with unmistakable accuracy by Professor Walter R. Agard in *Classical Philology* of July, 1937.)

These insane or obsessed people of Sophocles all display a perverse kind of nobility. I have spoken of the authority of expiation which emanates from the blasted Oedipus. Even the virulence of Electra's revenge conditions the intensity of her tenderness for Orestes. And so the maniacal fury which makes Ajax run amok, the frenzy of Heracles in the Nessus robe, terribly though they transform their victims, can never destroy their virtue of heroes. The poor disgraced Ajax will receive his due of honor after his suicide and will come to stand higher in our sympathies than Menelaus and Agamemnon, those obtuse and brutal captains, who here as in the *Philoctetes* are obviously no favorites of Sophocles'. Heracles in his final moments bids his spirit curb his lips with steel to keep him from crying out, and carry him through his self-destructive duty as a thing that is to be desired.

Some of these maladies are physical in origin, others are psychological; but they link themselves with one another. The case of Ajax connects psychological disorder as we get it in Electra, for example, with the access of pain and rage that causes Heracles to kill the herald Lichas; the case of Heracles connects a poisoning that produces a murderous fury with an infection that, though it distorts the personality, does not actually render the victim demented: the wound of Philoctetes, whose agony comes in spasms like that of Heracles. All these cases seem intimately related.

It has been the misfortune of Sophocles to figure in academic tradition as the model of those qualities of coolness and restraint which that tradition regards as classical. Those who have never read him—remembering the familiar statue—are likely to conceive something hollow and marmoreal. Actually, as C. M. Bowra says, Sophocles is 'passionate and profound.' Almost everything that we are told about him by the tradition of the ancient world suggests equanimity and amiability and the enjoyment of unusual good fortune. But there is one important exception: the anecdote in Plato's *Republic* in which Sophocles is represented as saying that the release from amorous desire which had come to him in his old age had been like a liberation from an insane and cruel master. He *has* balance and logic, of course: those qualities that the classicists admire; but these qualities only count because they master so much savagery and madness. Somewhere even in the fortunate Sophocles there had been a sick and raving Philoctetes.

And now let us go back to the *Philoctetes* as a parable of human character. I should interpret the fable as follows. The victim of a malodorous disease which renders him abhorrent to society and periodically degrades him and makes him helpless is also the master of a superhuman art which everybody has to respect and which the normal man finds he needs. A practical man like Odysseus, at the same time coarse-grained and clever, imagines that he can somehow get the bow without having Philoctetes on his hands or that he can kidnap Philoctetes the bowman without regard for Philoctetes the invalid. But the young son of Achilles knows better. It is at the moment when his sympathy for Philoctetes would naturally inhibit his cheating him—so the supernatural influences in Sophocles are often made with infinite delicacy to shade into subjective motivations—it is at this moment of his natural shrinking that it becomes clear to him that the words of the seer had meant that the bow would be useless without Philoctetes himself. It is in the nature of things—of this world where the divine and the human fuse—that they cannot have the irresistible weapon without its loathsome owner, who upsets the processes of normal life by his curses and his cries, and who in any case refuses to work for men who have exiled him from their fellowship.

It is quite right that Philoctetes should refuse to come to Troy. Yet it is also decreed that he shall be cured when he shall have been able to forget his grievance and to devote his divine gifts to the service of his own people. It is right that he should refuse to submit to the purposes of Odysseus, whose only idea is to exploit him. How then is the gulf to be got over between the ineffective plight of the bowman and his proper use of his bow, between his ignominy and his destined glory? Only by the intervention of one who is guileless enough and human enough to treat him, not as a monster, nor yet as a mere magical property which is wanted for accomplishing some end, but simply as another man, whose sufferings elicit his sympathy and whose courage and pride he admires. When this human relation has been realized, it seems at first that it is to have the consequence of frustrating the purpose of the expedition and ruining the Greek campaign. Instead of winning over the outlaw, Neoptolemus has outlawed himself as well, at a time when both the boy and the cripple are desperately needed by the Greeks. Yet in taking the risk to his cause which is involved in the recognition of his common humanity with the sick man, in refusing to break his word, he dissolves Philoctetes' stubbornness, and thus cures him and sets him free, and saves the campaign as well.

Art and Neurosis

The question of the mental health of the artist has engaged the attention of our culture since the beginning of the Romantic Movement. Before that time it was commonly said that the poet was "mad," but this was only a manner of speaking, a way of saying that the mind of the poet worked in different fashion from the mind of the philosopher; it had no real reference to the mental hygiene of the man who was the poet. But in the early nineteenth century, with the development of a more elaborate psychology and a stricter and more literal view of mental and emotional normality, the statement was more strictly and literally intended. So much so, indeed, that Charles Lamb, who knew something about madness at close quarters and a great deal about art, undertook to refute in his brilliant essay, "On the Sanity of True Genius," the idea that the exercise of the imagination was a kind of insanity. And some eighty years later, the idea having yet further entrenched itself, Bernard Shaw felt called upon to argue the sanity of art, but his cogency was of no more avail than Lamb's. In recent years the connection between art and mental illness has been formulated not only by those who are openly or covertly hostile to art, but also and more significantly by those who are most intensely partisan to it. The latter willingly and even eagerly accept the idea that the artist is mentally ill and go on to make his illness a condition of his power to tell the truth.

This conception of artistic genius is indeed one of the characteristic notions of our culture. I should like to bring it into question. To do so is to bring also into question certain early ideas of Freud's and certain conclusions which literary laymen have drawn from the whole tendency of the Freudian psychology. From the very start it was recognized that psychoanalysis was likely to have important things to say about art and artists. Freud himself thought so, yet when he first addressed himself to the subject he said many clumsy and misleading things. I have elsewhere and at length tried to separate the useful from the useless and even dangerous statements about art that Freud has made.[1] To put it briefly here, Freud had some illuminating and even beautiful insights into certain particular works of art which made complex use of the element of myth. Then, without specifically undertaking to do so, his "Beyond the Pleasure Principle" offers a brilliant and comprehensive explanation of our interest in tragedy. And what is of course most important of all—it is a point to which I shall return—Freud, by the whole tendency of his psychology,

[1] See "Freud and Literature."

establishes the *naturalness* of artistic thought. Indeed, it is possible to say of Freud that he ultimately did more for our understanding of art than any other writer since Aristotle; and this being so, it can only be surprising that in his early work he should have made the error of treating the artist as a neurotic who escapes from reality by means of "substitute gratifications."

As Freud went forward he insisted less on this simple formulation. Certainly it did not have its original force with him when, at his seventieth birthday celebration, he disclaimed the right to be called the discoverer of the unconscious, saying that whatever he may have done for the systematic understanding of the unconscious, the credit for its discovery properly belonged to the literary masters. And psychoanalysis has inherited from him a tenderness for art which is real although sometimes clumsy, and nowadays most psychoanalysts of any personal sensitivity are embarrassed by occasions which seem to lead them to reduce art to a formula of mental illness. Nevertheless Freud's early belief in the essential neuroticism of the artist found an all too fertile ground—found, we might say, the very ground from which it first sprang, for, when he spoke of the artist as a neurotic, Freud was adopting one of the popular beliefs of his age. Most readers will see this belief as the expression of the industrial rationalization and the bourgeois philistinism of the nineteenth century. In this they are partly right. The nineteenth century established the basic virtue of "getting up at eight, shaving close at a quarter-past, breakfasting at nine, going to the City at ten, coming home at half-past five, and dining at seven." The Messrs. Podsnap who instituted this scheduled morality inevitably decreed that the arts must celebrate it and nothing else. "Nothing else to be permitted to these . . . vagrants the Arts, on pain of excommunication. Nothing else To Be—anywhere!" We observe that the virtuous day ends with dinner—bed and sleep are naturally not part of the Reality that Is, and nothing must be set forth which will, as Mr. Podsnap put it, bring a Blush to the Cheek of a Young Person.

The excommunication of the arts, when it was found necessary, took the form of pronouncing the artist mentally degenerate, a device which eventually found its theorist in Max Nordau. In the history of the arts this is new. The poet was always known to belong to a touchy tribe—*genus irritabile* was a tag anyone would know—and ever since Plato the process of the inspired imagination, as we have said, was thought to be a special one of some interest, which the similitude of madness made somewhat intelligible. But this is not quite to say that the poet was the victim of actual mental aberration. The eighteenth century did not find the poet to be less than other men, and certainly the Renaissance did not. If he was a professional, there might be condescension to his social status, but in a time which deplored all professionalism whatever, this was simply a way of asserting the high value of poetry, which ought not to be compromised by trade. And a certain good nature marked even the snubbing of the professional! At any rate, no one was likely to identify the poet with the weakling. Indeed, the Renaissance ideal held poetry to be, like arms or music, one of the signs of manly competence.

The change from this view of things cannot be blamed wholly on the bourgeois or philistine public. Some of the "blame" must rest with the poets themselves. The Romantic poets were as proud of their art as the vaunting poets of the sixteenth century, but one of them talked with an angel in a tree and insisted that Hell was better than Heaven and sexuality holier than chastity; another told the world that he wanted to lie down like a tired child and weep away this life of care; another asked so foolish a question as "Why did I laugh tonight?"; and yet another explained that he had written one of his best poems in a drugged sleep. The public took them all at their word—they were not as other men. Zola, in the interests of science, submitted himself to examination by fifteen psychiatrists and agreed with their conclusion that his genius had its source in the neurotic elements of his temperament. Baudelaire, Rimbaud, Verlaine found virtue and strength in their physical and mental illness and pain. W. H. Auden addresses his "wound" in the cherishing language of a lover, thanking it for the gift of insight it has bestowed. "Knowing you," he says, "has made me understand." And Edmund Wilson in his striking phrase, "the wound and the bow," has formulated for our time the idea of the characteristic sickness of the artist, which he represents by the figure of Philoctetes, the Greek warrior who was forced to live in isolation because of the disgusting odor of a suppurating wound and who yet had to be sought out by his countrymen because they had need of the magically unerring bow he possessed.

The myth of the sick artist, we may suppose, has established itself because it is of advantage to the various groups who have one or another relation with art. To the artist himself the myth gives some of the ancient powers and privileges of the idiot and the fool, half-prophetic creatures, or of the mutilated priest. That the artist's neurosis may be but a mask is suggested by Thomas Mann's pleasure in representing his untried youth as "sick" but his successful maturity as senatorially robust. By means of his belief in his own sickness, the artist may the more easily fulfill his chosen, and assigned, function of putting himself into connection with the forces of spirituality and morality; the artist sees as insane the "normal" and "healthy" ways of established society, while aberration and illness appear as spiritual and moral health if only because they controvert the ways of respectable society.

Then too, the myth has its advantage for the philistine—a double advantage. On the one hand, the belief in the artist's neuroticism allows the philistine to shut his ears to what the artist says. But on the other hand it allows him to listen. For we must not make the common mistake —the contemporary philistine does want to listen, at the same time that he wants to shut his ears. By supposing that the artist has an interesting but not always reliable relation to reality, he is able to contain (in the military sense) what the artist tells him. If he did not want to listen at all, he would say "insane"; with "neurotic," which hedges, he listens when he chooses.

And in addition to its advantage to the artist and to the philistine, we must take into account the usefulness of the myth to a third group, the group of "sensitive" people, who, although not artists, are not philistines either. These people form a group by virtue of their passive impatience with philistinism, and also by virtue of their awareness of their own emotional pain and uncertainty. To these people the myth of the sick artist is the institutional sanction of their situation; they seek to approximate or acquire the character of the artist, sometimes by planning to work or even attempting to work as the artist does, always by making a connection between their own powers of mind and their consciousness of "difference" and neurotic illness.

The early attempts of psychoanalysis to deal with art went on the assumption that, because the artist was neurotic, the content of his work was also neurotic, which is to say that it did not stand in a correct relation to reality. But nowadays, as I have said, psychoanalysis is not likely to be so simple in its transactions with art. A good example of the psychoanalytical development in this respect is Dr. Saul Rosenzweig's well-known essay, "The Ghost of Henry James."[2] This is an admirable piece of work, marked by accuracy in the reporting of the literary fact and by respect for the value of the literary object. Although Dr. Rosenzweig explores the element of neurosis in James's life and work, he nowhere suggests that this element in any way lessens James's value as an artist or moralist. In effect he says that neurosis is a way of dealing with reality which, in real life, is uncomfortable and uneconomical, but that this judgment of

[2] First published in *Character and Personality*, December 1943, and reprinted in *Partisan Review*, Fall, 1944.

neurosis in life cannot mechanically be transferred to works of art upon which neurosis has had its influence. He nowhere implies that a work of art in whose genesis a neurotic element may be found is for that reason irrelevant or in any way diminished in value. Indeed, the manner of his treatment suggests, what is of course the case, that every neurosis deals with a real emotional situation of the most intensely meaningful kind.

Yet as Dr. Rosenzweig brings his essay to its close, he makes use of the current assumption about the causal connection between the psychic illness of the artist and his power. His investigation of James, he says, "reveals the aptness of the Philoctetes pattern." He accepts the idea of "the sacrificial roots of literary power" and speaks of "the unhappy sources of James's genius." "The broader application of the inherent pattern," he says, "is familiar to readers of Edmund Wilson's recent volume *The Wound and the Bow*. . . . Reviewing the experience and work of several well-known literary masters, Wilson discloses the sacrificial roots of their power on the model of the Greek legend. In the case of Henry James, the present account . . . provides a similar insight into the unhappy sources of his genius. . . ."

This comes as a surprise. Nothing in Dr. Rosenzweig's theory requires it. For his theory asserts no more than that Henry James, predisposed by temperament and family situation to certain mental and emotional qualities, was in his youth injured in a way which he believed to be sexual; that he unconsciously invited the injury in the wish to identify himself with his father, who himself had been similarly injured—"castrated": a leg had been amputated—and under strikingly similar circumstances; this resulted for the younger Henry James in a certain pattern of life and in a preoccupation in his work with certain themes which more or less obscurely symbolize his sexual situation. For this I think Dr. Rosenzweig makes a sound case. Yet I submit that this is not the same thing as disclosing the roots of James's power or discovering the sources of his genius. The essay which gives Edmund Wilson's book its title and cohering principle does not explicitly say that the roots of power are sacrificial and that the source of genius is unhappy. Where it is explicit, it states only that "genius and disease, like strength and mutilation, may be inextricably bound up together," which of course, on its face, says no more than that personality is integral and not made up of detachable parts; and from this there is no doubt to be drawn the important practical and moral implication that we cannot judge or dismiss a man's genius and strength because of our awareness of his disease or mutilation. The Philoctetes legend in itself does not suggest anything beyond this. It does not suggest that the wound is the price of the bow, or that without the wound the bow may not be possessed or drawn. Yet Dr. Rosenzweig has accurately summarized the force and, I think, the intention of Mr. Wilson's whole book; its several studies do seem to say that effectiveness in the arts does depend on sickness.

An examination of this prevalent idea might well begin with the observation of how pervasive and deeply rooted is the notion that power may be gained by suffering. Even at relatively high stages of culture the mind seems to take easily to the primitive belief that pain and sacrifice are connected with strength. Primitive beliefs must be treated with respectful alertness to their possible truth and also with the suspicion of their being magical and irrational, and it is worth noting on both sides of the question, and in the light of what we have said about the ambiguous relation of the neurosis to reality, that the whole economy of the neurosis is based exactly on this idea of the *quid pro quo* of sacrificial pain: the neurotic person unconsciously subscribes to a system whereby he gives up some pleasure or power, or inflicts pain on himself in order to secure some other power or some other pleasure.

In the ingrained popular conception of the relation between suffering and power there are actually two distinct although related ideas. One is that there exists in the individual a fund of power which has outlets through various organs or faculties, and that if its outlet through one organ or faculty be prevented, it will flow to increase the force or sensitivity of another. Thus it is popularly believed that the sense of touch is intensified in the blind not so much by the will of the blind person to adapt himself to the necessities of his situation as, rather, by a sort of mechanical redistribution of power. And this idea would seem to explain, if not the origin of the ancient mutilation of priests, then at least a common understanding of their sexual sacrifice.

The other idea is that a person may be taught by, or proved by, the endurance of pain. There will easily come to mind the ritual suffering that is inflicted at the tribal initiation of youths into full manhood or at the admission of the apprentice into the company of journeyman adepts. This idea in sophisticated form found its way into high religion at least as early as Aeschylus, who held that man achieves knowledge of God through suffering, and it was from the beginning an important element of Christian thought. In the nineteenth century the Christianized notion of the didactic suffering of the artist went along with the idea of his mental degeneration and even served as a sort of countermyth to it. Its doctrine was that the artist, a man of strength and health, experienced and suffered, and thus learned both the facts of life and his artistic craft.

"I am the man, I suffered, I was there," ran his boast, and he derived his authority from the knowledge gained through suffering.

There can be no doubt that both these ideas represent a measure of truth about mental and emotional power. The idea of didactic suffering expresses a valuation of experience and of steadfastness. The idea of natural compensation for the sacrifice of some faculty also says something that can be rationally defended: one cannot be and do everything and the wholehearted absorption in any enterprise, art for example, means that we must give up other possibilities, even parts of ourselves. And there is even a certain validity to the belief that the individual has a fund of undifferentiated energy which presses the harder upon what outlets are available to it when it has been deprived of the normal number.

Then, in further defense of the belief that artistic power is connected with neurosis, we can say that there is no doubt that what we call mental illness may be the source of psychic knowledge. Some neurotic people, because they are more apprehensive than normal people, are able to see more of certain parts of reality and to see them with more intensity. And many neurotic or psychotic patients are in certain respects in closer touch with the actualities of the unconscious than are normal people. Further, the expression of a neurotic or psychotic conception of reality is likely to be more intense than a normal one.

Yet when we have said all this, it is still wrong, I believe, to find the root of the artist's power and the source of his genius in neurosis. To the idea that literary power and genius spring from pain and neurotic sacrifice there are two major objections. The first has to do with the assumed uniqueness of the artist as a subject of psychoanalytical explanation. The second has to do with the true meaning of power and genius.

One reason why writers are considered to be more available than other people to psychoanalytical explanation is that they tell us what is going on inside them. Even when they do not make an actual diagnosis of their malaises or describe "symptoms," we must bear it in mind that it is their profession to deal with fantasy in some form or other. It is in the nature of the writer's job that he exhibit his unconscious. He may disguise it in various ways, but disguise is not concealment. Indeed, it may be said that the more a writer takes pains with his work to remove it from the personal and subjective, the more—and not the less—he will express his true unconscious, although not what passes with most for the unconscious.

Further, the writer is likely to be a great hand at personal letters, diaries, and autobiographies: indeed, almost the only good autobiographies are those of writers. The writer is more aware of what happens to him or goes on in him and often finds it necessary or useful to be articulate about his inner states, and prides himself on telling the truth. Thus, only a man as devoted to the truth of the emotions as Henry James was would have informed the world, despite his characteristic reticence, of an accident so intimate as his. We must not of course suppose that a writer's statements about his intimate life are equivalent to true statements about his unconscious, which, by definition, he doesn't consciously know; but they may be useful clues to the nature of an entity about which we can make statements of more or less cogency, although never statements of certainty; or they at least give us what is surely related to a knowledge of his unconscious—that is, an insight into his personality.[3]

But while the validity of dealing with the writer's intellectual life in psychoanalytical terms is taken for granted, the psychoanalytical explanation of the intellectual life of scientists is generally speaking not countenanced. The old myth of the mad scientist, with the exception of an occasional mad psychiatrist, no longer exists. The social position of science requires that it should cease, which leads us to remark that those partisans of art who insist on explaining artistic genius by means of psychic imbalance are in effect capitulating to the dominant mores which hold that the members of the respectable professions are, however dull they may be, free from neurosis. Scientists, to continue with them as the best example of the respectable professions, do not usually give us the clues to their personalities which writers habitually give. But no one who has ever lived observantly among scientists will claim that they are without an unconscious or even that they are free from neurosis. How often, indeed, it is apparent that the devotion to science, if it cannot be called a neurotic manifestation, at least can be understood as going very cozily with neurotic elements in the temperament, such as, for example, a marked compulsiveness. Of scientists as a group we can say that they are less concerned with the manifestations of personality, their own or others', than are writers as a group. But this relative indifference is

[3] I am by no means in agreement with the statements of Dr. Edmund Bergler about "the" psychology of the writer, but I think that Dr. Bergler has done good service in warning us against taking at their face value a writer's statements about himself, the more especially when they are "frank." Thus, to take Dr. Bergler's notable example, it is usual for biographers to accept Stendhal's statements about his open sexual feeling for his mother when he was a little boy, feelings which went with an intense hatred of his father. But Dr. Bergler believes that Stendhal unconsciously used his consciousness of his love of his mother and of his hatred of his father to mask an unconscious love of his father, which frightened him. ("Psychoanalysis of Writers and of Literary Productivity" in *Psychoanalysis and the Social Sciences*, vol. 1.)

scarcely a sign of normality—indeed, if we choose to regard it with the same sort of eye with which the characteristics of writers are regarded, we might say the indifference to matters of personality is in itself a suspicious evasion.

It is the basic assumption of psychoanalysis that the acts of *every* person are influenced by the forces of the unconscious. Scientists, bankers, lawyers, or surgeons, by reason of the traditions of their professions, practice concealment and conformity; but it is difficult to believe that an investigation according to psychoanalytical principles would fail to show that the strains and imbalances of their psyches are not of the same frequency as those of writers, and of similar kind. I do not mean that everybody has the same troubles and identical psyches, but only that there is no special category for writers.[4]

If this is so, and if we still want to relate the writer's power to his neurosis, we must be willing to relate all intellectual power to neurosis. We must find the roots of Newton's power in his emotional extravagances, and the roots of Darwin's power in his sorely neurotic temperament, and the roots of Pascal's mathematical genius in the impulses which drove him to extreme religious masochism—I choose but the classic examples. If we make the neurosis-power equivalence at all, we must make it in every field of endeavor. Logician, economist, botanist, physicist, theologian—no profession may be so respectable or so remote or so rational as to be exempt from the psychological interpretation.[5]

---

[4] Dr. Bergler believes that there is a particular neurosis of writers, based on an oral masochism which makes them the enemy of the respectable world, courting poverty and persecution. But a later development of Dr. Bergler's theory of oral masochism makes it *the* basic neurosis, not only of writers but of everyone who is neurotic.

[5] In his interesting essay, "Writers and Madness" (*Partisan Review*, January–February 1947), William Barrett has taken issue with this point and has insisted that a clear distinction is to be made between the relation that exists between the scientist and his work and the relation that exists between the artist and his work. The difference, as I understand it, is in the claims of the ego. The artist's ego makes a claim upon the world which is personal in a way that the scientist's is not, for the scientist, although he does indeed want prestige and thus "responds to one of the deepest urges of his ego, it is only that his prestige may come to attend his person through the public world of other men; and it is not in the end his own being that is exhibited or his own voice that is heard in the learned report to the Academy." Actually, however, as is suggested by the sense which mathematicians have of the *style* of mathematical thought, the creation of the abstract thinker is as deeply involved as the artist's—see *An Essay on the Psychology of Invention in the Mathematical Field* by Jacques Hadamard, Princeton University Press, 1945—and he quite as much as the artist seeks to impose *himself*, to *express* himself. I am of course not maintaining that the processes of

Further, not only power but also failure or limitation must be accounted for by the theory of neurosis, and not merely failure or limitation in life but even failure or limitation in art. Thus it is often said that the warp of Dostoevski's mind accounts for the brilliance of his psychological insights. But it is never said that the same warp of Dostoevski's mind also accounted for his deficiency in insight. Freud, who greatly admired Dostoevski, although he did not like him, observed that "his insight was entirely restricted to the workings of the abnormal psyche. Consider his astounding helplessness before the phenomenon of love; he really only understands either crude, instinctive desire or masochistic submission or love from pity."[6] This, we must note, is not merely Freud's comment on the extent of the province which Dostoevski chose for his own, but on his failure to understand what, given the province of his choice, he might be expected to understand.

And since neurosis can account not only for intellectual success and for failure or limitation but also for mediocrity, we have most of society involved in neurosis. To this I have no objection—I think most of society is indeed involved in neurosis. But with neurosis accounting for so much, it cannot be made exclusively to account for one man's literary power.

We have now to consider what is meant by genius when its source is identified as the sacrifice and pain of neurosis.

In the case of Henry James, the reference to the neurosis of his personal life does indeed tell us something about the latent intention of his work and thus about the reason for some large part of its interest for us. But if genius and its source are what we are dealing with, we must observe

---

scientific thought are the same as those of artistic thought, or even that the scientist's creation is involved with his total personality *in the same way* that the artist's is—I am maintaining only that the scientist's creation is as *deeply* implicated with his total personality as is the artist's.

This point of view seems to be supported by Freud's monograph on Leonardo. One of the problems that Freud sets himself is to discover why an artist of the highest endowment should have devoted himself more and more to scientific investigation, with the result that he was unable to complete his artistic enterprises. The particular reasons for this that Freud assigns need not be gone into here; all that I wish to suggest is that Freud understands these reasons to be the working out of an inner conflict, the attempt to deal with the difficulties that have their roots in the most primitive situations. Leonardo's scientific investigations were as necessary and "compelled" and they constituted as much of a claim on the whole personality as anything the artist undertakes; and so far from being carried out for the sake of public prestige, they were largely private and personal, and were thought by the public of his time to be something very like insanity.

[6] From a letter quoted in Theodor Reik's *From Thirty Years With Freud*, p. 175.

that the reference to neurosis tells us nothing about James's passion, energy, and devotion, nothing about his architectonic skill, nothing about the other themes that were important to him which are not connected with his unconscious concern with castration. We cannot, that is, make the writer's inner life exactly equivalent to his power of expressing it. Let us grant for the sake of argument that the literary genius, as distinguished from other men, is the victim of a "mutilation" and that his fantasies are neurotic.[7] It does not then follow as the inevitable next step that his ability to express these fantasies and to impress us with them is neurotic, for that ability is what we mean by his genius. Anyone might be injured as Henry James was, and even respond within himself to the injury as James is said to have done, and yet not have his literary power.

The reference to the artist's neurosis tells us something about the material on which the artist exercises his powers, and even something about his reasons for bringing his powers into play, but it does not tell us anything about the source of his power, it makes no causal connection between them and the neurosis. And if we look into the matter, we see that there is in fact no causal connection between them. For, still granting that the poet is uniquely neurotic, what is surely not neurotic, what indeed suggests nothing but health, is his power of using his neuroticism. He shapes his fantasies, he gives them social form and reference. Charles Lamb's way of putting this cannot be improved. Lamb is denying that genius is allied to insanity; for "insanity" the modern reader may substitute "neurosis." "The ground of the mistake," he says, "is, that men, finding in the raptures of the higher poetry a condition of exaltation, to which they have no parallel in their own experience, besides the spurious resemblance of it in dreams and fevers, impute a state of dreaminess and fever to the poet. But the true poet dreams being awake. He is not possessed by his subject but has dominion over it. . . . Where he seems most to recede from humanity, he will be found the truest to it. From beyond the scope of nature if he summon possible existences, he subjugates them to the law of her consistency. He is beautifully loyal to that sovereign directress, when he appears most to betray and desert her. . . . Herein the great and the little wits are

---

[7] I am using the word *fantasy*, unless modified, in a neutral sense. A fantasy, in this sense, may be distinguished from the representation of something that actually exists, but it is not opposed to "reality" and not an "escape" from reality. Thus the idea of a rational society, or the image of a good house to be built, as well as the story of something that could never really happen, is a fantasy. There may be neurotic or non-neurotic fantasies.

differenced; that if the latter wander ever so little from nature or natural existence, they lose themselves and their readers. . . . They do not create, which implies shaping and consistency. Their imaginations are not active—for to be active is to call something into act and form—but passive as men in sick dreams."

The activity of the artist, we must remember, may be approximated by many who are themselves not artists. Thus, the expressions of many schizophrenic people have the intense appearance of creativity and an inescapable interest and significance. But they are not works of art, and although Van Gogh may have been schizophrenic he was in addition an artist. Again, as I have already suggested, it is not uncommon in our society for certain kinds of neurotic people to imitate the artist in his life and even in his ideals and ambitions. They follow the artist in everything except successful performance. It was, I think, Otto Rank who called such people half-artists and confirmed the diagnosis of their neuroticism at the same time that he differentiated them from true artists.

Nothing is so characteristic of the artist as his power of shaping his work, of subjugating his raw material, however aberrant it be from what we call normality, to the consistency of nature. It would be impossible to deny that whatever disease or mutilation the artist may suffer is an element of his production which has its effect on every part of it, but disease and mutilation are available to us all—life provides them with prodigal generosity. What marks the artist is his power to shape the material of pain we all have.

At this point, with our recognition of life's abundant provision of pain, we are at the very heart of our matter, which is the meaning we may assign to neurosis and the relation we are to suppose it to have with normality. Here Freud himself can be of help, although it must be admitted that what he tells us may at first seem somewhat contradictory and confusing.

Freud's study of Leonardo da Vinci is an attempt to understand why Leonardo was unable to pursue his artistic enterprises, feeling compelled instead to advance his scientific investigations. The cause of this Freud traces back to certain childhood experiences not different in kind from the experiences which Dr. Rosenzweig adduces to account for certain elements in the work of Henry James. And when he has completed his study Freud makes this *caveat*: "Let us expressly emphasize that we have never considered Leonardo as a neurotic. . . . We no longer believe that health and disease, normal and nervous, are sharply distinguished from each other. We know today that neurotic symptoms are substitutive formations for certain repressive acts which must result in the course of our development from the child to the cultural man, that we all produce such substitutive formations, and that only the amount, intensity, and distribution of these substitutive formations justify the practical conception of illness. . . ." The statement becomes the more striking when we remember that in the course of his study Freud has had occasion to observe that Leonardo was both homosexual and sexually inactive. I am not sure that the statement that Leonardo was not a neurotic is one that Freud would have made at every point in the later development of psychoanalysis, yet it is in conformity with his continuing notion of the genesis of culture. And the *practical*, the quantitative or economic, conception of illness he insists on in a passage in the *Introductory Lectures*. "The neurotic symptoms," he says, ". . . are activities which are detrimental, or at least useless, to life as a whole; the person concerned frequently complains of them as obnoxious to him or they involve suffering and distress for him. The principal injury they inflict lies in the expense of energy they entail, and, besides this, in the energy needed to combat them. Where the symptoms are extensively developed, these two kinds of effort may exact such a price that the person suffers a very serious impoverishment in available mental energy which consequently disables him for all the important tasks of life. This result depends principally upon the amount of energy taken up in this way; therefore you will see that 'illness' is essentially a practical conception. But if you look at the matter from a theoretical point of view and ignore this question of degree, you can very well see that we are all ill, i.e., neurotic; for the conditions required for symptom-formation are demonstrable also in normal persons."

We are all ill: the statement is grandiose, and its implications—the implications, that is, of understanding the totality of human nature in the terms of disease—are vast. These implications have never been properly met (although I believe that a few theologians have responded to them), but this is not the place to attempt to meet them. I have brought forward Freud's statement of the essential sickness of the psyche only because it stands as the refutation of what is implied by the literary use of the theory of neurosis to account for genius. For if we are all ill, and if, as I have said, neurosis can account for everything, for failure and mediocrity—"a very serious impoverishment of available mental energy"—as well as for genius, it cannot uniquely account for genius.

This, however, is not to say that there is no connection between neurosis and genius, which would be tantamount, as we see, to saying that there is no connection between human nature and genius. But the connection lies wholly in a particular and special relation which the artist has to neurosis.

In order to understand what this particular and special connection is we must have clearly in mind what neurosis is. The current literary conception of neurosis as a *wound* is quite misleading. It inevitably suggests passivity, whereas, if we follow Freud, we must understand a neurosis to be an *activity*, an activity with a purpose, and a particular kind of activity, a *conflict*. This is not to say that there are no abnormal mental states which are not conflicts. There are; the struggle between elements of the unconscious may never be instituted in the first place, or it may be called off. As Freud says in a passage which follows close upon the one I last quoted, "If regressions do not call forth a prohibition on the part of the ego, no neurosis results; the libido succeeds in obtaining a real, although not a normal, satisfaction. But if the ego . . . is not in agreement with these regressions, conflict ensues." And in his essay on Dostoevski Freud says that "there are no neurotic complete masochists," by which he means that the ego which gives way completely to masochism (or to any other pathological excess) has passed beyond neurosis; the conflict has ceased, but at the cost of the defeat of the ego, and now some other name than that of neurosis must be given to the condition of the person who thus takes himself beyond the pain of the neurotic conflict. To understand this is to become aware of the curious complacency with which literary men regard mental disease. The psyche of the neurotic is not equally complacent; it regards with the greatest fear the chaotic and destructive forces it contains, and it struggles fiercely to keep them at bay.[8]

We come then to a remarkable paradox: we are all ill, but we are ill in the service of health, or ill in the service of life, or, at the very least,

---

[8] In the article to which I refer in the note on page [737], William Barrett says that he prefers the old-fashioned term "madness" to "neurosis." But it is not quite for him to choose—the words do not differ in fashion but in meaning. Most literary people, when they speak of mental illness, refer to neurosis. Perhaps one reason for this is that the neurosis is the most benign of the mental ills. Another reason is surely that psychoanalytical literature deals chiefly with the neurosis, and its symptomatology and therapy have become familiar; psychoanalysis has far less to say about psychosis, for which it can offer far less therapeutic hope. Further, the neurosis is easily put into a causal connection with the social maladjustments of our time. Other forms of mental illness of a more severe and degenerative kind are not so widely recognized by the literary person and are often assimilated to neurosis with a resulting confusion. In the present essay I deal only with the conception of neurosis, but this should not be taken to imply that I believe that other pathological mental conditions, including actual madness, do not have relevance to the general matter of the decision.

ill in the service of life-in-culture. The form of the mind's dynamics is that of the neurosis, which is to be understood as the ego's struggle against being overcome by the forces with which it coexists, and the strategy of this conflict requires that the ego shall incur pain and make sacrifices of itself, at the same time seeing to it that its pain and sacrifice be as small as they may.

But this is characteristic of all minds: no mind is exempt except those which refuse the conflict or withdraw from it; and we ask wherein the mind of the artist is unique. If he is not unique in neurosis, is he then unique in the significance and intensity of his neurosis? I do not believe that we shall go more than a little way toward a definition of artistic genius by answering this question affirmatively. A neurotic conflict cannot ever be either meaningless or merely personal; it must be understood as exemplifying cultural forces of great moment, and this is true of any neurotic conflict at all. To be sure, some neuroses may be more interesting than others, perhaps because they are fiercer or more inclusive; and no doubt the writer who makes a claim upon our interest is a man who by reason of the energy and significance of the forces in struggle within him provides us with the largest representation of the culture in which we, with him, are involved; his neurosis may thus be thought of as having a connection of concomitance with his literary powers. As Freud says in the Dostoevski essay, 'the neurosis . . . comes into being all the more readily the richer the complexity which has to be controlled by his ego." Yet even the rich complexity which his ego is doomed to control is not the definition of the artist's genius, for we can by no means say that the artist is pre-eminent in the rich complexity of elements in conflict within him. The slightest acquaintance with the clinical literature of psychoanalysis will suggest that a rich complexity of struggling elements is no uncommon possession. And that same literature will also make it abundantly clear that the devices of art—the most extreme devices of poetry, for example—are not particular to the mind of the artist but are characteristic of mind itself.

But the artist is indeed unique in one respect, in the respect of his relation to his neurosis. He is what he is by virtue of his successful objectification of his neurosis, by his shaping it and making it available to others in a way which has its effect upon their own egos in struggle. His genius, that is, may be defined in terms of his faculties of perception, representation, and realization, and in these terms alone. It can no more be defined in terms of neurosis than can his power of walking and talking, or his sexuality. The use to which he puts his power, or the manner and style of his power, may be discussed with reference to his particular neurosis, and so may such matters as the untimely diminution or cessation of its exercise. But its essence is irreducible. It is, as we say, a gift.

We are all ill: but even a universal sickness implies an idea of health. Of the artist we must say that whatever elements of neurosis he has in common with his fellow mortals, the one part of him that is healthy, by any conceivable definition of health, is that which gives him the power to conceive, to plan, to work, and to bring his work to a conclusion. And if we are all ill, we are ill by a universal accident, not by a universal necessity, by a fault in the economy of our powers, not by the nature of the powers themselves. The Philoctetes myth, when it is used to imply a causal connection between the fantasy of castration and artistic power, tells us no more about the source of artistic power than we learn about the source of sexuality when the fantasy of castration is adduced, for the fear of castration may explain why a man is moved to extravagant exploits of sexuality, but we do not say that his sexual power itself derives from his fear of castration; and further the same fantasy may also explain impotence or homosexuality. The Philoctetes story, which has so established itself among us as explaining the source of the artist's power, is not really an explanatory myth at all; it is a moral myth having reference to our proper behavior in the circumstances of the universal accident. In its juxtaposition of the wound and the bow, it tells us that we must be aware that weakness does not preclude strength nor strength weakness. It is therefore not irrelevant to the artist, but when we use it we will do well to keep in mind the other myths of the arts, recalling what Pan and Dionysius suggest of the relation of art to physiology and superabundance, remembering that to Apollo were attributed the bow and the lyre, two strengths together, and that he was given the lyre by its inventor, the baby Hermes—that miraculous infant who, the day he was born, left his cradle to do mischief: and the first thing he met with was a tortoise, which he greeted politely before scooping it from its shell, and, thought and deed being one with him, he contrived the instrument to which he sang "the glorious tale of his own begetting." These were gods, and very early ones, but their myths tell us something about the nature and source of art even in our grim, late human present.

The Keys to Dreamland

I have been trying to explain literature by putting you in a primitive situation on an uninhabited island, where you could see the imagination working in the most direct and simple way. Now let's start with our own society, and see where literature belongs in that, if it does. Suppose you're walking down the street of a North American city. All around you is a highly artificial society, but you don't think of it as artificial: you're so accustomed to it that you think of it as natural. But suppose your imagination plays a little trick on you of a kind that it often does play, and you suddenly feel like a complete outsider, someone who's just blown in from Mars on a flying saucer. Instantly you see how conventionalized everything is: the clothes, the shop windows, the movement of the cars in traffic, the cropped hair and shaved faces of the men, the red lips and blue eyelids that women put on because they want to conventionalize their faces, or "look nice," as they say, which means the same thing. All this convention is pressing toward uniformity or likeness. To be outside the convention makes a person look queer, or, if he's driving a car, a menace to life and limb. The only exceptions are people who have decided to conform to different conventions, like nuns or beatniks. There's clearly a strong force making toward conformity in society, so strong that it seems to have something to do with the stability of society itself. In ordinary life even the most splendid things we can think of, like goodness and truth and beauty, all mean essentially what we're accustomed to. As I hinted just now in speaking of female make-up, most of our ideas of beauty are pure convention, and even truth has been defined as whatever doesn't disturb the pattern of what we already know.

When we move on to literature, we again find conventions, but this time we notice that they are conventions, because we're not so used to them. These conventions seem to have somthing to do with making literature as unlike life as possible. Chaucer represents people as making up stories in ten-syllable couplets. Shakespeare uses dramatic conventions, which means, for instance, that Iago has to smash Othello's marriage and dreams of future happiness and get him ready to murder his wife in a few minutes. Milton has two nudes in a garden haranguing each other in set speeches beginning with such lines as "Daughter of God and Man, immortal Eve"—Eve being Adam's daughter because she's just been extracted from his ribcase. Almost every story we read demands that we accept as fact something that we know to be nonsense: that good people always win, especially in love; that murders are complicated and ingenious puzzles to be solved by logic, and so on. It isn't only popular literature that demands this: more highbrow stories are apt to be more ironic, but irony has its conventions too. If we go further back into literature, we run into such conventions as the king's rash promise, the enraged cuckold, the cruel mistress of love poetry—never anything that we or any other time would recognize as the normal behavior of adult people, only the maddened ethics of fairyland.

Even the details of literature are equally perverse. Literature is a world where phoenixes and unicorns are quite as important as horses and dogs—and in literature some of the horses talk, like the ones in *Gulliver's Travels*. A random example is calling Shakespeare the "swan of Avon"—he was called that by Ben Jonson. The town of Stratford, Ontario, keeps swans in its river partly as a literary allusion. Poets of Shakespeare's day hated to admit that they were writing words on a page: they always insisted that they were producing music. In pastoral poetry they might be playing a flute (or more accurately an oboe), but every other kind of poetic effort was called song, with a harp, a lyre or a lute in the background, depending on how highbrow the song was. Singing suggests birds, and so for their typical songbird and emblem of themselves, the poets chose the swan, a bird that can't sing. Because it can't sing, they made up a legend that it sang once before death, when nobody was listening. But Shakespeare didn't burst into song before his death: he wrote two plays a year until he'd made enough money to retire, and spent the last five years of his life counting his take.

So however useful literature may be in improving one's imagination or vocabulary, it would be the wildest kind of pedantry to use it directly as a guide to life. Perhaps here we see one reason why the poet is not only very seldom a person one would turn to for insight into the state of the world, but often seems even more gullible and simple-minded than the rest of us. For the poet, the particular literary conventions he adopts are likely to become, for him, facts of life. If he finds that the kind of writing he's best at has a good deal to do with fairies, like Yeats, or a white goddess, like Graves, or a life-force, like Bernard Shaw, or episcopal sermons, like T. S. Eliot, or bullfights, like Hemingway, or exasperation at social hypocrisies, as with the so-called angry school, these things are apt to take on a reality for him that seems badly out of proportion to his contemporaries. His life may imitate literature in a way that may warp or even destroy his social personality, as Byron wore himself out at thirty-four with the strain of being Byronic. Life and literature, then, are both conventionalized, and of the conventions of literature about all we can say is that they don't much resemble the conditions of life. It's when the two sets of conventions collide that we realize how different they are.

In fact, whenever literature gets too probable, too much like life, some self-defeating process, some mysterious law of diminishing returns, seems to set in. There's a vivid and expertly written novel by H. G. Wells called *Kipps*, about a lower-middle-class, inarticulate, very likeable Cockney, the kind of character we often find in Dickens. Kipps is carefully studied: he never says anything that a man like Kipps wouldn't say; he never sounds the "h" in home or head; nothing he does is out of line with what we expect such a person to be like. It's an admirable novel, well worth reading, and yet I have a nagging feeling that there's some inner secret in bringing him completely to life that Dickens would have and that Wells doesn't have. All right, then, what would Dickens have done? Well, one of the things that Dickens often does do is write *badly*. He might have given Kipps sentimental speeches and false heroics and all sorts of inappropriate verbiage to say; and some readers would have clucked and tut-tutted over these passages and explained to each other how bad Dickens's taste was and how uncertain his hold on character could be. Perhaps they'd be right too. But we'd have had Kipps a few times the way he'd look to himself or the way he'd sometimes wish he could be: that's part of his reality, and the effect would remain with us however much we disapproved of it. Whether I'm right about this book or not, and I'm not at all sure I am, I think my general principle is right. What we'd never see except in a book is often what we go to books to find. Whatever is completely lifelike in literature is a bit of a laboratory specimen there. To bring anything really to life in literature we can't be lifelike: we have to be literature-like.

The same thing is true even of the use of language. We're often taught that prose is the language of ordinary speech, which is usually true in literature. But in ordinary life prose is no more the language of ordinary speech than one's Sunday suit is a bathing suit. The people who actually speak prose are highly cultivated and articulate people, who've read a good many books, and even they can speak prose only to each other. If you read the beautiful sentences of Elizabeth Bennet's conversation in *Pride and Prejudice*, you can see how in that book they give a powerfully convincing impression of a sensible and intelligent girl. But any girl who talked as coherently as that on a street car would be stared at as though she had green hair. It isn't only the difference between 1813 and 1962 that's involved either, as you'll see if you compare her speech with her mother's. The poet Emily Dickinson complained that everybody said "What?" to her, until finally she practically gave up trying to talk altogether, and confined herself to writing notes.

All this is involved with the principle I've touched on before: the difference between literary and other kinds of writing. If we're writing to convey information, or for any practical reason, our writing is an act of will and intention: we mean what we say, and the words we use represent that meaning directly. It's different in literature, not because the poet doesn't mean what he says too, but because his real effort is one of putting words together. What's important is not what he may have meant to say, but what the words themselves say when they get fitted together. With a novelist it's rather the incidents in the story he tells that get fitted together—as D. H. Lawrence says, don't trust the novelist; trust his story. That's why so much of a writer's best writing is or seems to be involuntary. It's involuntary because the forms of literature itself are taking control of it, and these forms are what are embodied in the conventions of literature. Conventions, we see, have the same role in literature that they have in life: they impose certain patterns of order and stability on the writer. Only, if they're such different conventions, it seems clear that the order of words, or the structure of literature, is different from the social order.

The absence of any clear line of connection between literature and life comes out in the issues involved in censorship. Because of the large involuntary element in writing, works of literature can't be treated as embodiments of conscious will or intention, like people, and so no laws can be framed to control their behavior which assume a tendency to do this or an intention of doing that. Works of literature get into legal trouble because they offend some powerful religious or political interest, and this interest in its turn usually acquires or exploits the kind of social hysteria that's always revolving around sex. But it's impossible to give legal definitions of such terms as obscenity in relation to works of literature. What happens to the book depends mainly on the intelligence of the judge. If he's a sensible man we get a sensible decision; if he's an ass we get that sort of decision, but what we don't get is a legal decision, because the basis for one doesn't exist..The best we get is a precedent tending to discourage cranks and pressure groups from attacking serious books. If you read the casebook on the trial of *Lady Chatterley's Lover*, you may remember how bewildered the critics were when they were asked what the moral effect of the book would be. They weren't putting on an act: they didn't know. Novels can only be good or bad in their own categories. There's no such things as a morally bad novel: its moral effect depends entirely on the moral quality of its reader, and nobody can predict what that will be. And if literature isn't morally bad it isn't morally good either. I suppose one reason why *Lady Chatterley's Lover* dramatized this question so vividly was that it's a rather preachy and self-conscious book: like the Sunday-school novels of my childhood, it bores me a little because it tries so hard to do me good.

So literature has no consistent connection with ordinary life, positive or negative. Here we touch on another important difference between structures of the imagination and structures of practical sense, which include the applied sciences. Imagination is certainly essential to science, applied or pure. Without a constructive power in the mind to make models of experience, get hunches and follow them out, play freely around with hypotheses, and so forth, no scientist could get anywhere. But all imaginative effort in practical fields has to meet the test of practicability, otherwise it's discarded. The imagination in literature has no such test to meet. You don't relate it directly to life or reality: you relate works of literature, as we've said earlier, to each other. Whatever value there is in studying literature, cultural or practical, comes from the total body of our reading, the castle of words we've built, and keep adding new wings to all the time.

So it's natural to swing to the opposite extreme and say that literature is really a refuge or escape from life, a self-contained world like the world of the dream, a world of play or make-believe to balance the world of work. Some literature is like that, and many people tell us that they only read to get away from reality for a bit. And I've suggested myself that the sense of escape, or at least detachment, does come into everybody's literary experience. But the real point of literature can hardly be that. Think of such writers as William Faulkner or François Mauriac, their great moral dignity, the intensity and compassion that they've studied the life around them with. Or think of James Joyce, spending seven years on one book and seventeen on another, and having them ridiculed or abused or banned by the customs when they did get published. Or of the poets Rilke and Valéry, waiting patiently for years in silence until what they had to say was ready to be said. There's a deadly seriousness in all this that even the most refined theories of fantasy or make-believe won't quite cover. Still, let's go along with the idea for a bit, because we're not getting on very fast with the relation of literature to life, or what we could call the horizontal perspective of literature. That seems to block us off on all sides.

The world of literature is a world where there is no reality except that of the human imagination. We see a great deal in it that reminds us vividly of the life we know. But in that very vividness there's something unreal. We can understand this more clearly with pictures, perhaps. There are trick-pictures—*trompe l'oeil*, the French call them—where the resemblance to life is very strong. An American painter of this school played a joke on his bitchy wife by painting one of her best napkins so expertly that she grabbed at the canvas trying to pull it off. But a painting as realistic as that isn't a reality but an illusion: it has the glittering unnatural clarity of a hallucination. The real realities, so to speak, are things that don't remind us directly of our own experience, but are such things as the wrath of Achilles or the jealousy of Othello, which are bigger and more intense experiences than anything we can reach—except in our imagination, which is what we're reaching with. Sometimes, as in the happy endings of comedies, or in the ideal world of romances, we seem to be looking at a pleasanter world than we ordinarily know. Sometimes, as in tragedy and satire, we seem to be looking at a world more devoted to suffering or absurdity than we ordinarily know. In literature we always seem to be looking either up or down. It's the vertical perspective that's important, not the horizontal one that looks out to life. Of course, in the greatest works of literature we get both the up and down views, often at the same time as different aspects of one event.

There are two halves to literary experience, then. Imagination gives us both a better and a worse world than the one we usually live with, and demands that we keep looking steadily at them both. I said in my first talk that the arts follow the path of the emotions, and of the tendency of the emotions to separate the world into a half that we like and a half that we don't like. Literature is not a world of dreams, but it would be if we had only one half without the other. If we had nothing but romances and comedies with happy endings, literature would express only a wish-fulfilment dream. Some people ask why poets want to write tragedies when the world's so full of them anyway, and suggest that enjoying such things has something morbid or gloating about it. It doesn't, but it might if there were nothing else in literature.

This point is worth spending another minute on. You recall that terrible scene in *King Lear* where Gloucester's eyes are put out on the stage. That's part of a play, and a play is supposed to be entertaining. Now in what sense can a scene like that be entertaining? The fact that it's not really happening is certainly important. It would be degrading to watch a real blinding scene, and far more so to get any pleasure out of watching it. Consequently, the entertainment doesn't consist in its reminding us of a real blinding scene. If it did, one of the great scenes of drama would turn into a piece of repulsive pornography. We couldn't stop anyone from reacting in this way, and it certainly wouldn't cure him, much less help the public, to start blaming or censoring Shakespeare for putting sadistic ideas in his head. But a reaction of that kind has nothing to do with drama. In a dramatic scene of cruelty and hatred we're seeing cruelty and hatred, which we know are permanently real things in human life, from the point of view of the imagination. What the imagination suggests is horror, not the paralyzing sickening horror of a real blinding scene, but an exuberant horror, full of the energy of repudiation. This is as powerful a rendering as we can ever get of life as we don't want it.

So we see that there are moral standards in literature after all, even though they have nothing to do with calling the police when we see a word in a book that's more familiar in sound than in print. One of the things Gloucester says in that scene is: "I am tied to the stake, and I must stand the course." In Shakespeare's day it was a favourite sport to tie a bear to a stake and set dogs on it until they killed it. The Puritans suppressed this sport, according to Macaulay, not because it gave pain to the bear but because it gave pleasure to the spectators. Macaulay may have intended his remark to be a sneer at the Puritans, but surely if the Puritans did feel this way they were one hundred per cent right. What other reason is there for abolishing public hangings? Whatever their motives, the Puritans and Shakespeare were operating in the same direction. Literature keeps presenting the most vicious things to us as entertainment; but what it appeals to is not any pleasure in these things, but the exhilaration of standing apart from them and being able to see them for what they are because they aren't really happening. The more exposed we are to this, the less likely we are to find an unthinking pleasure in cruel or evil things. As the eighteenth century said in a fine mouth-filling phrase, literature refines our sensibilities.

The top half of literature is the world expressed by such words as sublime, inspiring, and the like, where what we feel is not detachment but absorption. This is the world of heroes and gods and titans and Rabelaisian giants, a world of powers and passions and moments of ecstasy far greater than anything we meet outside the imagination. Such forces would not only absorb but annihilate us if they entered ordinary life, but luckily the protecting wall of the imagination is here too. As the German poet Rilke says, we adore them because they disdain to destroy us. We seem to have got quite a long way from our emotions with their division of things into "I like this" and "I don't like this." Literature gives us an experience that stretches us vertically to the heights and depths of what the human mind can conceive, to what corresponds to the conceptions of heaven and hell in religion. In this perspective what I like or don't like disappears, because there's nothing left of me as a separate person: as a reader of literature I exist only as a representative of humanity as a whole. We'll see in the last talk how important this is.

No matter how much experience we may gather in life, we can never in life get the dimension of experience that the imagination gives us. Only the arts and sciences can do that, and of these, only literature gives us the whole sweep and range of human imagination as it sees itself. It seems to be very difficult for many people to understand the reality and intensity of literary experience. To give an example that you may think a bit irrelevant: why have so many people managed to convince themselves that Shakespeare did not write Shakespeare's plays, when there is not an atom of evidence that anybody else did? Apparently because they feel that poetry must be written out of personal experience, and that Shakespeare didn't have enough experience of the right kind. But Shakespeare's plays weren't produced by his experience: they were produced by his imagination, and the way to develop the imagination is to read a good book or two. As for us, we can't speak or think or comprehend even our own experience except within the limits of our own power over words, and those limits have been established for us by our great writers.

Literature, then, is not a dream-world: it's two dreams, a wish-fulfillment dream and an anxiety dream, that are focused together, like a pair of glasses, and become a fully conscious vision. Art, according to Plato, is a dream for awakened minds, a work of imagination withdrawn from ordinary life, dominated by the same forces that dominate the dream, and yet giving us a perspective and dimension on reality that we don't get from any other approach to reality. So the poet and the dreamer are distinct, as Keats says. Ordinary life forms a community, and literature is among other things an art of communication, so it forms a community too. In ordinary life we fall into a private and separate subconscious every night, where we reshape the world according to a private and separate imagination. Underneath literature there's another kind of subconscious, which is social and not private, a need for forming a community around certain symbols, like the Queen and the flag, or around certain gods that represent order and stability, or becoming and change, or death and rebirth to a new life. This is the myth-making power of the human mind, which throws up and dissolves one civilization after another.

I've taken my title for this talk, "The Keys to Dreamland," from what is possibly the greatest single effort of the literary imagination in the twentieth century, Joyce's *Finnegans Wake*. In this book a man goes to sleep and falls, not into the Freudian separate or private subconscious, but into the deeper dream of man that creates and destroys his own societies. The entire book is written in the language of this dream. It's a subconscious language, mainly English, but connected by associations and puns with the eighteen or so other languages that Joyce knew. *Finnegans Wake* is not a book to read, but a book to decipher: as Joyce says, it's about a dreamer, but it's addressed to an ideal reader suffering from an ideal insomnia. The reader or critic, then, has a role complementing the poet's role. We need two powers in literature, a power to create and a power to understand.

In all our literary experience there are two kinds of response. There is the direct experience of the work itself, while we're reading a book or seeing a play, especially for the first time. This experience is uncritical, or rather pre-critical, so it's not infallible. If our experience is limited, we can be roused to enthusiasm or carried away by something that we can later see to have been second-rate or even phony. Then there is the conscious, critical response we make after we've finished reading or left the theatre, where we compare what we've experienced with other things of the same kind, and form a judgment of value and proportion on it. This critical response, with practice, gradually makes our pre-critical responses more sensitive and accurate, or improves our taste, as we say. But behind our responses to individual works, there's a bigger response to our literary experience as a whole, as a total possession.

The critic has always been called a judge of literature, which means, not that he's in a superior position to the poet, but that he ought to know something about literature, just as a judge's right to be on a bench depends on his knowledge of law. If he's up against something the size of Shakespeare, he's the one being judged. The critic's function is to interpret every work of literature in the light of all the literature he knows, to keep constantly struggling to understand what literature as a whole is about. Literature as a whole is not an aggregate of exhibits with red and blue ribbons attached to them, like a cat-show, but the range of articulate human imagination as it extends from the height of imaginative heaven to the depth of imaginative hell. Literature is a human apocalypse, man's revelation to man, and criticism is not a body of adjudications, but the awareness of that revelation, the last judgment of mankind.

Pessimism

1

To the plain reader, any novel that does not end happily is a pessimistic novel. Hence modern fiction is notoriously pessimistic; serious writers are forever reminding the plain reader of the kind of thing that he thinks there is too much of in "real life" and that he wishes to escape in his reading. Yet as so often happens, despite the fuzziness of his thinking, he is right: the view of life reflected in most of the more important novels is pessimistic in the strict sense of the word. This is scarcely strange. Pessimism is the natural consequence and the most obvious sign of the widespread decay of faith. Simply because it raises such important issues, however, one must clear the air of a deal of sentimental or hysterical loose talk that befogs these issues. To listen to many who live in Heartbreak House, one would gather that they were its first tenants, and their gloom an altogether new development in human history. Shades of Ecclesiastes!

Actually, pessimism darkens literature from its beginnings. Some periods, like the eighteenth century, have been superficially given to a formal optimism—an optimism that reached its ultimate lunacy in the statements of Hartley, who declared that "all individuals are actually and always infinitely happy," and of Abraham Tucker, who worked with more scientific exactness and calculated that the sum of our suffering equals "a minute of pain once in every twenty-two years." Other periods, like the Victorian, have attempted to stifle the growing doubts of the perfection of their civilization by a morbid, precocious insistence on the wholesome moral and the happy ending. But the great poets of every age have almost uniformly taken a somber view of human life. Thomas Hardy himself never struck a note of more profound melancholy than that in the famous words of Sophocles: "Not to be born is, past all prizing, best; but, when a man hath seen the light, this is next by far, that with all speed he should go thither, whence he hath come."

Tragedy is a universal literary form simply because of the permanence of the inescapable tragic fact of human life: the eternal seeking and not finding, the eternal gap between aspiration and achievement. Those idealistic philosophers, like Hegel, who announce magisterially that destiny is always rationality, and that tragedy displays the eternal justice of the divine order, are arguing their own principles, not interpreting the actual practice of tragic poets. In the lofty and comfortable seclusion of their philosophical chambers they impose upon life a sublime reasonableness that the mere existence of tragedy refutes. Implicit in its existence is a recognition of an inexplicably harsh destiny. Although the poets do ultimately effect some kind of reconciliation with this destiny, there is even in the peace at the end of their works a residuum of the mysterious, the terrible, the seeming unjust.

As the modern pessimist is thus not a wholly new species on earth, similarly he seldom gives his views the logical and consistent application that might actually revolutionize human behavior. It is easy to exaggerate the influence of intellectual concepts in modern literature and life. Thomas Hardy lived with his gloomy notions to a ripe and apparently serene old age. Krutch announced that ours is a lost cause—and continued to be an assiduous critic of our letters. Their readers make the same discount of abstract theory. Some deal of absurdity clings to all pessimistic philosophers, however unquestionable their sincerity. Perhaps the only really genuine, consistent pessimists were the early Thracians, who, if we can believe Herodotus, greeted the new-born child with lamentations, pointing out the sufferings in store for him, and buried the dead with rejoicings and festivities.

Even in the purely intellectual realm, moreover, one hears curiously discordant notes. These same distracted moderns have given the world the idea of historical evolution, the ideal of Progress, and have been busiest fashioning Utopias. Early peoples put their Utopias behind them; they had rather the notion, still incorporated in orthodox Christianity, of a decline from a primitive state of happiness. Even the highly civilized Greeks did not seriously conceive the progress of mankind toward a higher state. As Irwin Edman has pointed out, to them intelligence was primarily a "faculty of vision"; they did not, like the moderns, cultivate it as an instrument of action, a technique of regeneration. And though in recent years the faith in intelligence has been going the way of older faiths, though hymns of progress have for many ears a sour note, something of the new hope persists. A number of our most distinguished scientists are rediscovering God, pointing out that He appears to be a super-mathematician and scientist whose ways may accordingly be fathomable; and in the political world the Communists, despite their materialistic philosophy, are battling to establish an ideal as profoundly optimistic as man has ever conceived. The very indignation in the social tragedies of confirmed pessimists like Hardy and Dreiser implies a belief in the possibility of a better society such as Sophocles apparently never dreamed of.

The movements in the symphony of modern literature are not, then, all *adagio lamentoso*. I say this, however, only to clear the way for a sober analysis; for there is no denying the pessimism of the modern temper. These very qualifications must in turn be qualified. The hope of a better society, for example, springs less often from a robust optimism than from a confusion and discontent at times almost hysterical; much of the enthusiasm that supports it is simply neurotic. The idea of Progress was at first a pure, shining revelation, either a new demonstration of the glorious powers of the human mind or a new manifestation of the glorious ways of God that brought the heavenly city within nearer view. But even the eighteenth-century philosophers insisted too much; and the Victorians, who insisted still more, were plainly trying to drown out their secret misgivings about what God and England had wrought. Today men often embrace the future chiefly to escape the horrors of the present. Like the persecuted Hebrews in the time of Daniel, they seek refuge in apocalyptic visions. Many cling to the idea of Progress as a hope; fewer build on it as a vital faith. And others contemplate chiefly its logical complement: decadence.

Underlying all such anxiety, however, lies the chaos of unbelief, from which the immediate practical problems are almost a blessed distraction. The pessimism of the past was largely an unreasoned pessimism. It was an emotional recognition of the mortality of man and the suffering that is his portion, and it appears as plainly in folk-music as in tragic poetry. But pessimism today has a more solid philosophical basis and emanates from a more compact body of uncongenial knowledge. As it diffuses, it becomes emotional and unphilosophical, but at its source it is more rational and systematic. Above all, it is more devastating. It plumbs still darker depths and raises still more awful phantoms than man had dreamed of.

The most obvious source of this pessimism is man's new notions about the universe and his position in it. The story of what has happened to his world is an all too familiar one. Briefly, he is no longer the very important fellow that once he was. He still feels himself a part of an immense order, which he may still capitalize and refer to as God, but he is no longer sure that he knows its purposes, and still less sure that those purposes are his purposes. He is no longer the special concern, "the pet and privy councillor," of deity. Life itself, once the unquestioned glorious end-product of creation, he now thinks may be, in the striking words of Sir James Jeans, no more than "a mere accidental and possibly unimportant by-product of natural processes which have some other and more stupendous end in view"—or even "a disease which affects matter in its old age."

Such notions man's common sense—or his egoism—is likely to dismiss as fantastic. It is again an old story, however, that from these remote and rarefied regions science has moved steadily toward the more intimate realms of human experience. From astronomy to biology to psychology its progress has been inexorable. If we can believe I. A. Richards, man's egoism will presently have to withstand still more terrific onslaughts, digest still more lumpish masses of uncongenial truth:

> The most dangerous of the sciences is only now beginning to come into action. I am thinking less of Psychoanalysis or of Behaviorism than of the whole subject which includes them. It is very probable that the Hindenberg Line to which the defense of our traditions retired as a result of the onslaughts of the last century will be blown up in the near future. If this should happen a mental chaos such as man has never experienced may be expected.

Still more corrosive than its specific discoveries, however, is the rationale of science, the modes of experience it has imposed. It has not only broken up many of the oldest emotional associations of the race but made difficult their necessary replacement. Few men can actually live in the world it continues to create with no day of rest—the world of electric charges whirling in a field of force, in which time and space are relative, and cause and effect perhaps an illusion.

> *Nature, and Nature's laws, lay hid in night:*
> *God said,* Let Newton be! *and all was light*

—so ran Pope's hymn in a happier day. Many would now answer with J. C. Squire:

> *It did not last: the Devil, howling Ho!*
> Let Einstein be! *restored the status quo.*

Yet men have at least caught the general idea. They live in a world that is no longer explained in terms of human hopes and desires; the essence of the scientific attitude is that such considerations are rigorously excluded. Of no type of thought, indeed, are contemporaries more conscious and more distrustful than of rationalization. At the outset of his *Quest for Certainty* John Dewey accordingly finds it necessary to discard all the philosophical systems of the past.

The difficulty, however, is that if men now think differently from their ancestors, they still feel very much the same. Intellectually they may grow rapidly more subtle and sophisticated; emotionally they do not. Like their primitive ancestors, for example, they are instinctively ritualists. Ritual regulates behavior and is the source of faith—as Sumner noted in *Folkways,* it *makes* religion, it is not made by it. Even the emancipated today unconsciously follow it and are steadied by its influence. Yet the whole way of life of modern men, their habits of thought and conduct, are hostile to it. They perceive chiefly flux and change, they feel chiefly the need of individual adjustment. They brush their teeth regularly, they go through the prescribed paces in office or factory, they make habits of their thousand mechanical gadgets—in their surface lives they are creatures of fashion and routine; but in their more deeply human relations there is no ordained ritual, no spirit of reverent conformity. Although the faith in science has itself become a religion, with high priests to conduct it, its abstract forms and symbols do not satisfy the deepest needs of the being, and are often, indeed, incompatible with the reverent emotions they are supposd to excite. Men still feel the basic need of building their lives on some system of natural pieties; it is difficult for any such system to take root in the habit of suspended judgement and "organized doubt," the insistence on taking life straight, that is considered the first duty of the intelligent modern.

Hence when Eddington, Jeans, and other leaders of science began to toy with metaphysics and find room for God, they found few grateful readers. They were greeted instead with derision, scorn, even indignation. They were suspected of softening of the brain, they were charged with apostasy. The layman has been by now only too well trained, and demands that all attitudes be supported by *fact*. Yet this makes for an impossible strain on man in his present state of knowledge, when there are insufficient objective references for all his emotions and instinctive responses. "The justification of any attitude *per se*," writes Richards as a practical psychologist, "is its success for the needs of the being." These needs vary with the individual and his situation; and to attempt to base all our attitudes on matters of fact is to "run extreme risks of later disorganization elsewhere."

One need not look far in modern literature to discover evidences of such disorganization. Writers have been forced to examine their premises anxiously, and this necessity is sobering even when their conclusions are not bleakly pessimistic. "In periods of firmly established meanings," Kenneth Burke observes, "one does not *study* them, one *uses* them: one frames his acts in accordance with them." Almost as sustaining as this unconscious acceptance of a set of meanings, it might be added, is a vigorous attack upon them in the cause of another positive set. But even such crusading has become difficult for the self-conscious modern. In the early 'twenties skepticism was fashionable and exciting. It was a kind of luxury that a society complacent in its seeming prosperity could afford to indulge. Now it is a drug on the market. "Organized bad taste" is no longer good taste; puncturing faiths is no longer good clean fun. Even intelligent men are now responding with pathetic eagerness to promises of security and light—to dictators in the world of affairs, to soul-healers in the world of literature.

2

The essential difference between pessimism today and the pessimism of the past appears most plainly in the modern conception of tragedy. Greek tragedy is at bottom an act of piety. Not merely is it permeated with a sense of the divine government of the world, but the adequacy of this government is not seriously questioned; the poets do not put embarrassing questions to the gods. Their characters are the hapless victims of monstrous fatalities ordained by the "dark, unfathomable mind of Zeus," and to a modern reader often appear innocent. One can justify even so horrible an act as Jocasta's exposure of her infant son, for it was committed to avert the still more horrible intention of the gods as expressed by the oracle. Yet the grief aroused by these spectacles was in the Greeks not a rebellious grief; with their fatalism they managed to reconcile a conviction of human responsibility for human suffering. There are grounds here for indignant protest, but the poets acquiesce. There are grounds for despair, but they somehow retain a faith in the fitness of things.

The world of Shakespeare, more "cheerless, dark, and deadly" than that of any other great poet before recent times, is indeed less orderly, less susceptible of comforting interpretation. As on the religious and ethical problems implicit in his tragedies he preserved a strange silence—possibly because his audience did not encourage him to speak out, possibly because he had no pat answers to offer—the reader is left to form his own impressions; and about impressions there can be no conclusive argument. Yet most readers have felt that Shakespeare does in the end reconcile himself to the controlling order. Its workings are manifestly complicated and often painfully incomprehensible. They involve an appalling waste of good; noble figures like Hamlet and Brutus and Othello are wantonly thrown away. Still, Shakespeare never definitely rejects the idea of a Providence, never definitely represents the ruling powers as merely blind or indifferent. His order is in its largest aspect a moral order, and its compulsion a moral compulsion. *Human evil* is always the chief disturbing element and the primary source of Shakespeare's tragedy. "We remain confronted," writes A. C. Bradley, "with the inexplicable fact . . . of a world travailing for perfection, but bringing to birth, together with glorious good, an evil which it is able to overcome only by self-torture and self-waste." But eventually this evil is eliminated, if at terrible cost, and a balance is struck, an equilibrium restored, with "all passions spent."

In a word, such pessimism as colors the tragedy of the past was qualified by some notion of a divine plan in the working out of which man was the chief actor, and to which his sufferings were referred and thus given dignity and meaning. This was a vital intuitive faith that preceded reasoning and went deeper than religious belief. Some were less conversant than others with the intentions of deity, but the humblest agreed with the glibbest prophets about the importance of man in the scheme of things. Behind all puzzled speculation and recurrent misgivings was a clear certainty by the light of which man could follow the paths to glory in this world if not the next. And this fundamental certainty of the greatness of man and the divinity that shapes his ends is what makes ancient tragedy never a confession of despair but an assertion of faith. As has often been remarked, the world's greatest tragedies were the products of two of the most confident ages man has known—the Periclean and the Elizabethan.

Here, then, is the peculiar characteristic of much tragedy that men now write: it no longer resolves its dissonances into a triumphant major chord. It insists not merely that great suffering is and under the unalterable conditions of human life always must be, but that it is compensated for by no ultimate good. It denies that behind this suffering is any exalted or intelligible purpose to which man can submit with pride. Submit he must, but to a blank necessity.

The essence of tragedy, Schlegel declared, is a conflict between necessity without and freedom within; the terms of this conflict are today radically altered. Men have had, in the first place, to temper their notions of the freedom within. They perceive how largely they are products of their environment, and they have learned how subterranean and amazingly tortuous are the workings of their minds. To be captain of one's soul, writes Irwin Edman, "has become impossible now that personality itself seems to be more like a river than a ship." But more troublesome is the form now assumed by the external necessity. Men can no longer respect the forces that crush them. An awful Fate has given way to the unsanctified compulsions of the social and natural environment; the decrees of the gods have dwindled into the commands of their neighbors and bosses, and the blind necessity of natural and economic laws. Thus where there was one solemn mystery there are now a hundred vexing riddles. Where the older poets saw an order whose larger purposes were reasonable or even benevolent, the modern writer can see only a "meaningless welter," an "immense indifference." Where, accordingly, the spirit of ancient tragedy is ultimately that of reverent acceptance, the spirit of the moderns is like Conrad's of ironic aloofness, like Hardy's of vehement protest, like Hemingway's of alcoholic bravado, like Dreiser's of complete confusion and dismay. There are few to justify the ways of God to man.

The dangers of such a pessimism are obvious enough. It may simply depress human vitality, dry up the springs of energy at their source. It may shrivel into sere and barren despair. And this is actually what one finds in much modern fiction: an insistence upon the merely painful, an utter joylessness, devoid of passion even in its negations. Some writers come to no sort of decent terms with life, make no sort of peace. They neither chant a solemn litany nor voice an indignant protest. The burden of such brilliant studies as Ernest Hemingway's *The Sun Also Rises* and Aldous Huxley's *Point Counterpoint* is chiefly world-weariness, disenchantment, futility. Still emptier of values or meanings is William Faulkner's *Sanctuary*, a riot of violence and horror for their own sake. A more remarkable work, Celine's *Journey to the End of Night*, is remarkable for a superior savagery; it is the apotheosis of downright disgust with life. And perhaps most dismal, if less striking, of this melancholy kind is Julian Green's *The Dark Journey*, a relentlessly objective, brilliantly "scientific" study of the mean struggles of mean souls, born seemingly of an entire lack of emotion. Here is tragedy at the last remove from a *Hamlet* or an *Antigone*, never warmed by compassion, never lighted by poetry, never lifted by a sense of greatness in pain or solemnity in mystery.

These novels are not, to be sure, fairly representative; one may reasonably doubt that the future is theirs. Yet throughout its range modern fiction has not the glamor, the sweep and pomp, the grand and compelling figures of ancient tragedy. As a more realistic and a prose performance, it could indeed scarcely be expected to deal in such heroics. More significant, however, than that the modern hero no longer sweeps the boards in purple robes or makes significant gestures, no longer sways the destiny of nations, is that he is often a base, miserable fellow. The mantle of Hamlet is now worn by a Clyde Griffiths, the splendor of Antigone has shriveled into the meanness of an Emma Bovary; and the comment of stately choruses has dwindled into the gossip of the neighbors. Modern novelists are less confident of the glorious possibilities of man and feel more at home when making absorbed studies of the ordinary, the weak, the morbid, or even the ignoble.

To this generalization there are notable exceptions—the men of Conrad's best work, for example, have much of the stature, force, and glamor of the Shakespearian heroes. But, on the whole, writers appear to be more often impressed by the pettiness than by the magnificence of man, by the futility of his efforts than by the splendor of his aspirations. They distrust the grand passions, and like the hero of *A Farewell to Arms*, who "was always embarrassed by the words sacred, glorious, and sacrifice, and the expression in vain," they are prone to feel a little uneasy and ridiculous when writing largely about life. "Rhetoric" has become a term of disparagement. The mere mention of the word "spiritual" makes men uncomfortable, and "soul" has become the property of ministers, as "heart" of the writers for the pulps. They shrink from passionate utterance as something adolescent; they live in fear of being somehow taken in. Chiefly they appear to be interested in the maladjustments of what we have recently discovered to be our highly complicated minds. They prefer subtlety to vehemence, the nuance to the flaming line, the minor to the major key.

This is another of the mixed blessings of that extraordinary "improvement in natural knowledge" in which Thomas Huxley had so fervid, joyous a confidence. It has made many distrustful of the inherited idealisms that could otherwise sustain them in the bleak immensities they have discovered. When the biologists and psychoanalysts have done with love, for example, they are less ready than their ancestors to think the world well lost for it. The terrible plight of Edipus, which the Greeks invested with all the majesty of tragedy, is now a symbol of one of the many ugly complexes from which they suffer. The behaviorists have turned their deepest emotions into conditioned reflexes, comparable to the salivations of a laboratory dog. No conclusion about behavior has more weight, William James once lamented, than one derived from the twitchings of a frog's leg—especially if the frog was decapitated. In general, the tendency of science has been to substitute physical and psychical compulsions for freedom of choice, to explain personality in terms of glands, hormones, and complexes, and to enforce an unpleasant awareness of the unlovely origins of human impulses. In *Point Counterpoint*, for instance, Aldous Huxley, a great lover of music, describes the rendition of a masterpiece. "The fiddlers drew their rosined horse-hair across the stretched intestines of lambs"—and what happened? "The hairy endings of the auditory nerve shuddered like weeds in a rough sea . . . and Lord Edward ecstatically whispered 'Bach!' " This is a professional irony and in itself of slight significance;

yet it is this kind of thought that curdles the idealisms of many artists—
and in some measure explains the torment in Huxley himself.

3

In the presence of these melancholy exhibits, one can more easily understand Krutch's famous pronouncement that it is impossible for the moderns to write Tragedy. Not only have they lost the vital faith that inspired the old masterpieces, but, he declared, they cannot recapture it by a mere intellectual conviction that it would be desirable to do so. And although *Mourning Becomes Electra* convinced him that he had been wrong, this clinical interpretation of an ancient legend only strengthened the fears of others that a glory has permanently departed this earth. Modern pessimism, we often hear, makes impossible a great literature. The conception of a universe purposeless or indifferent to human values cuts the ground from under these values, without which a great literature cannot exist. It makes of all idealism at best a gloomy consolation, a mere whistling in the dark.

This is clearly a serious issue, and the property not merely of clergymen or professional viewers-with-alarm. I shall return to it at the end. Yet I should meanwhile remark, again simply for the purposes of preliminary survey, that the growth of pessimism has not been uniformly cankerous, and that only the tender-minded should find modern tragedy an altogether sordid, ineffectual, and merely distressing performance. Man has had to surrender his flattering hopes of a magnificent destiny and accommodate himself to a lower range of dream and desire. In the immense drama of the spheres his own drama has come to seem an inconsequential and possibly alien interlude. But in being thus driven back upon himself he has sought new sources of inspiration and support, and often made virtues of his necessities. If only because of the predicament in which he finds himself, he has cultivated such values as tolerance, compassion, and charity.

One reason why modern literature rises less often to the level of the heroic and sublime is simply that it is so deeply rooted in our common humanity. The last hundred years have been marked by a growth in understanding and therefore in sympathy. In the everyday world this appears in the more humane treatment of paupers, delinquents, mental defectives, and the wayward and unfortunate generally; in the intellectual world in the rise of the social sciences; and in imaginative literature in a lively, sympathetic interest in all classes and types of men. This interest may be chiefly scientific, but more typically it is humanitarian. Despite their objective manner, many modern novels are saturated with pity—a pity that embraces the humblest creature in them.

Many contemporaries no doubt enjoy their glow of pity because, as William James said, it enables them to feel virtuous at the expense of very little effort. At its worst, this spirit of compassion melts into a facile, mawkish self-pity—a dispirited resignation, or a sniffling over a cold, cruel world. At times it attaches itself to paltry objects or softens into the sentimentalism that has provided us with so many pure-hearted prostitutes. It raises the difficult issue of "selective sympathy"; though one may distrust the specific criteria of the cloistered Paul Elmer More, or suspect any man who sets up as a stern judge of his fellows, there is a plain objection to an undiscriminating humanitarianism. At its best, however—as in the works of Dostoyevsky, Hardy, and Hauptmann—this compassion is a healthful, cleansing, and sustaining feeling. It has at least lightened the burden of the new knowledge, taken some of the curse off the depressing notions men have got.

This attitude has at any rate considerably altered the ethical content of modern literature. As Jehovah goes the way of Zeus, His commands naturally cease to command obedience or even respect. At the same time there is none (except perhaps the psychiatrist) to inherit the mantle of His authority. In an age that no longer pretends to know ultimate meanings, the moralist can no longer assume the comfortable posture of the oracle, no longer carry his case to a heavenly Court of Appeals. Such wisdom as he may express does not flow from a holy fount but must justify itself on empirical grounds. If he is realistic, he must accordingly recognize that his judgments can be only provisional and relative. In the absence either of complete knowledge (even the psychiatrist suffers from this) or of supernatural authority, moral laws are no longer immutable and no longer have absolute validity. For better or worse, the categorical imperative is no more.

A natural result of this confusion of the preachers' tongues has been much babble and angry polemics. We have again in our laps the whole immensely difficult problem brought by our emancipation from Prejudice and Superstition, the tyranny of priests and kings. The impulse of much modern fiction is accordingly an impersonal, undogmatic effort to understand life for what it inexorably is. Writers have cultivated the ideal, derived from the practice of science, of suspended judgment. They seldom write the tragedy merely of sin and retribution, seldom make out plain blacks and whites. In so far as they preach, they preach the doctrine of every man his own moralist.

Now, the moral world of ancient literature is indeed not so simple and tidy as it is often made out to be. Pedagogues seize too eagerly upon Aristotle's comfortable notion of the "tragic flaw." Aristotle was too little a poet, too much an orderly philosopher and logician, thoroughly to understand tragedy; he could find no place in his precise system for the grossly fortuitous and unreasonable elements in the fates of Edipus, Antigone, and Orestes. Imperfect though these characters are, their crimes followed almost inevitably the curse laid upon their families by the gods, a curse of which they were themselves guiltless; only by being less sensitive, less noble, could they have averted their tragedy. Similarly the destructive forces in Shakespeare are far too ruthless to be considered mere avenging deities, and they exact a penalty out of all proportion to the offense; if it is justice that an old king and all whom he loves should be brutally destroyed because of the mistakes of his dotage, it is justice by no civilized human standards. The chief fault is not in these great figures but in the world about them. In short, in the poetic as in the actual world, the little measuring rule of the tragic flaw is hopelessly inadequate.

Yet the old masterpieces at least lend themselves to a conventional moralistic interpretation. They are founded on relatively simple, fixed notions of right and wrong; the forces of good and the forces of evil are sharply opposed; and there is little serious disposition to question the essential rightness of the laws of man or of God by which their heroes live and die. The issues in modern fiction, however, are far more complicated. Most writers now regard volition and conscience as largely the product of external forces beyond the individual's control, derivatives of the social context, and his actions as therefore not susceptible of a downright judgment. They attempt to penetrate to underlying causes, distinguishing between the evil of a deed and the criminality of its perpetrator, and they question the theory of punishment—as even so humane a man as Henry Fielding did not. With him as with the Elizabethans a scoundrel existed only to be hanged, and his hanging was an edifying spectacle; now writers try to understand the scoundrel in terms of his environment, and to correct that environment. Hence society itself is often the evil force in their fictions. Such unfortunates as Tess Durbeyfield and Jennie Gerhardt suffer primarily because of the rigorous moral law imposed by the community; their authors question the law itself, the standard of judgment. And this is another reason why good, placid people are pained and bewildered by much modern fiction: it is forever asking questions that they prefer to think closed, disturbing the ordered serenity—or violence—of their moral judgments.

This wider humanity, if not greater veracity, of modern fiction is reflected as well in the banishment of the villain to melodrama. Shakespeare introduced these implausible figures less as a concession to a primitive moral sense than as the stock instrument for effecting the necessary complication and conflict; from either point of view, however, this conflict falls short of inevitability and universal truth. Modern realists have accordingly discarded this easy device. They feel that man's sufferings seldom result from a great sin or the machinations of a villain or any head-on collision of virtue and vice, but that they arise rather from a maladjustment with the social environment, or from the inevitable conflict of interest and desires in a group of characters upon no one of whom is especial guilt to be fastened. The reader of Shakespeare ordinarily identifies himself with the hero, as does the simple spectator of melodrama. But in modern tragedy he is asked to identify himself with all the characters at once—with Sue Bridehead as with Jude Fawley, with Soames and Irene as with young Jon and Fleur Forsyte, with Hurstwood as with Sister Carrie. Where he is urged to become partizan, it is on behalf rather of a principle than of an individual.

The pleasant way of describing this whole change is to say that modern novelists have subdued the violence of the primitive urge to damn heretics and deliver transgressors to an angry tribal god, and that out of a profound sense of the community of human frailty and suffering they have cultivated the ideal of tolerance. A rude critic, however, might call it but another symptom of the sickness of the age. He might point out that the growth of tolerance is usually the sign of the decay of faith, and that those today who do have a strong faith—the Communists, for instance, or the New Humanists—are much less charitable in their judgments. And he might also point out that others revel too luxuriously in their freedom from categorical imperatives. They junk too wantonly the accumulated wisdom of the past simply because it comes to them with the stamp of a discredited theological authority. They are too ready to suspend judgment, too eager to disclaim all personal responsibility. One yearns at times for the refreshing common sense or even the dogmatism of a Sam Johnson, and would like to say as plainly, "The woman's a whore, and there's an end on it." For despite their emancipation men have still to face the inexorable logic of facts. They may shift the responsibility for their deeds, but they cannot escape the consequences. The problem of evil in one form or another is still a fundamental concern of literature; and today as in the past we are finally called upon to make some sort of judgment.

Whether fortunate or unfortunate, this emphasis upon the values of catholicity, forbearance, and compassion is plainly a result of the skepticism and pessimism of the modern temper. If it is regarded as an essentially Christian spirit, it marks most conspicuously the work of novelists like Hardy and Dreiser who have utterly rejected the Christian faith. The pessimist often becomes a misanthrope; but he is also notoriously apt to be a more charitable fellow than the optimist who is in touch with the Absolute, and who has therefore a laudable eagerness to share the truth, a reasonable impatience with those who fail to see it.

JEAN-PAUL SARTRE

Existentialism

Man is nothing else but what he makes of himself. Such is the first principle of existentialism. It is also what is called subjectivity, the name we are labeled with when charges are brought against us. But what do we mean by this, if not that man has a greater dignity than a stone or table? For we mean that man first exists, that is, that man first of all is the being who hurls himself toward a future and who is conscious of imagining himself as being in the future. Man is at the start a plan which is aware of itself, rather than a patch of moss, a piece of garbage, or a cauliflower; nothing exists prior to this plan; there is nothing in heaven; man will be what he will have planned to be. Not what he will want to be. Because by the word "will" we generally mean a conscious decision, which is subsequent to what we have already made of ourselves. I may want to belong to a political party, write a book, get married; but all that is only a manifestation of an earlier, more spontaneous choice that is called "will." But if existence really does precede essence, man is responsible for what he is. Thus, existentialism's first move is to make every man aware of what he is and to make the full responsibility of his existence rest on him. And when we say that a man is responsible for himself, we do not only mean that he is responsible for his own individuality, but that he is responsible for all men.

The word "subjectivism" has two meanings, and our opponents play on the two. Subjectivism means, on the one hand, that an individual chooses and makes himself; and, on the other, that it is impossible for man to transcend human subjectivity. The second of these is the essential meaning of existentialism. When we say that man chooses his own self, we mean that every one of us does likewise; but we also mean by that that in making this choice he also chooses all men. In fact, in creating the man that we want to be, there is not a single one of our acts which does not at the same time create an image of man as we think he ought to be. To choose to be this or that is to affirm at the same time the value of what we choose, because we can never choose evil. We always choose the good, and nothing can be good for us without being good for all.

If, on the other hand, existence precedes essence, and if we grant that we exist and fashion our image at one and the same time, the image is valid for everybody and for our whole age. Thus, our responsibility is much greater than we might have supposed, because it involves all mankind. If I am a workingman and choose to join a Christian trade union rather than be a Communist, and if by being a member I want to show that the best thing for man is resignation, that the kingdom of man is not of this world, I am not only involving my own case—I want to be resigned for everyone. As a result, my action has involved all humanity. To take a more individual matter, if I want to marry, to have children, even if this marriage depends solely on my own circumstances or passion or wish, I am involving all humanity in monogamy and not merely myself. Therefore, I am responsible for myself and for everyone else. I am creating a certain image of man of my own choosing. In choosing myself, I choose man.

This helps us understand what the actual content is of such rather grandiloquent words as anguish, forlornness, despair. As you will see, it's all quite simple.

First, what is meant by anguish? The existentialists say at once that man is anguish. What that means is this: the man who involves himself and who realizes that he is not only the person he chooses to be, but also a lawmaker who is, at the same time, choosing all mankind as well as himself, cannot help escape the feeling of his total and deep responsibility. Of course, there are many people who are not anxious; but we claim that they are hiding their anxiety, that they are fleeing from it. Certainly, many people believe that when they do something, they themselves are the only ones involved, and when someone says to them, "What if everyone acted that way?" they shrug their shoulders and answer, "Everyone doesn't act that way." But really, one should always ask himself, "What would happen if everybody looked at things that way?" There is no escaping this disturbing thought except by a kind of double-dealing. A man who lies and makes excuses for himself by saying "not everybody does that," is someone with an uneasy conscience, because the act of lying implies that a universal value is conferred upon the lie.

Anguish is evident even when it conceals itself. This is the anguish that Kierkegaard called the anguish of Abraham. You know the story: an angel has ordered Abraham to sacrifice his son; if it really were an angel who has come and said, "You are Abraham, you shall sacrifice your son," everything would be all right. But everyone might first wonder, "Is it really an angel, and am I really Abraham? What proof do I have?"

There was a madwoman who had hallucinations; someone used to speak to her on the telephone and give her orders. Her doctor asked her, "Who is it who talks to you?" She answered, "He says it's God." What proof did she really have that it was God? If an angel comes to me, what proof is there that it's an angel? And if I hear voices, what proof is there that they come from heaven and not from hell, or from the subconscious, or a pathological condition? What proves that they are addressed to me? What proof is there that I have been appointed to impose my choice and my conception of man on humanity? I'll never find any proof or sign to convince me of that. If a voice addresses me, it is always for me to decide that this is the angel's voice; if I consider that such an act is a good one, it is I who will choose to say that it is good rather than bad.

Now, I'm not being singled out as an Abraham, and yet at every moment I'm obliged to perform exemplary acts. For every man, everything happens as if all mankind had its eyes fixed on him and were guiding itself by what he does. And every man ought to say to himself, "Am I really the kind of man who has the right to act in such a way that humanity might guide itself by my actions?" And if he does not say that to himself, he is masking his anguish.

There is no question here of the kind of anguish which would lead to quietism, to inaction. It is a matter of a simple sort of anguish that anybody who has had responsibilities is familiar with. For example, when a military officer takes the responsibility for an attack and sends a certain number of men to death, he chooses to do so, and in the main he alone makes the choice. Doubtless, orders come from above, but they are too broad; he interprets them, and on this interpretation depend the lives of ten or fourteen or twenty men. In making a decision he cannot help having a certain anguish. All leaders know this anguish. That doesn't keep them from acting; on the contrary, it is the very condition of their action. For it implies that they envisage a number of possibilities, and when they choose one, they realize that it has value only because it is chosen. We shall see that this kind of anguish, which is the kind that existentialism describes, is explained, in addition, by a direct responsibility to the other men whom it involves. It is not a curtain separating us from action, but is part of action itself.

When we speak of forlornness, a term Heidegger was fond of, we mean only that God does not exist and that we have to face all the consequences of this. The existentialist is strongly opposed to a certain kind of secular ethics which would like to abolish God with the least possible expense. About 1880, some French teachers tried to set up a secular ethics which went something like this: God is a useless and costly hypothesis; we are discarding it; but, meanwhile, in order for there to be an ethics, a society, a civilization, it is essential that certain values be taken seriously and that they be considered as having an *a priori* existence. It must be obligatory, *a priori*, to be honest, not to lie, not to beat your wife, to have children, etc., etc. So we're going to try a little device which will make it possible to show that values exist all the same, inscribed in a heaven of ideas, though otherwise God does not exist. In other words—and this, I believe, is the tendency of everything called reformism in France—nothing will be changed if God does not exist. We shall find ourselves with the same norms of honesty, progress, and humanism, and we shall have made of God an outdated hypothesis which will peacefully die off by itself.

The existentialist, on the contrary, thinks it very distressing that God does not exist, because all possibility of finding values in a heaven of ideas disappears along with Him; there can no longer be an *a priori* Good, since there is no infinite and perfect consciousness to think it. Nowhere is it written that the Good exists, that we must be honest, that we must not lie; because the fact is we are on a plane where there are only men. Dostoievsky said, "If God didn't exist, everything would be possible." That is the very starting point of existentialism. Indeed, everything is permissible if God does not exist, and as a result man is forlorn, because neither within him nor without does he find anything to cling to. He can't start making excuses for himself.

If existence really does precede essence, there is no explaining things away by reference to a fixed and given human nature. In other words, there is no determinism, man is free, man is freedom. On the other hand, if God does not exist, we find no values or commands to turn to which legitimize our conduct. So, in the bright realm of values, we have no excuse behind us, nor justification before us. We are alone, with no excuses.

That is the idea I shall try to convey when I say that man is condemned to be free. Condemned, because he did not create himself, yet, in other respects is free; because, once thrown into the world, he is responsible for everything he does. The existentialist does not believe in the power of passion. He will never agree that a sweeping passion is a ravaging torrent which fatally leads a man to certain acts and is therefore an excuse. He thinks that man is responsible for his passion.

The existentialist does not think that man is going to help himself by finding in the world some omen by which to orient himself. Because he thinks that man will interpret the omen to suit himself. Therefore, he thinks that man, with no support and no aid, is condemned every moment to invent man. Ponge, in a very fine article, has said, "Man is the future of man." That's exactly it. But if it is taken to mean that this future is recorded in heaven, that God sees it, then it is false, because it would really no longer be a future. If it is taken to mean that, whatever a man may be, there is a future to be forged, a virgin future before him, then this remark is sound. But then we are forlorn.

To give you an example which will enable you to understand forlornness better, I shall cite the case of one of my students who came to see me under the following circumstances: his father was on bad terms with his mother, and, moreover, was inclined to be a collaborationist; his older brother had been killed in the German offensive of 1940, and the young man, with somewhat immature but generous feelings, wanted to avenge him. His mother lived alone with him, very much upset by the half-treason of her husband and the death of her older son; the boy was her only consolation.

The boy was faced with the choice of leaving for England and joining the Free French forces—that is, leaving his mother behind—or remaining with his mother and helping her to carry on. He was fully aware that the woman lived only for him and that his going off—and perhaps his death—would plunge her into despair. He was also aware that every act that he did for his mother's sake was a sure thing, in the sense that it was helping her to carry on, whereas every effort he made toward going off and fighting was an uncertain move which might run aground and prove completely useless; for example, on his way to England he might, while passing through Spain, be detained indefinitely in a Spanish camp; he might reach England or Algiers and be stuck in an office at a desk job. As a result, he was faced with two very different kinds of action: one, concrete, immediate, but concerning only one individual; the other concerned an incomparably vaster group, a national collectivity, but for that very reason was dubious, and might be interrupted en route. And, at the same time, he was wavering between two kinds of ethics. On the one hand, an ethics of sympathy, of personal devotion; on the other, a broader ethics, but one whose efficacy was more dubious. He had to choose between the two.

Who could help him choose? Christian doctrine? No. Christian doctrine says, "Be charitable, love your neighbor, take the more rugged path, etc., etc." But which is the more rugged path? Whom should he love as a brother? The fighting man or his mother? Which does the greater good, the vague act of fighting in a group, or the concrete one of helping a particular human being to go on living? Who can decide *a priori?* Nobody. No book of ethics can tell him. The Kantian ethics says, "Never treat any person as a means, but as an end." Very well, if I stay with my mother, I'll treat her as an end and not as a means; but by virtue of this very fact, I'm running the risk of treating the people around me who are fighting, as means; and, conversely, if I go to join those who are fighting, I'll be treating them as an end, and, by doing that, I run the risk of treating my mother as a means.

If values are vague, and if they are always too broad for the concrete and specific case that we are considering, the only thing left for us is to trust our instincts. That's what this young man tried to do; and when I saw him, he said, "In the end, feeling is what counts. I ought to choose whichever pushes me in one direction. If I feel that I love my mother enough to sacrifice everything else for her—my desire for vengeance, for action, for adventure—then I'll stay with her. If, on the contrary, I feel that my love for my mother isn't enough, I'll leave."

But how is the value of a feeling determined? What gives his feeling for his mother value? Precisely the fact that he remained with her. I may say that I like so-and-so well enough to sacrifice a certain amount of money for him, but I may say so only if I've done it. I may say "I love my mother well enough to remain with her" if I have remained with her. The only way to determine the value of this affection is, precisely, to perform an act which confirms and defines it. But, since I require this affection to justify my act, I find myself caught in a vicious circle.

On the other hand, Gide has well said that a mock feeling and a true feeling are almost indistinguishable; to decide that I love my mother and will remain with her, or to remain with her by putting on an act, amount somewhat to the same thing. In other words, the feeling is formed by the acts one performs; so, I cannot refer to it in order to act upon it. Which means that I can neither seek within myself the true condition which will impel me to act, nor apply to a system of ethics for concepts which will permit me to act. You will say, "At least, he did go to a teacher for advice." But if you seek advice from a priest, for example, you have chosen this priest; you already knew, more or less, just about what advice he was going to give you. In other words, choosing your adviser is involving yourself. The proof of this is that if you are a Christian, you will say, "Consult a priest." But some priests are collaborating, some are just marking time, some are resisting. Which to choose? If the young man chooses a priest who is resisting or collaborating, he has already decided on the kind of advice he's going to get. Therefore, in coming to see me he knew the answer I was going to give him, and I had only one answer to give: "You're free, choose, that is, invent." No general ethics can show you what is to be done; there are no omens in in the world. The Catholics will reply, "But there are." Granted—but, in any case, I myself choose the meaning they have.

When I was a prisoner, I knew a rather remarkable young man who was a Jesuit. He had entered the Jesuit order in the following way: he had had a number of very bad breaks; in childhood, his father died, leaving him in poverty, and he was a scholarship student at a religious institution where he was constantly made to feel that he was being kept out of charity; then, he failed to get any of the honors and distinctions that children like; later on, at about eighteen, he bungled a love affair; finally, at twenty-two, he failed in military training, a childish enough matter, but it was the last straw.

This young fellow might well have felt that he had botched everything. It was a sign of something, but of what? He might have taken refuge in bitterness or despair. But he very wisely looked upon all this as a sign that he was not made for secular triumphs, and that only the triumphs of religion, holiness, and faith were open to him. He saw the hand of God in all this, and so he entered the order. Who can help seeing that he alone decided what the sign meant?

Some other interpretation might have been drawn from this series of setbacks; for example, that he might have done better to turn carpenter or revolutionist. Therefore, he is fully responsible for the interpretation. Forlornness implies that we ourselves choose our being. Forlornness and anguish go together.

As for despair, the term has a very simple meaning. It means that we shall confine ourselves to reckoning only with what depends upon our will, or on the ensemble of probabilities which make our action possible. When we want something, we always have to reckon with probabilities. I may be counting on the arrival of a friend. The friend is coming by rail or streetcar; this supposes that the train will arrive on schedule, or that the streetcar will not jump the track. I am left in the realm of possibility; but possibilities are to be reckoned with only to the point where my action comports with the ensemble of these possibilities, and no further. The moment the possibilities I am considering are not rigorously involved by my action, I ought to disengage myself from them, because no God, no scheme, can adapt the world and its possibilities to my will. When Descartes said, "Conquer yourself rather than the world," he meant essentially the same thing.

The Marxists to whom I have spoken reply, "You can rely on the support of others in your action, which obviously has certain limits because you're not going to live forever. That means: rely on both what others are doing elsewhere to help you, in China, in Russia, and what they will do later on, after your death, to carry on the action and lead it to its fulfillment, which will be the revolution. You even *have* to rely upon that, otherwise you're immoral." I reply at once that I will always rely on fellow-fighters insofar as these comrades are involved with me in a common struggle, in the unity of a party or a group in which I can more or less make my weight felt; that is, one whose ranks I am in as a fighter and whose movements I am aware of at every moment. In such a situation, relying on the unity and will of the party is exactly like counting on the fact that the train will arrive on time or that the car won't jump the track. But, given that man is free and that there is no human nature for me to depend on, I cannot count on men whom I do not know by relying on human goodness or man's concern for the good of society. I don't know what will become of the Russian revolution; I may make an example of it to the extent that at the present time it is apparent that the proletariat plays a part in Russia that it plays in no other nation. But I can't swear that this will inevitably lead to a triumph of the proletariat. I've got to limit myself to what I see.

Given that men are free and that tomorrow they will freely decide what man will be, I cannot be sure that, after my death, fellow-fighters will carry on my work to bring it to its maximum perfection. Tomorrow, after my death, some men may decide to set up Fascism, and the others may be cowardly and muddled enough to let them do it. Fascism will then be the human reality, so much the worse for us.

Actually, things will be as man will have decided they are to be. Does that mean that I should abandon myself to quietism? No. First, I should involve myself; then, act on the old saw, "Nothing ventured, nothing gained." Nor does it mean that I shouldn't belong to a party, but rather that I shall have no illusions and shall do what I can. For example, suppose I ask myself, "Will socialization, as such, ever come about?" I know nothing about it. All I know is that I'm going to do everything in my power to bring it about. Beyond that, I can't count on anything. Quietism is the attitude of people who say, "Let others do what I can't do." The doctrine I am presenting is the very opposite of quietism, since it declares, "There is no reality except in action." Moreover, it goes further, since it adds, "Man is nothing else than his plan; he exists only to the extent that he fulfills himself; he is therefore nothing else than the ensemble of his acts, nothing else than his life."

According to this, we can understand why our doctrine horrifies certain people. Because often the only way they can bear their wretchedness is to think, "Circumstances have been against me. What I've been and done doesn't show my true worth. To be sure, I've had no great love, no great friendship, but that's because I haven't met a man or woman who was worthy. The books I've written haven't been very good because I haven't had the proper leisure. I haven't had children to devote myself to because I didn't find a man with whom I could have spent my life. So there remains within me, unused and quite viable, a host of propensities, inclinations, possibilities, that one wouldn't guess from the mere series of things I've done."

Now, for the existentialist there is really no love other than one which manifests itself in a person's being in love. There is no genius other than one which is expressed in works of art; the genius of Proust is the sum of Proust's works; the genius of Racine is his series of tragedies. Outside of that, there is nothing. Why say that Racine could have written another tragedy, when he didn't write it? A man is involved in life, leaves his impress on it, and outside of that there is nothing. To be sure, this may seem a harsh thought to someone whose life hasn't been a success. But, on the other hand, it prompts people to understand that reality alone is what counts, that dreams, expectations, and hopes warrant no more than to define a man as a disappointed dream, as miscarried hopes, as vain expectations. In other words, to define him negatively and not positively. However, when we say, "You are nothing else than your life," that does not imply that the artist will be judged solely on the basis of his works of art; a thousand other things will contribute toward summing him up. What we mean is that a man is nothing else than a series of undertakings, that he is the sum, the organization, the ensemble of the relationships which make up these undertakings.

When all is said and done, what we are accused of, at bottom, is not our pessimism, but an optimistic toughness. If people throw up to us our works of fiction in which we write about people who are soft, weak, cowardly, and sometimes even downright bad, it's not because these people are soft, weak, cowardly, or bad; because if we were to say, as Zola did, that they are that way because of heredity, the workings of environment, society, because of biological or psychological determinism, people would be reassured. They would say, "Well, that's what we're like, no one can do anything about it." But when the existentialist writes about a coward, he says that this coward is responsible for his cowardice. He's not like that because he has a cowardly heart or lung or brain; he's not like that on account of his physiological make-up; but he's like that because he has made himself a coward by his acts. There's no such thing as a cowardly constitution; there are nervous constitutions; there is poor blood, as the common people say, or strong constitutions. But the man whose blood is poor is not a coward on that account, for what makes cowardice is the act of renouncing or yielding. A constitution is not an act; the coward is defined on the basis of the acts he performs. People feel, in a vague sort of way, that this coward we're talking about is guilty of being a coward, and the thought frightens them. What people would like is that a coward or a hero be born that way. . . .

From these few reflections it is evident that nothing is more unjust than the objections that have been raised against us. Existentialism is nothing else than an attempt to draw all the consequences of a coherent atheistic position. It isn't trying to plunge man into despair at all. But if one calls every attitude of unbelief despair, like the Christians, then the word is not being used in its original sense. Existentialism isn't so atheistic that it wears itself out showing that God doesn't exist. Rather, it declares that even if God did exist, that would change nothing. There you've got our point of view. Not that we believe that God exists, but we think that the problem of His existence is not the issue. In this sense existentialism is optimistic, a doctrine of action, and it is plain dishonesty for Christians to make no distinction between their own despair and ours and then to call us despairing.

CRITICAL APPROACHES

THEODORE SPENCER

The Central Problem in Literary Criticism

To define the central problem in literary criticism is not easy. When the critic is doing his job in the right way, he is performing a very elaborate act, which is important as a total act, so that it is in a sense false to say that any one part of it is more central than another. It is necessary to point this out at the beginning. For what is a man doing when he starts out in his task of literary criticism? Among other things he is doing the following:

1. He is trying to understand what the author says—in itself a very complicated business.
2. He is considering the form in which the author is saying it.
3. He is trying to distinguish between what is essential and what is nonessential in the author's presentation of his subject.
4. He is relating what the author says to his own experience of life.
5. He is comparing the author's success in carrying out his aims with the success of other authors in carrying out similar aims.
6. He is undergoing, or failing to undergo, a set of emotional and intellectual experiences which give him what he calls, for lack of a better word, enjoyment. And this enjoyment, while it includes the operations which I have just mentioned, is something more, and something different, from the sum of their parts.

Which of these activities is the essential one? On which should we concentrate if we are to discuss the central problem of criticism?

The first thing we must do, if we are to answer this question, is to make an artificial distinction, which, in spite of its artificiality, is nevertheless both valid and essential. We must distinguish between the work of art and our own response to it. We must first look at the work objectively, as something with an order of its own, and as an example, even, of certain principles of construction. We must first treat it, in other words, as Aristotle treated tragedy—we must ask ourselves to what class of work this particular work belongs, we must understand the relation of one part to another, we must understand the particular kind of structural organism of which it is an example. We must, as Arnold says, see the thing as it really is. Only later should we discuss our responses to it.

Most teachers of literature will disagree with this. They will use a lot of hard words like "formalism," "frigidity," "academic," and "pedantic," and they will say that to approach literature from the formal side is to kill appreciation, is to look at literature from the wrong angle, and that, even if a mature critic likes to imitate Aristotle, it will not work with students. Literature, they will say, is something to be felt, not something to be analyzed and hence killed.

There is, of course, some truth in those objections, and I would agree that unless some kind of initial pleasure is found in a work of art, there is little point in analysis. There is no use taking an automobile apart and putting it together again unless you are going to get the fun of riding in it. But, on the other hand, if mere undefined enjoyment is what is aimed at, then distinctions break down and criticism becomes impossible. The first problem that the artist himself is compelled to face in creation is the problem of form; the critic, who is a follower of the artist, should begin at the same place.

This has been easier in some generations than it has in others. In the eighteenth century, when certain recognized forms were in vogue and each kind of art had its own decorum (as life itself was supposed to have decorum), it was much easier to begin the critical act with a discussion of artistic form. At the present time experimentation has made form an individual matter, and, confronted with an enormous variety, the critic has great difficulty both in finding general principles and in using those principles in the discussion of an individual work. Many artists of the past generation have given critics an inferiority complex, so that too many false judgments have been made. The critic is so afraid of misunderstanding the artist's intention that he attributes more intention to a given work than the artist originally had in mind. The result has been a great deal of critical confusion, as the present state of American criticism only too clearly shows. For the critics have themselves been experimenting and have piled up all kinds of individual vocabularies and private critical terms to explain phenomena which in happier, less Alexandrian generations could be analyzed in a less individual fashion.

That is one reason why the critic, starting out with his analysis of form, should have more than the individual form of the particular work he is criticizing in mind. Classification is the beginning of thought, in criticism as in everything else, and no critic has given himself the right kind of training unless he has seriously discussed with himself the different classes and types of literature. That is why he must return again and again to Aristotle, not only because of what Aristotle says about a particular form, but because Aristotle's method is the most fruitful method yet devised for showing what the critic's business should be in distinguishing between what is essential and what is accidental in a given artistic form.

If he reads Aristotle correctly he will see that Aristotle does two things: he describes and he defines. There is a fundamental difference between these activities, and it is usually possible to separate the first-class critic from the second-class according to which activity he emphasizes. The second-class critic generally confines himself to description, and, though he is performing a useful function, and frequently acts as an invaluable intermediary between the work of art and the reader, he does not get at the core of the problem, which is the discovery of universals.

And that—for I have come to it at last—is the heart of our problem. How, in the morass of relativism, of impressionism, of individual response, are we to discover and define those principles of form which underlie works of literature? It will not do to deny their existence; to say that each work of art has its own laws, is the product of a particular set of circumstances—economic, social, or religious—and is the creation of a particular and unique individual. We cannot dismiss these things, of course—in fact, it would be fatal to do so, but it is even more fatal not to go beyond them. If, for example, we are considering the novel, we must begin with a large range of apparently diverse material, which includes *Don Quixote* and *Tristram Shandy*, *Martin Chuzzlewit* and *Ulysses*; it is a literary form which employs a large number of different technical devices and is the reflection of a great variety of individual temperaments. The descriptive critic should rightly be concerned with exploring such matters, with trying to understand what each author was trying to do, and with showing how he accomplished it. But the critic who is really doing his job must, when considering any one of these novels, keep in mind what all of them have in common; he must, like Aristotle, define as well as describe. If he has meditated on the subject sufficiently, he will have discovered for himself a set of general principles, similar to Aristotle's definition of tragedy, which will enable him to criticize any individual work with some pretentions to authority. He will no longer be merely an impressionist but will be able to examine the particular novel with that kind of objective attention which it is the primary function of the critic to employ.

I do not mean to suggest by this a merely authoritarian attitude, or to say that the critic should build a Procrustes bed and fit every work of art into it whether it is the right size or not. My point is simply this: I believe that intelligent human beings, trained along the same lines, have enough in common so that when two of them meditate seriously on the fundamental characteristics of a given set of phenomena they will arrive at similar conclusions. If the object to be studied is the novel, certain universals will be agreed upon; and these are the bases of criticism.

But criticism cannot stop with the discussion of form. Literature, to use Mr. I. A. Richards' phrase, "is a store house of recorded values," and the problem of values, the content which the form shapes, can never be separated from any critical discussion. And, since we are all teachers as well as critics, the responsibility of looking for universals in value as well as in form is a heavy one.

The tendency of many trends in contemporary education is not only to limit experience by concentrating on the personal but also to limit it by concentrating on the merely contemporary. For many reasons we are in danger, at the present time and in this country, of losing all sense of the past under the pressure of our immediate necessities. The past no longer seems to have any reality, and this may be one explanation, though cause and effect are hard to disentangle, why, when the past is taught, it is so often taught in a fashion that fails to bring it alive. But just as a man cannot be called wise unless he is aware of other emotions and thoughts than his own, so a man cannot be called educated unless he knows and understands how other periods than his own expressed themselves. To make these seem important in an age of stress is difficult, but if it can be accomplished the stress itself is lessened. Not that the imaginative awareness of other views and other periods than our own should be considered an escape—though, in spite of the abusive connotations around the word, "escape" does describe at least a part of what happens in any imaginative experience. We must at times be taken out of ourselves and enabled to see what is happening to us in the light of what has happened to other people—and in so doing we must not merely taste, as Pater would have had us do; we must also judge. And, if we are to judge, we must have a sense of values about both literary and nonliterary experience.

Here we come to the second aspect of our main problem. We may talk glibly about a standard of values, but to define what we mean by it at the present time is not easy, and any discussion of it involves much more than merely a discussion of literature. In the past two generations there has been an increasing tendency to consider any experience valuable in and for itself, and this has meant that the type of experience sought for has been increasingly outward rather than inward. Our whole civilization tends to that direction; our entertainment—the movies and the radio, for example—are made for us in a standardized fashion, and are made for us in such quantity that we have little time to contemplate or to judge. The great literature of the past seems slow and ponderous compared to this vivid and rapidly moving entertainment, and as experience and speed tend to become synonymous, the value of one kind of experience as compared to another tends to shrink, and each experience becomes like every other experience. From this lack of discrimination literature alone cannot save us, though there have been people, like Matthew Arnold, who thought it could. Literature is always an adjunct—a reflection, however profound—of the forces (social, philosophical, and religious) which lie behind it, and, if we are to achieve a hierarchy of value in literature, we must first have a hierarchy of value in life. And yet, since literature is the reflection of past values, a knowledge of it can help us to construct a hierarchy of our own, and we may approach the problem by asking ourselves what it is that the greatest works of literature have in common. What is it that is shared by the great masters—Homer, Sophocles, Dante, Cervantes, Shakespeare? Two things, obviously to begin with: a masterly and magical control of the medium of expression and a convincing and moving presentation of human beings. But we must go further than this and ask ourselves why it is that their presentation of human beings seems so close to the truth. Fundamentally it is because in these authors, expressed in very different ways, we find four things: a presentation in concrete terms of the contrast or conflict between good and evil; a sense of the essential dignity and nobility in individual human beings; an awareness of a reality other than that given by the senses; and an awareness of some kind of unity or order beyond the diversity of individual experience. It is because great literature presents instances of these general truths that we call it great, and we may even say that it is possible to judge literature according to how much of them it includes. Consequently, we would have one type of literature which is merely entertainment (the fairy story), another type which describes merely action (the detective story), a third which includes character on a realistic level (a novel like *Moll Flanders*), a fourth which describes contrast of characters and sees these characters as typical (the *Canterbury Tales*), and a fifth type, the greatest of all, which presents the four truths mentioned above and sees human action in their present terms: Homer, Sophocles, Dante, Cervantes, Shakespeare. In other words, what we must be aware of as critics is the existence of certain universals in value, as in form, by which we may not only define but also judge. If we fail to realize this we fail to perform our essential function; we are neither critics nor proper teachers of literature.

But at the present time we must go even more deeply into our subject than this. So far I have been speaking mainly about criticism in relation to literature. But both literature and criticism are dependent on the society of which they are a part; they reflect and they mold the world which produces them and which they shape. That is why the responsibility of the true critic and the teacher is so great. And we cannot properly assume it unless we recognize that there is one fact which faces us, as critics, as students and teachers of the best that has been thought and said in the world, as human beings—a fact which faces us with unmistakable force. It is this: We are living in a period which represents the end of one cycle of Western civilization. The sanctions upon which human action in the past has been based have lost their meaning. Partly through the development of science, partly through mistaken notions of progress, partly through the shortsightedness of well-meaning educators, our culture (not only in Europe) is falling in darkness to pieces. All cultures *do* fall to pieces when they abandon, as we (with the best intentions in the world) have abandoned, the tradition by which they have been upheld. It is our function to see that the tradition does not entirely disappear. In a previous dark age it did not disappear, due to the curiosity and devotion of a few secluded men who were cut off from the world. But the critic and the teacher are not cut off from the world as they were, which makes our situation both more difficult and more responsible. We have got to be both above the contemporary turmoil and a part of it; and we have got to keep alive, in an age that does everything it can (and in all sorts of disguises) to kill them, those universals which the great literature of our civilization has expressed, and which it is our business to rediscover and expound. The central problem in literary criticism is not only a problem of form, not only a problem of literary value—it is the problem of what it means to be a conscious being in a world that may darken to annihilation.

W. K. WIMSATT, JR.
M. C. BEARDSLEY

The Intentional Fallacy

The claim of the author's "intention" upon the critic's judgment has been challenged in a number of recent discussions, notably in the debate entitled *The Personal Heresy*, between Professors Lewis and Tillyard. But it seems doubtful if this claim and most of its romantic corollaries are as yet subject to any widespread questioning. The present writers, in a short article entitled "Intention" for a *Dictionary* of literary criticism, raised the issue but were unable to pursue its implications at any length. We argued that the design or intention of the author is neither available nor desirable as a standard for judging the success of a work of literary art, and it seems to us that this is a principle which goes deep into some differences in the history of critical attitudes. It is a principle which accepted or rejected points to the polar opposites of classical "imitation" and romantic expression. It entails many specific truths about inspiration, authenticity, biography, literary history and scholarship, and about some trends of contemporary poetry, especially its allusiveness. There is hardly a problem of literary criticism in which the critic's approach will not be qualified by his view of "intention."

"Intention," as we shall use the term, corresponds to *what he intended* in a formula which more or less explicitly has had wide acceptance. "In order to judge the poet's performance, we must know *what he intended*." Intention is design or plan in the author's mind. Intention has obvious affinities for the author's attitude toward his work, the way he felt, what made him write.

We begin our discussion with a series of propositions summarized and abstracted to a degree where they seem to us axiomatic.

1. A poem does not come into existence by accident. The words of a poem, as Professor Stoll has remarked, come out of a head, not out of a hat. Yet to insist on the designing intellect as a *cause* of a poem is not to grant the design or intention as a *standard* by which the critic is to judge the worth of the poet's performance.

2. One must ask how a critic expects to get an answer to the question about intention. How is he to find out what the poet tried to do? If the poet succeeded in doing it, then the poem itself shows what he was trying to do. And if the poet did not succeed, then the poem is not adequate evidence, and the critic must go outside the poem—for evidence of an intention that did not become effective in the poem.

"Only one *caveat* must be borne in mind," says an eminent intentionalist in a moment when his theory repudiates itself; "the poet's aim must be judged at the moment of the creative act, that is to say, by the art of the poem itself."

3. Judging a poem is like judging a pudding or a machine. One demands that it work. It is only because an artifact works that we infer the intention of an artificer. "A poem should not mean but be." A poem can *be* only through its *meaning*—since its medium is words—yet it *is*, simply *is*, in the sense that we have no excuse for inquiring what part is intended or meant. Poetry is a feat of style by which a complex of meaning is handled all at once. Poetry succeeds because all or most of what is said or implied is relevant; what is irrelevant has been excluded, like lumps from pudding and "bugs" from machinery. In this respect poetry differs from practical messages, which are successful if and only if we correctly infer the intention. They are more abstract than poetry.

4. The meaning of a poem may certainly be a personal one, in the sense that a poem expresses a personality or state of soul rather than a physical object like an apple. But even a short lyric poem is dramatic, the response of a speaker (no matter how abstractly conceived) to a situation (no matter how universalized). We ought to impute the thoughts and attitudes of the poem immediately to the dramatic *speaker*, and if to the author at all, only by an act of biographical inference.

5. There is a sense in which an author, by revision, may better achieve his original intention. But it is a very abstract sense. He intended to write a better work, or a better work of a certain kind, and now has done it. But it follows that his former concrete intention was not his intention. "He's the man we were in search of, that's true," says Hardy's rustic constable, "and yet he's not the man we were in search of. For the man we were in search of was not the man we wanted."

"Is not a critic," asks Professor Stoll, "a judge, who does not explore his own consciousness, but determines the author's meaning or intention, as if the poem were a will, a contract, or the constitution? The poem is not the critic's own." He has accurately diagnosed two forms of irresponsibility, one of which he prefers. Our view is yet different. The poem is not the critic's own and not the author's (it is detached from the author at birth and goes about the world beyond his power to intend about it or control it). The poem belongs to the public. It is embodied in language, the peculiar possession of the public, and it is about the human being, an object of public knowledge. What is said about the poem is subject to the same scrutiny as any statement in linguistics or in the general science of psychology.

A critic of our *Dictionary* article, Ananda K. Coomaraswamy, has argued that there are two kinds of inquiry about a work of art: (1) whether the artist achieved his intentions; (2) whether the work of art "ought ever to have been undertaken at all" and so "whether it is worth preserving." Number (2), Coomaraswamy maintains, is not "criticism of any work of art *qua* work of art," but is rather moral criticism; number (1) is artistic criticism. But we maintain that (2) need not be moral criticism: that there is another way of deciding whether works of art are worth preserving and whether, in a sense, they "ought" to have been undertaken, and this is the way of objective criticism of works of art as such, the way which enables us to distinguish between a skillful murder and a skillful poem. A skillful murder is an example which Coomaraswamy uses, and in his system the difference between the murder and the poem is simply a "moral" one, not an "artistic" one, since each if carried out according to plan is "artistically" successful. We maintain that (2) is an inquiry of more worth than (1), and since (2) and not (1) is capable of distinguishing poetry from murder, the name "artistic criticism" is properly given to (2).

II

It is not so much a historical statement as a definition to say that the intentional fallacy is a romantic one. When a rhetorician of the first century A.D. writes: "Sublimity is the echo of a great soul," or when he tells us that "Homer enters into the sublime actions of his heroes" and "shares the full inspiration of the combat," we shall not be surprised to find this rhetorician considered as a distant harbinger of romanticism and greeted in the warmest terms by Saintsbury. One may wish to argue whether Longinus should be called romantic, but there can hardly be a doubt that in one important way he is.

Goethe's three questions for "constructive criticism" are "What did the author set out to do? Was his plan reasonable and sensible, and how far did he succeed in carrying it out?" If one leaves out the middle question, one has in effect the system of Croce—the culmination and crowning philosophic expression of romanticism. The beautiful is the successful intuition-expression, and the ugly is the unsuccessful; the intuition or private part of art is *the* aesthetic fact, and the medium or public part is not the subject of aesthetic at all.

> The Madonna of Cimabue is still in the Church of Santa Maria Novella; but does she speak to the visitor of to-day as to the Florentines of the thirteenth century?
>
> *Historical interpretation* labours . . . to reintegrate in us the psychological conditions which have changed in the course of history. It . . . enables us to see a work of art (a physical object) as its *author saw it* in the moment of production.

The first italics are Croce's, the second ours. The upshot of Croce's system is an ambiguous emphasis on history. With such passages as a point of departure a critic may write a nice analysis of the meaning or "spirit" of a play by Shakespeare or Corneille—a process that involves close historical study but remains aesthetic criticism—or he may, with equal plausibility, produce an essay in sociology, biography, or other kinds of non-aesthetic history.

III

> I went to the poets; tragic, dithyrambic, and all sorts. . . . I took them some of the most elaborate passages in their own writings, and asked what was the meaning of them. . . . Will you believe me? . . . there is hardly a person present who would not have talked better about their poetry than they did themselves. Then I knew that not by wisdom do poets write poetry, but by a sort of genius and inspiration.

That reiterated mistrust of the poets which we hear from Socrates may have been part of a rigorously ascetic view in which we hardly wish to participate, yet Plato's Socrates saw a truth about the poetic mind which the world no longer commonly sees—so much criticism, and that the most inspirational and most affectionately remembered, has proceeded from the poets themselves.

Certainly the poets have had something to say that the critic and professor could not say; their message has been more exciting: that poetry should come as naturally as leaves to a tree, that poetry is the lava of the imagination, or that it is emotion recollected in tranquillity. But it is necessary that we realize the character and authority of such testimony. There is only a fine shade of difference between such expressions and a kind of earnest advice that authors often give. Thus Edward Young, Carlyle, Walter Pater:

> I know two golden rules from *ethics*, which are no less golden in *Composition*, than in life. 1. *Know thyself*; 2dly, *Reverence thyself*.
>
> This is the grand secret for finding readers and retaining them: let him who would move and convince others, be first moved and convinced himself.

Horace's rule, *Si vis me flere,* is applicable in a wider sense than the literal one. To every poet, to every writer, we might say: Be true, if you would be believed.

Truth! there can be no merit, no craft at all, without that. And further, all beauty is in the long run only *fineness* of truth, or what we call expression, the finer accommodation of speech to that vision within.

And Housman's little handbook to the poetic mind yields this illustration:

> Having drunk a pint of beer at luncheon—beer is a sedative to the brain, and my afternoons are the least intellectual portion of my life—I would go out for a walk of two or three hours. As I went along, thinking of nothing in particular, only looking at things around me and following the progress of the seasons, there would flow into my mind, with sudden and unaccountable emotion, sometimes a line or two of verse, sometimes a whole stanza at once.

This is the logical terminus of the series already quoted. Here is a confession of how poems were written which would do as a definition of poetry just as well as "emotion recollected in tranquillity"—and which the young poet might equally well take to heart as a practical rule. Drink a pint of beer, relax, go walking, think on nothing in particular, look at things, surrender yourself to yourself, search for the truth in your own soul, listen to the sound of your own inside voice, discover and express the *vraie vérité*.

It is probably true that all this is excellent advice for poets. The young imagination fired by Wordsworth and Carlyle is probably closer to the verge of producing a poem than the mind of the student who has been sobered by Aristotle or Richards. The art of inspiring poets, or at least of inciting something like poetry in young persons, has probably gone further in our day than ever before. Books of creative writing such as those issued from the Lincoln School are interesting evidence of what a child can do. All this, however, would appear to belong to an art separate from criticism—to a psychological discipline, a system of self-development, a yoga, which the young poet perhaps does well to notice, but which is something different from the public art of evaluating poems.

Coleridge and Arnold were better critics than most poets have been, and if the critical tendency dried up the poetry in Arnold and perhaps in Coleridge, it is not inconsistent with our argument, which is that judgment of poems is different from the art of producing them. Coleridge has given us the classic "anodyne" story, and tells what he can about the genesis of a poem which he calls a "psychological curiosity," but his definitions of poetry and of the poetic quality "imagination" are to be found elsewhere and in quite other terms.

It would be convenient if the passwords of the intentional school, "sincerity," "fidelity," "spontaneity," "authenticity," "genuineness," "originality," could be equated with terms such as "integrity," "relevance," "unity," "function," "maturity," "subtlety," "adequacy," and other more precise terms of evaluation—in short, if "expression" always meant aesthetic achievement. But this is not so.

"Aesthetic" art, says Professor Curt Ducasse, an ingenious theorist of expression, is the conscious objectification of feelings, in which an intrinsic part is the critical moment. The artist corrects the objectification when it is not adequate. But this may mean that the earlier attempt was not successful in objectifying the self, or "it may also mean that it was a successful objectification of a self which, when it confronted us clearly, we disowned and repudiated in favor of another." What is the standard by which we disown or accept the self? Professor Ducasse does not say. Whatever it may be, however, this standard is an element in the definition of art which will not reduce to terms of objectification. The evaluation of the work of art remains public; the work is measured against something outside the author.

IV

There is criticism of poetry and there is author psychology, which when applied to the present or future takes the form of inspirational promotion; but author psychology can be historical too, and then we have literary biography, a legitimate and attractive study in itself, one approach, as Professor Tillyard would argue, to personality, the poem being only a parallel approach. Certainly it need not be with a derogatory purpose that one points out personal studies, as distinct from poetic studies, in the realm of literary scholarship. Yet there is danger of confusing personal and poetic studies; and there is the fault of writing the personal as if it were poetic.

There is a difference between internal and external evidence for the meaning of a poem. And the paradox is only verbal and superficial that what is (1) internal is also public: it is discovered through the semantics and syntax of a poem, through our habitual knowledge of the language, through grammars, dictionaries, and all the literature which is the source of dictionaries, in general through all that makes a language and culture; while what is (2) external is private or idiosyncratic;

not a part of the work as a linguistic fact: it consists of revelations (in journals, for example, or letters or reported conversations) about how or why the poet wrote the poem—to what lady, while sitting on what lawn, or at the death of what friend or brother. There is (3) an intermediate kind of evidence about the character of the author or about private or semiprivate meanings attached to words or topics by an author or by a coterie of which he is a member. The meaning of words is the history of words, and the biography of an author, his use of a word, and the associations which the word had for *him*, are part of the word's history and meaning. But the three types of evidence, especially (2) and (3), shade into one another so subtly that it is not always easy to draw a line between examples, and hence arises the difficulty for criticism. The use of biographical evidence need not involve intentionalism, because while it may be evidence of what the author intended, it may also be evidence of the meaning of his words and the dramatic character of his utterance. On the other hand, it may not be all this. And a critic who is concerned with evidence of type (1) and moderately with that of type (3) will in the long run produce a different sort of comment from that of the critic who is concerned with (2) and with (3) where it shades into (2).

The whole glittering parade of Professor Lowes' *Road to Xanadu*, for instance, runs along the border between types (2) and (3) or boldly traverses the romantic region of (2). "'Kubla Khan,'" says Professor Lowes, "is the fabric of a vision, but every image that rose up in its weaving had passed that way before. And it would seem that there is nothing haphazard or fortuitous in their return." This is not quite clear—not even when Professor Lowes explains that there were clusters of associations, like hooked atoms, which were drawn into complex relation with other clusters in the deep well of Coleridge's memory, and which then coalesced and issued forth as poems. If there was nothing "haphazard or fortuitous" in the way the images returned to the surface, that may mean (1) that Coleridge could not produce what he did not have, that he was limited in his creation by what he had read or otherwise experienced, or (2) that having received certain clusters of associations, he was bound to return them in just the way he did, and that the value of the poem may be described in terms of the experiences on which he had to draw. The latter pair of propositions (a sort of Hartleyan associationism which Coleridge himself repudiated in the *Biographia*) may not be assented to. There were certainly other combinations, other poems, worse or better, that might have been written by men who had read Bartram and Purchas and Bruce and

Milton. And this will be true no matter how many times we are able to add to the brilliant complex of Coleridge's reading. In certain flourishes (such as the sentence we have quoted) and in chapter headings like "The Shaping Spirit," "The Magical Synthesis," "Imagination Creatrix," it may be that Professor Lowes pretends to say more about the actual poems than he does. There is a certain deceptive variation in these fancy chapter titles; one expects to pass on to a new stage in the argument, and one finds—more and more sources, more and more about "the streamy nature of association."

"Wohin der Weg?" quotes Professor Lowes for the motto of his book. "Kein Weg! Ins Unbetretene." Precisely because the way is *unbetreten*, we should say, it leads away from the poem. Bartram's *Travels* contains a good deal of the history of certain words and of certain romantic Floridian conceptions that appear in "Kubla Khan." And a good deal of that history has passed and was then passing into the very stuff of our language. Perhaps a person who has read Bartram appreciates the poem more than one who has not. Or, by looking up the vocabulary of "Kubla Khan" in the *Oxford English Dictionary*, or by reading some of the other books there quoted, a person may know the poem better. But it would seem to pertain little to the poem to know that *Coleridge* had read Bartram. There is a gross body of life, of sensory and mental experience, which lies behind and in some sense causes every poem, but can never be and need not be known in the verbal and hence intellectual composition which is the poem. For all the objects of our manifold experience, for every unity, there is an action of the mind which cuts off roots, melts away context—or indeed we should never have objects or ideas or anything to talk about.

It is probable that there is nothing in Professor Lowes' vast book which could detract from anyone's appreciation of either *The Ancient Mariner* or "Kubla Khan." We next present a case where preoccupation with evidence of type (3) has gone so far as to distort a critic's view of a poem (yet a case not so obvious as those that abound in our critical journals).

In a well known poem by John Donne appears this quatrain:

> *Moving of th' earth brings harmes and feares,*
>   *Men reckon what it did and meant,*
> *But trepidation of the spheares,*
>   *Though greater farre, is innocent.*

A recent critic in an elaborate treatment of Donne's learning has written of this quatrain as follows:

> He touches the emotional pulse of the situation by a skillful allusion to the new and the old astronomy. . . . Of the new astronomy, the "moving of the earth" is the most radical principle; of the old, the "trepidation of the spheres" is the motion of the greatest complexity. . . . The poet must exhort his love to quietness and calm upon his departure; and for this purpose the figure based upon the latter motion (trepidation), long absorbed into the traditional astronomy, fittingly suggests the tension of the moment without arousing the "harmes and feares" implicit in the figure of the moving earth.

The argument is plausible and rests on a well substantiated thesis that Donne was deeply interested in the new astronomy and its repercussions in the theological realm. In various works Donne shows his familiarity with Kepler's *De Stella Nova,* with Galileo's *Siderius Nuncius,* with William Gilbert's *De Magnete,* and with Clavious' commentary on the *De Sphaera* of Sacrobosco. He refers to the new science in his Sermon at Paul's Cross and in a letter to Sir Henry Goodyer. In *The First Anniversary* he says the "new philosophy calls all in doubt." In the *Elegy on Prince Henry* he says that the "least moving of the center" makes "the world to shake."

It is difficult to answer argument like this, and impossible to answer it with evidence of like nature. There is no reason why Donne might not have written a stanza in which the two kinds of celestial motion stood for two sorts of emotion at parting. And if we become full of astronomical ideas and see Donne only against the background of the new science, we may believe that he did. But the text itself remains to be dealt with, the analyzable vehicle of a complicated metaphor. And one may observe: (1) that the movement of the earth according to the Copernican theory is a celestial motion, smooth and regular, and while it might cause religious or philosophic fears, it could not be associated with the crudity and earthiness of the kind of commotion which the speaker in the poem wishes to discourage; (2) that there is another moving of the earth, an earthquake, which has just these qualities and is to be associated with the tear-floods and sigh-tempests of the second stanza of the poem; (3) that "trepidation" is an appropriate opposite of earthquake, because each is a shaking or vibratory motion; and "trepidation of the spheres" is "greater far" than an earthquake, but not much greater (if two such motions can be compared as to greatness) than the annual motion of the earth; (4) that reckoning what it "did and meant" shows that the event has passed, like an earthquake, not like the incessant celestial movement of the earth. Perhaps a knowledge of Donne's interest in the new science may add another shade of meaning, an overtone to the stanza in question, though to say even this runs against the words. To make the geocentric and heliocentric antithesis the core of the metaphor is to disregard the English language, to prefer private evidence to public, external to internal.

V

If the distinction between kinds of evidence has implications for the historical critic, it has them no less for the contemporary poet and his critic. Or, since every rule for a poet is but another side of a judgment by a critic, and since the past is the realm of the scholar and critic, and the future and present that of the poet and the critical leaders of taste, we may say that the problems arising in literary scholarship from the intentional fallacy are matched by others which arise in the world of progressive experiment.

The question of "allusiveness," for example, as acutely posed by the poetry of Eliot, is certainly one where a false judgment is likely to involve the intentional fallacy. The frequency and depth of literary allusion in the poetry of Eliot and others has driven so many in pursuit of full meanings to the *Golden Bough* and the Elizabethan drama that it has become a kind of commonplace to suppose that we do not know what a poet means unless we have traced him in his reading—a supposition redolent with intentional implications. The stand taken by F. O. Matthiessen is a sound one and partially forestalls the difficulty.

> If one reads these lines with an attentive ear and is sensitive to their sudden shifts in movement, the contrast between the actual Thames and the idealized vision of it during an age before it flowed through a megalopolis is sharply conveyed by that movement itself, whether or not one recognizes the refrain to be from Spenser.

Eliot's allusions work when we know them—and to a great extent even when we do not know them, through their suggestive power.

But sometimes we find allusions supported by notes, and it is a nice question whether the notes function more as guides to send us where we may be educated, or more as indications in themselves about the character of the allusions. "Nearly everything of importance . . . that is apposite to an appreciation of 'The Waste Land,'" writes Matthiessen of Miss Weston's book, "has been incorporated into the structure of the poem itself, or into Eliot's Notes." And with such an admission it may begin to appear that it would not much matter if Eliot invented his sources (as Sir Walter Scott invented chapter epigraphs from "old plays" and "anonymous" authors, or as Coleridge wrote marginal glosses for *The Ancient Mariner*) Allusions to Dante, Webster, Marvell, or Baudelaire doubtless gain something because these writers existed, but it is doubtful whether the same can be said for an allusion to an obscure Elizabethan:

> *The sound of horns and motors, which shall bring*
> *Sweeney to Mrs. Porter in the spring.*

"Cf. Day, *Parliament of Bees:*" says Eliot,

> *When of a sudden, listening, you shall hear,*
> *A noise of horns and hunting, which shall bring*
> *Actaeon to Diana in the spring,*
> *Where all shall see her naked skin.*

The irony is completed by the quotation itself; had Eliot, as is quite conceivable, composed these lines to furnish his own background, there would be no loss of validity. The conviction may grow as one reads Eliot's next note: "I do not know the origin of the ballad from which these lines are taken: it was reported to me from Sydney, Australia." The important word in this note—on Mrs. Porter and her daughter who washed their feet in soda water—is "ballad." And if one should feel from the lines themselves their "ballad" quality, there would be little need for the note. Ultimately, the inquiry must focus on the integrity of such notes as parts of the poem, for where they constitute special information about the meaning of phrases in the poem, they ought to be subject to the same scrutiny as any of the other words in which it is written. Matthiessen believes the notes were the price Eliot "had to pay in order to avoid what he would have considered muffling the energy of his poem by extended connecting links in the text itself." But it may be questioned whether the notes and the need for them are not equally muffling. F. W. Bateson has plausibly argued that Tennyson's "The Sailor Boy" would be better if half the stanzas were omitted, and the best versions of ballads like "Sir Patrick Spens" owe their power to the very audacity with which the minstrel has taken for granted the story upon which he comments. What then if a poet finds he cannot take so much for granted in a more recondite context and rather than write informatively, supplies notes? It can be said in favor of this plan that at least the notes do not pretend to be dramatic, as they would if written in verse. On the other hand, the notes may look like unassimilated material lying loose beside the poem, necessary for the meaning of the verbal symbol, but not integrated, so that the symbol stands incomplete.

We mean to suggest by the above analysis that whereas notes tend to seem to justify themselves as external indexes to the author's *intention*, yet they ought to be judged like any other parts of a composition (verbal arrangement special to a particular context), and when so judged their reality as parts of the poem, or their imaginative integration with the rest of the poem, may come into question. Matthiessen, for instance, sees that Eliot's titles for poems and his epigraphs are informative apparatus, like the notes. But while he is worried by some of the notes and thinks that Eliot "appears to be mocking himself for writing the note at the same time that he wants to convey something by it," Matthiessen believes that the "device" of epigraphs "is not at all open to the objection of not being sufficiently structural." "The *intention*," he says, "is to enable the poet to secure a condensed expression in the poem itself." "In each case the epigraph is *designed* to form an integral part of the effect of the poem." And Eliot himself, in his notes, has justified his poetic practice in terms of intention.

> The Hanged Man, a member of the traditional pack, fits my purpose in two ways: because he is associated in my mind with the Hanged God of Frazer, and because I associate him with the hooded figure in the passage of the disciples to Emmaus in Part V. . . . The man with Three Staves (an authentic member of the Tarot pack) I associate, quite arbitrarily, with the Fisher King himself.

And perhaps he is to be taken more seriously here, when off guard in a note, than when in his Norton Lectures he comments on the difficulty of saying what a poem means and adds playfully that he thinks of prefixing to a second edition of *Ash Wednesday* some lines from *Don Juan*:

> I don't pretend that I quite understand
> My own meaning when I would be very fine;
> But the fact is that I have nothing planned
> Unless it were to be a moment merry.

If Eliot and other contemporary poets have any characteristic fault, it may be in *planning* too much.

Allusiveness in poetry is one of several critical issues by which we have illustrated the more abstract issue of intentionalism, but it may be for today the most important illustration. As a poetic practice allusiveness would appear to be in some recent poems an extreme corollary of the romantic intentionalist assumption, and as a critical issue it challenges and brings to light in a special way the basic premise of intentionalism. The following instance from the poetry of Eliot may serve to epitomize the practical implications of what we have been saying. In Eliot's "Love Song of J. Alfred Prufrock," toward the end, occurs the line: "I have heard the mermaids singing, each to each," and this bears a certain resemblance to a line in a Song by John Donne, "Teach me to heare Mermaides singing," so that for the reader acquainted to a certain degree with Donne's poetry, the critical question arises: Is Eliot's line an allusion to Donne's? Is Prufrock thinking about Donne? Is Eliot thinking about Donne? We suggest that there are two radically different ways of looking for an answer to this question. There is (1) the way of poetic analysis and exegesis, which inquires whether it makes any sense if Eliot-Prufrock *is* thinking about Donne. In an earlier part of the poem, when Prufrock asks, "Would it have been worth while, . . . To have squeezed the universe into a ball," his words take half their sadness and irony from certain energetic and passionate lines of Marvell "To His Coy Mistress." But the exegetical inquirer may wonder whether mermaids considered as "strange sights" (to hear them is in Donne's poem analogous to getting with child a mandrake root) have much to do with Prufrock's mermaids, which seem to be symbols of romance and dynamism, and which incidentally have literary authentication, if they need it, in a line of a sonnet by Gérard de Nerval. This method of inquiry may lead to the conclusion that the given resemblance between Eliot and Donne is without significance and is better not thought of, or the method may have the disadvantage of providing no certain conclusion. Nevertheless, we submit that this is the true and objective way of criticism, as contrasted to what the very uncertainty of exegesis might tempt a second kind of critic to undertake: (2) the way of biographical or genetic inquiry, in which, taking advantage of the fact that Eliot is still alive, and in the spirit of a man who would settle a bet, the critic writes to Eliot and asks what he meant, or if he had Donne in mind. We shall not here weigh the probabilities—whether Eliot would answer that he meant nothing at all, had nothing at all in mind—a sufficiently good answer to such a question—or in an unguarded moment might furnish a clear and, within its limit, irrefutable answer. Our point is that such an answer to such an inquiry would have nothing to do with the poem "Prufrock"; it would not be a critical inquiry. Critical inquiries, unlike bets, are not settled in this way. Critical inquiries are not settled by consulting the oracle.

CLEANTH BROOKS

The Heresy of Paraphrase

The ten poems that have been discussed were not selected because they happened to express a common theme or to display some particular style or to share a special set of symbols. It has proved, as a matter of fact, somewhat surprising to see how many items they do have in common: the light symbolism as used in "L'Allegro-Il Penseroso" and in the "Intimations" ode, for example; or, death as a sexual metaphor in "The Canonization" and in *The Rape of the Lock*; or the similarity of problem and theme in the "Intimations" ode and "Among School Children."

On reflection, however, it would probably warrant more surprise if these ten poems did not have much in common. For they are all poems which most of us will feel are close to the central stream of the tradition. Indeed, if there is any doubt on this point, it will have to do with only the first and last numbers of the series—poems whose relation to the tradition I shall, for reasons to be given a little later, be glad to waive. The others, it will be granted, are surely in the main stream of the tradition.

As a matter of fact, a number of the poems discussed in this book were not chosen by me but were chosen for me. But having written on these, I found that by adding a few poems I could construct a chronological series which (though it makes no pretension to being exhaustive of periods or types) would not leave seriously unrepresented any important period since Shakespeare. In filling the gaps I tried to select poems which had been held in favor in their own day and which most critics still admire. There were, for example, to be no "metaphysical" poems beyond the first exhibit and no "modern" ones other than the last. But the intervening poems were to be read as one has learned to read Donne and the moderns. One was to attempt to see, in terms of this approach, what the masterpieces had in common rather than to see how the poems of different historical periods differed—and in particular to see whether they had anything in common with the "metaphysicals" and with the moderns.

The reader will by this time have made up his mind as to whether the readings are adequate. (I use the word advisedly, for the readings do not pretend to be exhaustive, and certainly it is highly unlikely that they are not in error in one detail or another.) If the reader feels that they are seriously inadequate, then the case has been judged; for the generalizations that follow will be thoroughly vitiated by the inept handling of the particular cases on which they depend.

If, however, the reader does feel them to be adequate, it ought to be readily apparent that the common goodness which the poems share will have to be stated, not in terms of "content" or "subject matter" in the usual sense in which we use these terms, but rather in terms of structure. The "content" of the poems is various, and if we attempt to find one *quality* of content which is shared by all the poems—a "poetic" subject matter or diction or imagery—we shall find that we have merely confused the issues. For what is it to be poetic? Is the schoolroom of Yeats's poem poetic or unpoetic? Is Shakespeare's "new-borne babe/ Striding the blast" poetic whereas the idiot of his "Life is a tale tolde by an idiot" is unpoetic? If Herrick's "budding boy or girl" is poetic, then why is not that monstrosity of the newspaper's society page, the "society bud," poetic too?

To say this is not, of course, to say that all materials have precisely the same potentialities (as if the various pigments on the palette had the same potentialities, any one of them suiting the given picture as well as another). But what has been said, on the other hand, requires to be said: for, if we are to proceed at all, we must draw a sharp distinction between the attractiveness or beauty of any particular item taken as such and the "beauty" of the poem considered as a whole. The latter is the effect of a total pattern, and of a kind of pattern which can incorporate within itself items intrinsically beautiful or ugly, attractive or repulsive. Unless one asserts the primacy of the pattern, a poem becomes merely a bouquet of intrinsically beautiful items.

But though it is in terms of structure that we must describe poetry, the term "structure" is certainly not altogether satisfactory as a term. One means by it something far more internal than the metrical pattern, say, or than the sequence of images. The structure meant is certainly not "form" in the conventional sense in which we think of form as a kind of envelope which "contains" the "content." The structure obviously is everywhere conditioned by the nature of the material which goes into the poem. The nature of the material sets the problem to be solved, and the solution is the ordering of the material.

Pope's *Rape of the Lock* will illustrate: the structure is not the heroic couplet as such, or the canto arrangement; for, important as is Pope's use of the couplet as one means by which he secures the total effect, the heroic couplet can be used—has been used many times—as an instrument in securing very different effects. The structure of the poem, furthermore, is not that of the mock-epic convention, though here, since the term "mock-epic" has implications of attitude, we approach a little nearer to the kind of structure of which we speak.

The structure meant is a structure of meanings, evaluations, and interpretations; and the principle of unity which informs it seems to be one of balancing and harmonizing connotations, attitudes, and meanings. But even here one needs to make important qualifications: the principle is not one which involves the arrangement of the various elements into homogeneous groupings, pairing like with like. It unites the like with the unlike. It does not unite them, however, by the simple process of allowing one connotation to cancel out another nor does it reduce the contradictory attitudes to harmony by a process of subtraction. The unity is not a unity of the sort to be achieved by the reduction and simplification appropriate to an algebraic formula. It is a positive unity, not a negative; it represents not a residue but an achieved harmony.

The attempt to deal with a structure such as this may account for the frequent occurrence in the preceding chapters of such terms as "ambiguity," "paradox," "complex of attitudes," and—most frequent of all, and perhaps most annoying to the reader—"irony." I hasten to add that I hold no brief for these terms as such. Perhaps they are inadequate. Perhaps they are misleading. It is to be hoped in that case that we can eventually improve upon them. But adequate terms—whatever those terms may turn out to be—will certainly have to be terms which do justice to the special kind of structure which seems to emerge as the common structure of poems so diverse on other counts as are *The Rape of the Lock* and "Tears, Idle Tears."

The conventional terms are much worse than inadequate: they are positively misleading in their implication that the poem constitutes a "statement" of some sort, the statement being true or false, and expressed more or less clearly or eloquently or beautifully; for it is from this formula that most of the common heresies about poetry derive. The formula begins by introducing a dualism which thenceforward is rarely overcome, and which at best can be overcome only by the most elaborate and clumsy qualifications. Where it is not overcome, it leaves the critic lodged upon one or the other of the horns of a dilemma: the critic is forced to judge the poem by its political or scientific or philosophical truth; or, he is forced to judge the poem by its form as conceived externally and detached from human experience. Mr. Alfred Kazin, for example, to take an instance from a recent and popular book, accuses the "new formalists"—his choice of that epithet is revealing—of accepting the latter horn of the dilemma because he notices that they have refused the former. In other words, since they refuse to rank poems by their messages, he assumes that they are compelled to rank them by their formal embellishments.

The omnipresence of this dilemma, a false dilemma, I believe, will also account for the fact that so much has been made in the preceding chapters of the resistance which any good poem sets up against all attempts to paraphrase it. The point is surely not that we cannot describe adequately enough for many purposes what the poem in general is "about" and what the general effect of the poem is: *The Rape of the Lock* is *about* the foibles of an eighteenth-century belle. The effect of "Corinna's going a-Maying" is one of gaiety tempered by the poignance of the fleetingness of youth. We can very properly use paraphrases as pointers and as shorthand references provided that we know what we are doing. But it is highly important that we know what we are doing and that we see plainly that the paraphrase is not the real core of meaning which constitutes the essence of the poem.

For the imagery and the rhythm are not merely the instruments by which this fancied core-of-meaning-which-can-be-expressed-in-a-paraphrase is directly rendered. Even in the simplest poem their mediation is not positive and direct. Indeed, whatever statement we may seize upon as incorporating the "meaning" of the poem, immediately the imagery and the rhythm seem to set up tensions with it, warping and twisting it, qualifying and revising it. This is true of Wordsworth's "Ode" no less than of Donne's "Canonization." To illustrate: if we say that the "Ode" celebrates the spontaneous "naturalness" of the child, there is the poem itself to indicate that Nature has a more sinister aspect—that the process by which the poetic lamb becomes the dirty old sheep or the child racing over the meadows becomes the balding philosopher is a process that is thoroughly "natural." Or, if we say that the thesis of the "Ode" is that the child brings into the natural world a supernatural glory which acquaintance with the world eventually and inevitably quenches in the light of common day, there is the last stanza and the drastic qualifications which it asserts: it is significant that the thoughts that lie too deep for tears are mentioned in this sunset stanza of the "Ode" and that they are thoughts, not of the child, but of the man.

We have precisely the same problem if we make our example *The Rape of the Lock*. Does the poet assert that Belinda is a goddess? Or does he say that she is a brainless chit? Whichever alternative we take, there are elaborate qualifications to be made. Moreover, if the simple propositions offered seem in their forthright simplicity to make too easy the victory of the poem over any possible statement of its meaning, then let the reader try to formulate a proposition that will say what the poem "says." As his proposition approaches adequacy, he will find, not only that it has increased greatly in length, but that it has begun to fill itself up with reservations and qualifications—and most significant of all—the formulator will find that he has himself begun to fall back upon metaphors of his own in his attempt to indicate what the poem "says." In sum, his proposition, as it approaches adequacy, ceases to be a proposition.

Consider one more case, "Corinna's going a-Maying." Is the doctrine preached to Corinna throughout the first four stanzas true? Or is it damnably false? Or is it a "harmlesse follie"? Here perhaps we shall be tempted to take the last option as the saving mean—what the poem really *says*—and my account of the poem at the end of the third chapter is perhaps susceptible of this interpretation—or misinterpretation. If so, it is high time to clear the matter up. For we mistake matters grossly if we take the poem to be playing with opposed extremes, only to point the golden mean in a doctrine which, at the end, will correct the falsehood of extremes. The reconcilement of opposites which the poet characteristically makes is not that of a prudent splitting of the difference between antithetical overemphases.

It is not so in Wordsworth's poem nor in Keats's nor in Pope's. It is not so even in this poem of Herrick's. For though the poem reflects, if we read it carefully, the primacy of the Christian mores, the pressure exerted throughout the poem is upon the pagan appeal; and the poem ends, significantly, with a reiteration of the appeal to Corinna to go a-Maying, an appeal which, if qualified by the Christian view, still, in a sense, has been deepened and made more urgent by that very qualification. The imagery of loss and decay, it must be remembered, comes in this last stanza after the admission that the May-day rites are not a real religion but a "harmless follie."

If we are to get all these qualifications into our formulation of what the poem says—and they are relevant—then, our formulation of the "statement" made by Herrick's poem will turn out to be quite as difficult as that of Pope's mock-epic. The truth of the matter is that all such formulations lead away from the center of the poem—not toward it; that the "prose-sense" of the poem is not a rack on which the stuff of the poem is hung; that it does not represent the "inner" structure or the "essential" structure or the "real" structure of the poem. We may use—and in many connections must use—such formulations as more or less convenient ways of referring to parts of the poem. But such formulations are scaffoldings which we may properly for certain purposes throw about the building: we must not mistake them for the internal and essential structure of the building itself.

Indeed, one may sum up by saying that most of the distempers of criticism come about from yielding to the temptation to take certain remarks which we make *about* the poem—statements about what it says or about what truth it gives or about what formulations it illustrates—for the essential core of the poem itself. As W. M. Urban puts it in his *Language and Reality*: "The general principle of the inseparability of intuition and expression holds with special force for the aesthetic institution. Here it means that form and content, or content and medium, are inseparable. The artist does not first intuit his object and then find the appropriate medium. It is rather in and through his medium that he intuits the object." So much for the process of composition. As for the critical process: "To pass from the intuitible to the nonintuitible is to negate the function and meaning of the symbol." For it "is precisely because the more universal and ideal relations cannot be adequately expressed directly that they are indirectly expressed by means of the more intuitible." The most obvious examples of such error (and for that reason those which are really least dangerous) are those theories which frankly treat the poem as propaganda. The most subtle (and the most stubbornly rooted in the ambiguities of language) are those which, beginning with the "paraphrasable" elements of the poem, refer the other elements of the poem finally to some role subordinate to the paraphrasable elements. (The relation between all the elements must surely be an organic one—there can be no question about that. There is, however, a very serious question as to whether the paraphrasable elements have primacy.)

Mr. Winters' position will furnish perhaps the most respectable example of the paraphrastic heresy. He assigns primacy to the "rational meaning" of the poem. "The relationship, in the poem, between rational statement and feeling," he remarks in his latest book, "is thus seen to be that of motive to emotion." He goes on to illustrate his point by a brief and excellent analysis of the following lines from Browning:

> So wore night; the East was gray,
> White the broad-faced hemlock flowers. . . .

"The verb *wore*," he continues, "means literally that the night passed, but it carries with it connotations of exhaustion and attrition which belong to the condition of the protagonist; and grayness is a color which we associate with such a condition. If we change the phrase to read: 'Thus night passed,' we shall have the same rational meaning, and a meter quite as respectable, but no trace of the power of the line: the connotation of *wore* will be lost, and the connotation of *gray* will remain in a state of ineffective potentiality."

But the word *wore* does not mean *literally* "that the night passed," it means literally "that the night *wore*"—whatever *wore* may mean, and as Winters' own admirable analysis indicates, *wore* "means," whether *rationally* or *irrationally*, a great deal. Furthermore, "So wore night" and "Thus night passed" can be said to have "the same rational meaning" only if we equate "rational meaning" with the meaning of a loose paraphrase. And can a loose paraphrase be said to be the "motive to emotion"? Can it be said to "generate" the feelings in question? (Or, would Mr. Winters not have us equate "rational statement" and "rational meaning"?)

Much more is at stake here than any quibble. In view of the store which Winters sets by rationality and of his penchant for poems which make their evaluations overtly, and in view of his frequent blindness to those poems which do not—in view of these considerations, it is important to see that what "So wore night" and "Thus night passed" have in common as their "rational meaning" is not the "rational meaning" of each but the lowest common denominator of both. To refer the structure of the poem to what is finally a paraphrase of the poem is to refer it to something outside the poem.

To repeat, most of our difficulties in criticism are rooted in the heresy of paraphrase. If we allow ourselves to be misled by it, we distort the relation of the poem to its "truth," we raise the problem of belief in a vicious and crippling form, we split the poem between its "form" and its "content"—we bring the statement to be conveyed into an unreal competition with science or philosophy or theology. In short, we put our questions about the poem in a form calculated to produce the battles of the last twenty-five years over the "use of poetry."[1]

If we allow ourselves to be misled by the heresy of paraphrase, we run the risk of doing even more violence to the internal order of the poem itself. By taking the paraphrase as our point of stance, we misconceive the function of metaphor and meter. We demand logical coherences where they are sometimes irrelevant, and we fail frequently to see imaginative coherences on levels where they are highly relevant. Some of the implications of the paraphrastic heresy are so stubborn and so involved that I have thought best to relegate them to an appendix. There the reader who is interested may find further discussion of the problem and, I could hope, answers to certain misapprehensions of the positive theory to be adumbrated here.

But what would be a positive theory? We tend to embrace the doctrine of a logical structure the more readily because, to many of us, the failure to do so seems to leave the meaning of the poem hopelessly up in the air. The alternative position will appear to us to lack even the relative stability of an Ivory Tower: it is rather commitment to a free balloon. For, to deny

---

[1] I do not, of course, intend to minimize the fact that some of these battles have been highly profitable, or to imply that the foregoing paragraphs could have been written except for the illumination shed by the discussions of the last twenty-five years.

the possibility of pinning down what the poem "says" to some "statement" will seem to assert that the poem really says nothing. And to point out what has been suggested in earlier chapters and brought to a head in this one, namely, that one can never measure a poem against the scientific or philosophical yardstick for the reason that the poem when laid along the yardstick, is never the "full poem" but an abstraction from the poem —such an argument will seem to such readers a piece of barren logic-chopping—a transparent dodge.

Considerations of strategy then, if nothing more, dictate some positive account of what a poem is and does. And some positive account can be given, though I cannot promise to do more than suggest what a person is, nor will my terms turn out to be anything more than metaphors.[2]

The essential structure of a poem (as distinguished from the rational or logical structure of the "statement" which we abstract from it) resembles that of architecture or painting: it is a pattern of resolved stresses. Or, to move closer still to poetry by considering the temporal arts, the structure of a poem resembles that of a ballet or musical composition. It is a pattern of resolutions and balances and harmonizations, developed through a temporal scheme.[3]

---

[2] For those who cannot be content with metaphors (or with the particular metaphors which I can give) I recommend René Wellek's excellent "The Mode of Existence of a Literary Work of Art" (*The Southern Review*, Spring, 1942). I shall not try to reproduce here as a handy, thumb-nail definition his account of a poem as "a stratified system of norms," for the definition would be relatively meaningless without the further definitions which he assigns to the individual terms which he uses. I have made no special use of his terms in this chapter, but I believe that the generalizations about poetry outlined here can be thoroughly accommodated to the position which his essay sets forth.

[3] In recent numbers of *Accent*, two critics for whose work I have high regard have emphasized the dynamic character of poetry. Kenneth Burke argues that if we are to consider a poem as a poem, we must consider it as a "mode of action." R. P. Blackmur asks us to think of it as gesture, "the outward and dramatic play of inward and imagined meaning." I do not mean to commit either of these critics to my own interpretation of dramatic or symbolic action; and I have, on my own part, several rather important reservations with respect to Mr. Burke's position. But there are certainly large areas of agreement among our positions. The reader might also compare the account of poetic structure given in this chapter with the following passage from Susanne Langer's *Philosophy in a New Key*: ". . . though the *material* of poetry is verbal, its import is not the literal assertion made in the words, but *the way the assertion is made*, and this involves the sound, the tempo, the aura of associations of the words, the long or short sequences of ideas, the wealth or poverty of transient imagery that contains them, the sudden arrest of fantasy by pure fact, or of familiar fact by sudden fantasy, the suspense of literal meaning by a sustained ambiguity resolved in a long-awaited key-word, and the unifying, all-embracing artifice of rhythm."

Or, to move still closer to poetry, the structure of a poem resembles that of a play. This last example, of course, risks introducing once more the distracting element, since drama, like poetry, makes use of words. Yet, on the whole, most of us are less inclined to force the concept of "statement" on drama than on a lyric poem; for the very nature of drama is that of something "acted out"—something which arrives at its conclusion through conflict—something which builds conflict into its very being. The dynamic nature of drama, in short, allows us to regard it as *an action* rather than as a formula for action or as a statement about action. For this reason, therefore, perhaps the most helpful analogy by which to suggest the structure of poetry is that of the drama, and for many readers at least, the least confusing way in which to approach a poem is to think of it as a drama.

The general point, of course, is not that either poetry or drama makes no use of ideas, or that either is "merely emotional"—whatever *that* is—or that there is not the closest and most important relationship between the intellectual materials which they absorb into their structure and other elements in the structure. The relationship between the intellectual and the nonintellectual elements in a poem is actually far more intimate than the conventional accounts would represent it to be: the relationship is not that of an idea "wrapped in emotion" or a "prose-sense decorated by sensuous imagery."

The dimension in which the poem moves is not one which excludes ideas, but one which does include attitudes. The dimension includes ideas, to be sure; we can always abstract an "idea" from a poem—even from the simplest poem—even from a lyric so simple and unintellectual as

Western wind, when wilt thou blow
    That the small rain down can rain?
Christ, that my love were in my arms
    And I in my bed again!

But the idea which we abstract—assuming that we can all agree on what that idea is—will always be *abstracted:* it will always be the projection of a plane along a line or the projection of a cone upon a plane.

If this last analogy proves to be more confusing than illuminating, let us return to the analogy with drama. We have argued that any proposition asserted in a poem is not to be taken in abstraction but is justified, in terms of the poem, if it is justified at all, not by virtue of its scientific or historical or philosophical truth, but is justified in terms of a principle analogous to that of dramatic propriety. Thus, the proposition that "Beauty is truth, truth beauty" is given its precise meaning and significance by its relation to the total context of the poem.

This principle is easy enough to see when the proposition is asserted overtly in the poem—that is, when it constitutes a specific detail of the poem. But the reader may well ask: is it not possible to frame a proposition, a statement, which will adequately represent the total meaning of the poem; that is, is it not possible to elaborate a summarizing proposition which will "say," briefly and in the form of a proposition, what the poem "says" as a poem, a proposition which will say it fully and will say it exactly, no more and no less? Could not the poet, if he had chosen, have framed such a proposition? Cannot we as readers and critics frame such a proposition?

The answer must be that the poet himself obviously did not—else he would not have had to write his poem. We as readers can attempt to frame such a proposition in our effort to understand the poem; it may well help toward an understanding. Certainly, the efforts to arrive at such propositions can do no harm *if we do not mistake them for the inner core of the poem*—if we do not mistake them for "what the poem *really says*." For, if we take one of them to represent the essential poem, we have to disregard the qualifications exerted by the total context as of no account, or else we have assumed that we can reproduce the effect of the total context in a condensed prose statement.[4]

But to deny that the coherence of a poem is reflected in a logical paraphrase of its "real meaning" is not, of course, to deny coherence to poetry; it is rather to assert that its coherence is to be sought elsewhere. The characteristic unity of a poem (even of those poems which may accidentally possess a logical unity as well as this poetic unity) lies in the unification of attitudes into a hierarchy subordinated to a total and governing attitude. In the unified poem, the poet has "come to terms" with his experience.

---

[4] We may, it is true, be able to adumbrate what the poem says if we allow ourselves enough words, and if we make enough reservations and qualifications, thus attempting to come nearer to the meaning of the poem by successive approximations and refinements, gradually encompassing the meaning and pointing to the area in which it lies rather than realizing it. The earlier chapters of this book, if they are successful, are obviously illustrations of this process. But such adumbrations will lack, not only the tension—the dramatic force—of the poem; they will be at best crude approximations of the poem. Moreover—and this is the crucial point they will be compelled to resort to the methods of the poem—analogy, metaphor, symbol, etc.—in order to secure even this near an approximation.

Urban's comment upon this problem is interesting: he says that if we expand the symbol, "we lose the 'sense' or value of the symbol *as symbol*. The solution . . . seems to me to lie in an adequate theory of interpretation of the symbol. It does not consist in substituting *literal* for symbol sentences, in other words substituting 'blunt' truth for symbolic truth, but rather in deepening and enriching the meaning of the symbol."

The poem does not merely eventuate in a logical conclusion. The conclusion of the poem is the working out of the various tensions—set up by whatever means—by propositions, metaphors, symbols. The unity is achieved by a dramatic process, not a logical; it represents an equilibrium of forces, not a formula. It is "proved" as a dramatic conclusion is proved: by its ability to resolve the conflicts which have been accepted as the *données* of the drama.

Thus, it is easy to see why the relation of each item to the whole context is crucial, and why the effective and essential structure of the poem has to do with the complex of attitudes achieved. A scientific preposition can stand alone. If it is true, it is true. But the expression of an attitude, apart from the occasion which generates it and the situation which it encompasses, is meaningless. For example, the last two lines of the "Intimations" ode,

*To me the meanest flower that blows can give
Thoughts that do often lie too deep for tears,*

when taken in isolation—I do not mean quoted in isolation by one who is even vaguely acquainted with the context—makes a statement which is sentimental if taken in reference to the speaker, and one which is patent nonsense if taken with a general reference. The man in the street (of whom the average college freshman is a good enough replica) knows that the meanest flower that grows does not give *him* thoughts that lie too deep for tears; and, if he thinks about the matter at all, he is inclined to feel that the person who can make such an assertion is a very fuzzy sentimentalist.

We have already seen the ease with which the statement "Beauty is truth, truth beauty" becomes detached from its context, even in the hands of able critics; and we have seen the misconceptions that ensue when this detachment occurs. To make one more instance: the last stanza of Herrick's "Corinna," taken in isolation, would probably not impress the average reader as sentimental nonsense. Yet it would suffer quite as much by isolation from its context as would the lines from Keats's "Ode." For, as mere statement, it would become something flat and obvious—of course our lives are short! And the conclusion from the fact would turn into an obvious truism for the convinced pagan, and, for the convinced Christian, equally obvious, though damnable, nonsense.

Perhaps this is why the poet, to people interested in hard-and-fast generalizations, must always seem to be continually engaged in blurring out distinctions, effecting compromises, or, at the best, coming to his conclusions only after provoking and unnecessary delays. But this last position is merely another variant of the paraphrastic heresy: to assume it is to misconceive the end of poetry—to take its meanderings as negative, or to excuse them (with the comfortable assurance that the curved line is the line of beauty) because we can conceive the purpose of a poem to be only the production, in the end, of a proposition—of a statement.

But the meanderings of a good poem (they are meanderings only from the standpoint of the prose paraphrase of the poem) are not negative, and they do not have to be excused; and most of all, we need to see what their positive function is; for unless we can assign them a positive function, we shall find it difficult to explain why one divergence from "the prose line of the argument" is not as good as another. The truth is that the apparent irrelevancies which metrical pattern and metaphor introduce do become relevant when we realize that they function in a good poem to modify, qualify, and develop the total attitude which we are to take in coming to terms with the total situation.

If the last sentence seems to take a dangerous turn toward some special "use of poetry"—some therapeutic value for the sake of which poetry is to be cultivated—I can only say that I have in mind no special ills which poetry is to cure. Uses for poetry are always to be found, and doubtless will continue to be found. But my discussion of the structure of poetry is not being conditioned at this point by some new and special role which I expect poetry to assume in the future or some new function to which I would assign it. The structure described—a structure of "gestures" or attitudes—seems to me to describe the essential structure of both the *Odyssey* and *The Waste Land*. It seems to be the kind of structure which the ten poems considered in this book possess in common.

If the structure of poetry is a structure of the order described, that fact may explain (if not justify) the frequency with which I have had to have recourse, in the foregoing chapters, to terms like "irony" and "paradox." By using the term irony, one risks, of course, making the poem seem arch and self-conscious, since irony, for most readers of poetry, is associated with satire, *vers de société*, and other "intellectual" poetries. Yet, the necessity for some such term ought to be apparent; and irony is the most general term that we have for the kind of qualification which the various elements in a context receive from the context. This kind of qualification, as we have seen, is of tremendous importance in any poem. Moreover, irony is our most general term for indicating that recognition of incongruities—which, again, pervades all poetry to a degree far beyond what our conventional criticism has been heretofore willing to allow.

Irony in this general sense, then, is to be found in Tennyson's "Tears,

Idle Tears" as well as in Donne's "Canonization." We have, of course, been taught to expect to find irony in Pope's *Rape of the Lock*, but there is a profound irony in Keats's "Ode on a Grecian Urn"; and there is irony of a very powerful sort in Wordsworth's "Intimations" ode. For the thrusts and pressures exerted by the various symbols in this poem are not avoided by the poet: they are taken into account and played, one against the other. Indeed, the symbols—from a scientific point of view—are used perversely: it is the child who is the best philosopher; it is from a kind of darkness—from something that is "shadowy"—that the light proceeds; growth into manhood is viewed, not as an extrication from, but as an incarceration within, a prison.

There should be no mystery as to why this must be so. The terms of science are abstract symbols which do not change under the pressure of the context. They are pure (or aspire to be pure) denotations; they are defined in advance. They are not to be warped into new meanings. But where is the dictionary which contains the terms of a poem? It is a truism that the poet is continually forced to remake language. As Eliot has put it, his task is to "dislocate language into meaning." And, from the standpoint of a scientific vocabulary, this is precisely what he performs: for, rationally considered, the ideal language would contain one term for each meaning, and the relation between term and meaning would be constant. But the word, as the poet uses it, has to be conceived of, not as a discrete particle of meaning, but as a potential of meaning, a nexus or cluster of meanings.

What is true of the poet's language in detail is true of the larger wholes of poetry. And therefore, if we persist in approaching the poem as primarily a rational statement, we ought not to be surprised if the statement seems to be presented to us always in the ironic mode. When we consider the statement immersed in the poem, it presents itself to us, like the stick immersed in the pool of water, warped and bent. Indeed, whatever the statement, it will always show itself as deflected away from a positive, straightforward formulation.

It may seem perverse, however, to maintain, in the face of our revived interest in Donne, that the essential structure of poetry is not logical. For Donne has been appealed to of late as the great master of metaphor who imposes a clean logic on his images beside which the ordering of the images in Shakespeare's sonnets is fumbling and loose. It is perfectly true that Donne makes a great show of logic; but two matters need to be observed. In the first place, the elaborated and "logical" figure is not Donne's only figure or even his staple one. "Telescoped" figures like "Made one anothers hermitage" are to be found much more frequently than the celebrated comparison of the souls of the lovers to the legs of a pair of compasses. In the second place, where Donne uses "logic," he regularly uses it to justify illogical positions. He employs it to overthrow a conventional position or to "prove" an essentially illogical one.

Logic, as Donne uses it, is nearly always an ironic logic to state the claims of an idea or attitude which we have agreed, with our everyday logic, is false. This is not to say, certainly, that Donne is not justified in using his logic so, or that the best of his poems are not "proved" in the only senses in which poems can be proved.

But the proof is not a logical proof. "The Canonization" will scarcely prove to the hard-boiled naturalist that the lovers, by giving up the world, actually attain a better world. Nor will the argument advanced in the poem convince the dogmatic Christian that Donne's lovers are really saints.

In using logic, Donne as a poet is fighting the devil with fire. To adopt Robert Penn Warren's metaphor (which, though I lift it somewhat scandalously out of another context, will apply to this one): "The poet, somewhat less spectacularly [than the saint], proves his vision by submitting it to the fires of irony—to the drama of the structure—in the hope that the fires will refine it. In other words, the poet wishes to indicate that his vision has been earned, that it can survive reference to the complexities and contradictions of experience."

The same principle that inspires the presence of irony in so many of our great poems also accounts for the fact that so many of them seem to be built around paradoxes. Here again the conventional associations of the term may prejudice the reader just as the mention of Donne may prejudice him. For Donne, as one type of reader knows all too well, was of that group of poets who wished to impress their audience with their cleverness. All of us are familiar with the censure passed upon Donne and his followers by Dr. Johnson, and a great many of us still retain it as our own, softening only the rigor of it and the thoroughness of its application, but not giving it up as a principle.

Yet there are better reasons than that of rhetorical vain-glory that have induced poet after poet to choose ambiguity and paradox rather than plain, discursive simplicity. It is not enough for the poet to analyse his experience as the scientist does, breaking it up into parts, distinguishing part from part, classifying the various parts. His task is finally to unify experience. He must return to us the unity of the experience itself as man knows it in his own experience. The poem, if it be a true poem is a simulacrum of reality—in this sense, at least, it is an "imitation"—by *being* an experience rather than any mere statement about experience or any mere abstraction from experience.

Tennyson cannot be content with *saying* that in memory the poet seems both dead *and* alive; he must dramatize its life-in-death for us, and his dramatization involves, necessarily, ironic shock and wonder. The dramatization demands that the antithetical aspects of memory be coalesced into one entity which—if we take it on the level of statement—is a paradox, the assertion of the union of opposites. Keats's Urn must express a life which is above life and its vicissitudes, but it must also bear witness to the fact that its life is not life at all but is a kind of death. To put it in other terms, the Urn must, in its role as historian, assert that myth is truer than history. Donne's lovers must reject the world in order to possess the world.

Or, to take one further instance: Wordsworth's light must serve as the common symbol for aspects of man's vision which seem mutally incompatible—intuition and analytic reason. Wordsworth's poem, as a matter of fact, typifies beautifully the poet's characteristic problem itself. For even this poem, which testifies so heavily to the way in which the world is split up and parceled out under the growing light of reason, cannot rest in this fact as its own mode of perception, and still be a poem. Even after the worst has been said about man's multiple vision, the poet must somehow prove that the child is father to the man, that the dawn light is still somehow the same light as the evening light.

If the poet, then, must perforce dramatize the oneness of the experience, even though paying tribute to its diversity, then his use of paradox and ambiguity is seen as necessary. He is not simply trying to spice up, with a superficially exciting or mystifying rhetoric, the old stale stockpot (though doubtless this will be what the inferior poet does generally and what the real poet does in his lapses). He is rather giving us an insight which preserves the unity of experience and which, at its higher and more serious levels, triumphs over the apparently contradictory and conflicting elements of experience by unifying them into a new pattern.

Wordsworth's "Intimations" ode, then, is not only a poem, but, among other things, a parable about poetry. Keats's "Ode on a Grecian Urn" is quite obviously such a parable. And, indeed, most of the poems which we have discussed in this study may be taken as such parables.

In one sense, Pope's treatment of Belinda raises all the characteristic problems of poetry. For Pope, in dealing with his "goddess," must face the claims of naturalism and of common sense which would deny divinity to her. Unless he faces them, he is merely a sentimentalist. He must do an even harder thing: he must transcend the conventional and polite attributions of divinity which would be made to her as an acknowledged belle. Otherwise, he is merely trivial and obvious. He must "prove" her divinity against the common-sense denial (the brutal denial) and against the conventional assertion (the polite denial). The poetry must be wrested from the context: Belinda's lock, which is what the rude young man wants and which Belinda rather prudishly defends and which the naturalist asserts is only animal and which displays in its curled care the style of a particular era of history, must be given a place of permanence among the stars.

PHILIP WHEELWRIGHT

Poetry, Myth and Reality

Poetry suffers today from at once too high and too low an appraisal. We burden Shakespeare with flatteries which his contemporaries would have reserved for royalty or for the ancients, but there is reason to believe that modern theater audiences are insensitive to much in his plays that the rowdier but more perceptive frequenters of the Globe Theater took in as an expected part of the entertainment. Charged language, language of associative complexity, is a rarity on the stage or in the cinema today, and when it occurs it is likely to embarrass by its artiness, its rather too evident snob appeal. We read poetry as a special discipline, becoming scholarly about it or ecstatic about it according to our profession, temperament and mood, but we deprecate its intrusion into the sober business of everyday living. Poetry seems to most of us something to be set upon a pedestal and left there, like one of those chaste heroines of medieval romance, high and dry.

Why is there this impoverishment of response toward poetry in present-day society? The question may be one of the most important we can ask, for it concerns not poetry and poetic response alone, but by implication the general sickness of our contemporary world. The symptoms, though diverse, are connected; and I suspect we shall not understand why great poetry is no longer written in an age which endows innumerable lecturers to talk about poetry, unless we also understand why it is that we must let our fellow-countrymen starve in an era of productive plenty, and why as Americans we spent twenty years professing our love of peace and democracy while helping to finance dictatorships and throttle democracies on three continents, and why as Christians we think it proper to build imposing churches while treating God as something out of last year's Sunday supplement. The question of poetry's status in the present-day world is interrelated with such questions as these, and it seems to me that we cannot adequately understand any one of the questions except in a perspective that catches at least the outlines of the others. The needed perspective is to my mind a mytho-religious one, without any of the clap-trap sometimes associated with either word; for it involves a rediscovery of the original and essentially unchangeable conditions of human insight and human blessedness. The aim of this lecture is to indicate the nature of that perspective and to discover its latent presence in some of the great poetry of past times.

Suppose we represent the dimensions of human experience, very tentatively, by means of a diagram,—where the horizontal line E-P represents the dimension of secular experience, *empirical* experience as I think we may call it without redundancy; of that trafficking with things, relations and ideas that makes up our everyday commonsense world. It has two poles: outwardly there are the phenomena (P) that constitute our physical universe; these are spacelike, are interrelated by causal laws,

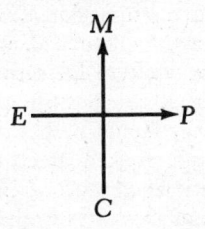

```
        M
        ↑
  E ————+————▶ P
        ↓
        C
```

and are the proper object of scientific inquiry. At the other pole of this horizontal axis stands the ego (E) which knows the phenomena—partly as a spectator and partly no doubt as a contributor to their connection and significance. The major philosophical movements of the past three centuries owe their character and their limitations to the stress, I think the undue stress, which they have put upon the horizontal axis. Descartes made the additional mistake of hypostatizing E and P, establishing the thinking self and the extended world of things over against each other as distinct substances; he "cut the universe in two with a hatchet," as Hegel said, separating it into two absolutely alien spheres, thought without extension and extension without thought: thereby settling the direction, perhaps the doom, of modern philosophy. Granted that the Cartesian bifurcation was immensely fruitful for the subsequent development of natural science, the benefit was purely one of conceptual efficiency, not of interpretive fulness. The general result was to alienate nature from man by denuding it of human significance, and thereby deprive man of his natural sense of continuity with the environing world, leaving him to face the Absolute alone. To this stark confrontation the Cartesian man brings a single talisman—pure reason, which, rightly used, can answer all questions, solve all mysteries, illumine every dark cranny in the universal scheme. All truth becomes to the unobstructed reason as clear and indubitable as the truth of an arithmetical sum. A child who performs an arithmetical sum correctly—so Descartes declares—knows the utmost, with respect to that sum, that the human mind, and by implication God's mind, can ever discover. Analogously a physicist, by confining himself to clear and distinct ideas, may come to know the utmost, with respect to any given problem, that can possibly be known;

and this would be true, on Cartesian principles, even of a psychologist or a theologian or a student of any field whatever who adhered to properly rational methods. Athene springs full-born from the head of Zeus; or to use a more modern simile, wisdom consists in a sort of klieg-light brilliance rather than in adjusting one's eyes to the chiaroscuro of the familiar world. For the familiar world—here is its essential defect to a rationalist like Descartes—has a past, it develops, is time-burdened, and draws much of its meaning from shared tradition; while to Descartes' view tradition, except so far as reason can justify it, is superstition, loyalties to the past are servile, and the philosopher should be like an architect who tears down the lovable old houses and crooked streets of a medieval town in order to erect a symmetrical city where no one can lose his way. Thus in this rationalistic philosophy of Descartes we have, close to its modern source, the deadliest of all heresies. It is the sin, or, if you prefer, the delusion, of intellectual pride, a reenactment of Adam's fall and of the building of Bab-el, and it leads in our time to the fallacy of hoping for a future without organically remembering a past, the imbecility of trying to build history out of an unhistorical present.

The influence of Descartes' dualistic rationalism has been far-flung. In subsequent philosophy, although various parts of his doctrine became modified or rejected, the Cartesian way of conceiving human experience, as an individual ego able by its own powers to know the world of phenomena confronting it, played a decisive rôle. British empiricists and positivists in particular, from Locke through Hume and Mill right down to Bertrand Russell and a majority of professional philosophers in our own day, have differed from one another not in any doubt as to the self-sufficiency of the horizontal axis of experience but in their particular ways of distinguishing or connecting or distributing the emphasis between the ego and its objects. Today the horizontal philosophy has reached its clearest and most intractable expression in the related doctrines of behaviorism, instrumentalism, and semantic positivism: behaviorism, which reduces the human mind to what can be experimentally observed of its bodily behavior; instrumentalism, which reduces the meaning of any concept to that set of experimental operations by which the denotation of the concept could be objectively shown; and semantic positivism, which aims at a one-to-one correspondence between units of language and the sets or types of objects and events which such language-units denote. These three doctrines, which may be grouped under the general name of positivistic materialism, have acquired great prestige in our time. Every honest and sane intellectual must, I believe, come to grips with them: must recognize both that they are the logically inescapable outcome and expression of our secular way of life, and that they are utterly disastrous. The only truth on this basis is experimental truth, structures built out of the common denominators of human experience; religious truth and poetic truth are dismissed as fictions, as misnomers. Religion ceases to have more than a tentative and subjective validity: it expresses the yearnings and fears and awe-struck impotence of human minds with respect to events and sequences in the external world which up to a given stage of human development have eluded scientific explanation and experimental control. Poetry, likewise, has no truth-value that is distinctive to it as poetry. It contains, on the one hand, a "subject" (in Matthew Arnold's sense), a "scenario," a literal meaning, which could be expressed without essential loss in the language of science; and beyond this there is only the pleasurable decoration and emotional heightening which the form and evocative language of the poem bestows. The poet is not in any sense a seer or a prophet; he is simply, in the jargon of advertising, an effective layout man. Science has thus become the Great Dictator, to whom the spiritual republics of religion and poetry are yielding up their autonomy in bloodless defeat. There is no help for it within the purely horizontal perspective of human experience: if we see the world only as patterns of phenomena, our wisdom will be confined to such truths as phenomena can furnish. And this situation is very barren and very unpromising, not only for religion and for poetry, but for expanding love and the sense of *radical significance* which are at the root of both.

Now my belief is that the problem as posited exclusively in terms of the horizontal consciousness is an unnatural problem, an intellectual monstrosity which leads away from, rather than toward, the greater and more enduring truths. No genuine religious teacher, and with the lone exception of Lucretius no great poet, has ever sought truth in exclusively empirical terms; and I must say I find deeper truths, richer and more relevant truths, in the mysticism of Lao-tse and Jesus, in the dramatic suggestiveness of Aeschylus and Shakespeare, than in the impersonal experiments of scientists or the voluminous literalism of scholars. How then are we to validate, and in what terms are we to discuss, the trans-empirical factor in truth which is presupposed in all religion and in all the profounder sort of poetry?

The thing required of us, I believe, if we are to escape the blind alley of empirical positivism, is a proper understanding of myth, and of mythical consciousness. It is the habit of secular thought to dismiss myth either as pure fiction, a set of fairy-tales with which the human race in childhood frittered away its time; or else as allegory—that is, as a roundabout and inexact way of expressing truths about physical and human nature which could be expressed just as pertinently and much more accurately by the language of science. On either interpretation myth becomes regarded as an archaism, a barren survival, with no function of its own which cannot be served more efficiently by more up-to-date language and methods; a kind of fiction that should be renounced as completely as possible by the serious truth-seeker. What I want to stress is that this secular, positivistic attitude toward myth appears to me quite inadequate to explain the facts—I mean, of course, the salient, the really interesting aspect of the facts. It ignores or deprecates that haunting awareness of transcendental forces peering through the cracks of the visible universe, that is the very essence of myth. It blandly overlooks the possibility, which to Aeschylus, Dante, Shakespeare and many others was an axiom of assured faith, that myth may have a non-exchangeable semantic function of its own—that myth may express visions of truth to which the procedures of the scientist are grossly irrelevant; that the mythical consciousness, in short, (to exploit a convenient mathematical metaphor) may be a dimension of experience cutting across the empirical dimension as an independent variable.

In the foregoing diagram I have represented the mythico-religious dimension of human experience by a vertical line C-M cutting across the horizontal axis E-P.

C represents the community mind, which is to myth more or less what the individual mind is to science; and the upper pole M represents Mystery, of which the community mind is darkly aware. Thus the semantic arrow points from C to M, as it points from E to P. This double relation should not be conceived too rigidly: scientific truth is admittedly established by some degree of social cooperation, and mythical truth is apprehended and given form by individuals. Nevertheless the distinction is basically sound. Myth is the expression of a profound sense of togetherness—a togetherness not merely upon the plane of intellect, as is primarily the case among fellow-scientists, but a togetherness of feeling and of action and of wholeness of living. Such togetherness must have, moreover, a history. Community mind is nothing so sporadic as the mass mind of a modern lynching party or a wave of war hysteria, nor even is it found to any considerable degree in a trade union. In such manifestations as these the collective mind possesses little or no significant pattern, for it has had no time to mature. It creates not myths but merely ideologies—an ideology being a sort of parvenu myth which expresses not the interests of the group as a cooperative organism but the interests of each member of the group reflected and repeated in each other member: to this extent it lacks also a transcendental reference. A mass cannot create myths, for it has had no real history. Myths are the expression of a community mind which has enjoyed long natural growth, so that the sense of togetherness becomes patterned and semantically significant. A patterned sense of togetherness develops its proper rhythms in cremony and prayer, dance and song; and just as the micro-rhythms of the eye project themselves as a visible world of trees and stones, and as the micro-rhythms of the ear project themselves as an audible world of outer sounds, so the larger rhythms of community life project themselves as a sense of enveloping Mystery. In cultures where the mythico-religious consciousness has developed freely, this sense of mystery tinges all cognition: whether called *mana* as by the Melanesians, or *wakonda* as by the Sioux Indians, or *brahma* as by the early Aryan invaders of India, there is felt to be a mysterious Other, a spirit or breath in the world, which is more real, more awful, and in the higher religions more reverenceable than the visible and obvious particulars of experience, while at the same time it may manifest or embody itself in persons, things, words and acts in unforeseeable ways. Sometimes this basic Mystery becomes dispersed and personified into a polytheism of gods and daemons, sometimes concentrated and exalted into a single majestic God. Whatever its eventual form, it appears to express on the one hand man's primordial way of knowing, before the individual has separated himself with clear critical awareness from the group; and on the other hand an indispensable element in the cognitive activity of every vital culture, primitive or civilized. What I am arguing, in short, is not merely that the consciousness which arises from group-life and group-memories is the original matrix of individual consciousness—that much is a sociological truism—but that when the consciousness of individuals separates itself too utterly from the sustaining warmth of the common myth-consciousness, the dissociated consciousness becomes in time unoriented and sterile, fit for neither great poetry nor great wisdom nor great deeds.

What concerns the student of poetry most directly is the relation of myth to speech, the characteristic forms in which the mythical consciousness finds utterance. Shelley declared truly that "in the infancy of society every author is a poet, because language itself is poetry"; and, we may add, the reason why primitive language is poetry lies in the fact that it is the spontaneous expression of a consciousness so largely, in our sense, mythical. There are two outstanding respects in which primitive language, and especially spoken language, tends to be poetic, or at any rate to have a natural kinship with poetry: first, in its manner of utterance, its rhythms and euphonies; second, in its manner of reference, in the delicacy and associative fulness with which it refers to various aspects of the all-encompassing Mystery. In short, primitive speech—for I am dealing here with language that is meant to be spoken—employs both rhythm and metaphor. The reasons for the possession of these characteristics by primitive speech are doubtless clear from the foregoing description of the mythical consciousness. Primitive speech is a more direct expression of the community mind than speech that has grown sophisticated, and rhythm is the vehicle by which the sense of community is projected and carried through time. Rhythm has furthermore a magical function: for since the primitive community mind is not limited to a society of actual living persons but embraces also the ghosts of ancestors and the souls of things in the environing world, the rhythms of gesture and speech are felt to include and to exert a binding effect not only upon men but, when conducted under auspicious conditions, upon ghosts, gods, and nature; which is the essence of magic. Such language thus possesses a naturally evocative quality: it is felt as having a tendency to endow the world with the qualities which it declares to be there. The metaphorical character of primitive language, on the other hand, consists in its tendency to be rather manifoldly allusive: it can be so, because of the varied associations with which communication within a closed society has gradually become charged; and it has a semantic necessity of being so, because only in language having multiple reference can the full, manifold, and paradoxical character of the primordial Mystery find fit expression. Owing to such referential plenitude the language of primitives tends to employ paradox freely: it makes use of statements contradicting each other and of statements contradicting an experientially accepted situation; for the Mystery which it tries to express cannot be narrowed down to logical categories.

The island of Fiji furnishes a particularly interesting illustration of uses to which primitive poetry can be put. When a Fijian dies, the legend is that his ghost spends three days traversing the fifty-mile path that leads from the principal Fijian city to the sacred mountain Naukavadra, situated on the western coast of the isle. This mountain has a ledge overlooking the sea, called Nai-thombo-thombo, "the jumping-off place," from which the departing ghost hurls itself down and swims to a distant paradise beyond the sunset, where it rejoins its ancestors. Before the final immersion, however, the ghost on arriving at the sacred mountain is received hospitably in a cave by the ghosts of ancient hero-ancestors, guardians of the tribe's morality and well-being. After a feast, partly cannibal, has been eaten in common and ancient tribal lays have been sung, the newcomer finds his spiritual eyes awakened, and realizing for the first time that death has befallen him he is overwhelmed with grief. To the accompaniment of native instruments, addressing the ancestors he chants these words:

> My Lords! In evil fashion are we buried,
> Buried staring up into heaven,
> We see the scud flying over the sky,
> We are worn out with the feet tramping on us.
>
> Our ribs, the rafters of our house, are torn asunder,
> The eyes with which we gazed on one another are destroyed,
> The nose with which we kissed has fallen in,
> The breast with which we embraced is ruined,
> The mouth with which we laughed at one another has decayed,
> The teeth with which we bit have showered down.
> Gone is the hand that threw the tinka stick.
> The testes have rolled away.
>
> Hark to the lament of the mosquito!
> It is well that he should die and pass onward.
> But alas for my ear that he has devoured.
>
> Hark to the lament of the fly!
> It is well that he should die and pass onward.
> But alas! he has stolen the eye from which I drank.
>
> Hark to the lament of the black ant!
> It is well that he should die and pass onward.
> But alas for my whale's-tooth[1] that he has devoured.

The dead man's meeting with the ancestors takes place on the third day after death, and is followed by the leap into the sea and the passage over into the afterworld. Thus far we are in the realm of myth. Parallel to the myth-pattern is a behavior-pattern which is traditional with the survivors. On the third day they bury the now putrefying corpse, and while doing so they chant ceremonially the same songs that the dead man hears and sings in the cave at Mt. Naukavadra. Evidently the cause-effect relation involved is complex. Sociological analysis will regard the belief as a fictional projection which has the function of explaining and justifying the tribal burial processes; while to the survivors, on the other hand, the matter appears in reverse, their ceremonies being designed to annotate,

---

[1] Whale's-tooth: the phallus; also used (in its literal sense) as a symbol of wealth and medium of exchange.

and by imitative magic to assist, the dead one's situation. In any case the dirge I have just quoted serves by its strongly marked rhythms, inescapable even in translation, to establish a sense of widened community, whereby, for the duration of the ceremony at least, the chanting survivors, the recently deceased, and the ancient ancestor-gods are brought into a strongly felt and tersely articulated togetherness. Such expressions of a widened community-sense, paced in the tribal calendar according to the occurrence of emotionally significant events like births and deaths, puberty, marriage, and war, are the most vitalizing forces in tribal cultural life.

In ancient Egypt a similar phenomenon was current, although in Egyptian death chants the magical elements is more explicit. The Pyramid Texts—those ancient inscriptions dating from the fourth millennium B.C. which are found on the inner walls of the pyramid tombs—are records of the royal chants by which bands of faithful subjects, led ceremonially by the high priests, helped the Pharaoh whom they were burying there to secure immortal divinity. Here, in part, is one of the noblest of these texts:

The flier flies from earth to sky.
Upward he soars like a heron,
Upward he leaps like a grasshopper,
Kissing the sky like a hawk.

Crowned with the headdress of the sun god,
Wearing the hawk's plumage,
Upward he flies to join his brothers the gods.
Joyously we behold him.

Now we give back your heart, Osiris.
Now we give back your feet, Osiris.
Now we give back your arms, Osiris.

Flying aloft like a bird,
He settles down like a beetle
On a seat in the ship of the sun-god.
Now he rows your ship across the sky, O Glowing One!

Now he brings your ship to land, O Glowing One!
And when again you ascend out of the horizon,
He will be there with staff in hand,
The navigator of your ship, O Glowing One!

The primordial gods, the ancient nine, are dazzled,
The Lords of Forms are shaken with terror
As he breaks the metallic sky asunder.
Older than the Great One, he issues commands.
Eternity is set before him,
Discernment is placed at his feet,
The horizon is given to his keeping.

The sky is darkened, the stars rain down,
The bones of the earth-god tremble
When this one steps forth as a god
Devouring his fathers and mothers,
With the sacred serpents on his forehead.

Men and gods he devours.
His sky-dwelling servants prepare the cooking-pots,
Wiping them out with the legs of their women.
The gods are cooked for him piece by piece
In the cooking-pots of the sky at evening.

Cracking the backbones he eats the spinal marrow,
He swallows the hearts and lungs of the Wise Ones.
Their wisdom and their strength has passed into his belly.
Their godhood is within him.

The community-sense expressed in this hymn has a definite but again complex pattern. On the plane of earthly actuality the celebrants feel their union in a shared joy at the heavenly prowess of their dead king. On the transcendental plane, the plane of myth, there is another sort of union—an identification of the dead king with Osiris, god of periodic and perpetual rebirth, and with Ra the sun god. Although a reverent distinction is observed between the worshippers and the "Osirified One," the exalted king-god whose deification they celebrate, nevertheless the surviving community enjoys a vicarious participation in godhood, since the Pharaoh is felt to be still the worshippers' representative and the symbol of their communal solidarity as he had been on earth. That sense of mystical community, in Egypt as elsewhere, found its natural expression in a type of poetry characterized by marked rhythms and transcendental imagery, which are the esthetic correlates of the lower and upper poles of myth-consciousness.

Thus the logic of myth proceeds on different assumptions from the logic of science and of secular realism, and moves by different laws.

Attempts to deal with myth by the methods of science fall inevitably short of the mark. While objective methods of inquiry can trace the occasions of myth, the conditions under which it may flourish, they are quite incapable of understanding the mythical consciousness itself. For science and myth are basically incommensurate ways of experiencing, and science cannot "explain" myth without explaining it away. Its explanations are not interpretive but pragmatically reductive. The questions which science poses about myth are never quite relevant, for the questions essential to myth are patterned on a different syntax. Always in scientific thinking there is the implicit assumption of an "either-or" situation. Is the Pharaoh identical with Osiris after death or is he not? If so, and if all the Pharaohs who ruled before him share the identity, it follows (by the logic of science) that they must be identical with each other; and in that case why are they buried and worshipped individually? Moreover, if identification with Osiris is the soul's final attainment, as the Pyramid Texts indicate, why is the corpse mummified as if to preserve symbolically, and perhaps magically, just this individual to whom the body had once belonged? Such questions as these do not admit of any logically clear answer, and it is important for the understanding both of myth and of poetry to see why they do not. Science seeks clarity of an outward, publicly recognizable kind; it can regard mysteries as but materials for its particular techniques of clarification. By scientific logic a thing is either A or B and not both; or, if both, its double character must mean either that the thing is complex and can be dissociated into A and B as its elements, or else that A and B share a common quality K which with sufficient care is susceptible of exact description. The tendency of science is always to think in terms of mechanical models—structures analyzable into parts which, added up, remake the originals. Mechanical operations do work in that way, but wholeness of experience does not, and myth is an expression of whole experiences that whole men have known and felt.

Passing from primitive poetry to the poetry of more civilized eras, we find that while a greater proportion of the poem is contributed by the genius of some individual poet, yet in those poems which carry the signature of greatness, myth still plays a prominent and usually a more deliberate role. Myth is invaluable to the poet, furnishing as it does a background of familiar reference by which the sensibilities of the poet and his readers are oriented and so brought into profounder communication than would otherwise have been possible. The ways in which myth is poetically employed, and the effects gained by its employment, depend not only upon the artistry of the individual poet but also upon the general attitude toward myth in the age in which he has the good or bad luck to be born. He may be born, like Aeschylus or Dante, in a period when a substantial body of myths enjoys wide acceptance as literally true: his greatest poems in such case will be poetic intensifications and elaborations of some of those myths. He may be born, like Virgil or Shakespeare, at a time when a more sophisticated attitude toward myths is beginning to set in but before it has made such headway as to drain the myths of all vitality: the poet will then employ his myths thematically, breaking them up and redistributing their elements as may best suit his esthetic purpose. Or he may be born, finally, in an age like our own, in the late afternoon of a culture, when the myths that once moved men to great deeds now survive as antiquarian curiosities: such a poet will feel himself to be living in a cultural wasteland, his materials will be fragmentary and unpromising, and while he may prove an ingenious renovator of ruined monuments or a resourceful practitioner of metajournalism, his contribution as a poet—the contribution of a whole man who speaks powerfully to whole men—will be small.

Aeschylus, the first great dramatic poet of the West, exemplifies the early condition of civilized poetry in its relation to myth. In his time the chorus of dancing priests, which probably stemmed from ancient religious rituals associated with Dionysus and the grain-goddess Demeter, had become partly secularized, until, although the religious background was still a vital part of the whole show and amply familiar to the playgoing Greeks, the predominant purpose of the great dramatic festivals had insensibly slipped from worship to entertainment. The spectators, who in an earlier age had no doubt participated in the ritualistic dance, were now become relatively immunized: their function is to sit still and at proper times to applaud and perhaps even to chant in unison some of the choric refrains—a practice apparently indicated by the closing exhortation of *The Eumenides*. But atavistically they are still religious celebrants, being led in their observances by the band of rhythmically chanting priests, which has now become the tragic chorus; their emotions pulsate synchronically with those which the chorus expresses by word and gesture, and their acceptance of the dramatic situations which unfold themselves is largely governed by this dramatic communion.

The characteristic problem of Aeschylean drama is human guilt and its consequences. In the Greek mind two conceptions of destiny and of guilt interplayed: the Olympian and the chthonic. According to the former conception man's cardinal guilt was *hybris*, pride, which consisted in trying to overstep the boundary that separated man's ordained lot from that of the blessed and deathless gods, while virtue consisted in observing due measure, remaining loyal to one's destined station in life, and especially to one's condition of earthbound mortal manhood. The Olympian conception was thus at bottom *spacelike*, a matter of observing boundaries, limits and middle paths: indeed, in Hesiod's *Works and Days* it is particularized, in what may have been its original form, as an admonition to till one's own soil and not trespass on one's neighbor's. The chthonic conception, on the other hand, related guilt to the earth (*chthôn*), which became infectiously polluted when innocent blood was spilled, and to the vengeful ancestor ghosts who, living within the earth, were offended by actions that weakened the power and prestige, or violated the moral code, of the tribe or nation to which they still in a manner belonged. Thus the ghost of King Darius, in *The Persians*, returns from the underworld to berate his royal son for leading the Persian host into a disastrous war; and thus too the three Furies (originally snakes and still wearing snaky locks at the beginning of *The Eumenides*) haunt Orestes for his crime of matricide; and thus again in Sophocles' *Oedipus Rex* a plague has fallen on the land and cannot be removed until the unwitting murder and incest have been brought to light and expiated. In all these cases the dominant motif is the rhythmic succession of guilt and expiation, which at once expresses the ingrained Greek sense of a rhythmically pulsating nature in which moral qualities like physical ones undergo seasonal alteration, while at the same time it provides a forceful and intelligible form into which tragic drama can be moulded. There is a clear sense, therefore, in which the chthonic conception of guilt tends to be *timelike*, a matter of working out the patterned destiny of an individual or family or city or nation.

Clearly the chthonic conception of destiny lends itself to representation most readily through the time-charged medium of tragic drama, the Olympian conception through the relatively static medium of the epic. The distinction is a shifting one, however: in the sculpturally conceived *Prometheus Bound* the Olympian conception appears to predominate, while in that one great surviving trilogy, the *Oresteia*, the chthonic theme of guilt and retribution is intertwined with Olympian imagery, until in the end both elements are sublimated in a magnificent patriotic finale, by which the dramatic community-sense is explicitly secularized. Nevertheless it is worth noting that in the *Oresteia*, which without much dispute may stand as his greatest work, Aeschylus is more respectful and attaches greater dramatic and moral importance to chthonic than to Olympian ideas. He dismisses gravely the Olympian myth that the gods envy human prosperity, while the chthonic myth of the inheritance of guilt haunts him right through to the end, and motivates the long tortured struggle that constitutes the three dramas. Again, in the final play of the trilogy, although Apollo is strangely ridiculed, the Furies are treated with exaggerated respect, as powers who must be placated and even reverenced since they are the life-germ of Athenian moral and political life. All in all, the time-myth, as Nietzsche's *The Birth of Tragedy* explosively demonstrates, is at the core of Greek as of every other vital culture, and when its rhythms become weakened or vulgarized the culture grows senile.

Magic, which has played so large and so explicit a rôle in primitive poetry, appears in Aeschylean drama in sublimated form. For what is magic but operation through a direct emotional congruence established between the operator and his object? The dramatist no longer operates like the primitive magician upon gods and daemons and unnamed mysterious forces of the outer world. His magic is turned, at least to a very large degree, upon the responsive feelings of his audience. We still speak today of a dramatist's "magic," but the compliment is usually vapid. In Greek tragedy the word was applicable more literally, as through the medium of rhythmic chants with musical and choreographic accompaniment, behind which lay the common heritage of mythological background that found stylized expression in plot and imagery, the vast throng that packed the City Dionysia was brought for a few hours into significant emotional unity. Aristotle has noted the katharsis of pity and terror which takes place on such occasions, but they do not exhaust the emotional effect. Deeper than they and deeper than any conscious recognition is the communally felt, ceremonially induced emotion of religious awe, by which the Greek spectators in a miraculous bubble of time are caught up and momentarily identified with the transcendental forces that envelop them and impregnate their culture.

Shakespeare was of course a more eclectic mythologer. As a master-dramatist he could adapt expertly to poetic and dramatic uses the myths that colored the popular consciousness of his time. And yet there is in Shakespeare's mythical consciousness a deep-lying unity, which becomes gradually visible as we trace in their varied expressions what I suggest are the two Shakespearean key-myths—the myth of love and the myth of divine and earthly governance. Every play that Shakespeare wrote shows a large concern with one or the other and usually both of these themes—if not in plot, at least in imagery and allusion.

The love myth enjoys a varied and imagistically colored career in its earlier expressions—*Venus and Adonis*, the Sonnets, such comedies as *Love's Labour's Lost*, and culminating in *Romeo and Juliet*. Love, as represented here, although often strikingly realistic—

> *He wrings her nose, he strikes her on the cheeks,*
> *He bends her fingers, holds her pulses hard, . . .*

is much more than a transient phenomenon of human experience. Unlike the anarchy of lust, love is a harmony, a sweet concord, a transcendently heard music; and Venus' consuming passion for Adonis strikes the reader as sufficiently redeemed and justified by its harmonization with the universal passion that throbs through nature. Venus' desire, allied by pedigree with the high concerns of the gods, becomes merged in the poem with such natural manifestations as the strong-necked stallion who breaks rein on espying a young breeding mare:

> *Imperiously he leaps, he neighs, he bounds,*
> *And now his woven girths he breaks asunder;*
> *The bearing earth with his hard hoof he wounds,*
> *Whose hollow womb resounds like heaven's thunder;*
> *   The iron bit he crusheth 'tween his teeth,*
> *   Controlling what he was controlled with.*
>
> *His ears up-prick'd; his braided hanging mane*
> *Upon his compass'd crest now stand on end;*
> *His nostrils drink the air, and forth again,*
> *As from a furnace, vapors doth he send;*
> *   His eye, which scornfully glisters like fire,*
> *   Shows his hot courage and his high desire.*

The sexual and procreative imagery of these stanzas needs no underlining. But the important thing is that love and procreation are joined—here by imagery as later, in the Sonnets, by explicit statement:

> *And nothing 'gainst Time's scythe can make defence*
> *Save breed, to brave him when he takes thee hence.*

This couplet introduces the villain of the love-myth: Time, who devours like a cormorant all of this present breath's endeavors. Or rather, all save one. For through the medium of art man can rise above his mortal existence, and making himself the heir of all eternity can bate the scythe's keen edge.

> *Yet do thy worst, old Time; despite thy wrong,*
> *My love shall in my verse ever live young.*

Poetry and music uphold the immortality of love in all Shakespeare's plays; love's frailty or perversion is announced by jangling discordant rhythms, with the frequent imagistic accompaniment of tempests as indicative of discord in nature.

The myth of universal governance, divine and earthly, has its double source in Christianity and in Elizabethan patriotic consciousness; like the love-myth it expresses a harmony that joins mankind with divinity and with ordered nature.

> *The heavens themselves, the planets, and this center*
> *Observe degree, priority, and place.*
> *. . . But when the planets*
> *In evil mixture to disorder wander,*
> *What plagues and what portents! what mutiny!*
> *What raging of the sea! shaking of earth!*
> *Commotion in the winds! Frights, changes, horrors,*
> *Divert and crack, rend and deracinate*
> *The unity and married calm of states*
> *Quite from their fixture.*

These plagues and portents, tempests and deracinations, symbolize the inverse side of the governance-myth: they accompany—at first in verbal imagery, then later in actual stage-presentation—not only the regicide of a Caesar and a Duncan, but the insurrections of man's inner state which are always the most crucial motivation of Shakespearean tragedy. The myth of governance affirms "degree, priority and place" at once in the political order, in nature, in the soul of man, and in the divine government of the world; now one, now another of these aspects is given foremost emphasis, and at times the last of them is denied, according to the contextual requirements of the individual drama. But in the king-god imagery of *Richard II*, in the allegorical overtones of *Measure for Measure* and *The Tempest*, in the demonology of *Macbeth*, and most subtly of all in the tragic katharsis of *King Lear*, the unity is reaffirmed: earthly and divine government, the order of nature, and the nobility of man are brought again and again into symbolic and always somewhat incomplete identification.

Running through and giving form to the other mythical material, there is, in the greater achievements of Shakespeare, the myth of tragedy itself. This myth, which attains increasingly full realization in Shakespeare's successive experiments with tragedy up to and including *Lear*, finally receives brief explicit utterance in Edmund's cry:

> *The wheel is come full circle; I am here.*

We today have lost this sense of cyclical fulness and therewith of transcendental significance in human affairs; accordingly we no longer produce great tragedy, because we no longer believe in the tragic myth. In its place we have substituted the shabbier myth of comedy, which Shakespeare utilized for a time and then, when it had lost its power to move him dramatically, unleashed his contempt by expressing it as the title of one of his worst and weakest plays, "All's Well That Ends Well." This wretched quarter-truth is exploited in most of the novels and nearly all of the movies of our day—no longer as healthy comedy merely, but decked out with false sentimentality in the trappings that once belonged to tragedy. Our failure in tragic intuition, our substitution for it of bathos and business practicality in loose-wedded conjunction, is not least among the disastrous factors of the contemporary world.

These considerations of the rôle of myth in great poetry of the past may throw some light upon the predicament of the poet and the unpromising estate of poetry in our non-mythological present. The poet of today—and by that I mean the poetic impetus in all of us today—is profoundly inhibited by the dearth of shared consciousness of myth. Our current motivating ideas are not myths but ideologies, lacking transcendental significance. This loss of myth-consciousness I believe to be the most devastating loss that humanity can suffer; for as I have argued, myth-consciousness is the bond that unites men both with one another and with the unplumbed Mystery from which mankind is sprung and without reference to which the radical significance of things goes to pot. Now a world bereft of radical significance is not long tolerated; it leaves men radically unstable, so that they will seize at any myth or pseudo-myth that is offered. There have been ages of scepticism in the past, and they have always succumbed in time to new periods of belief, sometimes of violent fanaticism. It appears to me historically probable that whether we like it or not, our own present philosophy of liberal democratic scepticism will be succeeded within the next generation, perhaps sooner, by a recrudescence of myth-consciousness in America, although we can only dimly foresee what form that consciousness will take. Probably it will include a strong consciousness of America and the American destiny, but the important question is whether it will include something more— whether America will become a genuine symbol or merely a dogma. The myth of the nation must be shot through with a larger, transcendent mythological consciousness, or it lacks sanctity and in the long run will not satisfy the deeper human cravings. But we have to reckon with the possibility that this development will not take place at once. History does serve human needs, but not on the table d'hote plan; the preparations are slow and we have to expect a certain amount of bungling in the kitchen. Perhaps our immediate prospect is one of darkness, and waiting, and wholesale liquidation of much that has seemed indispensable to us, spiritual as well as material. We do not know what is to come; we can only try to learn what we must do. I suspect we must be like starving men who keep a little from their meager store to plant it in the ground for a future crop. The poetry of our time doesn't matter much, it is a last echo of something important that was alive long ago. What matters is the myth-consciousness of the next generations, the spiritual seed that we plant in our children; their loves and insights and incubating sense of significant community. On that depend the possibilities of future greatness—in poetry and in everything else.

Literature and Psychology

I must begin by explaining a drastic simplification of my topic. Despite the fact that psychoanalysis has weaker empirical credentials than the experimental schools that prevail in American universities, "psychology" will here be contracted to mean psychoanalysis. There are several reasons for this, beyond a wish to avoid the spirit of meandering tourism. Psychoanalysis is the only psychology to have seriously altered our way of reading literature, and this alteration is little understood by the affected parties. To dwell at length on the possible literary implications of physiological psychology, of perception and cognition psychology, or of learning theory would be to say more than the psychologists themselves have been able to say. Even Gestalt psychology, which does promise enlightenment about the perception of artistic form, has told us virtually nothing about literature. We must give our attention here to those who have claimed it.

The historical prominence of psychoanalysis in literary studies is readily understandable. Literature is written from and about motives, and psychoanalysis is the only thoroughgoing theory of motives that mankind has devised. The moment we perceive that works of art can express emotional conflict, or that they contain latent themes, or that their effect on us is largely subliminal, we have entered the realm of interest that is uniquely occupied by Freudianism and its offshoots. The psychoanalyst offers us, with a presumption we are likely to resent, a view of the writer's innermost preoccupations, a technique for exposing those preoccupations behind the defenses erected against them, and a dynamic explanation of how the literary work is received and judged. It is not merely that literature illustrates psychoanalytic ideas, as it does the ideas of other systems, but that the psychoanalyst alone undertakes to find motives for every rendered detail.

Needless to say, literary people have been anxious to debate the validity of such awesome claims. Much of the debate, however, has been acrimonious and irrelevant, thanks partly to the embarrassing subject matter of psychoanalysis and partly to professional rivalry. The traditional critic sees the analyst as an uninvited guest whose muddy boots will smudge the figure in the carpet; the analyst pities the critic his inhibitions and offers him sexual enlightenment free of charge. And both of them frequently speak of psychoanalysis as if it were contained in the personality and tastes of its founder, who still evokes obedience or hostility nearly three decades after his death. If we are to do any better here, it might be well to review the nature of Freud's interest in literature and make a sharp distinction between this interest and the independent possibilities of psychoanalysis in the hands of a literary critic.

We may say that literary people have taken offense at both the special presumptions and the special successes of Freud. Profoundly influenced though he was by Sophocles, Shakespeare, Dostoevsky, and Ibsen, Freud had little patience with what we like to call the integrity of the work of art. The work, in Philip Rieff's explanation, "is something to see through; it is presumably best explained by something other than—even contradicting —itself. Every work of art is to Freud a museum piece of the unconscious, an occasion to contemplate the unconscious frozen into one of its possible gestures."

Thus Freud was interested not in art but in the latent meaning of art, and then only for illustrative purposes. Like dreams, myths, and fairy tales, works of art supplied useful evidence of the primordial and monotonous fantasies of mankind, and of the processes of condensation, displacement, and symbolism through which those fantasies are both expressed and disguised. Such an emphasis is insulting to the artist, who *thought* he knew what he meant to say, and to the moral or formal critic, who prefers to dwell on what Freud regards as peripheral "manifest content" and "secondary elaboration." And the insult is compounded by its success. We may assume that if Freud had been wholly mistaken in his notion of buried themes, he would long since have ceased to provoke defenders of literary tradition into outbursts against "reductionism," "pan-sexualism," and "psychoanalyzing the dead."

Freud's challenge to the creator and the lover of literature is not contained merely in his undermining of surface effects and stated intentions. The artist, Freud tells us, has "an introverted disposition and has not far to go to become neurotic. He is one who is urged on by instinctual needs which are too clamorous; he longs to attain to honour, power, riches, fame, and the love of women; but he lacks the means of achieving these gratifications. So . . . he turns away from reality and transfers all his interest, and all his libido too, on to the creation of his wishes in the life of phantasy, from which the way might readily lead to neurosis." If, as an heir of the Romantic movement, Freud sometimes credited art with visionary truth, as a bourgeois, a scientist, and a utilitarian he suspected it of unreality and evasion.

Thus the literary critic is not altogether wrong in seeing Freud as a disrespectful intruder. Yet to move from perceiving this to denying the relevance of dynamic psychology to criticism is, to say the least, a hasty step. We are free to use Freud's interpretive techniques without endorsing his competitive and ambivalent remarks about artists. Post-Freudian psychoanalysis, furthermore, offers theoretical grounds for taking the consciously "adaptive" aspects of literature more seriously than Freud did, and Freud's own views lead us beyond the static "museum piece" criticism he usually practiced. Tempting as it is to dispose of a complex and disturbing subject by means of *ad hominem* ridicule, such a method of argument is unworthy of scholars.

Everything hinges on whether psychoanalysis gives a true or sufficiently inclusive account of mental processes—a question that obviously cannot be settled here. Certainly it would be futile to cajole the reader who has decided that his own common sense is psychology enough. Yet most literary students, I feel, are of two minds about psychoanalysis; they may be impressed by its wide acceptance but reluctant to undertake an arduous and confusing course of reading. To justify this reluctance they vaguely entertain some of the many persisting grievances against psychoanalysis and psychoanalytic criticism. In order to put the matter on more rational grounds I propose to review the most common of these grievances and ask whether they do in fact warrant the theoretical neglect of a field which has already influenced our critical practice—often, to be sure, in a surreptitious or ignorantly popularized way. Before turning to literary applications I shall deal with prevalent objections to psychoanalysis as a body of knowledge:

1. *Being unverified and unverifiable by experiment, psychoanalysis cannot be called a science at all. It is simply a technique of therapy, or a system of metaphors.*

It is the nature of all experiments that variables be kept to a minimum and that the path of inference from effect to cause be fairly direct. Any theory of complex and dynamic mental acts, and especially one that includes an idea of unconscious "overdetermination," must therefore remain largely unverified by experiment. Yet it is questionable whether this is a telling point against psychoanalysis. The psychological school which most insists on laboratory verification, namely Behaviorism, has necessarily confined most of its researches to animals and to relatively simple problems of stimulus and response. The gain in verifiability is achieved at the cost of never approaching the complexity of uniquely human motives.

In any case it is incorrect to say that psychoanalysis remains wholly unverified. Certain of its aspects *have* been tested by experiment, and have withstood as much scrutiny as experiment could cast on them. Despite some overpublicized defections, furthermore, the confirmation and refinement of Freud's discoveries have been proceeding in a fairly orderly way for many years; the essential concepts of psychoanalysis have been adequate to characterize the findings of innumerable independent workers. Corroboration of unconscious themes and processes is also offered by an abundance of materials external to the analytic experience: jokes and errors, primitive institutions and ritual, myths, and of course literature itself. For an unverified science psychoanalysis has had a remarkably profound effect on such apparently unrelated disciplines as anthropology, sociology, and educational theory. While the literary scholar is righteously declaring himself free of Freudian influence, his wife may be absorbing it in homeopathic doses from Dr. Spock.

The charge that psychoanalysis is metaphorical is true but easily misinterpreted. Such concepts as id, ego, and superego are not meant to describe physiological entities but spheres of interest that must be postulated to account for the observed fact that mental acts express compromised intentions. Curiously enough, the most questionable part of psychoanalysis in the eyes of many post-Freudians is its least metaphorical, most biological side, namely the theory of instinctual psychic energy. The strength of psychoanalysis may be said to lie in the precision of its metaphors—by which I mean their capacity for economically describing a vast range of evidence for which no other descriptive terms have been found. Where those metaphors need further refinement, as in the unwieldy overlapping of "topographic" and "structural" systems, the task will not be to adopt a more physical vocabulary but to achieve a parsimony of inferred concepts.

2. *The layman has no basis for choosing among the many schismatic sects of psychoanalysis, and so should ignore them until they settle their differences.*

This would be sound advice if there were any likelihood that individual psychoanalysts, ambitious of glory, would stop founding new ideologies on isolated portions of theory. The student who cannot wait forever to decide what to think about human motivation must try as best he can to discriminate between such popular ideologies and genuinely empirical critiques of psychoanalysis. . . . If, for example, a rival system has had no medical consequences and has become a program of secular salvation rather than of therapy; if it has abandoned or attenuated the idea of dynamic conflict in favor of a monolithic and omnipresent explanation (trauma of birth, inferiority complex, collective unconscious, etc.); if it depends upon the support of religious and literary pieties and moral commonplaces divorced from clinical evidence—then, I think, suspicion is demanded. The literary student seems peculiarly vulnerable to pseudoscientific improvements of psychoanalysis which dispense with sexual nastiness and glorify creativity. "Of the artist's relations to the psychologist," Edward Glover has written, "it can be said with some justice that their cordiality is in inverse ratio to their depth."

This is not to say that one may fall back on Freudian orthodoxy as if it were revealed truth. Like all systems originating in a feeling for the indescribable, psychoanalysis has seen its metaphors reified, its hypotheses hardened into dogma, and its particular area of interest mistaken for total existence. Freud himself was not always above these tendencies, and few of his followers have shared his grasp of the difference between psychological reality and the conceptual framework needed for discussing that reality. Furthermore, on the positive side, present-day psychoanalysis has passed beyond Freud's almost exclusive emphasis on instinctual demands and infantile traumas to consider adaptive functions at all stages of development. The result remains "Freudian"—nearly all the principles of ego psychology are derived from hints in Freud's later writings—but not in the reductive sense that has most frequently alienated non-Freudians. By reference to the so-called "conflict-free sphere of the ego," analysts now take better account of normal mental processes. Mastery of conflict is now as prominent as submission to conflict—a fact of moment for students of artistic creativity.

When this shift is considered along with Freud's own reformulations from decade to decade, the layman will feel properly discouraged from using any single text as his guide to psychoanalysis. If he intends to involve himself in the subject at all he had better be resigned to plodding through a certain amount of dreary polemics. Fortunately, however, clear explanations of the progress and quarrels of psychoanalysis are readily available and may be used to supplement a reading of one of Freud's sets of introductory lectures, which remain the most engaging means of initiation.

I turn now to objections to the effect of psychoanalytic ideas and methods on literary criticism:

3. *The psychoanalytic view of the writer as a neurotic is presumptuous and condescending. Psychoanalysis is unequipped to describe the way writers really work.*

Even Freud was careful never to say that the artist is directly neurotic, and he admitted—perhaps hastily, many now feel—that psychoanalysis "can do nothing towards elucidating the nature of the artistic gift, nor can it explain the means by which the artist works—artistic technique." Certainly Freud's disproportionate emphasis on unconscious factors had a pernicious effect on the first ventures into psychoanalytic criticism. Ludicrous diagnoses of writers' mental diseases, uninfluenced by historical or biographical knowledge or by literary taste, continue to appear regularly in the pages of clinical journals. Yet these efforts are more than bad criticism, they are bad psychology as well. It cannot be too strongly affirmed that psychoanalytic theory, especially in recent years, finds no necessary connection—at the most a useful analogy—between artistic production and the production of neurotic symptoms.

This analogy rests on the supposition that both art and neurosis originate in conflict and may be conceived as ways of managing it. But whereas the neurotic's solution is the helplessly regressive and primitive one of allowing repressed ideas to break into a disguised expression which is satisfying neither to the neurotic himself nor to others, the artist has the power to sublimate and neutralize conflict, to give it logical and social coherence through conscious elaboration, and to reach and communicate a sense of catharsis. The chief insistence on creative strength—on the artist's innate capacity for sublimation, his ability to handle dangerous psychic materials successfully—has come from within the psychoanalytic movement, not from outraged traditionalists. In truth, the theory that the artist is an especially morbid type antedates psychoanalysis and serves the very un-Freudian purpose of exaggerating the non-artist's freedom from conflict. It is thus a form of philistinism—one to which bad psychoanalysts have been susceptible but which is contrary to the whole spirit of the movement. "Of all mental systems," Lionel Trilling has justly written, "the Freudian psychology is the one which makes poetry indigenous to the very constitution of the mind. Indeed, the mind, as Freud sees it, is in the greater part of its tendency exactly a poetry-making organ."

In a psychoanalytic view the artist is exceptionally able to make imaginative use of capacities which are present in everyone, but which are largely unavailable to expression in the non-creative man and are bound to self-destructive strife in the neurotic. The artist may, of course, be impelled by a certain degree of neurotic conflict to submit himself to unconscious dictates; this corresponds to the undeniable observation that great numbers of artists *are* neurotic. But neurosis alone cannot produce art and is inimical to the preconscious elaboration and the sublimation that make art possible. Insofar as he is neurotic, therefore, the artist is deficient in the functions that distinguish art from symptom-formation.

This is not to say, of course, that we are free after all to treat artistic creation and the aesthetic experience as special events in which the laws of mental dynamics are suspended. Many literary scholars are eager to believe those psychologists who, like C. G. Jung and his followers, sweep the element of personal conflict out of view and thus prepare the way for a mystic reverence for artistic truth. But the literary work which is completely free from its biographical determinants is not to be found, and in many of the greatest works—the prime example is *Hamlet*—unresolved emotion and latent contradiction are irreducibly involved in the aesthetic effect. To appreciate why there are gaps in the surface we must be prepared to inspect what lies beneath them.

An aesthetic theory which ignores the possibility that latent and manifest content, unconscious and conscious purpose may be imperfectly harmonized is, to my mind, more reductive than a theory in which art represents a complex, "overdetermined" adjustment of varying psychic interests. One must decide whether to see art as a mental activity or as a direct apprehension of truth and beauty. The former attitude is less exalted, but it leaves the critic freer to trace the actual shape of a work, including its possible double meanings or confusions and its shifts of intensity and mood. The final word on the tiresome debate about art and neurosis should be that art need not express neurotic traits, but may very well do so in any individual case; the critic must wait and see.

4. *Psychoanalytic criticism neglects literary form, reduces all writers to an undifferentiated substratum of sexual obsession, and discards a writer's stated intention for a supposed unconscious one.*

If this is taken as a description of much psychoanalytic criticism to date, rather than a statement of inherent limitations in the psychoanalytic attitude, then I must agree that it is accurate. Unfortunately, most literary people do not recognize this distinction; the "Freudian reductionist" is used as a scarecrow to protect the scholar's private harvest of literary history or factual detail or didactic moralism. It is true, of course, that a critical method which seizes upon a few unconscious themes and pronounces them the whole meaning of the work is grossly levelling; it is also true that Freud's technique of dream interpretation lends a certain inadvertent sanction to this approach. But the difference between dream and literature have long been recognized, as have the differences of purpose between the psychoanalyst, who is interested only in the mind that produced the dream or poem, and the critic, who must respect the object itself—including the elements in it which the analyst would regard merely as subterfuge. To say that psychoanalytic criticism *cannot* do justice to literary complexity is to suppose, as the worst psychoanalytic critics do, that an interest in psychological evidence can have no other purpose than to explain away manifest emphasis.

In shifting toward ego psychology, psychoanalytic theory has become better adapted to a study of the higher mental processes that enter into artistic creation, and to recognition of a communicative as well as a self-expressive function. It was a psychoanalyst, Ernst Kris, who insisted that the "reality" from which a literary creation proceeds is not only the reality of the author's drives and fantasies, but also the structure of his artistic problem and the historical state of his genre. Indeed, nothing (other than inadequate acquaintance with tradition) prevents the psychoanalytic critic from considering exactly the same factors that concern the literary, the social, and the intellectual historian. As psychoanalysis has approached a point of reconciliation with social psychology, so too have psychoanalytic critics begun to turn their attention to broader matters than the unconscious fixations of a few unhappy writers. There have been numerous recent attempts to define the psychological quality of entire genres and movements, and even to take a psychological view of forces operating through history. Nor has the psychology of form and style remained unexamined. Kenneth Burke—himself a Freudian of a maverick sort—once defined form as "an arousing and fulfillment of desires." The idea has been pursued by several investigators, perhaps most successfully by Simon O. Lesser. Form is being increasingly recognized not only as an aid to perception but as a vehicle of pleasure, including the pleasure of reducing the anxieties that other aspects of the work bring into play.

As for the author's stated intention, the subtlest modern critics have rightly placed little value on it—but not always for good reasons. The most celebrated dogma of the New Criticism has been that statements made before or after the literary fact must be considered less reliable than statements inferred from the text. All too often, however, this sound principle allows the critic to overstate the work's unity of effect or to drain off its passion and leave behind only a fragile tissue of symbols. By invoking the Intentional Fallacy the critic may fail to consider divisions of intention that are intrinsic to the work's structure and effect. I submit that we are entitled to consider *both* overt purpose and the perhaps contradictory purpose (or purposes) that may emerge from imagery or the shape of a plot. Psychoanalytic criticism has customarily occupied itself with the latter sort alone, but here too the historical reasons for this bias have lost their strength. In principle at least, the theory of overdetermination should enable us to feel more at home with literary tensions and contradictions than the critic who is searching only for leading ideas or unitary "meaning."

5. *It is impossible to psychoanalyze dead writers, and anachronistic to apply Freudian rules to writers who lived before Freud.*

Freud himself maintained the former truism, though he egregiously violated it in his study of Leonardo. There is a difference, however, between guessing at the infantile sources of trauma in an absent figure and identifying general psychological themes in a literary document. Freud's brilliant essay on Dostoevsky provides a model of the latter, more legitimate, kind of investigation. To be sure, Freud draws on biographical materials and his own clinical knowledge to arrive at a speculation about the source of Dostoevsky's dominant theme; but our apprehension of Dostoevsky's literary qualities is richer for the speculation. An analysis of imagery or a repeated theme, when handled with discretion, can supply for the critic part of what the practicing analyst might gather more reliably from the patient's associations. It is a risky business, as countless pratfalls by psychoanalytic critics remind us. Most recent Freudians have acknowledged the dangers of biographical inference and have turned their attention to the structure of the literary work at hand, or to the varying responses it elicits from the reader.

One may also detect a new caution about ascribing a psychological prehistory to literary characters—the most ridiculed of all Freudian practices. Much early psychoanalytic criticism, especially the efforts by physicians who were only dabbling in literature, perpetuated the quaint Victorian error of treating *homo fictus* as a completely knowable person. There is a qualitative gap between Mrs. Clarke's *Girlhood of Shakespeare's Heroines* and Ernest Jones's *Hamlet and Oedipus* (London, 1949), but they are connected by an embarrassing thread of tradition. Still, Jones is more faithful to the genuine puzzle of *Hamlet* than are the circumspect followers of E. E. Stoll, who solve essentially psychological problems by recourse to theatrical convention. What psychoanalytic criticism needs, in my opinion, is not an injunction against seeing arrested development in literary heroes, but a vocabulary for describing a work's implied psychological pattern without mistaking that pattern for the hero's case-history. Hamlet may not have an Oedipus complex, but *Hamlet* does.

The charge of anachronism is easy to refute. It implies that at a certain moment in time Freud made human nature Freudian. To say that preFreudian men cannot illustrate psychoanalytic principles is simply to say that psychoanalysis is wrong—a position which ought to be argued without recourse to the sophistry of anachronism. Academic logic has never been shakier than in recent efforts to prove that the psychological insight of certain writers may be completely explained by the mental theories current in their day. The reader must be dull of soul who can be persuaded that Shakespeare is contained in Timothy Bright, or that Hawthorne and Melville were disciples of the sunny moralist Thomas C. Upham. Perhaps we need to be reminded of Freud's own discovery that the essential features of his system were anticipated by poets and novelists—or, more simply, perhaps we should have some faith in the literary imagination.

6. *Psychoanalytic criticism identifies unconscious content with literary value.*

Like other objections we have reviewed, this one is historically but not theoretically warranted. The psychoanalytic movement has carried with it a fringe of zealots—we may include in this category such otherwise diverse persons as the Surrealist painters, D. H. Lawrence, Wilhelm Reich, and Norman O. Brown—who have preached a total escape from repression. This is not the goal of psychoanalysis, nor is it the *summum bonum* of Freudian criticism. Freud's aim was not to celebrate and release the unconscious but to bring its destructive tendency under rational control. While treasuring the evidence of unconscious processes in literature, he did not imagine that mere seizure by unconscious forces made a good writer or a good work. On the contrary, he complained of Dostoevsky that "his insight was entirely restricted to the workings of the abnormal psyche," and he showed how this narrowness warped Dostoevsky's representation of love. Psychoanalytic critics have naturally been tempted to place aesthetic value on what they have brought to light, and more often than not it has been some compulsive pattern. But psychoanalytic theory clearly states that art depends on the ability to manage and shape unconscious materials, not on those materials alone.

7. *Psychoanalytic criticism is jargon-ridden.*

Here too we may grant the charge but deny that it will inevitably apply to subsequent efforts. For several reasons the temptation to write in technical jargon has been greater for psychoanalytic critics than for most others. They have been subject both to a pride in sounding scientific and to a despair of placating the inevitable academic reviewers who will decry all technical language not drawn from the humanistic sewing-circle. One detects a Thersites-like pleasure in the analysts' declaration that the heart of some beloved classic is rotten with polysyllabic fixations which the reader will not be able to find in his college dictionary. Such tendencies can of course be kept in check.

At the same time, it seems to me doubtful that psychoanalytic criticism can ever be, as one of its distinguished advocates would like, "rendered completely acceptable to the non-psychologically oriented scholars." Beyond a certain point the disguise of one's premises amounts to abandonment of them. How, for example, can one substitute the term "conscience" for "superego" without blurring the irrationality—even the savagery—with which self-punishment is often inflicted in literary plots? How can one substitute "self" for "ego" without losing the often necessary sense of conflicting interests *within* a character's "self"? True jargon is technical language used imprecisely or unnecessarily. The real danger is not that the critic will have to resort to clinical terms (thereby offending those who would have rejected his argument anyway), but that he will allow his focus to stray from the literary work to the psychological system (thereby using the system as a club rather than a tool).

I would not want this essay to be taken as a plea for recruits to a militantly Freudian criticism. While psychoanalytic ideas have permeated our intellectual life, attempts at relating psychoanalysis to literature in a programmatic way have been handicapped by the need for cumbersome explanations of theory and for rapid passage from one example to the next. Our most respected critics—I think offhand of I. A. Richards, Edmund Wilson, W. H. Auden, William Empson, Kenneth Burke, Alfred Kazin, Lionel Trilling—have neither ignored Freudianism nor made it a battle-cry; they have absorbed it into their literary sense, along with other complementary approaches. I would urge, however, that such eclecticism be distinguished from indifference to theory. Something more than intellectual fashion is involved in the choice of psychological premises; the critic who disavows any taint of Freudianism usually ends by concocting his own psychology, a home-brew of conscious "experience" and moral prejudice. What Allen Tate once said of philosophy must therefore be said of psychological theory as well: by pretending not to use it in literary studies we are using it badly.

E. M. W. TILLYARD

The Personal Heresy, II

In his brilliant essay on *The Personal Heresy in Criticism* printed in last year's *Essays and Studies of the English Association*, Mr. C. S. Lewis mentioned my *Milton* as a book in which poetry was treated as the expression of personality. And up to a point he may have been right. But as he is hostile to my supposed way of thinking, and as I agree with a good deal of his essay, it seems either that I did not make myself clear or that Mr. Lewis is not entirely right. So I welcome this opportunity of saying what I mean by personality in literature. However, though certain cross-purposes may be straightened by further discussion, I do not say that much of Mr. Lewis's essay is not extremely provocative and controversial. With some of it I disagree; and as the matters of disagreement seem to me well worth dwelling on, I offer the comments that follow. I hope that my being stirred to argue the point with Mr. Lewis may be taken as my warm tribute to his essay's excellence.

As a preliminary, I must express surprise that Mr. Lewis considers the Personal Heresy, as he calls it, a sign of modernity. I should have thought it slightly shop-soiled. Mr. Lewis quotes an ambiguous passage from Mr. T. S. Eliot as supporting it: yet what weight can this passage have in the face of so uncompromising an attack on the Personal Heresy as that author's essay on *Tradition and the Individual Talent?* Here Mr. Eliot says that 'the progress of an artist is a continual self-sacrifice, a continual extinction of personality', and that 'honest criticism and sensitive appreciation is directed not upon the poet but upon the poetry'. And he comes to the conclusion that for the poet the mind of Europe and of his own country is much more important than his own private mind. Now these sentiments are not only close to Mr. Lewis's but they agree with a strong modern tendency, whose limits are not easily drawn, to belittle the individual in comparison with the race, the personal in comparison with the abstract, the Renaissance in comparison with Byzantium. Whatever the fate of this tendency—it may peter out in a few years for all we can tell—at the moment it is modern, and the opposite tendency to cling to the personal, even if fated shortly to prevail, just fails to be modern.

As a second preliminary let me say I entirely accept Mr. Lewis's contention that in the matter of personality you can draw no line between lyric and dramatic poetry. I believe with him that there is a difference between (for example) the poet's feeling towards personal pain and towards pain pictured in his poetry; but within the latter category it makes no difference whether the pain is pictured as happening to the poet speaking for himself in a lyric or to a fictitious personage in a drama.

To turn now to the words 'personal' and 'personality', it is plain how easy misunderstanding may be if we consider the following sentence of Mr. Lewis's. In commenting on the passage from Keats's *Hyperion* beginning—

As when, upon a tranced summer-night,
Those green-rob'd senators of mighty woods,
Tall oaks . . .

he writes:

> It is not relevant that Keats first read about senators (let us say) in a little brown book, in a room smelling of boiled beef, the same day that he pulled out a loose tooth; it is relevant that the senators sat still when the invading Gauls entered the Senate House; it is relevant that Rome really established an empire.

In this passage Mr. Lewis implies that 'personal' as a critical term includes every accident however trivial connected with the author. No one can complain that he does so, but I should guess that not a few supporters of the 'personal heresy' would simply ignore such trivialities in their conception of personality. They would attach them to the sphere of literary gossip, not to that of criticism. Certainly I should never dream of giving them any critical value in themselves and I should agree that to recall such things when reading poetry would be grossly inappropriate. The most that literary gossip can do in the way of criticism is to keep people off a wrong track. There is a story about Milton that once after his blindness, hearing a lady sing, he said, 'Now I swear this lady is handsome'. Such an anecdote might have had a critical use at the time when Milton was imagined to be insusceptible to female charm. Now that this error has been generally discarded, the anecdote has no critical value—it is no more than a pleasant piece of literary gossip, and to be conscious of it when we read, for instance, the Chorus's description of Dalila entering like a ship with streamers flying is to abuse both the anecdote and the poetry. If Mr. Lewis in attacking the personal heresy is wishing to point out that some of the labour spent in recent years on Johnson and Lamb, for instance, is anecdotal rather than critical, and that to confound the two spheres is a heresy, then he has my support.

Of course Mr. Lewis does not confine 'personal' to this trivial or accidental sense. He grants that it is possible through poetry to come into contact with a poet's temperament in the most intimate way. The reader shares the poet's consciousness. But, according to Mr. Lewis, even so the personal contact involved is relatively unimportant: first, because the personality with which the reader achieves contact is not the poet's normal personality but a heightened, temporary, perhaps alien, personality; secondly, because that personality is a means of vision rather than the thing ultimately seen. The personal heresy consists in the reader's seeing the poet's *normal* personality in his poetry, and in focusing his eyes on that personality instead of letting them contemplate the universe in a particular way.

Now if it is heretical to hold that part of the value of poetry consists in gaining contact with the normal personality of the poet, then I am a heretic. But I shall probably be using the word 'normal' in a way Mr. Lewis would disclaim. When he imagines Keats reading about senators in a little brown book in a room smelling of boiled beef he attaches these supposed facts to Keat's normal personality. I should do nothing of the sort, but call them as irrelevant to his normal personality as to the passage of *Hyperion* under discussion. In other words by 'personality' or 'normal personality' I do not mean practical or everyday personality, I mean rather some mental pattern which makes Keats Keats and not Mr. Smith or Mr. Jones. (Pattern is of course a bad word because it implies the static, whereas personality cannot remain fixed: the poet's personality is in the pattern of the sea rather than in that of a mosaic pavement.) And I believe we read Keats in some measure because his poetry gives a version of a remarkable personality of which another version is his life. The two versions are not the same but they are analogous. Part of our response to poetry is in fact similar to the stirring we experience when we meet some one whose personality impresses us. Such a person may startle us by the things he does, but quite outside anything he does there will be a distinction about him which, though difficult to define, we prize and which has the faculty of rousing us to some extent from our quotidian selves. This person may be subject to accidents, such as toothache, irregular habits, or an uncertain temper, which interfere with our enjoying this distinguished mental pattern of his; yet we know that the pattern is there. Though subject to change it is definite enough to be called habitual; it can indeed be looked on as his normal self underlying the accidents of quotidian existence.

One of the readiest ways of pointing to the function of personality in poetry is by means of the word style. 'Style' readily suggests the mental pattern of the author, the personality realized in words. Style in poetry is partly a matter of rhythm; and rhythm, Dr. Richards says very truly in *Science and Poetry*, 'is no matter of tricks with syllables, but directly reflects personality'. Mr. Lewis would probably define style as the poet's credentials certifying him a person whom you can trust in the quest of bringing back true reports on the universe; and consider the report far more important than the credentials. But I should assert myself that experience shows how directly personality revealed through style can constitute the major appeal of poetry. It is pleasant to choose an example from a modern poet who considers poetry an escape from personality rather than an expression of it. In Mr. T. S. Eliot's latest work, *The Rock*, the most successful passages are those where the author's characteristic rhythms and word-arrangements have freest scope, where his style is most obviously recognizable, in other words when he is most himself.

> *A Cry from the North, from the West and from the South:*
> *Whence thousands travel daily to the timekept City;*
> *Where My Word is unspoken,*
> *In the land of lobelias and tennis flannels*
> *The rabbit shall burrow and the thorn revisit,*
> *The nettle shall flourish on the gravel court,*
> *And the wind shall say: 'Here were decent godless people:*
> *Their only monument the asphalt road*
> *And a thousand lost golf balls.'*

Here the style *is* the poetry. The rhythm has a tense pregnant hush, simple in seeming, however subtle in the attainment, that sets off, that exploits to the utmost, the startling mixture of biblical reference and golf balls. It is entirely individual to the author, it reflects a poetical personality that quickens our pulses, and we value it far more than any heightened apprehension the passage may give us of the things of which it speaks. Mr. Lewis might retort by attaching Mr. Eliot, for all his professions of classicism, to the romantic tradition, and by pointing to his admission that for that tradition the personal theory does not work too badly. So I had better choose a second example not open to this retort; and I cannot do better in illustrating how widely I differ from Mr. Lewis in my conception of the personal sphere in literature than choose the passage from Isaiah to which he refuses all personal quality whatsoever:

> And Babylon, the glory of kingdoms, the beauty of the Chaldees' excellency, shall be as when God overthrew Sodom and Gomorrah. It shall never be inhabited, neither shall it be dwelt in from generation to generation: neither shall the Arabian pitch tent there: neither shall the shepherds make their fold there. But wild beasts of the deserts shall lie there; and their houses shall be full of doleful creatures; and owls shall dwell there, and satyrs shall dance there. And the wild beasts of the islands shall cry in their desolate houses, and dragons in their pleasant palaces.

First, I am willing to admit with Mr. Lewis that we do not through this passage get in touch with the personality of the original author, or at least, if we see him, it is at best through a mist. But with his remarks on the translator I disagree. Mr. Lewis considers that he was so preoccupied with philological and theological matters that his own personality could find no entrance. This to my mind is to misunderstand not only translation but any art that appears to consist in getting a job of work done. Rule out the possibility of the translator mediating his own self, and you turn much early painting and sculpture, where the artist is fighting to render (as he thinks) a convincing likeness, into a mere technical exercise. On the contrary, it is precisely when a translator has worked himself up into an excited desire to do justice to a fine passage or a primitive sculptor is growing triumphant at surmounting a technical difficulty that his own mental pattern has the chance of manifesting itself. The artist will probably think his personality is lost in his non-personal activity, but the result may quite belie his own expectations. The sculptor of the Delphic Charioteer would have been incredulous if he had been told that his 'personality' had in any way entered into the figure of that impassive, severely draped young man; he probably thought he had done a good job of work and made a good imitation of the sort of driver who ought to win a chariot race for an illustrious prince. Yet the statue is like no other statue on earth, and I believe this unlikeness to be both an important element in the statue's excellence and to be connected with the sculptor's personality. Similarly the passage from Isaiah has a quite individual ferocity of rhythm which, if we heed it, will make the passage far less remote and romantic than Mr. Lewis would have it be, and incidentally, not too far removed from the immediacy which he very justly postulates for the original. 'For us', says Mr. Lewis, 'Babylon is far away and long ago': possibly, but was it so for a Protestant divine writing not long after the Gunpowder Plot? Not that the translator consciously or literally thought the passage a prophecy of the fall of the Papacy, and that he believed dragons would writhe in the ruined halls of the Vatican, but I suspect that Babylon evoked the Protestant fervour which was a motive in the translator's mental pattern. Of course a modern reader may let his mind be guided by the associations that the various evocative words in the passage have got for him: but this is rather an indulgence of the reader's own personal proclivities than a proper reading; 'personal' in a far less legitimate sense than in that of trying to establish contact with the mental pattern of the author.

When I spoke of the sculptor of the Delphic Charioteer having no notion that his own personality had anything to do with a statue, I was hinting at a paradox that may go a good way to explaining why people who may agree at bottom appear to think so differently about personality in literature. When Mr. Eliot calls poetry 'an escape from personality', he means more than an escape from the accidents that attend a person in everyday life. He is trying to describe what it feels like when a man succeeds in writing poetry. The feeling (and other poets confirm Mr. Eliot) brings with it the impression of a complete abandonment of personality, analogous to the feeling of 'getting out of yourself' that may occur in many non-literary contexts. Mr. Eliot speaks of the poet 'surrendering himself wholly to the work to be done'. The paradox consists in the poet often producing the most characteristic and personal work through this very process of self-surrender. The more the poet experiences this abandonment of personality, the more likely is the reader to hail the poet's characteristic, unmistakable self. In fact the poet is *ipsissimus cum minime ipse*. Nor will it make the poet any less personal, if he carefully avoids every vestige of private emotion, if he seeks the utmost objectification. On the contrary, the pattern into which these apparently alien objects are fitted will express all the more clearly, with the least risk of encumbrance, the characteristic lines of the poet's mental pattern. Herein lies the reason why the following passage from Mr. Lewis's essay is no valid argument against the personal theory. In commenting on the lines from *Hyperion* he writes:

> It is absolutely essential that each word should suggest not what is private and personal to the poet but what is public, common, impersonal, objective. The common world with its nights, its oaks, and its stars, which we have all seen, and which mean at least *something* the same to all of us, is the bank on which he draws his cheques.

Here Mr. Lewis is assuming that what is true of communication is true of the experience communicated. As far as the former goes, his doctrine is sound, containing the legitimate reproof of the kind of modern verse that draws its cheque on the banks of Albi or Florence or Timbuctoo rather than on the Bank of England. But as regards experience Mr. Lewis is not always right. However public the means of communication, the experience conveyed may (among other things or even chiefly) be a mental pattern peculiar to the poet. Anyhow it is plain enough that those who choose to see only one half of the paradox will never agree with those who choose to see only the other.

However, granted the paradox, there remains another critical sense of the word personal. It is best set forth through Coleridge's comparison of Shakespeare and Milton in the fifteenth chapter of the *Biographia Literaria*:

> While the former darts himself forth, and passes into all the forms of human character and passion, the one Proteus of the fire and blood; the other attracts all forms and things to himself, into the unity of his own ideal. All things and modes of action shape themselves anew in the being of Milton; while Shakespeare becomes all things, yet for ever remaining himself.

Now in a sense Shakespeare was just as thorough as Milton in impressing his own personality on the reader. But just because Shakespeare's own mental pattern largely consisted of an almost unexampled power of adapting itself to the shifting experiences of life so as to extract the utmost mental nourishment from them, his personality makes a much less precise effect on us than does the more rigid personality of Milton. When then we talk of the poetry of Milton or of Wordsworth being more personal than that of Shakespeare or of Keats we may be meaning that it expresses a more austerely rigid nature. Now these fluid and rigid natures, although they may both be transmuted into poetry and become thereby accessible, do react differently on the relation between the poet's life and the poet's art. The fluid, adaptable, receptive natures, granted power, are likely to be pure artists and to empty their lives for the sake of their art. Their power, their fierceness go to solving their artistic problems. Flaubert is habitually quoted as an author of this kind. The more rigid natures, who insist, for all their sensibility to impressions, on imposing their own very definite patterns on the world of their vision are likely to be interesting persons in their private lives, apt to do more notable things and to impress themselves on those around them. Thus Wordsworth must needs poke his nose into the French Revolution.

Before drawing some critical deductions from these statements, I wish to say that the above general division of authors into the fluid and empty-lived on the one hand, and the rigid and full-lived on the other, does not invalidate the analogy I postulated above between the mind-pattern as expressed in art and the mind-pattern as expressed in life. True, the analogy between a biography composed of a few dry facts supplemented by a few trivial anecdotes and a beautifully proportioned body of poetry can appear ridiculous. But it may be that the two versions differ less in kind than in completeness. One is a perfect volume; the other consists of a few mutilated pages. The mind-pattern is fully revealed in the poetry; from the biographical material its main lines are indecipherable. And yet the fact that we cannot decipher them does not prove that their trend is not similar to that purged, clarified, and intensified pattern that shows up in the poetry. Even when an author distils almost the whole of himself into his writing (as Flaubert did), what is left of the man, ghost-like and bloodless as it may be, can repeat in some vague sort the mental pattern that has been presented so perfectly in the works. Contact with him might inform us that here is a remarkable personality, but so abstract from active living as to be unprofitable to pursue. In other words, even the author most depersonalized or sucked dry by his art is potentially a man of note outside the literary sphere.

Still, though the life of the man who has yielded himself to his art should present some analogy with that art, it may, however closely scrutinized, be entirely useless in heightening the appreciation of that art. In fact biographical study will in this case insist on staying on the hither side of criticism in the province of literary anecdotage. It is very likely that Shakespeare's biography, even with the fullest knowledge, would remain as at present in that province. But with the other class, the biography, the *facts* of personality, the data for the mental pattern of the man's life, may substantially help our understanding of the mental pattern as revealed in his art. An extreme example would be William Morris, a much less extreme one, Milton. And if, in writing of Milton, I have forsaken the safe Johnsonian example of not confounding biography and criticism, I would say in defence that I did so because I was writing of Milton, not because I thought they should invariably be so confounded. Yet I grant that the mixture of biography and criticism, even when most justified by the nature of the author, has its besetting danger: it is all too easy for the reader to use biography as an illegitimate short cut into the poet's mental pattern as revealed in his poems. He may arrive thereby at what seems a place higher up on the more difficult road of intensive study of the isolated word, but he will have missed the the essential revelation that could only be obtained by the very journey he has shirked. He will, in fact, have been doing something like looking up the answers to a problem when tired of trying to solve it, or using a crib when reading a foreign text. It is when a man believes that the intense study of the isolated word has gone astray or has been brought to a standstill that he is justified in seeking guidance from biography.

Mr. Lewis's essay raises the whole question of what poetry is about. From the hints he drops I gather that for him poetry is about objects outside the poet's mind, about racial perception, and about God. My business is not with this topic, nor am I clear enough about Mr. Lewis's views to be able to use them as a starting-point. But I wish to make two observations on it before I close. First, I disclaim any intention of limiting the value of poetry to establishing contact with an important personality; and I would refer the reader to an early chapter in my recent book, *Poetry Direct and Oblique*, in which I discuss the things poetry tends to concern. Some of these things, though we accept information about them only because we trust the person who gives it, are different from the personality or mental pattern of the author, described above. They are nearer, at any rate, to the discoveries about the universe that Mr. Lewis expects the poet to make. Secondly, although I have departed from the doctrines of Dr. Richards so far as to admit that the poet tells us things as well as imposes valuable equilibria on our minds, I find Mr. Lewis too rigidly concerned with things and too little heedful of states of mind when he discusses his examples. My disagreement from him can best be illustrated by discussing one of his own instances, Herrick's *Upon Julia's Clothes*. Mr. Lewis discusses half the poem. It may be fairer to take the whole:

Whenas in silks my Julia goes,
Then, then, methinks, how sweetly flows
That liquefaction of her clothes.
Next, when I cast mine eyes, and see
That brave vibration each way free;
Oh, how that glittering taketh me!

Commenting on the first three lines, Mr. Lewis calls them 'poetry of an unusually sensuous and simple type', and says that in them 'the only experience which has any claim to be poetical experience is an apprehension not of the poet, but of silk'. The poet has presented an idea of silk and one of unusual vividness. Now Mr. Lewis expressly excludes from the poetic value of the lines the notion, 'With what eyes the poet must have seen silk': that is merely an irrelevant afterthought. I can only conclude that in his opinion the lines concern not a state of mind but a substance called silk, and that they reveal hitherto unapprehended qualities of silk. What are these qualities? Mr. Lewis suggests that the world liquefaction is responsible for the vividness with which silk is apprehended. In other words Herrick has made the discovery that compared with certain other textures (felt, for instance) silk resembles in its suppleness a liquid rather than a solid. I cannot believe that Mr. Lewis really holds that the poem's virtue can reside in so elementary an observation, an observation in the power of so many people and not at all requiring the superior penetration of poetic genius. Yet what is the alternative? I can only see (granted silk as the concern of the poem) the vaguely mystical or Platonic notion (common enough in the late nineteenth century) that objects have some essential quality, some true self, which the artist can in some way reveal. Now such interpretations of poetry seem to me justified only if backed by the complete philosophy which they imply. Usually they imply no philosophy; and I doubt, from Mr. Lewis's remarks, whether he really wishes to attach this particular poem to any comprehensive creed. If he does, I have no quarrel with him. If he does not, I think he has failed to attach any value to Herrick's lines.

What I cannot accept in Mr. Lewis's interpretation of the poem is the value he puts on 'things'. I do not say that the poem does not tell us something, but I do say that what it tells us about silk has a very subordinate share in the poem's total meaning. Silk may have considerable importance as a means, as an end it is negligible. Even the claim of temporal priority made for silk (a claim whose importance I do not admit) is not justified; for before the silk is made vivid to us, we are given through the excited repetition of the words 'then, then', the statement of the speaker's excitement at the sight of his Julia in motion. Far from containing the virtue of the poem, the apprehension of silk is but one of a number of factors that go to express a state of mind which readers have somehow shared, and which they have considered in some way valuable. Here are a few of these factors. A fresh and unaffected sensuality pervades the poem. Not only is the speaker's excitement expressed by 'then, then', but from the flow of the clothes and their vibration the hint of the body beneath is not absent. The full emphasis and the fall of the third line express how well the spectator's excitement is satisfied by the downward flow of the silk. We may even derive from 'liquefaction' a hint of the word 'satisfaction'. 'Liquefaction' is a sophisticated word, and as such is more important than as describing a quality of silk which (incidentally) had been already indicated in the word 'flows'. More important, probably, than any of the factors noted above is the contrast on which the poem is constructed. The spectator first sees the downward flow of Julia's silks and he experiences satisfaction. He then sees the silks vibrating, perhaps moving in little horizontal eddies, and he is captivated. Even if this contrast means no more than a sense of balance or decorum it is not unimportant in the poem; and anyhow it is something very different from an isolated apprehension of silk.

Now few readers will accept all these observations on Herrick's poem, but I hope most of them will agree that it is complicated and not so very simple and sensuous. And I should be glad to think that they found it initially more reasonable to consider that poem in terms of a state of mind than in terms of a substance called silk. For it is not by any laborious process of induction *after* we have read the poem that we apprehend the qualities of unaffected sensuality, keen observation, sophistication, and sense of decorum. We apprehend them from the rhythm, the vocabulary, the word-arrangement, the pattern of the poem, in fact from the poem's most intimate poetical features. And the fact that such an enumeration is critically only of the most trivial value does not preclude its being on sounder lines than seeing the poem in terms of 'things'.

To go further, to describe the state of mind these qualities compose is luckily not necessary to my argument, nor need I reopen the question of how far it is the poet's personality we get in touch with through the poem. But I should like to add that seeing a poem in terms of a state of mind need not preclude 'Theism or Platonism or Absolute Idealism'. If you wish to see God in poetry, you can see Him as readily in the mind of a human being as in a piece of silk.

The Jinnee in the Well-Wrought Urn

This is the age which has repudiated books about the girlhood of Shakespeare's heroines. Criticism within the past few decades has made it its business to guarantee the autonomy of the work of art as constituted within its own limits. Every effort has been made to clear the art object of accretions, to focus attention on it as freed of irrelevancies concerning the author's life, his friends and his problems, or of errant speculation about the previous or subsequent history of characters, if any—from all that might be styled the personalist irrelevancies adventitious to the work of art in its own totality. The effort has been reasonably successful. The once undisputed popularity of biographical excursion has been severely curtailed. It maintains itself with effort even in concert programme notes.

The compulsions responsible for the present emphasis are many and complex, and they operate in quite diverse quarters simultaneously. The conviction that it is neither the potter who made it nor the people, real or fictional, to whose lives it is tangent, but the well-wrought urn itself which counts, has been fed indifferently out of studies of Donne or Pope or Coleridge, out of trenchant criticism working through contemporary literature, out of theory spun from clues picked up in St. Thomas Aquinas, and from innumerable other sources. Indeed, the ability it manifests to pick up nourishment almost anywhere at all is convincing testimony to the essential truth of the conviction in question: it is in accord with facts as they are.

In a sense, the current emphasis on the work of art as such simply exploits by reaction a special weakness of nineteenth-century criticism such as Hazlitt's or Lamb's. Associated with commitments of rhetorical theory through long centuries, this weakness was not even new. But the present age found it singularly ripe for attack, and the past few decades have, by a kind of inner compulsion, set themselves to forging weapons for the anti-personalist armory. This compulsion is discernible in T. S. Eliot's submersion of the individual's subjective talent in an objective tradition (of which, to be sure, the subjective talent is simultaneously the expression), and in the attack launched by F. R. Leavis and others against a criticism based on measuring fictional characters by 'real life'—by their seeming adaptability to ultra-fictional projection. The same compulsion is seen everywhere in the persistent emphasis of American criticism as represented by such work as that of Cleanth Brooks or Kenneth Burke.

But a change of heart, however carefully defined, is setting in, as a close reading of recent critical credos, such as those of Leslie Fiedler or of Richard Chase, shows. The compulsion to beat the personalist horse loses force as the impression gains ground that he has shown no unambiguous signs of life for a long while. Beating him becomes a bore, and we want something newer and more interesting to do.

However, it is not quite clear to me, nor perhaps to many others, that the horse is really dead. A phenomenon so universal and persistent as the personalist deviation in criticism, it would seem, still deserves rather more explicit consideration than it has received. It has been written off in places at which it might well have been looked into. Personalist deviationism is, after all, not merely the last infirmity of feeble sensibilities. Dr. Johnson, who is honestly admired by most objectivist critics and is cited by Mr. Fiedler as a practitioner commonly acknowledged as extraordinarily good, not only stands for an approach to literature that is frankly moral, in a distressingly simplified fashion, but could state bluntly to Boswell that 'the biographical part of literature is what I love most'. (The personalist horse does seem dead and shrunk to a heap of bones when we try to imagine a present-day critical collection with *that* for a title-page motto.)

This is not to say that the personalist approach to a work of art is to be advocated. If I may be permitted a personal deviation of my own, I myself subscribe wholeheartedly to the practice and theory of focusing primarily on the work of art itself and feel no desire to defend the personalist approach as a substitute technique. It is not defence of the personalist drift, but explanation, that is needed. The personalist deviation is here to stay, not only in programme notes but in serious discussions of literature which, apparently unaffected by recent critical trends, continue to pour from the presses. For some it may be a racking experience to own that the personalist approach is still established as the dominant approach in most classrooms. But there it is, all the same.

However objectionable, the personalist approach manifests a persistency that itself clamours for explanation. If the urn really is the issue, why is it always in peril of being overlooked or tossed aside? If you so much as whisper that there is a jinnee in the urn, most onlookers will be only too willing to drop the urn without further ado. Broken, it will let the jinnee out, and they can ask him a few questions. While decrying the tendency to behave this way, we may be excused for asking what accounts for the presence of the tendency in the first place.

II

There are countless ways in which works of art fray out into personalities and thus give the personalist distraction a foothold within the art object itself. The most obvious, that of character in literature or even in the plastic arts, is both so straightforward and so complicated—with the curious susceptibility characters exhibit even for getting themselves psycho-analysed—that it hardly need be mentioned. But there are other footholds, some closely approximating to this. There is the autobiographical strain which persistently fertilizes fiction. Or there is the obverse autobiography of a Scott Fitzgerald, where not only are the novels cut to the measure of the author's life, but this life itself is lived to the measure of the novels—type and antitype are generated not only simultaneously but reciprocally as well.

Or there is the fact that groupings of works by author have a tough and ready viability not found in groupings by classes. The body of works by Shakespeare—plays, sonnets, and other poems all together—forms a whole in a way more integrated than that formed by the body of Elizabethan sonnets or by Elizabethan drama. *Sweeney Agonistes* belongs with *Tradition and the Individual Talent* in a way it does not with Pound's *Cantos* or with a poem by Auden.

Or again, there is the fact that the final stage of interest in a poet's work creates inevitably the poet's shrine, which is consecrated to the poet's person and thus may as well be his birthplace as something more readily connected with his works. The Shakespeare Memorial Theatre is at Stratford, not on the south bank of the Thames. Or, once more, the personalist distraction intrudes itself by reason of the sense of communion which rides through the contemplation of a work of art. At the threshold of consciousness, there hovers the awareness that others, or at least another, knows this work in the intimate way that I do. What would be an intrusion on our attention if only an object were concerned, is thus transmuted into a sharing in terms of this injection of personality, however vague it may be. One wonders if there could be any artistic experience at all if the contemplator were a human being entirely alone in the universe.

This is not all. The very genesis of works of art is often—perhaps always and necessarily—derivative from personal relations and tensions. That the muses are conceived of as persons and not as clouds or waves bears testimony to a state of mind elusive but real. Certainly the artistic impulse is at a kind of peak when the person-to-person relationship takes possession of the whole field of life in a crisis terminating ordinarily in marriage. For the great majority of persons, this is the only time anything like artistic creativity even remotely threatens in their lives. Even those whose creative activity persists testify to the earlier period of intensification of impulse and the readjustment demanded for continuation. There is Villon's verse testament executed 'en l'an de mon trentiesme aage', or Mr. Eliot's pertinent remarks about those who want to continue to write poetry after their early youth. The crisis adverted to here is one which hardly exerts itself so immediately in the case of scientists.

Even where there is readjustment and the period of artistic impulse associated in one way or another with entrance upon the plenary personal relationship of marriage is past, the personal drive continues in the production of works of art. Frank accounts of artistic development, such as Stephen Spender's recent account, throughout are replete with personal relations and tensions, which, again, would have an entirely different status in the life of a mathematician or physicist or perhaps even a metaphysician.

It would be hard to disprove the statement that the impulse to produce a work of fine art simply cannot arise except within a framework of personal give-and-take, a *you-me* situation, set up within the artist's mind. The lack of artistic impulse among animals is a simple corollary of the dead quiet which Rilke found so terrifying in the animal eye. J. S. Mill's attempt to define poetry as something not heard but *over*heard is largely traceable to the impulse of the abstractionist, scientific mind to extricate poetry from the network of personality in which it is involved. But the attempt is successful, or at least titillating, precisely in so far as it removes the sensorily ascertainable audience and replaces it with a mysterious audience suggesting the bottomless depths of a pure personality, disengaged from the crudities of sense perception and existing only in the vibrant tension which makes a *me* separate from a *you*.

Creative activity is often—again, perhaps always—powered by the drive to accomplish, in terms of the production of an object of art, an adjustment or readjustment in certain obscure relationships with other persons. The state of protest in which artistic activity is so often framed is evidence of how matters stand here. Only persons are liable to protest. You cannot protest to a fact or to an object. Although you speak of protesting against it, you can only protest about it to some *one*. In a discussion of Lionel Trilling's recent book, R. P. Blackmur very properly suggests the artistic sterility of a feeling for systems—impersonal things—and the fact that existing politics is good not *for* literature, but 'to *aggravate* literature'. These sensitively conceived remarks underscore the value of high-potential person-to-person situations in generating the artist's product.

Even critical activity is dependent on this person-to-person situation for its coming into being. Another way of putting this is to say, as it is commonly said, that criticism is a social activity in a way in which scientific activity is not. Although in science there is question of background, there seems to be no question of a personal *mise en scène* as a condition of scientific activity in the way in which there is in critical activity. Even when questions as to who says what about whom are not obvious at the surface, issues involving such questions are likely to be found in the depths, where the wells of criticism, like those of the poem, are driven deep in the personal situation in which the critic finds himself. The goddess of criticism is a kind of in-law of the muses, and there is some question of an underground passage between the watering places to which she brings her devotees and the springs of Helicon.

III

The artistic situation differs from the scientific, against which it is helpful to set it here, precisely in centring about an externalized, man-made object. The persuasion that the object itself must be primary is thus both sound and promising. But the object is not free of involvement in tragedy simply because of its primacy as object. Although it stands solidly—or pretty solidly—on its own feet, it is none the less a harbinger of disappointment and of death. For once we have granted to the work of art the kind of autonomy which the artistic situation demands, once we have decided to allow it to slough its irrelevancies, which would dissipate its own objective being in the confusion of personal issues out of which it perhaps arose, a further question presents itself: Is it not in the last analysis cruel to face a human being with merely an object as such, a being which is less than a person? As soon as contemplation enters beyond a certain stage of awareness, is not the human being going to be unsatisfied if he cannot find another, a person, a *you*, in whatever it is he is concerned with?

It seems that he is going to be unsatisfied, precisely in so far as he drives this contemplation of the object to its ultimate—in so far as he takes it in its maximum of seriousness. We consider here the case not of passing attention to a work of art but the case of plenary attention, serious and protracted and repeated. Contemplation of this sort involves love, and the question is whether it can be carried on, or how far it can be carried on, without some suggestion of reciprocity. Projected into an unpeopled void, love becomes only the ultimate refinement of self-torture. And while it is true that contemplation of a minor object of art may not involve the full psychological mechanism of love in all its complications, still, in proportion as the object of art pretends to be serious, it at least set in motion this tremendous mechanism, which demands for full satisfaction the reciprocity of another person.

Man's deepest orientation is personal. He cannot give himself fully in an outpouring of love unless someone else is *there*, with at least the capability of giving a self in return. Otherwise, psychological disaster threatens—the disaster which takes such heavy toll of serious writers or artists.

The morass of personality which surrounds the work of art in ways only briefly hinted at here establishes the personalist aberration as a permanent threat. As contemplation enters upon a more serious stage, the human being is driven by the whole economy of what it is to be man to find opposite himself, in that which he contemplates, a person capable of reacting in turn. This drive is primordial and will not be denied. It can be deflected from the object, as it ordinarily is, by a refusal to take the object in total seriousness, by a smile, a shrug of the shoulders, by an acknowledgment, if only subconscious, that somewhere or other the poem will break down, will ultimately reach a point at which it is incapable of eliciting further love—unlike a person, who can go on eliciting love without limit.

When the personalist aberration sets in, or in so far as it sets in, the resolution of the state of tension is otherwise effected. The movement of love goes on, but persons—the characters of the novel, the artist himself responsible for the object, the peopled parlour where the Ming vase was displayed, or the woman who ran her fingers over the cool jade—will begin to haunt the attention, not as within the work of art itself but as constituted more and more in their own right. This personalization is, of course, unsatisfactory, even to the compulsion from which it derives. It is only an evanescent appeasement, for these persons do not exist in the present situation controlled by the object, and it is an existent and responsive person that human nature demands. But the personalist drive, if still frustrated, has had a kind of say.

The nature of the frustration here can be misunderstood. It turns not on the fact that the work of art is man-made but on the fact that it is an object. Drilled at least from the time of Walter Pater to focus all aesthetic questions on the man-made art object, we are likely to overlook the fact that the fundamental impasse here presents itself at a more basic level than that of art itself, and that the impulse to focus the difficulty at the level of art is only another manifestation of the tendency to keep the potential of personality around an object at a maximum. The art object, with its immediate social context, is an easier point than the natural object at which both to study and to project the personalist aberration. That for both operations we today automatically avail ourselves of the object of art rather than of the natural object testifies perhaps to the waning power of the imagination in our present culture.

In more primitive cultures, it has been otherwise. It has been otherwise in the earlier history of the culture of the West. The nature cults react to the impasse created by the person-object situation not only on the artistic, but upon the natural level as well. Hebrew and early Christian critiques of the nature cults of antiquity attack the cults precisely on such ground. In the analysis offered by the writer of the Book of Wisdom, it is man's orientation towards personality which has betrayed him in his contemplation of natural objects, so that he pretends that the objects themselves are persons, imagining 'either the fire, or the wind, or the swift air, or the circle of the stars, or the great water, or the sun and the moon, to be the gods that rule the world'. The pre-Hellenic nature cults are accused of pretending to close a circuit where it cannot be closed, of failing to own that the person-to-person drive must push on past the person-object situation to find a response which plays back. While the objects of nature are indeed redolent of Person, the Person must be not in, but beyond them. The error lies in the self-deception which tries to turn the object into a person instead of squarely facing the impasse.

Centuries later, this same critique is extended to the Graeco-Roman world and given additional dimensions by Paul in the opening of his Letter to the Romans. Men have allowed themselves to be misled in imputing what is proper to the invisible and incorruptible God (personality as such is not visible, the human person, in so far as merely visible, being rather like an object) not only to human beings but to birds and four-footed animals and creeping things. Here the aberration of idolatry, of misplaced personalism, is presented as intimately connected with other deep psychological displacements. The deterioration of the sexual aspect of marriage in an idolatrous society is not a mere accident, for treating objects like persons and persons like objects suggests a basic imbalance sure to make itself felt in this deepest of human personal relationships.

IV

It would be difficult to assign the precise differences between the place of the artist and the art object in contemporary society and their place in the Judaeo-Hellenistic world. It is, however, certain that the shifts that have produced the modern world have radically altered the focus of the personalist crisis. Men are less and less inclined to impregnate inanimate nature with personality, at least in any crass fashion, although it is well to recall that in Mr. Eliot's later poems, as H. Marshall McLuhan has recently pointed out, the quite convincing speakers seem to be sections of the landscape. Even apart from reflections suggested by this and the many related phenomena which everyone can think of, it would be too simple to maintain that the old apotheosis of natural objects has simply been removed and the apotheosis of the objects of human art put into its place. But it is certain that a great shift has taken place from the former to the latter kind of apotheosis.

Between Graeco-Roman times and the present, the crudity—indeed, the childishness—of almost all medieval and Renaissance purely rhetorical theory, which stands in such strange contrast to the sophistication of theological, philosophical, and even, within its limits, what we might today call the para-physical or para-medical theory of the same periods, and which lags far behind rhetorical practice, betrays the fact that through the Middle Ages and the Renaissance the object of art had not aggregated to itself any large concentration of serious intellectual issues. No especially crucial questions attached to objects of art, not because earlier ages had an adequate apparatus of theory for explaining away the questions, but rather because the object of art failed, it would seem even in the case of serious artists, to become in any urgent way the psychological crux for things. It was idolatry of nature, implemented indeed by art, but only implemented, which long remained the real threat. The idolatry of art seems only during the Renaissance to have begun to appear as something more than a mist on the horizon.

Whatever the complete details of its history, the shift in emphasis from nature to art has matured today in connection with several related phenomena. There is the elaboration of rhetorical and esthetic theory which has marked the past few centuries, there is the cult, half-explicit but quite real, of the artist who is martyr to his craft and burnt up wholly in its service, and, finally, there is the present insistence on focusing the object of art itself to the careful exclusion of its personalized periphery.

The first of these phenomena, the elaboration of theory, is simply testimony to the fact that the work of art itself is now somehow capable of focusing the central issues of human existence. The second points immediately to the personalized aspect of these issues, for in figures such as those of Kafka or Proust or Joyce—at least as they exist as symbols in men's minds, for, as to their persons, we cannot presume to frame a definitive answer—we find the human being who has given himself to the work of art so completely as to blur the distinction between himself and it, presenting himself to it, as though it were a person, in an act of total abandonment, and thus endowing it, by what must be the ultimate fiction, with the marrow of his own abrogated personality. For the devotee of the martyr-artist, the blurring here is accomplished not at the periphery of the work of art by shading this periphery out into personalities, but rather at the very centre of the work, where the personality of the artist has so annihilated itself as to be defined by nothing more than the work. The autobiographical bias in the work here does not stand in relationship to a life retained in its own right as real. The autobiography has consumed the life in its telling. The real life has been terminated in a foundation sacrifice: a human being has been put to death in order to serve as the ultimate substructure of the artistic edifice. To serve even the cause of the natural fertility which underlies the fertility of art, neither Moloch nor any other Baal could ask for more.

It is in association with such phenomena as these that the present insistence on the autonomy of the art object acquires its high seriousness. The concentration on the object is hardly a passing infatuation of a school of critics. It is a specialized focus of a persistent problem at the centre of human life. If the object of art has become less religious today in being less often explicitly directed towards an extra-temporal goal, it has also become more religious in bearing more directly the weight of religious issues. The object-person question pressing on the art object today is not a mere prop tangential to human living. It is the axis, the quiet pole that bears the weight and movement of all.

The assertion that in works of art it is the object itself which counts thus treads such crucial ground that it must be made with great honesty, which means with circumspection and humility. Not only the truth of the situation, but its awkwardness as well, must be faced. This awkwardness derives from the fact that, far fetched as it may seem when applied to less important works of art, the principle apparently holds that, in a valid but not exclusive sense, each work of art is not only an object but a kind of surrogate for a person. Anything that bids for attention in an act of contemplation is a surrogate for a person. In proportion as the work of art is capable of being taken in full seriousness, it moves further and further along an asymptote to the curve of personality.

The very insistence on the object-existence of the work of art, the insistence that it be set off from another reality, clean and self-possessed, involves an anomaly. For it is not an object, but a person who is self-possessed. It is only persons who, in their deep interiors where no other creature can enter, are cut off clean from the rest of the world, poised alone. The object situation itself is really the crux, the ultimate impossibility—a situation which by its very structure points away from itself to another world of persons, which carries in itself its own dissolution. The very way in which we envision the object-situation as clean, cut off, is derived not so much from the object as from our own personalist bias. We have forgotten the lesson of Gestalt-psychology. This is humiliating for those who must deal with objects, as we all must. But it will do no good to blink the facts and pretend that they are otherwise. And it will perhaps do no harm to understand and sympathize with the recurrent impulse—shall we say, of the undergraduate?—to get away from it all and back into the vibrant world of personalities again.

The fact is that, in the last analysis, as a matter of full, serious, protracted contemplation and love, it is unbearable for a man or woman to be faced with anything less than a person—and thus, tragically, even part-way unbearable to be faced only with other human persons, where the personal relationship is inevitably enmeshed in material situations involving objects, and where even the human being, measurable, definable, partakes of the nature of object at the same time that he is person. In all our moves, our motivation, perhaps in secret and by indirection, bears towards the counter-move, hopes to find itself really a counter-move. Our great fear is that we are not being loved. Our gaze on the object, we peep anxiously from the corners of our eyes, alert for someone's response somewhere.

This situation keeps the jinnee in the urn and promises to keep him there for good. Try as you may, he will not be exorcized. What is worse, he will always threaten to prove more interesting than the urn itself. For he is a person, or—since it is hard to be certain about jinn, themselves folklore creatures grown out of the person-object crisis and representing an ambiguous and unsatisfactory compromise, for some Moslem writers make them angelic or demonic persons, but others mere diaphanous animals—at any rate, if he is not a person, he behaves enough like one to betray the bias of the human heart.

Tradition and the Individual Talent

In English writing we seldom speak of tradition, though we occasionally apply its name in deploring its absence. We cannot refer to "the tradition" or to "a tradition"; at most we employ the adjective in saying that poetry of So-and-so is "traditional" or even "too traditional." Seldom, perhaps, does the word appear except in a phrase of censure. If otherwise, it is vaguely approbative, with the implication, as to the work approved, of some pleasing archaeological reconstruction. You can hardly make the word agreeable to English ears without this comfortable reference to the reassuring science of archaeology.

Certainly the word is not likely to appear in our appreciations of living or dead writers. Every nation, every race, has not only its own creative, but its own critical turn of mind; and is even more oblivious of the shortcomings and limitations of its critical habits than of those of its creative genius. We know, or think we know, from the enormous mass of critical writing that has appeared in the French language the critical method or habit of the French; we only conclude (we are such unconscious people) that the French are "more critical" than we, and sometimes even plume ourselves a little with the fact, as if the French were the less spontaneous. Perhaps they are; but we might remind ourselves that criticism is as inevitable as breathing, and that we should be none the worse for articulating what passes in our minds when we read a book and feel an emotion about it, for criticizing our own minds in their work of critcism. One of the facts that might come to light in this process is our tendency to insist, when we praise a poet, upon those aspects of his work in which he least resembles any one else. In these aspects or parts of his work we pretend to find what is individual, what is the peculiar essence of the man. We dwell with satisfaction upon the poet's difference from his predecessors, especially his immediate predecessors; we endeavour to find something that can be isolated in order to be enjoyed. Whereas if we approach a poet without this prejudice we shall often find that not only the best, but the most individual parts of his work may be those in which the dead poets, his ancestors, assert their immortality most vigorously. And I do not mean the impressionable period of adolescence, but the period of full maturity.

Yet if the only form of tradition, of handing down, consisted in following the ways of the immediate generation before us in a blind or timid adherence to its successes, "tradition" should positively be discouraged. We have seen many such simple currents soon lost in the sand; and novelty is better than repetition. Tradition is a matter of much wider significance. It cannot be inherited, and if you want it you must obtain it by great labour. It involves, in the first place, the historical sense, which we may call nearly indispensable to any one who would continue to be a poet beyond his twenty-fifth year; and the historical sense involves a perception, not only of the pastness of the past, but of its presence: the historical sense compels a man to write not merely with his own generation in his bones, but with a feeling that the whole of the literature of Europe from Homer and within it the whole of the literature of his own country has a simultaneous existence and composes a simultaneous order. This historical sense, which is a sense of the timeless as well as of the temporal and of the timeless and of the temporal together, is what makes a writer traditional. And it is at the same time what makes a writer most acutely conscious of his place in time, of his own contemporaneity.

No poet, no artist of any art, has his complete meaning alone. His significance, his appreciation is the appreciation of his relation to the dead poets and artists. You cannot value him alone; you must set him, for contrast and comparison, among the dead. I mean this as a principle of aesthetic, not merely historical, criticism. The necessity that he shall conform, that he shall cohere, is not onesided; what happens when a new work of art is created is something that happens simultaneously to all the works of art which preceded it. The existing monuments form an ideal order among themselves, which is modified by the introduction of the new (the really new) work of art among them. The existing order is complete before the new work arrives; for order to persist after the supervention of novelty, the *whole* existing order must be, if ever so slightly, altered; and so the relations, proportions, values of each work of art toward the whole are readjusted; and this is conformity between the old and the new. Whoever has approved this idea of order, of the form of European, of English literature will not find it preposterous that the past should be altered by the present as much as the present is directed by the past. And the poet who is aware of this will be aware of great difficulties and responsibilities.

In a peculiar sense he will be aware also that he must inevitably be judged by the standards of the past. I say judged, not amputated, by them; not judged to be as good as, or worse or better than, the dead; and certainly not judged by the canons of dead critics. It is a judgment, a comparison, in which two things are measured by each other. To conform merely would be for the new work not really to conform at all; it would not be new, and would therefore not be a work of art. And we do not quite say that the new is more valuable because it fits in; but its fitting in is a test of its value—a test, it is true, which can only be slowly and cautiously applied, for we are none of us infallible judges of conformity. We say: it appears to conform, and is perhaps individual, or it appears individual, and many conform; but we are hardly likely to find that it is one and not the other.

To proceed to a more intelligible exposition of the relation of the poet to the past: he can neither take the past as a lump, an indiscriminate bolus, nor can he form himself wholly on one or two private admirations, nor can he form himself wholly upon one preferred period. The first course is inadmissible, the second is an important experience of youth, and the third is a pleasant and highly desirable supplement. The poet must be very conscious of the main current, which does not at all flow invariably through the most distinguished reputations. He must be quite aware of the obvious fact that art never improves, but that the material of art is never quite the same. He must be aware that the mind of Europe—the mind of his own country—a mind which he learns in time to be much more important than his own private mind—is a mind which changes, and that this change is a development which abandons nothing *en route*, which does not superannuate either Shakespeare, or Homer, or the rock drawing of the Magdalenian draughtsmen. That this development, refinement perhaps, complication certainly, is not, from the point of view of the artist, any improvement. Perhaps not even an improvement from the point of view of the psychologist or not to the extent which we imagine; perhaps only in the end based upon a complication in economics and machinery. But the difference between the present and the past is that the conscious present is an awareness of the past in a way and to an extent which the past's awareness of itself cannot show.

Some one said: "The dead writers are remote from us because we *know* so much more than they did." Precisely, and they are that which we know.

I am alive to a usual objection to what is clearly part of my programme for the *métier* of poetry. The objection is that the doctrine requires a ridiculous amount of erudition (pedantry), a claim which can be rejected by appeal to the lives of poets in any pantheon. It will even be affirmed that much learning deadens or perverts poetic sensibility. While, however, we persist in believing that a poet ought to know as much as will not encroach upon his necessary receptivity and necessary laziness, it is not desirable to confine knowledge to whatever can be put into a useful shape for examinations, drawing-rooms, or the still more pretentious modes of publicity. Some can absorb knowledge, the more tardy must sweat for it. Shakespeare acquired more essential history from Plutarch than most men could from the whole British Museum. What is to be insisted upon is that the poet must develop or procure the consciousness of the past and that he should continue to develop this consciousness throughout his career.

What happens is a continual surrender of himself as he is at the moment to something which is more valuable. The progress of an artist is a continual self-sacrifice, a continual extinction of personality.

There remains to define this process of depersonalization and its relation to the sense of tradition. It is in this depersonalization that art may be said to approach the condition of science. I, therefore, invite you to consider, as a suggestive analogy, the action which takes place when a bit of finely filiated platinum is introduced into a chamber containing oxygen and sulphur dioxide.

II

Honest criticism and sensitive appreciation are directed not upon the poet but upon the poetry. If we attend to the confused cries of the newspaper critics and the *susurrus* of popular repetition that follows, we shall hear the names of poets in great numbers; if we seek not Blue-book knowledge but the enjoyment of poetry, and ask for a poem, we shall seldom find it. I have tried to point out the importance of the relation of the poem to other poems by other authors, and suggested the conception of poetry as a living whole of all the poetry that has ever been written. The other aspect of this Impersonal theory of poetry is the relation of the poem to its author. And I hinted, by an analogy, that the mind of the mature poet differs from that of the immature one not precisely in any valuation of "personality," not being necessarily more interesting, or having "more to say," but rather by being a more finely perfected medium in which special, or very varied, feelings are at liberty to enter into new combinations.

The analogy was that of the catalyst. When the two gases previously mentioned are mixed in the presence of a filament of platinum, they form sulphurous acid. This combination takes place only if the platinum is present; nevertheless the newly formed acid contains no trace of platinum, and the platinum itself is apparently unaffected; has remained inert, neutral, and unchanged. The mind of the poet is the shred of platinum. It may partly or exclusively operate upon the experience of the man himself; but, the more perfect the artist, the more completely separate in him will be the man who suffers and the mind which creates;

the more perfectly will the mind digest and transmute the passions which are its material.

The experience, you will notice, the elements which enter the presence of the transforming catalyst, are of two kinds: emotions and feelings. The effect of a work of art upon the person who enjoys it is an experience different in kind from any experience not of art. It may be formed out of one emotion, or may be a combination of several; and various feelings, inhering for the writer in particular words or phrases or images, may be added to compose the final result. Or great poetry may be made without the direct use of any emotion whatever: composed out of feelings solely. Canto XV of the *Inferno* (Brunetto Latini) is a working up of the emotion evident in the situation; but the effect, though single as that of any work of art, is obtained by considerable complexity of detail. The last quatrain gives an image, a feeling attaching to an image, which "came," which did not develop simply out of what precedes, but which was probably in suspension in the poet's mind until the proper combination arrived for it to add itself to. The poet's mind is in fact a receptacle for seizing and storing up numberless feelings, phrases, images, which remain there until all the particles which can unite to form a new compound are present together.

If you compare several representative passages of the greatest poetry you see how great is the variety of types of combination, and also how completely any semi-ethical criterion of "sublimity" misses the mark. For it is not the "greatness," the intensity, of the emotions, the components, but the intensity of the artistic process, the pressure, so to speak, under which the fusion takes place, that counts. The episode of Paolo and Francesca employs a definite emotion, but the intensity of the poetry is something quite different from whatever intensity in the supposed experience it may give the impresssion of. It is no more intense, furthermore, than Canto XXVI, the voyage of Ulysses, which has not the direct dependence upon an emotion. Great variety is possible in the process of transmutation of emotion: the murder of Agamemnon, or the agony of Othello, gives an artistic effect apparently closer to a possible original than the scenes from Dante. In the *Agamemnon*, the artistic emotion approximates to the emotion of an actual spectator; in *Othello* to the emotion of the protagonist himself. But the difference between art and the event is always absolute; the combination which is the murder of Agamemnon is probably as complex as that which is the voyage of Ulysses. In either case there has been a fusion of elements. The ode of Keats contains a number of feelings which have nothing particular to do with the nightingale, but which the nightingale, partly, perhaps, because of its attractive name, and partly because of its reputation, served to bring together.

The point of view which I am struggling to attack is perhaps related to the metaphysical theory of the substantial unity of the soul: for my meaning is, that the poet has, not a "personality" to express, but a particular medium, which is only a medium and not a personality, in which impressions and experiences combine in peculiar and unexpected ways. Impressions and experiences which are important for the man may take no place in the poetry, and those which become important in the poetry may play quite a negligible part in the man, the personality.

I will quote a passage which is unfamiliar enough to be regarded with fresh attention in the light—or darkness—of these observations:

> *And now methinks I could e'en chide myself*
> *For doating on her beauty, though her death*
> *Shall be revenged after no common action.*
> *Does the silkworm expend her yellow labours*
> *For thee? For thee does she undo herself?*
> *Are lordships sold to maintain ladyships*
> *For the poor benefit of a bewildering minute?*
> *Why does yon fellow falsify highways,*
> *And put his life between the judge's lips,*
> *To refine such a thing—keeps horse and men*
> *To beat their valours for her?* . . .

In this passage (as is evident if it is taken in its context) there is a combination of positive and negative emotions: an intensely strong attraction toward beauty and an equally intense fascination by the ugliness which is contrasted with it and which destroys it. This balance of contrasted emotion is in the dramatic situation to which the speech is pertinent, but that situation alone is inadequate to it. This is, so to speak, the structural emotion, provided by the drama. But the whole effect, the dominant tone, is due to the fact that a number of floating feelings, having an affinity to this emotion by no means superficially evident, have combined with it to give us a new art emotion.

It is not in his personal emotions, the emotions provoked by particular events in his life, that the poet is in any way remarkable or interesting. His particular emotions may be simple, or crude, or flat. The emotion in his poetry will be a very complex thing, but not with the complexity of the emotions of people who have very complex or unusual emotions in life. One error, in fact, of eccentricity in poetry is to seek for new human emotions to express; and in this search for novelty in the wrong place it discovers the perverse. The business of the poet is not to find new emotions, but to use the ordinary ones and, in working them up into poetry, to express feelings which are not in actual emotions at all. And emotions which he has never experienced will serve his turn as well as those familiar to him. Consequently, we must believe that "emotion recollected in tranquillity" is an inexact formula. For it is neither emotion, nor recollection, nor, without distortion of meaning, tranquillity. It is a concentration, and a new thing resulting from the concentration, of a very great number of experiences which to the practical and active person would not seem to be experiences at all; it is a concentration which does not happen consciously or of deliberation. These experiences are not "recollected," and they finally unite in an atmosphere which is "tranquil" only in that it is a passive attending upon the event. Of course this is not quite the whole story. There is a great deal, in the writing of poetry, which must be conscious and deliberate. In fact, the bad poet is usually unconscious where he ought to be conscious, and conscious where he ought to be unconscious. Both errors tend to make him "personal." Poetry is not a turning loose of emotion, but an escape from emotion; it is not the expression of personality, but an escape from personality. But, of course, only those who have personality and emotions know what it means to want to escape from these things.

III

δ δὲ νοῦς ἴσως θειότερόν τι χαὶ ἀπαθές ἐστιν.[1]

This essay proposes to halt at the frontier of metaphysics or mysticism, and confine itself to such practical conclusions as can be applied by the responsible person interested in poetry. To divert interest from the poet to the poetry is a laudable aim: for it would conduce to a juster estimation of actual poetry, good and bad. There are many people who appreciate the expression of sincere emotion in verse, and there is a smaller number of people who can appreciate technical excellence. But very few know when there is an expression of *significant* emotion, emotion which has its life in the poem and not in the history of the poet. The emotion of art is impersonal. And the poet cannot reach this impersonality without surrending himself wholly to the work to be done. And he is not likely to know what is to be done unless he lives in what is not merely the present, but the present moment of the past, unless he is conscious, not of what is dead, but of what is already living.

[1] "Perhaps the Mind is something divine and [therefore] unaffected [by outside impressions]." Aristotle, *On the Soul*, ch. 4.

GEORG LUKÁCS

The Ideology of Modernism

It is in no way surprising that the most influential contemporary school of writing should still be committed to the dogmas of 'modernist' anti-realism. It is here that we must begin our investigation if we are to chart the possibilities of a bourgeois realism. We must compare the two main trends in contemporary bourgeois literature, and look at the answers they give to the major ideological and artistic questions of our time.

We shall concentrate on the underlying ideological basis of these trends (ideological in the above-defined, not in the strictly philosophical, sense). What must be avoided at all costs is the approach generally adopted by bourgeois-modernist critics themselves: that exaggerated concern with formal criteria, with questions of style and literary technique. This approach may appear to distinguish sharply between 'modern' and 'traditional' writing (i.e. contemporary writers who adhere to the styles of the last century). In fact it fails to locate the decisive formal problems and turns a blind eye to their inherent dialectic. We are presented with a false polarization which, by exaggerating the importance of stylistic differences, conceals the opposing principles actually underlying and determining contrasting styles.

To take an example: the *monologue intérieur*. Compare, for instance, Bloom's monologue in the lavatory or Molly's monologue in bed, at the beginning and at the end of *Ulysses*, with Goethe's early-morning monologue as conceived by Thomas Mann in his *Lotte in Weimar*. Plainly, the same stylistic technique is being employed. And certain of Thomas Mann's remarks about Joyce and his methods would appear to confirm this.

Yet it is not easy to think of any two novels more basically dissimilar than *Ulysses* and *Lotte in Weimar*. This is true even of the superficially rather similar scenes I have indicated. I am not referring to the—to my mind—striking difference in intellectual quality. I refer to the fact that with Joyce the stream-of-consciousness technique is no mere stylistic device; it is itself the formative principle governing the narrative pattern and the presentation of character. Technique here is something absolute; it is part and parcel of the aesthetic ambition informing *Ulysses*. With Thomas Mann, on the other hand, the *monologue intérieur* is simply a technical device, allowing the author to explore aspects of Goethe's world which would not have been otherwise available. Goethe's experience is not presented as confined to momentary sense-impressions. The artist reaches down to the core of Goethe's personality, to the complexity of his relations with his own past, present, and even future experience. The stream of association is only apparently free. The monologue is composed with the utmost artistic rigour: it is a carefully plotted sequence gradually piercing to the core of Goethe's personality. Every person or event, emerging momentarily from the stream and vanishing again, is given a specific weight, a definite position, in the pattern of the whole. However unconventional the presentation, the compositional principle is that of the traditional epic; in the way the pace is controlled, and the transitions and climaxes are organized, the ancient rules of epic narration are faithfully observed.

It would be absurd, in view of Joyce's artistic ambitions and his manifest abilities, to qualify the exaggerated attention he gives to the detailed recording of sense-data, and his comparative neglect of ideas and emotions, as artistic failure. All this was in conformity with Joyce's artistic intentions; and, by use of such techniques, he may be said to have achieved them satisfactorily. But between Joyce's intentions and those of Thomas Mann there is a total opposition. The perpetually oscillating patterns of sense- and memory-data, their powerfully charged—but aimless and directionless—fields of force, give rise to an epic structure which is *static*, reflecting a belief in the basically static character of events.

These opposed views of the world—dynamic and developmental on the one hand, static and sensational on the other—are of crucial importance in examining the two schools of literature I have mentioned. I shall return to the opposition later. Here, I want only to point out that an exclusive emphasis on formal matters can lead to serious misunderstanding of the character of an artist's work.

What determines the style of a given work of art? How does the intention determine the form? (We are concerned here, of course, with the intention realized in the work; it need not coincide with the writer's conscious intention). The distinctions that concern us are not those between stylistic 'techniques' in the formalistic sense. It is the view of the world, the ideology or *weltanschauung* underlying a writer's work, that counts. And it is the writer's attempt to reproduce this view of the world which constitutes his 'intention' and is the formative principle underlying the style of a given piece of writing. Looked at in this way, style ceases to be a formalistic category. Rather, it is rooted in content; it is the specific form of a specific content.

Content determines form. But there is no content of which Man himself is not the focal point. However various the *données* of literature (a particular experience, a didactic purpose), the basic question is, and will remain: what is Man?

Here is a point of division: if we put the question in abstract, philosophical terms, leaving aside all formal considerations, we arrive—for the realist school—at the traditional Aristotelian dictum (which was also reached by other than purely aesthetic considerations): Man is *zoon politikon*, a social animal. The Aristotelian dictum is applicable to all great realistic literature. Achilles and Werther, Oedipus and Tom Jones, Antigone and Anna Karenina: their individual existence—their *Sein an sich*, in the Hegelian terminology; their 'ontological being', as a more fashionable terminology has it—cannot be distinguished from their social and historical environment. Their human significance, their specific individuality cannot be separated from the context in which they were created.

The ontological view governing the image of man in the work of leading modernist writers is the exact opposite of this. Man, for these writers, is by nature solitary, asocial, unable to enter into relationships with other human beings. Thomas Wolfe once wrote: 'My view of the world is based on the firm conviction that solitariness is by no means a rare condition, something peculiar to myself or to a few specially solitary human beings, but the inescapable, central fact of human existence.' Man, thus imagined, may establish contact with other individuals, but only in a superficial, accidental manner; only, ontologically speaking, by retrospective reflection. For 'the others', too, are basically solitary, beyond significant human relationship.

This basic solitariness of man must not be confused with that individual solitariness to be found in the literature of traditional realism. In the latter case, we are dealing with a particular situation in which a human being may be placed, due either to his character or to the circumstances of his life. Solitariness may be objectively conditioned, as with Sophocles' Philoctetes, put ashore on the bleak island of Lemnos. Or it may be subjective, the product of inner necessity, as with Tolstoy's Ivan Ilyitsch or Flaubert's Frédéric Moreau in the *Education Sentimentale*. But it is always merely a fragment, a phase, a climax or anticlimax, in the life of the community as a whole. The fate of such individuals is characteristic of certain human types in specific social or historical circumstances. Beside and beyond their solitariness, the common life, the strife and togetherness of other human beings, goes on as before. In a word, their solitariness is a specific social fate, not a universal *condition humaine*.

The latter, of course, is characteristic of the theory and practice of modernism. I would like, in the present study, to spare the reader tedious excursions into philosophy. But I cannot refrain from drawing the reader's attention to Heidegger's description of human existence as a 'thrownness-into-being' (*Geworfenheit ins Dasein*). A more graphic evocation of the ontological solitariness of the individual would be hard to imagine. Man is 'thrown-into-being'. This implies, not merely that man is constitutionally unable to establish relationships with things or persons outside himself; but also that it is impossible to determine theoretically the origin and goal of human existence.

Man, thus conceived, is an ahistorical being. (The fact that Heidegger does admit a form of 'authentic' historicity in his system is not really relevant. I have shown elsewhere that Heidegger tends to belittle historicity as 'vulgar'; and his 'authentic' historicity is not distinguishable from ahistoricity). This negation of history takes two different forms in modernist literature. First, the hero is strictly confined within the limits of his own experience. There is not for him—and apparently not for his creator —any pre-existent reality beyond his own self, acting upon him or being acted upon by him. Secondly, the hero himself is without personal history. He is 'thrown-into-the-world': meaninglessly, unfathomably. He does not develop through contact with the world; he neither forms nor is formed by it. The only 'development' in this literature is the gradual revelation of the human condition. Man is now what he has always been and always will be. The narrator, the examining subject, is in motion; the examined reality is static.

Of course, dogmas of this kind are only viable in philosophical abstraction, and then only with a measure of sophistry. A gifted writer, however extreme his theoretical modernism, will in practice have to compromise with the demands of historicity and of social environment. Joyce uses Dublin, Kafka and Musil the Hapsburg Monarchy, as the locus of their masterpieces. But the locus they lovingly depict is little more than a backcloth; it is not basic to their artistic intention.

This view of human existence has specific literary consequences. particularly in one category, of primary theoretical and practical importance, to which we must now give our attention: that of *potentiality*. Philosophy distinguishes between *abstract* and *concrete* (in Hegel, 'real') *potentiality*. These two categories, their interrelation and opposition, are rooted in life itself. *Potentiality*—seen abstractly or subjectively—is richer than actual life. Innumerable possibilities for man's development are imaginable, only a small percentage of which will be realized. Modern subjectivism, taking these imagined possibilities for actual complexity of life, oscillates between melancholy and fascination. When the world declines to realize these possibilities, this melancholy becomes tinged with contempt. Hofmannsthal's Sobeide expressed the reaction of the generation first exposed to this experience:

The burden of those endlessly poured-over
And now forever perished possibilities . . .

How far were those possibilities even concrete or 'real'? Plainly, they existed only in the imagination of the subject, as dreams or day-dreams. Faulkner, in whose work this subjective potentiality plays an important part, was evidently aware that reality must thereby be subjectivized and made to appear arbitrary. Consider this comment of his: 'They were all talking simultaneously, getting flushed and excited, quarrelling, making the unreal into a possibility, then into a probability, then into an irrefutable fact, as human beings do when they put their wishes into words.' The possibilities in a man's mind, the particular pattern, intensity and suggestiveness they assume, will of course be characteristic of that individual. In practice, their number will border on the infinite, even with the most unimaginative individuals. It is thus a hopeless undertaking to define the contours of individuality, let alone to come to grips with a man's actual fate, by means of potentiality. The *abstract* character of potentiality is clear from the fact that it cannot determine development—subjective mental states, however permanent or profound, cannot here be decisive. Rather, the development of personality is determined by inherited gifts and qualities; by the factors, external or internal, which further or inhibit their growth.

But in life potentiality can, of course, become reality. Situations arise in which a man is confronted with a choice; and in the act of choice a man's character may reveal itself in a light that surprises even himself. In literature—and particularly in dramatic literature—the denouement often consists in the realization of just such a potentiality, which circumstances have kept from coming to the fore. These potentialities are, then, 'real' or concrete potentialities. The fate of the character depends upon the potentiality in question, even if it should condemn him to a tragic end. In advance, while still a subjective potentiality in the character's mind, there is no way of distinguishing it from the innumerable abstract potentialities in his mind. It may even be buried away so completely that, before the moment of decision, it has never entered his mind even as an abstract potentiality. The subject, after taking his decision, may be unconscious of his own motives. Thus Richard Dudgeon, Shaw's Devil's Disciple, having sacrificed himself as Pastor Andersen, confesses: 'I have often asked myself for the motive, but I find no good reason to explain why I acted as I did.'

Yet it is a decision which has altered the direction of his life. Of course, this is an extreme case. But the qualitative leap of the denouement, cancelling and at the same time renewing the continuity of individual consciousness, can never be predicted. The concrete potentiality cannot be isolated from the myriad abstract potentialities. Only actual decision reveals the distinction.

The literature of realism, aiming at a truthful reflection of reality, must demonstrate both the concrete and abstract potentialities of human beings in extreme situations of this kind. A character's concrete potentiality once revealed, his abstract potentialities will appear essentially inauthentic. Moravia, for instance, in his novel *The Indifferent Ones*, describes the young son of a decadent bourgeois family, Michel, who makes up his mind to kill his sister's seducer. While Michel, having made his decision, is planning the murder, a large number of abstract—but highly suggestive —possibilities are laid before us. Unfortunately for Michel the murder is actually carried out; and, from the sordid details of the action, Michel's character emerges as what it is—representative of that background from which, in subjective fantasy, he had imagined he could escape.

Abstract potentiality belongs wholly to the realm of subjectivity; whereas concrete potentiality is concerned with the dialectic between the individual's subjectivity and objective reality. The literary presentation of the latter thus implies a description of actual persons inhabiting a palpable, identifiable world. Only in the interaction of character and environment can the concrete potentiality of a particular individual be singled out from the 'bad infinity' of purely abstract potentialities, and emerge as the determining potentiality of just this individual at just this phase of his development. This principle alone enables the artist to distinguish concrete potentiality from a myriad abstractions.

But the ontology on which the image of man in modernist literature is based invalidates this principle. If the 'human condition'—man as a solitary being, incapable of meaningful relationships—is identified with reality itself, the distinction between abstract and concrete potentiality becomes null and void. The categories tend to merge. Thus Cesare Pavese notes with John Dos Passos, and his German contemporary, Alfred Döblin, a sharp oscillation between 'superficial *verisme*' and 'abstract Expressionist schematism'. Criticizing Dos Passos, Pavese writes that fictional characters 'ought to be created by deliberate selection and description of individual features'—implying that Dos Passos' characterizations are transferable from one individual to another. He describes the artistic consequences: by exalting man's subjectivity, at the expense of the objective reality of his environment, man's subjectivity itself is impoverished.

The problem, once again, is ideological. This is not to say that the ideology underlying modernist writings is identical in all cases. On the contrary: the ideology exists in extremely various, even contradictory forms. The rejection of narrative objectivity, the surrender to subjectivity, may take the form of Joyce's stream of consciousness, or of Musil's 'active passivity', his 'existence without quality', or of Gide's *'action gratuite'*, where abstract potentiality achieves pseudo-realization. As individual character manifests itself in life's moments of decision, so too in literature. If the distinction between abstract and concrete potentiality vanishes, if man's inwardness is identified with an abstract subjectivity, human personality must necessarily disintegrate.

T. S. Eliot described this phenomenon, this mode of portraying human personality, as

> *Shape without form, shade without colour,*
> *Paralysed force, gesture without motion.*

The disintegration of personality is matched by a disintegration of the outer world. In one sense, this is simply a further consequence of our argument. For the identification of abstract and concrete human potentiality rests on the assumption that the objective world is inherently inexplicable. Certain leading modernist writers, attempting a theoretical apology, have admitted this quite frankly. Often this theoretical impossibility of understanding reality is the point of departure, rather than the exaltation of subjectivity. But in any case the connection between the two is plain. The German poet Gottfried Benn, for instance, informs us that 'there is no outer reality, there is only human consciousness, constantly building, modifying, rebuilding new worlds out of its own creativity'. Musil, as always, gives a moral twist to this line of thought. Ulrich, the hero of his *The Man without Qualities*, when asked what he would do if he were in God's place, replies: 'I should be compelled to abolish reality.' Subjective existence 'without qualities' is the complement of the negation of outward reality.

The negation of outward reality is not always demanded with such theoretical rigour. But it is present in almost all modernist literature. In conversation, Musil once gave as the period of his great novel, 'between 1912 and 1914'. But he was quick to modify this statement by adding: 'I have not, I must insist, written a historical novel. I am not concerned with actual events. . . . Events, anyhow, are interchangeable. I am interested in what is typical, in what one might call the ghostly aspect of reality.' The word 'ghostly' is interesting. It points to a major tendency in modernist literature: the attenuation of actuality. In Kafka, the descriptive detail is of an extraordinary immediacy and authenticity. But Kafka's artistic ingenuity is really directed towards substituting his *angst*-ridden vision of the world for objective reality. The realistic detail is the expression of a ghostly un-reality, of a nightmare world, whose function is to evoke *angst*.

The same phenomenon can be seen in writers who attempt to combine Kafka's techniques with a critique of society—like the German writer, Wolfgang Koeppen, in his satirical novel about Bonn, *Das Treibhaus*. A similar attenuation of reality underlies Joyce's stream of consciousness. It is, of course, intensified where the stream of consciousness is itself the medium through which reality is presented. And it is carried *ad absurdum* where the stream of consciousness is that of an abnormal subject or of an idiot—consider the first part of Faulkner's *Sound and Fury* or, a still more extreme case, Beckett's *Molloy*.

Attenuation of reality and dissolution of personality are thus interdependent: the stronger the one, the stronger the other. Underlying both is the lack of a consistent view of human nature. Man is reduced to a sequence of unrelated experiential fragments; he is as inexplicable to others as to himself. In Eliot's *Cocktail Party* the psychiatrist, who voices the opinions of the author, describes the phenomenon:

Ah, but we die to each other daily
What we know of other people
Is only our memory of the moments
During which we knew them. And they have changed since then.

To pretend that they and we are the same
Is a useful and convenient social convention
Which must sometimes be broken. We must also remember
That at every meeting we are meeting a stranger.

The dissolution of personality, originally the unconscious product of the identification of concrete and abstract potentiality, is elevated to a deliberate principle in the light of consciousness. It is no accident that Gottfried Benn called one of his theoretical tracts '*Doppelleben*'. For Benn, this dissolution of personality took the form of a schizophrenic dichotomy. According to him, there was in man's personality no coherent pattern of motivation of behaviour. Man's animal nature is opposed to his denaturized, sublimated thought-processes. The unity of thought and action is 'backwoods philosophy'; thought and being are 'quite separate entities'. Man must be either a moral or a thinking being—he cannot be both at once.

These are not, I think, purely private, eccentric speculations. Of course, they are derived from Benn's specific experience. But there is an inner connection between these ideas and a certain tradition of bourgeois thought. It is more than a hundred years since Kierkegaard first attacked the Hegelian view that the inner and outer world form an 'objective dialectical unity, that they are indissolubly married in spite of their apparent opposition. Kierkegaard denied any such unity. According to Kierkegaard, the individual exists within an opaque, impenetrable 'incognito'.

This philosophy attained remarkable popularity after the Second World War—proof that even the most abstruse theories may reflect social reality. Men like Martin Heidegger, Ernst Jünger, the lawyer Carl Schmitt, Gottfried Benn and others passionately embraced this doctrine of the eternal incognito which implies that a man's external deeds are no guide to his motives. In this case, the deeds obscured behind the mysterious incognito were, needless to say, these intellectuals' participation in Nazism: Heidegger, as Rector of Freiburg University, had glorified Hitler's seizure of power at his Inauguration; Carl Schmitt had put his great legal gifts at Hitler's disposal. The facts were too well-known to be simply denied. But, if this impenetrable incognito were the true *'condition humaine'*, might not—concealed within their incognito—Heidegger or Schmitt have been secret opponents of Hitler all the time, only supporting him in the world of appearances? Ernst von Salomon's cynical frankness about his opportunism in *The Questionnaire* (keeping his reservations to himself or declaring them only in the presence of intimate friends) may be read as an ironic commentary on this ideology of the incognito as we find it, say, in the writings of Ernst Jünger.

This digression may serve to show, taking an extreme example, what the social implications of such an ontology may be. In the literary field, this particular ideology was of cardinal importance; by destroying the complex tissue of man's relations with his environment, it furthered the dissolution of personality. For it is just the opposition between a man and his environment that determines the development of his personality. There is no great hero of fiction—from Homer's Achilles to Mann's Adrian Leverkühn or Sholochov's Grigory Melyekov—whose personality is not the product of such an opposition. I have shown how disastrous the denial of the distinction between abstract and concrete potentiality must be for the presentation of character. The destruction of the complex tissue of man's interaction with his environment likewise saps the vitality of this opposition. Certainly, some writers who adhere to this ideology have attempted, not unsuccessfully, to portray this opposition in concrete terms. But the underlying ideology deprives these contradictions of their dynamic, developmental significance. The contradictions co-exist, unresolved, contributing to the further dissolution of the personality in question.

It is to the credit of Robert Musil that he was quite conscious of the implications of his method. Of his hero Ulrich he remarked: 'One is faced with a simple choice: either one must run with the pack (when in Rome, do as the Romans do); or one becomes a neurotic.' Musil here introduces the problem, central to all modernist literature, of the significance of psychopathology.

This problem was first widely discussed in the Naturalist period. More than fifty years ago, that doyen of Berlin dramatic critics, Alfred Kerr, was writing: 'Morbidity is the legitimate poetry of Naturalism. For what is poetic in everyday life? Neurotic aberration, escape from life's dreary routine. Only in this way can a character be translated to a rarer clime and yet retain an air of reality.' Interesting, here, is the notion that the poetic necessity of the pathological derives from the prosaic quality of life under capitalism. I would maintain—we shall return to this point—that in modern writing there is a continuity from Naturalism to the Modernism of our day—a continuity restricted, admittedly, to underlying ideological principles. What at first was no more than dim anticipation of approaching catastrophe developed, after 1914, into an all-pervading obsession. And I would suggest that the ever-increasing part played by psychopathology was one of the main features of the continuity. At each period—depending on the prevailing social and historical conditions—psychopathology was given a new emphasis, a different significance and artistic function. Kerr's description suggests that in naturalism the interest in psychopathology sprang from an aesthetic need; it was an attempt to escape from the dreariness of life under capitalism. The quotation from Musil shows that some years later the opposition acquired a moral slant. The obsession with morbidity had ceased to have a merely decorative function, bringing colour into the greyness of reality, and become a moral protest against capitalism.

With Musil—and with many other modernist writers—psychopathology became the goal, the *terminus ad quem*, of their artistic intention. But there is a double difficulty inherent in their intention, which follows from its underlying ideology. There is, first, a lack of definition. The protest expressed by this flight into psychopathology is an abstract gesture; its rejection of reality is wholesale and summary, containing no concrete criticism. It is a gesture, moreover, that is destined to lead nowhere; it is an escape into nothingness. Thus the propagators of this ideology are mistaken in thinking that such a protest could ever be fruitful in literature. In any protest against particular social conditions, these conditions themselves must have the central place. The bourgeois protest against feudal society, the proletarian against bourgeois society, made their point of departure a criticism of the old order. In both cases the protest—reaching out beyond the point of departure—was based on a concrete *terminus ad quem*: the establishment of a new order. However indefinite the structure and content of this new order, the will towards its more exact definition was not lacking.

How different the protest of writers like Musil! The *terminus a quo* (the corrupt society of our time) is inevitably the main source of energy, since the *terminus ad quem* (the escape into psychopathology) is a mere abstraction. The rejection of modern reality is purely subjective. Considered in terms of man's relation with his environment, it lacks both content and direction. And this lack is exaggerated still further by the character of the *terminus ad quem*. For the protest is an empty gesture, expressing nausea, or discomfort, or longing. Its content—or rather lack of content—derives from the fact that such a view of life cannot import a sense of direction. These writers are not wholly wrong in believing that psychopathology is their surest refuge; it is the ideological complement of their historical position.

This obsession with the pathological is not only to be found in literature. Freudian psychoanalysis is its most obvious expression. The treatment of the subject is only superficially different from that in modern literature. As everybody knows, Freud's starting point was 'everyday life'. In order to explain 'slips' and day-dreams, however, he had to have recourse to psychopathology. In his lectures, speaking of resistance and repression, he says: 'Our interest in the general psychology of symptom-formation increases as we understand to what extent the study of pathological conditions can shed light on the workings of the normal mind.' Freud believed he had found the key to the understanding of the normal personality in the psychology of the abnormal. This belief is still more evident in the typology of Kretschmer, which also assumes that psychological abnormalities can explain normal psychology. It is only when we compare Freud's psychology with that of Pavlov, who takes the Hippocratic view that mental abnormality is a deviation from a norm, that we see it in its true light.

Clearly, this is not strictly a scientific or literary-critical problem. It is an ideological problem, deriving from the ontological dogma of the solitariness of man. The literature of realism, based on the Aristotelean concept of man as *zoon politikon*, is entitled to develop a new typology for each new phase in the evolution of a society. It displays the contradictions within society and within the individual in the context of a dialectical unity. Here, individuals embodying violent and extraordinary passions are still within the range of a socially normal typology (Shakespeare, Balzac, Stendhal). For, in this literature, the average man is simply a dimmer reflection of the contradictions always existing in man and society; eccentricity is a socially-conditioned distortion. Obviously, the passions of the great heroes must not be confused with 'eccentricity' in the colloquial sense: Christian Buddenbrook is an 'eccentric'; Adrian Leverkühn is not.

The ontology of *Geworfenheit* makes a true typology impossible; it is replaced by an abstract polarity of the eccentric and the socially-average. We have seen why this polarity—which in traditional realism serves to increase our understanding of social normality—leads in modernism to a fascination with morbid eccentricity. Eccentricity becomes the necessary complement of the average; and this polarity is held to exhaust human potentiality. The implications of this ideology are shown in another remark of Musil's: 'If humanity dreamt collectively, it would dream Moosbrugger.' Moosbrugger, you will remember, was a mentally-retarded sexual pervert with homicidal tendencies.

What served, with Musil, as the ideological basis of a new typology—escape into neurosis as a protest against the evils of society—becomes with other modernist writers an immutable *condition humaine*. Musil's statement loses its conditional 'if' and becomes a simple description of reality. Lack of objectivity in the description of the outer world finds its complement in the reduction of reality to a nightmare. Beckett's *Molloy* is perhaps the *ne plus ultra* of this development, although Joyce's vision of reality as an incoherent stream of consciousness had already assumed in Faulkner a nightmare quality. In Beckett's novel we have the same vision twice over. He presents us with an image of the utmost human degradation—an idiot's vegetative existence. Then, as help is imminent from a mysterious unspecified source, the rescuer himself sinks into idiocy. The story is told through the parallel streams of consciousness of the idiot and of his rescuer.

Along with the adoption of perversity and idiocy as types of the *condition humaine*, we find what amounts to frank glorification. Take Montherlant's *Pasiphae*, where sexual perversity—the heroine's infatuation with a bull—is presented as a triumphant return to nature, as the liberation of impulse from the slavery of convention. The chorus—i.e. the author—puts the following question (which, though rhetorical, clearly expects an affirmative reply): 'Si l'absence de pensée et l'absence de morale ne contribuent pas beaucoup à la dignité des bêtes, des plantes et des eaux . . .?' Montherlant expresses as plainly as Musil, though with different moral and emotional emphasis, the hidden—one might say repressed—social character of the protest underlying this obsession with psychopathology, its perverted Rousseauism, its anarchism. There are many illustrations of this in modernist writing. A poem of Benn's will serve to make the point:

O that we were our primal ancestors,
Small lumps of plasma in hot, sultry swamps;
Life, death, conception, parturition
Emerging from those juices soundlessly.

A frond of seaweed or a dune of sand,
Formed by the wind and heavy at the base;
A dragonfly or gull's wing—already, these
Would signify excessive suffering.

This is not overtly perverse in the manner of Beckett or Montherlant. Yet, in his primitivism, Benn is at one with them. The opposition of man as animal to man as social being (for instance, Heidegger's devaluation of the social as 'das Man', Klages' assertion of the incompatibility of *Geist* and *Seele,* or Rosenberg's racial mythology) leads straight to a glorification of the abnormal and to an undisguised anti-humanism.

A typology limited in this way to the *homme moyen sensuel* and the idiot also opens the door to 'experimental' stylistic distortion. Distortion becomes as inseparable a part of the portrayal of reality as the recourse to the pathological. But literature must have a concept of the normal if it is to 'place' distortion correctly; that is to say, to see it *as* distortion. With such a typology this placing is impossible, since the normal is no longer a proper object of literary interest. Life under capitalism is, often rightly, presented as a distortion (a petrification or paralysis) of the human substance. But to present psychopathology as a way of escape from this distortion is itself a distortion. We are invited to measure one type of distortion against another and arrive, necessarily, at universal distortion. There is no principle to set against the general pattern, no standard by which the petty-bourgeois and the pathological can be seen in their social context. And these tendencies, far from being relativized with time, become ever more absolute. Distortion becomes the normal condition of human existence; the proper study, the formative principle, of art and literature.

I have demonstrated some of the literary implications of this ideology. Let us now pursue the argument further. It is clear, I think, that modernism must deprive literature of a sense of *perspective.* This would not be surprising; rigorous modernists such as Kafka, Benn, and Musil have always indignantly refused to provide their readers with any such thing. I will return to the ideological implications of the idea of perspective later. Let me say here that, in any work of art, perspective is of overriding importance. It determines the course and content; it draws together the threads of narration; it enables the artist to choose between the important and the superficial, the crucial and the episodic. The direction in which characters develop is determined by perspective, only those features being described which are material to their development. The more lucid the perspective—as in Molière or the Greeks—the more economical and striking the selection.

Modernism drops this selective principle. It asserts that it can dispense with it, or can replace it with its dogma of the *condition humaine*. A naturalistic style is bound to be the result. This state of affairs—which to my mind characterizes all modernist art of the past fifty years—is disguised by critics who systematically glorify the modernist movement. By concentrating on formal criteria, by isolating technique from content and exaggerating its importance, these critics refrain from judgment on the social or artistic significance of subject-matter. They are unable, in consequence, to make the aesthetic distinction between *realism* and *naturalism*. This distinction depends on the presence or absence in a work of art of a 'hierarchy of significance' in the situations and characters presented. Compared with this, formal categories are of secondary importance. That is why it is possible to speak of the basically *naturalistic* character of modernist literature—and to see here the literary expression of an ideological continuity. This is not to deny that variations in style reflect changes in society. But the particular form this principle of naturalistic arbitrariness, this lack of hierarchic structure, may take is not, decisive. We encounter it in all-determining 'social conditions' of Naturalism, in Symbolism's impressionist methods and its cultivation of the exotic, in the fragmentation of objective reality in Futurism and Constructivism and and the German *Neue Sachlichkeit*, or, again, in Surrealism's stream of consciousness.

These schools have in common a basically static approach to reality. This is closely related to their lack of perspective. Characteristically, Gottfried Benn actually incorporated this in his artistic programme. One of his volumes bears the title, *Static Poems*. The denial of history, of development, and thus of perspective, becomes the mark of true insight into the nature of reality.

The wise man is ignorant
of change and development

*his children and children's children
are no part of his world.*

The rejection of any concept of the future is for Benn the criterion of wisdom. But even those modernist writers who are less extreme in their rejection of history tend to present social and historical phenomena as static. It is, then, of small importance whether this condition is 'eternal', or only a transitional stage punctuated by sudden catastrophes (even in early Naturalism the static presentation was often broken up by these catastrophes, without altering its basic character). Musil, for instance, writes in his essay, *The Writer in our Age:* 'One knows just as little about the present. Partly, this is because we are, as always, too close to the present. But it is also because the present in which we were plunged some two decades ago is of a particularly all-embracing and inescapable character.' Whether or not Musil knew of Heidegger's philosophy, the idea of *Geworfenheit* is clearly at work here. And the following reveals plainly how, for Musil, this static state was upset by the catastrophe of 1914: 'All of a sudden, the world was full of violence. . . . In European civilization, there was a sudden rift. . . .' In short: thus static apprehension of reality in modernist literature is no passing fashion; it is rooted in the ideology of modernism.

To establish the basic distinction between modernism and that realism which, from Homer to Thomas Mann and Gorky, has assumed change and development to be the proper subject of literature, we must go deeper into the underlying ideological problem. In *The House of the Dead* Dostoevsky gave an interesting account of the convict's attitude to work. He described how the prisoners, in spite of brutal discipline, loafed about, working badly or merely going through the motions of work until a new overseer arrived and allotted them a new project, after which they were allowed to go home. 'The work was hard,' Dostoevsky continues, 'but, Christ, with what energy they threw themselves into it! Gone was all their former indolence and pretended incompetence.' Later in the book Dostoevsky sums up his experiences: 'If a man loses hope and has no aim in view, sheer boredom can turn him into a beast. . . .' I have said that the problem of perspective in literature is directly related to the principle of selection. Let me go further: underlying the problem is a profound ethical complex, reflected in the composition of the work itself. Every human action is based on a presupposition of its inherent meaningfulness, at least to the subject. Absence of meaning makes a mockery of action and reduces art to naturalistic description.

Clearly, there can be no literature without at least the appearance of change or development. This conclusion should not be interpreted in a narrowly metaphysical sense. We have already diagnosed the obsession with psychopathology in modernist literature as a desire to escape from the reality of capitalism. But this implies the absolute primacy of the *terminus a quo*, the condition from which it is desired to escape. Any movement towards a *terminus ad quem* is condemned to impotence. As the ideology of most modernist writers asserts the unalterability of outward reality (even if his is reduced to a mere state of consciousness) human activity is, *a priori*, rendered impotent and robbed of meaning.

The apprehension of reality to which this leads is most consistently and convincingly realized in the work of Kafka. Kafka remarks of Josef K., as he is being led to execution: 'He thought of flies, their tiny limbs breaking as they struggle away from the fly-paper.' This mood of total impotence, of paralysis in the face of the unintelligible power of circumstances, informs all his work. Though the action of *The Castle* takes a different, even an opposite, direction to that of *The Trial*, this view of the world, from the perspective of a trapped and struggling fly, is all-pervasive. This experience, this vision of a world dominated by *angst* and of man at the mercy of incomprehensible terrors, makes Kafka's work the very type of modernist art. Techniques, elsewhere of merely formal significance, are used here to evoke a primitive awe in the presence of an utterly strange and hostile reality. Kafka's *angst* is the experience *par excellence* of modernism.

Two instances from musical criticism—which can afford to be both franker and more theoretical than literary criticism—show that it is indeed a universal experience with which we are dealing. The composer, Hanns Eisler, says of Schönberg: 'Long before the invention of the bomber, he expressed what people were to feel in the air raid shelters.' Even more characteristic—though seen from a modernist point of view—is Theodor W. Adorno's analysis (in *The Ageing of Modern Music*) of symptoms of decadence in modernist music: 'The sounds are still the same. But the experience of *angst*, which made their originals great, has vanished.' Modernist music, he continues, has lost touch with the truth that was its *raison d'être*. Composers are no longer equal to the emotional presuppositions of their modernism. And that is why modernist music has failed. The diminution of the original *angst*-obsessed vision of life (whether due, as Adorno thinks, to inability to respond to the magnitude of the horror or, as I believe, to the fact that this obsession with *angst* among bourgeois intellectuals has already begun to recede) has brought about a loss of substance in modern music, and destroyed its authenticity as a modernist artform.

This is a shrewd analysis of the paradoxical situation of the modernist artist, particularly where he is trying to express deep and genuine experience. The deeper the experience, the greater the damage to the artistic whole. But this tendency towards disintegration, this loss of artistic unity, cannot be written off as a mere fashion, the product of experimental gimmicks. Modern philosophy, after all, encountered these problems long before modern literature, painting or music. A case in point is the problem of *time*. Subjective Idealism had already separated time, abstractly conceived, from historical change and particularity of place. As if this separation were insufficient for the new age of imperialism, Bergson widened it further. Experienced time, subjective time, now became identical with real time; the rift between this time and that of the objective world was complete. Bergson and other philosophers who took up and varied this theme claimed that their concept of time alone afforded insight into authentic, i.e. subjective, reality. The same tendency soon made its appearance in literature.

The German left-wing critic and essayist of the Twenties, Walter Benjamin, has well described Proust's vision and the techniques he uses to present it in his great novel: 'We all know that Proust does not describe a man's life as it actually happens, but as it is remembered by a man who has lived through it. Yet this puts it far too crudely. For it is not actual experience that is important, but the texture of reminiscence, the Penelope's tapestry of a man's memory.' The connection with Bergson's theories of time is obvious. But whereas with Bergson, in the abstraction of philosophy, the unity of perception is preserved, Benjamin shows that with Proust, as a result of the radical disintegration of the time sequence, objectivity is eliminated: 'A lived event is finite, concluded at least on the level of experience. But a remembered event is infinite, a possible key to everything that preceded it and to everything that will follow it.'

It is the distinction between a philosophical and an artistic vision of the world. However hard philosophy, under the influence of Idealism, tries to liberate the concepts of space and time from temporal and spatial particularity, literature continues to assume their unity. The fact that, nevertheless, the concept of subjective time cropped up in literature only shows how deeply subjectivism is rooted in the experience of the modern bourgeois intellectual. The individual, retreating into himself in despair at the cruelty of the age, may experience an intoxicated fascination with his forlorn condition. But then a new horror breaks through. If reality cannot be understood (or no effort is made to understand it), then the individual's subjectivity—alone in the universe, reflecting only itself—takes on an equally incomprehensible and horrific character. Hugo von Hofmannsthal was to experience this condition very early in his poetic career:

> It is a thing that no man cares to think on,
> And far too terrible for mere complaint,
> That all things slip from us and pass away,
>
> And that my ego, bound by no outward force—
> Once a small child's before it became mine—
> Should now be strange to me, like a strange dog.

By separating time from the outer world of objective reality, the inner world of the subject is transformed into a sinister, inexplicable flux and acquires—paradoxically, as it may seem—a static character.

On literature this tendency towards disintegration, of course, will have an even greater impact than on philosophy. When time is isolated in this way, the artist's world disintegrates into a multiplicity of partial worlds. The static view of the world, now combined with diminished objectivity, here rules unchallenged. The world of man—the only subject-matter of literature—is shattered if a single component is removed. I have shown the consequences of isolating time and reducing it to a subjective category. But time is by no means the only component whose removal can lead to such disintegration. Here, again, Hofmannsthal anticipated later developments. His imaginary 'Lord Chandos' reflects: 'I have lost the ability to concentrate my thoughts or set them out coherently.' The result is a condition of apathy, punctuated by manic fits. The development towards a definitely pathological protest is here anticipated—admittedly in glamorous, romantic guise. But it is the same disintegration that is at work.

Previous realistic literature, however violent its criticism of reality, had always assumed the unity of the world it described and seen it as a living whole inseparable from man himself. But the major realists of our time deliberately introduce elements of disintegration into their work—for instance, the subjectivizing of time—and use them to portray the contemporary world more exactly. In this way, the once natural unity becomes a conscious, constructed unity (I have shown elsewhere that the device of the two temporal planes in Thomas Mann's *Doctor Faustus* serves to emphasize its historicity). But in modernist literature the disintegration of the world of man—and consequently the disintegration of personality—coincides with the ideological intention. Thus *angst*, this basic modern experience, this by-product of *Geworfenheit*, has its emotional origin in the experience of a disintegrating society. But it attains its effects by evoking the disintegration of the world of man.

To complete our examination of modernist literature, we must consider for a moment the question of allegory. Allegory is that aesthetic genre which lends itself par excellence to a description of man's alienation from objective reality. Allegory is a problematic genre because it rejects that assumption of an immanent meaning to human existence which—however unconscious, however combined with religious concepts of transcendence—is the basis of traditional art. Thus in medieval art we observe a new secularity (in spite of the continued use of religious subjects), triumphing more and more, from the time of Giotto, over the allegorizing of an earlier period.

Certain reservations should be made at this point. First, we must distinguish between literature and the visual arts. In the latter, the limitations of allegory can be the more easily overcome in that transcendental, allegorical subjects can be clothed in an aesthetic immanence (even if of a merely decorative kind) and the rift in reality in some sense be eliminated—we have only to think of Byzantine mosaic art. This decorative element has no real equivalent in literature; it exists only in a figurative sense, and then only as a secondary component. Allegorical art of the quality of Byzantine mosaic is only rarely possible in literature. Secondly, we must bear in mind in examining allegory—and this is of great importance for our argument—a historical distinction: does the concept of transcendence in question contain within itself tendencies towards immanence (as in Byzantine art or Giotto), or is it the product precisely of a rejection of these tendencies?

Allegory, in modernist literature, is clearly of the latter kind. Transcendence implies here, more or less consciously, the negation of any meaning immanent in the world or the life of man. We have already examined the underlying ideological basis of this view and its stylistic consequences. To conclude our analysis, and to establish the allegorical character of modernist literature, I must refer again to the work of one of the finest theoreticians of modernism—to Walter Benjamin. Benjamin's examination of allegory was a product of his researches into German Baroque drama. Benjamin made his analysis of these relatively minor plays the occasion for a general discussion of the aesthetics of allegory. He was asking, in effect, why it is that transcendence, which is the essence of allegory, cannot but destroy aesthetics itself.

Benjamin gives a very contemporary definition of allegory. He does not labour the analogies between modern art and the Baroque (such analogies are tenuous at best, and were much overdone by the fashionable criticism of the time). Rather, he uses the Baroque drama to criticize modernism, imputing the characteristics of the latter to the former. In so doing, Benjamin became the first critic to attempt a philosophical analysis of the aesthetic paradox underlying modernist art. He writes:

> In Allegory, the *facies hippocratica* of history looks to the observer like a petrified primeval landscape. History, all the suffering and failure it contains, finds expression in the human face—or, rather, in the human skull. No sense of freedom, no classical proportion, no human emotion lives in its features—not only human existence in general, but the fate of every individual human being is symbolized in this most palpable token of mortality. This is the core of the allegorical vision, of the Baroque idea of history as the passion of the world; History is significant only in the stations of its corruption. Significance is a function of mortality—because it is death that marks the passage from corruptibility to meaningfulness.

Benjamin returns again and again to this link between allegory and the annihilation of history:

> In the light of this vision history appears, not as the gradual realization of the eternal, but as a process of inevitable decay. Allegory thus goes beyond beauty. What ruins are in the physical world, allegories are in the world of the mind.

Benjamin points here to the aesthetic consequences of modernism—though projected into the Baroque drama—more shrewdly and consistently than any of his contemporaries. He sees that the notion of objective time is essential to any understanding of history, and that the notion of subjective time is a product of a period of decline. 'A thorough knowledge of the problematic nature of art' thus becomes for him—correctly, from his point of view—one of the hall-marks of allegory in Baroque drama. It is problematic, on the one hand, because it is an art intent on expressing absolute transcendence that fails to do so because of the means at its disposal. It is also problematic because it is an art reflecting the corruption of the world and bringing about its own dissolution in the process. Benjamin discovers 'an immense, anti-aesthetic subjectivity' in Baroque literature, associated with a theologically-determined subjectivity'. (We shall presently show—a point I have discussed elsewhere in relation to Heidegger's philosophy—how in literature a 'religious atheism' of this kind can acquire a theological character.) Romantic—and, on a higher plane, Baroque—writers were well aware of this problem, and gave their understanding, not only theoretical, but artistic—that is to say allegorical—expression. 'The image,' Benjamin remarks, 'becomes a rune in the sphere of allegorical intuition. When touched by the light of theology, its symbolic beauty is gone. The false appearance of totality vanishes. The image dies; the parable no longer holds true; the world it once contained disappears.'

The consequences for *art* are far-reaching, and Benjamin does not hesitate to point them out: 'Every person, every object, every relationship can stand for something else. This transferability constitutes a devastating, though just, judgment on the profane world—which is thereby branded as a world where such things are of small importance.' Benjamin knows, of course, that although details are 'transferable', and thus insignificant, they are not banished from art altogether. On the contrary. Precisely in modern art, with which he is ultimately concerned, descriptive detail is often of an extraordinary sensuous, suggestive power—we think again of Kafka. But this, as we showed in the case of Musil (a writer who does not consciously aim at allegory) does not prevent the materiality of the world from undergoing permanent alteration, from becoming transferable and arbitrary. Just this, modernist writers maintain, is typical of their own apprehension of reality. Yet presented in this way, the world becomes, as Benjamin puts it, 'exalted and depreciated at the same time'. For the conviction that phenomena are *not* ultimately transferable is rooted in a belief in the world's rationality and in man's ability to penetrate its secrets. In realistic literature each descriptive detail is both *individual* and *typical*. Modern allegory, and modernist ideology, however, deny the *typical*. By destroying the coherence of the world, they reduce detail to the level of mere particularity (once again, the connection between modernism and naturalism is plain). Detail, in its allegorical transferability, though brought into a direct, if paradoxical connection with transcendence, becomes an abstract function of the transcendence to which it points. Modernist literature thus replaces concrete typicality with abstract particularity.

We are here applying Benjamin's paradox directly to aesthetics and criticism, and particularly to the aesthetics of modernism. And, though we have reversed his scale of values, we have not deviated from the course of his argument. Elsewhere, he speaks out even more plainly—as though the Baroque mask had fallen, revealing the modernist skull underneath:

> Allegory is left empty-handed. The forces of evil, lurking in its depths, owe their very existence to allegory. Evil is, precisely, the non-existence of that which allegory purports to represent.

The paradox Benjamin arrives at—his investigation of the aesthetics of Baroque tragedy has culminated in a negation of aesthetics—sheds a good deal of light on modernist literature, and particularly on Kafka. In interpreting his writings allegorically I am not, of course, following Max Brod, who finds a specifically religious allegory in Kafka's works. Kafka refuted any such interpretation in a remark he is said to have made to Brod himself: 'We are nihilistic figments, all of us; suicidal notions forming in God's mind.' Kafka rejected, too, the gnostic concept of God as an evil demiurge: 'The world is a cruel whim of God, an evil day's work.' When Brod attempted to give this an optimistic slant, Kafka shrugged off the attempt ironically: 'Oh, hope enough, hope without end—but not, alas, for us.' These remarks, quoted by Benjamin in his brilliant essay on Kafka, point to the general spiritual climate of his work: 'His profoundest experience is of the hopelessness, the utter meaninglessness of man's world, and particularly that of present-day bourgeois man.' Kafka, whether he says so openly or not, is an atheist. An atheist, though, of that modern species who regard God's removal from the scene not as a liberation—as did Epicurus and the Encyclopedists—but as a token of the 'God-forsakenness' of the world, its utter desolation and futility. Jacobsen's *Niels Lyhne* was the first novel to describe this state of mind of the atheistic bourgeois intelligentsia. Modern religious atheism is characterized, on the one hand, by the fact that unbelief has lost its revolutionary *élan*—the empty heavens are the projection of a world beyond hope of redemption. On the other hand, religious atheism shows that the desire for salvation lives on with undiminished force in a world without God, worshipping the void created by God's absence.

The supreme judges in *The Trial*, the castle administration in *The Castle*, represent transcendence in Kafka's allegories: the transcendence of Nothingness. Everything points to them, and they could give meaning to everything. Everybody believes in their existence and omnipotence; but nobody knows them, nobody knows how they can be reached. If there is a God here, it can only be the God of religious atheism: *atheos absconditus*. We become acquainted with a repellent host of subordinate authorities; brutal, corrupt, pedantic—and, at the same time, unreliable and irresponsible. It is a portrait of the bourgeois society Kafka knew, with a dash of Prague local colouring. But it is also allegorical in that the doings of this bureaucracy and of those dependent on it, its impotent victims, are not concrete and realistic, but a reflection of that Nothingness which governs existence. The hidden, non-existent God of Kafka's world derives his spectral character from the fact that his own non-existence is the ground of all existence; and the portrayed reality, uncannily accurate as it is, is spectral in the shadow of that dependence. The only purpose of transcendence—the intangible *nichtendes Nichts*—is to reveal the *facies hippocratica* of the world.

That abstract particularity which we saw to be the aesthetic consequence of allegory reaches its high mark in Kafka. He is a marvellous observer; the spectral character of reality affects him so deeply that the simplest episodes have an oppressive, nightmarish immediacy. As an artist, he is not content to evoke the surface of life. He is aware that individual detail must point to general significance. But how does he go about the business of abstraction? He has emptied everyday life of meaning by using the allegorical method; he has allowed detail to be annihilated by his transcendental Nothingness. This allegorical transcendence bars Kafka's way to realism, prevents him from investing observed detail with typical significance. Kafka is not able, in spite of his extraordinary evocative power, in spite of his unique sensibility, to achieve that fusion of the particular and the general which is the essence of realistic art. His aim is to raise the individual detail in its immediate particularity (without generalizing its content) to the level of abstraction. Kafka's method is typical, here, of modernism's allegorical approach. Specific subject-matter and stylistic variation do not matter; what matters is the basic ideological determination of form and content. The particularity we find in Beckett and Joyce, in Musil and Benn, various as the treatment of it may be, is essentially of the same kind.

If we combine what we have up to now discussed separately we arrive at a consistent pattern. We see that modernism leads not only to the destruction of traditional literary forms; it leads to the destruction of literature as such. And this is true not only of Joyce, or of the literature of Expressionism and Surrealism. It was not André Gide's ambition, for instance, to bring about a revolution in literary style; it was his philosophy that compelled him to abandon conventional forms. He planned his *Faux-Monnayeurs* as a novel. But its structure suffered from a characteristically modernist schizophrenia: it was supposed to be written by the man who was also the hero of the novel. And, in practice, Gide was forced to admit that no novel, no work of literature could be constructed in that way. We have here a practical demonstration that—as Benjamin showed in another context—modernism means not the enrichment, but the negation of art.

The Esthetic Judgment and the Ethical Judgment

I

"We, it seems, are critical; we are embarrassed with second thoughts; we cannot enjoy anything for hankering to know whereof the pleasure consists; we are lined with eyes; we see with our feet; the time is infected with Hamlet's unhappiness—'Sicklied o'er with the pale cast of thought.'" These are the words in which Emerson, a hundred years ago, characterized our modern age, an age of criticism.

It is sometimes remarked that there is something wrong with an age which goes in predominantly for criticism. Unhappily there are many other reasons for thinking that there is something wrong with our age. That is precisely why we need criticism. Our modern age, bent upon a return to Nature, has more and more prostituted the humanities—the civilizing forces of religion, philosophy, literature and the arts; and now the totalitarian states, employing with sinister effect the one great creative force of the modern world, science, are intent upon completing the return to Nature, the return to the primitive. These are the times that try men's souls, to see whether we still have souls. These are the times that try men's minds, to see whether we can clarify the phrases we glibly repeat to summon up courage, phrases such as "preserving the values of civilization," "preserving the democratic way of life," "preserving the dignity of man." Without a keener and more earnestly affirmative criticism than we have had, we shall not even know what we wish to preserve, or why it is worth preserving.

Because there is nearly everything wrong with our age, the kind of criticism which can render the greatest service is a general criticism, taking into account that whole of our civilization. Granted that our civilization is highly complex, still we shall have to deal with it in the light of a few simple ideas firmly established. The greater the degree of specialization—the more men are sundered from each other by their preoccupations—to the same extent the need grows for some kind of intellectual and spiritual clearing-house. I refer to the kind of criticism, ranging into diverse fields and vitally connecting them, exemplified in the nineteenth century by Carlyle, Ruskin, Arnold, and Emerson, in the early twentieth century by Chesterton, Babbitt, and More, and in the present day by Jacques Maritain and Lewis Mumford. Such men are not merely critics of literature, they are critics of the foundations of our whole culture.

II

I am to deal in this paper, however, not with general but with literary criticism. What is the task of literary criticism? Let me begin with some negations.

Literary criticism is not concerned with literary works in respect to their *causes*. In our scientific age, it has been customary to think of the intention of a literary work as the sum of many and diverse causes. These causes lie in the author's experience, external and internal, the relation between the world in which he lives, which spreads round him and also back into the past, and his own inner constitution, his developing capacities as man and artist. For each of his works, it is conceived, there is an intricate complex of causes, but we can never be sure that we have found all of them. The study of these causes is a form of history, a blend of literary history, intellectual history, and social history. As scholars know, it is a fascinating study in itself, and it may offer valuable hints to the literary critic, who must use all means to understand the work with which he is dealing. Possibly it is capable of offering more help to the critic than has sometimes been allowed for it by those, including myself, who have reacted against the exaggerated estimate of its services by the sons of Taine; no one, admittedly, has thought through with any finality the relations of the two fields of activity. Clearly, however, the historical study of literature is not literary criticism but at best a preparation for it.

Nor is literary criticism concerned with literary works in respect to their ulterior *effects*. When a work is published—given to the public—it produces (or so the author hopes) some effect upon the public. It may influence the direction of thought or feeling, as in the case of Emerson's *Essays*. It may even lead to more or less change in the realm of practical affairs, ethical, social, political. Thus, *Uncle Tom's Cabin* became one of the causes of the War Between the States, and latterly *The Grapes of Wrath* has begotten a vigorous social response. The high potency of the effects of literary works was a vital concern with Plato, who expelled from his republic all poets except those singing hymns to the gods and praises of famous men, and it is today a vital concern with the dictators of Europe. It has also been a vital concern with American Humanists and Neo-Scholastics, who, since Babbitt's book on *Literature and the American College*, have given fresh life to Matthew Arnold's contention that not science but great literature is the central instrument in the educational process of making men human. And it has been a vital concern with Marxist and other Leftist critics, who realize that literature may become one instrument in the process of making men socialists. Yet it must be admitted that all practical effects, whether good, bad, or indifferent, are extrinsic to the literary work, carrying us away from the work. As causes take us back, effects take us forward. The literary critic must not go either way: he must stay with the work itself: he must deal with its values intrinsically.

Now if there is any sense at all in the history of criticism from Greek antiquity to the present century, two kinds of value are inherent in literature, esthetic and ethical. Let it be granted at once that esthetic value and ethical value are interdependent and, in all strictness, blended inseparably; still, it has not been found possible to discuss them both adequately at one and the same time. Let it be granted also that, logically if not practically, esthetic value must come first, since this determines whether a piece of writing is literature or a piece of non-literary writing.

III

An essential task of the literary critic is to contemplate, analyze, and judge a literary work as a work of art, as a thing of beauty, in its esthetic character. Literature is an art, a form of skill in making, the thing made being a thing of beauty and therefore "a joy forever." The critic is interested, like the artist, in technique, the process of making, but especially he is interested in structure, the esthetic properties of the thing made, its architectonic features such as unity, balance, emphasis, rhythm, and the like, the shapely pattern resulting when all the materials, that is, the emotions, sense perceptions, images, allusions, ideas, ethical insights, have been brought into more or less complete interplay and fullness of tension. When the whole work finally springs to life in his mind, the critic experiences a delight, a joy in the thing of beauty, akin to that of the artist when his vision at length fell into shape. He has a revel similar to that of Mozart, who tells us that musical ideas came streaming to him, began to join one another and kindle his imagination, and formed in his mind into a larger and larger piece till the composition, though unwritten, was complete, and could be seen at a glance. "Then," he said, "I don't hear the notes one after another, as they are hereafter to be played, but it is as if in my fancy they were all at once. And that *is* a revel (*das ist nun ein Schmaus*)." Inferior works of art do not afford this esthetic experience, and in the greatest art the excitement is imperfect. The critic thus has esthetic exaltations, satisfactions, annoyances, boredoms, which it is his business, as a rational judge, to justify in terms of the esthetic qualities of the works themselves.

I need not say more concerning esthetic judgment; no responsible person questions that it is the business of the literary critic, as of all art critics. A suggestive fact must now be noted: that whereas criticism in the other arts is usually esthetic, criticism in the art of literature is usually not. Why this is I shall inquire presently. Here let me pay tribute to a group of distinguished critics who have so earnestly concentrated upon the esthetic aspect that they have developed a new expertness in the analysis of poetic patterns. Never before, at least in English and American letters, have we had so much close reading, sensitive discrimination, free-ranging alertness expressed in a subtle style suited to the task. I refer, of course, to men like T. S. Eliot, William Empson, John Crowe Ransom, Allen Tate, Cleanth Brooks, and R. P. Blackmur, who, though they have had other interests as well, have excelled in practical criticism of the esthetic aspect of poems. That I am not disposed to underrate their achievement, or the importance of the esthetic point of view, I have perhaps indicated by sponsoring, at the University of Iowa, the recognition of imaginative writing as an art in the graduate school, taking the stand that a play, a novel, a book of verse is as pertinent and honorable in the training of a literary doctor as an academic study in language or literary history or literary criticism.

Having said this, I feel the freer to attack the heresy to which our esthetic critics are inclined, the heresy of the esthetic to which Poe, for example, subscribed. The heresy of the esthetic seems to me as bad as the heresy of the didactic. Both endeavor to make partial truth serve as the whole truth.[1] Both tend to take us away from literature, the one into problems of morals, the other into problems of esthetics. Indeed, esthetic critics, judging from their line of argument, appear to have scant interest in literature. They begin by speaking of literature; then they turn to the art of literature; then to the art of poetry; then to one kind of poetry, the lyric; and then to one kind of lyric, the metaphysical, in which the poem, as they put it, must not *mean* but *be*, in which substance and form are one, as in the art of music. Now, the view that music, the great modern art, is also the purest art came into vogue with romanticism, along with the corollary view that the essence of literature is lyricism. If music is the purest art, literature is obviously the impurest, so impure that we

---

[1] Heresies of many sorts have thrived in modern culture because it is so divisive and specialist. The concept of the "economic man," whose activity is independent of moral and political considerations, is but one instance of our tendency to seek purity of thought and achieve unreality. The esthetic man is as artificial as the economic man, as George F. Thomas pointed out in his inaugural lecture at Princeton, "Religion in an Age of Secularism," 1940.

actually speak of "literature and the arts," as if literature were not an art at all.

But there is another way of ranking the arts, according to their degree of articulateness. From this point of view music is the least and literature the most articulate art. While literature often strives in vain to equal music in wedding form and substance, its special perfection is an articulateness for which the other arts often strive in vain. Whereas music, in the line of Sidney Lanier, is "Love in search of a word," literature begins with the word, and builds its structures in terms of sentences, that is to say, propositions. In literature, reason and the ethical imagination, contemplating man and the grounds of his happiness and unhappiness, speak to us with an incomparable fulless and clarity; and they do this with maximum facility in the drama, because the essence of drama, as of human life, is action, external action in relation to the inner springs of action. Conceived as the most articulate art, literature has its center, not in the lyric, but rather in the drama, which lies about midway between works like *The Education of Henry Adams* or *The Flowering of New England*, where literature begins to be differentiated from non-literary prose, and the poems of Vachel Lindsay or Gertrude Stein, where literature is on the verge of passing over into music. Or we might reasonably say that literature has its center in the narrative poem or in the novel, since such works as the *Iliad* and *Wilhelm Meister*, like *Hamlet* and *Ghosts*, are, whatever their personal content and accent, primarily imaginative representations of life.[2]

IV

We have now come upon the explanation of the fact which I remarked a while ago, that whereas criticism in the other arts is generally esthetic, criticism in the field of literature tends to neglect the esthetic aspect. I deplore the neglect, but the reason for it seems plain enough: that the ethical or philosophic aspect of literature is not only a legitimate but an indispensable concern of the literary critic. I believe that Aristotle was right in thinking of imaginative literature as not only an art giving pleasure or delight, but as a reasonable imitation of life, of human action

---

[2] Works like these, in their rich articulation, would be more competent than lyrics to enlighten the proverbial Martian as to the nature of literature and the nature of mundane life. The lyric, as a fine distillate, a terse comment or gloss upon the text of life, is capable of an articulateness which is incisive rather than abundant. Its special character is, however, unlimited implication, an inexhaustible indeterminateness approaching that of music.

and human nature; in thinking of imaginative literature as philosophical in a way in which history and science are not. I do not find it necessary to follow Max Eastman and some of his successors in conceiving that all we *know* about life is what science tells us and that the area in which poetry may disport is fast shrinking to nothing. There is, and will always be, not only scientific but human knowledge, the sort of knowledge that we derive from the humanities, notably from literature, knowledge such as we may secure, as Dr. Johnson recognized, by reading Shakespeare, "by reading human sentiments in human language, by scenes from which a hermit may estimate the transactions of the world, and a confessor predict the progress of the passions." Not a little of Johnson's wisdom, which exceeded that of most of our psychologists and sociologists of today, came from great literature.

That poetry contains wisdom was well understood not only by Johnson, but also by Sidney, Dryden, Coleridge, Shelley, Arnold, Emerson, indeed pretty much everybody till we arrive at a few esthetic specialists of the present day. Traditionally they thought of wisdom as instruction, and conceived of the poet as a teacher, an unfortunate terminology because it seems to emphasize the effects of literature, which are the province of the sociological and moral critic. The literary critic is concerned rather with the wisdom *inherent* in literature, with the judgment of its ethical soundness, the firmness and range of its imitation of life. He repeats the Horatian formula not because it is traditional but because its soundness has made it traditional, saying with Robert Frost, the wisest of our contemporary poets, that a poem "begins in delight and ends in wisdom," or with Paul Engle that a poem affords a "wise excitement" or "intense wisdom." He is content to say, if you insist, that delight is all, but in that case he will add at once that the delight comes from the wisdom expressed as well as from the expression of the wisdom.

If, then, literary criticism is an esthetic judgment, it is equally an ethical judgment, and both judgments are needed to determine the "greatness" of literary works. A poem like "A Psalm of Life" falls short on both counts: it is bungling in its art, stereotyped in its wisdom. A poem like "Tintern Abbey" is great esthetically; as we have come increasingly to see, it is ethically vital but unsound; in sum, this poem is a superb expression of unwisdom. On the other hand, the poem which Wordsworth addressed to Milton (along with some of his other sonnets deeply inspired by the nobility of the English tradition) has greatness on the two counts, is both finely formed and wisely conceived.

To estimate the greatness of literary works, which is the main business of literary criticism, what is needed is a rounded estimate, esthetic and ethical. In a truly rounded estimate, the two tasks will be inseparable, will interpenetrate as intimately as in the organic unity of the literary work itself. But in fact such an organic criticism is impossible, and indeed all interpretation and evaluation is, strictly speaking, inept. Change the words and you change the thought. Paraphrase and you rob the text of much of its meaning. Translate and you impoverish or else create a new thing. Say anything whatever about a piece of literature in either its esthetic or its ethical aspect and you dilute or denature what is there. The only completely scrupulous critic is, therefore, the completely silent critic. Since this asceticism is more than critic flesh can endure, critics may be permitted to go on criticizing as well as they can, turning, again and again, consciously or not, from one kind of judgment to the other, violating the simultaneity of literature by resorting to alternation. Or they may be permitted to let one kind of judgment preponderate, because it is the kind in which they are interested or gifted, provided that they leave room, in their total theory, for others to practise more fully the other kind of judgment. Unfortunately some critics will be tempted to go farther, to become exclusive and intolerant, to employ one of the two judgments and decry the other. Preoccupied with a half-truth, such critics will fall into the heresy of estheticism or the heresy of didacticism.[3]

V

The theory of literary criticism I have sketched is that of the so-called Neo-Humanists. Why have they so inadequately practised it? Why has their interest in the esthetic properties of literature always been so definitely secondary, their interest in its ethical properties so definitely primary? Why did Babbitt and More, the leaders of the group, display an increasing aloofness even from literature? Why did the author of so many accomplished literary studies in the Shelburne series select as his crowning achievement a profound study of the Christian religion? And why did Babbitt, one of whose first books was on the modern

[3] From the Greeks till the late nineteenth century, the greater peril was didacticism; since the *Décadents* it has been estheticism.

Treating the ethical quality of the artifact as but one element in a system of relationships on a par with such other elements as rhythm, imagery, and diction, an accomplished group of critics today has tended to a confined and unwholesome estheticism which contrasts with the wide and free humanity of literature itself. As I. A. Richards suggests, many naturally superior critical minds, reacting against the "wild asses" who crudely applied the criterion of moral effect, "have virtually shut themselves up in a paddock."

confusion of the arts, attain his most substantial achievement in a book on democracy and close his career with a book on Hindu religion?

I have already answered these questions by saying that More and Babbitt were general critics. They were convinced that there is nearly everything wrong with modern civilization. Living in a time of complacent naturalism, when the idea of progress promised a Utopia, and science a method for attaining it, they made themselves unpopular by asserting that such a deluded program could only lead to the destruction of our civilization. To others, such as the socialists, who saw something fundamentally wrong in our civilization but who sought a remedy in a new economic system, they replied that the higher issues must be faced before the lower, since "the economic problem will be found to run into the political problem, and the political problem in turn into the philosophical problem, and the philosophical problem itself to be almost indissolubly bound up at last with the religious problem." Believing that our civilization had gone wrong on first principles, they were not content to be literary critics; they were general critics, and finally religious critics.

That it is possible to serve the same high ends without leaving the field of literary criticism has been shown most clearly, perhaps, by a scholar deeply influenced by them, G. R. Elliott of Amherst College. His *Cycle of Modern Poetry*, published in that year of economic hubris and nemesis, 1929, is not a work of philosophy, nor a work in which literature is merely used as material for philosophic purposes; it is a genuine piece of literary criticism, in which a sensitive esthetic discrimination interplays with keen ethical insight. With this double awareness Mr. Elliott considers the whole cycle of English poetry since the eighteenth century, beginning with Shelley and Byron, ending with Hardy, Frost, and their immediate successors. This great poetic impulse, as he conceives, is "now pretty well exhausted": "Poetry today, in England and America, is groping for a fresh direction." Mr. Elliott's prevailing theme is the subjection of modern poetry; his purpose, to show how it may attain freedom. "Perhaps never before," he says, "has poetry been so widely eager and experimental and, at the same time, so shortly tethered." He finds it tethered on one side to art because of a mistaken notion of the relation of poetry to art, and on the other side to something which is lacking large human meanings. His conclusion is that our poetry can rewin its freedom only by traversing anew "the great zones of the religious and moral imagination" with the aid of Milton "as a living classic and as our chief guide." A serious effort at poetic freedom will compel us to transcend modern ideas of human freedom. To illustrate, Mr. Elliott contrasts Whitman's declaration at the close of the Civil War: "Be not disheartened, affection shall solve the problems of freedom yet," with what Milton wrote at the close of the English Civil War: "Instead of fretting with vexation, or thinking that you can lay the blame on anyone but yourselves, know that to be free is the same thing as to be pious, to be wise, to be temperate and just, to be frugal and abstinent, and lastly, to be magnanimous and brave." Whitman's sentence, Mr. Elliott comments, "is the theme of nineteenth century poetry: its social unreality is now glaring; it is a worn-out imagining." But the passage from Milton "speaks to us, in our post-war era, like the voice of destiny close to our ear."

There may be many reasons, as the general critic could point out, why we need to deepen our notion of freedom, but Mr. Elliott, as literary critic, is concerned with one reason only: to restore the health of modern poetry. He wishes to free poetry from its deforming aberrations by returning it to the great tradition. Once reconnected with a truly usable past, it will have some chance to move forward to a central creativeness, instead of deploying barrenly in technical experiment. To become great once more, poetry needs a humane philosophy.[4]

VI

Now, the prominence given by humanist critics—even by Mr. Elliott—to the philosophical aspect of literature has been frequently condemned, sometimes by those who happen to prefer a different philosophy, sometimes by those who assert that the literary critic has no business trafficking with philosophy at all. I wish to answer the latter charge.

The answer lies, I think, in a distinction between systematic and literary philosophy. By systematic philosophy I mean, of course, the kind of philosophy which is outlined in the histories of philosophy, the kind with which university departments of philosophy busy themselves. With philosophy in this sense the literary critic should seek friendship but not wedlock. In the equipment of a critic, as W. C. Brownell put it, "a tincture at least of philosophic training may be timidly prescribed. . . . Drenched in philosophy, the critical faculty is almost certain to drown." Perhaps it would be better to say that the more philosophy a

---

[4] In the decade since *The Cycle of Modern Poetry* appeared, efforts have been extended to find a usable past in the poetry of Milton's century, especially in that of Donne, but with emphasis on a shift in technique rather than on a return to a humane philosophy.

Literature needs also, as Mr. Elliott is well aware, a humane society, a usable present, since writers absorb their age into their lives and work and are nourished by it.

critic can carry without altering his center of gravity, the sharper his criticism will be in its logical niceties, the tighter and richer in its intellectual texture. An excess of philosophy, however, may easily betray him into a rigid application of ideas to a field which is, after all, not amenable to philosophic standards. This is why the professional philosopher is so rarely a good literary critic. He is simply not at home. Despite all his training in thought, he is likely to manhandle thought in literary works. He is handicapped not merely because of his ineptness in the realm of the concrete and sensuous, but, far more seriously, because of his inclination to want a writer to look as firmly philosophic as possible and then to belabor him when he is literary, that is to say the greater part of the time. It is the very nature of literary philosophy to be loose, to be unsystematic, to be open not closed, to be generous not exclusive, to be suggestive not decisive. While the most articulate of the arts, literature does not aim at the specialized articulation of philosophy, the perfect web of abstract thought. Writers, like people in general, have a philosophy of life, not a formulated scheme such as professional philosophers require. The informal philosophies of our writers can be appropriately judged only by literary critics, who, being literary, share the writers' distrust of fixed systems, the writers' assumption that reason cannot exhaust the whole of reality, the conviction of a man like Plato, who was man of letters as well as philosopher, that logical explication must give way to symbol and myth when the highest truths are to be adumbrated.

Literature is not philosophy; it is, if I may quote what I have said elsewhere, "the record, in terms of beauty, of the striving of Mankind to know and express itself." Blending its love of beauty with its love of truth, it aims at nothing more than a working philosophy, enough articulation to give it firmness. Its subject is, essentially, the inner nature of man; it offers a working philosophy of man, or that "philosophy of wisdom" of which Erasmus spoke. It is not a parasitic but an independent growth. It may feed upon the works of systematic thinkers, but somewhat casually, not strictly following their logic. It could, in fact, get along without them, for literature has its own philosophic life and would go on even if philosophy had never been or should cease to be. Writers are thinkers, unsystematic thinkers, for whom everything is grist: experience here and now, the traditions of literature and the arts, history, science, religion, philosophy, all the concerns of man.

This is equally true of literary critics. Their activity is that of the writers; they too achieve some sort of working philosophy, but with them the end aimed at is different since they are not makers but judges. For them a working philosophy is requisite, not for informing works of art with significance, but for evaluating the significance of works of art. And in order to evaluate, they must be a great deal more conscious of their working philosophy than the artist. To the artist a philosophy is ideally an ardent faith, something so profoundly felt that it no longer needs reflection, something given which only asks to be formed or made, so that he is free to bestow upon it his full attention as an artist. Sound, therefore, is the advice which Jacques Maritain addresses to the artist: "Do not *separate* your art from your faith. But leave *distinct* what is distinct. Do not try to blend by force what life unites so well. If you were to make your esthetic an article of faith, you would spoil your faith. If you were to make your devotion a rule of artistic operation, or turn the desire to edify into a method of your art, you would spoil your art." But this unanalyzed integrity which M. Maritain recommends to the artist is not for the critic as well. His task is not to shape a symbol but to separate elements, to distinguish, to explain, to classify, to compare and contrast, to weigh, to reach a palpable conclusion, and for this rational task he needs a rational control of his philosophy.

There are those, to be sure, who would have the literary critic set aside his philosophy if it happens to be different from that of the work he is criticizing. They would have him suppress his disbelief. For the time being he should be like a guileless child, willing to credit the fairy tale. This I think is often impossible, and in any case absurd. But not wholly absurd. Let me explain by describing how, it seems to me, a good critic will read a book new to him. He will read it in two ways, first one way and then the other, or else in the two ways simultaneously. One way we may speak of as "feeling the book," the other as "thinking the book." By feeling the book I mean passively responding to the will of the author, securing the total impression aimed at. If the book accords with the critic's tastes and beliefs, this will be easy; otherwise, he will have to attempt an abeyance of disbelief, a full acceptance of the work for the time being, in order to understand it. But understanding is not criticism, and therefore he must read it another way, "thinking the book," that is, analyzing closely the esthetic pattern and the ethical burden, and reflecting upon these in terms of his criteria until he is ready with a mature opinion of the book's value. If obliged to suspend disbelief when reading the first way, he is now obliged to state and justify his disbelief.

A good critic will read in this double fashion, I think, no matter what his working philosophy may be. How much of extant literature a critic can genuinely accept and admire will depend on his particular philosophy. To the thoroughgoing naturalist of the present day, the great bulk of literature from Homer to the middle nineteenth century is, on the ethical side, misguided, dated, of antiquarian interest. To the humanist, on the other hand, this same body of literature represents, on the ethical side, the "wisdom of the ages" as opposed to the brief unwisdom of the romantics and the naturalists. Since the romantics pretended to high wisdom and the naturalists have proclaimed their austere love of truth, the humanist deems it appropriate to meet them on their own ground and to try to demonstrate their philosophic immaturity. Today, when a crude naturalism runs rampant in literature and the arts, as well as in the realm of political thought and action, the humanist conceives that he may be forgiven his comparative indifference to the esthetic aspects of contemporary writings, may be permitted to dwell upon the subversiveness of their ethical significance, their celebration of the indignity of man, their basic defeatism.

How much of the dignity of man of which we prate is symbolized in our literature, the true mirror of our thoughts? Sometimes it is travestied by the lingering formulas of romanticism, more often it is drably belied by books and plays in which man is pictured as irrational and unfree, in ugly bondage to heredity and environment. To the pale cast of our thought, what a piece of nature is a man! How ignoble in rationalizing! How infinite in blundering! Here is something to which the literary critic may well apply a humane philosophy, bringing his literary judgment into relation with a general or final judgment, if he would not be numbered among those "Irresponsibles" whom Archibald MacLeish has excoriated.

If the life of man is indeed as nasty and brutish as the most typical literature of our time represents it, the victory of the organized, mechanized evil which is now loose in the world will only confirm a disaster that has already taken place. As Walter Lippmann declared with unwonted fervor in an address to his Harvard Class, what has made possible the victories of this scientized evil is "the lazy, self-indulgent materialism, the amiable, lackadaisical, footless, confused complacency of the free nations of the world. They have dissipated, like wastrels and drunkards, the inheritance of freedom and order that came to them from hard-working, thrifty, faithful, believing, and brave men. The disaster in the midst of which we are living is a disaster in the character of men."

I think that Mr. Lippmann is right. Vast armaments alone will not save us. We must also rewin our all but lost inheritance of freedom and order, and with freedom and order that on which they depend, belief in the dignity of man. And this in turn can come only through a religious renewal of belief in man as a spiritual being, or if that is beyond our attainment, a humanistic renewal of belief in man as a rational and free animal, a belief still richly current in the time of Washington and Jefferson, a belief that comes down to us all the way from ancient Greece. We have had our "return to Nature"; it is time for another great historical return, the "return to Man."

If the literary critic has no concern with such problems, he might as well close up shop and let the tempest ride.

Periods and Movements in Literary History

Every book of literary history is subdivided into periods or movements and uses terms designating specific periods freely and frequently. Nevertheless, only a very few writers of literary history indicate the principles which underlie the formation of periods in literary history. I cannot find an express discussion of our problem in English, though many historians make, of course, incidental remarks and reflect on the nature of specific periods such as "Romanticism." I have found, however, three German papers devoted to a theoretical discussion of our problem: one by Richard Moritz Meyer, dating from 1901, which is a defense of his division of German literature of the nineteenth century according to decades, and two more recent by Herbert Cysarz and Benno von Wiese, which approach the problem in a highly metaphysical manner. Cysarz wants us even to conceive of a period as an almost metaphysical entity, whose nature we have to intuit.[1]

It will be best to start with the opposite point of view. One frequently hears that the term "period" (I leave the discussion of "movement" for a moment) is nothing given or discoverable in reality, but merely a linguistic label for any section of time which we want to consider in isolation for the practical purpose of analysis and description. If this were so, I might as well declare the question closed. The extreme "nominalist" point of view which assumes that "period" is merely an arbitrary superimposition on a material which in reality is a continuous, directionless flux, leaves us with a chaos of concrete events on the one hand and purely subjective labels on the other. It must lead to barren skepticism, to an abandonment of the whole problem, which is precisely that of discovering crests and troughs in the undulatory stream of literature.

"Period" is a term which cannot be discussed in isolation: a single period, though we may elect to study it to the exclusion of others, is a period only within a series of periods which together make up the development of literature. Our conception of a period is thus inextricably bound up

---

[1] R. M. Meyer. "Prinzipien der wissenschaftlichen Periodenbildung," *Euphorion,* VIII (1901), 1 ff.; Herbert Cysarz, "Das Periodenprinzip in der Literaturwaissenschaft" in *Philosophie der Literaturwissenschaft* (ed. by Emil Ermatinger, Berlin, 1930); Benno von Wiese, "Zur Kritik des geistesgeschichtlichen Epochenbegriffes," *Deutsche Vierteljahrschrift für Literaturwissenschaft und Geistesgeschichte,* XI, (1933), 130 ff. As my article was passing through the press, my attention was called to Max Foerster's "The Psychological Basis of Literary Periods," in *Studies for William H. Read,* 1940, pp. 254 ff. This is an attempt, similar to Cazamian's, to establish a "law of polar reaction" (p. 261) in the mental development of mankind.

with our conception of the whole process of literature. If we conceive of this development as a directionless flux, then obviously it does not matter where we put a cross section through a reality which is essentially uniform in its manifold variety. If we hold this view (and it is held consciously and unconsciously by many) it is of no importance what scheme of periods, however arbitrary and mechanical, we adopt. We can write literary history by calendar centuries, by decades, or year by year in an annalistic fashion. We might even adopt such a criterion as Arthur Symons did in his book on the *Romantic Movement in English Poetry* (1909). He discusses only authors born before 1800 and only those who died after 1800. Period is then merely a convenient label: a necessity for subdividing a book or choosing a topic. This view underlies, though frequently unconsciously, the practice of literally hundreds of books which respect the date lines between centuries religiously or which set to a topic exact limitations of date (for example, 1710–1730, 1700–1775) which are not justified by any other reason except the purely practical consideration that their authors have to begin somewhere and stop somewhere else. Of course, such a respect for calendar dates is perfectly legitimate in purely bibliographical compilations, where it serves for orientation as the Dewey decimal system helps us to arrange a library. But it seems to me that one should not pretend that such periodical divisions have anything to do with literary history proper.

If we ignore the worshippers of calendar dates, I think we have to come to the conclusion that most histories of literature divide their periods in accordance with political changes and thus conceive of literature as completely determined by the political or social revolutions of a nation. The problem of determining periods is thus nicely shifted to the shoulders of the political and social historians: their divisions and periods are usually taken over without question. If we look into older histories of English literature, we shall find that they are either written according to number divisions or according to one simple political criterion—the reigns of the English sovereigns. I do not think we need to show how misleading the cutting up of the course of English literature is, if we follow the chance dates of the deaths of the English rulers: nobody thinks seriously of distinguishing in early nineteenth-century literature between the reigns of George III, George IV, and William IV, but the equally artificial distinction between the reigns of Elizabeth, James I, and Charles I still survive, though scarcely anybody would ascribe any value to them.

Rather, if we look into more recent histories of English literature, we find that the old divisions by calendar centuries or reigns of kings have disappeared almost completely and have been replaced by a series of periods whose names, at least, are derived from the most divers activities of the human mind. We still use the terms "Elizabethan" and "Victorian," which are survivals of the old distinctions between reigns: but they have assumed a new meaning inside a scheme of intellectual history. We keep them because we feel that the two queens seem to symbolize the character of their times. We no longer cling to a rigid chronological framework actually determined by the ascent to the throne and the deaths of these monarchs. We use the term "Elizabethan" to include writers before the closing of the theaters, almost forty years after the death of the queen, and, on the other hand, we rarely speak of a man like Oscar Wilde as a Victorian, though his life falls well within the chronological limits of the reign of Queen Victoria. The terms, originally of political origin, have thus assumed a definite meaning in intellectual and even in literary history. But still the motley derivation of our current labels is somewhat disconcerting. "Reformation" comes from ecclesiastical history; "humanism," mainly from the history of scholarship; "Renaissance" from art history; "Commonwealth" and "Restoration" refer to definite political events. The term "eighteenth century" is an old numerical term which has assumed some of the functions of literary terms such as "Augustan" and "neoclassic." "Pre-romanticism" and "romanticism" are primarily literary terms, while Victorian, Edwardian, and Georgian are derived from the reigns of the sovereigns. The same bewildering picture is presented by almost any other literature: for example, the "colonial period" in American literature is a political term, "romanticism" and "realism" are literary, and so forth.

In defense of this mixture of terms it may, of course, be urged that this apparent confusion was caused by history itself. We, as literary historians, have first of all to pay heed to the ideas and conceptions, the programs and names of the writers themselves, and thus we have to be content with accepting their own divisions. I would not want to minimize the value of the evidence supplied by consciously formulated programs, factions, and self-interpretations in the history of literature. I think the term "movement" might well be reversed for such self-conscious and self-critical activities, which we must, of course, describe as we would any other historical sequence of events and pronouncements. But, I think, they are merely materials for our study of a period, just as much as the whole history of criticism will be a running commentary to any history of literature. They may give us suggestions and hints, but they should not prescribe our own methods and divisions, not because our views are necessarily more penetrating than theirs, but because we have the benefit of seeing the past in the light of the future.

Besides, it must be pointed out, it is simply not true that this welter of terms of different origin was established in their own time. In English the term "humanism" occurs first in 1832; "Renaissance" in 1840; "Elizabethan" in 1817; "Augustan" in 1819; and "Romanticism" in 1844. These dates, which I derive from the *Oxford Dictionary*, are probably not quite reliable, for I have found the term "Augustan" applied to English literature by Leonard Welsted as early as 1724;[2] but they indicate the time lag between the labels and the periods which they designate. We all know that the Romanticists did not call themselves Romanticists, at least in England. So far as I know, the German scholar Alois Brandl, in his book on Coleridge (1887), first connected Coleridge and Wordsworth definitely with the Romantic movement and grouped them with Shelley, Keats, and Byron. In her *Literary History of England between the End of the Eighteenth and the Beginning of the Nineteenth Century* (1882) Mrs. Oliphant never uses the term, nor does she conceive of the "Lake" poets, the "Cockney" school, and the "Satanic" Byron as one movement. There is thus no historical justification for the present usually accepted periods of English literature. One cannot escape the conclusion that it is a motley collection of political, literary, or artistic labels picked up here and there without much rhyme or reason.

I would, however, go further. Even if we had a series of periods neatly following any one periodical division of any cultural activity of man—politics, philosophy, the other arts, and so forth—literary history should not be content to accept a scheme arrived at on the basis of various materials with different aims in mind. This, of course, is a topic far beyond the confines of a short paper: it would require a solution of the whole question of the relation of literature to all the other cultural activities of man. I can only state somewhat dogmatically that literature is not merely the passive reflection or copy of the political, social, or even intellectual development of mankind. It is, no doubt, in constant interrelation with all the other activities. It is influenced by them profoundly, and (what is frequently forgotten) it influences them. But literature has its own autonomous development irreducible to any other activity or even to a sum of all these activities. Otherwise it would cease to be literature and would lose its *raison d'être*. As to politics, it is easy to show that the courses of literature and of political fortune do not run parallel. It suffices to cite as an example Germany during the Napoleonic epoch, when a period of political impotence coincided with the greatest flowering of literature. The

---

[2] *Epistles, Odes* . . . (1724), p. 45, in "An Epistle to the Duke of Chandos."

arts of painting and music developed differently from literature for the simple reason that neither painting nor music had the support or dead weight of a tradition of classical antiquity. Technical philosophy does not necessarily run parallel with the ideology embodied or implied in the poetry of its time, as witness the rule of Scottish Commonsense philosophy and of Utilitarianism during the English Romantic period. Thus I would merely argue that the usual affirmative answer to the question whether political, social, philosophical, or artistic periods coincide with literary periods is too hastily given. I would not deny that there is such a problem as that of the "time spirit," but it seems to me that this unity has to be established with much more careful arguments than are usually given in the German *Geistesgeschichte*. The practical examples one has seen, for instance, Paul Meissner's *Englisches Literaturbarock* (1934), indulge in extravagant speculations which frequently do not amount to more than the construction of an ingenious, but arbitrary, pattern of antithetical concepts.[3] The supposed similarities between the arts are frequently based on little more than elaborate equivocations or extended metaphors, and most of the work seems as far away from the actual process of literature as anything in the more humble studies of social or intellectual historians. I do not, of course, deny the problem of a general history of mankind and its spiritual evolution. I would only plead that this problem is distinct from our aim: the establishment of the development of literature.

This, I think, should be done first by purely literary criteria. If our results should coincide with those of political, social, artistic, and intellectual historians, well and good. But our starting point must be the development of literature as literature. There seem to be great differences with this concept. In this stimulating book on *English Poetry and the English Language* (1934) F. W. Bateson comes to the conclusion that a "flux is unintelligible except in reference to something outside itself."[4] As he rejects the usual view of literature as dependent on social evolution, he adopts another equally one-sided causal explanation, that is, linguistic evolution. But the very fact that we can conceive of a universal history of literature (which would be also a history of literary forms and genres) cutting across all linguistic boundaries shows that literature is not a simple reflex of linguistic evolution. We must try to envisage an autonomous

---

[3] See the criticism by R. S. Crane in the *Philological Quarterly*, XIV (1935), 152–54.
[4] Page 7.

development of literature, distinct from its reflection of social change or change of intellectual atmosphere. Few would doubt the possibility of such a history of painting or music. It suffices to walk through any art gallery arranged in chronological order or in accordance with "schools" to see that there is a history of the art of painting which is quite distinct from either the lives of painters or an appreciation of individual pictures. It suffices to listen to a concert in which compositions are arranged in chronological order to realize that there is a history of music which has scarcely anything to do with the biographies of composers, the social conditions under which the works were produced, or the appreciation of individual pieces. Literary history is confronted with the analogous problem of tracing the history of literature in comparative isolation from its social history, the biographies of its authors, or the appreciation of individual works.

There are, however, scholars who simply deny that literature has a history. W. P. Ker argued that we do not need literary history, since the materials on which the history is based are always present, are "eternal," and therefore have no proper history at all.[5] "Art," one could quote Schopenhauer, "has always reached its goal." It never improves; it cannot be superseded or repeated. In art we need not find out "what it was that actually happened"—as Ranke puts the aim of historiography—because we can experience directly how things are. So literary history is, it has been argued, no proper history, as it is merely the knowledge of the present, the omnipresent, the eternally present. According to this theory, advocated, for instance, by Herbert Cysarz, periods are merely abstract types, not time sections in a historical process. We can therefore speak of Greek romanticism or medieval classicism, as we mean only that this or another work of art shows certain characteristics which we traditionally have come to call "classical" or "romantic" or "realistic."

I think one cannot deny that there is some real difference between political history and the history of art. There is a distinction between that which is historical and past and that which is historical and still somewhat present. The battle of Waterloo is definitely past, though its effects may be felt even today and though its course may be reconstructed accurately; but the *Iliad*, the Parthenon, and a mass by Palestrina are still somehow present. Granting this, I think this distinction by no means refutes the fact that there is real history in the constant changes which literary tradition undergoes. It could be shown that even an individual work of art does

[5] *Thomas Warton*, Oxford, 1910, p. 6; also in *Essays*, I, 92.

not remain unchanged in the course of history. Besides, there is constant development of literature, if we contemplate it is a whole fluctuating, growing process. Genres, stylistic types, motifs, linguistic traditions, and periods grow, flower, and decay. It is not a uniform progress toward one aim; it is a patchy development of this art form, of that ideology, of this system of critical values, or of that national talent.

But the concept of development of a series of works of art seems an extraordinarily difficult one. In a sense, at first sight each work of art is a structure or system of signs discontinuous with each neighboring work of art. One could argue that there is no development from one individuality to another. Homer does not change into Shakespeare, nor does Marlowe. One meets even with the objection that there is no history of literature, but only of men writing. According to the same argument we should have to give up writing a history of language, as there are only men uttering words, and a history of philosophy, since there are only men thinking. Such extreme "personalism" must lead to anarchy, to a complete isolation of every individual work of art which in practice would mean that it would be both incommunicable and incomprehensible. We must conceive rather of literature as a whole system of works which is, with the accretion of new ones, constantly changing its relationships and growing as a changing whole.

The mere fact, however, that the literary situation of one decade or century differs from that of the preceding decade or century is still insufficient to establish a process of actual historical evolution, as the concept of change applies to any series of natural phenomena. It merely means repeated reshufflings of a kaleidoscope, which are "meaningless" and "incomprehensible." Thus the study of change, as recommended by F. J. Teggart in his *Theory of History* (1925), would lead merely to the abolishment of all differences between historical and natural processes and would leave the historian helplessly thrown back upon borrowings from natural science. If changes recurred with absolute regularity, we should arrive at the concept of law in the physicist's sense of the word. But such predictable changes have never been discovered in any historical process, in spite of the brilliant speculations of Spengler and Toynbee. Those literary historians who have hunted this chimera of literary law have arrived only at a few psychological uniformities (as the supposed "law" of action and reaction or of convention and revolt), which cannot tell us anything significant about the individual historical process. It would lead me into too much detail to show that the one ambitious attempt to arrive at such a law of English literature, Cazamian's "accelerated oscillation of the rhythm of the English national mind," is merely an ingenious construction which at every point does violence to the actual evolution of English literature.[6]

Thus development means something else and something more than change—even regular, predictable change. It seems obvious that the term should be used in the sense elaborated by biology. In biology, if we look closely, there are two very different concepts of evolution.[7] First, the process exemplified by the growth of a hen from an egg or a butterfly from a caterpillar; second, the change exemplified by the evolution of the brain of a fish to that of man. In the latter case no series of brains ever develops, but rather some conceptual abstraction, the brain, which can be defined only by its function. The individual stages of development are conceived as different approximations to an ideal, derived from the human brain. In what sense can one speak of evolution with either of these two meanings in literature? Ferdinand Brunetière and, in England, John Addington Symonds assumed that we can speak in both senses of the evolution of literature.[8] Brunetière and Symonds considered literary genres as analogous to species in nature. According to Brunetière, as soon as a literary genre reaches a certain degree of perfection it must wither, languish, and finally disappear. A genre grows, reaches perfection, declines, and dies, just as the life cycle of an individual; also genres become transformed into higher and more differentiated genres, just as species in the Darwinian conception of evolution. I hardly need to show that the use of the term "evolution" in the first sense is little more than a fanciful metaphor. According to Brunetière, for example, French tragedy was born, grew, declined, and died. But the *tertium comparationis* for the birth of tragedy is merely the fact that there were no tragedies written in French before Jodelle. Tragedy died only in the sense that no important tragedies conforming to a certain ideal pattern were written after Voltaire. But there is always the possibility that such a tragedy will be written in French in the future. According to Brunetière, Racine's *Phèdre* stands at the

---

[6] L. Cazamian, *L'Évolution psychologique de la littérature en Angleterre*, Paris, 1920, and the *History of English Literature* (together with E. Legouis), English translation, London, 1929.

[7] See Hans Driesch, *Studien über Entwicklung*, Sitzungsberichte der Heidelberger Akademie, Philosophisch-Historische Klasse, 1918, No. 3, p. 60.

[8] See especially Brunetière's *L'Évolution des genres dans l'histoire de la littérature*, I (Paris, 1890), 18 and 277–78, and John Addington Symonds: *Shakespere's Predecessors in the English Drama* (1884) and "On the Application of Evolutionary Principles to Art and Literature," in *Essays Speculative and Suggestive*, London, 1890, I, 42–84.

beginning of the decline of tragedy, somewhere near its old age, but it strikes us as young and fresh compared to the learned and dull Renaissance tragedies which according to this theory represent the "youth" of French tragedy. Even less defensible is the idea that genres become transformed into other genres. French pulpit oratory of the seventeenth and eighteenth centuries was, according to Brunetière, transformed into the lyrical poetry of the romantic movement. Actually no real "transmutation" has, however, taken place: all one can say is that the same or similar emotions were expressed once in oratory and later in lyrical poetry and that possibly the same or similar social purposes were served.

While we must reject the biological analogy between the development of literature and the closed evolutionary process from birth to death, the concept of evolution in the second sense seems to me much nearer to the real concept of historical evolution. It recognizes that a mere series of changes does not suffice, and that a direction of this series must be postulated. The different parts of the series must be the necessary conditions for the achievement of the aim. The concept of evolution toward a specific goal (for instance, the human brain) makes a series of changes into a real concatenation with a beginning and an end. Still there is an important distinction between this second meaning of biological evolution and historical evolution in the proper sense. In order to grasp historical evolution as distinct from evolution in biology we must somehow succeed in preserving the individuality of the historical event, while the historical process must not be left as a collection of sequent but unrelated events.

The solution lies in the attempt to relate the historical process to a scheme of values or norms. Only then can the apparently meaningless series of events be split into its essential and unessential elements. Only then can we speak of historical evolution which still leaves the individuality of the single event unimpaired. In relating an individual event to a general value we do not consider the individual as a mere specimen of a general concept, but we give significance to the individual. The point of view here advocated implies that history does not simply exemplify general values (nor is it, of course, a discontinuous meaningless flux), but that the historical process will produce ever new forms of value, hitherto unknown and unpredictable. The relativity of the individual work of art to a scale of values is thus nothing else than the necessary correlative of its individuality. The series of developments will be constructed in reference to a scheme of values or norms, but these values themselves emerge only from the contemplation of this process. There is, one has to admit, a logical circle in this fact that the historical process has to be judged by values, while the scale of values is itself derived from history. But this seems unavoidable, because otherwise we must either resign ourselves to the idea of a meaningless flux of change or apply some extra-literary set of standards: some absolute derived from religion, ethics, philosophy, or even politics, which is extraneous to the process of literature. Such a judgment by non-literary absolutes may very well be one of the tasks of criticism which need not be strictly literary, but it scarcely could be called literary history.

All this seems to have led us far afield. But only apparently, because in solving the problem of development (or at least bringing it nearer to a solution) we have solved the problem of periods. A period is after all only a sub-section of the universal development. History can be written with reference to a variable scheme of values, and this scheme of values has to be abstracted from history itself. Such a scheme of values dominates a period. We can, of course, conceive of other historical schemes of values: genres, ideals of versifications, and so forth. A period, therefore, is no metaphysical entity nor an arbitrary cross-section, but rather a time section dominated by a system of literary norms, whose introduction, spread, diversification, integration, and disappearance can be traced. This does not, of course, mean that we have to accept this system of norms as binding for ourselves. We must extract it from history itself: we have to discover it there in reality. For instance, "romanticism" is not a unitary quality which spreads like an infection or a plague (nor is it, of course, merely a verbal label), but a historical category or, if one prefers this Kantian term, a "regulative idea" (or rather a whole system of ideas) with the help of which we interpret the historical process. But we have found this scheme of ideas in the process itself. This concept of the term "period" differs thus from one in frequent use: its expansion into a psychological type which can be taken out of its historical context and transferred anywhere else. I would not necessarily condemn the use even of established historical terms as names for such psychological or artistic types. But it seems to me that such a typology of literature is something very different from the matter we are discussing: it does not belong to literary history in the narrow sense.

Thus a period is not a type or a class, but a time section defined by a system of norms embedded in the historical process, irremovable from its temporal place. If it were merely a general concept, it could be defined exhaustively. But the many futile attempts to define "romanticism" show that a period is not a concept similar to a class in logic. If it were, all individual works could be subsumed under it. But this is manifestly impossible. An individual work of art is not an instance in a class, but a part which, together with all the other works makes up the concept of the period. It thus itself modifies the concept of the whole. The discrimination of different "romanticisms" or multiple definitions, however valuable they are as indications of the complexity of the scheme to which they refer, seems to me mistaken on theoretical grounds. It should be, I think, frankly realized that a period is not an ideal type or an abstract pattern or a series of class concepts, but a time section, dominated by a whole system of norms, which no work of art will ever realize in its entirety. The history of a period will consist in the tracing of the changes from one system of norms to another. While a period is thus a section of time to which some sort of unity is ascribed, it is obvious that this unity can be only relative. It means merely that during this period a certain scheme of norms has been realized most fully. If the unity of any one period were absolute, the periods would lie next to each other like blocks of stone. There would be no continuity of development. Thus the survival of a preceding scheme of norms and also anticipations of a following scheme are inevitable, as a period is historical only if every event is considered as a result of the whole preceding past and if its effects can be traced into the whole future. One could elaborate on this conception in some detail, but possibly this outline is sufficient here.

Let me sum up some of the results of my reflections:

1. A period is comprehensible only as a section inside the process of development. Thus we have to consider the question of development first. "Movement" is a term which should perhaps be reserved for a self-conscious, collective striving, a series of events and pronouncements, the description of which does not offer particular problems. With a slightly different meaning "movement" is used for the one dominant scheme of values in any one period.

2. The development of literature should be conceived as autonomous. This means merely that the development of literature is not simply a passive reflection or a copy of the political, social, intellectual, or linguistic evolution of mankind. This does not, of course, imply that literature does not have vital relationships with all the other activities of humanity; its course will be, in fact, the resultant of social forces modifying an internal evolution.

3. This development should not, of course, be conceived as a uniform progress toward one model, nor should it be interpreted as analogous to the life cycle of an individual or a species. It is rather a process of continuous evolution toward different and divers specific aims which it is best to conceive as so many systems of norms or values. These have to be discovered in the literary process itself and, as to the future, are still unknown and quite unpredictable.

4. A "period" is a time section in which such a system of norms is

dominant. Every individual work of art can be understood as an approximation to one of these systéms. Thus "period" is a dynamic "regulative" concept and is not either a metaphysical essence or a purely verbal label.

5. If we take our second point seriously, we must try to derive our system of norms, our "regulative ideas," from the art of literature, not merely from the norms of some related activity. Only then can we have a series of periods which would divide the stream of literary development by literary categories. Thus a series of literary periods can alone make up, as parts of a whole, the continuous process of literature, which is, after all, the central topic in the study of literary history.

6. Only after we have arrived at a series of literary periods does the further question arise how far these periods coincide with those determined by political, sociological, philosophical, linguistic, and other criteria. I am not answering this question, as I am convinced that the answers cannot be merely in the negative or in the affirmative. We must, I think, weigh the pros and cons in every individual instance. But this is a highly speculative topic—one which should be left to historians of the whole spiritual development of humanity. Literary history has not yet achieved its immediate ideal: the description in literary terms of a series of periods.[9]

---

[9] Part of this paper is a version of my "Theory of Literary History," in the *Travaux du Cercle Linguistique de Prague*, VI (Prague, 1936), 173 ff.

SPECIFIC WORKS

HENRY A. MURRAY

Bartleby and I

For some time now it has been *de rigueur* in some quarters for a writer to be tantalizingly obscure, unintelligible to all but the gifted few who are disposed to spend what time it takes to decipher his secret code of symbols. If his sentences are structured and coherent and their meanings unmistakable, he is a Square or squarish fellow-traveler who is serving to perpetuate the basic cultural currency of the established order, the order that is headed for oblivion. In view of this, I shouldn't tell you who is meant by the "I" in the title I have chosen. I should weave around this first person pronoun at entangling spider's web of recondite allusions and insinuations, with unannounced shifts from one level to another. Initially you would naturally be led to think that "I" referred to the "I" in Melville's story, the only person who had a face-to-face relationship with Bartleby. Then you might come to the idea that I, the commentator, had myself in mind since, for better or for worse, whatever I say about the scrivener must be the result of an emphatic and cognitive transaction between him and me. Bartleby *per se* is meaningless so long as no reader can either discover or drive a bit of sense in him. In one respect at least it is not difficult for me to identify with Bartleby, since both of us have a wall to face: in my case it is that wall of legitimate aesthetic principles or laws—instead of Wall Street laws—which is there in some of you literary scholars to protect your domain against those who carry in their heads the weapons of analytical psychology. But the next minute you might be thinking No, the "I" refers to Melville, since it is only he who knows to what extent, if any, the scrivener was consciously created in his own image. My identification with Melville is facilitated by the approximation of our initials, HAM and HM: to arrive at a momentary, sort of Christ-like state of mind, if that's what's necessary, I have only to delete the middle A, which stands for the Old Adam of original sin at the center of my nature.

At this point—if my paper were written with any particle of subtlety—some of you would undoubtedly become convinced that I, the commentator, was punning: the single letter "I" in my title must be a kind of camouflage for "Eye" in three letters, and you, ever-alert to esoteric significancies, might well surmise that the referent I had in mind was some all-seeing Eye; and from here on the opportunities for projection would be boundless. Might it not be the ominiscient Eye behind the pasteboard mask, the Eye whose incessant gaze was Melville's prime source of tribulation for so many years? or possibly the Evil Eye? or, let us say, the Eye of History? or the Eye of Criticism? or maybe the Eye of some special cult or doctrine—theosophy, Marxism, Freudian infantology, Jungian archetypology, existentialism, Zen Buddhism—whose penetrating rays could supposedly bring to light the locked-up secret that Bartleby took with him to the grave. But, of course, wherever you might locate the all-seeing, three-letter "Eye," you would have to include the single-letter "I" on this page, since willy-nilly it is I, the commentator, who, with all my liabilities to error, must be its mouthpiece for the length of this paper. And so, since some of you have classified me as a would-be biographer—one who, whenever urged to publish, baffles your good-will with a measly "I would prefer not to"— there is ground for the conjecture that one of the seeing Eyes that wants to use me as its mouthpiece is what could be called the Documentary Eye, say, of the biographer, of the critic or historian. Far more widely familiar to most of you than it is to me, the Documentary Eye may be defined as the power that resides in the knowledge of certain facts to make visible some previously invisible determinants of the mood, the themes, the episodes, the allusions, or the underlying meaning of a literary work. Finally, since certain features of Melville's mind can be seen in the vacillating mental processes of the attorney he created, we return to the point from which we started, the "I" of the imaginary narrator of the story. So you see I have ended by proving myself a veritable Square by dispelling all the mystery from my title. Now everything is clear. You have been introduced to most of my cast of spirit characters, the fantastic participants in the symposium to be reported here. The attorney has the floor.

The attorney. "As I was being molded in the womb of my creator's mind I had certain disquieting premonitions as to the outcome of the on-going generative process; but not until I was delivered and could see the reflection of myself in the looking-glass of the novella, did I fully realize, after an initial shock of unrecognition, that my composer had intended from the start—and there must have been some malice sinewing that intention—to make a laughing-stock of me. For a week or so this distortion of my true nature rankled and festered in my heart. I kept thinking: if only *I* could wield a pen as *he* can, I would wreak my vengeance on him. But then I was reminded of Long Ghost and a score of other persons who had been similarly outraged by published caricatures of their peculiarities and conduct. The idea that we had all been sacrificed, one by one, on the altar of our creator's art engendered a sort of fellow-feeling which brought comfort to my wounded vanity. Later, hearing of the story's completely favorable reception by the elder Richard H. Dana, for example—I began to feel a touch of pride that I was in it. This might be my only chance for immortality. After further thought, however, recalling Dana's two adjectives "ludicrous and pathetic," it became apparent that nobody could doubt that ludicrous applied to me and pathetic to my copyist. For awhile I couldn't decide which was better: no life at all after death or life as a symbol of absurdity or sheer mediocrity. Anyhow, although it is against my grain to indulge in dangerous indignation (my creator was fair enough to admit that) I am still to this day nursing a grudge against him, mainly on one score: he confounded me with an insoluble problem. This is proved by the fact that for a hundred years, no critic, so far as I know, has come out with a definite statement as to what I should have done or what he himself would have done in my place."

The psychologist. "Let me interrupt you for a minute to make a bid for the distinction of being the first to say what he would have done in your place: call Bellevue Hospital."

The attorney. "Well, Ginger Nut didn't hesitate to say that Bartleby was 'a little *luny*,' and eventually I too came to the conclusion that he was the victim of some 'innate and incurable disorder.' And so, in my own proper person I would naturally have thought of Bellevue or the Bloomingdale Asylum; but Mr. Melville did not offer me those tranquillizers of a bad conscience. The only available option of this sort was the city Tombs with all its associated images of brutality and misery. It is true that I could not bear the thought of consigning the defenseless Bartleby to the inhumanities of the existing penal system. That being repugnant to me, what resources did I have except the mental functions that constitute the basis of my profession, in fact the very basis of democracy? In other words, what could I do but trust to the power of reason? What else is there as a substitute for force?"

The psychologist. "In your day there was virtually nothing else. Most of the doctors who tried to cope with mental disorders used persuasion and suggestion very much as you did and with no greater success. The esteemed Dr. Brown at Bloomingdale, for example, was not able to liberate Mr. Melville's friend, George Adler, from paranoid schizophrenia. Hypnotism, or what was known to you as Mesmerism, had proved temporarily remedial in some cases; but Bartleby would never have permitted himself to succumb to that procedure."

The attorney. "I welcome your support of my case against the author, which in summary is this, first, that he faced me, as I have said, with a problem that not even a trained psychiatrist could solve. Second, that he made Bartleby so meek and mild, that if I had forcefully ejected him from my chambers I would have gone down in literary history as just another striking proof of the heartlessness of the cold and wolfish world which my creator so thoroughly detested and would someday teach others to detest. Third, having limited me to unaided reason as an instrument of action, he caricatured and mocked the utter futility of all my well-meaning efforts. Fourth, although he endowed me with some propensity for sympathy, he made it evident that this was but one subordinate part of a calculating prudential philosophy, and that the spring of whatever benevolence I may have manifested was not a compassionate concern for the welfare of Bartleby, but dread of the suffering that a punishing conscience would inflict on me if I, on my own initiative, called the constables and had that inflexible irritant removed from my office. In other words, my creator was publicly announcing that so long as I didn't have to shoulder the abrasive burden of that amount of guilt, all would be nice and snug inside. Let the scrivener be handled—roughly if need be—by somebody who was not encumbered by my paralyzing scruples. That was not my business. Finally, when I visited my former employee in jail—it was kind of me to do so, wasn't it?—my maker went out of his way to unveil my dominating motive by having me too hastily announce my innocence: 'It was not I that brought you here, Bartleby.' But my profoundest, all-embracing grievance comes from an uneasy feeling, or suspicion, that Mr. Melville was out to flog me with the Sermon on the Mount, as if to say, you should have given the full measure of your love to Bartleby, all of it, every atom's atom of it, without reservations, qualifications, or reflections as to the consequences of so selfless a commitment of compassion. You should have sacrificed your profession, deserted your clients, set aside your duties to the High Court of Chancery, and taken Bartleby to live with you at home. Is not the author implying this and nothing less? If he is, I'd like to ask, what right has he to judge me from that unearthly and inhuman pinnacle of ethics?"

The author. "I will answer your question only so far as to assert that for me the Sermon on the Mount was the 'greatest real miracle of all religions. . . . This is of God! cries the heart, and in that cry ceases all inquisition.' In my youth I felt with my whole enthusiastic soul that those divine sentences 'embody all the love of the Past, and all the love which can be imagined in any conceivable Future.' From then on this was my topmost truth, the absolute standard which perpetually assured me that the world in which we live is 'saturated and soaking with lies.' This truth constituted my main justification for disliking 'all mankind—in the mass,' that is to say, the public, this generation of vipers, as distinguished from certain particular individuals. You, attorney, belong to the public in my mind, though you may be better than the vast majority of that class. You see, you're always playing safe, working your head in behalf of your conservative self-interests. You're the kind of man who would wince if he heard my bold declaration 'that a thief in jail is as honorable as General George Washington.' This declaration, like the Sermon on the Mount, is ludicrous to the head; and so I say 'To the dogs with the head! . . . I stand for the heart,' a heart which carries me but a step beyond the Sermon in ascribing a certain 'august dignity' to a prisoner in jail, even to 'the most mournful, perchance the most abased' of men. And so, when it came to Bartleby, I was sure that God would bear me out in it if I 'spread a rainbow over his disastrous set of sun.' "

The attorney. "I protest. You have virtually admitted to an irrational prejudice against me in favor of the scrivener, just because I was reasonably well-adjusted, responsible and happy, and that lazy scrivener was maladjusted, irresponsible, and mournful. But look, it was not I who abased Bartleby, but Bartleby who abased me. My grievance is unalleviated."

The author. "Would it console you at all if I said that a man can truly sympathize only with another person in similar circumstances. I have been as full of grief as Bartleby ever since those early days when I was 'rubbed, curried, and ground down to fine powder in the hopper of an evil fortune.' You, on the other hand, having never actually experienced anything like the woe with which the scrivener was burdened, were in no position to proffer sympathy with grace. My story could not help but make this evident."

The scrivener. "Let me speak! I would prefer to. Who's got a better right? I'm the hero, ain't I? First I should tell you that I was a very ordinary fellow before Mr. Melville began the job of re-creating me. As you might suspect, I was about the unhappiest human being in the whole world with the idea of suicide almost continuously in mind, and Mr. Melville's heart went out to me with unquestioning and unerring understanding. His eyes expressed a tenderness that was more feminine than masculine. But he didn't act on it as Jesus would have done. Christ's fated role was to drive out devils, not to make books. That's the crux of the matter. What Mr. Melville did was to take me into himself to be reshaped with affectionate concern, and to give me a rebirth as a personage with far more drawing power than I ever had in real life. If in the flesh of my first birth I could have had a quarter of the sympathy I have received when presented to the world in the form of my second birth, I would never have landed in the Asylum with what they would call today, schizophrenia, catatonic type. There I refused to eat; but unhappily I was physically forced to submit to the indignity of being fed by stomach tube until a year or so later the Comforter came and terminated my soul's agony. Mr. Melville was truthful in ascribing to me a state of absolute misanthropy, or alienation, coupled with the hardihood to persist in affirming a sovereign nature in myself, amid all the institutionalized powers of society. But beyond that everything was of his invention. Look at the combination of strategies he gave me to defend the integrity of my being. First, silence combined with a stance of impassive immobility, the only effective tactic for a cornered person who is faced by the rage of a dangerous human being, mob, or beast. It was precisely this posture, combined with my pathetic look, which repeatedly dissolved the anger of my employer. Compared to a vehement No, my mild 'I would prefer not to' sounded as if it were no more than the expression of a personal choice, which in a democratic society is accepted as the inalienable right of every citizen. That was a very clever trick of Mr. Melville's. And, then, by having me withhold the reasons for my stubbornly-held decision, the attorney was deprived of all possible points of entry for rational counter-arguments; and, furthermore, by having me refuse to answer his personal questions, I was able to frustrate his humane attempts to understand me. Indeed I cut him dead, spiritually speaking, virtually killed him so far as I was concerned, as a man unworthy of my trust, just another self-complacent member of that hateful world which I had totally and permanently rejected. By remaining mysterious, I implanted in the lawyer's mind a sticky riddle that called for some solution, a magnet to his thoughts; and partly by my meek exterior, but more especially by the disdain implicit in my unshakeable refusal to converse with him, I gained an appreciable ascendancy over my employer, which so undermined what confidence he had in his own powers that a reversal of status was effected: I, the forlorn squatter compelled the legitimate owner to desert his own domain, leaving me, a little Bonaparte, as its solitary occupant. 'Blessed are the meek: for they shall inherit the earth.'"

The psychologist. "What were your innermost feelings through all those experiences?"

The scrivener. "As I have said, utterly misanthropic, a kind of hate-grief with pride to bolster it. Tired of everything, I had resigned myself to—well, a sort of death in life, and then to no life, the last resource of an insulted and unendurable existence. But yet, now that it's all over, I can confess to feeling a little lift of secret, spiteful enjoyment every time my employer laid down his arms before my wall of self-containment, my meekly-voiced negation. I also derived some hidden pleasure from witnessing the disturbance I produced in the office, seeing to what extent I became the center of attention, and how, one after the other, they adopted my word 'prefer.' Nothing is sweeter than revenge, you know, and to tell the truth, my deepest satisfaction—rising in the very midst of my pervasive melancholy—came when I discovered how much guilt I could arouse in my employer. He had given me no good reason to abase him in his own proper person; but, seeing him as a pasteboard mask of the world that had humiliated me, I felt justified in making his conscience prick him till it hurt. And now looking back on the whole course of events I am very grateful to Mr. Melville's embracing sympathy in representing me as he did. I haven't been able to make out what there was in me—a very ordinary man as I have said—that fetched him."

The author. "Evidently, you haven't read my books. It was your sorrow: 'that mortal man who hath more of joy than sorrow in him, that mortal cannot be true.' And then your silence: 'Silence is at once the most harmless and the most awful thing in all nature. . . . Silence is the only Voice of our God.' And then your forlornness that was irresistible to me. I used to call my favorite sister, Augusta, the Forlorn One. In short, I recognized in you a humble fellow-misanthrope."

The psychologist. "When did *your* misanthropy begin, Mr. Melville?"

The author. "When I wrote 'Bartleby' I was a confirmed misanthrope. But it was much earlier, about 1837—I'm not precise about dates—that I had my first acute and critical attack of it, at the time that my soul's ship, which I later called the *Pequod*, was irrecoverably sunk. But even before that, as far back as I can remember in my childhood, I was prone to melancholy moods. My father used to say I was morose."

The biographer. "I have an overlooked document from the New York Public Library which may be pertinent at this point. Other biographers have started with Herman's birth, but I chose to start with his conception which, as it happens, can be definitely placed sometime during the first week in November, 1818, just after the Melvilles arrived in New York and took up lodgings at Mrs. Bradish's stylish boardinghouse on State Street. Mrs. Melville was keenly looking forward to the grand dinners and parties for which this center of fashion was renowned. Family friends who had known her in Albany and were living in the neighborhood of State Street, were notified of her arrival. But nothing happened, and less than a month later, when the future grief-stricken author of *Moby Dick* was a sensitive, three-weeks embryo within her body, Maria Melville wrote an unusually long letter to her brother Peter Gansevoort in Albany, which may be veridically abbreviated as follows:

Dear Brother:
. . . I do think the inhabitants of New York, the most ungrateful, inasmuch, as many have been at our house partaken of our hospitality, & now that a return can be expected, feign not to know me, I am in a fair way of becoming a Misanthrope . . .
. . . The Mayors Lady Visits every Lady that comes to the City, She has Given half A dozen large Parties, all go, invitations to all except us, Mrs. Bartley an actress is carress'd, visited, visited, invited, to the first houses in this City, while I am worse than forgotten, shuned, It is next to impossible that people, should not enquire and know who we are, altogether, this is a Selfish hateful Place . . . I have too much pride to allow it to Mr. M—, but really the inhabitants of this Place, will not see merit they shut their Eyes, against everything but wealth, Wealth is their reigning God & if you have not wealth, you must have patience to put up with every slight, & many mortifications . . .

           Maria

Here we have it in a nutshell: Everybody is invited to parties except me. I am worse than forgotten, shunned. This is a hateful place. The inhabitants must know who we are but they will not see merit. I have too much pride to admit it even to my husband, but I am in a fair way of becoming a misanthrope."

The first critic. "This is the kind of thing that makes me boil! What has embryology got to do with the texture and structure of a work of art? Are you expecting us to take some purely hypothetical prenatal influence into account in our appreciation of Mr. Melville's consummate skill and poise in writing the superb story that we have before us?"

The biographer. "I stand corrected. But before backing out, I should say first, that Maria Melville seems to have persisted in this attitude for many years, and second, that she was the most influential person in her son's entire life. Mr. Melville and his mother had a terribly profound, reciprocal, love-hate relationship almost, I would guess, from start to finish."

The author. "By the way, gentleman, let's not stand on any ceremony here. It's proper for the characters I immortalized to call me 'Mister'; but you critics and biographers had better talk as you do when I'm not present. In view of the neglect I experienced in my lifetime, to be the center at this symposium of so much devoted attention and reflection is all that my scarred vanity requires to make it purr delightedly. The 'Mister' is superfluous."

The first critic. "Thank you, Mr. Melville—oh, I should say Melville. Now, let's return to our proper province. So far none of the discussants have placed the novella in a historic literary context. No one has mentioned Dickens and Kafka and the comedy-of-the-absurd. And we haven't discussed the meaning of the story. We all know that most of Melville's stories have a hidden meaning."

The scrivener. "His meaning is hidden from me. I can only say that ever since my resurrection in this novella, most of my old sorrow has given way to a divine content. There is nothing like world-wide recognition and acclaim to cheer a fellow up. It seems that I have been virtually canonized as a kind of saint, because almost everyone has assumed that I am Herman Melville in disguise. By silencing me to the bitter end, he succeded somehow in hanging a Christ-like halo over my head as if I had been crucified by society because I was too good for them. Actually I did no good to anybody and, as I've told you, my soul was chock-full of pent-up bitterness and hate."

The biographer. "It's hard to avoid the inference that Melville had himself in mind to some extent when he turned you into the hero of his story. In the novella, remember, it is Bartleby himself who asks for the job of copyist. He is not forced to it; and there is not the slightest intimation that he is capable of greater works. This corresponds to the apparent fact that by 1853 Melville had written himself out—mostly in *Moby Dick* and *Pierre*—just as he predicted to Hawthorne that he would. Those two No-in-thunder books were what he had most wanted to write, indeed had been impelled to write. But after two or three explosions of his volcano, he was left, like a burnt-out crater, with only a mild No to energize his composing a number of symbolic stories, pretty much as a copyist, we could say, of Hawthorne, whose No had never come with thunder, as Melville once said it did, but with mildness such as Bartleby's. Bartleby's preference for *not* correcting copy corresponds to Melville's preference for *not* correcting proof. Finally, analogous to the attorney's attempts to get the copyist out of his chambers, we have the efforts of Hawthorne and a score of lawyers, with Allan Melville in Wall Street as co-ordinator, to obtain a consulship for Melville—chiefly to get him *out* of the room in which he wrote at Arrowhead. These efforts were initially instigated by Melville's mother who attributed her son's increasingly patent signs of mental illness to his 'constant indoor confinement—constant working of the brain & excitement of the imagination' (as we learn from our unexampled source book, *The Melville Log* by Jay Leyda). This gives us three rough correspondences between Bartleby and the Melville of 1853: both at first prefer to copy, both prefer not to correct copy, and both have lawyers trying to move them from their preferred location. Furthermore, both prefer solitude, both are suspected of being mentally unbalanced, and both are inclined toward suicide. We have, for example, as one of many bits of evidence, Sarah Morewood's account of a conversation with Melville in 1851 in which she says: I 'told him that the recluse life he was leading made his friends think that he was slightly insane—he replied that long ago he came to the same conclusion himself.' And, as for suicide, we have, among other things, Melville's admission in a letter to Samuel Shaw that: 'I once, like other spoonies, cherished a loose sort of notion that I did not care to live very long'; which sounds as if he had once been saying to himself: 'I would *prefer* not to live very long.' It all fits."

The first critic. "Well, if that's it, if the story is just veiled autobiography, Melville is a lesser artist than I thought he was. According to my view the scrivener stands for the writer in America and Wall Street for the capitalistic system which had no use for him."

The second critic. "That's looking at the story through the eyes of a twentieth-century writer. If *you* are right, Melville is a lesser artist than I thought, because as a parable or manifesto in behalf of the profession of letters it is a total failure. What capitalist could possibly get the idea that a young man who applied for the humble position of copyist and had nothing at all to say for himself was meant to represent a typical American writer or a great genius who was fuller than a city and capable of scaling great heights out of his present lowest depths? I don't believe that any living American author except Melville himself, or conceivably Hawthorne, would have seen any part of himself in Bartleby. Not Washington Irving, Cooper, Longfellow, Lowell, Thoreau, or Emerson certainly. Furthermore, the Wall Street lawyer is far more appreciative and benevolent than his copyist. If one condemns all forms of autobiography in literature, one must chuck out Shakespeare's sonnets and a hundred other great masterpieces."

The biographer. "The question of better or worse is not the issue here. The primary question is, who or what did Melville have in mind when he shaped the character of Bartleby. According to my divining rod, the secret title of the Wall Street story is, 'I and my Wall,' and it could stand as a companion piece to 'I and my Chimney,' for the perfect elucidation of which we are indebted to the intuition and scholarship of Merton Sealts. Without the knowledge which assures us that in 'I and my Chimney,' Melville was representing the disturbance that was created in his household by what his mother took to be evidences of insanity in her son—without that knowledge-grounded intuition, a good deal of the charm, subtlety, humor, and pathos of the story would be wasted on us. I would wager that the spirit of Herman Melville, who always vainly hoped for worthy readers, fully and gratefully appreciates the perspicacity of Merton Sealts."

The author. "You're right there."

The second critic. "But, even if we had the relevant autobiographic facts, this in itself would not define the meaning of the story; and since none of the rest of you seem to be disposed to tackle this problem, let me hazard these three related propositions in regard to Melville's conscious intention: first, to use today's terminology, it is a comedy-of-the-absurd marked by the surprising and unprecedented perversity of Bartleby's simple yet adamant refusal to perform his duties, in conjunction with the agitation and indecisiveness that is engendered in his baffled, conscience-ridden employer by the reiteration of this negative response to every one of his justified demands and by the frustration of each of his endeavors to reason this seemingly innocuous young man out of his unreasonable willfulness. Coupled with this continuously humorous aspect of the encounters between employer and employee is a tragic aspect which I shall call the second theme. This is determined by the impossibility of the attorney's empathetically comprehending the nature of Bartleby's entrenched grief. As Melville expressed it in *Pierre:* 'in the inexorable and unhuman eye of mere undiluted reason, all grief, whether on our own account, or that of others, is the sheerest unreason and insanity.' Here we might be reminded of Starbuck's attempt to dissuade Ahab from pursuing the White Whale: 'It will not fetch thee much in our Nantucket market.' To which Ahab replies: 'My vengeance will fetch a great premium here,' smiting his chest. Likewise with Bartleby inwardly considered. He is driven by a similar emotional necessity, and although his will is capable of executing the actions that have been chosen for him by that necessity, it is no longer free to choose and execute a different course of action. Finally, there is the theme of fortitude marked by Bartleby's adherence, despite everything, to the principle of self-sovereignty, the last stand of an oppressed ego. Given intense and irremediable suffering there is nothing irrational about the act of suicide. It is irrational only to those who stand outside of it."

The historian. "At this moment that strikes me as a fitting summary of Melville's probable intentions in this novella. But there is a larger issue, namely that of the history of alienation in the West. Bartleby is a precursor of those fictional characters which have become predominant in recent years. It is all condensed in Malraux's dictum: 'Man is dead,' presumably because God is dead, as Hegel, Heine, Nietzsche, and Sartre announced. Melville was pretty close to this conclusion, wasn't he?"

The first critic. "Bartleby is certainly as near to being dead, in this sense, as a man could be, more dead than alive: more dead than Camus's 'Stranger,' more dead than any of Beckett's non-heroes, for the scrivener has stopped talking, and there is no hint that he is waiting for any semblance of Godot. When we first meet him he has already committed social suicide and he is on his way to an organic suicide. The wall might stand for the meaninglessness of life, no future prospect or purpose to be seen."

The second critic. "Let's ask Mr. Melville himself."

The author. "I'm not required to expose what I took pains to hide when writing 'Bartleby,' am I? Have you by any chance read my whaling story for boys? If you have, you will remember Captain Ahab exclaiming: 'To me the White Whale is that wall, shoved near to me. . . . How can the prisoner reach outside except by thrusting through the wall?' In that narrative, you may recall, Ahab fails in his attempt to kill the whale, that is, he fails to effect a breakthrough. So you find in the story you are now considering the very same wall shoved even closer to the hero. But in contrast to Ahab, Bartleby has concluded that the wall is impregnable, and, acknowledging his defeat, is resigned to pallid hopelessness. He ends his career as an impotent, though noble, prisoner."

The psychologist. "Would you say, Mr. Melville, that the aggressive, destructive force which the sadistic Ahab directed outwardly at the whale is now directed inwardly at him, or what remains of him, namely, the partly masochistic Bartleby who is Ahab's shadowy antithesis or counterpart?"

The author. "If you like that kind of language, you can have it. I won't contradict you."

The biographer. "My impression is that the majority of critics have pretty well agreed that the White Whale, besides being a real biological whale in the Pacific Ocean, represents the prohibiting and punishing, Calvinistic and puritanical aspect of God that was implanted in Melville's soul at an early age. In short, the wall of the White Whale is the wall of an imprisoning, punishing, and mutilating conscience; and, if the Wall Street wall is of the same moral texture, the chances are that it represents those laws, in Melville's day, whose prohibitions and penalties reinforced the ordinances of Calvinism. In which case, Wall Street does not refer to the stock exchange and the economic system, but to the seat of the legal system, where Melville's brother, Allan, his friend Daniel Shepherd, and the scrivener's employer had their offices. We are dealing, then, with a wall buttressed by two formidable establishments: the Church and the Law. Now, when you consider the extreme degree to which Melville valued the open independence of his way, and consider that after his father's death his life was marked for nearly fifteen years by recurrent egressions—departures, escapes, flights, or whatever you choose to call them—from a confining space or job, you might surmise that in the late forties he found himself imprisoned to an intolerable extent in a way that he had never been before. He dropped out of school at twelve, a little later abandoned his job at the bank, then gave up working at Gansevoort's fur store, then left his uncle's farm at Pittsfield, then dropped the studies that were preparing him for teaching, then suddenly quit the Sykes School at Pittsfield, then dropped his studies at Lansingburgh Academy, then left home to be a sailor on a merchant ship to Liverpool, etc., etc. until he reached a total of seventeen egressions. Then in 1847—after starting *Mardi* I would guess—he was married to Elizabeth Shaw, *period*. I would like to ask Mr. Melville whether or not marriage was his wall, his prison, in 1850, and, if so, why did he tantalize his readers with so many references to a wall without giving a few decipherable clues as to what it stood for."

The author. "Why should I put so private and delicate a matter before the eyes of a 'bantering, barren, and prosaic, heartless age,' a generation of censorious, nominally-Christian hypocrites? To my world, with its pride of purity, marriage was a sacred, inviolable institution, guarded and walled-in by the most powerful moral sentiments. You people, with your permissive attitude toward sex and your lenient divorce laws, cannot possibly imagine what it feels like to be in the position I was in in 1850. Divorce was practically impossible. But since I had to be frank with *myself*, I could not omit the wall. Besides, I did give a few hints. For instance, I made it clear enough, for any knowledgeable reader, that passionate love for my gentle, innocent little wife dissolved within the first month of marriage. In *Mardi*, not long after I was married, speaking of Taji and Yillah, I wrote: 'For a time we were happy in Odo; Yillah and I in our islet. . . . Often I thought that Paradise had overtaken me on earth, and that Yillah was verily an angel . . . But how fleeting our joys. Storms follow bright mornings . . . Long memories of short-lived scenes, sad thoughts of joyous hours . . . Sped the hours, the days, the one brief moment of our joys . . . Oh Yillah, Yillah!' What could be more patent than this? And yet academic critics, whose heads are apt to suffocate their hearts, seem to have come to the conclusion that Yillah was meant to represent some transcendent entity, such as absolute truth or wisdom. They should pay more attention to the elucidation of that *Mardi* passage which I offered them in *Pierre* when I wrote of: 'That nameless and infinitely delicate aroma of inexpressible tenderness and attentiveness which, like the bouquet of the costliest German wines, too often evaporates upon pouring love out to drink, in the disenchanting glasses of the matrimonial days and nights . . .' And then, in that novel, didn't I have the hero abandon his Lucy? I had them engaged instead of married, because I didn't think that the public would stand for a hero who deserted a devoted wife, and, as it turned out, the public's tolerance was much less than I anticipated: they condemned with blasts of moral indignation everything that my hero felt, and thought, and did. So you can see what I was up against. Besides, as I made plain in *Pierre*, my wife's 'sympathetic mind and person had both been cast in one mold of wondrous delicacy.' Her nature was permeated by 'what may be artistically styled angelicalness,' which, in my scales, is 'the highest essence compatible with created being.' I couldn't bring myself to hurt her any more than I did in that book."

The biographer. "Didn't you rage at her occasionally in real life? I was told by a member of your family that once you clutched her by the throat and exclaimed: 'Now I know what a man feels like who wants to kill his wife.' And after that didn't she leave you and return to her family's house in Boston, taking her children with her?"

The author. "Yes, but I was overcome with remorse and pity and in a week or so—I don't remember how long it was exactly—I went up there and persuaded her to come back to me and try again. Nobody like you on the outside can possibly understand the anguish of these years for both of us. Do not judge, lest you be judged; and so the less said the better. 'Ladies are like creeds; if you cannot speak well of them, say nothing.' "

First critic. "I protest again, biographer. You have gone too far with your probings into the secret recesses of Melville's stricken heart. Numberless other artists, such as D. H. Lawrence and Eugene O'Neill, have attacked their wives with greater fury than Melville ever did. That's all too human. You may or you may not have hit on the best explanation of Melville's wall as cause of his own hopelessness, the state of mind which he portrays in Bartleby. But, whether right or wrong, this hypothesis is scarcely relevant to the work of art we are surveying, the basic theme of which is the inevitable opposition between the requirements of the on-going social system and the requirements of the individual with his innate need for autonomy. In Melville's narrative we have a miniature social system with its traditions and customs, laws and regulations, rewards and penalties, operating within the frame of the Protestant ethic and the utilitarian philosophy, in terms of which, as usual, rationality and sanity are defined. Buck the system, dissent, and you're 'straightway handled with a chain,' as Emily Dickinson has put it. The administrator of this system is a lawyer of good will who, believing 'that the easiest way of life is the best,' has chosen 'the cool tranquillity of a snug retreat' to perform his professional duties, confident that his two great virtues, prudence and method, will insure a smooth and regular routine of office work. But these peaceful expectations are destined—or, as the lawyer eventually concludes, *predestined*—first, to be shaken by his two clerks with their regular irregularities of conduct, and finally to be completely cancelled by the cadaverous Bartleby, who seems to be set on carrying Emerson's advocacy of nonconformity to the point of ultimate insanity as judged by the system he disrupts. Whatever principle or right Bartleby may be secretly defending, he prefers to die rather than to compromise and enjoy whatever scraps of pleasure would be then accessible to him. Since it can't be All (the wall prohibits it), it will be Nothing; and from that wall there will be retreat through him. That's the key to this superb story, perfectly wrought out of simple, realistic elements, a compact gem which embodies a whole world of complementary meanings, prophetic of much that will come later. Today we have the Squares and the Beats, another version of the archetypal situation."

The second critic. "I agree with everything you've said; but before we leave the author and his wall, I would like to expound a little thesis which not only supports the biographer's emphasis on Melville's marital despair, but explicates the symbolism of the Dead Letter Office where Bartleby worked previous to his engagement as a copyist in Wall Street. My thesis starts with the observation that Melville's mental excitement usually reached its peak in conjunction with his writing of the last phase or chapters of a book; and, furthermore, as he progressed with the series of works that he wanted to write, those dictated by his daemon—*Mardi*, *Moby Dick*, and *Pierre*—his terminal agitation increased from book to book. Now, in late November, 1852—four months after the publication of *Pierre*—Melville informed Hawthorne with evident zest that he was about to begin the story of Agatha, that is, his fictional version of a true story about a Quakeress of that name, the details of which, as you all know, were obtained by Melville from a New Bedford lawyer on his trip to Nantucket in July. It must have been this work, then—since there is mention of no other possibility—which, as his mother put it, 'completely absorbed' Melville during the succeeding winter of 1853, and which, in the spring of that year, was said to be 'nearly ready for the press.' That Melville's agitation in finishing the Agatha story was even greater than it had been in finishing *Pierre* is suggested by his wife's note in her memoir of her husband, which reads: 'We all felt anxious about the strain on his health in spring of 1853,' as well as by the fact that it was at this time that his mother most urgently pressed her brother Peter Gansevoort, an Albany lawyer, to exert himself ('hoping that you will lose no time, as every day counts') in enlisting the support of influential friends, most of whom were lawyers, in procuring from President Pierce, Hawthorne's old friend, a consulship abroad for her son Herman. In short, what little evidence we have points to the conclusion that the writing of the Agatha story was attended by another—the last—outburst of Melville's existential daemon. Fitting this conclusion, as hand in glove, is the nature of Melville's material, the series of actual events and situations which awakened 'the most lively interest' in him and kindled his creative imagination. In other words, the history of the repeated desertions of the forbearing, patient, and permissive Agatha of Pembroke, Massachusetts, by her errant and erratic sailor-husband, combined with his two bigamous marriages, the second with Agatha's virtual consent—all this provided Melville with a compelling skeleton for one more last story of 'the intrepid effort of the soul' to break through her imprisoning wall and attain 'the open independence of her sea.' Among other things, Melville called Hawthorne's attention to the facility with which Robertson had first left his wife and then taken another one. Evidently the 'sense of the obligation of the marriage-vow to Agatha had little weight with him at first,' a moral condition which the former seaman Melville attributed to the likelihood that Robertson in his previous sailor life 'had found a wife (for a night) in every port.' Not until he had spent some years ashore did Robertson experience enough remorse to act on it to some extent. But I surmise, in agreement with Leon Howard, that what particularly appealed to Melville as something of profound significance was the wholly feminine, 'angelic' nature of Agatha, very similar to that of Pierre's selflessly devoted Lucy. As the New Bedford lawyer expressed it, it was Agatha's 'long continued & uncomplaining submission to wrong and anguish' which 'made her in his eyes a heroine.' This is about all I have to offer that is calculated not only to buttress the biographer's notion that the wall is Melville's marriage vow in the eyes of God and of the Law, but also to account for the author's excessive agitation in the spring of 1853."

The first critic. "That's off the target of our main objective here. I've been paying attention to you all this time because I thought you were going to elucidate the passage about the Dead Letter Office in the sequel to 'Bartleby.'"

The second critic. "Yes, to be sure. I'm glad you reminded me. My thesis is simply this: that since a 'new work' by Melville—and what could it be but the story of Agatha?—was said by his mother to be 'nearly ready for the press' on April 20th, 1853, and since no such story was ever published or found in manuscript form, the chances are it was destroyed, probably burnt by Melville himself in a moment of self-negating desperation. In any event, the melancholy fact that this product of a long winter of creative toil never reached a single reader is quite comparable to the fate of the dead letters which were assorted for the flames by Bartleby during his previous employment. Without stretching credulity too much we can imagine that the dead Agatha manuscript contained 'hope for those who died unhoping; good tidings for those who died stifled by unrelieved calamities.' My thesis ends here with the death of the two prime hopes of Melville's soul: the hope of embracing another love (represented by Isabel in *Pierre*) and the hope of writing another spirit-driven book. These two defeats account for the pallid hopelessness of Bartleby, the silent copyist."

The biographer. "Not bad. And now, to return for a moment to the question of how much of the 1853 Melville is represented in the figure of Bartleby, I would like to remind you of a few more correspondences besides the three just mentioned and the six I listed earlier. Melville and Bartleby are similar insofar as both write all day long and, being seldom in the sunlight, Melville must have been nearly as pallid as his scrivener. It was thought that Bartleby had over-strained his eyes and impaired his vision much as Melville had; and both are unusually silent. In a letter to George Duyckinck, Mrs. Morewood reports that Melville, engaged in writing *Pierre,* frequently does not 'leave his room till quite dark in the evening—when he for the first time during the day partakes of solid food'; and the attorney tells us that Bartleby, 'ran a day and night line, copying by sun-light and by candle-light.' The much-traveled cosmopolitan, Maunsell B. Field, wrote of a drive with Darley in 1855 to see Melville 'whom I had always known as the most silent man of my acquaintance'; but later, when joined by Oliver Wendell Holmes, this most silent man opened up and became engaged in a discussion with the doctor 'which was conducted with the most amazing skill and brilliancy on both sides. . . . I never chanced to hear better talking in my life.' This shows that the always-silent Bartleby is no more than one aspect of Melville. A few convivial friends gathered in New York could count on a 'good stirring evening' whenever Melville arrived 'fresh from his mountain' in the Berkshires and 'charged to the muzzle with his sailor metaphysics and jargon of things unknowable,' as Evert Duyckinck, with his two-dimensional gentility of mind, characterized the abundance of his friend's thought. This gives us an enormous major difference and thirteen minor similarities between Melville and his scrivener. Finally, one more item that bears on the hypothesis that Bartleby-Melville is a copyist of Hawthorne, namely, the fact that initially Melville offered the Agatha material to his friend on the ground 'that this thing lies very much in a vein, with which you are peculiarly familiar . . . the thing seems naturally to gravitate towards you.' Having said to him, 'I think that in this matter you would make a better hand at it than I would,' the chances are that, when Hawthorne decided not to accept his offer, Melville carried out his treatment of the narrative with Hawthorne's vein and style prominently in mind, a step or transition, one might say, toward the Hawthornesque symbolism of his later short stories. But even when all this is said and done, the character of Bartleby remains a riddle."

The psychologist. "I have often been asked in what psychological or psychiatric category Bartleby belongs and I always answer that there is none made for him. Bartleby is unprecedented, an invention of Melville's creative spirit, the author's gift to psychology, a mythic figure who deserves a category in his own name. I see the scrivener as a composite of several very human dispositions, the first of which is silence, the refusal to speak; and here I could tell you of numerous cases of children as well as adults who, feeling insulted by something that was said to them by a parent or relative, vowed, in a vengeful spirit, never to speak to that person again, and some of these have stubbornly adhered to their vow for many years. But in such cases the verbal ostracism is specific; in Bartleby it is general, with occasional lapses as seen in patients with catatonic schizophrenia. Bartleby's absence of initiative, the immobility accompanying his wall-reveries is often indicative of an inhibiting dread of punishment or guilt, engendered by a surplus of pent-up hostility. It is related to the aboulia one finds in some cases of obsessional neurosis and to the paralysis of will associated with severe depressions. The most accentuated of Bartleby's dispositions is an unswerving negativism which could be interpreted as a regression to the phase of normal development that commonly occurs in the latter half of the second year of life. The nay-saying characteristic of this stage marks the child's initial efforts to attain autonomy and self-sufficiency. Bartleby's refusal of food is indicative of regression to an even earlier stage, illustrated by those resentful and distrustful babies who pucker up their tightly-closed lips when offered the bottle after being accustomed to the breast. I wouldn't put it beyond Melville—who had a 4-months-old daughter at the time—to have derived the name of Bartleby from bottle or bottle baby. Finally, let us note, that Melville had the scrivener end his life with his body huddled in the embryonic position at the base of the prison wall, with 'his head touching the cold stones,' which suggests a web of too many additional ideas for this symposium. That will do as a 5-cent sketch of what I have in mind on this topic. I will end by crediting Mr. Melville with the discovery of the Bartleby complex."

The author. "Is this meant to be a compliment? a prize for my remaining silent and unobtrusive throughout the length of your dissection of my heart and head? No ill-will; but I've had about as much as I can take today of that line of talk. Let's have some brandy and cigars, and reason of Providence and futurity."

I, the commentator. "All right, gentlemen, the meeting is adjourned. This fantasy has ended. All these I's, as I foretold you, were spirits, and are 'melted into air, into thin air.' They were 'such stuff as dreams are made on,' and now the time has come to rub our eyes, get up, and face the world of embodied actualities."

FRANCIS FERGUSSON

Ghosts: *The Theater of Modern Realism*

The Plot of Ghosts: *Thesis, Thriller, and Tragedy*

Ghosts is not Ibsen's best play, but it serves my purpose, which is to study the foundations of modern realism, just because of its imperfections. Its power, and the poetry of some of its effects, are evident; yet a contemporary audience may be bored with its old-fashioned iconoclasm and offended by the clatter of its too-obviously well-made plot. On the surface it is a *drame à thèse*, of the kind Brieux was to develop to its logical conclusion twenty years later: it proves the hollowness of the conventional bourgeois marriage. At the same time it is a thriller with all the tricks of the Boulevard entertainment: Ibsen was a student of Scribe in his middle period. But underneath this superficial form of thesis-thriller—the play which Ibsen started to write, the angry diatribe as he first conceived it—there is another form, the shape of the underlying action, which Ibsen gradually made out in the course of his two-years' labor upon the play, in obedience to his scruple of truthfulness, his profound attention to the reality of his fictive characters' lives. The form of the play is understood according to two conceptions of the plot, which Ibsen himself did not at this point clearly distinguish: the rationalized concatenation of events with a univocal moral, and the plot as the "soul" or first actualization of the directly perceived action.

Halvdahn Khot, in his excellent study *Henrick Ibsen*, has explained the circumstances under which *Ghosts* was written. It was first planned as an attack upon marriage, in answer to the critics of *A Doll's House*. The story of the play is perfectly coherent as the demonstration and illustration of this thesis. When the play opens, Captain Alving has just died, his son Oswald is back from Paris where he had been studying painting, and his wife is straightening out the estate. The Captain had been accepted locally as a pillar of society but was in secret a drunkard and debauchee. He had seduced his wife's maid, and had a child by her; and this child, Regina, is now in her turn Mrs. Alving's maid. Mrs. Alving had concealed all this for something like twenty years. She was following the advice of the conventional Pastor Manders and endeavoring to save Oswald from the horrors of the household: it was for this reason she had sent him away to school. But now, with her husband's death, she proposes to get rid of the Alving heritage in all its forms, in order to free herself and Oswald for the innocent, unconventional "joy of life." She wants to endow an orphanage with the Captain's money, both to quiet any rumors there may be of his sinful life and to get rid of the remains of his power over her. She encounters this power, however, in many forms, through the Pastor's timidity and through the attempt by Engstrand (a local carpenter who was bribed to pretend to be Regina's father) to blackmail her. Oswald wants to marry Regina and has to be told the whole story. At last he reveals that he has inherited syphilis from his father— the dead hand of the past in its most sensationally ugly form—and when his brain softens at the end, Mrs. Alving's whole plan collapses in unrelieved horror. It is "proved" that she should have left home twenty years before, like Nora in *A Doll's House*; and that conventional marriage is therefore an evil tyranny.

In accordance with the principles of the thesis play, *Ghosts* is plotted as a series of debates on conventional morality, between Mrs. Alving and the Pastor, the Pastor and Oswald, and Oswald and his mother. It may also be read as a perfect well-made thriller. The story is presented with immediate clarity, with mounting and controlled suspense; each act ends with an exciting curtain which reaffirms the issues and promises important new developments. In this play, as in so many others, one may observe that the conception of dramatic form underlying the thesis play and the machine-made Boulevard entertainment is the same: the logically concatenated series of events (intriguing thesis or logical intrigue) which the characters and their relationships merely illustrate. And it was this view of *Ghosts* which made it an immediate scandal and success.

But Ibsen himself protested that he was not a reformer but a poet. He was often led to write by anger and he compared the process of composition to his pet scorpion's emptying of poison; Ibsen kept a piece of soft fruit in his cage for the scorpion to sting when the spirit moved him. But Ibsen's own spirit was not satisfied by the mere discharge of venom; and one may see, in *Ghosts*, behind the surfaces of the savage story, a partially realized tragic form of really poetic scope, the result of Ibsen's more serious and disinterested brooding upon the human condition in general, where it underlies the myopic rebellions and empty clichés of the time.

In order to see the tragedy behind the thesis, it is necessary to return to the distinction between plot and action, and to the distinction between the plot as the rationalized series of events, and the plot as "the soul of the tragedy." The action of the play is "to control the Alving heritage for my own life." Most of the characters want some material or social advantage from it—Engstrand money, for instance, and the Pastor the security of conventional respectability. But Mrs. Alving is seeking a true and free human life itself—for her son, and through him, for herself. Mrs. Alving sometimes puts this quest in terms of the iconoclasms of the time, but her spiritual life, as Ibsen gradually discovered it, is at a deeper level; she tests everything—Oswald, the Pastor, Regina, her own moves—in the light of her extremely strict if unsophisticated moral sensibility: by direct perception and not by ideas at all. She is tragically seeking; she suffers a series of pathoses and new insights in the course of the play; and this rhythm of will, feeling, and insight underneath the machinery of the plot is the form of the life of the play, the soul of the tragedy.

The similarity between *Ghosts* and Greek tragedy, with its single fated action moving to an unmistakable catastrophe, has been felt by many critics of Ibsen. Mrs. Alving, like Oedipus, is engaged in a quest for her true human condition; and Ibsen, like Sophocles, shows on-stage only the end of this quest, when the past is being brought up again in the light of the present action and its fated outcome. From this point of view Ibsen is a plot-maker in the first sense: by means of his selection and arrangement of incidents he defines an action underlying many particular events and realized in various modes of intelligible purpose, of suffering, and of new insight. What Mrs. Alving sees changes in the course of the play, just as what Oedipus sees changes as one veil after another is removed from the past and the present. The underlying form of *Ghosts* is that of the tragic rhythm as one finds it in *Oedipus Rex*.

But this judgment needs to be qualified in several respects: because of the theater for which Ibsen wrote, the tragic form which Sophocles could develop to the full, and with every theatrical resource, is hidden beneath the clichés of plot and the surfaces "evident to the most commonplace mind." At the end of the play the tragic rhythm of Mrs. Alving's quest is not so much completed as brutally truncated, in obedience to the requirements of the thesis and the thriller. Oswald's collapse, before our eyes, with his mother's screaming, makes the intrigue end with a bang, and hammers home the thesis. But from the point of view of Mrs. Alving's tragic quest as we have seen it develop through the rest of the play, this conclusion concludes nothing: it is merely sensational.

The exciting intrigue and the brilliantly, the violently clear surfaces of *Ghosts* are likely to obscure completely its real life and underlying form. The tragic rhythm, which Ibsen rediscovered by his long and loving attention to the reality of his fictive lives, is evident only to the histrionic sensibility. As Henry James put it, Ibsen's characters "have the extraordinary, the brilliant property of becoming when represented at once more abstract and more living": i.e., both their lives and the life of the play, the spiritual content and the form of the whole, are revealed in this medium.

A Nazimova, a Duse, could show it to us on the stage. Lacking such a performance, the reader must endeavor to respond imaginatively and directly himself if he is to see the hidden poetry of *Ghosts*.

Mrs. Alving and Oswald: The Tragic Rhythm in a Small Figure

As Ibsen was fighting to present his poetic vision within the narrow theater admitted by modern realism, so his protagonist Mrs. Alving is fighting to realize her sense of human life in the blank photograph of her own stuffy parlor. She discovers there no means, no terms, and no nourishment; that is the truncated tragedy which underlies the savage thesis of the play. But she does find her son Oswald, and she makes of him the symbol of all she is seeking: freedom, innocence, joy, and truth. At the level of the life of the play, where Ibsen warms his characters into extraordinary human reality, they all have moral and emotional meanings for each other; and the pattern of their related actions, their partially blind struggle for the Alving heritage, is consistent and very complex. In this structure, Mrs. Alving's changing relation to Oswald is only one strand, though an important one. I wish to consider it as a sample of Ibsen's rediscovery, through modern realism, of the tragic rhythm.

Oswald is of course not only a symbol for his mother, but a person in his own right, with his own quest for freedom and release, and his own anomalous stake in the Alving heritage. He is also a symbol for Pastor Manders of what he wants from Captain Alving's estate: the stability and continuity of the bourgeois conventions. In the economy of the play as a whole, Oswald is the hidden reality of the whole situation, like Oedipus' actual status as son-husband: the hidden fatality which, revealed in a series of tragic and ironic steps, brings the final peripety of the action. To see how this works, the reader is asked to consider Oswald's role in Act I and the beginning of Act II.

The main part of Act I (after a prologue between Regina and Engstrand) is a debate, or rather agon, between Mrs. Alving and the Pastor. The Pastor has come to settle the details of Mrs. Alving's bequest of her husband's money to the orphanage. They at once disagree about the purpose and handling of the bequest; and this disagreement soon broadens into the whole issue of Mrs. Alving's emancipation versus the Pastor's conventionality. The question of Oswald is at the center. The Pastor wants to think of him, and to make of him, a pillar of society such as the Captain was supposed to have been, while Mrs. Alving wants him to be her masterpiece of liberation. At this point Oswald himself wanders in, the actual but still mysterious truth underlying the dispute between his mother and the Pastor. His appearance produces what the Greeks would have called a complex recognition scene, with an implied peripety for both Mrs. Alving and the Pastor, which will not be realized by them until the end of the act. But this tragic development is written to be acted; it is to be found, not so much in the actual words of the characters, as in their moral-emotional responses and changing relationships to one another.

The Pastor has not seen Oswald since he grew up; and seeing him now he is startled as though by a real ghost; he recognizes him as the very reincarnation of his father: the same physique, the same mannerisms, even the same kind of pipe. Mrs. Alving with equal confidence recognizes him as her own son, and she notes that his mouth-mannerism is like the Pastor's. (She had been in love with the Pastor during the early years of her marriage, when she wanted to leave the Captain.) As for Oswald himself, the mention of the pipe gives him a Proustian intermittence of the heart: he suddenly recalls a childhood scene when his father had given him his own pipe to smoke. He feels again the nausea and the cold sweat, and hears the Captain's hearty laughter. Thus in effect he recognizes himself as his father's, in the sense of his father's *victim*; a premonition of the ugly scene at the end of the play. But at this point no one is prepared to accept the full import of these insights. The whole scene is, on the surface, light and conventional, an accurate report of a passage of provincial politeness. Oswald wanders off for a walk before dinner, and the Pastor and his mother are left to bring their struggle more into the open.

Oswald's brief scene marks the end of the first round of the fight, and serves as prologue for the second round, much as the intervention of the chorus in the agon between Oedipus and Tiresias punctuates their struggle, and hints at an unexpected outcome on a new level of awareness. As soon as Oswald has gone, the Pastor launches an attack in form upon Mrs. Alving's entire emancipated way of life, with the question of Oswald, his role in the community, his upbringing and his future, always at the center of the attack. Mrs. Alving replies with her whole rebellious philosophy, illustrated by a detailed account of her tormented life with the Captain, none of which the Pastor had known (or been willing to recognize) before. Mrs. Alving proves on the basis of this evidence that her new freedom is right; that her long secret rebellion was justified; and that she is now about to complete Oswald's emancipation, and thereby her own, from the swarming ghosts of the past. If the issue were merely on this rationalistic level, and between her and the Pastor, she would triumph at this point. But the real truth of her situation (as Oswald's appearance led us to suppose) does not fit either her rationalization or the Pastor's.

Oswald passes through the parlor again on his way to the dining room to get a drink before dinner, and his mother watches him in pride and pleasure. But from behind the door we hear the affected squealing of Regina. It is now Mrs. Alving's turn for an intermittence of the heart: it is as though she heard again her husband with Regina's mother. The insight which she had rejected before now reaches her in full strength, bringing the promised pathos and peripety; she sees Oswald, not as her masterpiece of liberation, but as the sinister, tyrannical, and continuing life of the past itself. The basis of her rationalization is gone; she suffers the breakdown of the moral being which she had built upon her now exploded view of Oswald.

At this point Ibsen brings down the curtain in obedience to the principles of the well-made play. The effect is to raise the suspense by stimulating our curiosity about the facts of the rest of the story. What will Mrs. Alving do now? What will the Pastor do—for Oswald and Regina are half-brother and sister; can we prevent the scandal from coming out? So the suspense is raised, but the attention of the audience is diverted from Mrs. Alving's tragic quest to the most literal, newspaper version of the facts.

The second act (which occurs immediately after dinner) is ostensibly concerned only with these gossipy facts. The Pastor and Mrs. Alving debate ways of handling the threatened scandal. But this is only the literal surface: Ibsen has his eye upon Mrs. Alving's shaken psyche, and the actual dramatic form of this scene, under the discussion which Mrs. Alving keeps up, is her pathos which the Act I curtain broke off. Mrs. Alving is suffering the blow in courage and faith; and she is rewarded with her deepest insight: "I am half inclined to think we are all ghosts, Mr. Manders. It is not only what we have inherited from our fathers and mothers that exists again in us, but all sorts of dead ideas and all kinds of old dead beliefs and things of that kind. They are not actually alive in us; but they are dormant all the same, and we can never be rid of them. Whenever I take up a newspaper and read it, I fancy I see ghosts creeping between the lines. There must be ghosts all over the world. They must be as countless as the grains of sand, it seems to me. And we are so miserably afraid of the light, all of us."[1] This passage, in the fumbling phrases of Ibsen's provincial lady, and in William Archer's translation, is not by itself the poetry of the great dramatic

---

[1] *Ghosts*, by Henrik Ibsen. Translated by William Archer.

poets. It does not have the verbal music of Racine, nor the freedom and sophistication of Hamlet, nor the scope of the Sophoclean chorus, with its use of the full complement of poetic and musical and theatrical resources. But in the total situation in the Alving parlor which Ibsen has so carefully established, and in terms of Mrs. Alving's uninstructed but profoundly developing awareness, it has its own hidden poetry: a poetry not of words but of the theater, a poetry of the histrionic sensibility. From the point of view of the underlying form of the play—the form as "the soul" of the tragedy—this scene completes the sequence which began with the debate in Act I: it is the pathos-and-epiphany following that agon.

It is evident, I think, that insofar as Ibsen was able to obey his realistic scruple, his need for the disinterested perception of human life beneath the clichés of custom and rationalization, he rediscovered the perennial basis of tragedy. The poetry of *Ghosts* is under the words, in the detail of action, where Ibsen accurately sensed the tragic rhythm of human life in a thousand small figures. And these little "movements of the psyche" are composed in a complex rhythm like music, a formal development sustained (beneath the sensational story and the angry thesis) until the very end. But the action is not completed: Mrs. Alving is left screaming with the raw impact of the calamity. The music is broken off, the dissonance unresolved—or, in more properly dramatic terms, the acceptance of the catastrophe, leading to the final vision or epiphany which should correspond to the insight Mrs. Alving gains in Act II, is lacking. The action of the play is neither completed nor placed in the wider context of meanings which the disinterested or contemplative purposes of poetry demand.

The unsatisfactory end of *Ghosts* may be understood in several ways. Thinking of the relation between Mrs. Alving and Oswald, one might say that she had romantically loaded more symbolic values upon her son than a human being can carry; hence his collapse proves too much—more than Mrs. Alving or the audience can digest. One may say that, at the end, Ibsen himself could not quite dissociate himself from his rebellious protagonist and see her action in the round, and so broke off in anger, losing his tragic vision in the satisfaction of reducing the bourgeois parlor to a nightmare, and proving the hollowness of a society which sees human life in such myopic and dishonest terms. As a thesis play, *Ghosts* is an ancestor of many related genres: Brieux's arguments for social reform, propaganda plays like those of the Marxists, or parables *à la* Andreev, or even Shaw's more generalized plays of the play-of-thought about social questions. But this use of the theater of modern realism for promoting or discussing political and social ideas never appealed to Ibsen. It did not solve his real problem, which was to use the publicly accepted theater of his time for poetic purposes. The most general way to understand the unsatisfactory end of *Ghosts* is to say that Ibsen could not find a way to represent the action of his protagonist, with all its moral and intellectual depth, within the terms of modern realism. In the attempt he truncated this action, and revealed as in a brilliant light the limitations of the bourgeois parlor as the scene of human life.

The End of *Ghosts*:
The Tasteless Parlor and the Stage of Europe

Oswald is the chief symbol of what Mrs. Alving is seeking, and his collapse ends her quest in a horrifying catastrophe. But in the complex life of the play, all of the persons and things acquire emotional and moral significance for Mrs. Alving; and at the end, to throw as much light as possible upon the catastrophe, Ibsen brings all of the elements of his composition together in their highest symbolic valency. The orphanage has burned to the ground; the Pastor has promised Engstrand money for his "Sailor's Home" which he plans as a brothel; Regina departs, to follow her mother in the search for pleasure and money. In these eventualities the conventional morality of the Alving heritage is revealed as lewdness and dishonesty, quickly consumed in the fires of lust and greed, as Oswald himself (the central symbol) was consumed even before his birth. But what does this wreckage mean? Where are we to place it in human experience? Ibsen can only place it in the literal parlor, with lamplight giving place to daylight, and sunrise on the empty, stimulating, virginal snow-peaks out the window. The emotional force of this complicated effect is very great; it has the searching intimacy of nightmare. But it is also as disquieting as a nightmare from which we are suddenly awakened; it is incomplete, and the contradiction between the inner power of dream and the literal appearances of the daylight world is unresolved. The spirit that moved Ibsen to write the play, and which moved his protagonist through her tragic progress, is lost to sight, disembodied, imperceptible in any form unless the dreary exaltation of the inhuman mountain scene conveys it in feeling.

Henry James felt very acutely the contradiction between the deep and strict spirit of Ibsen and his superb craftsmanship on one side, and the little scene he tried to use—the parlor in its surrounding void—on the other. "If the spirit is a lamp within us, glowing through what the world and the flesh make of us as through a ground-glass shade, then such pictures as *Little Eyolf* and *John Gabriel* are each a chassez-croisez of lamps burning, as in tasteless parlors, with the flame practically exposed," he wrote in *London Notes*.[2] "There is a positive odor of spiritual paraffin. The author nevertheless arrives at the dramatist's great goal—he arrives for all his meagerness at intensity. The meagerness, which is after all but an unconscious, an admirable economy, never interferes with that: it plays straight into the hands of his rare mastery of form. The contrast between this form—so difficult to have reached, so 'evolved,' so civilized—and the bareness and bleakness of his little northern democracy is the source of half the hard frugal charm he puts forth."

James had rejected very early in his career his own little northern democracy, that of General Grant's America, with its ugly parlor, its dead conventions, its enthusiastic materialism, and its "non-conducting atmosphere." At the same time he shared Ibsen's ethical preoccupation, and his strict sense of form. His comments on Ibsen are at once the most sympathetic and the most objective that have been written. But James's own solution was to try to find a better parlor for the theater of human life; to present the quest of his American pilgrim of culture on the wider "stage of Europe" as this might still be felt and suggested in the manners of the leisured classes in England and France. James would have nothing to do with the prophetic and revolutionary spirit which was driving the great continental authors, Ibsen among them. In his artistry and his moral exactitude Ibsen is akin to James; but this is not his whole story, and if one is to understand the spirit he tried to realize in Mrs. Alving, one must think of Kierkegaard, who had a great influence on Ibsen in the beginning of his career.

Kierkegaard (in *For Self-Examination*) has this to say of the disembodied and insatiable spirit of the times: ". . . thou wilt scarcely find anyone who does not believe in—let us say, for example, the spirit of the age, the *Zeitgeist*. Even he who has taken leave of higher things and is rendered blissful by mediocrity, yea, even he who toils slavishly for paltry ends or in the contemptible servitude of ill-gotten gains, even he believes, firmly and fully too, in the spirit of the age. Well, that is natural enough, it is by no means anything very lofty he believes in, for the spirit of the age is after all no higher than the age, it keeps close to the ground, so that it is the sort of spirit which is most like will-o'-the-wisp; but yet he believes in spirit. Or he believes in the world-spirit (*Weltgeist*) that strong spirit (for allurements, yes), that ingenious spirit (for deceits, yes); that spirit which Christianity calls an evil spirit—so that, in consideration of this, it is by no means anything very lofty he believes in

---

[2] Jan.–Aug., 1897.

when he believes in the world-spirit; but yet he believes in spirit. Or he believes in 'the spirit of humanity,' not spirit in the individual, but in the race, that spirit which, when it is god-forsaken for having forsaken God, is again, according to Christianity's teaching, an evil spirit—so that in view of this it is by no means anything very lofty he believes in when he believes in this spirit; but yet he believes in spirit.

"On the other hand, as soon as the talk is about a holy spirit—how many, dost thou think, believe in it? Or when the talk is about an evil spirit which is to be renounced—how many, dost thou think, believe in such a thing?"[3]

This description seems to me to throw some light upon Mrs. Alving's quest, upon Ibsen's modern-realistic scene, and upon the theater which his audience would accept. The other face of nineteenth century positivism is romantic aspiration. And Ibsen's realistic scene presents both of these aspects of the human condition: the photographically accurate parlor, in the foreground, satisfies the requirements of positivism, while the empty but stimulating scene out the window—Europe as a moral void, an uninhabited wilderness—offers as it were a blank check to the insatiate spirit. Ibsen always felt this exhilarating wilderness behind his cramped interiors. In *A Doll's House* we glimpse it as winter weather and black water. In *The Lady from the Sea* it is the cold ocean, with its whales and its gulls. In *The Wild Duck* it is the northern marshes, with wildfowl but no people. In the last scene of *Ghosts* it is, of course, the bright snow-peaks, which may mean Mrs. Alving's quest in its most disembodied and ambivalent form; very much the same sensuous moral void in which Wagner, having totally rejected the little human foreground where Ibsen fights his battles, unrolls the solitary action of passion. It is the "stage of Europe" before human exploration, as it might have appeared to the first hunters.

There is a kinship between the fearless and demanding spirit of Kierkegaard, and the spirit which Ibsen tried to realize in Mrs. Alving. But Mrs. Alving, like her contemporaries whom Kierkegaard describes, will not or cannot accept any interpretation of the spirit that drives her. It may look like the *Weltgeist* when she demands the joy of living, it may look like the Holy Ghost itself when one considers her appetite for truth. And it may look like the spirit of evil, a "goblin damned," when we see the desolation it produces. If one thinks of the symbols which Ibsen brings together in the last scene: the blank parlor, the wide unex-

---

[3] Kierkegaard, *For Self-Examination and Judge for Yourselves* (Princeton University Press, 1944), p. 94.

plored world outside, the flames that consumed the Alving heritage and the sunrise flaming on the peaks, one may be reminded of the condition of Dante's great rebel Ulysses. He too is wrapped in the flame of his own consciousness, yet still dwells in the pride of the mind and the exhilaration of the world free of people, *il mondo senza gente*. But this analogy also may not be pressed too far. Ulysses is in hell; and when we explore the Mountain on which he was wrecked, we can place his condition with finality, and in relation to many other human modes of action and awareness. But Mrs. Alving's mountains do not place her anywhere: the realism of modern realism ends with the literal. Beyond that is not the ordered world of the tradition, but *Unendlichkeit*, and the anomalous "freedom" of undefined and uninformed aspiration.

Perhaps Mrs. Alving and Ibsen himself are closer to the role of Dante than to the role of Ulysses, seeing a hellish mode of being, but free to move on. Certainly Ibsen's development continued beyond *Ghosts*, and toward the end of his career he came much closer to achieving a consistent theatrical poetry within the confines of the theater of modern realism. He himself remarked that his poetry was to be found only in the series of his plays, no one of which was complete by itself.

But my purpose is, of course, not to do justice to Ibsen but to consider the potentialities of modern realism; and for this purpose Chekhov's masterpiece is essential. Chekhov did not solve the problem which Ibsen faced in *Ghosts*. He was not trying to show a desperate quest like Mrs. Alving's, with every weapon of the mind and the will. By his time the ambitious machinery of thesis and thriller had begun to pall; the prophetic-revolutionary spirit, grown skeptical and subtle, had sunk back into the flesh and the feelings, into the common beggarly body, for a period of pause, in hope and foreboding. Chekhov does not have Isben's force and intellect but he can accept the realistic stage much more completely, and use it with greater mastery for the contemplative purpose of art.

C. S. LEWIS

Donne and Love Poetry in the Seventeenth Century

Little of Manfred (but not very much of him) —W. S. GILBERT

I have seen an old history of literature in which the respective claims of Shelley and Mrs. Hemans to be the greatest lyrist of the nineteenth century were seriously weighed; and Donne, who was so inconsiderable fifty years ago, seems at the moment to rank among our greatest poets.

If there were no middle state between absolute certainty and what Mr. Kellett calls the whirligig of taste, these fluctuations would make us throw up criticism in despair. But where it is impossible to go quite straight we may yet resolve to reel as little as we can. Such phenomena as the present popularity of Donne or the growing unpopularity of Milton are not to be deplored; they are rather to be explained. It is not impossible to see why Donne's poetry should be overrated in the twentieth and underrated in the eighteenth century; and in so far as we detect these temporary disturbing factors and explain the varying appearances of the object by the varying positions of the observers, we shall come appreciably nearer to a glimpse of Donne *simpliciter*. I shall concern myself in what follows chiefly with his love poetry.

In style this poetry is primarily a development of one of the two styles which we find in the work of Donne's immediate predecessors. One of these is the mellifluous, luxurious, 'builded rhyme,' as in Spenser's *Amoretti*: the other is the abrupt, familiar, and consciously 'manly' style in which nearly all Wyatt's lyrics are written. Most of the better poets make use of both, and in *Astrophel and Stella* much of Sidney's success depends on deliberate contrast between such poetry as

That golden sea whose waves in curls are broken

and such poetry as

He cannot love: no, no, let him alone.

But Wyatt remains, if not the finest, yet much the purest example of the plainer manner, and in reading his songs, with their conversational openings, their surly (not to say sulky) defiances, and their lack of obviously poetic ornament, I find myself again and again reminded of Donne. But of course he is a Donne with most of the genius left out. Indeed, the first and most obvious achievement of the younger poet is to have raised this kind of thing to a much higher power; to have kept the vividness of conversation where Wyatt too often had only the flatness; to sting like a lash where Wyatt merely grumbled. The difference in degree between the two poets thus obscures the similarity in kind. Donne has so far surpassed not only Wyatt but all the Elizabethans in what may be called their Wyatt moments, and has so generally abstained from attempting to rival them in their other vein, that we hardly think of him as continuing one side of their complex tradition; he appears rather as the innovator who substituted a realistic for a decorated kind of love poetry.

Now this error is not in itself important. In an age which was at all well placed for judging the comparative merits of the two styles, it would not matter though we thought that Donne had invented what in fact he only brought to perfection. But our own age is not so placed. The mellifluous style, which we may agree to call Petrarchan though no English poet is very like Petrarch, has really no chance of a fair hearing. It is based on a conception of poetry wholly different from that of the twentieth century. It descends from old Provençal and Italian sources and presupposes a poetic like that of Dante. Dante, we may remember, thinks of poetry as something to be made, to be 'adorned as much as possible', to have its 'true sense' hidden beneath a rich vesture of 'rhetorical colouring'. The 'Petrarchan' sonneteers are not trying to make their work sound like the speaking voice. They are not trying to communicate faithfully the raw, the merely natural, impact of actual passion. The passion for them is not a specimen of 'nature' to be followed so much as a lump of ore to be refined: they ask themselves not 'How can I record it with the least sophistication?' but 'Of its bones what coral can I make?', and to accuse them of insincerity is like calling an oyster insincere because it makes its disease into a pearl. The aim of the other style is quite different. It wishes to be convincing, intimate, naturalistic. It would be very foolish to set up these two kinds of poetry as rivals, for obviously they are different and both are good. It is a fine thing to hear the living voice, the voice of a man like ourselves, whispering or shouting to us from the printed page with all the heat of life; and it is a fine thing, too, to see such life—so pitiably like our own, I doubt not, in the living—caught up and transfigured, sung by the voice of a god into an ecstasy no less real though in another dimension.[1] There is no necessary quarrel between the two. But there

---

[1] Those who object to 'emotive terms' in criticism may prefer to read '.... used by an accomplished poet to produce an attitude relevant not directly to outer experience but to the central nucleus of the total attitude-and-belief-feeling system'. It must not be supposed, however, that the present writer's theory of either knowledge or value would permit him, in the long run, to accept the restatement.

are many reasons why one of them should start with overwhelming odds in its favour at the present moment. For many years our poetics have been becoming more and more expressionistic. First came Wordsworth with his theory, and we have never quite worked it out of our system; even in the crude form that 'you should write as you talk', it works at the back of much contemporary criticism. Then came the final break-up of aristocracy and the consequent, and still increasing, distaste for arduous disciplines of sentiment—the wholesale acceptance of the merely and unredeemedly natural. Finally, the psychological school of criticism overthrew what was left of the old conception of a poem as a construction and set up instead the poem as 'document'. In so far as we admire Donne for being our first great practitioner in one of the many possible kinds of lyric, we are on firm ground; but the conception of him as liberator, as one who substituted 'real' or 'live' or 'sincere' for 'artificial' or 'conventional' love lyric, begs all the questions and is simply a prejudice *de siècle*.

But of course when we have identified the Wyatt element in Donne, we have still a very imperfect notion of his manner. We have described 'Busie old foole' and 'I wonder by my troth' and 'For Godsake hold your tongue, and let me love'; but we have left out the cleaving remora, the triple soul, the stiff twin compasses, and a hundred other things that were not in Wyatt. There were indeed a great many things not in Wyatt, and his manly plainness can easily be overpraised—'pauper videri Cinna vult et est pauper'. If Donne had not reinforced the style with new attractions it would soon have died of very simplicity. An account of these reinforcements will give us a rough notion of the unhappily named 'metaphysical' manner.

The first of them is the multiplication of conceits—not conceits of any special 'metaphysical' type but conceits such as we find in all the Elizabethans. When Donne speaks of the morning coming from his mistress's eyes, or tells how they wake him like the light of a taper, these fanciful hyperboles are not, in themselves, a novelty. But, side by side with these, we find, as his second characteristic, what may be called the difficult conceit. This is clearly a class which no two readers will fill up in quite the same way. An example of what I mean comes at the end of *The Sunne Rising* where the sun is congratulated on the fact that the two lovers have shortened his task for him. Even the quickest reader will be checked, if only for an infinitesimal time, before he sees how and why the lovers have done this, and will experience a kind of astonished relief at the unexpected answer. The pleasure of the thing, which can be paralleled in other artistic devices, perhaps in rhyme itself, would seem to depend on recurrent tension and relaxation. In the third place, we have Donne's characteristic choice of imagery. The Petrarchans (I will call them so for convenience) had relied for their images mainly on mythology and on natural objects. Donne uses both of these sparingly—though his sea that 'Leaves embroider'd works upon the sand' is as fine an image from nature as I know—and taps new sources such as law, science, philosophy, and the commonplaces of urban life. It is this that has given the Metaphysicals their name and been much misunderstood. When Johnson said that they were resolved to show their learning he said truth in fact, for there is an element of pedantry, or dandyism, an *odi profanos* air, about Donne—the old printer's address not to the *readers* but to the *understanders* is illuminating. But Johnson was none the less misleading. He encouraged the idea that the abstruse nature of some of Donne's similes was poetically relevant for good or ill. In fact, of course, when we have once found out what Donne is talking about—that is, when Sir Herbert Grierson has told us—the learning of the poet becomes unimportant. The image will stand or fall like any other by its intrinsic merit—its power of conveying a meaning 'more luminously and with a sensation of delight.' The matter is worth mentioning only because Donne's reputation in this respect repels some humble readers and attracts some prigs. What is important for criticism is his avoidance of the obviously poetical image; whether the intractable which he is determined to poetize is fetched from Thomas Aquinas or from the London underworld, the method is essentially the same. Indeed it would be easy to exaggerate the amount of learned imagery in his poems and even the amount of his learning. He knows much, but he seems to know even more because his knowledge so seldom overlaps with our own; and some scraps of his learning, such as that of angelic consciousness or of the three souls in man, come rather too often—like the soldiers in a stage army, and with the same result. This choice of imagery is closely connected with the surprising and ingenious nature of the connexions which Donne makes between the image and the matter in hand, thus getting a double surprise. No one, in the first place, expects lovers to be compared to compasses; and no one, even granted the comparison, would guess in what respect they are going to be compared.

But all these characteristics, in their mere enumeration, are what Donne would have called a 'ruinous anatomie.' They might all be used—indeed they all are used by Herbert—to produce a result very unlike Donne's. What gives their peculiar character to most of the *Songs and Sonets* is that they are dramatic in the sense of being addressed to an imagined hearer in the heat of an imagined conversation, and usually addresses of a violently argumentative character. The majority of lyrics, even where nominally addressed to a god, a woman, or a friend, are meditations or introspective narratives. Thus Herbert's 'Throw away thy rod' is formally an apostrophe; in fact, it is a picture of Herbert's own state of mind. But the majority of the *Songs and Sonets*, including some that are addressed to abstractions like Love, present the poet's state of mind only indirectly and are ostensibly concerned with badgering, wheedling, convincing, or upbraiding an imagined hearer. No poet, not even Browning, buttonholes us or, as we say, "goes for" us like Donne. There are, of course, exceptions. *Goe and catche a falling starre*, though it is in the form of an address, has not this effect; and *Twicknam Garden* or the *Nocturnall* are in fact, as well as in pretension, soliloquies. These exceptions include some of Donne's best work; and indeed, one of the errors of contemporary criticism, to my mind, is an insufficient distinction between Donne's best and Donne's most characteristic. But I do not at present wish to emphasize this. For the moment it is enough to notice that the majority of his love lyrics, and of the *Elegies*, are of the type I have described. And since they are, nearly always, in the form of arguments, since they attempt to extort something from us, they are poetry of an extremely exacting kind. This exacting quality, this urgency and pressure of the poet upon the reader in every line, seems to me to be the root both of Donne's weakness and his strength. When the thing fails it exercises the same dreadful fascination that we feel in the grip of the worst kind of bore—the hot-eyed, unescapable kind. When it succeeds it produces a rare intensity in our enjoyment—which is what a modern critic meant (I fancy) when he claimed that Donne made all other poetry sound less 'serious.' The point is worth investigation.

For, of course, in one sense these poems are not serious at all. Poem after poem consists of extravagant conceits woven into the preposterous semblance of an argument. The preposterousness is the point. Donne intends to take your breath away by the combined subtlety and impudence of the steps that lead to his conclusion. Any attempt to overlook Donne's 'wit' in this sense, or to pretend that his rare excursions into the direct expression of passion are typical, is false criticism. The paradox, the surprise, are essential; if you are not enjoying these you are not enjoying what Donne intended. Thus *Womans Constancy* is of no interest as a document of Donne's 'cynicism'—any fool can be promiscuously unchaste and any fool can say so. The merit of the poem consists in the skill with which it leads us to expect a certain conclusion and then gives us precisely the opposite conclusion, and that, too, with an appearance of reasonableness. Thus, again, the art of *The Will* consists in keeping us guessing through each stanza what universal in the concluding triplet will bind together the odd particulars in the preceding six lines. The test case is *The Flea*. If you think this very different from Donne's other poems you may be sure that you have no taste for the real Donne. But for the accident that modern cleanliness by rendering this insect disgusting has also rendered it comic, the conceit is exactly on the same level as that of the tears in *A Valediction: of weeping*.

And yet the modern critic was right. The effect of all these poems is somehow serious. 'Serious' indeed is the only word. Seldom profound in thought, not always passionate in feeling, they are none the less the very opposite of gay. It is as though Donne performed in deepest depression those gymnastics which are usually a sign of intellectual high spirits. He himself speaks of his '*concupiscence* of wit'. The hot, dark word is well chosen. We are all familiar—at least if we have lived in Ireland—with the type of mind which combines furious anger with a revelling delight in eloquence, nay grows more rhetorical as anger increases. In the same way, wit and the delight in wit are, for Donne, not only compatible with, but actually provoked by, the most uneasy passions—by contempt and self-contempt and unconvinced sensuality. His wit is not so much the play as the irritability of intellect. But none the less, like the angry Irishman's *clausulae*, it is still enjoyed and still intends to produce admiration; and if we do not hold our breaths as we read, wondering in the middle of each complication how he will resolve it, and exclaiming at the end 'How ever did you think of *that*?' (Carew speaks of his 'fresh invention'), we are not enjoying Donne.

Now this kind of thing can produce a very strong and a very peculiar pleasure. Our age has nothing to repent of in having learned to relish it. If the Augustans, in their love for the obviously poetical and harmonious, were blind to its merits, so much the worse for them. At the same time it is desirable not to overlook the special congeniality of such poetry to the twentieth century, and to beware of giving to this highly specialized and, in truth, very limited kind of excellence, a place in our scheme of literary values which it does not deserve. Donne's rejection of the obviously poetical image was a good method—for Donne; but if we think that there is some intrinsic superiority in this method, so that all poetry about pylons and *non obstantes* must needs be of a higher order than poetry about lawns and lips and breasts and orient skies, we are deceived—deceived by the fact that we, like

Donne, happen to live at the end of a great period of rich and nobly obvious poetry. It is natural to want your savoury after your sweets; but you must not base a philosophy of cookery on that momentary preference. Again, Donne's obscurity and occasional abstruseness have sometimes (not always) produced magnificent results, and we do well to praise them. But, as I have hinted, an element of dandyism was present in Donne himself—he 'would have no such readers as he could teach'—and we must be very cautious here lest shallow call to shallow. There is a great deal of dandyism (largely of Franco-American importation) in the modern literary world. And finally, what shall we say of Donne's 'seriousness', of that persistency, that nimiety, that astringent quality (as Boehme would have said) which makes him, if not the saddest, at least the most uncomfortable, of our poets? Here, surely, we find the clearest and most disturbing congeniality of all. It would be foolish not to recognize the growth in our criticism of something that I can only describe as literary Manichaeism—a dislike of peace and pleasure and heartsease simply as such. To be bilious is, in some circles, almost the first qualification for a place in the Temple of Fame.[2] We distrust the pleasures of imagination, however hotly and unmerrily we preach the pleasures of the body. This seriousness must not be confused with profundity. We do not like poetry that essays to be wise, and Chaucer would think we had rejected 'doctryne' and 'solas' about equally. We want, in fact, just what Donne can give us—something stern and tough, though not necessarily virtuous, something that does not conciliate. Born under Saturn, we do well to confess the liking complexionally forced upon us; but not to attempt that wisdom which dominates the stars is pusillanimous, and to set up our limitation as a norm—to believe, against all experience, in a Saturnocentric universe—is folly.

Before leaving the discussion of Donne's manner I must touch, however reluctantly, on a charge that has been brought against him from the time of Ben Jonson till now. Should he, or should he not, be hanged for not keeping the accent? There is more than one reason why I do not wish to treat this subject. In the first place, the whole nature of Donne's stanza, and of what he does within the stanza, cannot be profitably discussed except by one who knows much more than I do about the musical history of the time. *Confined Love*, for example, is metrically meaningless without the tune. But I could make shift with

---

[2] In this we have been anticipated. See *Emma*, ch. 25: 'I know what worthy people they are. Perry tells me that Mr. Cole never touches malt liquor. You would not think it to look at him, but he is bilious—Mr. Cole is very bilious.'

that difficulty: my real trouble is of quite a different kind. In discussing Donne's present popularity, the question of metre forces me to a statement which I do not make without embarrassment. Some one must say it, but I do not care for the office, for what I have to say will hardly be believed among scholars and hardly listened to by any one else. It is simply this—that the opinions of the modern world on the metre of any poet are, in general, of no value at all, because most modern readers of poetry do not know how to scan. My evidence for this amazing charge is twofold. In the first place I find that very many of my own pupils—some of them from excellent schools, most of them great readers of poetry, not a few of them talented and (for their years) well-informed persons—are quite unable, when they first come to me, to find out from the verse how Marlowe pronounced Barabas or Mahomet. To be sure, if challenged, they will say that they do not believe in syllable-counting or that the old methods of scansion have been exploded, but this is only a smoke screen. It is easy to find out that they have not got beyond the traditional legal fiction of longs and shorts and have never even got so far: they are in virgin ignorance. And my experience as an examiner shows me that this is not peculiar to my own pupils. My second piece of evidence is more remarkable. I have heard a celebrated belle-lettrist—a printed critic and poet—repeatedly, in the same lecture, so mispronounce the name of a familiar English poem as to show that he did not know a decasyllabic line when he met it. The conclusion is unavoidable. Donne may be metrically good or bad, in fact; but it is obvious that he might be bad to any degree without offending the great body of his modern admirers. On that side, his present vogue is worth precisely nothing. No doubt this widespread metrical ignorance is itself a symptom of some deeper change; and I am far from suggesting that the appearance of *vers libre* is simply a result of the ignorance. More probably the ignorance, and the deliberate abandonment, of accentual metres are correlative phenomena, and both the results of some revolution in our whole sense of rhythm—a revolution of great importance reaching deep down into the unconscious and even perhaps into the blood. But that is not our business at the moment.

The sentiment of Donne's love poems is easier to describe than their manner, and its charm for modern readers easier to explain. No one will deny that the twentieth century, so far, has shown an extraordinary interest in the sexual appetite and has been generally marked by a reaction from the romantic idealization of that appetite. We have agreed with the romantics in regarding sexual love as a subject of overwhelming importance, but hardly in anything else. On the purely literary side we are wearied with the floods of uxorious bathos which the romantic conception undoubtedly liberated. As psychologists we are interested in the new discovery of the secreter and less reputable operations of the instinct. As practical philosophers we are living in an age of sexual experiment. The whole subject offers us an admirable field for the kind of seriousness I have just described. It seems odd, at first sight, that a sixteenth-century poet should give us so exactly what we want; but it can be explained.

The great central movement of love poetry, and of fiction about love, in Donne's time is that represented by Shakespeare and Spenser. This movement consisted in the final transmutation of the medieval courtly love or romance of adultery into an equally romantic love that looked to marriage as its natural conclusion. The process, of course, had begun far earlier—as early, indeed, as the *Kingis Quhair*—but its triumph belongs to the sixteenth century. It is most powerfully expressed by Spenser, but more clearly, and philosophically by Chapman in that under-estimated poem, his *Hero and Leander*. These poets were engaged, as Professor Vinaver would say, in reconciling Carbonek and Camelot, virture and courtesy, divine and human love; and incidentally in laying down the lines which love poetry was to follow till the nineteenth century. We who live at the end of the dispensation which they inaugurated and in reaction against it are not well placed for evaluating their work. Precisely what is revolutionary and creative in it seems to us platitudinous, orthodox, and stale. If there were a poet, and a strong poet, alive in their time who was failing to move with them, he would inevitably appear to us more 'modern' than they.

But was Donne such a poet? A great critic has assigned him an almost opposite role, and it behooves us to proceed with caution. It may be admitted at once that Donne's work is not, in this respect, all of a piece; no poet fits perfectly into such a scheme as I have outlined—it can be true only by round and by large. There are poems in which Donne attempts to sing a love perfectly in harmony with the moral law, but they are not very numerous and I do not think they are usually his best pieces. Donne never for long gets rid of a medieval sense of the sinfulness of sexuality; indeed, just because the old conventional division between Carbonek and Camelot is breaking up, he feels this more continously and restively than any poet of the Middle Ages.

Donne was bred a Roman Catholic. The significance of this in relation to his learned and scholastic imagery can be exaggerated; scraps of Calvin, or, for that matter, of Euclid or Bacon, might have much the same poetical effect as his scraps of Aquinas. But it is all-important for his treatment of love. This is not easily understood by the modern reader, for later-day conceptions of the Puritan and the Roman Catholic stand in the way. We have come to use the word 'Puritan' to mean what should rather be called 'rigorist' or 'ascetic', and we tend to assume that the sixteenth-century Puritans were 'puritanical' in this sense. Calvin's rigorist theocracy at Geneva lends colour to the error. But there is no understanding the period of the Reformation in England until we have grasped the fact that the quarrel between the Puritans and the Papists was not primarily a quarrel between rigorism and indulgence, and that, in so far as it was, the rigorism was on the Roman side. On many questions, and specially in their view of the marriage bed, the Puritans were the indulgent party; if we may without disrespect so use the name of a great Roman Catholic, a great writer, and a great man, they were much more Chestertonian than their adversaries. The idea that a Puritan was a repressed and repressive person would have astonished Sir Thomas More and Luther about equally. On the contrary, More thought of a Puritan as one who 'loved no lenten fast nor lightly no fast else, saving breakfast and eat fast and drink fast and luske fast in their lechery'—a person only too likely to end up in the 'abominable heresies' of the Anabaptists about communism of goods and wives. And Puritan theology, so far from being grim and gloomy, seemed to More to err in the direction of fantastic optimism. 'I could for my part', he writes, 'be very well content that sin and pain and all were as shortly gone as Tindall telleth us: but I were loth that he deceved us if it be not so.' More would not have understood the idea, sometimes found in the modern writers, that he and his friends were defending a 'merry' Catholic England against sour precisions; they were rather defending necessary severity and sternly realistic theology against wanton labefaction—penance and 'works' and vows of celibacy and mortification and Purgatory against the easy doctrine, the mere wish-fulfillment dream, of salvation by faith. Hence when we turn from the religious works of More to Luther's *Table-talk* we are at once struck by the geniality of the latter. If Luther is right, we have waked from nightmare into sunshine: if he is wrong, we have entered a fools' paradise. The burden of his charge against the Catholics is that they have needlessly tormented us with scruples; and, in particular, that 'Antichrist will regard neither God nor the love of women'. 'On what pretence have they forbidden us marriage? 'Tis as though we were forbidden to eat, to drink, to sleep.' 'Where women are not honoured, temporal and domestic government are despised.' He praises women repeatedly: More, it will be remembered, though apparently an excellent husband and father, hardly ever mentions a woman save to ridicule her. It is easy to see why Luther's marriage (as he called it) or Luther's 'abominable bichery' (if you prefer) became almost a symbol. More can never keep off the subject for more than a few pages.

This antithesis, if once understood, explains many things in the history of sentiment, and many differences, noticeable to the present day, between the Protestant and the Catholic parts of Europe. It explains why the conversion of courtly love into romantic monogamous love was so largely the work of English, and even of Puritan, poets; and it goes far to explain why Donne contributes so little to that movement.

I trace in his poetry three levels of sentiment. On the lowest level (lowest, that is, in order of complexity), we have the celebration of simple appetite, as in *Elegy XIX*. If I call this a pornographic poem, I must be understood to use that ugly word as a descriptive, not a dyslogistic, term. I mean by it that this poem, in my opinion, is intended to arouse the appetite it describes, to affect not only the imagination but the nervous system of the reader.[3] And I may as well say at once—but who would willingly claim to be a judge in such matters?—that it seems to me to be very nearly perfect in its kind. Nor would I call it an immortal poem. Under what conditions the reading of it could be an innocent act is a real moral question; but the poem itself contains nothing intrinsically evil.

On the highest, or what Donne supposed to be the highest, level we have the poems of ostentatiously virtuous love, *The Undertaking*, *A Valediction: forbidding mourning*, and *The Extasie*. It is here that the contrast between Donne and his happier contemporaries is most marked. He is trying to follow them into the new age, to be at once passionate and innocent; and if any reader will make the experiment of imagining Beatrice or Juliet or Perdita, or again, Amoret or Britomart, or even Philoclea or Pamela, as the auditress throughout these poems, he will quickly feel that something is wrong. You may deny, as perhaps some do, that the romantic conception of 'pure' passion has any meaning; but certainly, if there is such a thing, it is not like this. It does not prove itself pure by talking about purity. It does not keep on drawing distinctions between spirit and flesh to the detriment of the latter and then explaining why the flesh is, after all, to be used. This is what Donne

---

[3] The restatement of this in terms acceptable to the Richardian school (for whom all poetry equally is addressed to the nervous system) should present no difficulty. For them it will be a distinction between parts, or functions, of the system.

does, and the result is singularly unpleasant. The more he labours the deeper 'Dun is in the mire', and it is quite arguable that *The Extasie* is a much nastier poem than the nineteenth *Elegy*. What any sensible woman would make of such a wooing it is difficult to imagine—or would be difficult if we forgot the amazing protective faculty which each sex possesses of not listening to the other.

Between these two extremes falls the great body of Donne's love poetry. In certain obvious, but superficial, respects, it continues the medieval tradition. Love is still a god and lovers his 'clergie'; oaths may be made in 'reverentiall feare' of his 'wrath'; and the man who resists him is 'rebell and atheist'. Donne can even doubt, like Soredamors, whether those who admit Love after a struggle have not forfeited his grace by their resistance, like

> *Small townes which stand stiffe, till great shot*
> *Enforce them.*

He can personify the attributes of his mistress, the 'enormous gyant' her Disdain and the 'enchantress *Honor*', quite in the manner of *The Romance of the Rose*. He writes *Albas* for both sexes, and in the *Holy Sonnets* repents of his love poetry, writing his palinode, in true medieval fashion. A reader may wonder, at first, why the total effect is so foreign to the Middle Ages: but Donne himself has explained this when he says, speaking of the god of Love,

> *If he wroung from mee a teare, I brin'd it so*
> *With scorne or shame, that him it nourish'd not.*

This admirable couplet not only tells us, in brief, what Donne has effected but shows us that he knew what he was doing. It does not, of course, cover every single poem. A few pieces admittedly express delighted love and they are among Donne's most popular works; such are *The Good-morrow* and *The Anniversarie*—poems that again remind us of the difference between his best and his typical. But the majority of the poems ring the changes on five themes, all of them grim ones— on the sorrow of parting (including death), the miseries of secrecy, the falseness of the mistress, the fickleness of Donne, and finally on contempt for love itself. The poems of parting stand next to the poems of happy love in general popularity and are often extremely affecting. We may hear little of the delights of Donne's loves, and dislike what we hear of their 'purity'; the pains ring true. The song *Sweetest love, I do not goe* is remarkable for its broken, but haunting, melody, and nowhere else has Donne fused argument, conceit, and classical imitation into a more perfect unity. *The Feaver* is equally remarkable, and that for a merit very rare in Donne—its inevitability. It is a single jet of music and feeling, a straight flight without appearance of effort. The remaining four of our five themes are all various articulations of the 'scorne or shame' with which Donne 'brines' his reluctantly extorted tributes to the god of Love; monuments, unparalleled outside Catallus, to the close kinship between certain kinds of love and certain kinds of hate. The faithlessness of women is sometimes treated, in a sense, playfully; but there is always something—the clever surprise in *Womans Constancy* or the grotesque in *Goe and catche a fallinge starre*—which stops these poems short of a true anacreontic gaiety. The theme of faithlessness rouses Donne to a more characteristic, and also a better, poetry in such a hymn of hate as *The Apparition*, or in the sad mingling of fear, contempt, and self-contempt in A *Lecture upon the Shadow*. The pains of secrecy give opportunity for equally fierce and turbulent writing. I may be deceived when I find in the sixteenth *Elegy*, along with many other nauseas and indignations, a sickened male contempt for the whole female world of nurses and 'midnight startings' and hysterics; but *The Curse* is unambiguous. The ending here is particularly delicious just because the main theme—an attack on *Jalosie* or the 'lozengiers'—is so medieval and so associated with the 'honour of love.' Of the poet's own fickleness one might expect, at last, a merry treatment; and perhaps in *The Indifferent* we get it. But I am not sure. Even this seems to have a sting in it. And of *Loves Usury* what shall I say? The struggle between lust and reason, the struggle between love and reason, these we know; but Donne is perhaps the first poet who has ever painted lust holding love at arm's length, in the hope 'that there's no need to trouble himself with any such thoughts yet'—and all this only as an introduction to the crowning paradox that in old age even a reciprocated love must be endured. The poem is, in its way, a masterpiece, and a powerful indirect expression of Donne's habitual 'shame and scorne'. For, in the long run, it must be admitted that 'the love of hatred and the hate of love' is the main, though not the only, theme of the *Songs and Sonets*. A man is a fool for loving and a double fool for saying so in 'whining poetry'; the only excuse is that the sheer difficulty of drawing one's pains through rhyme's vexation 'allays' them. A woman's love at best will be only the 'spheare' of a man's—inferior to it as the heavenly spheres are to their intelligences or air to angels. Love is a spider that can transubstantiate all sweets into bitter: a devil who differs from his fellow devils at court by taking the soul and giving nothing in exchange. The mystery which the Petrarchans or their medieval predecessors made of it is 'imposture all', like the claims of alchemists. It is a very simple matter (*foeda et brevis voluptas*), and all it comes to in the end is

> that my man
> Can be as happy as I can.

Unsuccessful love is a plague and tyranny; but there is a plague even worse—Love might try

> A deeper plague, to make her love mee too!

Love enjoyed is like gingerbread with the gilt off. What pleased the whole man now pleases one sense only—

> And that so lamely, as it leaves behinde
> A kinde of sorrowing dulnesse to the minde.

The doctors say it shortens life.

It may be urged that this is an unfair selection of quotations, or even that I have arrived at my picture of Donne by leaving out all his best poems, for one reason or another, as 'exceptions', and then describing what remains. There is one sense in which I admit this. Any account of Donne which concentrates on his love poetry must be unfair to the poet, for it leaves out much of his best work. By hypothesis, it must neglect the dazzling sublimity of his best religious poems, the grotesque charm of *The Progresse of the Soule*, and those scattered, but exquisite, patches of poetry that appear from time to time amidst the insanity of *The First and Second Anniversaries*. Even in the *Epistles* there are good passages. But as far as concerns his love poetry, I believe I am just. I have no wish to rule out the exceptions, provided that they are admitted to be exceptions. I am attempting to describe the prevailing tone of his work, and in my description no judgment is yet implied.

To judgement let us now proceed. Here is a collection of verse describing with unusual and disturbing energy the torments of a mind which has been baffled in its relation to sexual love by certain temporary and highly special conditions. What is its value? To admit the 'unusual and disturbing energy' is, of course, to admit that Donne is a poet; he has, in the modern phrase, 'put his stuff across'. Those who believe that criticism can separate inquiry into the success of communication from that into the value of the thing communicated will demand that we should now proceed to evaluate the 'stuff'; and if we do so, it would not be hard to point out how transitory and limited and, as it were, accidental the appeal of such 'stuff' must be. But something of the real problem escapes under this treatment. It would not be impossible to imagine a poet dealing with this same stuff, marginal and precarious as it is, in a way that would permanently engage our attention. Donne's real limitations is not that he writes *about*, but that he writes *in*, a chaos of violent and transitory passions. He is perpetually excited and therefore perpetually cut off from the deeper and more permanent springs of his own excitement. But how is this to be separated from his technique— the nagging, nudging, quibbling stridency of his manner? If a man writes thus, what can he communicate but excitement? Or again, if he finds nothing but excitement to communicate, how else should he write? It is impossible here to distinguish cause from effect. Our concern, in the long run, must be with the actual poetry (the 'stuff' *thus* communicated, this communication of *such* 'stuff') and with the question how far that total phenomenon is calculated to interest human imagination. And to this question I can see only one answer: that its interest, save for a mind specially predisposed in its favour, must be short-lived and superficial, though intense. Paradoxical as it may seem, Donne's poetry is too simple to satisfy. Its complexity is all on the surface—an intellectual and fully conscious complexity that we soon come to the end of. Beneath this we find nothing but a limited series of 'passions'—explicit, mutually exclusive passions which can be instantly and adequately labelled as such— things which can be readily talked about, and indeed, must be talked about because, in silence, they begin to lose their hard outlines and overlap, to betray themselves as partly fictitious. That is why Donne is always arguing. There are puzzles in his work, but we can solve them all if we are clever enough; there is none of the depth and ambiguity of real experience in him, such as underlies the apparent simplicity of *How sleep the brave* or *Songs of Innocence*, or even Αἰαῖ Λευψύδριον.[4] The same is true, for the most part, of the specifically 'metaphysical' comparisons. One idea has been put into each and nothing more can come out of it. Hence they tend to die on our hands, where some seemingly banal comparison of a woman to a flower or God's anger to flame can touch us at innumerable levels and renew its virginity at every reading. Of all literary virtues 'originality', in the vulgar sense, has, for this reason, the shortest life. When we have once mastered a poem by Donne there is nothing more to do with it. To use his own simile, he deals in earth-

---

[4] The superficial simplicity here is obvious; the deeper ambiguity becomes evident if we ask whether Lipsydrion is an object of detestation or of nostalgic affection.

quakes, not in that 'trepidation of the spheres' which is so much less violent but 'greater far'.

Some, of course, will contend that his love poems should interest me permanently because of their 'truth'. They will say that he has shown me passion with the mask off, and catch at my word 'uncomfortable' to prove that I am running away from him because he tells me more truth than I can bear. But this is the mere frenzy of antiromanticism. Of course, Donne is true in the sense that passions such as he presents do occur in human experience. So do a great many other things. He makes his own selection, like Dickens, or Gower, or Herrick, and his world is neither more nor less 'real' than theirs; while it is obviously less real than the world of Homer, or Virgil, or Tolstoy. In one way, indeed, Donne's love poetry is less true than that of the Petrarchans, in so far as it largely omits the very thing that all the pother is about. Donne shows us a variety of sorrows, scorns, angers, disgusts, and the like which arise out of love. But if any one asked 'What is all this *about*? What is the attraction which makes these partings so sorrowful? What is the peculiarity about this physical pleasure which he speaks of so contemptuously, and how has it got tangled up with such a storm of emotions?', I do not know how we could reply except by pointing to some ordinary love poetry. The feeblest sonnet, almost, of the other school would give us an answer with coral lips and Cupid's golden wings and the opening rose, with perfumes and instruments of music, with some attempt, however trite, to paint that iridescence which explains why people write poems about love at all. In this sense Donne's love poetry is parasitic. I do not use this word as a term of reproach; there are so many good poets, by now, in the world that one particular poet is entitled to take for granted the depth of a passion and deal with its froth. But as a purely descriptive term, 'parasitic' seems to me true. Donne's love poems could not exist unless love poems of a more genial character existed first. He shows us amazing shadows cast by love upon the intellect, the passions, and the appetite; to learn of the substance which casts them we must go to other poets, more balanced, more magnanimous, and more humane. There are, I well remember, poems (some two or three) in which Donne himself presents the substance; and the fact that he does so without much luxury of language and symbol endears them to our temporarily austere taste. But in the main, his love poetry is *Hamlet* without the prince.

Donne's influence on the poets of the seventeenth century is a commonplace of criticism. Of that influence at its best, as it is seen in the great devotional poetry of the period, I have not now to speak. In love poetry he was not, perhaps, so dominant. His *nequitiae* probably encouraged the cynical and licentious songs of his successors, but, if so, the imitation is very different from the model. Suckling's impudence, at its best, is light-hearted and very unlike the ferocity of Donne; and Suckling's chief fault in this vein—a stolid fleshliness which sometimes leads him to speak of his mistress's body more like a butcher than a lecher—is entirely his own. The more strictly metaphysical elements in Donne are, of course, lavishly reproduced; but I doubt if the reproduction succeeds best when it is most faithful. Thus Carew's stanzas *When thou, poor Excommunicate* or Lovelace's *To Lucasta, going beyond the Seas* are built up on Donne's favourite plan, but both, as it seems to me, fail in that startling and energetic quality which this kind of thing demands. They have no edge. When these poets succeed it is by adding something else to what they have learned from Donne—in fact by reuniting Donne's manner with something much more like ordinary poetry. Beauty (like cheerfulness) is always breaking in. Thus the conceit of asking where various evanescent, beautiful phenomena go when they vanish and replying that they are all to be found in one's mistress is the sort of conceit that Donne might have used; and, starting from that end, we could easily work it up into something tolerably like bad Donne. As thus:

> *Oh fooles that aske whether of odours burn'd*
> *The seminall forme live, and from that death*
> *Conjure the same with chymique arte—'tis turn'd*
> *To that quintessence call'd her Breath!*

But if we use the same idea as Carew uses it we get a wholly different effect:

> *Ask me no more where Jove bestows*
> *When June is past, the fading rose:*
> *For in your beauty's orient deep*
> *These flowers, as in their causes, sleep.*

The idea is the same. But the choice of the obvious and obviously beautiful rose, instead of the recondite seminal form of vegetables, the great regal name of Jove, the alliteration, the stately voluptuousness of a quatrain where all the accented syllables are also long in quantity (a secret little known)—all this smothers the sharpness of thought in sweetness. Compared with Donne, it is almost soporific; compared with it, Donne is shrill. But the conceit is there; and 'as in their causes, sleep' which looks at first like a blunder, is in fact a paradox that Donne might have envied. So again, the conceit that the lady's hair outshines the sun, though not much more than an Elizabethan conceit, might well have appeared in the *Songs and Sonets*; but Donne would neither have wished, nor been able, to attain the radiance of Lovelace's

But shake your head and scatter day!

This process of enchanting, or, in Shakespeare's sense, 'translating' Donne was carried to its furthest point by Marvell. Almost every element of Donne—except his metrical roughness—appears in the *Coy Mistress*. Nothing could be more like Donne, both in the grimness of its content and in its impudently argumentative function, than the conceit that

worms shall try
That long preserved virginity.

All the more admirable is the art by which this, and everything else in that poem, however abstruse, dismaying, or sophistical, is subordinated to a sort of golden tranquility. What was death to Donne is mere play to Marvell. 'Out of the strong', we are tempted to say, 'has come sweetness', but in reality the strength is all on Marvell's side. He is an Olympian, ruling at ease for his own good purposes, all that intellectual and passionate mobility of which Donne was the slave, and leading Donne himself, bound, behind his chariot.

From all this we may conclude that Donne was a 'good influence'—a better influence than many greater poets. It would hardly be too much to say that the final cause of Donne's poetry is the poetry of Herbert, Crashaw, and Marvell; for the very qualities which make Donne's kind of poetry unsatisfying poetic food make it a valuable ingredient.

The Later Poetry of W. B. Yeats

The later poetry of William Butler Yeats is certainly great enough in its kind, and varied enough within its kind, to warrant a special approach, deliberately not the only approach, and deliberately not a complete approach. A body of great poetry will awaken and exemplify different interests on different occasions, or even on the same occasions, as we may see in the contrasting and often contesting literatures about Dante and Shakespeare: even a relation to the poetry is not common to them all. I propose here to examine Yeats's later poetry with a special regard to his own approach to the making of it; and to explore a little what I conceive to be the dominant mode of his insight, the relations between it and the printed poems, and—a different thing—the relations between it and the readers of his poems.

The major facts I hope to illustrate are these: that Yeats has, if you accept his mode, a consistent extraordinary grasp of the reality of emotion, character, and aspiration; and that his chief resort and weapon for the grasping of that reality is magic; and that if we would make use of that reality for ourselves we must also make some use of the magic that inspirits it. What is important is that the nexus of reality and magic is not by paradox or sleight of hand, but is logical and represents, for Yeats in his poetry, a full use of intelligence. Magic performs for Yeats the same fructifying function that Christianity does for Eliot, or that ironic fatalism did for Thomas Hardy; it makes a connection between the poem and its subject matter and provides an adequate mechanics of meaning and value. If it happens that we discard more of Hardy than we do of Yeats and more of Yeats than we do of Eliot, it is not because Christianity provides better machinery for the movement of poetry than fatalism or magic, but simply because Eliot is a more cautious craftsman. Besides, Eliot's poetry has not even comparatively worn long enough to show what parts are permanent and what merely temporary. The point here is that fatalism, Christianity, and magic are not of them disciplines to which many minds can consciously appeal today, as Hardy, Eliot, and Yeats do, for emotional strength and moral authority. The supernatural is simply not part of our mental furniture, and when we meet it in our reading we say: Here is debris to be swept away. But if we sweep it away without first making sure what it is, we are likely to lose the poetry as well as the debris. It is the very purpose of a supernaturally derived discipline, as used in poetry, to set the substance of natural life apart, to give it a form, a meaning, and a value which cannot be evaded. What is excessive and unwarranted in the discipline we indeed ought to dismiss; but that can be determined only when what is integrating and illuminating is known first. The discipline will in the end turn out to have had only a secondary importance for the reader; but its effect will remain active even when he no longer considers it. That is because for the poet the discipline, far from seeming secondary, had an extraordinary structural, seminal, and substantial importance to the degree that without it he could hardly have written at all.

Poetry does not flow from thin air but requires always either a literal faith, an imaginative faith, or, as in Shakespeare, a mind full of many provisional faiths. The life we all live is not alone enough of a subject for the serious artist; it must be life with a leaning, life with a tendency to shape itself only in certain forms, to afford its most lucid revelations only in certain lights. If our final interest, either as poets or as readers, is in the reality declared when the forms have been removed and the lights taken away, yet we can never come to the reality at all without the first advantage of the form and lights. Without them we should *see* nothing but only glimpse something unstable. We glimpse the fleeting but do not see what it is that fleets.

So it was with Yeats; his early poems are fleeting, some of them beautiful and some that sicken, as you read them, to their own extinction. But as he acquired for himself a discipline, however unacceptable to the bulk of his readers, his poetry obtained an access to reality. So it is with most of our serious poets. It is almost the mark of the poet of genuine merit in our time—the poet who writes serious works with an intellectual aspect which are nonetheless poetry—that he performs his work in the light of an insight, a group of ideas, and a faith, with the discipline that flows from them, which taken together form a view of life most readers cannot share, and which, furthermore, most readers feel as repugnant, or sterile, or simply inconsequential.

All this is to say generally—and we shall say it particularly for Yeats later—that our culture is incomplete with regard to poetry; and the poet has to provide for himself in that quarter where authority and value are derived. It may be that no poet ever found a culture complete for his purpose; it was a welcome and arduous part of his business to make it so. Dante, we may say, completed for poetry the Christian culture of his time, which was itself the completion of centuries. But there was at hand for Dante, and as a rule in the great ages of poetry, a fundamental agreement or convention between the poet and his audience about the validity of the view of life of which the poet deepened the reality and spread the scope. There is no such agreement today. We find poets either using the small conventions of the individual life as if they were great conventions, or attempting to resurrect some great convention of the past, or, finally, attempting to discover the great convention that must lie, willy-nilly, hidden in the life about them. This is a labor, whichever form it takes, which leads as often to subterfuge, substitution, confusion, and failure, as to success; and it puts the abnormal burden upon the reader of determining what the beliefs of the poet are and how much to credit them before he can satisfy himself of the reality which those beliefs envisage. The alternative is to put poetry at a discount—which is what has happened.

This the poet cannot do who is aware of the possibilities of his trade: the possibilities of arresting, enacting, and committing to the language through his poems the expressed value of the life otherwise only lived or evaded. The poet so aware knows, in the phrasing of that prose-addict Henry James, both the sacred rage of writing and the muffled majesty of authorship; and knows, as Eliot knows, that once to have been visited by the Muses is ever afterward to be haunted. These are qualities that once apprehended may not be discounted without complete surrender, when the poet is no more than a haunt haunted. Yeats has never put his poetry at a discount. But he has made it easy for his readers to do so—as Eliot has in his way—because the price he has paid for it, the expense he has himself been to in getting it on paper, have been a price most readers simply do not know how to pay and an expense, in time and labor and willingness to understand, beyond any initial notion of adequate reward.

The price is the price of a fundamental and deliberate surrender to magic as the ultimate mode for the apprehension of reality. The expense is the double expense of, on the one hand, implementing magic with a consistent symbolism, and on the other hand, the greatly multiplied expense of restoring, through the *craft* of poetry, both the reality and its symbols to that plane where alone their experience becomes actual—the plane of the quickened senses and the concrete emotions. That is to say, the poet (and, as always, the reader) has to combine, to fuse inextricably into something like an organic unity the constructed or derived symbolism of his special insight with the symbolism animating the language itself. It is, on the poet's plane, the labor of bringing the representative forms of knowledge home to the experience which stirred them: the labor of keeping in mind *what* our knowledge is of: the labor of craft. With the poetry of Yeats this labor is, as I say, doubly hard, because the forms of knowledge, being magical, do not fit naturally with the forms of knowledge that ordinarily preoccupy us. But it is possible, and I hope to show it, that the difficulty is, in a sense, superficial and may be overcome with familiarity, and that the mode of magic itself, once familiar, will even seem rational for the purposes of poetry—although it will not thereby seem inevitable. Judged by its works in the representation of emotional reality—and that is all that can be asked in our context—magic and its burden of symbols may be a major tool of the imagination. A tool has often a double function; it performs feats for which it was designed, and it is heuristic, it discovers and performs new feats which could not have been anticipated without it, which it indeed seems to instigate for itself and in the most unlikely quarters. It is with magic as a tool in its heuristic aspect—as an agent for discovery—that I wish here directly to be concerned.

One of the finest, because one of the most appropriate to our time and place, of all Yeats's poems, is his "The Second Coming."

> Turning and turning in the widening gyre
> The falcon cannot hear the falconer;
> Things fall apart; the centre cannot hold;
> Mere anarchy is loosed upon the world,
> The blood-dimmed tide is loosed, and everywhere
> The ceremony of innocence is drowned;
> The best lack of all conviction, while the worst
> Are full of passionate intensity.
>
> Surely some revelation is at hand;
> Surely the Second Coming is at hand.
> The Second Coming! Hardly are those words out
> When a vast image out of Spiritus Mundi
> Troubles my sight: somewhere in sands of the desert
> A shape with lion body and the head of a man,
> A gaze blank and pitiless as the sun,
> Is moving its slow thighs, while all about it
> Reel shadows of the indignant desert birds.
> The darkness drops again; but now I know
> That twenty centuries of stony sleep
> Were vexed to nightmare by a rocking cradle,
> And what rough beast, its hour come round at last,
> Slouches towards Bethlehem to be born?

There is about it, to any slowed reading, the immediate conviction of pertinent emotion; the lines are stirring, separately and in their smaller groups, and there is a sensible life in them that makes them seem to combine in the form of an emotion. We may say at once then, for what it is worth, that in writing his poem Yeats was able to choose words which to an appreciable extent were the right ones to reveal or represent the emotion which was its purpose. The words deliver the meaning which was put into them by the craft with which they were arranged, and that meaning is their own, not to be segregated or given another arrangement without diminution. Ultimately, something of this sort is all that can be said of this or any poem, and when it is said, the poem is known to be good in its own terms or bad because not in its own terms. But the reader seldom reaches an ultimate position about a poem; most poems fail, through craft or conception, to reach an ultimate or absolute position: parts of the craft remain machinery and parts of the conception remain in limbo. Or, as in this poem, close inspection will show something questionable about it. It is true that it can be read as it is, isolated from the rest of Yeats's work and isolated from the intellectual material which it expresses, and a good deal gotten out of it, too, merely by submitting to it. That is because the words are mainly common, both in their emotional and intellectual senses; and if we do not know precisely what the familiar words drag after them into the poem, still we know vaguely what the weight of it feels like; and that seems enough to make a poem at one level of response. Yet if an attempt is made at a more complete response, if we wish to discover the precise emotion which the words mount up to, we come into trouble and uncertainty at once. There is an air of explicitness to each of the separate fragments of the poem. Is it, in this line or that, serious? Has it a reference?—or is it a rhetorical effect, a result only of the persuasive overtones of words?—or is it a combination, a mixture of reference and rhetoric?

Possibly the troubled attention will fasten first upon the italicized phrase in the twelfth line: *Spiritus Mundi;* and the question is whether the general, the readily available senses of the words are adequate to supply the specific sense wanted by the poem. Put another way, can the poet's own arbitrary meaning be made, merely by discovering it, to participate in and enrich what the "normal" meanings of the words in their limiting context provide? The critic can only supply the facts; the poem will in the end provide its own answer. Here there are certain facts that may be extracted from Yeats's prose writings which suggest something of what the words symbolize for him. In one of the notes to the limited edition of *Michael Robartes and the Dancer,* Yeats observes that his mind, like another's, has been from time to time obsessed by images which had no discoverable origin in his waking experience. Speculating as to their origin, he came to deny both the conscious and the unconscious memory as their probable seat, and finally invented a doctrine which traced the images to sources of supernatural character. I quote only that sentence which is relevant to the phrase in question:

"Those [images] that come in sleep are (1) from the state immediately preceding our birth; (2) from the *Spiritus Mundi*—that is to say, from a general storehouse of images which have ceased to be a property of any personality or spirit." It apparently follows, for Yeats, that images so derived have both an absolute meaning of their own and an operative force in determining meaning and predicting events in this world. In another place (the Introduction to "The Resurrection" in *Wheels and Butterflies*) he describes the image used in this poem, which he had seen many times, "always at my left side just out of the range of sight, a brazen winged beast that I associated with laughing, ecstatic destruction." Ecstasy, it should be added, comes for Yeats just before death, and at death comes the moment of revelation, when the soul is shown its kindred dead and it is possible to see the future.

Here we come directly upon that central part of Yeats's magical beliefs which it is one purpose of this poem emotionally to represent: the belief in what is called variously *Magnus Annus*, The Great Year, The Platonic Year, and sometimes in a slightly different symbolism, The Great Wheel. This belief, with respect to the history of epochs, is associated with the precession of the equinoxes, which bring, roughly every two thousand years, a Great Year of death and rebirth, and this belief, with respect to individuals, seems to be associated with the phases of the moon; although individuals may be influenced by the equinoxes and there may be a lunar interpretation of history. These beliefs have a scaffold of geometrical figures, gyres, cones, circles, etc., by the application of which exact interpretation is secured. Thus it is possible to predict, both in biography and history, and in time, both forward and backward, the character, climax, collapse, and rebirth in antithetical form of human types and cultures. There is a subordinate but helpful belief that signs, warnings, even direct messages, are always given, from *Spiritus Mundi* or elsewhere, which the poet and the philosopher have only to see and hear. As it happens, the Christian era, being nearly two thousand years old, is due for extinction and replacement, in short for the Second Coming, which this poem heralds. In his note to its first publication (in *Michael Robartes and the Dancer*) Yeats expresses his belief as follows:

> At the present moment the life gyre is sweeping outward, unlike that before the birth of Christ which was narrowing, and has almost reached its greatest expansion. The revelation which approaches will however take its character from the contrary movement of the interior gyre. All our scientific, democratic, fact-accumulating, heterogeneous civilisation belongs to the outward gyre and prepares not the continuance of itself but the revelation as

in a lightning flash, though in a flash that will not strike only in one place, and will for a time be constantly repeated, of the civilisation that must slowly take its place.

So much for a major gloss upon the poem. Yeats combined, in the best verse he could manage, the beliefs which obsessed him with the image which he took to be a specific illustration of the beliefs. Minor and buttressing glosses are possible for many of the single words and phrases in the poem, some flowing from private doctrine and some from Yeats's direct sense of the world about him, and some from both at once. For example: The "ceremony of innocence" represents for Yeats one of the qualities that made life valuable under the dying aristocratic social tradition; and the meaning of the phrase in the poem requires no magic for completion but only a reading of other poems. The "falcon and the falconer" in the second line has, besides its obvious symbolism, a doctrinal reference. A falcon is a hawk, and a hawk is symbolic of the active or intellectual mind; the falconer is perhaps the soul itself or its uniting principle. There is also the apposition which Yeats has made several times that "Wisdom is a butterfly/And not a gloomy bird of prey." Whether the special symbolism has actually been incorporated in the poem, and in which form, or whether it is private debris merely, will take a generation of readers to decide. In the meantime it must be taken provisionally for whatever its ambiguity may seem to be worth. Literature is full of falcons, some that fly and some that lack immediacy and sit, archaic, on the poet's wrist; and it is not always illuminating to determine which is which. But when we come on such lines as

The best lack all conviction, while the worst
Are full of passionate intensity.

we stop short, first to realize the aptness of the statement to every plane of life in the world about us, and then to connect the lines with the remote body of the poem they illuminate. There is a dilemma of which the branches grow from one trunk but which cannot be solved; for these lines have, not two meanings, but two sources for the same meaning. There is the meaning that comes from the summary observation that this is how men are—and especially men of power—in the world we live in; it is knowledge that comes from knowledge of the "fury and the mire in human veins"; a meaning the contemplation of which has lately (April, 1934) led Yeats to offer himself to any government or party that, using force and marching men, will "promise not this or that measure but a discipline, a way of life." And there is in effect the same meaning, at least at the time the poem was written, which comes from a different source and should have, one would think, very different consequences in prospective party loyalties. Here the meaning has its source in the doctrines of the Great Year and the Phases of the Moon; whereby, to cut exegesis short, it is predicted as necessary that, at the time we have reached, the best minds, being subjective, should have lost all faith though desiring it, and the worst minds, being so nearly objective, have no need of faith and may be full of "passionate intensity" without the control of any faith or wisdom. Thus we have on the one side the mirror of observation and on the other side an imperative, magically derived, which come to the conclusion of form in identical words.

The question is, to repeat, whether the fact of this double control and source of meaning at a critical point defeats or strengthens the unity of the poem; and it is a question which forms itself again and again in the later poems, sometimes obviously but more often only by suggestion. If we take another poem on the same theme, written some years earlier, and before his wife's mediumship gave him the detail of his philosophy, we will find the question no easier to answer in its suggested than in its conspicuous form. There is an element in the poem called "The Magi" which we can feel the weight of but cannot altogether name, and of which we can only guess at the efficacy.

> Now as at all times I can see in the mind's eye,
> In their stiff, painted clothes, the pale unsatisfied ones
> Appear and disappear in the blue depths of the sky
> With all their ancient faces like rain-beaten stones,
> And all their helms of silver hovering side by side,
> And all their eyes still fixed, hoping to find once more,
> Being by Calvary's turbulence unsatisfied,
> The uncontrollable mystery on the bestial floor.

I mean the element which, were Yeats a Christian, we could accept as a species of Christian blasphemy or advanced heresy, but which since he is not a Christian we find it hard to accept at all: the element of emotional conviction springing from intellectual matters without rational source or structure. We ought to be able, for the poem's sake, to accept the conviction as an emotional possibility, much as we accept *Lear* or Dostoevski's *Idiot* as valid, because projected from represented experience. But Yeats's experience is not represented consistently on any one plane. He constantly indicates a supernatural validity for his images of which the authority cannot be reached. If we come nearer to accepting "The Magi" than "The Second Coming" it is partly because the familiar Christian paradigm is more clearly used, and, in the last two lines, what Yeats constructs upon it is given a more immediate emotional form, and partly because, *per contra*, there is less demand made upon arbitrary intellectual belief. There is, too, the matter of scope; if we reduce the scope of "The Second Coming" to that of "The Magi" we shall find it much easier to accept; but we shall have lost much of the poem.

We ought now to have enough material to name the two radical defects of magic as a tool for poetry. One defect, which we have just been illustrating, is that it has no available edifice of reason reared upon it conventionally independent of its inspiration. There is little that the uninspired reader can naturally refer to for authority outside the poem, and if he does make a natural reference he is likely to turn out to be at least partly wrong. The poet is thus in the opposite predicament; he is under the constant necessity of erecting his beliefs into doctrines at the same time that he represents their emotional or dramatic equivalents. He is, in fact, in much the same position that Dante would have been had he had to construct his Christian doctrine while he was composing *The Divine Comedy:* an impossible labor. The Christian supernaturalism, the Christian magic (no less magical than that of Yeats), had the great advantage for Dante, and imaginatively for ourselves, of centuries of reason and criticism and elaboration: it was within reason a consistent whole; and its supernatural element had grown so consistent with experience as to seem supremely *natural*—as indeed it may again. Christianity has an objective form, whatever the mysteries at its heart and its termini, in which all the phenomena of human life may find place and meaning. Magic is none of these things for any large fraction of contemporary society. Magic has a tradition, but it is secret, not public. It has not only central and terminal mysteries but has also peripheral mysteries, which require not only the priest to celebrate but also the adept to manipulate. Magic has never been made "natural." The practical knowledge and power which its beliefs lead to can neither be generally shared nor overtly rationalized. It is in fact held to be dangerous to reveal openly the details of magical experience: they may be revealed, if at all, only in arbitrary symbols and equivocal statements. Thus we find Yeats, in his early and innocuous essay on magic, believing his life to have been imperiled for revealing too much. Again, the spirits or voices through whom magical knowledge is gained are often themselves equivocal and are sometimes deliberately confusing. Yeats was told to remember, "We will deceive you if we can," and on another occasion was forbidden to record anything that was said, only to be scolded later because he had failed to record every word. In short, it is of the essence of magical faith that the supernatural cannot be brought into the natural world except through symbol. The distinction between natural and supernatural is held to be substantial instead of verbal. Hence magic may neither be criticized nor institutionalized; nor can it ever reach a full expression of its own intention. This is perhaps the justification of Stephen Spender's remark that there is more magic in Eliot's "The Hollow Men" than in any poem of Yeats; because of Eliot's Christianity, his magic has a rational base as well as a supernatural source: it is the magic of an orthodox, authoritative faith. The dogmas of magic, we may say, are all heresies which cannot be expounded except each on its own authority as a fragmentary insight; and its unity can be only the momentary unity of association. Put another way, magic is in one respect in the state of Byzantine Christianity, when miracles were quotidian and the universal frame of experience, when life itself was held to be supernatural and reason was mainly a kind of willful sophistication.

Neither Yeats nor ourselves dwell in Byzantium. At a certain level, though not at all levels, we conceive life, and even its nonrational features, in rational terms. Certainly there is a rational bias and a rational structure in the poetry we mainly agree to hold great—though the content may be what it will; and it is the irrational bias and the confused structure that we are mainly concerned to disavow, to apologize or allow for. It was just to provide himself with the equivalent of a rational religious insight and a predictable rational structure for the rational imagination that in his book, A Vision (published, in 1925, in a limited edition only, and then withdrawn), he attempted to convert his magical experience into a systematic philosophy. "I wished," he writes in the Dedication to that work, "for a system of thought that would leave my imagination free to create as it chose and yet make all that it created, or could create, part of the one history, and that the soul's." That is, Yeats hoped by systematizing it to escape from the burden of confusion and abstraction which his magical experience had imposed upon him. "I can now," he declares in this same Dedication, "if I have the energy, find the simplicity I have sought in vain. I need no longer write poems like 'The Phases of the Moon' nor 'Ego Dominus Tuus,' nor spend barren years, as I have done three or four times, striving with abstractions that substitute themselves for the play that I had planned."

"Having inherited," as he says in one of his poems, "a vigorous mind," he could not help seeing, once he had got it all down, that his system was something to disgorge if he could. Its truth as experience would be all the stronger if its abstractions could be expunged. But it could not be disgorged; its thirty-five years of growth was an intimate part of his own growth, and its abstractions were all of a piece with his most objective experience. And perhaps we, as readers, can see that better from outside than Yeats could from within. I suspect that no amount of will could have rid him of his magical conception of the soul; it was by magic that he knew the soul; and the conception had been too closely associated with his profound sense of his race and personal ancestry. He has never been able to retract his system, only to take up different attitudes toward it. He has alternated between granting his speculations only the validity of poetic myth and planning to announce a new deity. In his vacillation—there is a poem by that title—the rational defect remains, and the reader must deal with it sometimes as an intrusion, of indeterminate value, upon the poetry and sometimes as itself the subject of dramatic reverie or lyric statement. At least once he tried to force the issue home, and in a section of *A Packet for Ezra Pound* called "Introduction to the Great Wheel" he meets the issue by transforming it, for the moment, into wholly poetic terms. Because it reveals a fundamental honesty and clarity of purpose in the midst of confusion and uncertainty the section is quoted entire.

> Some will ask if I believe all that this book contains, and I will not know how to answer. Does the word belief as they will use it, belong to our age, can I think of the world as there and I here judging it? I will never think any thoughts but these, or some modification or extension of these; when I write prose or verse they must be somewhere present though it may not be in the words; they must affect my judgment of friends and events; but then there are many symbolisms and none exactly resembles mine. What Leopardi in Ezra Pound's translation calls that 'concord' wherein 'the arcane spirit of the whole mankind turns hardy pilot'—how much better it would be without that word 'hardy' which slackens speed and adds nothing—persuades me that he has best imagined reality who has best imagined justice.

The rational defect, then, remains; the thought is not always in the words; and we must do with it as we can. There is another defect of Yeats's magical system which is especially apparent to the reader but which may not be apparent at all to Yeats. Magic promises precisely matters which it cannot perform—at least in poetry. It promises, as in "The Second Coming," exact prediction of events in the natural world; and it promises again and again, in different poems, exact revelations of the supernatural, and of this we have an example in what has to many seemed a great poem, "All Souls' Night," which had its first publication as an epilogue to *A Vision*. Near the beginning of the poem we have the explicit declaration: "I have a marvelous thing to say"; and near the end another: "I have mummy truths to tell." "Mummy truths" is an admirable phrase, suggestive as it is of the truths in which the dead are wrapped, ancient truths as old as Egypt perhaps, whence mummies commonly come, and truths, too, that may be unwound. But there, with the suggestion, the truths stop short; there is, for the reader, no unwinding, no revelation of the dead. What Yeats actually does is to summon into the poem various of his dead friends as "characters"—and this is the greatness, and only this, of the poem: the summary, excited, even exalted presentation of character. Perhaps the rhetoric is the marvel and the evasion the truth. We get an impact as from behind, from the speed and weight of the words, and are left with an ominous or terrified frame of mind, the revelation still to come. The revelation, the magic, was in Yeats's mind; hence the exaltation in his language; but it was not and could not be given in the words of the poem.

It may be that for Yeats there was a similar exaltation and a similar self-deceit in certain other poems, but as the promise of revelation was not made, the reader feels no failure of fulfillment. Such poems as "Easter, 1916," "In Memory of Major Robert Gregory," and "Upon a Dying Lady" may have buried in them a conviction of invocation and revelation; but if so it is no concern of ours: we are concerned only, as the case may be, with the dramatic presentations of the Irish patriots and poets, Yeats's personal friends, and Aubrey Beardsley's dying sister, and with, in addition, for minor pleasure, the technical means—the spare and delicate language, the lucid images, and quickening rhymes—whereby the characters are presented as intensely felt. There is no problem in such poems but the problem of reaching, through a gradual access of intimacy, full appreciation; here the magic and everything else are in the words. It is the same, for bare emotion apart from character, in such poems as "A Deep-Sworn Vow," where the words accumulate by the simplest means an intolerable excitement, where the words are, called as they may be from whatever source, in an ultimate sense their own meaning.

> *Others because you did not keep*
> *That deep-sworn vow have been friends of mine;*
> *Yet always when I look death in the face,*
> *When I clamber to the heights of sleep,*
> *Or when I grow excited with wine,*
> *Suddenly I meet your face.*

Possibly all poetry should be read as this poem is read, and no poetry greatly valued that cannot be so read. Such is one ideal toward which reading tends; but to apply it as a standard of judgment we should first have to assume for the poetic intelligence absolute autonomy and self-perfection for all its works. Actually, autonomy and self-perfection are relative and depend upon a series of agreements or conventions between the poet and his readers, which alter continually, as to what must be represented by the fundamental power of language (itself a relatively stable convention) and what, on the other hand, may be adequately represented by mere reference, sign, symbol, or blueprint indication. Poetry is so little autonomous from the technical point of view that the greater part of a given work must be conceived as the manipulation of conventions that the reader will, or will not, take for granted; these being crowned, or animated, emotionally transformed, by what the poet actually represents, original or not, through his mastery of poetic language. Success is provisional, seldom complete, and never permanently complete. The vitality or letter of a convention may perish although the form persists. *Romeo and Juliet* is less successful today than when produced because the conventions of honor, family authority, and blood-feud no longer animate and justify the action; and if the play survives it is partly because certain other conventions of human character do remain vital, but more because Shakespeare is the supreme master of representation through the reality of language alone. Similarly with Dante; with the cumulative disintegration, even for Catholics, of medieval Christianity as the ultimate convention of human life, the success of *The Divine Comedy* comes more and more to depend on the exhibition of character and the virtue of language alone—which may make it a greater, not a lesser poem. On the other hand, it often happens that a poet's ambition is such that, in order to get his work done at all, he must needs set up new conventions or radically modify old ones which fatally lack that benefit of form which can be conferred only by public recognition. The form which made his poems available was only gradually conferred upon the convention of evil in Baudelaire and, as we may see in translations with contrasting emphases, its limits are still subject to debate; in his case the more so because the life of his language depended more than usual on the viability of the convention.

Let us apply these notions, which ought so far to be commonplace, to the later work of Yeats, relating them especially to the predominant magical convention therein. When Yeats came of poetic age he found himself, as Blake had before him, and even Wordsworth but to a worse extent, in a society whose conventions extended neither intellectual nor moral authority to poetry; he found himself in a rational but deliberately incomplete, because progressive, society. The *emotion* of thought, for poetry, was gone, along with the emotion of religion and the emotion of race—the three sources and the three aims of the great poetry of the past. Tyndall and Huxley are the villains, Yeats records in his *Autobiographies*, as Blake recorded Newton; there were other causes, but no matter, these names may serve as symbols. And the dominant aesthetics of the time were as rootless in the realm of poetic import and authority as the dominant conventions. Art for Art's sake was the cry, the Ivory Tower the retreat, and Walter Pater's luminous langour and weak Platonism the exposition. One could say anything but it would mean nothing. The poets and society both, for opposite reasons, expected the poet to produce either exotic and ornamental mysteries or lyrics of mood; the real world and its significance were reserved mainly to the newer sciences, though the novelists and the playwrights might poach if they could. For a time Yeats succumbed, as may be seen in his early work, even while he attempted to escape; and of his poetic generation he was the only one to survive and grow in stature. He came under the influence of the French Symbolists, who gave him the clue and the hint of an external structure but nothing much to put in it. He read, with a dictionary, Villiers de l'Isle-Adam's *Axel*, and so came to be included in Edmund Wilson's book *Axel's Castle*—although not, as Wilson himself shows, altogether correctly. For he began in the late 'nineties, as it were upon his own account, to quench his thirst for reality by creating authority and significance and reference in the three fields where they were lacking. He worked into his poetry the substance of Irish mythology and Irish politics and gave them a symbolism, and he developed his experiences with Theosophy and Rosicrucianism into a body of conventions adequate, for him, to animate the concrete poetry of the soul that he wished to write. He did not do these things separately; the mythology, the politics, and the magic are conceived, through the personalities that reflected them, with an increasing unity of apprehension. Thus more than any poet of our time he has restored to poetry the actual emotions of race and religion and what we call abstract thought. Whether we follow him in any particular or not, the general poetic energy which he liberated is ours to use if we can. If the edifice that he constructed seems personal, it is because he had largely to build it for himself, and that makes it difficult to understand in detail except in reference to the peculiar unity which comes from their mere association in his life and work. Some of the mythology and much of the politics, being dramatized and turned into emotion, are part of our common possessions. But where the emphasis has been magical, whether successfully or not, the poems have been misunderstood, ignored, and the actual emotion in them which is relevant to us all decried and underestimated, merely because the magical mode of thinking is foreign to our own and when known at all is largely associated with quackery and fraud.

We do not make that mistake—which is the mistake of unwillingness—with Dante or the later Eliot, because, although the substance of their modes of thinking is equally foreign and magical, it has the advantage of a rational superstructure that persists and which we can convert to our own modes if we will. Yeats lacks, as we have said, the historical advantage and with it much else; and the conclusion cannot be avoided that this lack prevents his poetry from reaching the first magnitude. But there are two remedies we may apply, which will make up, not for the defect of magnitude, but for the defect of structure. We can read the magical philosophy in his verse *as if* it were converted into the contemporary psychology with which its doctrines have so much in common. We find little difficulty in seeing Freud's preconscious as a fertile myth and none at all in the general myth of extroverted and introverted personality; and these may be compared with, respectively, Yeats's myth of *Spiritus Mundi* and the Phases of the Moon: the intention and the scope of the meaning are identical. So much for a secular conversion. The other readily available remedy is this: to accept Yeats's magic literally as a machinery of meaning, to search out the prose parallels and reconstruct the symbols he uses on their own terms in order to come on the emotional reality, if it is there, actually in the poems—when the machinery may be dispensed with. This method has the prime advantage over secular conversion of keeping judgment in poetic terms, with the corresponding disadvantage that it requires more time and patience, more "willing suspension of disbelief," and a stiffer intellectual exercise all around. But exegesis is to be preferred to conversion on still another ground, which may seem repellent: that magic, in the sense that we all experience it, is nearer the represented emotions that concern us in poetry than psychology, as a generalized science, can ever be. We are all, without conscience, magicians in the dark.

But even the poems of darkness are read in the light. I cannot, of course, make a sure prognosis; because in applying either remedy the reader is, really, doctoring himself as much as Yeats. Only this much is sure: that the reader will come to see the substantial unity of Yeats's work, that it is the same mind stirring behind the poems on Crazy Jane and the Bishop, on Cuchulain, on Swift, the political poems, the biographical and the doctrinal—a mind that sees the fury and the mire and the passion of the dawn as contrary aspects of the real world. It is to be expected that many poems will fail in part and some entirely, and if the chief, magic will not be the only cause of failure. The source of a vision puts limits upon its expression which the poet cannot well help overpassing. "The limitation of his view," Yeats wrote of Blake, "was from the very intensity of his vision; he was a too-literal realist of imagination, as others are of nature"; and the remark applies to himself. But there will be enough left to make the labor of culling worth all its patience and time. Before concluding, I propose to spur the reader, or inadvertently dismay him, by presenting briefly a few examples of the sort of reconstructive labor he will have to do and the sort of imaginative assent he may have to attempt in order to enter or dismiss the body of the poems.

As this is a mere essay in emphasis, let us bear the emphasis in, by repeating, on different poems, the sort of commentary laid out above on "The Second Coming" and "The Magi," using this time "Byzantium" and "Sailing to Byzantium." Byzantium is for Yeats, so to speak, the heaven of man's mind; there the mind or soul dwells in eternal or miraculous form; there all things are possible because all things are known to the soul. Byzantium has both a historical and an ideal form, and the historical is the exemplar, the dramatic witness, of the ideal. Byzantium represents both a dated epoch and a recurrent state of insight, when nature is magical, that is, at the beck of mind, and magic is natural—a practical rather than a theoretic art. If with these notions in mind we compare the two poems named we see that the first, called simply "Byzantium," is like certain cantos in the *Paradiso* the poetry of an intense and condensed declaration of doctrine; not emotion put into doctrine from outside, but doctrine presented as emotion. I quote the second stanza.

> *Before me floats an image, man or shade,*
> *Shade more than man, more image than a shade;*
> *For Hades' bobbin bound in mummy-cloth*
> *May unwind the winding path;*
> *A mouth that has no moisture and no breath*
> *Breathless mouths may summon;*
> *I hail the superhuman;*
> *I call it death-in-life and life-in-death.*

The second poem, "Sailing to Byzantium," rests upon the doctrine but is not a declaration of it. It is, rather, the doctrine in action, the doctrine actualized in a personal emotion resembling that of specific prayer. This is the emotion of the flesh where the other was the emotion of the bones. The distinction should not be too sharply drawn. It is not the bones of doctrine but the emotion of it that we should be aware of in reading the more dramatic poem: and the nearer they come to seeming two reflections of the same thing the better both poems will be. What must be avoided is a return to the poem of doctrine with a wrong estimation of its value gained by confusion of the two poems. Both poems are serious in their own kind, and the reality of each must be finally in its own words whatever clues the one supplies to the other. I quote the third stanza.

> O sages standing in God's holy fire
> As in the gold mosaic of a wall,
> Come from the holy fire, perne in a gyre,
> And be the singing-masters of my soul.
> Consume my heart away; sick with desire
> And fastened to a dying animal
> It knows not what it is; and gather me
> Into the artifice of eternity.

We must not, for example, accept "perne in a gyre" in this poem merely because it is part of the doctrine upon which the poem rests. Its magical reference may be too explicit for the poem to digest. It may be merely part of the poem's intellectual machinery, something that will *become* a dead commonplace once its peculiarity has worn out. Its meaning, that is, may turn out not to participate in the emotion of the poem: which is an emotion of aspiration. Similarly a note of aspiration would have been injurious to the stanza quoted from "Byzantium" above.

Looking at other poems as examples, the whole problem of exegesis may be put another way; which consists in joining two facts and observing their product. There is the fact that again and again in Yeats's prose, both in that which accompanies the poems and that which is independent of them, poems and fragments of poems are introduced at strategic points, now to finish off or clinch an argument by giving it as proved, and again merely to balance argument with witness from another plane. A *Vision* is punctuated by five poems. And there is the complementary fact that, when one has read the various autobiographies, introductions, and doctrinal notes and essays, one continually finds echoes, phrases, and developments from the prose in the poems. We have, as Wallace Stevens says, the prose that wears the poem's guise at last; and we have, too, the poems turning backward, re-illuminating or justifying the prose from the material of which they sprang. We have, to import the dichotomy which T. S. Eliot made for his own work, the prose writings discovering and buttressing the ideal, and we have the poems which express as much as can be actualized—given as concrete emotion—of what the prose discovered or envisaged. The dichotomy is not so sharp in Yeats as in Eliot. Yeats cannot, such is the unity of his apprehension, divide his interests. There is one mind employing two approaches in the labor of representation. The prose approach lets in much that the poetic approach excludes; it lets in the questionable, the uncertain, the hypothetic, and sometimes the incredible. The poetic approach, using the same material, retains, when it is successful, only what is manifest, the emotion that can be made actual in a form of words that need only to be understood, not argued. If props of argument and vestiges of idealization remain, they must be felt as qualifying, not arguing, the emotion. It should only be remembered and repeated that the poet invariably requires more machinery to secure *his* effects—the machinery of his whole life and thought—than the reader requires to secure what he takes as the *poem's* effects; and that, as readers differ, the poet cannot calculate what is necessary to the poem and what is not. There is always the debris to be cut away.

In such a fine poem as "A Prayer for My Son," for example, Yeats cut away most of the debris himself, and it is perhaps an injury to judgment provisionally to restore it. Yet to this reader at least the poem seems to richen when it is known from what special circumstance the poem was freed. As it stands we can accept the symbols which it conspicuously contains—the strong ghost, the devilish things, and the holy writings—as drawn from the general stock of literary conventions available to express the evil predicament in which children and all innocent beings obviously find themselves. Taken so, it is a poem of natural piety. But for Yeats the conventions were not merely literary but were practical expressions of the actual terms of the predicament, and his poem is a prayer of dread and supernatural piety. The experience which led to the poem is recounted in *A Packet for Ezra Pound*. When his son was still an infant Yeats was told through the mediumship of his wife that the Frustrators or evil spirits would henceforth "attack my health and that of my children, and one afternoon, knowing from the smell of burnt feathers that one of my children would be ill within three hours, I felt before I could recover self-control the mediaeval helpless horror of witchcraft." The child *was* ill. It is from this experience that the poem seems to have sprung, and the poem preserves all that was actual behind the private magical conventions Yeats used for himself. The point is that the reader has a richer poem if he can substitute the manipulative force of Yeats's specific conventions for the general literary conventions. Belief or imaginative assent is no more difficult for either set. It is the emotion that counts.

That is one extreme to which the poems run—the extreme convention of personal thought. Another extreme is that exemplified in "A Prayer for My Daughter," where the animating conventions *are* literary and the piety *is* natural, and in the consideration of which it would be misleading to introduce the magical convention as more than a foil. As a foil it is nevertheless present; his magical philosophy, all the struggle and warfare of the intellect, is precisely what Yeats in this poem *puts out of mind,* in order to imagine his daughter living in innocence and beauty, custom and ceremony.

A third extreme is that found in the sonnet "Leda and the Swan," where there is an extraordinary sensual immediacy—the words meet and move like speaking lips—and a profound combination of the generally available or literary symbol and the hidden, magical symbol of the intellectual, philosophical, impersonal order. Certain longer poems and groups of poems, especially the series called "A Woman Young and Old," exhibit the extreme of combination as well or better; but I want the text on the page.

A sudden blow: the great wings beating still
Above the staggering girl, her thighs caressed
By the dark webs, her nape caught in his bill,
He holds her helpless breast upon his breast.

How can those terrified vague fingers push
The feathered glory from her loosening thighs?
And how can body, laid in that white rush,
But feel the strange heart beating where it lies?

A shudder in the loins engenders there
The broken wall, the burning roof and tower
And Agamemnon dead.
               Being so caught up,
So mastered by the brute blood of the air,
Did she put on his knowledge with his power
Before the indifferent beak could let her drop?

It should be observed that in recent years new images, some from the life of Swift, and some from the Greek mythology, have been spreading through Yeats's poems; and of Greek images he has used especially those of Oedipus and Leda, of Homer and Sophocles. But they are not used as we think the Greeks used them, nor as mere drama, but deliberately, after the magical tradition, both to represent and hide the myths Yeats has come on in his own mind. Thus "Leda and the Swan" can be read on at least three distinct levels of significance, none of which interferes with the others: the levels of dramatic fiction, of condensed insight into

Greek mythology, and a third level of fiction and insight combined, as we said, to represent and hide a magical insight. This third level is our present concern. At this level the poem presents an interfusion among the normal terms of the poem two of Yeats's fundamental magical doctrines in emotional form. The doctrines are put by Yeats in the following form in his essay on magic: "That the borders of our mind are ever shifting, and that many minds can flow into one another, as it were, and create or reveal a single mind, a single energy. . . . That this great mind can be evoked by symbols." Copulation is the obvious nexus for spiritual as well as physical seed. There is also present I think some sense of Yeats's doctrine of Annunciation and the Great Year, the Annunciation, in this case, that produced Greek culture. It is a neat question for the reader, so far as this poem is concerned, whether the poetic emotion springs from the doctrine and seizes the myth for a safe home and hiding, or whether the doctrine is correlative to the emotion of the myth. In neither case does the magic matter as such; it has become poetry, and of extreme excellence in its order. To repeat the interrogatory formula with which we began the commentary on "The Second Coming," is the magical material in these poems incorporated in them by something like organic reference or is its presence merely rhetorical? The reader will answer one way or the other, as, to his rational imagination, to all the imaginative understanding he can bring to bear, it either seems to clutter the emotion and deaden the reality, or seems rather, as I believe, to heighten the emotional reality and thereby extend its reference to what we call the real world. Once the decision is made, the magic no longer exists; we have the poetry.

Other approaches to Yeats's poetry would have produced different emphases, and this approach, which has emphasized little but the magical structure of Yeats's poetic emotions, has made that emphasis with an ulterior purpose: to show that magic may be a feature of a rational imagination. This approach should be combined with others, or should have others combined with it, for perspective and reduction. No feature of a body of poetry can be as important as it seems in discussion. Above all, then, this approach through the magical emphasis should be combined with the approach of plain reading—which is long reading and hard reading—plain reading of the words, that they may sink in and do as much of their own work as they can. One more thing: When we call man a rational animal we mean that reason is his great myth. Reason is plastic and takes to any form provided. The rational imagination in poetry, as elsewhere, can absorb magic as a provisional method of evocative and heuristic thinking, but it cannot be based upon it. In poetry, and largely elsewhere, imagination is based upon the reality of words and the emotion of their joining. Yeats's magic, then, like every other feature of his experience, is rational as it reaches words; otherwise it is his privation, and ours, because it was the rational defect of our society that drove him to it.

BABETTE DEUTSCH
STANLEY KUNITZ

A Symposium on Roethke's "In a Dark Time"

Babette Deutsch: Essay

Contemporary poems so often seem anonymous that one which readily allows us to identify the author makes a special claim upon us. In the stanzas of "In a Dark Time" Theodore Roethke's voice is clear. It is recognizable in the cadences, which make grave lyricism of normal iambic pentameter, in imagery taken from the natural world to signify the climates of the soul—movement and metaphor together exploring the more obscure regions of consciousness and, with equal boldness, pointing to the emergence of an exalted awareness. The poem declares a misery that appalls, a rescue that demands spiritual athleticism in the teeth of continued threat.

The paradoxical truth stated in the opening line, "In a dark time, the eye begins to see," announces the theme. It is one touched upon in a lyric by Goethe, that most hale of poets:

Wer nie die kummervollen Nächte
Auf seinem Bette weinend sass,
Der kennt euch nicht, ihr himmlischen Mächte!

When, however, Roethke follows his initial affirmation with the words: "I meet my shadow in the deepening shade," the reader may find matter for wonder. But only if he reads hastily. "Shade" is a dusk all the gloomier for being amorphous. A shadow is usually well defined and is cast by a definite object; it may nonetheless be terrifying. This one is cast by the speaker. As he advances into "the deepening shade," suggestive both of the encroachment of physical death and of the mind's beclouding, he may well be afraid to meet his own shadow. If it does not take on the aspect of a ghost, it is yet mutely eloquent of unreality. Certainly it is a darker self. The sense of a hovering Double is immediately adumbrated again: "I hear my echo in the echoing wood"—where "echo" and "echoing" carry a weird resonance. Nor can we escape here the further "echo" of the poet who, soon to venture into Hell, found himself

per una selva oscura,
che la diritta via era smarrita.

The connotation of "the echoing wood" is, of course, not the sunless brambles of political life in thirteenth-century Florence, but a more general Wood of Error, where there is no trace of the right path. And the reader may also remember the cry in an earlier poem of Roethke's, "The Lost Son":

> *Tell me:*
> *Which is the way I take?* . . .

Here the lost man is not so bewildered as to be unable to comment ironically on his situation: "A lord of nature weeping to a tree." Yet his self-mockery leaves him no less sadly alone, with the trees, the birds of the air, the "beasts of the hill and serpents of the den."

The birds that he names, "the heron and the wren," are creatures of nature, yet they have fabulous kindred. The first, present only as the invisible thunder of the Great Herne, symbolized Deity for Yeats in *The Herne's Egg*. What he called his "strangest and wildest" play was too wild to be staged. It deals with man's war upon God. The image of the heron, a recurrent one in Yeats's poems, has its nobler prototype in the avatar of Zeus in "Leda and the Swan." The heron is also notably prominent in *Calvary*, where, however differently, it again seems linked to the theme of man's opposition to God. In a note to that play Yeats spoke of the bird, along with the hawk, the eagle, and the swan, as "a natural symbol for subjectivity" and so, by implication, of the poet himself. Is it a like symbol here? And what of the wren? It used to be known as the king of the birds, and was annually hunted, killed, carried in triumph from one house to another, and ceremoniously buried, in villages in the British Isles, in many countries of Europe, in southern France as recently as the first half of the nineteenth century. Roethke may have had no thought of these matters when he wrote: "I live between the heron and the wren." Yet Yeats is one of his masters, and he is familiar with folklore; in any event, the reader is aware, however vaguely, of the beating of supernatural wings.

The second stanza opens with abstractions infused with vigorous life. The question so forcibly posed seems italicized for us here and now.

> *What's madness but nobility of soul*
> *At odds with circumstance?*

Roethke is clearly not referring to Socrates' observation, à propos of the inspired poet: "The sane man is nowhere at all when he enters into rivalry with the madman." Nor is he recalling the passage in *A Midsummer Night's Dream* in which the poet, being "of imagination all compact," is equated with the lover and the lunatic. This is a more radical madness, not to be confused, either, with the insanity of powerful criminals. True, it has seized upon men who never made a verse, but when Roethke names it he summons up for us those poets who have been forced to take asylum from a world they never made. Not all of them have shown the "nobility of soul" of a Christopher Smart or a Friedrich Hölderlin, but the noble among them continue to bear witness to the outrage that the world perpetrates upon the sensitive mind. The stanza does more than imply that by the cultivation of callousness men save themselves from madness. The power of the lines lies largely in the presentation:

> *The day's on fire!*
> *I know the purity of pure despair,*
> *My shadow pinned against a sweating wall.*

What response is there but the cry of recognition: "Why, this is hell . . . ?"

Yet as long as a question can be asked, the purity of despair may be impugned. And a question *is* asked:

> *That place among the rocks—is it a cave*
> *Or winding path?*

A "place among the rocks" is almost inevitably associated for us with the parched landscape of the Waste Land, the more so here because it recalls "Rock and no water and the sandy road/ The road winding above among the mountains/ Which are mountains of rock . . ." For all the bleakness of this scene, Roethke's mention of a "cave," with its promise of shelter, offers hope; provided, of course, that the place is not inhabited by the "serpents of the den" or, if it is, that they can be overcome. Even the "winding path," in spite of its intimation of arduous climbing ahead, seems to point toward freedom. "On a huge hill,/ Cragged and steep," we remember, "Truth stands, and hee that will/ Reach her, about must, and about must goe." He who achieves truth, the assurance goes, will be set free. But there is another and more pressing association here; indeed, in "Byzantium" we find the very phrase that Roethke uses:

> *. . . Hades' bobbin bound in mummy-cloth*
> *May unwind the winding path. . . .*

The reference, as every reader of Yeats knows, is to the idea that the dead, living in their memories, unwind the thread of past experience. The "winding path" is the serpentine course that it is natural for men to take, as distinct from the straight path followed by saint or sage. If Roethke is harking back to Yeats here, as seems not unlikely, then "That place among the rocks" may be supposed to set him again on the tortuous road of real life, with its miseries that have no origin in fantasy, and that allow no escape, except madness. At this point one thing seems clear: "The edge is what I have."

It is a risky having. As we discover again when the third stanza opens with "A steady storm of correspondences!—" For one who has nothing but an edge to cling to, a "steady storm" is an unwelcome phenomenon. Not less so when the "correspondences" fling wildly out of the echoing forest of symbols familiar to another haunted poet. Terror mounts in "A night flowing with birds"—one imagines neither heron nor wren, but darker shapes against "a ragged moon." Then the thunderclap: "And in broad day the midnight come again!" Yet on the heels of horror there is another glimmer of hope. The assumption is that he will find out what he is, though the discovery must come during the dark night of the soul:

> *Death of the self in a long tearless night,*
> *All natural shapes blazing unnatural light.*

The strangeness of the light becomes more frightening in the final stanza, as darkness thickens:

> *Dark, dark my light, and darker my desire.*
> *My soul, like some heat-maddened fly*
> *Keeps buzzing at the sill.*

The epithet "heat-maddened," since the fly is a simile for the soul, is a reminder of the earlier horror, when the day is on fire and the desperate man sees his shadow "pinned against a sweating wall." The homely image of the insect "buzzing at the sill" calls up as well, for me, the deathbed scene, indelibly drawn by Emily Dickinson, when a fly "With blue, uncertain, stumbling buzz" interposed between one dying and the light, till at the last he "could not see to see." Thus, after another fashion, in "broad day" was "midnight come again." Possibly the Dickinson poem came to mind not only because of the buzzing fly, but also because the death wish looms in the opening line of Roethke's last stanza.

The fight for identity is sharpened as the poem proceeds. In this last stanza it takes shape in the shrilling cry: "Which I is *I?*" But relief comes at the close:

> *A fallen man, I climb out of my fear.*
> *The mind enters itself, and God the mind,*
> *And one is One, free in the tearing wind.*

There is something subdued in the tone of this affirmation. It seems to speak of the stunned aftermath of a confrontation not wholly unlike the struggle between Jacob and the Angel, at least in its terror and in the hardly wrung blessing of its conclusion. But the release is less fully realized than the conflict and the dread that haunts it, and so haunts the major part of the poem. The change from appalled uncertainty to what one might call "the comfort of the resurrection" (with a lower-case "r") is too sudden to be quite convincing, especially since it comes directly after that piercing cry. Another reader might not be disturbed as I am by the abruptness of this reversal. The last three lines, taken by themselves, I find wholly acceptable, and the phrase, "free in the tearing wind" is a fine and moving conclusion, and one way of defining the human condition.

Not the least notable feature of the poem is that, dealing with madness in so intimately revealing a fashion, it exhibits such extraordinary control. The simplicity of the language—most of the words are monosyllables and the fewest have more than two syllables, the quiet tone in which the drama is set forth, help to make it impressive. The pattern of the rhymes, and the use of consonance and internal rhyme, delight the ear, as the tendency to repetition in the placing of the caesura gives the phrasing the quality of insistent speech. The poem is the story of a purgation. One of its virtues is that it purges the reader, alike by what it says and by what it intimates.

Stanley Kunitz: Essay—The Taste of Self

"Searching nature," noted Gerard Manley Hopkins in 1880, "I taste *self* but at one tankard, that of my own being." Comparably, Theodore Roethke searches for a language, a lyric process, in and through a world of multiple appearances, to convey the sensation of the torment of identity. Logic told Hopkins that he was doomed to fail in his effort to distill "this taste of myself, of *I* and *me* above and in all things, which is more distinctive than the taste of ale or alum, more distinctive than the smell of walnut leaf or camphor, and is incommunicable by any means to another man (as when I was a child I used to ask myself: What must it be to be someone else?)." But logic did not prevent him from writing "in blood" the sonnet beginning "I wake and feel the fell of dark, not day," with its harrowing lines from the far side of anguish, "I am gall, I am heartburn. God's most deep decree/ Bitter would have me taste: my taste was me." In Roethke the self is divided, and the hostile parts are seen as voraciously cannibalistic: "My meat eats me."

Like much of Roethke's recent work, "In a Dark Time" is marked by a style of oracular abstraction. The vocabulary is plain, predominantly monosyllabic; the pentameters are strictly measured and often balanced; the stanzaic units, with their formalized combination of true and off-rhyme, adhere to a tight pattern. If these fiercely won controls were to break down at any point, the whole poem would collapse in a cry, a tremendous outpouring of wordless agitation.

With lesser poets we are inclined to stay in the poem itself, as in a closed society that satisfies our public needs. Roethke belongs to that superior order of poets who will not let us rest in any one of their poems, who keep driving us back through the whole body of their work to that live cluster of images, ideas, memories, and obsessions that constitutes the individuating source of the creative personality, the nib of art, the very selfhood of the imagination. In my reading of "In a Dark Time" I shall try to indicate, selectively, how its configurations are illuminated by the totality of the poet's vision and intuition. Page references are to *Words for the Wind* (Doubleday, 1958), Roethke's most comprehensive collection.

STANZA I

The poem begins with a paradox, the first of a series of seeming contradictions to establish the dialectic of the structure. The "dark time," like Hopkins' "fell of dark," bespeaks the night of spiritual desolation, that *noche oscura del alma*, in which, according to the testimony of the mystics, the soul is tortured by the thought "that God has abandoned it . . . that He cast it away into darkness as an abominable thing," in the classic description by St. John of the Cross. "The shadow of death and the pains and torments of hell are most acutely felt, that is, the sense of being without God. . . . All this and even more the soul feels now, for a fearful apprehension has come upon it that thus it will be with it for ever." Such desolation is not an obsolescent state, nor one reserved only for the religious. Modern philosophy and psychiatry have been much concerned with the condition of anxiety, defined by Dr. Rollo May as "the subjective state of the individual's becoming aware that his existence can become destroyed, that he can lose himself and his world, that he can become nothing." In simpler terms, "anxiety is the experience of the threat of imminent non-being."

Roethke's first words inform us that the speaker has already entered into his land of desolation. If a poem is to be made, which is tantamount to saying if a spirit is to be saved, it will only be by a turning to the light, by a slow recognition of the beloved diurnal forms. As is true of Roethke's major sequence, *Praise to the End!* (pp. 63–110),* the archetypal journey of the poem is from darkness into light, from blindness into vision, from death into life. The emergent landscape is already familiar to us: "Eternity howls in the last crags,/ The field is no longer simple:/ It's a soul's crossing time" (p. 101). We have listened before to this poet's invocation of the creatures of earth that arose out of the original deep and that alone can show him the way back to the baptismal source: "Wherefore, O birds and small fish, surround me./ Lave me, ultimate waters" (p. 100).

His first encounters, as he struggles to recover his identity, are not with things in themselves or even with himself as object, but with shadow and echo, the evidences at one remove of his existence. "Once I could touch my shadow, and be happy" (p. 205). In his need for self-esteem he describes himself as a lord, though only "a lord of nature weeping to a tree": he is not ready for the world of human sympathy. His place is in the lower order of creation, in the kingdom where he is most at home. One of Roethke's earliest poems celebrated the heron (p. 24), not as the philosopher bird, in the manner of Yeats, but as the antic lord of his observed amphibian environment. The leg on which the heron balances in the marsh is his visible connection with the primordial element. As for wrens, they are forever flitting through Roethke's poems. They belong to his world of "lovely diminutives" (page 91), the most blessed and light-hearted of God's creatures, free as they almost are of the gross burden of corporeality. "The small" are associated with beginnings; they invariably excite the poet's tenderness (p. 37) or his joy, not always unalloyed with dread (p. 178). The implicit question in this passage is spelt out in another poem (p. 203):

Where was I going? Where?
What was I running from?
To these I cried my life—
The loved fox, and the wren.

Roethke's quadrupeds, except for those who live in holes, such as the bear and the fox, are not usually "loved"; most of the time they appear as rabid and predatory, "dogs of the groin" (p. 81), the running pack of sex. Reptiles are either overtly phallic (p. 136) or emblematic of "pure, sensuous form" (p. 181).

---

* Editor's note: All subsequent page numbers refer to Theodore Roethke, *Words for the Wind*, New York: Doubleday, 1958.

STANZA II

As if in reply to an accusing voice, the poet launches into an impassioned self-justification. The world may call him mad, but it is only because he refuses to compromise with the world that he suffers this sacred disorder. Madness knows an ecstasy, a burning revelation, that is denied to reason. "Reason? That dreary shed, that hutch for grubby schoolboys!" (p. 104). In his ordeal of despair and terror he has faced the absolute. "Who else sweats light from a stone?" (p. 207). "Tell me, body without skin, does a fish sweat?" (p. 101). The momentary clarity of vision, born of the authenticity of suffering, fades. "That place among the rocks" would seem to be suggested by the "sweating wall" in the previous line. In one sense it is Golgotha, the place of suffering; in another, it is a place beyond, but dimly apprehended, as through a clouded window—a habitation fit for one who identifies himself with the "beasts of the hill." Is it a promise of rest, of hiding, of Being? Or of departure, journeying, Becoming? Caves and nests, in Roethke, are womb images, representing the sub-world of intuition and the unconscious. Conversely, the "winding path" signifies the world of one's unfolding fate, realizable only in terms of action. The "edge" that the poet lays claim to, in an abrupt return of certainty, is expounded in several other contexts:

> *I was always one for being alone,*
> *Seeking in my own way, eternal purpose;*
> *At the edge of the field waiting for the pure moment* . . . (*p. 205*)

> *I have gone into the waste lonely places*
> *Behind the eye; the lost acres at the edge of smoky cities* . . . (*p. 195*)

> *The edges of the summit still appall*
> *When we brood on the dead or the beloved* . . . (*p. 190*).

> *On love's worst ugly day*
> *The weeds hiss at the edge of the field* . . .
> *The bleak wind eats at the weak plateau,*
> *And the sun brings joy to some.*
> *But the rind, often, hates the life within* (*p. 193*).

As evidence of the presence of a creative syndrome, it should be noted that in writing "The Shape of the Fire" more than a decade before "In a Dark Time," Roethke introduced the figure of "the edge" in recognizably the same fixed constellation of images.

> *The wasp waits.*
>   *The edge cannot eat the center.*
> *The grape glistens.*
>   *The path tells little to the serpent.*
> *An eye comes out of the wave.*
>   *The journey from flesh is longest.*
> *A rose sways least.*
>   *The redeemer comes a dark way* (p. 95).

If I read Roethke aright, he is differentiating between the spiritual life, which is achievable through discipline, prayer, and revelation, and "the life within," which is the soul locked inside the cabinet of flesh, the cave, and not locked in alone but with the central devouring worm. Hell is the trap where one is forever tasting oneself. To be saved one must undertake in the dark the long journey from flesh, that is, from the country of one's birth and bondage, that bloody incestuous ground, to the other side of the field, or to the appalling height, the jumping-off place, where the clean light falls on everything one has learned to love. Is this a parable for art? Blake tells us that "the road of excess leads to the palace of wisdom," and again, that "improvement makes straight roads; but the roads without improvement are roads of Genius." There is a kind of poetry that, in its creative excess, insists on pushing itself to the edge of the absurd, as to the edge of a cliff, at which point only two eventualities remain conceivable: disaster or miracle. The real and beautiful absurdity, as every artist knows, is that the miracle sometimes occurs.

STANZA III

The voice is one of growing assurance, as the things of this world emerge more and more sharply, not only in their bold lineaments but in their metaphorical radiations as well. No contemporary poet can use the word "correspondences" without harking back to Baudelaire and his Symbolist heirs. For Roethke, nature is the wayward source of joys and illuminations, the great mother of secrets, from whom they must be wooed or pried, out of urgent necessity, and at any cost.

> *Sing, sing, you symbols! All simple creatures,*
> *All small shapes, willow-shy,*
> *In the obscure haze, sing!* (p. 102).

> *The moon, a pure Islamic shape, looked down.*
> *The light air slowed: It was not night or day.*
> *All natural shapes became symbolical* (p. 203).

At the visionary climax of the poem, under the transformations of the cloud-torn moon, the air becomes electric with the agitated flight of birds. Everything is in motion, plunged beyond the syntax of time, to the brink of incoherence, where there are no divisions between night and day, reason and unreason, ecstasy and despair. The steadying thought is that "a man goes far to find out what he is"; in other words, that the life justifies the journey to the "edge." Elsewhere, in a variant of this maxim, Roethke has written, "I learn by going where I have to go" (p. 124). The last two lines of the stanza are a triumphant collocation of the spiritual and phenomenal levels of this total experience: the self dying, the world revealed. Past pity for himself and past tears, our "lord of nature weeping to a tree" hardens to a man arrived "in a long tearless night." The light that he sees blazing from "all natural shapes" is termed "unnatural," largely in the sense of "supernatural," transcending nature, but certainly also with the force of an epithet transferred from witness to object. Roethke has answered for himself the question that he posed in an earlier poem:

Before the moon draws back,
Dare I blaze like a tree? (p. 209).

The answer may well be: Yes, by becoming like a tree.

STANZA IV

As the transcendent moment fades, the poet returns to the prison-house of his senses. The slow rhythm, the massed percussive effects suggest the heaviness of his tread, the weight of his body. He can scarcely untrack himself from the word "dark." Where once he wrote, "The dark has its own light" (p. 108), he now asserts the counter-truth. In the blindness of desire is the deepest dark. Even the soul is seen as contemptible, an insect frenzied with heat (desire) that keeps batting itself at the window of perception, trying to get out.

In the slow coming-out of sleep,
On the sill of the eyes, something flutters,
A thing we feel at evening, and by doors,
Or when we stand at the edge of a thicket . . . (p. 199).

The true ancestor of this ominous apparition can be found in "The Lost Son":

> Sat in an empty house
> Watching shadows crawl,
> Scratching.
> There was one fly (*p. 79*).

As Yeats asked, "How can we know the dancer from the dance?" and as Hopkins when a child puzzled, "What must it be to be someone else?", Roethke inquires, pressing the same question of identity, "How can I find myself in the confusion of my separate and divided selves?" What desolates him is the thought that he has no true identity, and what makes him whole again is the recognition and confession that he is "a fallen man," whose quintessential taste is that of being lost. To embrace this knowledge is to overcome the dread of non-being, is to be redeemed or, so to speak, reborn. In the final couplet the separation between mind and God is dissolved in the mystery of interpenetration. Having found the divinity in himself, man is free—free to fly, like the birds of the preceding stanza—in the chancy wind that will leave him "torn and most whole."

"In a Dark Time" recalls the lamentation that more than a century ago John Clare wrote in madness, beginning "I am: yet what I am none cares or knows." The parallelism extends to the sestet structure as well as to the theme, whose history of explicit formulation runs back through Descartes and Iago to the eternal Yahwe's "I am that I am." Roethke's poem seems to me more solid, more profound, more terrible than Clare's, altogether finer, but I must grant that it is curiously less affecting, perhaps for the simple reason that it is less naive, more ambitious. Amid so much nobility and injured pride one longs for the artless human touch. At his infrequent best when Clare writes, "I am the self-consumer of my woes"; when he speaks of living "like vapours tost/ Into the nothingness of scorn and noise"; when he deplores "the vast shipwreck of my life's esteems," we cannot doubt that he is eating dust without an inch over his head; his long sigh overrides the beat and surges through to the final word. Roethke's admirable restraints on his cold rage have not permitted him the liberty of sustained action. Each self-enclosed stanza is conceived as a separate stage for which new scenery must be set up for a repetition of the drama of rebirth. Only an extraordinary creative energy, such as is manifestly present here, could set the stages rolling, like a procession of pageants in a medieval mystery. Roethke succeeds, for me, in effecting this illusion through three complete stanzas of mounting intensity and almost halfway through the fourth, where I stumble on his rhetorical question. The fussy grammar of "Which I is I?" is only part of the trouble; I am more concerned with the clinically analytic tone, which jars on the ear that has been listening to a stranger music. Furthermore, I am not wholly persuaded by the final couplet, superbly turned as it is. It may be my own deficiency that leads me to resist whatever seems to smack of conventional piety, but I cannot agree that anything in the poem prepares me for so pat a resolution. The "natural" climax remains, marvelous though unresolved, in Stanza III.

Despite the foregoing, "In a Dark Time" is one of a handful of contemporary poems to which I am most attached. What it says and the grandeur of the saying are important to me, as much after thirty or forty readings as after the first. If it required an epigraph, I should be happy to supply one in the form of a sentence by Paul Tillich: "The self-affirmation of a being is the stronger the more non-being it can take into itself."

BIOGRAPHICAL NOTES

The Authors

ARNOLD, MATTHEW (1822–1888), was the son of Thomas Arnold, famous Headmaster of Rugby. Soon after his graduation from Oxford, he was appointed inspector of schools, a position he held from 1851 until nearly the end of his life. His duties required extensive travel in England and on the Continent, and on one occasion in 1883 he toured the United States. Though not a prolific poet, he was elected professor of poetry at Oxford in 1857, a title he retained for 10 years. Among all his poetry, "Dover Beach" ranks as one of the finest poems of the Victorian period. Of concern to scholars are his erudite works of literary criticism and cultural philosophy, the best known entitled *Essays in Criticism, First Series* (1865), and *Culture and Anarchy* (1869).

AUDEN, W(YSTAN) H(UGH) (1907–   ), was born in York, England, but in 1939 came to the United States where he gained American citizenship. Educated at Oxford and associated with such younger poets as Stephen Spender, Louis MacNeice, and Christopher Isherwood, he published his first poetry in 1930 and another volume of poetry in 1935. In 1935 he married Erika Mann, daughter of Thomas Mann, the greatest German novelist of the first half of the century. After crystallizing many of his social and political ideas while serving as an ambulance driver in the Spanish Civil War, Auden collaborated with Isherwood in the plays *The Ascent of F.6* (1936), *On the Frontier* (1938), and *Journey to a War* (1939). Still an active writer, he has also written a critical work entitled *The Enchafèd Flood* (1950), two books on Kierkegaard, and *The Dyer's Hand* (1962).

BALDWIN, JAMES (1924–   ), was born in New York City and attended high school there. His first novel, *Go Tell It on the Mountain* (1953), tells of the religious awakening of a 14-year-old Negro boy in Harlem. It is a novel of great intensity, one which immediately established Baldwin's reputation. Other fiction includes *Giovanni's Room* (1958), set in Paris where he exiled himself for several years, and *Another Country* (1961). He is also important as an essayist; his nonfiction includes *Notes of a Native Son* (1955), *Nobody Knows My Name* (1960), and *The Fire Next Time* (1963), all powerful statements about the American Negro's plight. His successful venture into drama is *Blues for Mr. Charlie* (1964).

BLAKE, WILLIAM (1757–1827), was the son of a London hosier whose sufficiently comfortable circumstances allowed young Blake, at age 10, to enroll in Par's drawing school—the best of its day. At 14 he became an apprentice to James Basire, engraver to the Society of Antiquaries.

Not until he was 26 did he publish his first poetry, a thin volume entitled *Poetical Sketches*, followed six years later by *Songs of Innocence*. The poems in this second collection mark his interest in mysticism and divine love. In contrast is his next volume, *Songs of Experience* (1794), published when he was 37. Pervaded by a sense of evil and gloom, these poems treat the enigmas of life, illustrated in his most famous poem, "The Tiger." After this date his poetry consists of vast and complex explorations into a self-created mythology, sometimes only thinly veiling his observation upon the moral and social times. Adorned with many beautiful engravings from his own hand, his later volumes include *The Book of Urizen* (1794), *Europe* (1794), *The Book of Ahania* (1795), *The Book of Los* (1795), *Jerusalem* (1804).

BLY, ROBERT (1926–   ), was born in Minnesota, graduated *magna cum laude* from Harvard in 1950, and received his M.A. from the University of Iowa in 1956. Apart from a few years in New York and one in Norway, he has spent most of his life in Minnesota, where he now lives with his wife and children. As founder-editor of *The Sixties*, he has devoted much effort to the translation and publication of South American and European poetry in the belief that languages other than English are better suited to poetic expression. The emphasis of his own work is on simplicity and purity of language, a conscious revolt against what he calls the "tortured-self" rhetoric of current poets. His first collection of verse, *Silence in the Snowy Fields* (1962), brought him the Amy Lowell Travelling Fellowship in poetry (1964), and he later received a Guggenheim Fellowship (1965). Subsequent publications of verse have been *The Light Around the Body* (1967), for which he received the National Book Award in 1968, and *The Morning Glory* (1969). One of the most effective of the antiwar intellectuals, he launched the American Writers Against the Vietnam War.

BORGES, JORGE LUIS (1899–   ), is an Argentine short-story writer, essayist, and poet. Until 1930 he devoted himself mainly to verse, rich in nostalgic and nationalistic treatments of Argentine themes. Later, with failing eyesight and poor health, he turned to fiction for which he is best known today. Resembling Kafka, Gide, Faulkner, and Virginia Woolf—all of whom he translated—his fiction treats the fantastic and esoteric world of the inner self and the bestial world outside, best illustrated in *Ficciones* (1945, 1956), a collection of short stories which includes "The South," Borges' own preferred story. In 1962 another English translation of some of his stories and essays appeared under the title *Labyrinths*. His latest work is *Dr. Brodies' Report* (1972).

BROOKS, GWENDOLYN (1917–   ), a resident of Chicago since infancy, has created a wealth of poetic description of urban Negro life. Her first poem was published when she was 13; later published work appeared in *Poetry*, and between 1943 and 1945 she won poetry prizes at the Midwestern Writers' Conferences at Northwestern University. She has won major critical acclaim for *A Street in Bronzeville* (1945) and the Pulitzer Prize in 1950 for *Annie Allen*. Since then she has published *Bronzeville Boys and Girls* (1956), *The Bean Eaters* (1960), and a novel, *Maude Martha*; she has received an American Academy of Arts and Letters award and two Guggenheim Fellowships. Her lectures and succinct book reviews also have been acclaimed.

CRANE, STEPHEN (1871–1900), lived less than 29 years, but in that short time brought American literary realism to full bloom. The fourteenth child of a Methodist clergyman, he studied a year at Lafayette College and another year at Syracuse University. His interest in journalism took him to New York where, at the age of 20, he started writing articles for the New York *Tribune* and *Herald* about his slumming in the Bowery. In 1893 he borrowed enough money to publish *Maggie: A Girl of the Streets*, his first literary piece of genuine distinction. Desperate from poverty and ill health, he borrowed money from William Dean Howells to have *The Red Badge of Courage* typed. This novel, published in 1894, is a masterful description of the cavernous fears deep within Henry Fleming, a soldier in the Civil War. After publishing two collections, one of poetry called *The Black Riders* (1895) and the other of Civil War stories entitled *The Little Regiment* (1896), he went to Cuba as a correspondent. His experiences of being shipwrecked en route are told in "The Open Boat," the title story of another collection published in 1898. After a stint as war correspondent on the Greco-Turkish front, he married and lived for a short time in England. He died of tuberculosis.

CULLEN, COUNTEE (1903–1946), grew up in New York, graduated from New York University in 1925, and the same year published *Color*, his first book of verse. The next year he received a master's degree from Harvard. As Assistant Editor of *Opportunity, Journal of Negro Life*, he became acquainted with the major writers of the Harlem renaissance. In 1928 he received a Guggenheim Fellowship, which enabled him to study in Paris. Though he tried his hand at writing a children's book, a novel, and a musical play, his lyric poetry remained his best work. In 1947 his best poems, including "Heritage," were published posthumously in the collection, *On These I Stand*.

CUMMINGS, E(DWARD) E(STLIN) (1894–1962), was born in Cambridge, Massachusetts, where his father was a Congregational minister. Shortly after graduating from Harvard in 1915, he served with an American ambulance corps in France where, in 1917, he was confined in a concentration camp on an unfounded charge of treasonable correspondence. From this experience he wrote *The Enormous Room* (1922). After the war he lived with American expatriates in Paris and later moved to Greenwich Village in New York City. He published many volumes of poetry with such intriguing titles as *Tulips and Chimneys* (1923), *XLI Poems* (1925), *&* (1925), *is 5* (1926), *Vi Va* (1931), *No Thanks* (1935), *IXI* (1944). In these and other volumes, his verse is best known for its typographical distortions, unconventional spacing, slang dialect, and—throughout—for an acute sensitivity and lyricism. He wrote two plays—*him* (1928), an expressionist drama in verse and prose, and *Santa Claus* (1946), a morality play—and "six nonlectures," delivered at Harvard. A painter as well, he has exhibited with the Society of Independent Artists.

DICKINSON, EMILY (1830–1886), is now, along with Walt Whitman, considered one of America's greatest nineteenth-century poets. Born in Amherst, Massachusetts, into a close and highly respected New England family, she grew up honoring her family and adoring her father, a lawyer and legislator. She considered her home a "holy thing" where her life's work was "to make everything pleasant for father and Austin" (her brother). An acute and often painful emotional responsiveness led to a self-imposed seclusion in adult life. Writing letters was her only medium of communication with the world outside her home. Many of these letters were sent to Thomas Wentworth Higginson, her literary advisor. Her poems exhibited a boldness with meter, rhyme, grammar, and punctuation, which precluded her success as a popular poet. Only three of her poems were published before she died of Bright's disease at the age of 56, after which more than 1500 poems were discovered wrapped in boxes and stuffed away in drawers.

DONNE, JOHN (1572–1631), the son of a wealthy London merchant, gained a reputation during his younger years as a swashbuckling rake in the world of wit and fashion. After attending both Oxford and Cambridge but taking a degree from neither university, he studied law at the Inns of Court, and took part in two naval expeditions in 1596 and 1597. Sojourning in Europe, marrying, and writing lyrical gems about love, collected posthumously in *Songs and Sonnets* (1633), led to a painful spiritual struggle with himself which resulted in his taking holy orders in the Anglican Church. During this inner turmoil, between 1607 and 1615, he wrote most of his religious verse including the twenty-six "holy" *Sonnets*. Six years after his ordination in 1615, he was appointed Dean of St. Paul's in London, and achieved a widespread reputation as an intensely passionate and clarion preacher.

DOSTOEVSKY, FYODOR (1821–1881), a Russian novelist once sentenced to death for revolutionary activities, was reprieved and sent to Siberia. He returned a changed man, devoted to the Church and to recurrent themes of social criticism and moral possibilities. His *Notes from Underground* (1864) deals with the creative and destructive powers of man, and his need to suffer—themes which later appeared in his finest works. Of these, the first was *Crime and Punishment* (1866), which influenced Nietzsche's idea of the superman. His other great novels were *The Idiot* (1868–1869), *The Possessed* (1871), and *The Brothers Karamazov* (1880), rich in social, psychological, and religious themes, with a pre-Freudian understanding of the subconscious.

ELIOT, T(HOMAS) S(TEARNS) (1888–1965), like Henry James, left the country of his birth to become a British citizen. He was born in St. Louis, Missouri, and educated at Harvard, the Sorbonne, and Oxford. His early poems "The Love Song of J. Alfred Prufrock" (1917), and "The Waste Land" (1922) marked the beginning of a literary career which has remained foremost among twentieth-century poets. Retaining his complex elliptical style, he infused *Ash Wednesday* (1930) and the *Four Quartets* (1943) with a deeply religious, Anglo-Catholic spirit. In addition to poetry, plays like *Murder in the Cathedral* (1935) and *The Cocktail Party* (1949) and such critical works as *The Sacred Wood* (1920) all have contributed to his monumental reputation.

FAULKNER, WILLIAM (1897–1962), left New Albany, Mississippi, early in his childhood and grew up forty miles away in Oxford, his home almost uninterruptedly thereafter. As a member of the Canadian Flying Corps he served with the R.A.F. in France during World War I. When he returned home he attended the University of Mississippi for one year. He lived for awhile in New Orleans, sharing an apartment with Sherwood Anderson, and in 1925 took a walking tour of Europe. Back in Oxford, isolated from the clamor of the times, he wrote *Soldier's Pay* (1926) and *Mosquitoes* (1927) and then began writing a southern saga unmatched for its virtuosity and extravagance. The saga unfolds in fictional Yoknapatawpha County—"William Faulkner sole owner and proprietor," as he described it. In more than a dozen novels placed in Yoknapatawpha County, he intricately wove together such themes as violence, degeneration, heroism, and endurance. Of these novels, his most famous are *The Sound and the Fury* (1929), *Light in August* (1932), *Absalom, Absalom!* (1936), *The Hamlet* (1940), *Intruder in the Dust* (1948), and *The Fable* (1954). In 1949 he won the Nobel Prize for literature.

FROST, ROBERT (1875–1963), though born in San Francisco, has traditionally been considered the poet of New England. Educated at Dartmouth and Harvard, he worked in a textile mill, taught school in New Hampshire, and even tried his hand at shoemaking. Finding no publisher for his poetry, he lived in England for a short time where he published *A Boy's Will* (1913) and *North of Boston* (1914), his first volumes of verse. In 1916 he joined the English faculty at Amherst where he taught, with brief leaves of absence, until 1938. Always direct and lucid, his writing has counterbalanced much modern poetry which is often characterized by its radical unconventionality frequently leading to obscurity. For his many volumes of poetry, collected into the *Complete Poems* (1949), he has received four Pulitzer Prizes and the gold medal of the National Institute of Arts and Letters.

HANSBERRY, LORRAINE (1930–1965), grew up in Chicago, where her father was a successful real estate agent. Her ambition was to be a painter, although she had been captivated by the theater. After attending the University of Wisconsin and Chicago's Art Institute, she abandoned her desire to be a painter and, in 1950, moved to New York. She married Robert Nemiroff, song writer and music publisher, and began to write plays. *A Raisin in the Sun* (1958) was the first play written by a black woman to be produced on Broadway and the first play by a black to win the New York Drama Critics' Award. Her work is concerned not so much with the problems of her race as with the basic daily problems of people who happen to be black Americans. Her next, and last, play was *The Sign in Sidney Brustein's Window*, produced on Broadway by her husband in 1964.

HAYDEN, ROBERT (1913–   ), was born in Detroit, earned degrees from Wayne State University and the University of Michigan, and is now a professor of English at Fisk University. His poetry has brought him numerous honors, including a Ford Foundation Fellowship (1945–1955) and the Grand Prize for Poetry at the First World Festival of Negro Arts in 1965, awarded for *A Ballad for Remembrance*. Other collections of his verse are *Heart-Shape in the Dust* (1940), *The Lion and the Archer* (1948), and *Selected Poems* (1966). The source and subject matter of his poems range from direct personal observation ("The Whipping") to events in the history of his race ("Frederick Douglass").

HEMINGWAY, ERNEST (1898–1961), born in Oak Park, Illinois, where he was graduated from high school in 1917, worked as a reporter for the Kansas City *Star* before going to Italy to serve as an ambulance driver in World War I. Badly wounded, he returned home, then went to the Near East as a correspondent for the Toronto *Star*. In 1921 he settled in Paris, living with other American expatriates including Gertrude Stein and Ezra Pound who both influenced him greatly. His first important literary work was *In Our Time* (1924), a group of stories climaxed by "Big Two-Hearted River: Parts I and II." With *The Sun Also Rises* (1926) he became the voice of the "lost generation," Miss Stein's term to designate post-war Americans whose values had been destroyed by the kind of war Hemingway depicted in *Farewell to Arms* (1929). In 1936 he went to Spain as a newspaper correspondent; the Civil War which he observed was the subject of another great novel, *For Whom the Bell Tolls* (1940). After World War II service as a correspondent, he lived in Cuba where he wrote *The Old Man and the Sea* (1952). He made frequent trips away from Cuba, and while in Idaho he died of a gunshot wound.

HERBERT, GEORGE (1593–1633), was born into an aristocratic family at Montgomery Castle, Wales. He was educated by his mother, whom he fondly characterizes in his poetic *Parentalia*, his only published volume during his lifetime. After his graduation from Cambridge in 1613, he stayed on until 1626 when he was ordained deacon in Lincoln Cathedral. Four years later he was ordained as an Anglican priest and assigned to the rectory of Fulston St. Peter's in Wiltshire, where he became one of the most sought-after preachers in England. Izaak Walton called him "holy Herbert," and because of his profoundly metaphysical poetry he was referred to as "God's troubadour." Published after his death, his collection of sacred poems entitled *The Temple: Sacred Poems and Private Ejaculations* (1633) contains, in 129 poems, the record of his spiritual experiences.

HERRICK, ROBERT (1591–1674), the fourth son of Nicholas Herrick, a London goldsmith, received his early education at Westminster School. After his father's death, he contracted a ten-year apprenticeship with his uncle, but before the term expired he enrolled in St. John's College, Cambridge. He transferred later to Trinity Hall from where he was graduated in 1617. For many years he lived at Dean Prior, near Ashburton, Devonshire, where he wrote his chief work, *Hesperides* (1648), which is a collection of some 1200 poems. His poetry shows great diversity of form, ranging from imitations of Horace to epistles, love poetry, and simple folk songs. In 1647 Herrick, a devoted royalist, was ejected from his vicarage at Devonshire. He lived in London until 1662 when he returned to Devonshire, there to live for the rest of his life.

HOUSMAN, A(LFRED) E(DWARD) (1859–1936), born at Fockbury in Worcestershire County, England, was graduated from Oxford in 1881 and took a position the following year in the Patent Office in London. A classical scholar while at Oxford, he continued to devote his spare time to Latin and Greek studies. Ten years later, in 1892, he was offered a Latin professorship at University College, London, where he stayed until 1911. In that year he was chosen from among England's best scholars to go to Cambridge as professor of Latin. Erudite, withdrawn, and single, he spent his remaining years at the University. His most famous collection of poems, *A Shropshire Lad* (1896), was followed by *Last Poems* (1922) and *More Poems* (1936). His poems show classical restraint and concentration. They center on a single theme: the brevity and tragedy of life.

IBSEN, HENRIK (1828–1906), is recognized today as the father of modern drama. Born in Skien, Norway, and accustomed to poverty and loneliness, he made his way to Oslo where his first play, *Catiline*, was published in 1850. There and in Bergen he studied dramaturgy and in 1857 became Director of The Norwegian Theater in Oslo. Overworked and unhappy, he resigned in 1862 to have the leisure to write. Up to this time he had written nine plays, none of them successful; now one masterpiece followed another. *Brand* (1866) and *Peer Gynt* (1867) preceded *A Doll's House* (1879) and *Ghosts* (1881), the last two of such startlingly new realism that the public was outraged. *An Enemy of the People* (1882) re-established his reputation with his audiences, who missed the irony of his comedy. *The Wild Duck* (1884) and *Rosmersholm* (1886) contain exquisite poetry and deep soundings into the unconscious mind. *Hedda Gabler* (1890), a profound character study, and *The Master Builder* (1892), ironic and pessimistic, concluded his creative work. Shortly afterward, he suffered a paralytic stroke which disabled him until his death.

IONESCO, EUGENE (1912–   ), was born in Rumania, but he spent most of his childhood in France. He graduated from the University of Bucharest and there lectured and taught French until 1938, when he moved to Paris out of revulsion for the fascism of the Iron Guard and Nazi ideology. His first play, *The Bald Soprano*, was inspired by his experience in attempting to learn the English language with the help of a primer. This parody of human utterances was to eventuate in a revolution of dramatic form: in presenting truth not as literal reality but as the substance of dreams. He expressed his love of paradox and ambiguity in subsequent plays such as *The Lesson* (1951), which merges the simple relationship of teacher and pupil to that of murderer and victim, *The Chairs* (1952), *Victims of Duty* (1953), *Amédée or How to Get Rid of It* (1954), *Jack or the Submission* (1955), *The New Tenant* (1956), and *The Future Is in Eggs* (1959). His most successful play, *Rhinoceros* (1960), brutally presents man as beast and best conveys his preoccupation with the existential premise of the absurdity of the universe.

JOYCE, JAMES (1882–1941), more than any writer of our century, experimented with the craft of fiction and, as a result, created one of the most controversial novels of all time. In a stream-of-consciousness style, *Ulysses* (1922) deals with the events and countless psychological entanglements of a middle-class Dubliner and his wife during a single day. Full of blasphemy and obscenity, the book was banned for many years in the United States and England, but it has since been acclaimed by both critics and artists as a vastly monumental work. In *Finnegans Wake* (1939), recording the subconscious mind in sleep, he extended his ambitious experiments in writing fiction to the point that he lost all but his most persevering readers. Born and educated in Dublin, he sensitively reacted to the poverty and squalor of the large city and to the pathos in the lives of its inhabitants. From this background he wrote *Dubliners* (1914), a collection of exquisite short stories. Two years later he wrote his first novel, *A Portrait of the Artist as a Young Man*, describing with incredible artistry the inner torments of Stephen Dedalus attempting to free himself from the inhibiting loyalties of family, church, and nation.

KAFKA, FRANZ (1883–1924), remains a literary enigma; certainly he is among the most neurotic of artists—and one of the most penetrating interpreters of neurosis. Scholars still puzzle over his weird tales. He was born in Prague of Jewish parentage and in 1906 received his degree in law at the German University in Prague. To his father's satisfaction, he obtained a position in an accident-insurance company. Caught between wanting to please his father, who was a forceful and thoroughly bourgeois businessman, and wanting to write fiction, he spent years of torment ineffectually doing both. Filled with guilt and wild discontent, he wrote in 1912 his famous story, "The Judgment," which explores this terrible struggle between father and son. This story marks the beginning of his brief literary career, madly dedicated to the existential problems of man lonely and guilt-ridden in a neutral universe. In addition to several short stories—"The Metamorphosis," "In the Penal Colony," "The Hunger Artist" among his most famous—he also wrote three posthumously published novels: *The Trial* (1925), *The Castle* (1926), and *Amerika* (1927). He died at the age of 41 of tuberculosis.

KEATS, JOHN (1795–1821), greatest of the so-called second generation of Romantic poets, grew up in London where his father managed a livery stable. After his father's death in 1804 and his mother's in 1810, the four children were subjected to the haphazard care of guardians. Keats was apprenticed to a surgeon and passed his examinations before the Court of Apothecaries in 1816. Vastly more interested in poetry than chemistry, he showed one of his first poems—"On First Looking into Chapman's Homer"—to Leigh Hunt, who promptly published it in his London newspaper in 1815. His first modest collection entitled *Poems* (1817) received little of the abusive criticism which followed the publication of *Endymion* in 1818, the same year he developed tuberculosis. Blackwood's *Edinburgh Monthly Magazine* called him a mere Cockney rhymer, a charge voiced also by the London *Quarterly Review*. He went to live at Hampstead where he fell in love with Fanny Brawne, a 17-year-old coquette who understood nothing of her lover's anguish until after his death. During a flush of creative energy late in 1818, he wrote his most delicately beautiful poetry including his Odes "To a Nightingale," "On a Grecian Urn," "On Melancholy," and "To Autumn." In February, 1820, he realized his illness was fatal. In September he went to Italy with Joseph Severn and died in Rome the following February.

LAWRENCE, D(AVID) H(ERBERT) (1885–1930), was born in Nottingham, England, the son of a coal miner who would have been satisfied with his rugged life had it not been for his wife's complaints. Resentful toward her social inferiority, she insisted that her children get some education and leave the working-class life. Lawrence attended the University of Nottingham and taught school for a short time, but his overruling interest was in literature. In rapid order he wrote *The White Peacock* (1911), *The Trespassers* (1912), and *Sons and Lovers* (1913), which is his best book. After marrying Frieda von Richthofen, wife of Ernest Weekly, who was one of his university teachers, he boldly explored the problems of successful mating in *The Rainbow* (1915). Embittered by the public's suppression of this novel, he wrote as a more explicit sequel *Women in Love* which no publisher accepted till 1921. So, thoroughly hostile toward social hypocrisy, with its scientific education and pursuit of wealth, he left England permanently, hoping to rediscover the deep sources of imagination and spontaneity which modern civilization had blighted. First to Italy, then Australia, Mexico, and southwestern United States—he wandered continually looking for cultures in which one's emotional life could harmonize with social life. Expressive of these anxieties are several novels written during this time, most notably *Aaron's Rod* (1922), *Kangaroo* (1923), and the mystical *The Plumed Serpent* (1926). His strongest repudiation of emotionless, mechanized civilization was *Lady Chatterley's Lover* (1929), written in Italy where he died a year later of tuberculosis.

LOWELL, ROBERT (1917–   ), one of the famous Lowell family of Boston, was born in this same city but was graduated from Kenyon College (Ohio) in 1940. Many of his poems, however, are set in New England, and several of them deal with his early ancestors. Perhaps the leading American poet of his generation, he has received numerous awards including the Academy of Arts and Letters Prize, the Pulitzer Prize, a Guggenheim Fellowship, and the Guinness Poetry Award. *Land of Unlikeness* (1944), his first collection of poems, reflects his conversion to Catholicism in 1940; a number of poems in this privately printed volume were included in *Lord Weary's Castle* (1946). *The Mills of Kavanaugh*, of which the title poem is a narrative set in Maine, appeared in 1951. *Life Studies* (1959) is an autobiographical work in prose and verse; *The Old Glory* (1964) is a verse drama. For *Imitations* he received the Bollingen translation prize in 1962.

MALAMUD, BERNARD (1914–   ), grew up in Brooklyn where he was born. In 1936 he received his Bachelor of Arts degree from City College of New York, in 1942 his Master of Arts degree from Columbia University. During the 1940s he taught evening English classes in New York high schools. In 1949 he joined the faculty at Oregon State University where he stayed until 1961 when he moved to Bennington College in Vermont. Much of his fiction recaptures Jewish life in New York, most notably in *The Assistant* (1957) and in short stories included in *The Magic Barrel* (1958) and *Idiots First* (1963). His first novel, *The Natural* (1952), is an allegorical baseball story; *A New Life* (1961) is a satiric treatment of a young professor who goes west to teach. For his novel, *The Fixer* (1967), Malamud won both the National Book Award and the Pulitzer Prize.

MARVELL, ANDREW (1621–1678), the son of an Anglican clergyman, was born at Winestead, Yorkshire, England. He spent most of his life at Cambridge University after his graduation in 1638. Few of his love lyrics were published during his life, though "To His Coy Mistress" has since become one of the best known in English lyric poetry. His contemporary fame as a writer came with his sharp satires against Charles II and his government. After his death from an accidental overdose of opiates, the main substance of his poetry was published in 1681.

MCCULLERS, CARSON (1917–   ), was born in Columbus, Georgia, where she began writing at the age of 16. At 17 she moved to New York, attended Columbia University and New York University, and married in 1937. At this time she began her writing career in earnest with *The Heart Is a Lonely Hunter* (1940) and *Reflections in a Golden Eye* (1941). Recipient of the American Academy of Arts & Letters Award (1943) and twice winner of a Guggenheim Fellowship (1942, 1946), she went on to write *The Member of the Wedding* (1946), for which she received the New York Critics' Award in 1950; *The Ballad of the Sad Cafe* (1951); *Square Root of Wonderful* (1958); *Clock Without Hands* (1961); and the play *The Ballad of the Sad Cafe* (1963).

MELVILLE, HERMAN (1819–1891), was born in New York City and, when only 17, ran away to sea, leaving his widowed and destitute mother with seven other children. When he returned the following year (he had sailed to England), he looked for employment but found little except school teaching jobs at Pittsfield and East Albany. With a "damp, drizzly November" in his soul, he signed aboard the whaler *Acushnet* in 1841 and sailed for the south seas. In 1845 he was back home, ready to begin an incredibly prolific period of creative work: ten books in eleven years. His first books—*Typee* (1846) and *Omoo* (1847)—made him widely popular as a man who had lived among exotic savages. *Mardi* (1849) puzzled its readers, who could not understand why he had veered from the plot to devote over half the book to seemingly incoherent philosophy and exasperating satire. He returned to more conventional writing in *Redburn* (1849) and in *White Jacket* (1850). His masterpiece, *Moby Dick* (1851), dedicated to Nathaniel Hawthorne, whose vision of blackness reinforced his own, was not popular, and *Pierre: or the Ambiguities* (1852) in its intense treatment of guilt alienated his readers even further. In 1855 he published *Israel Potter*, followed by *The Piazza Tales* in 1856, *The Confidence Man* in 1857, and three volumes of verse. From 1866 to 1885 he worked as a U.S. customs inspector on the New York docks. Just before his death in 1891 he wrote one of his greatest short stories, "Billy Budd," published posthumously in 1924.

MILTON, JOHN (1608–1674), born in London, attended St. Paul's public school and, at the age of 16, matriculated into Christ's College, Cambridge, where he took his B.A. degree and, in 1632, his M.A. degree. He had intended to become a clergyman, but he grew so disgusted with Archbishop Laud's rule of the Church of England that he decided the only possible life for him was one dedicated to scholarship and literature. Among his early writings are sonnets, *Comus* (a masque), and "Lycidas," written in 1637 to commemorate the death of Edward King, one of Milton's closest friends at Cambridge. When Civil War broke out in 1642 Milton's pen became as powerful as Cromwell's sword. He wrote his greatest prose during the 1640s, and when Charles I was beheaded in 1649 Milton was the first Englishman of fame to attach himself openly to the new republic. Under Cromwell he served as Latin Secretary of the Council of State, mysteriously escaping execution in 1660 when the monarchy was restored with Charles II. Totally blind in 1652 and left with three small children after the death of his second wife, he served Cromwell's government until the Restoration, at which time he began work on *Paradise Lost*, finished in 1665 and published two years later. In 1671 he published *Paradise Regained* and *Samson Agonistes*.

MOORE, MARIANNE (1887–1972), was born in St. Louis and educated at Bryn Mawr. She spent most of her life in New York City. From 1921 to 1925 she worked in the New York Public Library, then served as editor of *The Dial* until this "little magazine" came to an end in 1929. She was frequently linked with the Imagist poets whose concentrated, metaphoric style and free range of subject ushered in a renaissance in American poetry a decade earlier. Her own poetry shows an unconventional use of metrics, frequently ironic in tone and always brilliantly polished. In 1945 she won a Guggenheim Memorial Fellowship and six years later, when her many volumes of poetry were brought together in *Collected Poems*, she won both the National Book Award and a Pulitzer Prize.

O'CONNOR, (MARY) FLANNERY (1925–1964), was born in Savannah, Georgia, graduated from Georgia Woman's College, and published her first story in 1946 while studying on a scholarship at the Writers' Workshop of the University of Iowa. She published two novels—*Wise Blood* (1952) and *The Violent Bear It Away* (1960)—but her best work is found in her short stories, collected in two volumes: *A Good Man Is Hard To Find* (1955) and *Everything That Rises Must Converge* (1965). A devout Roman Catholic, she learned in 1950 that she had inherited from her father a fatal blood disease. The faith that sustained her in the following years of slow and painful physical deterioration is evident in her fiction's recurrent theme of grotesque and perverted Christianity, as in "Good Country People."

PLATH, SYLVIA (1932–1963), was born in Boston of German parentage and saw, at the age of 8, her first poem published in a newspaper. She attended Smith College, from which she graduated *summa cum laude*. A Fulbright Scholar, she married the British poet Ted Hughes in 1956 and they had two children. Her poetry is especially significant for its revelation of the compulsive and troubled aspects of her life: the death of her beloved father when she was 10, an unsuccessful attempt at suicide during her college years, the breakup of her marriage in 1962, and finally her death by suicide. Her first collection of poems, *The Colussus*, was published in 1960; however, her second volume, *Ariel*, and later *Crossing the Water*, both published posthumously, and her novel *The Bell Jar* reveal more powerfully the frenzied self-analysis of her final years.

PORTER, KATHERINE ANNE (1894–   ), once remarked, "I have written and destroyed manuscripts quite literally by the trunkfuls." She attempted no publications before she was 30 and chose to associate with none of her contemporary writers. Born in Indian Creek, Texas, and educated in small Southern convent schools in both Texas and Louisiana, she worked as a journalist for a short time in this country and Europe. Her first literary success was *Flowering Judas* (1930), a group of stories set in Mexico and the United States. The intense psychological penetration marking these stories is evident throughout her later writing. In her short novel *Noon Wine* (1937), she handled subjects of murder and suicide with extreme and ironic restraint. Two years later she published *Pale Horse, Pale Rider* which consisted of three novelettes: *Noon Wine, Old Mortality*, and the title piece. Her last major work was *Ship of Fools* (1962), a long novel which resulted in wide critical controversy.

RANSOM, JOHN CROWE (1888–   ), is best known as poet and critic who helped initiate New Criticism in this country. A Tennessean by birth, he spent a year at Oxford as a Rhodes Scholar in 1913 and the following year joined the faculty of Vanderbilt University in Nashville. Except for a year as field artilleryman in France during World War I, he remained at Vanderbilt until 1937. During this time he was one of seven who founded and edited the *Fugitive*, a strongly agrarian journal devoted to literary criticism and poetry. As Professor of English he moved to Kenyon College in 1937, where he helped edit *The Kenyon Review* and contributed regularly to it. Through the years he has published several volumes of criticism including *God Without Thunder* (1930), *The World's Body* (1938), *The New Criticism* (1941), and poetry.

ROETHKE, THEODORE (1908–1963), was born in Saginaw, Michigan, and educated at the University of Michigan and Harvard. Before going to his last teaching post at the University of Washington, he taught English at Lafayette College, Pennsylvania State College, and Bennington College. For his several volumes of poetry he had received both the Pulitzer Prize and the National Book Award.

ROTH, PHILIP (1933–   ), well known for his fictional treatment of contemporary Jewish life in America, was born in Newark, New Jersey, and was graduated from Bucknell University in 1954. The following year he earned a Master of Arts degree from the University of Chicago. First as an English teacher in Chicago, then an instructor at the Iowa Writer's Workshop, and later as writer-in-residence at Princeton University, he combined teaching with his creative writing, his stories first appearing in such periodicals as *Harper's, The New Yorker, Epoch*, and *Commentary*. For this work he received the Aga Khan prize for fiction in 1958 and a Guggenheim Fellowship in 1959. For *Goodbye, Columbus*, which contains his story, "The Conversion of the Jews," he received the National Book Award in 1960. His other books of fiction include *Letting Go* (1962) and *Portnoy's Complaint* (1969).

SARTRE, JEAN-PAUL (1905–   ), is the most famous modern existentialist. Born in Paris, he finished his formal education in Berlin where he studied the writings of Husserl, Heidegger, and Kierkegaard—all philosophical existentialists. In his first novel, *Nausea* (1938), he probed into the meaning of existence, finding nothing except reasons for nausea. He continued in "The Wall," published the following year, to explore the meaning of life that lacked essence. During World War II he was taken prisoner on the Maginot Line and repatriated nine months later. *The Flies* (1942) and *No Exit* (1944) established him as a bold and skillful playwright, and his long philosophical work entitled *Being and Nothingness* (1943) made him the leading spokesman of atheistic existentialism. In fiction, drama, and philosophy, he has continued to represent French intellectualism in its most brilliant and fluent aspects.

SHAKESPEARE, WILLIAM (1564–1616), probably the greatest writer of all time, was born in Stratford-upon-Avon and, 52 years later, died in the same city. He married Anne Hathaway, who bore him three children. Most of his literary life was spent in London where, from 1594 on, he was associated exclusively with the Lord Chamberlain's Company which later became the King's Company; financially well off, it built the Globe Theater in 1599. From 1590 to 1600 he wrote his main chronicle plays, romances, and comedies. After 1600 his titanic plays appeared: *Hamlet* (1602), *Othello* (1604), *Macbeth* (1606), *King Lear* (1607), *Coriolanus* (1609). Of several volumes of poetry, his *Sonnets* (1609) are the best known. During a period of "reposeful contemplation" he wrote *Cymbeline* (1610), *The Tempest* (1611), and *The Winter's Tale* (1611), preceding his return to the city of his birth.

STAFFORD, WILLIAM (1914–   ), has lived in the Pacific Northwest for over twenty years, most of this time as a professor of English at Lewis and Clark College in Portland, Oregon. Born in Hutchinson, Kansas, he received both his Bachelor of Arts and Master of Arts degrees from the University of Kansas; he earned his doctorate in 1954 at the State University of Iowa. His published books include *Down in My Heart* (1947), *West of Your City* (1960), *Traveling through the Dark* (1962) for which he won the National Book Award, and *The Rescued Year* (1966). Recipient of a Guggenheim grant for creative writing, he has also served as consultant in poetry for the Library of Congress.

STEVENS, WALLACE (1879–1955), was both a wealthy insurance executive and, according to Allen Tate, "the most finished poet of his age." He was born in Reading, Pennsylvania, attended Harvard and the New York Law School, and in 1904 was admitted to the bar. He lived most of his life in Hartford, Connecticut, the heart of America's insurance business. His first published poetry was collected in *Harmonium* (1923), when he was 44, but he wrote most of his poetry after his 50th birthday. His collected poems appeared in 1954 just prior to his death. They contain richly sensuous imagery and the kind of aesthetic insight by which he attempted to give order to life. His work amply corroborates his own conviction that writing poetry, as he said, "is a damned serious affair."

STRINDBERG, AUGUST (1849–1912), was a Swedish dramatist, novelist, short-story writer, and poet. His works reveal his own antithetical nature: an early recluse and a later man of the world, a realist and an idealist, an atheist and a free-thinking Christian. His prolific writings deal with these contradictory themes, and some works indicate symptoms of his own paranoia. With Ibsen, he is considered an initiator of modern drama, his expressionistic plays serving as models for the modern theater. Best known are *The Father* (1887), *Miss Julie* (1888), *The Dream Play* (1902), and *The Ghost Sonata* (1907).

SYNGE, JOHN MILLINGTON (1871–1909), an Irish poet and playwright, completed five plays, all dealing with the Irish peasant. Encouraged by William Butler Yeats, for several years he lived in Galway and the Aran Islands, studying the life and speech of the peasants. The fruits of his efforts were articles in periodicals, a book (*The Aran Islands*), and—best known—his folk plays. These include *In the Shadow of the Glen* (1903), a great modern comedy, *The Playboy of the Western World* (1907), and *Riders to the Sea* (1904).

TATE, ALLEN (JOHN ORLEY) (1899–   ), was born and reared in Kentucky and graduated from Vanderbilt University in 1923, where he studied under John Crowe Ransom. Like Ransom, Tate is known as both poet and New Critic. For his first collection of poetry, *Mr. Pope and Other Poems* (1928), he received a Guggenheim Fellowship, which took him and his wife, novelist Caroline Gordon, to Paris, where they joined other expatriate artists of the era. He has also published numerous short stories and a novel but is best known for his criticism. His first volume of criticism, *Reactionary Essays on Poetry and Ideas*, was published in 1936; in 1968 his collected criticism was published in *Essays of Four Decades*.

TENNYSON, ALFRED, LORD (1809–1892), England's most popular late nineteenth-century poet, was born in Somersby where his father was a rector. At Trinity College, Cambridge, he became acquainted with A. H. Hallam who later figured so importantly in his work. In 1827 he published his first poetry entitled *Poems, by Two Brothers*, followed three years later by *Poems, Chiefly Lyrical*. In 1832 he and Hallam traveled on the Continent. The next year Hallam was dead, the even marking the beginning of Tennyson's "In Memoriam" (1850), one of the greatest elegies in English literature. After 1842 he became a prolific poet, publishing in that year a two-volume work which included

"Morte d'Arthur," "Locksley Hall," and "Ulysses." When four "Idylls of the King" (Enid, Vivien, Elaine, Guinevere) were published in 1859, his popularity was widespread and his reputation secure. He continued writing until his death. He was buried in the poets' corner of Westminster Abbey.

THOMAS, DYLAN (1914–1953), born in Swansea, Wales, served as an antiaircraft gunner during World War II and also read his poetry over the BBC. Contained in his poetry are the acute contrasts between the romantic lyricism about nature and the agonized horror about war, death, and meaninglessness. His poetry was brought together in his *Collected Poems* (1953), but he is also remembered for such works as his play *Under Milk Wood* (1954) and his sprightly, anecdotal autobiography entitled *Portrait of the Artist as a Young Dog* (1940). Frequently reading his poetry to public audiences, he was well known on many American college campuses. Some critics believe his last four years of extensive touring and public readings wasted his creative energy. His tragic death in New York City resulted from acute alcoholism.

TOLSTOY, LEO (1828–1910), despite the fact that he came from a background of aristocratic landowners, was chiefly interested in the primitive living conditions and simplicity of the Russian peasants. He described the Cossack settlers in his first novel, *The Cossacks*, written in 1854 and published nine years later. He traveled extensively in Russia and Europe, returning to his estate each time with a greater respect for the serfs. On his estate he started a school for peasant children whom he paternally taught. In 1862 he was married and in that same year started writing his great novel *War and Peace* which he finished nine years later. After more years of work he completed *Anna Karenina* in 1877. Deeply moral in his search for the meaning of life, found he said in the Sermon on the Mount, he wrote several more haunting masterpieces: *The Death of Iván Ilých* (1884), *The Kreutzer Sonata* (1889), and his last great novel, *The Resurrection* (1899).

UNAMUNO, MIGUEL DE (1864–1936), a Spanish philosopher, essayist, poet, and novelist, was a self-avowed iconoclast, desiring to make everyone live "fearfully and hungrily." His writing reveals the Spanish dilemma between the sacred and profane, and it attempts to reconcile them in a way that his countrymen could live with integrity. He struggled against the dogmatism of Church, school, and state, and for six years was banished from Spain for his political involvement. His chief work is *Ensayos* (8 vols., 1916–1918), abounding in themes related to contemporary issues.

VAUGHAN, HENRY (1622–1695), a British mystic poet, was known as "the Silurist" because he was born in South Wales, home of the ancient Silures. First a student of law in London, then of medicine, he returned to Wales to live and practice among his own people. After a prolonged illness his heightened spiritual awareness led to his writing the deeply moving sacred poetry in *Silex Scintillans* (1650). His mystical poetry immediately linked him with the work of George Herbert, another metaphysical poet. Two centuries later scholars noticed similarities in Vaughan's mysticism and love of nature with these same qualities in Wordsworth's poetry.

WELTY, EUDORA (1909–   ), was born in Jackson, Mississippi, and, apart from having received her degree from the University of Wisconsin in 1929, has spent most of her life there. She is best known for her short stories, the first of which was "Death of a Travelling Salesman," published in 1936. Her stories, collected in *A Curtain of Green* (1941), *The Wide Net* (1943), *The Golden Apples* (1949), and *The Bride of Innisfallen* (1955), all deal with the South she knows so well. She has received an American Academy of Arts and Letters award (1944), and, for *The Ponder Heart*, the Howells Medal for "the most distinguished work of American fiction" (1955). In addition, she has written two other novels and a series of essays on the problems of the fiction writer.

WHITMAN, WALT(ER) (1819–1892), was born in Huntington, Long Island, New York. Four years later his parents, with their nine children, moved to Brooklyn, where his father, a carpenter, built and sold houses and where Walt, after leaving school in 1830, first worked as office boy and printer's assistant to help supplement his father's meager earnings. By 1841 he had become a full-time editor of newspapers both on Long Island and in New York City. His most important editorship, from 1846 to 1848, was for the Brooklyn *Eagle*. His gigantic contribution to American literature occurred in 1855, the publication date of his first edition of *Leaves of Grass* containing 12 untitled poems. This one major volume, enlarged and revised through ten subsequent editions, appeared in its final eleventh edition in 1892 and contained 383 titled poems. Few other American writers have been as controversial—as abused and as heralded—as Whitman. Several prose works including *Democratic Vistas* (1871) and *Specimen Days* (1883) reveal further dimensions to his enormous power of expression. Nothing he wrote, however, has the broad grandeur and poignancy of his poems such as "Song of Myself," "Out of the Cradle Endlessly Rocking," "When Lilacs Last in the Dooryard Bloom'd," "Crossing Brooklyn Ferry," "Passage to India," and poems in *Drum-Taps* including "A March in the Ranks Hard-Prest." In 1873, after a paralytic stroke which left him a semi-invalid, he moved to Camden, New Jersey, where he spent his remaining years.

WILLIAMS, TENNESSEE (Thomas Lanier Williams) (1914–   ), first became interested in the theater when, as a University of Missouri student, he saw a performance of Ibsen's *Ghosts*. As a child in Columbus, Mississippi, his birthplace, he spent much time with his grandfather who was an Episcopal clergyman. His mother was of Southern aristocratic background. His family moved to St. Louis where he attended high school. He stayed at the University of Missouri only a year, then went to work in the same shoe factory where his father was employed. Disheartened by the oppressive monotony of the factory, he returned to school, going first to Washington University in St. Louis and then to the University of Iowa where he received his Bachelor of Arts degree. Restless in odd jobs and travel, he wrote constantly but received little notice until 1945 when *The Glass Menagerie* won the Drama Critics Circle Award. Far more violent in its treatment of sexual frustration and dream-world fantasies was *A Streetcar Named Desire*, his next play, which won the Pulitzer Prize in 1947. He received another Pulitzer Prize in 1955 for *Cat on a Hot Tin Roof*. Considered one of America's major twentieth-century dramatists, he continues as a prolific playwright. Less well known are his short stories collected in *One Arm* (1948, revised 1950) and *Hard Candy* (1954).

WILLIAMS, WILLIAM CARLOS (1883–1963), spent most of his life in New Jersey, where he was a physician by profession. Though he was a friend of Ezra Pound's and admired Pound's use of symbolism, Williams' daily contact with sickness and ordinary reality led him to seek exactness and simplicity in language. His first volume, *Poems*, was published in 1909; the second, *The Tempers*, in 1913. He subsequently produced several more volumes of verse. In his later years he attempted an autobiographical epic poem, *Paterson*, concerning an industrial city, but his best poetry remains the earlier direct, immediate, realistic works. He received several honorary degrees—the *Dial* award for "service to American literature" (1926), the Bollingen Poetry Award (1953), and the National Book Prize. In addition to poetry, he produced novels, short fiction, a play, and several volumes of essays.

WORDSWORTH, WILLIAM (1770–1850), and the Lake District of Cumberland recall England's greatest romantic poetry. Born in Cockermouth, he was dependent upon his uncles for his education after his mother died when he was 8, his father when he was 13. After leaving Cambridge in 1787, he went to France where his two great passions were the French Revolution and Annette Vallon, whom he never married but whose daughter, Anne Caroline, was born from this relationship. Another important phase in his life was meeting Samuel Taylor Coleridge in 1795 and collaborating with him on *Lyrical Ballads* (1798). This slender volume of verse, including Wordsworth's "Tintern Abbey" and Coleridge's "The Rime of the Ancient Mariner," is highly important for its rebellion against the contorted and artificially stylized contemporary verse. In 1799 Wordsworth and his sister Dorothy settled at Dove Cottage by Grasmere where he and Coleridge worked on an enlarged edition of *Lyrical Ballads* (1800). During the next five years Wordsworth reached the pinnacle of his creative work. He wrote much poetry after this period, but it was anticlimactic. With Mary Hutchinson, whom he married in 1802, he spent his remaining years in the Lake District. He became Poet Laureate of England in 1843, long after his best poetry had been written.

WRIGHT, RICHARD (1908–1960), was born in Natchez, Mississippi, and became a very influential Afro-American novelist. He moved to Chicago in 1927. His first book, *Uncle Tom's Children* (1938), was a collection of stories about southern Negroes. His most famous work, *Native Son* (1940), dealt with American racism. Hailed as a work of art by critics, it gave new direction to the work of black writers. Other works include four novels, a collection of short stories, and two nonfiction books about racial problems. Deeply troubled by the dilemmas of his race, he became an expatriate and spent his last years in Paris.

YEATS, WILLIAM BUTLER (1865–1939), who was born near Dublin, enjoyed as a child the west country of Ireland, especially the lakes of Sligo, which inspired his early poem "The Lake Isle of Innisfree." As the leading poet of the Irish Literary Revival, he was determined to create a literature purely Irish. To this end, he studied Irish folk tales before publishing his first poem of importance, *The Wanderings of Oisin* (1889). With the same nationalistic spirit he collaborated with Isabella Augusta, Lady Gregory, in founding the Irish National Theatre Society in 1899. For two decades he loved Maud Gonne, but he was finally rejected in marriage by both her and her daughter Iseult. In 1917 he married Georgie Hyde-Lees. His poetry in later years was inspired by occult and prophetic depths, manifested with tremendous splendor in such poems as "The Magi" and "Sailing to Byzantium." His pronouncements of gloom and destruction assume an eerie power in "The Second Coming" and "Leda and the Swan." For his numerous plays, published essays, criticisms, and volumes of verse, he was awarded the Nobel Prize for literature in 1923.

The Critics

BEARDSLEY, MONROE C. (1915–   ), professor of philosophy at Swarthmore College, is the author of books on logic and aesthetics and, with W. K. Wimsatt, Jr., coauthor of the two widely known essays, "The Intentional Fallacy" and "The Affective Fallacy."

BLACKMUR, R. P. (1904–1965), American poet and literary critic, was on the faculty of Princeton University for many years before his death. His important critical works include *The Double Agent* (1935), *Language and Gesture* (1952), *The Lion and the Honeycomb* (1955), and *Form and Value in Modern Poetry* (1957).

BROOKS, CLEANTH (1906–   ), professor at Yale, was editor (with Robert Penn Warren) of *The Southern Review* from 1935 to 1942. He later served as Honorary Consultant to the Library of Congress. His critical works include *Modern Poetry and the Tradition* (1939), *The Well Wrought Urn* (1947), and *William Faulkner: The Yoknapatawpha Country* (1963). With W. K. Wimsatt, Jr., he wrote *Literary Criticism: A Short History* (1957).

CREWS, FREDERICK C. (1933–   ), was educated at Yale and Princeton and is now Professor of English at the University of California, Berkeley. His works include *E. M. Forster: The Perils of Humanism*, *The Pooh Perplex*, *The Patch Commission*, and *The Sins of the Fathers: Hawthorne's Psychological Themes*.

DEUTSCH, BABETTE (1895–   ), is an American critic and poet; she is also a lecturer at Columbia University and a member of the National Institute of Arts and Letters. Collaborating with her husband, Avrahm Yarmolinsky, she has translated German and Russian verse.

ELIOT, T. S. See above ("The Authors").

FERGUSSON, FRANCIS (1904–   ), received his undergraduate degree from Oxford University, and he has taught at both Bennington College and Princeton University. A critic of dramatic performance and literature, his most important book is *The Idea of a Theater* (1949).

FOERSTER, NORMAN (1887–   ), American critic and educator, was the long-time director of the School of Letters at the University of Iowa. His critical writing is based largely upon a humanistic and sociological approach to literature.

FRYE, NORTHROP (1912–   ), a Canadian scholar and educator, is professor of English at Victoria College, Toronto. Known best as a myth-critic, his monumental *Anatomy of Criticism* was published in 1957.

HEILMAN, ROBERT B. (1906–   ), received his Ph.D. from Harvard and is Professor of English at the University of Washington. Among his numerous awards for scholarship and criticism are a Huntington Library grant and a Guggenheim Fellowship. His writings include two critical works on Shakespeare; *America in English Fiction, 1760–1800;* and *Tragedy and Melodrama: Versions of Experience.* In addition, he has published a number of critical essays and has edited several anthologies.

KUNITZ, STANLEY J. (1905–   ), received the Pulitzer Prize in 1959 for his *Selected Poems, 1928–1958.*

LEWIS, C. S. (1898–1963), an English novelist and essayist, wrote many works (including fiction) dealing with Christian theology. One such novel, *The Screwtape Letters,* brought him wide acclaim in 1942. His main work of criticism is *The Allegory of Love* (1936), a study of the medieval courtly tradition.

LUKÁCS, GEORG (1885–   ), grew up in Budapest, has written in German since 1910, and is a leading literary scholar behind the Iron Curtain. A proponent of Critical Realism, he rejects both the modernism of the West and the propagandism of eastern European literature. His most famous work, which he has since repudiated, is *History and Class Consciousness* (1923). A more recent work is *The Historical Novel* (1955).

MULLER, HERBERT J. (1905–   ), critic and scholar who teaches at the University of Illinois, has written many books on history and literary criticism, including *Modern Fiction* (1937).

MURRAY, HENRY A. (1893–   ), received his doctorate in biochemistry from Cambridge University and for many years was a professor of clinical psychology at Harvard. However, Melville's writings have influenced him since 1925, when, he says, the reading of *Moby Dick* "catapulted him out of the field of biochemistry into the landless sea of the unconscious mental processes."

ONG, WALTER J. (1912–   ), a Jesuit priest, has received degrees from Harvard University and St. Louis University, where he is now Professor of English. He was a member of the White House Task Force on Education, 1966–67, and was a Guggenheim Fellow, 1949–50 and 1951–52. His many articles and books include *Frontiers in American Catholicism* and *The Presence of the Word.*

ROETHKE, THEODORE. See above ("The Authors").

SARTRE, JEAN-PAUL. See above ("The Authors").

SLATOFF, WALTER J. (1922–   ), was born in New York and was educated at Columbia University and the University of Michigan. He is presently Professor of English at Cornell University. His critical works include *With Respect to Readers*, which is concerned with methods of reading and teaching literature, and *Quest for Failure: A Study of William Faulkner*.

SPENCER, THEODORE (1902–1949), American poet, critic, and professor of English at Harvard, was primarily concerned with Shakespearean dramatic technique and the philosophical implications of literature.

SPENDER, STEPHEN (1909–   ), a British writer of poetry and criticism, has served as coeditor of *Horizon* and *Encounter* and has translated works of Toller and Schiller. His collected poems appeared in 1954; his critical works include *The Destructive Element* (1935), *The Creative Element* (1953), and *The Making of a Poem* (1962).

TILLYARD, E. M. W. (1889–1962), long associated with Cambridge University, was particularly interested in Shakespeare and Milton and the background of thought in their periods. In 1939 he collaborated with C. S. Lewis in writing *The Personal Heresy*. Other works include *The Elizabethan World Picture* (1944), *Shakespeare's History Plays* (1946), and *Studies in Milton* (1951).

TRILLING, LIONEL (1905–   ), on the faculty at Columbia University, has written *Matthew Arnold* (1939), *The Liberal Imagination* (1950), and *The Opposing Self* (1955), as well as the novel, *The Middle of the Journey* (1947), and several short stories which have been frequently anthologized.

WELLEK, RENÉ (1903–   ), is a naturalized American citizen who was born in Vienna. He was educated at Charles University in Prague and at Princeton. He has taught comparative literature at Smith, Princeton, and the University of London and has been at Yale since 1948. Recipient of numerous honorary degrees and prizes, he has been a Fulbright Scholar and Lecturer and a Guggenheim Fellow. A prolific writer, his work includes *Concepts of Criticism*, *Essays on Czech Literature*, and *History of Modern Criticism*.

WHEELWRIGHT, PHILIP (1901–   ), was educated at Princeton University and Union Theological Seminary. His writings, concerned mainly with philosophy and ethics, also include studies of symbolism and literature, the chief of which is *The Burning Fountain* (1954).

WILSON, EDMUND (1895–   ), is an American editor and writer of plays, verse, fiction, and criticism. He has served on the editorial staff of *Vanity Fair* and *The New Republic*. Among his many volumes of literary criticism are *Axel's Castle* (1931), *The Wound and the Bow* (1941), and *Patriotic Gore* (1962).

WIMSATT, WILLIAM K., JR. (1907–   ), professor at Yale University since 1939, is known for his studies in eighteenth-century literature and for such critical studies as *The Verbal Icon: Studies in the Meaning of Poetry* (1954) and, with Cleanth Brooks, *Literary Criticism: A Short History* (1957).

INDEX

After Apple-Picking, 680–681
Ah Sun-Flower!, 621
The Altar, 610
Among School Children, 675–677
And Death Shall Have No Dominion, 731–732
Apparently with No Surprise, 662
Araby, 39–43
Arnold, Matthew, 655–658
Art and Neurosis, 793–808
At the round earth's imagined corners, 607
Auden, W. H., 711

Baldwin, James, 70–97
Bartleby and I, 983–1002
Bartleby the Scrivener, 324–355
Batter my heart, three-personed God, 608
Beardsley, M. C., 849–861
Because I Could Not Stop for Death, 660–661
Bells for John Whiteside's Daughter, 699
Big Two-Hearted River: Part I, 152–159
Big Two-Hearted River: Part II, 159–167
Blackmur, R. P., 1032–1052
Blake, William, 620–622
Blue Girls, 699–700
Bly, Robert, 742–743
Borges, Jorge Luis, 245–250
Brooks, Cleanth, 862–877
Brooks, Gwendolyn, 733–735
Buffalo Bill's, 701
The Buried Life, 655–657
The Bustle in a House, 661–662
Byzantium, 677–678

the Cambridge ladies, 701
The Canonization, 601–602
The Central Problem in Literary Criticism, 843–848
The Chestnut Casts His Flambeaux, 665–666
Come with Me, 743

Composed upon Westminster Bridge, September 3, 1802, 626–627
The Conversion of the Jews, 107–119
Corinna's Going A-Maying, 613–615
Crane, Stephen, 3–24
Crazy Jane Talks with the Bishop, 679
Crews, Frederick C., 896–906
Crossing the Water, 750
Cullen, Countee, 708–710
Cummings, E. E., 701–704

Death, be not proud, 607–608
The Death of Iván Ilých, 275–323
Delight in Disorder, 613
Desert Places, 683
Deutsch, Babette, 1053–1057
Dickinson, Emily, 659–662
Disillusionment of Ten O'Clock, 684–685
Do Not Go Gentle into That Good Night, 730–731
Dolor, 713–714
Donne, John, 599–608
Donne and Love Poetry in the Seventeenth Century, 1014–1031
Dostoevsky, Fyodor, 120–137
Dover Beach, 658
The Dream, 715–716
The Drunken Fisherman, 740

Easter, 1916, 669–671
Easter Wings, 610
The Ecstasy, 603–605
Elegy for Jane, 714
Eliot, T. S., 695–698, 928–934
Essay, 1053–1057
Essay—The Taste of Self, 1057–1064
The Esthetic Judgment and the Ethical Judgment, 958–970
The Executive's Death, 742
Existentialism, 833–842

Faulkner, William, 44–58
Fergusson, Francis, 1003–1013
Fern Hill, 729–730
Fire and Ice, 682
The Fish, 692–693

1089

The Flea, 602–603
Flowering Judas, 168–178
Foerster, Norman, 958–970
The Force That Through the Green Fuse Drives the Flower, 728
Frederick Douglass, 722
Frost, Robert, 680–683
Frye, Northrup, 809–818
The Full Man and the Fullness Thereof, 772–778
The Funeral, 606

The Gap, 588–594
Ghosts, 359–415
Ghosts: The Theater of Modern Realism, 1003–1013
The Glass Menagerie, 457–513
Good Country People, 179–196
The Grand Inquisitor, 120–137
Gulls, 689

Hansberry, Lorraine, 514–587
Hayden, Robert, 720–724
Heilman, Robert B., 772–778
Hemingway, Ernest, 152–167
Herbert, George, 609–610
The Heresy of Paraphrase, 862–877
Heritage, 708–710
Herrick, Robert, 613–615
A High-Toned Old Christian Woman, 684
Holy Sonnets, 607–608
Housman, A. E., 663–666

I am a little world made cunningly, 607
I Like a Look of Agony, 660
i thank You God, 704
Ibsen, Henrik, 359–415
The Ideology of Modernism, 935–957
Idiots First, 266–274
if there are any heavens, 703–704
Immortal Is an Ample Word, 662
In a Dark Time, 716–717
In Evening Air, 717–718
In the Days of Prismatic Colour, 693–694
The Indifferent, 600–601
Insomniac, 747–748

The Intentional Fallacy, 849–861
Ionesco, Eugene, 138–151, 588–594
An Irish Airman Foresees His Death, 668
It Is a Beauteous Evening, Calm and Free, 627

The Jinnee in the Well-Wrought Urn, 918–927
Joyce, James, 39–43
The Judgment, 98–106

Kafka, Franz, 98–106
Keats, John, 629–636
The Keys to Dreamland, 809–818
kitchenette building, 733
Kunitz, Stanley, 1057–1064

La Belle Dame Sans Merci, 629–630
The Lake Isle of Innisfree, 667
The Lamb, 620
The Later Poetry of W. B. Yeats, 1032–1052
Lawrence, D. H., 25–38
Leda and the Swan, 673–674
Lewis, C. S., 1014–1031
Literature and Psychology, 896–906
London, 622
London, 1802, 627
The Love Song of J. Alfred Prufrock, 695–698
Loveliest of Trees, 663
Love's Deity, 605–606
Lowell, Robert, 736–741
Lukács, Georg, 935–957

The Magi, 667
Malamud, Bernard, 266–274
Man and Wife, 741
The Man Who Was Almost a Man, 59–69
A March in the Ranks Hard-Prest, and the Road Unknown, 642–643
Marvell, Andrew, 616–617
McCullers, Carson, 251–257
Medgar Evers, 734
Melville, Herman, 324–355
Milton, John, 618–619
Mirror, 748
Miss Julie, 416–446

Monet's "Waterlilies," 722–723
Moore, Marianne, 692–694
Moss-Gathering, 712–713
Mourning Poem for the Queen of Sunday, 720
Muller, Herbert J., 819–832
Murray, Henry A., 983–1002
Musée des Beaux Arts, 711
My Papa's Waltz, 713
my sweet old etcetera, 702–703

A Narrow Fellow in the Grass, 661
Nocturne, 700

O'Connor, Flannery, 179–196
Ode on a Grecian Urn, 631–633
Ode on Melancholy, 630–631
Ode to a Nightingale, 633–635
Ode to the Confederate Dead, 705–707
On First Looking into Chapman's Homer, 629
On His Blindness, 619
On His Having Arrived at the Age of Twenty-three, 618
Ong, Walter J., 918–927
The Open Boat, 3–24
Open House, 712
Our City Is Guarded by Automatic Rockets, 727
Our Lady of Walsingham, 739
Out of the Cradle Endlessly Rocking, 637–642
"Out, Out—," 681–682

The Pause, 691
Periods and Movements in Literary History, 978–982
The Personal Heresy, II, 907–917
Pessimism, 819–832
Philoctetes: The Wound and the Bow, 779–792
A Plague of Starlings, 723–724
Plath, Sylvia, 744–750
Poetry, Myth and Reality, 878–895
Poppies in October, 745
Porter, Katherine Anne, 168–178
A Prayer for My Daughter, 671–673
the preacher: ruminates behind the sermon, 734

Prelude to Winter, 691
The Pulley, 609

The Quaker Graveyard in Nantucket, 736–740

A Raisin in the Sun, 514–587
Ransom, John Crowe, 699–700
The Red Wheelbarrow, 689
A Refusal to Mourn the Death, by Fire, of a Child in London, 728–729
Reluctance, 680
Requiem, 726
Requiescat, 657
Riders to the Sea, 447–456
The Right Thing, 719
Roethke, Theodore, 712–719, 753–754
Roth, Philip, 107–119

Safe in Their Alabaster Chambers, 659–660
Sailing to Byzantium, 674–675
Saint Emmanuel the Good, Martyr, 197–227
Sartre, Jean-Paul, 228–244, 833–842
The Second Coming, 671
The Sequel, 718–719
The Shades of Spring, 25–38
Shakespeare, William, 597–598
The Sick Rose, 620
the skinny voice, 701–702
Slatoff, Walter J., 755–771
Slime, 138–151
Some Self-Analysis, 753–754
Song, 599
a song in the front yard, 733
Sonnets, 597–598
Sonny's Blues, 70–97
A Sort of a Song, 691
The South, 245–250
Spencer, Theodore, 843–848
Stafford, William, 725–727
Stevens, Wallace, 684–688
Stopping by Woods on a Snowy Evening, 683
Strindberg, August, 416–446
Success Is Counted Sweetest, 659
The Sun Rising, 599–600

Sunday Morning, 685–688
A Symposium on Roethke's "In a Dark Time," 1053–1064
Synge, John Millington, 447–456

Tate, Allen, 705–707
Tennyson, Alfred, Lord, 651–654
Terence, This Is Stupid Stuff, 663–665
That Evening Sun, 44–58
Thomas, Dylan, 728–732
Those Winter Sundays, 721–722
The Tiger, 620–621
The Tillamook Burn, 725
Tillyard, E. M. W., 907–917
Tintern Abbey, 623–626
Tithonus, 652–654
To a Winter Squirrel, 735
To Autumn, 635–636
To His Coy Mistress, 616–617
To My Sister, 712
To the Nightingale, 618
Tolstoy, Leo, 275–323
Tradition and the Individual Talent, 928–934
Traveling through the Dark, 725
A Tree, A Rock, A Cloud, 251–257
Trilling, Lionel, 793–808
Tulips, 744–745

Ulysses, 651–652
Unamuno, Miguel de, 197–227

Varieties of Involvement, 755–771
Vaughan, Henry, 611–612

Vocation, 726

The Waking, 714–715
The Wall, 228–244
Wanting to Experience All Things, 743
Watching Television, 742
Wellek, René, 971–982
Welty, Eudora, 258–265
What Are Years?, 694
Wheelwright, Philip, 878–895
When Lilacs Last in the Dooryard Bloom'd, 643–650
The Whipping, 721
Whitman, Walt, 637–650
Whitsun, 749
The Wild Swans at Coole, 667–668
Williams, Tennessee, 457–513
Williams, William Carlos, 689–691
Wilson, Edmund, 779–792
Wimsatt, W. K., Jr., 849–861
Witch Burning, 749–750
With Rue My Heart Is Laden, 663
Words, 746–747
Wordsworth, William, 623–628
The World, 611–612
The World Is Too Much with Us; Late and Soon, 628
A Worn Path, 258–265
Wright, Richard, 59–69

The Yachts, 690
Years, 746
Yeats, William Butler, 667–679